HOLT

CALL TO FREEDOM

Sterling Stuckey ■ Linda Kerrigan Salvucci
Reading Consultant • Judith Irvin

HOLT, RINEHART AND WINSTON
A Harcourt Education Company
Austin • New York • Orlando • Atlanta • San Francisco • Boston • Dallas • Toronto • London

About the Authors

Sterling Stuckey is Professor of History and holds the Presidential Chair at the University of California, Riverside. Dr. Stuckey is the author of *Slave Culture: Nationalist Theory and the Foundations of Black America* and *Going Through the Storm: The Influence of African American Art in History.*

Linda Kerrigan Salvucci is Associate Professor of History at Trinity University, San Antonio, Texas. Dr. Salvucci is currently working on a book entitled *Ironies of Empire: The United States–Cuba Trade Under Spanish Rule.*

Editorial
Sue Miller, *Director*
Steven L. Hayes, *Executive Editor*
Robert Wehnke, *Managing Editor*
Rhonda Haynes, *Senior Editor*

Pupil's Edition
Doug Sims, *Project Editor*
Laura M. Shankland, *Associate Editor*

Teacher's Edition
Kristie L. Kelly, *Associate Editor*

Ancillaries
Jeffrey C. Herndon, *Associate Editor*

Technology Resources
Rob Hrechko, *Internet Editor*

Fact Checking
Bob Fullilove, *Editor*
Jenny Rose, *Assistant Editor*

Copy Editing
Julie Beckman, *Senior Copy Editor*
Katelijne A. Lefevere, *Copy Editor*

Support
Gina Tasby-Rogers, *Administrative Assistant*
Sue Minkler, *Assistant Editorial Coordinator*

Editorial Permissions
Ann B. Farrar, *Senior Permissions Editor*

Art, Design, and Photo
Book Design
Diane Motz, *Senior Design Director*
Christine Stanford, *Design Manager*
Candace Moore, *Senior Designer*
Lori Male, *Senior Designer*
Cathy Jenevein, *Designer*
Bob Prestwood, *Designer*
Ed Diaz, *Design Associate*

Image Acquisitions
Joe London, *Director*
Tim Taylor, *Photo Research Supervisor*
Andy Christiansen, *Photo Researcher*
Stephanie Morris, *Photo Researcher*
Michelle Rumpf, *Art Buyer Supervisor*
Julie Kelly, *Art Buyer*

Technology Design
Susan Michael, *Design Director*
Kimberly Cammerata, *Design Manager*
Grant Davidson, *Designer*

Media Design
Curtis Riker, *Design Director*
Richard Chavez, *Designer*

Graphic Services
Kristen Darby, *Manager*
Cathy Murphy, *Senior Image Designer*
Linda Wilbourn, *Image Designer*
Jane Dixon, *Image Designer*
Jeff Robinson, *Senior Ancillary Designer*

Design and Production
DECODE, Inc.

Prepress and Manufacturing
Gene Rumann, *Production Manager*
Nancy Hargis, *Production Supervisor*
Leanna Ford, *Production Coordinator*
Cyntia Munoz, *Production Coordinator*
Antonella Posterino, *Coordinator*
Jevara Jackson, *Manufacturing Coordinator, Book*
Rhonda Farris, *Inventory Planner*
Kim Harrison, *Manufacturing Coordinator, Media*

For acknowledgments, see page R77, which is an extension of the copyright page.

Printed in the United States of America

ISBN 0-03-064679-0

2 3 4 5 6 7 8 9 48 05 04 03 02

COVER: *Originally known as "Liberty Enlightening the World," the Statue of Liberty soars over the New York Harbor. The statue has long represented American opportunity and liberty.*

Content Reviewers

Dr. Richard Abbott
Eastern Michigan University
Reconstruction

Dr. Larry Conyers
University of Denver
Anthropology

Dr. R. Douglas Cope
Brown University
Colonial Latin America

Dr. Paul A. Gilje
University of Oklahoma
U.S., 1492–1865

Dr. Christopher Hendricks
Armstrong Atlantic State University
Early U.S.

Dr. Melvin Holli
University of Illinois at Chicago
U.S. urban and ethnic

Dr. Raymond Hyser
James Madison University
Gilded Age and Progressive Era

Dr. Elizabeth Jameson
University of New Mexico
American West and U.S. social

Dr. Beverly Jones
North Carolina Central University
Reconstruction

Dr. Yasuhide Kawashima
University of Texas at El Paso
Colonial and revolutionary America, American legal

Dr. F. Daniel Larkin
State University of New York-Oneonta
19th-century U.S.

Dr. Helen Nader
University of Arizona
Renaissance, Spain

Dr. Edward Peters
University of Pennsylvania
Medieval European

Dr. Jack Rakove
Stanford University
American Revolution, early American political

Dr. Leonard Richards
University of Massachusetts
Jacksonian America

Dr. Joel Silbey
Cornell University
19th-century U.S.

Dr. David Switzer
Plymouth State College
Civil War and Reconstruction

Dr. Jesús F. de la Teja
Southwest Texas State University
Spanish Borderlands

Dr. Patricia Tracy
Williams College
Colonial America

Dr. Clarence E. Walker
University of California at Davis
African American 1450–present

Dr. John R. Wunder
University of Nebraska
American West

Educational Reviewers

Anistacio Asuncion
Piedmont Middle School
San Jose, California

Michelle Bohanek
Orozco Academy
Chicago, Illinois

Jeri Goodspeed-Gross
Minnetonka Middle School West
Chaska, Minnesota

Cynthia Gore
Castillero Middle School
San Jose, California

Tom Harris
Oak Park Middle School
Leesburg, Florida

Valerie Hill
Gaston Middle School
Dallas, Texas

Robert Jones
Perry Junior High School
New Hartford, New York

Marilyn Kretzer
Johnston Middle School
Houston, Texas

Janie Maldanado
Lanier High School
Austin, Texas

Barbara Mayo
Program Facilitator
Austin Independent School District
Austin, Texas

Steve Munzel
Jane Lathrop Stanford Middle School
Palo Alto, California

Milt Perlman
Junior High School 185
Flushing, New York

Pat Tobbe
Newburg Middle School
Louisville, Kentucky

Helen Webb
Wynn Seale Middle School
Corpus Christi, Texas

George Wood
Gregory-Portland Junior High School
Portland, Texas

Field Test Teachers

Sandra Poe Borowiecki
New Hartford Perry Junior High School
New Hartford, New York

Mary Beth Breshears
Wood Middle School
Fort Leonard Wood, Missouri

Richard J. Giannicchi
West Seneca Junior High School
West Seneca, New York

Kim Gravell
Dripping Springs Middle School
Dripping Springs, Texas

Deborah K. Lofton
Charles F. Blackstock Junior High School
Port Hueneme, California

Stan Mendenhall
Broadmoor Junior High School
Pekin, Illinois

Daniel Murray
Hackett Middle School
Albany, New York

Martha Potter
John Jay Middle School
Katonah, New York

Linda B. Rothrock
Harlandale Middle School
San Antonio, Texas

Amy Thompson
Union Middle School
San Jose, California

Call to Freedom

CONTENTS

Pottery made by Native Americans

UNIT 2 Colonies in the Americas

Colonists build their first settlement in New England.

CHAPTER 3 The English Colonies

CHAPTER 4 Life in the English Colonies

CHAPTER 5 Conflicts in the Colonies

Benjamin Franklin

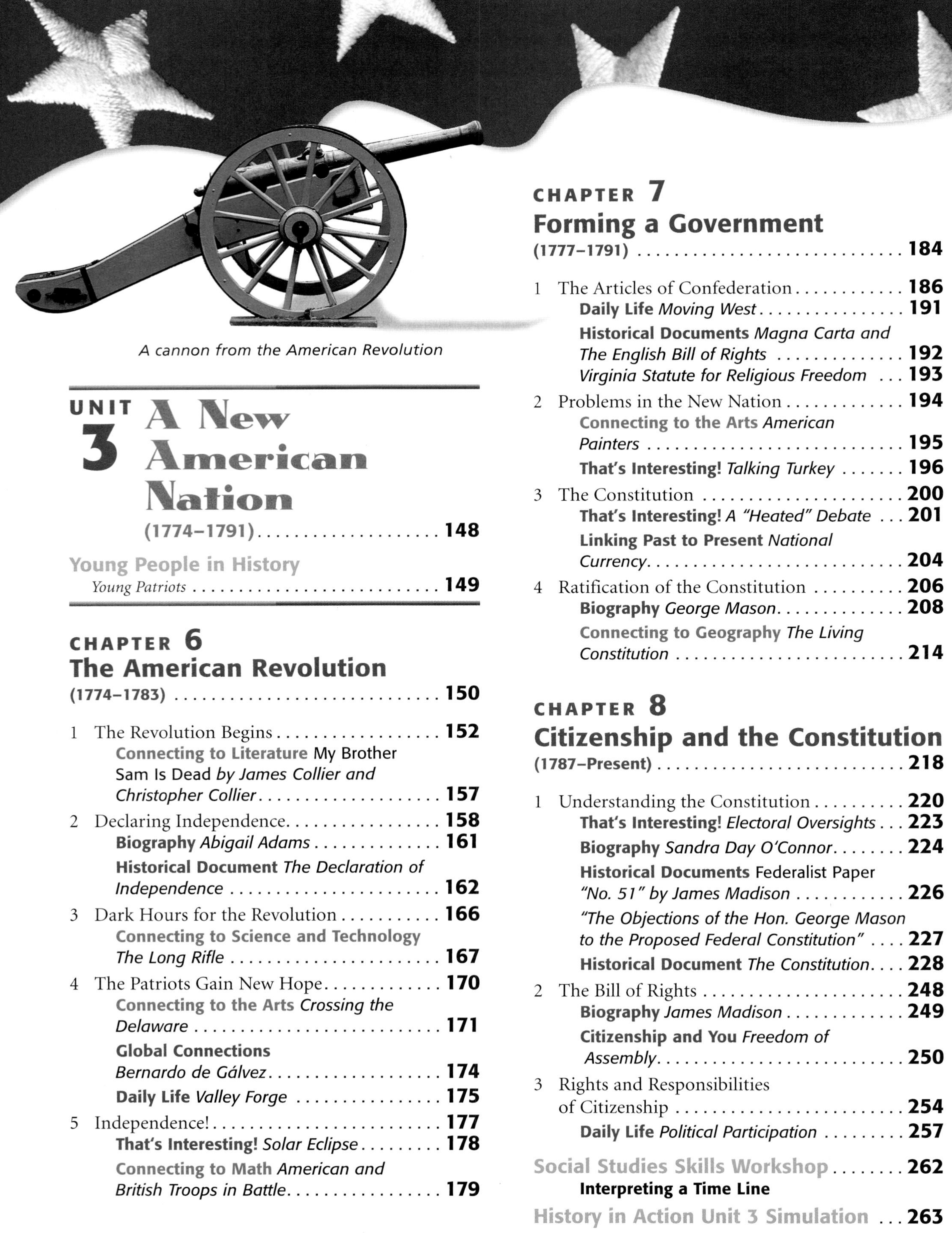

A cannon from the American Revolution

UNIT 4 Building a Strong Nation

CHAPTER 9 Launching the Nation

CHAPTER 10 The Expanding Nation

CHAPTER 11 A New National Identity

Washington's cabinet

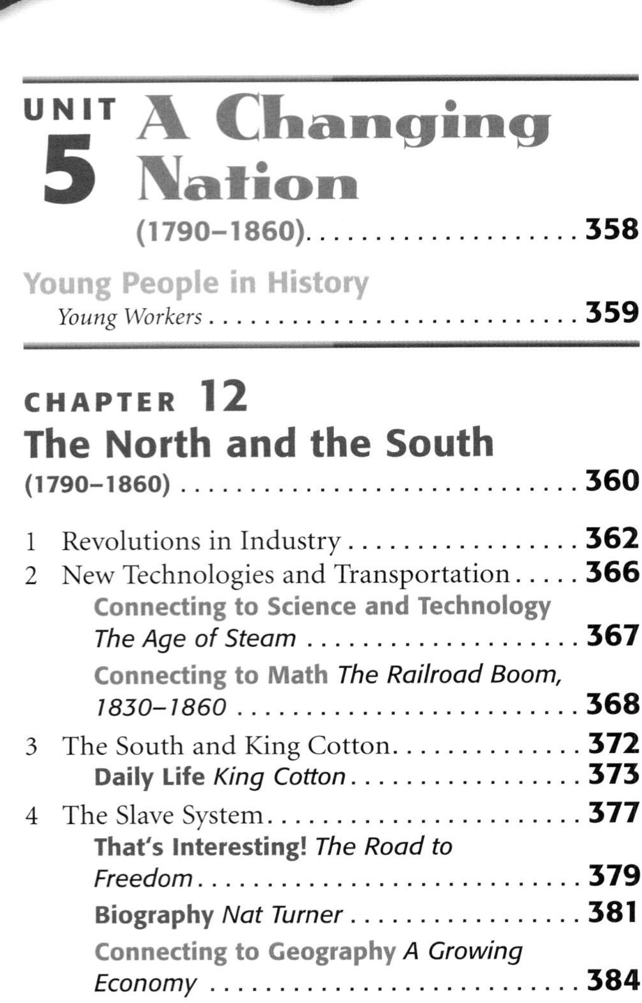

Cotton gin

UNIT 5 A Changing Nation

Conestoga wagon

UNIT 6 The Nation Breaks Apart

A Civil War soldier and his family

Susan B. Anthony

CHAPTER 22 World War I

CHAPTER 23 The Roaring Twenties

UNIT 9 A World in Crisis

CHAPTER 24 The Great Depression

Newspaper headlines announcing the 1929 crash of the stock market

STAGE BROADWAY SCREEN
VARIETY PRICE 25¢
NEW YORK, WEDNESDAY, OCTOBER 30, 1929
WALL ST. LAYS AN EGG
Going Dumb Is Deadly to Hostess In Her Serious Dance Hall Profesh
DROP IN STOCKS ROPES SHOWMEN
Kidding Kissers in Talkers Burns Up Fans of Screen's Best Lovers

ARETHA: LADY SOUL

BOB DYLAN HIGHWAY 61 REVISITED

Popular music from the 1960s

A commemorative bicentennial patch

Primary Sources

The bald eagle

History Makers Speak

Primary Sources, *continued*

Frederick Douglass

Primary Sources

Historical Documents

Political Cartoons

History and Your World

WHY IT MATTERS TODAY and CNNfyi.com

National Guard members helping a community

History and Your World *continued*

A quill pen from the 1700s

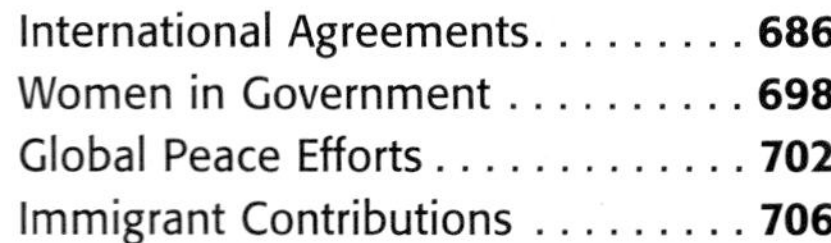

Supreme Court justice Ruth Bader Ginsburg speaking to a group of students

Young People IN HISTORY

LINKING PAST to PRESENT

Interdisciplinary Activities

Connecting to Geography

Connecting to The Arts

Connecting to Literature

Connecting to Science and Technology

Connecting to Math

Historical Highlights

Early pioneers used wagons such as this one to settle the frontier.

THE GRANGER COLLECTION, NEW YORK

That's Interesting!

Daily Life

BIOGRAPHIES and PRESIDENTIAL PROFILES

GLOBAL CONNECTIONS

Technology Activities

Research on the ROM

internet connect

go.hrw.com

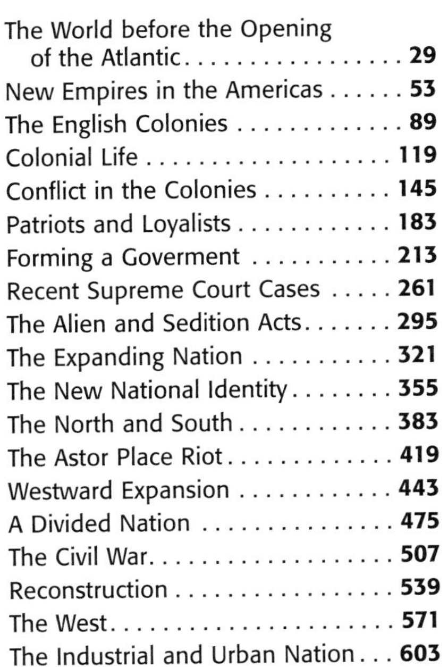

Skill-Building Activities

Social Studies Skills WORKSHOPS

History in Action UNIT SIMULATIONS

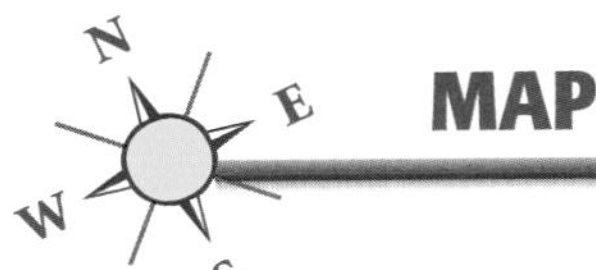

MAPS

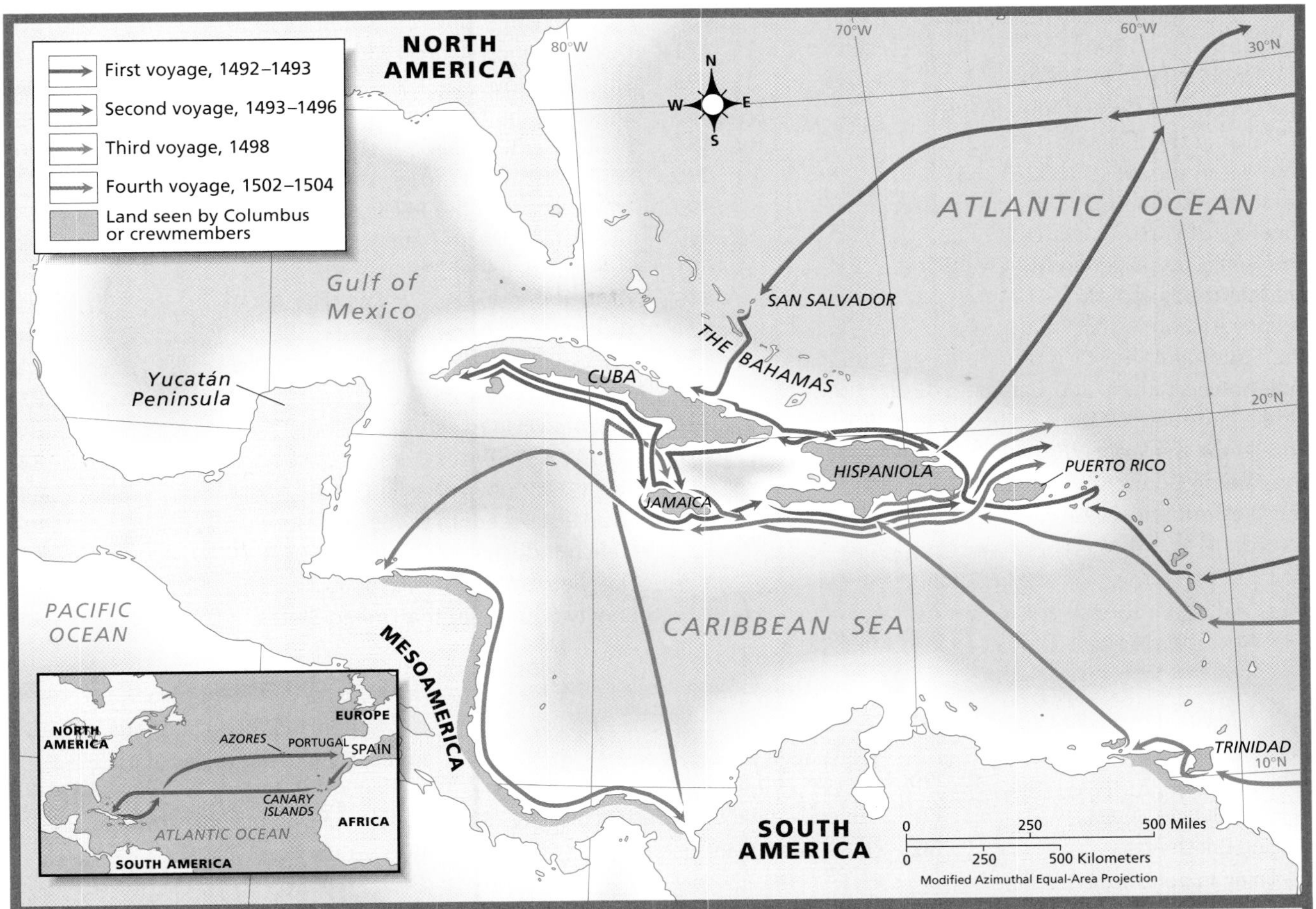

Columbus's Voyages, 1492–1504

Interpreting Maps Christopher Columbus made four trips to the Americas over a 12-year period. During these voyages, Columbus learned much about the lands and waters of the Caribbean Sea.

Skills Assessment **Places and Regions** On which voyage did Columbus reach the southwest edge of Cuba?

An astrolabe

THE GRANGER COLLECTION, NEW YORK

Skill-Building Activities *continued*

GRAPHS AND CHARTS

TIME LINES

VISUALIZING HISTORY

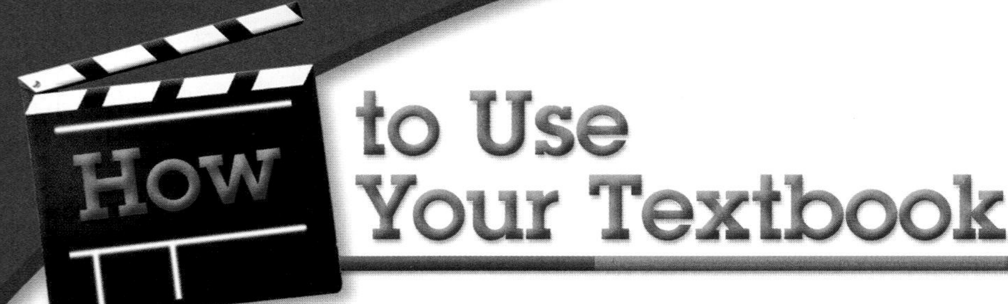

Use the chapter opener to get an overview of the time period.

The Chapter Time Line shows you a comparison of U.S. and global events.

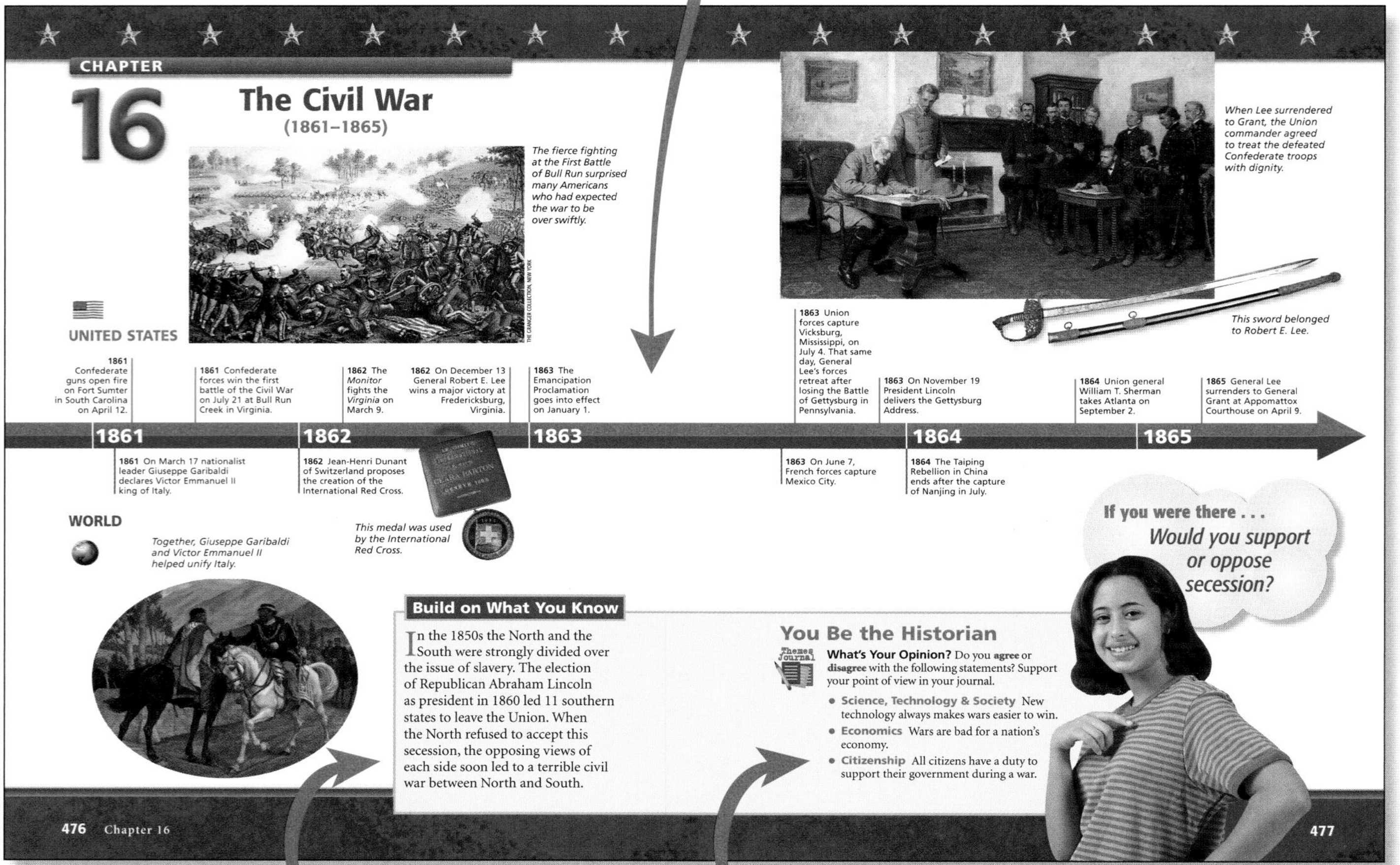

CHAPTER

16

The Civil War

(1861–1865)

The fierce fighting at the First Battle of Bull Run surprised many Americans who had expected the war to be over swiftly.

THE GRANGER COLLECTION, NEW YORK

When Lee surrendered to Grant, the Union commander agreed to treat the defeated Confederate troops with dignity.

This sword belonged to Robert E. Lee.

UNITED STATES

1861 Confederate guns open fire on Fort Sumter in South Carolina on April 12.

1861 Confederate forces win the first battle of the Civil War on July 21 at Bull Run Creek in Virginia.

1862 The *Monitor* fights the *Virginia* on March 9.

1862 On December 13 General Robert E. Lee wins a major victory at Fredericksburg, Virginia.

1863 The Emancipation Proclamation goes into effect on January 1.

1863 Union forces capture Vicksburg, Mississippi, on July 4. That same day, General Lee's forces retreat after losing the Battle of Gettysburg in Pennsylvania.

1863 On November 19 President Lincoln delivers the Gettysburg Address.

1864 Union general William T. Sherman takes Atlanta on September 2.

1865 General Lee surrenders to General Grant at Appomattox Courthouse on April 9.

1861 | 1862 | 1863 | 1864 | 1865

1861 On March 17 nationalist leader Giuseppe Garibaldi declares Victor Emmanuel II king of Italy.

1862 Jean-Henri Dunant of Switzerland proposes the creation of the International Red Cross.

1863 On June 7, French forces capture Mexico City.

1864 The Taiping Rebellion in China ends after the capture of Nanjing in July.

WORLD

Together, Giuseppe Garibaldi and Victor Emmanuel II helped unify Italy.

This medal was used by the International Red Cross.

If you were there . . .
Would you support or oppose secession?

Build on What You Know

In the 1850s the North and the South were strongly divided over the issue of slavery. The election of Republican Abraham Lincoln as president in 1860 led 11 southern states to leave the Union. When the North refused to accept this secession, the opposing views of each side soon led to a terrible civil war between North and South.

You Be the Historian

Themes Journal

What's Your Opinion? Do you **agree** or **disagree** with the following statements? Support your point of view in your journal.

- **Science, Technology & Society** New technology always makes wars easier to win.
- **Economics** Wars are bad for a nation's economy.
- **Citizenship** All citizens have a duty to support their government during a war.

476 Chapter 16 | 477

Build on What You Know bridges the material you have studied in previous chapters with the material you are about to begin. As you read the Build on What You Know feature, take a few minutes to think about the topics that might apply to the chapter you are starting.

You Be the Historian puts you in the place of a historian looking at the past. In this feature you will be asked to respond to three general statements about the chapter. Each statement is tied to one of the key themes of the program. You should respond based on your own knowledge and then record your responses in your journal. There are no right or wrong answers, just your informed opinion.

Use these built-in tools to read for understanding.

Read to Discover questions begin each section of *Call to Freedom.* These questions serve as your guide as you read through the section. Keep them in mind as you explore the section content.

Define and Identify terms are introduced at the beginning of each section. The terms will be defined in context.

Why It Matters Today is an exciting way for you to make connections between what you are reading in your history book and the world around you. In each section you will be invited to explore a topic that is relevant to our lives today by using **CNNfyi.com** connections.

The Story Continues features an interesting episode from American history that shows you that history is not just a collection of facts but a blend of many individual stories and adventures.

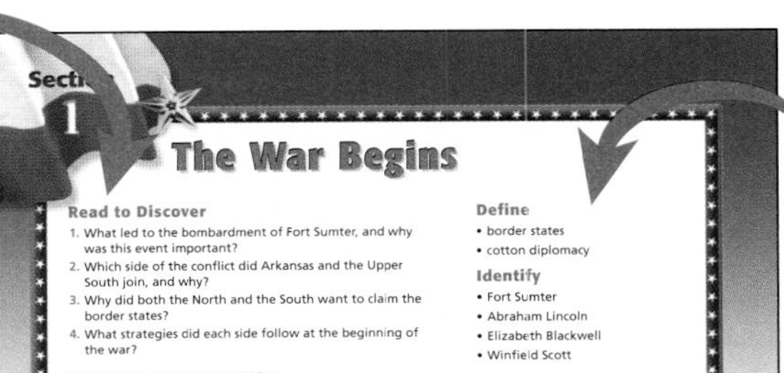

Section 1

The War Begins

Read to Discover

1. What led to the bombardment of Fort Sumter, and why was this event important?
2. Which side of the conflict did Arkansas and the Upper South join, and why?
3. Why did both the North and the South want to claim the border states?
4. What strategies did each side follow at the beginning of the war?

Define

- border states
- cotton diplomacy

Identify

- Fort Sumter
- Abraham Lincoln
- Elizabeth Blackwell
- Winfield Scott

WHY IT MATTERS TODAY

Many countries around the world are currently experiencing civil wars. Use CNNfyi.com or other **current events** sources to find out about some of these places. Record your findings in your journal.

The Spirit of '61 was used as a symbol of Union pride on recruiting posters.

The Story Continues

When Abraham Lincoln took office, seven states had already left the Union. He wanted to keep more southern states from seceding. Lincoln gave his inaugural address on March 4, 1861. He pledged that he would not try to end slavery in the South. He also promised the South that the federal "government will not assail [attack] you. You can have no conflict without being yourselves the aggressors." At the same time, however, Lincoln spoke of his intention to preserve the Union.

Lincoln Faces a Crisis

The South did not respond to these calls for unity. Confederate officials were already taking over many federal mints, arms storehouses, and forts. One important federal post was **Fort Sumter**, located near Charleston, South Carolina. The fort controlled the entrance to Charleston Harbor. By early March 1861 the federal troops at Fort Sumter were running low on supplies. Instead of ordering the troops to surrender, President **Abraham Lincoln** decided to resupply them.

478 Chapter 16

History Makers Speak quotations appear frequently throughout the book. These exciting primary source quotations give you a glimpse into the lives of actual people who made history. Many of these quotations are accompanied by an Analyzing Primary Sources question to help you better interpret the sources and draw inferences about their importance.

Interpreting the Visual Record features accompany many of the book's rich images. Pictures are one of the most important primary sources historians can use to help analyze the past. These features invite you to examine the images and to interpret their content.

THE GRANGER COLLECTION, NEW YORK

Interpreting the Visual Record

Fort Detroit *Pontiac's forces tried for months to capture Fort Detroit from the British.* ***What in the image suggests the difficulties of attacking the fort?***

These leaders had not signed any treaties with Britain and would not give up their land because of an agreement between Britain and France. Chippewa leader Minavavana expressed this view to a trader in 1761. "Englishman, although you have conquered the French, you have not yet conquered us!"

In the 1760s American Indian tribes began to join together to resist the British. Chief Pontiac of the Ottawa led forces that included the Delaware, Huron, Miami, Ottawa, and Shawnee peoples. Pontiac followed the teachings of the so-called Delaware Prophet. This leader called on Indians to drive out the white settlers and give up all European practices. In 1763 Pontiac shared these ideas with a gathering of American Indians.

History Makers Speak

> **"How comes it that you suffer the whites on your lands? Can't you do without them? You might live wholly [completely] as you did before you knew them. . . . Those who come to trouble your country, drive them out, make war [on] them! . . . They are my enemies and the enemies of your brothers!"**
>
> —Pontiac, quoted in *The World Turned Upside Down,* edited by Colin G. Calloway

Analyzing Primary Sources

Identifying Points of View How does Pontiac describe white settlers?

Pontiac's Rebellion began in May 1763 when American Indians attacked British forts on the frontier. Within a month Pontiac's forces had destroyed or captured seven forts. Pontiac then led the attack on Fort Detroit, Britain's political and trading center in the Great Lakes area. Despite the best efforts of Pontiac and his allies, the British held out for months. The American Indians following Pontiac grew tired of attacking the fort and returned to their villages. An Indian attack on the important British position at Fort Pitt also failed. Both sides suffered many casualties. As more Indians left Pontiac, he surrendered in 1766.

✔ Reading Check: **Identifying Cause and Effect** Why did Pontiac and his followers fight the British, and what happened as a result?

Conflicts in the Colonies 133

Reading Check questions appear throughout the book to allow you to check your comprehension while you are reading. As you read each section, pause for a moment to consider each Reading Check. If you have trouble answering the question, go back and examine the material you just read.

Use these review tools to pull together all the information you have learned.

Graphic Organizers will help you review important information from the section. You can complete the graphic organizer as a study tool to prepare for a test or writing assignment.

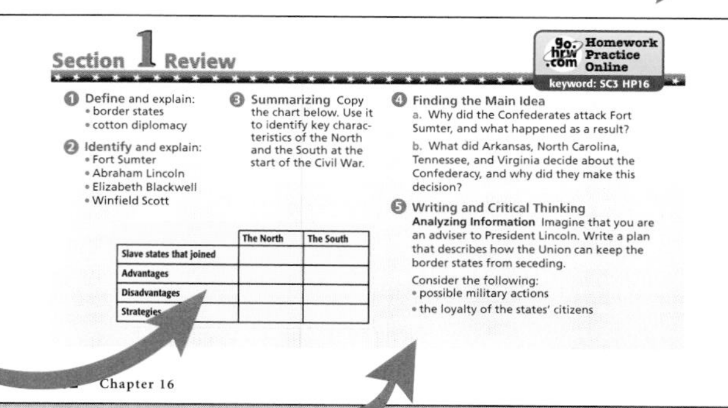

Section 1 Review

go.hrw.com Homework Practice Online
keyword: SC3 HP16

1. Define and explain:
   - border states
   - cotton diplomacy
2. Identify and explain:
   - Fort Sumter
   - Abraham Lincoln
   - Elizabeth Blackwell
   - Winfield Scott
3. Summarizing Copy the chart below. Use it to identify key characteristics of the North and the South at the start of the Civil War.

	The North	The South
Slave states that joined		
Advantages		
Disadvantages		
Strategies		

4. Finding the Main Idea
   a. Why did the Confederates attack Fort Sumter, and what happened as a result?
   b. What did Arkansas, North Carolina, Tennessee, and Virginia decide about the Confederacy, and why did they make this decision?
5. Writing and Critical Thinking
   Analyzing Information Imagine that you are an adviser to President Lincoln. Write a plan that describes how the Union can keep the border states from seceding.
   Consider the following:
   - possible military actions
   - the loyalty of the states' citizens

Chapter 16

Homework Practice Online lets you log on to the go.hrw.com Web site to complete an interactive self-check of the material covered in the section.

Writing and Critical Thinking activities allow you to explore a section topic in greater depth and to build your skills.

The Chapter at a Glance is an interesting visual summary of the main ideas of the chapter.

Social Studies Skills Workshop is a way for you to build your skills at analyzing information and to practice answering standardized-test questions.

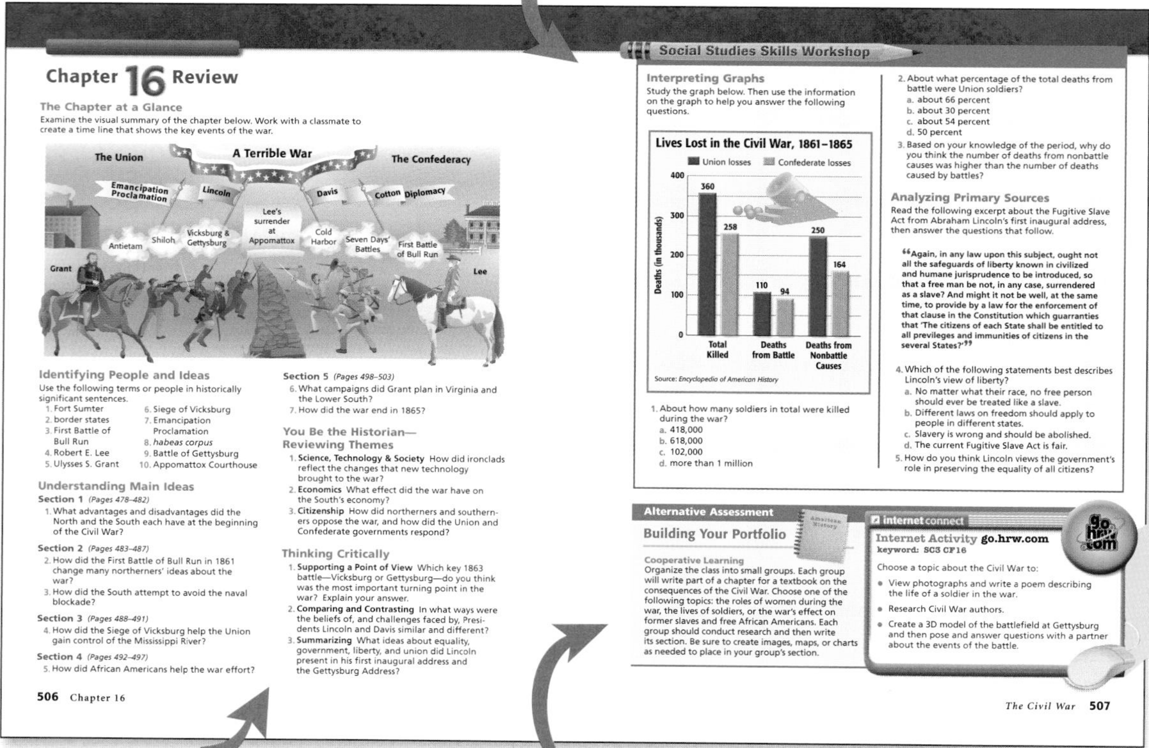

Chapter 16 Review

The Chapter at a Glance

Examine the visual summary of the chapter below. Work with a classmate to create a time line that shows the key events of the war.

Identifying People and Ideas

Use the following terms or people in historically significant sentences.

1. Fort Sumter
2. border states
3. First Battle of Bull Run
4. Robert E. Lee
5. Ulysses S. Grant
6. Siege of Vicksburg
7. Emancipation Proclamation
8. *habeas corpus*
9. Battle of Gettysburg
10. Appomattox Courthouse

Understanding Main Ideas

Section 1 *(Pages 478–482)*

1. What advantages and disadvantages did the North and the South each have at the beginning of the Civil War?

Section 2 *(Pages 483–487)*

2. How did the First Battle of Bull Run in 1861 change many northerners' ideas about the war?
3. How did the South attempt to avoid the naval blockade?

Section 3 *(Pages 488–491)*

4. How did the Siege of Vicksburg help the Union gain control of the Mississippi River?

Section 4 *(Pages 492–497)*

5. How did African Americans help the war effort?

Section 5 *(Pages 498–503)*

6. What campaigns did Grant plan in Virginia and the Lower South?
7. How did the war end in 1865?

You Be the Historian— Reviewing Themes

1. **Science, Technology & Society** How did ironclads reflect the changes that new technology brought to the war?
2. **Economics** What effect did the war have on the South's economy?
3. **Citizenship** How did northerners and southerners oppose the war, and how did the Union and Confederate governments respond?

Thinking Critically

1. **Supporting a Point of View** Which key 1863 battle—Vicksburg or Gettysburg—do you think was the most important turning point in the war? Explain your answer.
2. **Comparing and Contrasting** In what ways were the beliefs of, and challenges faced by, Presidents Lincoln and Davis similar and different?
3. **Summarizing** What ideas about equality, government, liberty, and union did Lincoln present in his first inaugural address and the Gettysburg Address?

506 Chapter 16

Social Studies Skills Workshop

Interpreting Graphs

Study the graph below. Then use the information on the graph to help you answer the following questions.

1. About how many soldiers in total were killed during the war?
   a. 418,000
   b. 618,000
   c. 102,000
   d. more than 1 million
2. About what percentage of the total deaths from battle were Union soldiers?
   a. about 66 percent
   b. about 30 percent
   c. about 54 percent
   d. 50 percent
3. Based on your knowledge of the period, why do you think the number of deaths from nonbattle causes was higher than the number of deaths caused by battles?

Analyzing Primary Sources

Read the following excerpt about the Fugitive Slave Act from Abraham Lincoln's first inaugural address, then answer the questions that follow.

> "Again, in any law upon this subject, ought not all the safeguards of liberty known in civilized and humane jurisprudence to be introduced, so that a free man be not, in any case, surrendered as a slave? And might it not be well, at the same time, to provide by a law for the enforcement of that clause in the Constitution which guarranties that 'The citizens of each State shall be entitled to all previleges and immunities of citizens in the several States?'"

4. Which of the following statements best describes Lincoln's view of liberty?
   a. No matter what their race, no free person should ever be treated like a slave.
   b. Different laws on freedom should apply to people in different states.
   c. Slavery is wrong and should be abolished.
   d. The current Fugitive Slave Act is fair.
5. How do you think Lincoln views the government's role in preserving the equality of all citizens?

Alternative Assessment

Building Your Portfolio

Cooperative Learning

Organize the class into small groups. Each group will write part of a chapter for a textbook on the consequences of the Civil War. Choose one of the following topics: the roles of women during the war, the lives of soldiers, or the war's effect on former slaves and free African Americans. Each group should conduct research and then write its section. Be sure to create images, maps, or charts as needed to place in your group's section.

internet connect

Internet Activity go.hrw.com
keyword: SC3 CF16

Choose a topic about the Civil War to:

- View photographs and write a poem describing the life of a soldier in the war.
- Research Civil War authors.
- Create a 3D model of the battlefield at Gettysburg and then pose and answer questions with a partner about the events of the battle.

The Civil War 507

Thinking Critically questions ask you to use the information you have learned in the chapter to extend your knowledge. These critical thinking skills will help you prepare for the TAKS test.

Building Your Portfolio is an exciting and creative way to demonstrate your understanding of history.

Use these online tools to review and complete online activities.

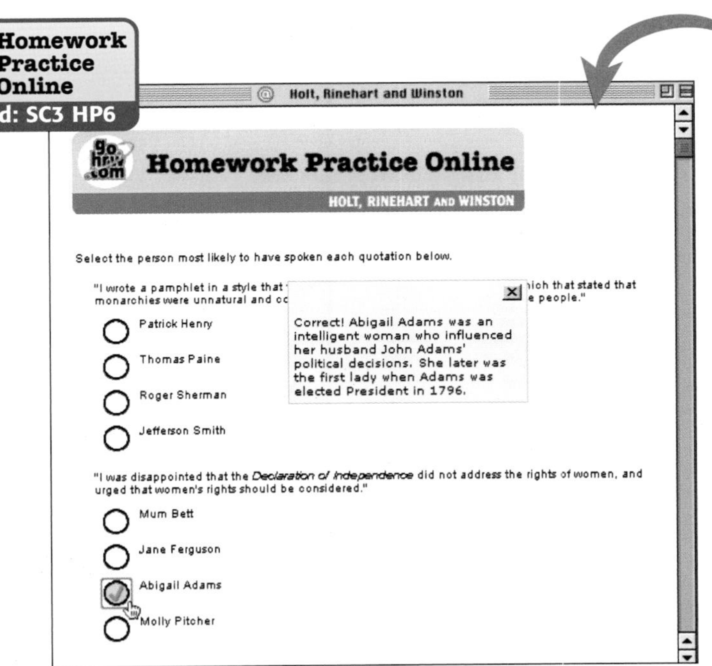

Homework Practice Online lets you log on for review anytime.

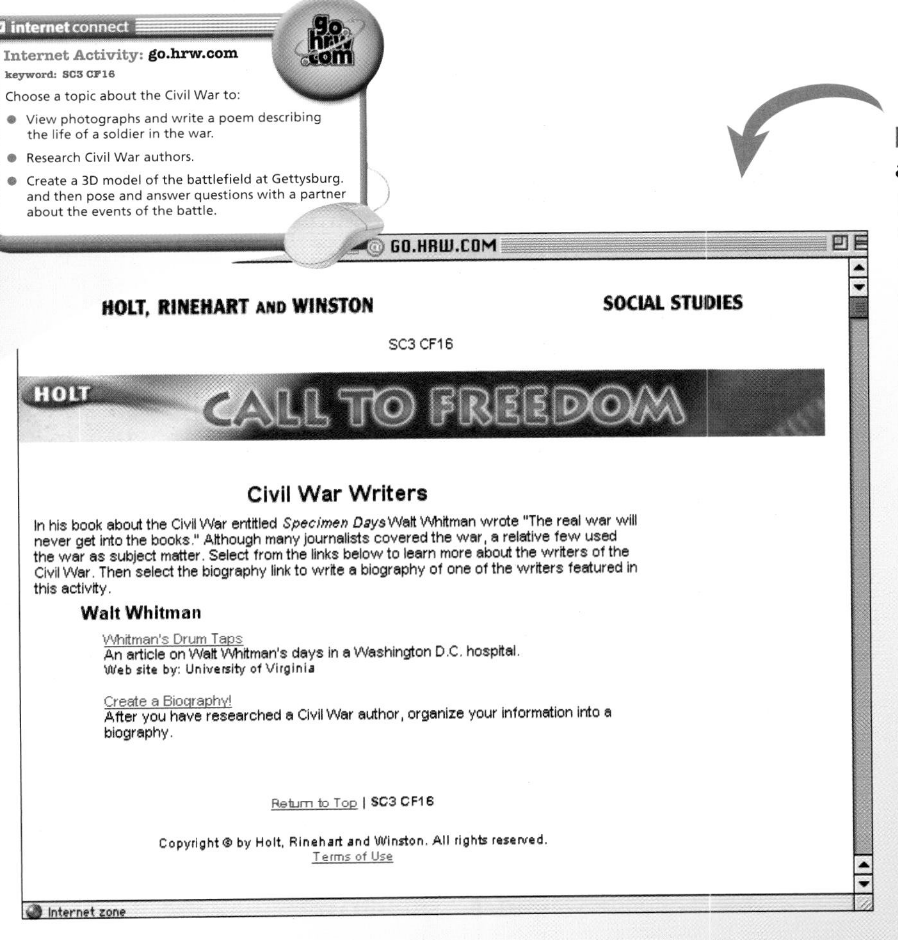

Internet Connect activities are just one part of the world of online learning experiences that awaits you on the go.hrw.com Web site. By exploring these online activities, you will take a journey through some of the richest American history materials available on the World Wide Web. You can then use these resources to create real-world projects, such as newspapers, brochures, reports, and even your own Web site!

Why History Matters Today

"History and destiny have made America the leader of the world that would be free. And the world that would be free is looking to us for inspiration."

—Colin Powell

Right now at this very second, somewhere in the United States, someone is making history. It is impossible to know whom or in what way, but the actions of people today may become the history of tomorrow.

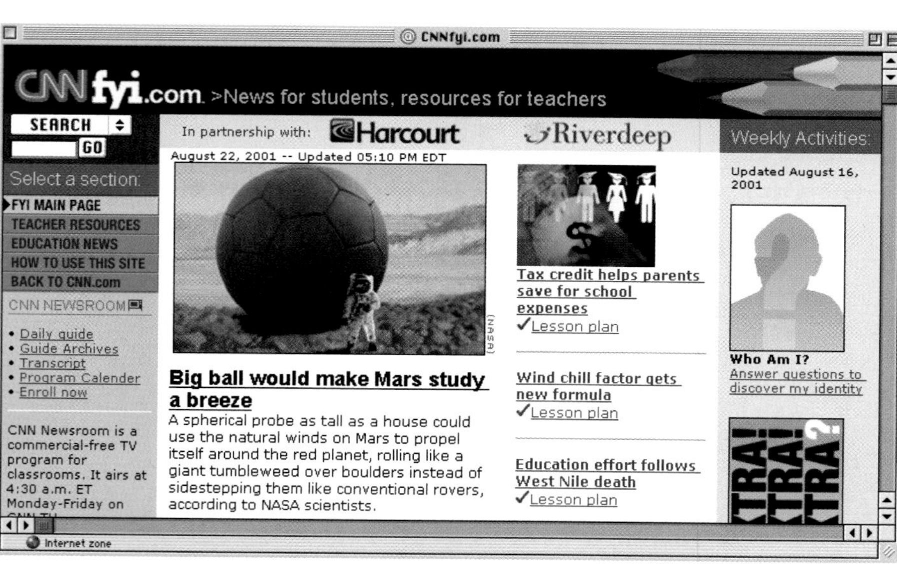

History and Your World

All you need to do is watch or read the news to see history unfolding. How many news stories do you see or hear about ordinary people doing extraordinary things? The Why It Matters Today feature beginning every section of *Call to Freedom* invites you to use the vast resources of **CNNfyi.com** or other current events sources to examine the links between past and present. Through this feature you will be able to draw connections between what you are studying in your history book and the events that are taking place today.

Anyone Can Be a History Maker

When you think of the word *history*, what comes to mind? Do you picture politicians sitting around a table deciding the future of the nation? Or do you see a long list of dates and boring facts to be memorized? Of course, politicians, dates, and facts are part of history, but there is actually much more to understanding and exploring our past. Our nation has developed through the efforts of many different people, from all backgrounds and walks of life. Many of them were teenagers like yourself. Did you know that teenagers helped settle the West? It's true. For example, teenager Nancy Kelsey was among the first pioneers to arrive in California in 1841.

*Student reporters contribute to **CNNfyi.com.***

Student visiting the Vietnam Veterans Memorial

History Makes Us Who We Are

There is no one single "story" in history. Instead, the combined experiences of millions of people across time have come together to form the foundation of American society today.

"So when someone asks you 'Why does history matter today?' you might answer, 'Because in our past, we see a reflection of ourselves.'"

Teenagers also played a role in the Civil War. Thousands of soldiers, like 15-year-old Thomas Galway, fought in this bloody conflict, which shaped the nation's future. You might also be interested to know that young Americans in the Civilian Conservation Corps played a key role in keeping the nation going during the darkest hours of the Great Depression. These are just a few of the many examples of how people about the same age as yourself have helped shape our nation's past. What contributions do you think your generation will make to our national history?

These young people are participating in a reenactment to celebrate the unveiling of the African American Civil War Memorial at Arlington National Cemetery.

Themes in American History

Call to Freedom begins every chapter with a set of theme statements under the heading "You Be the Historian." These statements are drawn from several broad themes central to American history: Geography; Economics; Government; Citizenship; Culture; Science, Technology & Society; Constitutional Heritage; and Global Relations. As you begin each chapter of *Call to Freedom,* you will be asked to respond to the theme statements in a general way, based on your own knowledge. At the end of the chapter, you will be asked to respond to more specific questions about the themes, based on the chapter content.

Geography

The Geography theme explores ways in which the nation's vast and diverse geography has played an important role in American history. The theme examines how the development of the nation's resources has helped shape its economy, society, and politics. In addition, the Geography theme traces how public and government attitudes about resources and the environment have changed over time.

The American West

Economics

President Calvin Coolidge once said that "the business of America is business." The Economics theme asks you to explore the relationship between history and economics in the United States. The theme traces the changing relationship between government, business, and labor in America. It examines how the growth of a strong national free-enterprise economic system has influenced the country's domestic and global politics as well as individual lives and American society.

Catalogs display hundreds of goods for consumers.

Government

Even before the nation had won its independence from Great Britain in the Revolution, the founders saw the need to establish a national government. The Government theme asks you to explore the workings of the American system of government—from the Articles of Confederation up to the present. This theme also examines the relationships between federal, state and local governments and how the system is designed to serve the people.

Scientists such as these underwater archaeologists search for clues about the distant past.

Citizenship

Throughout our history, Americans have struggled to define, possess, and protect individual rights and personal freedoms, such as the freedoms of speech and of religion, the right to vote, and the right to privacy. Americans have also worked to uphold the responsibilities of citizenship that accompany participation in our democracy. The Citizenship theme explores how changing social, economic, and political conditions have influenced the theory and practices of these rights, freedoms, and responsibilities. This theme also examines the many conflicts that have arisen over these democratic values as well as Americans' attempts to resolve these conflicts.

Science, Technology & Society

From the building of the transcontinental railroad and the construction of skyscrapers during the Second Industrial Revolution, to the computers that help you with your school assignments and personal projects today, science and technology have influenced every aspect of our culture and society. The Science, Technology & Society theme explores scientific and technological developments and their influence on the U.S. economy and life.

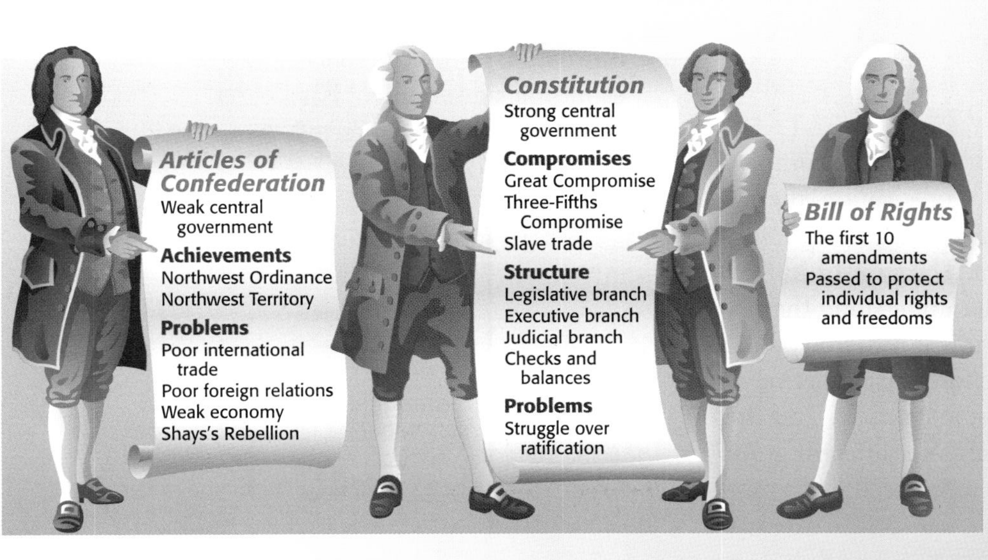

Immigrants to the United States take an oath to become citizens.

The Constitution

Culture

Our nation's rich and unique cultural heritage comes from its many ethnic, racial, and religious groups. The Culture theme examines the influences of diverse culture groups, from before the time of the European explorers to recent immigrants from around the world.

Constitutional Heritage

No study of American history would be complete without examining the U.S. Constitution, the document that provides the legal framework for our democratic government. The Constitutional Heritage theme will help you understand the Constitution's origins and how it has evolved through constitutional amendments, Supreme Court rulings, and congressional action. This theme also explores how individuals and different groups in the nation's history have influenced the Constitution.

Global Relations

Since the first Asian nomads crossed a land bridge to this continent thousands of years ago, America has been involved in global events. The Global Relations theme invites you to trace ways in which our nation's political, social, and economic development has affected—and been affected by—other countries and their people.

International Red Cross medal

Essential Elements of Geography

History and geography share many elements. History describes important events that have taken place from ancient times until the present day. Geography describes how physical environments affect human events. It also examines how people's actions influence the environment around them. One way to look at geography is to identify essential elements of its study. The following six essential elements, developed from the National Geography Standards, will be used throughout Call to Freedom.

The World in Spatial Terms This essential element refers to the way geographers view the world. They look at where things are and how they are arranged on Earth's surface. For example, geographers might be interested to learn why certain cities developed where they did.

Places and Regions Geographers often focus on the physical and human characteristics that make particular parts of Earth special. A region is an area with common characteristics that make it different from surrounding areas. People create regions as a convenient way to study the world. Regions can be large, like North America, or small like a neighborhood.

Physical Systems
Geographers study the physical processes and interactions between four physical systems—Earth's atmosphere, land, water, and life. Physical processes shape and change Earth's physical features and environments.

Human Systems As with physical systems, studying human systems can tell geographers much about the world around us. For example, studying population growth, distribution, and movement helps in understanding human events and their effects on the environment.

Environment and Society One of the most important topics in geography is how people interact with the environment. People depend on the environment's natural resources for survival. However, human activities can have both positive and negative effects on Earth's environment.

The Uses of Geography Historians use geography to understand the past. They look not only at when things happened but where and why they happened. But geography is important to the present as well as the past. People use geography every day to explore how to use Earth's limited resources, such as water and minerals, more effectively and in a way that ensures the success of future generations.

Anasazi homes were built of stone and sun-dried clay bricks. Some were built in openings in high cliffs.

Skills Handbook

The first battle of the American Revolution took place in Lexington.

Critical Thinking

Throughout *Call to Freedom,* you will be asked to think critically about the events and issues that have shaped U.S. history. Critical thinking is the reasoned judgment of information and ideas. The development of critical thinking skills is essential to effective citizenship. Such skills empower you to exercise your civic rights and responsibilities. Helping you develop critical thinking skills is an important goal of *Call to Freedom.* The following critical thinking skills appear in the section reviews and chapter reviews of the book.

1 Analyzing Information is the process of breaking something down and examining the relationships between its parts. Analyzing enables you to better understand the whole. For example, to analyze the outcome of the 1876 presidential election, you might study how, since the election results were disputed, both sides had to come to an agreement before Rutherford B. Hayes could become president.

2 Sequencing is the process of placing events in correct chronological order to better understand the historical relationships between the events. You can sequence events in two basic ways: according to absolute or relative chronology. Absolute chronology means that you pay close attention to the exact dates on which events took place. Placing events on a time line would be an example of absolute chronology. Relative chronology refers to the way events relate to one another. To put events in relative order, you need to know which one happened first, which came next, and so forth.

Coat of arms granted to Christopher Columbus

3 Categorizing is the process by which you group things together by the characteristics they have in common. By putting things or events into categories, it is easier to make comparisons and see differences among them.

4 Identifying Cause and Effect is a part of interpreting the relationships between historical events. A *cause* is an action that leads to an event. The outcome of the action is an *effect.* To explain historical events, historians often point out multiple causes and effects. For example, economic and political differences between the North and South, as well as the issue of slavery, brought about the Civil War—which in turn had many far-reaching effects.

Emancipation Proclamation

5 Comparing and Contrasting is examining events, situations, or points of view for their similarities and differences. *Comparing* focuses on both the similarities and the differences. *Contrasting* focuses only on the differences. For example, a comparison of early Irish and Chinese immigrants to the United States shows that both groups were recruited to help build railroads and that both groups faced discrimination. In contrast, language and racial barriers generally proved more of a problem for Chinese immigrants.

6 **Finding the Main Idea** is combining and sifting through information to determine what is most important. Historical writing often uses many examples and details to support the author's main ideas. Throughout *Call to Freedom,* you will find numerous Reading Checks and questions in section reviews to help you focus on the main ideas in the text.

7 **Summarizing** is the process of taking a large amount of information and boiling it down into a short and clear statement. Summarizing is particularly useful when you need to give a brief account of a longer story or event. For example, the story of the Battle of Gettysburg during the Civil War is an exciting but detailed one. Many different events came together to make up this story. You could summarize these events by saying something like, "In 1863 General Lee led his army north into Pennsylvania where he met the Union forces under General Meade at Gettysburg. After several days of bloody fighting, Lee was forced to retreat. Lee's defeat at Gettysburg was a major turning point in the war."

Lee's surrender at Appomattox Courthouse

8 **Making Generalizations and Predictions** is the process of interpreting information to form more general statements and to guess about what will happen next. A *generalization* is a broad statement that holds true for a variety of historical events or situations. Making generalizations can help you see the "big picture" of historical events, rather than just focusing on details. It is very important, however, that when making generalizations you try not to include situations that do not fit the statement. When this occurs, you run the risk of creating a stereotype, or overgeneralization. A *prediction* is an educated guess about an outcome. When you read history, you should always be asking yourself questions like, "What will happen next? If this person does this, what will that mean for . . . ?", and so on. These types of questions help you draw on information you already know to see patterns throughout history.

9 **Drawing Inferences and Conclusions** is forming possible explanations for an event, a situation, or a problem. When you make an *inference,* you take the information you know to be true and come up with an educated guess about what else you think is true about that situation. A *conclusion* is a prediction about the outcome of a situation based on what you already know. Often, you must be prepared to test your inferences and conclusions against new evidence or arguments. For example, a historian might conclude that women's leadership roles in the abolition movement led to the development of the early women's movement. The historian would then organize the evidence needed to support this conclusion and challenge other arguments.

Women's suffrage supporter

10 **Identifying Points of View** is the process of identifying factors that influence the outlook of an individual or group. A person's point of view includes beliefs and attitudes that are shaped by factors such as age, gender, religion, race, and economic status. This critical thinking skill helps you examine why people see things as they do, and it reinforces the realization that people's views may change over time or with a change in circumstances.

11 Supporting a Point of View involves choosing a viewpoint on a particular event or issue and arguing persuasively for that position. Your argument should be well organized and based on specific evidence that supports the point of view you have chosen. Supporting a point of view often involves working with controversial or emotional issues. For example, you might consider the points of view involved in the struggles between labor unions and businesses in the late 1800s. Whether you choose a position in favor of unions or in favor of businesses, you should state your opinion clearly and give reasons to defend it.

Labor union booklet

12 Identifying Bias is the process of evaluating the opinions of others about events or situations. Bias is an opinion based on prejudice or strong emotions, rather than on fact. It is important to identify bias when looking at historical sources, because biased sources often give you a false sense of what really happened. When looking at both primary and secondary sources, it is always important to keep the author's or speaker's point of view in mind and to adjust your interpretation of the source when you detect any bias.

13 Evaluating is assessing the significance or overall importance of something, such as the success of a reform movement, the actions of a president, or the results of a major conflict. You should base your judgment on standards that others will understand and are likely to share. For example, you might consider the outcome of the Mexican War and evaluate its importance to U.S. politics and expansion. You could also evaluate the effect of the war on the peoples already living in the West.

14 Problem Solving is the process by which you pose workable solutions to difficult situations. The first step in the process is to identify a problem. Next you will need to gather information about the problem, such as its history and the various factors that contribute to the problem. Once you have gathered information, you should list and consider the options for solving the problem. For each of the possible solutions, weigh their advantages and disadvantages and, based on your evaluation, choose and implement a solution. Once the solution has been tried, go back and evaluate the effectiveness of the solution you selected.

15 Decision Making is the process of reviewing a situation and then making decisions or recommendations for the best possible outcome. To complete the process, first identify a situation that requires a solution. Next, gather information that will help you reach a decision. You may need to do some background research to study the history of the situation. Once you have done your research, identify options that might resolve the situation. For each option, predict what the possible consequences might be if that option were followed. Once you have identified the best option, take action by making a recommendation and following through on any tasks that option requires.

Becoming a Strategic Reader

by Dr. Judith Irvin

Everywhere you look, print is all around us. In fact, you would have a hard time stopping yourself from reading. In a normal day, you might read cereal boxes, movie posters, notes from friends, T-shirts, instructions for video games, song lyrics, catalogs, billboards, information on the Internet, magazines, the newspaper, and much, much more. Each form of print is read differently depending on your purpose for reading. You read a menu differently from the way you read poetry, and a motorcycle magazine is read differently than a letter from a friend. Good readers switch easily from one type of text to another. In fact, they probably do not even think about it, they just do it.

When you read, it is helpful to use a strategy to remember the most important ideas. You can use a strategy before you read to help connect information you already know to the new information you will encounter. Before you read, you can also predict what a text will be about by using a previewing strategy. During the reading you can use a strategy to help you focus on main ideas, and after reading you can use a strategy to help you organize what you learned so that you can remember it later. *Call to Freedom* was designed to help you more easily understand the ideas you read. Important reading strategies employed in *Call to Freedom* include the following:

1. Methods to help you **anticipate** what is to come
2. Tools to help you **preview and predict** what the text will be about
3. Ways to help you **use and analyze visual information**
4. Ideas to help you **organize the information** you have learned

1. Anticipate Information

How Can I Use Information I Already Know to Help Me Understand What a New Chapter Will Be About?

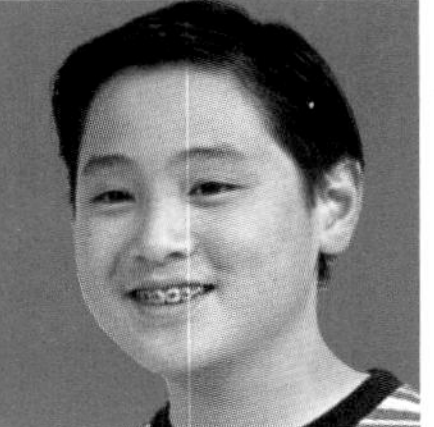

Anticipating what a new chapter will be about helps you connect the upcoming information to what you already know. By drawing on your background knowledge, you can build a bridge to the new material.

1 Each chapter of *Call to Freedom* asks you to explore the main themes of the chapter before you start reading by forming opinions based on your current knowledge.

> **You Be the Historian**
>
> 
>
>
> **What's Your Opinion?** Do you **agree** or **disagree** with the following statements? Support your point of view in your journal.
>
> - **Science, Technology & Society** New technology always makes wars easier to win.
> - **Economics** Wars are bad for a nation's economy.
> - **Citizenship** All citizens have a duty to support their government during a war.

Create a chart like this one to help you analyze the statements.

A Before Reading Agree/Disagree		B After Reading Agree/Disagree
2	New technology always makes wars easier to win.	4
	Wars are bad for a nation's economy.	
	All citizens have a duty to support their government during a war.	

3 Read the text and discuss your answers with classmates.

5 You can also refine your knowledge by answering the You Be the Historian—Reviewing Themes questions in the chapter review.

> **You Be the Historian—Reviewing Themes**
>
> 1. **Science, Technology & Society** How did ironclads reflect the changes that new technology brought to the war?
> 2. **Economics** What effect did the war have on the South's economy?
> 3. **Citizenship** How did northerners and southerners oppose the war, and how did the Union and Confederate governments respond?

Anticipating Information

Step 1 Identify the major concepts of the chapter. In *Call to Freedom*, these are presented in the **You Be the Historian** feature at the beginning of each chapter.

▼

Step 2 Agree or disagree with each of the statements and record your opinions in your journal.

▼

Step 3 Read the text and discuss your responses with your classmates.

▼

Step 4 After reading the chapter, revisit the statements and respond to them again based on what you have learned.

▼

Step 5 Go back and check your knowledge by answering the You Be the Historian—Reviewing Themes questions in the chapter review.

2. Preview and Predict

How Can I Figure out What the Text Is about before I Even Start Reading a Section?

Previewing and Predicting

Step 1 Identify your purpose for reading. Ask yourself what will you do with this information once you have finished reading.

Step 2 Ask yourself what the main idea of the text is and what key vocabulary words you need to know.

Step 3 Use signal words to help identify the structure of the text.

Step 4 Connect the information to what you already know.

Previewing and **predicting** are good methods to help you understand the text. If you take the time to preview and predict before you read, the text will make more sense to you during your reading.

1 Usually, your teacher will set the purpose for reading. After reading some new information, you may be asked to write a summary, take a test, or complete some other type of activity.

2 As you preview the text, use *graphic signals* such as headings, subheadings, and boldfaced type to help you determine what is important in the text. Each section of *Call to Freedom* opens by giving you important clues to help you preview the material.

Looking at the section's **main heading** and **subheadings** can give you an idea of what is to come.

Read to Discover questions give you clues as to the section's main ideas.

Define and Identify terms let you know the key vocabulary you will encounter in the section.

The War in the East

Read to Discover

1. What battles did the Confederates win in Virginia, and why were they important?
2. What stopped the northward advance of the Confederate army?
3. What was the significance of the *Monitor* and the *Virginia*?

Define

- ironclad

Identify

- Thomas "Stonewall" Jackson
- First Battle of Bull Run
- George B. McClellan
- Robert E. Lee
- Seven Days' Battles
- Second Battle of Bull Run
- Battle of Antietam

WHY IT MATTERS TODAY

During the Civil War, powerful new types of warships were developed. Use CNNfyi.com or other **current events** sources to find out about the types of ships used by the U.S. Navy today. Record your findings in your journal.

3 Other tools that can help you in previewing are **signal words**. These words prepare you to think in a certain way. For example, when you see words such as *similar to, same as,* or *different from,* you know that the text will probably compare and contrast two or more ideas. Signal words indicate how the ideas in the text relate to each other. Look at the list below of some of the most common signal words grouped by the type of text structures they indicate.

Signal Words

Cause and Effect	Compare and Contrast	Description	Problem and Solution	Sequence or Chronological Order
• because • since • consequently • this led to…so • if…then • nevertheless • accordingly • because of • as a result of • in order to • may be due to • for this reason	• different from • same as • similar to • as opposed to • instead of • although • however • compared with • as well as • either…or • but • on the other hand • unless	• for instance • for example • such as • to illustrate • in addition • most importantly • another • furthermore • first, second…	• the question is • a solution • one answer is	• not long after • next • then • initially • before • after • finally • preceding • following • on (date) • over time • today • when

4 Learning something new requires that you connect it in some way with something you already know. This means you have to think before you read and while you read. You may want to use a chart like this one to remind yourself of the information already familiar to you and to come up with questions you want answered in your reading. The chart will also help you organize your ideas after you have finished reading.

What I know	What I want to know	What I learned

3. Use and Analyze Visual Information

How Can All the Pictures, Maps, Graphs, and Time Lines with the Text Help Me Be a Stronger Reader?

Analyzing Visual Information

Step 1 As you preview the text, ask yourself how the visual information relates to the text.

Step 2 Generate questions based on the visual information.

Step 3 After reading the text, go back and review the visual information again.

Step 4 Make connections to what you already know.

Using visual information can help you understand and remember the information presented in *Call to Freedom*. Good readers form a picture in their minds when they read. The pictures, charts, graphs, cartoons, time lines, and diagrams that occur throughout *Call to Freedom* are placed strategically to increase your understanding.

1 You might ask yourself questions like:

Why did the author include this information with the text? What details about this visual are mentioned in the text?

After you have read the text, see if you can answer your own questions.

2

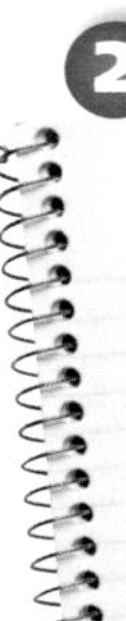

Why is the train important?

Are those people going to get on the train?

Why is the town right beside the railroad tracks?

3 After reading, take another look at the visual information.

4 Try to make connections to what you already know.

4. Organize Information

Once I Learn New Information, How Do I Keep It All Straight So That I Will Remember It?

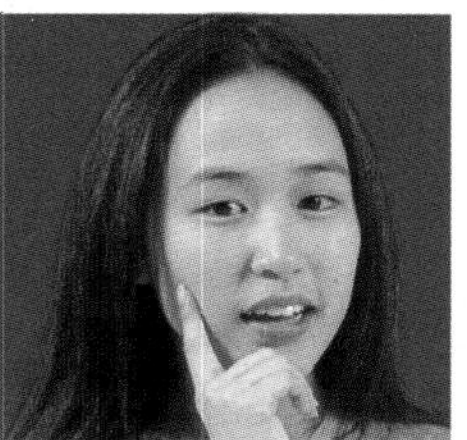

To help you remember what you have read, you need to find a way of **organizing information**. Two good ways of doing this are by using graphic organizers and concept maps. **Graphic organizers** help you understand important relationships—such as cause-and-effect, compare/contrast, sequence of events, and problem/solution—within the text. **Concept maps** provide a useful tool to help you focus on the text's main ideas and organize supporting details.

Constructing Graphic Organizers

Step 1 Preview the text, looking for signal words and main ideas.

Step 2 Form a hypothesis as to which type of graphic organizer would work best to display the information presented.

Step 3 Work individually or with your classmates to create a visual representation of what you read.

Identifying Relationships

Using graphic organizers will help you recall important ideas from the section. They are also study tools you can use to prepare for a quiz or test or to help with a writing assignment. Some of the most common types of graphic organizers are shown below.

Cause and Effect

Events in history cause people to react in certain ways. Cause-and-effect patterns show the relationship between results and the ideas or events that made the results occur. You may want to represent cause-and-effect relationships as one cause leading to multiple effects,

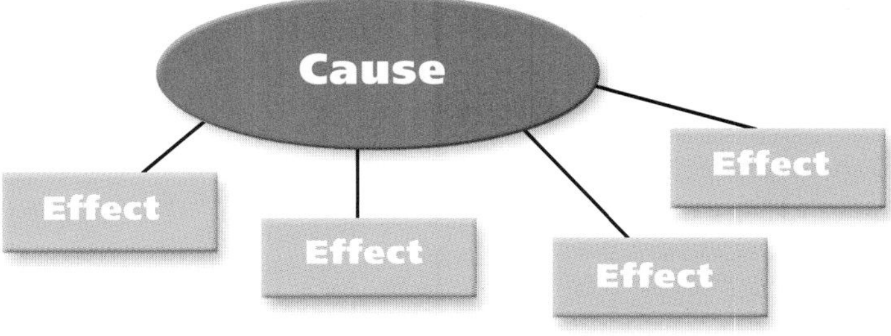

or as a chain of cause-and-effect relationships.

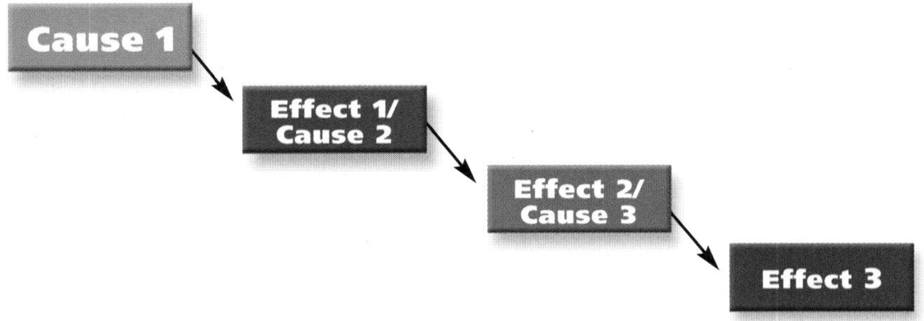

Comparing and Contrasting

Graphic organizers are often useful when you are comparing or contrasting information. Compare-and-contrast diagrams point out similarities and differences between two concepts or ideas.

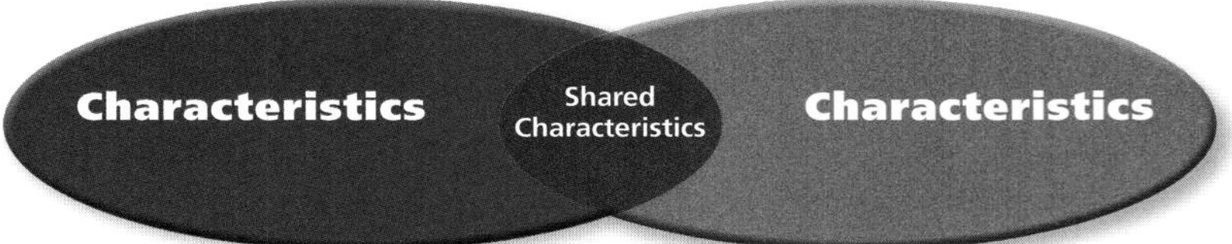

Sequencing

Keeping track of dates and the order in which events took place is essential to understanding history. Sequence or chronological-order diagrams show events or ideas in the order in which they happened.

Problem and Solution

Problem/solution patterns identify at least one problem, offer one or more solutions to the problem, and explain or predict outcomes of the solutions.

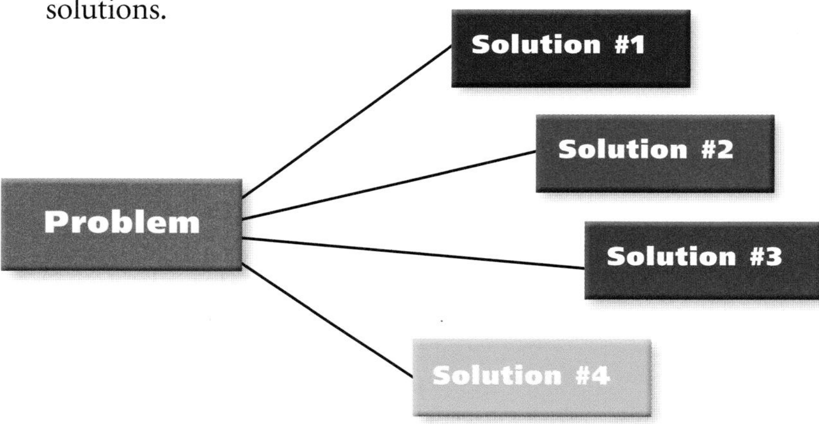

Identifying Main Ideas and Supporting Details

One special type of graphic organizer is the concept map. A concept map, sometimes called a semantic map, allows you to zero in on the most important points of the text. The map is made up of lines, boxes, circles, and/or arrows. It can be as simple or as complex as you need it to be to accurately represent the text.

Here are a few examples of concept maps you might use.

Constructing Concept Maps

Step 1 Preview the text, looking for what type of structure might be appropriate to display a concept map.

Step 2 Taking note of the headings, boldfaced type, and text structure, sketch a concept map you think could best illustrate the text.

Step 3 Using boxes, lines, arrows, circles, or any shapes you like, display the ideas of the text in the concept map.

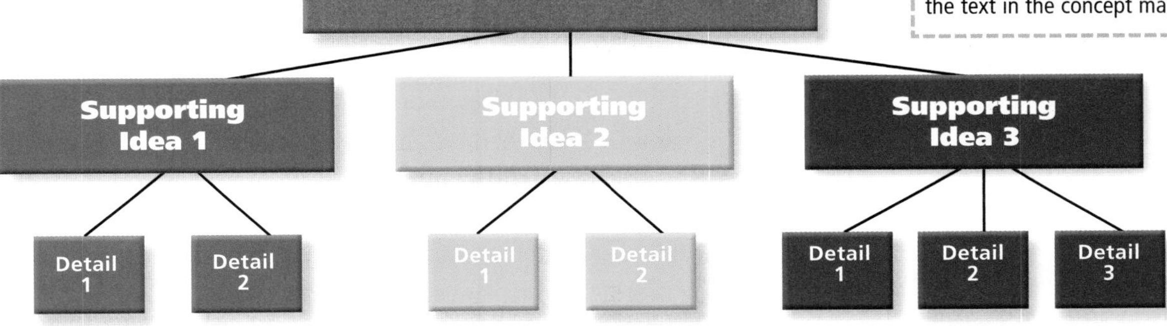

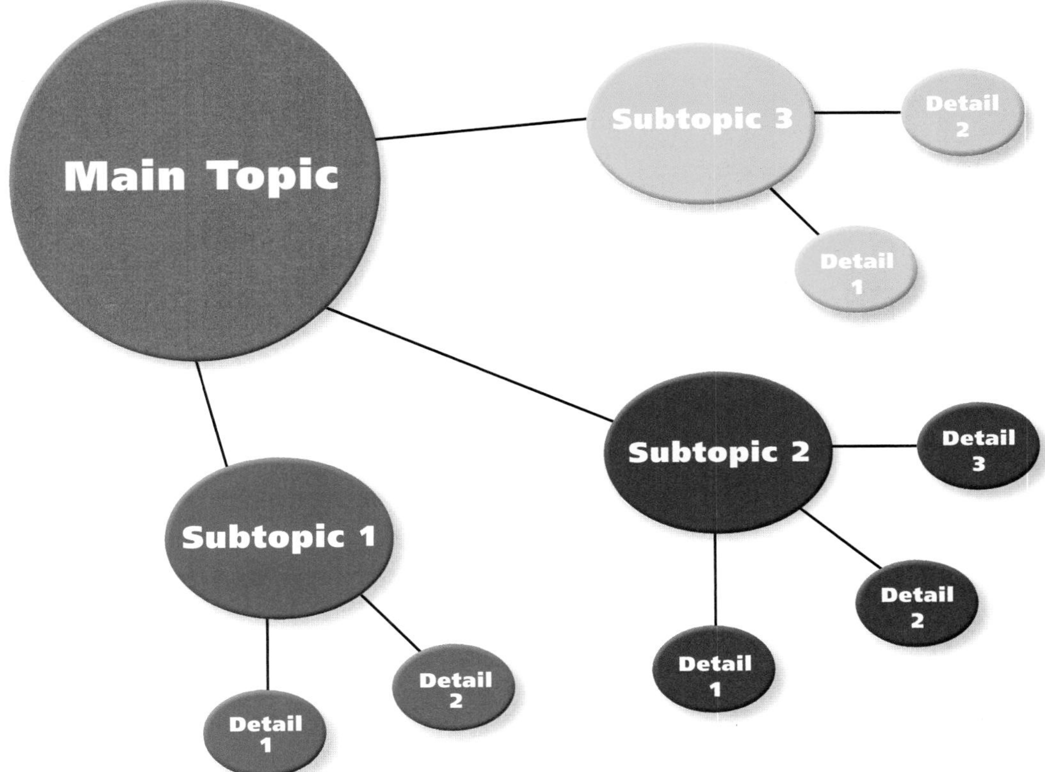

Standardized Test–Taking Strategies

A number of times throughout your school career, you may be asked to take standardized tests. These tests are designed to demonstrate the content and skills you have learned. It is important to keep in mind that in most cases the best way to prepare for these tests is to pay close attention in class and to take every opportunity to improve your general social studies, reading, writing, and mathematical skills.

Tips for Taking the Test

1. Be sure that you are well rested.
2. Be on time and be sure that you have the necessary materials.
3. Listen to the instructions of the teacher.
4. Read directions and questions carefully.
5. **DON'T STRESS!** Just remember what you have learned in class, and you should do well.

▶ **Practice the strategies at go.hrw.com.**

go.hrw.com **Standardized Test–Prep Online**
keyword: SC3 STP

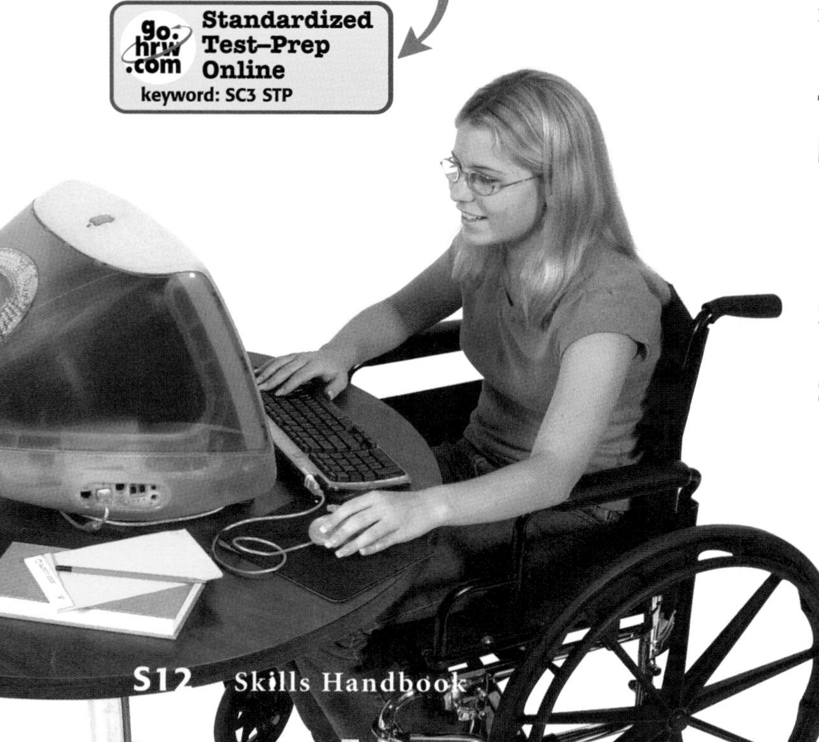

Tackling Social Studies

The social studies portions of many standardized tests are designed to test your knowledge of the content and skills that you have been studying in one or more of your social studies classes. Specific objectives for the test vary, but some of the most common include the following:

1. Demonstrate an understanding of issues and events in history.
2. Demonstrate an understanding of geographic influences on historical issues and events.
3. Demonstrate an understanding of economic and social influences on historical issues and events.
4. Demonstrate an understanding of political influences on historical issues and events.
5. Use critical thinking skills to analyze social studies information.

Standardized tests usually contain multiple-choice and, sometimes, open-ended questions. The multiple-choice items will often be based on maps, tables, charts, graphs, pictures, cartoons, and/or reading passages and documents.

Tips for Answering Multiple-Choice Questions

1. If there is a written or visual piece accompanying the multiple-choice question, pay careful attention to the title, author, and date.
2. Then read through or glance over the content of the piece accompanying the question.
3. Next, read the multiple-choice question for its general intent. Then reread it carefully, looking for words that give clues. For example, words such as *most* or *best* tell you that there may be several correct answers, but you should look for the most appropriate answer.

4. Always read all of the possible answer choices, even if the first one seems like the correct answer. There may be a better choice farther down in the list.
5. Reread the accompanying information (if any is included) carefully to determine the answer to the question. Again, note the title, author, and date of primary-source selections. The answer will rarely be stated exactly as it appears in the primary source, so you will need to use your critical thinking skills to read between the lines.
6. Use your knowledge of the time in history or person involved to help limit the answer choices.
7. Finally, reread the question and selected answer to be sure that you made the best choice and that you marked it correctly on the answer sheet.

Strategies for Success

There are many strategies you can use to help you feel more confident about answering questions on social studies standardized tests. Here are a few suggestions:

1. Adopt an acronym—a word formed from the first letters of other words—that you will always use for analyzing a document or visual that might accompany a question.

Helpful Acronyms

For a document, use **SOAPS**, which stands for

S Subject
O Occasion
A Audience
P Purpose
S Speaker/author

For a picture, cartoon, map, or other visual piece of information, use **OPTIC**, which stands for

O Overview
P Parts (labels or details of the visual)
T Title
I Interrelations (how the different parts of the visual work together)
C Conclusion (what the visual means)

2. Form visual images of maps and try to draw them from memory. The standardized test will most likely include important maps from the time period and subjects you have been studying. For example, in early U.S. history, be able to see in your mind's eye such things as where the New England, middle, and southern colonies were located, what land the Louisiana Purchase and Mexican Cession covered, and the dividing line for slave and free states. Know major physical features, such as the Mississippi River, the Appalachian and Rocky Mountains, the Great Plains, and the various regions of the United States, and be able to place them on a map.
3. When you have finished studying any historical era, try to think of who or what might be important enough for the test. You may want to keep your ideas in a notebook to refer to when it is almost time for the test.
4. Pay particular attention to the Constitution and its development. Many standardized tests contain questions about this all-important document and the period during which it was written. Questions may include Magna Carta, the English Bill of Rights, the Declaration of Independence, and *Common Sense,* as well as many other important historical documents.
5. For the skills area of the tests, practice putting major events and personalities in order in your mind. Sequencing people and events by dates can become a game you play with a friend who also has to take the test. Always ask yourself why this event is important.
6. Follow the tips under "Ready for Reading" on the next page when you encounter a reading passage in social studies, but remember that what you have learned about history can help you in answering reading-comprehension questions.

Ready for Reading

The main goal of the reading sections of most standardized tests is to determine your understanding of different aspects of a reading passage. Basically, if you can grasp the main idea and the author's purpose, then pay attention to the details and vocabulary so that you are able to draw inferences and conclusions, you will do well on the test.

Tips for Answering Multiple-Choice Questions

1. Read the passage as if you were not taking a test.
2. Look at the big picture. Ask yourself questions like, "What is the title?", "What do the illustrations or pictures tell me?", and "What is the author's purpose?"
3. Read the questions. This will help you know what information to look for.
4. Reread the passage, underlining information related to the questions.

Types of Multiple-Choice Questions

1. **Main Idea** This is the most important point of the passage. After reading the passage, locate and underline the main idea.
2. **Significant Details** You will often be asked to recall details from the passage. Read the question and underline the details as you read. But remember that the correct answers do not always match the wording of the passage precisely.
3. **Vocabulary** You will often need to define a word within the context of the passage. Read the answer choices and plug them into the sentence to see what fits best.
4. **Conclusion and Inference** There are often important ideas in the passage that the author does not state directly. Sometimes you must consider multiple parts of the passage to answer the question. If answers refer to only one or two sentences or details in the passage, they are probably incorrect.

5. Go back to the questions and try to answer each one in your mind before looking at the answers.
6. Read all the answer choices and eliminate the ones that are obviously incorrect.

Tips for Answering Short-Answer Questions

1. Read the passage in its entirety, paying close attention to the main events and characters. Jot down information you think is important.
2. If you cannot answer a question, skip it and come back later.
3. Words such as *compare, contrast, interpret, discuss,* and *summarize* appear often in short-answer questions. Be sure you have a complete understanding of each of these words.
4. To help support your answer, return to the passage and skim the parts you underlined.
5. Organize your thoughts on a separate sheet of paper. Write a general statement with which to begin. This will be your topic statement.
6. When writing your answer, be precise but brief. Be sure to refer to details in the passage in your answer.

Targeting Writing

On many standardized tests, you will occasionally be asked to write an essay. In order to write a concise essay, you must learn to organize your thoughts before you begin writing the actual composition. This keeps you from straying too far from the essay's topic.

Tips for Answering Composition Questions

1. Read the question carefully.
2. Decide what kind of essay you are being asked to write. Essays usually fall into one of the following types: persuasive, classificatory, compare/contrast, or "how to." To determine the type of essay, ask yourself questions like, "Am I trying to persuade my audience?", "Am I comparing or contrasting ideas?", or "Am I trying to show the reader how to do something?"
3. Pay attention to key words, such as *compare, contrast, describe, advantages, disadvantages, classify,* or *speculate.* They will give you clues as to the structure that your essay should follow.
4. Organize your thoughts on a separate sheet of paper. You will want to come up with a general topic sentence that expresses your main idea. Make sure this sentence addresses the question. You should then create an outline or some type of graphic organizer to help you organize the points that support your topic sentence.
5. Write your composition using complete sentences. Also, be sure to use correct grammar, spelling, punctuation, and sentence structure.
6. Be sure to proofread your essay once you have finished writing.

Gearing up for Math

On most standardized tests you will be asked to solve a variety of mathematical problems that draw on the skills and information you have learned in class. If math problems sometimes give you difficulty, use the tips below to help yourself work through the problems.

Tips for Solving Math Problems

1. Decide what the goal of the question is. Read or study the problem carefully and determine what information must be found.
2. Locate the factual information. Decide what information represents key facts—the ones you must use to solve the problem. You may also find facts you do not need to reach your solution. In some cases, you may determine that more information is needed to solve the problem. If so, ask yourself, "What assumptions can I make about this problem?" or "Do I need a formula to help solve this problem?"
3. Decide what strategies you might use to solve the problem, how you might use them, and what form your solution will be in. For example, will you need to create a graph or chart? Will you need to solve an equation? Will your answer be in words or numbers? By knowing what type of solution you should reach, you may be able to eliminate some of the choices.
4. Apply your strategy to solve the problem and compare your answer to the choices.
5. If the answer is still not clear, read the problem again. If you had to make calculations to reach your answer, use estimation to see if your answer makes sense.

The Geographer's Tool Kit

A map is an illustration drawn to scale of all or part of Earth's surface. Knowing how to read and interpret maps is one of the most valuable tools you can use to study history.

Types of Maps

Types of maps include physical maps, political maps, and thematic (special-purpose) maps.

Physical maps illustrate the natural landscape of an area—the landforms that mark Earth's surface. Physical maps often use shading to show relief—the existence of mountains, hills, and valleys—and colors to show elevation, or height above sea level. The map of the United States on pages A2–A3 is strictly a physical map.

Political maps illustrate political units, such as states and nations, and use color variations and lines to mark boundaries, dots for major cities, and stars or stars within circles for capitals. Political maps show information such as territorial changes or military alliances. The map of the United States on page A1 is a political map.

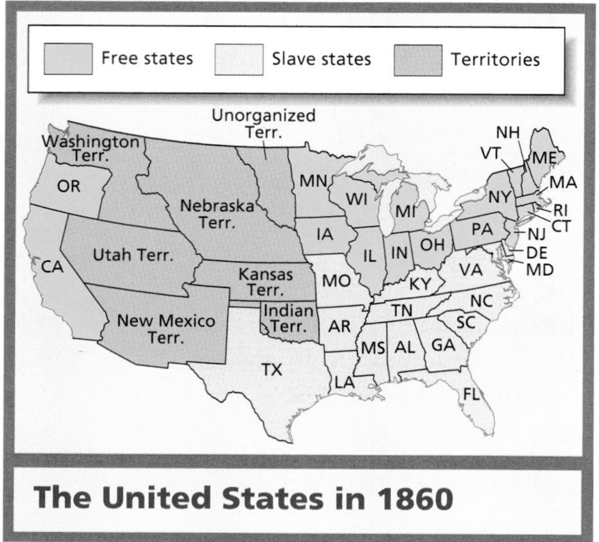

The United States in 1860

Thematic (special-purpose) maps present specific information, such as the routes of explorers or the outcome of an election. Both the maps shown on these two pages are thematic maps.

Map Features

Most maps have some features in common. Familiarity with these elements makes reading maps easier.

Titles, legends, and labels A map's title tells you what the map is about, what areas are shown, and usually what time period is represented. The legend, or key, explains any special symbols, colors, or shadings used on the map. Labels designate political and geographic place-names as well as physical features like mountain ranges and rivers.

The global grid The absolute location of any place on Earth is given in terms of latitude (degrees north or south of the equator) and longitude (degrees east or west of the prime meridian). The symbol for a degree is °. Degrees are divided into 60 equal parts called minutes, which are represented by the symbol ′. The global grid is created by the intersecting lines of latitude (parallels) and lines of longitude (meridians). Lines of latitude and longitude may sometimes be indicated by tick marks near the edge of a map or by lines across an entire map.

Directions and distance Most maps in *Call to Freedom* have a compass rose, or directional indicator. The compass rose indicates the four cardinal points—*N* for north, *S* for south, *E* for east, and *W* for west. You can also find intermediate directions—northeast, southeast, southwest, and northwest—using the compass rose. This helps in describing the relative location of a place. (If a map has no compass rose, assume that north is at the top, east is to the right, and so on.) Many maps in this textbook include a scale, showing both miles and kilometers, to help you relate distances on the map to actual distances on Earth's surface.

Map projections Because Earth is a sphere, it is best represented by a three-dimensional globe. Although a flat map is an imperfect representation of Earth's surface, mapmakers have devised various ways of showing Earth two dimensionally. These different flat views of Earth's surface are called projections.

Every map projection, and therefore every map, distorts to some extent at least one of the following aspects: (1) the shape of land areas, (2) their relative sizes, (3) directions, or (4) distances. Mapmakers choose the projection that least distorts what they wish to show. For example, an equal-area projection shows the relative sizes of different countries or continents quite accurately but distorts shapes somewhat.

How to Read a Map

1. **Determine the focus of the map.** Read the map's title and labels to determine the map's focus—its subject and the geographic area it covers.
2. **Study the map legend.** Read the legend and become familiar with any special symbols, lines, colors, and shadings used on the map.
3. **Check directions and distance.** Use the directional indicator and scale as needed to determine direction, location, and distance between various points on the map.
4. **Check the grid lines.** Refer to lines of longitude and latitude or to a locator map to place the area on the map in a larger context.
5. **Study the map.** Study the map's basic features and details, keeping its purpose in mind. If it is a special-purpose map, study the specific information being presented.

The War in the East, 1861–1862

Interpreting Maps One Union objective was to capture the Confederate capital of Richmond.

Skills Assessment **Locate** What battle took place in Maryland? What was the outcome?

United States of America: Political

WASHINGTON
Seattle
Tacoma
Olympia
Spokane
Puget Sound
Strait of Juan de Fuca
Franklin D. Roosevelt Lake
Portland
Columbia River
OREGON
Salem
Eugene
Goose Lake
IDAHO
Boise
Sun Valley
Pocatello
Snake River
Pend Oreille
Flathead Lake
MONTANA
Great Falls
Helena
Billings
Missouri River
Fort Peck Lake
Yellowstone River
Yellowstone Lake
NORTH DAKOTA
Lake Sakakawea
Grand Forks
Bismarck
Fargo
Lake Oahe
SOUTH DAKOTA
Pierre
Rapid City
Sioux Falls
Sioux City
WYOMING
Cheyenne
NEBRASKA
Omaha
Lincoln
Platte River
PACIFIC OCEAN
Cape Mendocino
CALIFORNIA
Shasta Lake
Sacramento River
Sacramento
Berkeley
Oakland
San Francisco
San Francisco Bay
San Jose
Monterey Bay
San Joaquin River
Fresno
Santa Barbara
Ventura
Los Angeles
Long Beach
Channel Islands
Riverside
Palm Springs
Anaheim
Santa Ana
Salton Sea
San Diego
NEVADA
Pyramid Lake
Reno
Carson City
Lake Tahoe
Las Vegas
Lake Mead
UTAH
Great Salt Lake
Ogden
Salt Lake City
Utah Lake
Provo
Green River
Lake Powell
COLORADO
Boulder
Denver
Vail
Aspen
Colorado Springs
Pueblo
KANSAS
Topeka
Wichita
Arkansas River
ARIZONA
Colorado River
Flagstaff
Phoenix
Gila River
Casa Grande
Tucson
NEW MEXICO
Taos
Santa Fe
Albuquerque
Las Cruces
OKLAHOMA
Canadian River
Keystone Lake
Tulsa
Oklahoma City
Eufaula Lake
Lawton
Lake Texoma
TEXAS
Amarillo
Lubbock
Abilene
Fort Worth
Dallas
Midland
Odessa
El Paso
Pecos River
Brazos River
Colorado River
Waco
Austin
Houston
Rio Grande
Amistad Reservoir
San Antonio
Laredo
Corpus Christi
PADRE ISLAND
MEXICO
GULF OF CALIFORNIA
130°W
125°W
120°W
45°N
40°N
35°N
30°N
25°N

To understand the relative locations of Alaska and Hawaii, as well as the vast distances separating them from the rest of the United States, see the world map.

HAWAII
KAUAI
NIIHAU
OAHU
Honolulu
MOLOKAI
MAUI
LANAI
KAHOOLAWE
PACIFIC OCEAN
Hilo
HAWAII
22°N
19°N
160°W
155°W
0 75 150 Miles
0 75 150 Kilometers

ALASKA
ARCTIC OCEAN
RUSSIA
Arctic Circle
Bering Strait
65°N
Nome
ST. LAWRENCE ISLAND
ST. MATTHEW ISLAND
NUNIVAK ISLAND
Yukon River
Fairbanks
CANADA
BERING SEA
Anchorage
Valdez
ATTU ISLAND
ALEUTIAN ISLANDS
KODIAK ISLAND
Gulf of Alaska
Skagway
Juneau
ALEXANDER ARCHIPELAGO
PACIFIC OCEAN
60°N
55°N
50°N
170°E
180°
170°W
160°W
150°W
140°W
0 250 500 Miles
0 250 500 Kilometers
Projection: Albers Equal Area

CANADA
MINNESOTA
WISCONSIN
MICHIGAN
IOWA
ILLINOIS
INDIANA
OHIO
PENNSYLVANIA
NEW YORK
MAINE
VT
NH
MA
CT
RI
NJ
DE
MD
WEST VIRGINIA
VIRGINIA
KENTUCKY
MISSOURI
TENNESSEE
NORTH CAROLINA
SOUTH CAROLINA
ARKANSAS
MISSISSIPPI
ALABAMA
GEORGIA
LOUISIANA
FLORIDA
ATLANTIC OCEAN
GULF OF MEXICO
THE BAHAMAS
CUBA
National capital
State capitals
Other cities
0 250 500 Miles
0 250 500 Kilometers
Projection: Albers Equal Area
Robinson Projection

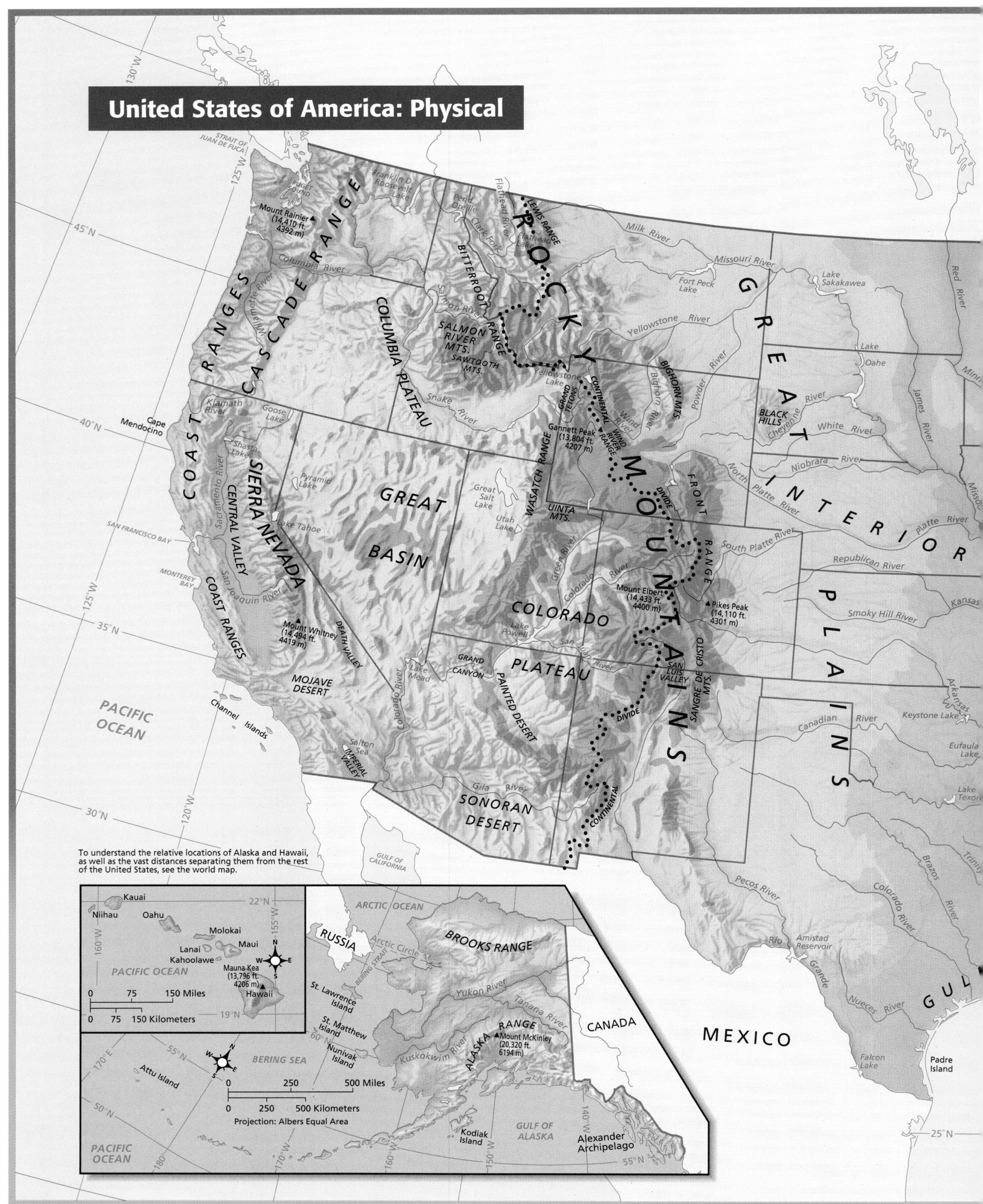
United States of America: Physical
STRAIT OF JUAN DE FUCA
PUGET SOUND
Mount Rainier (14,410 ft. 4392 m)
CASCADE RANGE
COAST RANGES
Franklin D. Roosevelt Lake
Pend Oreille Lake
Flathead River
LEWIS RANGE
Flathead Lake
Clark Fork
BITTERROOT RANGE
ROCKY MOUNTAINS
Milk River
Missouri River
Fort Peck Lake
Lake Sakakawea
GREAT INTERIOR PLAINS
Red River
Columbia River
Willamette River
COLUMBIA PLATEAU
Salmon River
SALMON RIVER MTS.
SAWTOOTH MTS.
Yellowstone River
Yellowstone Lake
Lake Oahe
BIGHORN MTS.
Bighorn River
Powder River
Snake River
GRAND TETONS
CONTINENTAL DIVIDE
WIND RIVER RANGE
Gannett Peak (13,804 ft. 4207 m)
Wind River
BLACK HILLS
Cheyenne River
White River
James River
Klamath River
Goose Lake
Cape Mendocino
Shasta Lake
SIERRA NEVADA
Sacramento River
CENTRAL VALLEY
Pyramid Lake
GREAT BASIN
Great Salt Lake
Utah Lake
WASATCH RANGE
UINTA MTS.
FRONT RANGE
Niobrara River
North Platte River
Platte River
SAN FRANCISCO BAY
Lake Tahoe
MONTEREY BAY
San Joaquin River
Green River
Colorado River
South Platte River
Republican River
Mount Elbert (14,433 ft. 4400 m)
Pikes Peak (14,110 ft. 4301 m)
Smoky Hill River
Kansas
Mount Whitney (14,494 ft. 4419 m)
DEATH VALLEY
COLORADO PLATEAU
Lake Powell
San Juan River
Lake Mead
GRAND CANYON
PAINTED DESERT
SAN LUIS VALLEY
SANGRE DE CRISTO MTS.
MOJAVE DESERT
PACIFIC OCEAN
Channel Islands
Canadian River
Keystone Lake
Arkansas
Eufaula Lake
Salton Sea
IMPERIAL VALLEY
Gila River
SONORAN DESERT
Lake Texoma
GULF OF CALIFORNIA
Pecos River
Brazos River
Colorado River
Trinity
Rio Grande
Amistad Reservoir
Nueces River
Falcon Lake
Padre Island
MEXICO
GULF
45°N
40°N
35°N
30°N
25°N
130°W
125°W
120°W
To understand the relative locations of Alaska and Hawaii, as well as the vast distances separating them from the rest of the United States, see the world map.
Kauai
Niihau
Oahu
Molokai
Maui
Lanai
Kahoolawe
Mauna Kea (13,796 ft. 4206 m)
Hawaii
PACIFIC OCEAN
0 75 150 Miles
0 75 150 Kilometers
22°N
19°N
160°W
155°W
ARCTIC OCEAN
RUSSIA
Arctic Circle
BERING STRAIT
BROOKS RANGE
St. Lawrence Island
St. Matthew Island
Nunivak Island
Yukon River
Tanana River
CANADA
ALASKA RANGE
Mount McKinley (20,320 ft. 6194 m)
Kuskokwim River
BERING SEA
Attu Island
0 250 500 Miles
0 250 500 Kilometers
Projection: Albers Equal Area
Kodiak Island
GULF OF ALASKA
Alexander Archipelago
PACIFIC OCEAN
60°N
55°N
50°N
170°E
180°
170°W
160°W
150°W
140°W

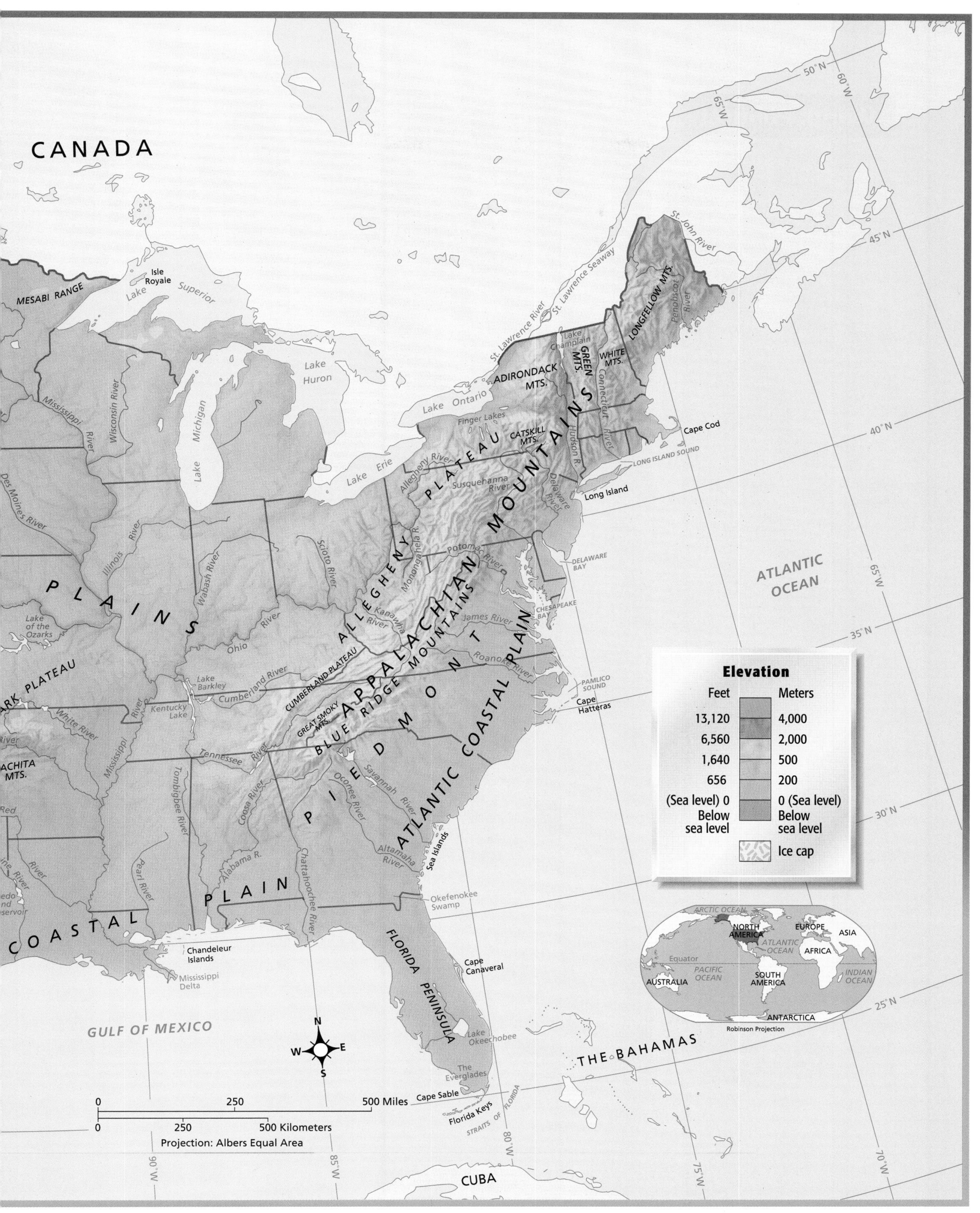

CANADA
MESABI RANGE
Isle Royale
Lake Superior
Lake Huron
Lake Michigan
Lake Ontario
Lake Erie
St. Lawrence River
St. Lawrence Seaway
St. John River
LONGFELLOW MTS.
Penobscot River
Lake Champlain
GREEN MTS.
WHITE MTS.
ADIRONDACK MTS.
Connecticut River
Finger Lakes
CATSKILL MTS.
Hudson R.
Cape Cod
LONG ISLAND SOUND
Long Island
Allegheny River
Susquehanna River
Delaware River
ALLEGHENY PLATEAU
APPALACHIAN MOUNTAINS
Monongahela R.
Potomac River
DELAWARE BAY
CHESAPEAKE BAY
James River
Kanawha River
Scioto River
Wabash River
Illinois River
Mississippi River
Wisconsin River
Des Moines River
PLAINS
Lake of the Ozarks
Ohio River
OZARK PLATEAU
Lake Barkley
Cumberland River
CUMBERLAND PLATEAU
Kentucky Lake
White River
OUACHITA MTS.
Red River
GREAT SMOKY MTS.
BLUE RIDGE MOUNTAINS
PIEDMONT
Roanoke River
PAMLICO SOUND
Cape Hatteras
ATLANTIC COASTAL PLAIN
Tennessee River
Tombigbee River
Coosa River
Oconee River
Savannah River
Alabama R.
Chattahoochee River
Altamaha River
Sea Islands
Pearl River
COASTAL PLAIN
Okefenokee Swamp
Chandeleur Islands
Mississippi Delta
FLORIDA PENINSULA
Cape Canaveral
Lake Okeechobee
The Everglades
Cape Sable
Florida Keys
STRAITS OF FLORIDA
GULF OF MEXICO
THE BAHAMAS
CUBA
ATLANTIC OCEAN
N
E
S
W
0
250
500 Miles
0
250
500 Kilometers
Projection: Albers Equal Area
Elevation
Feet
Meters
13,120
4,000
6,560
2,000
1,640
500
656
200
(Sea level) 0
0 (Sea level)
Below sea level
Below sea level
Ice cap
ARCTIC OCEAN
NORTH AMERICA
EUROPE
ASIA
ATLANTIC OCEAN
AFRICA
Equator
PACIFIC OCEAN
SOUTH AMERICA
AUSTRALIA
INDIAN OCEAN
ANTARCTICA
Robinson Projection
50° N
45° N
40° N
35° N
30° N
25° N
60° W
65° W
70° W
75° W
80° W
85° W
90° W

World: Political

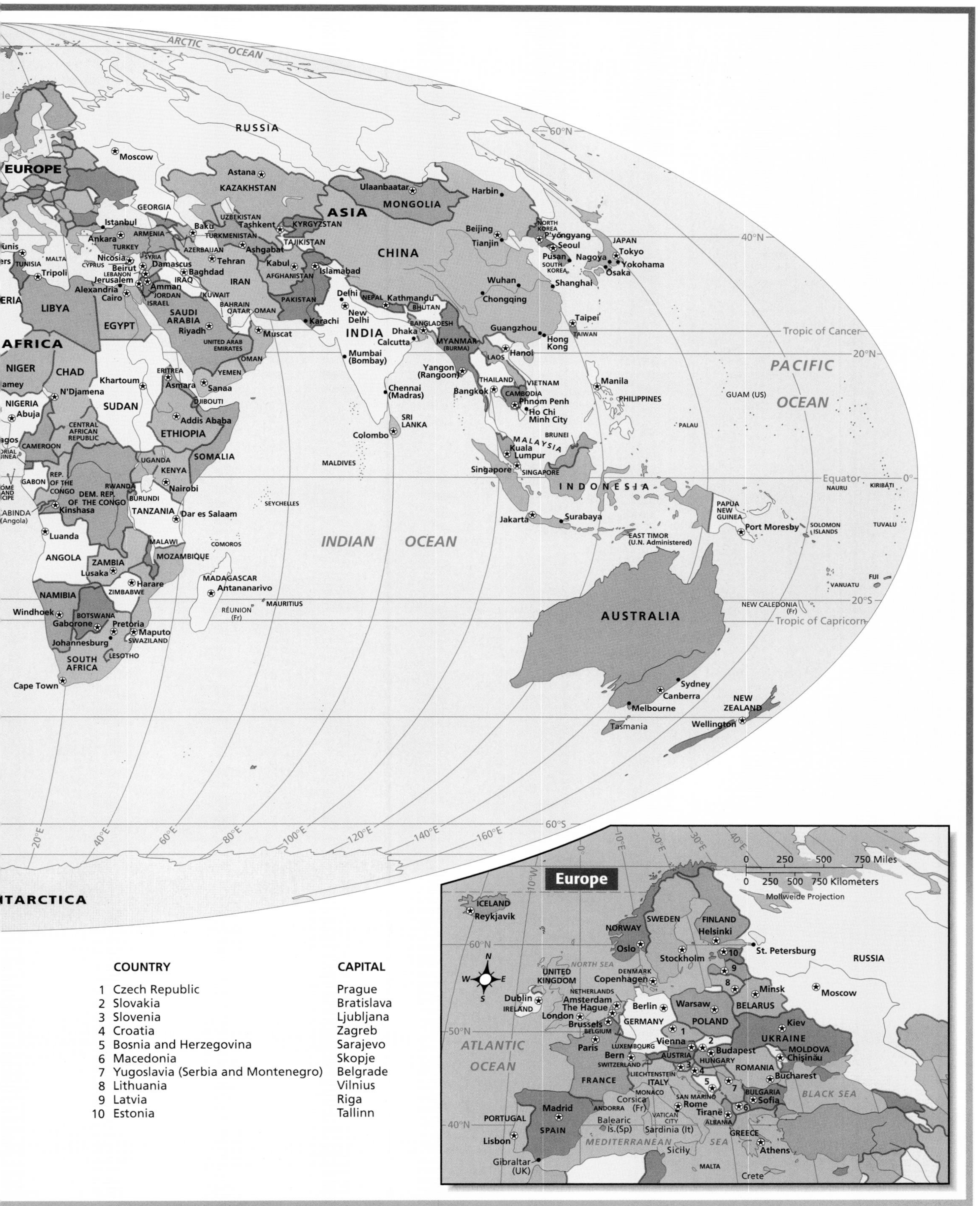

	COUNTRY	CAPITAL
1	Czech Republic	Prague
2	Slovakia	Bratislava
3	Slovenia	Ljubljana
4	Croatia	Zagreb
5	Bosnia and Herzegovina	Sarajevo
6	Macedonia	Skopje
7	Yugoslavia (Serbia and Montenegro)	Belgrade
8	Lithuania	Vilnius
9	Latvia	Riga
10	Estonia	Tallinn

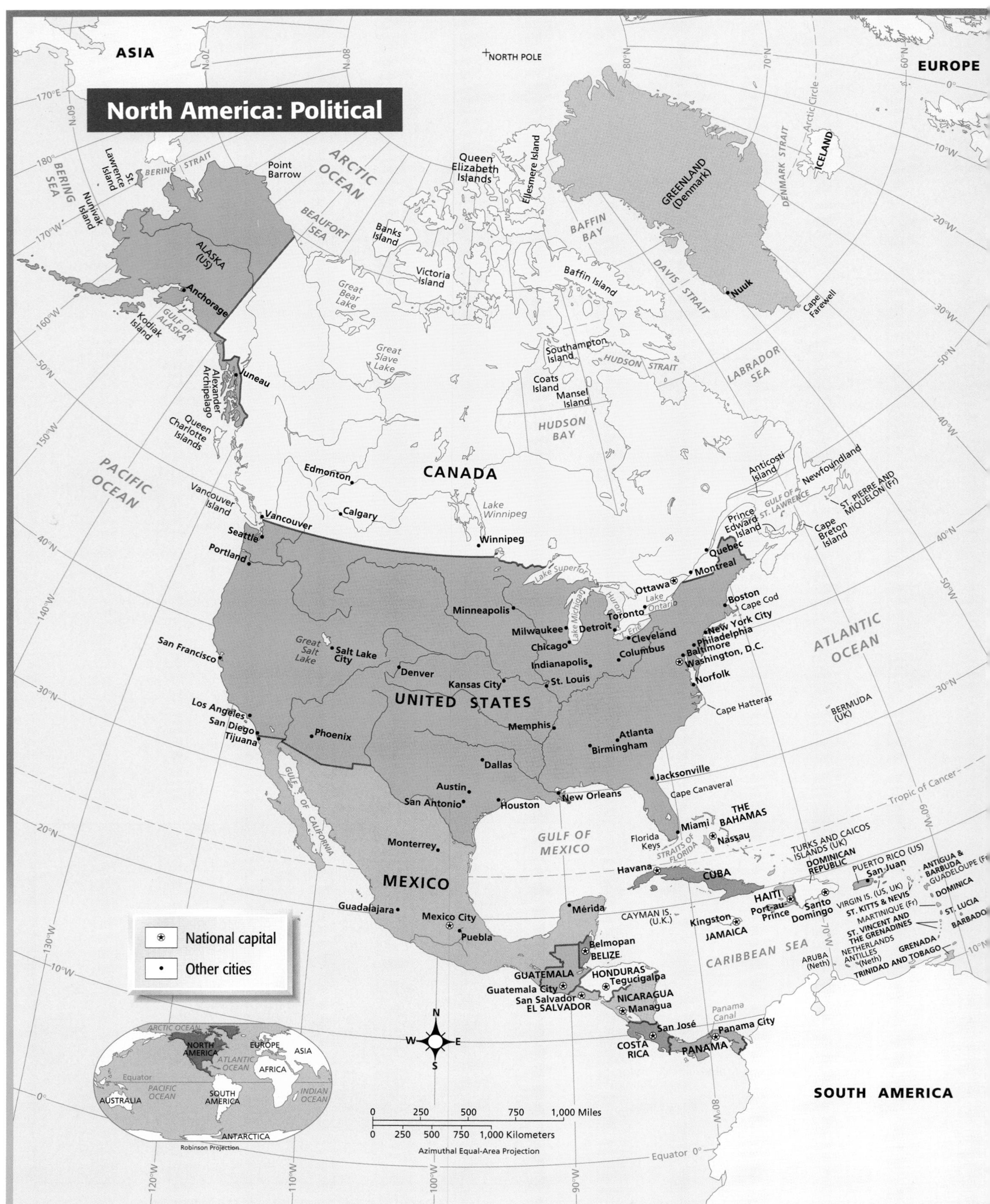
North America: Political
ASIA
EUROPE
NORTH POLE
ARCTIC OCEAN
BERING SEA
BERING STRAIT
BEAUFORT SEA
BAFFIN BAY
DAVIS STRAIT
DENMARK STRAIT
HUDSON STRAIT
LABRADOR SEA
HUDSON BAY
GULF OF ALASKA
PACIFIC OCEAN
ATLANTIC OCEAN
GULF OF MEXICO
CARIBBEAN SEA
GULF OF CALIFORNIA
GULF OF ST. LAWRENCE
STRAITS OF FLORIDA
CANADA
UNITED STATES
MEXICO
GREENLAND (Denmark)
ICELAND
ALASKA (US)
CUBA
JAMAICA
HAITI
DOMINICAN REPUBLIC
THE BAHAMAS
BELIZE
GUATEMALA
HONDURAS
EL SALVADOR
NICARAGUA
COSTA RICA
PANAMA
SOUTH AMERICA
National capital
Other cities
0 250 500 750 1,000 Miles
0 250 500 750 1,000 Kilometers
Azimuthal Equal-Area Projection
Robinson Projection

South America: Political
CENTRAL AMERICA
CARIBBEAN SEA
ATLANTIC OCEAN
PACIFIC OCEAN
COLOMBIA
VENEZUELA
GUYANA
SURINAME
FRENCH GUIANA (Fr)
ECUADOR
PERU
BRAZIL
BOLIVIA
PARAGUAY
CHILE
ARGENTINA
URUGUAY
Barranquilla
Cartagena
Medellín
Bogotá
Cali
Caracas
Lake Maracaibo
Orinoco River
Georgetown
Paramaribo
Cayenne
Malpelo Island (Colombia)
Quito
Guayaquil
Galápagos Islands (Ecuador)
Río Negro
Amazon River
Belém
Marañón River
Ucayali River
Trujillo
Callao
Lima
Arequipa
Lake Titicaca
La Paz
Lake Poopó
Sucre
Recife
Salvador
Brasília
São Francisco River
Belo Horizonte
Campinas
São Paulo
Rio de Janeiro
Curitiba
Paraguay River
Asunción
Paraná River
Uruguay River
Pôrto Alegre
San Ambrosio Island (Chile)
San Félix Island (Chile)
Juan Fernández Islands (Chile)
Córdoba
Rosario
Valparaíso
Santiago
Buenos Aires
Morón
San Justo
Lomas de Zamora
Montevideo
RÍO DE LA PLATA
STRAIT OF MAGELLAN
Tierra del Fuego
FALKLAND ISLANDS (UK)
SOUTH GEORGIA ISLAND (UK)
Equator 0°
Tropic of Capricorn
20°N
10°N
10°S
20°S
30°S
40°S
50°S
110°W
100°W
90°W
80°W
70°W
60°W
50°W
40°W
30°W
20°W
N
S
E
W
National capital
Other cities
0 250 500 750 1,000 Miles
0 250 500 750 1,000 Kilometers
Azimuthal Equal-Area Projection
ARCTIC OCEAN
NORTH AMERICA
EUROPE
ASIA
ATLANTIC OCEAN
AFRICA
Equator
PACIFIC OCEAN
SOUTH AMERICA
INDIAN OCEAN
AUSTRALIA
ANTARCTICA
Robinson Projection

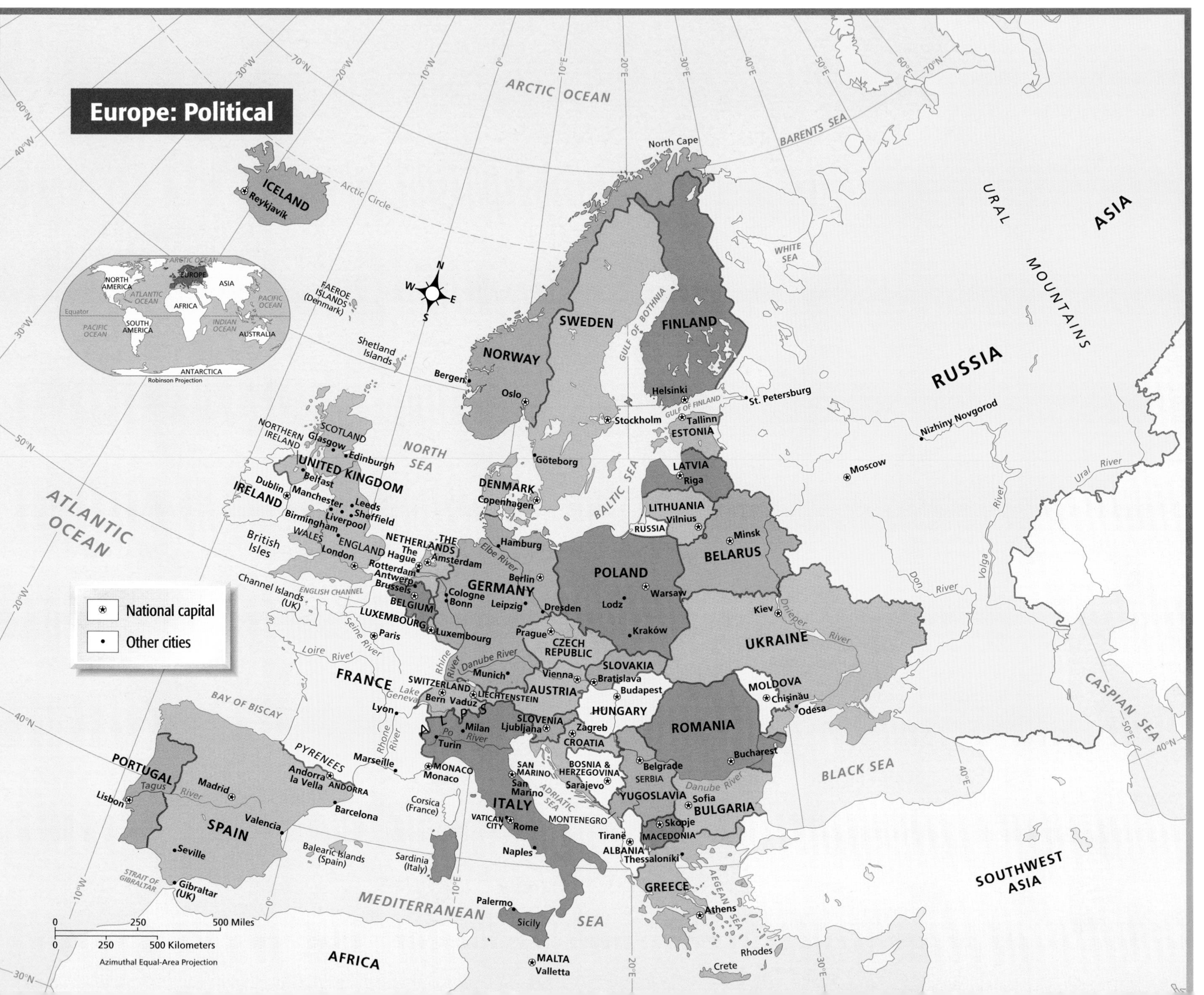
Europe: Political
ARCTIC OCEAN
BARENTS SEA
North Cape
Arctic Circle
ICELAND
Reykjavik
NORTH AMERICA
EUROPE
ASIA
AFRICA
SOUTH AMERICA
AUSTRALIA
ANTARCTICA
ARCTIC OCEAN
ATLANTIC OCEAN
PACIFIC OCEAN
INDIAN OCEAN
Equator
Robinson Projection
FAEROE ISLANDS (Denmark)
Shetland Islands
WHITE SEA
URAL MOUNTAINS
ASIA
RUSSIA
St. Petersburg
Nizhniy Novgorod
Moscow
Ural River
Volga River
Don River
NORWAY
Bergen
Oslo
SWEDEN
Stockholm
Göteborg
GULF OF BOTHNIA
FINLAND
Helsinki
GULF OF FINLAND
Tallinn
ESTONIA
LATVIA
Riga
LITHUANIA
Vilnius
RUSSIA
BELARUS
Minsk
NORTH SEA
BALTIC SEA
DENMARK
Copenhagen
SCOTLAND
NORTHERN IRELAND
Glasgow
Edinburgh
UNITED KINGDOM
Belfast
Dublin
IRELAND
Manchester
Leeds
Sheffield
Liverpool
Birmingham
WALES
ENGLAND
London
British Isles
ATLANTIC OCEAN
Channel Islands (UK)
ENGLISH CHANNEL
THE NETHERLANDS
The Hague
Amsterdam
Rotterdam
Antwerp
Brussels
BELGIUM
LUXEMBOURG
Luxembourg
Hamburg
Elbe River
Berlin
GERMANY
Cologne
Bonn
Leipzig
Dresden
POLAND
Warsaw
Lodz
Kraków
Kiev
Dnieper River
UKRAINE
National capital
Other cities
Paris
Seine River
Loire River
Rhine River
Danube River
Prague
CZECH REPUBLIC
SLOVAKIA
Munich
Vienna
Bratislava
Budapest
MOLDOVA
Chişinău
Odesa
CASPIAN SEA
FRANCE
SWITZERLAND
Lake Geneva
Bern
Vaduz
LIECHTENSTEIN
AUSTRIA
HUNGARY
ROMANIA
BAY OF BISCAY
Lyon
ALPS
Milan
Po River
Turin
SLOVENIA
Ljubljana
Zagreb
CROATIA
Bucharest
Rhone River
PYRENEES
Marseille
MONACO
Monaco
SAN MARINO
San Marino
BOSNIA & HERZEGOVINA
Sarajevo
Belgrade
SERBIA
BLACK SEA
PORTUGAL
Tagus River
Madrid
Andorra la Vella
ANDORRA
Lisbon
Barcelona
Corsica (France)
ADRIATIC SEA
YUGOSLAVIA
Sofia
BULGARIA
ITALY
Valencia
SPAIN
VATICAN CITY
Rome
MONTENEGRO
Skopje
Tiranë
MACEDONIA
ALBANIA
Thessaloníki
Seville
Balearic Islands (Spain)
Sardinia (Italy)
Naples
SOUTHWEST ASIA
STRAIT OF GIBRALTAR
Gibraltar (UK)
GREECE
AEGEAN SEA
MEDITERRANEAN SEA
Palermo
Sicily
Athens
0 250 500 Miles
0 250 500 Kilometers
Azimuthal Equal-Area Projection
AFRICA
MALTA
Valletta
Rhodes
Crete

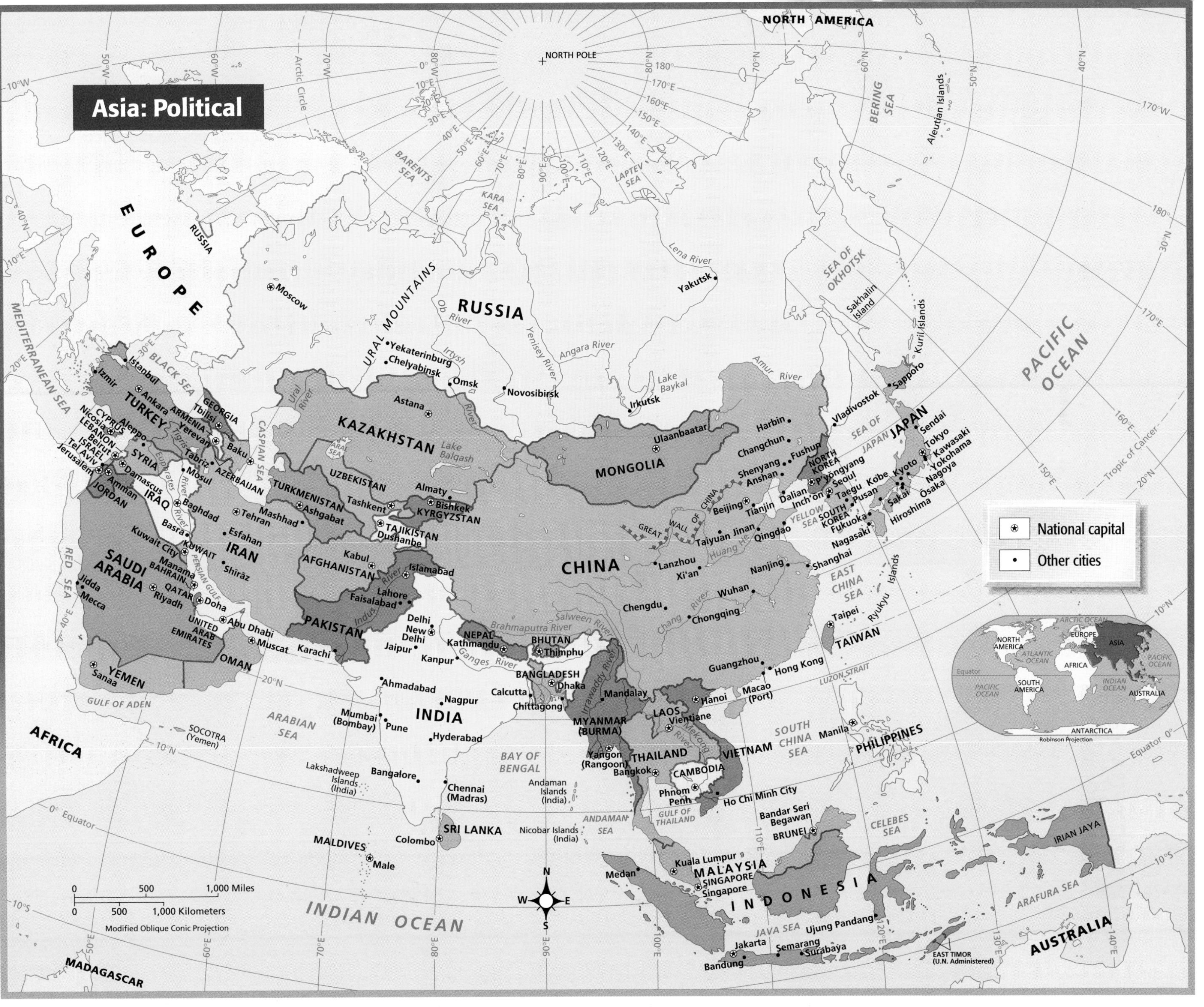

Asia: Political
National capital
Other cities
Modified Oblique Conic Projection
1,000 Miles
1,000 Kilometers
Robinson Projection
EUROPE
RUSSIA
KAZAKHSTAN
MONGOLIA
CHINA
INDIA
JAPAN
NORTH KOREA
SOUTH KOREA
TAIWAN
PHILIPPINES
VIETNAM
LAOS
THAILAND
CAMBODIA
MYANMAR (BURMA)
BANGLADESH
BHUTAN
NEPAL
PAKISTAN
AFGHANISTAN
TAJIKISTAN
KYRGYZSTAN
UZBEKISTAN
TURKMENISTAN
IRAN
IRAQ
SYRIA
TURKEY
GEORGIA
ARMENIA
AZERBAIJAN
CYPRUS
LEBANON
ISRAEL
JORDAN
KUWAIT
BAHRAIN
QATAR
UNITED ARAB EMIRATES
OMAN
YEMEN
SAUDI ARABIA
SRI LANKA
MALDIVES
MALAYSIA
SINGAPORE
BRUNEI
INDONESIA
IRIAN JAYA
EAST TIMOR (U.N. Administered)
AUSTRALIA
AFRICA
MADAGASCAR
NORTH AMERICA
NORTH POLE
PACIFIC OCEAN
INDIAN OCEAN
BERING SEA
SEA OF OKHOTSK
SEA OF JAPAN
YELLOW SEA
EAST CHINA SEA
SOUTH CHINA SEA
CELEBES SEA
JAVA SEA
ARAFURA SEA
BAY OF BENGAL
ANDAMAN SEA
ARABIAN SEA
GULF OF ADEN
RED SEA
PERSIAN GULF
CASPIAN SEA
BLACK SEA
MEDITERRANEAN SEA
ARAL SEA
BARENTS SEA
KARA SEA
LAPTEV SEA
GULF OF THAILAND
LUZON STRAIT
URAL MOUNTAINS
GREAT WALL OF CHINA
Aleutian Islands
Kuril Islands
Ryukyu Islands
Sakhalin Island
Andaman Islands (India)
Nicobar Islands (India)
Lakshadweep Islands (India)
SOCOTRA (Yemen)
Arctic Circle
Tropic of Cancer
Equator
Ob River
Irtysh River
Yenisey River
Angara River
Lena River
Amur River
Ural River
Huang He
Chang River
Mekong River
Salween River
Irrawaddy River
Brahmaputra River
Ganges River
Indus River
Tigris River
Euphrates River
Lake Baykal
Lake Balqash
Moscow
Yekaterinburg
Chelyabinsk
Omsk
Novosibirsk
Irkutsk
Yakutsk
Vladivostok
Astana
Almaty
Bishkek
Tashkent
Dushanbe
Ashgabat
Ulaanbaatar
Beijing
Tianjin
Shanghai
Harbin
Changchun
Shenyang
Anshan
Fushun
Dalian
Qingdao
Jinan
Taiyuan
Lanzhou
Xi'an
Chengdu
Chongqing
Wuhan
Nanjing
Guangzhou
Hong Kong
Macao (Port)
Taipei
P'yongyang
Seoul
Inch'on
Taegu
Pusan
Tokyo
Sendai
Sapporo
Yokohama
Kawasaki
Nagoya
Kyoto
Osaka
Kobe
Sakai
Hiroshima
Fukuoka
Nagasaki
Manila
Hanoi
Vientiane
Bangkok
Phnom Penh
Ho Chi Minh City
Mandalay
Yangon (Rangoon)
Dhaka
Chittagong
Thimphu
Kathmandu
Calcutta
Delhi
New Delhi
Kanpur
Jaipur
Nagpur
Hyderabad
Ahmadabad
Mumbai (Bombay)
Pune
Bangalore
Chennai (Madras)
Colombo
Male
Islamabad
Lahore
Faisalabad
Karachi
Kabul
Tehran
Mashhad
Esfahan
Shiraz
Baghdad
Mosul
Basra
Kuwait City
Manama
Doha
Abu Dhabi
Muscat
Riyadh
Jidda
Mecca
Sanaa
Damascus
Aleppo
Beirut
Amman
Jerusalem
Tel Aviv
Nicosia
Ankara
Istanbul
Izmir
Tbilisi
Yerevan
Baku
Tabriz
Kuala Lumpur
Singapore
Bandar Seri Begawan
Jakarta
Bandung
Semarang
Surabaya
Ujung Pandang
Medan

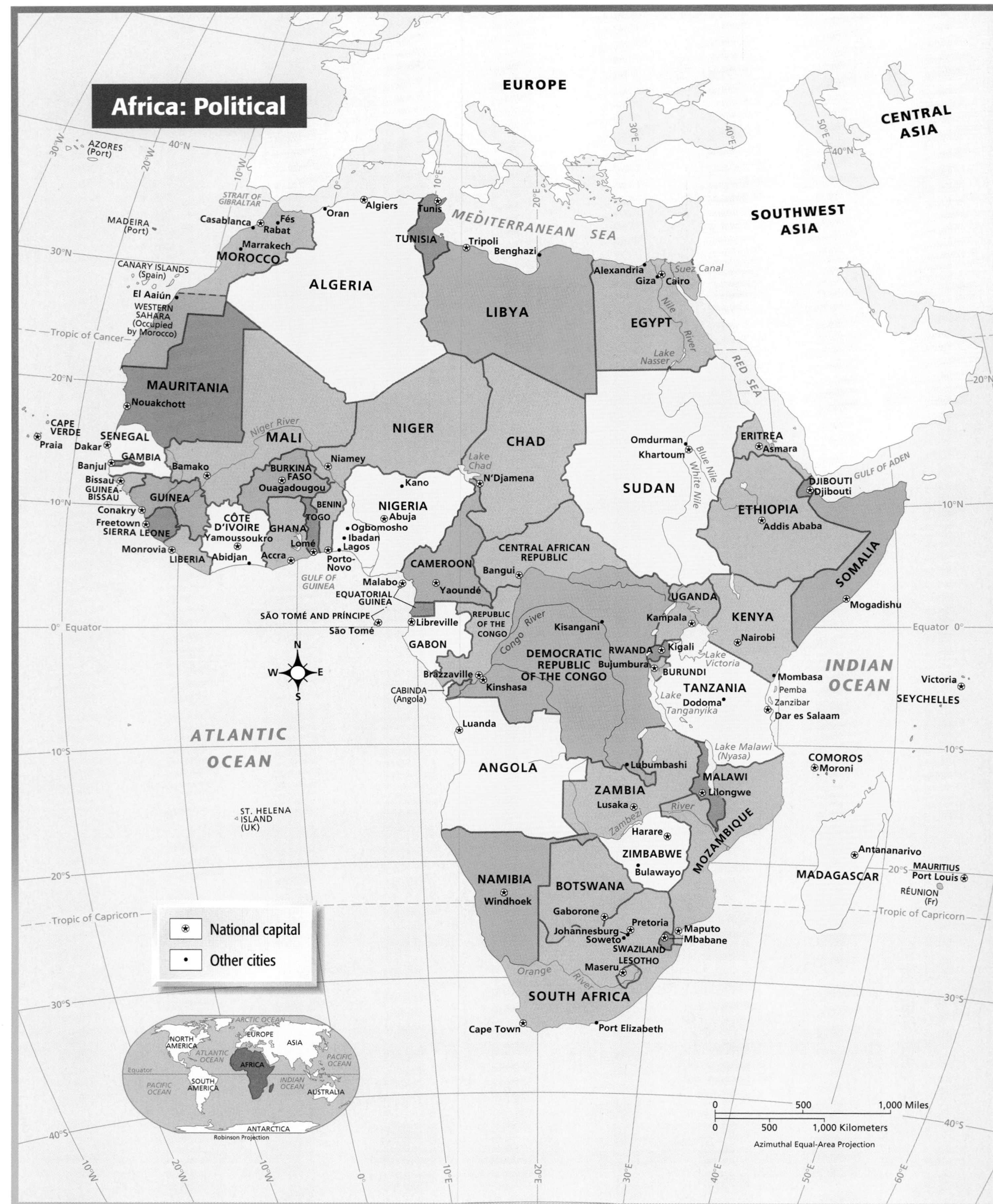
Africa: Political
EUROPE
CENTRAL ASIA
SOUTHWEST ASIA
AZORES (Port)
MADEIRA (Port)
CANARY ISLANDS (Spain)
STRAIT OF GIBRALTAR
MEDITERRANEAN SEA
Casablanca
Fés
Rabat
Marrakech
MOROCCO
Oran
Algiers
Tunis
TUNISIA
ALGERIA
Tripoli
Benghazi
LIBYA
Alexandria
Giza
Cairo
Suez Canal
EGYPT
Nile River
Lake Nasser
RED SEA
El Aaiún
WESTERN SAHARA (Occupied by Morocco)
Tropic of Cancer
MAURITANIA
Nouakchott
CAPE VERDE
Praia
SENEGAL
Dakar
GAMBIA
Banjul
Bissau
GUINEA-BISSAU
GUINEA
Conakry
Freetown
SIERRA LEONE
Monrovia
LIBERIA
CÔTE D'IVOIRE
Yamoussoukro
Abidjan
GHANA
Accra
TOGO
Lomé
BENIN
Porto-Novo
MALI
Niger River
Bamako
BURKINA FASO
Ouagadougou
Niamey
NIGER
NIGERIA
Kano
Abuja
Ogbomosho
Ibadan
Lagos
GULF OF GUINEA
Malabo
EQUATORIAL GUINEA
SÃO TOMÉ AND PRÍNCIPE
São Tomé
CAMEROON
Yaoundé
Libreville
GABON
CHAD
Lake Chad
N'Djamena
CENTRAL AFRICAN REPUBLIC
Bangui
REPUBLIC OF THE CONGO
Congo River
Brazzaville
Kinshasa
CABINDA (Angola)
DEMOCRATIC REPUBLIC OF THE CONGO
Kisangani
SUDAN
Omdurman
Khartoum
Blue Nile
White Nile
ERITREA
Asmara
DJIBOUTI
Djibouti
GULF OF ADEN
ETHIOPIA
Addis Ababa
SOMALIA
Mogadishu
UGANDA
Kampala
KENYA
Nairobi
RWANDA
Kigali
Bujumbura
BURUNDI
Lake Victoria
TANZANIA
Dodoma
Lake Tanganyika
Mombasa
Pemba
Zanzibar
Dar es Salaam
INDIAN OCEAN
Victoria
SEYCHELLES
Equator
ATLANTIC OCEAN
Luanda
ANGOLA
Lubumbashi
Lake Malawi (Nyasa)
MALAWI
Lilongwe
ZAMBIA
Lusaka
Zambezi River
COMOROS
Moroni
ST. HELENA ISLAND (UK)
Harare
ZIMBABWE
Bulawayo
MOZAMBIQUE
Antananarivo
MADAGASCAR
MAURITIUS
Port Louis
RÉUNION (Fr)
NAMIBIA
Windhoek
BOTSWANA
Gaborone
Pretoria
Johannesburg
Soweto
Maputo
Mbabane
SWAZILAND
LESOTHO
Maseru
Orange River
SOUTH AFRICA
Cape Town
Port Elizabeth
Tropic of Capricorn
National capital
Other cities
N
S
E
W
ARCTIC OCEAN
NORTH AMERICA
EUROPE
ASIA
ATLANTIC OCEAN
AFRICA
PACIFIC OCEAN
Equator
SOUTH AMERICA
INDIAN OCEAN
AUSTRALIA
ANTARCTICA
Robinson Projection
0 500 1,000 Miles
0 500 1,000 Kilometers
Azimuthal Equal-Area Projection

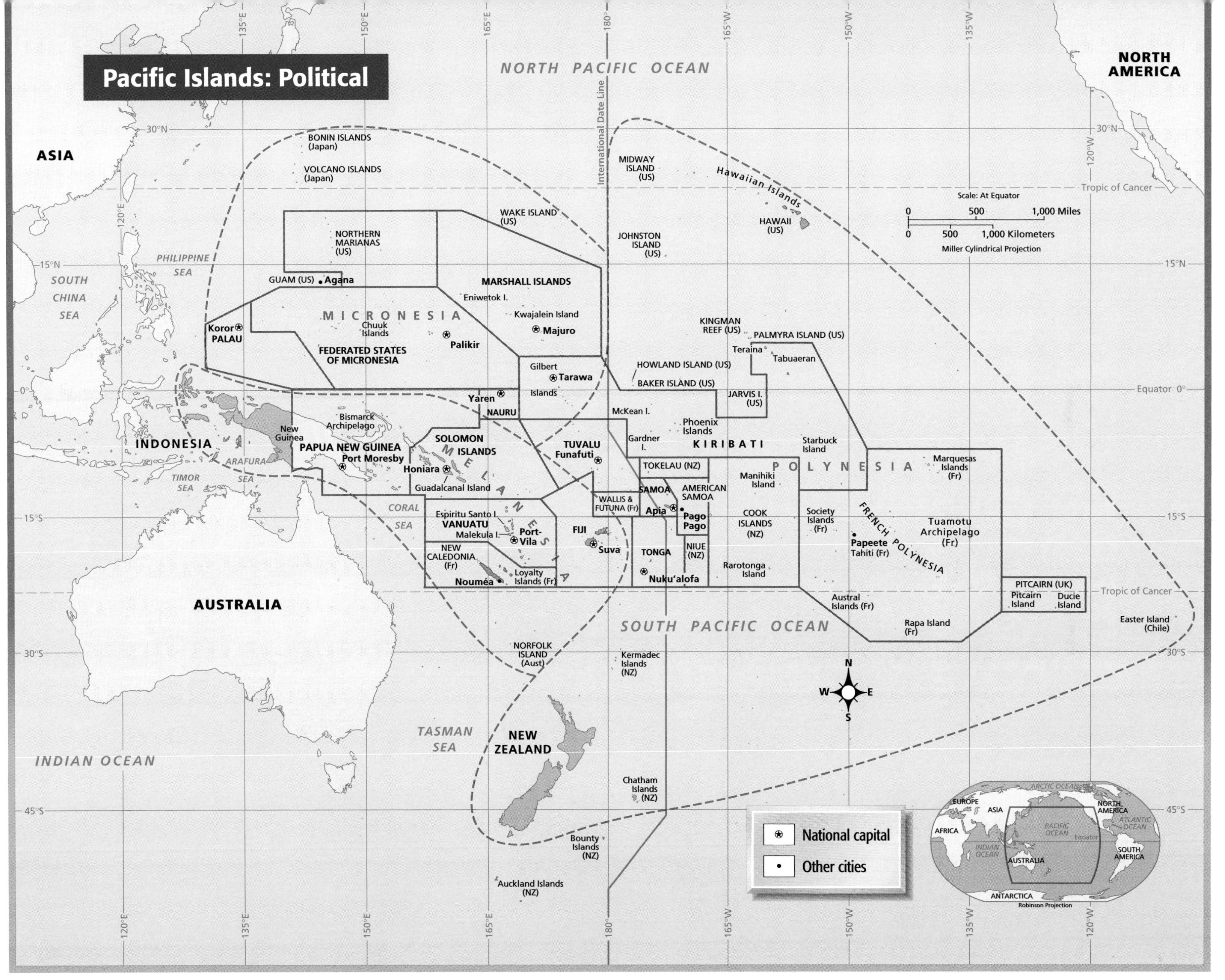
Pacific Islands: Political
NORTH AMERICA
ASIA
AUSTRALIA
NEW ZEALAND
INDONESIA
NORTH PACIFIC OCEAN
SOUTH PACIFIC OCEAN
INDIAN OCEAN
SOUTH CHINA SEA
PHILIPPINE SEA
CORAL SEA
TASMAN SEA
ARAFURA SEA
TIMOR SEA
International Date Line
Tropic of Cancer
Equator 0°
Tropic of Cancer
MICRONESIA
MELANESIA
POLYNESIA
Hawaiian Islands
HAWAII (US)
MIDWAY ISLAND (US)
JOHNSTON ISLAND (US)
WAKE ISLAND (US)
BONIN ISLANDS (Japan)
VOLCANO ISLANDS (Japan)
NORTHERN MARIANAS (US)
GUAM (US)
Agana
MARSHALL ISLANDS
Eniwetok I.
Kwajalein Island
Majuro
FEDERATED STATES OF MICRONESIA
Chuuk Islands
Palikir
Koror
PALAU
PAPUA NEW GUINEA
Port Moresby
New Guinea
Bismarck Archipelago
SOLOMON ISLANDS
Honiara
Guadalcanal Island
NAURU
Yaren
Gilbert Islands
Tarawa
KIRIBATI
TUVALU
Funafuti
HOWLAND ISLAND (US)
BAKER ISLAND (US)
McKean I.
Gardner I.
Phoenix Islands
JARVIS I. (US)
KINGMAN REEF (US)
PALMYRA ISLAND (US)
Teraina
Tabuaeran
Starbuck Island
TOKELAU (NZ)
SAMOA
Apia
AMERICAN SAMOA
Pago Pago
WALLIS & FUTUNA (Fr)
FIJI
Suva
TONGA
Nuku'alofa
NIUE (NZ)
Manihiki Island
COOK ISLANDS (NZ)
Rarotonga Island
VANUATU
Espiritu Santo I.
Malekula I.
Port-Vila
NEW CALEDONIA (Fr)
Nouméa
Loyalty Islands (Fr)
NORFOLK ISLAND (Aust)
Kermadec Islands (NZ)
Chatham Islands (NZ)
Bounty Islands (NZ)
Auckland Islands (NZ)
FRENCH POLYNESIA
Society Islands (Fr)
Papeete
Tahiti (Fr)
Marquesas Islands (Fr)
Tuamotu Archipelago (Fr)
Austral Islands (Fr)
Rapa Island (Fr)
PITCAIRN (UK)
Pitcairn Island
Ducie Island
Easter Island (Chile)
Scale: At Equator
0 500 1,000 Miles
0 500 1,000 Kilometers
Miller Cylindrical Projection
National capital
Other cities
EUROPE
ASIA
AFRICA
NORTH AMERICA
SOUTH AMERICA
AUSTRALIA
ANTARCTICA
ARCTIC OCEAN
ATLANTIC OCEAN
PACIFIC OCEAN
INDIAN OCEAN
Equator
Robinson Projection

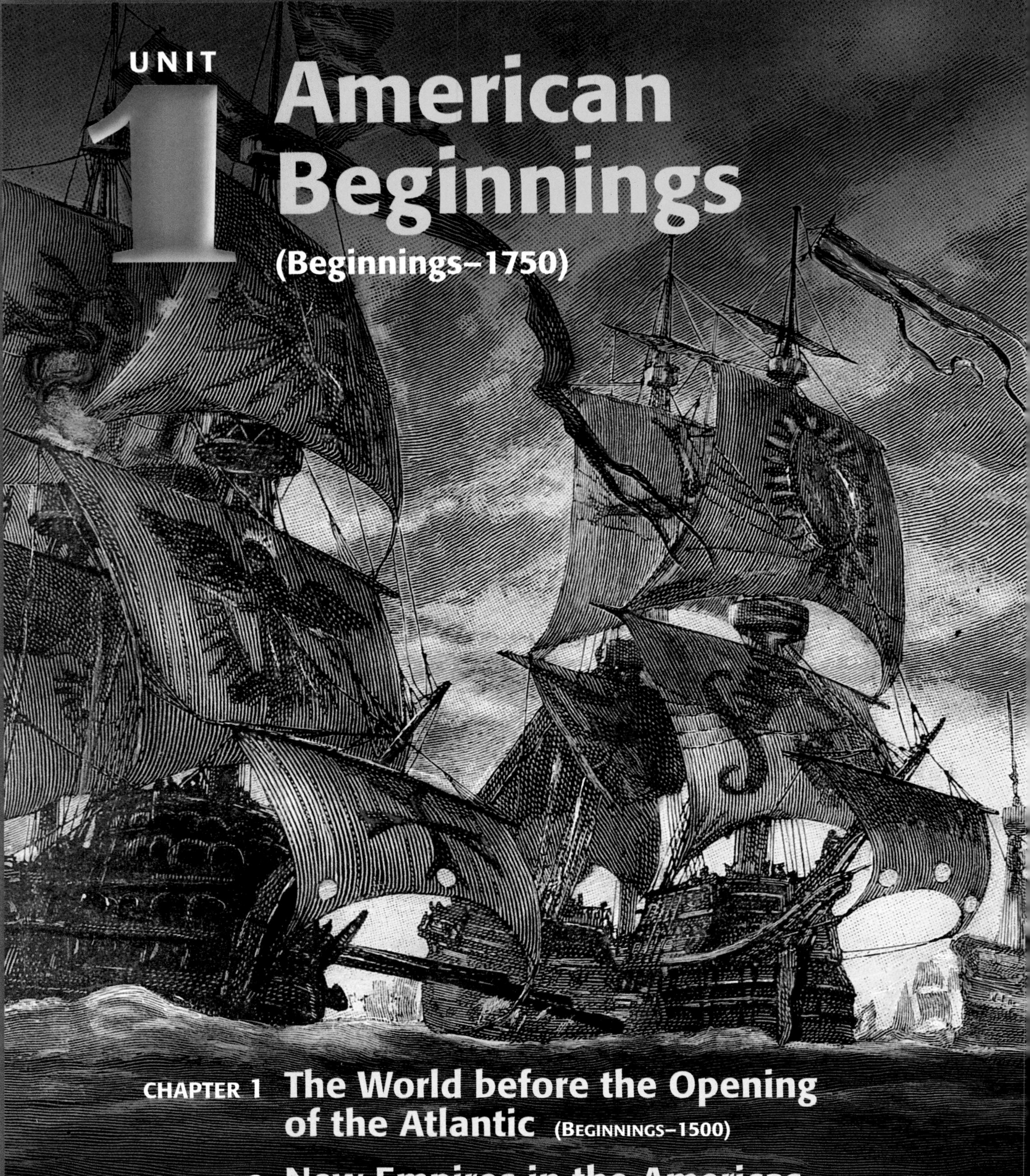

UNIT 1

American Beginnings

(Beginnings–1750)

Young People

IN HISTORY

Young Sailors

During the early days of European exploration, sailors kept track of time with sand-filled hourglasses. They turned them over every half hour. On Spanish ships, some crew members would stand watch, or serve as lookouts. As they did, a young boy would announce that watch's eighth turning of the glass.

"Good is that which passeth,
better that which cometh,
seven is past and eight floweth,
more shall flow if God willith."

The boys who sang these verses were sailors-in-training called *gromets*. These boys often served as cabin boys and pages on their first voyages. The youngest ones helped with the ship's religious ceremonies. They sang the blessing every morning and led the hymns.

Gromets also helped take care of the ship. They maintained the ship's compass and made materials to help keep water out of the ship. *Gromets* also swept the decks and served as lookouts. Late at night, when the sea was calm and there was little danger, *gromets* could take the ship's steering wheel. Although some *gromets* were too small to see over the ship's railing, they learned to keep a steady course for the ship.

After a crew mutiny in 1611, explorer Henry Hudson, his young son, and seven others were set adrift in a small boat.

On his first voyage to the Americas, Christopher Columbus gave orders not to allow *gromets* to steer. He believed that it was too risky. The ships, he felt, were too far from home and in unknown waters. Not all the sailors followed these orders. Columbus reported in his log on December 25, 1492, that there had been an accident involving the *Santa María,* his flagship. "The sailor who was steering the ship decided to go away to sleep and left the [steering] to a ship's boy. . . . The currents of water carried the ship upon one of those banks [coral reefs]." Soon after that collision, the *Santa María* sank.

If You Were There ***How would you contribute as a crew member on a sailing ship?***

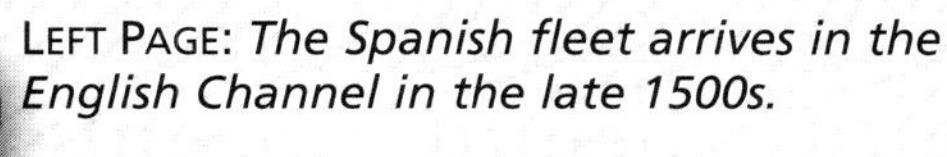

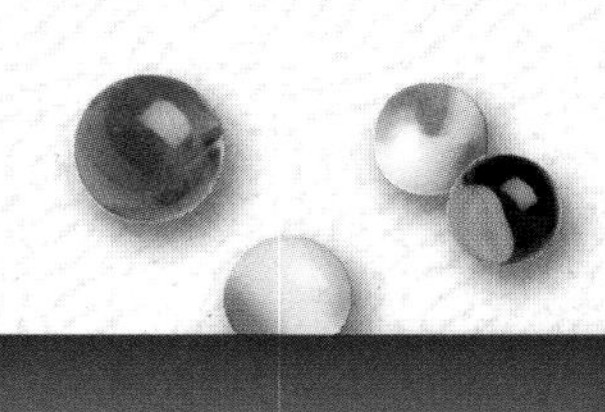

LEFT PAGE: *The Spanish fleet arrives in the English Channel in the late 1500s.*

CHAPTER

1 The World before the Opening of the Atlantic (Beginnings–1500)

The Maya created many complex wall carvings.

Maize was an important crop for many early Americans.

UNITED STATES

c. 38,000–10,000 B.C. Paleo-Indians migrate to the Americas.

c. 5000 B.C. Communities in Mexico cultivate corn.

c. 1200 B.C. The Olmec civilization appears in Mesoamerica.

c. A.D. 300 The Maya civilization begins a period of great development in Mesoamerica.

10,000 B.C. — **5000 B.C.** — **1 B.C. / A.D. 1**

WORLD

c. 8000 B.C. The Ice Age ends.

c. 2600 B.C. The Great Pyramid is built at Giza, Egypt, as the tomb for the pharaoh Cheops.

509 B.C. The Roman Republic is established.

A.D. 800s Vikings invade England, France, Iceland, and Ireland.

The Egyptian pyramids were considered wonders of the ancient world.

The Romans built aqueducts like this one to carry water to their towns.

Build on What You Know

Native Americans lived in the Americas for thousands of years before the first Europeans arrived after A.D. 1000. During this time, merchants and adventurers around the world traveled great distances in search of land and riches. Trade brought many different cultures into contact with one another.

Tenochtitlán was the capital of the mighty Aztec Empire.

This Inca knife is made of gold.

A.D. 1000 | A.D. 1100 | A.D. 1200 | A.D. 1300 | A.D. 1400

A.D. 1066 William the Conqueror wins the Battle of Hastings.

A.D. 1099 The crusaders capture Jerusalem.

A.D. 1100 The Anasazi people begin moving into protected cliff dwellings.

A.D. 1215 England's King John agrees to Magna Carta—one of the first documents to protect individuals' rights.

c. A.D. 1250 The ceremonial center of the Mississippi culture in North America begins to decline.

c. A.D. 1325 The Aztec build the great city of Tenochtitlán in Mesoamerica.

A.D. 1368 The Ming dynasty begins in China.

c. A.D. 1400 The Inca begin expanding in South America.

c. A.D. 1400 The African kingdom of Mali breaks apart.

If you were there . . .
What part of the world would you choose to visit in the early 1000s?

You Be the Historian

What's Your Opinion? Do you **agree** or **disagree** with the following statements? Support your point of view in your journal.

- **Culture** A group's culture is heavily influenced by its environment.
- **Geography** A group's survival depends on its ability to adjust to its environment.
- **Global Relations** Trade is the cause of most contact between cultures.

Section 1

The Earliest Americans

Read to Discover

1. How did the first people arrive in the Americas?
2. Why was the development of agriculture important?
3. What were some aspects of early Mesoamerican cultures?
4. What early societies existed in North America, and what were their accomplishments?

Define

- archaeology
- artifacts
- migration
- hunter-gatherers
- environments
- societies
- culture
- domestication
- maize
- glyphs

Identify

- Paleo-Indians

WHY IT MATTERS TODAY

People continue to move to new places in search of better living conditions. Use CNNfyi.com or other **current events** sources to identify a group that is currently migrating to a new home. Record your findings in your journal.

The Raven was an important figure in some Native American myths.

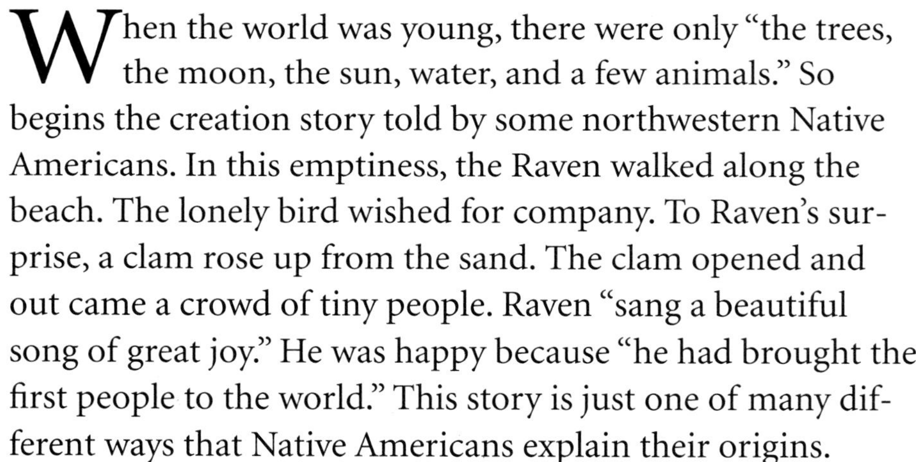

The Story Begins

When the world was young, there were only "the trees, the moon, the sun, water, and a few animals." So begins the creation story told by some northwestern Native Americans. In this emptiness, the Raven walked along the beach. The lonely bird wished for company. To Raven's surprise, a clam rose up from the sand. The clam opened and out came a crowd of tiny people. Raven "sang a beautiful song of great joy." He was happy because "he had brought the first people to the world." This story is just one of many different ways that Native Americans explain their origins.

The First Migration to the Americas

Many scientists believe that people first arrived in North America during the last Ice Age. At the start of the Ice Age, the world grew colder. Water froze into huge moving ice sheets called glaciers, which locked up large amounts of water. As a result, ocean levels dropped more than 300 feet lower than they are today. When the water level fell, a land bridge appeared between northeastern Asia and present-day Alaska. Geographers call this landmass Beringia.

No one knows exactly when people crossed into North America. The travelers from Asia left no written records. Instead, historians rely on **archaeology**—the study of the unwritten past. Archaeologists look at **artifacts**, or remains of objects made by humans. Artifacts suggest that **Paleo-Indians**, or the first Americans, crossed into Alaska sometime between 38,000 and 10,000 B.C.

This **migration**—a movement of people from one region to another—took place over a long period of time. Most archaeologists believe the Paleo-Indians first crossed over the land bridge in search of animals to hunt. One archaeologist described what the land crossing might have looked like.

> **"The low lying land bridge was no landscape of gently waving grass. . . .[it] was a treeless, arctic land, covered with a patchwork of very different types of vegetation."**
>
> —Brian M. Fagan, *Ancient North America*

Analyzing Primary Sources

Drawing Inferences and Conclusions What does this quote suggest about the harshness of the journey across the Beringia land bridge?

Most Paleo-Indians and their descendants traveled into present-day Canada, the United States, and Mexico. Eventually their descendants reached as far as the tip of South America. The Paleo-Indians were **hunter-gatherers.** They lived by hunting animals and gathering wild plants. They also made stone tools to hunt large animals such as mammoths.

✔ **Reading Check: Finding the Main Idea** When and how did the first people come to the Americas?

Migration to the Americas

During the Ice Age much of the world grew very cold. Water froze into huge moving ice sheets called glaciers. Ocean levels dropped more than 300 feet lower than they are today.

Visualizing History

1. **Geography** Where did the Paleo-Indians come from?
2. **Connecting to Today** What methods do people use to come to the Americas today?

Bering Strait

ALASKA

A A land bridge known as Beringia appeared between Asia and present-day Alaska. Paleo-Indians crossed Beringia in search of food.

NORTH AMERICA

PACIFIC OCEAN

ATLANTIC OCEAN

Gulf of Mexico

MESOAMERICA

B The Paleo-Indians and their descendants traveled throughout North and South America.

SOUTH AMERICA

Adapting to a New Climate

When the Ice Age ended about 8000 B.C., the world's climate changed. Rising temperatures melted glaciers. The oceans rose, covering Beringia with water. As late as 1000 B.C. people continued to come to North America using small boats.

The warmer weather at the end of the Ice Age created many new **environments**—climates and landscapes that surround living things. Short grasses replaced the taller grasses that had fed giant animals such as the mammoth. These animals either died out naturally or were hunted to extinction by Native Americans. However, large herds of smaller animals such as buffalo and deer ate the new short grasses. Paleo-Indians adapted to the changes by hunting these animals. People also ate more berries, roots, and seeds.

Different environments influenced the development of Native American **societies**. A society is a group that shares a common **culture**—a set of common values and traditions. These traits include language, government, and family relationships. Like all societies, Native American groups changed over time.

The earliest farming societies in the Americas began in Mesoamerica, or Middle America, and South America. Mesoamerica includes southern Mexico and northern Central America. People in this region learned to breed and grow wild plants to create food crops. This process of breeding plants or animals to meet human needs is called **domestication**.

Archaeologists in Mexico have found signs of the first **maize**, or corn, grown by people. People in Mesoamerica also grew beans and peppers. In eastern North America, Native Americans domesticated plants by about 2000 B.C. In the Southwest, agricultural methods were introduced from Mesoamerica between 1000 and 750 B.C. Agriculture allowed many Native American groups to settle in villages. It thus led to the rise of larger and more complex societies.

✔ Reading Check: **Analyzing Information** How did the end of the Ice Age help make the rise of civilizations in North America possible?

CONNECTING TO SCIENCE AND TECHNOLOGY

Discovering the Distant Past

Archaeologists use scientific tests to determine the age of artifacts. In 1949 Willard Libby developed carbon-14 dating. This highly accurate test measures the amount of carbon 14—a form of carbon atom—that exists in an artifact. Before the use of carbon-14 dating, archaeologists used unreliable methods to guess the age of artifacts.

Scientists know that half the carbon 14 in a dead plant or animal decays about every 5,000 years. After 50,000 years almost all the carbon 14 is gone. Knowing this, archaeologists measure the amount of carbon 14 in a fossil or artifact. This measurement is then used to figure out its age. Today scientists can also use other advanced methods to date objects older than 50,000 years. How do scientists use carbon 14 to determine the age of artifacts?

Mesoamerica and South America

Some of the earliest American civilizations developed in Mesoamerica. The Olmec society was one of the first. It has been called the "mother culture" because it highly influenced most later civilizations in Mesoamerica. The Olmec developed along the Mexican Gulf Coast between about 1200 and 400 B.C. During that time Olmec priests created number and calendar systems. They invented a method of writing that used **glyphs**, or symbols that represent ideas.

The Maya civilization thrived in southeastern Mesoamerica from about A.D 300 to 900. The Maya built many large stone temples, palaces, and bridges. The city of Tikal was an important Maya center. The Maya created several calendars. They also studied mathematics and astronomy. By about A.D. 900 the Maya civilization started to decline. Historians are not sure why this took place.

About A.D. 1200, Aztec invaders came south and occupied the central valley of Mexico. The center of Aztec civilization was Tenochtitlán (tay-nawch-teet-LAHN). Present-day Mexico City was built on the site of this ancient city. Tenochtitlán stood in the middle of a huge lake, with raised highways connecting the city to the shore. It is thought that as many as 300,000 people may have lived in this great capital.

The Aztec created a large empire by conquering most of their neighbors. The empire had a vast trading network involving goods such as cocoa, gold, and jade. However, the Aztec knew that their success might not last. They expressed this idea in their poetry.

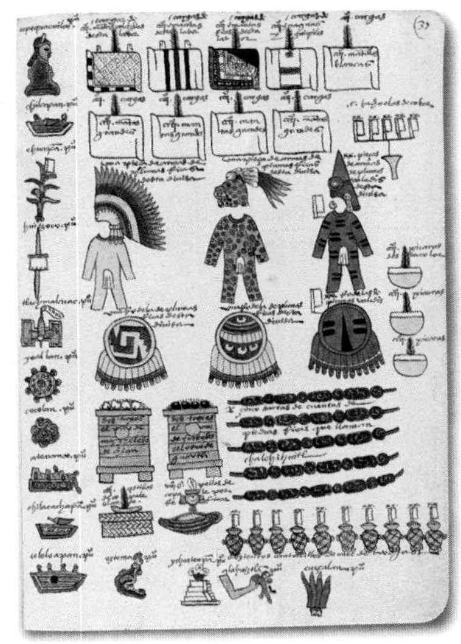

The Aztec used tax records like this one to keep track of their wealth.

"Truly do we live on earth?
Not forever on earth; only a little
while here.
Although it be jade, it will be
broken,
Although it be gold, it is
crushed. . . .
Not forever on earth; only a little
while here."

—King Nezahualcóyotl, quoted in *Aztec Thought and Culture* by Miguel León-Portilla

While the Aztec were thriving in Mexico, the Inca created their own civilization in South America. The Inca civilization began high in the Andes. In the A.D. 1400s they started to conquer surrounding lands. Eventually, the Inca ruled an area stretching from present-day Ecuador to central Chile. Across this empire the Inca built a network of roads some 25,000 miles long. These roads let armies and messengers move quickly. The Inca built palaces and temples in their capital city of Cuzco (KOO-skoh). Decorated with gold and silver, the palaces had beautiful gardens and bathrooms with running water. Most Inca subjects lived in villages. They were allowed to keep their own land and many of their customs. But families did have to dig canals and grow crops to help feed the Inca Empire.

✔ **Reading Check: Comparing** List some cultural developments of the Mesoamerican and South American civilizations.

Interpreting the Visual Record

Machu Picchu *The Inca built the great city of Machu Picchu high in the Andes of present-day Peru.* ***What would be the advantages and disadvantages of building in such a location?***

Early North American Societies

Although less populated than South America and Mesoamerica, North America had several farming cultures. These cultures had to adapt to very different environments. For example, in the southwestern region of the present-day United States there was little rainfall for farming. As a result, Native Americans created irrigation systems to bring water to crops, allowing groups to build permanent settlements.

The Anasazi (ah-nuh-SAH-zee) lived in the Four Corners region, where present-day Arizona, Colorado, New Mexico, and Utah meet. They built their pueblos, or villages, among high hills and deep canyons. Anasazi pueblos were made mostly of cut stone or adobe—sun-baked clay and straw. Many pueblos were multistory buildings with ladders connecting the different levels. Pueblo Bonito in New Mexico's Chaco Canyon has five stories and 800 rooms.

The Anasazi built their early pueblos on mesas, or flat-topped hills. Later, about A.D. 1100, they began building their homes into cliffsides for defense. By A.D. 1300, some Anasazi began to leave the larger pueblos. Drought or war may have driven them away.

In eastern and midwestern North America, advanced cultures developed between 1000 B.C. and A.D. 1250. The Hopewell culture arose between 300 and 200 B.C. The Hopewell lived along the Mississippi,

Interpreting the Visual Record

Mesa Verde *Southwestern Indians built cliff dwellings, like this one in Mesa Verde, to protect themselves from harsh weather and enemy attacks.* ***Why would the location of these buildings have offered protection?***

Interpreting the Visual Record

Burial mounds *The ancient mound builders constructed the Great Serpent Mound near what is now Hillsboro, Ohio.* ***How do you think this mound got its present name?***

Ohio, and lower Missouri River valleys. They built large burial mounds, some 30 feet tall, to honor their dead. The Hopewell supported their large populations with agriculture and trade. However, by about A.D. 400, the Hopewell no longer dominated the region. Archaeologists have yet to discover why the Hopewell culture declined.

The Mississippians were another widespread farming culture that relied on trade. Like the Hopewell, the Mississippians also had religious practices honoring the dead. From about A.D. 700 to the early 1500s, the Mississippian people lived along the Ohio and Mississippi Rivers. Mississippians built pyramid mounds out of solid earth. Religious ceremonies were held on top of these pyramids. The largest of these is Monks Mound, near Cahokia (kuh-HOH-kee-uh), Illinois. Monks Mound covers 16 acres and stands 98 feet tall.

✔ **Reading Check: Summarizing** What were some features of early North American cultures?

Section 1 Review

go.hrw.com **Homework Practice Online**
keyword: SC3 HP1

1. **Define** and explain:
   - archaeology
   - artifacts
   - migration
   - hunter-gatherers
   - environments
   - societies
   - culture
   - domestication
   - maize
   - glyphs

2. **Identify** and explain:
   - Paleo-Indians

3. **Summarizing** Copy the chart below. Use it to identify the early societies in the Americas, where they were located, and one major accomplishment of each society.

Early American Societies	Location	Accomplishments

4. **Finding the Main Idea**
   a. What events made it possible for Paleo-Indians to migrate to North America?
   b. Why do you think that growing crops such as maize was important to many early Native American civilizations?

5. **Writing and Critical Thinking**
   Analyzing Information Imagine that you are a visitor to one of the early Mesoamerican cultures. Write a letter to a friend describing the society you encounter.
   Consider the following:
   - the time period of the culture
   - the location and physical environment of the society
   - the society's cultural accomplishments

Section 2

Cultural Areas in North America

Read to Discover

1. How did the environment influence Native American cultures in North America?
2. What types of housing did Native Americans build?
3. What were various traits of Native Americans in different culture areas?

Define

- kayaks
- igloos
- totems
- potlatches
- kivas
- wigwams
- longhouses

Identify

- Iroquois League

WHY IT MATTERS TODAY

Many Native Americans still practice ancient cultural traditions. Use CNNfyi.com or other **current events** sources to find out about a Native American tradition being followed today. Examples might include storytelling, art, or dance. Record your findings in your journal.

The Story Continues

Native Americans developed customs based on their close ties to the land. Many tribes in the American Southwest held dances that celebrated the importance of the Sun and rain. One Native American song called the Southwest "a House Made of Dawn . . . made of pollen and of rain." The Inuit of the Far North lived on land too cold to grow crops. They held ceremonies to help them hunt wild game. Native Americans across the continent adapted their lifestyles to their surroundings.

Southwestern Native Americans often decorated their pottery with animal symbols.

The Far North

Researchers use culture areas—the geographic locations that influenced societies—to help them describe ancient Native American peoples. The Far North of North America is divided into the Arctic and Subarctic culture areas. Few plants grow in the Arctic because the ground is always frozen. The Aleut and the Inuit adapted to these harsh conditions. The Inuit lived in present-day northern Alaska and Canada, and the Aleut lived in western Alaska. The two groups shared many cultural traits,

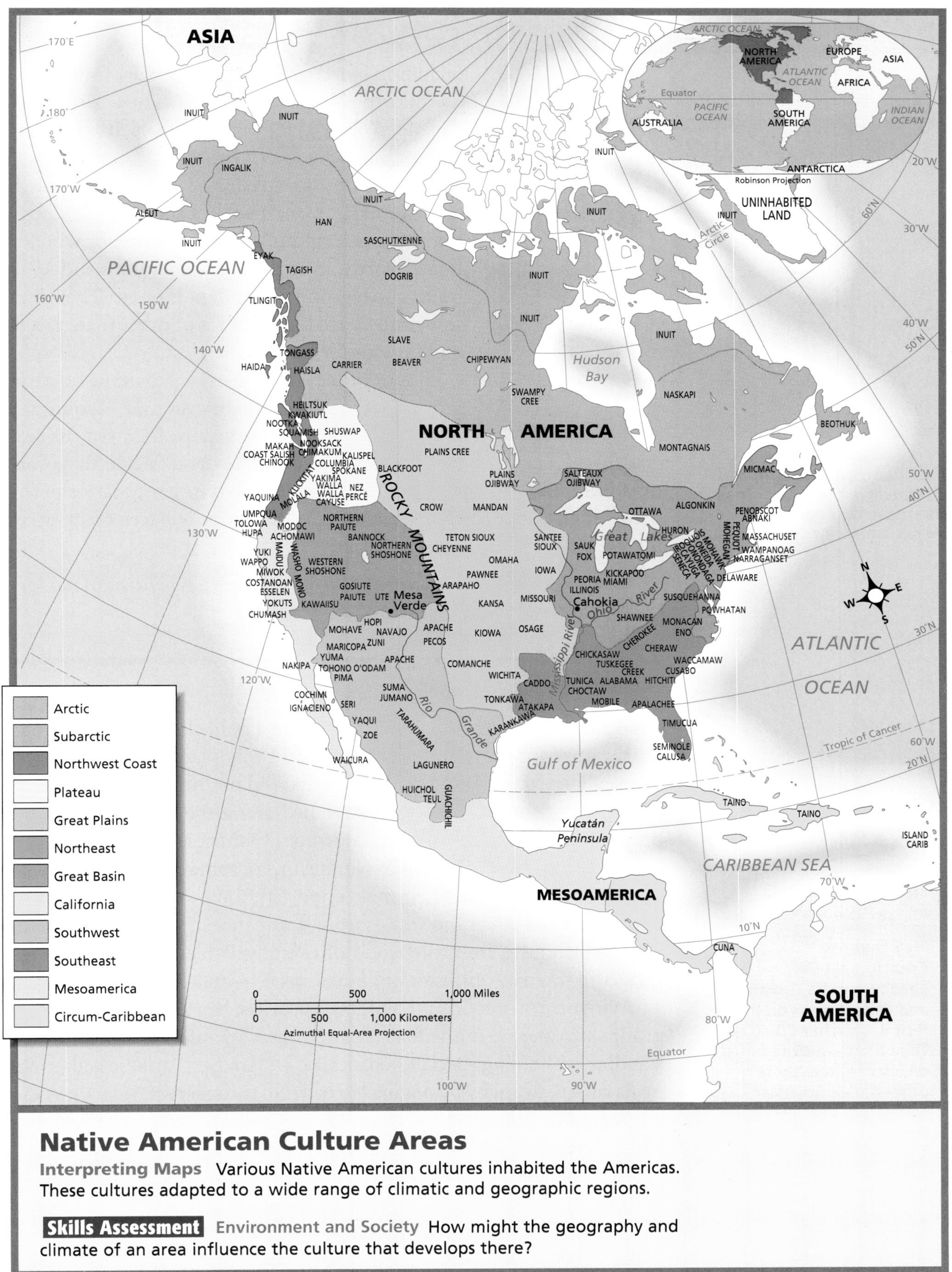

Native American Culture Areas

Interpreting Maps Various Native American cultures inhabited the Americas. These cultures adapted to a wide range of climatic and geographic regions.

Skills Assessment **Environment and Society** How might the geography and climate of an area influence the culture that develops there?

The Inuit used kayaks to cross icy waters in the Arctic. They also made carvings from walrus bones.

including language. Both survived by fishing and by hunting large mammals. They also both depended on dogs for many tasks, such as hunting and pulling sleds.

In addition to dogsleds, the Inuit and Aleut used **kayaks**, or one-person canoes covered with skins. Some Inuit built earthen, stone, or wooden houses partly underground. Other Inuit and Aleut built aboveground wooden houses. The Inuit sometimes used blocks of ice or other materials to build **igloos** for housing.

South of the Arctic lies the Subarctic, home to groups such as the Athabascan and Algonquian peoples. Each year these groups followed the seasonal migrations of the caribou. When they went on a hunt, the Athabascan and Algonquian lived in temporary shelters made of animal skins. At other times they lived in villages made up of log houses.

✔ **Reading Check: Summarizing** How did the Native Americans of the Far North get their food?

The Pacific Coast

Unlike the Far North, the Pacific Coast had a mild climate. The area had a rich supply of game animals, sea life, and wild plants. These resources allowed large populations to develop that did not need to rely on farming. The Northwest Coast area stretched along the shoreline between present-day southern Alaska and northern California.

The Tlingit, Nootka, and Skokomish were some of the peoples who lived in the Northwest. Their most important food was salmon, but they also hunted sea otters and whales from large canoes. People in the Northwest built houses from the wood of evergreen trees. They also carved images of **totems**—ancestor or animal spirits—on tall wooden poles.

With plenty of food and building materials, Northwest Coast culture groups prospered. Individuals showed their wealth and earned social standing by holding special events called **potlatches**. At these gatherings hosts gave away many belongings in order to gain respect.

Farther south along the coast was the California region, which had several climates. Native Americans living in this area had many food sources available year-round, so farming was not necessary. Their major food plant was acorns, which they ground into a flour. They also fished and hunted deer and other game. Most Native Americans in the California region lived in isolated groups of families. Each of these groups had

Free Find:
Creation Myths
Read about the Tuskegee and Caddo myths on the **Holt Researcher CD-ROM**. Then draw a picture based on a scene from these or other Native American creation myths.

a small population of only 50 to 300. Among these Native Americans—which included the Pomo, Hupa, and Yurok—more than 100 different languages were spoken.

✔ **Reading Check: Finding the Main Idea** How did the environment influence the food sources for Native Americans in the California and Northwest Coast regions?

The West and Southwest

The West and Southwest of the present-day United States received less rain than the Far West. As a result, the people had fewer resources than their neighbors on the Pacific Coast. Although they did not practice agriculture, groups in the dry Columbia Plateau region lived in permanent villages. Native Americans living near rivers fished for salmon, hunted small game, and gathered plants. These groups included the Flathead, Modoc, and Nez Percé.

Native Americans faced more difficulties surviving in the much drier Great Basin region. They adapted to the dry climate by gathering seeds, digging roots, and trapping small animals for food. They also ate ants, crickets, lizards, and rabbits. Rabbits were highly valued because they provided meat as well as fur and skins for blankets and clothing. Most Native Americans of the Great Basin lived in small family groups that moved often in search of food. Most groups in this region spoke variations of the same language. These groups included the Paiute, Shoshone, and Ute.

Native Americans of the Southwest also had to adapt to a dry climate. This region's landscape varied from deserts to evergreen forests. Southwestern culture groups included the Apache, Navajo, and Pueblo. The

CONNECTING TO THE ARTS

Totems In parts of Alaska and British Columbia, Native Americans practice a unique and striking ancient tradition. Artists carve images of ravens, bears, fish, and human beings into towering totem poles. The Tlingit, Nootka, and other groups have long used these poles to tell important stories.

To create the poles, the artist first listens to the story that the purchaser wants to have shown. These tales can be personal, family, or tribal stories. Then the artist designs and carves the work. After the totem pole's completion, the buyer hosts a potlatch to dedicate it and raise it into place. During the potlatch, singers and actors often perform the pole's story. **How do totem poles reflect the relationship between people in the Northwest Coast culture area and their environment?**

Interpreting the Visual Record

Kachinas *Southwestern Native Americans such as the Zuni believed in ancestral spirits called kachinas, who were often represented in ceremonies by costumed dancers. This wooden doll is a model of a kachina dancer. Sandpaintings also had important ceremonial uses. This Navajo blanket was based on a sandpainting design.* ***What is similar and different about the figures shown in these two images?***

Pueblo were farmers who irrigated their land to grow crops. Other tribes, such as the Apache, hunted game and gathered plants for food. These groups also raided the villages of farming groups such as the Pueblo.

The Pueblo people had many religious festivals. These rituals focused on the two key areas of Pueblo life—rain and maize. Pueblo religious activities were held in **kivas**—round ceremonial rooms.

✔ **Reading Check:** **Finding the Main Idea** How did Native Americans adapt to the dry environment of the West and Southwest?

The Great Plains

The huge Great Plains region stretches south from Canada into Texas. This culture area is bounded by the Mississippi Valley on the east and the Rocky Mountains on the west. The Plains were mainly grassland, on which millions of buffalo and other game grazed in herds. The Mandan lived in the northern Plains, while the Pawnee lived on the central Plains. Both groups grew crops such as beans, maize, and squash. Like some other Native American groups, the Pawnee society was matrilineal. This means that people traced their ancestry through their mothers, rather than through their fathers. In addition, when a couple married, the husband moved into the wife's home.

Several Native American groups, such as the Apache, lived in the southern Plains. People in this area hunted buffalo on foot and gathered berries, nuts, and vegetables. Some groups grew to depend largely on the buffalo for clothing, food, and shelter.

Many other Native Americans lived on the eastern or western borders of the Plains. These groups included the Arapaho, Blackfoot, Comanche, and Teton Sioux. Hunters among the Blackfoot sometimes killed huge numbers of buffalo by chasing the animals over steep cliffs.

The East

Unlike the Great Plains, eastern North America was rich in sources for food and shelter. The East was mainly forest. The Mississippi River and the Everglades—a huge swamp in what is now Florida—also provided many resources.

Native Americans of the Southeast included the Cherokee, Creek, Natchez, and Seminole. The Natchez were direct descendants of the ancient Mississippian people. Most southeastern groups lived in villages along river valleys. They relied mainly on farming but also hunted game, gathered plants, fished, and traded. Each of these groups was led by a village council.

Northeastern tribes lived in a broad area stretching west from the Atlantic Ocean to the Mississippi Valley. This area extended north to the Great Lakes region and south into present-day Virginia and North Carolina. The Algonquian and Iroquois peoples were the two main groups of the Northeast. Some Algonquian peoples lived north of the Great Lakes. These groups could not farm all year-round because the climate in this northern region was too cold. They survived by hunting and by gathering edible plants.

Other Algonquian peoples, including the Wampanoag and Pequot, lived farther south. In the warmer areas they farmed, hunted, gathered plants, and fished in rivers and the ocean. These groups lived in

Daily Life

Hunting buffalo Buffalo are large, powerful animals that once roamed the Great Plains in huge herds. Hunting these creatures was not an easy task for early Native Americans. But the buffalo could provide for so many needs, including food and clothing, that it was worth the risk to hunt them. Here two Native American hunters wearing wolf skins try to get close enough to bring down a buffalo. **Why do you think these hunters are wearing wolf skins?**

Iroquois warriors such as the one shown here had great success in warfare.

permanent villages. Some built large multifamily lodges, while others lived in small **wigwams**, or round huts.

To the east of the Algonquian lived the Iroquois. Unlike other Native American women, Iroquois women controlled the material goods of their people. They also oversaw most parts of community life. The Iroquois relied mostly on farming for food, although they also hunted and traded with other tribes. Men were responsible for hunting and trading. Women grew and harvested crops.

The Iroquois lived in **longhouses**, or rectangular homes made from logs and bark. Longhouses ranged from 50 to 100 feet long and housed 8 to 10 families each. Fences of pointed stakes surrounded longhouses for defense. Neighboring tribes feared the military skills of the Iroquois.

The Iroquois also developed the **Iroquois League**. This political confederation was made up of the Cayuga, Mohawk, Oneida, Onondaga, and Seneca. The League was responsible for waging war and making peace with non-Iroquois peoples. Women selected the male members of the League council. Women could overrule decisions made by the council and could remove its members. The League helped the Iroquois become one of the most powerful peoples in North America.

✔ **Reading Check: Comparing and Contrasting** What were some of the similarities and differences between the cultures of Native Americans in the Great Plains and the East?

Section 2 Review

go.hrw.com Homework Practice Online
keyword: SC3 HP1

1. **Define** and explain:
   - kayaks
   - igloos
   - totems
   - potlatches
   - kivas
   - wigwams
   - longhouses

2. **Identify** and explain:
   - Iroquois League

3. **Identifying Cause and Effect** Copy the graphic organizer below. Use it to show how the environments of the Far North, the Southwest, and the East affected the cultures of the Native Americans who lived in each area.

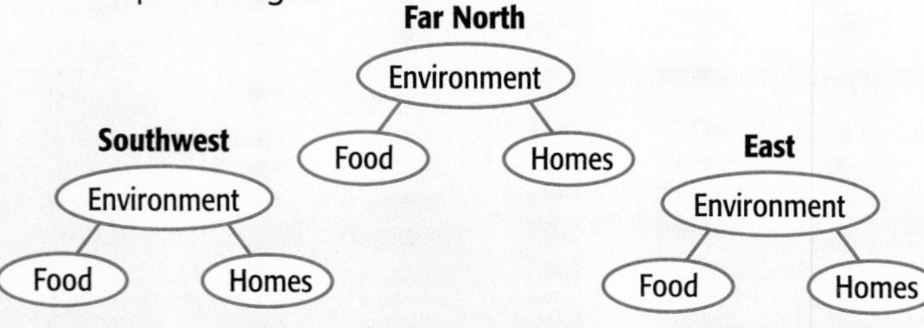

4. **Finding the Main Idea**
   a. Compare and contrast the major cultural traits of the Far North and the Southwest culture groups.
   b. Why do you think that Native Americans who practiced agriculture were more likely than hunter-gatherers to establish permanent homes?

5. **Writing and Critical Thinking**
   Summarizing Imagine that you are living in an early Native American society. Write a paragraph describing your life as a member of this group.
   Consider the following:
   - how you obtain your food
   - the type of shelter in which you live
   - other cultural traits your group shares

Section 3

Europe during the Middle Ages

Read to Discover

1. What new lands did the Vikings explore?
2. What were society and daily life like during the Middle Ages?
3. How did the Catholic Church affect people's lives during the Middle Ages?
4. What events brought about major change in the late Middle Ages?

Define

- feudalism
- manors

Identify

- Leif Eriksson
- Middle Ages
- Eleanor of Aquitaine
- William of Normandy
- King John
- Magna Carta

WHY IT MATTERS TODAY

A person who rules over a kingdom or empire is known as a monarch. Use CNNfyi.com or other **current events** sources to find information about a country that has a monarch today. Record your findings in your journal.

The Story Continues

The bold Vikings described their adventures in sagas—long, heroic stories that mixed myth and fact. "Erik's Saga" tells how Leif Eriksson heard tales of a land across the sea. Seeking fame and fortune, he went in search of the mysterious land. Eriksson and his crew were tossed by the seas as they set sail from his home in Iceland. According to the saga, the Vikings eventually "came upon lands whose existence he [Eriksson] had never suspected." They saw "fields of flowing wheat there, and vines" with wild grapes. Eriksson, who had landed on the shore of North America, called this place Vinland.

This replica of a Viking ship shows the unique design used.

 The Viking Explorations

The Vikings were from Scandinavia, which includes the present-day countries of Denmark, Norway, and Sweden. The Vikings were skilled sailors who developed a new style of ship that curved up at both ends. These ships traveled on the rough North Atlantic seas better than

Vikings led by Leif Eriksson attack a Native American camp in Vinland.

earlier designs. The Vikings raided and traded throughout Europe. Evidence shows that the Vikings reached the British Isles, the northern European coast, and as far away as the Mediterranean and the Black Sea. In many places their raids caused great fear. "Never before had such a terror appeared in Britain," noted Anglo-Saxon scholar Alcuin in A.D. 793.

Eventually the Vikings sailed west into the North Atlantic. Much of what historians know about these explorations comes from Viking stories called sagas. According to the sagas, the Vikings founded a settlement on the island of Iceland about A.D. 874. More than 100 years later, the Viking Erik the Red left Iceland to settle Greenland.

Leif Eriksson, son of Erik the Red, shared his father's love of adventure. About A.D. 1000 he gathered a crew and launched his own expedition, sailing west from Greenland. After a difficult journey, they reached North America, landing on Labrador Peninsula and the island of Newfoundland in present-day Canada. This landing represented the first time Europeans made contact with the North American continent. The Vikings then sailed farther south, perhaps as far as what is now New England. According to the sagas, they saw forests, meadows, and rivers that held "larger salmon than they had ever seen."

Eriksson settled in a coastal area he called Vinland. The Vikings left Vinland after only a few years, however. As one Viking reported, "they would always live in dread" of attacks by Native Americans. Vinland may also have simply been too far from other Viking settlements to be supported. In the 1400s the Vikings left Greenland as well. The settlers remained in Iceland, however.

That's Interesting!

Fire and Ice Did you know that Iceland has more than 200 volcanoes? That's right! While icy glaciers cover one tenth of the island, large numbers of volcanoes erupt from the island's surface. There are also many geysers and hot springs, which supply energy used today to heat homes. And despite being located just south of the Arctic Circle, Iceland's average daily temperatures are only slightly below freezing in the winter. Iceland's unusually fair weather made it an inviting spot for the Vikings to start a settlement.

✔ **Reading Check: Sequencing** What were the stages of Viking exploration that led to their landing in North America, and when did the landing take place?

The Middle Ages

While the Vikings were exploring, Europe was struggling through a difficult period. Beginning in the late A.D. 300s, the Roman Empire had suffered serious political and economic problems. The vast empire soon crumbled under continued invasion by groups such as the Huns. The fall of the Roman Empire marked the beginning of Europe's **Middle Ages**. This historical period lasted roughly from A.D. 500 to 1500. During the Middle Ages, trade and communication were limited. City populations also dropped as people moved into the countryside.

During the Middle Ages a new system of government called **feudalism** emerged. Under this system people known as vassals pledged their loyalty to a lord in exchange for land. Acquiring land was an important step to achieving power and wealth in the Middle Ages. The lord benefited by gaining the military services of his vassals. These vassals often included mounted warriors called knights. Feeding knights and their horses and equipping them with weapons and armor was expensive. However, nobles needed knights to defend their **manors**, or large estates, against attack. The feudal system relied on the loyalty of vassals.

Unlike the nobility, peasants—free tenants and serfs—farmed the land. Tenants rented land from lords and could leave when their rental agreements were over. In contrast, serfs lived on one manor for life, farming the lord's land or performing other services. In return they received the protection of the lord. The degree of personal freedom enjoyed by serfs varied in different parts of Europe. In addition to peasants, there were a small number of slaves in Europe.

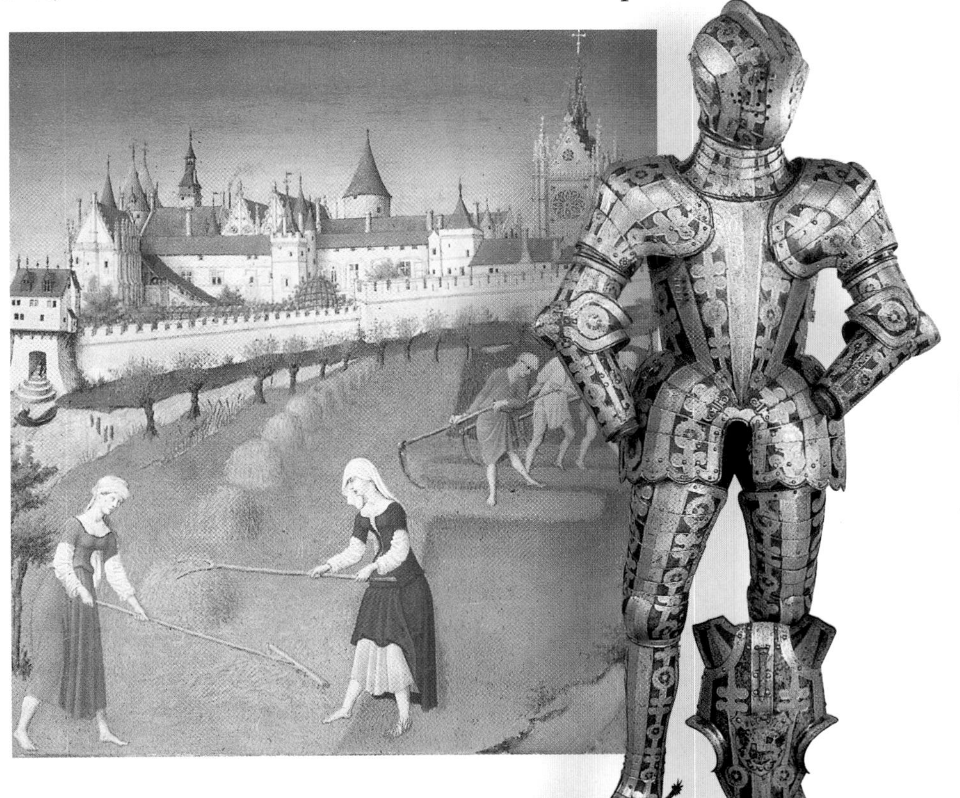

Interpreting the Visual Record

Society in the Middle Ages *While peasants such as those shown here working in the fields had few belongings, wealthy nobles might own fine goods such as this beautifully decorated suit of armor.* ***What types of buildings can be seen behind the peasants?***

Life on a Manor

Manors provided most of what their inhabitants needed to live. Lords ruled their manors with little interference. Lords and their families lived in large wooden or stone houses or castles. These were often surrounded by water-filled trenches—called moats—and high walls for defense. Noblemen spent their time ruling, fighting in battles, and managing their farmland. Noblewomen usually ran the home and raised children. Noblemen and noblewomen also spent a large amount of time carrying out their duties as Christians. For example, women often prayed daily for the well-being of the household. In 1190 Richard of Devizes listed some of the qualities of **Eleanor of Aquitaine**, whom he considered an ideal noblewoman. He described her as "beautiful yet virtuous [moral], powerful yet gentle, humble yet keenwitted [intelligent]."

Life for peasants was very different. Whole families often slept and ate in a single room. Women and men worked in the fields from before sunrise until after sunset. From an early age, children were also expected to work. Children grew up knowing that they would have little chance to move ahead in life. Under feudalism, a person's birth usually determined his or her place in society.

✔ **Reading Check: Contrasting** How did daily life differ for nobles and peasants during the Middle Ages?

Interpreting the Visual Record

Medieval architecture *This French cathedral built in the 1200s reflects the beauty of medieval architecture.* ***How might the design of such a building have affected those who worshiped there?***

The Catholic Church

The Catholic Church was the center of religious and social life in the Middle Ages. Both peasants and nobles attended church services led by the local priest. Priests also cared for the sick and poor, counseled the rich, and taught the young. Frequent religious festivals offered everyone a chance to celebrate.

Many religious groups existed during the Middle Ages, but most Europeans were Roman Catholic. Christianity influenced culture and politics across Europe. By the late 800s, the Church owned large amounts of land. In addition, church leaders often advised rulers on important matters. The Catholic Church paid for many art and architecture projects. One example is the Notre Dame cathedral in Paris, France.

Monasteries were important during the early Middle Ages. These were religious communities in which men called monks devoted their lives to practicing Christianity. Monks gave up all personal possessions, but monasteries themselves often owned large estates. Monasteries became centers of learning, and some produced books.

Similar religious centers for women were called convents. The women who lived in these convents were known as nuns. Nuns spent most of their time running convent lands, reading religious texts, and writing. They also created works of art and earned money selling crafts such as woven goods. Many women joined convents because they wanted to devote their lives to learning and prayer. Convents gave women an alternative to getting married and having children. In other cases, families encouraged elderly or unmarried women to become nuns.

Convents offered women a rare chance to pursue an education. Some nuns wrote history, poetry, and plays. Others even advised leaders. Saint Hilda, who founded a religious community, received praise from an early historian of England.

"So great was her prudence [good judgment] that not only ordinary folk, but kings and princes used to come and ask her advice in their difficulties and take it."

Bede, *A History of the English Church and People*

BIOGRAPHY

William of Normandy

(c. 1028–1087)

William of Normandy, also known as William the Conqueror, was born in what is now France. When the English king Edward the Confessor died in 1066, Duke William invaded England. He fought and defeated the new English king, Harold, at the Battle of Hastings.

William brought many changes to English society. He and his nobles established the feudal system in England and built the first English castles. William's court also introduced the English to French customs, laws, and language. What were some of the ways that William changed English society?

✔ **Reading Check:** **Analyzing Information** What role did the Catholic Church play in people's lives during the Middle Ages?

The Rise of Nations

During the mid- and late Middle Ages, some nobles began losing power to growing kingdoms. These kingdoms, including England and France, became some of the first nations in the world. In 1066 **William of Normandy** conquered England. (Normandy is an area in present-day France.) He later ordered a survey of the entire kingdom. The result was the enormous Domesday Book, or Day of Judgment Book. A writer recorded the process used to collect the information.

"William, king of the English, sent [his men] through all the provinces of England and caused it to be inquired [asked] . . . how much the king had in lands and cattle and livestock in each province. . . . And so thoroughly was all this carried out that there did not remain in the whole of England . . . an ox or cow or a pig which was not written in that return [document]. And all the writings of all these things were brought back to the king."

—Anonymous, quoted in *English Historical Documents, 1042–1189*, edited by David C. Douglas and George W. Greenaway

Analyzing Primary Sources

Making Generalizations and Predictions Why would the information from this survey have been important to the king?

The Bayeux Tapestry shows the Norman invasion of England.

As trade brought greater riches to Europe, wealthy couples could enjoy fine weddings such as the one shown here.

During the rule of William's great-great-grandson **King John**, the nobles rebelled against his misuse of royal power. In 1215 they forced John to agree to **Magna Carta**, or the Great Charter. The charter addressed the land rights of nobles. It also required the king to gain the agreement of the nobility before raising new taxes. In addition, Magna Carta was one of the first documents to protect some of the rights of free people.

The early 1200s brought other major changes to Europe. Trade greatly increased. One major cause for this was that Italian cities began expanding their trade connections. Eventually Italian merchants were trading regularly with nations around the Mediterranean Sea and northern Europe.

Across Europe, advances in farming led to increased food production and rising populations. Farmers began using horses instead of oxen to pull plows. They also learned to fertilize soil and to rotate crops. As the population grew, landowners cleared more land for farming. Many people began using new technology, such as windmills and watermills. These devices provided power for grinding grain, working with metals, and pumping water.

More people and more trade meant new towns and larger cities. With the growth of technology, trade, and kingdoms, by 1500 Europe's Middle Ages were drawing to a close.

✔ **Reading Check: Summarizing** How did countries change in the late Middle Ages?

go.hrw.com **Homework Practice Online**
keyword: SC3 HP1

1. **Define** and explain:
   - feudalism
   - manors
2. **Identify** and explain:
   - Leif Eriksson
   - Middle Ages
   - Eleanor of Aquitaine
   - William of Normandy
   - King John
   - Magna Carta
3. **Comparing and Contrasting** Copy the diagram below. Use it to explain the similarities and differences between peasants' and nobles' daily lives under feudalism.

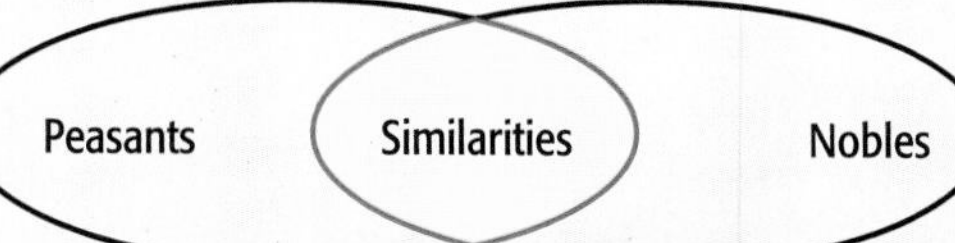

4. **Finding the Main Idea**
   a. What technology enabled the Vikings to explore new lands, and what were the results of their explorations?
   b. How did the Catholic Church influence daily life and culture during the Middle Ages?
5. **Writing and Critical Thinking**
   Identifying Cause and Effect Imagine that you are a monk or a nun during the Middle Ages and you are recording the history of your time. Write a paragraph explaining the major changes of the late Middle Ages and their effects.
   Consider the following:
   - the significance of Magna Carta
   - the expansion of trade
   - advances in agricultural technology

Section 4

Trade across Continents

Read to Discover

1. How did Islam affect the Mediterrean region?
2. What led the Chinese to join in and then withdraw from international trade?
3. How did trade influence African kingdoms?

Why It Matters Today

Trade remains an important way for cultures around the world to interact with one another. Use CNNfyi.com or other **current events** sources to find information about some of the products that the United States trades with other countries. Record your findings in your journal.

Identify

- Muhammad
- Islam
- Crusades
- Kublai Khan
- Silk Road
- Zheng He
- Mansa Musa

The Story Continues

The city of Mecca, in what is now Saudi Arabia, was a thriving trade center. One of its residents was Muhammad, a successful Arab merchant. In A.D. 610 Muhammad's life changed dramatically. That year he recorded having a vision of an angel, who ordered him to teach the word of God, or Allah. Muhammad dedicated his life to this task, spreading his faith first in Mecca and later in other communities. He overcame many obstacles and founded the religion known as Islam.

This Turkish miniature shows an Islamic scene.

The Spread of Islam

Muhammad devoted his life to preaching the messages of Allah. After his death, Muhammad's followers wrote these messages in the Qur'an (kuh-RAN), the holy book of **Islam**. Islam gained many followers, called Muslims, who swiftly spread their faith. Muslims took Jerusalem, Syria, the Persian Empire, and Egypt. Once they held the seaports of Syria and Egypt, Muslims built a powerful navy. By the late 600s they dominated the eastern Mediterranean Sea. Before long, North Africa, Sicily, and much of present-day Spain had come under Muslim control.

Muslim traders helped spread Islam. Trade also allowed people to exchange new ideas. Muslims valued learning highly. Muslim mathematicians adopted a numeral system from India, including the concept of zero. Using this system, they developed algebra. Muslim scholars also studied medicine, philosophy, astronomy, and physics. Some of this they learned from ancient Greek writings. Muslim doctors improved surgical methods and the understanding of diseases. One teacher gave the following advice to young students. "He who has not endured the stress of study will not taste the joy of knowledge."

✔ **Reading Check: Drawing Inferences and Conclusions** Besides the spread of knowledge, in what other ways do you think the Muslim empire benefited from trade?

The Crusades

Like Jews and Christians, Muslims showed their faith by visiting the Holy Land. This area included the city of Jerusalem and the land surrounding it. Muslims conquered Jerusalem in 637 but continued to let people of other religions visit. However, about 1077 the Seljuk Turks, who were also Muslims, took over the city and began to prevent Christians from visiting holy places. In 1095 Pope Urban II called on all Christians to start a holy war to seize control of Jerusalem.

History Makers Speak

"Jerusalem is the center of the earth; the land is fruitful above all others, like another paradise of delights. . . . This royal city . . . is now held captive by the enemies of Christ. . . . When an armed attack is made upon the enemy, let this one cry be raised by all the soldiers of God: it is the will of God! It is the will of God!"

Pope Urban II, quoted in *The Medieval Reader,* edited by Norman Cantor

Interpreting the Visual Record

Crusaders *A group of crusaders is preparing to travel to the Holy Land. The banners of different noble families fly above the ships.* ***What does this image suggest about the difficulty of reaching the Holy Land?***

With these words, the pope asked Christians across Europe to take back the Holy Land. The resulting military expeditions to the Holy Land, which continued off and on for more than 150 years, were called the **Crusades**. Many knights, soldiers, and nobles joined the holy wars. According to William of Malmesbury, the Crusades greatly changed the European population. The "lands were deserted of their husbands-men, houses of their inhabitants, even whole cities migrated."

The crusaders captured Jerusalem in 1099 and controlled it for nearly 90 years. However, in 1187 Saladin, a Muslim sultan, arrived with a massive army. At the end of the battle that followed, the city was back in Muslim hands. Future Crusades were unable to recapture Jerusalem.

✔ **Reading Check: Finding the Main Idea** Why did the Crusades take place?

Empires in Asia

While fighting continued in the Holy Land, China faced an invasion by the Mongols of Central Asia. Chinese emperors had built the Great Wall—which stretched some 4,500 miles—to defend against such attacks. But Mongol leader Genghis Khan could not be stopped. By 1279 his grandson **Kublai Khan** (koo-bluh-KAHN) ruled an Asian empire that stretched to the Black Sea from China's southern coast. Kublai Khan used his large navy to expand trade. In addition, merchants used the **Silk Road**, an overland trade route running from China to the Black Sea.

In 1368 the Ming dynasty overthrew the Mongol Empire in China. Zhu Di seized the Ming throne in 1402. He soon built a large fleet of ships. This fleet allowed China to exchange silk and porcelain for spices and other goods. China established new trade with India and Arabia. Admiral **Zheng He** commanded the fleet's 317 brightly painted ships and more than 27,000 men. His expeditions brought wealth and knowledge of other cultures to China.

After Zheng He's death, the Ming dynasty reduced its long-distance ocean trade. By the mid-1400s, China had abandoned its command of the seas. Political conflicts, piracy, a lack of tax money, and other events led the country to refocus on internal affairs.

✔ **Reading Check Summarizing** What role did China play in international trade between the 1200s and 1400s?

African Trading Kingdoms

Well before Chinese merchants established trade contacts with East Africa, several African kingdoms had grown wealthy from long-distance trade. The Aksum kingdom began in present-day Ethiopia. Aksum gained much of its wealth by trading with Egypt and ports in the Indian Ocean.

GLOBAL CONNECTIONS

The Silk Road

In the 100s B.C. Chinese emperor Wu Di opened up China's western trade routes. Chinese merchants began sending goods to Central Asia along a great highway known as the Silk Road. It eventually stretched about 5,000 miles from eastern China to the Black Sea. Harsh weather and bandits made the Silk Road dangerous.

The promise of wealth kept traders on the Silk Road. By A.D. 100, large caravans made regular journeys from western China. Chinese merchants carried furs, ceramics, jade, cinnamon, and silk. Caravans returning to China carried valuables like gold, glass, and linen fabrics.

Trade along the Silk Road slowed in the 800s, renewed in the 1300s, and then ended. Today, adventurers explore parts of what was once the Silk Road. **Why was the Silk Road important?**

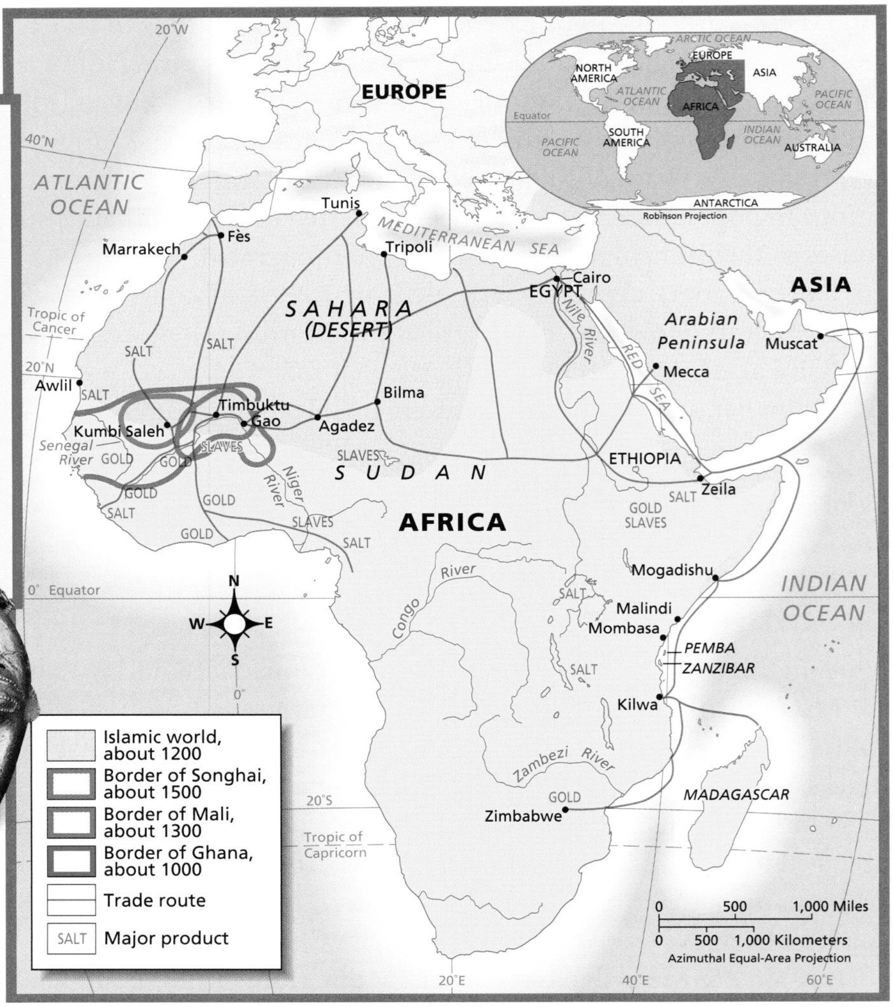

African Trading Kingdoms

Interpreting Maps The African trade routes allowed the exchange of goods between regions and cultures.

Skills Assessment

1. **Places and Regions** According to the map, what products came from the African region south of the equator?
2. **Comparing** Which African kingdom was larger: Ghana, Mali, or Songhai?

Islamic world, about 1200
Border of Songhai, about 1500
Border of Mali, about 1300
Border of Ghana, about 1000
Trade route
SALT Major product

Important port cities were built along the Red Sea, which separates Africa from Southwest Asia. Aksum's most valuable trade good was ivory. Many Aksumites converted to Christianity after North African and Middle Eastern Christians introduced the religion.

Farther down the East African coast, Arab traders came into contact with Bantu-speaking peoples. They traded in market centers that grew into about 30 separate city-states. Each competed for control of the trade in gold, ivory, and slaves in southern Africa. Among the most important city-states were Mogadishu (moh-guh-DEE-shoo), Mombasa (mohm-BAH-sah), and Kilwa. Bantu and Arab influences in the region combined to create a unique culture. The people shared a common religion, Islam, and a new language, Swahili (swah-HEE-lee).

Long-distance trading networks also developed in West Africa. Traders eventually used camels to carry goods across the desert. These nomads from North Africa and the northern Sahara—called Berbers—brought salt south and gold north. Several kingdoms and empires grew wealthy and powerful from this trade. Ghana (GAH-nuh) ruled an area between the Niger (NY-juhr) and Senegal Rivers to the south and the

Free Find:
Two Views of Africa
After reading al-Mas'udi's and Ibn Battuta's accounts of traveling in Africa on the **Holt Researcher CD–ROM**, create a travel guide to these areas during the times the authors were there.

Sahara to the north. Most of Ghana's wealth came from trading gold. Berber merchants carried the gold north to the Mediterranean.

Mali emerged in the early 1200s, long after Ghana had collapsed. Mali stretched more than 1,000 miles inland from Africa's west coast. The empire of Mali included the important trading city of Timbuktu (tim-buhk-TOO). The Muslim traveler Ibn Battuta described the empire.

This mosque in Timbuktu, Mali, dates from the early 1300s.

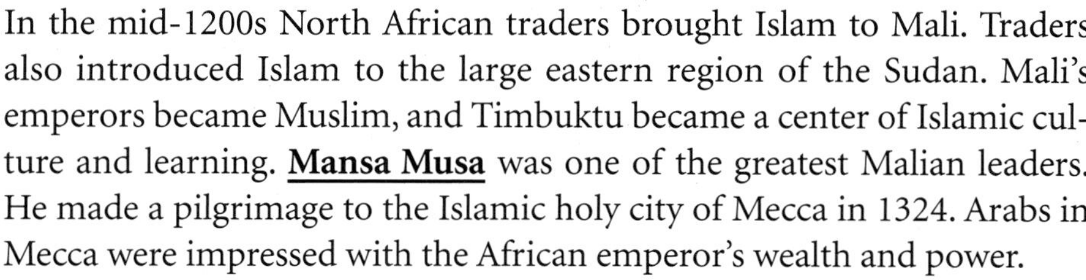

"[The Malians] are seldom unjust, and have a greater horror of injustice than other people. Their [ruler] shows no mercy to anyone who is guilty of the least act of it. There is complete security in their country. Neither traveler nor inhabitant in it has anything to fear from robbers or men of violence."

Ibn Battuta, quoted in *A Short History of Africa,* by Roland Oliver and J. D. Fage

In the mid-1200s North African traders brought Islam to Mali. Traders also introduced Islam to the large eastern region of the Sudan. Mali's emperors became Muslim, and Timbuktu became a center of Islamic culture and learning. **Mansa Musa** was one of the greatest Malian leaders. He made a pilgrimage to the Islamic holy city of Mecca in 1324. Arabs in Mecca were impressed with the African emperor's wealth and power.

The large Songhai (SAWNG-hy) Empire also had great influence in the region. Songhai's Muslim rulers encouraged the spread of Islamic culture throughout their vast territory. The Songhai Empire remained powerful until the late 1500s.

✔ **Reading Check: Summarizing** What effect did trade have on different empires in Africa?

Section 4 Review

go.hrw.com Homework Practice Online
keyword: SC3 HP1

1. **Identify** and explain:
   - Muhammad
   - Islam
   - Crusades
   - Kublai Khan
   - Silk Road
   - Zheng He
   - Mansa Musa

2. **Summarizing** Copy the chart below. Use it to list the benefits of global trade for Africa, China, and the Muslim empire.

	Traded with	Benefits
Africa		
China		
Muslim empire		

3. **Finding the Main Idea**
   a. How was Islam spread through much of the Mediterranean region?
   b. When did China reopen trading networks with other countries, and what led to the decline of Chinese participation in international trade?

4. **Writing and Critical Thinking**
   Supporting a Point of View Imagine that you are a noble lord in Europe at the time of the first Crusades. Write a speech to give to your vassals explaining why you think joining the Crusade is or is not a good idea.
   Consider the following:
   - Pope Urban's call to protect Jerusalem
   - the risks of war so far from home
   - the potential benefits of occupying the Holy Land

Chapter 1 Review

The Chapter at a Glance

Examine the visual summary of the chapter below. Then use it to create a graphic organizer covering the chapter's main ideas that you might give to a classmate.

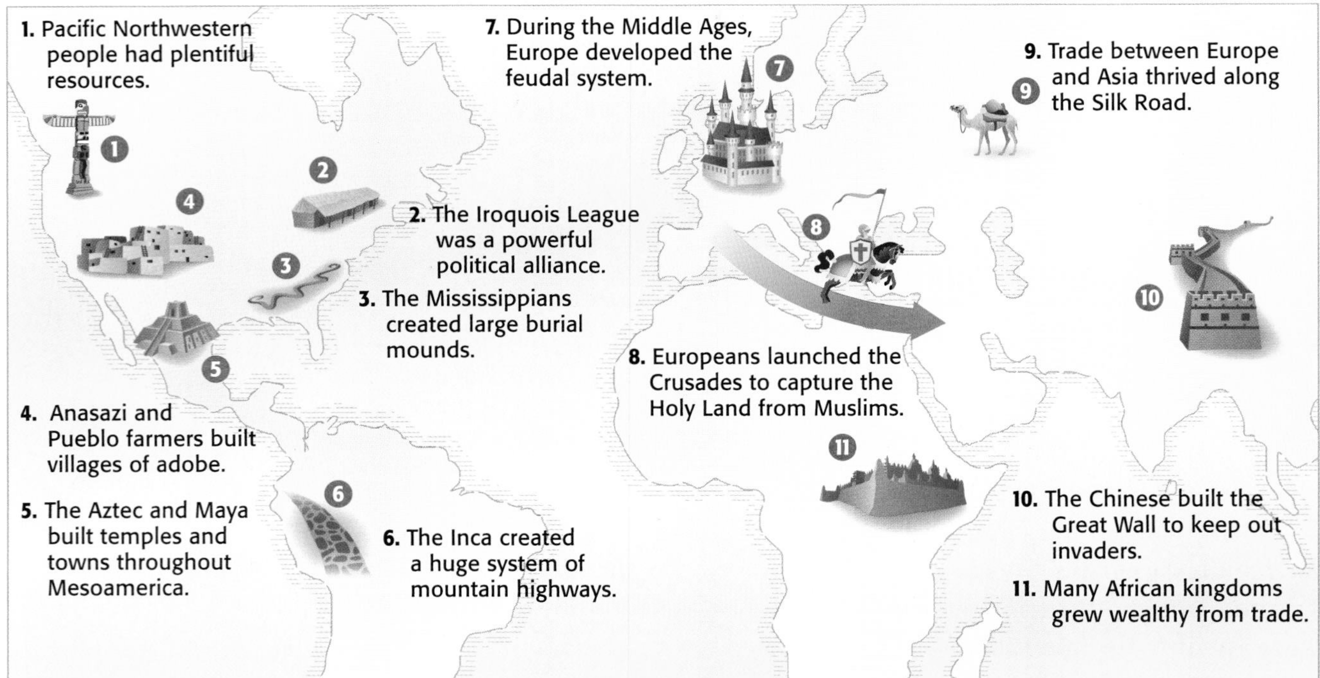

Identifying People and Ideas

Use the following terms and people in historically significant sentences.

1. archaeology
2. domestication
3. totems
4. Leif Eriksson
5. feudalism
6. Eleanor of Aquitaine
7. Magna Carta
8. Crusades
9. Silk Road
10. Zheng He

Understanding Main Ideas

Section 1 *(Pages 4–9)*

1. How did Paleo-Indians adapt to the widespread environmental changes caused by the end of the Ice Age?
2. What were some of the major achievements of Mesoamerican civilizations?

Section 2 *(Pages 10–16)*

3. How did the different environments in North America affect the ways that Native Americans gained food?
4. What was the Iroquois League?

Section 3 *(Pages 17–22)*

5. What role did the Catholic Church play in the Middle Ages?

Section 4 *(Pages 23–27)*

6. What were the Crusades, and why did they take place?
7. What were some of Africa's major kingdoms?

You Be the Historian— Reviewing Themes

1. **Culture** In what ways were Native American societies in the same region often similar?
2. **Geography** What types of housing did Native Americans build and why?
3. **Global Relations** How did trade networks benefit civilizations in Africa, Asia, and Europe?

Thinking Critically

1. **Comparing and Contrasting** How were the early Native American groups in the Northwest and Northeast culture areas similar and different?
2. **Finding the Main Idea** How did the development of agriculture change the way Native Americans lived?
3. **Supporting a Point of View** Do you think that all members of European society benefited from the feudal system during the Middle Ages? Explain your answer.

Social Studies Skills Workshop

Interpreting Maps

Study the map below. Then use the information on the map to help you answer the questions that follow.

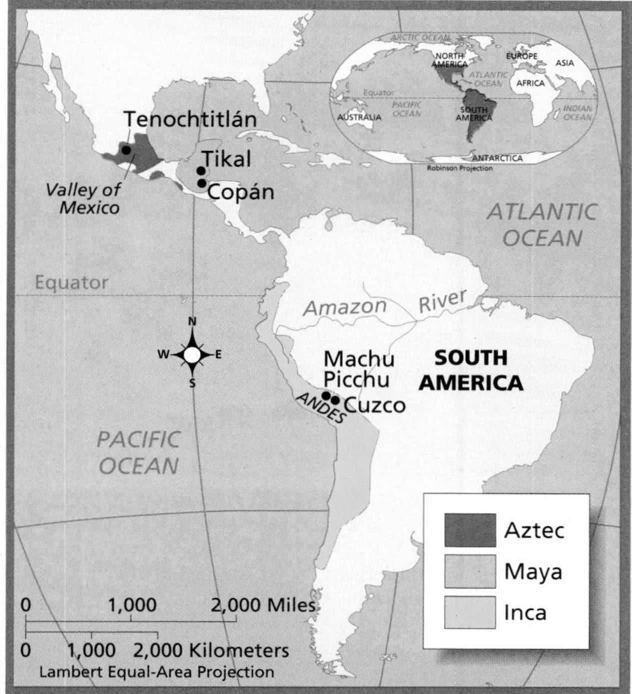

1. Which of the following is a fair statement based on the information provided on the map?
   a. The Maya Empire developed along the Pacific Coast.
   b. The Inca Empire developed along the Amazon River.
   c. Tenochtitlán was the capital of the Maya Empire.
   d. The Inca Empire controlled more land than the Aztec or Maya Empires.

2. Using the map, locate and identify the major geographic features within the Aztec and Inca Empires. How might these different environments have led to differences between the two civilizations?

Analyzing Primary Sources

Read the following pledge of loyalty by the knight Bernard Atton, then answer the questions.

> **"I swear upon these four gospels of God that I will always be a faithful vassal to thee and to thy successors . . . in all things in which a vassal is required to be faithful to his lord; and I will defend thee, my lord, and all thy successors . . . and the castles and manors and all your men and their possessions against all malefactors [criminals] and invaders, of my own free will."**

3. Which of the following best sums up what Bernard Atton is promising?
   a. to provide land and money to his lord
   b. to protect the lord and his possessions
   c. to be faithful to the Church
   d. to capture criminals

4. Whom does Atton promise to serve?
   a. only his lord
   b. his lord and the king
   c. his lord and the Catholic Church
   d. his lord and all his lord's successors

5. Historians carefully examine the historical context in which a source was written. Why might a ruler during Europe's Middle Ages have needed the services of a knight like Bernard Atton?

Alternative Assessment

Building Your Portfolio

American History

Cooperative Learning

Complete the following activity in small groups. Your group is responsible for creating a detailed map of a manor during the Middle Ages. Assign each group member the role of one of the following members of feudal society: lord, vassal, peasant, or church official. Each member should study his or her role and make suggestions for how it should be represented on the map. Your map should show where different groups lived, public buildings such as a church, and images of daily activity.

internet connect

Internet Activity: go.hrw.com
keyword: SC3 CF1

Choose a topic about the World before the Opening of the Atlantic:

- Model Maya mathematics by solving a math problem.
- Learn about Paleolithic culture at the Clovis site.
- Research modern Africa and Asia.

CHAPTER

2 New Empires in the Americas

(1450–1750)

Columbus encountered the Taino Indians when he reached the Americas.

An ancient Aztec drawing

UNITED STATES

1492 Christopher Columbus and his crew reach the Americas on October 12.

1497 John Cabot reaches the coast of North America.

1450 1470 1480 1490

WORLD

1469 Isabella of Castile and Ferdinand II of Aragon marry.

1488 Portuguese explorer Bartolomeu Dias is blown off course and passes the Cape of Good Hope at the southern tip of Africa.

1494 The Treaty of Tordesillas between Spain and Portugal divides the world's unexplored lands.

1495 Leonardo da Vinci begins painting his masterpiece *The Last Supper*.

Portuguese explorers used astrolabes like this one to navigate the seas.

Build on What You Know

During the Middle Ages communication and trade between Europe and other areas slowed. By the 1300s, however, feudal society in Europe had formed trading relationships with merchants from Africa and Asia. During the Renaissance, Europeans began to seek out new sea routes to Asia. While trying to find a new route, Christopher Columbus reached the Americas in 1492.

Explorer Samuel de Champlain allied with some American Indians against their enemies. This illustration shows him leading an attack on an Indian fort in what is now western New York.

Canoes were a common means of travel in the Great Lakes region.

1500 Portuguese explorer Pedro Álvars Cabral lands in South America.

1504 Columbus returns to Spain from his fourth and final voyage to the Americas.

1513 Juan Ponce de León lands in Florida.

1522 Survivors of Ferdinand Magellan's expedition for Spain complete the first voyage around the world.

1535 Jacques Cartier of France sails up the St. Lawrence River to the site of present-day Montreal.

1615 French explorer Samuel de Champlain reaches the Great Lakes.

1500 | 1510 | 1520 | 1530 | 1750

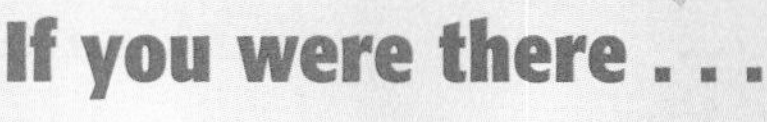

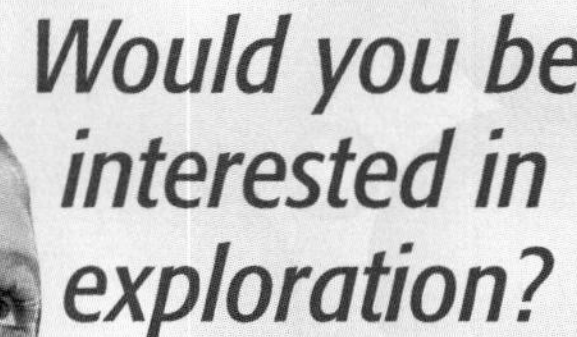

If you were there . . .
Would you be interested in exploration?

You Be the Historian

What's Your Opinion? Do you **agree** or **disagree** with the following statements? Support your point of view in your journal.

- **Economics** Exploration improves a country's economy.
- **Geography** Lands that are dangerous can never be settled.
- **Culture** Conflicts arise when people with different languages, religions, and cultures meet.

Section 1

Early Voyages of Exploration

Read to Discover

1. How did the Portuguese seek direct trade with Asia?
2. Why did Christopher Columbus make his voyage across the Atlantic Ocean?
3. How did Europeans react to Columbus's voyages?

Why it Matters Today

Christopher Columbus was the first European to explore the Caribbean. Today many Caribbean countries have a mix of European, American Indian, and African cultures. Use CNNfyi.com or other **current events** sources to learn about some of the foods, languages, music, or sports that are common in the Caribbean today. Record your findings in your journal.

Define

- monopoly
- astrolabe
- caravel

Identify

- Prince Henry
- Bartolomeu Dias
- Christopher Columbus
- King Ferdinand
- Queen Isabella
- Line of Demarcation
- Treaty of Tordesillas

Columbus was inspired by travelers' tales, such as Marco Polo's Description of the World.

The Story Continues

In 1488 Christopher Columbus traveled to Portugal to meet with King John II. The Italian explorer wanted to sail across the Atlantic Ocean to Asia. He hoped that the king would give him money and ships to achieve his dream. King John had called Columbus "a big talker . . . full of fancy and imagination." However, King John was still interested in Columbus's idea. Just as Columbus arrived in Lisbon, Bartolomeu Dias returned with news of sailing around the tip of Africa. King John decided that reaching Asia by way of Africa was the best idea. Columbus left Portugal without support for his plan.

The Search for a Sea Route

In the 1400s the Italian city of Venice held a **monopoly**, or sole control, on European trade with Asia. Goods were carried from Asia on the Silk Road and shipped to Venice across the Mediterranean Sea. Wanting a share of this profitable trade, other European nations looked for a sea route to the East. Under the guidance of **Prince Henry**, known as the Navigator, Portugal led the way.

Sailors traveled the open seas by charting the position of the stars with an ancient invention called the **astrolabe.** To improve sailing techniques, Prince Henry gathered experts in navigation, mapmaking, shipbuilding, and sailing. His team designed the **caravel,** a small sturdy ship made to be fast and easy to manage. He also paid for expeditions along the west coast of Africa, hoping that his sailors would discover a water route to Asia. One person made this observation about Prince Henry.

> **"It seemed to him that if he or some other lord did not endeavor [try] to gain that knowledge, no mariners [sailors] or merchants would ever dare to attempt it."**
>
> —Gomes Eannes de Zurara, quoted in *The Chronicles of the Discovery and Conquest of Guinea,* by C. Raymond Beasley and Edgar Prestage

By the time Prince Henry died in 1460, the Portuguese were successfully exploring the west coast of Africa.

In 1487 Portuguese captain **Bartolomeu Dias** led an expedition along the African coast. A terrible storm blew his ships far out to sea. When Dias sighted land again, he learned that he had passed the southern tip of Africa. He returned to Portugal and reported the good news to King John. The tip of Africa was named the Cape of Good Hope "for the promise it gave of the finding of India."

The Portuguese set up small trading posts along the coast of Africa. There they traded cloth, armor, and guns for gold, ivory, and slaves. The Portuguese got slaves from Arab or African merchants, who traded people who had been captured during wars or raids. Most Europeans felt that it was acceptable to enslave non-Christians. Many enslaved Africans worked on farms in Portuguese colonies where they endured hard labor and bad living conditions. For these people and their communities, the European explorations had disastrous results.

✔ **Reading Check: Contrasting** What were the positive and negative effects of European exploration?

Columbus's Bold Idea

Christopher Columbus was an experienced Italian sailor from the town of Genoa. He was convinced that he could reach Asia by sailing west over the Atlantic Ocean—a very daring idea at the time. Some scholars believed that the Atlantic was more than 10,000 miles across from Europe to the Indies. (The Indies was a common European name for all Asian lands.) Traveling such a distance seemed impossible, and crews would need food and water to last for months. Columbus, however, believed the Atlantic was much smaller than this.

Free Find:
Henry the Navigator
After reading information about Prince Henry on the **Holt Researcher CD–ROM**, imagine what he studied. Make a list of classes that students hoping to become explorers would need to take.

Modern Explorers

Hundreds of years after Christopher Columbus set out on his first voyage, modern explorers continue to search the seas. Today deep-sea explorers have the help of underwater video cameras, robots, and remote-controlled vehicles. Many of these explorers hunt for shipwrecks. Divers have used Alvin, a vehicle that can carry three people 15,000 feet below the surface of the ocean, to explore the wreck of the *Titanic.* Some explorers hope to find lost treasure, while others are in search of historical knowledge. **How do you think exploration during Christopher Columbus's time was different than it is today?**

Columbus eventually convinced **King Ferdinand** and **Queen Isabella** of Spain to fund his voyage. At the time, Spain was fighting the kingdom of Granada, which was held by the Moors. These North African Muslims had conquered the area in the early Middle Ages. Finally, in January 1492 Spain won Granada, and the *Reconquista* (re-kawng-KEE-stah)—the ongoing struggle to drive the Moors from Spain—ended.

Ferdinand and Isabella ordered Columbus to bring back any "Pearls, Precious Stones, Gold, Silver, Spiceries, and other Things." They told Columbus to claim for Spain any lands he explored. In return, he could keep one tenth of all the gold he found and profits from any trading.

On August 3, 1492, Columbus's three ships set sail. The *Niña* and the *Pinta* were small fast caravels. Columbus sailed in the larger *Santa María.* The cramped ships were filled with some 90 sailors in all and carried a year's worth of supplies.

From Portugal's Canary Islands off the west coast of Africa, a favorable wind blew the three ships west across the Atlantic Ocean. Despite quick travel, after a month with no land in sight, the crew became very nervous and complained to Columbus. One Spaniard recalled:

Analyzing Primary Sources

Drawing Inferences and Conclusions Do you think Columbus would have given up before he reached the Indies? Explain your answer.

"The Admiral [Columbus] cheered them as best he could, holding out good hope of the benefits they would have. And he added that it was useless to complain since he had come to find the Indies, and so had to continue until he found them."

—Bartolomé de Las Casas, quoted in *The Conquest of America,* by Tzvetan Todorov

On October 12, 1492, a lookout saw land. The journey from the Canary Islands had taken 33 days. Exactly where Columbus landed is still a mystery, but most scholars believe he landed in the Bahamas. Columbus called the island San Salvador, which means "Holy Savior." He believed that San Salvador was near China or Japan. Columbus did not realize that he had actually landed between Europe and Asia.

Interpreting the Visual Record

Columbus's voyage *The small fleet that Columbus led faced great risks on its voyage across the Atlantic Ocean.* ***What dangers do you think the fleet encountered?***

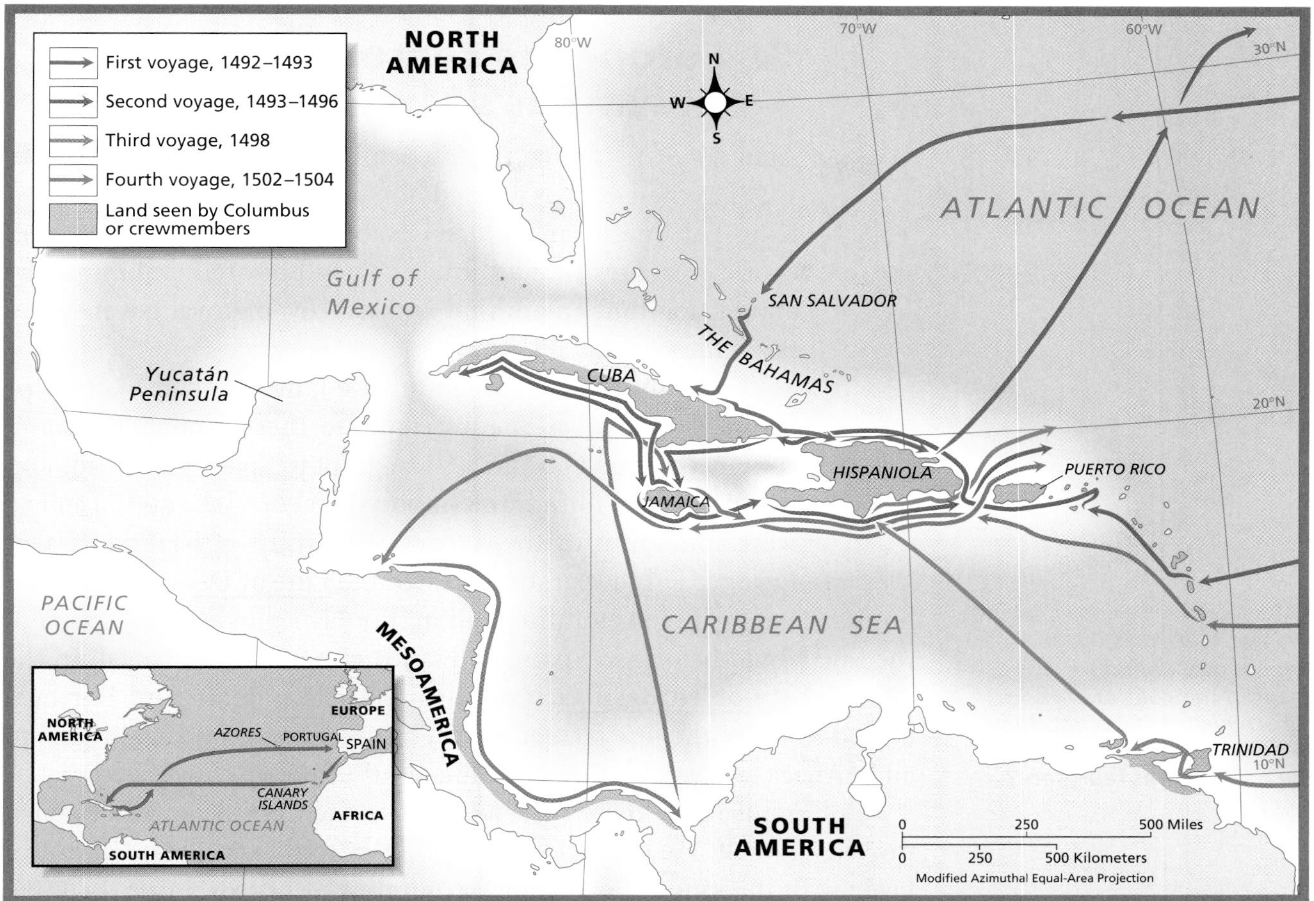

First voyage, 1492–1493
Second voyage, 1493–1496
Third voyage, 1498
Fourth voyage, 1502–1504
Land seen by Columbus or crewmembers

Columbus's Voyages, 1492–1504

Interpreting Maps Christopher Columbus made four trips to the Americas over a 12-year period. During these voyages, Columbus learned much about the lands and waters of the Caribbean Sea.

Skills Assessment **Places and Regions** On which voyage did Columbus reach the southwest edge of Cuba?

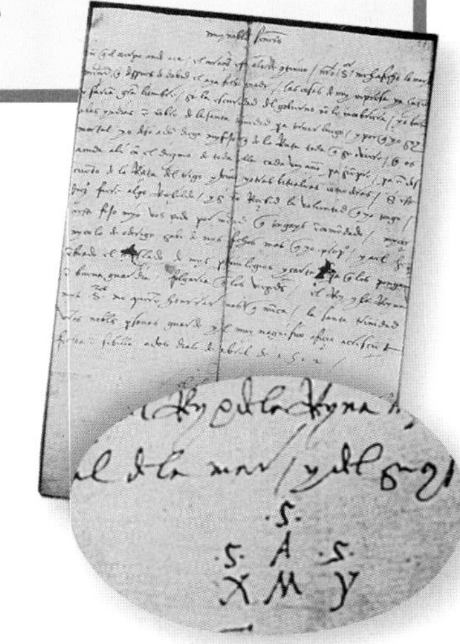
A letter that is believed to have been written by Columbus

In search of riches, Columbus explored other islands. He met the Taino (TY-noh) on an island he named Hispaniola. Believing he had landed in the Indies, he called the inhabitants of the islands Indians. Columbus explored the islands for several months and gathered unusual plants and animals and small amounts of gold. When Columbus decided that he had found enough gold and local treasures, he prepared to return to Spain. Before he and his men left, however, the *Santa María* struck a coral reef and sank. Because there was not enough room for all of the sailors on the *Niña* and *Pinta*, Columbus and his men built a small colony on the north coast of Hispaniola. They called it La Navidad, the Spanish word for Christmas. Columbus left about 40 of his men at La Navidad and promised to return for them soon. He then boarded the *Niña* and set sail for Spain in January 1493.

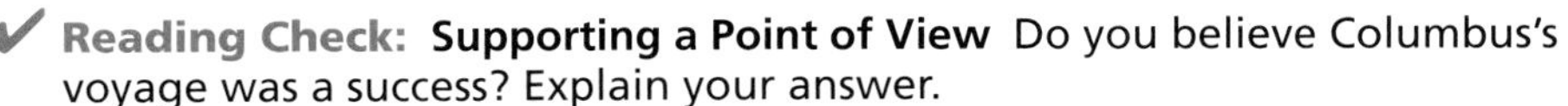
✔ **Reading Check: Supporting a Point of View** Do you believe Columbus's voyage was a success? Explain your answer.

Interpreting the Visual Record

A royal gift *Columbus was granted this coat of arms for his achievements.* ***What do you think the different images on the coat of arms represent?***

Europeans Learn of Columbus's Voyage

After a stormy return trip, Columbus finally reached Spain in 1493. Excited crowds greeted him as a hero. Columbus showed King Ferdinand and Queen Isabella the gold nuggets and exotic treasures he had found. They honored Columbus by appointing him an admiral and viceroy, or royal governor, of the Indies.

Columbus had claimed all the lands he had visited for Spain. To establish Spain's rights to these lands, Ferdinand convinced Pope Alexander VI to grant to Spain "all islands and mainlands . . . found one hundred leagues [about 300 miles] west and south of the Azores"—a group of islands west of Europe. This declaration created the **Line of Demarcation**, the boundary of Spain's exploration and monopoly rights. All lands west of the line would belong to Spain, and lands east of it to Portugal. In the 1494 **Treaty of Tordesillas** (tawrd-uh-SEE-uhs), Spain and Portugal agreed to move the line farther west. This treaty gave Portugal rights to all of Africa and what is now Brazil in South America.

Columbus made three more voyages to the Caribbean, all of which proved difficult. He quarreled with other officials and soon fell out of favor with the king, who stripped Columbus of his royal title. In 1506, after two years of very poor health, Columbus died "unnoticed and unsung," according to one modern historian. Years would pass before Europeans realized how much Columbus had changed their world.

✔ **Reading Check: Finding the Main Idea** Did the Spanish think that Columbus's first voyage was a success? Explain your answer.

Section 1 Review

keyword: SC3 HP2

1. **Define** and explain:
   - monopoly
   - astrolabe
   - caravel
2. **Identify** and explain:
   - Prince Henry
   - Bartolomeu Dias
   - Christopher Columbus
   - King Ferdinand
   - Queen Isabella
   - Line of Demarcation
   - Treaty of Tordesillas
3. **Identifying Cause and Effect** Copy the graphic organizer below. Use it to explain how Christopher Columbus made his voyage, why he chose that route, and what the results were.

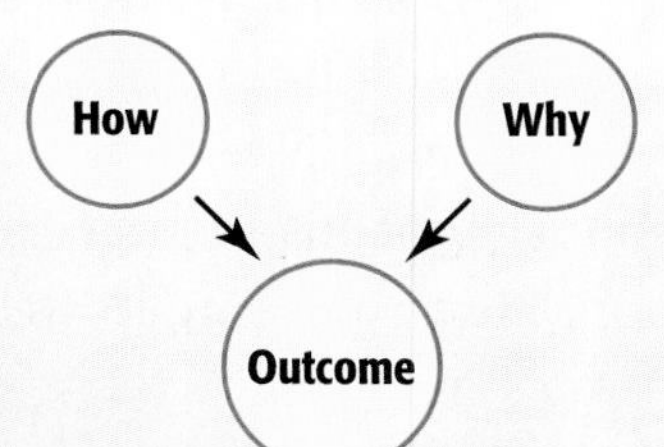

4. **Finding the Main Idea**
   a. How did Portugal try to begin trade with the East?
   b. What was the reaction in Europe to Columbus's voyages?
5. **Writing and Critical Thinking**
   Summarizing Imagine that you are a sailor serving under Christopher Columbus on his first voyage. Write three journal entries describing the events of the voyage.
   Consider the following:
   - travel conditions
   - concerns of the crew
   - Columbus's response

Section 2

Europe Looks to the Americas

Read to Discover

1. Where did the Portuguese explore, and what were the outcomes of their voyages?
2. Who explored for Spain after Columbus, and what were the results?
3. How did the Columbian Exchange affect the world?

Define

- strait
- circumnavigate

Identify

- Vasco da Gama
- Amerigo Vespucci
- Vasco Núñez de Balboa
- Ferdinand Magellan
- Columbian Exchange

WHY IT MATTERS TODAY

Today some countries are interested in exploring space instead of Earth. Use CNNfyi.com or other **current events** sources to find images related to recent space explorations. Record your findings in your journal.

The Story Continues

Christopher Columbus always believed that he had landed just off the coast of China. However, he knew that many people did not accept his claims. King Manuel had become ruler of Portugal in 1495. Manuel was one of those who thought that an eastern sea route to Asia, not Columbus's proposed western route, made more sense.

Chinese porcelain was a highly valued trade item in Europe.

Early Explorations

Portugal's King Manuel believed that the best route to Asia would follow Bartolomeu Dias's course south and east around Africa. The king chose **Vasco da Gama**, a minor noble and skilled sailor, to lead an expedition around the Cape of Good Hope. Da Gama spent two years planning the long dangerous journey.

In 1498 da Gama's fleet successfully rounded Africa's Cape of Good Hope and sailed across the Indian Ocean to southwestern India. The Portuguese began to build trading forts in Africa, India, and China. Wanting their share of the trade, other European nations sent sailors to explore Columbus's western route to Asia.

CONNECTING TO THE ARTS

Images of the Americas In the 1500s few Europeans had the chance to visit the Americas. Instead they relied on illustrated maps. Such maps often recorded where explorers went and what they found. The map of North and South America shown here is surrounded by pictures of explorers such as Columbus. As well as landmasses and names of places, the map includes decorations such as a sea monster. These early maps were often not very accurate, but they helped feed people's curiosity about new lands. **What major geographic errors can you find on this early map of the Americas?**

In 1501 Italian explorer **Amerigo Vespucci** (ve-SPOO-chee) reached the coast of what is now South America with a Spanish expedition. Vespucci believed that these were not just islands blocking the way to China. He wrote many exaggerated stories about his travels. A German mapmaker, impressed with Vespucci's writings, published a book with a large map showing new continents across the ocean. He labeled them "America" in honor of Vespucci. The book and map became popular, and Europeans soon began referring to these lands as North America and South America.

Europeans began to accept the idea that Columbus had not found a sea route to Asia after all. Instead, they realized, Asia lay somewhere to the west beyond the Americas. Spain began to search for a water passage through or around its American land claims. One Spanish explorer, **Vasco Núñez de Balboa** (NOON-yays day bahl-BOH-uh), had come to the Americas as Spain began to settle colonies there. While bargaining with a powerful American Indian nation in what is now Panama, he heard some fascinating news from an Indian leader.

Analyzing Primary Sources

Identifying Points of View What does this statement say about the American Indians' knowledge of the Europeans?

> **"I will shewe [show] you a region flowing with golde, where you may satisfie your ravening [hungry] appetites. . . . When you are passing over [the] mountains . . . you shall see another sea . . . with shippes as bigge as yours."**
>
> —Peter Martyr quoting an anonymous speaker, quoted in *The Discoverers,* by Daniel J. Boorstin

In 1513 Balboa gathered soldiers and Indian guides to find this mysterious sea. After weeks of travel he saw a great sparkling body of water that he called the South Sea. There was no way for ships to cross Panama to reach these waters, but Balboa believed that he might find a way into the South Sea. Balboa decided to build a fleet to explore the area around the coast. But his success threatened some Spanish authorities. Balboa's enemies charged him with treason and executed him in 1519.

✔ **Reading Check:** **Identifying Cause and Effect** Why did Spain and Portugal continue exploring, and what was the result of these explorations?

Sailing around the World

Portuguese sea captain **Ferdinand Magellan** (muh-JEL-uhn) soon learned of Balboa's discovery. Magellan became convinced that he could sail west to Asia by way of the South Sea. However, the Portuguese king refused to back Magellan's proposed voyage. Gradually, his confidence and experience as a sailor convinced Spanish officials to fund his trip and give him five ships.

Magellan set sail in September 1519. He reached the eastern coast of South America after a difficult trip across the Atlantic. Magellan went farther south, looking for a channel through the continent. The weather grew colder, and supplies ran low. Finally Magellan came upon a **strait**—a narrow sea passage—winding through the cliffs along the coast. Battling fierce winds, the crew took more than a month to pass through the narrow rock-filled strait. Finally, Magellan's crew spotted open sea. The passageway became known as the Strait of Magellan. As the ships sailed past the strait, the weather changed and the sea turned so calm that the crew renamed Balboa's South Sea, calling it the Pacific, or peaceful, Ocean.

The crew had lost two ships and used up much of its food and water while passing through the strait. Magellan thought they would reach Asia in a few weeks. Instead, the journey took more than 100 days. Finding food and water became key to survival. One of the sailors described the crew's hardships.

"We were three months and twenty days without getting any kind of fresh food. We ate . . . powder of biscuit swarming with worms. We drank yellow water that had been putrid [spoiled] for many days. . . . Often we ate sawdust."

—Antonio Pigafetta, quoted in *The Discoverers,* by Daniel J. Boorstin

Using instinct and skill, Magellan crossed the world's largest ocean and reached the Indies. Searching for islands not claimed by the Portuguese, he landed in what is now the Philippines. There, while helping the ruler of the Philippines in a war with another kingdom, Magellan was killed in battle.

BIOGRAPHY

Ferdinand Magellan

(c. 1480–1521)

Ferdinand Magellan was an explorer driven by a natural curiosity to search out distant lands. Yet the characteristics that made Magellan a great captain put him at a disadvantage with kings. King Manuel of Portugal dismissed Magellan's proposal to sail westward to Asia because of reports of Magellan's misconduct. Magellan then took his plan to the king of Spain. As a result, the Portuguese explorer was sponsored by Spain, which benefited from his discovery of a new route to Asia. **In what ways was Magellen's toughness useful, and how did it get in his way?**

That's Interesting!

"Golden Apples" Did you know that for many years some Europeans thought tomatoes were poisonous? It's true! Tomatoes originated in South America and later spread to Mesoamerica. The word *tomato* comes from the Aztec word *tomatl*. Tomatoes were first brought back to Europe by Spanish explorers. Northern Europeans grew tomato plants for decoration but were not sure that eating them was safe. In Italy and Spain, however, people soon began cooking with the new fruits. The Italians called tomatoes "golden apples," perhaps because some of the early varieties were yellow. Many years later, European settlers brought tomatoes back across the Atlantic Ocean to North America.

Juan Sebastián de Elcano led the crew home, traveling west. Only one of the three remaining ships made it back. In September 1522 the lucky ship *Vittoria* reached Spain with a cargo of cloves. The sale of the cloves paid for the cost of the entire trip and made a profit for the Crown, crew, and investors. However, this profit came at a terrible cost. Only 18 of the approximately 240 original crew had survived the long journey around the world.

Magellan's sailors were the first people to **circumnavigate**, or sail completely around, Earth. Their 40,000-mile journey took them across three oceans and gave Spain the all-water route to Asia that Columbus had searched for.

✔ **Reading Check: Sequencing** List the key events of the first circumnavigation of Earth in the order that they took place.

A Shift in Trade

The voyages of Columbus, da Gama, Magellan, and others turned the Atlantic Ocean into a gateway to Africa, the Americas, and India. Nations in western and northern Europe moved from the sidelines of world trade to the center. One Spaniard explained this change to the city council of Cordova. "Formerly we were at the end of the world; now we are in the middle of it, with an unprecedented [never before known] change in our fortunes."

With new sea routes, Spain's and Portugal's trade with Asia and Africa grew. The Portuguese controlled as much as 75 percent of the spice trade between Asia and Europe in the 1500s. They made huge profits on each round-trip trading voyage. As Spain and Portugal became richer, their influence in European affairs grew. Other European nations near the Atlantic wanted more wealth and power. They began to search for their own sea routes to China, India, and Japan.

Europeans also began to view the Atlantic as more than just a way to reach Africa and Asia. Explorers reported that the lands on the other side of the Atlantic were full of wealth. Columbus and Vespucci had told of lush forests, clear streams, and many natural resources in the Americas. In the 1500s some Europeans used these resources. For example, many Europeans crossed the northern Atlantic to catch huge schools of cod that lived off the coast of present-day Newfoundland.

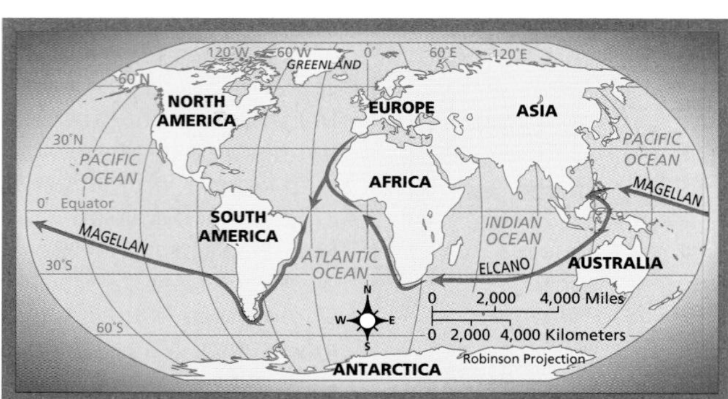

The Voyage of Magellan and Elcano, 1519–1522

Interpreting Maps After Ferdinand Magellan died, Juan Sebastián de Elcano became the leader of the fleet.

Skills Assessment The World in Spatial Terms What is the last ocean Magellan's ship crossed?

✔ **Reading Check: Identifying Cause and Effect** How did European countries react to Spain's new wealth, and what was the result?

The Columbian Exchange

In their travels, explorers transferred plants, animals, and diseases between the "Old World"—Europe, Asia, and Africa—and the "New World" of the Americas. This transfer, known as the **Columbian Exchange**, changed the world dramatically.

European explorers in the Americas found many new species of plants and animals. "All the trees were as different from ours as day from night," Columbus noted in his journal. American plants such as corn, potatoes, and tomatoes proved valuable to Europeans.

European settlers and explorers also brought plants and animals from Africa, Asia, and Europe to the American continents. Cattle, horses, and pigs soon ran wild in the Americas. European farmers also brought grains such as wheat and barley.

The explorers also brought diseases such as smallpox, measles, and typhus with them. Most adult Europeans had developed immunity, or natural resistance, to these sicknesses. However, American Indians had never dealt with these illnesses before and had no resistance to them. No one knows how many Indians of North and South America died from foreign diseases, but the loss of life was staggering.

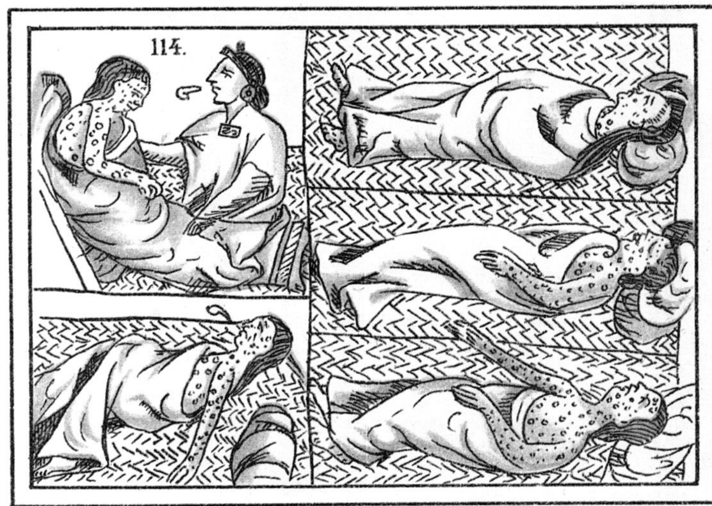

Interpreting the Visual Record

Deadly diseases *This illustration from a history of Spanish settlements in the Americas written in the 1500s shows the effects of smallpox on the Aztec of Mexico.* ***What feeling do you think the artist was trying to create in this illustration?***

✔ **Reading Check: Analyzing Information** How did the Columbian Exchange alter the world?

Section 2 Review

go.hrw.com **Homework Practice Online** keyword: SC3 HP2

1. **Define** and explain:
   - strait
   - circumnavigate
2. **Identify** and explain:
   - Vasco da Gama
   - Amerigo Vespucci
   - Vasco Núñez de Balboa
   - Ferdinand Magellan
   - Columbian Exchange
3. **Categorizing** Copy the chart below. Use it to show the positive and negative effects of the Columbian Exchange.

Positive	Negative

4. **Finding the Main Idea**
   a. What areas did Portugal send explorers to, and what was the result of their explorations?
   b. Who did Spain send to explore after the voyages of Columbus, and what did they discover?
5. **Writing and Critical Thinking**
   Making Predictions and Generalizations Imagine that you are a historian reflecting upon the voyages of explorers such as Ferdinand Magellan. Write a short magazine article explaining how you feel they changed the way people viewed the world.
   Consider the following:
   - Portuguese and Spanish explorations
   - increased global trade and world power
   - the Columbian Exchange

Section 3

The Spanish in America

Read to Discover

1. What led to the fall of the Aztec and Inca Empires?
2. How did Spain organize and govern its empire in the Americas?
3. How were the economy and society of New Spain structured?

Define

- conquistadores
- pueblos
- missions
- presidios
- *encomienda* system
- plantations
- borderlands

Identify

- Hernán Cortés
- Moctezuma II
- Francisco Pizarro
- Hernando de Soto
- Francisco Vásquez de Coronado
- Council of the Indies
- Bartolomé de Las Casas

Why It Matters Today

People from different cultures still fight against each other because their beliefs are different. Use CNNfyi.com or other **current events** sources to learn about a world conflict involving cultures with different beliefs. Record your findings in your journal.

Hernán Cortés came to the Americas as a young man hoping to gain wealth and power.

The Story Continues

The *Reconquista* was a time of constant warfare in Spain. From this struggle, a class of Spanish soldiers arose, experienced in fighting but with little land or money. Military leader Hernán Cortés explained, "Since this harsh land will yield us no living, we must rely on our swords and lances. For the same reason, we must move on." In the 1500s many Spanish soldiers went to the Americas to find their fortunes.

The Conquistadores

The **conquistadores** (kahn-kees-tuh-DAWR-eez) were Spanish soldiers who brought the spirit of the *Reconquista* to the Americas. After conquering Cuba, Jamaica, and Puerto Rico, they led military expeditions into the interior of the Americas, searching for riches and fame.

In 1519 the governor of Cuba sent conquistador **Hernán Cortés** to what is now Mexico, where Cortés heard stories of a wealthy land ruled by a king named **Moctezuma II** (MAWK-tay-soo-mah). Moctezuma ruled the

Interpreting the Visual Record

Tenochtitlán *The battle for Tenochtitlán destroyed much of the city.* ***What advantages does each army in the battle appear to have?***

Aztec Empire. The Aztec had a rich civilization. The empire also had fierce armies and demanded heavy taxes of crops and treasure from people they had conquered in central Mexico.

Cortés began his expedition with only about 500 soldiers, 16 horses, some guns, and thousands of Indian allies in his march to the Aztec capital city, Tenochtitlán. When the fighting ended, Moctezuma was dead and Tenochtitlán lay in ruins. As Cortés conquered other Aztec cities, the Aztec people began to die from diseases that the Spanish had brought to Mexico. Hundreds of thousands of Indians died from smallpox alone, quickening the fall of the Aztec Empire.

Cortés's conquest inspired other conquistadores. In the early 1530s **Francisco Pizarro** (pee-SAHR-roh) invaded the Inca Empire, a vast area of South America stretching from present-day central Chile to Colombia. With the help of Indian allies, Pizarro conquered the Inca by 1534. He gained huge amounts of gold and silver for himself and Spain. Even before Pizarro's conquest, Spain sent explorers to what is now Florida. In 1513 Juan Ponce de León (PAWN-say day lay-AWN) explored Florida in search of gold and a legendary Fountain of Youth.

In 1527 Pánfilo de Narváez led an unsuccessful expedition to the west coast of Florida. Two of the expedition's survivors, Álvar Núñez Cabeza de Vaca (kah-BAY-sah day BAH-kah) and a Moor named Estevanico (e-stay-bah-NEE-koh), crossed the Gulf of Mexico and landed in Texas in 1528. They spent eight years exploring Texas and New Mexico.

Eventually, de Vaca traveled to Mexico with a group of Spanish soldiers that he had found. His legends about cities of gold convinced yet another conquistador, **Hernando de Soto**, to explore Florida. De Soto found no gold, but he explored as far north as what is now North Carolina. He became the first European to cross the Mississippi River. Conquistador **Francisco Vásquez de Coronado** was drawn to western North America by legends of the golden Seven Cities of Cíbola. He never found gold, but he enabled Spain to claim vast areas of North America.

✔ **Reading Check: Identifying Cause and Effect** What motivated many of the explorers, and what were the results of their travels?

That's Interesting!

Mistaken Identity Can you imagine arriving in a new land and having strangers treat you like a legendary king? Indeed, some of the Aztec treated Cortés this way. Their reaction was based on Aztec legends about Quetzalcoatl (kwet-suhl-kuh-WAH-tuhl). In some Aztec accounts, this being was a god who would return from beyond the sea. In other stories he was a powerful king. Images of him showed a man with pale skin and dark hair. Aztec historians wrote that when Moctezuma first heard of Cortés, "it was as if he thought the new arrival was our prince Quetzalcoatl."

Spanish Exploration and Conquests, 1513–1542

Interpreting Maps Spanish explorers claimed lands from Peru in South America to the interior of North America.

Skills Assessment **Places and Regions** Which Spanish explorer first claimed the western coast of South America?

Governing New Spain

By the mid-1500s Spain's focus changed from conquering new lands to settling and controlling an empire. Spain used royal officials to rule its American territories. At the top was the **Council of the Indies**, formed in 1524. Based in Spain, the Council of the Indies wrote laws, appointed officials, and oversaw all government in Spanish America. Beneath the council were two viceroys. The viceroy of Peru governed a South American region stretching from what is now Chile to Colombia. New Spain's viceroy governed the North American area that extended from Mexico to what is now California and Florida. The viceroys also chose many local leaders.

In New Spain, the Spanish started three kinds of settlements to handle the region's economic, religious, and military needs. **Pueblos**, or towns, served as trading posts and sometimes as centers of local government. A pueblo usually had a central plaza with homes, a church, and businesses around it. Farms lay outside the pueblo. **Missions** were settlements started by the Catholic Church to convert American Indians to Christianity. Priests and Indians built mission compounds around a central church building. **Presidios**, or military settlements, were built to protect towns and missions from attacks. Most presidios were located in faraway, or frontier, areas, particularly in Florida and Texas.

✔ **Reading Check:** **Summarizing** How did the Spanish organize to meet economic, religious, and military needs in New Spain?

La Conquistadora upon her altar at St. Francis Cathedral, Santa Fe

Colonial Economy and Class Structure

In New Spain's early days, many settlers depended on American Indians to work their fields and mines. As a reward for settlers who moved to the new lands, Spain developed the ***encomienda*** (en-koh-mee-EN-duh) **system.** This system gave many settlers, known as *encomenderos* (en-koh-muhn-DE-rohs), the right to tax or demand labor from American Indians. Although settlers were not permitted to enslave Indians, they often forced them to work in harsh conditions. As a result, many Indians died of disease and exhaustion.

A few Spaniards, such as the priest **Bartolomé de Las Casas**, who had once taken part in the *encomienda* system, defended Indians' rights.

"The natural laws and rules and rights of men are common to all nations . . . whatever their sect [religious faith], law, state, color, and condition, without any difference."

—Bartolomé de Las Casas, quoted in *The Conquest of America,* by Tzvetan Todorov

Analyzing Primary Sources

Drawing Inferences and Conclusions How do you think Las Casas felt about the *encomienda* system?

Las Casas's work against the *encomienda* system did lead to some reforms. The Spanish created rules to free Indians from the system after one generation. However, many settlers violated this law.

The Spanish found the *encomienda* system less successful in Florida and the Caribbean. There American Indians resisted the *encomienda* system and died in great numbers from diseases. As a result, in 1501 the Spanish began to bring enslaved Africans to work on **plantations**, large farms that specialized in one crop.

By 1650 between 3 and 4 million people lived in Spain's American empire. About 80 percent of those were American Indians. The rest were whites, Africans, and people of mixed racial background. Spanish law split the population into social groups based on their place of birth and race. The *peninsulares* (pah-neen-soo-LAHR-es), Spaniards born in Spain, held the highest political offices. Next in status were the Spanish people born in the Americas, or *criollos* (kree-OHL-yohs), and the mestizos (me-STEE-zohs), who were born to Spanish and American Indian parents. Mestizos were the largest group of European descent in Spanish America and often worked for *criollos* as laborers or craftspeople. American Indians also had only limited rights. Enslaved African people had few legal rights and struggled to survive under harsh living and working conditions.

Women in each social class usually had fewer opportunities than men, even though they shared the difficult work of starting settlements. Unlike married women in many European countries, married women in Spanish America could own private property and pass it on to their children. The high death rates for men often left women with added responsibilities.

✔ **Reading Check: Analyzing Information** Describe the economy and class structure of New Spain.

"World, in Hounding Me"

Sor Juana Inés de la Cruz

The nun Sor Juana Inés de la Cruz spoke out on a woman's right to education and independence. In the following poem she defends her choice to defy the traditional role of women in New Spain.

World, in hounding me, what do you gain?
How can it harm you if I choose, **astutely,**[1]
rather to stock my mind with things of beauty,
than waste its stock on every beauty's claim?

Costliness and wealth bring me no
pleasure;
the only happiness I care to find
derives from setting treasure in my mind,
and not from mind that's set on winning
treasure.

I prize no **comeliness.**[2]
All fair things pay to time, the victor, their
appointed fee and
treasure cheats even the practiced eye.
Mine is the better and truer way:
to leave vanities of life aside,
not to throw my life away on vanity.

[1] **astutely:** wisely [2] **comeliness:** beauty

Understanding What You Read

Literature and History What choices has the poet made in her life that were unusual for her time?

Interpreting the Visual Record

Missions *San José Mission was established in 1720 in what is now Texas.* ***What materials from the region do you think were used to construct the mission?***

Expanding into the Borderlands

During the first 100 years of Spain's American empire, most settlers of New Spain went wherever they could gain the most wealth. Few Europeans lived in the area that historians call the **borderlands**, which included northern Mexico, Florida, and parts of present-day Arizona, California, New Mexico, and Texas.

The Spanish founded their first permanent settlements in Florida in 1565. About 1609 Santa Fe, New Mexico, was founded by Spain, becoming one of the most important European settlements in the borderlands. In Texas the Spanish built their first mission in El Paso in 1659. In the early 1700s Spanish officials began hearing reports of French forts in what is now Louisiana. The Spanish responded by setting up more forts and missions in eastern Texas. California was one of the last borderland areas settled by the Spanish.

✔ **Reading Check: Finding the Main Idea** Why did Spain set up forts and missions in eastern Texas?

Section 3 Review

go.hrw.com Homework Practice Online
keyword: SC3 HP2

1. **Define** and explain:
   - conquistadores
   - pueblos
   - missions
   - presidios
   - *encomienda* system
   - plantations
   - borderlands

2. **Identify** and explain:
   - Hernán Cortés
   - Moctezuma II
   - Francisco Pizarro
   - Hernando de Soto
   - Francisco Vásquez de Coronado
   - Council of the Indies
   - Bartolomé de Las Casas

3. **Comparing and Contrasting** Copy the diagram below. Use it to compare and contrast the circumstances that led to the fall of the Aztec and Inca Empires.

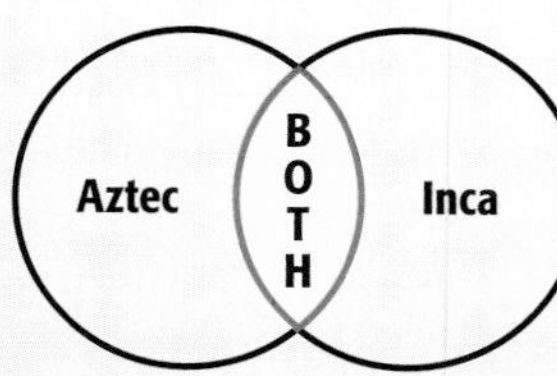

4. **Finding the Main Idea**
   a. Describe the government and settlements in New Spain.
   b. Describe the structure of the economy and society of New Spain.

5. **Writing and Critical Thinking**
   Supporting a Point of View Imagine that you are an American Indian working for an *encomendero*. Prepare a speech protesting or supporting this system. Include reasons to support your position.
   Consider the following:
   - life prior to colonization
   - your rights and status under the *encomienda* system
   - the rights and status of others under the system

Section 4

The Race for Empires

Read to Discover

1. Why and how did the Protestant Reformation affect ties between Spain and England?
2. What factors led to the decline of Spain?
3. What early experiences did Europeans have in colonizing North America?

Define

- sea dogs
- inflation
- charter

Identify

- Martin Luther
- Protestant Reformation
- Protestants
- Philip II
- Elizabeth I
- Spanish Armada
- Northwest Passage
- Henry Hudson
- Walter Raleigh
- John White

Why It Matters Today

In many countries today, religion plays a key role in political issues and events. Use CNNfyi.com or other **current events** sources to learn about the influence of religion on a key present-day political issue or event. Record your findings in your journal.

The Story Continues

On October 31, 1517, a priest named Martin Luther nailed a paper to the door of Castle Church in Wittenberg, Germany. The paper contained 95 theses, or ideas, criticizing some common practices of the Roman Catholic Church. Luther charged that the Church was too wealthy and abused its great power. When Charles V, emperor of the Holy Roman Empire, asked Luther to take back his views, Luther replied, "I cannot and will not recant anything. . . . On this I take my stand. I can do no other."

Martin Luther helped begin a movement to change the Catholic Church's practices.

Conflict between Spain and England

In the 1500s the divisions over religion led to conflicts between people and nations in Europe. **Martin Luther** and others started a religious movement known as the **Protestant Reformation** in 1517. This movement began as an effort to reform the Roman Catholic Church. The reformers were called **Protestants** because they protested some practices of the Catholic Church. The Protestant Reformation began in Germany and soon spread to France, the Netherlands, Switzerland, and England. Throughout Europe, fighting between Catholics and Protestants often led to civil war and widespread destruction.

This fighting eventually drew England and Spain into war. During the late 1500s King **Philip II** of Spain used much of his country's new wealth to combat the Protestant Reformation. His chief enemy was Queen **Elizabeth I** of England, whose father, Henry VIII, had founded the Anglican Church, or Church of England. Elizabeth secretly encouraged a group of English sailors called **sea dogs** to fight Philip.

July 1588
A British fleet defeats the Spanish Armada.

In 1588 King Philip put together a huge fleet, the **Spanish Armada**, to try to overthrow Queen Elizabeth and the Anglican Church. However, smaller faster English ships sank much of the Armada in battle and stormy weather destroyed many of the remaining ships.

The Armada's defeat was a sign of Spain's declining power. Wealth from the Americas had made Spain the most powerful nation in Europe, but also hurried its downfall. The great flow of wealth from the Americas created high **inflation**—an increase in prices—in Spain's economy. To avoid high local prices, many Spaniards bought goods like food and manufactured products from abroad. Buying imported products discouraged the Spanish from making their own goods. Eventually, Spain could neither buy nor produce the goods needed to maintain its power. As Spain's power declined, other European nations began to found colonies in the Americas.

✔ **Reading Check:** **Finding the Main Idea** What led to the decline of Spain's power?

Interpreting the Visual Record

Declining power *The defeat of the Armada was a disaster for Spain.* ***How does this painting show the effect of the battle?***

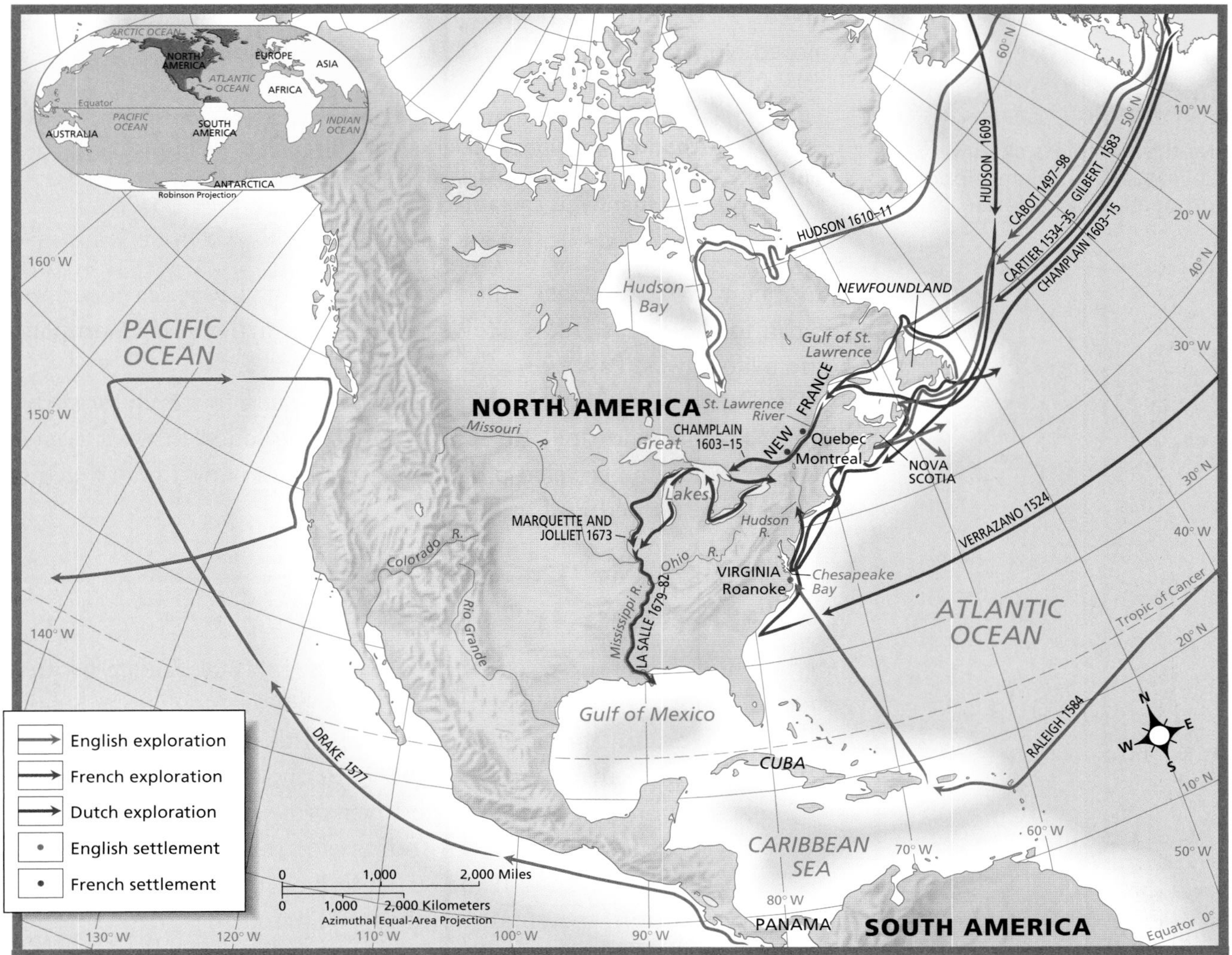

English exploration
French exploration
Dutch exploration
English settlement
French settlement

Dutch, English, and French Exploration of North America

Interpreting Maps Spain's rivals sent their own explorers to claim land in the Americas and the riches those lands might hold.

Skills Assessment **Places and Regions** What country's explorers claimed the Great Lakes region?

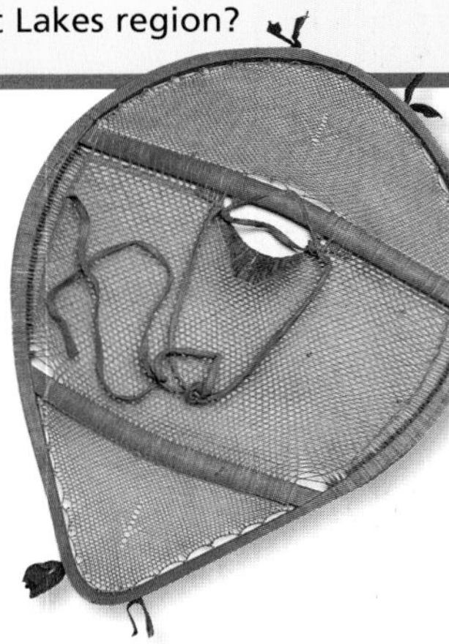

American Indians in the cold northern regions taught Europeans how to make and use snowshoes, like the one shown above, to travel in the winter.

Searching for a Northwest Passage

Spain and Portugal were not the only nations exploring the Americas. Other European nations began exploring North America. Some hoped to find a **Northwest Passage** through or around the continent to sail from the Atlantic to the Pacific.

As early as 1497, England sent John Cabot, a Genoese sailor like Columbus, to search the northern coastline of North America for passage to the Indies. In 1534 France sent Jacques Cartier (kahr-tyay) to find a Northwest Passage. Cartier made three voyages to North America and explored areas along the Atlantic coast of what is now Canada, including Newfoundland and the St. Lawrence River.

Nearly 70 years later, French sailor Samuel de Champlain also explored North America. He wrote about it in his journal.

Analyzing Primary Sources

Identifying Points of View Why does Champlain support European exploration?

"Through [exploration] we gain knowledge in different countries, regions and kingdoms; through it we attract and bring into our countries all kinds of riches; through it . . . Christianity [is spread] in all parts of the earth."

—Samuel de Champlain, quoted in *The Canadian Frontier, 1534–1760,* by W. J. Eccles

Champlain made repeated journeys along the St. Lawrence River and sailed into the Great Lakes. However, neither Cartier nor Champlain found a Northwest Passage.

The Dutch hired English captain **Henry Hudson** to search for such a passage. Hudson did not find it, but in 1609 he sailed to what is now New York. There he traveled past Manhattan Island and up a river that would later be named for him.

Early French Settlements

Based on the explorations of Jacques Cartier, in 1604 France formed permanent North American settlements in what are now Nova Scotia, New Brunswick, and parts of Maine. Samuel de Champlain founded Quebec on the St. Lawrence River in 1608. Because of the fur trade, the Great Lakes region and St. Lawrence River proved valuable to France. The French traded with American Indians for furs, and then shipped the furs to France. The fur trade strengthened ties between the two groups. In addition, the small number of French in North America helped them avoid conflicts with Indians over land.

In the late 1600s the French began spreading out from the Great Lakes region. Some headed south toward the lands of New Spain. In 1673 explorer Louis Jolliet (jahl-ee-ET) and missionary Jacques Marquette traveled down the Mississippi River as far as present-day Arkansas. Nine years later, René-Robert de La Salle followed the Mississippi River to the Gulf of Mexico. He claimed the Mississippi River valley for King Louis XIV of France, naming it Louisiana.

The French eventually called all their North American territory New France. Starting in the early 1700s, they founded forts—such as Detroit, St. Louis, and New Orleans—on the Great Lakes and along the Mississippi.

Interpreting the Visual Record

Louisiana *Louisiana, which was claimed for the French by René-Robert de La Salle, became a royal colony in 1731.* ***What important geographic features might the French find in Louisiana?***

✔ **Reading Check: Analyzing Information** Why did the English, French, and Dutch explore the Great Lakes region and the St. Lawrence River?

Dutch and English Settlements

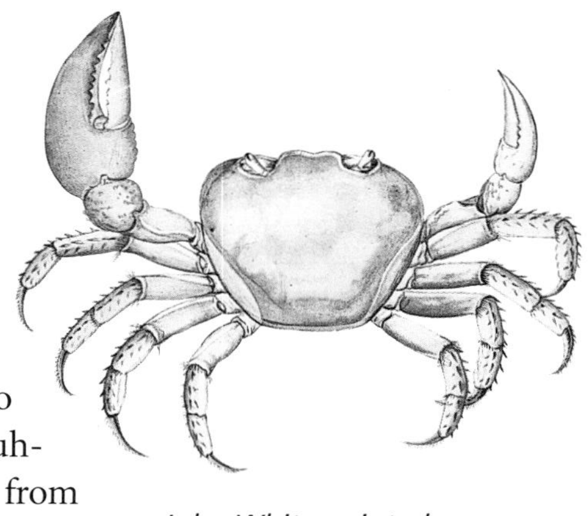

John White painted many American plants and animals. His works are among the earliest known European pictures of North American wildlife.

The fur trade also drew the Dutch to North America. They based their claims to the land between the Delaware and Connecticut Rivers on Henry Hudson's explorations. This area, which they called New Netherland, included parts of what are now Connecticut, Delaware, New Jersey, and New York. In 1624 the newly formed Dutch West India Company sent about 30 families to settle in New Netherland. Two years later, Peter Minuit (MIN-yuh-wuht), the director of New Netherland, bought Manhattan Island from the American Indians who lived there. He then founded the settlement of New Amsterdam. To attract more settlers, the Dutch West India Company allowed other Europeans to settle in New Netherland. The Dutch practiced religious toleration, which attracted colonists.

England also wanted its own settlements. In 1578 Sir Humphrey Gilbert got a **charter**, or written permission to form a colony, from Queen Elizabeth. His settlement in Newfoundland failed, however, when he drowned in 1583.

Gilbert's half-brother, Sir **Walter Raleigh**, funded another expedition to what is now Virginia and North Carolina. Raleigh sent a group to found a colony on Roanoke Island, but the settlers fought with American Indians and had trouble finding food. In 1586 sea dog Sir Francis Drake stopped at Roanoke and took the remaining settlers home to England.

John White resettled the Roanoke colony in the spring of 1587. In 1590, White returned to Roanoke after getting more supplies from England and found the colony deserted.

✔ **Reading Check: Summarizing** What were the results of England's early colonization efforts?

go.hrw.com Homework Practice Online
keyword: SC3 HP2

1 Define and explain:
- sea dogs
- inflation
- charter

2 Identify and explain:
- Martin Luther
- Protestant Reformation
- Protestants
- Philip II
- Elizabeth I
- Spanish Armada
- Northwest Passage
- Henry Hudson
- Walter Raleigh
- John White

3 Identifying Cause and Effect Copy the graphic organizer below. Use it to identify what caused the Protestant Reformation and the changes that resulted.

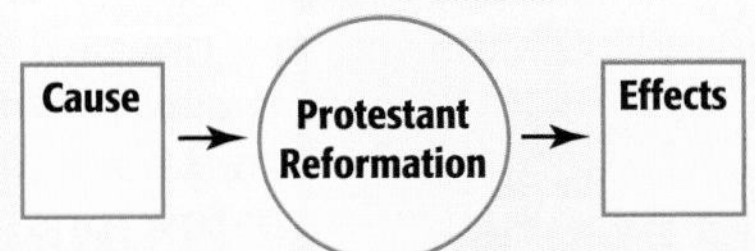

4 Finding the Main Idea

a. What were some of the early experiences that French, Dutch, and English settlers had in colonizing North America?

b. What economic factors caused Spain's power to decline in the late 1500s and the early 1600s?

5 Writing and Critical Thinking

Drawing Inferences and Conclusions Imagine that you are a historian. Write a half-page story about what might have happened to the settlers at the second Roanoke colony.

Consider the following:
- Sir Walter Raleigh's failed attempt
- conditions on Roanoke

Chapter 2 Review

The Chapter at a Glance

Examine the visual summary of the chapter below. Create a five-question multiple choice quiz covering the chapter's main ideas that you might give to a classmate.

Identifying People and Ideas

Use the following terms or people in historically significant sentences.

1. astrolabe
2. Christopher Columbus
3. Treaty of Tordesillas
4. Ferdinand Magellan
5. conquistadores
6. Moctezuma II
7. Council of the Indies
8. Bartolomé de Las Casas
9. Elizabeth I
10. Henry Hudson

Understanding Main Ideas

Section 1 *(Pages 32–36)*

1. How did Portugal seek direct trade with Asia?
2. What did Columbus expect to find by sailing west, and why did he believe this?

Section 2 *(Pages 37–41)*

3. Where did Portugal explore, and what were the results of Portuguese exploration?
4. Where did Spain explore after Columbus's first voyage, and how did these discoveries affect Spain?

Section 3 *(Pages 42–46)*

5. How did Spain's colonial government, communities, economy, and society function?

Section 4 *(Pages 47–51)*

6. What factors led to the decline of Spain's power?
7. Why were France, the Netherlands, and England interested in settling North America?

You Be the Historian— Reviewing Themes

1. **Economics** Describe the effects that global exploration and trade had on the economic development of Spain.
2. **Geography** What geographic difficulties did Europeans experience during their explorations and settlement of the Americas?
3. **Culture** What were the effects of the Portuguese and Spanish explorations on the peoples of Africa and the Americas?

Thinking Critically

1. **Summarizing** List some of the long-term effects that Columbus's discoveries had on Spain, Europe, and the Americas.
2. **Comparing** Compare Columbus's voyage and Cortés's expedition. Which do you think more fully met its goals? Which do you think had the greatest long-term effect on the world?
3. **Supporting a Point of View** Do you agree with the idea of naming the Americas after Amerigo Vespucci? Explain your answer.

Social Studies Skills Workshop

Interpreting Charts

Study the chart below. Then use the information on the chart to help you answer the following questions.

1. Which of the following inventions were important to sea travel?
   a. the astrolabe and the compass
   b. the heavy plow and the horse collar
   c. paper and the printing press
   d. none of the above
2. Using the information from the chart and your knowledge of the time period, create a map showing the place of origin of each invention.

Technology of the Middle Ages

INVENTION	PLACE OF ORIGIN	BENEFIT TO EUROPE
Astrolabe	Europe	Enabled sailors to determine their north-south position on Earth—that is, their degree of latitude—by using the location of the stars
Compass	China	Enabled people to determine their direction of travel even when the stars were hidden
Heavy plow	Europe	Enabled farming in the hard soils of northern Europe
Horse collar	Central Asia	Enabled horses to pull the heavy plow
Paper	China	Served as a cheap replacement for parchment
Printing Press	China	Johannes Gutenberg refined Asian printing techniques, which allowed the quick and cheap printing of large quantities of material

Analyzing Primary Sources

Read the following quotation from Bartolomé de Las Casas, a Spanish priest who wrote about Columbus's journey to the Americas, and then answer the following questions.

> **"The Admiral [Columbus] cheered them [his crew] as best he could, holding out good hope of the benefits they would have. And he added that it was useless to complain since he had come to find the Indies, and so had to continue until he found them."**

3. Which of the following statements best describes Columbus's point of view?
   a. He was worried about where he was going.
   b. He was willing to give up if difficulties arose.
   c. He did not care how his crew felt.
   d. He was determined to find the Indies.
4. In what ways did Columbus try to motivate his crew?
   a. He cheered them and reminded them of the rewards of the journey.
   b. He threatened to dismiss anyone who did not remain loyal to him.
   c. He promised to include them in future explorations.
   d. He told them that the journey would soon be over.
5. What sorts of benefits might Columbus have promised his crew if their journey was successful?

Alternative Assessment

Building Your Portfolio

American History

Linking to Community

A new school can seem like a new land to incoming students. You can help by doing the exploring for them. Work with your teacher to create an orientation packet for your school. Create a map listing important places in the building and the neighborhood. Include a brief description of the environment and the customs of the people who live there. This description could include rules as well as school traditions.

internet connect

Internet Activity: go.hrw.com
keyword: SC3 CF2

Choose an activity on New Empires in the Americas to:

- Research the impact of Columbus on the Americas.
- Write a biography of Sor Juana Inés de la Cruz.
- Create an annotated map showing Dutch, English, French, and Spanish claims and settlements in North America.

Connecting to Geography

The Columbian Exchange

On the morning of October 12, 1492, a lookout aboard the Pinta, *one of three ships in Christopher Columbus's fleet, sighted land. That day Columbus and his crew landed on an island in the Bahamas, starting the European settlement of the Americas. Columbus's landing also started a long process known today as the Columbian Exchange.*

In this process, explorers brought plants and animals from Europe, Africa, and Asia to the Americas. They often returned home with American plants and animals. These plants and animals were later spread throughout the Eastern Hemisphere.

Origins of Food Crops

When Columbus returned to the Americas in 1493, he brought with him a number of plants, including wheat. European explorers also took home some plants raised by American Indians, such as corn, potatoes, and tomatoes.

Origins and Production Areas of Food Crops

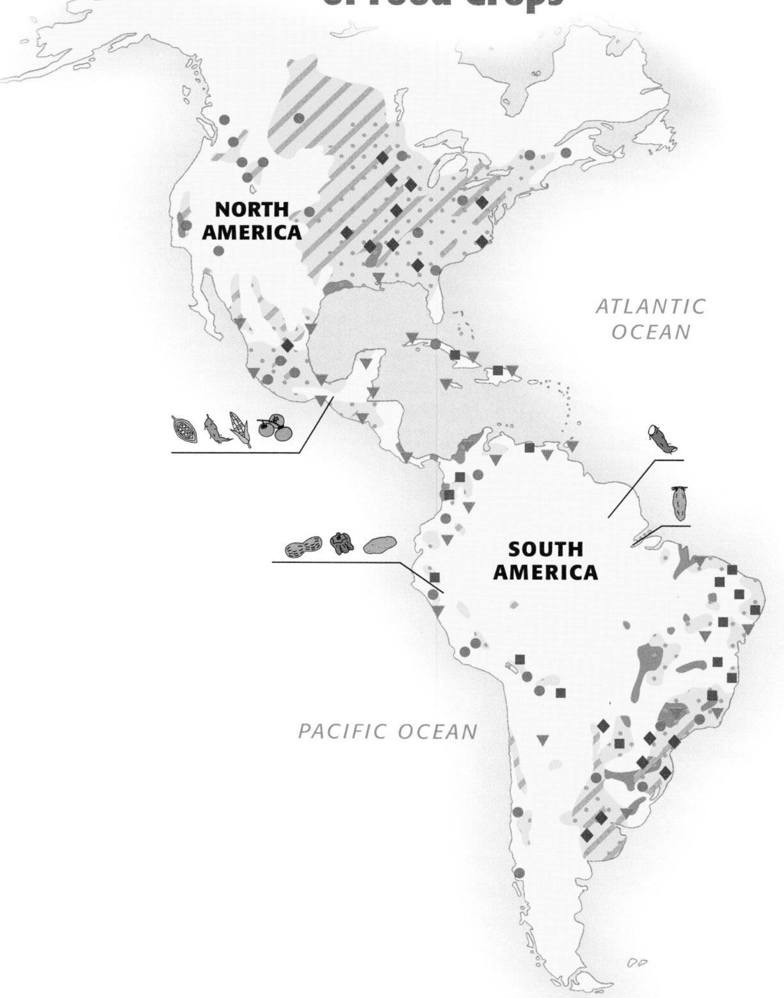

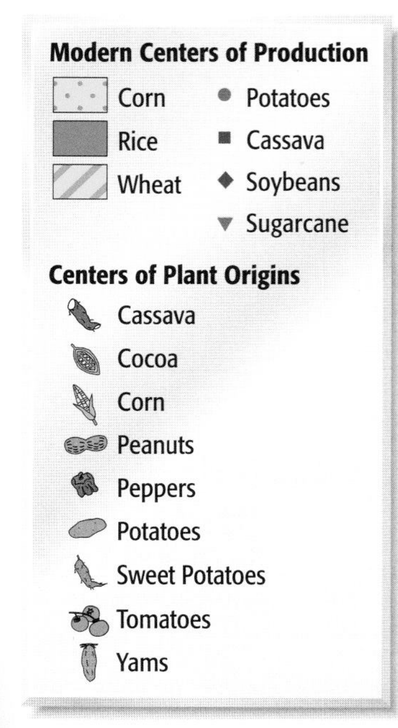

Origins and Production Areas of Food Crops

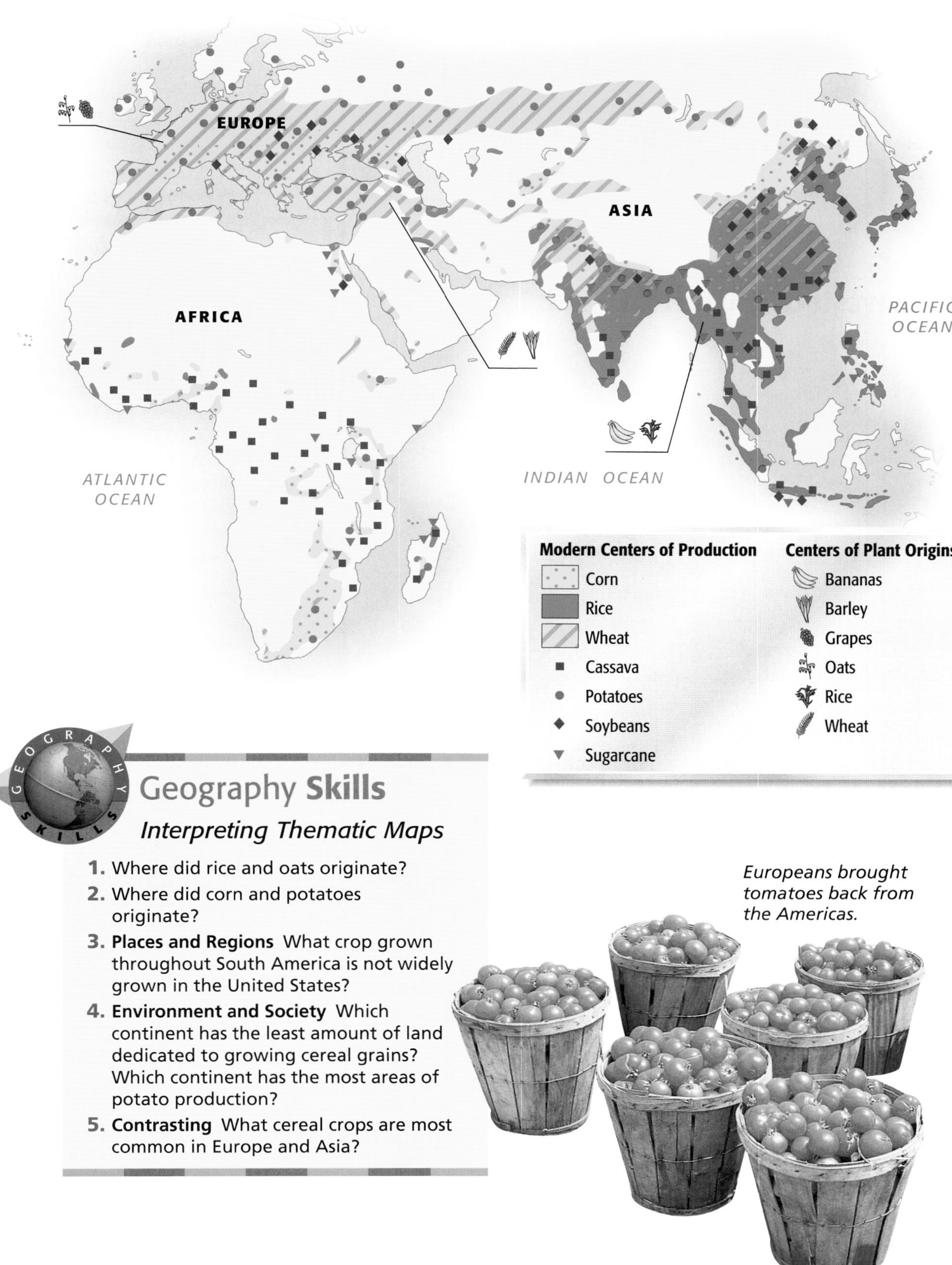

Geography Skills

Interpreting Thematic Maps

1. Where did rice and oats originate?
2. Where did corn and potatoes originate?
3. **Places and Regions** What crop grown throughout South America is not widely grown in the United States?
4. **Environment and Society** Which continent has the least amount of land dedicated to growing cereal grains? Which continent has the most areas of potato production?
5. **Contrasting** What cereal crops are most common in Europe and Asia?

Europeans brought tomatoes back from the Americas.

Origins of Animals

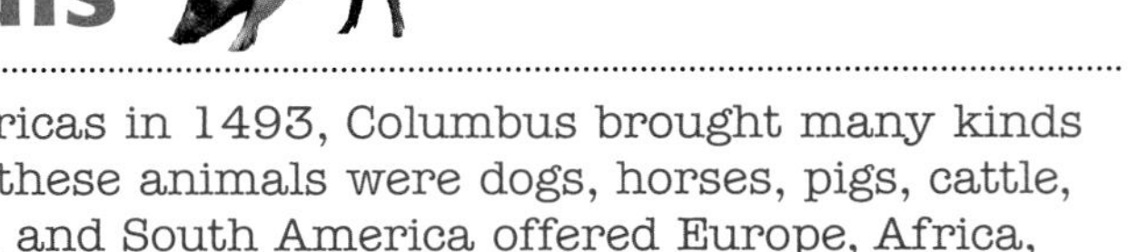

On his second voyage to the Americas in 1493, Columbus brought many kinds of domesticated animals. Among these animals were dogs, horses, pigs, cattle, chickens, sheep, and goats. North and South America offered Europe, Africa, and Asia fewer types of animals. The animals that the Americas offered included the turkey and the llama. Such animals had less economic importance.

Origins of Various Animals and Livestock Production Areas

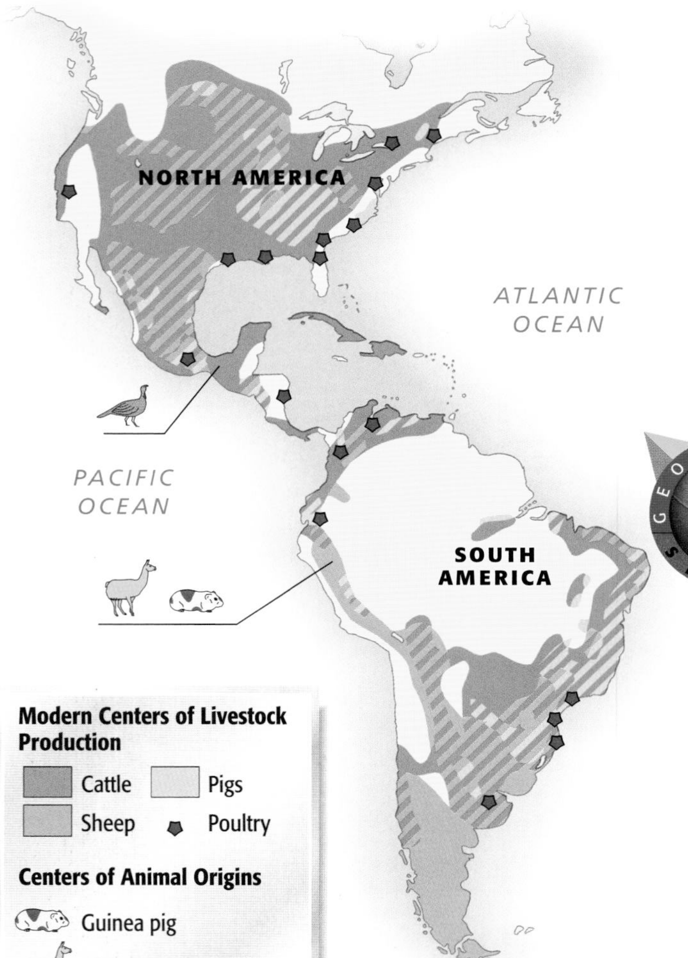

History Note 1

During the 1500s and 1600s, Spanish colonists raised horses throughout the Americas. Runaway horses multiplied and formed wild herds. Gradually, horse herds spread throughout the grasslands of central and northern South America. Eventually they roamed from the plains of Mexico all the way north to Canada. By the early 1700s American Indians of the western Great Plains had learned to train and ride these horses. They made horses an important part of their culture.

Geography Skills

Interpreting Thematic Maps

1. Which type of animal is most common to the southern tip of South America?
2. **The World in Spatial Terms** In what part of the world did turkeys originate?
3. **Drawing Inferences and Conclusions** Why do you think settlers from Europe brought their own livestock, seeds, and plant clippings to the Americas?

History Note 2

Pigs had the easiest time adapting to the hot wet climate of the Caribbean and present-day southeastern United States. It even became common practice for explorers to leave pigs behind on islands as food for future expeditions.

Origins of Various Animals and Livestock Production Areas

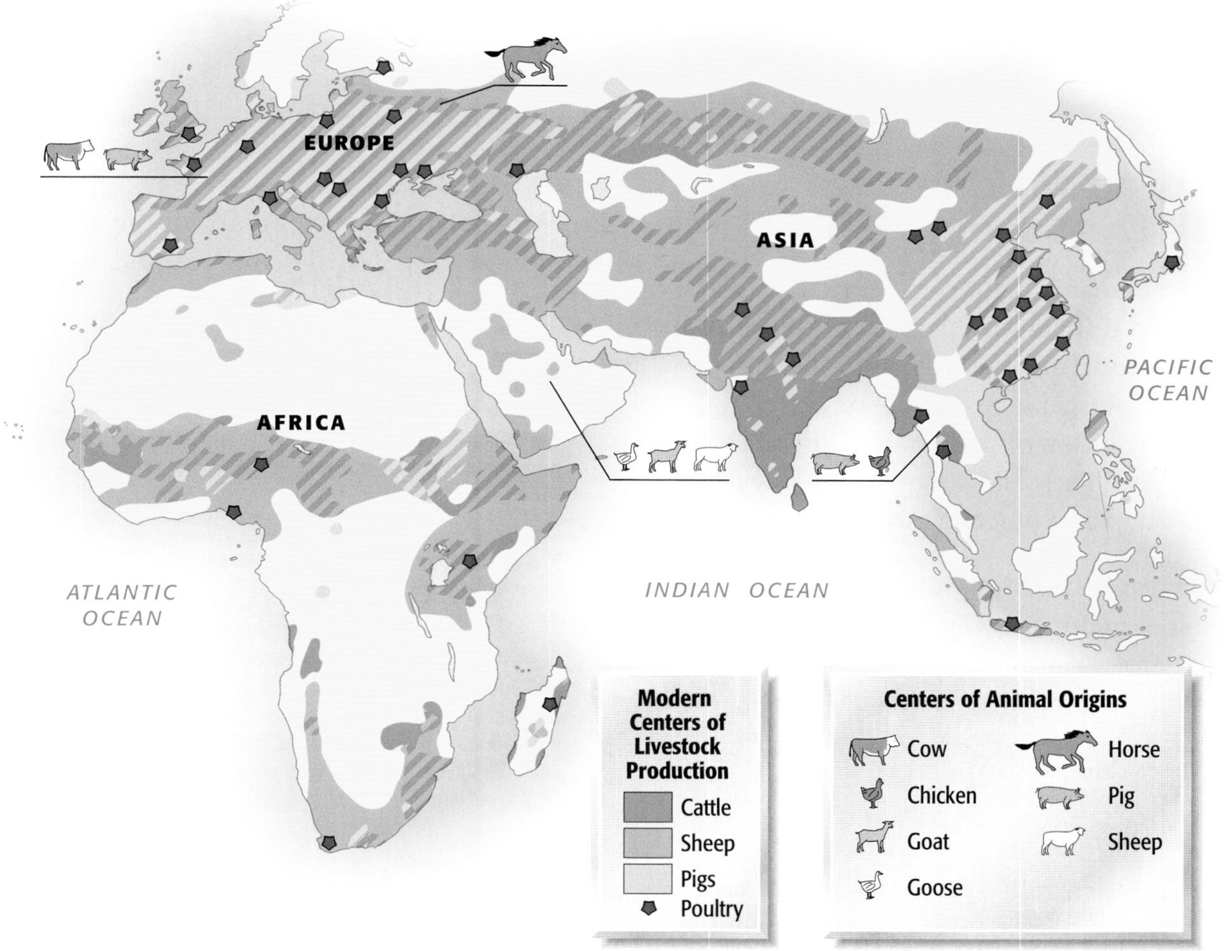

EUROPE

ASIA

AFRICA

ATLANTIC OCEAN

INDIAN OCEAN

PACIFIC OCEAN

Modern Centers of Livestock Production

- Cattle
- Sheep
- Pigs
- Poultry

Centers of Animal Origins

- Cow
- Chicken
- Goat
- Goose
- Horse
- Pig
- Sheep

Geography **Skills**

Interpreting Thematic Maps

1. Which animals originated in Europe?
2. **Physical Systems** Which animal originated in both Europe and Asia?
3. **Summarizing** What are the geographic origins of the plants and animals involved in the Columbian Exchange? Create a chart or table that will help a fellow student organize this information. Then exchange charts with a partner and fill them in using the information in your textbook and notes.

History Note 3

The Africanized, or "killer," bee is an example of how intercontinental exchanges continue in modern times. In the 1950s research scientists brought African honeybees to Brazil. African bees accidentally escaped from Brazilian laboratories and mixed with South American bees to produce the so-called killer bee. These bees then began to spread north. Today swarms of killer bees live in both Texas and California.

Social Studies Skills
WORKSHOP

Decision-Making and Problem-Solving Skills

Like you, many figures in American history have faced difficult problems and decisions. By using appropriate skills such as problem solving and decision making, you will be better able to choose a solution or make a decision on important issues. The following activities will help you develop and practice these skills.

Decision Making

Decision making involves choosing between two or more options. Listed below are guidelines to help you with making decisions.

1. **Identify a situation that requires a decision.** Think about your current situation. What issue are you faced with that requires you to take some sort of action?

2. **Gather information.** Think about the issue. Examine the causes of the issue or problem and consider how it affects you and others.

3. **Identify your options.** Consider the actions that you could take to address the issue. List these options so that you can compare them.

4. **Make predictions about consequences.** Predict the consequences of taking the actions listed for each of your options. Compare these possible consequences. Be sure the option you choose produces the results you want.

5. **Take action to implement a decision.** Choose a course of action from your available options, and put it into effect.

Problem Solving

Problem solving involves many of the steps of decision making. Listed below are guidelines to help you solve problems.

1. **Identify the problem.** Identify just what the problem or difficulty is that you are facing. Sometimes you face a difficult situation made up of several different problems. Each problem may require its own solution.

2. **Gather information.** Conduct research on any important issues related to the problem. Try to find the answers to questions like the following: What caused this problem? Who or what does it affect? When did it start?

3. **List and consider options.** Look at the problem and the answers to the questions you asked in Step 2. List and then think about all the possible ways in which the problem could be solved. These are your options—possible solutions to the problem.

4. **Examine advantages and disadvantages.** Consider the advantages and disadvantages of all the options that you have listed. Make sure that you consider the possible long-term effects of each possible solution. You should also determine what steps you will need to take to achieve each possible solution. Some suggestions may sound good at first but may turn out to be impractical or hard to achieve.

5. **Choose and implement a solution.** Select the best solution from your list and take the steps to achieve it.

6. **Evaluate the effectiveness of the solution.** When you have completed the steps needed to put your plan into action, evaluate its effectiveness. Is the problem solved? Were the results worth the effort required? Has the solution itself created any other problems?

Practicing the Skill

1. Chapter 2, Section 4: The Race for Empires, describes the search for a Northwest Passage to Asia. Imagine that you are an explorer who is aware of the failed attempts to find this passage. Use the decision-making guidelines to help you decide whether to continue searching for such a passage. Be prepared to defend your decision.
2. Identify a similar problem discussed in Chapters 1 or 2 and apply the problem-solving process to come up with a solution.

History in Action

UNIT 1 SIMULATION

You Solve the Problem . . .

How Do You Convince a Monarch to Finance Your Expedition?

Complete the following activity in small cooperative groups. It is the era of exploration, 1492–1534. You and your crew wish to petition your country's monarch for more funds to further explore distant lands. Your group is not the only one that would like more money. The monarch does not want only personal presentations. He or she has requested that a brochure be submitted also. The ship that will transport the brochure to the monarch leaves with the next tide. Follow these steps to solve your problem.

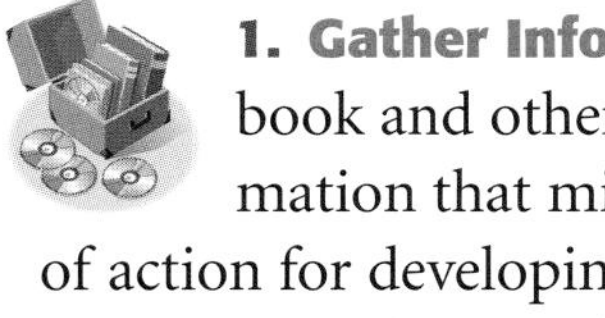

1. Gather Information. Use your textbook and other resources to find information that might influence your plan of action for developing a brochure. Be sure to use what you learned from this unit's Skills Workshop on Decision Making and Problem Solving to help you find an effective solution to this problem. You may want to divide different parts of the research among group members.

2. List and Consider Options. After reviewing the information you have gathered, list and consider the options you might use as justifications for your request that the monarch fund further explorations. Your final solution to the problem may be easier to reach if you consider as many options as possible. Be sure to record your possible options for the preparation of your brochure.

3. Consider Advantages and Disadvantages. Now consider the advantages and disadvantages of taking each option. Ask yourselves questions like: "Will this information convince the monarch that your expedition will benefit his or her country?" Once you have considered the advantages and disadvantages, record them as notes for use in preparing your brochure.

4. Choose, Implement, and Evaluate a Solution. After considering the advantages and disadvantages, you should plan and create your brochure. Be sure to make your proposal very clear. You will need to support your reasons for exploration by including information you gathered and by explaining why you rejected other options or reasons for exploration. Your brochure needs to be visually appealing to attract the attention of the monarch. When you are ready, decide which group members will present the brochure, and then take your brochure to the monarch (the rest of the class). Good luck!

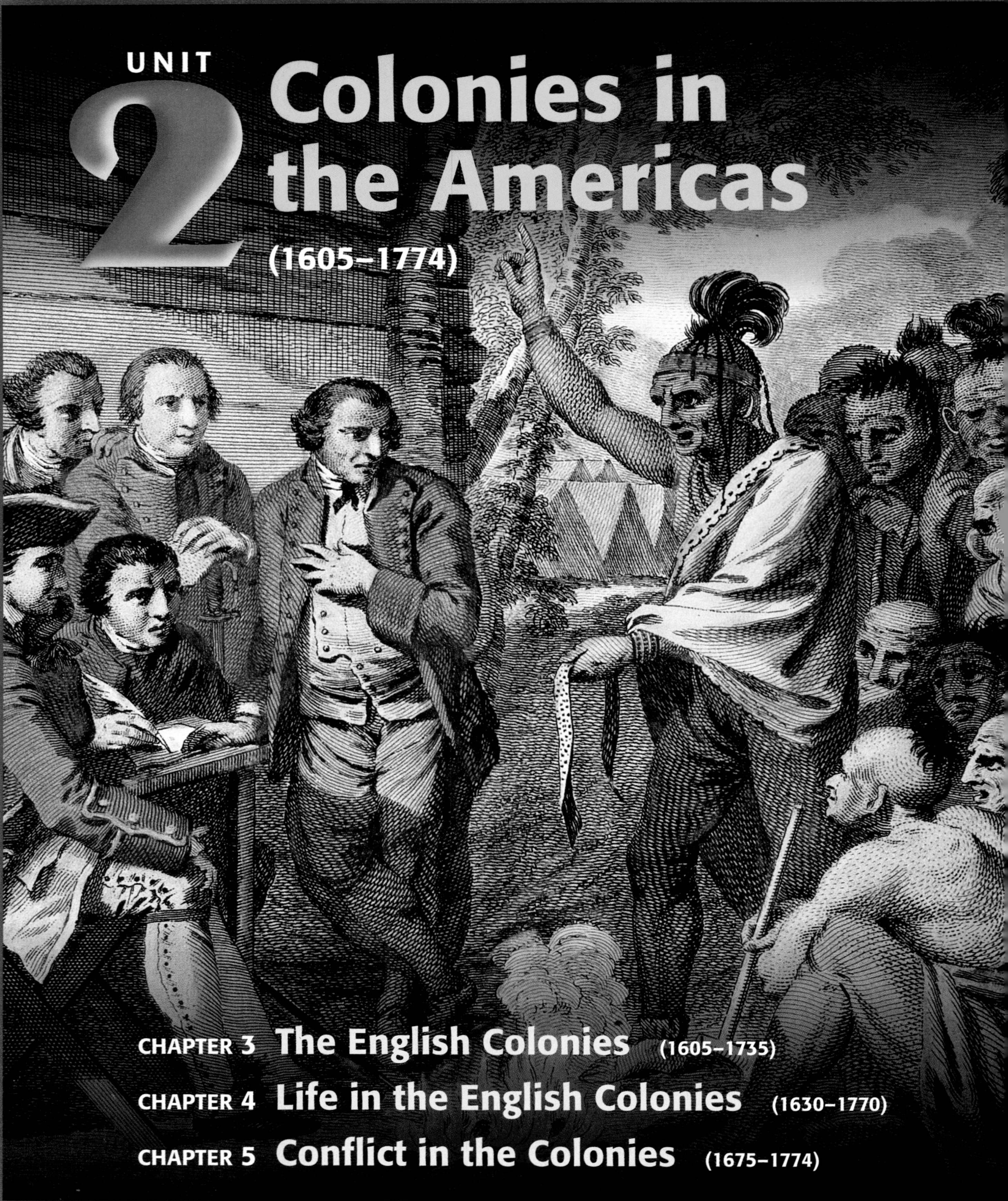

UNIT 2

Colonies in the Americas

(1605–1774)

Young People

IN HISTORY

Young American Indians

Many different American Indian peoples lived in the eastern woodlands region of North America. Teenagers from the various peoples shared similar responsibilities and experiences. Girls learned how to grow and harvest beans, corn, and squash in their own gardens and also in larger community fields. Girls also collected wild plants for food and medicine. They took care of household chores, such as collecting firewood and making clothes. Boys learned how to hunt and fish for survival. The Delaware people, who lived in what is now New York, required their teenage boys to stay alone in the woods for several days. These boys depended on their hunting and woodcraft skills to find food and build shelters.

Life for young American Indians was not all about work, however. Many peoples in eastern North America played ball games similar to lacrosse and soccer. The Cherokee of the Southeast liked to play a game called *anetsa*. In this rough physical game, players used netted sticks to carry a ball and throw it toward a goal. Only the most athletic young men played *anetsa,* and many suffered broken bones. Every Cherokee village had a team. The Cherokee believed that great honor and good fortune would come to the winner.

By their early teenage years most American Indians were considered adults. Among the Powhatan, who lived around Chesapeake Bay, boys took part in a special coming-of-age ritual. This ceremony required boys between the ages of about 10 and 15 to live in the woods for several months. They were tested with hardships and fasting. Those boys who proved their strength and bravery were declared worthy as future leaders. Virginia colonist Robert Beverly explained that the intention of the ritual was educational. The ritual encouraged the boys' progress into adulthood. Beverly observed, "Thus they unlive their former lives, and [become] men, by forgetting that they ever have been boys."

Young American Indians, like this boy, often played sports similar to some of those played today, such as lacrosse.

If You Were There *How would you survive on your own in the woods?*

LEFT PAGE: *In October 1764, British colonists met with American Indian leaders in what is now Ohio.*

CHAPTER

3 The English Colonies (1605–1735)

THE GRANGER COLLECTION, NEW YORK

Puritan colonists built their first settlement in New England.

THE GRANGER COLLECTION, NEW YORK

John Smith was an early leader at Jamestown.

UNITED STATES

1607 English colonists found the Jamestown settlement in present-day Virginia.

1619 The first representative assembly in North America is formed in Virginia.

1620 The Pilgrims sign the Mayflower Compact.

1630 Puritans found the Massachusetts Bay Colony.

1639 Thomas Hooker helps draft the Fundamental Orders of Connecticut.

1610 | 1620 | 1630 | 1640

WORLD

1611 The first edition of the King James Version of the Bible is published.

1630s The Great Migration begins as thousands of people leave England to settle in colonies or other European countries.

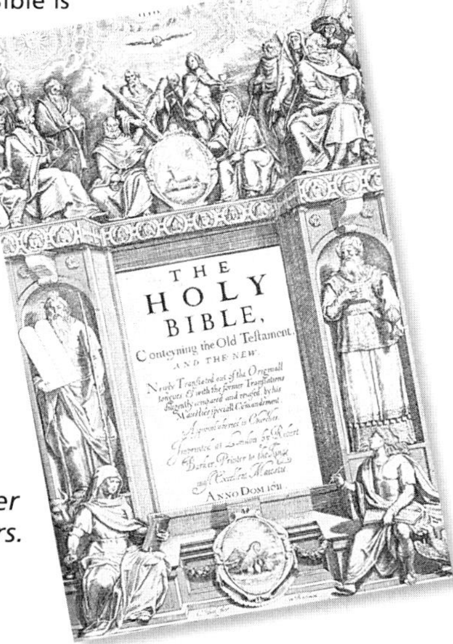

The King James Version of the Bible was produced by dozens of scholars over a period of seven years.

Build on What You Know

By the early 1600s, European exploration of the Americas had led to great interest in colonization. At first, the English wanted to colonize North America because they hoped to have a better quality of life there. However, many English colonists quickly found that merely surviving in their harsh new environment took most of their efforts.

COURTESY OF THE PENNSYLVANIA ACADEMY OF THE FINE ARTS, PHILADELPHIA. GIFT OF MRS. SARAH HARRISON (THE JOSEPH HARRISON, JR. COLLECTION)

Pennsylvania proprietor William Penn signs a peace treaty with local Indians on one of his trips to America.

The Puritans placed people's head and arms in stocks such as these as a form of punishment.

1649 Maryland passes the Toleration Act, which promotes religious freedom.

1649 King Charles I of England is overthrown and executed.

1650

1670 The Hudson Bay Company is formed to trade in the Hudson Bay region of North America.

1675

1676 Bacon's Rebellion begins in Virginia.

1682 Peter the Great becomes czar of Russia.

1692 The Salem witch trials take place in Massachusetts.

1700

1702 East and West Jersey are united into the single royal colony of New Jersey.

1725

1733 James Oglethorpe founds Savannah, Georgia.

If you were there . . .
What factors would lead you to settle in a new country?

You Be the Historian

What's Your Opinion? Do you **agree** or **disagree** with the following statements? Support your point of view in your journal.

- **Geography** Weather and geography determine a people's way of life—how they work, where they live, and how wealthy they can become.
- **Economics** A colony cannot survive unless the colonists find a way to make money.
- **Culture** Religious freedom is a basic right of all people.

Section 1

The Virginia Colony

Read to Discover

1. Why were people in England interested in founding Jamestown, and when was the colony established?
2. How did the Jamestown colonists interact with local American Indians?
3. How did the English plantation system begin?
4. What role did indentured servants and enslaved Africans have in Virginia's economy?

Define

- headright
- indentured servants
- planters

Identify

- John Smith
- Powhatan Confederacy
- John Rolfe
- Pocahontas
- Nathaniel Bacon
- Bacon's Rebellion

WHY IT MATTERS TODAY

Many important historical places in the United States have been protected and preserved. Use CNNfyi.com or other **current events** sources to find out about a historical site in the United States today. Record your findings in your journal.

THE GRANGER COLLECTION, NEW YORK

Posters like this one promoted the opportunities that were to be found in the colonies.

The Story Continues

In 1605 a company of English merchants asked the Crown for the right to found a new settlement in North America. They asked to settle in a region called Virginia. At the time, Virginia extended from present-day Maine to South Carolina. In 1606 King James I granted the request. He promised the London Company the rights to "all the lands . . . rivers . . . [and] commodities [goods]" along part of the Virginia coast. The company's efforts, wrote King James, "may in time bring . . . a settled and quiet government."

Settlement in Jamestown

The members of the London Company knew about the Roanoke colony's failure. They wanted to start a settlement without depending on the wealth of just one person. Instead, investors formed a joint-stock company, which allowed a group to share the cost and risk of founding a colony. Colonies formed in this way were called company colonies. To attract investors and settlers, the London Company printed advertisements praising Virginia.

"The land yields . . . [an] abundance of fish, infinite store [endless supply] of deer, and hares, with many fruits and roots. . . . There are hills and mountains making a sensible proffer [offer] of hidden treasure, never yet searched."

—The Virginia Company of London, quoted in *Ordinary Americans*, edited by Linda R. Monk

Analyzing Primary Sources

Identifying Bias What might this report have left out of its description of Virginia?

The promise of such wealth attracted adventurers and people who were suffering economic hardship in England.

On April 26, 1607, the first three ships sent by the London Company arrived off the Virginia coast. The fleet brought 105 male colonists to found a settlement. The ships sailed into Chesapeake Bay and up the James River. About 40 miles upstream, the colonists founded their first settlement, named Jamestown after the English king.

April 26, 1607

The London Company founds Jamestown.

The men who came to Jamestown were poorly prepared to start a settlement. Most were adventurers interested in making their fortune and returning to England. One of the colonists, Captain **John Smith**, complained that "ten good workmen would have done more substantial work in a day than ten of these [colonists] in a week." In fact, very few colonists had farming experience or useful skills such as carpentry. Jamestown was also a poor site for a settlement. The settlement was surrounded by marshes full of disease-carrying mosquitoes. In addition, the river water was too salty to drink safely. These conditions proved deadly. By the time winter arrived, two thirds of the original colonists had died. The few survivors were hungry and sick. The situation temporarily improved after Smith took control of the colony in September 1608. He forced the settlers to work and to build better housing. This reduced the number of deaths from starvation and exposure.

Interpreting the Visual Record

Jamestown *The settlers at Jamestown settled close by the James River.* ***Why do you think the colonists built their settlement in the manner shown here?***

COLONIAL WILLIAMSBURG FOUNDATION

The Powhatan Confederacy

The colonists also received help from the powerful **Powhatan Confederacy**. Wahunsonacock (wah-hoohn-SUH-nuh-kahk) led this alliance of Algonquian Indians. At times, the Powhatan brought food to aid the colonists. The Powhatan also taught them how to grow corn.

The relationship between the Powhatan and the Virginia colonists was not entirely peaceful, however. The colonists at times took food from the Powhatan by force. These actions led Wahunsonacock to say:

"Why will you take by force what you may obtain by love? Why will you destroy us who supply you with food? What can you get by war? . . . We are unarmed, and willing to give you what you ask, if you come in a friendly manner."

—Wahunsonacock, quoted in *The Portable North American Indian Reader,* edited by Frederick W. Turner III

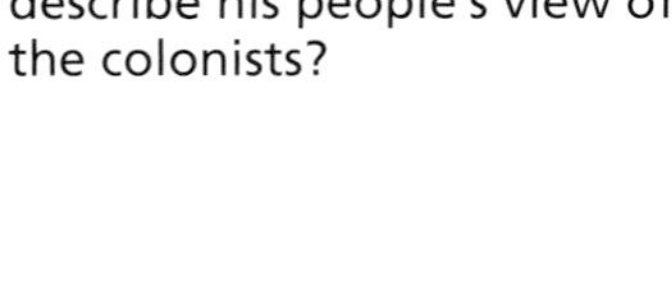

Identifying Points of View How does Wahunsonacock describe his people's view of the colonists?

In 1609 some 400 more settlers arrived in Jamestown. An injury from an accident forced John Smith to return to England, leaving the settlers without a strong leader. That winter, disease and famine once again hit the colony. The colonists called this period the "starving time." By the spring of 1610, only 60 colonists were still alive.

Because the colony struggled to survive, Jamestown failed to make a profit for the London Company. Colonist **John Rolfe** helped solve this problem in 1612. Smoking tobacco had been a favorite pastime in England since the 1560s. Tobacco grew well in Virginia. However, the local variety grown by the Powhatan was too bitter for European tastes, so Rolfe introduced a sweeter West Indian variety. Soon the colonists were able to export tobacco to England successfully. As Virginia colonist John Pory wrote in 1619, "All our riches for the present doe consiste in [come from] Tobacco." Another important change in the colony was a shift in land ownership from the London Company to individual colonists. The possibility of owning land attracted new settlers and thus helped the colony survive.

✔ Reading Check: **Finding the Main Idea** When did English settlers arrive in Virginia, and what challenges did they face?

Free Find:
Pocahontas
After reading about Pocahontas on the **Holt Researcher CD–ROM,** write a short essay describing the way the Powhatan treated the English settlers of Jamestown.

War in Virginia

John Rolfe married **Pocahontas**, Wahunsonacock's daughter, in 1614. Their marriage helped the Jamestown colony form more peaceful relations with the Powhatan. However, in 1617 Pocahontas died while visiting England, and Wahunsonacock died the next year. By that time, the colonists no longer depended on the Powhatan for food. They lost interest in allying with their American Indian neighbors. Many colonists also wanted to grow tobacco on American Indian lands. As the colony grew, the Powhatan and the Virginia colonists came into greater conflict.

In 1622, colonists killed a Powhatan leader. Opechancanough (OH-puh-chan-kuh-noh), the brother of Wahunsonacock, responded by attacking the Virginia settlers later that year. The Powhatan killed about 350 men, women, and children. Among the dead was John Rolfe. Angry survivors then burned American Indian villages. Fighting between the colonists and the Powhatan continued for the next 20 years.

The war in Virginia showed that the London Company could not help its colonists. Settlers were running short of supplies and were angry that the Company failed to send them any military support. These problems persuaded the English Crown to cancel the London Company's charter in 1624. Virginia became a royal colony under the authority of a governor chosen by the king.

Pocahontas had this portrait painted when she visited England with John Rolfe in 1616.

✔ **Reading Check: Sequencing** List the events that marked the Jamestown colonists' changing relationship with American Indians in the proper sequence.

Daily Life in Virginia

In early Virginia, people lived on scattered farms rather than in towns. Tobacco farmers soon began founding large farms called plantations. These plantations were made possible in part by use of the **headright** system. Under this system, colonists who paid their own way to Virginia received 50 acres of land. A colonist could earn 50 acres more for every

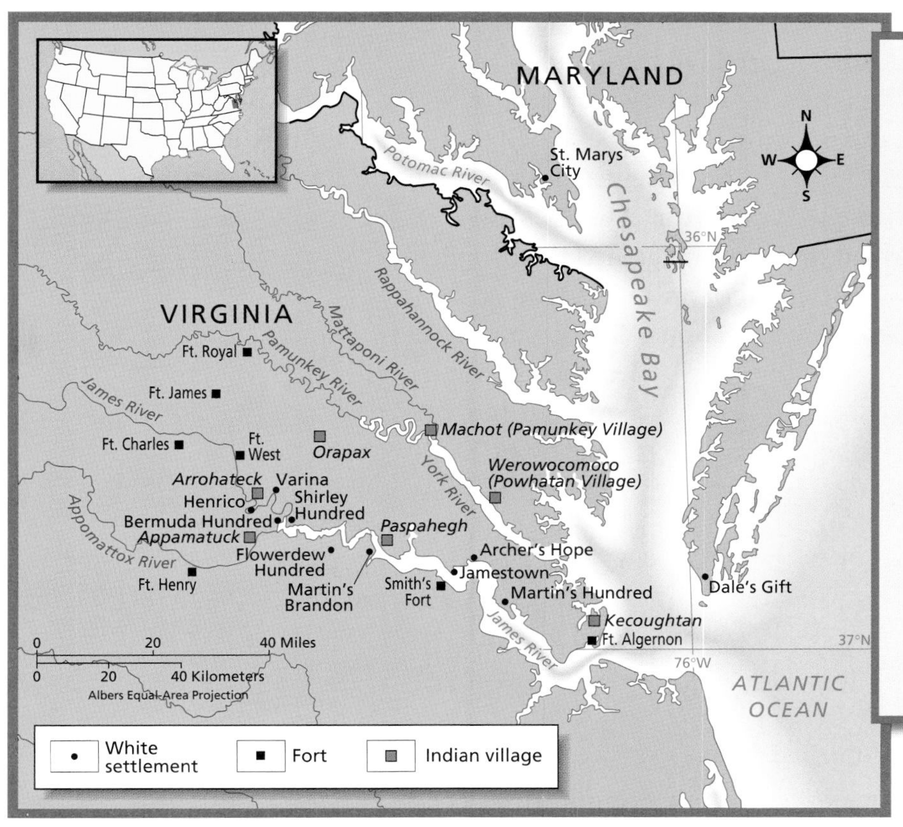

English Settlement in the Chesapeake Region, 1607–1675

Interpreting Maps English colonies in the Chesapeake Bay area were often located near American Indian villages. The contact between the two cultures was sometimes cooperative but often turned violent.

Skills Assessment

1. **The World in Spatial Terms** What Indian villages were located on the York River?
2. **Analyzing Information** Near what geographic features were most English settlements located? Why do you think settlers chose these areas?

additional person brought from England. Rich colonists brought servants or relatives to Virginia and gained large amounts of land.

Those who brought relatives to Virginia found that raising a family was difficult. Loved ones often died of deadly diseases, such as malaria. The London Company tried to bring women to the colony by offering promises of marriage. However, during the early years of the settlement men outnumbered women seven to one. Colonial families in Virginia focused on providing the basic necessities for themselves. Most colonists provided their own food and shelter. They also made eating utensils, tools, furniture, and clothing by hand. Parents gave lessons in reading and religion at home because there were no schools and few churches.

✔ **Reading Check** **Summarizing** How and why did the plantation system develop in the South?

Labor in Virginia

Colonists in Virginia faced a hard life. They suffered very high death rates, which led to labor shortages in the colony. More laborers were needed to work on plantations and farms. The majority of these workers were **indentured servants**. These colonists signed a contract to work from four to seven years for those who paid their ship fare to America. Of the early Virginia colonists, some 75 percent arrived as indentured servants. In one such contract, Margarett Williams promised to work for plantation owner Richard Smyth for four years. Smyth agreed "to pay for her [ocean] passing, and to find and allow [provide] her meate, drinke, apparrel [clothes] and lodging."

Living conditions were poor, and sickness was common. As a result, many indentured servants died before their term had ended. One servant wrote to his parents: "I have eaten more in a day at home than I have [had] here for a week." However, servants who survived their period of indenture gained their freedom and were able to claim land.

Not all laborers in Virginia came from Europe. The first Africans came to Virginia on a Dutch ship in 1619. Some Africans were indentured servants. Others had been enslaved. African indentured servants worked and lived side by side with white indentured servants and had similar contracts. Some of them became successful farmers when their contracts ended.

At first, indentured servants were more common than slaves in Virginia. These servants were clearly less expensive to bring to the colonies than slaves. However, the demand for workers was greater than the supply of people willing to work as indentured servants under the harsh conditions. Over time the cost of slaves fell.

The first enslaved Africans to arrive in the English colonies were brought in the early 1600s.

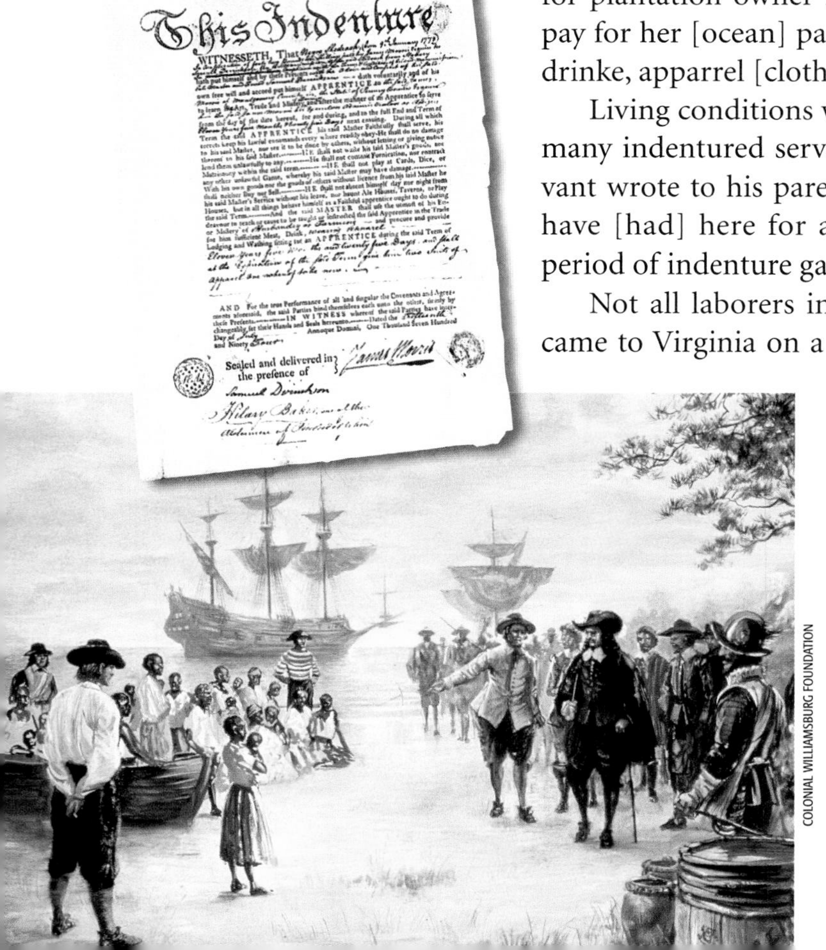
Philadelphia--Printed by E. Story, opposite I. Queen.

This Indenture

WITNESSETH, That

Sealed and delivered in the presence of

COLONIAL WILLIAMSBURG FOUNDATION

These factors led some colonists, particularly **planters**—wealthy farmers with large plantations—to turn to slave labor. By the late 1600s most Africans in Virginia were being kept in lifelong slavery. The widespread use of slave labor helped some tobacco plantation owners become rich. However, this wealth came at a great cost in human life and liberty.

Bacon's Rebellion

During the mid-1600s many colonists grew increasingly unhappy with conditions in the colony. They were angered by the governor's tight control over the colony and his refusal to call elections. Poor colonists also believed that members of Virginia's assembly were ignoring their concerns. They complained about higher taxes and the lack of available farmland. Many of them began farming on land belonging to American Indians. In doing so, they ignored treaties between the government and local American Indians.

In 1676 a group of former indentured servants attacked some peaceful American Indians. These angry colonists were led by **Nathaniel Bacon**, a wealthy frontier planter and a relative of the governor. When the governor tried to stop Bacon, he and his followers attacked and burned Jamestown. The uprising was known as **Bacon's Rebellion**. At one point Bacon controlled much of the colony. After he died of fever, however, the rebellion soon ended, and 23 of the remaining rebels were eventually hanged. Following the rebellion, the Virginia colonists found it difficult to make peace with American Indians. In addition, fears of future uprisings by former indentured servants led some planters in Virginia to depend more on slavery.

✔ **Reading Check: Analyzing Information** What factors led to the increased use of slave labor in Virginia?

Interpreting the Visual Record

Bacon's Rebellion *This scene shows a confrontation between Nathaniel Bacon at the right and Governor William Berkeley on the left.* ***What is threatening about Bacon's appearance in this image?***

Section 1 Review

go.hrw.com **Homework Practice Online**
keyword: SC3 HP3

1. **Define** and explain:
   - headright
   - indentured servants
   - planters
2. **Identify** and explain:
   - John Smith
   - Powhatan Confederacy
   - John Rolfe
   - Pocahontas
   - Nathaniel Bacon
   - Bacon's Rebellion
3. **Summarizing** Copy the graphic organizer below. Use it to explain the reasons people from England decided to establish the Jamestown colony in 1607.

   Problems in England → Jamestown Colony, 1607 ← Advantages of America

4. **Finding the Main Idea**
   a. Provide examples of the cooperation and conflict between American Indians and Virginia colonists.
   b. Why did the plantation system develop in Virginia, and what economic role did tobacco play?
5. **Writing and Critical Thinking**
   Supporting a Point of View Imagine that you are a wealthy planter in colonial Virginia. Create a pamphlet for investors in England explaining why indentured servants and enslaved Africans are important for the colonial economy.
   Consider the following:
   - the headright system
   - the development of tobacco plantations
   - high death rates in the colony

Section 2

The Pilgrims' Experience

Read to Discover

1. Why did the Pilgrims come to America?
2. What was the Mayflower Compact, and why was it important?
3. What was life like in the Plymouth colony?

Define

- sect
- immigrants

Identify

- Puritans
- Separatists
- Pilgrims
- William Bradford
- Mayflower Compact
- Squanto

WHY IT MATTERS TODAY

Religious intolerance is still present in many parts of the world. Use CNNfyi.com or other **current events** sources to identify a religious group that recently faced intolerance. Record your findings in your journal.

King James I disagreed with many proposed Puritan religious reforms.

The Story Continues

England's King James I held a conference in 1604 to meet with Protestant leaders. They wanted to reform the Church of England, also known as the Anglican Church. The leaders criticized the power held by Anglican bishops. As they talked, the king grew restless. Finally, he interrupted one of the reformers and began shouting furiously. "While I am in England I will have bishops to govern the Church." The king had plans for those who asked for reform, too. James stated, "I will make them conform themselves [become Anglicans] or I will harry [drive] them out of this land."

Puritans and Pilgrims

Religious tension in England remained high after the Protestant Reformation. A Protestant group called the **Puritans** wanted to reform, or purify, the Church of England. The Puritans thought that bishops and priests had too much power over church members. They believed that the Bible was the most reliable source of authority. The most extreme **sect**, or religious group, of Puritans wanted to separate from the Church of England. These **Separatists** formed their own churches and cut all ties with the Church of England. In response, English leaders began to punish Separatists.

One group of Separatists who faced such treatment became known as the **Pilgrims**. In 1608 the Pilgrims left England to escape this persecution and moved to the Netherlands. The Pilgrims were **immigrants**—people who came to a new country after leaving the land of their birth. Dutch officials welcomed the Pilgrims and allowed them to practice their religion freely.

The Pilgrims were glad to be able to practice their faith. They were not happy, however, that their children were learning the Dutch language and culture. The Pilgrims feared that their children would forget their English traditions. They were also disappointed by the types of jobs available to them. These concerns led the Pilgrims to leave the Netherlands. First, they formed a joint-stock company with some merchants. Then, they returned to England to apply for permission to settle in Virginia.

DETAIL, COURTESY OF THE PILGRIM SOCIETY, PLYMOUTH, MASSACHUSETTS

Interpreting the Visual Record

Plymouth Rock *After the Pilgrims arrived at Plymouth Rock, their ship, the* Mayflower, *stayed with them as they struggled through the winter to build their settlement.* ***What does this image suggest about the condition of the Pilgrims when they arrived in America?***

✔ **Reading Check: Summarizing** What factors led the Pilgrims to leave England and come to America?

 The Founding of Plymouth

On September 16, 1620, a ship called the *Mayflower* left England with more than 100 men, women, and children aboard. Not all of these colonists were Pilgrims. However, Pilgrim leaders such as **William Bradford** were in charge. The Pilgrims also hired Captain Miles Standish to help organize the defense of their colony.

After two months of rough ocean travel, the Pilgrims sighted land. Soon they realized that they were far north of present-day Virginia. The Pilgrims realized that they were outside the boundaries of their English charter. They decided to establish basic laws and social rules to govern their colony. On November 21, 1620, 41 of the male passengers on board the *Mayflower* signed a legal contract. They called this contract the **Mayflower Compact**. In it they agreed to have fair laws to protect the general good. This was one of the first attempts at self-government in the English colonies.

In late 1620 the Pilgrims landed at Plymouth Rock in present-day Massachusetts. Bradford described the scene. "They [the Pilgrims] fell upon their knees and blessed the God of Heaven who had brought them over the vast and furious ocean." As they struggled to build the Plymouth settlement, nearly half the tired Pilgrims died from cold and sickness during the first winter.

✔ **Reading Check: Finding the Main Idea** Why was the Mayflower Compact created, and why is it significant?

Historical Document

The Mayflower Compact

In November 1620, the Pilgrim leaders aboard the *Mayflower* drafted the Mayflower Compact. This was the first document in the English colonies to establish guidelines for self-government. This excerpt from the Mayflower Compact describes the principles of the Pilgrim colony's government.

The Pilgrims arrived in the Mayflower.

> We whose names are underwritten, . . . having undertaken, for the glory of God, and advancement of the Christian faith, and the honour of our King and country, a voyage to plant the first colony in the northern parts of Virginia, do by these **presents**[1] solemnly and mutually in the presence of God, and one of another, **covenant**[2] and combine ourselves together into a civil body **politic**[3] for our better ordering and preservation and furtherance of the ends **aforesaid**[4]; and by **virtue**[5] hereof, to enact, constitute, and frame such just and equal laws, **ordinances**[6], acts, constitutions, and offices . . . as shall be thought most **meet**[7] and convenient for the general good of the colony unto which we promise all due . . . obedience. In witness whereof, we have . . . subscribed our names at Cape Cod, the eleventh of November, 1620.

Analyzing Primary Sources

1. Why do you think the colonists felt the need to establish a government for themselves?
2. How do you think the Mayflower Compact influenced later governments in America?

---

[1] **by these presents:** by this document
[2] **covenant:** promise
[3] **civil body politic:** group organized for government
[4] **aforesaid:** mentioned above
[5] **virtue:** authority
[6] **ordinances:** regulations
[7] **meet:** fitting

Pilgrims and American Indians

European fishing boats had already visited the Plymouth area before the Pilgrims' arrival. These European fishermen brought new diseases to the region. These sicknesses killed most of the local American Indians, such as the Patuxet. For some time the Pilgrims met no American Indians. Occasionally they came across deserted American Indian villages and empty cornfields. The Pilgrims used these empty fields in the spring to plant their crops.

"such just and equal laws . . . as shall be thought most . . . convenient for the general good of the colony . . ."

Then, according to Bradford, in March 1621 an American Indian walked boldly into the settlement. He "spoke to them in broken English, which they could well understand, but marveled at it." The man's name was Samoset. He came from a Pemaquid tribe that lived in the area. Samoset had learned some English from the crews of fishing boats. He gave the Pilgrims useful information about the peoples and places surrounding Plymouth. Later he introduced them to a Patuxet Indian named **Squanto**.

Squanto had lived in Europe and spoke English. He was a great help to the colonists. Bradford described Squanto's contributions.

> **"Squanto continued with them and was their interpreter. . . . He directed them how to set [plant] corn, where to take [catch] fish, and procure [get] other commodities [goods], and was also their pilot [guide] to bring them to unknown places."**
>
> —William Bradford, *History of Plymouth Plantation*

Analyzing Primary Sources
Identifying Points of View How did Bradford regard Squanto?

From Squanto the Pilgrims learned to fertilize the soil on their farms with fish remains. Squanto also helped the Pilgrims establish relations with Massasoit, the chief of the local Wampanoag Indians.

Conditions in the Plymouth colony began to improve. William Bradford described the Pilgrims' first harvest.

> **"They began now to gather in the small harvest that they had, and to fit up their houses and dwellings against winter, being all well recovered in health and strength and had all things in good plenty."**
>
> —William Bradford, *History of Plymouth Plantation*

The Pilgrims invited Chief Massasoit and 90 other Wampanoag guests to celebrate their harvest. This feast, held to thank God, became known as the first Thanksgiving. For the event, the Pilgrims killed wild turkeys. For three days the two groups feasted with each other. This event marked the survival of the Pilgrims in the new colony.

✔ **Reading Check: Summarizing** What was the relationship like between Pilgrims and American Indians, and what did this mean for the colony?

That's Interesting!

Squanto's Journey Did you know that Squanto had traveled even farther than the Pilgrims when they first met in America? It's true! Squanto had been kidnapped by English explorers in 1605. He lived in England until 1614, when he returned to New England. Squanto was captured once again in 1615 and sold into slavery in Spain. He managed to escape the Spanish and make his way to England, returning to New England in 1619. When Squanto finally reached his home, however, he discovered that his tribe had been wiped out by disease. He then lived with the Wampanoag until Samoset introduced him to the Pilgrims.

The Pilgrim Community

Although the Pilgrims overcame many problems, their small settlement still struggled. Most Pilgrims tried farming, but the farmland around their settlement was poor. They had hoped to prosper by trading furs and by fishing. Unfortunately, fishing and hunting conditions were not good in their area. Some colonists traded corn with American Indians for beaver furs. The Pilgrims were not wealthy but were able to form a strong community. The colony began to grow stronger in the mid-1620s after new settlers arrived and, as in Jamestown, colonists began to have more rights to farm their own land.

The Pilgrim settlement was different from Virginia in that families were common there. Most people hoped to have many children, who were needed to help with the work. If parents died, Pilgrim families quickly adopted children left behind. They raised them as their own. The Pilgrims taught their children to read and offered some education to their indentured servants. The family served as the center of religious life, health care, and community well-being. All family members worked together to survive during the early years of the colony. Women generally cooked, spun

THE GRANGER COLLECTION, NEW YORK

Interpreting the Visual Record

Homework *This woman works a spinning wheel in her kitchen. Colonial women made the family's clothing, often including shoes.* ***What can you learn from the image about the different jobs that women had to do?***

and wove wool, and sewed clothing. They also made soap and butter, carried water, dried fruit, and cared for livestock. Men spent most of their time repairing tools and working in the fields. They also chopped wood and built shelters.

In Plymouth, women had more legal rights than they did in England. In England women were not allowed to make contracts, to sue, or to own property. In America, Pilgrim women had the right to sign contracts and to bring certain cases before local courts. Widows could also own property. A widow often received one third of her husband's land and belongings. In addition, married and widowed women could get licenses to run inns and to sell liquor.

From time to time, local courts recognized the ways women helped the business community. Widow Naomi Silvester received a large share of her husband's estate. The court called her "a frugal [thrifty] and laborious [hardworking] woman in the providing of the said estate." Widow Elizabeth Warren's business ability convinced colonial leaders to make her a purchaser for the colony. She took the place of her late husband. The hard work of such women helped the Plymouth colony to survive.

✔ **Reading Check: Analyzing Information** How did the Pilgrims view the importance of women and children to the colony?

Section 2 Review

go.hrw.com **Homework Practice Online**
keyword: SC3 HP3

1. **Define** and explain:
   - sect
   - immigrants

2. **Identify** and explain:
   - Puritans
   - Separatists
   - Pilgrims
   - William Bradford
   - Mayflower Compact
   - Squanto

3. **Identifying Cause and Effect** Copy the web diagram below. Use it to describe the problems that the Pilgrims faced in Europe, and explain how they responded to these problems.

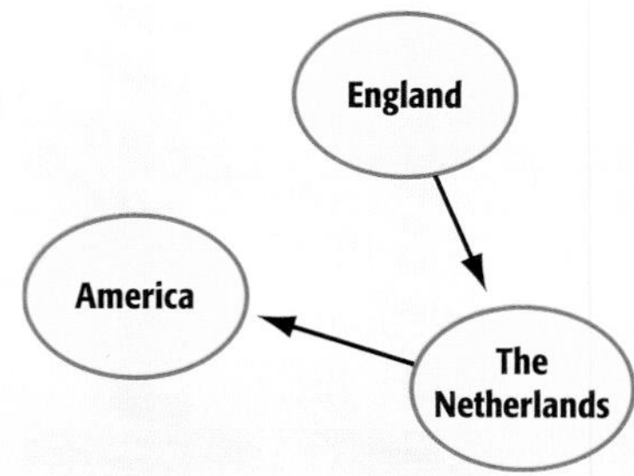

4. **Finding the Main Idea**
   a. How were family relations and religion important to the Plymouth colony?
   b. How did American Indians help the Plymouth colonists survive the early years?

5. **Writing and Critical Thinking**
   Summarizing Imagine that you are Pilgrim leader William Bradford. Write an essay describing the Mayflower Compact to place in the official records of the Plymouth colony.
   Consider the following:
   - why the Compact was necessary
   - who signed the document
   - the influence of the document on government

Section 3

The New England Colonies

Read to Discover

1. What was the Great Migration, and why did it occur?
2. What role did religion and the Church play in the Massachusetts Bay Colony?
3. How did the Puritans respond to dissenters?

Define

- dissenters
- covenant

Identify

- Great Migration
- John Winthrop
- Thomas Hooker
- Fundamental Orders of Connecticut
- Roger Williams
- Anne Hutchinson

Why It Matters Today

The Puritans made education an important part of their community. Many colleges founded in colonial times still operate today. Use CNNfyi.com or other **current events** sources to identify ways in which colleges and universities affect our lives today. Record your findings in your journal.

The Story Continues

In the early 1600s John Winthrop wrote to his wife, Margaret. He worried that "this land [England] grows weary of her inhabitants." As an Englishman, John Winthrop was fond of his country. As a Puritan, however, he believed that the members of his church were no longer welcome in England. Winthrop believed that the time was coming when they would have to leave their comfortable life behind. He later wrote that the Puritans would have to seek a new home to "be better preserved from the common corruptions [sins] of this evil world."

THE GRANGER COLLECTION, NEW YORK

John Winthrop was one of many Puritans who left England in search of religious freedom.

The Massachusetts Bay Colony

Beginning about 1620, England experienced an economic downturn, costing many people their jobs. Charles I, who became king in 1625, made the situation worse by raising taxes. This unpopular act led to a political crisis. At the same time, the Church of England began to punish Puritans because they were **dissenters**—people who disagree with official opinions. Charles I refused to allow Puritans to criticize Church actions.

These economic, political, and religious problems in England led to the **Great Migration**. Between 1630 and 1640 tens of thousands of English men, women, and children left England. More than 40,000 English emigrants moved to colonies in the Caribbean and New England. In 1629 a group of Puritans and merchants began planning a Puritan colony in North America. King Charles I granted the group a charter, allowing its members to establish a colony in the area known as New England. They formed the Massachusetts Bay Company.

In 1630 a fleet of ships carrying Puritan colonists left England for Massachusetts. There they hoped to have the freedom to practice their religion freely. While on board the flagship, *Arbella,* the colony's governor, **John Winthrop**, wrote about the Puritans' goals.

Analyzing Primary Sources

Identifying Points of View
What did Winthrop believe should be the focus of the Puritan colony?

History Makers Speak

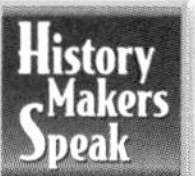

"We must delight in each other, make others' conditions our own and rejoice together, mourn together, labor and suffer together, always having before our eyes . . . our community . . . . For we must consider that we shall be like a City upon a Hill; the eyes of all people are on us."

—John Winthrop, quoted in *The Annals of America*

Winthrop's speech reflected the Puritans' belief that they had made a **covenant** with God. Under this covenant, or sacred agreement, Puritans agreed to build an ideal Christian community.

The Puritans arrived in New England well prepared to start their colony. They brought large numbers of tools and livestock. Trade with the colony of Plymouth helped them too. Like the Pilgrims, the Puritans faced little resistance at first from local American Indians. In addition, the Massachusetts region, unlike coastal Virginia, had a healthy climate. Thus, few Puritans died from sickness. All of these factors helped the Puritan colony do well.

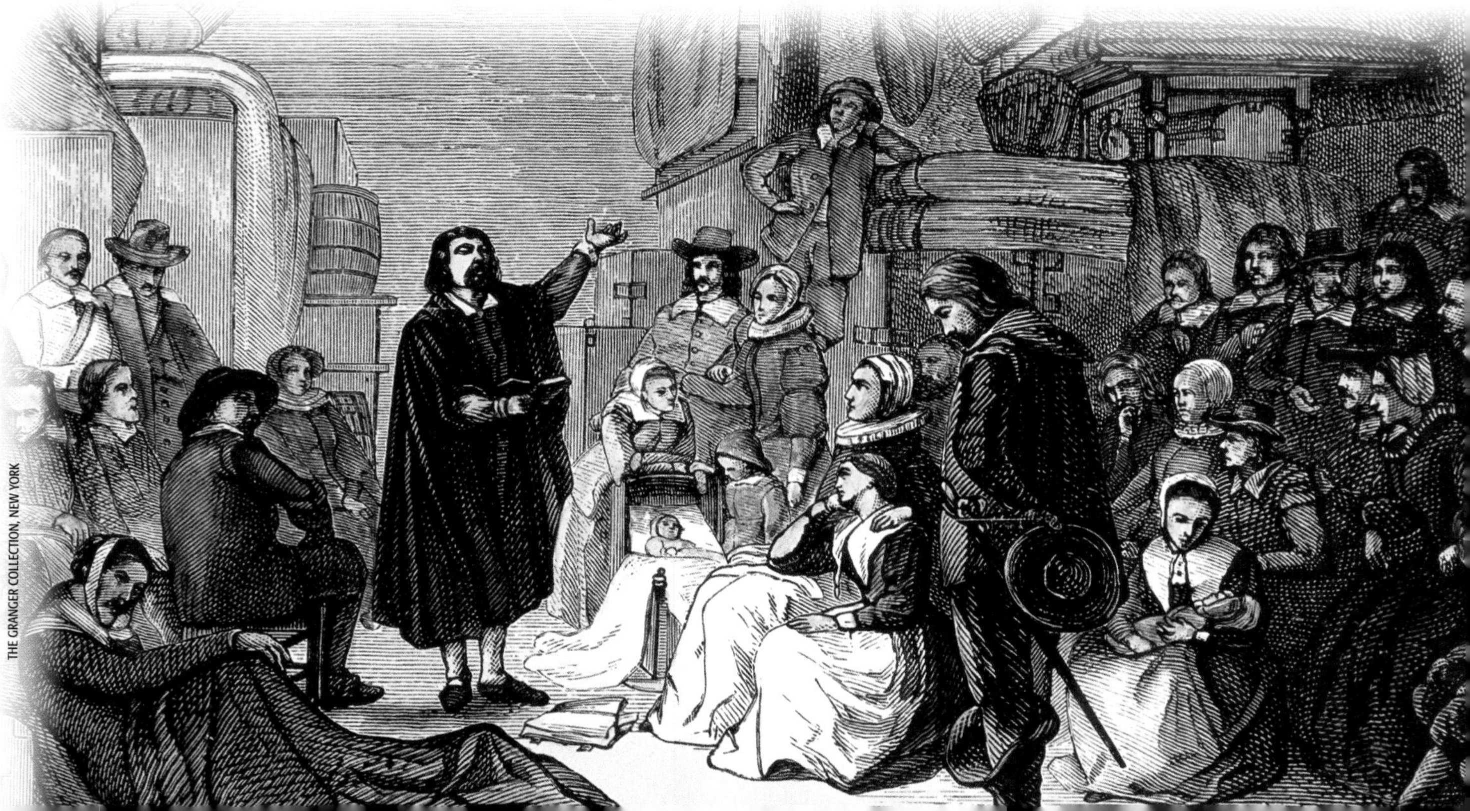

Religious services were a key part of community life for both the Pilgrim and Puritan colonies in New England.

By the end of 1630, about 1,000 more men, women, and children had joined the first settlers. These immigrants established the towns of Salem, Mystic, Newton, Watertown, and Dorchester. In addition, they built Boston, which became the colony's chief city and capital. Colonists also settled to the north, in present-day New Hampshire. In 1679 New Hampshire became a royal colony.

✔ **Reading Check:** **Summarizing** In what ways was religion an important factor in the establishment of the Massachusetts Bay Colony?

Church and State in New England

According to its company charter, Massachusetts was subject to English laws. However, the company charter provided more independence than did the royal charter of Virginia. The company charter created a General Court to help run the colony. The Puritan colonists turned this court into a type of self-government that tried to represent the needs of the people. Each town sent two or three delegates to the Court. After John Winthrop served as the first governor of Massachusetts, the General Court elected the governor and his assistants. In 1644 the General Court became a two-house legislature. This meant that the lawmaking body had two groups, and all decisions required a majority in each house.

Politics and religion were closely linked in Puritan New England. Government leaders were also church members. Although ministers were not political officials, they often had a great deal of power in Puritan communities. Male church members were the only colonists who could vote. Colonists became full members in the church by becoming what the Puritans called God's "elect," or chosen. Reaching this status was a difficult process. Individuals had to pass a public test to prove that their faith was strong.

In 1636 minister **Thomas Hooker** and his followers decided to leave Massachusetts to help found Connecticut, another New England colony. In 1639 Hooker helped draft the **Fundamental Orders of Connecticut**, a set of principles that made Connecticut's government more democratic. For example, the Orders allowed men who were not church members to vote. As a result of his role, some historians have called Hooker "the father of American democracy." The Fundamental Orders of Connecticut also outlined the powers of the general courts.

> **"General courts . . . shall have power to make laws or repeal them, to grant levies, to admit . . . freemen, dispose of [distribute] lands undisposed of to several towns or persons."**
>
> —The Fundamental Orders of Connecticut

✔ **Reading Check:** **Finding the Main Idea** What was distinctive about Connecticut's government?

Fundamental Orders of Connecticut

This excerpt describes the structure of the government adopted by the citizens of Connecticut in 1639. The Fundamental Orders are an example of the development of representative democracy in the colonies.

It is ordered . . . that there shall be yearly two general assemblies or courts: . . . The first shall be called the Court of Election, wherein shall be yearly chosen . . . public officers . . . which choice shall be made by all that are admitted freemen and have taken the oath of **fidelity**[1]. . . . It is ordered . . . that . . . [each town] shall have power . . . to send four of their freemen as their deputies to every general court; . . . which deputies shall have the power . . . to give their votes . . . as may be for the public good, and unto which the said towns are to be bound.

[1] **fidelity:** faithfulness

Analyzing Primary Sources

1. Who elected the public officials in Connecticut?
2. How are the people represented in the General Court?

Daily Life and Customs

New England colonists' lives centered around religion, family duties, and public work. Puritan religion strongly shaped everyday life in colonial New England. On Sundays, Puritans often heard two sermons. These weekly church meetings brought all members of the community together. In general, community life was more stable than in Virginia. Colonists in Virginia tended to be either wealthy or poor. Most colonists who immigrated to New England, however, were somewhere in between. Many New England colonists were skilled workers, and some were experienced farmers. Others had success with fishing enterprises or fur trading.

This is how a Puritan couple might be dressed for walking to church.

New England farmers grew food mainly for their own use rather than crops like tobacco for sale. Most New England farms were owned and run entirely by families. These small farms did not bring great wealth to their owners but also did not need as many laborers as did southern plantations. New England thus had little need for indentured servants or slaves.

Most colonists came to New England in family groups. As the colony grew, couples often had many children, who helped run the family farm. Parents helped choose their children's marriage partners in colonial New England in part because marriage involved a transfer of property from one family to another. Puritans believed that women had three main duties to fulfill in marriage. They had to obey their husbands, have children, and run the household. Husbands were expected in turn to treat their wives "with the greatest love, gentleness, kindness, [and] tenderness."

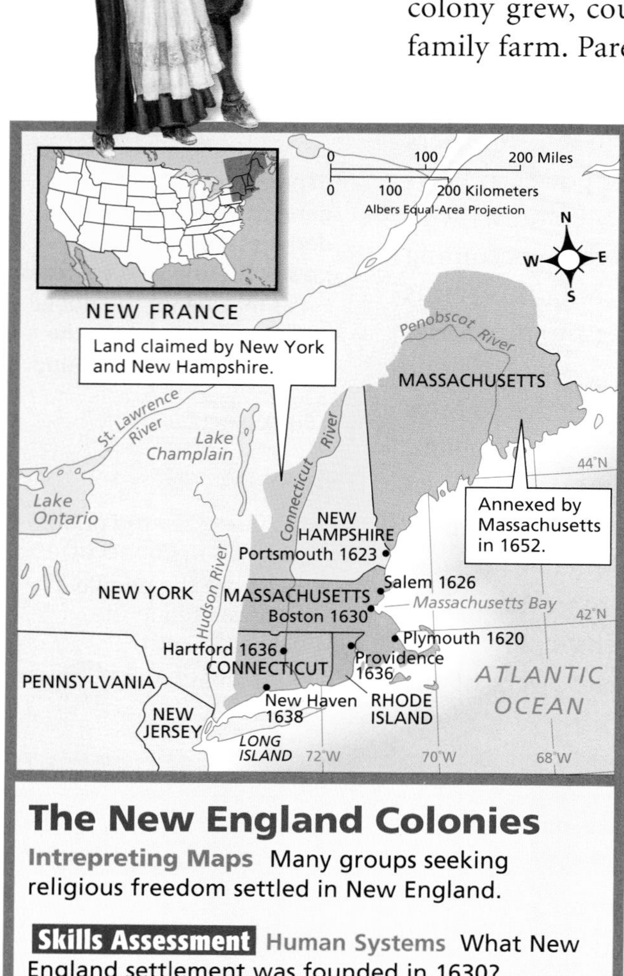

The New England Colonies

Intrepreting Maps Many groups seeking religious freedom settled in New England.

Skills Assessment **Human Systems** What New England settlement was founded in 1630?

Education was an important part of New England society, largely because mothers and fathers wanted their children to be able to read the Bible. The Massachusetts Bay Colony passed some of the first laws requiring parents to provide instruction for their children. In 1636 John Harvard and the General Court founded Harvard College. Harvard taught ministers and met the colony's need for higher education. By 1700 about 70 percent of the men and 45 percent of the women in New England could read and write. Figures for literacy were much lower in Virginia.

✔ **Reading Check: Contrasting** In what ways were the Massachusetts Bay Colony and the Virginia colony different?

CONNECTING TO Literature

THE GRANGER COLLECTION, NEW YORK

"To My Dear and Loving Husband"

Anne Bradstreet

In 1650 Puritan Anne Bradstreet published her poetry collection The Tenth Muse Lately Sprung Up in America. *She was the first published American poet. She wrote the following poem to her husband, Simon Bradstreet.*

If ever two were one, then surely we.
If ever man were loved by wife, then thee;
If ever wife was happy in a man,
Compare with me, ye women, if you can.
I prize thy love more than whole mines of gold
Or all the riches the East doth hold.
My love is such that rivers cannot quench,
Nor ought but love from thee, give **recompense**[1].
Thy love is such I can no way repay,
The heavens reward thee **manifold**[2] I pray.
Then while we live, in love let's so **persevere**[3]
That when we live no more, we may live ever.

[1] **recompense:** pay or satisfy
[2] **manifold:** many times
[3] **persevere:** continue on

Understanding What You Read

1. Literature and History How did Anne Bradstreet feel about her marriage?
2. Literature and You Do you think most colonial women would share Bradstreet's view of marriage? Explain your answer.

 Dissent in Massachusetts

Not all Puritans shared the same religious views. Minister **Roger Williams** did not agree with the leadership of Massachusetts. He called for his church to separate completely from the other New England congregations. Williams also criticized the General Court for taking land from American Indians without paying them.

Puritan leaders worried that Williams's ideas might hurt the colony and made him leave Massachusetts forever. Williams took his supporters to southern New England where they formed a new settlement called Providence. This settlement later became the colony of Rhode Island. Williams received a charter for his small settlement in 1644. In Providence, Williams supported the separation of the church from politics and promoted religious tolerance for all members of the community. In addition, he wanted to deal with American Indians fairly.

In Boston, **Anne Hutchinson** angered Puritan church leaders by publicly discussing religious ideas that some leaders thought radical. For example, Hutchinson believed that God speaks directly to people, apart from the Bible. A group of important community members often met at her home for religious discussions.

Hutchinson's views alarmed Puritan leaders such as John Winthrop. Puritan officials therefore put Hutchinson on trial for her ideas. The court decided to force Hutchinson out of the colony. With a group of followers, Hutchinson helped found the new colony of Portsmouth on Aquidneck Island (Rhode Island).

✔ **Reading Check: Identifying Cause and Effect** What led to religious disagreements among the Puritans, and what was the result?

Anne Hutchinson's beliefs led to her exile from Massachusetts.

The Salem Witch Trials

Perhaps the worst community conflicts in New England involved the witchcraft trials of the early 1690s. The largest number of trials were held in Salem, Massachusetts. In Salem a group of girls had accused people of casting spells on them. Most of the accused were women. The community formed a special court to judge the witchcraft cases. During the trials the young girls often screamed and fainted when someone accused of witchcraft entered the room. Witnesses reported they had seen witches speaking with the devil. The court often pressured the suspected witches to confess. One woman accused of witchcraft protested, "There was no other way to save our lives . . . but by our confessing."

The Salem witch trials led to 19 people being put to death. By the next year, many of the local officials and clergymen involved regretted their acts. Judge Samuel Sewall became one of the first to apologize publicly for his role in the wrongs committed by the Salem court.

✔ **Reading Check: Drawing Inferences and Conclusions** What effect do you think the witch trials had on Puritan communities?

Research on the ROM

Free Find:
Anne Hutchinson
After reading about Anne Hutchinson on the **Holt Researcher CD–ROM,** create a news report that explains both sides of her conflict with religious leaders.

Section 3 Review

go.hrw.com Homework Practice Online
keyword: SC3 HP3

1. **Define** and explain:
   - dissenters
   - covenant
2. **Identify** and explain:
   - Great Migration
   - John Winthrop
   - Thomas Hooker
   - Fundamental Orders of Connecticut
   - Roger Williams
   - Anne Hutchinson
3. **Summarizing** Copy the chart below. Use it to show how religious beliefs influenced the founding of various New England colonies and their systems of government.

Colony	Founded By	Reason for Founding	Form of Government

4. **Finding the Main Idea**
   a. How did religion and the Church influence the government and daily life of the Massachusetts Bay Colony?
   b. How did Puritan leaders treat dissenters such as Roger Williams and Anne Hutchinson?
5. **Writing and Critical Thinking**
   Analyzing Information Imagine that you are a Dutch citizen living in London during the time of the Great Migration. Write a letter to your friends in the Netherlands describing the Great Migration and why it is taking place.
   Consider the following:
   - freedom of religion
   - economic and political unrest in England
   - the number of English citizens leaving for the Americas

Section 4

The Southern and Middle Colonies

Read to Discover

1. What role did religion play in the founding and development of Maryland?
2. How were the Carolinas established, and how did their economies develop?
3. How were the middle colonies founded?

Define

- proprietors

Identify

- Cecilius Calvert
- Toleration Act of 1649
- Peter Stuyvesant
- Quakers
- William Penn
- James Oglethorpe

Why it Matters Today

The United States continues to receive thousands of immigrants each year. Use CNNfyi.com or other **current events** sources to find information on one or more groups of immigrants coming to the United States today. Record your findings in your journal.

The Story Continues

The English ship the *Ark* sailed into Chesapeake Bay. As it did, one passenger, Father Andrew White, looked out in wonder. He called the Potomac the "greatest river I have seene, so that the Thames is but a little finger to it." The *Ark* and its sister ship, the *Dove,* landed along the banks of the Potomac in March 1634. Most of the colonists on board were Catholic. On the riverbank, the colonists made a cross out of a large tree to celebrate their first Catholic mass in the new colony.

Maryland's St. Ignatius Church was established in 1641.

 Tolerant Maryland

Many English Catholics came to America for the same reason that many Puritans did. They wanted to escape religious persecution. English Catholics had long been against England's separation from the Roman Catholic Church. For this reason, they were not allowed by the Church of England to worship freely. England's leaders also feared that English

Cecilius Calvert never visited the colony that he founded.

Catholics would aid Catholic countries, such as France and Spain. In 1632 King Charles I gave **Cecilius Calvert** a charter to found a new colony. Also known as Lord Baltimore, Calvert intended the colony to be a refuge for English Catholics. He named the southern colony Maryland in honor of England's queen, Henrietta Maria.

Maryland was a proprietary colony. This meant that **proprietors**, or owners, controlled the government. Maryland was located just north of Virginia in the Chesapeake Bay area. In 1634 about 200 colonists arrived in Maryland to start a settlement.

Settlers in Maryland benefited from the lessons learned by the Jamestown colonists. They spent their time raising corn, cattle, and hogs. This way they would have enough to eat. Before long, however, many colonists turned their energies to growing tobacco for profit. Most of the colonists were men, and there were few families in Maryland at first.

Although Catholics founded Maryland, a growing number of Protestants began moving there in the 1640s. Soon religious conflicts between the two groups arose. To reduce tensions, Lord Baltimore presented a bill to the colonial assembly that became known as the **Toleration Act of 1649**. It made restricting the religious rights of Christians a crime. This act was one of the first laws supporting religious tolerance passed in the English colonies.

Analyzing Primary Sources

Drawing Inferences and Conclusions What historical events in Europe might have caused Lord Baltimore to introduce the Toleration Act?

"No person or persons whatsoever within this province . . . professing [claiming] to believe in Jesus Christ shall . . . be any way troubled, molested [persecuted], or . . . any way compelled [forced] to the belief or exercise of any other religion against his or her consent."

—Lord Baltimore, quoted in *Colonial America,* by Richard Middleton

The Toleration Act did not put an end to all religious conflict. However, it did show that the government wanted to offer some religious freedom and to protect the rights of minority groups.

✔ Reading Check: **Finding the Main Idea** How did religion shape the Maryland colony?

The Carolinas

In 1663 Charles II gave much of the land between Virginia and Spanish Florida to eight of his supporters. These colonial proprietors named the new southern colony Carolina, which is a Latin form of the name *Charles.* For many years Carolina was a single colony. However, the settlements within the colony were widely divided, making it hard for leaders to govern them all. Finally, in 1712 North and South Carolina became separate colonies. Most of the colonists in North Carolina were farmers who had moved south from Virginia. Unlike Virginia, North Carolina had few plantations. The colony had no towns and few churches until the early 1700s.

Colonial settlement in South Carolina began in 1670. That year three ships arrived from London with about 100 settlers. The colonists founded the port of Charles Town, which later became Charleston. Colonists who paid their own way to South Carolina received large grants of land. South Carolina drew many settlers from other English colonies, particularly from the British West Indies. These Caribbean colonists brought enslaved Africans with them. Because of this, South Carolina became one of the first colonies to depend mainly on the work of slaves.

Some colonists thought that rice might grow well in South Carolina's lowland swamps. However, they had little experience growing the crop. Many historians believe that African laborers taught the colonists how to raise rice in the 1690s. By the mid-1700s South Carolina's royal governor James Glen saw a change. He reported that "the only Commodity of Consequence [importance] produced in South Carolina is Rice."

Rice production required many workers, and plantation owners chose to meet their growing labor needs by using slaves. By 1730 about 20,000 enslaved Africans were living in the colony, compared to half as many white settlers. South Carolina was the only mainland colony with a higher population of enslaved Africans than free whites.

The proprietors' poor management of the Carolinas displeased the colonists. In 1719 the British government bought South Carolina from the original proprietors. The Crown then bought North Carolina in 1729, making it a royal colony as well.

✔ **Reading Check: Analyzing Information** How was South Carolina different from the other colonies, and why was this the case?

Daily Life

Charleston Charleston was the commercial, political, and social center of South Carolina. Because of the city's climate and location, many planters and officials chose to make it home. Soon, the wealth of merchants and planters helped build Charleston's cultural life. Cultural attractions included the city's library society and one of two newspapers published in the southern colonies. Over the years, Charleston's architecture has become another famous feature. Instead of using official buildings, government officials met in the large private homes of political leaders. **What features do you see in the image that might have drawn people to Charleston?**

THE GRANGER COLLECTION, NEW YORK

Diversity in New York and New Jersey

The Dutch founded New Netherland on the Hudson River in 1613 as a trading post for exchanging furs with the Iroquois. The town of New Amsterdam became the center of the fur trade in New Netherland. This settlement was founded on Manhattan Island. Most colonists in New Amsterdam were fur traders and farmers. Generous land grants and religious tolerance soon brought Jews, French Huguenots, Puritans, and others to the colony. Director General **Peter Stuyvesant** took control of the colony beginning in 1647. Stuyvesant was an experienced soldier with a wooden leg who ruled the colony as a dictator.

In 1664 the English took control of New Netherland when an English fleet captured New Amsterdam without a shot. New Netherland became an English colony and was renamed New York, the first of the middle colonies. Many Dutch settlers remained in the colony, shaping colonial life in different ways. For example, the Dutch contributed words such as *boss, cookie,* and *stoop* to the English language.

Soon after the conquest in 1664, the Duke of York made Sir George Carteret and John Lord Berkeley proprietors of New Jersey. This colony occupied lands between the Hudson and Delaware Rivers. It had a diverse population, including Dutch, Swedes, Finns, and Scots.

The fur trade remained important to New York's economy, and overseas trade grew over time. Both New York and New Jersey also produced large amounts of wheat.

✔ **Reading Check: Sequencing** List in their proper order the steps that established the colonies of New York and New Jersey.

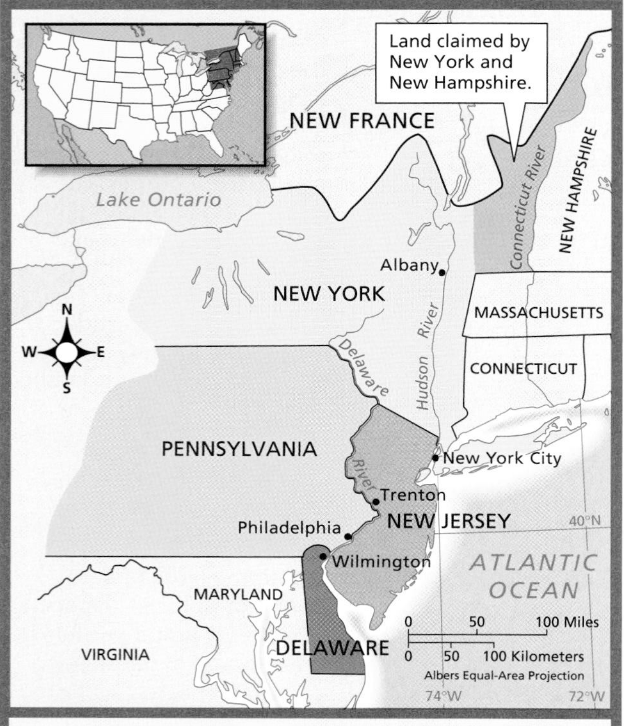

The Middle Colonies

Interpreting Maps The middle colonies were formed from land grants given by King Charles II.

Skills Assessment The World in Spatial Terms What river connects major cities in Delaware, New Jersey, and Pennsylvania?

After the English captured New Amsterdam, they renamed it New York, in honor of the Duke of York.

THE GRANGER COLLECTION, NEW YORK

Interpreting the Visual Record

Quaker meeting *Many of the colonists in Pennsylvania were farmers and helped create a peaceful and stable society there.* ***What does this image suggest about life in Pennsylvania?***

The Pennsylvania Experiment

The Society of Friends, or the **Quakers**, made up one of the largest religious groups in New Jersey. The Quakers were a Protestant sect founded by George Fox in the mid-1600s in England. Quakers believed that all people had an "inner light" that could help them experience God. They rejected formal religious practices and dressed plainly. The Quakers supported nonviolence as well as religious tolerance for all peoples. Such views differed from those of many Christians. As a result, Quakers were persecuted in both England and the American colonies.

One proprietor of the New Jersey colony was a Quaker named **William Penn**. Penn wished to found a larger colony under his own control that would provide a safe home for Quakers. In 1681 King Charles II agreed to grant Penn a charter to begin a colony west of New Jersey.

Known as Pennsylvania, this middle colony grew rapidly. Penn tried to create a government that was fair to all its people. He limited his own powers so that "the will of one man may not hinder [harm] the good of a whole country." He also provided a means of changing the colony's laws to reflect the will of the people. Penn sold land to colonists at low prices, and he also promised religious freedom to all Christians. In addition, Penn said that the government would care for the poor. His work

BIOGRAPHY

William Penn

(1644–1718)

William Penn was born in London, the son of a wealthy admiral. Penn joined the Quakers in 1666 and became an active preacher and writer of religious works. He supported toleration for dissenters. In 1681 he received a charter to establish a new colony called Pennsylvania. There Penn put his beliefs into practice. He insisted on fair dealings with local American Indians, welcomed immigrants, and promised religious toleration. Because he believed in nonviolence, he did not require settlers to serve in a colonial militia. Although Penn played a major role in establishing Pennsylvania, he lived there only a few years.

How did William Penn put his Quaker beliefs into practice when he founded Pennsylvania?

made Pennsylvania a key example of representative self-government in the colonies. Some of the largest groups to arrive in the colony were Welsh and Irish Quakers, and Germans. After arriving, many became farmers. These groups helped create a peaceful and stable society in Pennsylvania. Penn described one type of colonist he was seeking.

"Another sort of person [who is] . . . necessary in the colonies is the person of universal spirits. These people are concerned about the future. They both understand and promote good discipline and just government. Such persons . . . may find a place in the colonies for their good advice. These people deserve our esteem and should be encouraged to settle here."

—William Penn, "Some Account of the Province of Pennsylvania in America"

Penn named the capital of his colony Philadelphia, or the City of Brotherly Love. Penn designed the city himself. He laid it out in a checkerboard pattern that became a model for city planners in other colonies. Pennsylvania grew a great deal in 1682. That year the Duke of York sold Penn a region to the south of Pennsylvania. This area, called Delaware, remained part of Pennsylvania until 1776.

✔ **Reading Check: Finding the Main Idea** Why did William Penn establish Pennsylvania, and how did he influence its government?

The Ideal of Georgia

The English also founded the southern colony of Georgia. In 1732 King George II granted a charter to **James Oglethorpe** and other trustees. They received permission to start a colony for poor English citizens. Among the group were people who had been jailed for unpaid debts. The king hoped that Georgia would also serve as a shield between South Carolina and Spanish Florida.

In 1733 Oglethorpe and 120 other English colonists founded the city of Savannah on the coast of Georgia. Many of the early colonists were German, Swiss, and Welsh Protestants. Jewish settlers also moved to Savannah. Oglethorpe had high hopes for the Georgia settlement.

"The examples of other colonies suggest that the new colony will succeed. . . . Georgia is even more likely to succeed than either Virginia or Pennsylvania were."

James Oglethorpe, quoted in *Voices of America*, edited by Thomas R. Frazier

Oglethorpe wanted his colony to be different from the other southern colonies. He did not want Georgia to have large plantations ruled by a few wealthy individuals. He hoped that the colony would draw small farmers and avoid the rise of a class of wealthy planters. To reach this goal, Oglethorpe outlawed slavery and limited the size of land grants. He also gave poor colonists free passage to Georgia. Colonists received cattle, land, and food until they could provide their own. Soon, however,

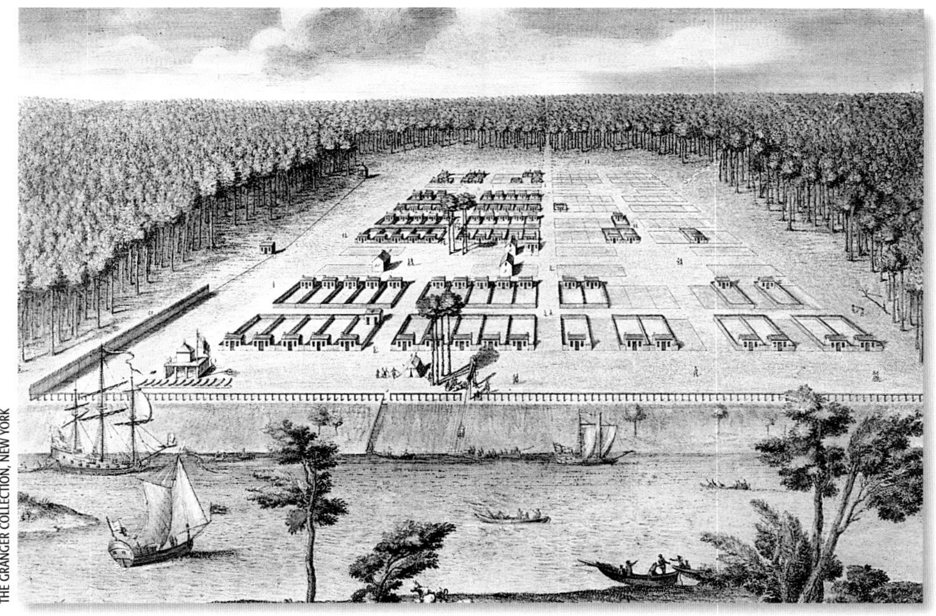

THE GRANGER COLLECTION, NEW YORK

Interpreting the Visual Record

An orderly community *James Oglethorpe carefully planned the town of Savannah, Georgia.* ***What suggests that this town has been planned?***

the settlers grew unhappy with Oglethorpe's strict rules. For example, many settlers wanted to allow slavery. They also wanted to have larger farms.

Finally, in 1752 the trustees of Georgia gave up their charter. The English government then made Georgia a royal colony with new laws. Coastal Georgia was soon filled with large rice plantations worked by thousands of slaves.

✔ **Reading Check: Analyzing Information** How did James Oglethorpe hope to make Georgia's population different from the other colonies?

Section 4 Review

go.hrw.com Homework Practice Online
keyword: SC3 HP3

1. **Define** and explain:
   - proprietors

2. **Identify** and explain:
   - Cecilius Calvert
   - Toleration Act of 1649
   - Peter Stuyvesant
   - Quakers
   - William Penn
   - James Oglethorpe

3. **Comparing and Contrasting** Copy the chart below. Use it to compare and contrast the reasons why each of the colonies discussed in this section was founded. Include the type of charter given to each colony and its main economic pursuit.

Colony	Reason for Founding	Type of Charter	Economic Pursuit
MD			
NC			
SC			
NY			
NJ			
PA			
GA			

4. **Finding the Main Idea**
   a. In what ways did religion affect settlement and law in the Maryland colony?
   b. When were the Carolinas founded, and how were their economies different from each other?

5. **Writing and Critical Thinking**
   Summarizing Imagine that you are a colonial historian. Create a pamphlet describing the founding and development of the middle colonies.
   Consider the following:
   - the capture of New Netherland
   - the role of William Penn
   - the economies of the middle colonies

Chapter 3 Review

The Chapter at a Glance

Examine the visual summary of the chapter below. Use the visual summary to create a chart comparing the thirteen colonies that shows which were founded for economic, political, or social reasons. If a colony was founded for more than one reason, list it in all appropriate columns on the chart.

New England Colonies

Massachusetts: Founded for religious freedom; Plymouth, 1620; Massachusetts Bay, 1630
New Hampshire: Founded for farming in 1623
Connecticut: Founded for political and religious freedom in 1635
Rhode Island: Founded for religious freedom in 1636

Middle Colonies

New York: Originally New Netherland; captured by England in 1664
New Jersey: Founded for farming and trade in 1664
Pennsylvania: Founded for religious freedom in 1682
Delaware: Established in 1776

Southern Colonies

Virginia: Jamestown founded in 1607 to find wealth
Maryland: Founded in 1634 for religious freedom
North and South Carolina: Founded in 1670 for farming and trade; divided into two colonies in the 1700s
Georgia: Founded in 1733 to provide relief for poor and protection from Spanish Florida

Identifying People and Ideas

Use the following terms or people in historically significant sentences.

1. Bacon's Rebellion
2. Pilgrims
3. Mayflower Compact
4. Squanto
5. John Winthrop
6. covenant
7. Fundamental Orders of Connecticut
8. Anne Hutchinson
9. Toleration Act of 1649
10. William Penn

Understanding Main Ideas

Section 1 *(Pages 64–69)*

1. What factors made it difficult for the Jamestown settlement to survive?

Section 2 *(Pages 70–74)*

2. In what ways did American Indians help the Pilgrims survive in Plymouth?

Section 3 *(Pages 75–80)*

3. How did Puritan dissenters such as Roger Williams contribute to the development of self-government in the colonies?

Section 4 *(Pages 81–87)*

4. Contrast the founding and settlement of the Carolinas, Georgia, and Maryland.

You Be the Historian— Reviewing Themes

1. **Geography** How did climate and geography affect the colonies' development?
2. **Economics** Why were indentured servants and enslaved Africans more important to the southern colonies' economies than to New England's?
3. **Culture** Why did Catholics, Puritans, and Quakers immigrate to America, and what colonies did they establish?

Thinking Critically

1. **Evaluating** Why was it important for members of colonial families to support each other?
2. **Comparing and Contrasting** Compare and contrast the economic reasons for founding each of the thirteen colonies.
3. **Categorizing** What were the social differences between the colonies at Jamestown and Plymouth, and what caused those differences?

Interpreting Maps

Study the map below. Then use the information on the map to help you answer the questions that follow.

The Thirteen Colonies

1. Using your knowledge of the period, explain why it would have been important for major towns to be located along rivers or along the coast.

2. Which colonies were known as the middle colonies?
   a. Georgia, Maryland, North Carolina, South Carolina, and Virginia
   b. Connecticut, Massachusetts, New Hampshire, and Rhode Island
   c. Delaware, New Jersey, New York, and Pennsylvania
   d. New Hampshire and New York

Analyzing Primary Sources

Read the following quotation by a woman accused of witchcraft in Massachusetts, and then answer the questions that follow.

> **"There was no other way to save our lives, . . . but by our confessing. . . . Indeed, that confession, that it is said we made, was no other than what was suggested to us by some gentlemen, they telling us that we were witches, and they knew it and we knew it, which made us thinking that it was so. . . . Some time after, when we were better composed, they telling us what we had confessed, we did profess that we were innocent and ignorant of such things."**

3. Which of the following statements best describes the claim being made by the accused woman?
   a. She and her friends are now convinced that they are witches.
   b. She and her friends confessed out of confusion and to save their lives.
   c. The confessions were given freely and fairly.
   d. There was a lot of evidence to back up the confessions.
4. Based on the information in this quote, do you think the woman and her friends received a fair trial? Explain your answer.

Alternative Assessment

Building Your Portfolio

Interdisciplinary Connection to Geography

Imagine that you are an English merchant traveling through the thirteen colonies to find new trade goods. Create a travel journal of your trip through the colonies. Include a map showing your route and descriptions of the people, places, and types of goods you encounter. Your journal should have at least one entry for each of the thirteen colonies.

internet connect

Internet Activity: go.hrw.com
keyword: SC3 CF3

Choose a topic about the English colonies to:

- Research settlement in Jamestown and create a graph to illustrate your information.
- Construct a scale model of a colonial home.
- Learn about colonial cuisine.

CHAPTER

4 Life in the English Colonies (1630–1770)

This scene shows Harvard College in Cambridge, Massachusetts, some 100 years after it was founded.

Puritan leaders of the Massachusetts Bay Colony had the Bay Psalm Book *printed.*

UNITED STATES

1636 Harvard College, located in Massachusetts, is the first college in the colonies.

1640 The *Bay Psalm Book* is the first book published in the English colonies.

1661 Virginia passes an act recognizing African slavery.

1686 The Dominion of New England is founded.

1630 1650 1670 1690

1648 Work is finished on India's Taj Mahal.

1653 Oliver Cromwell becomes Lord Protector of England.

1660 King Charles II is crowned as ruler of England.

1687 Sir Isaac Newton publishes the first volume of *Principia,* a new theory of physics.

WORLD

The crowning of Charles II was known as the Restoration because it returned the English monarchy to power.

Build on What You Know

English colonists began settling in North America in the 1600s. Some people came to America hoping to make their fortunes. Others came to escape religious persecution. Each region of the colonies developed its own economy. All of the colonies were still closely tied to England, but a unique colonial culture also began to develop.

Benjamin Franklin flew a kite in a thunderstorm during one of his experiments with electricity.

These bifocals are based on Benjamin Franklin's design.

1710 — **1730** — **1750** — **1770**

1721 Regular postal service begins between London and New England.

1727 Coffee is first planted in Brazil.

1730 John Smibert holds the first art exhibition in America.

1734 John Peter Zenger is arrested for publishing criticisms of the governor of New York.

1748 The Treaty of Aix-la-Chapelle ends the War of the Austrian Succession in Europe.

1752 Benjamin Franklin proves that lightning is a form of electricity.

If you were there . . .

What occupation would you choose as a colonist?

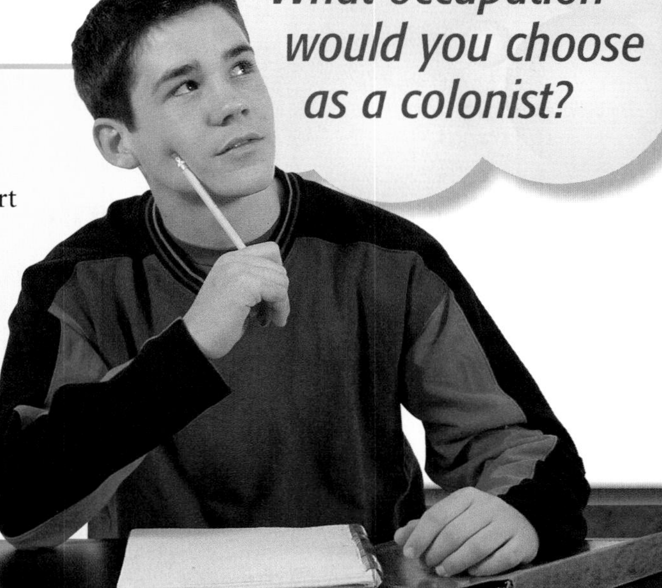

You Be the Historian

What's Your Opinion? Do you **agree** or **disagree** with the following statements? Support your point of view in your journal.

- **Economics** Colonies should trade only with their home country.
- **Geography** A colony must have good weather and many natural resources to be successful.
- **Science, Technology & Society** Scientific discoveries are always good for everyone.

Section 1

Forms of Government

Read to Discover

1. How did representative government develop in the colonies?
2. How did colonists influence the rulings of colonial courts?
3. How did the Dominion of New England affect the New England colonies?
4. How did the English Bill of Rights influence colonists?

Define

- bicameral legislature
- town meeting
- libel

Identify

- Privy Council
- Parliament
- House of Burgesses
- John Peter Zenger
- Dominion of New England
- Edmund Andros
- Glorious Revolution
- English Bill of Rights

WHY IT MATTERS TODAY

Many citizens participate in their local governments today. Use CNNfyi.com or other **current events** sources to find examples of ways citizens voice their opinions to their local governments. Record your findings in your journal.

The Story Continues

One September morning, William Byrd II rose at 5 A.M. to begin the business of running his Virginia plantation. After a few hours, he met Colonel Bassett, and the two men rode into Williamsburg. In the busy colonial capital, Byrd met with several members of the Council of State. These men were an important part of the colony's government. That day he was sworn in as a member of the Council—a major step in his political career. He wrote in his diary, "God grant I may distinguish myself with honor and good conscience."

The colonial Capitol Building in Williamsburg, Virginia, still stands.

Colonial Governments

The English colonies in America all had their own governments when they were first founded. Each government was given power by a charter. The three charter types were proprietary—meaning that one or more individuals had authority over the colony—company, and royal. The English monarch owned all of the colonies and had the sole power to grant charters. A group of royal advisers called the **Privy Council** set English policies in the colonies. However, the Privy Council allowed most colonies to run their own affairs. For example, Rhode Island's 1644 charter stated that all of the colony's laws should agree with those of England. At the same time, the charter stated that the colonists had "full Power and Authority to rule themselves."

Each colony had a governor who served as head of the government. Most governors were assisted by an advisory council. In royal colonies the English king or queen selected the governor and the council members. In proprietary colonies the proprietors chose all of these officials. In a few colonies, such as Connecticut, the people elected the governor. No matter who chose them, governors often possessed significant powers. It was their job to carry out the policies set by England.

✔ **Reading Check: Summarizing** What were the three types of colonial charters?

Colonial Assemblies

In the colonies the people also elected representatives to help make laws and set policy. These officials served in assemblies. Colonists based their assemblies on **Parliament**, England's national legislature, or lawmaking body. Parliament is a **bicameral legislature**—a lawmaking body made up of two houses, or groups. Colonial assemblies worked like the lower house of Parliament. They had the power to raise taxes and organize local governments. They also shared control of the military with the governor. The laws passed by each assembly had to be approved first by the advisory council and then by the governor. Then the Privy Council reviewed the colonial laws to make sure that they followed English laws.

Interpreting the Visual Record

Virginia's assembly *This scene shows an early meeting of Virginia's legislature.* ***What does this image suggest about the wealth and social status of these representatives? Explain your answer.***

Virginia's assembly, founded in Jamestown in 1619, was the first colonial legislature in North America. At first it met as a single body, but it was later split into two houses. The first house was known as the Council of State. The governor's advisory council and the Virginia Company selected its members. The **House of Burgesses** was the assembly's second house. The members of this house were elected by colonists to represent Virginia's plantations and towns.

Sometimes assemblies and governors disagreed. In such cases the governor had the final say on whether a law was passed. But assemblies could influence governors' actions by refusing to pay their salaries. William Byrd II described the relationship between the House of Burgesses and the royal governor of Virginia.

"Our government . . . is so happily constituted [designed] that a governor must first outwit us before he can oppress [subdue] us. And if he ever squeezes money out of us he must first take care to deserve it."

—William Byrd II, quoted in *Albion's Seed,* by David Hackett Fischer

Legislatures were not the only important political bodies in the colonies. The center of New England politics was the **town meeting**. In town meetings people talked about and decided issues of local interest, such as paying for schools. They also regulated other important issues, including the ownership and use of unsettled lands. The men in the community met one or more times every year. They would also select the group of officials who would carry out the town's decisions.

In the southern colonies people typically lived farther away from one another. Therefore, many decisions were made at the county level. The middle colonies used a combination of county meetings and town meetings in their local governments.

✔ **Reading Check: Analyzing Information** Why were colonial assemblies and town meetings created, and what did they do?

Colonial Courts

Colonial courts made up another important part of colonial governments. Royal officials could have a strong influence on the courts. Whenever possible, however, colonists used the courts to control local affairs. In general, the courts supported the interests and ideas of their communities. For example, many laws in Massachusetts enforced the Puritans' religious views.

Sometimes colonial courts also protected individual freedoms. For example, the court case of **John Peter Zenger** dealt with the issue of freedom of the press. In 1733 Zenger began criticizing the royal governor of New York in his newspaper. Officials charged him with committing **libel** against a public official. They accused him of printing a false

Citizenship and You

Town Meetings

Watertown, Massachusetts, is known as the "cradle of the town meeting." It held its first town meeting in the 1630s. In colonial times, the town meeting was the preferred form of local government in New England. Today any gathering open to the public to discuss community issues may be called a town meeting. The U.S. government has held such meetings so that citizens can discuss issues ranging from nuclear science to ways to improve neighborhoods.

Presidential candidates also have held town meetings to let voters ask questions and make their views known. Historian John Hope Franklin declared, "The town meeting movement seems to me a magnificent opportunity to catch the whole country up in a common effort." **Do you think town meetings are a good way for people to participate in government? Explain your answer.**

A town meeting in Hebron, Massachusetts

THE GRANGER COLLECTION, NEW YORK

Interpreting the Visual Record

Freedom of the Press *Attorney Andrew Hamilton argued that John Peter Zenger could publish the truth even if it offended people.* ***In what ways does this courtroom scene look different from the trial system used in the United States today?***

written statement that damaged the governor's reputation. Zenger was arrested in 1734.

Andrew Hamilton served as Zenger's attorney at the trial. He said that Zenger could publish whatever he wished as long as it was true. Even damaging facts could be printed, Hamilton said. The chief justice of the court did not agree with this view. He explained his opinion to the jury. "Nothing can be worse to any government than to have people attempt to create distrust and dislike of the management of it." The jury, however, found Zenger not guilty. The jury's decision showed its dislike of the royal governor. The jury's agreement with Hamilton's argument also reflected their support for the idea that colonists had a right to express their views openly.

✔ **Reading Check: Finding the Main Idea** Why might colonists support freedom of the press?

The Dominion of New England

In 1685 James II became king of England. He was determined to take more control over the English government, both in England and in the colonies. James believed that the northern colonies were too independent. He wanted them to be more connected to each other and to England. In 1686 James united the northern colonies under one government called the **Dominion of New England**. The Dominion eventually included the colonies of Connecticut, Maine, Massachusetts, New Hampshire, New Jersey, New York, and Rhode Island. James appointed Sir **Edmund Andros** as royal governor of the Dominion. James also chose a royal council for the Dominion.

The Dominion government took the place of the northern colonies' original charters. The king's actions greatly upset many of the colonists. As one colonist grumbled, the Dominion was "without any liberty for an Assembly."

In December 1686 Sir Edmund Andros arrived in Boston. Andros was a former governor of New York. The colonists disliked him, as one pamphlet writer explained.

Analyzing Primary Sources
Identifying Points of View Why does the speaker think the colonists dislike Andros?

"Sir Edmund Andros arrived as our governor; who besides his power, with the advice and consent of his Council, to make laws and raise taxes as he pleased, had also authority by himself to muster [gather for military duty] and employ all persons residing in the territory. . . . And several companies of soldiers were now brought from Europe to support what was to be imposed upon us."

—"A. B.," quoted in *The Annals of America*

In 1687 many residents of Ipswich, Massachusetts, protested Andros's taxation policy. Five were arrested and jailed. To prevent further protests, Andros used his royal authority to limit the powers of town meetings in 1688.

✔ **Reading Check: Summarizing** How did James II and Governor Andros limit New England colonists' participation in government?

The Glorious Revolution

The new policies of James II were unpopular in England as well as in the colonies. Parliament felt threatened when he tried to change England from a Protestant country back to a Catholic one. To stop the king, leaders of Parliament asked James's Protestant daughter, Mary, and her husband, William of Orange, to rule England. William, the leader of the Netherlands, landed in England with his army in the fall of 1688. James left the country. The overthrow of James II became known as the **Glorious Revolution**.

Protestant colonists celebrated the crowning of King William and Queen Mary with songs and pictures.

THE GRANGER COLLECTION, NEW YORK

When residents of the Dominion first learned about the Glorious Revolution in 1689, they removed Andros as governor. The delighted colonists sent Andros to England to answer for his actions. The individual colonies left the Dominion and quickly formed new assemblies. They then sent declarations of support for William and Mary. In time, William and Mary replaced the canceled colonial charters. The new charters were like the original ones, except in Massachusetts. The colonists there had originally elected the governor. However, the Crown now chose this person. In addition, men no longer had to be full church members to vote. Instead, they had to own a certain amount of property. Massachusetts also grew in size with the addition of Plymouth and Maine to its territory.

The political ideas of the Glorious Revolution led Parliament to pass the **English Bill of Rights** in 1689. Under this act, the powers of the English monarchy were reduced. At the same time, Parliament gained power. American colonists were greatly interested in this shift in power from the monarch to a representative governing body. As time went on, the colonists valued their own right to elect the representatives that governed them. (See pages 192–93.)

THE GRANGER COLLECTION, NEW YORK

The English Bill of Rights gave greater powers to Parliament, shown here meeting in London's Westminster Hall about 1700.

✔ **Reading Check: Finding the Main Idea** How did the Glorious Revolution and the English Bill of Rights affect the political views of colonists?

Section 1 Review

go.hrw.com **Homework Practice Online**
keyword: SC3 HP4

1. **Define** and explain:
   - bicameral legislature
   - town meeting
   - libel
2. **Identify** and explain:
   - Privy Council
   - Parliament
   - House of Burgesses
   - John Peter Zenger
   - Dominion of New England
   - Edmund Andros
   - Glorious Revolution
   - English Bill of Rights
3. **Contrasting** Copy the chart below. Use it to compare and contrast the powers that different institutions of colonial government held.

Privy Council	
Governors	
Assemblies	
Town Meetings	
Courts	

4. **Finding the Main Idea**
   a. Provide at least two examples of how colonists began to develop representative governments.
   b. Make a time line that describes the creation of the Dominion of New England, its actions and their effects on the colonies, and the Dominion's end.
5. **Writing and Critical Thinking**
   Making Generalizations and Predictions Imagine that you publish a colonial newspaper. Write an editorial announcing the passage of the English Bill of Rights and predicting its effect on the colonies.
   Consider the following:
   - reaction to the Glorious Revolution
   - the shift toward representative government in England
   - the document's guarantee of rights

Section 2

The Growth of Trade

Read to Discover

1. What effects did the Navigation Acts have on colonial economies?
2. What types of trade took place in the colonies during the 1700s?
3. Why did the colonies participate in the slave trade?

Define

- mercantilism
- balance of trade
- imports
- exports
- duties
- free enterprise
- triangular trade

Identify

- Navigation Acts
- Middle Passage
- Olaudah Equiano

Why It Matters Today

Many countries around the world have formed trading networks. Use CNNfyi.com or other **current events** sources to identify a trading network involving the United States. Record your findings in your journal.

The Story Continues

The beat of a drum began trade at the slave market. African slaves stood terrified as buyers rushed in to make their choices. Cries were heard from people who were separated from their family and friends. Such scenes led Olaudah Equiano (oh-LOW-duh ek-wee-AHN-oh), once a slave himself, to ask, "Why are parents to lose their children, brothers their sisters, or husbands their wives?" The answer was money and greed. The slave trade had become an important part of the colonial economy.

After gaining his freedom, Olaudah Equiano spoke out against slavery and published an account of his life.

English Trade Laws

Trade was one of England's main reasons for founding its American colonies. In 1689 an English official pointed out that the colonies made up "a full third part of the whole Trade and Navigation of England." In the late 1600s England, like most western European nations, practiced **mercantilism**. Using this economic system, nations created and maintained wealth by carefully controlling trade. A nation could be self-sufficient if it had a good **balance of trade**. This meant a country had fewer **imports**—goods bought from other countries—than **exports**—goods sold to other countries. Between 1650 and 1696 Parliament passed a series of **Navigation Acts**. These acts required colonists to do the bulk of their trading with England. The Navigation Acts also set **duties**, or import taxes, on some trade products.

England claimed that the Navigation Acts were good for the colonies. After all, the colonies had a steady market in England for their goods. But not everyone agreed. Many colonists wanted more freedom to buy or sell goods in whatever markets offered the best prices. Within the colonies many merchants practiced **free enterprise**—economic competition with little government control. But local demand for colonial goods was small compared to foreign demand for colonial products. English laws limited free enterprise by preventing colonists from selling or buying goods directly to or from many foreign countries. This led to an unfavorable balance of trade for the colonies.

✔ **Reading Check: Analyzing Information** In what ways did mercantilism and the Navigation Acts limit free enterprise in the colonies?

Mercantilism and the Colonies

Under the system of mercantilism, nations such as England tried to control what goods were traded to and from their colonies.

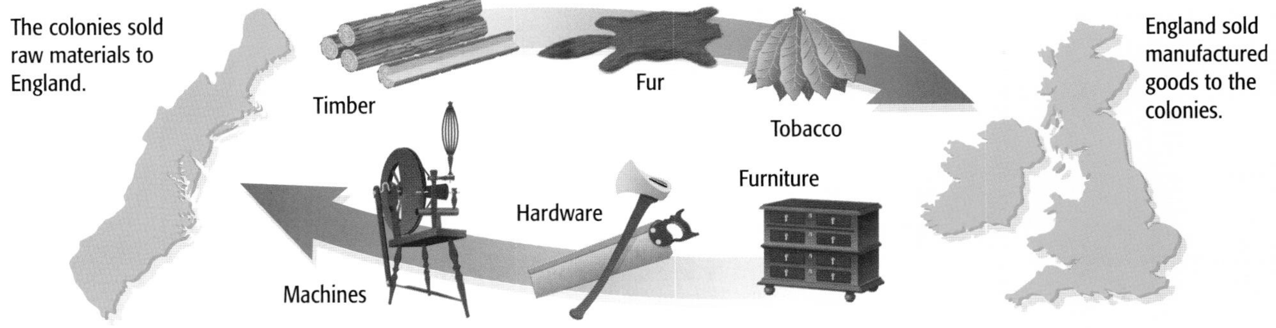

Colonists were not allowed to trade many of these goods with other countries. They had to buy from and sell only to England.

Visualizing History

1. **Economics** What were some of the disadvantages that colonists experienced under mercantilism?
2. **Connecting to Today** Do you think American businesses would support such a system today? Why or why not?

Colonial Trade

Despite colonial complaints, trade restrictions continued into the 1700s. In 1733 Parliament passed the Molasses Act, which placed duties on sugar, molasses, and rum. In response, some colonists began to bring these goods into the colonies illegally, a practice known as smuggling. However, British officials rarely punished these smugglers. One colonial official in Massachusetts complained that he could only enforce the law "with great delay and too many difficulties."

Legal trade was much more significant than smuggling. By the early 1700s the newly unified kingdom of Great Britain was trading around the world. Most American merchants traded directly with Britain or with its colonies in the West Indies. The West Indies produced large amounts of sugar. Writer and economist Adam Smith commented on the wealth that the sugar trade brought to the British West Indies.

Analyzing Primary Sources

Supporting a Point of View Why does Smith suggest that sugar plantations are particularly important?

"The profits of a [sugar] plantation in any of our West Indian colonies are generally much greater than those of any other cultivation [crop] that is known either in Europe or America."

—Adam Smith, *The Wealth of Nations*

Some merchants also took part in the **triangular trade**, which could follow several different routes. In one route the colonies sold goods like fish, grain, beef, and horses to plantation owners in the West Indies. In exchange, merchants received sugar and molasses. Some of these goods were then shipped to Britain. This was just one example of how colonial merchants sought the best markets for their products. This colonial participation in trade all across the Atlantic Ocean was an early form of free enterprise.

✔ **Reading Check: Finding the Main Idea** In what ways were colonists beginning to practice free enterprise?

Interpreting the Visual Record

Sugar refining *Slaves in the West Indies refined sugar by boiling sugarcane and drying the sugar in bins.* ***What do you think working conditions in such a refinery would be like?***

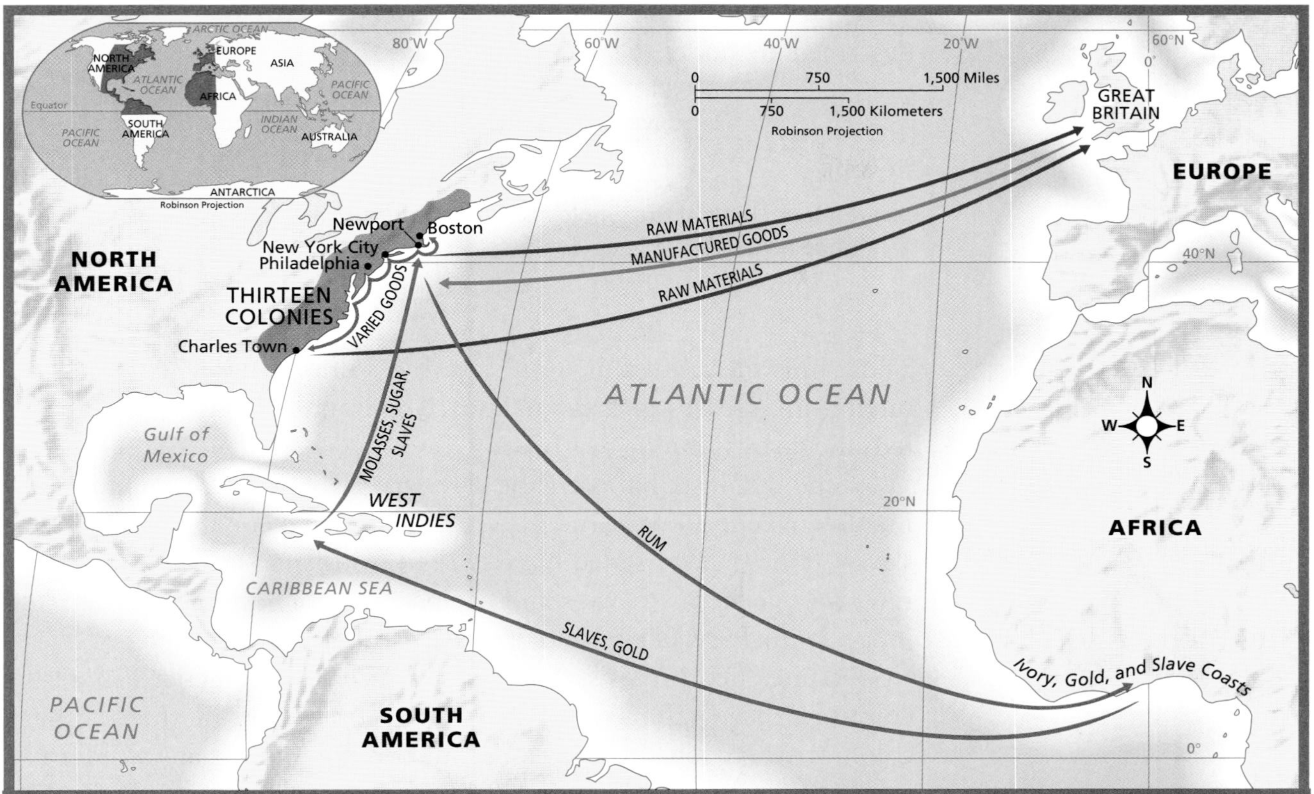

NORTH AMERICA
THIRTEEN COLONIES
Newport
Boston
New York City
Philadelphia
Charles Town
VARIED GOODS
RAW MATERIALS
MANUFACTURED GOODS
RAW MATERIALS
GREAT BRITAIN
EUROPE
ATLANTIC OCEAN
Gulf of Mexico
MOLASSES, SUGAR, SLAVES
WEST INDIES
RUM
AFRICA
CARIBBEAN SEA
SLAVES, GOLD
Ivory, Gold, and Slave Coasts
PACIFIC OCEAN
SOUTH AMERICA
0 750 1,500 Miles
0 750 1,500 Kilometers
Robinson Projection

Triangular Trade

Interpreting Maps The colonies supplied Great Britain with raw materials such as furs, timber, and tobacco. They also supplied the West Indies with food, importing molasses and sugar in return.

Skills Assessment **Human Systems** What did Great Britain export to its colonies?

The Middle Passage

One version of the triangular trade had a much greater cost in human suffering. It began with New England traders exchanging rum for slaves on the West African coast. The traders then sold the enslaved Africans in the West Indies for molasses or brought them back to sell in the mainland American colonies.

The slave trade brought around 10 million Africans across the Atlantic Ocean. This terrifying and often deadly voyage was called the **Middle Passage**. The journey could last as long as three months. Enslaved Africans were chained by the neck and legs. They lived between the upper and lower decks of the ship, in spaces just a few feet high. Even the sailors remarked on the terrible conditions enslaved Africans faced on the voyage. "They [the Africans] had not so much room as a man in his coffin," wrote one slave ship captain. Slave traders carried as many slaves as possible so they could earn greater profits when they sold their human cargo in North or South America.

Free Find:
Olaudah Equiano
After reading about Olaudah Equiano on the **Holt Researcher CD–ROM**, create a brochure for a museum exhibition on Equiano that shows the different stages of his life.

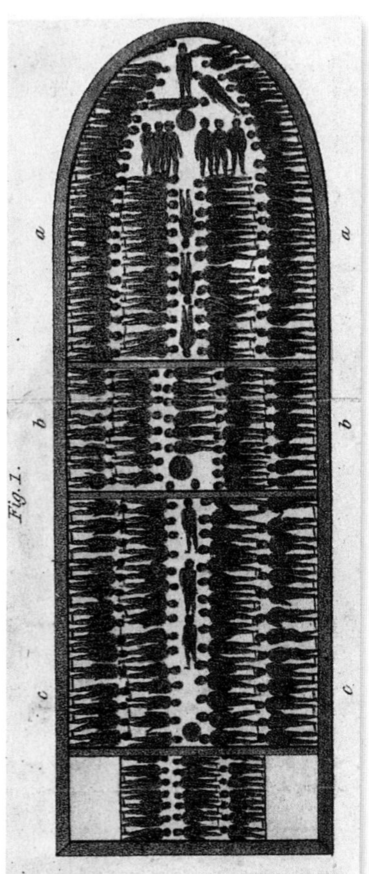

On slave ships like this, each African was confined in a space only about 16 inches wide and 5 ½ feet long.

Olaudah Equiano was sold into slavery when he was about 11. He described life under the decks of the slave ships.

> **"I received such a salutation [smell] in my nostrils, as I had never experienced in my life; . . . I became so sick and low that I was not able to eat. . . . The groans of the dying rendered [made] the whole a scene of horror almost inconceivable [unbelievable]."**
>
> —Olaudah Equiano, *The Interesting Narrative of the Life of Olaudah Equiano, or Gustavus Vassa, the African*

Thousands of captives died on slave ships during the Middle Passage, often from diseases such as smallpox. Thousands of slaves also committed suicide by jumping overboard.

Some colonists opposed the slave trade. In 1688 Quakers in Germantown, Pennsylvania, made the first recorded colonial protest against slavery. One Quaker stated his view: "To bring men hither [here], or to rob and sell them . . . we stand against." Massachusetts merchant and judge Samuel Sewall also criticized slavery in a 1700 pamphlet.

Despite such protests, slavery continued to be practiced in all the colonies. Slave labor was particularly important in the southern colonies, where tobacco and rice production required many workers. As southern farmers relied increasingly on slave workers instead of indentured servants, the demand for slaves grew. The slave trade also brought wealth to areas that used little slave labor. For example, some of the slave ships were built and owned by people in New England.

✔ **Reading Check: Identifying Cause and Effect** What factors caused the slave trade to grow, and how did this affect conditions on the Middle Passage?

Section 2 Review

go.hrw.com **Homework Practice Online**
keyword: SC3 HP4

1. **Define** and explain:
   - mercantilism
   - balance of trade
   - imports
   - exports
   - duties
   - free enterprise
   - triangular trade

2. **Identify** and explain:
   - Navigation Acts
   - Middle Passage
   - Olaudah Equiano

3. **Summarizing** Copy the web diagram below. Fill in each circle with goods and people that came from that region. Use arrows to show what goods were exchanged between the four regions.

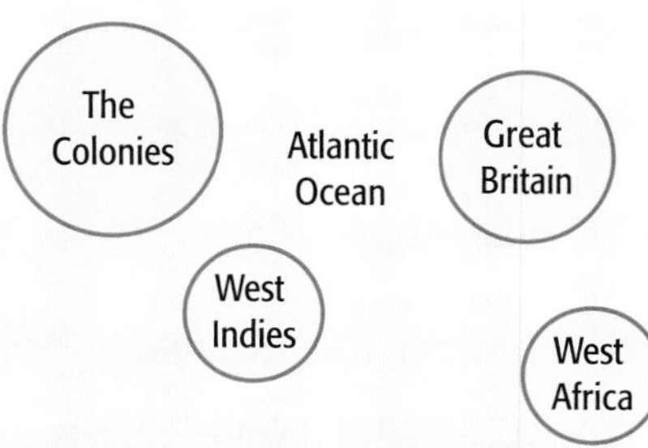

4. **Finding the Main Idea**
   a. Why did colonists participate in the slave trade?
   b. Imagine that you are a British official. How would you address the problem of colonial smuggling?

5. **Writing and Critical Thinking**
   Supporting a Point of View Imagine that you are a New England merchant who supports a freer market in the colonies. Create a handbill that explains the Navigation Acts and mercantilism and that calls for an end to both.
   Consider the following:
   - the economic effects of the Navigation Acts
   - the overseas demand for colonial products
   - the benefits of free enterprise

Section 3

The Colonial Economy

Read to Discover

1. Why were enslaved Africans the main workforce in the southern colonies?
2. How were New England's economic activities different from those of the southern colonies?
3. How did the middle colonies combine economic aspects of the southern and New England colonies?

Define

- cash crops
- slave codes
- apprentices
- staple crops

Identify

- Eliza Lucas Pinckney

WHY IT MATTERS TODAY

The different parts of the United States still have different economies. Use CNNfyi.com or other **current events** sources to find out about the major economic activities of a region of the United States. Record your findings in your journal.

The Story Continues

In 1647 Leonard Calvert, the governor of Maryland, lay dying. He asked that Margaret Brent be brought to his bedside. Brent had left England in 1638 to escape religious persecution. She now owned a Maryland plantation. Before witnesses, Governor Calvert said to Brent, "I make you my sole executrix [woman who carries out a will]. Take all and pay all." Brent was well known for her business skills and the management of her plantation. Calvert trusted her to handle his estate wisely.

Leonard Calvert was sent by his older brother, Cecilius Calvert, to rule the Maryland colony.

Agriculture in the Southern Colonies

The economies of the southern colonies depended on agriculture. They also exported materials for building ships, such as wood and tar. Some colonies also traded with local American Indians for deerskins to sell.

The colonies had many small farms and some large plantations. Farms did well because the South enjoyed a warm climate and long growing season. Many farms grew **cash crops** that were sold for profit. Tobacco, rice, and indigo—a plant used to make blue dye—were the

THE GRANGER COLLECTION, NEW YORK

Daily Life

Tobacco Industry Many of the slaves in the Chesapeake Bay area worked on tobacco plantantions, as shown in this 1670 painting. The tremendous demand for tobacco led planters to increase greatly their production. By the early 1700s the American colonies were exporting millions of pounds of tobacco to Europe. The demand for slave labor also increased. The growing slave trade led to more slave auctions such as the one listed on the poster above. **What does this image suggest about the effort it took to produce tobacco?**

most important cash crops. Virginia specialized in tobacco, and South Carolina specialized in rice and indigo. Eliza Lucas (later **Eliza Lucas Pinckney**) introduced indigo to the colony after she learned how to grow it on her family's plantation.

Crops such as indigo and rice required many workers to grow and harvest. By the 1700s the indentured servants who had first done this labor had been largely replaced by enslaved Africans. Unlike indentured servants, slaves and their children had to work for life.

Slaves performed most of the plantation labor. In his diary, William Byrd II described his daily life as a plantation owner.

> **"I said my prayers and ate milk for breakfast. I walked out to see my people [slaves] at work at the ditch. I read a little geometry. I ate mutton [sheep] for dinner. I walked to the ditch again. In the evening I said my prayers."**
>
> —William Byrd II, *The Secret Diary of William Byrd of Westover, 1709–1712*

When a job was finished, slaves might be allowed to do their own work. A few slaves were able to earn enough money to buy their freedom.

Most of the southern colonies passed **slave codes**, or laws to control slaves. Colonies with large numbers of slaves had the most extensive slave codes. South Carolina's slaveholders feared that slaves would revolt. As a result, South Carolina's code said slaves could not hold meetings or own weapons. Some colonies did not allow slaveholders to free their slaves. The Virginia Assembly claimed that runaway slaves committed "injuries to the inhabitants of this dominion [colony]." Assembly members passed a law allowing people to kill a runaway slave who resisted capture.

✔ **Reading Check: Summarizing** What role did slavery play in the southern plantation economy, and how was slavery regulated?

Industry and Trade in New England

Connecticut, Massachusetts, New Hampshire, and Rhode Island were very different from the southern colonies. The often harsh climate and rocky soil meant that few New England farms grew cash crops. They had little demand for large numbers of farm laborers. Although some people held slaves, slavery did not become as important to this region.

Trade was vital to New England's economy. New England entrepeneurs—people who undertake new businesses to make a profit—traded goods locally, with other colonies, and overseas. Many entrepeneurs traded local products such as furs, pickled beef, and pork.

Fishing and shipbuilding became two of the region's leading industries. One of the earliest settlers in Massachusetts exclaimed, "Here is a good store of fish, if we had boats to go 8 or 10 leagues [about 25 to 30 miles] to sea to fish in." Merchants exported dried fish. Whaling provided valuable oil for lighting. In addition, whale meat became an important part of the colonial diet.

The shipbuilding industry prospered in New England for several reasons. The region had plenty of forests and the local fishing industry needed ships. In addition, as trade in the New England seaports grew, more merchant ships were built. Shipyards throughout New England towns made high-quality, valuable vessels. Shipowners sometimes even told their captains to sell the ship along with the cargo when they reached their destination.

The diverse economy of New England needed skilled craftspeople. Families often sent younger sons off to learn skilled trades such as blacksmithing, weaving, shipbuilding, and printing. The young boys who learned skilled trades were known as **apprentices**. They lived with a master craftsman and learned from him. In exchange, the boys performed simple tasks. Gabriel Ginings was an apprentice in Portsmouth, Rhode Island. He received "sufficient food and raiment [clothing] suitable for such an apprentice," as his 1663 contract stated.

✔ **Reading Check: Contrasting** How were New England's economic activities different from those in the southern colonies, and why was this the case?

CONNECTING TO

SCIENCE AND TECHNOLOGY

Indigo Dye

During colonial times, the finest blue dyes came from an Asian plant called indigo. Indigo was not grown in the American colonies, however, until the mid-1700s. In 1740 Eliza Lucas (later Eliza Lucas Pinckney) began growing indigo on her family's plantation in South Carolina.

Removing the blue compounds from indigo was hard work. Skilled workers—usually slaves—had to soak, whip, and strain the plants for many hours. It took around 100 pounds of indigo plants to make a single four-ounce indigo bar!

By 1747 South Carolina was exporting more than 135,000 pounds of indigo each year. Today artificial indigo dye is used to color clothes such as blue jeans. **How did Eliza Lucas Pinckney contribute to indigo production?**

THE GRANGER COLLECTION, NEW YORK

Tremendous labor went into building sailing ships such as these three vessels in a New England shipyard.

The Middle Colonies

The middle colonies—Delaware, Pennsylvania, New Jersey, and New York—combined qualities of the New England and southern colonies. With a good growing season and rich land, farmers there could grow large amounts of food. The middle colonies grew **staple crops**, or crops that are always needed. Some of these crops were wheat, barley, and oats. Farmers also raised and sold livestock.

Slaves were more important to the middle colonies than they were to New England. They worked in cities as skilled laborers, such as blacksmiths and carpenters. Other slaves also worked on farms, in dockyards, on board ships, and in the growing shipbuilding industry. However, indentured servants largely filled the middle colonies' growing labor needs. Between 1700 and 1775 about 135,000 indentured servants came to the middle colonies from Britain and Germany. About half of them moved to Pennsylvania. By the mid-1700s Philadelphia had become one of the largest British colonial cities. Other cities in the middle colonies, such as New York City, also grew quickly.

Trade and free enterprise were important to the economy of the middle colonies. Merchants in Philadelphia and New York City exported colonial goods to markets in Britain and the West Indies. These products included wheat from New York. Colonial merchants also sold wheat and flour from Pennsylvania and New Jersey. Through hard work, they could make a comfortable living. A Philadelphia merchant noted this in a letter he wrote in 1768. He said that he was able "to live well, but [I] have not been able to lay up such a Stock, as would maintain me without daily labor."

✔ **Reading Check: Comparing** How did geography factors affect agriculture in each colonial region?

Just the Facts

African American Population in the American Colonies

Year	Population of African Ancestry	Total Population
1660	2,920	75,058
1680	6,971	151,507
1700	27,817	250,888
1720	68,839	466,185
1740	150,024	905,563
1760	325,806	1,593,625
1780	575,420	2,780,369

Using Mathematical Skills

1. About what percent of the colonial population in 1660 were people of African ancestry? About what percent were they in 1760?
2. Create a line graph showing these population figures.
3. Imagine that you are a colonial Quaker who opposes slavery. Prepare a pamphlet attacking the rise of slavery in the colonies, using these statistics to support your argument.

Philadelphia was a major center of colonial trade.

RARE BOOK DEPARTMENT, THE FREE LIBRARY OF PHILADELPHIA

Women and the Economy

Throughout the colonies, women made important contributions to the economy. They ran farms and businesses, such as clothing and grocery stores, bakeries, and drugstores. A few female shopkeepers used their business success to call for a voice in colonial politics. One group of women wrote to a New York newspaper in 1733.

"We are House keepers, Pay our taxes, carry on Trade, and most of us are the Merchants, and as we in some measure contribute to the Support of Government, we ought to be Intitled to some of the Sweets of it."

—New York shopkeepers, quoted in *Colonial Women of Affairs,* by Elisabeth Anthony Dexter

MARYLAND HISTORICAL SOCIETY, BALTIMORE

Plantation manager Margaret Brent—shown here speaking to colonial officials—was respected for her business skills.

Some women also practiced medicine, often as nurses and midwives. However, colonial laws and customs limited women's economic activities. Typically, a married woman could not work outside the home without her husband's permission. A husband also had the right to keep the money his wife earned.

Most colonial women worked in the home. Married women managed households and raised children. Sometimes they earned money for their families by washing clothes or selling products such as butter. Many women made items that their family needed, such as clothing.

✔ **Reading Check: Finding the Main Idea** How did women play important roles in the colonial economy?

Section 3 Review

go.hrw.com Homework Practice Online
keyword: SC3 HP4

1. **Define** and explain:
   - cash crops
   - slave codes
   - apprentices
   - staple crops
2. **Identify** and explain:
   - Eliza Lucas Pinckney
3. **Comparing and Contrasting** Copy the graphic organizer below. Use it to compare and contrast the characteristics of the economies of the three major colonial regions.

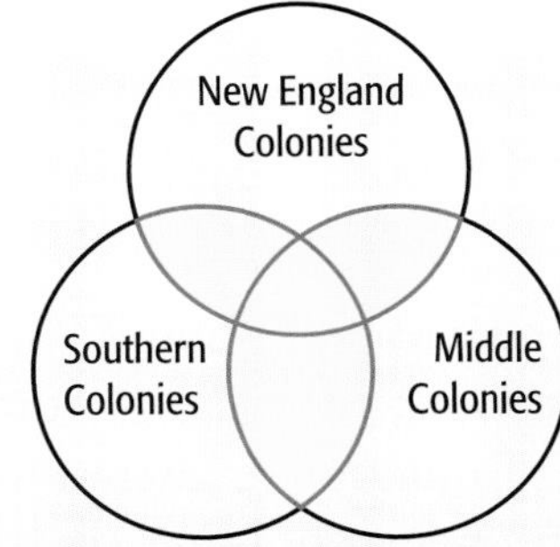

4. **Finding the Main Idea**
   a. Why was slavery common on southern plantations, and how did it affect laws in the southern colonies?
   b. What types of contributions did women make to the colonial economy?
5. **Writing and Critical Thinking**
   Summarizing Imagine that you are going to participate in a debate about the different colonial economic regions. Write a speech explaining how and why the middle colonies are similar to and different from the southern and New England colonies.
   Consider the following:
   - the economic activities of each region
   - the labor required by each region
   - the physical features of each region

Section 4

The Great Awakening

Read to Discover

1. What was the message of the Great Awakening?
2. How did the Great Awakening change colonial religious organizations and leaders?
3. How did the Great Awakening change colonial society?

Define

- revivals

Identify

- Great Awakening
- Jonathan Edwards
- George Whitefield
- Gilbert Tennent

WHY IT MATTERS TODAY

In some countries religious differences have led to conflict. Use CNNfyi.com or other **current events** sources to find out about a country where groups with different religious beliefs are either involved in or resolving a conflict. Record your findings in your journal.

The Story Continues

A beautifully decorated colonial Bible like this one would have been a prized possession.

One morning a Connecticut farmer and his wife heard that George Whitefield would be preaching in a nearby town. They quickly dropped their work. As fast as they could, they rushed to make the 12-mile journey. Still several miles from the meeting site, the couple met a line of horses carrying fellow travelers. To the farmer, each horse appeared "to go with all his might to carry his rider to hear news from heaven for the saving of souls." After hearing Whitefield's message, the inspired farmer joined others who had religious conversions. "I was born on Feb 15th 1711 and born again Octo 1741," he later wrote in the first line of his autobiography.

Words of the Great Awakening

In the early 1700s many church leaders worried that colonists were losing their religious faith. These leaders wanted to bring back the sense of religious duty held by previous generations. Some believed that emotional and inspiring sermons would revive interest in religion. Several ministers in the middle colonies began holding **revivals**, emotional gatherings where people came together to hear sermons and declare their faith.

Because of these ministers' work, many colonists experienced "a great awakening" in their religious lives. This **Great Awakening** reached its height in the 1730s and 1740s. It was a widespread Christian movement involving sermons and revivals that emphasized faith in God. The Great Awakening changed not only colonial religion but also social and political life. **Jonathan Edwards** was one of the most important leaders of the Great Awakening. He was a pastor of the Congregational Church in Northampton, Massachusetts. Edwards's dramatic sermons urged sinners to seek forgiveness for their sins or face punishment in Hell forever.

Interpreting the Visual Record

Revival *The Great Awakening preacher George Whitefield could draw crowds of thousands to his outdoor revival meetings.* ***How does this image suggest the power of Whitefield's preaching?***

In 1739 British minister **George Whitefield** made the second of his seven trips to America. On this visit he held revivals from Georgia to New England. Whitefield became one of the most popular ministers of the Great Awakening. Because of Whitefield, thousands of colonists found new faith in Christianity. New England farmer Nathan Cole was one of many people who found Whitefield's message inspiring.

"When I saw Mr. Whitefield come upon the scaffold [platform], he looked almost angelical [like an angel]. . . . And my hearing how God was with him everywhere as he came along, it solemnized [made serious] my mind and put me into a trembling fear before he began to preach; for he looked as if he was clothed with authority from the Great God . . . and my hearing him preach gave me a heart wound."

—Nathan Cole, quoted in *The Great Awakening,* edited by Alan Heimert and Perry Miller

Analyzing Primary Sources

Identifying Points of View Why does Cole feel that Mr. Whitefield's words are important?

The ministers of the Great Awakening preached that all people were born sinners who could only be saved by the will of God. However, the opportunity to be saved was available to all—rich and poor alike—who confessed their sins and accepted God's grace. This message brought hope to many people. However, the ministers of the Great Awakening could use a threatening tone. Jonathan Edwards's 1741 sermon *Sinners in the Hands of an Angry God* called up frightening images. "God . . . holds you over the pit of hell, much as one holds a spider, or some loathsome [disgusting] insect over the fire."

✔ **Reading Check: Finding the Main Idea** What did preachers of the Great Awakening and their followers believe?

Old and New Lights

THE GRANGER COLLECTION, NEW YORK

Minister Jonathan Edwards was known for sermons such as Sinners in the Hands of an Angry God.

Not all colonists believed in these new religious ideas. Eventually, some church congregations divided because of disagreements. There were traditionalists and those who followed the new ministers. In New England the traditionalists were called the "Old Lights." The followers of the Great Awakening were called the "New Lights."

Old Light ministers did not believe that the enthusiasm of the Great Awakening could truly awaken one's spirituality. Charles Chauncy of Boston's First Church agreed with this view. He stated that anyone who took part in such revivals was "under no other influence than that of an over-heated imagination." Chauncy thought that this excited form of religion was not a proper way to try to save one's soul.

Free Find:
Jonathan Edwards
After reading about Jonathan Edwards on the **Holt Researcher CD–ROM**, imagine that you had attended one of his sermons. Write a letter to a friend. In the letter, explain how Edwards's ideas were different from what other Protestants of the time believed.

The Great Awakening also changed the Presbyterian Church in the middle colonies. Presbyterian minister **Gilbert Tennent** was a leader of the new movement. His sermons attacked the traditionalists. As a result of Tennent's efforts, the Presbyterian Church split into two groups with opposing views on the revival movement. These became known as the "Old Side" and the "New Side."

In the middle and southern colonies, particularly Virginia, the Great Awakening greatly increased church membership. Much of this growth took place among the Baptists and Methodists. The Great Awakening was also influential on the frontier, where traveling preachers held revivals in small towns. There were few churches on the frontier. Therefore, these ministers were important to settlers.

Traditional and new ideas were in conflict even in these distant areas, however. Frontier missionary Charles Woodmason tried to oppose the changes brought about by the Great Awakening. He expressed his frustration.

Analyzing Primary Sources

Drawing Inferences and Conclusions Why might ministers of the Great Awakening want to follow Woodmason to places he was going to deliver sermons?

"If I give out [announce] to be at such a Place at such a Time, three or four of these fellows [Great Awakening ministers] are constantly at my Heels—They either get there before me, and hold forth—or after I have finish'd, or the next Day, or for days together. Had I a hundred Tongues, or as many Pairs of Legs, I could not singly [alone] oppose such a Numerous Crew."

—Charles Woodmason, quoted in *The Power of Words,* edited by T. H. Breen

✔ **Reading Check: Identifying Cause and Effect** What conflicts did the Great Awakening cause, and what were some of the effects of these conflicts?

The Great Awakening and Society

The Great Awakening attracted people of different classes and races. Women, members of minority groups, and poor people often took part in services. Women in particular welcomed the message of the Great Awakening. Many women sought spiritual renewal around the time of childbirth. They were interested in part because their lives were at risk during this time. One woman explained that her faith "would wear off again 'till the time of my first Lying in [labor]; and then I was . . . brought to the very brink of eternity." Both free and enslaved African Americans were drawn to the Great Awakening's message of acceptance and spiritual equality. Despite the stated belief in equality, however, some revivals were separated by race.

Before the Great Awakening, there was little communication between people living in different colonies. This changed as ministers began moving about and exchanging ideas. Educational opportunities also improved as many colleges were founded to provide religious instruction. Such efforts helped bring together the different colonial regions.

The Great Awakening promoted ideals that may also have affected colonial politics. Sermons about the spiritual equality of all people led some colonists to begin demanding more political equality. Revivals became popular places to talk about political and social issues. As a result of sharing new ideas, some colonists began to question the authority of existing institutions.

This illustration shows the First Baptist Church of Providence, Rhode Island. Baptist congregations were among those that grew rapidly during the Great Awakening.

✔ **Reading Check: Summarizing** How did the Great Awakening change colonial communities and society?

go.hrw.com Homework Practice Online
keyword: SC3 HP4

1. **Define** and explain:
   - revivals

2. **Identify** and explain:
   - Great Awakening
   - Jonathan Edwards
   - George Whitefield
   - Gilbert Tennent

3. **Identifying Cause and Effect** Copy the cause-and-effect chart below. Fill in at least three causes and effects relating to why the Great Awakening came about and how it affected society.

   Great Awakening

Cause		Effect
	→	
	→	
	→	

4. **Finding the Main Idea**
   a. What message did preachers of the Great Awakening tell their followers?
   b. Why might the teachings of the Great Awakening have led to a movement for greater democracy?

5. **Writing and Critical Thinking**
   Analyzing Information Imagine that you are a leader of a church that has become divided between New Lights and Old Lights. Write a story to share with church members that describes the problems faced by churches such as yours.
   Consider the following:
   - the beliefs of the Old Lights and New Lights
   - religion on the frontier
   - the splitting of some religious groups

Section 5

American Culture

Read to Discover

1. How did both the Scientific Revolution and the Enlightenment reflect new ways of thinking?
2. What was education like during colonial times?
3. What were Benjamin Franklin's key achievements?
4. What contributions were made to American culture in the 1700s?

Why It Matters Today

Scientists are always making new, important discoveries. Use CNNfyi.com or other **current events** sources to learn more about a new scientific discovery. Think about fields such as medicine or computer science. Record your findings in your journal.

Define

- scientific method

Identify

- Scientific Revolution
- Galileo Galilei
- Isaac Newton
- Enlightenment
- David Rittenhouse
- Benjamin Banneker
- Benjamin Franklin
- Anne Bradstreet
- Phillis Wheatley

Galileo built and decorated his first telescope by hand.

The Story Continues

Night after night in 1610 Italian scientist Galileo Galilei looked up at the sky. People had long believed that Earth was the center of the universe. Galileo, however, began to doubt this idea. He used his newly built telescope to view Jupiter and observed small moons around this planet. This discovery told him that not everything in the universe moved around Earth. Other scientists began to share Galileo's views. They thought that many other ideas about the natural world also needed to be reconsidered.

New Ideas in Europe

During the 1600s Western Europeans began to re-examine their world. As scientists performed more experiments, they made exciting discoveries. Scientists began to better understand the basic laws that govern nature. Their new ideas about the universe began what is known as the **Scientific Revolution**. This revolution began in mathematics and astronomy, but it later changed all areas of natural science.

Galileo Galilei was one of the leading figures in the Scientific Revolution. He demonstrated that the planets revolve around the Sun. In the late 1600s Sir **Isaac Newton** explained how objects on Earth and in the sky behaved. His theories proved that the same laws of physics govern both. He also developed much of the **scientific method** used today. The scientific method requires that scientists carefully study natural events. Scientists then form theories based on their observations and experiments. These ideas can be used to predict other behaviors or events. Scientists then test their theories as they learn new facts.

The Scientific Revolution also began changing the way people viewed human actions. This change in thought is often called the Age of Reason, or the **Enlightenment.** The Enlightenment took place during the 1700s. Enlightenment philosophers used reason and logic, much as scientists were doing. These thinkers, however, studied human nature and suggested ways to improve their world. Jean-Jacques Rousseau (roo-SOH), Voltaire, and Baron de Montesquieu (mohn-tes-kyoo) all formed ideas about how government should work to best serve the people.

Some Enlightenment thinkers believed that there was a social contract between government and citizens. With this contract, rulers needed the consent of the governed. Philosophers such as John Locke believed that people had natural rights such as equality and liberty. Locke stated that people should obey their rulers only if the state protected their life, liberty, and property. Eventually the ideas of the Scientific Revolution and the Enlightenment began to influence some colonial leaders.

✔ **Reading Check: Summarizing** What changes in ways of thinking took place in the 1600s and 1700s in Europe?

Colonial Education

In the colonies few people could afford a formal education. The availability of schooling also varied widely in the colonies. For example, there were more schools in New England than in the southern and middle colonies. New England colonists particularly valued the ability to read the Bible. They also wanted to make sure future generations had educated ministers. Therefore, communities founded and paid for town schools. Schoolchildren often used the *New England Primer*, which had characters and stories from the Bible. They learned to read at the same time that they learned about the community's religious values. In the middle and southern colonies, most children lived far from towns. They had to be taught by their parents or private tutors.

Most colonial children stopped their education after the elementary grades. Many went to work, either on the family farm or away from home. Some boys became apprentices. In New England and in the middle colonies, some girls became servants for other families.

LINKING PAST to PRESENT

Public Schools

Today most Americans consider public education to be a basic right. This was not the case in colonial America. In many places children received little or no formal education. Pennsylvania and most New England colonies were exceptions to this rule. In 1642 Massachusetts passed one of the first public education laws in Europe or the Americas. In 1683, Quaker officials passed laws requiring all children in Pennsylvania to learn how to read and write. Quaker leaders also decided to offer free schooling for poor children. In both Massachusetts and Pennsylvania male and female children received instruction. **How does current education compare with colonial public education? Use examples to support your answer.**

A page from the *New England Primer*, a colonial schoolbook

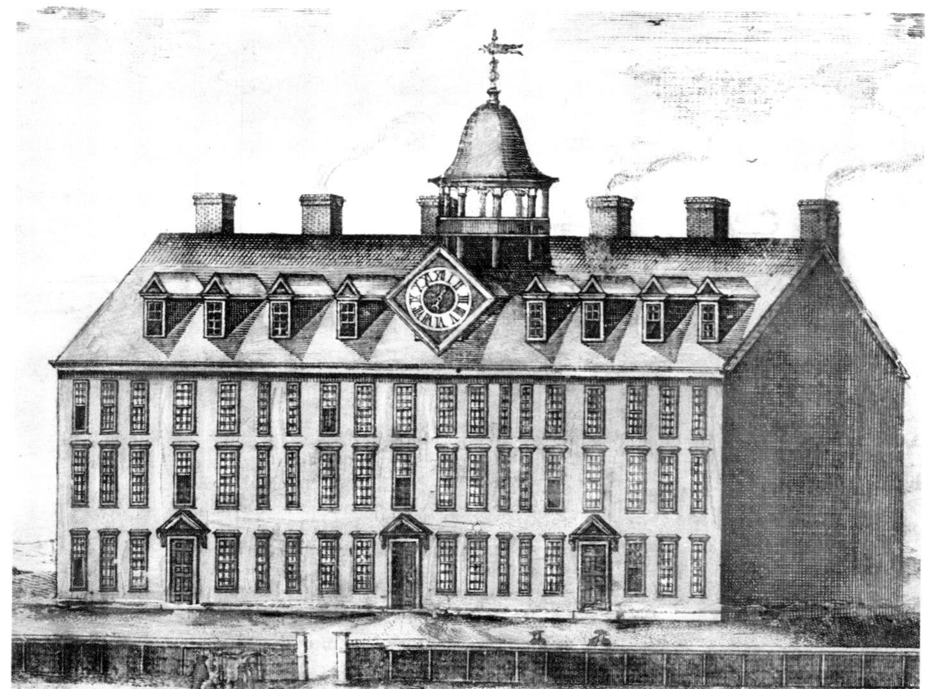

Yale College, in New Haven, Connecticut, was founded in 1701.

THE GRANGER COLLECTION, NEW YORK

A growing number of young men did attend universities. In 1636 colonists in Massachusetts founded Harvard College. Colonists went on to establish nine colleges, most of which were in the middle colonies and in New England. The classes at many of these colleges focused on religion. Some young men also went to English universities to study the sciences or law. Others studied at a colonial college and then trained with a professional in their field.

✔ **Reading Check: Contrasting** How did education in the New England colonies compare to schooling in the middle and southern colonies?

That's Interesting!

Banneker's Clock Did you know that Benjamin Banneker was the first colonist to build a clock? It's true! He did this even though he had never seen one before. In his early twenties, Banneker, who only had a few years of formal education, designed and built a clock. He used only a picture of a clock from an English journal and a geometry book for help. The clock kept time with great accuracy. His clock is said to have run for over 40 years.

THE GRANGER COLLECTION, NEW YORK

Colonial Scientists

Although few schools taught science, there were several talented scientists in the colonies. These scientists taught themselves by observing the world around them. In 1743 the American Philosophical Society was founded in Philadelphia for the study of science. Its members also wanted to improve communication among colonial scientists. **David Rittenhouse**, the society's second president, designed mathematical and astronomical instruments. Thomas Jefferson thought Rittenhouse was "second to no astronomer living."

Rittenhouse admired the astronomer and surveyor **Benjamin Banneker**, a free African American who lived in Maryland. In 1789 Banneker predicted a solar eclipse—when the Moon passes in front of the Sun. Banneker published his work in an almanac.

Botanist John Bartram was also self-taught. He traveled throughout the colonies studying plants and founded a botanical garden. Bartram also exchanged plants and information with scientists in Britain.

 Benjamin Franklin

Perhaps the most famous colonial scientist was **Benjamin Franklin**. A man with many interests, Franklin was one of the most important thinkers of his time. He was born in Boston in 1706 and worked first in his father's candle and soap shop. Later he became an apprentice in his brother's printing shop. In 1723 Franklin moved to Philadelphia. In his mid-20s, he started a newspaper, which quickly became the most successful paper in the colonies. Franklin published *Poor Richard's Almanack* between 1732 and 1757. He wrote the almanac under the made-up name of Richard Saunders. Franklin came up with sayings that are still used today, including "Early to Bed, and early to rise, makes a Man healthy, wealthy and wise." Poor Richard offered much additional advice.

"If you would be wealthy, think of Saving as well as of Getting: The Indies have not made Spain rich, because her Outgoes [expenses] are greater than her Incomes."

—Poor Richard (Benjamin Franklin), quoted in *Anthology of American Literature, Volume I*, 2nd edition

Analyzing Primary Sources

Identifying Points of View What does Franklin advise a person to do in order to get rich?

Franklin believed that reason could be used to make life better for people. During his life, he invented many useful devices. The lightning rod reduced the risk of fire started by electrical storms. The Franklin stove heated homes better than previous stoves had. Franklin also invented bifocals, eyeglasses with lenses that correct for both far- and nearsightedness. Franklin once said he was "glad of an opportunity to serve others" through his inventions. He did not take out patents on his work because he wanted all people to benefit from his good ideas.

Franklin also conducted many scientific experiments. He flew a kite during a thunderstorm in 1752 as an experiment to prove lightning is a form of electricity. He also found the positive and negative charges in electricity. These discoveries made him well known in the colonies and in Europe. Thomas Jefferson even boasted:

"We [Americans] have produced a Franklin, than whom no one of the present age has made more important discoveries, nor has enriched philosophy [improved scientific knowledge] with more, or more ingenious [clever] solutions of the phaenomena [events] of nature."

—Thomas Jefferson, quoted in *The Americans: The Colonial Experience*, by Daniel J. Boorstin

Franklin helped people in other ways as well. He started the first subscription library in the colonies, and opened an academy that later became the University of Pennsylvania. In addition, Franklin founded the American Philosophical Society.

✔ **Reading Check: Drawing Inferences and Conclusions** How are Franklin's many accomplishments alike?

Benjamin Franklin served as the first president of the American Philosophical Society, which he helped found.

BIOGRAPHY

Phillis Wheatley

c. 1753–1784

Phillis Wheatley was one of the first African Americans to be published. She was educated by the Boston family that bought her as a slave in 1761. Wheatley began writing poetry while still a teenager. Her first poem was published in 1770. In 1773 the Wheatleys freed Phillis so that she could go to England. While there she published a book of poetry. After both of the Wheatleys died, Phillis married John Peters. What is remarkable about Phillis Wheatley's career?

Colonial Writers and Artists

Self-taught writers and artists also contributed to colonial American culture. Religious speech and writing changed the colonies in many ways. Ministers such as John Cotton, Jonathan Edwards, and Cotton Mather developed a new American way of preaching, revealed in their dramatic sermons.

New England poet **Anne Bradstreet** wrote about her love for her family and her faith. Her poetry was published in *The Tenth Muse* in London in 1650. **Phillis Wheatley** also used religious language and imagery in her poetry. In "On Being Brought from Africa to America," Wheatley described how Christianity changed her life.

In the early 1700s the fine arts began to grow in the colonies. A few European artists came to America to paint and teach. British-born painter John Smibert held the first art exhibition in the English colonies in Boston in 1730. His pupil, American-born portrait artist Robert Feke, became a widely admired painter. Most colonial artists painted portraits because they were popular with colonists.

Colonial architecture and household furniture also improved in style and quality. The houses of the richest colonists were often made of brick, not wood, and were often built in fancy British styles. Inside these homes beautiful furniture showed the talents of highly skilled local carpenters and cabinetmakers. These changes reflected the general improvement in the colonists' lives.

✔ **Reading Check: Analyzing Information** What areas of the arts did colonists begin to pursue, and how did interest in the arts change over time in the colonies?

Section 5 Review

go.hrw.com Homework Practice Online
keyword: SC3 HP4

1. **Define** and explain:
   - scientific method
2. **Identify** and explain:
   - Scientific Revolution
   - Galileo Galilei
   - Sir Isaac Newton
   - Enlightenment
   - David Rittenhouse
   - Benjamin Banneker
   - Benjamin Franklin
   - Anne Bradstreet
   - Phillis Wheatley
3. **Summarizing** Copy the table below. Use it to list three important achievements made during colonial times for each category.

Science			
Writing			
Art			

4. **Finding the Main Idea**
   a. What new ways of thinking resulted from the Scientific Revolution and the Enlightenment?
   b. How does education in colonial times compare with modern schooling?
5. **Writing and Critical Thinking**
   Supporting a Point of View Imagine that you are a teenager living in colonial Philadelphia. You would like to serve as an apprentice to Benjamin Franklin. Write a letter to Franklin explaining why you would like to study with him and what you hope to learn.
   Consider the following:
   - Franklin's inventions and scientific experiments
   - Franklin's writings
   - Franklin's contributions to his community

CONNECTING TO

Literature

Benjamin Franklin's *Autobiography*

Benjamin Franklin's Autobiography *was not published until the year after his death. Many people believe Franklin's* Autobiography *to be a classic of American literature. Franklin's simple, clear writing influenced and inspired many American readers. The success of the* Autobiography *popularized the autobiography as a literary form.*

The Autobiography *also emphasized one of the values closely associated with the American character—self-reliance. In the following passage, Franklin shares his strategy for leading a successful life.*

Benajmin Franklin's Autobiography *was full of advice for readers.*

It was about this time that I **conceiv'd**[1] the bold and **arduous**[2] Project of arriving at moral Perfection. . . . As I knew, or thought I knew, what was right and wrong, I did not see why I might not always do the one and avoid the other. But I soon found I had undertaken a Task of more Difficulty than I have imagined. . . . I therefore **contriv'd**[3] the following Method. . . . I proposed to myself, for the sake of clearness, to use rather more names with fewer ideas **annexed**[4] to each than a few names with more ideas, and I included after . . . Names of Virtues all that at that time occurr'd to me as necessary or desirable, and annex'd to each a short **Precept**[5] . . . .

1. **Temperance** Eat not to Dulness. Drink not to Elevation.
2. **Silence** Speak not but what may benefit others or yourself. Avoiding **trifling**[6] Conversation.
3. **Order** Let all your Things have their Places. Let each Part of your Business have its Time.
4. **Resolution** Resolve to perform what you ought. Perform without fail what you resolve.
5. **Frugality** Make no Expense but to do good to others or yourself: **i.e.**[7], Waste nothing.
6. **Industry** Lose no Time. Be always employ'd in something useful. Cut off all unnecessary Actions.
7. **Sincerity** Use no hurtful Deceit. Think innocently and justly; and, if you speak, speak accordingly.
8. **Justice** Wrong none by doing Injuries or omitting the Benefits that are your Duty.
9. **Moderation** Avoid extremes. **Forbear**[8] resenting Injuries so much as you think they deserve.
10. **Cleanliness** Tolerate no Uncleanness in Body, Clothes or **Habitation.**[9]
11. **Tranquility** Be not disturbed at trifles or at accidents common or unavoidable.

Understanding What You Read

1. Literature and History What similarities exist among the virtues that Franklin lists?
2. Literature and You Do you think the virtues described by Franklin represent universal themes that still matter today? Explain your answer.

[1] **conceiv'd:** thought up
[2] **arduous:** difficult
[3] **contriv'd:** developed
[4] **annexed:** attached
[5] **precept:** rule
[6] **trifling:** unimportant
[7] **i.e.:** that is
[8] **forbear:** keep from
[9] **habitation:** home

Chapter 4 Review

The Chapter at a Glance

Examine the visual summary of the chapter below. Create a written summary of colonial events and achievements based on the drawing.

Government

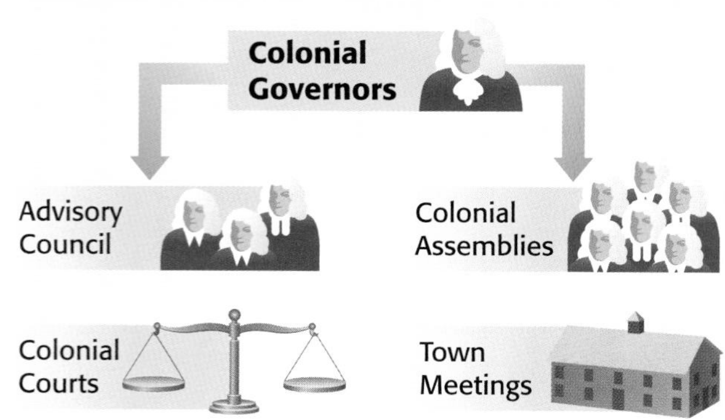

Economy

New England
Fishing, Manufacturing, Small Farms, Trade

Middle Colonies
Large Farms, Staple Crops, Trade

Southern Colonies
Cash Crops, Plantations, Slave System

Society

The Great Awakening

Identifying People and Ideas

Use the following terms or people in historically significant sentences.

1. House of Burgesses
2. English Bill of Rights
3. mercantilism
4. Middle Passage
5. cash crops
6. slave codes
7. Eliza Lucas Pinckney
8. Great Awakening
9. Benjamin Franklin
10. Anne Bradstreet

Understanding Main Ideas

Section 1 *(Pages 92–97)*

1. What roles did governors, assemblies, courts, and town meetings play in local governments?
2. Why were colonists interested in the Glorious Revolution and the English Bill of Rights?

Section 2 *(Pages 98–102)*

3. Why did mercantilism and English trade laws upset colonial merchants and farmers?
4. What items were part of the triangular trade?

Section 3 *(Pages 103–107)*

5. How did the economies of the New England, middle, and southern colonies differ?

Section 4 *(Pages 108–111)*

6. How did the Great Awakening change colonial society?

Section 5 *(Pages 112–116)*

7. Who were the most important writers and artists of the colonial period, and what were some of their accomplishments?

You Be the Historian—Reviewing Themes

1. **Economics** Why did England pass the Navigation Acts?
2. **Geography** How was the economy of each colonial region affected by its geography?
3. **Science, Technology & Society** In what ways did Benjamin Franklin's scientific discoveries and inventions benefit the colonies?

Thinking Critically

1. **Analyzing Information** Why did colonists begin thinking about representative government and political equality?
2. **Drawing Inferences and Conclusions** Why did much of the slave trade take place in northern ports?
3. **Evaluating** In what ways did the colonists practice free enterprise, and how did this benefit the colonies?

Social Studies Skills Workshop

Interpreting Graphs

Study the graph below. Then use the information in the graph to help you answer the following questions.

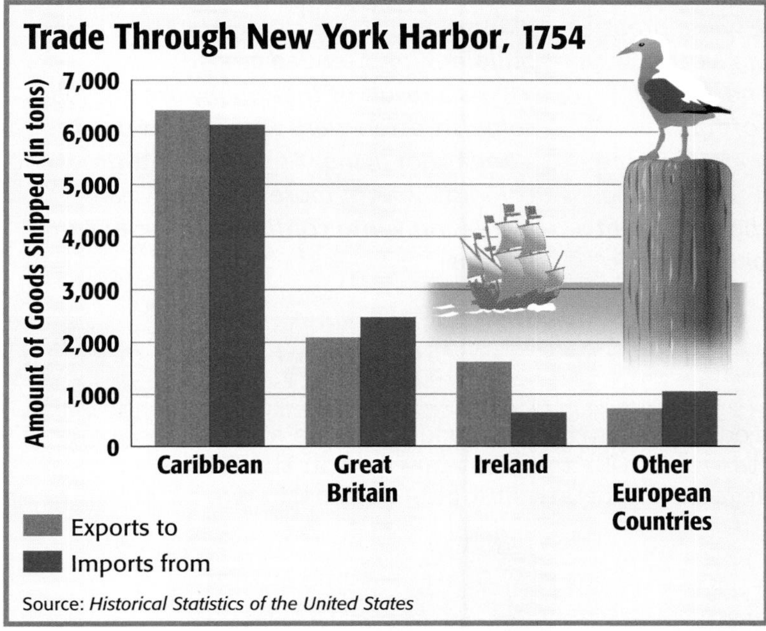

1. About how many tons of goods did the American colonies export to Great Britain through New York Harbor?
   a. less than 1,000
   b. more than 6,000
   c. about 4,400
   d. about 2,000
2. Based on your knowledge of the period, why do you think the amount of trade with the Caribbean was so much higher than with other areas?

Analyzing Primary Sources

Read the following quote about the rules of Harvard College written by the clergymen Hugh Peter and Thomas Weld. Then answer the questions that follow.

> **"Studiously redeem [make use of] the time, observe the general hours appointed for all the students, and the special hours for their own classes, and then diligently attend the lectures without any disturbance by word or gesture. . . . Every scholar shall be present in his tutor's chamber at the seventh hour in the morning, immediately after the sound of the bell . . . so also at the fifth hour at night, and then give account of his own private reading . . . and constantly attend lectures in the hall at the hours appointed."**

3. Which of the following statements best describes the schedule of the Harvard students?
   a. They could attend classes whenever they pleased and study on their own time.
   b. They had to report to tutors in the morning and evening and also go to other classes.
   c. They had to go to class from seven in the morning till five at night.
   d. Students had to attend classes regularly and were expected to ask many questions during lectures.
4. How do these requirements compare to a typical day at your school?

Alternative Assessment

Building Your Portfolio

Linking to Community

Private citizens still play an important part in local government. Using newspapers and other resources, find out about an issue in your community that has been raised at a town meeting or a council meeting. Learn about different opinions on the issue as well as what actions were taken. Then write a dramatization of the meeting showing the views of all the participants. Perform the dramatization with some of your classmates.

internet connect

Internet Activity: go.hrw.com
keyword: SC3 CF4

Choose a topic about life in the English colonies to:

- Analyze the impact of the Zenger case on the concept of freedom of the press.
- Create a model of a concept or theory from the Scientific Revolution.
- Explore modern trade in the original thirteen colonies and create a map.

Colonial Economies

Many settlers came to the American colonies for economic opportunities. For example, there was a great demand in Europe for furs from North America. Europeans explored north and west looking for new sources of furs.

As the colonies grew, they also became a rich source of farm products. The colonies exported tobacco, rice, and wheat to Great Britain. Plantation owners expanded agricultural production in the southern colonies. As they did so, they imported many enslaved Africans to work their plantations. Slaves cleared land, put up buildings, and tended crops.

As a result of their many efforts, many colonists often were able to improve their standard of living. As settlements grew and colonists sought more land, they came increasingly into conflict with American Indians.

Colonial Trade and Industry

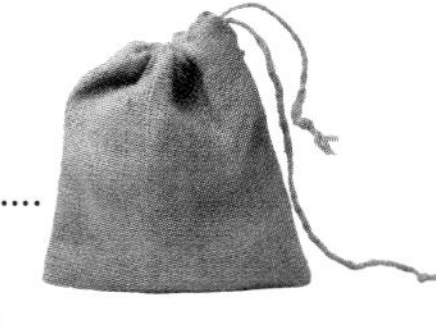

The British colonies produced a variety of goods for sale around the world. Most exports went to Britain, but markets in the West Indies and Europe were also important shipping destinations.

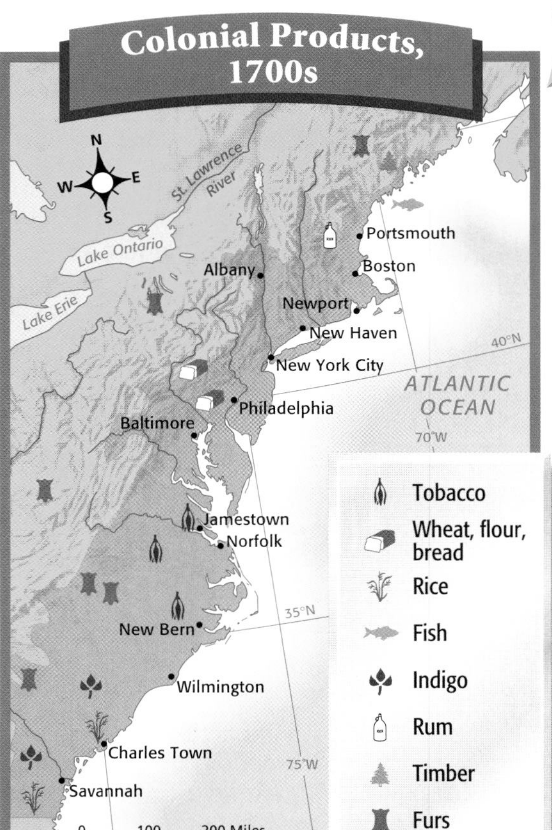

Geography **Skills**

Interpreting Thematic Maps

1. Where was fish an important colonial product?
2. **Places and Regions** In what area of the colonies was tobacco an important product?
3. **Drawing Inferences and Conclusions** Why do you think the towns shown on the map were important to colonial trade?

Colonial Boston Harbor

British Colonial Exports, 1770

Percentage of total value of exports from the British colonies by destination*

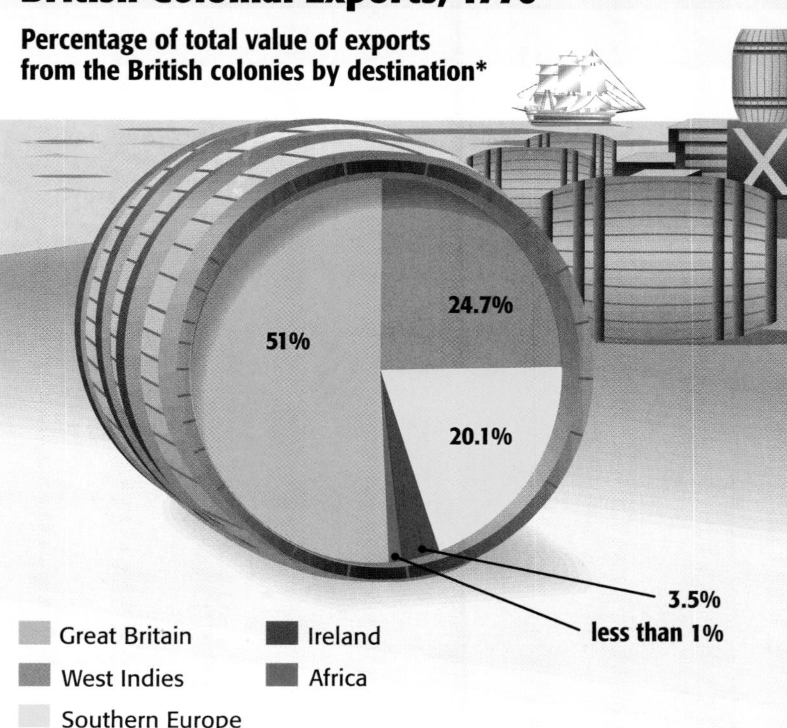

Source: *Historical Statistics of the United States*

*Includes Bahamas, Bermuda, and Newfoundland

History Note 1

In the 1700s, most exports from the thirteen colonies went to Great Britain. In recent years, however, most U.S. trade has stayed closer to home. Canada and Mexico are now major markets for U.S. exports. The United States also imports many goods from these two neighboring nations.

Many colonial goods were shipped in barrels.

Geography **Skills**

Interpreting Pie Graphs

1. What percentage of the total value of British exports from colonies in North America went to Britain in 1770?
2. **Human Systems** Which destination received the smallest percentage of the value of colonial exports?
3. **Analyzing Information** Rank each of the destinations shown on the pie graph in order of their importance to the colonial economy. Show your list to a fellow student. Ask him or her to explain why the colonists traded the most with the top two destinations on the list.

History Note 2

Which colony's settlers were the wealthiest? One way to address this question is to compare the average net worth per person in each area. Net worth equals the total value of a person's property, cash, and all other possessions of value minus the debts that they owe. In 1774 a free settler in the southern colonies had more than twice the net worth of a free settler in the middle colonies. A southern settler's net worth was about four times that of a free settler in New England.

The Growth of the Fur Trade in North America

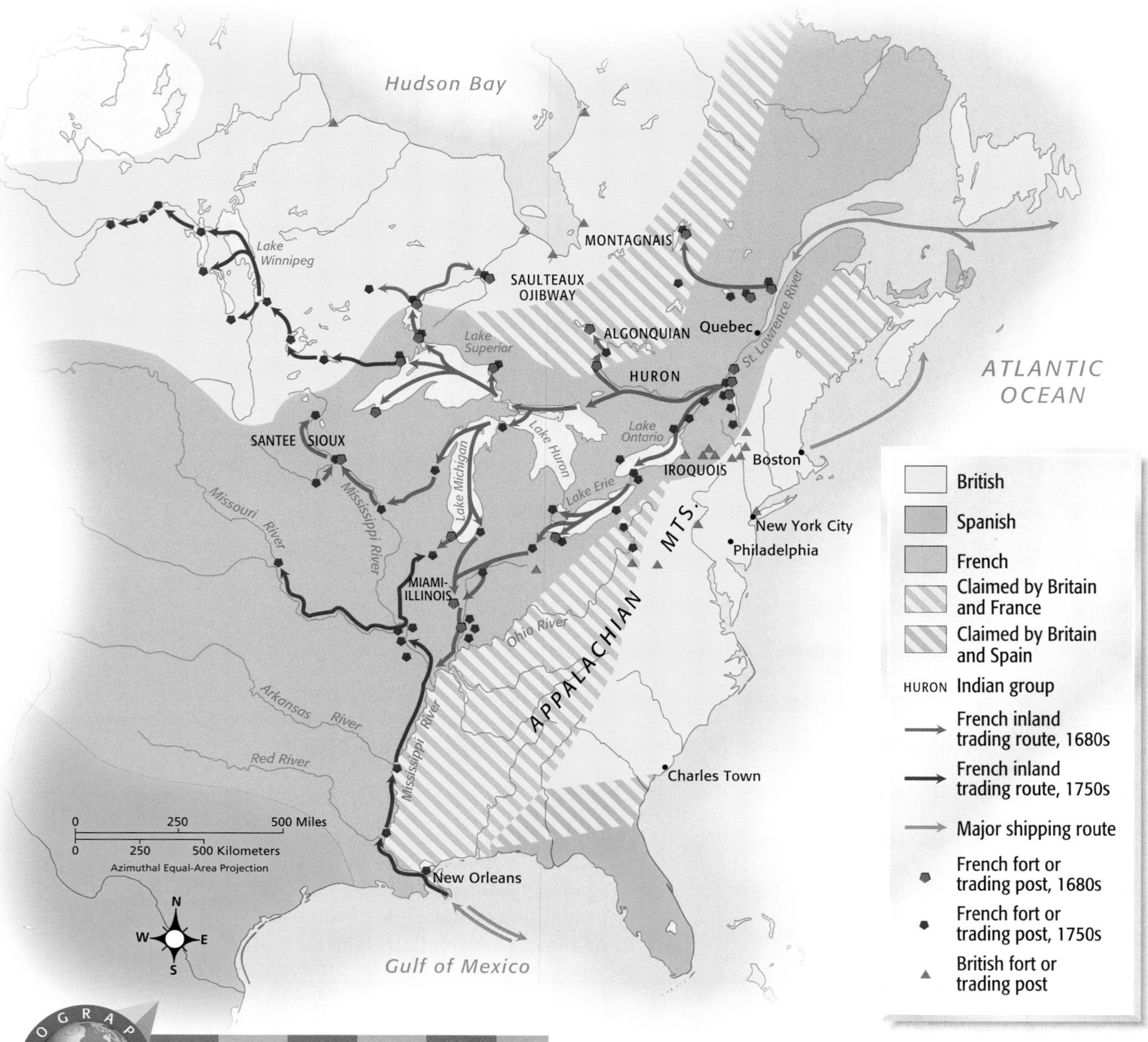

Geography Skills

Interpreting Thematic Maps

1. Which nation's trading posts were located farthest north?
2. **Human Systems** What French town was located farthest south? What British town was located farthest south?
3. **Evaluating** How would the location of these two southern towns have made them important to the French and the British?

History Note 3

The fur trade was very important to French Canada. The French built trading forts along rivers west of the British colonies to protect the fur trade. The thirteen colonies concentrated more on agriculture, although some British colonists traded in furs.

The Slave Trade 

Colonial settlers in the Americas imported many enslaved Africans to clear land and plant crops. Slaves were particularly important in the southern British colonies. In these colonies tobacco, rice, and indigo were often grown on large plantations.

The Atlantic Slave Trade

NORTH AMERICA
EUROPE
ATLANTIC OCEAN
Gulf of Mexico
CARIBBEAN SEA
AFRICA
SOUTH AMERICA

British North America 5.7%
Spanish America 9.1%
British West Indies 21.1%
Danish West Indies 0.5%
French West Indies 22.0%
Dutch West Indies 9.4%
Brazil 32.2%

N
W
E
S

Main areas of slave origin
Slave trade destinations

Percentages are based on numbers from the years 1701–1760

Source: *The Atlantic Slave Trade: A Census*

0 1,000 2,000 Miles
0 1,000 2,000 Kilometers
Robinson Projection

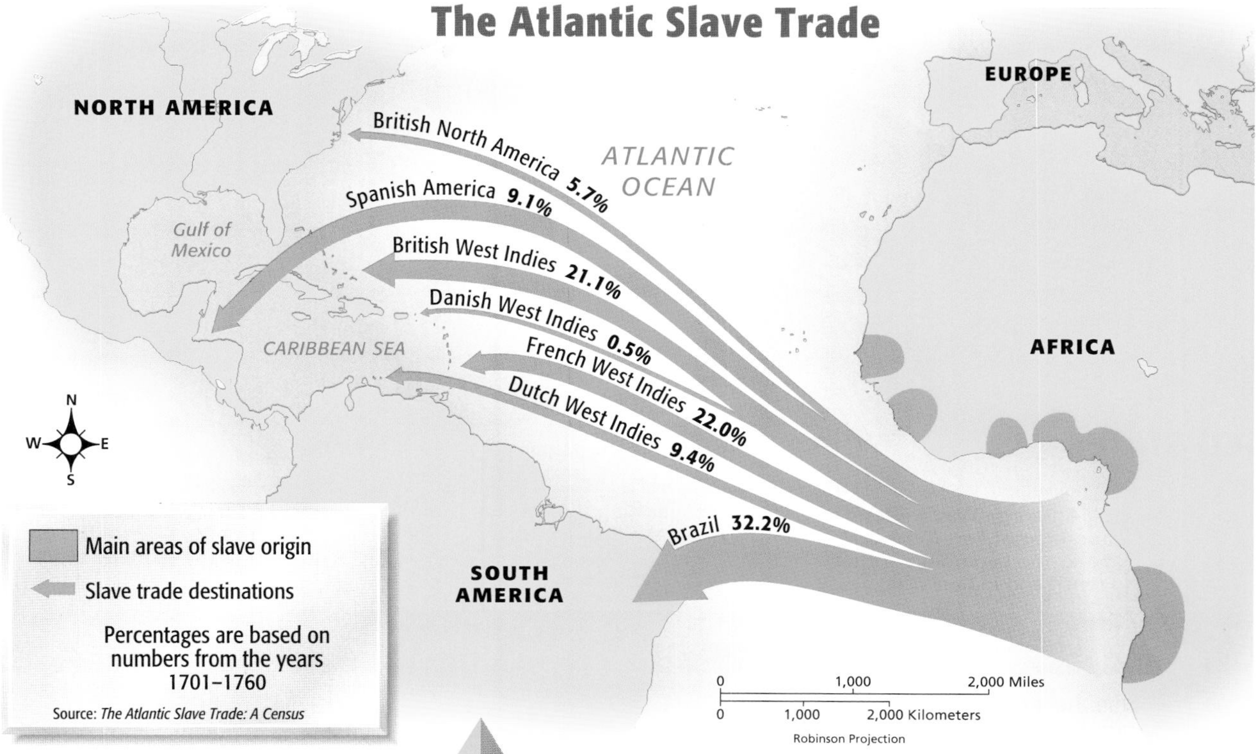

Geography **Skills**

Interpreting Thematic Maps

1. In what part of Africa did most slave trading take place?
2. **Human Systems** What percentage of slaves went to British North America during this period?
3. **Summarizing** Which destination received the highest percentage of slaves? Create a pie graph showing how the percentage of slaves brought across the Atlantic Ocean was divided among the regions shown on the map.

African slave market

History Note 4

Millions of Africans were taken to the Americas as slaves between the 1500s and 1800s. Enslaved Africans were the main labor force for large plantations in North America, South America, and the West Indies. Opposition to slavery grew gradually in the mid-1700s. Great Britain, once one of the world's largest traders in slaves, abolished the slave trade in 1807.

CHAPTER

5 Conflicts in the Colonies (1675–1774)

The Stamp Act required colonists to display stamps such as this one on nearly all paper documents.

THE GRANGER COLLECTION, NEW YORK

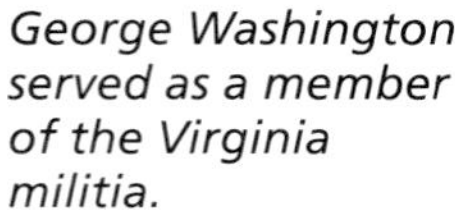

George Washington served as a member of the Virginia militia.

UNITED STATES

- **1676** King Philip's War ends.
- **1754** George Washington's surrender of Fort Necessity marks the beginning of the French and Indian War.
- **1763** Pontiac's Rebellion begins in March.
  In October King George III issues the Proclamation of 1763, limiting western expansion.
- **1765** Parliament passes the Stamp Act to raise revenue in the colonies.
- **1767** Parliament passes the Townshend Acts, which place import duties on many every-day items.

1675 | **1760** | **1765**

WORLD

- **1759** The British capture Quebec from the French.
- **1763** The Treaty of Paris ends the Seven Years' War.
- **1764** The British East India Company takes control of Bengal in India.

Colonial artist Benjamin West painted this scene of the Battle of Quebec entitled The Death of Wolfe.

Build on What You Know

A series of wars beginning in the late 1600s between France and Britain left the British as the major European power in eastern North America. As colonists began to move to the frontier, tensions rose between the settlers and American Indians. New British tax laws also upset the colonists.

On December 16, 1773, a group of colonists disguised as American Indians dumped British tea off of several ships while crowds watched from the shore.

This box contains the same brand of tea dumped by the colonists during the Boston Tea Party.

1768 British troops arrive in Boston.

1768 British explorer James Cook sets sail on his first trip to the South Pacific.

1770

1770 The Boston Massacre takes place.

1771 The first edition of the *Encyclopaedia Britannica* is published.

1773 Parliament passes the Tea Act in May, which allows the East India Company to sell tea cheaply in the colonies.

Patriots stage the Boston Tea Party in December.

1774 Parliament passes the Intolerable Acts, which restrict colonial power.

1774 Louis XVI becomes king of France.

1775

If you were there . . .

How would you respond to British efforts to increase control of the colonies?

You Be the Historian

What's Your Opinion? Do you **agree** or **disagree** with the following statements? Support your point of view in your journal.

- **Global Relations** A nation's colonies should fight on its behalf.
- **Geography** The growth of one nation will cause conflict with other nations.
- **Economics** People who are not represented in government will gladly pay taxes if they are protected from their enemies.

Section 1

Trouble on the Frontier

Read to Discover

1. How did English colonists and American Indians view each other?
2. What wars did the English colonists fight against other European colonists?
3. How did the French and Indian War affect the British colonies?

Define

- militia
- casualties

Identify

- Metacomet
- Albany Plan of Union
- Edward Braddock
- Treaty of Paris

WHY IT MATTERS TODAY

Nations still struggle against each other to control areas of the world. Use CNNfyi.com or other **current events** sources to find out where modern nations are in conflict over land or resources. Record your findings in your journal.

The Story Continues

Metacomet opposed further colonial expansion onto American Indian lands.

Chief Massasoit of the Wampanoag made a peace agreement with the Pilgrims in 1621.The agreement lasted his entire life. However, by the 1670s, Massasoit's son Metacomet had begun to distrust and dislike the English colonists. He said that they treated their Wampanoag neighbors poorly and were greedy for more land. Metacomet wanted the colonial leaders to treat him with respect. He finally told the colonists, "Your governor is but a subject. I shall treat [negotiate] only with my brother [equal], King Charles of England."

Colonists' Relations with American Indians

English settlers called **Metacomet** King Philip because he had compared himself to King Charles II. Metacomet opposed the colonists' efforts to take his people's land. At the same time, the colonists were afraid that Metacomet wanted to destroy them. In 1675 these tensions finally erupted into a conflict called King Philip's War. The colonial **militia**—civilians serving as soldiers—fought American Indian warriors.

Both sides also attacked each other's settlements, killing men, women, and children. The fighting finally ended in 1676, but only after about 600 colonists and some 3,000 Indians had been killed, including Metacomet.

Some American Indians allied with the colonists to fight against Metacomet's forces. This alliance was based on trade. Indian leaders wanted tools, weapons, and other goods that Europeans could provide. In exchange, the colonists wanted furs, which they sold for large profits in Europe. As a result, each side came to depend upon the other.

French colonists traded and allied with the Algonquian and Huron. English colonists traded and allied with the Iroquois League. This powerful group united American Indians from six different tribes. Many American Indians trusted the French more than they did the English. This was in part because the smaller French settlements were less threatening to Indians than the rapidly growing English colonies. No matter who their allies were, American Indian leaders took care to protect their people's independence.

"We are born free. We neither depend upon [the governor of New France] nor [the governor of New York]. We may go where we please, and carry with us whom we please, and buy and sell what we please."

—Garangula, an Iroquois leader, quoted in *The World Turned Upside Down*, edited by Colin G. Calloway

✔ **Reading Check: Finding the Main Idea** Why did some American Indians join Europeans in wars against other Indians?

Interpreting the Visual Record

Raiding party *During King Philip's War, colonists and American Indians raided each other's towns and forts.* ***Who are the defenders in this image, and what difficulties are the attackers facing?***

Conflicts with France

In the late 1600s France and England each wanted control over both Europe and North America. This conflict caused a series of wars between the two empires. The first, King William's War, lasted from 1689 to 1697 but did not change colonial boundaries in North America. Queen Anne's War began in 1702, with England fighting both France and Spain. In the colonies, English and French forces each had American Indian allies who raided the other side's frontier towns. English forces gained the upper hand in the war when they captured French Canada's Port Royal. Later they burned the Spanish settlement of St. Augustine in Florida. In 1713 a treaty ended Queen Anne's War. This time, Great Britain received what are now Hudson Bay, Newfoundland, and Nova Scotia from France. King George's War, fought against France in the 1740s, had little lasting effect on the colonies.

After King George's War, Great Britain and France were still competing for the Ohio Valley and the Great Lakes. British colonists wanted to settle the region. The French believed this settlement would harm their valuable fur trade with American Indians in the area. To protect their interests, the French built three forts in the Ohio Valley, on land claimed by the colony of Virginia. The British colonists felt that the French were keeping them from expanding west. In 1753 Virginia demanded that France give up its forts. When French officers refused, another war seemed likely.

British colonists knew that they were poorly organized and that fighting the French would be dangerous. In 1754 seven colonies sent delegates to Albany, New York. Colonial leaders wanted to make a treaty with the powerful Iroquois League. Soon the colonists were also talking about ways that the colonies could work together. Pennsylvania delegate Benjamin Franklin helped write the **Albany Plan of Union**, which called for all the colonies except Georgia to unite. Franklin based much of the proposal on the example of unified government that the Iroquois League represented.

"It would be a strange thing if Six Nations [of American Indians] should be capable of such a scheme [plan] for such a union, and be able to execute it in such a manner as that it has subsisted [lasted] ages . . . and yet that a like union should be impracticable [not practical] for ten or a dozen English colonies."

—Benjamin Franklin, quoted in *From Colonies to Country,* by Joy Hakim

However, the colonial governments did not want to give up their individual authority to form a union. They rejected the Albany Plan, as did Parliament.

✔ **Reading Check: Comparing and Contrasting** How were British and French goals for the Ohio Valley similar and different?

That's Interesting!

Following Orders Could you stand still while people shot at you? That's how the British and other Europeans fought during the 1600s and 1700s. Their old muskets were not very accurate. Soldiers were told to get close to the enemy, stand in one place, and shoot as quickly as possible. It could take dozens of shots to hit one enemy soldier! American colonists were not used to this style of fighting, and many had difficulty adjusting to it.

Free Find:
Iroquois Great Law of Peace
After reading about the Iroquois on the **Holt Researcher CD–ROM,** create a version of the Great Law of Peace for you and your classmates.

The French and Indian War

While the delegates were meeting in Albany, the British had begun building a fort along the Ohio River. However, the French drove them off and built Fort Duquesne (dooh-KAYN) on the site. A young Virginian named George Washington arrived with more soldiers and built a simple fort, which he named Fort Necessity. The French attacked, causing many **casualties**—killed, injured, or captured soldiers—and forcing Washington to surrender. Washington's defeat in 1754 was the start of the French and Indian War, between Britain and France. In 1756 fighting also began in Europe and elsewhere. This worldwide conflict was called the Seven Years' War.

This medallion commemorates the British victory at Quebec.

King George II sent General **Edward Braddock** to command British forces in North America. Braddock knew little about frontier fighting, which led to disaster when he decided to attack Fort Duquesne in 1755. His forces marched straight into a forest ambush

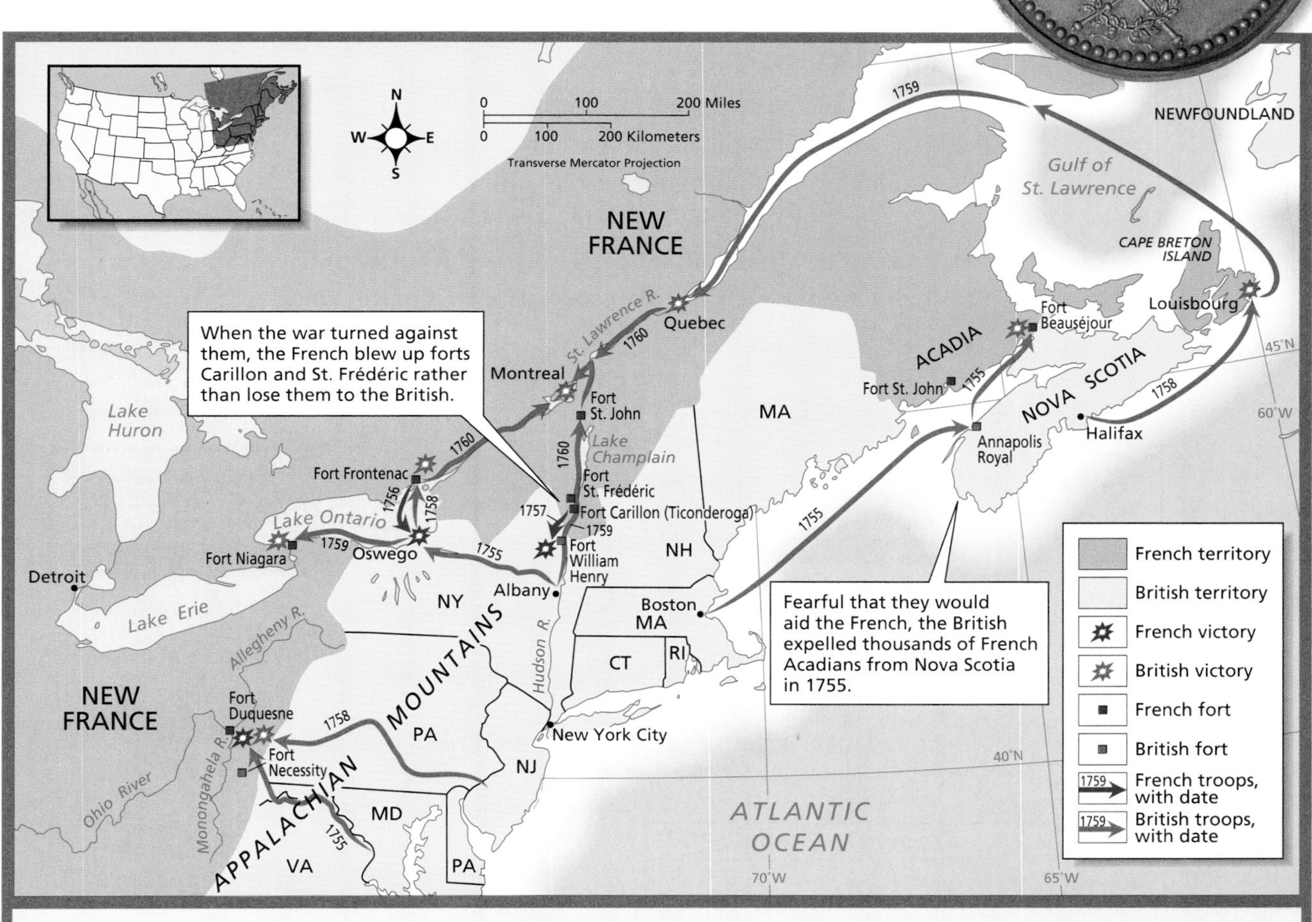

French and Indian War, 1754–1763

Interpreting Maps Great Britain gained most of France's North American lands at the end of the French and Indian War.

Skills Assessment The World in Spatial Terms Which French fort was located near Lake Erie?

Spain and the Seven Years' War

During the 1700s, kings from the Bourbon family ruled both France and Spain. These nations signed the Family Compact of 1761, which stated that "whoever attacked one crown, attacked the other." This Family Compact drew Spain into the conflict between France and Great Britain. Spain paid a high price for joining the war. In the Treaty of Paris, Britain gained control of Florida. Britain had become Spain's main enemy in North America. **Why did Spain enter the Seven Years' War?**

by French and American Indian troops. As one survivor explained, "The Enemy kept behind Trees, and cut down our Troops." The surprised British soon retreated. The British suffered almost 500 casualties, including Braddock himself, but the French and American Indians lost just 50.

The turning point of the war came in 1759, when British general James Wolfe captured Quebec, the capital of New France. Both Wolfe and the French commander were killed in the battle. Although fighting continued until 1763, Britain won most of the important battles.

The Treaty of Paris

Finally, in 1763 Great Britain and France signed the **Treaty of Paris**, officially ending the war. The treaty stated that the war "had spread trouble in the four parts of the world." Now the two sides wanted peace. In the process of ending their conflict, Britain and France redrew the political map of North America.

The terms of the treaty gave Canada to Britain, which also gained all French lands east of the Mississippi River except the city of New Orleans. From Spain, which had allied with France in 1762, Britain received Florida. (In an earlier treaty, Spain received Louisiana, the land that France had claimed west of the Mississippi River.) The Treaty of Paris changed the balance of power in North America. Britain had a claim to almost all land east of the Mississippi River. Spain was now the only other major European nation with lands in North America.

✔ **Reading Check: Identifying Cause and Effect** What caused the French and Indian War, and how did it affect North America?

Section 1 Review

go.hrw.com Homework Practice Online
keyword: SC3 HP5

1. **Define** and explain:
   - militia
   - casualties
2. **Identify** and explain:
   - Metacomet
   - Albany Plan of Union
   - Edward Braddock
   - Treaty of Paris
3. **Summarizing** Copy the table below. Use it to explain how each of the five wars that British colonists fought against Europeans and American Indians affected the American colonies.

War	Opponent	Effect on Colonies

4. **Finding the Main Idea**
   a. What was the main cause of the French and Indian War, and how did it affect the colonies?
   b. What do you think might have happened if France had won the French and Indian War?
5. **Writing and Critical Thinking**
   Evaluating Imagine that you are an American Indian leader living near the British and French colonies. Write a speech for your council that expresses your feelings about the British colonists.
   Consider the following:
   - worries about British expansion
   - the value of trade with the British
   - actions of the French compared to the British

Section 2

Consequences of the French and Indian War

Read to Discover

1. Why did many colonists move to the frontier?
2. What factors led to Pontiac's Rebellion?
3. What was the Proclamation of 1763, and how effective was it?

Define

- backcountry
- pioneers

Identify

- Pontiac's Rebellion
- King George III
- Proclamation of 1763

Why It Matters Today

Great Britain tried to tell its colonists where they could and could not live. Use CNNfyi.com or other **current events** sources to find an area that a modern government has made off-limits to growth. Record your findings in your journal.

The Story Continues

In 1759 British minister Andrew Burnaby decided to visit the American colonies to learn about their culture. He found life on the frontier interesting and kept a journal of his travels. To Burnaby, Americans seemed to want more and more new land. He wrote that families "will gradually retire [move] westward and settle upon fresh land."

THE GRANGER COLLECTION, NEW YORK

Early pioneers used wagons such as this one to settle the frontier.

The Frontier

Colonists set up most of the early settlements along the eastern coast or by major rivers. To the west was a huge frontier. Fur traders and a few forts were often the only signs of Europeans in this area. Yet European settlers slowly moved into the Virginia and Carolina **backcountry**. The backcountry was a thinly populated frontier area between the coastal settlements and the Appalachian Mountains. The first Europeans to settle the frontier were called **pioneers**. They risked attacks from American Indians who resisted this settlement on their land. There was little colonial settlement in what is now Tennessee and Kentucky until the 1770s.

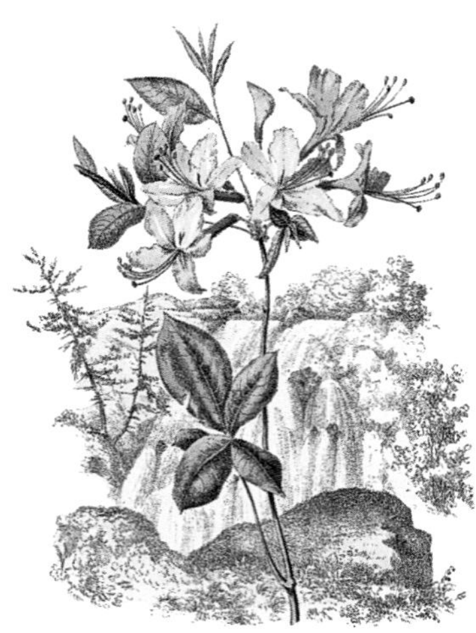

Wild honeysuckle was one of the many colorful plants that pioneers encountered in the Ohio Valley.

Some pioneers crossed the Appalachians farther to the north. They moved into the forested lands along the Ohio River in the 1750s. Pioneers found that the soil in the Ohio River valley was good for farming, and the valley was full of wild game such as turkey and deer. Although these were good conditions, fears of American Indian attacks kept British settlements small and isolated. However, this worry eased after the British won the French and Indian War. Then settlers began crossing the Appalachian Mountains in greater numbers.

✔ **Reading Check: Summarizing** When and why did pioneers begin settling in large numbers beyond the Appalachian Mountains?

Conflict in the Ohio River Valley

After the Treaty of Paris, Great Britain replaced France as the European power in the Ohio River valley. The British believed they were entitled to the land that France had controlled. This area included all of the American Indian lands in the Ohio River valley and the Great Lakes region. Unlike the French, the British wanted to build settlements in the area. This new policy led to problems between the British and American Indian leaders who opposed an increase in British settlements.

Pontiac's Rebellion

Interpreting Maps American Indians under the leadership of the Ottawa chief Pontiac won early battles, but their inability to capture key forts eventually doomed their rebellion.

Skills Assessment

1. **Locate** What British forts lay along Lake Erie?
2. **Analyzing Information** What British fort was not captured despite many nearby American Indian victories?

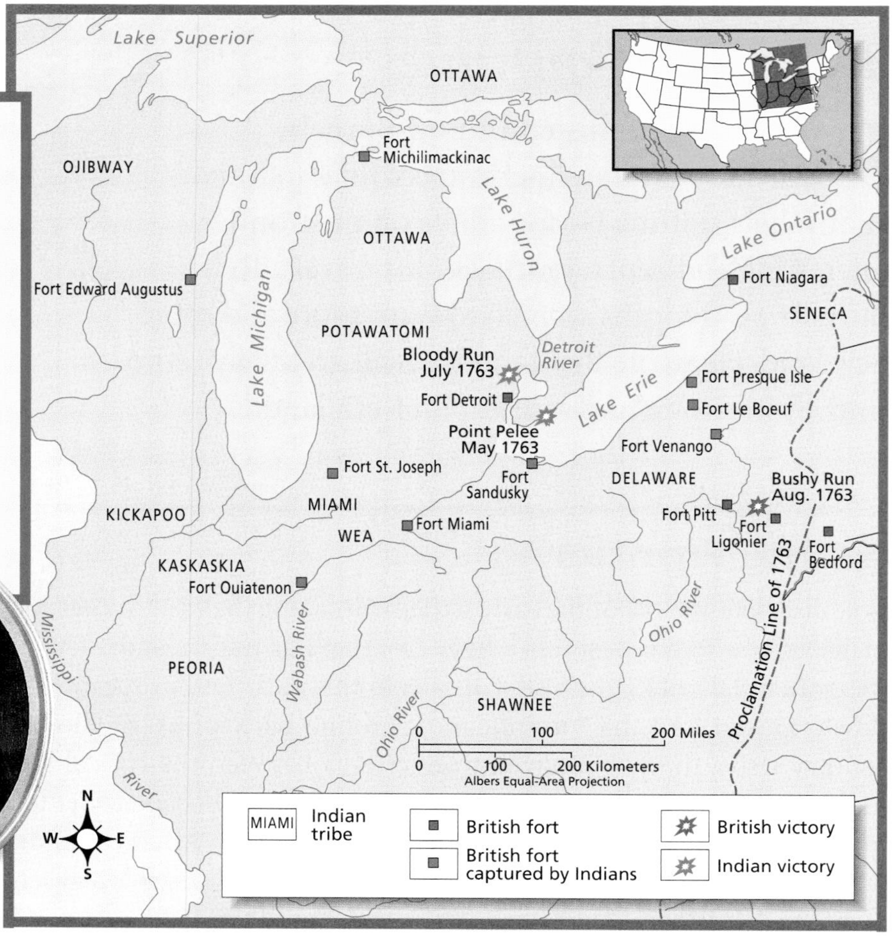

Chief Pontiac

THE GRANGER COLLECTION, NEW YORK

Interpreting the Visual Record

Fort Detroit *Pontiac's forces tried for months to capture Fort Detroit from the British.* ***What in the image suggests the difficulties of attacking the fort?***

These leaders had not signed any treaties with Britain and would not give up their land because of an agreement between Britain and France. Chippewa leader Minavavana expressed this view to a trader in 1761. "Englishman, although you have conquered the French, you have not yet conquered us!"

In the 1760s American Indian tribes began to join together to resist the British. Chief Pontiac of the Ottawa led forces that included the Delaware, Huron, Miami, Ottawa, and Shawnee peoples. Pontiac followed the teachings of the so-called Delaware Prophet. This leader called on Indians to drive out the white settlers and give up all European practices. In 1763 Pontiac shared these ideas with a gathering of American Indians.

History Makers Speak

"How comes it that you suffer the whites on your lands? Can't you do without them? You might live wholly [completely] as you did before you knew them. . . . Those who come to trouble your country, drive them out, make war [on] them! . . . They are my enemies and the enemies of your brothers!"

—Pontiac, quoted in *The World Turned Upside Down,* edited by Colin G. Calloway

Analyzing Primary Sources

Identifying Points of View How does Pontiac describe white settlers?

Pontiac's Rebellion began in May 1763 when American Indians attacked British forts on the frontier. Within a month Pontiac's forces had destroyed or captured seven forts. Pontiac then led the attack on Fort Detroit, Britain's political and trading center in the Great Lakes area. Despite the best efforts of Pontiac and his allies, the British held out for months. The American Indians following Pontiac grew tired of attacking the fort and returned to their villages. An Indian attack on the important British position at Fort Pitt also failed. Both sides suffered many casualties. As more Indians left Pontiac, he surrendered in 1766.

✔ **Reading Check: Identifying Cause and Effect** Why did Pontiac and his followers fight the British, and what happened as a result?

BIOGRAPHY

King George III

(1738–1820)

George III became king of Great Britain in 1760. King George had many rigid views. He wanted to assert his royal power and keep a strict rule over the colonies. But the economic and political changes that took place during his rule were beyond his control, and his harsh measures could not keep the thirteen colonies loyal. In 1788 King George began to show signs of mental illness, and by 1811 his son had to rule as king until George's death in 1820.

What did King George III hope to achieve?

The Proclamation of 1763

Tensions with American Indians worried officials in the British government. Leaders feared that more fighting would take place on the frontier if colonists kept moving onto American Indian lands. These conflicts would disrupt trade in the region and force Britain to spend more money on defense. To avoid these problems, Britain's **King George III** issued the **Proclamation of 1763**. This law banned the British from settling west of the Appalachian Mountains. The Proclamation created a border between colonial and American Indian lands. King George stated his position.

"It is just and reasonable and essential to our interest and the security of our colonies that the several nations or tribes of Indians with whom we are connected, and who live under our protection should not be . . . [attacked] or disturbed."

—Proclamation of 1763, from *The Annals of America*

The Proclamation also ordered colonists in the upper Ohio River valley "to remove themselves from such settlements." Many colonists defied the Proclamation. Some felt that Britain should allow the colonies to grow rapidly following France's defeat.

The Proclamation proved difficult to enforce. Most people who wanted to settle or trade in the Ohio River valley ignored it. As explorers like Daniel Boone led people west of the Appalachians, colonial settlement expanded. The colonists' disregard for the Proclamation showed their increasing unhappiness with British attempts to control them.

✔ Reading Check: **Summarizing** Why did King George III issue the Proclamation of 1763, and how did colonists respond to it?

Section 2 Review

keyword: SC3 HP3

1. **Define** and explain:
   - backcountry
   - pioneers

2. **Identify** and explain:
   - Pontiac's Rebellion
   - King George III
   - Proclamation of 1763

3. **Identifying Cause and Effect** Copy the diagram below. Use it to show the reasons that Great Britain issued the Proclamation of 1763 and how it affected the colonies.

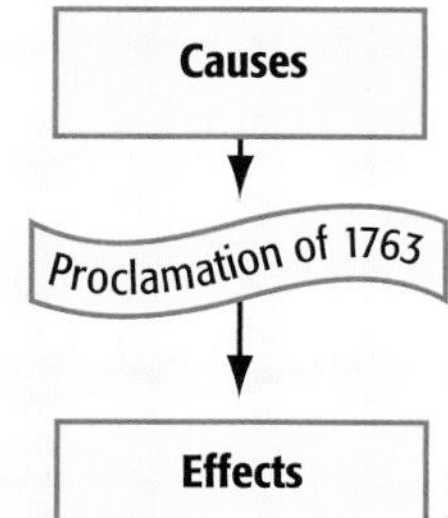

4. **Finding the Main Idea**
   a. Why did colonists move west of the Appalachians?
   b. Why did American Indians in the Ohio River valley unite and join Pontiac to fight the British?

5. **Writing and Critical Thinking**
   Supporting a Point of View Imagine that you are a settler on the frontier in the 1760s. Write a letter to relatives back East explaining what you do or do not like about living on the frontier.
   Consider the following:
   - relations between pioneers and American Indians
   - the British victory in the French and Indian War
   - the Proclamation of 1763

Section 3

Trouble over Colonists' Rights

Read to Discover

1. Why did Great Britain create new taxes for the colonies?
2. Why did colonists dislike the new tax laws?
3. How did colonists challenge these new taxes?

Why it Matters Today

Colonists formed organizations to protest British abuses of colonial rights. Use CNNfyi.com or other **current events** sources to research a modern organization that protests violations of certain rights. Record your findings in your journal.

Define

- boycott
- repeal

Identify

- George Grenville
- Sugar Act
- James Otis
- Samuel Adams
- Committees of Correspondence
- Stamp Act
- Sons of Liberty
- Patrick Henry

The Story Continues

Great Britain had heavy debts from its recent war against France. Prime Minister and Lord of the Treasury George Grenville set out to pay these debts. After taking office in 1763, he spared no one in his search for money. Grenville turned his attention to the American colonists.

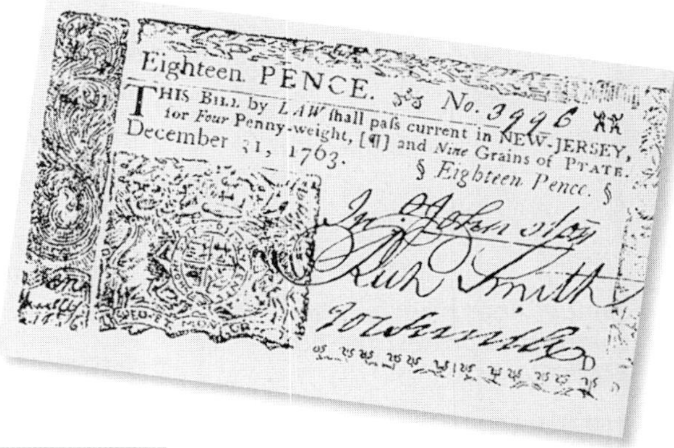

The colonies used bills such as this New Jersey 18-pence note for currency.

Raising Taxes

Great Britain had won the French and Indian War, but Parliament still had to pay for it. In addition, Britain kept an army in North America to protect the colonists against American Indian attacks. To help pay for this standing army, Prime Minister **George Grenville** asked Parliament to tax the colonists. In 1764 Parliament passed the **Sugar Act**. This law set duties, or taxes, on molasses and sugar imported by colonists. This was the first act passed specifically to raise money in the colonies, rather than to regulate trade.

In addition to passing new taxes, the British would not let the colonies print their own money. Parliament also made life much harder for

Parliament's New Tax Policies

Parliament made great efforts to force colonists to obey mercantile laws and pay the new taxes.

Colonial merchants had to give royal officials a list of all the trade goods on their ships. This made it hard for traders to avoid paying duties.

The British also began to stop and search ships for smuggled goods.

Traders caught smuggling could have their goods and ships taken from them.

Visualizing History

1. **Government** How did the British punish smugglers?
2. **Connecting to Today** Why is it important for a government to stop smugglers?

smugglers by giving the vice-admiralty courts greater powers. These courts had no juries, and their judges treated suspected smugglers as guilty until proven innocent. In regular British courts, accused persons were treated as innocent until proven guilty. In addition, trial by jury was a recognized right of British citizens.

✔ **Reading Check: Finding the Main Idea** In what ways did Parliament's new laws increase British control of the American colonies?

Samuel Adams encouraged colonists to protest the new British taxes.

Taxation without Representation

Parliament's actions upset many colonists who had grown used to being independent. Merchants thought the taxes were unfair and hurt business. **James Otis**, a lawyer from Boston, was one of the first colonists to protest taxation by Parliament. Otis argued that Parliament could not "take from any man any part of his property, without his consent in person or by representation." No one in Britain had asked the colonists if they wanted to be taxed. The colonists had no direct representatives in Parliament. In addition, colonial assemblies had little influence on Parliament's decisions. Therefore, Otis said, the tax was unfair and violated colonists' rights.

At a Boston town meeting in May 1764, leader **Samuel Adams** agreed with Otis. He believed that Parliament could not tax the colonists without their consent and said that agreeing to the tax would be dangerous.

"For if our trade may be taxed, why not our lands? Why not the produce of our lands and, in short, everything we possess or make use of?"

—Samuel Adams, quoted in *Patriots,* by A. J. Langguth

Analyzing Primary Sources

Identifying Points of View What did Adams fear would happen if Americans did not protest the new British taxes?

The ideas of Otis and Adams helped spread the slogan "No Taxation without Representation" throughout the colonies.

Adams also helped found the **Committees of Correspondence**, groups that contacted other towns and colonies. They shared ideas and information about the new British laws and ways to challenge them. A popular protest method was the **boycott**, in which people refuse to buy certain goods. In many homes women made substitutes for British goods. The boycott began in Massachusetts and soon spread to other colonies. Colonists hoped such efforts would hurt the British economy, perhaps convincing Parliament to end the new taxes.

"No Taxation without Representation"

✔ **Reading Check: Analyzing Information** How did Samuel Adams and James Otis influence colonial protests against new taxes?

The Stamp Act

By early 1765 Prime Minister Grenville had heard the complaints about the Sugar Act. He asked the colonists if they had a better plan for paying their share of military costs. Some colonists suggested taxing themselves, but Grenville rejected the idea. Grenville then proposed the **Stamp Act**, which Parliament passed in March 1765. This act affected most colonists. It required them to pay for an official stamp, or seal, whenever they bought paper items. The tax had to be paid on legal documents, licenses, newspapers, pamphlets, and even playing cards. Colonists who refused to buy stamps could be fined or sent to jail.

Grenville thought this tax was fair. After all, in Britain people already paid similar taxes. But colonists saw it differently. The Stamp Act was Parliament's first effort to raise money by taxing them directly. Protests against the Stamp Act began almost immediately.

In places such as New York and Massachusetts, colonists formed secret societies called the **Sons of Liberty**. Samuel Adams helped organize the Sons of Liberty in Boston. These groups sometimes used violence to frighten tax collectors. They told tax collector Andrew Oliver that "his house would be destroyed and his life [would be] in continual danger" unless he quit his job. Oliver quit. Many colonial courts shut down because people refused to buy the stamps required for legal documents. Businesses openly ignored the law by refusing to buy stamps.

This teapot was one of many ways in which the colonists opposed the Stamp Act.

COLONIAL WILLIAMSBURG FOUNDATION

In May 1765 **Patrick Henry** presented a series of resolutions to the House of Burgesses in Virginia. These resolutions stated that the Stamp Act violated the rights of the colonists as British citizens. In addition to taxation without representation, the Stamp Act denied the accused trial

COURTESY OF THE JOHN CARTER BROWN LIBRARY AT BROWN UNIVERSITY

Interpreting the Visual Record

The end of the Stamp Act *This cartoon shows members of Parliament giving a funeral for the Stamp Act.* ***Do you think the artist was pleased or upset at the repeal of the act? Explain your answer.***

by jury. The leader of the House, John Robinson, interrupted Henry's speech by crying, "Treason! Treason!" "If this be treason," replied Henry, "make the most of it!" Henry's speech convinced the assembly to support some of his ideas.

Repealing the Stamp Act

Word of Virginia's action reached Boston. There the members of the Massachusetts legislature called for a Stamp Act Congress. In October 1765, delegates from nine colonies met in New York. They issued a declaration that the Stamp Act violated their rights and liberties. They then asked Parliament to **repeal**, or end, the act.

Pressure to repeal the Stamp Act began to grow. A group of London merchants said that their trade suffered from the colonial boycott and asked Parliament to repeal the Stamp Act. Benjamin Franklin, serving as an official agent for Pennsylvania, spoke before Parliament. Repeal the stamp tax, he said, and colonists would buy British goods again. William Pitt, an important member of Parliament, also believed that the Stamp Act was unfair. Pitt led Parliament in repealing the act in 1766.

The members of Parliament were still upset that colonists had challenged their authority. Thus, Parliament issued the Declaratory Act, which stated that Parliament had the power to make laws for the colonies "in all cases whatsoever." In other words, Parliament made the rules, not the colonists.

✔ Reading Check: **Summarizing** What methods did the colonists use to protest the Sugar and Stamp Acts, and what were the results of their efforts?

Section 3 Review

1. **Define** and explain:
   - boycott
   - repeal
2. **Identify** and explain:
   - George Grenville
   - Sugar Act
   - James Otis
   - Samuel Adams
   - Committees of Correspondence
   - Stamp Act
   - Sons of Liberty
   - Patrick Henry
3. **Summarizing** Copy the graphic organizer below. Use it to show why the British taxed the American colonists, what the British tax laws were, and how the colonists responded.

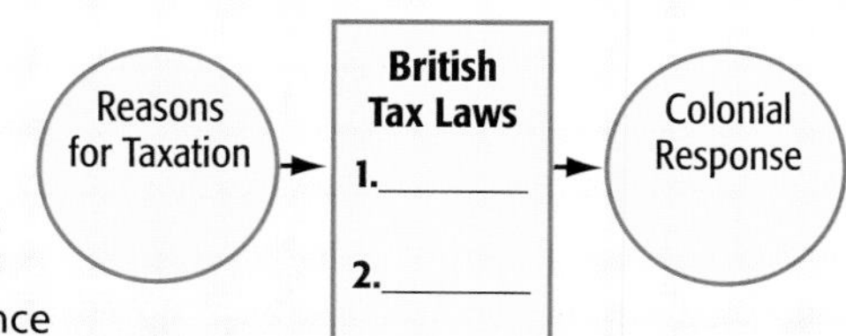

4. **Finding the Main Idea**
   a. Why did colonists dislike the Sugar Act, the vice-admiralty courts, and the Stamp Act?
   b. Compare and contrast the ways in which colonists challenged new taxes.
5. **Writing and Critical Thinking**
   Supporting a Point of View Imagine that you are a colonist upset by new taxes. Write a newspaper editorial persuading colonists to protest these new taxes.
   Consider the following:
   - reasons for British taxes
   - ideas of James Otis and Samuel Adams
   - Benjamin Franklin's testimony before Parliament

Section 4

New Taxes and Tensions

Read to Discover

1. How did colonists respond to the Townshend Acts?
2. Why were the Boston Massacre and the Boston Tea Party significant events?
3. What was the purpose of the Intolerable Acts?

Define

- writs of assistance
- propaganda

Identify

- Townshend Acts
- Daughters of Liberty
- Boston Massacre
- Tea Act
- Boston Tea Party
- Intolerable Acts
- Mercy Otis Warren

Why It Matters Today

The British government taxed the colonies to pay for the French and Indian War. Today our government uses taxes to pay for many services. Use CNNfyi.com or other **current events** sources to learn about a U.S. government program that uses tax dollars. Record your findings in your journal.

The Story Continues

People in cities across the colonies celebrated the repeal of the Stamp Act with fireworks. In Boston the people built a giant pyramid lit by 280 lamps. The Massachusetts legislature thanked King George III and promised to be loyal to him. However, Parliament and the colonies still disagreed on many issues.

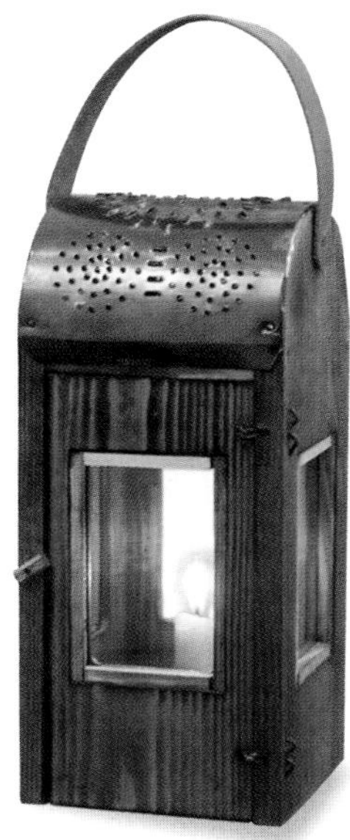

Colonial lanterns and lamps were often lit by candles or oil.

The Townshend Acts

In June 1767 Parliament passed the **Townshend Acts**, which placed duties on imported glass, lead, paint, paper, and tea. The money from these duties paid for military costs and the salaries of colonial governors. These payments violated the guarantee of having no standing army in peacetime without the colonists' consent. To enforce the Townshend Acts, British officials used **writs of assistance**. These special forms allowed tax collectors to search for smuggled goods. Colonists hated the new laws because they violated colonists' constitutional rights.

The colonists responded to the Townshend Acts by once again boycotting British goods. Women calling themselves the **Daughters of Liberty** supported the boycott. One leader explained their actions.

"I hope [we] would sooner wrap ourselves in sheep and goatskin than buy English goods of a people who have insulted us in such a scandalous [shocking] way."

—Anonymous Daughter of Liberty, quoted in *A History of Women in America,* by Carol Hymowitz and Michaele Weissman

Analyzing Primary Sources
Identifying Points of View How did this leader view the Townshend Acts?

Colonial legislatures also protested the Townshend Acts. In February 1768 Samuel Adams wrote a letter stating that the acts violated the legal rights of the colonists. The Massachusetts legislature sent this letter to other colonies, asking for their help. In a few months several legislatures voted to join the protest against the Townshend Acts.

At the same time, tax collectors in Massachusetts seized the ship *Liberty* on suspicion of smuggling. This action angered the ship's owner, Boston merchant John Hancock, who accused the tax collectors of punishing him because he opposed the Townshend Acts. The Sons of Liberty supported Hancock. They began to attack the houses of customs officials in protest. In response, Governor Francis Bernard broke up the Massachusetts legislature. He also asked troops to restore order. British soldiers arrived in Boston in October 1768.

The Sons of Liberty displayed posters like this one calling for a boycott against a Boston merchant.

WILLIAM JACKSON,
an *IMPORTER*; at the
BRAZEN HEAD,
North Side of the TOWN-HOUSE,
and *Oppofite the Town-Pump*, *in*
Corn-hill, BOSTON.

It is defired that the SONS and DAUGHTERS of *LIBERTY*, would not buy any one thing of him, for in fo doing they will bring Difgrace upon *themfelves*, and their *Pofterity*, for *ever* and *ever*, AMEN

✔ **Reading Check: Sequencing** What series of events led to the arrival of British troops in Boston in 1768?

 The Boston Massacre

Many Bostonians believed that the British government had sent the troops to silence its critics. Local leader Samuel Adams declared, "I look upon [British soldiers] as foreign enemies." Both sides disliked each other—name-calling and fights between locals and the soldiers were common.

The tension exploded on March 5, 1770, when a lone British soldier standing guard got into a fight with a colonist. A crowd gathered around the soldier, throwing snowballs and shouting insults. Soon a small group of troops arrived. The mob grew louder and angrier by the moment. Suddenly, the soldiers fired into the crowd killing several colonists.

Samuel Adams and others used the event as a form of **propaganda**—information giving only one side in an argument—against the British. Colonists called the shootings the **Boston Massacre**. The soldiers and their officer, Thomas Preston, were charged with murder. Two Boston lawyers, Josiah Quincy and John Adams—Samuel Adams's cousin—agreed to defend the soldiers. They argued that the troops had acted in self-defense. The Boston jury agreed. The jury found Preston and six soldiers not guilty. Two soldiers were convicted of killing people in the crowd by accident. These men were branded on the hand and then released. The trial helped calm people down, but many colonists were still angry at the British.

✔ **Reading Check: Contrasting** How did Samuel Adams and John Adams differ in their response to the Boston Massacre?

Research on the ROM

Free Find:
Samuel Adams
After reading about Samuel Adams on the **Holt Researcher CD–ROM**, imagine that you are a reporter for a Boston newspaper. Write a set of questions you might ask Adams about British treatment of the colonies. Include the answers you think Adams would give.

CONNECTING TO THE ARTS

Colonial Art Colonial artists often tried to show what daily life was like. Some used art to make a political point. Paul Revere's engraving of the Boston Massacre was one example. The picture shows British soldiers attacking unarmed colonists. The *Boston Gazette* advertised it as "A Print . . . of the late horrid [terrible] Massacre in King St." Revere's engraving sold many copies. It became a symbol of Great Britain's injustice toward the colonies. **How does Paul Revere's picture reveal changing colonial attitudes toward the British?**

A Tax on Tea

To reduce tensions in the colonies, Parliament repealed almost all of the Townshend Acts—but it kept the tax on tea. British officials knew that the colonial demand for tea was high despite the boycott. But the colonies were smuggling most of this imported tea and paying no duty on it. The British East India Company offered Parliament a solution. If allowed to sell its tea directly to the colonies, the company could charge low prices and still profit. Cheaper tea might lead to less smuggling and the collection of more money in taxes.

Parliament agreed and passed the **Tea Act** in 1773. Many colonial merchants and smugglers feared that cheap British tea would put them out of business. Other colonists worried that the British East India Company would monopolize—or gain complete control of—the tea trade. Other British companies might follow its example and threaten colonial businesses. As a result, colonists united against the Tea Act.

A ship carrying British tea arrived in Boston Harbor in November 1773. Two other tea ships soon joined it. The Sons of Liberty demanded that the ships leave immediately. But Thomas Hutchinson, governor of Massachusetts since 1771, would not let the ships leave without paying

Battling British Acts

ACT	COLONIAL RESPONSE	BRITISH REACTION
The **Sugar Act (1764)** replaced the Molasses Act and was aimed specifically at raising revenues from the colonies.	Colonists protested the act and called for a boycott on items with duties.	After asking colonists for a plan to pay military expenses and not receiving a satisfactory one, the prime minister proposed the Stamp Act.
The **Stamp Act (1765)** required colonists to purchase a stamp for newspapers, pamphlets, legal documents, and other items.	Colonists formed the Sons of Liberty, boycotted goods, and used violence to frighten tax collectors; Stamp Act Congress asked Parliament to repeal the act.	Parliament repealed the Stamp Act in March 1766, then issued the Declaratory Act.
The **Townshend Acts (1767)** placed duties on imported glass, lead, paint, paper, and tea and made it easier for tax collectors to get writs of assistance.	Colonists used boycotts, colonial legislatures circulated a letter protesting the acts, and the Sons of Liberty attacked homes of tax collectors.	Soldiers were sent to Boston in October 1768; colonists were killed in the Boston Massacre on March 5, 1770; most of the acts were repealed by Parliament; troops were removed from Boston.
The **Tea Act (1773)** kept in place duties on imported tea and allowed the British East India Company to export directly to the colonies.	Colonists used boycotts and propaganda, held the Boston Tea Party, and destroyed tea shipments in some colonies.	Parliament passed the Coercive Acts, also called the Intolerable Acts by colonists.
The **Intolerable Acts (1774)** closed Boston Harbor, canceled the Massachusetts charter, moved trials of colonial officials to Britain, allowed quartering of British troops in all colonies, and gave Canada control of the Ohio region.	Colonists called for large-scale boycotts, published propaganda, and convened the First Continental Congress.	King George III rejected the suggestions of the First Continental Congress.

the tea duty. On the night of December 16, colonists disguised as American Indians snuck onto the three tea-filled ships. One participant recalled his experience.

Analyzing Primary Sources

Drawing Inferences and Conclusions Based on George Hewes's statement, how organized does the Boston Tea Party seem? Explain your answer.

"In about three hours from the time we went on board, we had thus broken and thrown overboard every tea chest to be found in the ship, while those in the other ships were disposing of the tea in the same way, at the same time. . . . No attempt was made to resist us."

—George Hewes, quoted in *The Spirit of 'Seventy-Six,* edited by Henry Steele Commager and Richard B. Morris

After dumping 342 tea chests into Boston Harbor, the colonists headed home to remove their disguises. Word of this **Boston Tea Party** spread. Soon the streets echoed with shouts of "Boston harbour [is] a teapot tonight!"

✔ **Reading Check: Finding the Main Idea** Why did colonists oppose the Tea Act?

The Intolerable Acts

Lord North, the new British prime minister, was furious when he heard about the Boston Tea Party. "Can we remain in this situation long?" he asked Parliament. Parliament decided to punish Massachusetts. In the spring of 1774 Britain passed the Coercive Acts, which colonists called the **Intolerable Acts**. The acts had several effects.

1. Boston Harbor was closed until Boston paid for the lost tea.
2. The Massachusetts charter was canceled. The governor decided if and when the legislature could meet.
3. Royal officials accused of crimes were sent to Britain for trial. This let them face a more friendly judge and jury.
4. The Quartering Act forced colonists to quarter, or house and supply, British soldiers.
5. General Thomas Gage became the new governor of Massachusetts.

The British hoped that these steps would bring back order in the colonies by making an example of Massachusetts. But the acts simply made more people angry. The acts went against many of the traditional rights of British citizens, such as freedom of travel in peacetime and no quartering of troops in private homes. Some colonists wrote essays and poems critical of the British government's actions. **Mercy Otis Warren** wrote plays such as *The Group* and *The Blockheads*. In *The Group*, Warren gave British supporters names such as Hum Humbug to make them look foolish.

Colonial leaders in Boston proposed a boycott of all British goods in the colonies. They also tried to bring together leaders from each colony to decide the best way to respond to Britain's abuses of colonial rights.

✔ **Reading Check: Summarizing** What were the major effects of the Intolerable Acts, and what methods did colonists use to protest them?

BEQUEST OF WINSLOW WARREN, COURTESY MUSEUM OF FINE ARTS, BOSTON MA

Playwright Mercy Otis Warren was the daughter of James Otis and a friend of John Adams and Abigail Adams.

Section 4 Review

go.hrw.com Homework Practice Online
keyword: SC3 HP5

1. **Define** and explain:
   - writs of assistance
   - propaganda
2. **Identify** and explain:
   - Townshend Acts
   - Daughters of Liberty
   - Boston Massacre
   - Tea Act
   - Boston Tea Party
   - Intolerable Acts
   - Mercy Otis Warren
3. **Sequencing** Copy the graphic organizer below. Use it to explain the sequence of major events that led to the Intolerable Acts of 1774.

Event	Results
1. 2. 3. 4. 5. Intolerable Acts	→

4. **Finding the Main Idea**
   a. In what ways did colonists react to the Townshend Acts?
   b. How did the Boston Massacre and the Boston Tea Party affect relations between Great Britain and the colonies?
5. **Writing and Critical Thinking**
   Evaluating Imagine that you are a colonist. Write a brief pamphlet explaining what you think Parliament hopes to achieve with the Intolerable Acts.
   Consider the following:
   - the Boston Tea Party
   - the writings of Mercy Otis Warren
   - colonial boycott efforts

Chapter 5 Review

The Chapter at a Glance

Examine the visual summary of the chapter below. Write a one-paragraph summary of the main ideas covered in the chapter. Share your summary with a classmate to compare and contrast your ideas.

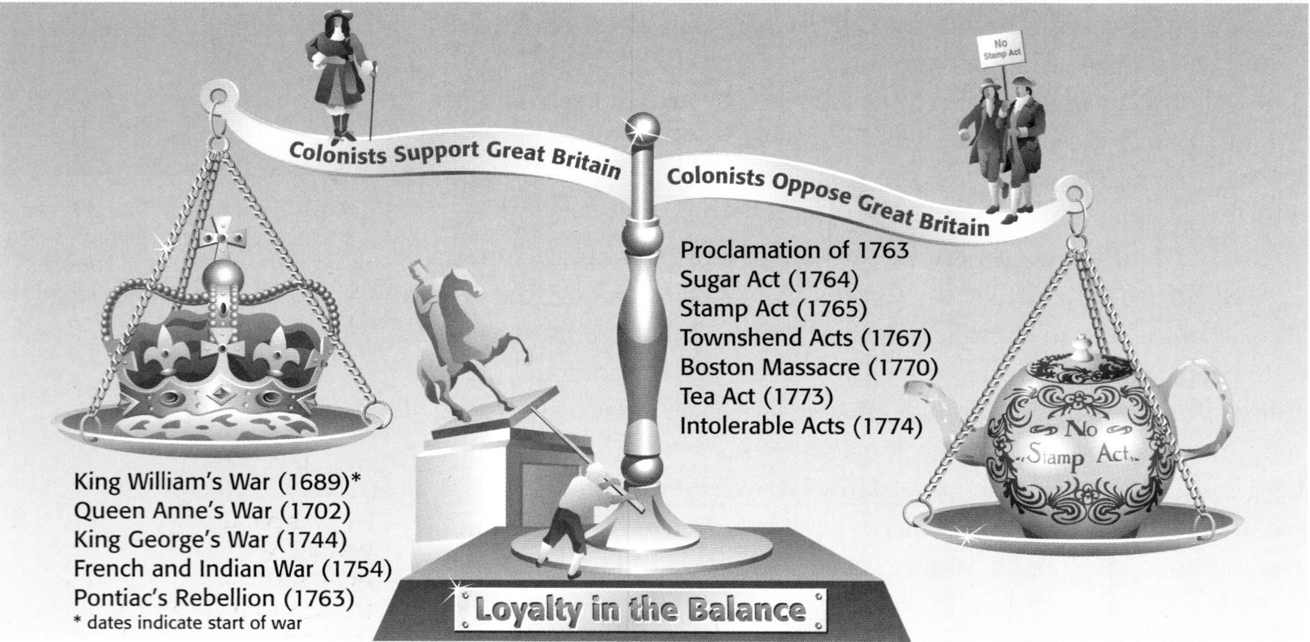

Identifying People and Ideas

Use the following terms or people in historically significant sentences.

1. Albany Plan of Union
2. pioneers
3. King George III
4. Proclamation of 1763
5. Samuel Adams
6. Committees of Correspondence
7. Stamp Act
8. Patrick Henry
9. writs of assistance
10. Mercy Otis Warren

Understanding Main Ideas

Section 1 *(Pages 126–130)*

1. What events led to the French and Indian War?
2. What were the terms of the Treaty of Paris?

Section 2 *(Pages 131–134)*

3. Why and how did King George III and Parliament try to limit colonial expansion?

Section 3 *(Pages 135–138)*

4. Why did colonists oppose new taxes?
5. How did colonists try to change the new taxes?

Section 4 *(Pages 139–143)*

6. How did colonists view the Townshend Acts?
7. Why did Parliament pass the Intolerable Acts?

You Be the Historian— Reviewing Themes

1. **Global Relations** How did the wars between France and Great Britain affect the British colonists in North America?
2. **Geography** What region did American pioneers settle during the 1760s, and what happened as a result?
3. **Economics** How did Americans react when they were taxed by Parliament, in which they were not represented?

Thinking Critically

1. **Supporting a Point of View** Imagine that you are a British colonist during the 1760s. Would you be willing to settle on the frontier? Explain your answer.
2. **Drawing Inferences and Conclusions** Why do you think British leaders felt the need to take greater control of the colonies?
3. **Identifying Cause and Effect** What were the main causes of the Boston Massacre and the Boston Tea Party, and how did these two events affect the relationship between Great Britain and the colonies?

Social Studies Skills Workshop

Interpreting Graphs

Study the graph below. Then use the information on the graph to help you answer the questions that follow.

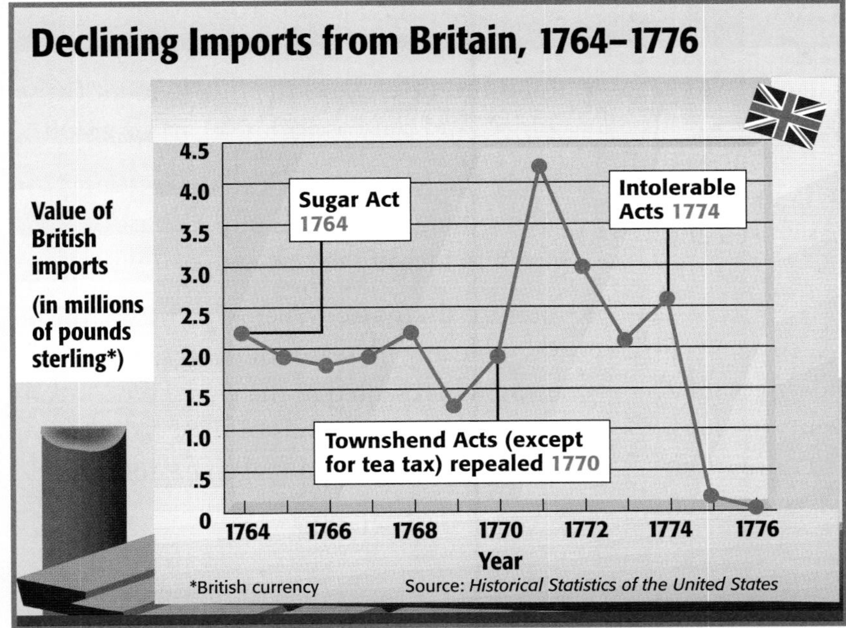

1. What happened to the value of British imports in the colonies between 1770 and 1771, and 1774 and 1775?
   a. Imports increased during both periods.
   b. Imports decreased during both periods.
   c. Imports fell in 1771 and rose in 1775.
   d. Imports rose in 1775 and fell in 1771.

2. Based on the graph and your knowledge of the period, do you think that the colonial boycotts against British goods were effective? Explain your answer.

Analyzing Primary Sources

Read the following quote by colonial militia member David Perry, and then answer the questions that follow.

> **"We had proceeded but a short distance into the woods before we were met by the enemy. . . . It was the first engagement I had ever seen, and the whistling of balls [bullets] and roar of musquetry [guns] terrified me not a little. At length our regiment formed among the trees, behind which the men kept stepping from their ranks for shelter. Colonel Preble, who, I well remember, was a harsh man, swore he would knock the first man down who should step out of his ranks, which greatly surprised me, to think that I must stand still to be shot at."**

3. Which of the following statements best describes Perry's reaction to this style of fighting?
   a. He was pleased that the militia was allowed to take cover behind trees.
   b. He was frightened by the fighting and confused by his orders.
   c. He was eager to fight against the French and American Indians.
   d. He was angry that Colonel Preble knocked him down.

4. What would be some of the disadvantages of the style of fighting described by Perry?

Alternative Assessment

Building Your Portfolio

American History

Cooperative Learning

Complete this activity in small groups. Imagine that you are attending a meeting of the Sons of Liberty after the Stamp Act has been passed. Write a skit that explains why you are upset with the British government and what actions you might take. Have at least one character in the skit urge the group to proceed with caution. Perform your skit for the class.

internet connect

Internet Activity: go.hrw.com
keyword: SC3 CF5

Choose an activity on conflict in the colonies to:

- Research battles of the French and Indian War, and create a map of the major engagements.
- Examine the fur trade in New France, and create a pamphlet on settlements.
- Research the life of Daniel Boone, and write a biography.

Social Studies Skills

WORKSHOP

Interpreting Charts and Graphs

Charts and graphs categorize and display data in a variety of ways. How the data is displayed depends on the type of chart or graph used and the subject matter.

Charts There are various types of charts. *Flowcharts,* used to show cause-and-effect relationships, display a sequence of events or steps. *Organizational charts* show the structure of an organization. *Tables* are columned charts that present data in categories.

Graphs There are several different types of graphs. A *line graph* often plots changes in quantities over time and has a horizontal axis and a vertical axis. A *bar graph* can also be used to display changes in quantities over time. Most often, however, bar graphs compare quantities within categories. A *pie graph,* or *circle graph,* shows sections of a whole graph as if they were slices of a pie. Taken together, all the sections of this circular graph total 100 percent.

How to Read a Chart or Graph

1. **Read the title.** Read the title to identify the subject and purpose of the chart or graph.
2. **Study the key parts.** Read the headings, subheadings, and labels of the chart or graph to identify the categories used.
3. **Analyze the data.** When reading quantities, note any increases or decreases in amounts presented in the chart. When reading dates, note intervals of time. When viewing an organizational chart, follow the direction of the arrows or lines.

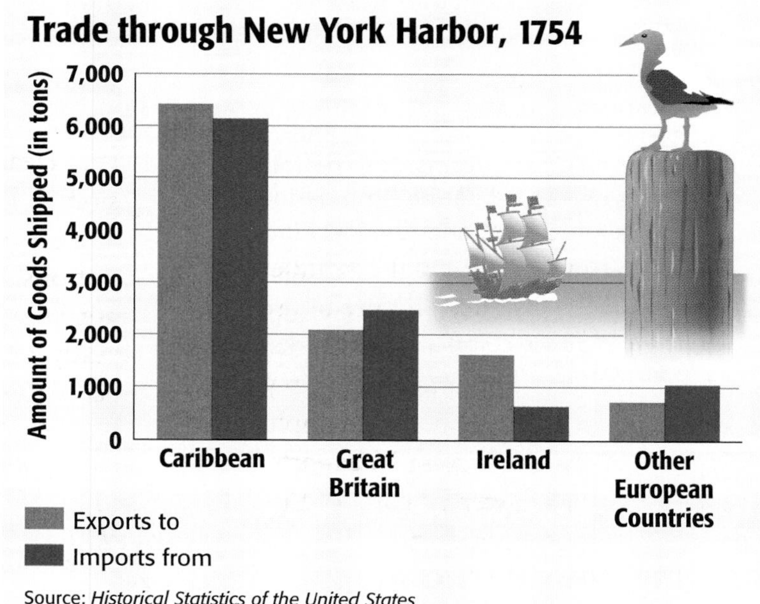

Practicing the Skills

Study the graph above. Then answer the following questions.

1. What labels are used for each axis?
2. What was the total amount of goods shipped through New York Harbor in 1754?
3. Using the information in this graph, what generalizations or conclusions can you draw about colonial trade in 1754?

History in Action

UNIT 2 SIMULATION

You Make the Decision . . .

Which Colonies Should Receive Financial Support from Great Britain?

Complete the following activity in small cooperative groups. It is 1755. George II is king of England. Britain and France are fighting each other for control of North American colonies and trade routes in the French and Indian War. In order to increase the cash flow for his country, King George II has to cut finances to the colonies. Your group has been asked to help the king decide which colonies Britain should not continue funding. Follow these steps to reach your decision.

1. Gather Information. Use your textbook and other resources to find information that might help you decide which colonies are least valuable to Great Britain. These colonies will not continue to receive financial assistance. Be sure to use what you learned from this unit's Skills Workshop on Interpreting Charts and Graphs to help you make an informed decision. For example, you might refer to charts on colonial exports. You may want to divide different parts of the research among group members.

2. Identify Options. After reviewing the information you have gathered, consider the options you might recommend to the king about which colonies should not get financial assistance. Your final decision may be easier to reach if you consider as many options as possible. Be sure to record your possible options for your presentation.

3. Predict Consequences. Now take each option you and the members of your group came up with and consider what might be the outcome of each course of action. Ask yourselves questions like: "How will not giving financial support to the colony affect Great Britain?" Once you have predicted the consequences, record them as notes for your presentation.

4. Take Action to Implement Your Decision. After you have considered your options, you should create your presentation. Be sure to make your decision on which colonies should receive financial aid very clear. You will need to support your decision by including information you gathered and by explaining why you rejected other options. Your presentation needs to be visually appealing to convince the king. When you are ready, decide which group members will make each part of the presentation, and then take your decision to the king (the rest of the class). Good luck!

UNIT 3 A New American Nation

(1774–1791)

Young People

IN HISTORY

Young Patriots

Jonathan Nickerson had quite a story to tell. At age 14 he volunteered to join the Continental Army during the Revolutionary War. Years after serving his country, he told of an event that happened outside of White Plains, New York. The year was 1782. About 80 British cavalrymen rode up to a group of American soldiers, including Nickerson. The British demanded, "Surrender, you . . . rebels, surrender!" Outnumbered, Nickerson and several American Patriots laid down their muskets to surrender. However, the British wanted blood and attacked the unarmed men. Nickerson was knocked to the ground and trampled by a horse. Then the British struck him repeatedly in the head and body with a sword. He recalled a soldier asking, "Shall we kill him?" The British commander replied, "No, let him alone. He will die soon himself." Nickerson proved the British captain wrong. He recovered from his wounds and lived to tell about his dramatic brush with death.

Young battlefield drummers, like the boy shown on the left, helped boost soldiers' morale during the Revolutionary War.

Among those who bravely contributed to the revolutionary struggle was 16-year-old Sybil Luddington. In April 1777, Luddington rode some 40 miles through the night to warn American colonists that British forces had landed at Danbury, Connecticut.

Another teenager to fight for American independence was 16-year-old Michael Smith. Smith's regiment served on a gunboat on the Hudson River in New York. The gunboat crew was ordered to protect Americans living in the area from British raiding parties. When a British warship approached the shore to land its raiding party, the gunboat's crew opened fire. The cannon shots that Smith and two of his fellow crew members fired successfully turned the British away. Smith and his crewmates were declared heroes.

If You Were There *How would you help the Patriots?*

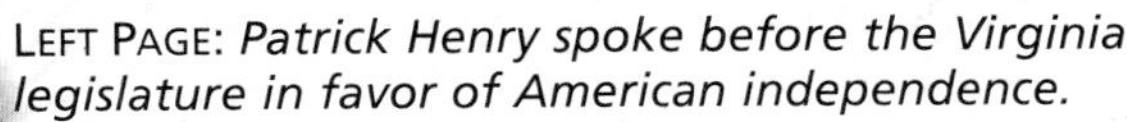

LEFT PAGE: *Patrick Henry spoke before the Virginia legislature in favor of American independence.*

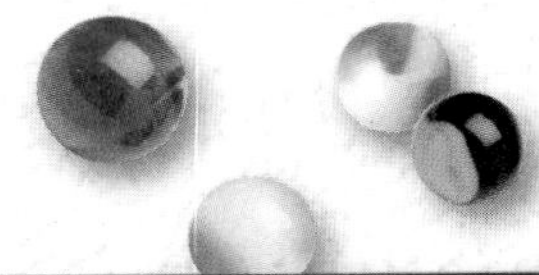

CHAPTER 6

The American Revolution

(1774–1783)

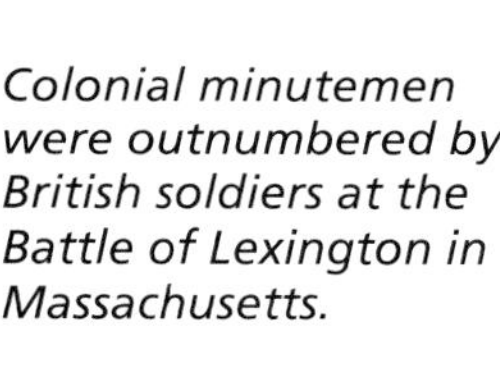

Colonial minutemen were outnumbered by British soldiers at the Battle of Lexington in Massachusetts.

Patriot Thomas Jefferson was the author of the Declaration of Independence.

UNITED STATES

1774 The First Continental Congress meets.

1775 On April 19 the Revolutionary War begins with the fighting at Lexington and Concord.

1776 On July 4 the thirteen colonies issue the Declaration of Independence and break away from Great Britain.

1776 On December 26 General George Washington wins the Battle of Trenton.

1777 On October 17 a British army surrenders to the Patriots after the Battle of Saratoga.

1778 The Continental Army suffers through the end of a harsh winter while stationed at Valley Forge, Pennsylvania.

1774	1775	1776	1777	1778

WORLD

1776 Scottish economist Adam Smith writes *The Wealth of Nations* about open economic markets and competition.

A gold British guinea coin

1778 France allies with the Americans and joins the war against Great Britain.

French allies supplied the Patriots with much-needed weapons such as this cannon.

Build on What You Know

By 1774 many colonists were angry with the British government. These colonists believed that Parliament had repeatedly violated their rights. Eventually their protests led to battles with British troops and a war for independence from Great Britain. The American Revolution marked the birth of the United States of America.

George Washington looks on as American forces accept the British surrender at Yorktown, Virginia.

COLONIAL WILLIAMSBURG FOUNDATION

The early U.S. flag had a star and a stripe for each state.

1779 Patriot George Rogers Clark and his forces recapture Vincennes.

1780 The British defeat the southern Patriot army at Camden, South Carolina.

1781 On October 19 the British surrender to George Washington at Yorktown, securing the American victory in the Revolutionary War.

1783 The Treaty of Paris is signed, ending the war.

1779 | 1780 | 1781 | 1782 | 1783

1779 Spain declares war on Britain.

1780 Great Britain declares war on the Netherlands.

1783 Great Britain agrees to return Florida to Spain.

If you were there . . .

Would you support the Revolution?

You Be the Historian

What's Your Opinion? Do you **agree** or **disagree** with the following statements? Support your point of view in your journal.

- **Citizenship** Citizens have the right to rebel against an unjust government.
- **Constitutional Heritage** All human beings possess certain natural rights that should be protected.
- **Global Relations** A powerful nation will always defeat a weaker country in war.

Section 1

The Revolution Begins

Read to Discover

1. What actions did the First Continental Congress take?
2. How did the fighting at Lexington and Concord affect the colonies' conflict with Great Britain?
3. What did the Second Continental Congress accomplish?
4. How did geography influence the early battles of the war?

Define

- minutemen
- siege

Identify

- First Continental Congress
- Thomas Gage
- Redcoats
- Second Continental Congress
- Continental Army
- George Washington
- Olive Branch Petition
- Battle of Bunker Hill

Why it Matters Today

At times Americans still have to defend their liberties. Sometimes the United States also helps protect the freedoms of people in other countries. Use CNNfyi.com or other **current events** sources to find a country in which the United States is helping to protect basic human rights. Record your findings in your journal.

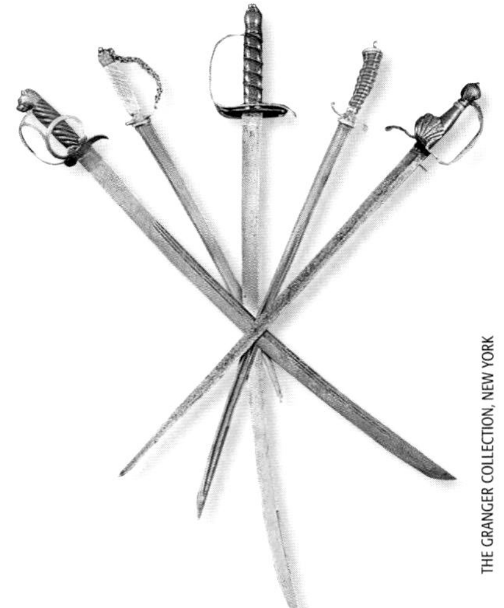

THE GRANGER COLLECTION, NEW YORK

This is a collection of swords used during the Revolutionary War.

The Story Continues

By the fall of 1774 the colonists had to do something about their problems with Great Britain. Cousins John and Samuel Adams were part of the debate. Samuel Adams was the rebel who had organized the Boston Tea Party. John Adams had defended the British soldiers who took part in the Boston Massacre. Both cousins thought that colonial leaders needed to respond to British acts. They agreed to represent Massachusetts at a colonial assembly taking place in Philadelphia.

The First Continental Congress

In September 1774 the **First Continental Congress** met in Philadelphia. The Congress had 56 colonial delegates, including John and Samuel Adams. Georgia was the only colony that did not send representatives. The delegates at the meeting debated the best way to respond to the crisis taking place in Boston. Delegate John Dickinson thought that the colonists should make peace with Great Britain. Delegate Patrick Henry said that there was no way to avoid a fight. "Arms [weapons] are a resource to which we shall be forced," he declared.

In the end, the delegates reached a compromise. They recommended that colonists continue to boycott British goods but also warned colonial militias to be prepared to fight. Meanwhile, they assembled a list of 10 resolutions to present to King George III. This Declaration of Rights listed freedoms that the delegates believed colonists should possess, including the right to "life, liberty, and property." The delegates agreed to meet again in May 1775 if the king did not agree.

✔ **Reading Check:** **Summarizing** Describe the accomplishments of the First Continental Congress.

GIFT OF JOSEPH W. REVERE, WILLIAM B. REVERE, AND EDWARD H.R. REVERE, COURTESY, MUSEUM OF FINE ARTS, BOSTON

Paul Revere's heroic ride helped warn the Patriots of the British advance toward Concord.

The "Shot Heard round the World"

Tensions remained high in Boston. Local militia members began calling themselves **minutemen** because they were ready to fight on a minute's notice. In April 1775 British general **Thomas Gage** decided to take away the minutemen's weapons and ammunition. These weapons were stored in Concord, a town about 20 miles west of Boston.

The Sons of Liberty learned of the British plan. On the evening of April 18, 1775, spies brought serious news to Paul Revere and William Dawes. British troops were heading toward Concord. The two men raced on their horses through the countryside, warning minutemen that the British were coming! Isaac Davis was one of the minutemen who heard the warning. His wife later described his response to Revere's call.

History Makers Speak

> **"The alarm was given early in the morning, and my husband lost no time in making ready to go to Concord with his company. . . . [he] said but little that morning. He seemed serious and thoughtful; but never seemed to hesitate. . . . He only said, 'Take good care of the children.'"**
>
> —Mrs. Isaac Davis, quoted in *From Colonies to Country,* by Joy Hakim

On the morning of April 19, fewer than 70 minutemen gathered at the Lexington village green, near Concord. There they met a much larger force of British troops. The colonial commander shouted to his soldiers,

Interpreting the Visual Record

The first battle *The fighting at Lexington was fierce but brief. The colonists suffered their first casualties of the war.* ***What differences does this image show between the fighting style of the minutemen and that of the British regular troops?***

THE GRANGER COLLECTION, NEW YORK

"Don't fire unless fired upon. But if they mean to have a war, let it begin here!" Suddenly a shot rang out. No one knows who fired this "shot heard round the world"—but once the soldiers heard it, the fight began. The battle ended in minutes. When the smoke cleared, the badly outnumbered colonists had suffered 8 dead and 10 wounded.

The British marched on to Concord, where they found few weapons because the colonists had already removed them. In anger, British troops set fire to a few buildings. One of the colonists shouted, "Will you let them burn the town down?" In response, the minutemen charged forward.

As the British retreated back to Boston, the minutemen fired upon them from behind trees and buildings. The British soldiers' bright red uniforms made easy targets. The colonists called the British soldiers **Redcoats** because of these uniforms. By the time the British reached Boston, they had suffered more than 250 casualties. Fewer than 100 colonists were killed or wounded. Isaac Davis was among those who died that day.

Word of the fighting at Lexington and Concord spread. Many people responded with shock and anger. Dr. James Thacher noted the effect on one Massachusetts town.

Analyzing Primary Sources

Identifying Bias Do you think Dr. Thacher supports the minutemen or the Redcoats? Why?

"This tragical event seems to have electrified all classes of people. . . . The sword is now unsheathed [drawn], and our friends are slaughtered by our cruel enemies. Expresses [messengers] are hastening from town to town, in all directions through the country . . . rousing the people To Arms! To Arms!"

—Dr. James Thacher, quoted in *Military Journal of the American Revolution*

✔ **Reading Check: Identifying Cause and Effect** What led to the fighting at Lexington and Concord, and how did it affect the colonies' conflict with Great Britain?

George Washington had fought in the French and Indian War.

The Second Continental Congress

In May 1775, representatives from 12 of the colonies met in the city of Philadelphia for the **Second Continental Congress**. The leaders of the Congress had to decide how to react to the fighting. They decided not to break away from Great Britain. The Congress did make plans to create a **Continental Army** to defend the colonies and chose Virginian **George Washington** to command this army.

As Washington began gathering his troops, the Congress tried one last time to keep the peace. On July 5 the delegates signed the **Olive Branch Petition**. This petition was so named because the olive branch is a symbol of peace. In November the colonists learned that King George III had angrily rejected the peace offer. By that time the fighting in the colonies had spread.

✔ **Reading Check: Drawing Inferences and Conclusions** Why do you think King George III rejected the Olive Branch Petition?

Early Battles

While the Second Continental Congress was meeting, some colonists were striking at the British. Their target was Fort Ticonderoga in northern New York. This fort guarded access to Lake Champlain, a key waterway. Colonel Benedict Arnold joined Ethan Allen, from present-day Vermont, to lead the effort. On May 10, 1775, the colonists surprised the British by attacking during an early morning storm. They quickly took the fort and its large supply of weapons, including cannons.

Back in Massachusetts, minutemen held Boston under **siege**—a situation in which soldiers surround a city or fort. In mid-June 1775 the British prepared to take Charlestown, an area that overlooks Boston from the north. Warned of the plan, colonial forces rushed to build defenses on nearby Bunker Hill and Breed's Hill. The British were surprised when they saw the colonial soldiers already on the hills. Still, the Redcoats tried to capture the colonists' positions. The colonial forces were well protected from attack, but they were low on gunpowder. The colonial commander ordered his troops not to fire on the Redcoats "until you see the whites of their eyes."

Research on the ROM

Free Find:
George Washington
After reading about George Washington on the **Holt Researcher CD–ROM**, list the information you think led the Second Continental Congress to select him to command the Continental Army.

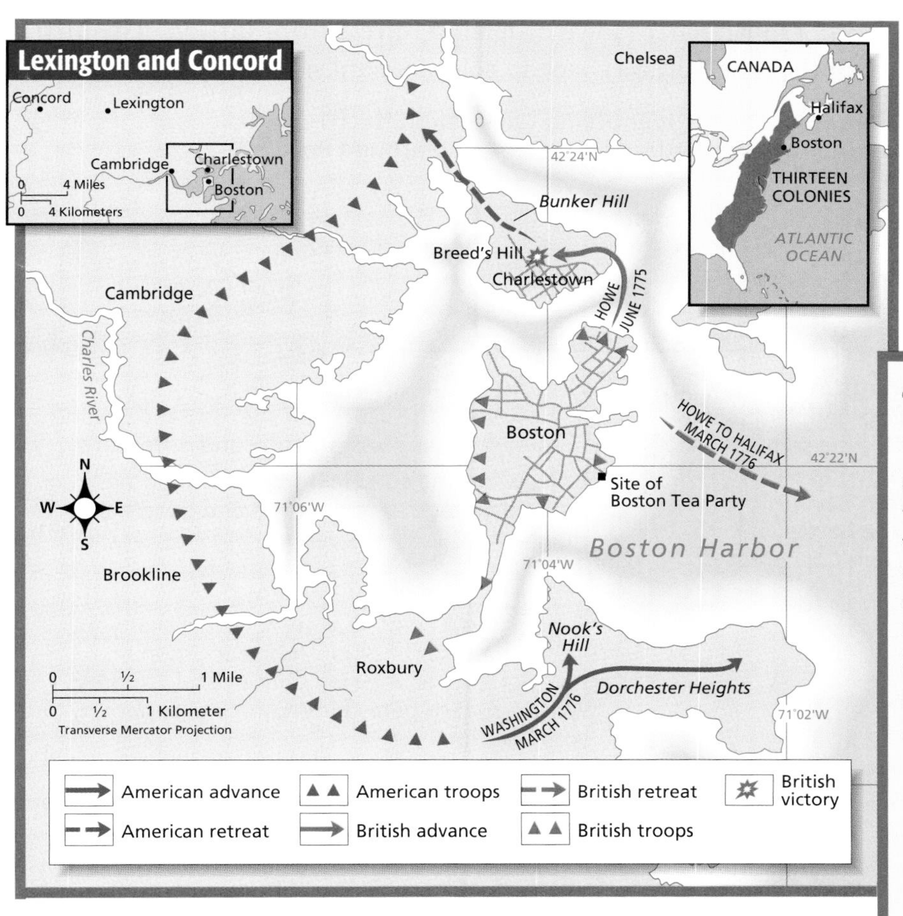

The Siege of Boston, 1775–1776

Interpreting Maps After the fighting at Lexington and Concord, the British retreated to the safety of Boston. It was not long, however, before the American forces moved closer to threaten the British positions.

Skills Assessment

1. **Locate** Find the location of Boston, Breed's Hill, and Bunker Hill on the map.
2. **Drawing Inferences and Conclusions** Why do you think the British did not retreat by land?

THE GRANGER COLLECTION, NEW YORK

As the British attacked Breed's Hill, Bostonians climbed onto city rooftops to watch the battle unfold.

Most of the fighting took place on Breed's Hill. The outnumbered colonists turned back several assaults. Yet, they eventually ran out of ammunition and had to retreat. The British suffered more than 1,000 casualties, compared to about 400 for the colonists. The **Battle of Bunker Hill** showed the colonists that they could hold their own against the British.

General Washington soon arrived to command the siege of Boston. To drive out the British, Washington needed the cannons from Fort Ticonderoga. In November he gave the task of transporting these guns to officer Henry Knox. Knox managed to haul the guns 300 miles in the middle of winter.

In March 1776 Washington used the cannons to fire on the British from Dorchester Heights, a hill overlooking southern Boston. The British were in trouble. The situation astonished British general William Howe. "The rebels have done more in one night than my whole army could do in months," he declared. On March 7 Howe ordered a retreat from Boston. The birthplace of the rebellion was back in colonial hands.

✔ **Reading Check: Identifying Cause and Effect** How did geography influence the early battles in New York and around Boston?

Section 1 Review

go.hrw.com **Homework Practice Online**
keyword: SC3 HP6

1. **Define** and explain:
   - minutemen
   - siege

2. **Identify** and explain:
   - First Continental Congress
   - Thomas Gage
   - Redcoats
   - Second Continental Congress
   - Continental Army
   - George Washington
   - Olive Branch Petition
   - Battle of Bunker Hill

3. **Analyzing Information** Copy the graphic organizer below. Use it to describe some of the factors that led to the start of the American Revolution, including the battles of Lexington and Concord.

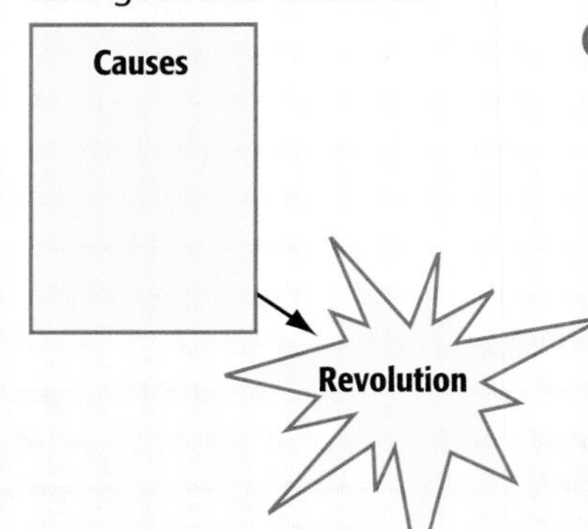

4. **Finding the Main Idea**
   a. How were the actions of the First and Second Continental Congresses similar and different?
   b. How did the colonial forces use geography to their advantage at Bunker Hill and Dorchester Heights?

5. **Writing and Critical Thinking**
   Supporting a Point of View Imagine that you are a supporter of either John Dickinson or Patrick Henry at the First Continental Congress. Write a speech persuading others to support your position.
   Consider the following:
   - the abuses committed by British authorities
   - the colonies' economic and social ties to Great Britain
   - the risks of fighting against the British

CONNECTING TO Literature

My Brother Sam Is Dead

James Collier and Christopher Collier

James and Christopher Collier describe the Revolutionary War in their book My Brother Sam Is Dead. *They write from the viewpoint of young Connecticut colonist Timmy Meeker. Tim's father is a Loyalist, or Tory, but his older brother Sam has joined the Patriots. In the following excerpt, Tim and Sam talk with Betsy Read about the possibility of war between the Americans and the British.*

Tim Meeker's family is divided by the Revolutionary War.

"Is your grandfather going to fight the Lobsterbacks [Redcoats]?"

"I don't think so," Betsy said. "He's too old. He said he would probably resign his **commission**[1] to some younger man. Anyway he doesn't think we ought to fight unless we really have to. He says there ought to be some way of working it out with the King and Parliament without having to fight."

"There isn't any way to work it out," Sam said. "The British government is determined to keep us their slaves. We're going to fight."

"A lot of people aren't going to fight," I said.

"Around here they aren't. This is Tory country. Father, Mr. Beach, the Lyons, the Couches—most of them in our church are Tories. And they think it's the same everywhere, but it isn't. Down in New Haven they're ready to fight, and Windham's already marched their militia to Boston." He was being **scornful**.[2] Sam always got scornful when other people disagreed with him, because he always thought he was right, although to be honest, a lot of the time he was right, because of being so smart. But still it was hard for me to think that Father was wrong.

"Sam, Father says for most people it isn't being free, it's only a few **pence**[3] in taxes."

"That's Father for you, it's the money that counts. There are principles involved, Tim. Either you live up to your principles or you don't and maybe you have to take a chance on getting killed."

"Who wants to get killed?"

"Nobody *wants* to get killed," Sam said. "But you should be willing to die for your principles."

"That's right," Betsy said.

"But Betsy, you don't have to take a chance on getting killed," I said.

"I'd fight if I could," she said.

I hated arguing about it. "Well maybe the King will change his mind and get the Lobsterbacks out."

Sam shook his head. "He won't. He thinks he's going to teach us a lesson. But we're going to teach him one. We already taught him one at Lexington."

"That's what I mean," I said. "Maybe he'll give up now."

Betsy shook her head. "He won't. Not according to my father."

Everybody was quiet for a minute. Then Sam said, "There's going to be war. Which side are you going to be on?"

I couldn't answer. . . .

[1] **commission:** rank [2] **scornful:** insulting [3] **pence:** pennies

Understanding What You Read

1. **Literature and History** Why does Sam believe the colonists should fight the British?
2. **Literature and You** Why do you think Tim cannot say which side he will be on? Which side would you choose?

Section 2

Declaring Independence

Read to Discover

1. How did Thomas Paine's *Common Sense* influence the colonies?
2. What were the main ideas stated in the Declaration of Independence?
3. How did Americans react to the Declaration of Independence?

Define

- unalienable rights

Identify

- *Common Sense*
- Thomas Paine
- Thomas Jefferson
- Declaration of Independence
- Patriots
- Loyalists
- Abigail Adams

Why It Matters Today

The Declaration of Independence established the basic principles of our individual freedoms. Use CNNfyi.com or other **current events** sources to find an example of how we experience these freedoms today. Record your findings in your journal.

Thomas Paine became well known throughout the colonies for his political pamphlet Common Sense.

The Story Continues

On January 9, 1776, a 47-page pamphlet hit the streets of Philadelphia. The author was 38-year-old Thomas Paine, a self-educated British Quaker. About two years before, Paine had met Benjamin Franklin in London and impressed the colonist with his sharp mind. Franklin had helped Paine come to Philadelphia, where Paine became the editor of the *Pennsylvania Magazine.* Then in 1776 Paine produced a work that changed the course of American history.

Paine's *Common Sense*

In his pamphlet ***Common Sense***, **Thomas Paine** argued for breaking away from Great Britain. News of the work spread through the thirteen colonies, and it eventually sold some 500,000 copies. *Common Sense* became popular because of its message and style. Most pamphlets of the time were written by lawyers in a style that only well-educated people could understand. Paine wrote as a common person speaking to common people, which allowed him to reach a wider audience.

Paine stated in *Common Sense* that the system of monarchy in countries such as Britain was not fair. He said that the people, not kings and queens, should make the laws. "A government of our own is our natural right," he wrote. At a time when monarchs ruled most countries of the world, this was a fairly new idea. Paine said that the colonies should demand their independence.

Paine's *Common Sense* helped change the way many colonists viewed Britain. With war now under way, the idea of independence gained more and more supporters.

✔ **Reading Check:** **Identifying Points of View** How did many colonists react to the ideas Thomas Paine expressed in *Common Sense*?

Declaring Independence

Many colonial leaders agreed with Paine that the colonies should be free. In June 1776 the Second Continental Congress created a committee to write a document declaring the colonies' independence. The committee members were John Adams, Benjamin Franklin, **Thomas Jefferson**, Robert R. Livingston, and Roger Sherman. Jefferson was the main author of the document.

The **Declaration of Independence** expresses three main ideas. First, Jefferson argued that all men possess **unalienable rights.** He stated that these basic rights include "life, liberty, and the pursuit of happiness." The writings of Enlightenment philosophers such as John Locke inspired the idea of unalienable rights.

Jefferson's second point was that King George III had violated the colonists' rights. Like Thomas Paine, he charged the king with passing unfair laws and interfering with colonial self-government. He also accused the king of taxing colonists without their consent. In addition, the presence of a large British army in the colonies upset Jefferson.

". . . life, liberty, and the pursuit of happiness."

Interpreting the Visual Record

Independence *Delegate Thomas Jefferson and the other members of his committee present the Declaration of Independence before the Second Continental Congress.* ***Who are some of the colonial leaders shown in this image?***

Third, Jefferson argued that the colonies had the right to break away from Great Britain. Jefferson was influenced by the Enlightenment idea of the social contract, which states that rulers should protect the rights of their citizens. In exchange, the people agree to be governed. Jefferson said that because King George III had broken the social contract, the colonists need no longer obey him.

July 4, 1776
The United States of America is formed.

On July 4, 1776, the Continental Congress approved the Declaration of Independence. This act broke all ties to the British Crown. The United States of America was born.

✔ Reading Check: **Finding the Main Idea** What are the key ideas stated by Jefferson in 1776 in the Declaration of Independence?

Choosing Sides

Colonists who chose to fight for independence became known as **Patriots**. Those who remained loyal to Great Britain were called **Loyalists** or Tories. Many other colonists remained neutral, choosing neither side. People on both sides often felt very strongly about their views. In March 1775, before the fighting had even started, Patriot Patrick Henry spoke before the Virginia House of Burgesses.

"Is life so dear or peace so sweet as to be purchased at the price of chains and slavery? Forbid it, Almighty God! I know not what course others may take; but as for me, give me liberty, or give me death!"

—Patrick Henry, quoted in *The Annals of America*

Interpreting the Visual Record

Rebellion *Patriots pull down a statue of King George III in New York.* ***How do you think these colonists feel about King George and Great Britain?***

Once the Declaration of Independence was signed, Loyalists became targets of abuse by Patriots. It is estimated that more than 100,000 Loyalists fled the colonies during the Revolution. Most of them went to Canada.

Many Loyalists shared the feelings of Samuel Curwen of Massachusetts. He was a merchant who believed that the colonies did not need independence. To Curwen, British rule was the best way to maintain peace and prosperity in the colonies. He refused to blame the fighting at Lexington and Concord entirely on the British. Patriot neighbors called him a Tory. Curwen had to flee his home to escape "the looks, words, and actions of the mad rabble [masses]."

The divisions caused by the war also affected some key Patriot leaders. For example, Thomas Fairfax, one of George Washington's closest friends, fled to Britain because he was a Loyalist. Even the great Patriot Benjamin Franklin had a Loyalist son, William.

✔ Reading Check: **Identifying Points of View** Why did some colonists remain Loyalists?

Other Reactions to the Declaration

Some people pointed out that the Declaration ignored many colonists. Although many women were Patriots, the Declaration did not address their rights. The phrase "all men are created equal" failed to mention women at all. This issue worried **Abigail Adams**, the wife of John Adams. In a letter she asked her husband to protect the rights of women.

> **"In the new code of Laws which I suppose it will be necessary for you to make I desire you would Remember the Ladies. . . . If particular care and attention is not paid to the Ladies we . . . will not hold ourselves bound by any Laws in which we have no voice, or Representation."**
>
> —Abigail Adams, quoted in *Notable American Women*

In addition, the Declaration did not recognize the rights of enslaved African Americans. In July 1776 slavery was legal in all the colonies. In his first draft of the Declaration, Thomas Jefferson—a slaveholder himself—had included a passage that attacked the slave trade. However, southern delegates insisted that the passage be removed.

The Revolution raised questions about whether slavery should exist in a land that valued liberty. Some Patriots had compared living under British rule to living as slaves. These writers could not ignore the difference between the ideals of liberty and the practice of slavery. Some colonists wanted the principle "all men are created equal" to apply to all people. Massachusetts abolished slavery in 1783, and by 1784 the rest of New England also had taken steps to end slavery. Even so, the conflict over slavery continued long after the Revolutionary War had ended.

✔ **Reading Check: Finding the Main Idea** What groups felt ignored by the Declaration of Independence?

BIOGRAPHY

Abigail Adams

(1744–1818)

Abigail Adams was born in Massachusetts in 1744. Educated at home by her parents, she developed a great love of reading and writing. She married John Adams in 1764, and they raised five children. Abigail Adams ran most of the family's businesses and advised her husband on political issues. Many of her letters to family and friends were saved long after her death in 1818. Some historians have called her "one of the great letter writers of all time." **How have historians been able to learn about the life of Abigail Adams?**

Section 2 Review

Homework Practice Online

keyword: SC3 HP6

1. **Define** and explain:
   - unalienable rights
2. **Identify** and explain:
   - *Common Sense*
   - Thomas Paine
   - Thomas Jefferson
   - Declaration of Independence
   - Patriots
   - Loyalists
   - Abigail Adams
3. **Comparing** Copy the graphic organizer below. Use it to compare the arguments that colonists offered for and against independence, including Thomas Jefferson's arguments in the Declaration of Independence.

Arguments for Independence		Arguments against Independence
	vs.	

4. **Finding the Main Idea**
   a. Why did colonists find Thomas Paine's arguments in *Common Sense* so persuasive?
   b. Why was 1776 significant for the colonies, and what major events took place that year?
5. **Writing and Critical Thinking**
   Identifying Points of View Imagine that you are living in the colonies in 1776. Write an essay explaining how colonists reacted to the Declaration of Independence.
   Consider the following:
   - the views of Loyalists and Patriots
   - the contributions of women to society
   - the meaning of the phrase "all men are created equal"

1776

THE DECLARATION of INDEPENDENCE

Exploring the Document

Thomas Jefferson wrote the first draft of the Declaration in a little more than two weeks. **How is the Declaration's idea about why governments are formed still important to our country today?**

In Congress, July 4, 1776
The unanimous Declaration of the thirteen united States of America,

When in the Course of human events, it becomes necessary for one people to dissolve the political bands which have connected them with another, and to assume among the Powers of the earth, the separate and equal station to which the Laws of Nature and of Nature's God entitle them, a decent respect to the opinions of mankind requires that they should declare the causes which impel[1] them to the separation.

[1] **impel:** force

Natural Rights

We hold these truths to be self-evident, that all men are created equal, that they are **endowed**[2] by their Creator with certain unalienable Rights, that among these are Life, Liberty, and the pursuit of Happiness. That to secure these rights, Governments are instituted among Men, deriving their just powers from the consent of the governed,

That whenever any Form of Government becomes destructive of these ends, it is the Right of the People to alter or to abolish it, and to institute new Government, laying its foundation on such principles and organizing its powers in such form, as to them shall seem most likely to effect their Safety and Happiness. Prudence, indeed, will dictate that Governments long established should not be changed for light and transient causes; and accordingly all experience hath shown, that mankind are more disposed to suffer, while evils are sufferable, than to right themselves by abolishing the forms to which they are accustomed. But when a long train of abuses and **usurpations**,[3] pursuing invariably the same Object **evinces**[4] a design to reduce them under absolute **Despotism**,[5] it is their right, it is their duty, to throw off such Government, and to provide new Guards for their future security.—

[2] **endowed:** provided

[3] **usurpations:** wrongful seizures of power

[4] **evinces:** clearly displays

[5] **despotism:** unlimited power

LEFT: *Thomas Jefferson*

Colonists' Complaints against the King

Such has been the patient sufferance of these Colonies; and such is now the necessity which constrains them to alter their former Systems of Government. The history of the present King of Great Britain is a history of repeated injuries and usurpations, all having in direct object the establishment of an absolute **Tyranny**[6] over these States. To prove this, let Facts be submitted to a **candid**[7] world.

He has refused his Assent to Laws, the most wholesome and necessary for the public good.

He has forbidden his Governors to pass Laws of immediate and pressing importance, unless suspended in their operation till his Assent should be obtained; and when so suspended, he has utterly neglected to attend to them.

He has refused to pass other Laws for the accommodation of large districts of people, unless those people would **relinquish**[8] the right of Representation in the Legislature, a right **inestimable**[9] to them and **formidable**[10] to tyrants only.

He has called together legislative bodies at places unusual, uncomfortable, and distant from the depository of their Public Records, for the sole purpose of fatiguing them into compliance with his measures.

He has dissolved Representative Houses repeatedly, for opposing with manly firmness his invasions on the rights of the people.

He has refused for a long time, after such dissolutions, to cause others to be elected; whereby the Legislative Powers, incapable of **Annihilation**,[11] have returned to the People at large for their exercise; the State remaining in the mean time exposed to all the dangers of invasion from without, and **convulsions**[12] within.

He has endeavored to prevent the population of these States; for that purpose obstructing the Laws of **Naturalization of Foreigners**;[13] refusing to pass others to encourage their migration hither, and raising the conditions of new **Appropriations of Lands**.[14]

He has obstructed the Administration of Justice, by refusing his Assent to Laws for establishing Judiciary Powers.

He has made Judges dependent on his Will alone, for the **tenure**[15] of their offices, and the amount and payment of their salaries.

He has erected **a multitude of**[16] New Offices, and sent hither swarms of Officers to harass our people, and eat out their substance.

He has kept among us, in times of peace, Standing Armies without the Consent of our legislature.

He has affected to render the Military independent of and superior to the Civil Power.

He has combined with others to subject us to a jurisdiction foreign to our constitution, and unacknowledged by our laws; giving his Assent to their Acts of pretended legislation:

[6]**tyranny:** oppressive power exerted by a government or ruler

[7]**candid:** fair

Exploring the Document

Here the Declaration lists the charges that the colonists had against King George III. **How might the language and content of the list appeal to people's emotions?**

[8]**relinquish:** release, yield

[9]**inestimable:** priceless

[10]**formidable:** causing dread

[11]**annihilation:** destruction

[12]**convulsions:** violent disturbances

[13]**naturalization of foreigners:** the process by which foreign-born persons become citizens

[14]**appropriations of land:** setting aside land for settlement

[15]**tenure:** term

[16]**a multitude of:** many

[17]**quartering:** lodging, housing

Exploring the Document

Colonists had been angry over British tax policies since just after the French and Indian War. **Why were the colonists protesting British tax policies?**

[18]**arbitrary:** not based on law

[19]**render:** make

[20]**abdicated:** given up

[21]**foreign mercenaries:** soldiers hired to fight for a country not their own

[22]**perfidy:** violation of trust

[23]**insurrections:** rebellions

[24]**petitioned for redress:** asked formally for a correction of wrongs

[25]**unwarrantable jurisdiction:** unjustified authority

[26]**magnanimity:** generous spirit

[27]**conjured:** urgently called upon

[28]**consanguinity:** common ancestry

[29]**acquiesce:** consent to

For **quartering**[17] large bodies of armed troops among us:

For protecting them, by a mock Trial, from Punishment for any Murders which they should commit on the Inhabitants of these States:

For cutting off our Trade with all parts of the world:

For imposing taxes on us without our Consent:

For depriving us in many cases, of the benefits of Trial by Jury:

For transporting us beyond Seas to be tried for pretended offences:

For abolishing the free System of English Laws in a neighboring Province, establishing therein an **Arbitrary**[18] government, and enlarging its Boundaries so as to **render**[19] it at once an example and fit instrument for introducing the same absolute rule into these Colonies:

For taking away our Charters, abolishing our most valuable Laws, and altering fundamentally the Forms of our Governments:

For suspending our own Legislature, and declaring themselves invested with Power to legislate for us in all cases whatsoever.

He has **abdicated**[20] Government here, by declaring us out of his Protection and waging War against us.

He has plundered our seas, ravaged our Coasts, burnt our towns, and destroyed the lives of our people.

He is at this time transporting large armies of **foreign mercenaries**[21] to complete the works of death, desolation and tyranny, already begun with circumstances of Cruelty & **perfidy**[22] scarcely paralleled in the most barbarous ages, and totally unworthy the Head of a civilized nation.

He has constrained our fellow Citizens taken Captive on the high Seas to bear Arms against their Country, to become the executioners of their friends and Brethren, or to fall themselves by their Hands.

He has excited domestic **insurrections**[23] amongst us, and has endeavored to bring on the inhabitants of our frontiers, the merciless Indian Savages, whose known rule of warfare, is an undistinguished destruction of all ages, sexes and conditions.

In every stage of these Oppressions We have **Petitioned for Redress**[24] in the most humble terms: Our repeated Petitions have been answered only by repeated injury. A Prince, whose character is thus marked by every act which may define a Tyrant, is unfit to be the ruler of a free People.

Nor have We been wanting in attention to our British brethren. We have warned them from time to time of attempts by their legislature to extend an **unwarrantable jurisdiction**[25] over us. We have reminded them of the circumstances of our emigration and settlement here. We have appealed to their native justice and **magnanimity**,[26] and we have **conjured**[27] them by the ties of our common kindred to disavow these usurpations, which, would inevitably interrupt our connections and correspondence. They too have been deaf to the voice of justice and of **consanguinity**.[28] We must, therefore, **acquiesce**[29] in the necessity, which denounces our Separation, and hold them, as we hold the rest of mankind, Enemies in War, in Peace Friends.

An Independent and United Nation

We, therefore, the Representatives of the united States of America, in General Congress, Assembled, appealing to the Supreme Judge of the world for the **rectitude**[30] of our intentions, do, in the Name, and by Authority of the good People of these Colonies, solemnly publish and declare, That these United Colonies are, and of Right ought to be Free and Independent States; that they are Absolved from all Allegiance to the British Crown, and that all political connection between them and the State of Great Britain, is and ought to be totally dissolved; and that as Free and Independent States, they have full Power to levy War, conclude Peace, contract Alliances, establish Commerce, and to do all other Acts and Things which Independent States may of right do. And for the support of this Declaration, with a firm reliance on the Protection of Divine Providence, we mutually pledge to each other our Lives, our Fortunes and our sacred Honor.

John Hancock
President of Massachusetts

GEORGIA
Button Gwinnett
Lyman Hall
George Walton

NORTH CAROLINA
William Hooper
Joseph Hewes
John Penn

SOUTH CAROLINA
Edward Rutledge
Thomas Heyward, Jr.
Thomas Lynch, Jr.
Arthur Middleton

MARYLAND
Samuel Chase
William Paca
Thomas Stone
Charles Carroll of Carrollton

VIRGINIA
George Wythe
Richard Henry Lee
Thomas Jefferson
Benjamin Harrison
Thomas Nelson, Jr.
Francis Lightfoot Lee
Carter Braxton

PENNSYLVANIA
Robert Morris
Benjamin Rush
Benjamin Franklin
John Morton
George Clymer
James Smith
George Taylor
James Wilson
George Ross

DELAWARE
Caesar Rodney
George Read
Thomas McKean

NEW YORK
William Floyd
Philip Livingston
Francis Lewis
Lewis Morris

NEW JERSEY
Richard Stockton
John Witherspoon
Francis Hopkinson
John Hart
Abraham Clark

NEW HAMPSHIRE
Josiah Bartlett
William Whipple
Matthew Thorton

MASSACHUSETTS
Samuel Adams
John Adams
Robert Treat Paine
Elbridge Gerry

RHODE ISLAND
Stephen Hopkins
William Ellery

CONNECTICUT
Roger Sherman
Samuel Huntington
William Williams
Oliver Wolcott

[30] **rectitude:** rightness

Exploring the Document

On July 4, 1776, Congress adopted the final draft of the Declaration of Independence. A formal copy written on parchment paper was signed on August 2, 1776. **From whom did the Declaration's signers receive their authority to declare independence in 1776?**

Exploring the Document

The following is part of a passage that the Congress removed from Jefferson's original draft: "He has waged cruel war against human nature itself, violating its most sacred rights of life and liberty in the persons of a distant people who never offended him, captivating and carrying them into slavery in another hemisphere, or to incur miserable death in their transportation thither." **Why do you think the Congress deleted this passage?**

Section 3

Dark Hours for the Revolution

Read to Discover

1. What were the Patriots' advantages and disadvantages at the beginning of the Revolutionary War?
2. How did different groups contribute to the war effort?
3. What problems did the Patriots face in Canada and New York?

Define

- mercenaries

Identify

- Lord Dunmore's Proclamation
- Thayendanegea
- Molly Pitcher
- William Howe

Why it Matters Today

When the colonies rebelled against Britain, they did not have a navy and a professional army. Today U.S. leaders consider it vital to have a well-equipped and prepared military. Use CNNfyi.com or other **current events** sources to learn where U.S. military forces are serving today. Record your findings in your journal.

COURTESY OF MOUNT VERNON LADIES' ASSOCIATION

During the winters, Martha Washington joined her husband wherever his army was camped.

The Story Continues

General George Washington faced a challenging task when he took command of the Continental Army. The Patriots were up against a mighty enemy in Britain. Washington wrote to his wife, Martha, that he did not know if he could build a strong enough army. "I shall hope that my undertaking is designed to answer some good purpose," he said. He did not know what to expect when he led his men into the field.

Comparing Strengths and Weaknesses

At the beginning of the war, the British seemed much stronger than the Patriots. Great Britain had more money and resources than the colonies. Britain also had a powerful military. Its navy was the largest in the world. British soldiers were mostly well-trained professionals. In contrast, when the war began, the colonists had no navy at all. The colonial army was made up of poorly trained local militias. Few of these groups had ever fought together.

However, the colonists did have some advantages. Many Americans supported the Revolution. As a result, the British army often had to deal with hostile citizens. The British also had to ship their supplies across the Atlantic Ocean. This process slowed down their war effort. Finally, the Patriots were fighting for a cause in which they believed. On the other hand, some British soldiers were **mercenaries**, or hired foreign soldiers.

✔ **Reading Check: Categorizing** What advantages and disadvantages did the Patriots have when the war began?

Colonial soldiers often used horns such as this one to store their gunpowder.

A Call to Arms

General Washington's first task was to organize and raise more troops for the Continental Army. During the course of the war, more than 230,000 soldiers served in the Continental Army. Another 145,000 Americans joined local militias. These volunteers came from many backgrounds. Many were teenagers, such as 14-year-old James Forten, who served in the Continental Navy. Some officers had fought in the French and Indian War, but few of the volunteers had combat experience. General Charles Lee hoped that their courage would be enough.

"They are admirable—young, stout, healthy, zealous [eager], good-humored and sober [serious]. . . . I really believe a very little time and pains would render [make] 'em the most invincible [unbeatable] army that have appeared."

—General Charles Lee, quoted in *Voices of 1776*, by Richard Wheeler

One question facing Washington was whether to recruit African Americans. Many African Americans, including some slaves, were already serving in local militias. African Americans like Peter Salem and Salem Poor had already fought in battles. But many southerners did not want the American forces to include black soldiers. Washington soon banned African Americans from serving in the army.

The British reacted quickly. Lord Dunmore, Virginia's governor, issued a proclamation on November 7, 1775. **Lord Dunmore's Proclamation** promised freedom to any slave who fought for the British. Thousands of slaves agreed. In response, the Continental Army began allowing free African Americans to enlist, and eventually some 5,000 joined.

Other Sources of Help

American Indian groups fought on both sides during the war. The British had many Indian allies. One of Great Britain's key allies was Mohawk leader **Thayendanegea** (thah-yuhn-dah-ne-GAY-uh), also known as Joseph Brant. He persuaded many of the Iroquois to support the British. However, the Patriots worked hard just to keep American Indians neutral. This effort was very important on the frontier.

CONNECTING TO SCIENCE AND TECHNOLOGY

The Long Rifle

Many Patriots from the frontier used a gun known as the long rifle or Kentucky rifle. A rifle is a type of gun with a grooved barrel. The grooves spin the ball, or bullet, as it is shot. Compared to a musket, a long rifle can shoot a ball farther and with greater accuracy. However, soldiers could fire and reload muskets faster than rifles. Rifles also lacked bayonets for use in hand-to-hand combat.

General Washington used rifle units for special missions such as sharpshooting and scouting. These groups impressed the British with their accuracy at long range. By the end of the war, the long rifle was well known. Over time, it became one of the most common weapons in North America. **How were rifles different from muskets?**

THE GRANGER COLLECTION, NEW YORK

This painting shows Molly Pitcher fighting alongside other Patriots at the Battle of Monmouth.

Many women also helped the Patriot cause. Women often ran farms and businesses while men served as soldiers. Other women helped support the army by raising money for supplies or joining sewing groups to make uniforms.

Analyzing Primary Sources

Summarizing How are women supporting the war effort according to this speaker?

> **"At every house Women and children [are] making Cartridges, running Bullets . . . and at the same time animating [encouraging] their Husbands and Sons to fight."**
>
> —Anonymous, quoted in *Born for Liberty,* by Sara M. Evans

Some women served as messengers, nurses, or spies. A few women, such as Deborah Sampson, even disguised themselves as men to fight in the war. The woman who perhaps became best known for her wartime service was Mary Ludwig Hays. She earned the nickname **Molly Pitcher** by bringing water to thirsty Patriot troops. When her husband was wounded in a 1778 battle, she quickly took his place loading cannons.

✔ **Reading Check: Summarizing** How did different groups living in the colonies contribute to the war effort?

British Victories

Many Patriot leaders favored fighting a defensive war. This would help the army's limited supplies last longer. However, other, more aggressive leaders wanted to make British-controlled Canada the "fourteenth colony." In November 1775, Patriot troops led by General Richard Montgomery took the town of St. John's, Canada. Shortly afterward Montgomery captured the nearby town of Montreal.

The next major target was the well-defended city of Quebec. General Benedict Arnold led his troops on a long march north through what is now Maine. When Arnold's forces reached Quebec, he waited for Montgomery's troops to arrive. Together, the commanders planned their attack. The American troops were cold and far from home. Many of the soldiers also had enlistments that would soon end. This meant that the Patriots had to act quickly, but the Americans had no cannons to knock down Quebec's walls. Arnold and Montgomery decided to wait for a snowstorm. They hoped the storm would provide cover while the Patriots got close to the city's defenses.

During a fierce blizzard on New Year's Eve, the Patriots attacked Quebec. The Americans suffered a crushing defeat. General Montgomery was killed early in the battle. More than half of the American troops were captured, killed, or wounded. Patriots' hopes of taking Canada soon faded.

Soldiers in the Continental Army (left) often wore the tricornered hat shown here.

British soldiers (below) were nicknamed Redcoats because of their uniforms.

COLLECTION OF THE NEW YORK HISTORICAL SOCIETY

Farther south, General Washington had moved his troops to New York. In early July 1776, Patriots spotted a large fleet of British ships nearing New York Bay. Led by General **William Howe**, the British drove the Continental Army off of Long Island. Washington's troops retreated to Manhattan Island. The British force was much larger and better equipped than that of the Patriots. Washington had to use all his leadership skills just to save his outnumbered army. In a series of battles, Howe forced the Continental Army to keep retreating. The Redcoats captured many Patriots as well as valuable supplies. After several months they pushed Washington out of New York. Howe's revenge for his defeat at Boston was complete.

✔ **Reading Check: Contrasting** Describe the different problems faced by the Continental Army in Canada and New York.

Section 3 Review

go.hrw.com Homework Practice Online
keyword: SC3 HP6

1 Define and explain:
- mercenaries

2 Identify and explain:
- Lord Dunmore's Proclamation
- Thayendanegea
- Molly Pitcher
- William Howe

3 Comparing Copy the chart below. Use it to compare the military advantages of the British and the Patriots.

British Advantages	Patriots' Advantages

4 Finding the Main Idea

a. Explain the roles that some young white men, African Americans, American Indians, and women played in supporting the Patriots during the American Revolution.

b. Why did the American invasion of Canada fail while the British attack on New York succeeded?

5 Writing and Critical Thinking

Analyzing Information Imagine that you are a British officer on the frontier. Write a brief report to your commander explaining why you think that many American Indians will side with the British.

Consider the following:
- which side Indian leaders think will win the war
- conflicts on the frontier
- alliances between American Indians and the British

Section 4

The Patriots Gain New Hope

Read to Discover

1. What were Washington's strategies at Trenton and Princeton?
2. Why was the Battle of Saratoga a turning point in the war?
3. How did foreign nations and individuals aid the Patriots?
4. How did the Patriots carry out the naval war?

Identify

- Battle of Trenton
- Battle of Princeton
- John Burgoyne
- Battle of Brandywine Creek
- Battle of Saratoga
- Bernardo de Gálvez
- Marquis de Lafayette
- Friedrich von Steuben
- John Paul Jones

Why It Matters Today

Foreign allies helped the Patriots fight the Revolutionary War. The United States still has close alliances with many countries. Use CNNfyi.com or other **current events** sources to learn more about a nation that is a U.S. ally today. Record your findings in your journal.

The Story Continues

In November 1776 General Howe took the last Patriot fort on Manhattan Island. Patriot Alexander Graydon was among those captured. He later recalled a British officer warning the prisoners, "Young men, ye should never fight against your king!" Graydon and other Patriots like him survived their capture. But they began to fear that the British were getting close to complete victory in the war.

General Howe was confident that the British would win the war quickly.

Victory in New Jersey

General Howe sent troops to take New Jersey in November 1776. After the British victories in Canada and New York, Howe thought the war would be over soon. So he gave his troops a rest and settled in New York City for the winter. Howe left New Jersey in the hands of Hessians. These were German mercenaries, many from the state of Hesse, hired to fight for the British.

Howe's delay allowed Washington to gather reinforcements. The Patriots were still in trouble, however. Writer Thomas Paine described the difficult situation in the first of his *Crisis* papers. "These are the times that try men's souls," he wrote. Paine urged the Patriots to stay loyal to their cause.

CONNECTING TO

THE ARTS

Crossing the Delaware

George Washington and his troops crossed the partially frozen Delaware River on the night of December 25, 1776. This daring act led to a key Patriot victory. German-American artist Emanuel Leutze created this famous painting of the event in 1851. *Washington Crossing the Delaware* now hangs in the Metropolitan Museum of Art in New York City. In 1999 Leutze's painting was used as the basis for the image on the back of the New Jersey state quarter. **What feelings do you think Leutze wanted to inspire with this painting?**

Washington decided to attack the Hessians at Trenton, New Jersey. He believed he could take them by surprise while they celebrated the holiday. On Christmas night in 1776, Washington and 2,400 soldiers silently crossed the icy Delaware River. The troops were short on supplies—many had no shoes. But, they were ready to fight. After landing early on the morning of December 26, the Patriots marched to Trenton. The **Battle of Trenton** lasted less than an hour. The Patriot forces captured more than 900 Hessians with just five American casualties. The impressive victory boosted the Patriots' spirits.

Washington was not satisfied with only one victory. As British general Charles Cornwallis rushed to stop him, Washington marched to the town of Princeton, northeast of Trenton. Washington planned another surprise for the enemy. On the night of January 2, the Patriots kept their campfires burning for the British to see. Most of the Patriots then left camp under cover of darkness and circled behind the British troops. The Patriots attacked the next morning. An 85-year-old civilian described the battle.

History Makers Speak

"The battle was plainly seen from our door . . . and the guns went off so quick and many together that they could not be numbered. We presently went down into the cellar to keep out of the way of the shot. There was a neighbor woman down in the cellar with us that was so affrighted [frightened]. . . . Almost as soon as the firing was over, our house was filled and surrounded with General Washington's men."

—Anonymous, quoted in *Voices of 1776,* by Richard Wheeler

The hard-fought **Battle of Princeton** ended in another victory for the Patriots. As he watched the Redcoats flee, Washington cheered, "It is a fine fox chase, my boys!"

✔ **Reading Check: Summarizing** Explain General Washington's strategy at Trenton and Princeton.

THE GRANGER COLLECTION, NEW YORK

Interpreting the Visual Record

Patriot victory *British general John Burgoyne surrenders his army to American Patriot general Horatio Gates at Saratoga, New York, on October 17, 1777.* ***What is Burgoyne handing over to the Americans?***

Turning Point at Saratoga

The defeats at Trenton and Princeton embarrassed the British. In the spring of 1777, they decided to strike back. They planned to cut New England off from the rest of the colonies. The plan called for British troops in Canada to take back Fort Ticonderoga. General **John Burgoyne** would lead this effort. He would then march south. Meanwhile, a second force would march east from Lake Ontario. Finally, General Howe's troops in New York City would move north. All three groups would come together at Albany, New York.

Burgoyne recaptured Fort Ticonderoga by early July. However, his route across New York cut through thick forests. Colonists chopped down large trees across his path to slow his progress. Another problem with the plan soon arose. General Howe decided to attack Philadelphia before marching to Albany. Washington raced to stop Howe, and the two sides met at the **Battle of Brandywine Creek**. On September 11, 1777, Howe's forces won a convincing victory. The Patriots suffered almost twice as many casualties as the British. Howe probably could have crushed the Continental Army completely, but he allowed many soldiers to escape.

Burgoyne did not know that Howe and the force from western Canada were both late. As a result, when Burgoyne neared Albany he found his army badly outnumbered by Patriot troops. At the **Battle of Saratoga** Burgoyne suffered a major defeat. Patriot troops led by General Horatio Gates drove back a British attack. American officer Benedict Arnold then led a bold charge that forced the British to retreat. Burgoyne soon found himself surrounded. On October 17, 1777, he surrendered to General Gates. The Patriots captured Burgoyne's entire army.

The victory at Saratoga was the greatest win yet for the American forces. It greatly boosted morale and led to increased foreign support for the Patriots. Patriot James Thacher wrote, "This event will make one of the most brilliant pages of American history."

✔ **Reading Check: Finding the Main Idea** Why was the Battle of Saratoga a turning point in the war for the Patriots?

Research on the ROM

Free Find:
Battle of Saratoga
After reading about the Battle of Saratoga on the **Holt Researcher CD–ROM**, create a fictional account of how the British might have won the battle.

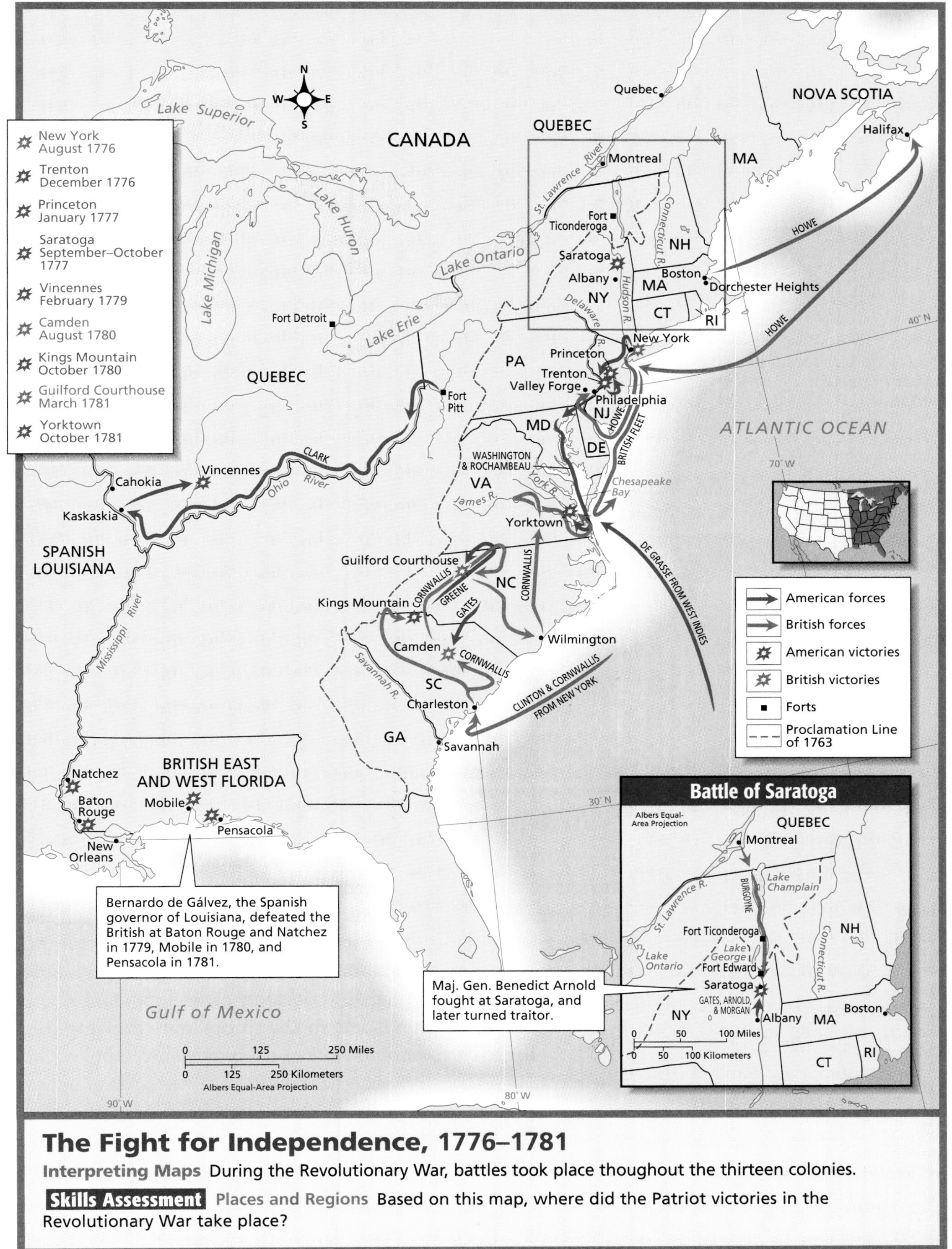

The Fight for Independence, 1776–1781

Interpreting Maps During the Revolutionary War, battles took place thoughout the thirteen colonies.

Skills Assessment **Places and Regions** Based on this map, where did the Patriot victories in the Revolutionary War take place?

The Marquis de Lafayette was an important ally of the Patriots.

Foreign Allies

France and Spain, who were enemies of Great Britain, had been secretly aiding the Patriots. In 1776 the Patriots had sent several delegates to France, including Benjamin Franklin. Franklin worked hard to increase French support for the Patriot cause. The victory at Saratoga convinced France that America could win the war. In May 1778 the Continental Congress approved an alliance with France that Franklin had helped arrange earlier in the year. Spain joined the war against Britain in 1779. The Spanish provided much of their help to the Patriots on the western frontier. **Bernardo de Gálvez**, the governor of Spanish Louisiana, was a key ally to the Patriots.

Individual foreigners also fought for the Patriots. One of the best-known was the **Marquis de Lafayette**. The wealthy, young Lafayette arrived in America from France in the summer of 1777. He spoke little English and lacked combat experience. However, his belief in the Patriot cause impressed General Washington. Lafayette said that "the welfare of America is closely bound up with the welfare of mankind." In his first battle, at Brandywine Creek, Lafayette was wounded in the leg. During the war he continued to aid the Patriots, even giving some $200,000 of his own money to support the Revolution.

Officers from countries not involved in the war also aided the Patriots. Tadeusz Kościuszko (kawsh-CHOOSH-kaw) and Kazimierz Pulaski came to America from Poland. Kościuszko brought army engineering skills to the war effort, and Pulaski helped train cavalry units.

✔ **Reading Check: Summarizing** Explain how foreign countries and individuals like the Marquis de Lafayette aided the Patriot war effort.

GLOBAL CONNECTIONS

THE HISTORIC NEW ORLEANS COLLECTION, COLOR ADDED

Bernardo de Gálvez

Bernardo de Gálvez, the governor of Spanish Louisiana, was an important ally to the Patriots. Gálvez allowed the Americans to use the Spanish port of New Orleans. Gálvez also attacked British forts along the Mississippi River and in Florida. These actions helped Patriots in the West. His efforts also kept Spain in command of the Gulf of Mexico. The city of Galveston in present-day Texas was named in his honor. **In what ways did Gálvez aid the Patriot cause?**

Winter at Valley Forge

The entry of France and Spain into the war came at a critical time for the Patriots because the Continental Army was running very low on supplies. In December 1777, Washington settled his troops at Valley Forge, Pennsylvania. There they suffered shortages of food and clothing. During the harsh winter of 1777–78, more than one fifth of the soldiers died of disease and malnutrition.

By the end of the winter, some of the troops were growing frustrated. They chanted "No pay, no clothes, no provisions [supplies]." In February 1778 a veteran Prussian army officer came to Washington's aid. Baron **Friedrich von Steuben** spoke no English. He led with a combination of respect and fear, teaching the American troops basic military skills. Von Steuben's drills worked. Soon he turned the Continental Army into a well-trained group of soldiers.

✔ **Reading Check: Finding the Main Idea** What challenges did the Continental Army face at Valley Forge?

THE GRANGER COLLECTION, NEW YORK

Daily Life

Valley Forge Soldiers in the Continental Army had to deal with many shortages throughout the Revolutionary War. They went for long periods of time without pay and often lacked needed supplies. Some of the most difficult conditions they faced came during the harsh winter of 1777–78 at Valley Forge, Pennsylvania. Short on food, clothing, and shelter, about 2,500 of Washington's soldiers died in the camp. **How does this picture show the hardships faced by soldiers at Valley Forge?**

The War at Sea

The Americans also faced difficult odds in the war at sea. The Continental Congress had created the Continental Navy and the marines in 1775. However, by February 1776, the navy had only eight fighting ships. This small fleet was no match for the much larger British one. The British navy could easily transport troops and attack American ports.

Instead of fighting large battles, the Patriots tried to attack individual British ships. The Patriots also attacked British supply ports and merchant ships. During the war the British lost hundreds of ships to small American raiding vessels. Many of these raiders were not officially part of the American navy. Their crews fought because they were allowed to sell any British cargo that they captured.

One of the most successful American captains was **John Paul Jones**. Jones was born John Paul in Scotland. He began working on ships at a young age. After accidentally killing the leader of a mutiny, he fled to America and added "Jones" to his name.

When the war broke out, Jones joined the newly created navy. He quickly established himself as a brave and clever sailor, capturing many British supply ships. The French greatly admired Jones. In 1779, French leaders gave him a small fleet of seven vessels to command. He named his flagship *Bonhomme Richard* ("Gentleman Richard") in honor of Benjamin Franklin's *Poor Richard's Almanack*.

One of Jones's most famous victories came against the British warship *Serapis* on September 23, 1779. Early in the battle, the British did heavy damage to the *Bonhomme Richard*. Captain Richard Pearson of the *Serapis* then called out to Jones, "Has your ship struck [surrendered]?" Jones replied, "I have not yet begun to fight!" More than two hours later, the British surrendered. Captain Pearson described the battle.

The Bonhomme Richard *defeated the* Serapis *in a long and bloody battle.*

Ships of the Continental Navy flew this flag during the war.

Analyzing Primary Sources

Drawing Inferences and Conclusions According to the British captain, why did the Americans win the battle?

"Long before the close of the action, it became clearly apparent that the American ship was dominated by a command will . . . and there could be no doubt that the intention of her commander was, if he could not conquer, to sink alongside."

—Captain Richard Pearson, quoted in *Voices of 1776*, by Richard Wheeler

The Continental Navy used fewer than 100 ships during the war. Yet the British navy lost almost 200 ships to the small but effective American naval forces.

✔ **Reading Check: Making Generalizations and Predictions** How did the achievements of John Paul Jones demonstrate the Patriots' naval strategy?

Section 4 Review

go.hrw.com Homework Practice Online
keyword: SC3 HP6

1. **Identify** and explain:
   - Battle of Trenton
   - Battle of Princeton
   - John Burgoyne
   - Battle of Brandywine Creek
   - Battle of Saratoga
   - Bernardo de Gálvez
   - Marquis de Lafayette
   - Friedrich von Steuben
   - John Paul Jones

2. **Summarizing** Copy the graphic organizer below. Use it to explain why the battles at Trenton, Princeton, and Saratoga helped turn the tide for the Patriots in the Revolutionary War.

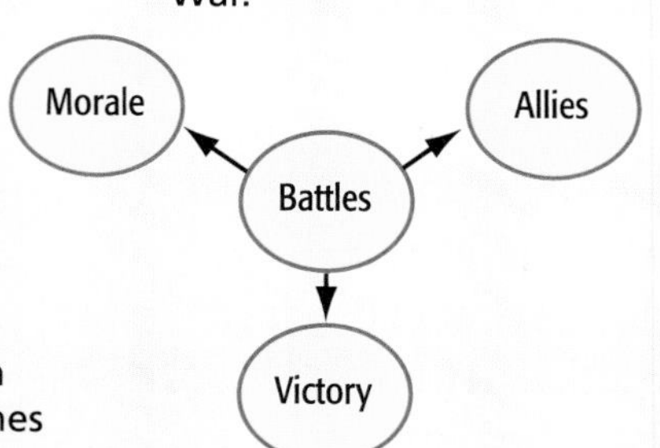

3. **Finding the Main Idea**
   a. What was Washington's strategy for capturing Trenton and Princeton?
   b. Explain how the achievements of John Paul Jones demonstrated the ways in which American captains fought the war at sea.

4. **Writing and Critical Thinking**
   Supporting a Point of View Imagine that you are a foreign officer like the Marquis de Lafayette who has come to assist the Patriots against the British. Write a letter home explaining to a friend how and why you have chosen to help the Patriot cause.
   Consider the following:
   - your military experience
   - your belief in the Patriot cause
   - any economic help you might be able to provide

Section 5

Independence!

Read to Discover

1. How did geography affect the Patriot strategy in the West?
2. How did the war take place in the southern colonies?
3. What events finally ended the war?

Define

- guerrilla warfare

Identify

- George Rogers Clark
- Battle of Vincennes
- Horatio Gates
- Francis Marion
- Comte de Rochambeau
- Battle of Yorktown
- Treaty of Paris of 1783

Why It Matters Today

The United States has grown from a small country to one of the most powerful nations in the world. Use CNNfyi.com or other **current events** sources to find an example that illustrates the strength of the United States today. Record your findings in your journal.

The Story Continues

Eventually the Revolutionary War reached the western frontier. Most of the fighting consisted of small battles between colonists and Britain's Indian allies. This situation changed when a young Virginian named George Rogers Clark stepped forward. Though only 24 years old at the time, Clark was a natural leader. His intelligence and forceful personality gained him the trust of men ranging from frontier fighters to Patriot Patrick Henry. Even the Indian leaders on the frontier viewed Clark with respect.

George Rogers Clark was a key American leader in the West.

 The War in the West

George Rogers Clark had spent years exploring and mapping the frontier, and he had a plan for capturing some small forts and Indian villages. Clark's goal was to build an army while weakening the British. He traveled across the frontier, gathering soldiers from small towns. Clark's first target was the British trading village of Kaskaskia, located along the Mississippi River. Clark thought the small post had great strategic value, which he explained to his superiors.

That's Interesting!

Solar Eclipse Can a solar eclipse affect people's lives? You bet it can. George Rogers Clark was an experienced frontiersman. He knew that the route he had chosen to Kaskaskia would be difficult. But not even he expected the surprise his troops received on June 26, 1778. While crossing river rapids they viewed a total eclipse of the Sun! Clark guided his soldiers safely through the dangerous rapids and told them that the eclipse was a good sign. A week later his troops captured Kaskaskia without firing a shot.

"The remote situation of this town . . . enables [the British] to . . . keep up a strict friendship with the Indians. . . . If it was in our possession it would distress the garrison [soldiers] at Detroit for provisions [supplies], it would fling [throw] the command of the two great rivers [Mississippi and Ohio] into our hands."

—George Rogers Clark, quoted in *Encyclopedia of the American Revolution,* by Mark M. Boatner III

In June 1778 Clark and 175 soldiers set out toward Kaskaskia. To surprise the enemy, they took a difficult route. Clark's troops had to cross river rapids before marching more than 120 miles through thick forests and open prairies. The plan worked. On July 4, 1778, the surprised leaders of Kaskaskia surrendered to Clark without a fight.

News of Clark's achievement spread, and the town of Vincennes on the Wabash River also surrendered to the Patriots. Clark then organized meetings with American Indian leaders on the frontier. He persuaded some of them to be temporarily neutral in the war. During this period the British recaptured Vincennes. Clark's forces returned and took back the town at the **Battle of Vincennes** in late February 1779. Clark was never able to capture Fort Detroit, Britain's major base on the frontier, but his efforts greatly weakened the British army in the West.

✔ **Reading Check: Finding the Main Idea** Explain how geography affected Clark's campaign in the West.

The War in the South

After the American victory at Saratoga, the British focused more of their efforts on the southern colonies. General Henry Clinton led their campaign. The British strategy of freeing slaves who joined them worked well in the South. In Georgia a slave named Quamino Dolly showed the British a secret trail to the port city of Savannah. The British used the trail to surprise the Patriots and capture the city. The next major

THE GRANGER COLLECTION, NEW YORK

Interpreting the Visual Record

Guerrilla war *A band of southern Patriots crosses a river in South Carolina.* ***How does this image show the difficult conditions that Patriots fought under in the South?***

southern city to fall to the British was the port of Charleston, South Carolina. Following months of hard-fought battles, the Patriots there surrendered on May 12, 1780. The British took more than 5,000 prisoners of war.

As the British marched through the South, they destroyed Patriot property. For example, in South Carolina they seized the plantation of indigo developer Eliza Lucas Pinckney. They stole her valuables, destroyed her crops, and killed her farm animals.

One of the most serious Patriot defeats was at Camden, South Carolina. In August 1780, Patriot forces led by **Horatio Gates** tried to drive out the British. The attack was poorly planned, however. Gates had only half as many soldiers as he first thought. In addition, most of his troops were hungry and tired from the march. In an attempt to raise their spirits, Gates fed the troops large amounts of molasses and cornmeal. This effort backfired, however, when the food made many of the troops sick.

When the weakened Patriots faced the British at Camden, a large group of Americans panicked and ran. The Patriot attack quickly fell apart. By the time the fighting ended, the British army had crushed Gates's forces. Only about 700 of approximately 4,000 American troops made it to safety. The Patriots had lost their southern army.

The southern Patriots did not stop fighting. Instead, they switched to **guerrilla warfare**—swift, hit-and-run attacks. No Patriot was better at this style of fighting than **Francis Marion**. He organized Marion's Brigade, a group of guerrilla soldiers that used surprise attacks to destroy British communications and supply lines. Despite great effort by the British, they could not catch Marion and his men. One frustrated British general claimed, "As for this . . . old fox, the devil himself could not catch him." From that point on, Marion was known as the Swamp Fox.

✔ **Reading Check: Sequencing** Describe the events of the war in the southern colonies in their proper order.

Victory at Yorktown

In early 1781 the war was going badly for the Patriots. They were low on money to pay soldiers and buy supplies. The entry of their foreign allies had not ended the war quickly. The army's morale took a blow when Benedict Arnold, one of America's most gifted officers, turned traitor. Arnold felt that the Continental Congress had treated him poorly and that Britain would reward his treachery. In addition to these problems, the British controlled most of the South.

British general Charles Cornwallis wanted to tighten his hold on the southern colonies. He therefore moved his forces into Yorktown, Virginia. Yorktown lies on a peninsula bounded by the Chesapeake Bay and the James and York Rivers. There Cornwallis prepared to attack a small Patriot force led by the Marquis de Lafayette.

CONNECTING TO MATH

Just the Facts

American and British Troops in Battle

Year	American	British
1775	9,173	7,555
1776	47,993	78,918
1777	67,790	67,737
1778	19,922	21,159
1779	14,682	8,575
1780	16,652	27,089
1781	35,829	28,590
Total	212,041	239,623

Using Mathematical Skills

1. How many more British troops than American troops served in 1776?
2. Create a graph comparing the number of American and British forces during each year of the war.
3. Imagine that you are a Continental Army officer in 1776. Write a letter using these statistics to argue that the Continental Congress needs to raise a larger army.

During the siege at Yorktown, the Patriots made a daring attack that captured part of the British fortifications.

Meanwhile, General Washington was in New York. There he planned strategy with a French general, the **Comte de Rochambeau** (roh-shhn-boh). Rochambeau had recently arrived in New York with a large French army. A French fleet commanded by the naval officer Comte de Grasse was also sailing from the West Indies to aid the Patriots and challenge the mighty British navy. It could also prevent any British ships from entering Chesapeake Bay to bring reinforcements to Yorktown.

Washington saw a chance to trap Cornwallis. As the French fleet was taking control of Chesapeake Bay, Washington and Rochambeau moved their troops south. They surrounded Cornwallis with a Patriot army of some 16,000 soldiers. This was more than twice the size of Cornwallis's own forces. Suddenly the Patriots had the upper hand.

For weeks the Patriots held Yorktown under siege. During the **Battle of Yorktown** the Patriots steadily wore down the British defenses. The British navy tried to rescue Cornwallis's army, but the French fleet drove them away. In early October Washington prepared for a major attack on the weakened British troops. Fearing a defeat, Cornwallis surrendered. After negotiating for several days, the two sides agreed to terms of surrender for Cornwallis and his troops. The British marched out of Yorktown in defeat on October 20, 1781. Lord North, the British prime minister, received word of the Yorktown surrender in November. In shock he declared, "It is all over!"

✔ **Reading Check: Finding the Main Idea** How did Washington win the Battle of Yorktown?

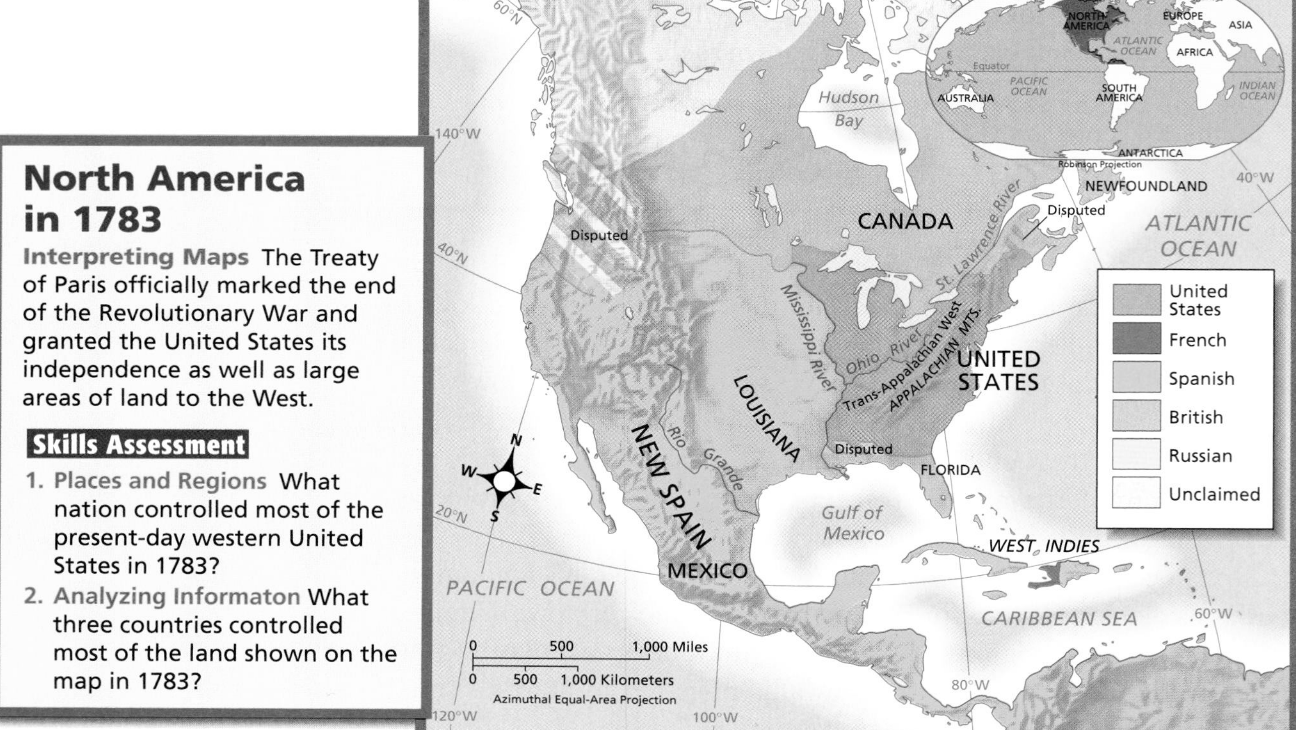

North America in 1783

Interpreting Maps The Treaty of Paris officially marked the end of the Revolutionary War and granted the United States its independence as well as large areas of land to the West.

Skills Assessment

1. **Places and Regions** What nation controlled most of the present-day western United States in 1783?
2. **Analyzing Informaton** What three countries controlled most of the land shown on the map in 1783?

The Treaty of Paris

At Yorktown the Patriots captured the largest British army in America. Only a few small battles took place afterward. In June 1781 a committee from the Continental Congress began peace negotiations with the British. The American delegates were John Adams, Benjamin Franklin, John Jay, and Henry Laurens. Franklin had played a key role in gaining French aid during the war. He was also influential in the peace talks. He expressed his feelings in a letter to a British friend.

"Let us now forgive and forget. . . . America will, with God's blessing, become a great and happy Country; and England, if she has at length gained Wisdom, will have gained something."

—Benjamin Franklin, from *The Autobiography and Other Writings,* edited by L. Jesse Lemisch

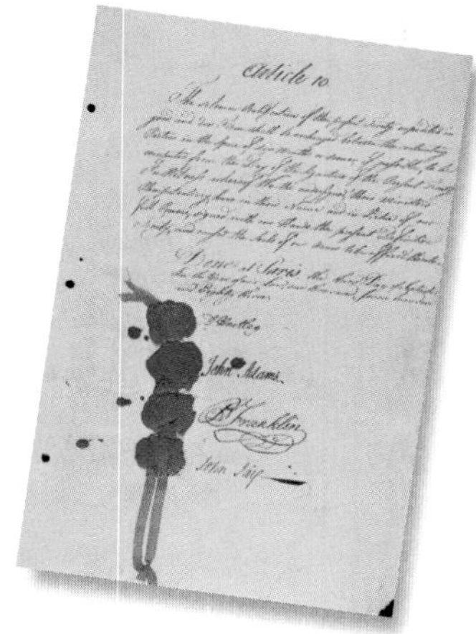

This is a signed copy of the Treaty of Paris.

Analyzing Primary Sources

Identifying Points of View How did Franklin think Great Britain and America should treat each other after the war?

The delegates took more than two years to come to an agreement, but in the **Treaty of Paris of 1783** Great Britain recognized the independent United States. The treaty also set the new nation's borders. The Great Lakes bounded the North. The Mississippi River served as the western border. A line at 31° North latitude formed the southern border. The British also accepted American rights to settle and trade west of the original thirteen colonies. With the war over, Patriot soldiers returned to their homes and families. The courage of soldiers and civilians had made America's victory possible. As the Continental Army's soldiers returned home, General Washington reflected on the triumph of his new country. "The citizens of America," he said, "are . . . acknowledged to be possessed of absolute freedom and independency."

✔ **Reading Check: Summarizing** Explain how the Revolutionary War finally ended.

Section 5 Review

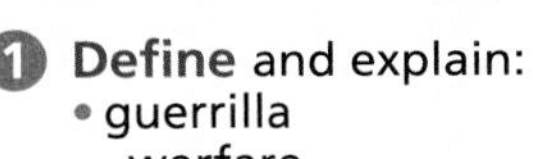

go.hrw.com **Homework Practice Online**
keyword: SC3 HP6

1. **Define** and explain:
   - guerrilla warfare

2. **Identify** and explain:
   - George Rogers Clark
   - Battle of Vincennes
   - Horatio Gates
   - Francis Marion
   - Comte de Rochambeau
   - Battle of Yorktown
   - Treaty of Paris of 1783

3. **Sequencing** Copy the graphic organizer below. Use it to list the major events that led to the end of the Revolutionary War.

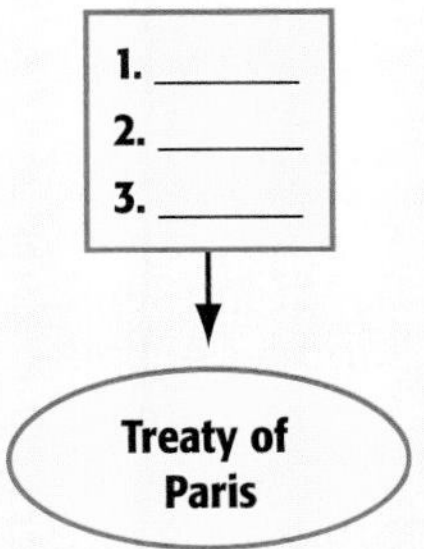

4. **Finding the Main Idea**
   a. How did geography affect the Patriot strategy on the western frontier?
   b. How did the war progress in the southern colonies up to Washington's victory at Yorktown?

5. **Writing and Critical Thinking**
   Summarizing Imagine that you are a colonial diplomat. Create a pamphlet announcing the war's end. Your pamphlet should include a summary of the war's final events.
   Consider the following:
   - the Battle of Yorktown
   - the terms of the Treaty of Paris of 1783
   - how you think the United States will fare after the war

Chapter 6 Review

The Chapter at a Glance

Examine the visual summary of the chapter below. Use it to help you create a five-question quiz that you might give to a classmate.

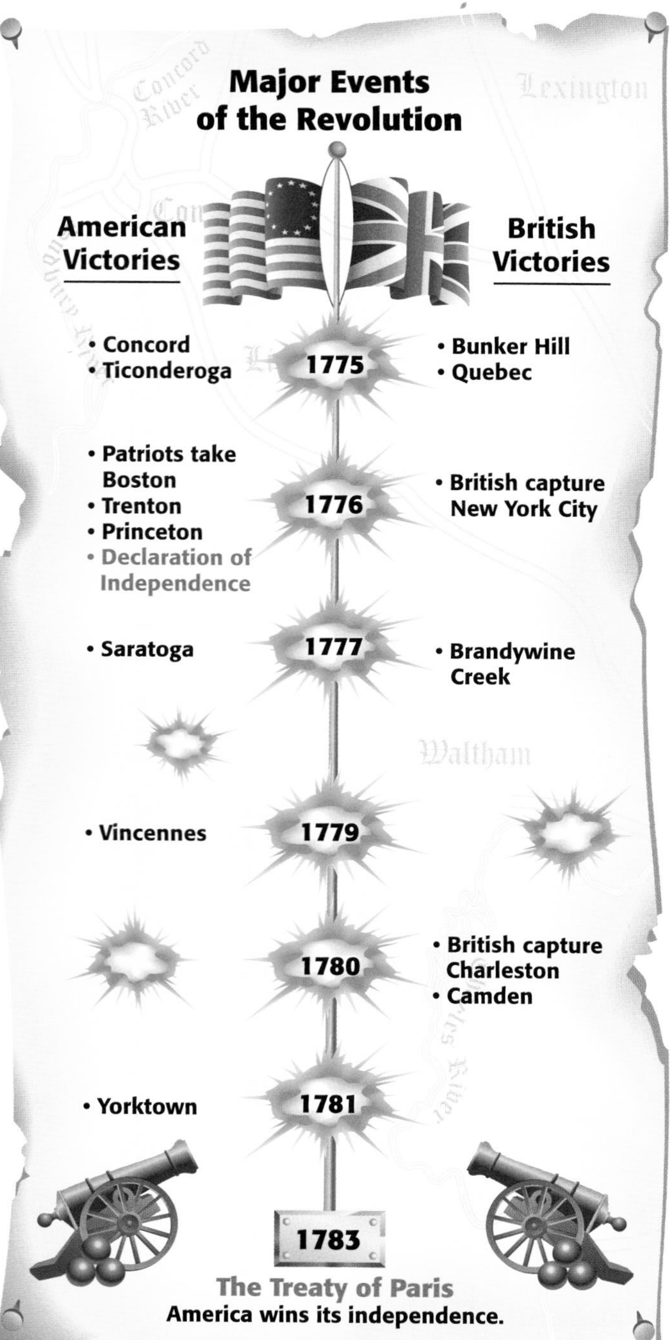

Identifying People and Ideas

Use the following terms or people in historically significant sentences.

1. minutemen
2. George Washington
3. *Common Sense*
4. Thomas Jefferson
5. Declaration of Independence
6. Abigail Adams
7. Marquis de Lafayette
8. John Paul Jones
9. Battle of Yorktown
10. Treaty of Paris of 1783

Understanding Main Ideas

Section 1 *(Pages 152–156)*

1. How did the fighting at Lexington and Concord affect the relationship between the colonies and Great Britain?
2. What did the First and Second Continental Congresses achieve?

Section 2 *(Pages 158–161)*

3. What effect did Thomas Paine's *Common Sense* have on colonial attitudes toward Britain?

Section 3 *(Pages 166–169)*

4. What advantages and disadvantages did the Patriots have when the Revolutionary War began?

Section 4 *(Pages 170–176)*

5. How did Washington defeat the British at Trenton and Princeton?
6. Why was the Battle of Saratoga important?

Section 5 *(Pages 177–181)*

7. How did the Patriots fight the war in the West and in the South?

You Be the Historian— Reviewing Themes

1. **Citizenship** Why did the colonies declare their independence from Britain?
2. **Constitutional Heritage** What are three rights that all men have according to the Declaration of Independence?
3. **Global Relations** Why did some foreign countries help the Patriots, and what role did Patriots such as Benjamin Franklin play in gaining this support?

Thinking Critically

1. **Supporting a Point of View** Did the Patriots' belief in their cause make up for their lack of supplies? Explain your answer.
2. **Summarizing** What key events occurred in 1776?
3. **Drawing Inferences and Conclusions** What do you think were the most significant causes of the American Revolution? Explain your answer.

Interpreting Charts

Study the chart below. Then use the information on the chart to help you answer the questions that follow.

Causes and Effects of the Revolution

Long-Term Causes

Proclamation of 1763

Increased taxation without representation

Increased British military presence and abuse of colonists' rights

Immediate Causes

Fighting at Lexington and Concord

Declaration of Independence

American Revolution
1775–1783

Effects

British recognition of U.S. independence

Boundaries of the United States extended west to the Mississippi River and south to Florida

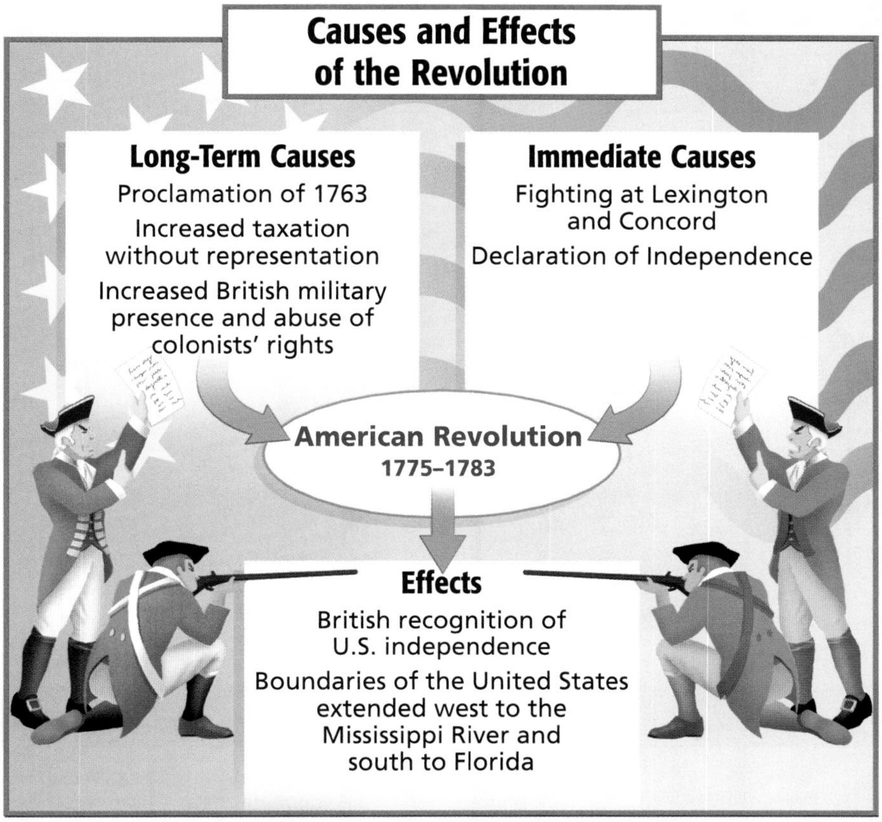

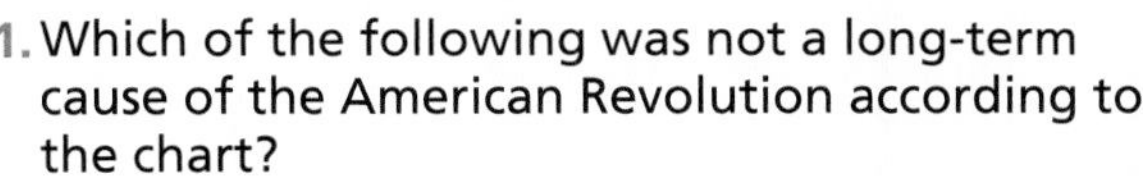

1. Which of the following was not a long-term cause of the American Revolution according to the chart?
   a. the Proclamation of 1763
   b. taxation without representation
   c. abuse of colonial rights
   d. French attacks on the colonies

2. Based on the chart and your knowledge of the period, how do you think the long-term causes of the Revolution contributed to the immediate causes of the war?

Analyzing Primary Sources

Read the following excerpt from *Common Sense* by Thomas Paine, then answer the questions that follow.

> **"A government of our own is our natural right; and when a man seriously reflects on the precariousness [uncertainness] of human affairs, he will become convinced that it is infinitely [completely] wiser and safer to form a constitution of our own in a cool deliberate manner, while we have it in our power, than to trust such an interesting event to time and chance."**

3. Which of the following best describes Paine's viewpoint?
   a. Americans should rush to form a new nation.
   b. Americans would be better off independent.
   c. Americans should remain British citizens.
   d. It is best to take risks.

4. Why do you think that Paine's message was popular with many colonists?

Alternative Assessment

Building Your Portfolio

American History

Linking to Community

John Paul Jones was a hero of the American Revolution. Present an oral report on a war hero from your community. This hero can be someone living in your community today or someone who lived there in the past. If the person still lives in your community, you may want to interview the individual for your report.

internet connect

Internet Activity: go.hrw.com
keyword: SC3 CF6

Access the Internet through the HRW Go site to conduct research on the differing viewpoints of Loyalists and Patriots. Then create a newspaper that shows bias to the Loyalist or Patriot position on the Revolution. Make sure you use at least three examples of biased reporting in your newspaper. On a separate sheet of paper, explain where the bias occurs and why it is biased.

CHAPTER

7 Forming a Government
(1777–1791)

Members of the Second Continental Congress knew that the former colonies needed to create a central government.

States such as New York minted their own coins.

UNITED STATES

1777 The Continental Congress approves the Articles of Confederation on November 15.

1781 On March 1 the Articles of Confederation go into effect after being ratified by all 13 states.

1777 | **1779** | **1781** | **1783**

WORLD

1781 German philosopher Immanuel Kant publishes his *Critique of Pure Reason,* a major theoretical work.

1782 Spain completes its conquest of British Florida.

1783 The Montgolfier brothers of France make the first flight in a hot-air balloon.

Early hot-air balloons, which were often decorated, delighted crowds in the late 1700s.

Build on What You Know

The United States declared its independence in 1776. But then Americans were faced with the difficult task of forming a new government. After a first attempt at national government failed to solve many of the nation's problems, many Americans wanted a change. In 1787, leaders from around the country came to Philadelphia to find a solution.

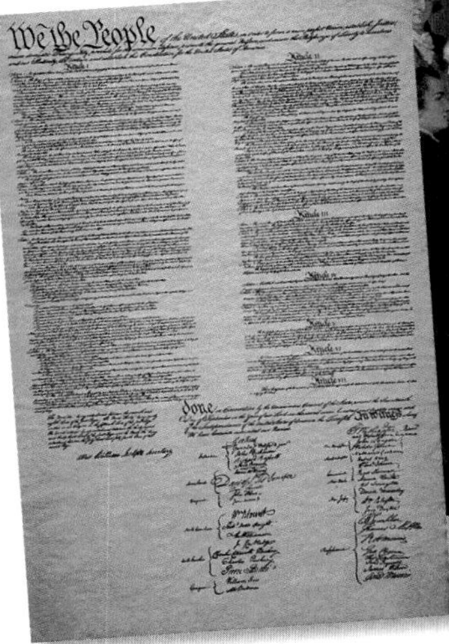

A signed copy of the Constitution

George Washington served as president of the Constitutional Convention.

1785 The United States begins using the dollar currency.

1786 Shays's Rebellion breaks out in Massachusetts.

1787 On May 14, state delegates begin to arrive at the Constitutional Convention in Philadelphia.

Congress passes the Northwest Ordinance on July 13.

The final draft of the Constitution is signed on September 17.

1789 James Madison submits possible amendments to the Constitution.

1790 Rhode Island becomes the final state to ratify the Constitution.

1791 The Bill of Rights is ratified by the states in December.

1785 — 1787 — 1789 — 1791

1786 Mennonites from central Europe settle in Canada.

1787 The Ottoman Empire declares war on Russia.

1791 Austrian composer Wolfgang Amadeus Mozart dies.

You Be the Historian

What's Your Opinion? Do you **agree** or **disagree** with the following statements? Support your point of view in your journal.

- **Global Relations** New nations will be taken advantage of by other countries.
- **Citizenship** Governments must protect certain rights of their citizens.
- **Constitutional Heritage** The power of the government must be limited.

Section 1

The Articles of Confederation

Read to Discover

1. What ideas and documents shaped American beliefs about government?
2. How did state constitutions contribute to the development of representative government?
3. What powers did the central government have under the Articles of Confederation?
4. What did the Northwest Ordinance accomplish?

Define

- constitution
- republicanism
- limited government
- suffrage
- ratification

Identify

- Virginia Statute for Religious Freedom
- Articles of Confederation
- Land Ordinance of 1785
- Northwest Ordinance of 1787
- Northwest Territory

Why It Matters Today

Many countries have modeled their political systems on American and European ideas of representative government. Use CNNfyi.com or other **current events** sources to learn about how a foreign nation elects its leaders. Record your findings in your journal.

The Story Continues

The bald eagle is one of the symbols of the United States.

In 1776 a short essay by an unknown author appeared. The essay called for the newly independent states to take great care when building their new governments. "They [the people] are now planting a seed," it stated. The author predicted that the seed would grow into a tree, whose branches would "shelter the liberty of succeeding ages." Many Americans agreed with this idea. They hoped that a strong republic could be formed in America.

Ideas about Government

The American colonies had taken a bold step in declaring their independence from Great Britain in July 1776. Their next political goal was to form new governments. To do so, the American people drew from a wide range of political ideas.

One source of inspiration was English law. England had limited the power of its kings and queens in two documents—Magna Carta and the English Bill of Rights. Magna Carta, signed by King John in 1215, required the king to follow the rule of law like other English people. The English Bill of Rights, passed in 1689, kept the king or queen from passing new taxes or changing laws without Parliament's approval. As a result, the people's representatives had a stronger voice in government.

Americans were also influenced by the Enlightenment. Writers of that period had called for the use of reason and expressed a belief in human goodness. Enlightenment philosopher John Locke believed that a social contract, or agreement, existed between political leaders and the people they ruled. One side of this contract was the government's duty to protect the people's unalienable rights. The rule of law, wrote Locke, was more important than the authority of any individual.

Interpreting the Visual Record

The Enlightenment *During the Enlightenment, philosophers often discussed their ideas at elegant social gatherings. British philosopher John Locke was widely respected.* ***How does the painting suggest the interest that the wealthy had in Enlightenment ideas?***

"Whosoever in authority exceeds the power given him by the law . . . may be opposed as any other man who by force invades the right of another."

—John Locke, *Two Treatises on Government*

Analyzing Primary Sources

Identifying Points of View
To whom does Locke compare a ruler who breaks the law?

Locke stated that leaders who broke the law or lost the approval of the people should be replaced.

Naturally American leaders looked to their own political traditions, such as the New England town meeting. At these meetings, townspeople addressed important issues in their community. Americans also looked to their own legislative assemblies, such as the Virginia House of Burgesses. These bodies offered models of representative governments. Christian traditions, such as the Great Awakening, may have also inspired colonists to question existing political institutions and look for more local control.

Americans also had written documents supporting the principles of self-government. In 1620 the Pilgrims had agreed to govern themselves at Plymouth colony by signing the Mayflower Compact. In 1639 the people of Connecticut had drawn up the Fundamental Orders of Connecticut. This plan was widely considered to be the first written **constitution** in the English colonies. A constitution is a set of basic principles and laws that state the powers and duties of the government. Finally, the Declaration of Independence clearly set forth the ideas on which Americans thought government should be based.

✔ **Reading Check: Summarizing** What influenced American ideas of government?

The State Constitutions

All of these political ideas were quickly put into practice after the United States declared independence. During the American Revolution nearly every colony wrote a new state constitution. These constitutions showed a belief in **republicanism**—that is, support for a system of government called a republic. In such a system, citizens elect representatives who are responsible to the people. Most Americans wanted to keep individual leaders from gaining too much power. Thus, each state constitution created a **limited government**. In a limited government all leaders have to obey the laws and no one has total power. For example, many states placed their courts outside of the governor's control.

Most state constitutions protected the individual rights of citizens. For example, George Mason wrote the Virginia Declaration of Rights. Some of the rights it defended were trial by jury, freedom of the press, and private ownership of property. In 1786 Thomas Jefferson's support for freedom of religion was included in the **Virginia Statute for Religious Freedom**. This law promoted the separation of church and state in Virginia. Other states soon followed, and by 1833 there were no state governments that supported an official church.

In addition, many state constitutions expanded **suffrage**, or voting rights. As one Virginian wrote, "The spirit of independence was converted into equality." Some states allowed any white man who was a taxpaying citizen to vote. Other states gave the vote only to white men who owned property. In most states people had to own property to hold an elected office. Seven of the first state constitutions gave voting rights to free African American men. However, by the 1860s these rights had been taken away or greatly limited by high property or residency requirements.

✔ **Reading Check: Analyzing Information** How did the first state constitutions promote the growth of democracy?

Interpreting the Visual Record

Female voters *The only state to give voting rights to women was New Jersey, though it took that right away in 1807.* ***From the way these women voters are dressed, do you think that they are property owners? Why or why not?***

THE GRANGER COLLECTION, NEW YORK

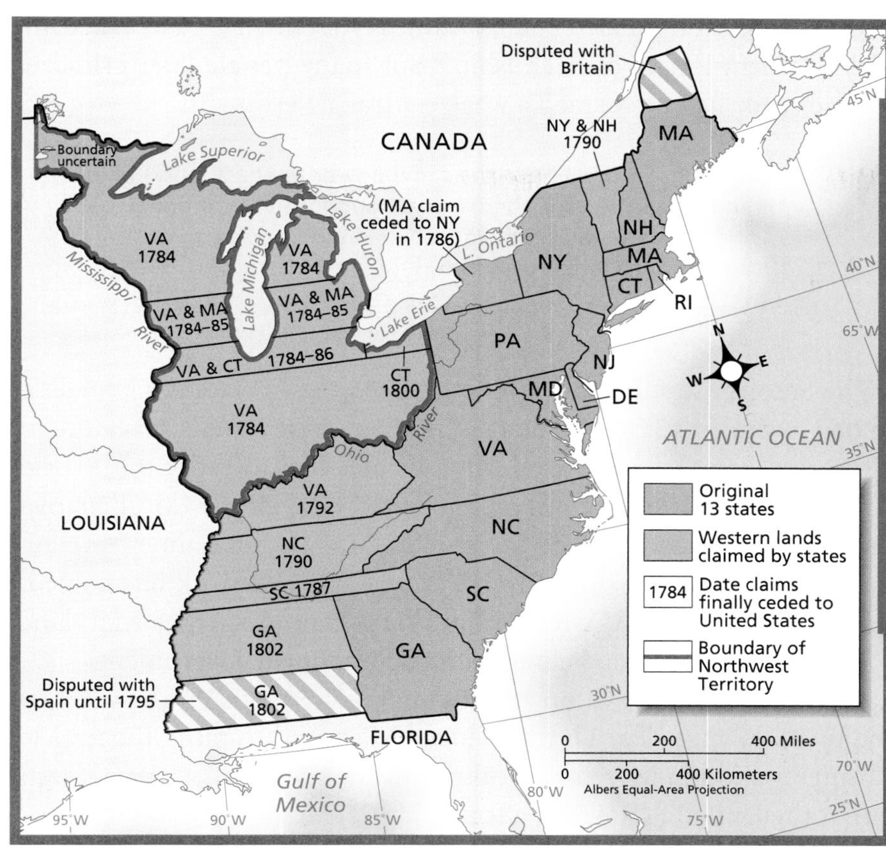

Western Land Claims, 1781–1802

Interpreting Maps Many of the original 13 states had claims to western lands that dated back to their colonial charters. It took several years for all the states to cede these lands to the United States.

Skills Assessment

1. **Places and Regions** What states claimed land within the boundaries of what became the Northwest Territory?
2. **Summarizing** Which states had no land claims?

Forming a Union

To many members of the Second Continental Congress, it was not enough for each state to have its own government. They believed that a national government was necessary in order to hold the country together. Some leaders of the Revolution disagreed. They worried that a new central government would be too powerful. After all, they were rebelling against Great Britain in part because of Parliament's abuse of authority.

On June 12, 1776, the Congress appointed a Committee of Thirteen, made up of one member from each colony. This group was assigned to create a national constitution. Committee members met for a month to discuss and draft the new document, called the **Articles of Confederation**. Under the Articles of Confederation, a new Confederation Congress would become the central national government. Each state would have one vote in the Congress. The national government did not have a president or a court system.

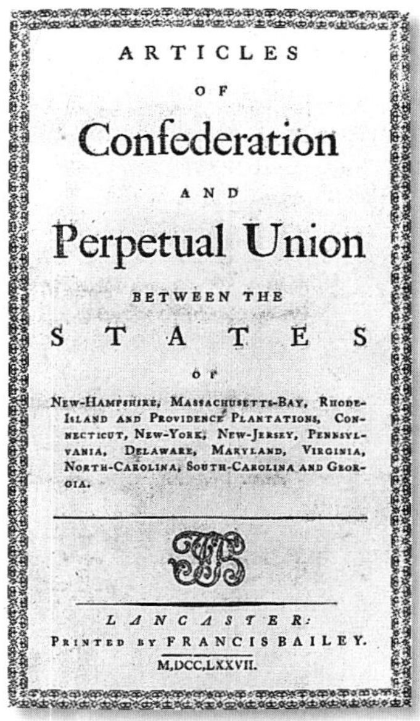

ARTICLES
OF
Confederation
AND
Perpetual Union
BETWEEN THE
STATES
OF
New-Hampshire, Massachusetts-Bay, Rhode-Island and Providence Plantations, Connecticut, New-York, New-Jersey, Pennsylvania, Delaware, Maryland, Virginia, North-Carolina, South-Carolina and Georgia.

LANCASTER:
Printed by FRANCIS BAILEY.
M,DCC,LXXVII.

The Articles of Confederation created a central government with limited powers.

The Confederation Congress had only limited powers. It could make coins and borrow money. It could negotiate and make treaties with other countries and with American Indians. Congress also could settle conflicts between the states and could ask states for money and soldiers. However, Congress could not force the states to provide money or troops, even in an emergency.

John Dickinson headed the Committee of Thirteen. He called the Articles "a firm league of friendship." But many people later criticized the Articles for having formed a weak central government.

Analyzing Primary Sources

Drawing Inferences and Conclusions Why might Webster have held this view?

"Congress must have the same power to enact [pass] laws and compel [force] obedience throughout the continent, as the legislatures of the States have in their respective jurisdictions [areas of authority]."

—Noah Webster, quoted in *The Growth of the American Republic*, by Samuel Eliot Morison, Henry Steele Commager, and William E. Leuchtenburg

The Second Continental Congress passed the Articles of Confederation on November 15, 1777. Then it sent them to each state legislature for **ratification**, or official approval. All 13 states had to ratify the Articles before the new national government could take effect. Conflicts over claims to western lands slowed the process. Many states claimed territory as far west as the Mississippi River. Virginia and New York had some of the largest land claims. States without land claims, such as Maryland, wanted these territories to belong to the new national government.

New York finally gave up its land claims in 1780. Virginia did the same the following year. This convinced Maryland to ratify the Articles of Confederation in March 1781, thus putting the first national government of the United States into effect.

Research on the ROM

Free Find:
Schooling
After reading about public schools on the **Holt Researcher CD–ROM**, imagine that you attend a public school in the late 1780s. Write a short account of your experiences.

✔ Reading Check: **Finding the Main Idea** What powers did the national government have under the Articles of Confederation?

The Northwest Territory

The new central government had to decide what to do with the western lands now under its control. It also had to raise money to pay war debts. The Confederation Congress hoped to solve both problems by selling western land to the public. It passed the **Land Ordinance of 1785**, which set up a system for surveying and dividing the public territory. First the land was split into townships of 36 square miles. Each township was divided into 36 lots of 640 acres each. One lot was set aside for a public school, with another 4 lots saved for Revolutionary War veterans. The remaining lots were for sale to the public.

To form a political system for the region north of the Ohio River, Congress passed the **Northwest Ordinance of 1787**. The ordinance created the **Northwest Territory**, which included the area that is now Illinois, Indiana, Michigan, Ohio, and Wisconsin.

The Northwest Ordinance also created a system for bringing new states into the Union. Congress agreed to divide the Northwest Territory into several smaller territories, each of which had a governor appointed by Congress. When the population of a territory reached 60,000, its settlers could draft their own constitution. The people could then ask Congress for permission to join the Union as a state.

Surveyors used tools like these to help them determine property boundaries.

Daily Life

Moving West After the Revolutionary War Americans began heading west in greater numbers. Thousands of people settled in the lands of the Northwest Territory. Many of these people were farmers from New England, where good farmland was scarce. As the population of the Northwest Territory grew and the region was divided into states, more settlers came from throughout the nation and from overseas. **Why do you think settlers would travel in a large group as shown here?**

In addition, the ordinance had a bill of rights. It also required that public education be provided for the citizens of the region. Finally, the Northwest Ordinance stated that "there shall be neither slavery nor involuntary servitude [forced labor] in the . . . territory." This last condition, based on a proposal by Thomas Jefferson, banned slavery in the Northwest Territory. However, the question of slavery would become more controversial as other new territories were formed.

✔ **Reading Check: Summarizing** How did the new Congress organize the nation's western lands?

Section 1 Review

go.hrw.com Homework Practice Online keyword: SC3 HP7

1. **Define** and explain:
   - constitution
   - republicanism
   - limited government
   - suffrage
   - ratification
2. **Identify** and explain:
   - Virginia Statute for Religious Freedom
   - Articles of Confederation
   - Land Ordinance of 1785
   - Northwest Ordinance of 1787
   - Northwest Territory
3. **Summarizing** Copy the graphic organizer below. Use it to identify the ideas and documents that influenced the U.S. state and national governments.

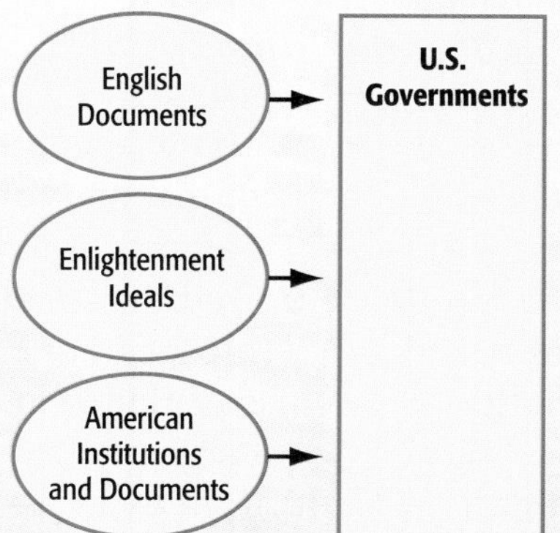

4. **Finding the Main Idea**
   a. In what ways did the first state constitutions support the growth of representative government?
   b. Why did Congress pass the Northwest Ordinance, and what did it achieve?
5. **Writing and Critical Thinking**
   Analyzing Information Imagine that you are a member of the Committee of Thirteen. Write a brief report for the states describing the powers given to the central government under the Articles of Confederation.
   Consider the following:
   - the structure of the national government
   - what the Confederation Congress could and could not do

A copy of Magna Carta

Magna Carta

England's King John angered many people with high taxes. In 1215 a group of English nobles joined the archbishop of Canterbury to force the king to agree to sign Magna Carta. This document stated that the king was subject to the rule of law, just as other citizens of England were. It also presented the ideas of a fair and speedy trial and due process of law. These principles are still a part of the U.S. Bill of Rights.

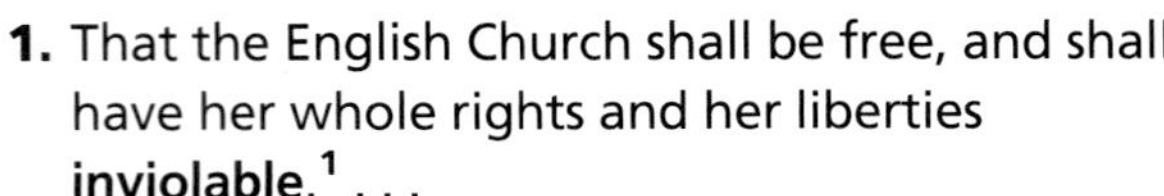

1. That the English Church shall be free, and shall have her whole rights and her liberties **inviolable.**[1] . . .

12. No **scutage**[2] nor aid shall be imposed in our kingdom, unless by the common council of our kingdom. . . .

38. No **bailiff,**[3] for the future, shall put any man to his law upon his own simple **affirmation,**[4] without **credible**[5] witnesses **produced for that purpose.**[6] . . .

39. No freeman shall be seized, imprisoned, **dispossessed,**[7] outlawed, or **exiled,**[8] or in any way destroyed; nor will we proceed against or prosecute him except by the lawful judgment of his **peers,**[9] or by the law of the land.

40. To none will we sell, to none will we deny, to none will we delay right or justice. . . .

Analyzing Primary Sources

1. How does Magna Carta allow for fair taxation?
2. Which of these rights supports the ideas of a fair trial and due process of law?

[1] **inviolable:** safe from sudden change
[2] **scutage:** tax for military purposes
[3] **bailiff:** sheriff
[4] **affirmation:** testimony
[5] **credible:** believable
[6] **produced for that purpose:** brought forward to testify
[7] **dispossessed:** deprived of his land
[8] **exiled:** forced to leave the country
[9] **peers:** equals

The English Bill of Rights

The seal of the House of Commons in Parliament

After the Glorious Revolution, Parliament passed the English Bill of Rights, which ensured that Parliament would have supreme power over the monarchy. The bill also protected the rights of English citizens.

1. That the pretended power of suspending of laws or the execution of laws by **regal**[1] authority without consent of Parliament is illegal; . . .

4. That **levying money**[2] for or to the use of the crown by pretense of **prerogative**[3] without grant of Parliament . . . is illegal;

5. That it is the right of the subjects to petition the king, and all commitments and prosecutions for such petitioning are illegal.

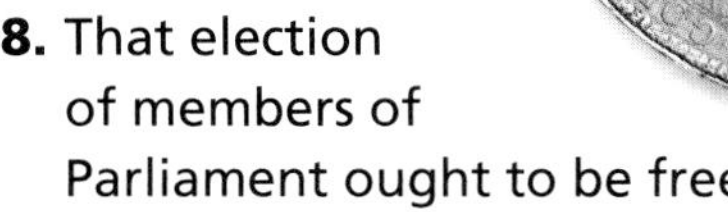

8. That election of members of Parliament ought to be free;

9. That the freedom of speech and debates or proceedings in Parliament ought not to be . . . questioned in any court or place out of Parliament;

10. That excessive bail ought not to be required, nor excessive fines imposed, nor cruel and unusual punishments inflicted.

11. That jurors ought to be duly **impaneled.**[4] . . .

13. And that, for **redress of**[5] all grievances and for the amending, strengthening, and preserving of the laws, Parliaments ought to be held frequently.

---

[1] **regal:** royal
[2] **levying money:** raising taxes
[3] **prerogative:** right
[4] **impaneled:** selected
[5] **redress of:** to make up for

Analyzing Primary Sources

1. What parts of this document describe the rights and powers of Parliament, and what are those rights and powers?
2. What parts of this document do you think Americans would want to use in their government?

Virginia Statute for Religious Freedom

Thomas Jefferson wrote the Virginia Statute for Religious Freedom. Jefferson hoped that by separating church and state, Virginians could practice their religion—whatever it might be—freely.

The Virginia Statute for Religious Freedom

I. Well aware that Almighty God has created the mind free; . . . that to **compel**[1] a man to **furnish contributions**[2] of money for the **propagation**[3] of opinions which he disbelieves is sinful and **tyrannical;**[4] that even . . . forcing him to support this or that teacher of his own religious **persuasion**[5] is depriving him of the comfortable liberty. . . . And, finally, that truth is great and will **prevail**[6] if left to herself . . . and has nothing to fear.

II. Be it **enacted**[7] by the General Assembly that no man shall be compelled to frequent or support any religious worship, place, or ministry whatsoever, nor shall be enforced, restrained, **molested,**[8] or burdened in his body or goods, nor shall otherwise suffer on account of his religious opinions or belief; but that all men shall be free to profess, and by argument to maintain, their opinion in matters of religion, and that the same shall in no wise **diminish,**[9] enlarge, or affect their civil capacities.

III. And though we well know that this assembly . . . [has] no power to restrain the acts of succeeding assemblies . . . we are free to declare, and do declare, that the rights hereby **asserted**[10] are of the natural rights of mankind, and that if any act shall hereafter be passed to repeal the present or to narrow its operation, such act will be an **infringement**[11] of natural rights.

Analyzing Primary Sources

1. How does this document protect freedom of religion?
2. Why do you think section III was included?

---

[1] **compel:** force
[2] **furnish contributions:** pay
[3] **propagation:** spreading
[4] **tyrannical:** unjust
[5] **persuasion:** belief
[6] **prevail:** win
[7] **enacted:** decided
[8] **molested:** injured
[9] **diminish:** reduce
[10] **asserted:** stated
[11] **infringement:** violation

Section 2

Problems in the New Nation

Read to Discover

1. How did other nations treat the new government of the United States?
2. What economic problems arose under the Articles of Confederation?
3. What were the causes and consequences of Shays's Rebellion?

Define

- tariffs
- interstate commerce
- inflation
- debtors
- creditors
- depression

Identify

- Shays's Rebellion
- Daniel Shays

WHY IT MATTERS TODAY

The United States today has a powerful central government. Use CNNfyi.com or other **current events** sources to learn about a way in which the U.S. government regulates business or trade. Record your findings in your journal.

The Story Continues

Merchants relied on barrels to ship many kinds of goods by land, river, and sea.

On June 7, 1786, Thomas Amis sailed his ship down the Mississippi River. He was carrying trade goods, as he had done many times before. This day was different, however. Amis's trip broke a new Spanish law, which greatly limited U.S. citizens' navigation rights along the lower part of the river. The Spanish troops at the town of Natchez—in present-day Mississippi—captured Amis. Then the Spanish stripped him of all his cargo, including 50 barrels of flour.

A Lack of Respect

Congress could do little to protect citizens like Thomas Amis against foreign threats. Under the Articles of Confederation, Congress could not force states to provide soldiers for an army. Without an army, the national government found it difficult to protect its citizens. It was also difficult to enforce the terms of international treaties. For example, Congress could do little to enforce the Treaty of Paris of 1783. The treaty called for the British to turn over "with all convenient speed" their forts on the U.S. side of the Great Lakes, but Great Britain was slow to leave these positions.

CONNECTING TO
THE ARTS

American Painters Artists John Singleton Copley, Gilbert Stuart, and Benjamin West all earned great success during the late 1700s. West was one of the most influential artists. Beginning his career as a portrait painter in America, West later moved to Britain and helped found the Royal Academy of Arts. West became known for his historical paintings, which showed people dressed in modern clothing instead of classical styles. West had to leave this painting of the signing of the Treaty of Paris unfinished when the British delegates refused to pose. **How is this unfinished painting symbolic of the relations between Britain and the United States?**

Spain also took advantage of the weakness of the United States. In 1784, Spanish officials closed the lower Mississippi River to U.S. shipping. Westerners who used the Mississippi to send goods to eastern markets were furious. But Spain refused to reopen the river to U.S. merchants.

Many state leaders began to criticize the weak Confederation Congress. Representatives from Rhode Island wrote to Congress. They said, "Our federal government is but a name; a mere shadow without substance [meaning]." Critics believed that a strong military would help the United States put pressure on Spain to open the Mississippi. For these political leaders, this failure showed that the national government needed to have more power.

✔ **Reading Check: Finding the Main Idea** How did the weaknesses of the Articles of Confederation affect U.S. relations with other countries?

Trouble with Trade

The United States also faced economic problems involving Great Britain. Before the Revolutionary War, colonial ships had traded a great deal with the British West Indies. But after the Treaty of Paris was signed, Britain closed many of its ports to American ships. In addition to shutting down this trade, Britain forced American merchants to pay high duties on U.S. exports. The tariffs applied to goods such as rice, tar, and tobacco, which colonial merchants wanted to sell in Britain.

The loss of trade with the British shook the U.S. economy. James Madison of Virginia wrote about the crisis.

Analyzing Primary Sources

Evaluating How did the end of the Revolutionary War affect the free enterprise system in the United States?

> **"The Revolution has robbed us of our trade with the West Indies . . . without opening any other channels to compensate [make up] for it. In every point of view, indeed, the trade of this country is in a deplorable [terrible] condition."**
>
> —James Madison, quoted in *Independence on Trial,* by Frederick W. Marks III

Farmers could no longer export their goods to the British West Indies. They also had to hire British ships to carry their goods to British markets, which was very expensive. Samuel Adams wrote about this to his cousin John Adams, "Our merchants are complaining bitterly that Great Britain is ruining their trade and there is good reason to complain." American exports dropped. At the same time, British goods flowed freely into the United States. This unequal trade caused serious economic problems for the new nation. British merchants could sell manufactured products in the United States at much lower prices than locally made goods. This competition hurt American businesses.

The Confederation Congress could not fix the problem because it did not have the power to pass **tariffs**—taxes on imports or exports. The states could offer little help. If one state passed a tariff, the British could simply sell their goods in another state. Most states did not cooperate when passing tariffs. Instead, each looked only to improve its own trade. In 1785 the situation led a British magazine to call the new nation the "Dis-United States." As a result of the trade problems with Britain, American merchants began looking for other new markets. Such new markets included China, France, and the Netherlands. Despite these attempts, Britain remained the most important trading partner of the United States.

That's Interesting!

Talking Turkey Did you know that Benjamin Franklin wanted the turkey, not the bald eagle, to be the national bird of the United States? It's true! He thought that the bald eagle was "a Bird of bad moral Character." He had more respect for the wild turkey. He lost his argument, and the bald eagle became an American symbol. But the turkey did not lose out completely. In the late 1900s Alabama, Massachusetts, Oklahoma, and South Carolina adopted the turkey as their official state game bird. Alabama recognized the turkey as "undoubtedly the most noble of all game birds upon the North American Continent."

✔ **Reading Check: Summarizing** What trade problems did the United States face with Great Britain, and why did these occur?

Economic Problems at Home

In addition to international trade issues, trade among the states became a major problem. The Confederation Congress had no power to regulate **interstate commerce**—trade between two or more states. Without such regulation, states followed their own commercial interests. As a result, trade laws differed from state to state. This situation made trade difficult for merchants whose businesses crossed state lines.

The ability of the states to print their own money caused more problems. After the Revolutionary War, most states had a hard time paying off war debts. They also struggled to collect overdue taxes. To ease economic hardships, some states at times printed large amounts of paper money. The result was **inflation**—increased prices for goods and services combined with the reduced value of money. Congress had no power to stop states from issuing more paper money. Thus, it could do little to stop inflation.

Inflation woes soon forced planters in North Carolina to sell tobacco to the state government in exchange for paper money. This money was worth almost nothing. In Rhode Island a similar problem arose. The state legislature printed large amounts of paper money worth very little. This made **debtors**—people who owe money—quite happy. They could pay back their debts with paper money worth less than the coins they had borrowed. However, **creditors**—people who lend money—were upset by the prospect of being paid back with worthless money. Similar situations took place in many states.

The rising inflation faced by the states combined with the loss of trade with Great Britain to cause a **depression.** A depression is a period of low economic activity combined with a rise in unemployment.

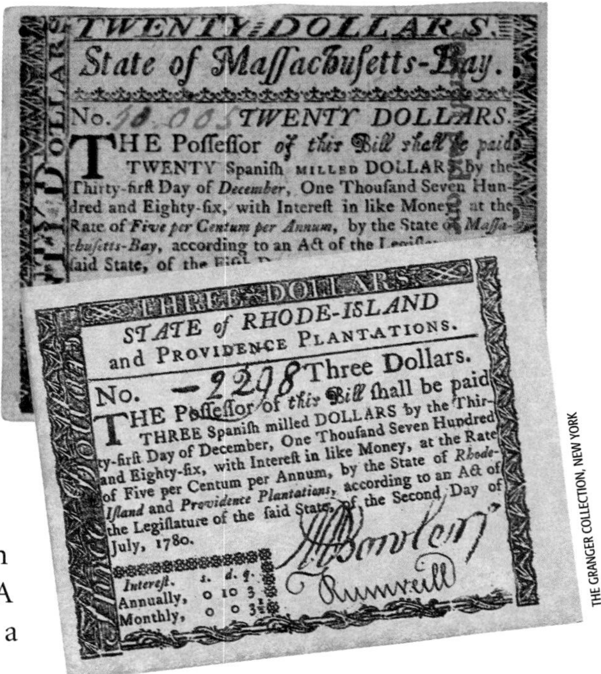

The states of Massachusetts and Rhode Island both suffered economic problems related to their currency policies.

✔ **Reading Check: Identifying Cause and Effect** What led to the economic differences between the states, and how did this affect the national economy?

Debt in Massachusetts

Each state handled its economic problems differently. Massachusetts refused to print paper money and tried to pay its war debts by collecting taxes on land.

The state's economic policy hit farmers particularly hard. As landowners, they had to pay the new taxes. With little gold or silver and no paper money, however, farmers had trouble paying their debts. When people could not pay their debts, the Massachusetts courts began forcing them to sell their property. Some farmers also had to serve terms in debtors' prison. Some even had to sell themselves as indentured servants. People soon began calling for change.

History Makers Speak

"We beg leave to inform your Honors that unless something takes place more favorable to the people, in a little time at least, one half of our inhabitants [people living in the state] in our opinion will become bankrupt [financially ruined] . . . . Sirs, in this situation what have we to live on—no money to be had; our estates [lands] daily posted and sold."

—Petition from a rural town, quoted in *The Growth of the American Republic*, by Samuel Eliot Morison, Henry Steele Commager, and William E. Leuchtenburg

Analyzing Primary Sources

Identifying Points of View What worries did farmers have?

However, many government leaders in Massachusetts had little sympathy for the problems of poor farmers. In some cases, farmers actually owed these politicians money.

THE GRANGER COLLECTION, NEW YORK

Interpreting the Visual Record

Shays's Rebellion *The followers of Daniel Shays, shown above at left, took possession of a Massachusetts courthouse during their rebellion.* ***Do you think this image portrays the rebels as dangerous? Why or why not?***

Shays's Rebellion

In September 1786, farmers in three western Massachusetts counties began a revolt. Bands of angry citizens armed with pitchforks and other farm tools closed down courts in the western part of the state. Their reasoning was simple—with the courts shut down, no one's property could be taken. This uprising became known as **Shays's Rebellion**. A poor farmer and Revolutionary War veteran named **Daniel Shays** was its main leader. The state government ordered the farmers to stop the revolt and threatened death to any captured rebel. However, these threats only made Shays and his followers more determined. Shays asked other citizens to join the rebellion. He signed a document stating, "The seeds of war are now sown. . . . Our cause is yours. Don't give yourself a rest and let us die here."

In September the rebels forced the state supreme court in the town of Springfield to close. Shays's forces returned to Springfield the next month, hoping to capture a federal weapons storehouse. This time, state troops defeated the rebels in a short battle in January 1787. By February many rebels had surrendered or been arrested. During their trials, 14 leaders were sentenced to death. However, the state soon freed most of the rebels, including Shays. State officials knew that many citizens in Massachusetts agreed with the rebels and their motives.

The rebellion greatly upset many political leaders. George Washington exclaimed, "I am mortified [embarrassed] beyond expression." He feared that the United States must look "ridiculous . . . in the eyes of all Europe." Not everyone saw the rebellion this way, however. Thomas Jefferson, serving as ambassador to France, also responded to the event. He said, "A little rebellion, now and then, is a good thing. . . . The tree of liberty must be refreshed from time to time with the blood of patriots and tyrants."

In the end, Shays's Rebellion helped reveal the weakness of the Confederation government. It led some Americans to admit that the Articles of Confederation were not working. When Massachusetts had asked the national government to help put down Shays's Rebellion, Congress could offer little help. More Americans began calling for a stronger central government. They wanted leaders who would be able to protect the nation in times of crisis.

✔ **Reading Check: Finding the Main Idea** What was Shays's Rebellion, and why was it important?

Alexander Hamilton was a lawyer with considerable influence in New York politics.

A Push for Change

In 1786 the Virginia legislature called for a national conference to talk about changing the Articles of Confederation. The meeting took place in Annapolis, Maryland, in September 1786. Only five states sent delegates to the Annapolis Convention, however. The New England states, the Carolinas, and Georgia were not represented. Even Maryland hesitated to send delegates.

James Madison and Alexander Hamilton attended the Annapolis Convention. At their urging, the Annapolis delegates called on all 13 states to send delegates to a Constitutional Convention at Philadelphia, in May 1787. They hoped this Convention would improve the national government. They wanted to make "the constitution of the Federal Government adequate to the exigencies [needs] of the Union."

✔ **Reading Check: Analyzing Information** How did the states address the problems of the central government?

Section 2 Review

go.hrw.com Homework Practice Online
keyword: SC3 HP7

1. **Define** and explain:
   - tariffs
   - interstate commerce
   - inflation
   - debtors
   - creditors
   - depression

2. **Identify** and explain:
   - Shays's Rebellion
   - Daniel Shays

3. **Categorizing** Copy the graphic organizer below. Use it to identify the domestic and international problems that arose under the Articles of Confederation.

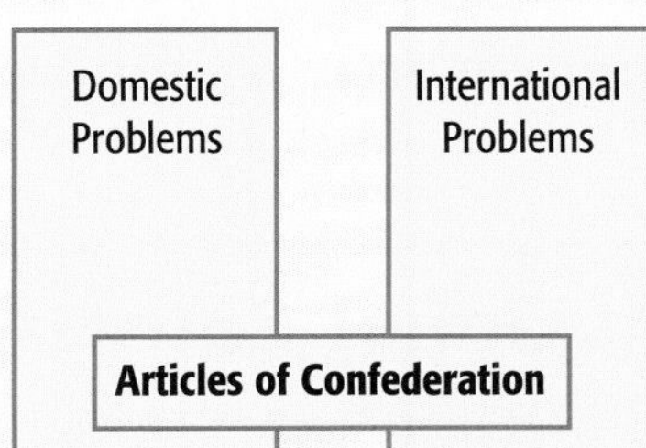

4. **Finding the Main Idea**
   a. In what ways did Great Britain and Spain take advantage of the weaknesses of the United States under its new government?
   b. Why did Massachusetts's farmers take part in Shays's Rebellion, and what was the result of the rebellion?

5. **Writing and Critical Thinking**
   Supporting a Point of View Imagine that you are a delegate to the Annapolis Convention. Write a letter to the states not attending the convention that explains why they should attend the next convention in Philadelphia.
   Consider the following:
   - economic problems under the Articles of Confederation
   - problems with defining the authority of the central government
   - social problems under the Articles of Confederation

Section 3

The Constitution

Read to Discover

1. Why did the delegates meet for the Constitutional Convention?
2. What were some of the main issues debated and compromises reached at the Constitutional Convention?
3. How is the federal government balanced under the U.S. Constitution?

Define

- popular sovereignty
- federalism
- legislative branch
- executive branch
- judicial branch
- checks and balances

Identify

- Constitutional Convention
- James Madison
- Virginia Plan
- William Paterson
- New Jersey Plan
- Great Compromise
- Three-Fifths Compromise

WHY IT MATTERS TODAY

Debate and compromise are still an important part of government in the United States. Use CNNfyi.com or other **current events** sources to learn about a recent political debate in the U.S. Congress. Record your findings in your journal.

The Story Continues

In 1786 a Pennsylvania newspaper printed an article about the U.S. government stating that the government could not afford to pay ambassador John Adams. The newspaper's editors were shocked. "Ought we not to blush . . . that the ambassadors of the states are . . . depending on foreign charity for their support?" John Adams's wife, Abigail, agreed. She felt that this was an embarrassment. She noted that "with the present salary and the present temper of the English no one need envy the [American] embassy." Such problems led some Americans to seek a more powerful national government.

John Adams served as U.S. ambassador to Great Britain.

The Constitutional Convention

By the mid-1780s most political leaders agreed that it was time to change the Articles of Confederation. In February 1787 the Confederation Congress invited each state to send delegates to a convention in Philadelphia. The delegates planned to discuss ways to improve the

Articles of Confederation. The **Constitutional Convention** was held in May 1787 in Philadelphia's State House, now called Independence Hall. It was in this same building that Americans had officially declared their independence. Twelve states sent a total of 55 delegates to the Convention. Only Rhode Island refused to send a delegation.

The delegates were a remarkable group. Most were well educated, and many of them had served in state legislatures or the Confederation Congress. Benjamin Franklin of Pennsylvania was the oldest delegate. **James Madison** proved to be one of the most important delegates to the Convention. Madison took good notes and joined many talks during the Convention. Revolutionary War hero George Washington was part of the Virginia delegation and was soon elected president of the whole Convention.

Several important American political leaders did not attend the Convention. John Adams and Thomas Jefferson were serving as ambassadors. Others, like Revolutionary hero Patrick Henry, chose not to attend because they were against such a meeting. The states did not choose any women, African Americans, or American Indians as delegates to the Convention. Members of these groups did not yet have the rights of full citizens, including the right to represent other citizens in government.

That's Interesting!

A "Heated" Debate Can you imagine sitting in a very hot room wearing a heavy suit and stockings? How about doing so in the middle of the summer with no air conditioning? That's what the framers of the Constitution did when they met in Philadelphia in 1787. Although it was hot, they kept the windows closed to keep out flies and so no one in the streets could hear their discussions. Despite the discomfort, the Founders were able to write a new Constitution for their country.

✔ **Reading Check: Finding the Main Idea** Who were some of the delegates at the Constitutional Convention, and what did they hope to accomplish?

The Great Compromise

Several issues divided the delegates to the Constitutional Convention. Some members wanted only to make small changes to the Articles of Confederation, while others wanted to rewrite the Articles. But the delegates who wanted major changes in the Articles had different goals. For example, small and large states had different concerns about representation. States also had different views about regional issues such as slavery. Economic issues such as tariffs also divided northerners from southerners. In addition, there was disagreement over how strong to make the national government.

After the delegates had met for four days, Edmund Randolph of Virginia presented the **Virginia Plan**. James Madison wrote most of this plan, also called the large-state plan. It offered a new federal constitution that would give sovereignty, or supreme power, to the central government. The Virginia Plan divided the national government into three branches: executive, judicial, and legislative.

Delegates from 12 of the 13 states gathered at Philadelphia's Independence Hall to revise the Articles of Confederation.

This engraving advised women that their proper place was in the home. Such attitudes were one reason that no female delegates were sent to the Constitutional Convention.

The legislature in this plan would be a bicameral, or two-house, legislature. This arrangement was similar to that used by several state assemblies. Representatives in the legislature would be chosen on the basis of state populations. Larger states would thus have more representatives than smaller states. Delegates from the smaller states did not like the Virginia Plan. They argued that it would give too much power to the larger states.

The delegates debated about the Virginia Plan for two weeks. New Jersey delegate **William Paterson** then presented the small-state or **New Jersey Plan**. This plan proposed keeping Congress's structure the same. It called for a unicameral, or one-house, legislature. In this case each state would have an equal number of votes, giving the smaller states an equal voice in the national government. The New Jersey Plan proposed that all acts passed by Congress "shall be the supreme law of the respective States." The plan gave the central government the power to tax citizens in all states. It also allowed the government to regulate commerce. Delegates from the large states were against the New Jersey Plan, which would give smaller states more influence.

After a month of debate, the delegates were still unable to agree. The Convention formed a committee to determine how states should be represented. The committee proposed a compromise—an agreement in which both sides give up some of their demands so that other demands can be met. Some historians call this agreement at the Convention the **Great Compromise**. Every state, regardless of its size, would have an equal vote in the upper house of the legislature. This would satisfy supporters of the New Jersey Plan. In the lower house, each state would have a number of representatives based on its population. This proposal would please those who liked the Virginia Plan. The delegates passed the Great Compromise, but there were still problems to settle.

✔ **Reading Check: Contrasting** What were the differences between the Virginia Plan and the New Jersey Plan, and how were these resolved?

Interpreting the Visual Record

Constitutional compromises *The delegates at the Constitutional Convention had to compromise to make progress.* ***How does this sculpture show delegates working together to address issues?***

NEBRASKA STATE HISTORICAL SOCIETY

The Three-Fifths Compromise

The debate over representation also involved some regional differences. Southern delegates wanted slaves to be counted as part of their state populations. This way they would have more representatives in Congress. Northerners disagreed. They wanted the number of slaves to determine taxes but not representation.

To resolve this problem, some delegates proposed counting three fifths of the slaves in each state as part of its population. This number would then decide how many representatives a state would have in the lower house. New York delegate Gouverneur Morris spoke with much emotion against this idea.

THE LIBRARY COMPANY OF PHILADELPHIA

Interpreting the Visual Record

Liberty *This antislavery painting shows a woman representing Liberty offering to aid freed slaves.* ***What does Liberty offer to the freed slaves in the painting?***

History Makers Speak

> **"The admission of slaves into the Representation . . . comes to this: that the inhabitant of [a state] who goes to the coast of Africa and . . . tears away his fellow creatures from their dearest connections and damns them to the most cruel bondage [slavery], shall have more votes in a Government [established] for protection of the rights of mankind."**
>
> —Gouverneur Morris, quoted in *Founding the Republic,* edited by John J. Patrick

However, the delegates voted to accept the so-called **Three-Fifths Compromise**. Under this agreement each slave would, in effect, be counted as three fifths of a person when determining representation.

Another major issue was the foreign slave trade. Some of the delegates wanted the federal government to end the slave trade. These people included George Mason of Virginia and John Dickinson of Delaware. Others said that the southern states' economies needed the slave trade. South Carolina delegate John Rutledge noted, "The people of these States will never be such fools as to give up so important an interest." Some of these southern delegates even threatened to leave the Union if the Constitution immediately ended the slave trade.

Worried delegates reached another compromise. Northern delegates agreed to wait 20 years before seeking to end the slave trade. Southern delegates agreed to stop insisting that laws in Congress be passed with a two-thirds majority vote. Oliver Ellsworth summed up the view of many delegates. He said, "The morality or wisdom of slavery . . . are considerations belonging to the states themselves."

✔ **Reading Check: Finding the Main Idea** What key compromises did delegates make about slavery at the Constitutional Convention?

Our Living Constitution

Most of the convention delegates wanted a strong national government to replace the Articles of Confederation. At the same time they wanted to protect **popular sovereignty**—the idea that political authority belongs to the people. They also wanted to balance the power of the national government with the powers of the states. Therefore, the delegates looked to **federalism**, or the sharing of power between a central government and the states that make up a country.

In this system, the federal government has power to enforce its laws in the states. This idea is stated in Article VI of the Constitution.

Analyzing Primary Sources
Evaluating How does this quotation support the principle of federalism?

"This Constitution and the Laws of the United States which shall be made in Pursuance thereof; and all Treaties made, or which shall be made, under the Authority of the United States, shall be the supreme Law of the Land; and the Judges in every State shall be bound thereby, any Thing in the Constitution or Laws of any State to the Contrary notwithstanding."

—The Constitution of the United States

Each state must obey the authority of the federal government. Article VI also notes that all state officials are required "by Oath . . . to support this Constitution." The federal government has the power to use the military to enforce its laws. These troops are under the command of the president.

Under the Constitution, states have control over government functions not specifically assigned to the federal government. For example, the states control local government, education, and the chartering of corporations. States also create and oversee civil and criminal law. States must also protect the welfare of their citizens.

✔ **Reading Check: Summarizing** What are some of the powers that belong to the states under the Constitution?

LINKING PAST to PRESENT

National Currency

The U.S. Constitution gives the federal government the sole power to issue legal currency, or money. Until the mid-1800s, however, many state banks could print banknotes. These notes could be exchanged at the bank that issued them for their value in gold or silver coins. However, banks often refused to accept notes from other banks, which interfered with trade. The federal government stopped the issuing of banknotes in the mid-1860s and created a national currency.

Recently, the Treasury has redesigned paper money to make it harder to copy. The U.S. Mint has also introduced new coins such as the state quarters and the Sacagawea gold dollar coin. **How does our national currency demonstrate the system of federalism?**

A Delicate Balance

The Constitution also balances the powers within the federal government. For this reason the federal government has three branches. Each is responsible for separate tasks. The first is the **legislative branch**, or Congress, which is responsible for proposing and passing laws. It is made up of two houses. The Senate, or upper house, has two members from each state, while in the House of Representatives, or lower house, each state is represented according to its population.

The second branch of the federal government is the **executive branch**. This branch includes the president and the departments that help run the government. The executive branch makes sure that laws are carried out. The third branch is the **judicial branch**, which is made up of all the national courts. This branch is responsible for interpreting laws, punishing criminals, and settling disputes between states. (*For the full text of the U.S. Constitution, see pages 228–47.*)

The framers of the Constitution created a system of **checks and balances** to keep any branch of government from becoming too powerful. For example, the framers gave Congress power to propose and pass legislation. The president has the power to veto, or reject, laws that Congress passes. However, Congress can override the president's veto with a two-thirds majority vote. Interpretation of the Constitution has provided the judicial branch with its own check. This check is the Supreme Court's power to review the laws passed by Congress. The Court may strike down a law that it finds unconstitutional—in violation of the Constitution.

This early draft of the Constitution shows corrections and comments by George Washington.

The delegates knew that the Constitution was not a perfect document. They believed, however, that they had founded a strong government that still protected the ideas of republicanism. The long and difficult debates at the Constitutional Convention lasted 16 weeks. Finally, in September 1787 the delegates signed a final draft of the Constitution. Only three of the 42 delegates who remained refused to sign. These three were Elbridge Gerry of Massachusetts and Edmund Randolph and George Mason of Virginia. The delegates then sent the Constitution to Congress, which sent it to the states for ratification.

September 1787
The final draft of the Constitution is signed.

✔ **Reading Check: Summarizing** How was the government structured under the new Constitution, and how was power balanced?

Section 3 Review

go.hrw.com Homework Practice Online
keyword: SC3 HP7

1. **Define** and explain:
   - popular sovereignty
   - federalism
   - legislative branch
   - executive branch
   - judicial branch
   - checks and balances

2. **Identify** and explain:
   - Constitutional Convention
   - James Madison
   - Virginia Plan
   - William Paterson
   - New Jersey Plan
   - Great Compromise
   - Three-Fifths Compromise

3. **Summarizing** Copy the graphic organizer below. Use it to explain the major compromises that took place at the Constitutional Convention.

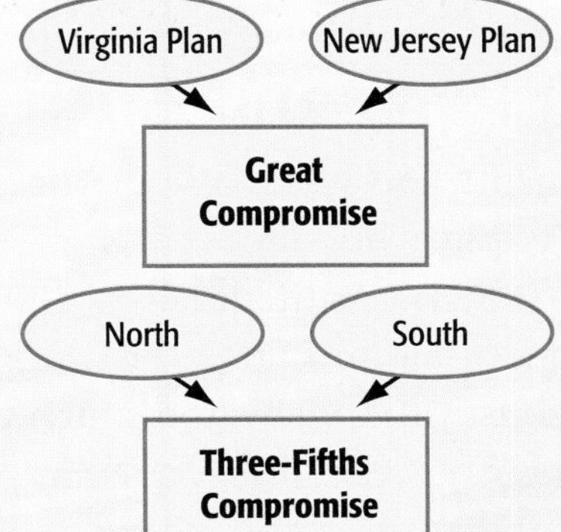

4. **Finding the Main Idea**
   a. What was the original purpose of the Constitutional Convention?
   b. How does the Constitution reflect the ideas of republicanism and limited government?

5. **Writing and Critical Thinking**
   Evaluating Imagine that you are a political scholar writing about the Constitutional Convention. Write an essay explaining how the actions of the Founding Fathers represented good citizenship.
   Consider the following:
   - the actions and beliefs of the Founding Fathers
   - what it means to be a good citizen

Section 4

Ratification of the Constitution

Read to Discover

1. Why were some people against the new Constitution?
2. What arguments for the Constitution did the *Federalist Papers* present?
3. When and how was the Constitution ratified?
4. Why did some people want a bill of rights, and how was it added to the Constitution?

Define

- amendments

Identify

- Antifederalists
- George Mason
- Federalists
- *Federalist Papers*
- Bill of Rights

Why It Matters Today

Debate still takes place over how much power the federal government has over the states. Use CNNfyi.com or other **current events** sources to study a recent dispute or legal case between a state and the federal government. Record your findings in your journal.

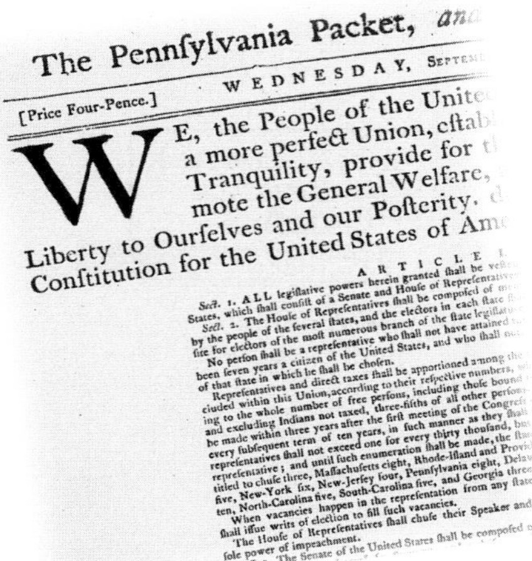
The Pennſylvania Packet, an

WEDNESDAY, Septem

[Price Four-Pence.]

WE, the People of the Unite
a more perfect Union, eſtab
Tranquility, provide for t
mote the General Welfare,
Liberty to Ourſelves and our Poſterity, d
Conſtitution for the United States of Am

ARTICLE I.

Sect. 1. ALL legiſlative powers herein granted ſhall be veſte
States, which ſhall conſiſt of a Senate and Houſe of Repreſentative
Sect. 2. The Houſe of Repreſentatives ſhall be compoſed of me
by the people of the ſeveral ſtates, and the electors in each ſtate ſh
ſite for electors of the moſt numerous branch of the ſtate legiſlatu
No perſon ſhall be a repreſentative who ſhall not have attained t
been ſeven years a citizen of the United States, and who ſhall no
of that ſtate in which he ſhall be choſen.
Repreſentatives and direct taxes ſhall be apportioned among the
cluded within this Union, according to their reſpective numbers, wh
ing to the whole number of free perſons, including thoſe bound
and excluding Indians not taxed, three-fifths of all other perſon
be made within three years after the firſt meeting of the Congreſs
every ſubſequent term of ten years, in ſuch manner as they ſhall
repreſentatives ſhall not exceed one for every thirty thouſand, but
repreſentative; and until ſuch enumeration ſhall be made, the ſtate
titled to chuſe three, Maſſachuſetts eight, Rhode-Iſland and Provid
five, New-York ſix, New-Jerſey four, Pennſylvania eight, Delaw
ten, North-Carolina five, South-Carolina five, and Georgia three.
When vacancies happen in the repreſentation from any ſtate,
ſhall iſſue writs of election to fill ſuch vacancies.
The Houſe of Repreſentatives ſhall chuſe their Speaker and o
ſole power of impeachment.
Sect. 3. The Senate of the United States ſhall be compoſed of

Newspapers supplied most Americans with their first look at the text of the Constitution.

The Story Continues

John Dunlap and David Claypoole stayed up well into the night on September 17, 1787. They reset type and filled all four pages of their Philadelphia newspaper. Dunlap and Claypoole had begun their work only hours after the end of the Constitutional Convention. The next morning, they presented the first printed copy of the U.S. Constitution.

Federalists and Antifederalists

When the Constitution was made public, a great debate began among Americans. People who opposed the Constitution were known as **Antifederalists**. Some Antifederalists thought that the Constitutional Convention had gone too far in creating a new government. Others thought the Constitution gave too much power to the central government. For some Antifederalists, the main problem was that the Constitution did not include a bill of rights. Constitutional Convention delegate **George Mason** became an Antifederalist for this reason.

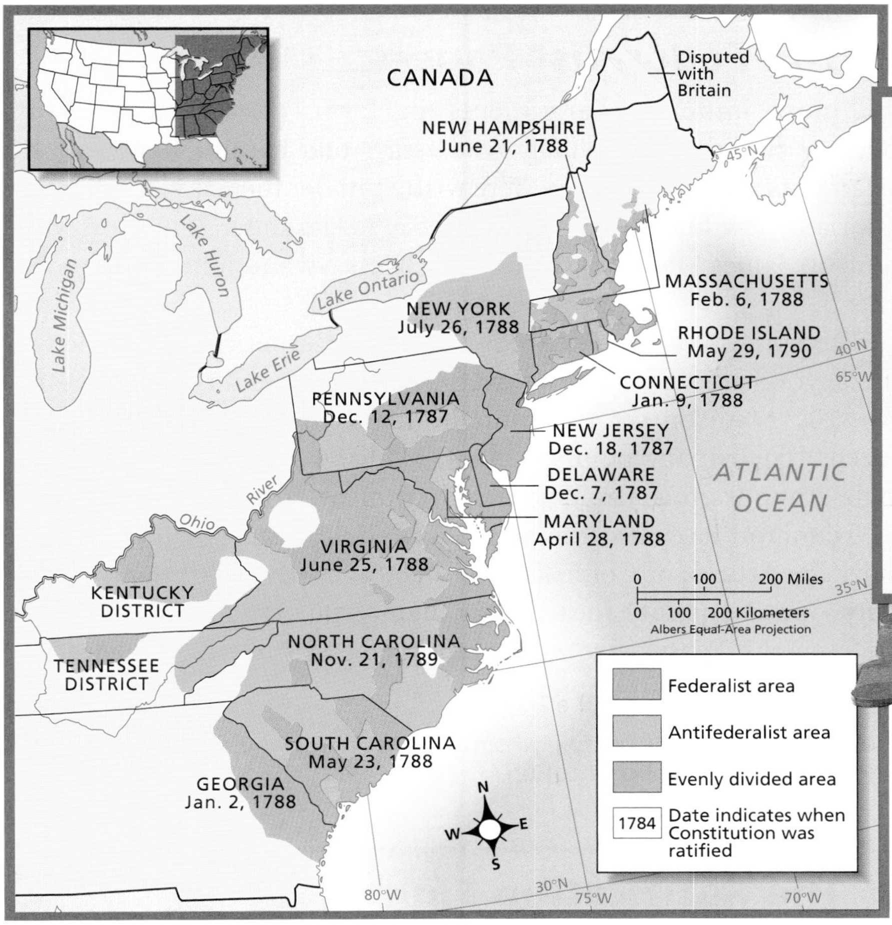

CANADA
Disputed with Britain
NEW HAMPSHIRE June 21, 1788
MASSACHUSETTS Feb. 6, 1788
RHODE ISLAND May 29, 1790
CONNECTICUT Jan. 9, 1788
NEW YORK July 26, 1788
NEW JERSEY Dec. 18, 1787
PENNSYLVANIA Dec. 12, 1787
DELAWARE Dec. 7, 1787
MARYLAND April 28, 1788
VIRGINIA June 25, 1788
KENTUCKY DISTRICT
NORTH CAROLINA Nov. 21, 1789
TENNESSEE DISTRICT
SOUTH CAROLINA May 23, 1788
GEORGIA Jan. 2, 1788
Lake Michigan
Lake Huron
Lake Ontario
Lake Erie
Ohio River
ATLANTIC OCEAN
0 100 200 Miles
0 100 200 Kilometers
Albers Equal-Area Projection
Federalist area
Antifederalist area
Evenly divided area
1784 Date indicates when Constitution was ratified

Federalists and Antifederalists

Interpreting Maps Federalists and Antifederalists often engaged in bitter debates over whether to ratify the new Constitution.

Skills Assessment

1. **Human Systems** According to the map, which states had the most complete Federalist support?
2. **Summarizing** In what month and year did the first states ratify the Constitution?

Many Antifederalists were small farmers and debtors, but some were wealthy. Some heroes of the American Revolution were also strong Antifederalists, such as Richard Henry Lee, Samuel Adams, and Patrick Henry. As the Constitution was debated in Virginia, George Mason warned against the power of a strong central government.

"The very idea of converting [changing] what was formerly a confederation to a consolidated [united] government, is totally subversive of [against] every principle which has hitherto [before] governed us. This power is calculated to annihilate [destroy] totally the state governments."

—George Mason, quoted in *Great Issues in American History,* edited by Richard Hofstadter

Analyzing Primary Sources

Identifying Points of View What did George Mason believe a strong central government would do to the states?

Antifederalists were challenged by many Americans who believed that the United States needed a stronger Constitution. Supporters of the Constitution called themselves **Federalists**. James Madison, George Washington, Benjamin Franklin, Alexander Hamilton, and John Jay were Federalists. Most Federalists believed that the Constitution offered a good balance of power. They thought it was a careful compromise between various political views.

✔ **Reading Check: Identifying Points of View** What were some of the Antifederalists' arguments against the Constitution?

BIOGRAPHY

George Mason

(1725–1792)

George Mason was a Virginia planter who turned to politics. He became devoted to limited government and the protection of human rights. His many speeches and writings greatly influenced the development of the U.S. government. One of his most important works was the Virginia Declaration of Rights, which served as a model for the bills of rights of many states. Although Mason served as a delegate to the Constitutional Convention, he refused to sign the Constitution because it did not include a bill of rights. What role did George Mason play in shaping American government?

The *Federalist Papers*

The most important arguments in favor of the Constitution appeared in a series of widely read essays that became known as the ***Federalist Papers***. The essays were written under the name Publius, but historians now know that of the 85 essays, Alexander Hamilton wrote about 50. James Madison wrote about 30 essays, and John Jay wrote the other 5.

The authors of the *Federalist Papers* told Americans that the new federal government would not overpower the states. In *Federalist Paper* "No. 10," Madison wrote about the many different groups of U.S. citizens. Their many points of view, Madison stated, would keep any single group from controlling the government. In *Federalist Paper* "No. 15," Hamilton discussed the need to fix the country's many problems under the Articles of Confederation. "Let us make a firm stand for our safety, our tranquillity [peace], our dignity, our reputation," he wrote. The *Federalist Papers* were widely reprinted and strongly influenced the debate over the Constitution.

✔ Reading Check: **Identifying Points of View** How did the *Federalist Papers* defend the Constitution?

The Ratification Fight

The true test of the Constitution's support came during the debate over state ratification, or approval. The Articles of Confederation had needed the approval of all 13 states to go into effect. However, the Constitution needed only 9 states to pass it. Each state except Rhode Island held special state conventions to give citizens the chance to discuss the Constitution. Then they could vote on whether the Constitution should be ratified.

Antifederalists also spoke out in state conventions. In New York one citizen said, "It appears that the government will fall into the hands of the few and the great." At the Virginia ratification convention, Patrick Henry spoke for many Antifederalists.

Analyzing Primary Sources

Identifying Points of View
What did Patrick Henry fear about the new form of government?

"If you make the citizens of this country agree to become the subjects of one great consolidated [united] empire of America, your government will not have sufficient energy to keep them together. . . . There will be no checks, no real balances, in this government."

—Patrick Henry, quoted in *Great Issues in American History,* edited by Richard Hofstadter

The Constitution had the support of heroes of the American Revolution such as Benjamin Franklin, Paul Revere, and George Washington. At the Massachusetts convention, Revere helped win the backing of other craftspeople.

On December 7, 1787, Delaware became the first state to ratify the Constitution. Throughout the rest of 1787 and the first half of 1788, eight other states ratified the Constitution. They did so in the following order: Pennsylvania, New Jersey, Georgia, Connecticut, Massachusetts, Maryland, South Carolina, and New Hampshire. The Constitution went into effect in June 1788 after New Hampshire became the ninth state to ratify it.

June 1788
The Constitution goes into effect.

However, there was still debate in New York, North Carolina, Rhode Island, and Virginia. Political leaders across America knew the new government needed the support of Virginia and New York. Virginia had the largest population in the nation. New York was an important center for business and trade. Finally, James Madison and the other Virginia Federalists convinced Virginia to ratify the Constitution in late June 1788. In New York, Federalists John Jay and Alexander Hamilton said that New York City would break away and join the new government if the Constitution was not ratified. New York State finally ratified the Constitution in

The Articles of Confederation and the Constitution

ARTICLES	CONSTITUTION
EXECUTIVE BRANCH	
No executive to administer and enforce legislation; Congress has sole authority to govern Executive committee to oversee government when Congress is out of session	President administers and enforces federal laws
LEGISLATIVE BRANCH	
A unicameral (one-house) legislature Each state has one vote, regardless of population Nine votes (of the original 13) to enact major legislation	A bicameral (two-house) legislature Each state has equal representation in the Senate; each state is represented according to population in the House of Representatives Simple majority to enact legislation
JUDICIAL BRANCH	
No national court system Congress to establish temporary courts to hear cases of piracy	National court system, headed by the Supreme Court Courts to hear cases involving national laws, treaties, and the Constitution as well as cases between states, between citizens of different states, or between a state and citizen of another state
OTHER MATTERS	
Admission to the Confederation by 9 votes (of 13) Amendment of the Articles by unanimous vote The states retain independence	Congress to admit new states; all must have a republican form of government Amendment of the Constitution by two-thirds vote of both houses of Congress or by national convention, followed by ratification by three fourths of the states The states accept the Constitution as the supreme law of the land

Interpreting the Visual Record

Political parade *Federalists held a parade to celebrate New York's ratification of the Constitution in July 1788.* ***Whose name is on the float, and why do you think this person was chosen to represent the Federalist cause?***

July 1788. North Carolina ratified the Constitution in November 1789. Rhode Island was the last state to ratify the Constitution in May 1790.

✔ **Reading Check: Sequencing** In what order did the states ratify the Constitution, and which states ratified the Constitution after it went into effect?

Demanding a Bill of Rights

Free Find:
James Madison
After reading about James Madison on the **Holt Researcher CD–ROM,** imagine that you are a newspaper editor. Write an obituary describing his political efforts to protect citizens' rights.

Several states ratified the Constitution only after they were promised that a bill of rights would be added to it. Many Antifederalists did not think that the Constitution would protect personal freedoms. The writer Mercy Otis Warren, an Antifederalist, expressed this concern in Boston's *Columbian Patriot.* "The whole constitution . . . appears a perversion [abuse] of the rights of particular states and of private citizens."

In the new Congress, some Federalists said that the nation did not need a federal bill of rights. They believed that state constitutions already promised these rights. Many Federalists also believed that the whole Constitution itself was a bill of rights. It was, they argued, written to protect the liberty of all U.S. citizens.

James Madison did not think that a bill of rights was necessary. However, he understood that the promise of such a bill had been key to ratification. He therefore wanted to make a bill of rights one of the new government's first priorities. Thomas Jefferson supported Madison's efforts. He wrote that "a bill of rights is what the people are entitled to against every government on earth, . . . and what no just government should refuse." In Congress's first session, Madison encouraged the legislators to put together a bill of rights. Then, the rights would be added to the Constitution as **amendments**—official changes, corrections, or additions. In Article V of the Constitution, the Founders had provided a way to change the document. They believed amendments would be necessary to reflect the will of the people. They designed the process to be difficult, however. Proposed amendments must be approved by a two-thirds majority of both houses of Congress. Then they must be ratified by three fourths of the states before taking effect.

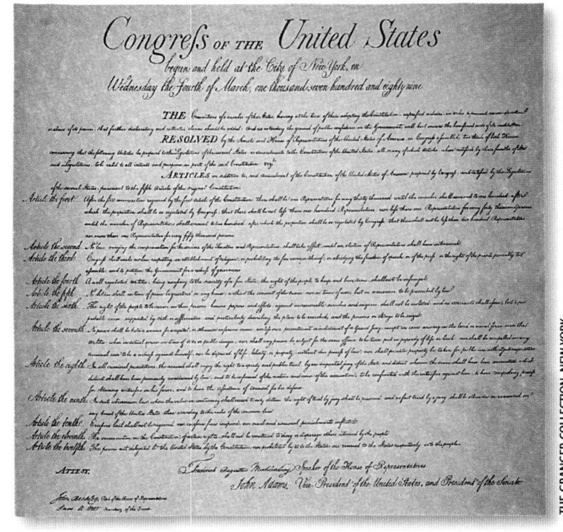
Congress of the United States
begun and held at the City of New-York, on
Wednesday the fourth of March, one thousand seven hundred and eighty nine

THE GRANGER COLLECTION, NEW YORK

The Bill of Rights assured many Americans that their new government would act to protect their liberties.

To create a list of possible amendments, the legislators took ideas from the state ratifying conventions. They also consulted the Virginia Declaration of Rights and the Declaration of Independence. Members of Congress worked to make sure that the abuses listed in the Declaration would be illegal under the new government. Congress debated the amendments for three months. Finally, in September 1789, Congress proposed 12 amendments, which were then sent to the states for ratification. By December 1791, the required three fourths of the states had ratified 10 of these proposed amendments. These first 10 amendments to the U.S. Constitution are known as the **Bill of Rights**. *(For a full discussion of the Bill of Rights, see Chapter 9.)*

These 10 amendments added to the strength and flexibility of the Constitution. The Bill of Rights also set a clear example of how to amend the Constitution to address the needs of the nation.

The Constitution is a remarkable document. It has clear guidelines and principles, yet can be changed to meet new challenges. The flexibility of the U.S. Constitution has allowed it to survive for more than 200 years. It is the world's oldest written national constitution.

✔ **Reading Check: Analyzing Information** Why did some people feel a bill of rights was necessary, and how was it added to the Constitution?

Section 4 Review

go.hrw.com Homework Practice Online
keyword: SC3 HP7

1. **Define** and explain:
   - amendments

2. **Identify** and explain:
   - Antifederalists
   - George Mason
   - Federalists
   - *Federalist Papers*
   - Bill of Rights

3. **Contrasting** Copy the chart below. Use it to identify the arguments for and against the Constitution.

U.S. Constitution

Federalist Views	Antifederalist Views

4. **Finding the Main Idea**
   a. Who wrote the *Federalist Papers*, and what were their arguments?
   b. How was the Constitution ratified, and when did it take effect?

5. **Writing and Critical Thinking**
   Summarizing Imagine that you are James Madison. Write an essay arguing why the Constitution should be amended with a bill of rights and explaining the amendment process.
   Consider the following:
   - the purpose of a Bill of Rights
   - those who supported a Bill of Rights in the Constitution
   - the process of amending the Constitution

Chapter 7 Review

The Chapter at a Glance

Examine the visual summary of the chapter below. Then create a poster illustrating the chapter's main ideas that you might present to the class.

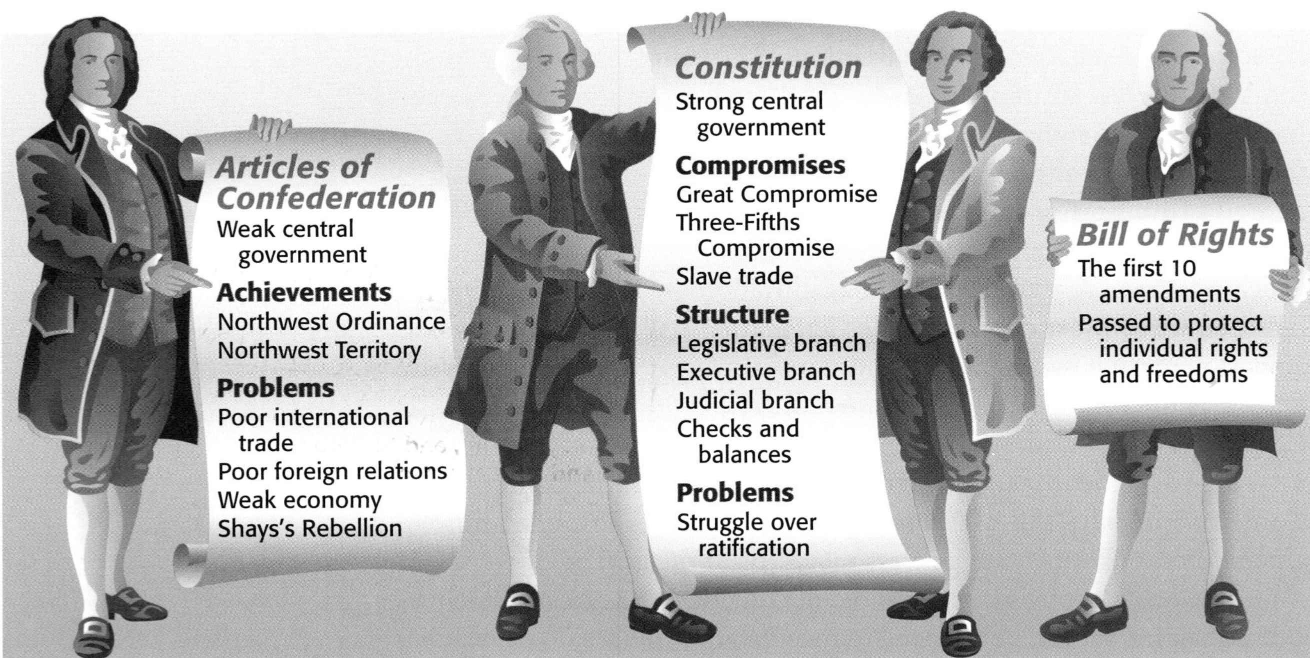

Identifying People and Ideas

Use the following terms or people in historically significant sentences.

1. Virginia Statute for Religious Freedom
2. Articles of Confederation
3. Northwest Ordinance of 1787
4. James Madison
5. Great Compromise
6. Three-Fifths Compromise
7. federalism
8. George Mason
9. *Federalist Papers*
10. amendments

Understanding Main Ideas

Section 1 *(Pages 186–191)*

1. What English and colonial examples of political ideas did Americans draw from when creating their new government?
2. What did the Northwest Ordinance of 1787 accomplish?

Section 2 *(Pages 194–199)*

3. How did a weak central government affect the American economy?

Section 3 *(Pages 200–205)*

4. What were the terms of the Great Compromise?
5. How is the federal government organized under the Constitution?

Section 4 *(Pages 206–211)*

6. What arguments did the Federalists and Antifederalists make regarding the Constitution?

You Be the Historian—Reviewing Themes

1. **Global Relations** How did the Articles of Confederation affect the new national government's ability to conduct foreign policy?
2. **Citizenship** Why did many Americans want a federal bill of rights?
3. **Constitutional Heritage** How does the Constitution guard against the misuse of power?

Thinking Critically

1. **Making Generalizations and Predictions** Without compromises, how do you think the Constitutional Convention would have turned out?
2. **Supporting a Point of View** Imagine that you are a delegate at a state ratifying convention. You have read the arguments made by Alexander Hamilton and Patrick Henry. Explain whose point of view you support and how you will vote.
3. **Drawing Inferences and Conclusions** In what ways did the Founding Fathers serve as examples of civic virtue?

Social Studies Skills Workshop

Interpreting Charts

Study the chart below. Then use the information from the chart to help you answer the questions that follow.

Ratifying the Constitution

STATE	RATIFICATION DATE
Delaware	December 7, 1787
Pennsylvania	December 12, 1787
New Jersey	December 18, 1787
Georgia	January 2, 1788
Connecticut	January 9, 1788
Massachusetts	February 6, 1788
Maryland	April 28, 1788
South Carolina	May 23, 1788
New Hampshire	June 21, 1788
Virginia	June 25, 1788
New York	July 26, 1788
North Carolina	November 21, 1789
Rhode Island	May 29, 1790

1. About how many months passed between the time that the first and last states ratified the Constitution?
   a. 31
   b. 33
   c. 6
   d. 3
2. During which year did the most states ratify the Constitution?
   a. 1787
   b. 1788
   c. 1789
   d. 1790
3. Based on your knowledge of the period and the information presented on the chart, when did the Constitution go into effect? Why was the support of New York and Virginia important?

Analyzing Primary Sources

Read the following quote by Benjamin Franklin, and then answer the questions that follow.

> **"Thus I consent, Sir, to this Constitution because I expect no better. . . . I hope therefore that for our own sakes as a part of the people, and for the sake of posterity [future generations], we shall act heartily and unanimously in recommending this constitution . . . wherever our influence may extend, and turn our future thoughts and endeavors to the means of having it well administered."**

4. Which of the following statements best describes Franklin's point of view?
   a. Future generations will like the Constitution more than the present one does.
   b. Americans should write a better constitution.
   c. The Constitution is as good as it can be, and the Founders should speak highly of it to Americans.
   d. The Constitution has broad influence.
5. Based on your knowledge of the period, do you think that Franklin's opinion would have been important to the other delegates at the Constitutional Convention? Explain your answer.

Alternative Assessment

Building Your Portfolio

Interdisciplinary Connection to Drama

Imagine that you are attending the Constitutional Convention. Think of an issue that was not addressed in the original Constitution (for example, suffrage for all Americans or the ending of slavery). Write a one-act play about the discussion that takes place at the Convention surrounding your issue. If possible, perform your play for the class using actors and appropriate props.

internet connect

Internet Activity: go.hrw.com
keyword: SC3 CF7

Choose an activity about forming a government to:

- Use graphic organizers to display global trade issues.
- Research a significant delegate to the Constitutional Convention and write a biography.
- Explore the political ideas of Federalists and Antifederalists.

The Living Constitution

The United States is governed by the Constitution, which was adopted by the original 13 states in 1789. The Constitution established a government in which the people choose their leaders. These officials make the nation's laws and run the government.

The framers of the Constitution created a federal system that is strong enough to enforce its authority. The principles and methods of governing that are outlined in the Constitution, however, are quite flexible. This flexibility has allowed the federal government to adjust to great change over more than 210 years. For example, the original nation of 13 states had a population of less than 4 million. Today the United States has 50 states and more than 280 million people.

The Union

The Northwest Ordinance was passed by the Confederation Congress in 1787, before the Constitution was written. The Ordinance established a method for admitting new states to the Union. The last states admitted to the Union were Alaska and Hawaii in 1959.

The Northwest Ordinance: Becoming a State

STEPS TO STATEHOOD

Congress specifies that three to five territories will be carved out of the Northwest Territory.

For each territory, Congress appoints a governor, a secretary, and three judges.

When a territory's population reaches 5,000 free male inhabitants of voting age, it elects a territorial legislature and sends a nonvoting delegate to Congress.

Once a territory's population increases to 60,000 free inhabitants, it becomes eligible for statehood and can draft a state constitution.

Congress approves the state constitution, and the territory becomes a state.

Sources: *Record of America; The Oxford Companion to American History*

Geography **Skills**

Interpreting Political Maps

1. When is a territory eligible for statehood?
2. **Human Systems** Under the Northwest Ordinance, who, or what, approves a territory's proposed constitution before the territory becomes a state?
3. **Sequencing** When did each state of the Northwest Territory join the Union?

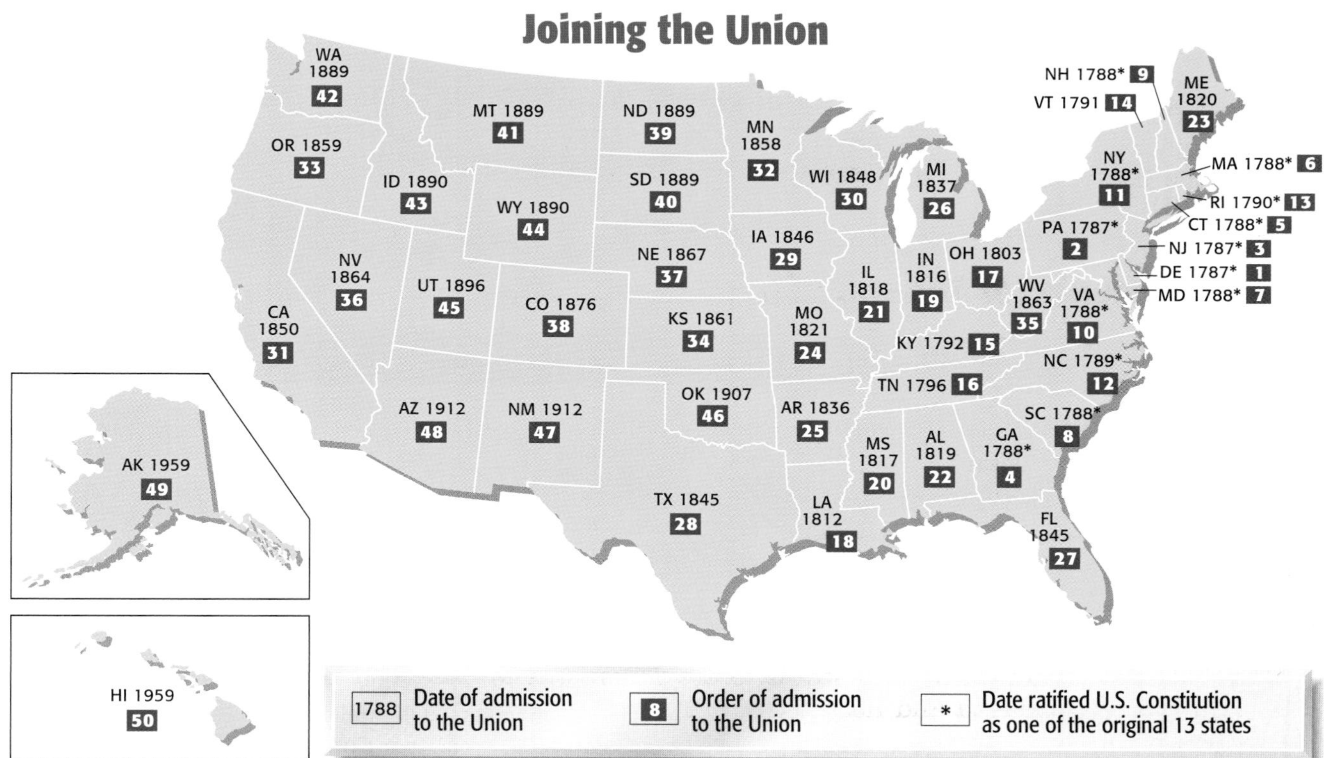

Geography **Skills**

Interpreting Thematic Maps

1. Which three states ratified the Constitution first?
2. **Places and Regions** What were the original 13 states of the Union?
3. **Summarizing** What states were admitted to the Union in the 1900s? In what years during this period were more than one state admitted?

History Note 1

Congress established the method for admitting new states to the Union in the Northwest Ordinance of 1787. Before that, however, some people in what is now the state of Tennessee made the first attempt to create a new state. In 1784 North Carolina turned over the Tennessee territory to the new government of the United States. Residents in northeastern Tennessee applied to Congress to form a new state named "Franklin" after Benjamin Franklin. However, North Carolina reclaimed the region before Congress could decide the issue. Finally, in 1790 North Carolina again gave the territory to the federal government. In 1796 the proposed state of Franklin became part of the new state of Tennessee.

Rocky Mount was the capital for the first territorial government of Tennessee.

Elected Officials and Voters

The Constitution sets the requirements for federal officials. The president, vice president, and members of Congress are all elected by the people. The percentage of the U.S. population that is eligible to vote has increased greatly over time.

Requirements for Federal Office

OFFICE	REQUIREMENTS	TERM	SELECTION
President **Vice President**	• 35 years old • Natural-born citizen • Live in United States 14 years	4 years	Elected by electoral college
Supreme Court Justice	• None	Life	Appointed by president and approved by Senate
Senator	• 30 years old • U.S. citizen 9 years • Live in state where elected	6 years	Originally chosen by state legislature (per Constitution); Currently elected by voters of state (per Seventeenth Amendment)
Representative	• 25 years old • U.S. citizen 7 years • Live in state where elected	2 years	Elected by voters of district

Geography **Skills**

Interpreting Charts

1. What are the age requirements for federal officials?
2. What are the terms of the federal officials listed?
3. **Comparing and Contrasting** Which federal office has the fewest requirements listed? Which position listed is not an elected office?

History Note 2

Franklin D. Roosevelt was the only president elected to more than two terms. He was elected president four times. In 1951 the Twenty-second Amendment was adopted, stating that no president can be elected more than twice. In 1995 the Supreme Court ruled that neither the states nor Congress could pass laws limiting the terms of members of Congress. A constitutional amendment that would allow term limits has been proposed. However, such an amendment has failed to pass in Congress.

The inauguration of President George W. Bush

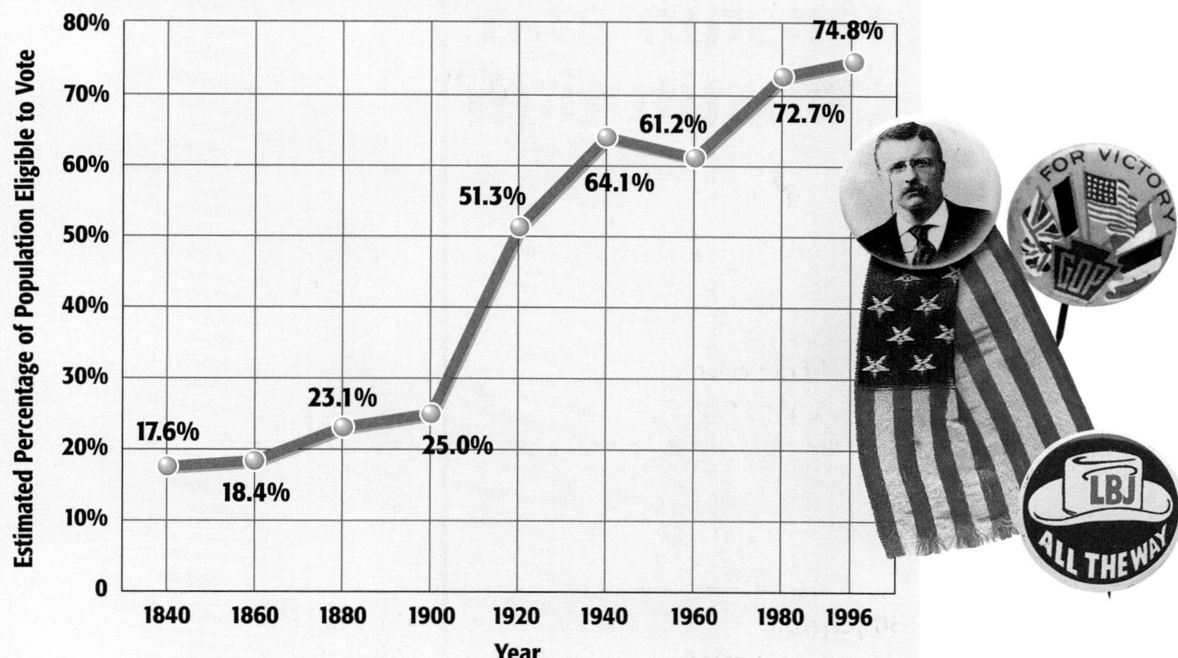

Sources: *Historical Statistics of the United States;* Federal Election Commission; *Congressional Quarterly's Guide to U.S. Elections; Datapedia of the United States, 1790–2000: America Year by Year*

Geography **Skills**

Interpreting Line Graphs

1. **Human Systems** What twenty-year interval on the graph shows the largest increase in the percentage of the U.S. population eligible to vote?
2. **Drawing Inferences and Conclusions** Show this graph to another student. Ask him or her to explain to you which amendments to the Constitution might account for the increases in voter eligibility seen in 1920 and 1980.

Presidential campaign buttons

History Note 3

The power to decide who is eligible to vote is reserved to the states under the Tenth Amendment. However, later constitutional amendments have extended the right to vote to more and more people. The Fifteenth Amendment, ratified in 1870, protects the right of people of any race to vote. In 1920 the Nineteenth Amendment gave women the right to vote in all states. The Twenty-sixth Amendment, ratified in 1971, lowered the legal voting age from 21 to 18.

CHAPTER

8 Citizenship and the Constitution

(1787–Present)

Congress sent the Constitution to the states for ratification in 1787.

THE GRANGER COLLECTION, NEW YORK

Suffragists parade down a street in Washington, D.C.

THE GRANGER COLLECTION, NEW YORK

UNITED STATES

1791 The Bill of Rights becomes part of the Constitution on December 15.

1920 The Nineteenth Amendment gives women the right to vote.

1954 The Supreme Court rules that segregated public schools are unconstitutional.

1800 // **1920** **1930** **1940** **1950**

WORLD

1917 Mexico adopts a new constitution.

1930 Mohandas K. Gandhi leads acts of civil disobedience to protest British rule in India.

1945 Delegates from 50 nations meet in San Francisco to found the United Nations.

1948 The United Nations adopts the Universal Declaration of Human Rights.

The United Nations was formed to resolve international conflicts peacefully.

Mohandas K. Gandhi (looking down at center) led many marches protesting British colonial rule in India.

Build on What You Know

After much discussion, the states ratified the new Constitution. For over 200 years the Constitution has provided the foundation of American democracy and freedom. Throughout recent history this document has been an example for many nations and democratic movements around the world.

Colin Powell led the organization America's Promise—The Alliance for Youth to promote volunteerism.

Immigrants take an oath to become U.S. citizens.

1967 Thurgood Marshall becomes the first African American justice on the Supreme Court.

1971 The Twenty-sixth Amendment is passed, giving the right to vote to all U.S. citizens aged 18 years or older.

1981 Sandra Day O'Connor becomes the first woman justice on the Supreme Court.

1990 The Americans with Disabilities Act is passed.

1997 Colin Powell starts a campaign for volunteerism.

1960 **1970** **1980** **1990** **2000**

1989 The East German government opens the Berlin Wall, allowing citizens of East Germany to travel to the West.

Demonstrators and celebrators gathered as the Berlin Wall was opened.

If you were there . . .

How would you educate Americans about their rights and responsibilities?

You Be the Historian

What's Your Opinion? Do you **agree** or **disagree** with the following statements? Support your point of view in your journal.

- **Constitutional Heritage** The government should be set up to make sure that the president does not have too much power.
- **Citizenship** One person's vote is not important to the outcome of an election.
- **Culture** The government should protect the rights of minorities over the interests of the majority.

Section 1

Understanding the Constitution

Read to Discover

1. How did the framers of the Constitution try to balance state and federal powers?
2. What are the three branches of the federal government, and what are the requirements for membership in each branch?
3. How is power divided between the three branches of government?

Why It Matters Today

The cabinet regularly advises the president on important issues. Use CNNfyi.com or other **current events** sources to identify a member of the presidential cabinet and read about some of the person's basic duties. Record your findings in your journal.

Define

- representative democracy
- delegated powers
- elastic clause
- reserved powers
- concurrent powers
- separation of powers
- apportionment
- impeach
- veto
- executive order
- pardon
- cabinet

Identify

- Thurgood Marshall
- Sandra Day O'Connor

The Story Continues

A sign on the Justice Department Building in Washington, D.C., describes the role of the Constitution. It reads, "No Free Government Can Survive That Is Not Based on the Supremacy of Law." This idea is central to the Constitution of the United States. The laws of our nation protect the freedom and the rights of our citizens.

The Department of Justice was established in 1870, with the attorney general as its head.

The Federal System

The United States is a **representative democracy**—a government led by officials who are chosen by the people. The Constitution created a federal system in which power is divided between the states and the federal government. The powers granted to the federal government are called **delegated powers**. Examples of these powers are coining money and regulating interstate and international trade. The federal government also runs the country's defense, declares war, and conducts diplomacy.

Federalism

POWERS DELEGATED TO THE NATIONAL GOVERNMENT	POWERS SHARED BY NATIONAL AND STATE GOVERNMENTS	POWERS RESERVED TO THE STATES
Declare war	Maintain law and order	Establish and maintain schools
Maintain armed forces	Levy taxes	Establish local governments
Regulate interstate and foreign trade	Borrow money	Regulate business within the state
Admit new states	Charter banks	Make marriage laws
Establish post offices	Establish courts	Provide for public safety
Set standard weights and measures	Provide for public welfare	Assume other powers not delegated to the national government or not prohibited to the states
Coin money		
Establish foreign policy		
Make all laws necessary and proper for carrying out delegated powers		

Sometimes, Congress has stretched its delegated powers to address new or unexpected issues. The "necessary and proper" clause of Article I, Section 8, of the Constitution makes this possible. The clause allows Congress to "make all Laws which shall be necessary and proper" for carrying out its duties. Because it provides flexibility for the government, this clause has become known as the **elastic clause**.

The powers kept by the state governments or by the citizens are **reserved powers**. These powers include creating local governments and holding elections. States also control education and trade within their borders. **Concurrent powers** are powers that the federal and state governments share. Taxing, borrowing money, enforcing laws, and providing for citizens' welfare are examples of these powers.

✔ **Reading Check: Categorizing** List at least two examples each of delegated, reserved, and concurrent powers.

The Legislative Branch

The federal government is divided into three separate branches, each with its own responsibilities and powers. This **separation of powers** is designed to balance each branch against the others. It keeps any single branch from becoming too powerful.

The legislative branch, or Congress, makes the nation's laws. "Members of Congress are the human connection between the citizen and . . . government," noted one member. Article I divides Congress into the House of Representatives and the Senate.

This is the seal of Congress, the lawmaking branch of the federal government.

Interpreting the Visual Record

Federal Hall *The first Congress under the Constitution met in Federal Hall in New York City.* ***Why might the Congress later need a new building?***

With 435 members, the House of Representatives is the larger of the two houses of Congress. The U.S. census, a population count taken every 10 years, decides the number of representatives for each state. To keep each state's total current, Congress uses **apportionment**, or planned distribution, of representatives. Under this system, no state can gain a representative unless another state loses one. House members represent a particular district of voters in a state. House members must be at least 25 years old, have been U.S. citizens for seven or more years, and be residents of the state in which they are elected. House members serve two-year terms.

The Senate is made up of two representatives, called senators, from each state. Senators represent the interests of their entire state. They must be at least 30 years old and have been U.S. citizens for nine or more years. Senators serve six-year terms and must be residents of the state they represent. The senator who has served longer is the state's senior senator. No law limits the number of times someone may be elected to either house of Congress.

The political party that has the most members in each house of Congress is called the majority party. The party with fewer members is the minority party. The leader of the House of Representatives is the Speaker of the House. House members select the Speaker, who is usually from the majority party. The vice president of the United States serves as the president of the Senate. The vice president does not join in Senate debates but can cast a vote to break a tie. When the vice president is absent, the president *pro tempore* leads the Senate.

Congress begins its regular session, or meeting, each year in the first week of January. Each house of Congress carries out most of its work in committees that specialize in certain types of bills, or proposed laws. For example, all bills about taxes begin in the House Ways and Means Committee.

✔ **Reading Check: Summarizing** What are the requirements and terms of office for members of the House and the Senate?

The Executive Branch

Article II of the Constitution specifies the powers of the executive branch. This branch enforces the laws that Congress passes. The president, as head of the executive branch, is the most powerful elected leader in the country. To become president, one must be a native-born U.S. citizen, at least 35 years old, and have been a U.S. resident for at least 14 years. The requirements are the same for the vice president.

Thus far, all U.S. presidents have been white men. In more recent elections, candidates for the nation's highest offices have been more diverse. African Americans such as Jesse Jackson and Alan Keyes have campaigned for nomination. In 1984 Geraldine Ferraro ran as the Democratic nominee for vice president. She was the first female candidate for a major political party. In 2000 Democrat Joseph Lieberman became the first Jewish nominee for vice president.

Every four years Americans elect a president and vice president. Franklin D. Roosevelt, who won four presidential elections, was the only president to serve more than two terms. Later, the Twenty-second Amendment limited presidents to two terms. If the president dies, resigns, or is removed from office, the vice president becomes president.

The House of Representatives can **impeach**, or vote to bring charges of "treason, bribery, or other high crimes and misdemeanors" against, a president. The Senate tries all impeachment cases. If a president is found guilty, Congress can remove him or her from office. In 1868 Andrew Johnson became the first president to be impeached. President Bill Clinton was impeached in 1998. In each case the Senate tried the president and found him not guilty. In 1974 President Richard Nixon resigned to avoid possible impeachment.

Working with Congress

The system of checks and balances often places the president against Congress. This problem is quite challenging when the president's party is different from that of the majority party in Congress. Despite their differences, the executive and legislative branches must cooperate. President Lyndon Johnson described the role Congress played in his work.

"What a President says and thinks is not worth five cents unless he has the people and Congress behind him. Without the Congress I'm just a six-feet-four Texan. With Congress I'm President of the United States in the fullest sense."

—President Lyndon Johnson, from *The Macmillan Dictionary of Political Quotations*

Although Congress passes laws, the president can ask members of Congress to pass or reject certain bills. The president also has the power to **veto**, or cancel, laws that Congress passes. Congress can override, or undo, a president's veto; however, doing so is very difficult. Overriding a veto requires a two-thirds majority vote. After Congress passes a law, federal agencies and departments often decide how to enforce it. In carrying out laws that affect parts of the Constitution, treaties, and statutes, the president may issue an **executive order**, a command that has the power of law. In an emergency the president might issue an executive order that stretches the definition of laws passed by Congress. The president also has the power to grant a **pardon**, or freedom from punishment. Pardons are sometimes given to persons convicted of federal crimes or who are facing criminal charges.

That's Interesting!

Electoral Oversights Did you know that the runner-up in a presidential election used to become vice president? It's true! Even if the top two finishers were from different policital parties, the candidate in second place served as vice president. To solve this problem, parties began choosing both a presidential and vice presidential candidate to run on the same ticket. But because electors cast only one ballot for both candidates, the two Democratic-Republican candidates in 1800 ended up tied with each other for president! In 1804, Congress passed the Twelfth Amendment, which directs electors to cast separate ballots for president and vice president.

Aaron Burr tied with Thomas Jefferson in the 1800 electoral vote.

THE GRANGER COLLECTION, NEW YORK

Analyzing Primary Sources

Drawing Inferences and Conclusions Why did President Johnson believe the support of Congress was important?

The president is also commander in chief of the armed forces. In an emergency, the president can send in U.S. troops, but only Congress can declare war. Some other executive duties are foreign relations and arranging treaties. Currently, 14 executive departments do most of the executive branch's work. The president chooses the department heads, whom Congress must then approve. The **cabinet**, made up of these department secretaries, advises the president on important matters.

✔ **Reading Check: Comparing** What powers do the executive and legislative branches have over each other?

Research on the ROM

Free Find:
Pendleton Civil Service Act
After reading about the Pendleton Civil Service Act on the **Holt Researcher CD–ROM**, write an editorial describing why it is important to have civil service jobs that are not appointed positions.

The Judicial Branch

The third branch of the government is the judicial branch. This branch is made up of a system of federal courts headed by the U.S. Supreme Court. Article III of the Constitution outlines the courts' duties. As an implied part of these duties, a federal court can strike down a state or federal law. However, a court can only do this if it finds a law unconstitutional. If Congress desires, it can propose an amendment to the Constitution that would make the law constitutional.

The president makes all appointments to federal courts. These judges receive the appointment for life to ensure that they will not be influenced by political parties. The lower courts in the federal system are divided according to the types of cases over which they have jurisdiction, or authority. Each state has at least one district court to handle federal cases. States with higher populations often have more than one district court. Today there are 94 U.S. district courts and 13 courts of appeals that review lower-court decisions.

At times, someone convicted of a crime believes that the original trial was unfair. That person can appeal his or her case to the higher court. Each of these courts of appeals has a panel of judges who decide whether the lower court tried the original case properly. If the judges uphold, or accept, the lower court's decision, then the case's original outcome stands. If not, the case may go back to the lower court for a new trial.

✔ **Reading Check: Analyzing Information** What check does the judicial branch have over the legislative branch?

BIOGRAPHY

Sandra Day O'Connor

1930–

Sandra Day O'Connor was born in El Paso, Texas, and attended law school at Stanford University in California. She served as Arizona's assistant attorney general and as a state legislator before becoming an Arizona state judge. In 1981 President Ronald Reagan chose O'Connor to serve on the Supreme Court. Although she was appointed by a conservative Republican president, at times O'Connor is often seen as a moderate justice. Her decisions show how Supreme Court justices can often be free from party politics. What experience did O'Connor have before becoming a judge?

The Supreme Court

After a case has been decided by the court of appeals, the losing side may appeal the decision to the Supreme Court. Thousands of cases are appealed to the Court each year. However, Supreme Court justices have time to review only about 100 of these cases. The justices carefully choose which cases to hear. Generally, cases that are chosen must involve an important constitutional or public interest issue. If the Court refuses to hear a case, the decision of the court of appeals is final. Most cases that are presented to the Supreme Court are review cases. However, some cases go directly to the Supreme Court. Some examples are cases that involve international diplomats or disputes between states.

Interpreting the Visual Record

The Supreme Court *Supreme Court justice Ruth Bader Ginsburg speaks to a group of students.* ***What would you ask Justice Ginsburg if you were one of the students in the picture?***

Congress decides how many justices sit on the Court. Traditionally that number has been fixed at nine. The chief justice of the United States leads the Supreme Court. Unlike the president and members of Congress, Court justices do not have specific requirements set by the Constitution. So far, however, every justice has been an attorney.

In the past few decades the makeup of the Supreme Court has become more diverse. In 1967 **Thurgood Marshall** became the first African American justice, with Clarence Thomas becoming the second in 1991. Right now two women sit on the high court—Ruth Bader Ginsburg and **Sandra Day O'Connor**. O'Connor became the first female Court justice after her 1981 appointment by President Ronald Reagan.

✔ **Reading Check: Finding the Main Idea** What types of cases does the Supreme Court usually review?

Section 1 Review

go.hrw.com **Homework Practice Online**
keyword: SC3 HP8

1. **Define** and explain:
   - representative democracy
   - delegated powers
   - elastic clause
   - reserved powers
   - concurrent powers
   - separation of powers
   - apportionment
   - impeach
   - veto
   - executive order
   - pardon
   - cabinet

2. **Identify** and explain:
   - Thurgood Marshall
   - Sandra Day O'Connor

3. **Categorizing** Copy the web diagram below. Use it to list the powers of the federal government's three branches.

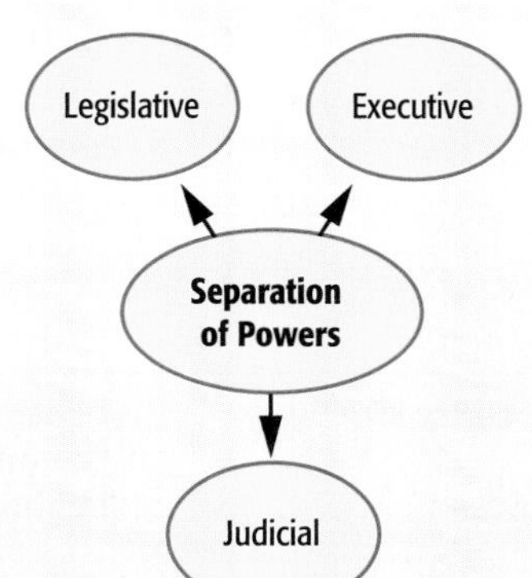

4. **Finding the Main Idea**
   a. What are the requirements for membership in the three branches of the federal government?
   b. Do you think the three branches of government share power equally? Explain your answer.

5. **Writing and Critical Thinking**
   Summarizing Imagine that you are one of the framers explaining the Constitution to U.S. citizens. Design a poster that explains how the Constitution balances state and federal powers. Your poster should define each power and provide examples.
   Consider the following:
   - delegated powers
   - reserved powers
   - concurrent powers

James Madison

FEDERALIST PAPER "NO. 51"

During the debates over the ratification of the Constitution, some New York newspapers printed essays favoring ratification. These essays answered Antifederalists' objections. The *Federalist Papers* were written by Alexander Hamilton, John Jay, and James Madison. In this excerpt from essay "No. 51," Madison describes the separation of powers. He also talks about how this separation would be preserved among the three branches of the government.

In order to lay a **due**[1] foundation for . . . the different powers of government, . . . it is evident that each department should have a will of its own; and consequently should be so **constituted**[2] that the members of each should have as little **agency**[3] as possible in the appointment of the members of the others. Were this principle **rigorously adhered to,**[4] it would require that all the appointments for the supreme executive, legislative, and judiciary **magistracies**[5] should be drawn from the same fountain of authority, the people, through channels having no communication whatever with one another. . . .

But the great security against a gradual concentration of the several powers in the same department [branch], consists in giving to those who administer each department the necessary constitutional means and personal motives to resist **encroachments**[6] of the others. The provision for defense must . . . be made **commensurate**[7] to the danger of attack. . . . It may be a reflection on human nature that such devices should be necessary to control the abuses of government. But what is government itself but the greatest of all reflections on human nature? If men were angels, no government would be necessary. If angels were to govern men, neither external nor internal controls on government would be necessary. In framing a government which is to be administered by men over men, the great difficulty lies in this: you must first enable the government to control the governed; and in the next place **oblige**[8] it to control itself.

The essays supporting the Constitution appeared in a book called The Federalist *in 1788.*

[1] **due:** proper
[2] **constituted:** set up
[3] **agency:** power
[4] **rigorously adhered to:** strictly followed
[5] **magistracies:** offices
[6] **encroachments:** improper advances
[7] **commensurate:** equal
[8] **oblige:** force

George Mason

"The Objections of the Hon. George Mason to the Proposed Federal Constitution"

George Mason played a behind-the-scenes role in the Revolutionary War and wrote Virginia's Declaration of Rights. He attended the Constitutional Convention in 1787. Mason criticized the proposed Constitution for allowing slavery, creating a strong central government, and lacking a Bill of Rights. As a result, he refused to sign the Constitution. However, after the Constitution was ratified, the government soon added a Bill of Rights. In addition to addressing Mason's concerns, the government used Virginia's Declaration of Rights as a model. In the following excerpt, George Mason explains why he will not sign the Constitution.

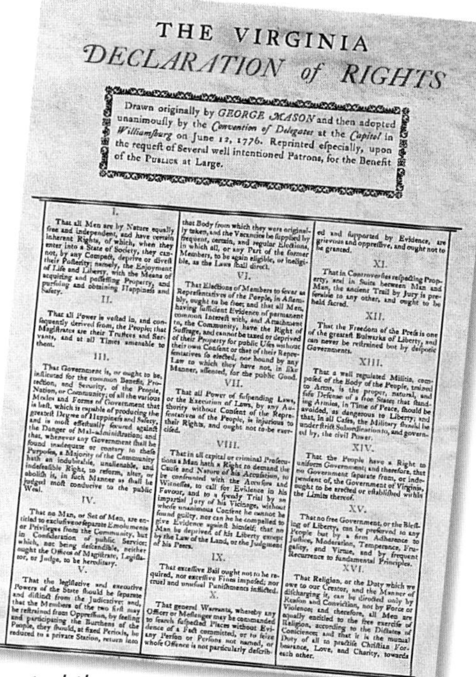
THE VIRGINIA
DECLARATION of RIGHTS

Drawn originally by GEORGE MASON and then adopted unanimously by the Convention of Delegates at the Capitol in Williamsburg on June 12, 1776. Reprinted especially, upon the request of Several well intentioned Patrons, for the Benefit of the Public at Large.

George Mason wanted the Constitution to include a Bill of Rights similar to Virginia's Declaration of Rights.

There is no declaration of rights: and the laws of the general government being **paramount**[1] to the laws and constitutions of the several states, the declarations of rights, in the separate states, are no security. Nor are the people secured even in the enjoyment of the benefit of the common law, which stands here upon no other foundation than its having been adopted by the respective acts forming the constitutions of the several states.

In the House of Representatives there is not the substance, but the shadow only of representation; which can never produce proper information in the legislature, or inspire confidence in the people. The laws will, therefore, be generally made by men little concerned in, and unacquainted with their effects and consequences. . . .

The President of the United States has no constitutional council. . . . He will therefore be unsupported by proper information and advice; and will generally be directed by **minions**[2] and favorites—or he will become a tool to the Senate. . . .

. . . There is no declaration of any kind for preserving the liberty of the press, the trial by jury in civil cases, nor against the danger of standing armies in time of peace. . . .

. . . [T]he general legislature is restrained from prohibiting the further importation of slaves for twenty odd years, though such importations render the United States weaker, more vulnerable, and less capable of defense.

Analyzing Primary Sources

1. How does Madison plan to "control the abuses of government"?
2. According to Mason, what rights were not protected by the Constitution?
3. In what ways do Madison and Mason agree?

[1] **paramount:** superior

[2] **minions:** servants

THE CONSTITUTION

"We the People of the United States, in Order to form a more perfect Union, establish Justice, insure domestic Tranquility, provide for the common defence, promote the general Welfare, and secure the Blessings of Liberty to ourselves and our Posterity, do ordain and establish this Constitution for the United States of America."

LEFT: Independence Hall, Philadelphia

ARTICLE I

Section 1. All legislative Powers herein granted shall be vested in a Congress of the United States, which shall consist of a Senate and House of Representatives.

Section 2. The House of Representatives shall be composed of Members chosen every second Year by the People of the several States, and the Electors in each State shall have the Qualifications requisite for Electors of the most numerous Branch of the State Legislature.

No Person shall be a Representative who shall not have attained to the Age of twenty five Years, and been seven Years a Citizen of the United States, and who shall not, when elected, be an Inhabitant of that State in which he shall be chosen.

Representatives and direct Taxes shall be apportioned among the several States which may be included within this Union, according to their respective Numbers~~, which shall be determined by adding to the whole Number of free Persons, including **those bound to Service**[1] for a Term of Years, and excluding Indians not taxed, three fifths of **all other Persons**~~.[2] The actual **Enumeration**[3] shall be made within three Years after the first Meeting of the Congress of the United States, and within every subsequent Term of ten Years, in such Manner as they shall by Law direct. The Number of Representatives shall not exceed one for every thirty Thousand, but each State shall have at Least one Representative~~; and until such enumeration shall be made, the State of New Hampshire shall be entitled to chuse three; Massachusetts eight; Rhode Island and Providence Plantations one; Connecticut five; New York six; New Jersey four; Pennsylvania eight; Delaware one; Maryland six; Virginia ten; North Carolina five; South Carolina five; and Georgia three~~.

When vacancies happen in the Representation from any State, the Executive Authority thereof shall issue Writs of Election to fill such Vacancies.

The House of Representatives shall chuse their Speaker and other Officers; and shall have the sole Power of Impeachment.

Section 3. The Senate of the United States shall be composed of two Senators from each State~~, chosen by the Legislature thereof~~, for six Years; and each Senator shall have one Vote.

Immediately after they shall be assembled in Consequence of the first Election, they shall be divided as equally as may be into three Classes. The Seats of the Senators of the first Class shall be vacated at the Expiration of the second Year, of the second Class at the Expiration of the fourth Year, and of the third Class at the Expiration of the sixth Year, so that one third may be chosen every second Year~~; and if Vacancies happen by~~

Legislative Branch
Article I explains how the legislative branch, called Congress, is organized. The chief purpose of the legislative branch is to make the laws. Congress is made up of the Senate and the House of Representatives.

The House of Representatives
The number of members each state has in the House is based on the population of the individual state. In 1929 Congress permanently fixed the size of the House at 435 members.

[1] **those bound to Service:** indentured servants

[2] **all other Persons:** slaves

[3] **Enumeration:** census or official population count

~~Resignation, or otherwise, during the Recess of the Legislature of any State, the Executive thereof may make temporary Appointments until the next Meeting of the Legislature, which shall then fill such Vacancies.~~

No Person shall be a Senator who shall not have attained to the Age of thirty Years, and been nine Years a Citizen of the United States, and who shall not, when elected, be an Inhabitant of that State for which he shall be chosen.

The Vice President
The only duty that the Constitution assigns to the vice president is to preside over meetings of the Senate. Modern presidents have usually given their vice presidents more responsibilities.

[4] **pro tempore:** temporarily

[5] **Impeachments:** official accusations of federal wrongdoing

The Vice President of the United States shall be President of the Senate, but shall have no Vote, unless they be equally divided.

The Senate shall chuse their other Officers, and also a President **pro tempore**,[4] in the Absence of the Vice President, or when he shall exercise the Office of President of the United States.

The Senate shall have the sole Power to try all **Impeachments**.[5] When sitting for that Purpose, they shall be on Oath or Affirmation. When the President of the United States is tried, the Chief Justice shall preside: And no Person shall be convicted without the Concurrence of two thirds of the Members present.

Exploring the Document

If the House of Representatives charges a government official with wrongdoing, the Senate acts as a court to decide if the official is guilty. **How does the power of impeachment represent part of the system of checks and balances?**

Judgment in Cases of Impeachment shall not extend further than to removal from Office, and disqualification to hold and enjoy any Office of honor, Trust or Profit under the United States: but the Party convicted shall nevertheless be liable and subject to Indictment, Trial, Judgment and Punishment, according to Law.

Section 4. The Times, Places and Manner of holding Elections for Senators and Representatives, shall be prescribed in each State by the Legislature thereof; but the Congress may at any time by Law make or alter such Regulations, except as to the Places of chusing Senators.

~~The Congress shall assemble at least once in every Year, and such Meeting shall be on the first Monday in December, unless they shall by Law appoint a different Day.~~

Section 5. Each House shall be the Judge of the Elections, Returns and Qualifications of its own Members, and a Majority of each shall constitute a **Quorum**[6] to do Business; but a smaller Number may **adjourn**[7] from day to day, and may be authorized to compel the Attendance of absent Members, in such Manner, and under such Penalties as each House may provide.

[6] **Quorum:** the minimum number of people needed to conduct business

[7] **adjourn:** to stop indefinitely

Each House may determine the Rules of its Proceedings, punish its Members for disorderly Behaviour, and, with the Concurrence of two thirds, expel a Member.

Each House shall keep a Journal of its Proceedings, and from time to time publish the same, excepting such Parts as may in their Judgment require Secrecy; and the Yeas and Nays of the Members of either House on any question shall, at the Desire of one fifth of those Present, be entered on the Journal.

Neither House, during the Session of Congress, shall, without the Consent of the other, adjourn for more than three days, nor to any other Place than that in which the two Houses shall be sitting.

Section 6. The Senators and Representatives shall receive a Compensation for their Services, to be ascertained by Law, and paid out of the Treasury of the United States. They shall in all Cases, except Treason, Felony and Breach of the Peace, be privileged from Arrest during their Attendance at the Session of their respective Houses, and in going to and returning from the same; and for any Speech or Debate in either House, they shall not be questioned in any other Place.

No Senator or Representative shall, during the Time for which he was elected, be appointed to any civil Office under the Authority of the United States, which shall have been created, or the **Emoluments**[8] whereof shall have been encreased during such time; and no Person holding any Office under the United States, shall be a Member of either House during his **Continuance**[9] in Office.

Section 7. All **Bills**[10] for raising Revenue shall originate in the House of Representatives; but the Senate may propose or concur with Amendments as on other Bills.

Every Bill which shall have passed the House of Representatives and the Senate, shall, before it become a Law, be presented to the President of the United States; If he approve he shall sign it, but if not he shall return it, with his Objections to that House in which it shall have originated, who shall enter the Objections at large on their Journal, and proceed to reconsider it. If after such Reconsideration two thirds of that House shall agree to pass the Bill, it shall be sent, together with the Objections, to the other House, by which it shall likewise be reconsidered, and if approved by two thirds of that House, it shall become a Law. But in all such Cases the Votes of both Houses shall be determined by yeas and Nays, and the Names of the Persons voting for and against the Bill shall be entered on the Journal of each House respectively. If any Bill shall not be returned by the President within ten Days (Sundays excepted) after it shall have been presented to him, the Same shall be a Law, in like Manner as if he had signed it, unless the Congress by their Adjournment prevent its Return, in which Case it shall not be a Law.

Every Order, Resolution, or Vote to which the Concurrence of the Senate and House of Representatives may be necessary (except on a question of Adjournment) shall be presented to the President of the United States; and before the Same shall take Effect, shall be approved by him, or being disapproved by him, shall be repassed by two thirds of the Senate and House of Representatives, according to the Rules and Limitations prescribed in the Case of a Bill.

[8] **Emoluments:** salary

[9] **Continuance:** term

[10] **Bills:** proposed laws

Exploring the Document

The framers felt that because members of the House are elected every two years, representatives would listen to the public and seek its approval before passing taxes. **How does Section 7 address the colonial demand of "no taxation without representation"?**

Exploring the Document

The veto power of the president is one of the important checks and balances in the Constitution. **Why do you think the Founding Fathers included the ability of Congress to override a veto?**

[11] **Duties:** tariffs

[12] **Imposts:** taxes

[13] **Excises:** internal taxes on the manufacture, sale, or consumption of a commodity

[14] **Rule of Naturalization:** a law by which a foreign-born person becomes a citizen

[15] **Securities:** bonds

[16] **Letters of Marque and Reprisal:** documents issued by governments allowing merchant ships to arm themselves and attack ships of an enemy nation

The Elastic Clause
The framers of the Constitution wanted a national government that was strong enough to be effective. This section lists the powers given to Congress. The last sentence in Section 8 contains the so-called "elastic clause," which has been stretched (like elastic) to allow Congress to meet changing circumstances.

Section 8. The Congress shall have Power To lay and collect Taxes, **Duties,**[11] **Imposts**[12] and **Excises,**[13] to pay the Debts and provide for the common Defence and general Welfare of the United States; but all Duties, Imposts and Excises shall be uniform throughout the United States;

To borrow Money on the credit of the United States;

To regulate Commerce with foreign Nations, and among the several States, and with the Indian Tribes;

To establish an uniform **Rule of Naturalization,**[14] and uniform Laws on the subject of Bankruptcies throughout the United States;

To coin Money, regulate the Value thereof, and of foreign Coin, and fix the Standard of Weights and Measures;

To provide for the Punishment of counterfeiting the **Securities**[15] and current Coin of the United States;

To establish Post Offices and post Roads;

To promote the Progress of Science and useful Arts, by securing for limited Times to Authors and Inventors the exclusive Right to their respective Writings and Discoveries;

To constitute Tribunals inferior to the supreme Court;

To define and punish Piracies and Felonies committed on the high Seas, and Offences against the Law of Nations;

To declare War, grant **Letters of Marque and Reprisal,**[16] and make Rules concerning Captures on Land and Water;

To raise and support Armies, but no Appropriation of Money to that Use shall be for a longer Term than two Years;

To provide and maintain a Navy;

To make Rules for the Government and Regulation of the land and naval Forces;

To provide for calling forth the Militia to execute the Laws of the Union, suppress Insurrections and repel Invasions;

To provide for organizing, arming, and disciplining, the Militia, and for governing such Part of them as may be employed in the Service of the United States, reserving to the States respectively, the Appointment of the Officers, and the Authority of training the Militia according to the discipline prescribed by Congress;

To exercise exclusive Legislation in all Cases whatsoever, over such District (not exceeding ten Miles square) as may, by Cession of particular States, and the Acceptance of Congress, become the Seat of the Government of the United States, and to exercise like Authority over all Places purchased by the Consent of the Legislature of the State in which the Same shall be, for the Erection of Forts, Magazines, Arsenals, dock-Yards, and other needful Buildings;—And

To make all Laws which shall be necessary and proper for carrying into Execution the foregoing Powers, and all other Powers vested by this

Constitution in the Government of the United States, or in any Department or Officer thereof.

Section 9. ~~The Migration or Importation of such Persons as any of the States now existing shall think proper to admit, shall not be prohibited by the Congress prior to the Year one thousand eight hundred and eight, but a Tax or duty may be imposed on such Importation, not exceeding ten dollars for each Person~~.

The Privilege of the **Writ of Habeas Corpus**[17] shall not be suspended, unless when in Cases of Rebellion or Invasion the public Safety may require it.

No **Bill of Attainder**[18] or **ex post facto Law**[19] shall be passed.

No **Capitation**,[20] or other direct, Tax shall be laid, unless in Proportion to the Census or Enumeration herein before directed to be taken.

No Tax or Duty shall be laid on Articles exported from any State.

No Preference shall be given by any Regulation of Commerce or Revenue to the Ports of one State over those of another: nor shall Vessels bound to, or from, one State, be obliged to enter, clear, or pay Duties in another.

No Money shall be drawn from the Treasury, but in Consequence of Appropriations made by Law; and a regular Statement and Account of the Receipts and Expenditures of all public Money shall be published from time to time.

No Title of Nobility shall be granted by the United States: And no Person holding any Office of Profit or Trust under them, shall, without the Consent of the Congress, accept of any present, Emolument, Office, or Title, of any kind whatever, from any King, Prince, or foreign State.

Section 10. No State shall enter into any Treaty, Alliance, or Confederation; grant Letters of Marque and Reprisal; coin Money; emit Bills of Credit; make any Thing but gold and silver Coin a Tender in Payment of Debts; pass any Bill of Attainder, ex post facto Law, or law impairing the Obligation of Contracts, or grant any Title of Nobility.

No State shall, without the Consent of the Congress, lay any Imposts or Duties on Imports or Exports, except what may be absolutely necessary for executing its inspection Laws: and the net Produce of all Duties and Imposts, laid by any State on Imports or Exports, shall be for the Use of the Treasury of the United States; and all such Laws shall be subject to the Revision and Controul of the Congress.

No State shall, without the Consent of Congress, lay any Duty of Tonnage, keep Troops, or Ships of War in time of Peace, enter into any Agreement or Compact with another State, or with a foreign Power, or engage in War, unless actually invaded, or in such imminent Danger as will not admit of delay.

[17] **Writ of Habeas Corpus:** a court order that requires the government to bring a prisoner to court and explain why he or she is being held

[18] **Bill of Attainder:** a law declaring that a person is guilty of a particular crime

[19] **ex post facto Law:** a law that is made effective prior to the date that it was passed and therefore punishes people for acts that were not illegal at the time

[20] **Capitation:** a direct uniform tax imposed on each head, or person

Exploring the Document

Although Congress has implied powers, there are also limits to its powers. Section 9 lists powers that are denied to the federal government. Several of the clauses protect the people of the United States from unjust treatment. **In what ways does the Constitution limit the powers of the federal government?**

ARTICLE II

Section 1. The executive Power shall be vested in a President of the United States of America. He shall hold his Office during the Term of four Years, and, together with the Vice President, chosen for the same Term, be elected, as follows.

Each State shall appoint, in such Manner as the Legislature thereof may direct, a Number of Electors, equal to the whole Number of Senators and Representatives to which the State may be entitled in the Congress: but no Senator or Representative, or Person holding an Office of Trust or Profit under the United States, shall be appointed an Elector.

~~The Electors shall meet in their respective States, and vote by Ballot for two Persons, of whom one at least shall not be an Inhabitant of the same State with themselves. And they shall make a List of all the Persons voted for, and of the Number of Votes for each; which List they shall sign and certify, and transmit sealed to the Seat of the Government of the United States, directed to the President of the Senate. The President of the Senate shall, in the Presence of the Senate and House of Representatives, open all the Certificates, and the Votes shall then be counted. The Person having the greatest Number of Votes shall be the President, if such Number be a Majority of the whole Number of Electors appointed; and if there be more than one who have such Majority, and have an equal Number of Votes, then the House of Representatives shall immediately chuse by Ballot one of them for President; and if no Person have a Majority, then from the five highest on the List the said House shall in like Manner chuse the President. But in chusing the President, the Votes shall be taken by States, the Representation from each State having one Vote; A quorum for this Purpose shall consist of a Member or Members from two thirds of the States, and a Majority of all the States shall be necessary to a Choice. In every Case, after the Choice of the President, the Person having the greatest Number of Votes of the Electors shall be the Vice President. But if there should remain two or more who have equal Votes, the Senate shall chuse from them by Ballot the Vice President.~~

The Congress may determine the Time of chusing the Electors, and the Day on which they shall give their Votes; which Day shall be the same throughout the United States.

No Person except a natural born Citizen~~, or a Citizen of the United States, at the time of the Adoption of this Constitution~~, shall be eligible to the Office of President; neither shall any Person be eligible to that Office who shall not have attained to the Age of thirty five Years, and been fourteen Years a Resident within the United States.

In Case of the Removal of the President from Office, or of his Death, Resignation, or Inability to discharge the Powers and Duties of the said Office, the Same shall devolve on the Vice President, and the Congress

Executive Branch
The president is the chief of the executive branch. It is the job of the president to enforce the laws. The framers wanted the president's and vice president's terms of office and manner of selection to be different from those of members of Congress. They decided on four-year terms, but they had a difficult time agreeing on how to select the president and vice president. The framers finally set up an electoral system, which varies greatly from our electoral process today.

Presidential Elections
In 1845 Congress set the Tuesday following the first Monday in November of every fourth year as the general election date for selecting presidential electors.

Exploring the Document

The youngest elected president was John F. Kennedy; he was 43 years old when he was inaugurated. (Theodore Roosevelt was 42 when he assumed office after the assassination of McKinley.) **What is the minimum required age for the office of president?**

may by Law provide for the Case of Removal, Death, Resignation or Inability, both of the President and Vice President, declaring what Officer shall then act as President, and such Officer shall act accordingly, until the Disability be removed, or a President shall be elected.

The President shall, at stated Times, receive for his Services, a Compensation, which shall neither be increased nor diminished during the period for which he shall have been elected, and he shall not receive within that Period any other Emolument from the United States, or any of them.

Before he enter on the Execution of his Office, he shall take the following Oath or Affirmation:—"I do solemnly swear (or affirm) that I will faithfully execute the Office of President of the United States, and will to the best of my Ability, preserve, protect and defend the Constitution of the United States."

Section 2. The President shall be Commander in Chief of the Army and Navy of the United States, and of the Militia of the several States, when called into the actual Service of the United States; he may require the Opinion, in writing, of the principal Officer in each of the executive Departments, upon any Subject relating to the Duties of their respective Offices, and he shall have Power to grant **Reprieves**[21] and **Pardons**[22] for Offenses against the United States, except in Cases of Impeachment.

He shall have Power, by and with the Advice and Consent of the Senate, to make Treaties, provided two thirds of the Senators present concur; and he shall nominate, and by and with the Advice and Consent of the Senate, shall appoint Ambassadors, other public Ministers and Consuls, Judges of the supreme Court, and all other Officers of the United States, whose Appointments are not herein otherwise provided for, and which shall be established by Law: but the Congress may by Law vest the Appointment of such inferior Officers, as they think proper, in the President alone, in the Courts of Law, or in the Heads of Departments.

The President shall have Power to fill up all Vacancies that may happen during the Recess of the Senate, by granting Commissions which shall expire at the End of their next Session.

Section 3. He shall from time to time give to the Congress Information of the State of the Union, and recommend to their Consideration such Measures as he shall judge necessary and expedient; he may, on extraordinary Occasions, convene both Houses, or either of them, and in Case of Disagreement between them, with Respect to the Time of Adjournment, he may adjourn them to such Time as he shall think proper; he shall receive Ambassadors and other public Ministers; he shall take Care that the Laws be faithfully executed, and shall Commission all the Officers of the United States.

Presidential Salary
In 1999 Congress voted to set future presidents' salaries at $400,000 per year. The president also receives an annual expense account. The president must pay taxes only on the salary.

Commander in Chief
Today, the president is in charge of the army, navy, air force, marines, and coast guard. Only Congress, however, can decide if the United States will declare war.

[21] **Reprieves:** delays of punishment

[22] **Pardons:** releases from the legal penalties associated with a crime

Appointments
Most of the president's appointments to office must be approved by the Senate.

The State of the Union
Every year the president presents to Congress a State of the Union message. In this message, the president introduces and explains a legislative plan for the coming year.

Section 4. The President, Vice President and all civil Officers of the United States, shall be removed from Office on Impeachment for, and Conviction of, Treason, Bribery, or other high Crimes and Misdemeanors.

ARTICLE III

Section 1. The judicial Power of the United States, shall be vested in one supreme Court, and in such inferior Courts as the Congress may from time to time ordain and establish. The Judges, both of the supreme and inferior Courts, shall hold their Offices during good Behaviour, and shall, at stated Times, receive for their Services, a Compensation, which shall not be diminished during their Continuance in Office.

Judicial Branch
The Articles of Confederation did not set up a federal court system. One of the first points that the framers of the Constitution agreed upon was to set up a national judiciary. In the Judiciary Act of 1789, Congress provided for the establishment of lower courts, such as district courts, circuit courts of appeals, and various other federal courts. The judicial system provides a check on the legislative branch: it can declare a law unconstitutional.

Section 2. The judicial Power shall extend to all Cases, in Law and Equity, arising under this Constitution, the Laws of the United States, and Treaties made, or which shall be made, under their Authority;—to all Cases affecting Ambassadors, other public Ministers and Consuls;—to all Cases of admiralty and maritime Jurisdiction;—to Controversies to which the United States shall be a Party;—to Controversies between two or more States;—~~between a State and Citizens of another State~~;—between Citizens of different States;—between Citizens of the same State claiming Lands under Grants of different States~~, and between a State, or the Citizens thereof, and foreign States, Citizens or Subjects~~.

In all Cases affecting Ambassadors, other public Ministers and Consuls, and those in which a State shall be Party, the supreme Court shall have original Jurisdiction. In all the other Cases before mentioned, the supreme Court shall have appellate Jurisdiction, both as to Law and fact, with such Exceptions, and under such Regulations as the Congress shall make.

The Trial of all Crimes, except in Cases of Impeachment, shall be by Jury; and such Trial shall be held in the State where the said Crimes shall have been committed; but when not committed within any State, the Trial shall be at such Place or Places as the Congress may by Law have directed.

Exploring the Document

In the Declaration of Independence, the colonists accused the British king of not allowing them trial by jury. **How does trial by jury differ from the vice-admiralty courts that colonists had faced?**

Section 3. Treason against the United States, shall consist only in levying War against them, or in adhering to their Enemies, giving them Aid and Comfort. No Person shall be convicted of Treason unless on the Testimony of two Witnesses to the same overt Act, or on Confession in open Court.

The Congress shall have Power to declare the Punishment of Treason, but no Attainder of Treason shall work **Corruption of Blood**,[23] or Forfeiture except during the Life of the Person attainted.

[23] **Corruption of Blood:** punishing the family of a person convicted of treason

ARTICLE IV

Section 1. Full Faith and Credit shall be given in each State to the public Acts, Records, and judicial Proceedings of every other State. And the

Congress may by general Laws prescribe the Manner in which such Acts, Records and Proceedings shall be proved, and the Effect thereof.

Section 2. The Citizens of each State shall be entitled to all Privileges and Immunities of Citizens in the several States.

A Person charged in any State with Treason, Felony, or other Crime, who shall flee from Justice, and be found in another State, shall on Demand of the executive Authority of the State from which he fled, be delivered up, to be removed to the State having Jurisdiction of the Crime.

~~No Person held to Service of Labour in one State, under the Laws thereof, escaping into another, shall, in Consequence of any Law or Regulation therein, be discharged from such Service or Labour, but shall be delivered up on Claim of the Party to whom such Service or Labour may be due~~.

Section 3. New States may be admitted by the Congress into this Union; but no new State shall be formed or erected within the Jurisdiction of any other State; nor any State be formed by the Junction of two or more States, or Parts of States, without the Consent of the Legislatures of the States concerned as well as of the Congress.

The Congress shall have Power to dispose of and make all needful Rules and Regulations respecting the Territory or other Property belonging to the United States; and nothing in this Constitution shall be so construed as to Prejudice any Claims of the United States, or of any particular State.

Section 4. The United States shall guarantee to every State in this Union a Republican Form of Government, and shall protect each of them against Invasion; and on Application of the Legislature, or of the Executive (when the Legislature cannot be convened) against domestic Violence.

ARTICLE V

The Congress, whenever two thirds of both Houses shall deem it necessary, shall propose Amendments to this Constitution, or, on the Application of the Legislatures of two thirds of the several States, shall call a Convention for proposing Amendments, which, in either Case, shall be valid to all Intents and Purposes, as Part of this Constitution, when ratified by the Legislatures of three fourths of the several States, or by Conventions in three fourths thereof, as the one or the other Mode of Ratification may be proposed by the Congress; Provided that ~~no Amendment which may be made prior to the Year One thousand eight hundred and eight shall in any Manner affect the first and fourth Clauses in the Ninth Section of the first Article; and that~~ no State, without its Consent, shall be deprived of its equal Suffrage in the Senate.

Exploring the Document

The framers wanted to ensure that the citizens could determine how the state governments would operate. **How does the need to respect the laws of each state support the principle of popular sovereignty?**

The States

States must honor the laws, records, and court decisions of other states. A person cannot escape a legal obligation by moving from one state to another.

Exploring the Document

In a republic, voters elect representatives to act in their best interest. **How does Article IV protect the practice of republicanism in the United States?**

Exploring the Document

America's founders may not have realized how long the Constitution would last, but they did set up a system for changing or adding to it. They did not want to make it easy to change the Constitution. **By what methods may the Constitution be amended? Under what sorts of circumstances do you think an amendment might be necessary?**

National Supremacy
One of the biggest problems facing the delegates to the Constitutional Convention was the question of what would happen if a state law and a federal law conflicted. Which law would be followed? Who would decide? The second clause of Article VI answers those questions. When a federal law and a state law disagree, the federal law overrides the state law. The Constitution and other federal laws are the "supreme Law of the Land." This clause is often called the supremacy clause.

Ratification
The Articles of Confederation called for all 13 states to approve any revision to the Articles. The Constitution required that 9 out of the 13 states would be needed to ratify the Constitution. The first state to ratify was Delaware, on December 7, 1787. Almost two and a half years later, on May 29, 1790, Rhode Island became the last state to ratify the Constitution.

ARTICLE VI

All Debts contracted and Engagements entered into, before the Adoption of this Constitution, shall be as valid against the United States under this Constitution, as under the Confederation.

This Constitution, and the Laws of the United States which shall be made in Pursuance thereof; and all Treaties made, or which shall be made, under the Authority of the United States, shall be the supreme Law of the Land; and the Judges in every State shall be bound thereby, any Thing in the Constitution or Laws of any State to the Contrary notwithstanding.

The Senators and Representatives before mentioned, and the Members of the several State Legislatures, and all executive and judicial Officers, both of the United States and of the several States, shall be bound by Oath or Affirmation, to support this Constitution; but no religious Test shall ever be required as a Qualification to any Office or public Trust under the United States.

ARTICLE VII

The Ratification of the Conventions of nine States, shall be sufficient for the Establishment of this Constitution between the States so ratifying the Same.

Done in Convention by the Unanimous Consent of the States present the Seventeenth Day of September in the Year of our Lord one thousand seven hundred and Eighty seven and of the Independence of the United States of America the Twelfth. In witness whereof We have hereunto subscribed our Names,

George Washington—
President and deputy from Virginia

NEW HAMPSHIRE
John Langdon
Nicholas Gilman

DELAWARE
George Read
Gunning Bedford, Jr.
John Dickinson
Richard Bassett
Jacob Broom

MASSACHUSETTS
Nathaniel Gorham
Rufus King

MARYLAND
James McHenry
Daniel of St. Thomas Jenifer
Daniel Carroll

CONNECTICUT
William Samuel Johnson
Roger Sherman

NEW YORK
Alexander Hamilton

VIRGINIA
John Blair
James Madison, Jr.

NEW JERSEY
William Livingston
David Brearley
William Paterson
Jonathan Dayton

NORTH CAROLINA
William Blount
Richard Dobbs Spaight
Hugh Williamson

PENNSYLVANIA
Benjamin Franklin
Thomas Mifflin
Robert Morris
George Clymer
Thomas FitzSimons
Jared Ingersoll
James Wilson
Gouverneur Morris

SOUTH CAROLINA
John Rutledge
Charles Cotesworth Pinckney
Charles Pinckney
Pierce Butler

GEORGIA
William Few
Abraham Baldwin

Attest:
William Jackson, Secretary

THE AMENDMENTS

Articles in addition to, and Amendment of the Constitution of the United States of America, proposed by Congress, and ratified by the Legislatures of the several States, pursuant to the fifth Article of the original Constitution.

[The First through Tenth Amendments, now known as the Bill of Rights, were proposed to the states for ratification on September 25, 1789, and declared in force on December 15, 1791.]

First Amendment

Congress shall make no law respecting an establishment of religion, or prohibiting the free exercise thereof; or abridging the freedom of speech, or of the press; or the right of the people peaceably to assemble, and to petition the Government for a redress of grievances.

Second Amendment

A well regulated Militia, being necessary to the security of a free State, the right of the people to keep and bear Arms, shall not be infringed.

Third Amendment

No Soldier shall, in time of peace, be **quartered**[24] in any house, without the consent of the Owner, nor in time of war, but in a manner to be prescribed by law.

Fourth Amendment

The right of the people to be secure in their persons, houses, papers, and effects, against unreasonable searches and seizures, shall not be violated, and no **Warrants**[25] shall issue, but upon probable cause, supported by Oath or affirmation, and particularly describing the place to be searched, and the persons or things to be seized.

Fifth Amendment

No person shall be held to answer for a capital, or otherwise **infamous**[26] crime, unless on a presentment or **indictment**[27] of a Grand Jury, except in cases arising in the land or naval forces, or in the Militia, when in actual service in time of War or public danger; nor shall any person be subject for the same offence to be twice put in jeopardy of life or limb; nor shall be compelled in any criminal case to be a witness against himself, nor be deprived of life, liberty, or property, without due process of law; nor shall private property be taken for public use, without just compensation.

Sixth Amendment

In all criminal prosecutions, the accused shall enjoy the right to a speedy and public trial, by an impartial jury of the State and district wherein the

Bill of Rights
One of the conditions set by several states for ratifying the Constitution was the inclusion of a bill of rights. Many people feared that a stronger central government might take away basic rights of the people that had been guaranteed in state constitutions.

Exploring the Document

The First Amendment forbids Congress from making any "law respecting an establishment of religion" or restraining the freedom to practice religion as one chooses. **Why is freedom of religion an important right?**

[24] **quartered:** housed

[25] **Warrants:** written orders authorizing a person to make an arrest, a seizure, or search

[26] **infamous:** disgraceful

[27] **indictment:** the act of charging with a crime

Rights of the Accused
The Fifth, Sixth, and Seventh Amendments describe the procedures that courts must follow when trying people accused of crimes.

Trials
The Sixth Amendment makes several guarantees, including a prompt trial and a trial by a jury chosen from the state and district in which the crime was committed.

[28] **ascertained:** found out

crime shall have been committed, which district shall have been previously **ascertained**[28] by law, and to be informed of the nature and cause of the accusation; to be confronted with the witnesses against him; to have compulsory process for obtaining witnesses in his favor, and to have the Assistance of Counsel for his defence.

Seventh Amendment

In Suits at common law, where the value in controversy shall exceed twenty dollars, the right of trial by jury shall be preserved, and no fact tried by a jury, shall be otherwise re-examined in any Court of the United States, than according to the rules of the common law.

Eighth Amendment

Excessive bail shall not be required, nor excessive fines imposed, nor cruel and unusual punishments inflicted.

Exploring the Document

The Ninth and Tenth Amendments were added because not every right of the people or of the states could be listed in the Constitution. **How do the Ninth and Tenth Amendments limit the power of the federal government?**

Ninth Amendment

The enumeration in the Constitution, of certain rights, shall not be construed to deny or disparage others retained by the people.

Tenth Amendment

The powers not delegated to the United States by the Constitution, nor prohibited by it to the States, are reserved to the States respectively, or to the people.

[29] **construed:** explained or interpreted

Eleventh Amendment

[Proposed March 4, 1794; declared ratified January 8, 1798]

The Judicial power of the United States shall not be **construed**[29] to extend to any suit in law or equity, commenced or prosecuted against one of the United States by Citizens of another State, or by Citizens or Subjects of any Foreign State.

President and Vice President
The Twelfth Amendment changed the election procedure for president and vice president.

Twelfth Amendment

[Proposed December 9, 1803; declared ratified September 25, 1804]

The Electors shall meet in their respective states, and vote by ballot for President and Vice-President, one of whom, at least, shall not be an inhabitant of the same state with themselves; they shall name in their ballots the person voted for as President, and in distinct ballots the person voted for as Vice-President, and they shall make distinct lists of all persons voted for as President, and of all persons voted for as Vice-President, and of the number of votes for each, which lists they shall sign and certify, and transmit sealed to the seat of the government of the United States, directed to the President of the Senate;—The President of the Senate shall, in the presence of the Senate and House of Representatives, open all the certificates and the votes shall then be counted;—The person having the greatest number of votes for President, shall be the President, if such number be a majority of the whole number of Electors appointed; and if no person have such majority, then from the persons having the highest numbers not exceeding three on the list of those voted for as President, the House of Representatives shall choose immediately, by ballot, the President. But in choosing the President, the votes shall be taken by states, the representation from each state having one vote; a quorum for this purpose shall consist of a member or members from two-thirds of the states, and a majority of all the states shall be necessary to a choice. ~~And if the House of Representatives shall not choose a President whenever the right of choice shall devolve upon them, before the fourth day of March next following, then the Vice-President shall act as President, as in the case of the death or other constitutional disability of the President.~~ —The person having the greatest number of votes as Vice-President, shall be the Vice-President, if such number be a majority of the whole number of Electors appointed, and if no person have a majority, then from the two highest numbers on the list, the Senate shall Choose the Vice-President; a quorum for the purpose shall consist of two-thirds of the whole number of Senators, and a majority of the whole number shall be necessary to a choice. But no person constitutionally ineligible to the office of President shall be eligible to that of Vice-President of the United States.

Thirteenth Amendment

[Proposed January 31, 1865; declared ratified December 18, 1865]

Section 1. Neither slavery nor **involuntary servitude**,[30] except as a punishment for crime whereof the party shall have been duly convicted, shall exist within the United States, or any place subject to their jurisdiction.

Section 2. Congress shall have power to enforce this article by appropriate legislation.

Abolishing Slavery
Although some slaves had been freed during the Civil War, slavery was not abolished until the Thirteenth Amendment took effect.

[30] **involuntary servitude:** being forced to work against one's will

Fourteenth Amendment

[Proposed June 13, 1866; declared ratified July 28, 1868]

Section 1. All persons born or naturalized in the United States, and subject to the jurisdiction thereof, are citizens of the United States and of the State wherein they reside. No State shall make or enforce any law which shall abridge the privileges or immunities of citizens of the United States; nor shall any State deprive any person of life, liberty, or property, without due process of law; nor deny to any person within its jurisdiction the equal protection of the laws.

Section 2. Representatives shall be apportioned among the several States according to their respective numbers, counting the whole number of per-

Protecting the Rights of Citizens
In 1833 the Supreme Court ruled that the Bill of Rights limited the federal government but not the state governments. This ruling was interpreted to mean that states were able to keep African Americans from becoming state citizens and keeping the Bill of Rights from protecting them. The Fourteenth Amendment defines citizenship and prevents states from interfering in the rights of citizens of the United States.

sons in each State~~, excluding Indians not taxed~~. But when the right to vote at any election for the choice of electors for President and Vice President of the United States, Representatives in Congress, the Executive and Judicial officers of a State, or the members of the Legislature thereof, is denied to any of the ~~male~~ inhabitants of such State, ~~being twenty-one years of age,~~ and citizens of the United States, or in any way abridged, except for participation in rebellion, or other crime, the basis of representation therein shall be reduced in the proportion which the number of such ~~male~~ citizens shall bear to the whole number of ~~male~~ citizens ~~twenty-one years of age~~ in such State.

Section 3. No person shall be a Senator or Representative in Congress, or elector of President and Vice President, or hold any office, civil or military, under the United States, or under any State, who, having previously taken an oath, as a member of Congress, or as an officer of the United States, or as a member of any State legislature, or as an executive or judicial officer of any State, to support the Constitution of the United States, shall have engaged in insurrection or rebellion against the same, or given aid or comfort to the enemies thereof. But Congress may by a vote of two-thirds of each House, remove such disability.

Section 4. The validity of the public debt of the United States, authorized by law, including debts incurred for payment of pensions and bounties for services in suppressing insurrection or rebellion, shall not be questioned. But neither the United States nor any State shall assume or pay any debt or obligation incurred in aid of insurrection or rebellion against the United States~~, or any claim for the loss of emancipation of any slave~~; but all such debts, obligations and claims shall be held illegal and void.

Section 5. The Congress shall have power to enforce, by appropriate legislation, the provisions of this article.

Fifteenth Amendment

[Proposed February 26, 1869; declared ratified March 30, 1870]

Section 1. The right of citizens of the United States to vote shall not be denied or abridged by the United States or by any State on account of race, color, or previous condition of servitude.

Section 2. The Congress shall have power to enforce this article by appropriate legislation.

Exploring the Document

The Fifteenth Amendment extended the vote to African American men. **Why is the right to vote guaranteed by the Fifteenth Amendment important?**

Sixteenth Amendment

[Proposed July 12, 1909; declared ratified February 25, 1913]

The Congress shall have power to lay and collect taxes on incomes, from whatever source derived, without apportionment among the several States, and without regard to any census or enumeration.

Seventeenth Amendment

[Proposed May 13, 1912; declared ratified May 31, 1913]

The Senate of the United States shall be composed of two Senators from each State, elected by the people thereof, for six years; and each Senator shall have one vote. The electors in each State shall have the qualifications requisite for electors of the most numerous branch of the State legislatures.

When vacancies happen in the representation of any State in the Senate, the executive authority of such State shall issue writs of election to fill such vacancies: *Provided,* That the legislature of any State may empower the executive thereof to make temporary appointments until the people fill the vacancies by election as the legislature may direct.

~~This amendment shall not be so construed as to affect the election or term of any Senator chosen before it becomes valid as part of the Constitution.~~

Exploring the Document

The Seventeenth Amendment requires that senators be elected directly by the people instead of by the state legislature. **What principle of our government does the Seventeenth Amendment protect?**

Eighteenth Amendment

[Proposed December 18, 1917; declared ratified January 29, 1919; repealed by the Twenty-first Amendment December 5, 1933]

~~Section 1. After one year from the ratification of this article the manufacture, sale, or transportation of intoxicating liquors within, the importation thereof into, or the exportation thereof from the United States and all territory subject to the jurisdiction thereof for beverage purposes is hereby prohibited.~~

~~Section 2. The Congress and the several States shall have concurrent power to enforce this article by appropriate legislation.~~

~~Section 3. This article shall be inoperative unless it shall have been ratified as an amendment to the Constitution by the legislatures of the several States, as provided in the Constitution, within seven years from the date of the submission hereof to the States by the Congress.~~

Prohibition

Although many people believed that the Eighteenth Amendment was good for the health and welfare of the American people, it was repealed 14 years later.

Nineteenth Amendment

[Proposed June 4, 1919; declared ratified August 26, 1920]

The right of citizens of the United States to vote shall not be denied or abridged by the United States or by any State on account of sex.

Congress shall have power to enforce this article by appropriate legislation.

Women's Suffrage

Abigail Adams and others were disappointed that the Declaration of Independence and the Constitution did not specifically include women. It took almost 130 years and much campaigning by groups before suffrage for women was finally achieved.

Twentieth Amendment

[Proposed March 2, 1932; declared ratified February 6, 1933]

Section 1. The terms of the President and Vice-President shall end at noon on the 20th day of January, and the terms of Senators and Representatives

Taking Office
In the original Constitution, a newly elected president and Congress did not take office until March 4, which was four months after the November election. The officials who were leaving office were called lame ducks because they had little influence during those four months. The Twentieth Amendment changed the date that the new president and Congress take office. Members of Congress now take office during the first week of January, and the president takes office on January 20.

at noon on the 3d day of January, of the years in which such terms would have ended if this article had not been ratified; and the terms of their successors shall then begin.

Section 2. The Congress shall assemble at least once in every year, and such meeting shall begin at noon on the 3d day of January, unless they shall by law appoint a different day.

Section 3. If, at the time fixed for the beginning of the term of the President, the President elect shall have died, the Vice-President elect shall become President. If a President shall not have been chosen before the time fixed for the beginning of his term, or if the President elect shall have failed to qualify, then the Vice-President elect shall act as President until a President shall have qualified; and the Congress may by law provide for the case wherein neither a President elect nor a Vice-President elect shall have qualified, declaring who shall then act as President, or the manner in which one who is to act shall be selected, and such person shall act accordingly until a President or Vice-President shall have qualified.

Section 4. The Congress may by law provide for the case of the death of any of the persons from whom the House of Representatives may choose a President whenever the right of choice shall have devolved upon them, and for the case of the death of any of the persons from whom the Senate may choose a Vice-President whenever the right of choice shall have devolved upon them.

~~**Section 5.** Sections 1 and 2 shall take effect on the 15th day of October following the ratification of this article.~~

~~**Section 6.** This article shall be inoperative unless it shall have been ratified as an amendment to the Constitution by the legislatures of three-fourths of the several States within seven years from the date of its submission.~~

Exploring the Document

The Twenty-first Amendment was the first amendment not ratified by state legislatures. **According to the crossed-out text, what method was used to ratify the Twenty-first Amendment?**

Twenty-first Amendment

[Proposed February 20, 1933; declared ratified December 5, 1933]

Section 1. The eighteenth article of amendment to the Constitution of the United States is hereby repealed.

Section 2. The transportation or importation into any State, Territory, or possession of the United States for delivery or use therein of intoxicating liquors, in violation of the laws thereof, is hereby prohibited.

~~**Section 3.** This article shall be inoperative unless it shall have been ratified as an amendment to the Constitution by conventions in the several States, as provided in the Constitution, within seven years from the date of the submission hereof to the States by the Congress.~~

Twenty-second Amendment

[Proposed March 21, 1947; declared ratified February 26, 1951]

Section 1. No person shall be elected to the office of the President more than twice, and no person who has held the office of President, or acted as President, for more than two years of a term to which some other person was elected President shall be elected to the office of the President more than once. ~~But this Article shall not apply to any person holding the office of President when this Article was proposed by the Congress, and shall not prevent any person who may be holding the office of President, or acting as President, during the term within which this Article becomes operative from holding the office of President or acting as President during the remainder of such term.~~

~~**Section 2.** This article shall be inoperative unless it shall have been ratified as an amendment to the Constitution by the legislatures of three-fourths of the several States within seven years from the date of its submission to the States by the Congress.~~

Exploring the Document

From the time of President George Washington's administration, it was a custom for presidents to serve no more than two terms in office. Franklin D. Roosevelt, however, was elected to four terms. The Twenty-second Amendment restricted presidents to no more than two terms in office. **Why do you think citizens chose to limit the power of the president in this way?**

Twenty-third Amendment

[Proposed June 16, 1960; ratified March 29, 1961]

Section 1. The District constituting the seat of Government of the United States shall appoint in such manner as the Congress may direct:

A number of electors of President and Vice-President equal to the whole number of Senators and Representatives in Congress to which the District would be entitled if it were a State, but in no event more than the least populous state; they shall be in addition to those appointed by the States, but they shall be considered, for the purposes of the election of President and Vice-President, to be electors appointed by a State; and they shall meet in the District and perform such duties as provided by the twelfth article of amendment.

Section 2. The Congress shall have power to enforce this article by appropriate legislation.

Voting Rights

Until the ratification of the Twenty-third Amendment, the people of Washington, D.C., could not vote in presidential elections.

Twenty-fourth Amendment

[Proposed August 27, 1962; ratified January 23, 1964]

Section 1. The right of citizens of the United States to vote in any primary or other election for President or Vice-President, for electors for President or Vice-President, or for Senator or Representative in Congress, shall not be denied or abridged by the United States or any State by reason of failure to pay any poll tax or other tax.

Section 2. The Congress shall have power to enforce this article by appropriate legislation.

Presidential Disability
The illness of President Eisenhower in the 1950s and the assassination of President Kennedy in 1963 were the events behind the Twenty-fifth Amendment. The Constitution did not provide a clear-cut method for a vice president to take over for a disabled president or upon the death of a president. This amendment provides for filling the office of the vice president if a vacancy occurs, and it provides a way for the vice president—or someone else in the line of succession—to take over if the president is unable to perform the duties of that office.

Twenty-fifth Amendment

[Proposed July 6, 1965; ratified February 10, 1967]

Section 1. In case of the removal of the President from office or of his death or resignation, the Vice-President shall become President.

Section 2. Whenever there is a vacancy in the office of the Vice-President, the President shall nominate a Vice-President who shall take office upon confirmation by a majority vote of both Houses of Congress.

Section 3. Whenever the President transmits to the President pro tempore of the Senate and the Speaker of the House of Representatives his written declaration that he is unable to discharge the powers and duties of his office, and until he transmits to them a written declaration to the contrary, such powers and duties shall be discharged by the Vice-President as Acting President.

Section 4. Whenever the Vice-President and a majority of either the principal officers of the executive departments or of such other body as Congress may by law provide, transmit to the President pro tempore of the Senate and the Speaker of the House of Representatives their written declaration that the President is unable to discharge the powers and duties of his office, the Vice-President shall immediately assume the powers and duties of the office as Acting President.

Thereafter, when the President transmits to the President pro tempore of the Senate and the Speaker of the House of Representatives his written declaration that no inability exists, he shall resume the powers and duties of his office unless the Vice-President and a majority of either the principal officers of the executive department or of such other body as Congress may by law provide, transmit within four days to the President pro tempore of the Senate and the Speaker of the House of Representatives their written declaration that the President is unable to discharge the powers and duties of his office. Thereupon Congress shall decide the issue, assembling within forty-eight hours for that purpose if not in session. If the Congress, within twenty-one days after receipt of the latter written declaration, or, if Congress is not in session, within twenty-one days after Congress is required to assemble, determines by two-thirds vote of both Houses that the President is unable to discharge the powers and duties of his office, the Vice-President shall continue to discharge the same as Acting President; otherwise, the President shall resume the powers and duties of his office.

Twenty-sixth Amendment

[Proposed March 23, 1971; ratified July 1, 1971]

Section 1. The right of citizens of the United States, who are eighteen years of age or older, to vote shall not be denied or abridged by the United States or by any State on account of age.

Section 2. The Congress shall have power to enforce this article by appropriate legislation.

Twenty-seventh Amendment

[Proposed September 25, 1789; ratified May 7, 1992]

No law, varying the compensation for the services of the Senators and Representatives, shall take effect, until an election of Representatives shall have intervened.

Expanded Suffrage
The Voting Act of 1970 tried to set the voting age at 18. However, the Supreme Court ruled that the act set the voting age for national elections only, not state or local elections. This ruling would make necessary several different ballots at elections. The Twenty-sixth Amendment gave 18-year-old citizens the right to vote in all elections.

Separation of Powers and Checks and Balances

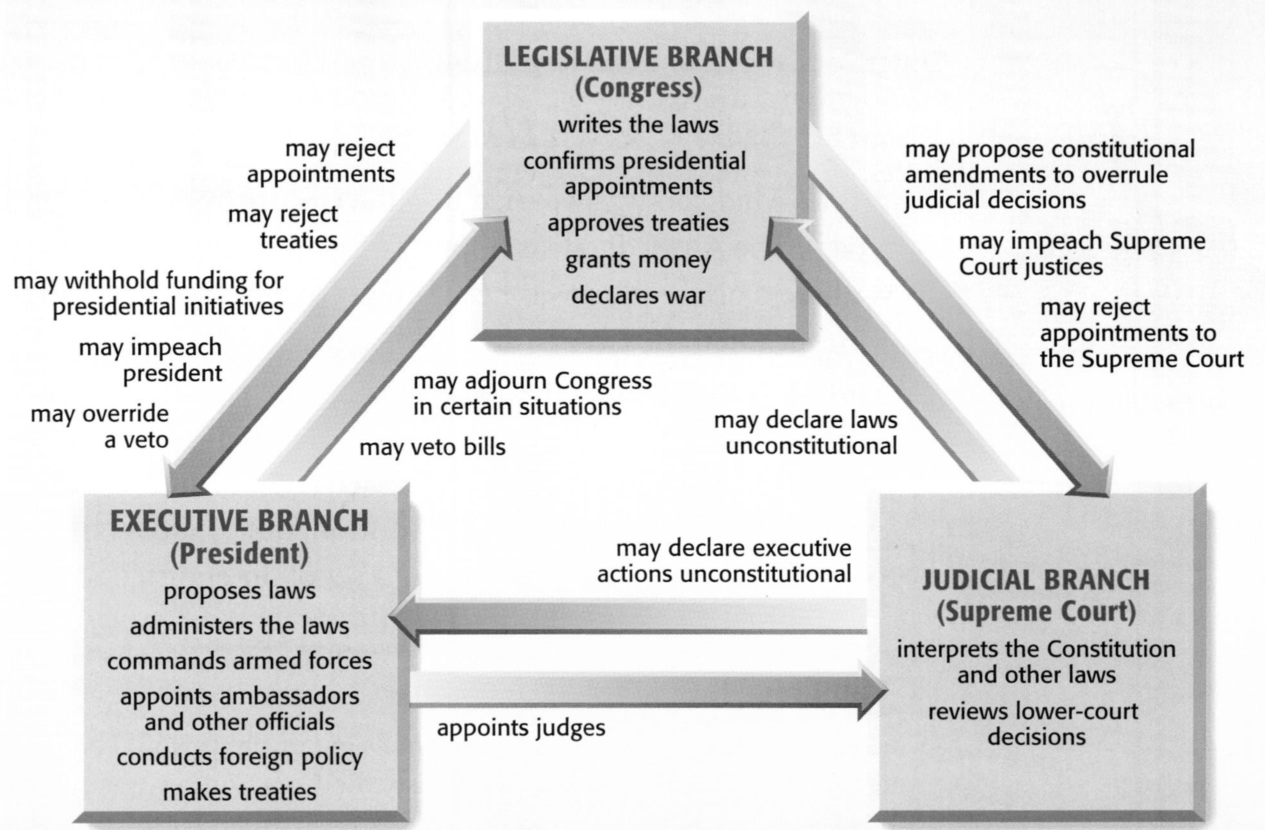

Section 2

The Bill of Rights

Read to Discover

1. What are the main freedoms outlined within the First Amendment, and why are they important?
2. How does the Bill of Rights address colonial grievances listed in the Declaration of Independence?
3. What protections does the Bill of Rights give to people accused of crimes?

Define

- petition
- search warrant
- due process
- indict
- double jeopardy
- eminent domain

Identify

- James Madison

Why it Matters Today

The Bill of Rights protects some of the basic rights that we enjoy in our daily lives. Not all countries let their citizens enjoy these same rights. Use CNNfyi.com or other **current events** sources to learn about people in another country who are trying to exercise some of the rights granted U.S. citizens in the Bill of Rights. Record your findings in your journal.

Quill pens like this one were used in the 1700s.

The Story Continues

James Madison was worried that the Constitution might not pass. The Antifederalists opposed it, and even Virginia, Madison's home state, was hesitating. Forceful speaker Patrick Henry wanted the Constitution to include a bill of rights before Virginia ratified it. The Virginia legislature rejected Henry's position and approved the Constitution on the condition that a bill of rights would be added later. At first, Madison had opposed amending the Constitution, but to satisfy the concerns of others, he put together a set of amendments.

The First Amendment

Federalist **James Madison** promised that a bill of rights would be added to the Constitution. With this promise, the Constitution was ratified. In 1789 Madison began narrowing down the huge list of proposed amendments. He then gave a shorter list of amendments to the House of Representatives. Of those, Congress approved 12 amendments. The states ratified 10. Those 10 amendments, called the Bill of Rights, protect U.S. citizens' individual liberties.

"The safety and happiness of society are the objects at which all political institutions aim and to which all such institutions must be sacrificed."

—James Madison, from *The Macmillan Dictionary of Political Quotations*

Analyzing Primary Sources

Identifying Points of View What does James Madison think the purpose of the government is?

The ideas within the First Amendment form the most basic rights of all U.S. citizens. These rights include freedom of religion, the press, speech, assembly, and to **petition**—make a request of the government. The First Amendment begins by stating that "Congress shall make no law respecting an establishment of religion, or prohibiting the free exercise thereof." In other words, the government cannot support or interfere with the practice of a religion. This amendment keeps the government from favoring any religion over others. When the Constitution was written, many countries had an official state religion. However, some Americans wanted to keep the government from establishing an official religion.

The First Amendment also guarantees freedom of speech and of the press. Americans have the right to express their own ideas and views and to hear the ideas and views of others. John Peter Zenger, the publisher of the *New York Weekly Journal,* was an example of why freedom of the press is important. Zenger had gone on trial in 1735 for criticizing New York's royal governor. The jury found Zenger not guilty because the statements he printed were true.

Freedom of speech does not mean that people can say anything they want to, however. The Constitution does not protect slander—false statements meant to damage someone's reputation. Libel, or intentionally publishing a lie that harms another person, is not protected either. The Supreme Court has also ruled that the First Amendment does not protect speech that endangers public safety. For example, Justice Oliver Wendell Holmes explained that falsely shouting "Fire!" in a crowded theater is not protected as free speech.

"The question in every case is whether the words used are used in such circumstances and are of such a nature to create a clear and present danger that . . . Congress has a right to prevent."

—Oliver Wendell Holmes, quoted in *A March of Liberty,* by Melvin I. Urofsky

Americans also have freedom of assembly, or to hold meetings. Any group may gather to discuss issues or to conduct business. If those people gather peacefully and are not involved in any illegal activity, the government cannot interfere. Any American can present a petition to a government official. This right lets Americans show their dissatisfaction with a law, as well as suggest new laws.

✔ **Reading Check: Finding the Main Idea** What are the freedoms protected by the First Amendment?

THE GRANGER COLLECTION, NEW YORK

BIOGRAPHY

James Madison

(1751–1836)

James Madison was born in Virginia in 1751. He attended the College of New Jersey, now Princeton University, before entering politics in Virginia. Early in his career, Madison became a strong supporter of religious freedom. Madison served in Congress until 1797. He later influenced politics from his family plantation. There he remained a slaveholder despite his stated belief in individual liberty. In 1801 Madison became secretary of state and went on to serve two terms as president. Madison played a central role in framing the Constitution and adding the Bill of Rights. For these reasons, he is often called the Father of the Constitution. **Why is Madison called the Father of the Constitution?**

Interpreting the Visual Record

Flood control *These members of the National Guard are helping local citizens prevent a river from flooding.* ***Why do you think it is important for community members to join together in such efforts?***

Protecting Citizens

The Second, Third, and Fourth Amendments all relate to colonial disputes with Great Britain before the Revolution. The Second Amendment deals with state militias. Colonial militias were vital to America's defense. The first battle of the Revolutionary War started when British troops tried to seize the Massachusetts militia's weapons. The framers believed that the states needed to keep their militias for emergencies. Today the National Guard has replaced state militias. National Guard members also serve in wars and help restore order during crises, such as natural disasters.

Some people believe that gun control laws violate the Second Amendment. This part of the Constitution states that "the right of the people to keep and bear arms shall not be infringed [violated]." In 1939 the Supreme Court passed rules for nonmilitary firearms. Years later, a U.S. court of appeals ruled that gun control laws do not violate the Second Amendment. The Supreme Court let that ruling stand in 1983.

The Third Amendment keeps the military from forcing citizens to give housing to soldiers. Before the Revolution, the British government pressured colonists to give food and shelter to its soldiers. British leaders also issued writs of assistance. These written orders let officials search any colonist's property for illegal goods. Anger over such actions led to the Fourth Amendment's rule against "unreasonable searches and seizures." Before authorities search someone's property, they must first get a **search warrant**, an order permitting them to look through someone's property. But authorities do not always need a warrant to conduct a search. Sometimes a suspect tries to destroy evidence or hide a weapon. When this happens, police can conduct an emergency search. This helps to protect both the officers and any evidence needed to prove criminal activity.

✔ **Reading Check: Contrasting** Contrast colonists' rights under British rule with the rights that Americans enjoy today under the Second, Third, and Fourth Amendments.

Citizenship and You

Freedom of Assembly

When Congress first talked about what should be in the Bill of Rights, some members argued that people in power should not be able to stop rival groups from meeting. Thus, freedom of assembly became part of the First Amendment. Over the years Americans have gathered to privately and publicly express their views on issues ranging from civil rights to education.

Americans do not have an unlimited right of assembly, however. Citizens must follow rules that protect public safety. For example, parades usually require a local permit so that traffic flow can be managed during the parade time. Such restrictions cannot be used to keep people or groups with unpopular beliefs from publicly expressing their views. **Should all groups have the same freedom of assembly? Explain your answer.**

The Rights of the Accused

The Fifth, Sixth, Seventh, and Eighth Amendments provide guidelines for trying people accused of crimes. The framers designed these amendments to protect the rights of the accused. According to the Fifth Amendment, the government cannot punish anyone for a crime without **due process** of law. This means that the law should always be fairly applied. A grand jury decides if there is enough evidence to **indict**, or formally accuse, the person. Without an indictment, the court cannot try someone for a serious crime. The Fifth Amendment also protects people from being forced to testify in their own criminal trial. To keep from testifying, the defendant "takes the Fifth." Anyone found not guilty in a criminal trial cannot face **double jeopardy**. In other words, that person cannot be tried again for the same crime.

The final clause of the Fifth Amendment addresses property rights. It states that no one will have property taken "without due process of law." The one exception to this principle is the government's power of **eminent domain**—the power to take personal property to benefit the public. An example would be the taking of private lands to build a public road. The government must pay the owners a fair price for their property. However, if the property that is taken was gained through illegal activities, then the person is not paid.

The Sixth Amendment protects the rights of someone who is indicted for a crime. It states that the accused must have a quick public trial by a jury. The accused person has the right to know the charges against him or her. The accused can also hear and question the witnesses testifying against him or her. The accused has the right to an attorney. If the person cannot afford legal services, the government provides an attorney.

Sometimes the accused refuses his or her Sixth Amendment rights. For example, some defendants refuse the services of an attorney. Others choose to have a trial in front of a judge alone instead of before a jury. Defendants can bypass a trial by agreeing to a plea bargain. In these cases, the individual pleads guilty to a lesser charge. By plea bargaining, defendants avoid the risk of conviction of a crime that may carry a greater sentence.

The Seventh Amendment states that juries can decide civil cases. Sometimes an individual causes physical or financial harm to another person without committing a crime. In such cases the injured party may sue, or seek justice, in civil court. Civil cases usually involve disputes over money or property. For example, someone might bring a civil suit against an individual who refuses to pay back a debt.

✔ **Reading Check: Summarizing** What rights do Americans have under the Fifth, Sixth, and Seventh Amendments?

A judge may issue a search warrant when it seems likely that someone's property contains evidence relating to a crime.

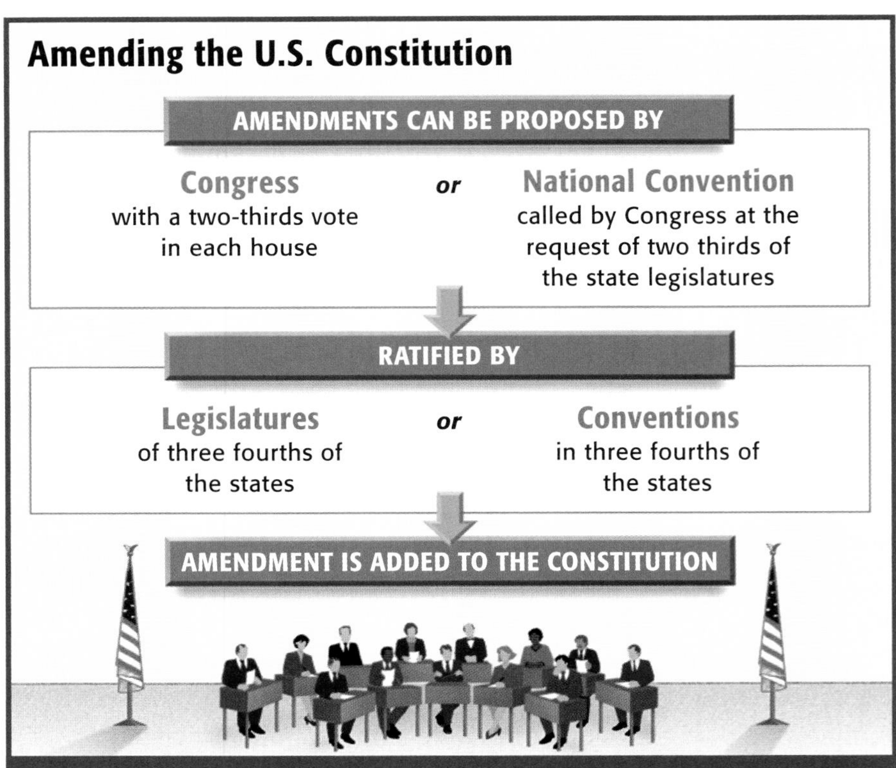

Bail and Punishment

The Eighth Amendment allows for defendants to post bail. Bail is money that defendants promise to pay the court if they do not appear in court at the proper time. Bail ensures that defendants do not have to stay in jail during the trial. Sometimes, a defendant does not show up for trial. If this happens, the court demands the bail money and issues a warrant for the defendant's immediate arrest. The Eighth Amendment prevents courts from setting unfairly high bail. However, the judge may refuse to set bail for individuals accused of very serious crimes or who the court believes may flee before trial.

The Eighth Amendment also bans "cruel and unusual punishments" of individuals convicted of a crime. For many years, Americans have debated exactly what this wording means. For example, in the 1972 case *Furman* v. *Georgia* the Supreme Court ruled that the methods by which most states carried out the death penalty were cruel and unusual. The Court also found that the processes used by many states to sentence people to death were unfair to the accused. As a result, executions were temporarily halted in those states that allowed the death penalty. However, in 1976 the Court ruled that not all executions are cruel and unusual. Today all states that allow the death penalty must establish guidelines to ensure that their methods are constitutional.

✔ **Reading Check: Finding the Main Idea** What rights does the Eighth Amendment protect?

The Rights of States and Citizens

The final two amendments in the Bill of Rights provide general protections for individual rights not addressed by the first eight amendments. The Ninth and Tenth Amendments also reserve some governmental powers for the states and people. The Ninth Amendment states that the rights listed in the Constitution are not the only rights citizens have. This amendment allows the courts and Congress to recognize other basic rights of citizens. For example, the Constitution does not address education, however most Americans believe education is a basic right. "Education is not just another consumer item. It is the bedrock [foundation] of our democracy," explained educational leader Mary Hatwood Futrell. Today state governments offer free public education—from elementary to high school—to all citizens.

These students benefit from free public education, which many Americans now consider a right of citizenship.

The Tenth Amendment recognizes that the states and the people have additional powers beyond those specifically mentioned in the Constitution. These include any powers that the Constitution does not specifically grant to Congress or deny to the states. Thus, the last amendment in the Bill of Rights protects citizens' rights in addition to helping keep the balance of power between the federal and state governments.

✔ **Reading Check: Analyzing Information** How do the Ninth and Tenth Amendments balance individual rights and governmental powers?

Section 2 Review

go.hrw.com Homework Practice Online
keyword: SC3 HP8

1. **Define** and explain:
   - petition
   - search warrant
   - due process
   - indict
   - double jeopardy
   - eminent domain

2. **Identify** and explain:
   - James Madison

3. **Summarizing** Copy the chart below. Use it to list the rights guaranteed to citizens by the first 10 amendments.

Amendment	Right
1	
2	
3	
4	
5	
6	
7	
8	
9	
10	

4. **Finding the Main Idea**
   a. Why are the rights protected by the First Amendment significant?
   b. How are the Constitution and the Bill of Rights related to the complaints against Great Britain made in the Declaration of Independence?

5. **Writing and Critical Thinking**
   Analyzing Information Imagine that you are a newspaper reporter covering a local trial. Write a brief article describing the rights of the accused as he or she faces trial.
   Consider the following:
   - due process
   - trial by jury
   - bail

Section 3

Rights and Responsibilities of Citizenship

Read to Discover

1. How can a person become a U.S. citizen?
2. What are some of the most important responsibilities of citizenship?
3. Why should citizens be involved with their community and government?

Define

- naturalized citizen
- deport
- draft
- political action committees

WHY IT MATTERS TODAY

Taxes are the responsibility of all U.S. citizens. Taxes help pay for services like roads, salaries of government employees, and schools. Use CNNfyi.com or other **current events** sources to research a current or proposed use of tax dollars that affects your area. Record your findings in your journal.

The Statue of Liberty is a symbol of freedom for many immigrants.

The Story Continues

Patrick Henry argued that the United States should be open to all people who wanted to become citizens. "Let . . . Liberty stretch forth her fair hand toward the people of the old world," he said. "Tell them to come, and bid them welcome." Many people desiring liberty have become U.S. citizens. Jozef Patyna immigrated to the United States in the early 1980s. He wanted to leave an unjust government in Poland. "The idea of freedom and democracy is what the people have an instinctive need for," explained Patyna.

Becoming a U.S. Citizen

People can become U.S. citizens in several ways. Anyone born in the United States or a territory it controls is a citizen. For example, people born in Puerto Rico are citizens because that island is a commonwealth that is still a U.S. territory. When a person of foreign birth is granted full citizenship, he or she has become a **naturalized citizen**. People born in a foreign country can become U.S. citizens if one of their parents is a U.S. citizen. Foreign-born people whose parents are not U.S. citizens must move to the United States if they want to become citizens. After completing a long process, they can apply for citizenship. The rights and responsibilities that naturalized citizens take on help create the sense of what it means to be an American.

This immigrant and the people standing around her are taking the oath of allegiance to complete the process of becoming U.S. citizens.

People who permanently move to a new country are called immigrants. In the United States, legal immigrants have many of the same rights and responsibilities as citizens. They cannot vote or hold public office, however. The U.S. government can **deport**, or return to their country of origin, any immigrant who breaks the law. Only two differences between naturalized and native-born citizens exist. Naturalized citizens can lose their citizenship, and they cannot become president or vice president. Many famous Americans have been naturalized citizens, including scientist Albert Einstein and former secretary of state Madeleine Albright.

Legal immigrants who are older than 18 may petition for naturalization. However, they may do this only after living in the United States for five years. All legal immigrants must be able to support themselves financially. If they cannot do this, someone must sponsor them and assume that financial responsibility. The U.S. Immigration and Naturalization Service (INS) oversees the process of becoming a citizen and sets a hearing to test the person's qualifications. The immigrants must prove that they are law-abiding and of good moral character. In addition, they must take a series of tests to show that they can read, write, and speak English. They must also have a basic understanding of U.S. history and government. The INS also conducts a background check to ensure that the candidates for naturalization have not hidden any information about themselves.

When all these steps are complete, the candidates appear before a naturalization court. There they take an oath of allegiance to the United States. Finally, they receive their certificate of naturalization. At that point all minors of the newly naturalized citizens also become citizens. Becoming a naturalized citizen takes dedication and effort. A Japanese immigrant wrote a poem to celebrate her naturalization.

**"Going steadily to study English,
Even through the rain at night,
I thus attain [acquire],
Late in life,
American citizenship."**

—Kiyoko Nieda, quoted in *Sounds from the Unknown*, edited by Lucille Nixon and Tomoe Tana

Analyzing Primary Sources

Identifying Points of View How do you think the author of this poem valued U.S. citizenship?

✔ **Reading Check: Identifying Cause and Effect** How does someone become a naturalized citizen, and what rights do they gain when they do?

Duties of Citizens

In addition to having certain rights, U.S. citizens have responsibilities. These duties are to other citizens, their government, and themselves. For representative democracy to work, citizens must fulfill their civic responsibilities. Former Texas representative Barbara Jordan explained why these duties are important. "The stakes . . . are too high for government to be a spectator sport," she stated.

Citizens elect leaders to make laws for them. In turn, citizens must obey the laws those leaders pass. If citizens do not agree with a law, they can try to change it in several ways. They can speak with their local, state, or national representatives or petition elected leaders to change the law. Electing new leaders who might change the law is another option. Citizens can also challenge a law in court. Citizens have a duty to know what the laws are. Thus, citizens need to stay informed of changes to laws that affect them. Ignorance of a certain law will not keep a person from being punished for breaking it.

Citizens also have an obligation to respect people in authority and to respect the rights of others. People in authority include parents, police officers, and teachers. Such people have been trusted to protect the welfare of others. Parents have a responsibility to meet their children's basic needs for clothing, education, food, and shelter. In return, children have a responsibility to obey their parents. Government authorities may step in to protect any children whose parents do not take proper care of them.

Upon turning 18, every male U.S. citizen must fill out a card like this one to register for a potential draft.

Responsibilities of Citizenship

In addition to having rights protected by the Constitution, citizens of the United States have important responsibilities to uphold.

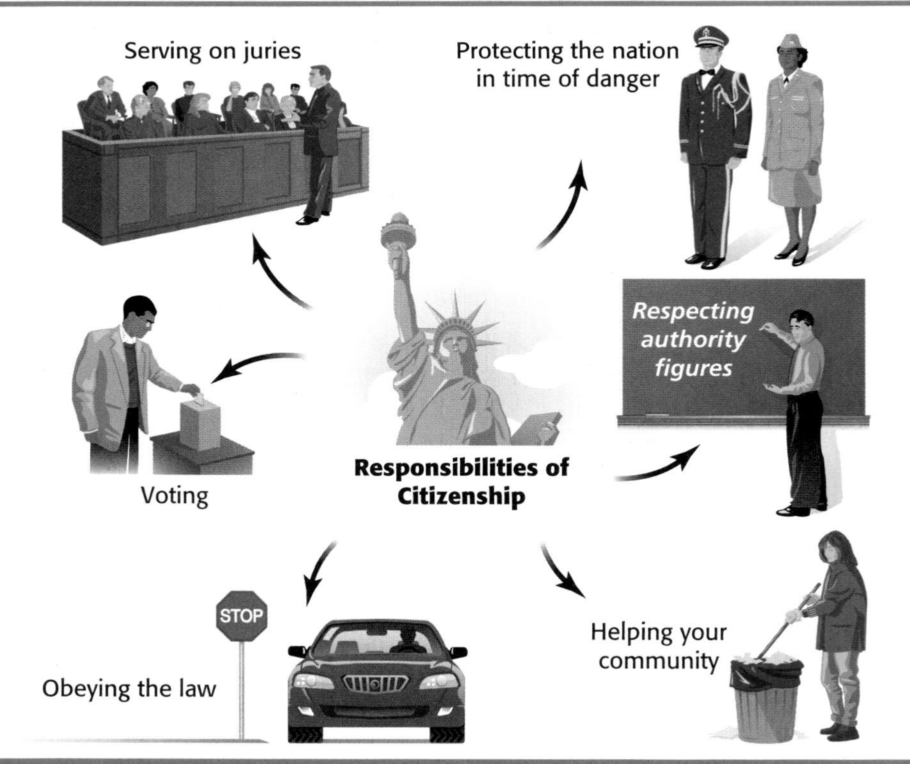

Visualizing History

1. **Citizenship** Which of the responsibilities of citizenship are related to the legal system?
2. **Connecting to Today** What responsibilities of citizenship can you fulfill?

Good citizenship also includes paying taxes. The government relies on taxes to pay for public roads, police and fire departments, and public schools. If Americans did not pay taxes, the government might be unable to provide these services. People pay many kinds of taxes, such as property taxes, sales taxes, and tariffs. For example, consumers often pay sales taxes when buying items at a store. Sales tax rates vary from place to place because state and local governments set and collect most sales taxes. People also pay a certain percentage of the value of their property to the government, called a property tax. Most school funding comes from property taxes.

April 15 of every year is income tax day. By that day all Americans who earned money the year before must pay a certain percentage of their income to the federal government. Some must pay their state government too. Income taxes are progressive—that is, the rate of income tax that people pay increases as their income level rises. Regressive taxes, such as city or state sales taxes, are applied equally to people regardless of income. Property taxes are based on the value of a person's property and may vary from area to area. Local governments gain much of their revenues from property taxes.

Citizens also have the duty to protect and defend the nation from harm. If a war breaks out, citizens should try to help in the war effort. In some war situations the federal government has set up a **draft**, or requirement of military service. A draft helps raise the needed number of soldiers. The United States has had all-volunteer armed forces since 1973. However, young men must register for the draft when they turn 18. This process gives the government a list of people who could be draftees if war were to break out. Women do not have to register for the draft, but many women serve in the armed forces.

All citizens can be called to serve on a jury. Jury duty involves listening to a court case and reaching a verdict on it. By serving as jurors, citizens help fulfill each person's Sixth Amendment right to a trial by jury. Americans also have a duty to testify in court if needed. For example, someone who witnesses a crime may be called to testify about it. Judges may issue subpoenas, or orders to appear in court, to force individuals to testify.

✔ **Reading Check: Summarizing** What are some of the responsibilities of citizenship?

Daily Life

Political participation Even individuals who are not old enough to vote can find ways to join in the political process. These students are volunteering their time to help run a candidate's campaign in a local election. There are many ways in which students can assist public officials or express their own views on issues important to their community or nation. **What do the students appear to be doing to participate in this local election?**

Research on the ROM

Free Find:
Taxes
After examining the Federal Budget Net Receipts from 1940 to 1995 on the **Holt Researcher CD–ROM**, create a bar graph that shows how much the federal government collected in taxes in the following years: 1940, 1950, 1960, 1970, 1980, and 1990.

These members of Students Against Driving Drunk visited Washington, D.C., to speak out against drinking and driving.

Citizens and Elections

Elections form the basis of representative democracy in the United States. Through free elections, citizens choose who will lead their government. Citizens should learn as much as they can about the issues and candidates before voting. Information is available through the Internet, newspapers, television, and other forms of media. However, voters should be beware of propaganda, or material that is biased deliberately to help or harm a cause.

In addition to voting, many Americans choose to campaign for a certain candidate or issue. Anyone can help campaign, even if he or she is not eligible to vote. Citizens can also give money to a candidate directly or through **political action committees** (PACs). These groups collect money to give to candidates who support certain issues.

To vote in the United States, one must be at least 18 years old. People younger than 18 can help campaigns by handing out pamphlets, making signs, or encouraging other citizens to vote. Many other members of political clubs get to know political leaders well. Some members stay active in politics as adults.

Citizens and Government

When colonists protested British rule in the 1700s, they formed committees and presented their views to political leaders. Today, people can influence officials by letting them know what the citizens want done.

Some U.S. citizens join interest groups. These groups are formed to lobby, or try to influence, politicians on behalf of certain issues. Some groups hold demonstrations to show the government how they feel and to gather public support. In 2000, for example, mothers in favor of gun control gathered in Washington, D.C., on Mother's Day. They called this demonstration the Million Mom March. Donna Dees-Thomases planned the march. She explained that the movement "started in my family room and has grown . . . across the nation." Not everyone agreed with her group. On the day of the Million Mom March, the Second Amendment Sisters held their own demonstration calling for gun-safety and education programs instead of gun control.

Citizens do not have to join a group to influence political leaders. People can and should share their views with leaders by writing letters and attending public meetings. These activities are ways that Americans exercise their First Amendment rights. Political participation is an important duty for U.S. citizens and immigrants alike.

This woman is showing her support for the Americans with Disabilities Act.

✔ **Reading Check: Drawing Inferences and Conclusions** How do you think the shared rights and responsibilities of citizenship help unite Americans who hold different views?

Community Service

Civic virtue, or the commitment to helping others, moves Americans to help their neighbors. Many of these Americans volunteer in community service groups. Some small communities rely on volunteers. These groups offer many public services, such as fire protection. Other volunteer groups help government-sponsored agencies, like police departments. For example, Citizens on Patrol and Neighborhood Watch are two groups that ask volunteers to walk their neighborhoods and report criminal activity. Neighborhoods with citizen patrols often have lower crime rates than other neighborhoods.

Other groups work along with the government. The American Red Cross aids citizens in times of natural disasters or other emergencies. Habitat for Humanity helps build houses for low-income families. The Boy Scouts and Girl Scouts plan many projects, such as planting trees to improve the environment.

Examples of community service could be found during the American Revolution, when patriotic women organized to make cloth and other goods for the colonists. Today the country's leaders want all citizens to serve others in their communities. Service projects can be simple acts like picking up trash or painting over graffiti.

Every day many Americans are in need. The nation is strengthened when all people do their part to help each other. Retired general Colin Powell, who was appointed secretary of state under President George W. Bush, launched a campaign in 1997 to promote volunteerism. He said, "This is the time for each and every one of us . . . to lift up a fellow American and put him on the road to success in this wonderful country of ours."

These volunteers are helping their neighbor by repainting a backyard fence.

✔ **Reading Check: Finding the Main Idea** What are some of the benefits of community service?

go.hrw.com Homework Practice Online
keyword: SC3 HP8

1. **Define** and explain:
   - naturalized citizen
   - deport
   - draft
   - political action committees

2. **Comparing and Contrasting** Copy the graphic organizer below. Use it to contrast the different ways that a person can become a U.S. citizen and to compare the responsibilities that all U.S. citizens share.

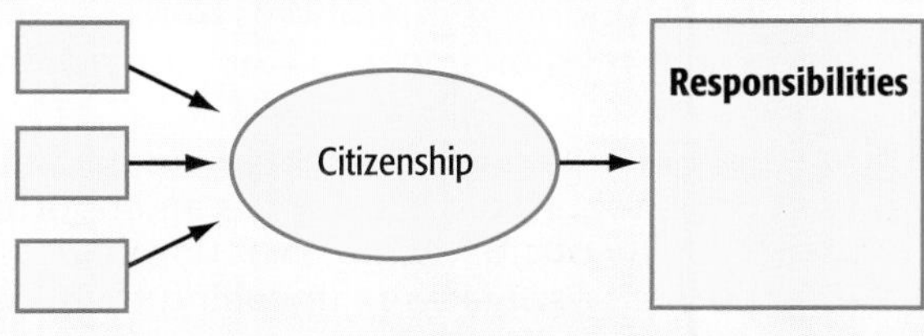

3. **Finding the Main Idea**
   a. Describe the steps in the naturalization process.
   b. How do responsibilities such as paying taxes, serving in the military, serving on juries, and voting help shape our national identity?

4. **Writing and Critical Thinking**
   Supporting a Point of View Imagine that you will be making a presentation at an awards ceremony honoring volunteers in your community. Write a poem honoring the volunteers.
   Consider the following:
   - civic virtue and citizens' responsibilities
   - how volunteerism benefits the community

Chapter 8 Review

The Chapter at a Glance

Examine the visual summary of the chapter below. Using information in the chapter, create a five-question quiz for one of your classmates to complete.

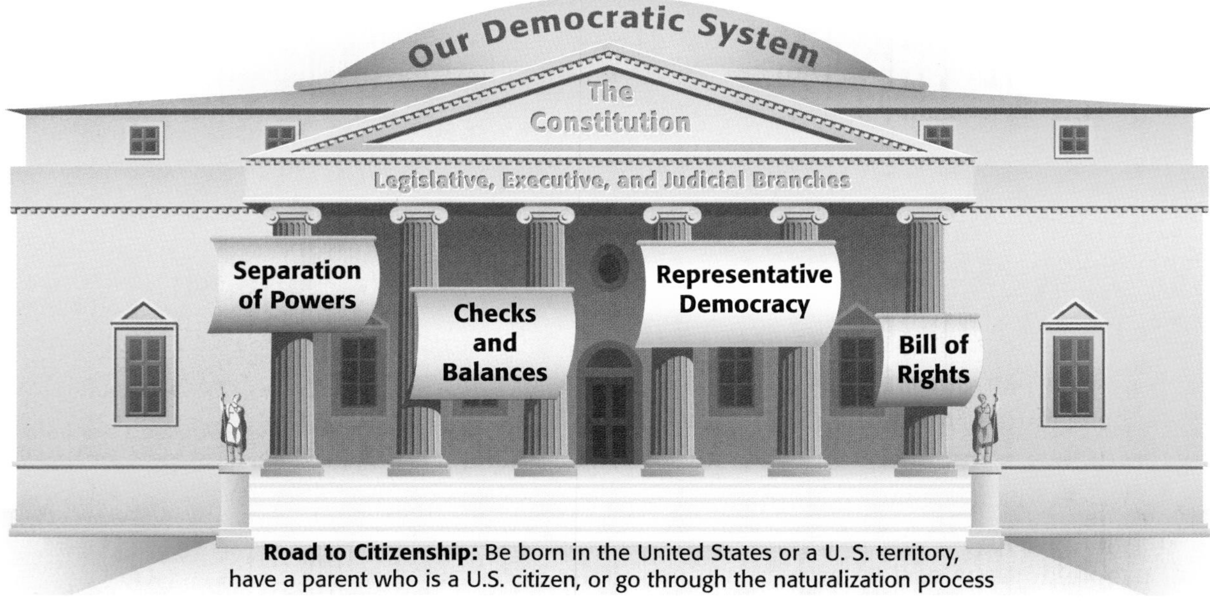

Identifying People and Ideas

Use the following terms or people in historically significant sentences.

1. representative democracy
2. separation of powers
3. Sandra Day O'Connor
4. James Madison
5. search warrant
6. due process
7. double jeopardy
8. naturalized citizen
9. draft
10. political action committees

Understanding Main Ideas

Section 1 *(Pages 220–225)*

1. What are the three branches of the federal government, and what are their primary responsibilities?
2. What are delegated powers, reserved powers, and concurrent powers?

Section 2 *(Pages 248–253)*

3. How did complaints against Great Britain made in the Declaration of Independence shape the Constitution and the Bill of Rights?
4. Which amendments focus on the rights of people accused of crimes, and what rights do these amendments guarantee?

Section 3 *(Pages 254–259)*

5. How does someone become a naturalized citizen?
6. What are the duties and responsibilities of citizenship?

You Be the Historian—Reviewing Themes

1. **Constitutional Heritage** How does the Constitution prevent any one branch of government from becoming too powerful? Be sure to consider all three branches of government.
2. **Citizenship** Why is voting an important responsibility in a representative democracy?
3. **Culture** In what ways does the U.S. government protect the rights of all Americans?

Thinking Critically

1. **Evaluating** How do you think the rights and duties of U.S. citizens reflect our identity as a nation?
2. **Drawing Inferences and Conclusions** How have the first amendment guarantees of freedom of speech and religion impacted the American way of life?
3. **Making Generalizations and Predictions** Serving on juries is required by law and is an important responsibility of citizenship. What problems might arise if people were unwilling to fulfill this responsibility?

Social Studies Skills Workshop

Interpreting Political Cartoons

Study the political cartoon below. Then use the information to help you answer the questions that follow.

FROM THE HERBLOCK GALLERY (SIMON & SCHUSTER, 1968)

1. What does the illustration suggest that President Johnson hopes to achieve by patting this Congressman on the back?
   a. Johnson wants the congressman to vote for his legislation.
   b. Johnson wants Congress to work harder.
   c. Johnson wants members of Congress to know how proud he is of their work.
   d. Johnson thinks Congress has too much power.
2. Based on your knowledge of the Constitution, why do you think President Johnson would find it necessary to encourage Congress to cooperate with him?

Analyzing Primary Sources

Read the following quote by President John F. Kennedy, and then answer the questions that follow.

> **"The right to vote in a free American election is the most powerful and precious right in the world—and it must not be denied on the grounds of race or color. It is a potent [powerful] key to achieving other rights of citizenship. For American history—both recent and past—clearly reveals that the power of the ballot has enabled those who achieve it to win other achievements as well, gain a full voice in the affairs of their state and nation, and to see their interests represented in the governmental bodies which affect their future. In a free society, those with the power to govern are necessarily responsive to those with the right to vote."**

3. Which of the following statements best describes Kennedy's point of view?
   a. The only way that people can influence their government is by writing letters to elected officials.
   b. You are not a citizen if you do not vote.
   c. Voting affects everyone's future.
   d. Government officials are more likely to respond to citizens if they know that citizens can vote them out of office.
4. Based on what you know about the Constitution of the United States, what amendment is President Kennedy probably referring to when he says that people of any race or color should not be denied the right to vote?

Alternative Assessment

Building Your Portfolio

American History

Linking to Community

Think about something in your community that is important to you, such as the creation of cross-walks or parks. Write a letter to a local official about this element of your community. Make sure the letter explains to the official why you are writing and what you want to be done. Then organize a campaign to get others to sign your letter. Support your campaign by creating signs, flyers, and other items.

internet connect

go.hrw.com

Internet Activity: go.hrw.com
keyword: SC3 CF8

Access the Internet through the HRW Go site to research Supreme Court cases heard during the recent term. Then write a brief summary that describes the main issues in the case, the Constitutional questions raised in the case, the Supreme Court's decision, and whether you agree with the Court's decision. Make sure your summary includes standard grammar, spelling, and punctuation.

Social Studies Skills

WORKSHOP

Interpreting a Time Line

Time lines display events in chronological order—the sequence in which the events occurred. Knowing the proper sequence of historical events helps you understand their significance. Time lines allow you to see relationships between events and help you to remember the dates of important events.

Sequence in a Time Line Time lines are meant to be read from left to right, with the oldest dates on the left. The lines of the time line mark the time period between each event. For example, the lines might mark 10-, 5-, or 1-year periods. Each entry on the time line lists an important event and when it took place. These entries provide you with a sequence of events and may suggest a relationship to one another.

B.C. and A.D. Sometimes a time line will contain the abbreviations B.C. and A.D. The abbreviation B.C. stands for "before Christ." A.D. stands for "anno Domini," which means "in the year of the Lord." The year 1 B.C. was followed by A.D. 1. There was no year "0." When you read dates marked B.C. or A.D., remember that the abbreviation B.C. appears after the year—for example, 100 B.C. The abbreviation A.D. appears before the year—for example, A.D. 100.

How to Read a Time Line

1. **Determine its framework.** Note the years covered and the intervals of time into which the time line is divided.
2. **Study the sequence of events.** Study the order of events on the time line and the length of time between events.
3. **Supply missing information.** Think about the people, places, and other events associated with each item on the time line.
4. **Note relationships.** Ask yourself how an event relates to earlier or later events. Look for cause-and-effect relationships and long-term developments.

1777 The Continental Congress approves the Articles of Confederation on November 15.

1781 On March 1 the Articles of Confederation go into effect after being ratified by all 13 states.

1787 On May 14, state delegates begin to arrive at the Constitutional Convention in Philadelphia. The final draft of the Constitution is signed on September 17.

1788 On June 21 the Constitution is ratified by the required 9 out of 13 states.

1776 | 1780 | 1784 | 1790

Practicing the Skills

Study the time line above, which lists some important events in the history of the United States between 1776 and 1790. Then answer the following questions.

1. Into what periods is the time line divided?
2. How much time passed between the ratification of the Articles of Confederation and the ratification of the Constitution?
3. Create your own time line, listing several significant events in U.S. history that occurred during a span of at least five years.

History in Action

UNIT 3 SIMULATION

You Solve the Problem . . .

How Should the President of the United States Be Selected?

Complete the following activity in small cooperative groups. It is early 1787. You are a delegate at the Constitutional Convention. The Convention has agreed upon the requirements for the candidates for the presidency: at least 35 years old, natural-born citizen, and a 14-year resident of the United States. Now you must give a presentation to the Constitutional Convention that suggests how the chief executive of the United States should be selected. Follow these steps to solve your problem.

1. Gather Information. Use your textbook and other resources to find information that might influence your plan of action for selecting a president. Be sure to use what you learned from this unit's Skills Workshop on Interpreting a Time Line to help you find an effective solution to the problem. For example, you might consider how often a new president should be selected. You may want to divide different parts of the research among group members.

2. List and Consider Options. Based on the information you have gathered, list and consider the options you might recommend for selecting a president. Your final solution to the problem may be easier to reach if you consider as many options as possible. Be sure to record your possible options for your presentation.

3. Consider Advantages and Disadvantages. Now consider the advantages and disadvantages of taking each option. Ask yourselves questions like: "Will all citizens be able to participate in the process?" Once you have considered the advantages and disadvantages, record them as notes for your presentation.

4. Choose, Implement, and Evaluate a Solution. After considering the advantages and disadvantages, you should plan and create a presentation. Be sure to make your proposal very clear. You will need to support your proposed method of selecting the president by including information you gathered and by explaining why you rejected other options. Your presentation needs to be visually appealing to the Constitutional Convention. When you are ready, decide which group members will make each part of the presentation, and then take your solution to Constitutional Convention (the rest of the class). Good luck!

UNIT 4 Building a Strong Nation

(1789–1840)

Young People

IN HISTORY

Young Explorers

In 1804 Meriwether Lewis and William Clark set out on an expedition to the western lands of the Louisiana Purchase. At age 18 George Shannon was the youngest member of their Corps of Discovery. Lewis described this group as the "best young woodsmen & Hunters in this part of the Countrey." Shannon excelled at his work and was put in charge of some expedition duties.

In late August 1804 Shannon failed to return after a day of hunting in Sioux Indian territory. Lewis and Clark sent out a search party, but it failed to find the young man, who had accidentally moved ahead of the group. Thinking he was actually behind the others, Shannon kept traveling westward as fast as he could.

Young frontiersmen, like those shown here, were an important part of the Lewis and Clark expedition.

Over time, he used all his bullets and was unable to hunt for food. He survived for a few weeks on plums and grapes. After becoming too weak to continue, Shannon sat down on a riverbank. He hoped that a trading boat might pass by. Instead, his friends rescued him! On September 11, 1804, the expedition rounded a bend in the Missouri River. To their surprise, they found an exhausted and hungry Shannon.

Shannon was one of many young adventurers who set their sights westward in the 1800s. William Swift and Titian Peale were two young men who accompanied Stephen Long on his expedition in 1819. Swift was 18 years old, and Peale was 19. They traveled along the Missouri River and into the western plains. Swift was hired to prepare a map of the territory, while Peale went along as an assistant naturalist.

Other teenagers explored the West as fur trappers. When he was about 18, Jim Bridger traveled to the upper Missouri River on a trapping expedition. Two years later, Bridger discovered what looked like a great shallow bay. Tasting the salty water, he reported he had found part of the Pacific Ocean. However, historians later determined that Bridger had actually seen the Great Salt Lake in what is now Utah.

If You Were There *What would you do if you got lost in the wilderness?*

LEFT PAGE: *Crossing the Rocky Mountains was one of the most difficult challenges facing western explorers.*

CHAPTER

9 Launching the Nation

(1789–1800)

Angry farmers tar and feather a tax collector during the Whiskey Rebellion.

President Washington with some members of his cabinet (left to right): Washington, Henry Knox, Alexander Hamilton, Thomas Jefferson, and Edmund Randolph

UNITED STATES

- **1789** George Washington is elected president on April 6.
- **1790** Washington is founded as the national capital.
- **1791** The Bank of the United States is formed.
- **1792** Kentucky becomes the 15th state.
- **1794** The Whiskey Rebellion begins in Pennsylvania.

1789 | **1791** | **1793**

- **1789** The French Revolution begins.
- **1791** Thomas Paine defends the French Revolution in *Rights of Man*.
- **1792** Austrian and Prussian armies invade France to try to end the Revolution.
- **1793** French revolutionaries behead King Louis XVI.

WORLD

The citizens of Paris storm the prison known as the Bastille during the French Revolution.

Build on What You Know

The Constitution created a new system of government for the United States. This federal system divided power between the states and a strong central government. Yet there was still much work left for the nation's leaders to do. Americans chose George Washington and other Founding Fathers to lead the new nation.

Mount Vernon, Washington's Virginia home, has been preserved as a historical landmark.

As first lady, Martha Washington tried to bring a sense of dignity and grace to the new government.

1795 American Indian leaders sign the Treaty of Greenville with the United States.

1796 Washington publishes his Farewell Address on September 19.

John Adams is elected president on December 7.

1798 Congress passes the Sedition Act on July 14.

1798 Agents of French foreign minister Talleyrand demand a bribe from U.S. diplomats, leading to the XYZ affair.

1799 George Washington dies at Mount Vernon, Virginia, on December 14.

1799 The Rosetta Stone is discovered in Egypt. Inscriptions on the stone make it possible for researchers to read Egyptian hieroglyphics.

1795 1797 1799

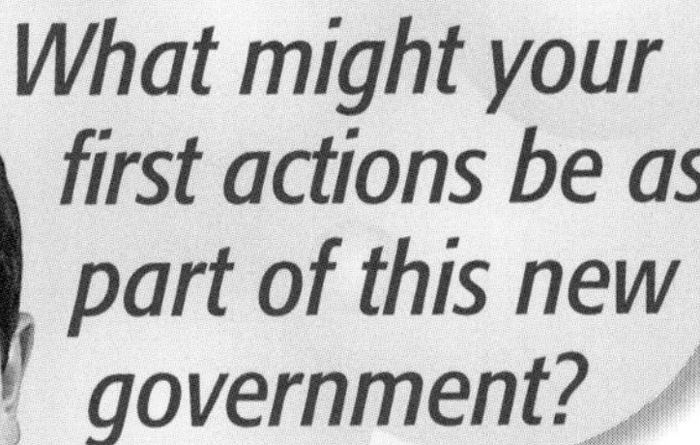

If you were there . . .

What might your first actions be as part of this new government?

You Be the Historian

What's Your Opinion? Do you **agree** or **disagree** with the following statements? Support your point of view in your journal.

- **Global Relations** A new country must stay away from conflicts and alliances.
- **Constitutional Heritage** There is one correct way to interpret the U.S. Constitution.
- **Economics** Countries should invest their money at home before paying their foreign debts.

Section 1

Laying the Foundations of Government

Read to Discover

1. Why did Americans elect George Washington as their first president?
2. What did Americans expect of their new government?
3. What steps did Congress and the president take to organize the new government?

Define

- electoral college
- precedent

Identify

- George Washington
- Martha Washington
- Judiciary Act of 1789

WHY IT MATTERS TODAY

Every day, leaders around the world try to serve their countries. Use CNNfyi.com or other **current events** sources to learn more about the president or leader of a country. Record your findings in your journal.

The Story Continues

George Washington looked forward to retiring from public life once the states had ratified the Constitution. However, his friends had other plans for him. They soon drew him into politics as a presidential candidate. When Washington hesitated, politician Gouverneur Morris helped convince him. "Should the idea prevail [win] that you would not accept the presidency, it should prove fatal . . . to the new government." Morris ended confidently, "Of all men, you are the best fitted to fill that office."

COURTESY OF THE JOHN CARTER BROWN LIBRARY AT BROWN UNIVERSITY

This 1788 print shows George Washington surrounded by the seal of the United States and the seals of the 13 states.

The First President

George Washington was concerned that his age and lack of political experience might make him a poor president. He also knew that he would have to deal with many difficult issues. Yet many Americans saw Washington as a great leader and hero of the Revolution. They believed that his strong character, honesty, and patriotism would make him an excellent leader. They thought he would be a model for all citizens.

In January 1789 the 11 states that had passed the Constitution each sent electors to choose the first president. These delegates formed the **electoral college.** Each state legislature had chosen electors who would represent the popular vote in their states. However, electors could vote for different candidates if they felt the public had not chosen the right person. On April 6, 1789, Congress declared that the electoral college had selected Washington unanimously. John Adams became his vice president.

Washington accepted the presidency because he felt it was his duty "to render [give] service to my country in obedience to its call." He traveled to New York City to be sworn into office. Along the roads he traveled and in the city, Americans cheered him on and celebrated. Ships in New York Harbor flew colorful flags and fired their cannons.

The presidency brought many changes for the Washington family. **Martha Washington** had to entertain guests and attend social events with her husband. Two weeks after arriving in New York, Martha described the scene to her niece. "I have not had one half-hour to myself since the day of my arrival," she wrote. Martha Washington ran the presidential household with grace and style. Abigail Adams once wrote, "I found myself much more deeply impressed [by George and Martha Washington] than I ever did before their majesties of Britain."

Patriot and author Judith Sargent Murray hoped women would play a different role in the new nation. Murray declared in newspaper essays that young women needed to be educated. "I expect to see our young women forming a new era in female history," she wrote. Murray, Abigail Adams, and other women helped share the idea of Republican Motherhood. This was the idea that women played an important role because they taught their children to be good citizens. Still, most women lacked the opportunity to take part equally in society.

✔ **Reading Check:** **Analyzing Information** What qualities made George Washington a good candidate for president?

Life in the New Republic

Hard work lay ahead for the new government. Few Americans had ever thought of themselves as citizens of a united nation. They expected the federal government to protect their liberty and hoped it would improve the economy by providing stability. However, they did not want the government to restrict trade as the British Parliament had done.

In 1790 the United States was home to almost 4 million people. Most Americans lived in the countryside and worked on farms. Farmers wanted fair tax laws and the right to settle western lands. Other Americans worked in towns as craftspeople, laborers, or merchants. These people knew that Americans had begun buying and selling goods across the country and around the world. As a result, they became more interested in trade laws. Merchants wanted simpler trade laws

Cheering crowds greeted Washington as he traveled to his inauguration.

The Electoral College

Under the system established by the Constitution, American voters do not directly elect the president. Instead, each state is represented by a number of electors equal to the total number of representatives and senators it has in Congress.

Electors are sworn to represent the interests of the people of their state. In most cases the candidate who wins a state's popular vote receives all of that state's electoral votes. Electors meet in December in election years in the capital of their home state to cast their votes for president and vice president. If no candidate receives an electoral majority, the House of Representatives chooses the president and the Senate chooses the vice president. **Why do you think that most states award all their electoral votes to the winner of the popular vote?**

Like these women, many Americans worked on farms in the early republic.

established by a unified government. Manufacturers wanted laws to protect them from foreign competition.

Only New York City and Philadelphia had populations greater than 25,000. New York City was the first capital of the United States, and in many ways it represented the spirit of the new nation. Badly damaged during the Revolutionary War, the city had already begun recovering. Citizens got rid of the signs of British rule. They changed Crown Street to Liberty Street, for example. International trade became more active, and business activity increased. A French visitor noted the city's energy.

Analyzing Primary Sources

Drawing Inferences and Conclusions What does this quote tell you about New York City's economic activities?

"Everything in the city is in motion; everywhere the shops resound [ring out] with the noise of workers. . . . One sees vessels arriving from every part of the world."

—A French visitor to New York, quoted in *New York in the American Revolution,* by Wilbur Abbott

By 1790 the city's population had topped 33,000 and was growing rapidly. Many leaders thought this lively community showed the country's potential. They believed it was a fitting place for the new administration to plan the country's future.

✔ **Reading Check: Finding the Main Idea** How did Americans expect the new government to help free enterprise?

Setting Precedents

The new federal government had to make important decisions about policies and procedures. President Washington noted this fact in a letter to James Madison. "The first of everything in our situation will serve to establish a precedent," he wrote. A **precedent** is an action or a decision that serves as an example for later generations.

Planning the government's executive branch was one of Congress's first tasks. Congress created several executive departments. Each department specialized in a different area of national policy, such as military affairs. Washington nominated the department heads, who required approval by the Senate. He picked Alexander Hamilton as secretary of the treasury and Thomas Jefferson as secretary of state. Washington began meeting with the department heads as a group, which became known as the cabinet. The cabinet members advised the president and talked about important issues. By 1792, cabinet meetings were common practice.

The judicial branch also needed organizing. The Constitution did not state the number or location of federal courts. In September 1789 Congress passed the **Judiciary Act of 1789**, which created a federal court system with three levels. It also outlined the powers of the federal courts and their relationship to the state courts. District courts were at the lowest level. Then came the courts of appeals, which reviewed district court decisions. At the top level was the Supreme Court, which had six justices.

The president nominated the candidates for federal judgeships at each level, who then needed congressional approval. John Jay served as the Supreme Court's first chief justice. Washington selected Edmund Randolph as attorney general. Washington wrote to the justices to explain the importance of their duties.

THE GRANGER COLLECTION, NEW YORK

Washington's cabinet members advised him on issues of national defense, diplomacy, and finance.

> **"I have always been persuaded that the stability and success of the national government, and consequently the happiness of the people of the United States, would depend in a considerable degree on the interpretation and execution of its laws. In my opinion, therefore, it is important that the judiciary system should not only be independent in its operations, but as perfect as possible in its formation."**
>
> —George Washington, from *The Real George Washington, Part 2,* edited by Andrew M. Allison, Jay A. Parry, and W. Cleon Skousen

With the parts of the federal government in place, leaders began addressing the problems that faced the country.

✔ **Reading Check: Summarizing** How did Washington and Congress set up the executive and judicial branches?

Section 1 Review

go.hrw.com Homework Practice Online
keyword: SC3 HP9

1. **Define** and explain:
   - electoral college
   - precedent

2. **Identify** and explain:
   - George Washington
   - Martha Washington
   - Judiciary Act of 1789

3. **Summarizing** Copy the chart below. Use it to show how three important positions in the new U.S. government, such as the president or Supreme Court justices, were selected.

Position	How Selected
1.	
2.	
3.	

4. **Finding the Main Idea**
   a. What did Americans want their government to do to help free enterprise?
   b. What problems did Washington and Congress face in organizing the executive branch and the judicial branch, and how did they work together to solve these problems?

5. **Writing and Critical Thinking**
   Supporting a Point of View Imagine that you are a member of the electoral college and that George Washington has not accepted his presidential nomination. Write a petition to persuade him to take office.
   Consider the following:
   - the needs of the nation
   - the expectations Americans had of the new government
   - Washington's civic and leadership qualities

Section 2

Hamilton and National Finances

Read to Discover

1. What challenge did Alexander Hamilton face as secretary of the treasury, and what issues did his plans raise?
2. What issues did Hamilton and Thomas Jefferson disagree on, and what were their views?
3. What questions were raised when the Bank of the United States was founded, and what different views did Hamilton and Jefferson have concerning the Bank?

Define

- national debt
- bonds
- speculators
- protective tariff
- loose construction
- strict construction

Identify

- Alexander Hamilton
- Thomas Jefferson
- Bank of the United States

WHY IT MATTERS TODAY

The U.S. government still imposes tariffs on some foreign goods. Use CNNfyi.com or other **current events** sources to learn more about a tariff that is in place today. Record your findings in your journal.

Alexander Hamilton had served as an aide to George Washington during the Revolutionary War.

The Story Continues

President Washington was worried about how to solve the nation's money problems. "There is but one man in the United States who can tell you," his friend Robert Morris suggested. "That is Alexander Hamilton." Hamilton's impressive reputation helped him become secretary of the treasury. But his skills were quickly put to the test. Within days of his appointment, Congress directed him to prepare a plan to improve the national economy.

Settling the Debt

Alexander Hamilton had a strong interest in business matters. He grew up on the island of Nevis in the British West Indies. When he was just a teenager he had helped run a shipping company there. Because of his intelligence and hard work, family friends sent him to the American colonies for an education. Hamilton eventually married into a very wealthy New York family and began practicing law.

As secretary of the treasury, Hamilton's biggest challenge was paying off the **national debt**. This was the amount of money owed by the United States to its lenders. Hamilton figured that the United States owed about $11.7 million to foreign countries such as France.

The United States also owed about $40.4 million to U.S. citizens. Some of the debt was in the form of **bonds**, or certificates that represent money owed. During the Revolutionary War the government sold bonds to raise money. Officials promised to buy back these bonds with interest, thus allowing buyers to make a profit. But the government had trouble keeping this promise. Eventually, bondholders began to doubt that the government would ever repay them. Many people sold their bonds for less than their original value to **speculators**. Speculators are people who buy items at low prices in the hope that the value will rise.

Hamilton wanted to put the federal government on a solid financial footing. He feared that otherwise the government would lose the trust of the American people. He also wanted to pay the country's foreign debt immediately and repay the full value of all bonds over time. This caused great argument among politicians, because paying full value would allow speculators to make a profit. Hamilton believed this was only fair. As he saw it, speculators "paid what the commodity [bond] was worth in the market and took the risks." **Thomas Jefferson** opposed Hamilton's plan. He thought that the idea cheated the original bondholders who had sold their bonds at low prices. Jefferson wrote, "Immense sums were thus filched [stolen] from the poor and ignorant." A majority in Congress agreed with Hamilton. In early 1790 the government started exchanging the old bonds for new, more reliable ones whose value was guaranteed by the federal government.

U.S. Government Finances, 1789–1791

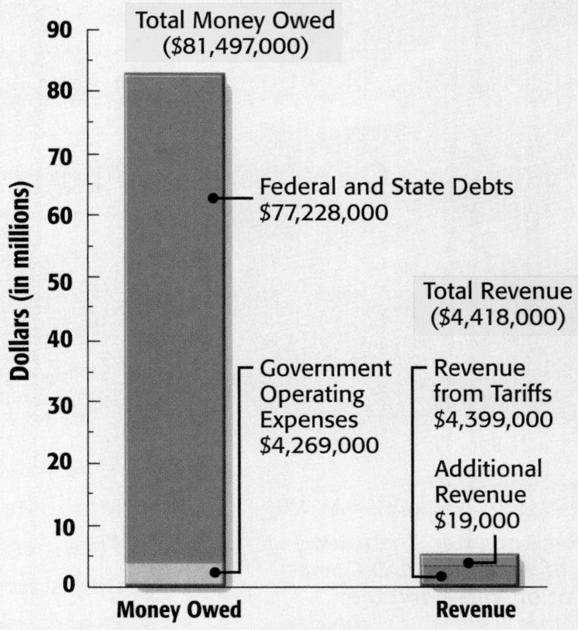

Source: *Historical Statistics of the United States*

Interpreting Graphs George Washington's administration had to deal with the federal government's financial problems.

Skills Assessment **Analyzing Information** What were the government's operating expenses from 1789 to 1791?

The value of government bonds such as this one varied greatly before Alexander Hamilton's efforts.

✔ **Reading Check: Finding the Main Idea** What domestic problem did Alexander Hamilton face, and how did he plan to solve it?

The States' Debts

The states owed $25 million for Revolutionary War expenses. Hamilton wanted the federal government to pay for $21.5 million of this debt. Hamilton believed that this aid would increase support for the federal government. He also thought that paying the state debts would help the national economy. Debtor states would not have to spend so much on

Interpreting the Visual Record

Before and after *The future site of Washington, D.C., was a plot of land along the Potomac River. Today the city is a cultural center filled with treasured historical artifacts and monuments.* ***Why do you think Congress chose to build a capital city rather than use an existing city for the national capital?***

repayment. Therefore, Hamilton said, they would have resources to develop business and trade.

Not all states agreed. Southern states such as Virginia and North Carolina had few war debts. Their representatives did not want to help the federal government pay the debts of other states. Patrick Henry did not even believe that the Constitution gave Congress the power to pay state debts. Hamilton knew that he needed the help of southern representatives to get his plan approved.

He got this help because southern officials wanted a new national capital. Many southerners did not like having the capital in New York. They thought this gave the northern states too much influence over national policy. Hamilton, Jefferson, and Representative James Madison met in June 1790. Hamilton promised to convince northern members of Congress to move the capital. In exchange, Jefferson and Madison agreed to gather support in the South for Hamilton's debt payment plan.

The compromise worked. In July the House of Representatives approved the plan. They chose an area along the Potomac River for the new national capital. This site would become present-day Washington, D.C. Philadelphia served as the temporary capital while architects began designing the new capital city.

✔ **Reading Check: Summarizing** What compromise did Hamilton and Jefferson reach to allow Congress to repay the state debts?

Research on the ROM

Free Find:
Alexander Hamilton
After reading about Alexander Hamilton on the **Holt Researcher CD–ROM,** write a short essay explaining his contributions to the new government of the United States.

Hamilton versus Jefferson

Hamilton and Jefferson did not cooperate for long. Instead, they began to disagree about how to define the authority of the central government. While Hamilton believed in a strong central government, Jefferson wanted to protect the powers of the states. Their conflict reflected basic differences in their opinions about democracy. Hamilton had little faith in the common person. He once said that "the people . . . seldom judge or determine [decide] right." He wanted a strong central government that balanced power between the "mass of the people" and wealthier citizens. He explained his beliefs.

"We must take man as we find him, and if we expect him to serve the public, [we] must interest his passions in doing so. A reliance on pure patriotism has been the source of many of our errors."

—Alexander Hamilton, quoted in *Odd Destiny: The Life of Alexander Hamilton,* by Marie B. Hecht

Analyzing Primary Sources

Identifying Points of View Does Hamilton believe that people are naturally good citizens? Explain your answer.

Hamilton believed that his approach would protect everyone's liberties while keeping the people from having too much power.

Jefferson disagreed strongly with Hamilton's views of the average citizen's ability. He did admit that "the people can not be all, and always, well informed." However, Jefferson firmly defended the right of the people to rule the country.

"It is my principle that the will of the Majority should always prevail [win]. . . . Above all things I hope the education of the common people will be attended to; [I am] convinced that on their good sense we may rely with the most security for the preservation of a due degree of liberty."

—Thomas Jefferson, quoted in *Thomas Jefferson,* edited by Joseph L. Gardner

Hamilton and Jefferson also argued over how the American economy should grow. Hamilton wanted new forms of economic growth. He also wanted to promote manufacturing and business. In a 1790 report he suggested that the government give prizes to certain American companies. These prizes would "reward some particular excellence or superiority" in the companies' products. In addition, Hamilton wanted to pass a higher tariff, or a tax on imported goods. Known as a **protective tariff**, this tax would raise the prices of foreign products. Hamilton hoped this would cause Americans to buy U.S. goods, which would protect American manufacturing from foreign competition.

CONNECTING TO THE ARTS

American Architecture and Classical Revival After the Revolution, American architects began to create buildings in the classical style of ancient Greece and Rome. Many Americans admired these civilizations because they had some of the same democratic ideals as the new American nation.

Thomas Jefferson started this trend in 1785 when he designed Virginia's capitol building. It was inspired by Roman architecture's use of columns, domes, and white stone. Architects designed banks, churches, colleges, and even the new U.S. Capitol Building in the same style. Shown here is William Thornton's winning design for the outside of the building. **What view is shown by Americans' new interest in classical architecture?**

George Washington

Many people consider George Washington to be the Father of Our Country. He entered the presidency as one of the great heroes of the American Revolution. He felt a great sense of responsibility to the nation. He wanted to be a dignified leader who also listened to the needs of the people. Yet the pressure of other people's expectations often made life difficult for him. Washington was very sensitive to attacks made against him in the press. Thomas Jefferson wrote, "I think he feels those things [criticisms] more than any person I ever met."

Washington left politics in 1797 and returned to his home in Mount Vernon. He died just two years later. His image is carved into the national monument at Mount Rushmore, South Dakota. Presidents' Day, a federal holiday, is held each year near his birthday, February 22. **Why do you think George Washington has been called the "Father of Our Country"?**

Jefferson, on the other hand, worried about depending too much on business and manufacturing. Jefferson believed that farmers were the most independent voters. They did not rely too much on other people's work to make a living. He wrote, "Our governments will remain virtuous [morally pure] for many centuries; as long as they are chiefly agricultural." Jefferson wanted lower tariffs, which would help farmers by keeping the price of imported goods low.

✔ **Reading Check: Comparing and Contrasting** Compare and contrast Hamilton's and Jefferson's ideas about government, the economy, and protective tariffs.

The Debate over the Bank

Hamilton's and Jefferson's differences came to the public's attention in early 1791. Hamilton wanted to start a national bank in which the government could safely deposit its money. The bank would also make loans to the government and businesses. Hamilton added that the United States should build a national mint—a place where coins are made. Then the country could begin issuing its own money. To limit the national bank's power, Hamilton asked for a 20-year charter. After this period of time, Congress could decide if it should extend the charter. Hamilton also asked each state to start its own bank so that the national bank would not have a monopoly.

The idea of establishing a national bank greatly worried both James Madison and Thomas Jefferson. They did not believe the U.S. Constitution gave Congress this power. In response, Hamilton and his supporters pointed to a clause in Article I, Section 8. This clause states that Congress has the power "to make all laws which shall be necessary and proper" for governing the nation. The passage later became known as the elastic clause because it has allowed the powers of the government to be stretched. Hamilton argued that this clause was meant to give the government the power to react to new situations. He saw the need for a national bank as an ideal example of such a situation. Hamilton's view became known as **loose construction** of the Constitution. According to loose construction, the federal government can take any reasonable actions that the Constitution does not specifically forbid it from taking.

Jefferson did not agree with Hamilton's argument. Jefferson believed that the "necessary and proper" clause should be used only in special cases. He wrote a letter explaining his view to President Washington. "The Constitution allows only the means which are 'necessary,' not those which are merely 'convenient.'" To Jefferson, the national bank was a convenience, not a necessity. Jefferson's view became known as **strict construction.** According to strict construction, the federal government should do only what the Constitution specifically says it can do.

THE GRANGER COLLECTION, NEW YORK

Interpreting the Visual Record

National finance *Both the Bank of the United States, shown at the left, and the U.S. Mint, which issued the coins shown below, were projects of Alexander Hamilton.* ***How are these two institutions similar?***

President Washington and Congress agreed with Hamilton. They hoped a bank would offer more security for the national economy. As a result, in February 1791 Congress chartered the **Bank of the United States**. The Bank helped offer stability during the next 20 years and played an important role in improving the U.S. economy.

✔ **Reading Check: Identifying Points of View** How did Hamilton interpret the Constitution during the Bank debate, and what problems did he face with this argument?

Section 2 Review

keyword: SC3 HP9

1 Define and explain:
- national debt
- bonds
- speculators
- protective tariff
- loose construction
- strict construction

2 Identify and explain:
- Alexander Hamilton
- Thomas Jefferson
- Bank of the United States

3 Contrasting Copy the graphic organizer below. Use it to contrast the ideas that Hamilton and Jefferson held about the topics listed.

Hamilton		Jefferson
	Bonds	
	Democracy	
	Economy	
	Tariffs	
	National Bank	
	Constitution	

4 Finding the Main Idea

a. What was Alexander Hamilton's biggest job, and what debate arose from his plans?

b. How did Hamilton win approval from Congress for the federal government to pay most of the states' war debts?

5 Writing and Critical Thinking

Summarizing Imagine that you are a member of Congress during Washington's administration. Write a speech to be delivered to the people of your home state that explains the conflict over the creation of a national bank.

Consider the following:
- different interpretations of the Constitution
- political differences between Hamilton and Jefferson
- the benefits of a national bank

Section 3

Troubles Abroad

Read to Discover

1. How did Americans and President Washington respond to events in France?
2. What policy did Washington follow toward foreign nations?
3. How did the United States settle its differences with Great Britain and Spain?

Why It Matters Today

The United States still signs treaties with other countries. Use CNNfyi.com or other **current events** sources to find out about an economic, military, or political treaty the United States has signed or considered signing in recent years. Record your findings in your journal.

Define

- privateers
- right of deposit

Identify

- French Revolution
- Neutrality Proclamation
- Edmond Genet
- John Jay
- Jay's Treaty
- Thomas Pinckney
- Pinckney's Treaty

THE GRANGER COLLECTION, NEW YORK

The fall of the Bastille is celebrated as a national holiday in France.

The Story Continues

On July 14, 1789, the citizens of Paris, France, challenged their corrupt government. Masses of people attacked the Bastille, a hated fortress and prison that held the enemies of the French Crown. Soldiers defending the walls were shocked. One of them described "the people . . . in a crowd, armed with muskets . . . swords . . . and shouting, 'We want the Bastille! Down with the troops.'" After hours of fighting, the crowd captured the fortress. The fall of this mighty symbol of royal power stunned the country.

The French Revolution

The storming of the Bastille was one of the first acts of the **French Revolution**. During this rebellion the French people overthrew their monarchy and created a republican government. The Declaration of the Rights of Man stated the French Revolution's principles: "liberty, equality, and fraternity [brotherhood]." As U.S. minister to France, Thomas Jefferson witnessed the early days of the Revolution. He wrote to friends back in America that the changes in France were "the first chapter of European liberty."

In 1789 King Louis XVI addressed the members of the French Legislature. Four years later revolutionaries beheaded the king using a guillotine like the one below.

News of the French Revolution spread quickly, gaining the support of many Americans. They believed France was founding a democratic republic similar to the United States. These Americans celebrated French independence by burning huge bonfires and singing French songs. Jefferson wrote to a friend about the scene. He said that he was fortunate "to see in the course of fourteen years two such revolutions as were never before seen."

Some Americans were not as pleased. They were very worried about the French Revolution's violent riots. They also feared the many attacks on all forms of traditional authority. The revolutionaries shocked many Americans by beheading King Louis XVI in January 1793 and Queen Marie-Antoinette later that year.

✔ **Reading Check: Contrasting** What differing opinions did Americans hold about the French Revolution?

U.S. Neutrality

A few months after the French Revolution started, France and Great Britain went to war. Some Americans backed the French, while others backed the British. The debate over U.S. foreign policy soon divided Congress and split President Washington's cabinet. After considering different arguments on the issue, Washington presented his own views to Congress on April 22, 1793.

"The duty and interest of the United States require that they should with sincerity and good faith adopt and pursue a conduct friendly and impartial [unbiased] towards the belligerent [fighting] powers."

—Proclamation of Neutrality

That's Interesting!

"Let them eat cake." Maybe you've heard the saying "Let them eat cake." Many people believe that the French queen Marie-Antoinette said this. As the story goes, this was her reply when a large mob of hungry women stormed the palace demanding bread. The story of the queen's heartless attitude became quite popular. The queen was probably out of touch with the needs of poor French citizens. But many historians believe that the French philosopher Jean-Jacques Rousseau actually made up the story to make the French monarchy look bad.

Patriots in France

The democratic goals of the French Revolution encouraged some former Patriots to take part. Two of the more well-known examples were Thomas Paine and the Marquis de Lafayette. Paine is shown above holding a copy of *Rights of Man,* which he wrote in support of the Revolution and the creation of democracies in Europe. When Paine went to France, however, he was jailed for protesting the new government's violent acts. In prison he wrote *The Age of Reason,* which attacked organized religion and cost him many of his supporters. The Marquis de Lafayette helped write the Declaration of the Rights of Man and the French Constitution of 1791. Lafayette then fled the country and took little part in French politics once Napoléon came to power.

How did Paine and Lafayette contribute to the French Revolution?

This **Neutrality Proclamation** stated that the United States would not take sides with countries at war in Europe. Washington believed that this plan would be the safest and most reasonable. However, not everyone agreed. Some newspaper editors and members of Congress criticized him. James Madison questioned Washington's right to issue the proclamation without Congress's approval.

Citizen Genet

At this time **Edmond Genet** (zhuh-ne), France's new representative to the United States, arrived. Citizen Genet, as he was known, traveled across the country seeking American support for France. He found four sea captains who agreed to command **privateers**—private ships allowed by a country to attack its enemies. Washington warned Genet that recruiting privateers on American soil hurt U.S. neutrality. In response, Genet said he would ask the American people to overrule Washington. At that point, even pro-French Jefferson agreed that Genet should be sent back home.

Although he wanted Genet to be removed, Jefferson was still upset by the U.S. policy toward France. He also felt that pro-British Hamilton was influencing the president's foreign policy. Hamilton's influence interfered with Jefferson's duties as secretary of state. As a result, Jefferson eventually decided to leave Washington's cabinet. In December 1793 Jefferson resigned. This decision disappointed Washington, who had a high opinion of Jefferson's honesty and talent. Some 30 years after he resigned, Jefferson expressed his view of President Washington. Although he disagreed with some of Washington's policies, Jefferson had great respect for the president.

"General Washington was himself sincerely a friend to the republican principles of our Constitution. . . . He repeatedly declared to me that he . . . would lose the last drop of his blood in its support."

—Thomas Jefferson, from *The Writings of Thomas Jefferson*, edited by Albert Ellery Bergh

✔ **Reading Check: Identifying Cause and Effect** What did President Washington do when France and Great Britain went to war, and how did Jefferson respond?

Jay's Treaty

Washington experienced other threats to U.S. neutrality. In late 1793 the British began seizing all ships carrying food to the French West Indies. In the process, the British captured hundreds of neutral American merchant ships. Rumors also flew that British officers on the western frontier were encouraging American Indian uprisings. The British had never abandoned these frontier forts, as the Treaty of Paris required. Now it looked as if the British might side with American Indians in a war against American settlers.

Even Alexander Hamilton recognized that the United States might be on the path to war. President Washington and Hamilton sent Chief Justice **John Jay** to London to work out a peaceful resolution. Jay's task was difficult. The British knew that the United States lacked a strong navy. Also, many American businesses relied on trade with Great Britain. However, the British did not want to fight another war in North America.

The two sides eventually reached an agreement in November 1794. **Jay's Treaty** was a compromise. The British agreed to pay damages for seized American ships. Small American merchant ships were allowed to continue trading certain items in the Caribbean. The British also said they would abandon their forts on the northwestern frontier. In exchange, the United States would pay the pre-Revolutionary debts it owed to British merchants.

Many congressional leaders argued that the treaty did not accomplish much. Critics pointed out that it ignored many important issues. The treaty did not prevent Britain from capturing large American ships or supporting American Indians on the frontier. It also did not make the British return slaves they had freed during the Revolutionary War. Although Washington disliked the treaty, he felt that it was the best that the United States could do. At his urging, the Senate approved the treaty.

Interpreting the Visual Record

Protest *Some critics of Jay's Treaty were so angry that they protested in the streets.* ***Whom does the figure being burned represent?***

✔ **Reading Check: Categorizing** Which aspects of Jay's Treaty benefited the United States, and which did not?

Pinckney's Treaty

Along the frontier with Spanish Florida and Louisiana, American settlers faced other problems. The Spanish disputed the border between the United States and Florida. As a result of this dispute, Spain closed the port of New Orleans to U.S. trade in 1784. New Orleans was an important port. All goods moving down the Mississippi to places in the East or overseas had to pass through the city. Closing the port separated settlers on the western frontier from their most important link with the outside world.

Washington asked U.S. ambassador **Thomas Pinckney** to help. Pinckney asked Spanish officials to reopen New Orleans to U.S. trade. Then he requested **right of deposit** at the port of New Orleans. This right would allow American boats to transfer their goods at New Orleans without paying fees on their cargo.

Interpreting the Visual Record

Western trade *The Mississippi River and the port of New Orleans were vital links to the wider world for settlers on the American frontier.* ***What parts of this image show trade taking place?***

Spanish minister Manuel de Godoy (goh-DOY) tried to delay reaching an agreement. He hoped that Pinckney would grow desperate and sign a treaty favorable to the Spanish. But Pinckney was patient. Godoy became worried that the United States and Great Britain might join against Spain after signing Jay's Treaty. So he agreed to **Pinckney's Treaty**, which was signed in October 1795. Under the treaty, Spain agreed to change the Florida border. Spain's government also reopened the port at New Orleans to American ships and gave them right of deposit. Because it opened the frontier to further expansion, Washington and most other Americans considered Pinckney's Treaty a success.

✔ **Reading Check: Analyzing Information** Why did most Americans believe Pinckney's Treaty was more successful than Jay's Treaty?

Section 3 Review

go.hrw.com **Homework Practice Online** keyword: SC3 HP9

1. **Define** and explain:
   - privateers
   - right of deposit

2. **Identify** and explain:
   - French Revolution
   - Neutrality Proclamation
   - Edmond Genet
   - John Jay
   - Jay's Treaty
   - Thomas Pinckney
   - Pinckney's Treaty

3. **Summarizing** Copy the web diagram below. Use it to show the dealings the United States had with each country, as well as any important politicians involved.

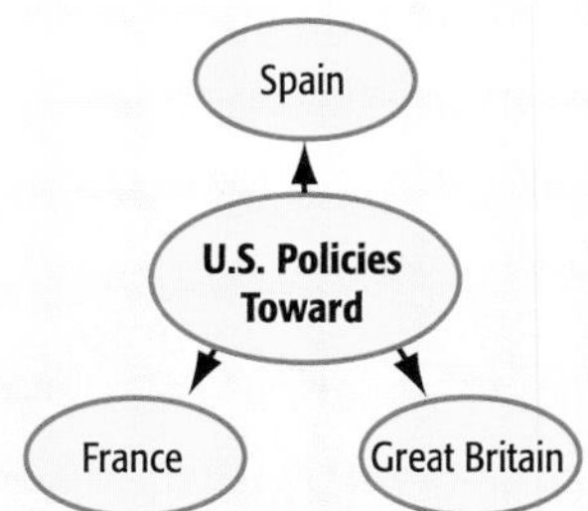

4. **Finding the Main Idea**
   a. Why did Washington want to pursue a policy of neutrality?
   b. What problems led to Jay's Treaty and Pinckney's Treaty, and what were the results of these treaties?

5. **Writing and Critical Thinking**
   Analyzing Information Imagine that news of the French Revolution has reached the U.S. capital. Write a script for a short skit that describes how the president and other individuals react to the news.
   Consider the following:
   - pro-French attitudes
   - pro-British attitudes
   - Washington's views on foreign policy

Section 4

Challenges at Home

Read to Discover

1. What domestic problems did the United States face?
2. What advice did Washington give the nation in his Farewell Address?

Identify

- Little Turtle
- Anthony Wayne
- Battle of Fallen Timbers
- Treaty of Greenville
- Whiskey Rebellion

Why It Matters Today

George Washington helped our country in many ways. Use CNNfyi.com or other **current events** sources to find out about another U.S. citizen who has made important contributions to the country. Record your findings in your journal.

The Story Continues

In November 1786 Mohawk leader Joseph Brant, or Thayendanegea, addressed a council of American Indian nations from the Ohio Valley. "The interests of any one [Indian] nation should be the welfare of all the others," he said. By uniting their efforts, they hoped to stop settlers from taking their land. Thayendanegea said that Indians must take action if they were to keep from being pushed farther west. The councilmembers agreed and formed a confederation of American Indian nations. The members promised to stop selling land to settlers and agreed to seek a new treaty from the U.S. government.

Thayendanegea had fought with the British against the United States in the Revolutionary War.

Conflict in the Northwest Territory

Despite the protests of American Indians, Americans continued to settle the Northwest Territory. Meetings between U.S. officials and American Indian leaders achieved little. Supplied with guns and ammunition by British traders, American Indians went to war. In 1790 and 1791 an American Indian confederation under Miami chief **Little Turtle** defeated U.S. forces. Washington then sent General **Anthony Wayne** to the frontier to take charge of the army.

Little Turtle asked his British allies for support, but they refused. He then quit his command and warned other American Indian leaders not to fight.

Analyzing Primary Sources
Identifying Points of View Why does Little Turtle give up the fight?

"The trail has been long and bloody; it has no end. The [whites] come from where the sun rises, and they . . . are many. They are like the leaves of the trees. When the frost comes they fall and are blown away. But when the sunshine comes again they come back more plentiful than ever before."

—Little Turtle, quoted in *The Ohio Frontier,* by Douglas Hurt

American Indian forces and the U.S. Army fought the **Battle of Fallen Timbers** on August 20, 1794. The victory went to Wayne's troops, who then burned the American Indians' villages and fields. The frontier war soon ended. In August 1795, Indian leaders signed the **Treaty of Greenville**. This treaty gave the United States access to American Indian lands in the Northwest Territory and guaranteed the safety of U.S. citizens there. In exchange, Indians received $20,000 worth of goods and a formal acknowledgment of their claim to the lands they still held.

✔ **Reading Check: Sequencing** List the events in the Northwest Territory that affected U.S. national security in the order that they took place.

The Whiskey Rebellion

More conflicts arose on the frontier when Congress passed a tax on American-made whiskey in March 1791. Farmers who produced small amounts of whiskey for trade argued that they could not afford the tax. After being fined for not paying the tax, farmer William Smith wrote, "I felt my blood boil." What began as the complaints of a few turned into the **Whiskey Rebellion** in 1794. Protesters refused to pay the tax and even tarred and feathered tax collectors. Some called themselves the new Sons of Liberty.

President Washington saw the rebels as a threat to federal authority. Under the Constitution, Congress had the power to pass the tax. He assembled some 13,000 men from state militias. The army approached western Pennsylvania in November 1794. By this time, most of the rebels had fled, and the Whiskey Rebellion ended without a battle.

✔ **Reading Check: Finding the Main Idea** What did farmers say and do in response to the whiskey tax, and why did this response worry Washington?

Interpreting the Visual Record

Whiskey Rebellion
Washington led an army into western Pennsylvania to put down the Whiskey Rebellion. ***Why do you think the government felt it was necessary to send such a large force for this task?***

THE METROPOLITAN MUSEUM OF ART, GIFT OF EDGAR WILLIAM AND BERNICE CHRYSLER GARBISCH, 1963 (63.201.2)

Washington's Farewell Address

In 1796 Washington decided not to run for a third presidential term. He wrote that he was "tired of public life" and "devoutly [strongly] wished for retirement." He also believed that by stepping down he would remind Americans that he was only a president, not a king. The people were the country's true leaders.

With the help of Alexander Hamilton and James Madison, the president wrote his Farewell Address. In it he spoke about what he believed were the greatest dangers to the American republic. Among these were the dangers of foreign ties and political divisions at home. Washington

Historical Document

George Washington

WASHINGTON'S FAREWELL ADDRESS

On September 19, 1796, President George Washington's Farewell Address first appeared in a Philadelphia newspaper. In it, he wrote about the nation's economy, foreign policy, and political parties.

I have already **intimated**[1] to you the danger of [political] parties in the state, with particular reference to the founding of them on geographical discriminations. Let me now take a more **comprehensive**[2] view and warn you in the most solemn manner against the **baneful**[3] effects of the spirit of party generally. . . .

If, in the opinion of the people, the distribution or **modification**[4] of the constitutional powers be in any particular wrong, let it be corrected by an amendment. . . .

Promote, then, as an object of primary importance, institutions for the general **diffusion**[5] of knowledge. . . . As the structure of a government gives force to public opinion, it is essential that public opinion should be enlightened. . . .

[Avoid] likewise the accumulation of debt, . . . not ungenerously throwing upon **posterity**[6] the burden which we ourselves ought to bear. . . .

Observe good faith and justice toward all nations. **Cultivate**[7] peace and harmony with all. . . .

It is our true policy to steer clear of permanent alliances with any portion of the foreign world. . . . There can be no greater error than to expect, or **calculate,**[8] upon real favors from nation to nation. It is an illusion which experience must cure, which a just pride ought to discard.

[1]**intimated:** told
[2]**comprehensive:** complete
[3]**baneful:** destructive
[4]**modification:** change
[5]**diffusion:** spreading
[6]**posterity:** future generations
[7]**cultivate:** seek
[8]**calculate:** plan

Analyzing Primary Sources

1. Under what circumstances does Washington propose changing the Constitution, and how should this be done?
2. Do you think Washington's advice on political parties and foreign policy is still appropriate today? Explain your answer.

Many Americans saw George Washington as a champion of liberty, represented by the woman standing by his statue.

also expressed his concerns about the public debt. He believed that the government should try not to borrow money. Such a policy would protect future generations from being saddled with debt.

Washington also wanted the country to be free from outside influences and to avoid diplomatic problems. He warned against forming permanent relationships, friendly or otherwise, with other countries.

History Makers Speak

"The nation which indulges [allows] toward another an habitual [regular] hatred or an habitual fondness is in some degree a slave. It is a slave to its animosity [hate] or to its affection, either of which is sufficient [enough] to lead it astray from its duty and its interest."

—George Washington, quoted in *The Annals of America*

Washington believed that disagreements between political groups weaken government. He worried that regional differences could lead too easily to political conflict that would harm the nation. Political unity, he said, was key to national success. Thus, Washington left office telling the nation to work out its differences and protect its independence. He concluded his speech by looking forward to his retirement and praising his country. "I anticipate . . . the sweet enjoyment . . . of good laws under a free government, the ever favorite object of my heart."

✔ **Reading Check: Summarizing** What were the key points of Washington's Farewell Address?

Section 4 Review

go.hrw.com Homework Practice Online
keyword: SC3 HP9

1. **Identify** and explain:
   - Little Turtle
   - Anthony Wayne
   - Battle of Fallen Timbers
   - Treaty of Greenville
   - Whiskey Rebellion

2. **Sequencing** Copy the graphic organizer below. Use it to describe, in order, the major domestic problems leading up to Washington's Farewell Address. Include Washington's views on the greatest threats that faced the United States.

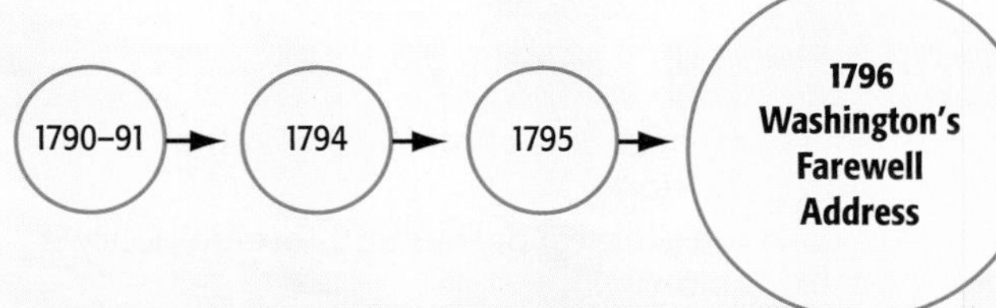

3. **Finding the Main Idea**
   a. What challenge did the United States face on the frontier, and what was its outcome?
   b. Do you think that the farmers in the Whiskey Rebellion were really like the Sons of Liberty? Why or why not?

4. **Writing and Critical Thinking**
   Making Generalizations and Predictions Imagine that you are a historian reading George Washington's Farewell Address. Think about what the country would be like today if Washington's advice was followed strictly. Write a journal entry expressing your thoughts.
   Consider the following:
   - political divisions and parties
   - the national debt
   - alliances with foreign nations

Section 5

John Adams's Presidency

Read to Discover

1. How did political parties form, and what role did they play in the presidential election of 1796?
2. What problems with foreign nations did John Adams face during his presidency?
3. What were the Alien and Sedition Acts, and how did Republicans respond to them?
4. What were the main issues in the election of 1800, and what were some of its outcomes?

Define

- political parties

Identify

- Federalist Party
- Democratic-Republican Party
- XYZ affair
- Alien and Sedition Acts
- Kentucky and Virginia Resolutions
- Twelfth Amendment

WHY IT MATTERS TODAY

Today the United States has two main political parties. These are the Democratic Party and the Republican Party. Use CNNfyi.com and other **current events** sources to learn about how one party or the other has made the news recently. Record your findings in your journal.

The Story Continues

When two-term vice president John Adams learned that President Washington was retiring, he thought about running for office. He asked his wife, Abigail, what she thought. She answered, "I would be second unto no Man but Washington." She thought that Adams should either run for president or quit politics. He considered her advice and chose to run for the presidency.

THE GRANGER COLLECTION, NEW YORK

Abigail Adams, a respected friend of several political figures, often gave her husband political advice.

 The Election of 1796

The election of 1796 began a new era in U.S. politics. For the first time, more than one candidate was running for president. **Political parties**, groups that help elect government officials and shape government policies, also had an important role. Two political parties had begun to form during Washington's presidency. Despite the warnings about party conflict given in Washington's Farewell Address, the rivalry between these two parties dominated the 1796 election.

Interpreting the Visual Record

Parties *This political cartoon shows members of the Federalist and Democratic-Republican Parties threatening to pull down the foundations of the government with their arguing.* ***Who is the person watching the party members and criticizing their actions?***

The **Federalist Party** wanted to make the federal government stronger and to promote industry and trade. This party was most popular in New England. Alexander Hamilton helped found the Federalist Party. However, he chose not to run for president. The Federalists chose former vice president John Adams and South Carolinian Thomas Pinckney as their candidates. Adams was not popular in the South or the West. But he and his wife Abigail hoped that voters would support him "as soon as they have had time to . . . consider and reflect [think about]" his years of loyal service to the nation.

The **Democratic-Republican Party** was started by such leaders as Thomas Jefferson and James Madison. The party's members were called Republicans. (This party is not related to the modern Republican Party.) Republicans wanted to limit the power of the federal government. The party was most popular in the South and along the western frontier. The Republicans chose former secretary of state Thomas Jefferson and New York politician Aaron Burr as their candidates.

Supporters of John Adams created this campaign button.

Both sides attacked each other during the election. Republicans called the Federalists the British party. Campaign posters for Jefferson called Adams a "Royalist." The Federalists answered that the Republicans were influenced too greatly by the French. They also questioned Jefferson's political skills. One Federalist wrote that Jefferson was "fit to be a professor in a College, [or] President of a Philosophical Society . . . but certainly not" president. Abigail Adams wrote to her son about the style of the campaign. "I fear America will never go through another Election without Blood Shed. We have had a paper War for six weeks past."

Hamilton, who did not like Adams, complicated matters by trying to get Pinckney elected instead. The plan failed, and Adams only narrowly defeated Jefferson. At the time, the person who took second place in a presidential election became vice president. This happened even if that person was not of the same political party as the president. So after months of running against each other, Adams and Jefferson took office together.

✔ **Reading Check: Summarizing** Explain how the Federalist and the Democratic-Republican Parties formed in the mid-1790s.

President Adams and the XYZ Affair

At first glance, John Adams did not appear well suited for the presidency. Adams had been a leading Patriot during the time of the American Revolution. He had later served as a foreign diplomat. Yet he lacked Washington's dignity, and most people saw him as a cold and distant person. Still, many people respected Adams—even his opponents. They recognized his hard work, honesty, and intelligence.

One of Adams's first goals as president was to improve relations between the United States and France. The French had been using privateers to attack American ships. In response, Adams sent U.S. diplomats Elbridge Gerry, John Marshall, and Charles C. Pinckney to Paris. Once in France, the diplomats learned that French foreign minister Charles-Maurice de Talleyrand-Périgord would not speak with them. Instead, three French agents paid them a secret visit. These agents said that Talleyrand would discuss a treaty only in exchange for a $250,000 bribe. The French government also wanted a loan of $12 million. The amazed diplomats refused this demand. In March 1798 President Adams told Congress that the peace-seeking mission had failed. He described the French terms, substituting the letters X, Y, and Z for the names of the French agents. Upon hearing the news, Federalists in Congress called for war with France.

Soon the story of the **XYZ affair**, as the requested bribe was called, spread across the country. "Millions for defense, but not one cent for tribute!" became the rallying cry of the American people. Fearing war, Adams asked Congress to expand the navy to a fleet of more than 30 ships. He also wanted to keep a peacetime army of several thousand troops. Congress approved both measures.

CONNECTING TO MATH

Just the Facts

Building the National Defense

Year	Total Federal Budget (in dollars)	Defense Spending (in dollars)
1792	5,080,000	1,101,000
1793	4,482,000	1,130,000
1794	6,991,000	2,700,000
1795	7,540,000	2,892,000
1796	5,727,000	1,535,000
1797	6,134,000	1,422,000
1798	7,677,000	3,391,000*
1799	9,666,000	5,325,000
1800	10,786,000	6,010,000

*The Department of the Navy was created in 1798.

Using Mathematical Skills

1. How much did military spending decrease from 1795 to 1796? How much did the total federal budget increase from 1796 to 1800? How much of this increase was military spending?
2. Create a line graph that compares the total federal budget from 1792 to 1800 with defense spending for those same years.
3. Imagine that you are a Federalist or Republican in 1800. Use these statistics to write a speech for your presidential candidate. Make your speech either in favor of or against President Adams's spending policies.

However, Adams did not ask Congress to declare war and instead tried to reopen peace talks. He believed that many people in the United States and France were against war. Adams was also worried about the cost of a war. Despite his efforts, American and French ships began fighting each other in the Caribbean.

Adams's opposition to a war stunned many Federalists. Some insulted him in speeches or essays. Hamilton even worked to weaken the president's power, but Adams refused to change his mind. In 1800 the United States and France finally signed a treaty that stopped fighting between American and French ships. Adams then forced two members of his cabinet to resign for trying to block his peace efforts.

✔ **Reading Check: Analyzing Information** What problems arose between France and the United States, and how did President Adams try to solve them?

The Alien and Sedition Acts

Republicans criticized Adams for making the military stronger. They also attacked the Federalists for supporting war with France. Many Federalists saw these attacks as disloyal. They said that the country needed to be protected from Republican traitors.

Federalists in Congress passed the **Alien and Sedition Acts** in the summer of 1798. The Alien Act allowed the president to have foreign residents removed from the country. They could be removed if the president believed they were involved "in any treasonable or secret machinations [plots] against the government." The Sedition Act stated that U.S. citizens could not join any plots against the government's policies. The act also made it illegal to "write, print, utter or publish" any false or hostile words against the government or its policies.

Interpreting the Visual Record

Alien and Sedition Acts *In 1798 Federalist congressman Roger Griswald attacked Republican Matthew Lyon during an angry debate over the Alien and Sedition Acts.* ***How are the other representatives responding to the fight?***

THE GRANGER COLLECTION, NEW YORK

These laws were applied mostly against Republican newspapers. In some cases the editors of newspapers were arrested. Federalists even had Republican representative Matthew Lyon arrested for speaking out against the government. French citizens living in the United States also began to leave the country.

Jefferson and Madison decided to strike back with the **Kentucky and Virginia Resolutions**. The states' legislatures passed these resolutions in 1798 and 1799. Madison wrote the Virginia Resolutions, and Jefferson wrote the Kentucky Resolutions.

They stated that the Alien and Sedition Acts were unconstitutional. Madison and Jefferson claimed that the federal government did not have the power to pass such laws and that the acts interferred with the state government. Jefferson explained their views. "Whensoever the general government assumes undelegated [unassigned] powers, its acts are unauthoritative [without authority], void, and of no force."

Madison and Jefferson said that state governments could ignore any federal laws that they found to be unconstitutional. To avoid such a conflict, they asked Congress to repeal the Alien and Sedition Acts. Congress refused. The acts remained in effect until a later Congress decided not to renew them. However, the resolutions had an important impact on the idea of states' rights. They gave support to the idea that state governments could challenge the federal government. This precedent would help other politicians who wanted to declare laws or actions of the federal government to be illegal.

✔ **Reading Check: Drawing Inferences and Conclusions** How did the Alien and Sedition Acts pose a threat to freedom of speech and freedom of the press, and why was this important?

CONNECTING TO
SCIENCE AND TECHNOLOGY

The USS *Constitution*

To protect American merchant ships, in 1794 Congress decided to create a small navy. The USS *Constitution* became the most famous ship of this first fleet. The ship's toughness in battle gained it the popular nickname "Old Ironsides." When the *Constitution* became too old for active duty, the U.S. Navy preserved it for future generations. After 200 years it remains the world's oldest commissioned warship afloat. Tourists now visit Old Ironsides to touch a part of history. **Why do you think Old Ironsides is respected today?**

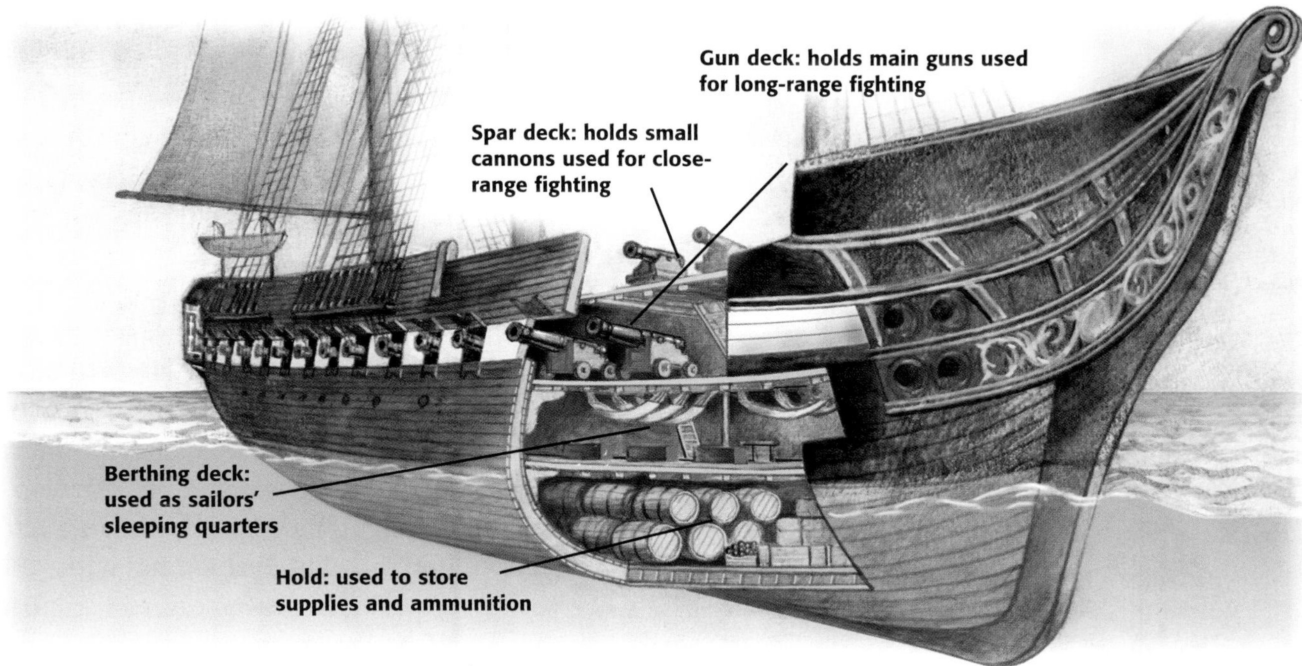

The Election Of 1800

Despite the problems his administration had faced, Adams decided to run for re-election. In the presidential election of 1800, Thomas Jefferson and Aaron Burr ran against Adams and Charles C. Pinckney. During the campaign the Republicans challenged the legality of the Alien and Sedition Acts. They criticized Adams's creation of a permanent army and the higher taxes needed to pay for it. In addition, Republicans said that Adams had hurt relations between France and the United States. The nation's leading Republican newspaper favored Jefferson.

Analyzing Primary Sources

Evaluating Sources Do you think the newspaper is making a fair statement? Explain your answer.

> **"The friends of *peace will vote for Jefferson*— the friends of war will vote for *Adams* or for *Pinckney*."**
>
> —The *Philadelphia Aurora,* quoted in *In Pursuit of Reason,* by Noble E. Cunningham Jr.

The Federalists answered by calling Jefferson a pro-French revolutionary. If elected, they said, he would ruin the country. They also said that Jefferson, who was deeply interested in science and philosophy, was against organized religion. In response, Republicans reminded voters that Jefferson was the author of the Declaration of Independence. He could certainly be trusted to protect the liberties of all Americans.

Jefferson actively sought support, while Adams took little part in his own campaign. He believed that the people would judge him on his political record. Alexander Hamilton again worked against Adams, publishing a highly critical essay. By doing this, he caused further division among the Federalists.

A Narrow Republican Victory

Jefferson and Burr won 73 electoral votes each to 65 for Adams and 64 for Pinckney. The Republicans had won the election, but the tie caused a problem. At that time there were no votes for the vice president—the runner-up won this office. Both Jefferson and Burr were eligible for the presidency. The decision went to the House of Representatives.

The Federalists in the House refused to vote for Jefferson as president and tried to elect Burr. Meanwhile, the Republicans voted for Jefferson, resulting in another tie and another vote. This process was repeated more than 30 times. Finally, about half of the Federalists simply refused to vote for anybody. Because he trusted Jefferson more than Burr, Hamilton worked on Jefferson's behalf. The Republicans were thus able to elect Jefferson. The problems with the voting system led Congress to propose the **Twelfth Amendment** in 1803. This

Bitterness between Hamilton and Burr over the 1800 election and other issues eventually led to this duel, in which Burr killed Hamilton.

amendment created a separate ballot for president and vice president. The states passed it in September 1804 before the next election.

Their loss in the presidential election weakened the Federalists, and Adams retired from public life. For many years following the election, Adams and Jefferson did not speak to each other. However, their respect for one another finally led them to renew their friendship.

Jefferson believed the transfer of power between parties showed the strengths of the U.S. system of government. Later, he wrote to a friend about the achievement that some Americans called the Revolution of 1800.

THE GRANGER COLLECTION, NEW YORK

This campaign banner was used by Jefferson's supporters in the election of 1800.

History Makers Speak

"[The election was] as real a revolution in the principles of our government as that of 1776 was in its form; not effected [caused] indeed by the sword, as that [was], but by the rational and peaceable instrument of reform, the suffrage [vote] of the people."

—Thomas Jefferson, quoted in *In Pursuit of Reason,* by Noble E. Cunningham Jr.

Analyzing Primary Sources

Identifying Points of View Why did Jefferson think the election was revolutionary?

To Jefferson, his victory was the triumph of the people. In addition, it proved that his faith in the intelligence of the everyday citizen was justified.

✔ **Reading Check: Finding the Main Idea** How did Jefferson win the presidency?

Section 5 Review

go.hrw.com Homework Practice Online keyword: SC3 HP9

1. **Define** and explain:
   - political parties
2. **Identify** and explain:
   - Federalist Party
   - Democratic-Republican Party
   - XYZ affair
   - Alien and Sedition Acts
   - Kentucky and Virginia Resolutions
   - Twelfth Amendment
3. **Identifying Cause and Effect** Use the diagram to explain why the Federalist and Republican Parties were formed and how they influenced the 1796 presidential election.

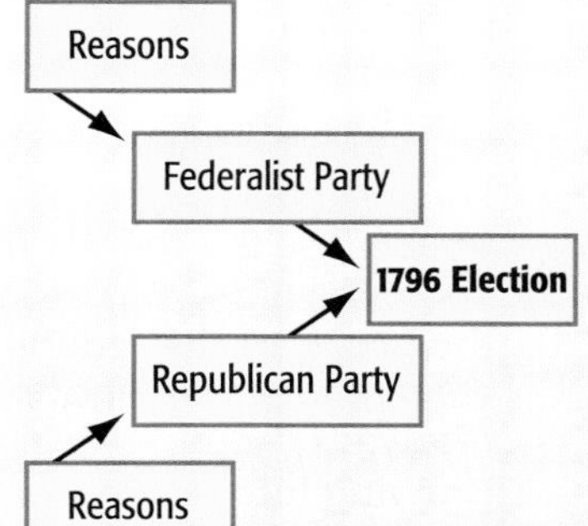

4. **Finding the Main Idea**
   a. How did John Adams address U.S. problems with France?
   b. What were the key issues of the election of 1800, and how did the outcome affect the political process?
5. **Writing and Critical Thinking**
   Supporting a Point of View Imagine that you are a newspaper editor who does not belong to either the Federalist or Republican Party. Write an editorial in response to the Alien and Sedition Acts and the Kentucky and Virginia Resolutions.
   Consider the following:
   - the extent of the powers of the federal government
   - how the Alien and Sedition Acts were used
   - the constitutional right to freedom of speech and freedom of the press

Chapter 9 Review

The Chapter at a Glance

Examine the visual summary of the chapter below. Write a paragraph describing the challenges that faced the new nation, leaving out the dates for key events. Have a classmate read the paragraph and fill in the missing dates.

Domestic Events

1789: Washington becomes president.

1790: The federal government assumes state debts. Washington, D. C., is declared the U.S. capital.

1791: The Bank of the United States is established.

1794: U.S. troops win the Battle of Fallen Timbers. The Whiskey Rebellion takes place.

1796: Washington gives his Farewell Address. John Adams is elected president.

1798: Congress passes the Alien and Sedition Acts.

1800: Thomas Jefferson is elected president.

International Events

1789: The French Revolution begins.

1794: Jay's Treaty is signed by Britain and the United States.

1795: Pinckney's Treaty with Spain reopens the port of New Orleans.

1798: The XYZ affair takes place in France.

Identifying People and Ideas

Use the following terms or people in historically significant sentences.

1. George Washington
2. Judiciary Act of 1789
3. protective tariff
4. Bank of the United States
5. Neutrality Proclamation
6. Jay's Treaty
7. Little Turtle
8. Whiskey Rebellion
9. political parties
10. XYZ affair

Understanding Main Ideas

Section 1 *(Pages 268–271)*

1. Describe how Washington and the first Congress organized the government.

Section 2 *(Pages 272–277)*

2. Why did Congress create a national bank, and what challenges did it face in doing this?

Section 3 *(Pages 278–282)*

3. What did Jay's Treaty and Pinckney's Treaty achieve?

Section 4 *(Pages 283–286)*

4. Why was the Whiskey Rebellion significant?
5. What issues concerned Washington when he retired?

Section 5 *(Pages 287–293)*

6. When were the Federalist Party and the Democratic-Republican Party formed, and what were their policies?
7. What effect did the Alien and Sedition Acts have on the Republicans?

You Be the Historian—Reviewing Themes

1. **Global Relations** How did Presidents Washington and Adams address foreign-policy issues?
2. **Constitutional Heritage** What constitutional issues did Alexander Hamilton confront when he proposed the creation of a national bank?
3. **Economics** How did Alexander Hamilton propose handling federal and state debts, and why?

Thinking Critically

1. **Supporting a Point of View** What qualities do you think made George Washington a good leader?
2. **Summarizing** What issues led to debates over the power of the federal government in the early republic, and how were these issues resolved?
3. **Drawing Inferences and Conclusions** Why do you think the Republican Party was more popular in the South and along the western frontier?

Interpreting Political Cartoons

Study the political cartoon of the XYZ affair below. Then answer the questions that follow.

THE GRANGER COLLECTION, NEW YORK

1. Which of the following statements best describes the main message of the cartoon?
   a. American diplomats are willing to take bribes and cannot be trusted.
   b. The Americans and the French were too different from each other to reach any kind of peace agreement.
   c. French officials are corrupt and dangerous but cannot frighten American officials.
   d. Americans should be willing to pay bribes to French agents if it will help achieve peace.
2. Why do you think the artist chose to portray the French agents as a many-headed monster? Do you think this cartoon supports going to war with France or not? Explain your answer.

Analyzing Primary Sources

Read the following quote by Secretary of the Treasury Alexander Hamilton, who argued that the Constitution allowed for the creation of a national bank. Then answer the questions that follow.

> **"A bank has a direct relation to the [constitutional] power of borrowing money. . . . The essentiality of such an institution . . . is exemplified at this very moment. An Indian expedition is to be prosecuted [performed]. The only fund out of which the money can arise . . . is a tax, which only begins to be collected in July next. The preparations, however, are instantly to be made. The money must, therefore, be borrowed—and of whom could it be borrowed if there were no public banks? It happens that there are institutions of this kind, but if there were none, it would be indispensable [necessary] to create one."**

3. Which of the following statements best describes the author's point of view?
   a. The Constitution gives the federal government the power to borrow money to pay for Indian expeditions.
   b. It would be easier to defend the United States if there were a national bank.
   c. A national bank is necessary because Congress might need to borrow money to provide for an emergency or for national defense.
   d. Congress has the power to collect taxes in July.
4. Why does Hamilton think that banks are important for the economy?
5. Based on what you know about the time, why might Congress need to use its constitutional power to borrow money?

Alternative Assessment

Building Your Portfolio

Interdisciplinary Connection to Geography

Learn more about the geographic history of present-day Washington, D.C. Discover what the area was like before the capital was founded and how the city has changed over time. Find the location of at least 10 major buildings or landmarks, such as the Capitol Building or the Washington Monument. Then create a city map that displays what you have learned.

internet connect

Internet Activity: go.hrw.com
keyword: SC3 CF9

Access the Internet through the HRW Go site to locate primary and secondary sources such as databases and media and news services. Use these resources to learn about the Alien and Sedition Acts of 1798 and the Pentagon Papers case during the Vietnam War. Then use a computer word-processing program to write a report outlining the connection between a free and a democratic society.

CHAPTER

10 The Expanding Nation (1800–1815)

Explorers Lewis and Clark kept several journals, including this one bound in elk skin.

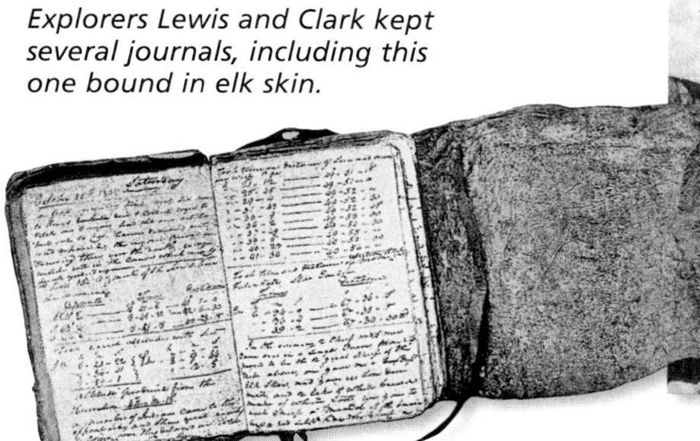

THE GRANGER COLLECTION, NEW YORK

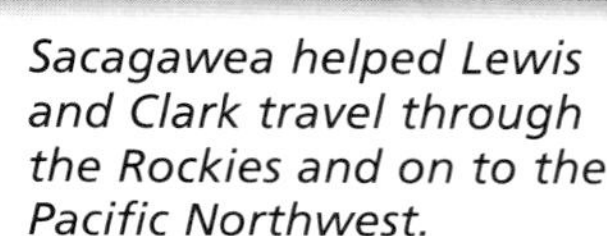

Sacagawea helped Lewis and Clark travel through the Rockies and on to the Pacific Northwest.

UNITED STATES

- **1801** Thomas Jefferson takes office as president.
- **1803** The U.S. Senate approves the Louisiana Purchase.
- **1804** Meriwether Lewis and William Clark set out to explore the Louisiana Territory.

1800 | **1802** | **1804** | **1806**

WORLD

- **1803** France and Great Britain go to war.
- **1804** Napoléon becomes emperor of France.
- **1806** The Holy Roman Empire officially ends.
- **1807** The slave trade is abolished in the British Empire.

At the last minute, Napoléon took the crown from Pope Pius VII and placed it on his own head.

Build on What You Know

By 1800, Federalists knew they had lost control of both the presidency and Congress to their Republican rivals. During his presidency, Thomas Jefferson greatly expanded the size of the United States. The young nation also came into conflict with France and Great Britain.

British forces charged the walls built by General Andrew Jackson's troops in the Battle of New Orleans.

Americans did not learn that the Treaty of Ghent had ended the War of 1812 until they had already fought the last battle.

1808 Napoléon names his brother Joseph as king of Spain.

1809 President Jefferson signs the Non-Intercourse Act.

1810

1811 William Henry Harrison's troops win the Battle of Tippecanoe against American Indian forces led by Tecumseh.

1811 Paraguay becomes the first Spanish colony in South America to gain independence.

1812 Congress declares war on Great Britain.

1814 On August 24, British soldiers burn the city of Washington.

Federalist delegates from New England hold the Hartford Convention on December 15.

1814 European nations meet at the Congress of Vienna to reorganize Europe after the fall of Napoléon.

1815 Andrew Jackson leads U.S. soldiers to victory over the British in the Battle of New Orleans.

If you were there . . .

How might you react to the election of Thomas Jefferson?

You Be the Historian

What's Your Opinion? Do you **agree** or **disagree** with the following statements? Support your point of view in your journal.

- **Constitutional Heritage** The Supreme Court should have power equal to the president and Congress.
- **Geography** Nations do not need to explore new territories that they acquire.
- **Global Relations** Nations that share borders are likely to fight wars against each other.

Section 1

Jefferson as President

Read to Discover

1. What views did Thomas Jefferson express about political parties in his first inaugural address?
2. What Republican policies did Jefferson introduce, and which Federalist policies did he accept?
3. Why was *Marbury* v. *Madison* an important court case?

Define

- judicial review

Identify

- Thomas Jefferson
- William Marbury
- John Marshall
- *Marbury* v. *Madison*

Why It Matters Today

Americans go to the polls to elect their president as well as many other officials. Use CNNfyi.com or other **current events** sources to learn about the policies of an elected official. Record your findings in your journal.

These coins celebrate Jefferson's inauguration.

The Story Continues

The day was March 4, 1801. Thomas Jefferson was about to become president of the United States. Washington and Adams had taken carriages to their inaugurations, or swearing-in ceremonies. Jefferson, however, chose to walk to the Capitol Building. Jefferson also decided not to wear fancy clothes. A reporter wrote, "His dress was, as usual, that of a plain citizen, without any distinctive badge of office."

The Republican Victory

A large crowd attended the inauguration of **Thomas Jefferson**, yet former president John Adams was absent. He was so upset by his defeat that he left the city. One observer who attended the inauguration called it "one of the most interesting scenes a free people can ever witness." The crowd was celebrating more than Jefferson's election. Along with his victory, the Republican Party had also won control of both houses of Congress. As a result, Jefferson would have the support of Congress for many of his plans. The inauguration marked the first time that one political party had replaced another in power in the United States. Many Americans saw the election of Jefferson as proof that the country could change leaders peacefully. That was a rare achievement for a government at the time.

Interpreting the Visual Record

Monticello *Among his many talents, President Jefferson was a fine architect. He designed his magnificent home, Monticello.* ***What does this image suggest about Jefferson's background?***

Jefferson read his carefully written speech in a quiet voice. He wanted to make it clear that he supported the will of the majority. However, he did not favor mob rule, as some Federalists had claimed. In his speech, Jefferson tried to comfort the Federalists still in the government by promising to run the government fairly.

Analyzing Primary Sources

Drawing Inferences and Conclusions Why do you think Jefferson said "We are all Republicans, we are all Federalists"?

"We are all Republicans, we are all Federalists. . . . Let us, then, with courage and confidence pursue our . . . attachment to union and representative government."

—Thomas Jefferson, First Inaugural Address

After taking the oath of office, Jefferson walked back down New Jersey Avenue to his boardinghouse. There he met with supporters and friends.

✔ **Reading Check: Finding the Main Idea** What was significant about the Republican victory in 1800?

Jefferson in Office

President Jefferson faced the task of putting his Republican ideas into practice. First, he selected the members of his cabinet. He chose James Madison as secretary of state and Albert Gallatin as secretary of the treasury. Together they set new Republican policies. Jefferson lowered military spending, reducing the size of the army to about 3,200 troops. The navy was cut to seven active ships. Jefferson and Gallatin hoped that the money saved would allow the government to repay the national debt. Jefferson also asked Gallatin to find ways to get rid of domestic taxes, like the tax on whiskey. They even wanted to close down the government agency that collected such taxes. The Republican-led Congress passed the laws needed to carry out these policies.

Jefferson did keep some programs established by the Federalists. Even though he had opposed the Bank of the United States, he agreed to let the Bank continue as it had under the Federalists. Whatever its faults, the banking system created by Hamilton seemed practical to Jefferson.

That's Interesting!

Capital under Construction
Did you know that when Jefferson became president, the city of Washington was not even finished? It's true! The streets of Washington were muddy and filled with tree stumps. Some people complained that the city had only "a few bad houses, [and] extensive swamps." The weather was also hot and humid. During the summers most people, including President Jefferson, left the capital to avoid the danger of disease. However, Washington went on to become a large and impressive city. Jefferson later said that he was proud to be a part of building the new U.S. capital.

Thomas Jefferson

Thomas Jefferson was born in 1743 to a family of Virginia plantation owners. He became a man of many talents. He attended private schools as a child and kept learning throughout his life. Jefferson loved architecture, art, farming, philosophy, and science. He put his studies to practical use. For example, he designed Monticello, his grand home on his Virginia plantation. Jefferson was a wealthy man who held more than 150 slaves. He became a member of the Virginia House of Burgesses in 1769. Jefferson was ambassador to France, secretary of state, and vice president before his two terms as president. Thomas Jefferson died on July 4, 1826, the 50th anniversary of the signing of the Declaration of Independence. In what ways did Thomas Jefferson serve his country?

This document presents the Supreme Court's decision in Marbury *v.* Madison.

FEBRUARY TERM, 1803.

WILLIAM MARBURY v. JAMES MADISON, Secretary of State of the United States.

Constitutional law.—Jurisdiction.—Mandamus.—Appointment and removal of officer.—Commission.

The president faced a difficult challenge soon after he was sworn into office. Jefferson had planned to keep many Federalists in their government jobs. However, many from his party expected the president to replace all Federalists with Republicans. The New York *American Citizen,* a pro-Republican newspaper, expressed this view. "If this should not be the case, for what . . . have we been contending [struggling]?" Federalists were equally unhappy with Jefferson. They complained that his military spending cuts put the country in danger.

Under pressure from both parties, Jefferson finally agreed to replace a number of Federalist officials with Republicans. However, he refused to replace them all. He also stuck to his ideas on government spending.

✔ **Reading Check: Summarizing** What problems did Jefferson face when he took office, and what Republican policies did Jefferson introduce to solve them?

Marbury v. *Madison*

Early in 1801, before Jefferson took office, Federalists in Congress passed a new law that created many new judgeships and other court offices. Before his term ended, President John Adams had appointed dozens of Federalists to fill these positions. Jefferson accused Adams of filling these positions "till 9 o'clock of the night, at 12 o'clock of which he was to go out of office." Other Republicans called the people chosen by Adams "midnight judges."

When Jefferson entered office on March 4, 1801, some Federalists chosen by Adams had not yet received their special commissions. Without these forms they could not begin working as judges. Jefferson took advantage of this fact. He ordered Secretary of State James Madison not to give out the papers. **William Marbury** was one of the people affected by this decision. He demanded that the Supreme Court force the executive branch to hand over his commission. The Court had never done such a thing. However, Marbury claimed that the Judiciary Act of 1789 gave the Supreme Court the right to do so.

The chief justice of the United States was **John Marshall**, a Federalist appointed by Adams. Marshall and President Jefferson disagreed about many political issues. When Marshall agreed to hear Marbury's case, Jefferson protested, complaining that the Federalists "have retired into the judiciary as a stronghold." He was concerned that Marshall would make sure that "all the works of republicanism are to be beaten down and erased."

The Supreme Court's decision in ***Marbury* v. *Madison*** surprised many people, including Jefferson. All the justices agreed that Marbury had been treated unfairly. But did the Supreme Court have the power to force Madison to give Marbury his commission? The Judiciary Act of 1789 said the Court did. Chief Justice Marshall said the Court did not.

His reason was simple. He did not think that the Constitution allowed Congress to give the Supreme Court new powers. The Judiciary Act of 1789, he believed, had wrongly given the Court such a power. In other words, the act was unconstitutional—meaning it did something not allowed by the Constitution. Therefore, the Supreme Court did not have the power to force the federal government to give Marbury his commission.

Marshall seemed to be giving up a power of the Supreme Court. But he was really claiming a much greater power. Marshall's ruling established the power of **judicial review.** This power allows the Supreme Court to declare an act of Congress to be unconstitutional. Such a law is then no longer in force. Marshall strongly defended judicial review in his written decision.

Interpreting the Visual Record

Chief Justice *John Marshall served as the first chief justice of the Supreme Court.* ***Why was Marshall's ruling in the*** **Marbury v. Madison** ***case so significant?***

> **"It is, emphatically [absolutely], the province and duty of the Judicial Department to say what the law is. . . . The Constitution is superior to any ordinary act of the legislature."**
>
> —John Marshall, *Marbury* v. *Madison*

Judicial review greatly increased the Supreme Court's legal authority. As a result, the Court became a much stronger branch within the national government.

✔ **Reading Check: Evaluating** What leadership qualities did Chief Justice John Marshall show in the *Marbury* v. *Madison* ruling?

Section 1 Review

go.hrw.com Homework Practice Online
keyword: SC3 HP10

1. **Define** and explain:
   - judicial review
2. **Identify** and explain:
   - Thomas Jefferson
   - William Marbury
   - John Marshall
   - *Marbury* v. *Madison*
3. **Categorizing** Copy the chart below. Use it to show how President Jefferson continued some Federalist policies while introducing Republican policies.

Jefferson as President

Federalist Policies	Republican Policies

4. **Finding the Main Idea**
   a. What were the major issues Thomas Jefferson discussed in his First Inaugural Address?
   b. What did Jefferson hope to accomplish by changing Federalist policies on military spending and taxes?
5. **Writing and Critical Thinking**
   Supporting a Point of View Imagine that you are a Supreme Court justice reviewing *Marbury* v. *Madison.* Write an opinion expressing your support for either Marbury or Madison.
   Consider the following:
   - "midnight judges"
   - Judiciary Act of 1789
   - judicial review

Section 2

The Louisiana Purchase

Read to Discover

1. How and why did the Louisiana Purchase take place?
2. What did the Lewis and Clark expedition achieve?
3. What was the purpose of Pike's expedition?

Identify

- Napoléon Bonaparte
- Toussaint-Louverture
- Louisiana Purchase
- Meriwether Lewis
- William Clark
- Lewis and Clark expedition
- Sacagawea
- Zebulon Pike

WHY IT MATTERS TODAY

People continue to explore Earth and beyond. Use CNNfyi.com or other **current events** sources to learn about one area being explored today. Record your findings in your journal.

The Story Continues

The Spanish flag flew over New Orleans after Spain took control of the city in 1762.

As Spain's rivals grew stronger, it struggled to hold on to its American empire. Spanish foreign minister Manuel de Godoy worried about how to keep American settlers out of the Spanish territory of Louisiana. "You can't put doors on open country," he said in despair. Years of effort failed to improve Spain's position. Under a secret treaty, Spain traded Louisiana to France, passing the problem on to someone else. One Spanish officer expressed his relief at leaving. "I can hardly wait to leave them [the Americans] behind me," he said.

French Louisiana

In 1800 France was led by General **Napoléon Bonaparte** (nuh-POH-lee-uhn BOH-nuh-pahrt). His political ambition and military skill caused fear across Europe. As he conquered neighboring countries, Napoléon also dreamed of rebuilding France's empire in North America. First, he wanted to send troops to Louisiana. Then France would replace Spain as the key European power in western North America.

Standing in the way of this plan was the former French colony of St. Domingue (present-day Haiti). The colony was located on the Caribbean island of Hispaniola. Enslaved Africans had gained their freedom by taking over the colony in the 1790s, and former slave

Toussaint-Louverture (too-san-loo-ver-toohr) ruled the island. Before sending troops to Louisiana, Napoléon needed to take back the island to use as a supply base. However, Toussaint's troops defeated the French forces sent to recapture St. Domingue in 1802. This defeat kept Napoléon from sending troops to Louisiana.

U.S. leaders became suspicious of Napoléon when they learned France once again owned Louisiana. President Jefferson knew that France could block the westward growth of the United States. The French could also interfere with American trade. Jefferson worried that from New Orleans, France could control American trade along the Mississippi River.

New Orleans was founded by the French in 1718 and came under Spanish rule in 1762. The city remained Spanish for some 40 years before returning to French control. Its busy docks were filled with settlers' farm products and valuable furs bought from American Indians. Many of these cargoes were then sent to Europe. At the same time, manufactured goods passed through the port on their way upriver. The city was also home to many languages and cultures, such as African, English, French, and Spanish. New Orleans soon became the focus of Jefferson's foreign policy.

THE GRANGER COLLECTION, NEW YORK

Toussaint-Louverture played a key role in the founding of the nation of Haiti.

✔ **Reading Check: Making Generalizations and Predictions** How do you think Napoléon's failure to regain control of Haiti would affect his plans for North America?

The Louisiana Purchase

President Jefferson wanted to keep the French from controlling New Orleans, but he did not want to start a war. He hoped that the United States could find a peaceful answer.

Jefferson told the U.S. ambassador to France, Robert R. Livingston, to try to buy New Orleans and West Florida. Jefferson sent James Monroe to help Livingston. Livingston met with Talleyrand, the French foreign minister, to discuss the offer. Talleyrand said that without New Orleans "the rest [of Louisiana] would be of little value" to France. Then he asked what the United States would "give for the whole." The stunned Americans realized that France was offering to sell all of Louisiana.

Napoléon was willing to sell Louisiana for a number of reasons. France was about to go to war against Great Britain. Napoléon also did not want to fight the United States and Britain at once. In addition, the French still had no troops in Louisiana. Instead of more territory, Napoléon now wanted money to buy supplies for his armies in Europe. He also realized that if the United States owned Louisiana, it could challenge Britain's power in North America. "I have given England a rival who, sooner or later, will humble her pride," he boasted.

Livingston and Monroe were eager to take advantage of this sudden opportunity. Congress had only authorized them to offer $10 million. However, the ambassadors agreed to buy Louisiana from France for about $15 million. They signed a treaty of purchase on May 2, 1803. Like Livingston and Monroe, Jefferson was pleased when he learned about the chance to buy all of Louisiana. But as a strict constructionist, Jefferson did not believe that the Constitution allowed him to buy the territory. However, Livingston and Monroe feared that the French might take back their offer, so they pushed the president to act quickly. Doing what he thought best for the country, Jefferson agreed to the purchase. On October 20, 1803, the Senate approved the treaty.

October 20, 1803
The U.S. Senate approves the Louisiana Purchase.

With the **Louisiana Purchase**, the size of the United States almost doubled. The Louisiana Territory was a huge region of land, stretching west from the Mississippi River all the way to the great Rocky Mountains. The exact boundaries of the territory were not yet clearly defined. President Jefferson was pleased that the land offered so much room for the United States to grow. He said proudly that the Louisiana Purchase expanded "the empire of liberty." He believed it would provide "a widespread field for the blessings of freedom."

✔ **Reading Check: Summarizing** What happened to U.S. territory in 1803, and why was this important to the future of the United States?

Louisiana Purchase treaty and seals

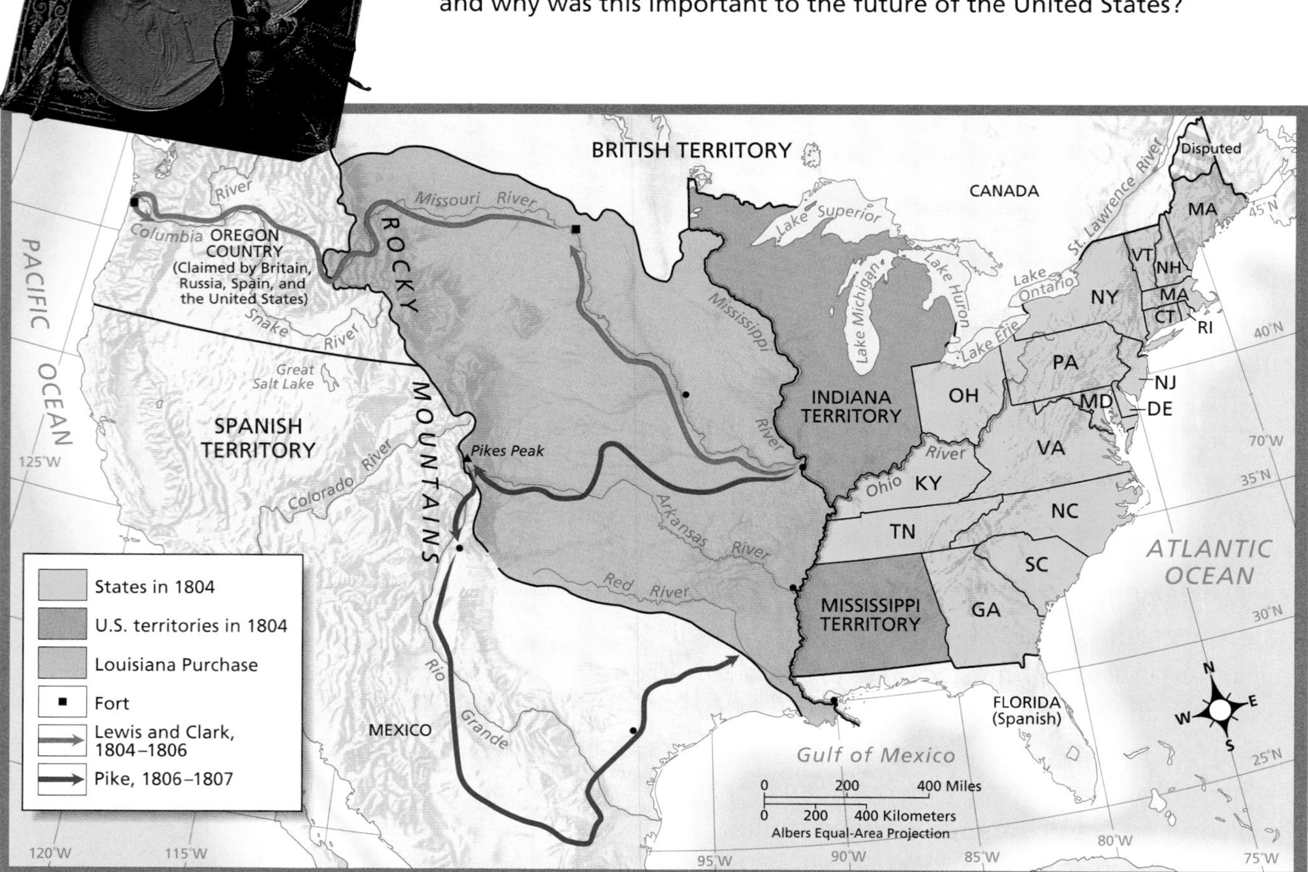

The Louisiana Purchase

Interpreting Maps Meriwether Lewis and William Clark, and later Zebulon Pike, led expeditions to explore the vast Louisiana Territory.

Skills Assessment **The World in Spatial Terms** From which city did both the Lewis and Clark and the Pike expeditions begin?

Interpreting the Visual Record

Lewis and Clark *Although Lewis and Clark tried to appear confident and powerful, they depended on the goodwill of American Indians they met.* ***With what kinds of situations do you think the Indian guides in the picture might help Lewis and Clark?***

Mission of Discovery

Americans knew little about western American Indians or the lands they inhabited. Jefferson wanted to learn more about the people and land of the West. He also wanted to see if there was a river route that could be taken to the Pacific Ocean. In January 1803 the president asked Congress to fund a small western expedition. To lead it, he chose former army captain **Meriwether Lewis**. Lewis had served as his presidential assistant. Jefferson described Lewis as "brave, prudent [careful], habituated [used] to the woods, and familiar with Indian manners and character." Lewis chose Lieutenant **William Clark** to be the co-leader of the expedition. Jefferson told Lewis and Clark to explore the Missouri River. He wanted them to form peaceful relations with American Indians they met. Jefferson added a long list of other directions.

History Makers Speak

"The commerce which may be carried on with the people inhabiting the line you will pursue, renders [makes] a knowledge of these people important. . . . Other objects worthy of notice will be the soil and face of the country, its growth and vegetable productions . . . the animals of the country . . . mineral productions of every kind . . . [and the area's] climate."

—Thomas Jefferson, quoted in *The Journals of Lewis and Clark,* edited by Frank Bergon

Analyzing Primary Sources

Summarizing What kind of information did Jefferson want Lewis and Clark to collect on their journey?

To prepare for the journey, Lewis spent weeks studying with experts about botany, surveying, and other subjects. This knowledge would allow him to take careful notes on what he saw. He also gathered supplies for the journey. With Clark, Lewis carefully selected skilled frontiersmen for their Corps of Discovery.

William Clark's journal contained illustrations and written descriptions of his travels.

Free Find:
From Lewis's Journal
After reading about Lewis's journal on the **Holt Researcher CD–ROM,** imagine that you are traveling with Lewis and Clark. Write your own journal entry for a typical day on the expedition.

The Lewis and Clark Expedition

In May 1804 the **Lewis and Clark expedition** began its long journey. The group set out from St. Louis, in present-day Missouri. The Corps of Discovery traveled up the Missouri River to the lands of the Mandan and the Sioux. Lewis used interpreters to talk to the leaders of each of the peoples they met. He told them that the United States now owned the land on which the American Indians lived. **Sacagawea** (sak-uh-juh-WEE-uh), a Shoshone from the Rocky Mountains, proved to be very helpful. Sacagawea's husband, a French fur trader who lived with the Mandan, offered to guide the expedition across the Great Plains.

Lewis and Clark kept journals describing the people, places, and animals that they encountered. Their journal entries are filled with wonder at things they saw for the first time. On the Great Plains, Lewis saw huge herds "of Buffaloe, Elk, deer, and Antelopes feeding in one common and boundless pasture." Their journals also revealed the many dangers of the journey. They told stories of sickness and conflicts with American Indians. They also described natural hazards, such as high mountains, raging rivers, and terrible storms.

After Lewis and Clark crossed the Plains, they came to the Rocky Mountains. The sight of this giant snowcapped mountain range amazed and worried Lewis. Fortunately for the explorers, the leader of the Shoshone who lived in the area was Sacagawea's brother. He provided horses and a guide to lead the expedition across the mountains. The journey was dangerous and difficult. An exhausted Lewis wrote, "We suffered everything Cold, Hunger, and Fatigue could impart [give]."

Leaving the mountains behind, Lewis and Clark followed the Columbia River, which forms the border between what are now Oregon and Washington. Along the way they met the powerful and friendly Nez Percé. Like the Shoshone, the Nez Percé provided the expedition with food. On November 7, 1805, Clark saw the Pacific Ocean. He wrote in his journal, "*Ocean in view!* O! the joy." The expedition stayed in the Pacific Northwest during the rough winter. They traded with the Clatsop and explored the coast.

In March 1806 Lewis and Clark set out on the long trip home. The party arrived by canoe in St. Louis in late September 1806. Many people from the town lined up along the river to greet them. Clark happily wrote, "Every person . . . seemed to express great pleasure at our return."

Lewis and Clark had not found a river route across the West to the Pacific Ocean. Yet they learned much about western lands and paths across the Rockies. The explorers also established contact with many American Indian groups. They had also collected a great deal of valuable scientific information on western plants and animals.

✔ **Reading Check: Summarizing** What regions did Lewis and Clark cross, and why was their expedition important?

Pike's Exploration

THE GRANGER COLLECTION, NEW YORK

Interpreting the Visual Record

Zebulon Pike *Explorer Zebulon Pike's report on his journey offered many Americans their first description of the Southwest.* ***What information do you think Pike's description contained?***

The year that Lewis and Clark returned home, young army officer **Zebulon Pike** was sent on another mission to the West. He was ordered to find the starting point of the Red River. This river runs through Louisiana and along some of the northern border of present-day Texas. The United States considered the Red River to be part of the Louisiana Territory's southwestern border with New Spain. Pike may also have had instructions to spy on Spanish outposts in the Southwest.

Pike led his small expedition to the Rocky Mountains, in present-day Colorado. There he tried to climb the mountain known today as Pikes Peak. In 1807 he headed south with a few expedition members into present-day New Mexico. They struggled across mountains in the bitter winter before reaching a tributary of the Rio Grande.

Although he had passed into Spanish-held lands, Pike continued exploring. He followed the river until a group of Spanish cavalry arrested him. When stopped, Pike pointed to the Rio Grande. "What, is not this the Red River?" The Spanish were not fooled, however. They suspected Pike of being a spy and put him in jail. When he was finally released, he returned to the United States and reported on his trip. Despite his imprisonment, Pike thought there were good business opportunities for Americans in the Southwest.

✔ Reading Check: **Supporting a Point of View** What would you do if you were Zebulon Pike and found yourself in Spanish territory?

Section 2 Review

go.hrw.com Homework Practice Online
keyword: SC3 HP10

1. **Identify** and explain:
   - Napoléon Bonaparte
   - Toussaint-Louverture
   - Louisiana Purchase
   - Meriwether Lewis
   - William Clark
   - Lewis and Clark expedition
   - Sacagawea
   - Zebulon Pike

2. **Sequencing** Copy the graphic organizer below. Use it to show what events led to the Louisiana Purchase and what steps the United States took to learn about the Louisiana Territory afterward.

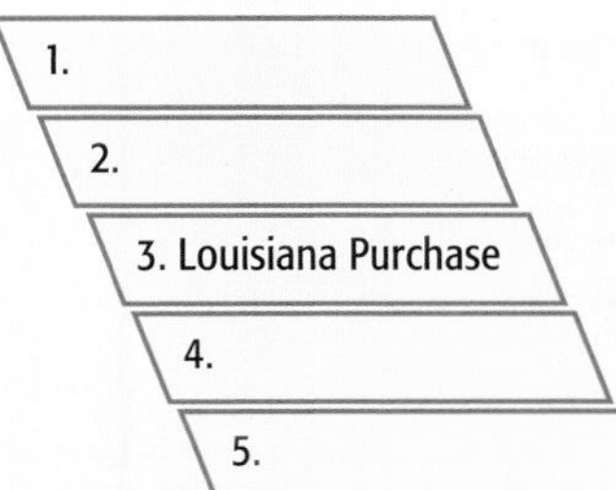

3. **Finding the Main Idea**
   a. Why was France willing to sell Louisiana, and why did the United States purchase it?
   b. What was the purpose of Pike's expedition, and where did he travel?

4. **Writing and Critical Thinking**
   Summarizing Imagine that you are a soldier on the Lewis and Clark expedition. Write a diary entry describing a specific adventure on the trip.
   Consider the following:
   - the dangers faced on the journey
   - the role of Sacagawea
   - scientific knowledge gained on the expedition

Section 3

The Coming of War

Read to Discover

1. Why did the United States place an embargo on France and Great Britain?
2. What did Tecumseh want to accomplish, and how successful was he?
3. Why did the United States declare war on Britain in 1812?

Define

- impressment
- embargo

Identify

- Embargo Act
- Non-Intercourse Act
- Tecumseh
- Battle of Tippecanoe
- War Hawks
- James Madison

WHY IT MATTERS TODAY

Nations continue to use trade restrictions in their dealings with other countries. Use CNNfyi.com or other **current events** sources to learn more about an embargo—a government's refusal to buy another country's goods. Record your findings in your journal.

The Barbary States were one of many threats to U.S. shipping in the late 1700s and early 1800s.

The Story Continues

In the fall of 1793 Samuel Calder wrote a desperate letter to the U.S. government. "I am very sorry to inform you of my present situation. . . . I was taken by an Algerian Cruzier [ship]." Calder went on to say that he and other Americans were being held prisoner by Algerian pirates. "We was immediately put into Chains and put to hard Labor," he wrote in despair. Calder begged for $100 so he could pay his ransom and be free again.

Danger on the High Seas

The state of Algiers was one of several North African lands known as the Barbary States. These countries practiced piracy and held foreign citizens captive for ransom. Many nations, including the United States, agreed to make payments to the Barbary States to protect their ships and citizens. However, U.S. officials eventually refused to pay any more and sent the U.S. Navy to end the pirate raids.

However, the United States faced greater threats on the high seas. When Great Britain and France went to war in 1803, the United States was drawn into the conflict. Each country wanted to stop the United States from supplying goods and war materials to the other. In the early 1800s Britain passed a series of acts allowing the British navy to search and seize ships carrying war supplies to France. The French quickly struck back, declaring that no country could ship goods to Britain.

Many American merchants ignored these foreign laws. As a result, the British and French navies captured many American merchant ships headed for Europe. The British also searched these ships for sailors who had run away from the British navy. The British then made these people return to British warships. This practice of pressing, or forcing, people to serve in the army or navy was called **impressment**. Sometimes U.S. citizens suffered impressment by accident.

One widely publicized example of impressment took place in June 1807. The British ship *Leopard* stopped the U.S. Navy ship *Chesapeake* and tried to remove four of its sailors. When the *Chesapeake*'s captain refused, the British opened fire and took the sailors by force. The *Chesapeake* incident angered many Americans. Attorney General Caesar A. Rodney declared that it "has excited the spirit of '76 and the whole country is literally in arms."

✔ **Reading Check: Finding the Main Idea** How did Great Britain's actions affect its relationship with the United States?

A Trade War

Debates raged about how the United States should respond to Great Britain's violations of U.S. neutrality. Some Americans wanted to go to war. Others favored an **embargo**, or the banning of trade, against Britain. A writer for the *Boston Chronicle* agreed. "Our trade is the most powerful weapon we can use in our defense."

Jefferson and the Republicans favored an embargo. In December 1807 Congress passed the **Embargo Act**. In effect, the law banned trade with foreign countries. Congress hoped to punish Britain and France and to protect American ships from capture. However, the act's main effect was to hurt American merchants. Without trade, they lost a great deal of money. The New England states and New York relied heavily on trade and were the most hard hit by the act.

The popularity of the Federalist Party rose, and Jefferson's support fell as the embargo continued. By December 1808 Jefferson had received 199 petitions asking him to repeal the Embargo Act. Meanwhile, the act had little effect on Britain or France. American merchants smuggled goods to Europe. The British also increased their trade with South America to replace lost U.S. trade. The U.S. minister in Paris noted that "here [the embargo] is not felt, and in England . . . it is forgotten."

GLOBAL CONNECTIONS

The Barbary Pirates

The small North African kingdoms of Algiers, Morocco, Tripoli, and Tunis—known as the Barbary States—operated pirate fleets. Like many European nations, the United States paid the Barbary States not to attack American ships. In 1801 Tripoli demanded a higher payment than normal. When the United States was slow to pay, Tripoli declared war. In response, Jefferson sent a small fleet to patrol the North African coast. Then in 1805, U.S. Marines and mercenaries marched across the desert to capture a Tripolitan town. Finally, the ruler of Tripoli signed a treaty and stopped attacks on American ships. The other Barbary States signed similar treaties in 1815. **How did the United States stop the Barbary pirates?**

CONNECTING TO MATH

Just the Facts

American Exports, 1800–1815

(in millions of dollars)

Year	Total Value All U.S. Exports	Total Value U.S. Exports to Great Britain
1800	71	19
1801	93	31
1802	72	16
1803	56	18
1804	78	13
1805	96	15
1806	102	16
1807	108	23
1808	22	3
1809	52	6
1810	67	12
1811	61	14
1812	39	6
1813	28	---
1814	7	---
1815	53	18

Using Mathematical Skills

1. What was the total value of U.S. exports to Great Britain from 1800 through 1815?
2. Create a graph that shows the value of all U.S. exports and the value of U.S. exports to Britain from 1800 through 1815.
3. Imagine that you are an economic adviser to President Madison in 1812. Prepare a presentation to show how the American economy has been affected by U.S. efforts to force Britain to respect American trade rights.

Congress replaced the unpopular law with the **Non-Intercourse Act** in 1809. This act banned trade only with Britain, France, and their colonies. It also stated that the United States would start trading with the first side that stopped violating U.S. neutrality. Congress wanted the new law to pressure Britain and France to stop taking American ships. In addition, Congress hoped that the Non-Intercourse Act would be less harmful to the nation's trade.

✔ Reading Check: **Comparing and Contrasting** How were the Embargo Act and the Non-Intercourse Act similar and different?

The Rise of Tecumseh

Disagreements between Great Britain and the United States went beyond the neutrality issue. In the West, the British, American Indians, and American settlers again clashed. In the early 1800s, thousands of American settlers were entering the Northwest Territory. They started farms and settlements on what had once been American Indian lands. The United States had gained control of much of this land through the Treaty of Greenville. The loss of this land had upset many Indians whose leaders had not agreed to the treaty.

Britain wanted to contain the rapid western growth of the United States and to protect its interests in Canada. British leaders did not want to fight the United States, however. Instead, the British government gave military aid to American Indian nations in the Northwest Territory.

One of the most influential and talented American Indian leaders of this period was **Tecumseh**. A Shawnee chief, Tecumseh was a skilled military leader and a brilliant speaker. He warned other American Indians about the dangers they faced from settlers.

"Where [today are] the Narranganset, the Mohican, the Pokanoket and many other once powerful tribes of our people? They have vanished before the avarice [greed] and oppression [domination] of the white man, as snow before a summer sun."

—Tecumseh, quoted in *Indian Wars,* by Robert M. Utley and Wilcomb E. Washburn

Tecumseh hoped to unite the American Indians of the Northwest Territory, the South, and the eastern Mississippi Valley. Aided by his brother, a religious leader called the Prophet, Tecumseh founded a village for his followers near the Wabash and Tippecanoe Rivers.

✔ Reading Check: **Analyzing Information** What was Tecumseh's goal?

Tecumseh hoped his union of American Indians might stop American settlers.

THE GRANGER COLLECTION, NEW YORK

Interpreting the Visual Record

Fighting on the frontier *The Battle of Tippecanoe broke the power of Tecumseh's American Indian confederation.* ***What advantages does each side have in the battle as shown in the image?***

War on the Frontier

William Henry Harrison, the governor of the Indiana Territory, believed that Tecumseh was a serious threat to American power. Tecumseh met Harrison face to face in 1810. The governor urged him to follow the treaties that had been signed. Tecumseh replied, "The white people have no right to take the land from the Indians, because the Indians had it first." No single chief, he insisted, could sell land belonging to all American Indians who used it. In response, Harrison warned Tecumseh not to resist the power of the United States.

Tecumseh then traveled south to ask the Creek nation to join his forces. Harrison decided to attack while Tecumseh was gone. Harrison raised an army and then marched his troops close to the village of Tecumseh's followers. The **Battle of Tippecanoe** began when the Prophet ordered an attack on Harrison's camp early on November 7. Indian forces broke through the camp lines. Yet Harrison remained "calm, cool, and collected," according to one observer. During the all-day battle, Harrison's soldiers forced the American Indian forces to retreat. Then they destroyed Tecumseh's village. Chief Shabonee said, "With the smoke of that town and the loss of the battle, I lost all hope." Although Tecumseh was safe, he had lost much of his support.

✔ **Reading Check: Finding the Main Idea** Why were U.S. officials worried by Tecumseh's actions?

Western politician Henry Clay was one of the leading War Hawks.

The War Debate

The frontier fighting angered many Americans. A Republican newspaper declared, "The war on the Wabash [River] is purely BRITISH." Many Americans believed that Britain had encouraged Tecumseh to attack settlers in the West.

The **War Hawks** were members of Congress who favored war against Great Britain. They saw war as the only answer to Britain's insults. Led by members of Congress such as Henry Clay of Kentucky and John C. Calhoun of South Carolina, the War Hawks were strongest in the West and the South. "If we submit," Calhoun warned, "the independence of this nation is lost." Philadelphia newspaper editor John Binns agreed with Calhoun. He insisted that "the honor of the Nation . . . will be sacrificed if war be not declared."

Some War Hawks believed that war would give the United States a chance to expand. Speaking to the House, Tennessee representative Felix Grundy explained his views. "I . . . feel anxious [eager] not only to add the Floridas to the South, but the Canadas to the North of this empire."

The strongest opponents of the War Hawks were New England Federalists. British trade restrictions and impressment were hurting New England's economy. But people there wanted to renew friendly business ties with Britain instead of fighting another war. Other politicians, such as John Randolph of Virginia, argued that war was foolish. Standing up in Congress, Randolph challenged the War Hawks.

Analyzing Primary Sources

Identifying Points of View
Why does Randolph oppose a war, and whom does he fear it would hurt?

"But is war the true remedy? Who will profit by it? . . . A few lucky merchants . . . and contractors. Who must suffer by it? The people. It is their blood, their taxes, that must flow to support it."

—John Randolph, quoted in *Annals of America*

Other antiwar politicians feared that the United States was not yet ready to fight powerful Britain. Senator Obadiah German of New York observed that the U.S. Army and Navy were small and poorly equipped. German pleaded with Congress to be patient. "Prior to any declaration of war . . . my plan would be . . . to put the country in complete armor."

✔ **Reading Check: Contrasting** Contrast the arguments of the opposing sides in the war debate.

A Declaration of War

President **James Madison**, a Republican elected in 1808, faced the difficulty of carrying on the trade war. He also felt growing pressure from the War Hawks. Speaking to Congress on June 1, 1812, Madison described Great Britain's conduct. He complained of Britain's impressment of American sailors and criticized Britain's continuing violation of

In 1812 the United States had only a small standing army to face its enemies.

U.S. neutrality. He concluded that Britain was in "a state of war against the United States." The president called on Congress to decide what the nation should do about this situation.

A few days later, representatives of southern and western states voted for war. Representatives of Delaware, the New England states, New Jersey, New York, and Pennsylvania voted for peace. When the votes were counted, the War Hawks had won. For the first time in U.S. history, Congress declared war. Months later, Madison was reelected. He would serve as commander in chief during the War of 1812.

✔ **Reading Check: Summarizing** Why did the United States declare war against Great Britain in 1812?

Section 3 Review

go.hrw.com **Homework Practice Online**
keyword: SC3 HP10

1. **Define** and explain:
   - impressment
   - embargo

2. **Identify** and explain:
   - Embargo Act
   - Non-Intercourse Act
   - Tecumseh
   - Battle of Tippecanoe
   - War Hawks
   - James Madison

3. **Identifying Cause and Effect** Copy the graphic organizer below. Use it to explain the causes and effects of the Embargo and Non-Intercourse Acts.

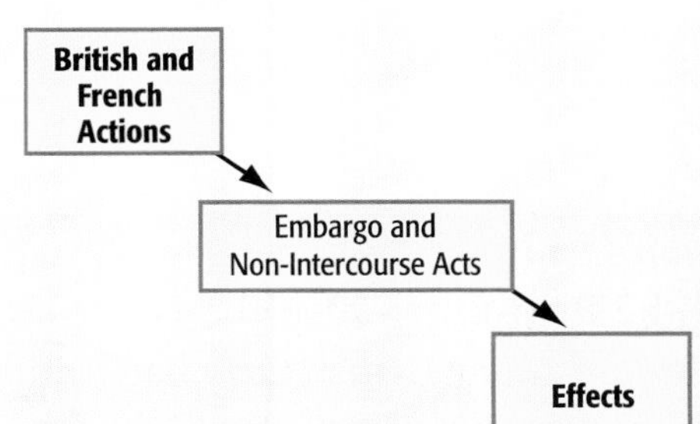

4. **Finding the Main Idea**
   a. What was Tecumseh's goal, and did he accomplish it?
   b. What led the United States to declare war on Great Britain?

5. **Writing and Critical Thinking**
   Analyzing Information Imagine that you are a reporter covering the War of 1812. Write an editorial on President Madison's foreign policy.
   Consider the following:
   - French and British interference with American ships
   - fighting against American Indians on the frontier
   - pressure from War Hawks

Section 4

The War of 1812

Read to Discover

1. How did the war progress at sea and in the Great Lakes region?
2. How did actions by American Indians aid the British during the war?
3. What strategy did the British pursue in the East?
4. How did the war come to an end?

Why It Matters Today

The Federalists protested the War of 1812, even though Congress had the power to declare it. People today continue to disagree with actions of the government. Use CNNfyi.com or other **current events** sources to find a political issue over which people disagree. Record your findings in your journal.

Identify

- Oliver Hazard Perry
- Battle of Lake Erie
- Battle of the Thames
- Red Eagle
- Andrew Jackson
- Battle of Horseshoe Bend
- Battle of New Orleans
- Hartford Convention
- Treaty of Ghent

The Story Continues

On August 19, 1812, the USS *Constitution* met the British ship *Guerrière* off the coast of Nova Scotia. The crews on both ships scrambled across the decks as the vessels circled each other. An observer said the *Constitution*'s first cannon blast rocked the *Guerrière* like "the shock of an earthquake." When the British returned fire, a U.S. sailor saw a cannonball bounce off the side of the *Constitution*. "Huzza, her sides are made of iron!" he cried. Soon "Old Ironsides" won one of the first battles of the War of 1812.

This is the captain's wheel of the USS Constitution, *which fought one of the first battles of the War of 1812.*

The War at Sea

The *Constitution*'s triumph over the *Guerrière* shocked many observers who expected the British to sweep the U.S. Navy from the seas. When the War of 1812 began, the British navy had hundreds of ships stationed around the world. In contrast, the U.S. Navy had fewer than 20. Republican Adam Seybert declared, "We cannot contend [compete] with Great Britain on the ocean."

Although outnumbered, the United States did have some advantages. The U.S. government licensed privately owned ships to attack British merchant ships. Equipping and operating these privateers cost less than building more naval ships. One Republican leader called the privateers "our cheapest & best Navy." The privateers captured hundreds of British ships. A London newspaper complained, "On the ocean, and even on our own coasts, we have been insulted."

Most of the British navy's ships were scattered around the globe and could not be called away to fight the United States. The U.S. Navy had well-trained sailors and new warships such as the *Constitution*. These well-built vessels carried more cannons than most British ships of the same size. U.S. captains proved their skill and the power of their ships early in the war, several times defeating British ships in one-on-one duels. These victories embarrassed the British and raised American morale. Eventually, the British brought more ships to the American coast. They began patrolling in large groups that the smaller U.S. Navy could not fight. The British blockaded American seaports and captured many American merchant ships.

The copper sheathing on the hull of the USS Constitution *was made by Patriot Paul Revere.*

✔ **Reading Check: Contrasting** What advantages did Great Britain and the United States have at the start of the war?

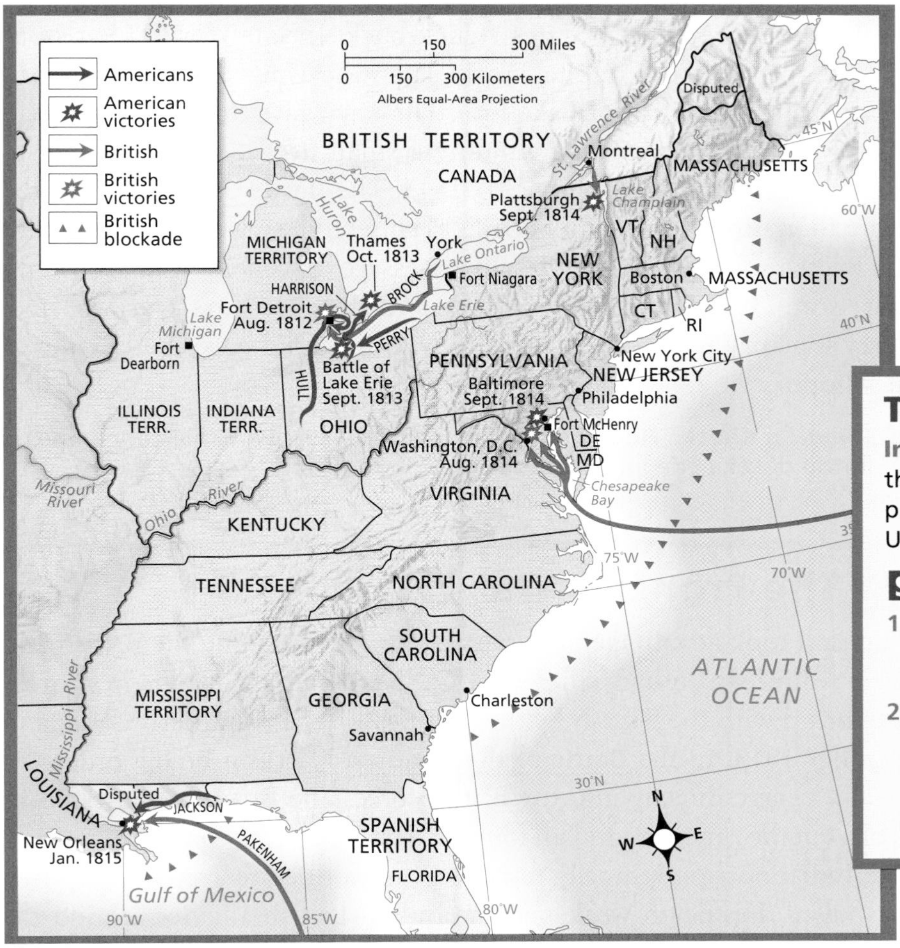

An American cannon

The War of 1812

Interpreting Maps During the War of 1812 battles took place in several regions of the United States.

Skills Assessment

1. **Places and Regions** What battle took place in the state of New York?
2. **Drawing Inferences and Conclusions** Why do you think there were so many battles along the Canadian border?

THE GRANGER COLLECTION, NEW YORK

Interpreting the Visual Record

The Battle of Lake Erie *Captain Oliver Hazard Perry was forced to abandon his damaged ship during the fighting and take command of a new one.* ***How does this image display Captain Perry's determination to win the battle?***

The Canadian Border

Hoping to equal the early success of the U.S. Navy, American leaders planned to invade Canada with three separate armies. They expected French Canadians to welcome U.S. troops. Former president Thomas Jefferson thought that conquering Canada would be "a mere matter of marching [there]."

These hopes were soon dashed. In July 1812 the British joined with American Indians led by Tecumseh to defeat an American army and capture Fort Detroit. The other American forces had to retreat when militia members refused to cross the Canadian border. By the end of 1812, Britain controlled the strategic Great Lakes region. The situation worried Treasury Secretary Albert Gallatin.

> **"The series of misfortunes exceeds [goes beyond] all anticipations made even by those who had least confidence in our inexperienced officers and undisciplined men."**
>
> —Albert Gallatin, quoted in *The War of 1812*, by Donald R. Hickey

In 1813, the United States struck back. In late April U.S. troops burned the Canadian capital, York. Then the United States moved to break Britain's control of Lake Erie. The navy gave the task to Captain **Oliver Hazard Perry**. After building a small fleet, Perry sailed out to meet the British on September 10, 1813. The **Battle of Lake Erie** lasted more than three hours, and both sides suffered heavy casualties. Finally, the British surrendered. Perry sent a message to General William Henry Harrison. "We have met the enemy and they are ours," he reported. Perry's victory forced the British to withdraw and gave the U.S. Army new hope.

✔ **Reading Check: Finding the Main Idea** Why was Perry's victory in the Battle of Lake Erie important to the U.S. war effort?

The Frontier War

Harrison took advantage of Perry's victory by pursuing the British and their American Indian allies into Canada. General Harrison's forces caught up with the British by the Thames River in southern Canada in October 1813. In the **Battle of the Thames**, Harrison boldly ordered a cavalry charge directly into the British force. The British defenses broke apart, but the American Indian forces, led by Tecumseh, continued to fight. The Indian forces eventually retreated, but not before Tecumseh himself was killed. His death weakened the Indian-British alliance around the

Great Lakes. The U.S. victory in the Battle of the Thames broke British power on the Northwest frontier and secured the U.S. border with Canada.

Two years before his death, Tecumseh had tried to enlist the Creek Indians in his confederacy. In 1813 the Creek finally decided to take up arms against the United States. Led by Chief **Red Eagle**, Creek forces destroyed Fort Mims in present-day Alabama. Close to 250 of the fort's defenders were killed. **Andrew Jackson**, a general in the Tennessee militia, led his soldiers south to fight the Creek.

After several bloody battles, Jackson attacked the main Creek base in 1814. It was a small fort on the Tallapoosa River in what is now Alabama. The **Battle of Horseshoe Bend** was a convincing victory for Jackson and his troops. Days later, Red Eagle came into Jackson's camp and surrendered. Jackson's victory ended the Creek War and led to a treaty that forced the Creek to give up millions of acres of their land.

✔ **Reading Check: Summarizing** What major battles did the United States win in Canada and present-day Alabama?

The British on the Offensive

Despite U.S. success on the western and southern frontiers, the situation in the East grew worse. Having defeated France in April 1814, the British sent more troops to America. They also strengthened their blockade of Atlantic seaports. Now reinforced, the British moved to attack the U.S. capital. President Madison and most of his cabinet were forced to flee when the British broke through U.S. defenses. The British marched

Interpreting the Visual Record

Washington *First Lady Dolley Madison heard about the British advance on Washington. Despite the danger, she stayed and saved a famous portrait of George Washington before escaping.* ***What threats would an American face trying to leave the capital?***

THE GRANGER COLLECTION, NEW YORK

THE GRANGER COLLECTION, NEW YORK

CONNECTING TO THE ARTS

The National Anthem In September 1814 American Francis Scott Key witnessed the British attack on Fort McHenry. Key could see the American flag flying over the fort as the battle began. He anxiously waited as the British fired their cannons throughout the night. At 7:00 A.M. the mist and smoke finally cleared. Key saw that the American flag still flew above the fort. The British had lost the battle. Key was so moved with joy that he wrote the words to "The Star-Spangled Banner," which became the national anthem in 1931. **Why do you think "The Star-Spangled Banner" became so popular?**

onward into the city setting fire to the White House and other government buildings.

This destruction was in response to the Americans' earlier burning of the British capital in Canada. After the British left the city, one observer surveyed the damage. All that was left of the president's home were "unroofed, marked walls, cracked, defaced [damaged], blackened with the smoke of fire." The British sailed on to Baltimore, Maryland, which was guarded by Fort McHenry. The British fleet shelled the fort and its defenders for 25 hours.

"The attack on Fort McHenry . . . was distinctly [clearly] seen from Federal Hill, and from the tops of houses which were covered with men, women, and children. The night . . . presented the whole awful spectacle [sight] of shot and shells, and rockets, shooting and bursting through the air."

—Reporter for the *Salem Gazette*, quoted in *The Rockets' Red Glare*, by Scott S. Sheads

The Americans refused to surrender Fort McHenry. The British chose to retreat instead of continuing to fight.

✔ **Reading Check: Sequencing** What did Great Britain's military forces do after destroying much of the nation's capital?

The Battle of New Orleans

After the attack on Washington, the British launched another offensive. From their Caribbean bases, they attacked New Orleans. They hoped to capture the city and thus take control of the Mississippi River. Andrew Jackson was in command of the U.S. forces around New Orleans. British troops advanced to within seven miles of the city. Startled, Jackson ordered his forces to make a stand. Jackson's troops were a mix of regular soldiers, state militia, and pirates led by Jean Laffite. They quickly constructed a wall of dirt and logs and waited for the attack.

The **Battle of New Orleans** began on the morning of January 8, 1815. Some 5,300 British troops attacked Jackson's force of 4,500. The British began marching toward the U.S. defenses under the cover of a thick morning fog. As they drew near, the air cleared. They were exposed to heavy fire from U.S. riflemen and artillery. Caught on an open field, the British were cut down with frightening speed. A militia member recalled the scene. "The field was entirely covered with . . . bodies. In some places they were lying in piles of several, one on top of the other." By the time the battle ended, more than 2,000 British soldiers had been killed or wounded. The Americans had suffered about 70 casualties.

✔ **Reading Check: Finding the Main Idea** What occurred at the Battle of New Orleans?

Ending the War

Before the battle at New Orleans, New England Federalists gathered at Hartford, Connecticut, to oppose the war. This gathering became known as the **Hartford Convention**. Some delegates to the convention wanted New England to withdraw from the United States. However, moderate members convinced the convention to send a delegation to meet with Congress to try to increase states' rights.

THE GRANGER COLLECTION, NEW YORK

Interpreting the Visual Record

Peace treaty *The signing of the Treaty of Ghent was a relief for two nations tired of war.* ***How does this image contrast with the battle scenes from the War of 1812?***

Before this delegation reached Washington, however, news reached North America that the war had ended. Some critics accused them of treason. The Federalists' attempt to challenge the power of the national government proved costly. Humiliated, the Federalists lost much of their political power.

The peace agreement that caught the Federalists by surprise was the **Treaty of Ghent**. It had been signed in Belgium on December 24, 1814, before the Battle of New Orleans took place. After months of frustrating negotiations, U.S. and British diplomats finally agreed to end the war. Each nation returned the territory it had conquered. However, the diplomats found no solutions to the problems of impressment or trade embargoes. Both sides agreed to address the remaining issues once there was peace. For the United States, the War of 1812 was a narrow escape from potential disaster. But Americans were proud that their young nation had stood up to the mighty British.

✔ **Reading Check: Identifying Cause and Effect** What led to the Hartford Convention, and what effect did it have on the political future of the Federalist Party?

Section 4 Review

go.hrw.com Homework Practice Online
keyword: SC3 HP10

1. **Identify** and explain:
   - Oliver Hazard Perry
   - Battle of Lake Erie
   - Battle of the Thames
   - Red Eagle
   - Andrew Jackson
   - Battle of Horseshoe Bend
   - Battle of New Orleans
   - Hartford Convention
   - Treaty of Ghent

2. **Comparing and Contrasting** Copy the chart below. Use it to compare and contrast the significant details of the major military battles fought on land and sea during the War of 1812.

Battle	Details (Winner, Location, Importance)

3. **Finding the Main Idea**
   a. What role did American Indians play in the War of 1812?
   b. How did the war progress in the East?

4. **Writing and Critical Thinking**
   Evaluating Imagine that you are a member of President Madison's cabinet in 1815. Write a diary entry describing the events that took place at the end of the War of 1812 and their significance.
   Consider the following:
   - the Hartford Convention
   - the Treaty of Ghent
   - the Battle of New Orleans

Chapter 10 Review

The Chapter at a Glance

Examine the visual summary of the chapter below. Create a set of flash cards listing the chapter's main events and the dates on which they occurred. Use your flash cards with a classmate to review the chapter content.

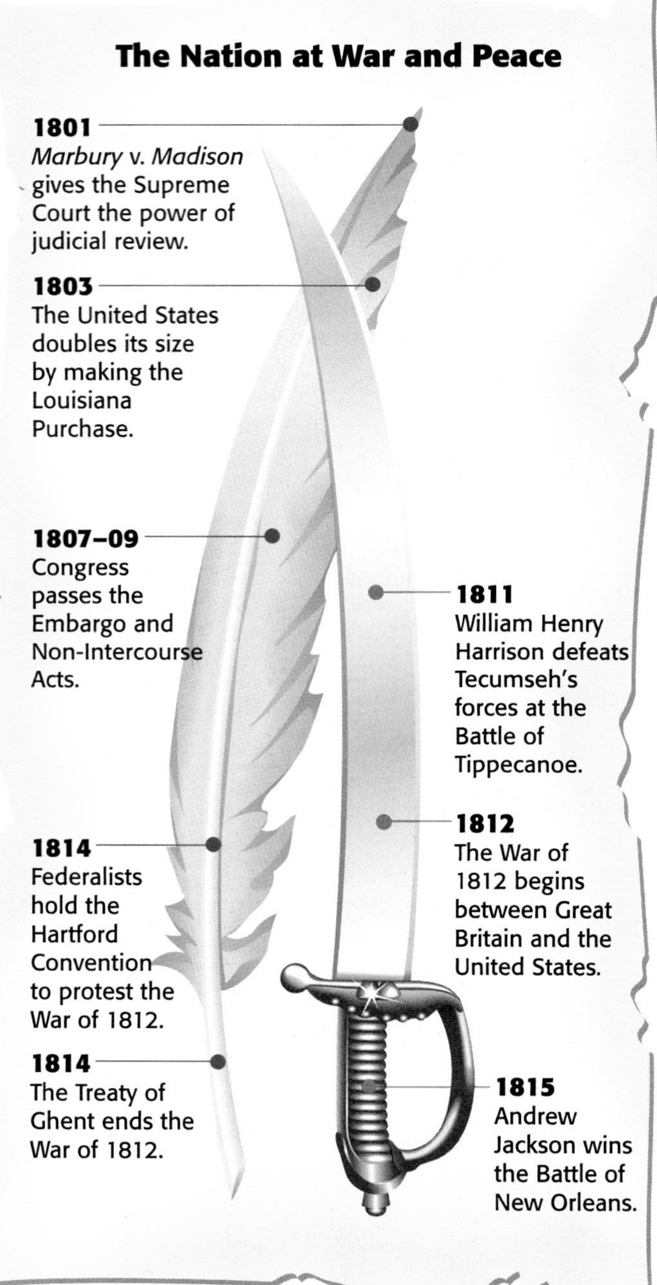

Identifying People and Ideas

Use the following terms or people in historically significant sentences.

1. John Marshall
2. judicial review
3. Louisiana Purchase
4. Lewis and Clark expedition
5. impressment
6. Tecumseh
7. War Hawks
8. Battle of New Orleans
9. Hartford Convention
10. Treaty of Ghent

Understanding Main Ideas

Section 1 *(Pages 298–301)*

1. What Federalist policy did President Jefferson leave in place?
2. Why did the Supreme Court review *Marbury* v. *Madison*?

Section 2 *(Pages 302–307)*

3. Why were New Orleans and the Mississippi River important to the United States?

Section 3 *(Pages 308–313)*

4. Starting with the war between Great Britain and France, list the series of events that led to the U.S. declaration of war on Britain in 1812.

Section 4 *(Pages 314–319)*

5. Was the War of 1812 a success from the American point of view? Explain your answer, considering the reasons why war was declared.

You Be the Historian— Reviewing Themes

1. **Constitutional Heritage** What was the significance of the *Marbury* v. *Madison* decision, and what issues did it resolve?
2. **Geography** Why did President Jefferson send Lewis and Clark to explore the West, and what important information did they bring back?
3. **Global Relations** What conflicts arose between the United States and American Indians along the western frontier?

Thinking Critically

1. **Evaluating** Do you think that Thomas Jefferson was right to purchase Louisiana despite his concerns that doing so was unconstitutional? Explain your answer.
2. **Supporting a Point of View** Write a speech arguing whether or not Congress should declare war on Great Britain in 1812.
3. **Drawing Inferences and Conclusions** What danger did the United States risk when it declared war on Britain in 1812?

Social Studies Skills Workshop

Interpreting Maps

Study the map below. Then use the information on the map to help you answer the questions that follow.

The Creek War

1. According to the map, where did the American victory in the Creek War take place?
   a. between the Alabama and Tallapoosa Rivers
   b. in Georgia near the border with the Mississippi Territory
   c. in Florida near the border with the Mississippi Territory
   d. in the Mississippi Territory near the border with Georgia

2. Based on your knowledge of the period, why was it significant that Jackson led his forces on to New Orleans after defeating the Creek?

Analyzing Primary Sources

Read the following quote from historian David Ramsay, who commented on the Louisiana Purchase in 1804, and then answer the questions that follow.

> **"History affords no example of the acquisition of such important benefits, at so moderate a price, and under such favorable circumstances. . . . [Aside from independence and the Constitution] the acquisition of Louisiana is the greatest political blessing ever conferred on these states."**

3. Which of the following best describes Ramsay's view of the Louisiana Purchase?
   a. The purchase was very valuable to the nation but still too expensive.
   b. The purchase was one of the most impressive achievements of the United States.
   c. The price of the purchase was fair, but the United States had little to gain from the new territory.
   d. The purchase was even more important than the Constitution.

4. What do you think Ramsay means when he calls the Louisiana Purchase "the greatest political blessing ever conferred on these states"?

5. Based on your knowledge of the period, do you agree or disagree with Ramsay's viewpoint on the importance of the Louisiana Purchase? Explain your answer.

Alternative Assessment

Building Your Portfolio

Interdisciplinary Connection to the Arts

Using the library and other available sources, research the role of the USS *Constitution* ("Old Ironsides") in the War of 1812. Use this information to build a model or make a sketch of the warship. Then use your model or sketch as a visual aid for a short oral report that you present to the class. Have a classmate ask and answer questions related to your work on the model.

internet connect

Internet Activity: go.hrw.com
keyword: SC3 CF10

Choose a topic on the Expanding Nation to:

- Explore the American West with Lewis and Clark.
- Research the causes and effects of the War of 1812, and write an analysis of its impact.
- Review the outcome of the last general election and compare it to the election of 1800.

The Growing Republic

In 1790 the United States was a new nation. The 13 states were all located on the eastern coast of North America. But pioneers had already begun to head west beyond the Appalachian Mountains. In 1803 the United States bought Louisiana from France. This Louisiana Purchase nearly doubled the size of the country.

The United States remained mostly a nation of farmers. Much of the young country's wealth, however, was based on trade with foreign nations.

Population and Trade

In 1790 the United States had nearly 4 million people. It stretched from the Atlantic Ocean to the Mississippi River. As the nation grew, so did its trade with other countries. But international conflicts sometimes caused foreign trade to rise or fall dramatically.

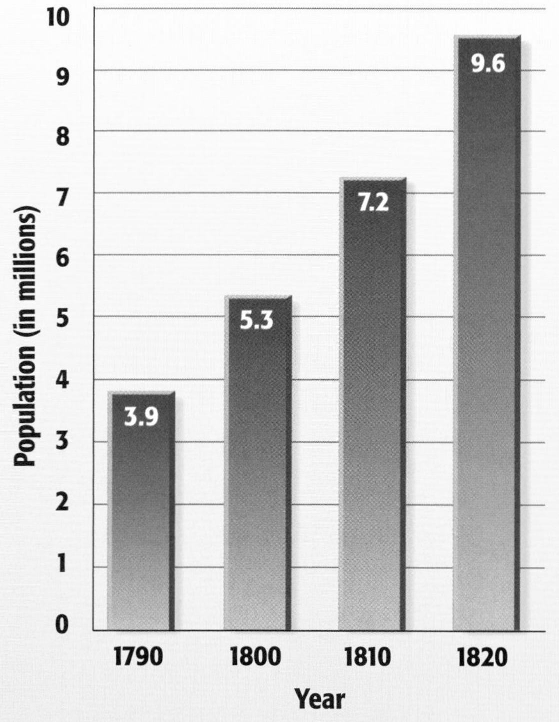

Source: *Historical Statistics of the United States*

Geography Skills
Interpreting Bar Graphs

1. **Human Systems** How much did the U.S. population increase between 1790 and 1820?
2. **Analyzing Information** During which ten-year periods did the U.S. population increase the most?

History Note 1

The U.S. population more than doubled between 1790 and 1820. The number of Americans in the West grew particularly fast. In 1790 about 4 percent of the U.S. population lived west of the Appalachian Mountains. By 1820 this figure had grown significantly.

Said-snow DEBBY,
burthen, 4 months old. April 20.
FOR SALE,
On board the Brig JAMES, oppofite No 67, South-fide Long-Wharf,
400 hhds Lifbon SALT afloat, &
a quantity of excellent LEMONS; only 35 days from Lifbon. april 20.
Brig Adventure's Cargo, from Trinidad.

Early American merchants sometimes listed their goods for sale in papers like this one. Decorated plates were one of many trade items.

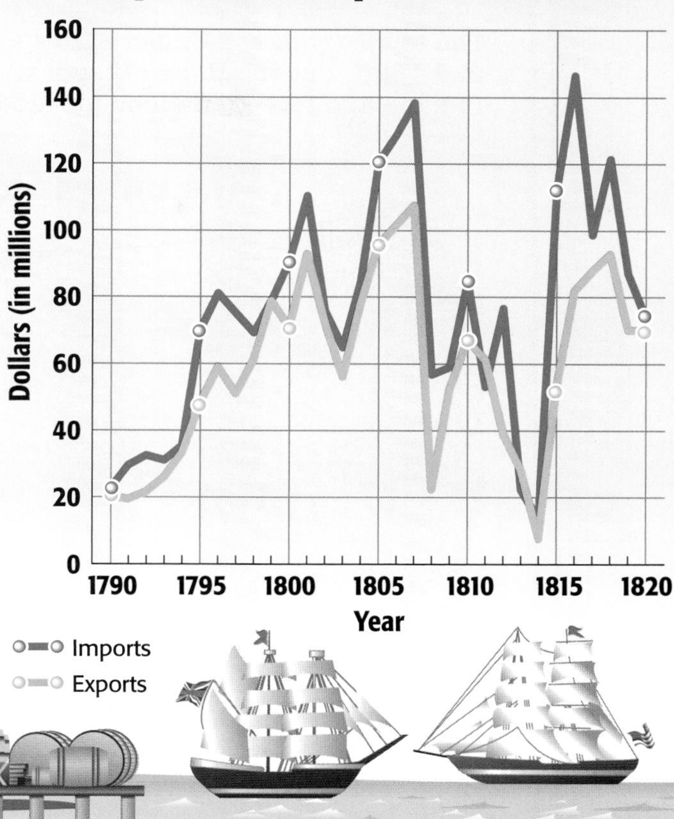

Source: *Historical Statistics of the United States*

History Note 2

Great Britain remained an important U.S. trading partner after the American Revolution. In 1790 more than a third of U.S. exports went to Britain. However, between 1790 and 1820 international conflicts sometimes made foreign trade difficult.

Geography **Skills**

Interpreting Line Graphs

1. Was the value of U.S. exports usually higher or lower than the value of imports from 1790 to 1820?
2. **Drawing Inferences and Conclusions** When were the values of U.S. exports and imports lowest? Why do you think trade was so low at those times?

ABBY ALDRICH ROCKEFELLER FOLK ART MUSEUM

This painting shows a scene of an ideal farm in the late 1700s.

The Expanding Nation 

The territory of the United States expanded greatly between 1790 and 1820. But the United States still competed with American Indians and foreign nations for land.

The United States, 1790

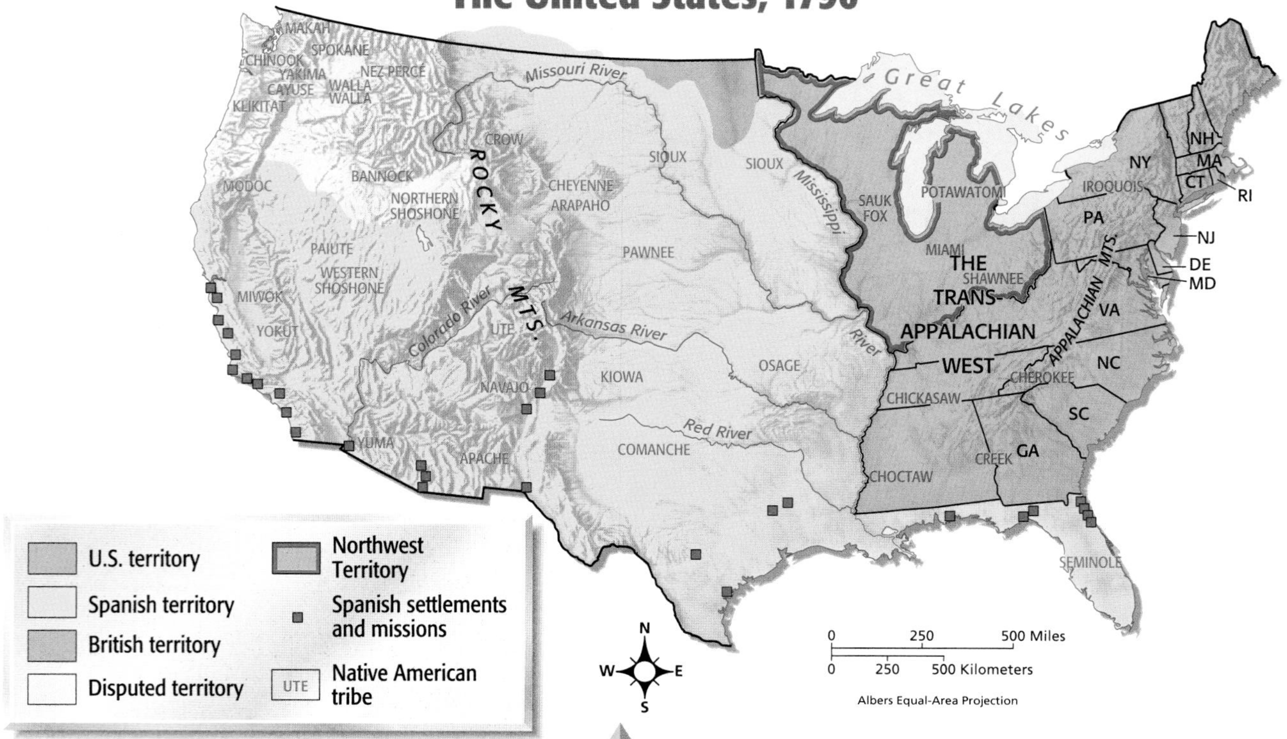

U.S. territory
Spanish territory
British territory
Disputed territory
Northwest Territory
Spanish settlements and missions
UTE Native American tribe

0 250 500 Miles
0 250 500 Kilometers
Albers Equal-Area Projection

History Note 3

The United States in 1790 was primarily a rural nation, with the vast majority of people living on farms. Only 24 U.S. cities had a population of more than 2,500.

Geography Skills

Interpreting Political Maps

1. What major American Indian peoples still populated U.S. territory in 1790?
2. **Physical Systems** In what ways was the physical geography of western North America different from the central and eastern parts of the continent?
3. **Summarizing** In what parts of the present-day United States were many Spanish settlements located?

History Note 4

Many American Indians in the West resisted the movement of settlers onto their lands. However, gradually most American Indian groups lost their lands to the expanding United States. By the 1790s treaties opened land to settlers throughout the Trans-Appalachian West. These areas included lands in Georgia, New York, North Carolina, and present-day Tennessee. A series of battles took place with American Indians in the Ohio Valley region. After a 1795 treaty, nearly two thirds of what is now the state of Ohio was opened for settlement.

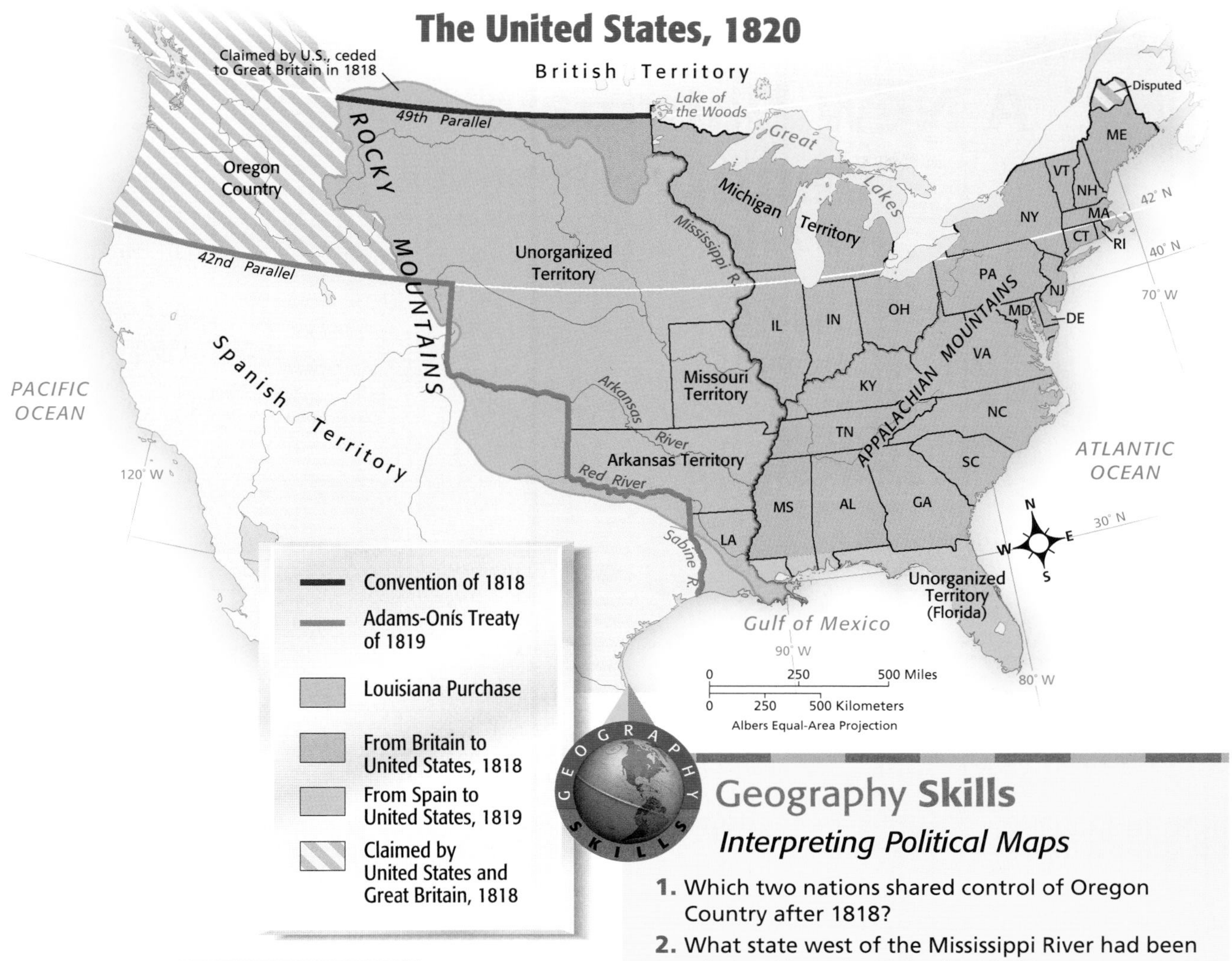

The United States, 1820

Claimed by U.S., ceded to Great Britain in 1818

British Territory

Lake of the Woods

49th Parallel

ROCKY MOUNTAINS

Oregon Country

42nd Parallel

Unorganized Territory

Michigan Territory

Great Lakes

Mississippi R.

Disputed

ME

VT

NH

MA

NY

CT

RI

42° N

40° N

70° W

PA

NJ

MD

DE

IL

IN

OH

VA

APPALACHIAN MOUNTAINS

KY

Missouri Territory

Spanish Territory

PACIFIC OCEAN

Arkansas River

TN

NC

Arkansas Territory

Red River

SC

ATLANTIC OCEAN

120° W

MS

AL

GA

LA

Sabine R.

Unorganized Territory (Florida)

30° N

Gulf of Mexico

90° W

80° W

0 250 500 Miles

0 250 500 Kilometers

Albers Equal-Area Projection

Convention of 1818

Adams-Onís Treaty of 1819

Louisiana Purchase

From Britain to United States, 1818

From Spain to United States, 1819

Claimed by United States and Great Britain, 1818

Geography Skills

Interpreting Political Maps

1. Which two nations shared control of Oregon Country after 1818?
2. What state west of the Mississippi River had been admitted into the Union by 1820?
3. **Places and Regions** Create a blank map of the United States. Ask a fellow student to draw in the U.S. borders established by the Convention of 1818 and the Adams-Onís Treaty of 1819.
4. **Analyzing Information** What physical features helped form the western boundary of the Louisiana Purchase and the Adams–Onís Treaty?

History Note 5

Immigration has always been an important contributor to the U.S. population. The original thirteen colonies that became the United States were mostly populated by immigrants from Great Britain. There were also sizable numbers of immigrants from Germany. After the Revolutionary War, overall immigration slowed. By 1820 more people were coming to the United States from Ireland than from Great Britain.

History Note 6

As American settlers moved westward, the abundance of land and other resources helped support large families. In fact, the average American household was significantly larger than households in Europe. An average free household in the United States had 6 members, compared to an average of 4.5 persons in British homes. A higher birthrate and rising standard of living in the United States help explain this difference in size.

CHAPTER

11 A New National Identity (1812–1840)

These five-dollar gold coins were issued by the U.S. Mint.

The Erie Canal was opened in 1825 and greatly reduced the cost of shipping goods from Buffalo to New York City.

UNITED STATES

1816 James Monroe is elected president.

1817 Work on the Erie Canal begins.

1819 Spain and the United States sign the Adams-Onís Treaty in February, giving Florida to the United States.

In March the Supreme Court establishes the constitutionality of the Second Bank of the United States in *McCulloch* v. *Maryland*.

1824 John Quincy Adams is elected president.

1812 **1815** **1818** **1821** **1824**

1815 Napoléon returns to power in France but is defeated at the Battle of Waterloo.

1819 Simon Bolívar becomes president of Gran Colombia.

1822 Brazil declares independence from Portugal.

1824 Simon Bolívar becomes president of Peru.

WORLD

The Brazilian Empire used this flag after it declared independence from Portugal.

The Duke of Wellington led an army of allied European nations to victory over Napoléon's French forces at the Battle of Waterloo.

Build on What You Know

The United States had survived a second war with Great Britain. Although the nation was at peace, there were still unresolved disputes with foreign powers. A rising sense of nationalism and an expansion of democracy played key roles in shaping American identity as the young nation began to assert itself.

THE GRANGER COLLECTION, NEW YORK

Andrew Jackson, shown standing before a crowd of well-wishers, received a record number of popular votes in 1828.

This picture of Jackson was carried by supporters during one of his presidential campaigns.

1827

1828 Andrew Jackson is elected president.

1829 The Ottoman Empire recognizes the independence of Greece.

1830

1830 Congress passes the Indian Removal Act.

1832 A British reform bill doubles the number of British men who can vote.

1833

1834 Opponents of Andrew Jackson form the Whig Party.

1835 Dutch colonists in Africa, known as the Boers, begin their Great Trek into the African interior.

1836

1836 Martin Van Buren is elected president.

1838 The Trail of Tears begins, as U.S. troops remove the Cherokee from Georgia.

1839

1839 The Opium War breaks out between Britain and China.

If you were there . . .
What would you do to help the country?

You Be the Historian

What's Your Opinion? Do you **agree** or **disagree** with the following statements? Support your point of view in your journal.

- **Global Relations** Disputes over land can be resolved without armed force.
- **Citizenship** Voting rights make a democracy stronger.
- **Constitutional Heritage** States should have the right to ignore federal laws with which they disagree.

Section 1

The Rise of Nationalism

Read to Discover

1. How did the United States settle its land disputes with Great Britain and Spain?
2. Why did President Monroe issue the Monroe Doctrine, and what were its most important points?

Identify

- James Monroe
- Rush-Bagot Agreement
- Convention of 1818
- Adams-Onís Treaty
- Simon Bolívar
- Monroe Doctrine

Why It Matters Today

Border disputes often lead to more serious international conflicts. Use CNNfyi.com or other **current events** sources to learn about a recent border dispute between countries. Record your findings in your journal.

The Story Continues

James Monroe was close friends with former presidents Thomas Jefferson and James Madison.

James Monroe greatly admired the French republic. Yet he believed that the United States could become the greatest republic ever. He shared these views with his daughter Eliza while they walked through the streets of Paris. When Eliza noted that the French had better roads, Monroe answered, "That's true, our country may be likened to a new house. We lack many things, but we possess the most precious of all—liberty!"

The Era of Good Feelings

After the War of 1812, the United States enjoyed a time of peace. National pride began to grow. By 1817, journalists had begun calling this time the Era of Good Feelings. The previous year **James Monroe**, a Republican, had easily won the presidency over Federalist Rufus King. Running unopposed, Monroe won re-election in 1820. During his presidency, the United States resolved several conflicts with foreign powers.

The Treaty of Ghent had ended the war with Britain. However, the United States and British Canada still disagreed about who controlled the waterways along their borders. Both countries wanted to keep their navies and fishing rights on the Great Lakes. In the spring of 1817, the two sides compromised by reaching the **Rush-Bagot Agreement**.

Secretary of State Richard Rush negotiated this treaty. It limited naval power on the Great Lakes for both the United States and British Canada. Another treaty, known as the **Convention of 1818**, gave the United States fishing rights off parts of the Newfoundland and Labrador coasts. It also set the border between the United States and Canada at the 49th parallel. This border extended as far west as the Rocky Mountains. In addition, both countries agreed to jointly occupy part of the Pacific Northwest.

✔ Reading Check: **Finding the Main Idea** How did the United States use compromise to settle its border disputes with British Canada?

That's Interesting!

Mistaken Identity Can you imagine the president of the United States being mistaken for a clerk? It happened to James Monroe. When a European diplomat paid a visit to the White House during Monroe's presidency, he came upon a man writing at a desk. The man had no wig and wore a dirty waistcoat spotted with ink. Ragged slippers hung on his feet. The diplomat was surprised that the president would hire such a messy assistant. Imagine his shock when he discovered this man was the president himself!

The Issue of Florida

Another dispute involved the U.S. border with Spanish Florida. Some Americans wanted to settle in the area. Others were angered by raids on U.S. towns made by Seminole Indians from Florida. The Seminole also aided runaway slaves. In 1818 Secretary of State John Quincy Adams held talks with Spanish diplomat Luis de Onís about allowing American settlers into Florida. Meanwhile, President Monroe sent troops under the command of General Andrew Jackson to secure the border.

In April 1818 Jackson's troops invaded Florida to capture Seminole raiders, thus beginning the First Seminole War. During the war, Jackson fought the Spanish as well as the Seminole. He took over most of Spain's important military posts and overthrew the governor of Florida. He commited these acts against Spain without receiving direct orders from President Monroe.

Jackson's actions upset both British and Spanish leaders. "We can hardly believe that any thing so offensive to public decorum [proper behavior] could be admitted, *even in America!*" reported one London

Interpreting the Visual Record

The Fourth of July *By 1819, when Joseph Krimmel painted* Fourth of July Celebration in Centre Square, *the Fourth of July had become a popular holiday celebrating the birth of the young United States.* ***What parts of this picture suggest that a national holiday is being celebrated?***

journal. Most Americans, however, were in favor of Jackson. One U.S. newspaper of the time described Jackson's popularity and power.

Analyzing Primary Sources

Drawing Inferences and Conclusions How would the reader know that Jackson is a powerful leader?

"Among the people of the West, his popularity is unbounded [unlimited]. . . . At his call, 50,000 of the most efficient warriors on this continent would rise, armed, and ready for any enemy."

—*Niles' Weekly Register,* quoted in *A Diplomatic History of the American People,* by Thomas A. Bailey

Jackson's presence in Florida helped convince Spanish leaders to settle all border disputes with the United States in the **Adams-Onís Treaty** of 1819. Under this treaty, Spain gave East Florida to the United States and gave up its claims to West Florida. In return, the United States gave up its claims to what is now Texas. The United States also agreed to take responsibility for up to $5 million of U.S. citizens' claims against Spain.

✔ **Reading Check: Summarizing** What disagreements did the United States have with Spain over Florida, and how were these settled?

The Monroe Doctrine

At the time of the Adams-Onís Treaty, Spain had other problems. The Spanish colonies of Central and South America began to challenge Spanish rule. By the early 1820s most of these Latin American countries had declared independence from Spain. Revolutionary fighter

Historical Document

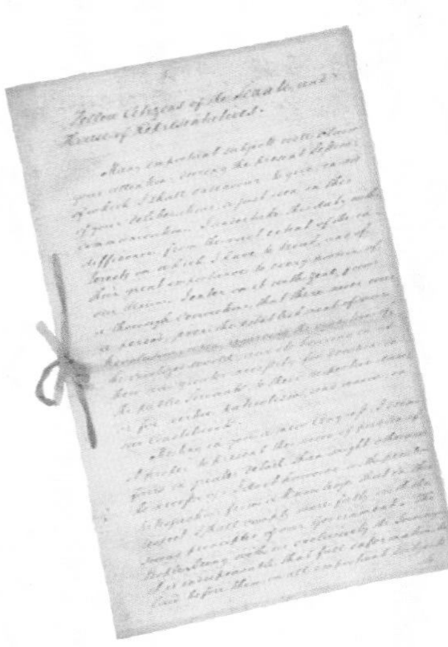

A replica of the Monroe Doctrine

The Monroe Doctrine

On December 2, 1823, President James Monroe issued what became known as the Monroe Doctrine. The following is an excerpt from the doctrine, which has had a significant effect on U.S. foreign policy.

We . . . declare that we should consider any attempt on their [European powers'] part to extend their [political] system to any portion of this hemisphere as dangerous to our peace and safety.

With the existing colonies or dependencies of any European power we have not interfered and shall not interfere. But with the governments who have declared their independence and maintained it, and whose independence we have . . . acknowledged, we could not view any **interposition**[1] for the purpose of **oppressing**[2] them, or controlling in any other manner their destiny, by any European power in any other light than as the **manifestation**[3] of an unfriendly disposition toward the United States.

[1] **interposition:** interference [2] **oppressing:** unjustly ruling [3] **manifestation:** evidence

Analyzing Primary Sources

1. What warning did President Monroe give to the European powers in the Monroe Doctrine?
2. What do you think is most important about this document?

Simon Bolívar, hailed as *the Liberator,* led many of these struggles. The revolutions in Latin America reminded most American leaders of the American Revolution. As a result, they supported the struggles for independence. In 1818 the *Nashville Whig* reported a toast given at a public dinner in Tennessee.

"*The patriots of South America:* palsied [paralyzed] be the arm that would wrest [take] from them the standard of liberty for which they have so nobly struggled. Six cheers!"

—*Nashville Whig,* quoted in *Life of Andrew Jackson* by James Parton

Simon Bolívar led the revolutions against Spanish rule in what are now the nations of Bolivia, Columbia, Ecuador, and Peru.

Yet Latin American independence worried President Monroe. He thought that European powers might try to take control of the newly independent Latin American countries. Secretary of State Adams and President Monroe decided to warn European powers not to interfere with the Americas. Delivered on December 2, 1823, this warning became known as the **Monroe Doctrine**. It stated that foreign powers should not create new colonies in North and South America. The United States would view any European interference with Latin American governments as a hostile act.

Some Europeans strongly criticized the Monroe Doctrine. The French foreign minister said that the doctrine "ought to be resisted by all the powers having commercial or territorial interests in the hemisphere." Despite such threats, few European countries challenged the Monroe Doctrine, which has played a major role in shaping U.S.–Latin American relations.

✔ **Reading Check: Analyzing Information** What did the Monroe Doctrine accomplish?

Section 1 Review

go.hrw.com **Homework Practice Online**
keyword: SC3 HP11

1. **Identify** and explain:
   - James Monroe
   - Rush-Bagot Agreement
   - Convention of 1818
   - Adams-Onís Treaty
   - Simon Bolívar
   - Monroe Doctrine

2. **Sequencing** Copy the graphic organizer below. Use it to describe how the United States responded to foreign-policy problems during Monroe's presidency. List the date of each response.

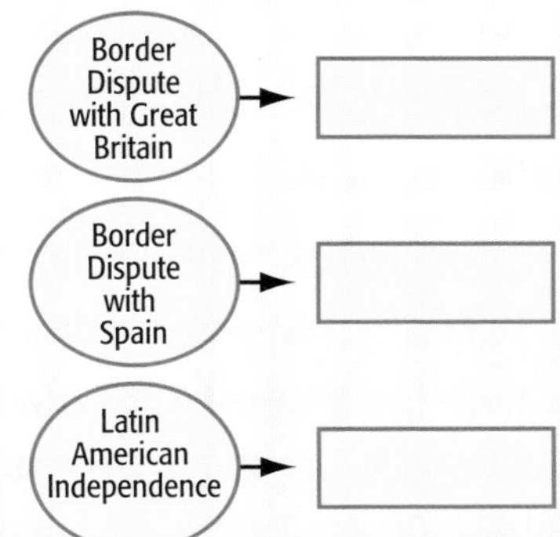

3. **Finding the Main Idea**
   a. How did the United States settle its conflict with Great Britain over Canada, and why was resolving the conflict important to both nations?
   b. What caused a dispute between the United States and Spain during Monroe's presidency, and how was this dispute settled?

4. **Writing and Critical Thinking**
   Supporting a Point of View Imagine that you are a U.S. ambassador. Write a memo to the secretary of state explaining your opinion of the Monroe Doctrine.
   Consider the following:
   - the main points of the doctrine
   - U.S. views on Latin American independence
   - the potential dangers of European involvement in Latin America

Section 2

Expansion and Improvements

Read to Discover

1. What issues was the Missouri Compromise supposed to address?
2. How did improvements in transportation affect the United States?
3. Why was the 1824 presidential election controversial?

Identify

- Henry Clay
- Missouri Compromise
- American System
- Cumberland Road
- Erie Canal
- John Quincy Adams

WHY IT MATTERS TODAY

Transportation is still very important in our daily lives. Use CNNfyi.com or other **current events** sources to learn about transportation issues in the United States. Record your findings in your journal.

Wagons were important for both settlement and trade on the western frontier.

The Story Continues

In the early 1800s, more Americans moved west. Most were looking for land and opportunity. An Ohio migrant described the scene in 1816. "The western country continues to rise in population and importance with unabated [unstoppable] rapidity." The writer mentioned the town of Mount Pleasant, Ohio. It grew from 7 families to about 90 families in just 10 years. As more Americans pushed west, debates arose over what laws would govern the newly settled lands.

The Missouri Compromise

A major regional conflict arose in 1819, when Congress considered the application of Missouri to enter the Union. Pro-slavery leaders in Missouri wanted to join the nation as a slave state. At the time, the Union included 11 free states and 11 slave states. Because free states in the North had a greater population, they controlled the House of Representatives. However, adding a new slave state would have tipped the balance in the Senate in favor of the South. Northern representatives in the House therefore passed a legislative amendment that would accept Missouri as a slave state with certain restrictions. Importing slaves into Missouri would become illegal. The amendment also required all children of Missouri slaves to be set free when they reached age 25. These proposed limits on slavery angered southern politicians.

Some senators, such as Rufus King of New York, opposed any expansion of slavery. "The existence of slavery impairs [harms] the industry and the power of a nation," he argued. North Carolina senator Nathaniel Macon wanted to continue adding slave states. "Why depart from the good old way, which has kept us in quiet, peace, and harmony?" he asked. Eventually, the Senate rejected the amendment. Missouri was still not a state.

Henry Clay had a long and distinguished political career and was noted for his efforts in Congress to achieve compromise between the North and the South.

To settle this dispute, Kentucky representative **Henry Clay** helped Congress reach the **Missouri Compromise**. This agreement had three main conditions.

1. Missouri would enter the Union as a slave state.
2. Maine would join the Union as a free state.
3. Slavery would be prohibited in any new territories or states formed north of 36°30' latitude—Missouri's southern border.

Another Kentucky representative, Benjamin Hardin, urged support for this compromise. He warned that regional differences over slavery threatened national unity.

"It is north and east against the south and the west. It is a great geographical line that separates the contending [competing] parties. And those parties, when so equally divided, shake mighty empires to their center, and break up the foundations of the great deep, that sooner or later, if not settled, will rend in twain [break in two] this temple of liberty."

—Benjamin Hardin, quoted in *Major Problems in the History of the American South, Volume I,* edited by Paul D. Escott and David R. Goldfield

Congress passed the Missouri Compromise in 1820. Maine became a state on March 15 of that year, and Missouri was admitted to the Union on August 10, 1821.

Clay earned the nickname the Great Pacificator, or peacemaker, for his efforts on behalf of the compromise. However, there were still strong disagreements between the North and the South over the expansion of slavery into the West. This controversial issue would continue to divide the nation.

✔ **Reading Check: Identifying Cause and Effect** Why did Henry Clay propose the Missouri Compromise, and what were its key points?

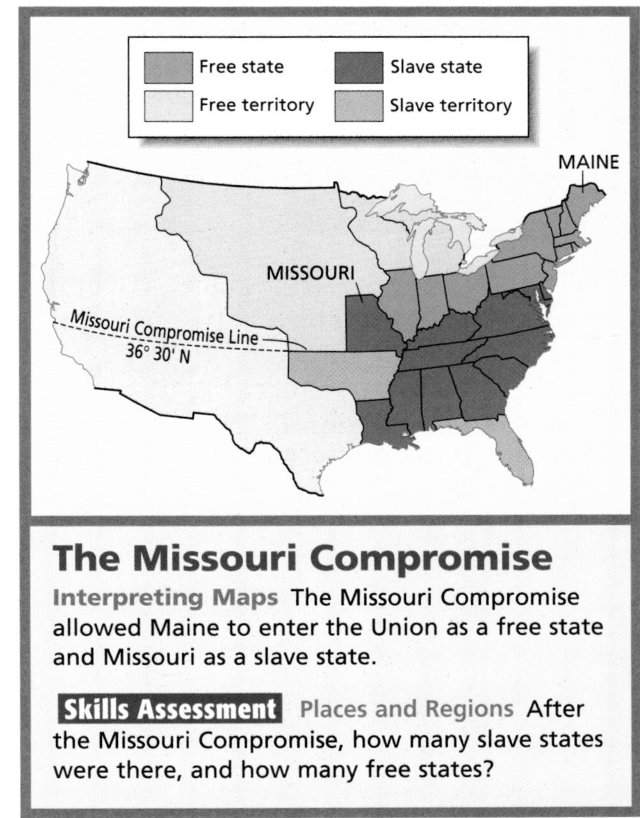

The Missouri Compromise

Interpreting Maps The Missouri Compromise allowed Maine to enter the Union as a free state and Missouri as a slave state.

Skills Assessment **Places and Regions** After the Missouri Compromise, how many slave states were there, and how many free states?

Research on the ROM

Free Find:
Henry Clay
After reading about Henry Clay on the **Holt Researcher CD–ROM,** create a poster in support of Clay for president. Be sure your poster shows his many accomplishments.

Internal Improvements

Henry Clay believed that a strong national economy would prevent regional conflicts. To strengthen the economy, he wanted a protective tariff. A tariff, Clay stated, would help domestic industries by keeping Americans from buying foreign goods. He wanted the tariff revenue to be used to improve roads and canals, or artificial waterways. These internal improvements would connect the regions of the country and make trade easier. Clay's plan became known as the **American System**.

Many people liked the idea of uniting the country through internal improvements. In 1816 a western citizen talked about these changes. "I believe the time [is] not very distant," he said, "when the wealth and resources of the western country will be brought almost to your doors." However, some members of Congress were against Clay's plan. They believed that the Constitution did not permit the federal government to spend money on internal improvements. Clay answered that the possible gains for the country justified federal action. Congress did pass a protective tariff, yet little of the money was used for internal improvements. Many state governments and private citizens continued to invest in improving the country's internal transportation systems.

✔ **Reading Check: Identifying Points of View** Why did some Americans believe the country needed internal improvements to build up the national economy?

The American System

The American System was Henry Clay's plan to strengthen the U.S. economy by protecting U.S. industries and improving national transportation.

An American-made fur hat might cost $1.50 to buy.

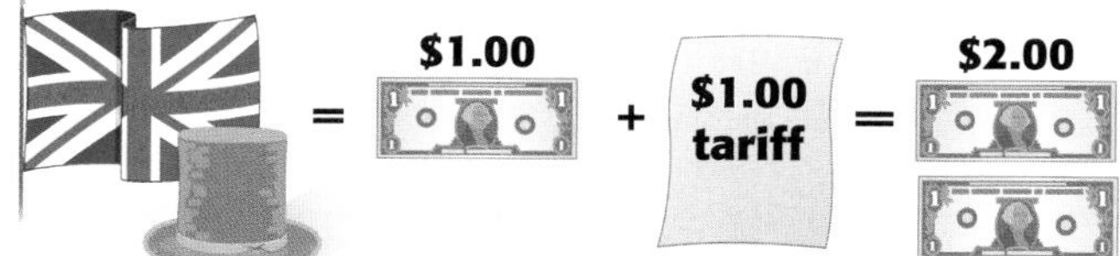

An imported British fur hat would be cheaper . . .

but the tariff would raise the cost.

Clay hoped such protective tariffs would encourage Americans to buy domestic goods and also provide money to build roads and canals.

Visualizing History

1. **Economics** Why did Henry Clay want a tariff?
2. **Connecting to Today** Do you think that the American System would work in today's economy? Explain your answer.

Interpreting the Visual Record

The National Road *The Fairview Inn was a stopping place for merchants and settlers traveling the National Road.* ***How busy does the road appear to be in this image?***

New Roads and Canals

In the early 1800s most roads in the United States were made of dirt, making land travel difficult. British actress Frances Kemble described one New York road on which she had struggled during a visit to the United States in the 1830s.

"The wickedest road, I do think, the cruellest, hard-heartedest road, that ever [a] wheel rumbled upon. Through bog [wet spongy ground] and marsh, and ruts [wheel tracks], wider and deeper than any . . . ruts I ever saw, with the roots of trees protruding [sticking out] across our path."

—Frances Anne (Kemble) Butler, *Journal*

Analyzing Primary Sources

Making Generalizations and Predictions How might travel over roads such as this one affect a nation?

The **Cumberland Road** was the first road built by the federal government. It ran from Cumberland, Maryland, to Wheeling, a town on the Ohio River in present-day West Virginia. Construction began in 1815, and by 1818 the road reached Wheeling. Then the Panic of 1819 hurt the economy, stopping further expansion. Construction on the road began again in the 1820s. In 1833 the National Road, as the extended road was called, stretched to Columbus, Ohio. It reached all the way to Illinois by 1850.

Water transportation was usually quicker, easier, and cheaper than overland travel. However, many areas of the country did not have rivers to connect them to other towns. Some Americans tried to make water transportation easier by building canals. During the early 1800s canal construction increased dramatically in the United States, particularly in the Northeast.

One of the largest projects was the **Erie Canal**, running from Albany to Buffalo, New York. Albany is located on the Hudson River, which feeds into New York Bay, and Buffalo is located on Lake Erie. Governor DeWitt Clinton of New York worked for many years to get approval for the project. Begun in 1817, it was completed in 1825. The Erie Canal

CONNECTING TO
SCIENCE AND TECHNOLOGY

Building the Erie Canal

In 1817 New York began building the Erie Canal to connect Buffalo to Albany. One early difficulty was that much of the land between the two cities is hilly. Engineers solved this problem by using locks. A lock is a section of a canal with large gates at either end. Water inside the lock can be raised or lowered, allowing boats to move up and down hills. Today the Erie Canal is a tourist attraction and carries sightseers. The canal has also become part of American folklore, inspiring songs such as "Fifteen Miles on the Erie Canal." **What challenges did engineers overcome in building the Erie Canal?**

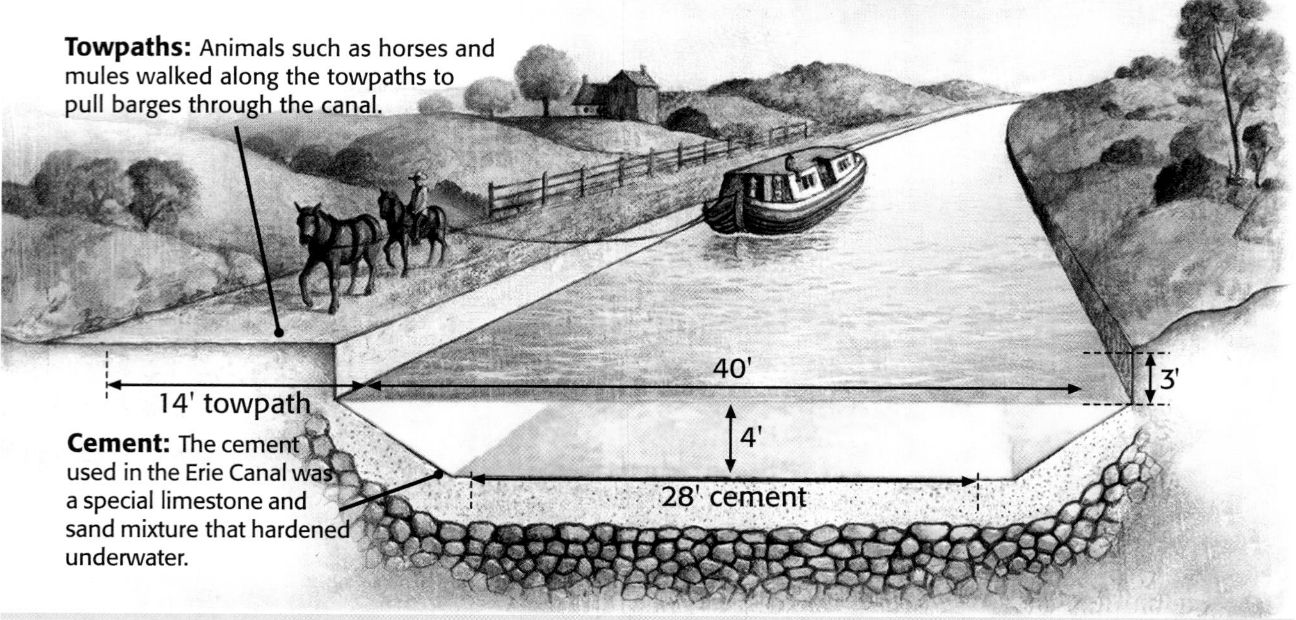

cost New York taxpayers millions of dollars, but it proved to be worth the expense. The canal allowed goods and people to move between all towns on Lake Erie and New York City. When the canal opened, a speaker at the opening ceremony called it a triumph of technology and praised its builders.

Analyzing Primary Sources

Identifying Points of View What qualities of the Erie Canal most impressed this speaker?

> **"They have built the longest canal in the world, in the least time, with the least experience, for the least money and to the greatest public benefit."**
>
> —Anonymous, quoted in *The Americans: The National Experience,* by Daniel Boorstin

The success of the Erie Canal helped start a canal-building boom across the country. South Carolina governor George McDuffie also sponsored a canal project. He hoped to make Charleston the center of southern Appalachian trade, wanting it to become "the New York of the South."

✔ **Reading Check: Summarizing** How did the creation of new roads and canals aid the economy?

The Election of 1824

Although Henry Clay had tried to build up a national economy, the country still faced many regional differences. The presidential election of 1824 showed these divisions. One of the two main candidates was Secretary of State **John Quincy Adams**. The other was Andrew Jackson, who had become a senator from Tennessee. Both men ran as Republicans. Jackson won the most popular votes, but he did not have enough electoral votes to win office. Under the rules set forth in the Constitution, the House of Representatives had to choose the winner. Speaker of the House Henry Clay influenced the vote by backing Adams. The House chose Adams as president. In response, Jackson's supporters claimed that Adams had made a "corrupt bargain" with Clay. These accusations only increased after Adams chose Clay to be his secretary of state.

The election controversy weakened President Adams's congressional and public support. He was already unpopular in the slaveholding South. He thus had little support when he asked for more federal money for canals, education, roads, and scientific research. Congress rejected most of these plans. However, it agreed to pay for some road and canal projects.

As president, John Quincy Adams supported higher education and tried unsuccessfully to establish a national university.

✔ **Reading Check: Finding the Main Idea** Why did John Quincy Adams have weak public and congressional support during his presidency?

Section 2 Review

go.hrw.com **Homework Practice Online**
keyword: SC3 HP11

1. **Identify** and explain:
   - Henry Clay
   - Missouri Compromise
   - American System
   - Cumberland Road
   - Erie Canal
   - John Quincy Adams

2. **Summarizing** Copy the graphic organizer below. Use it to describe how the debate over slavery affected the growth of the North, South, and West in the 1820s.

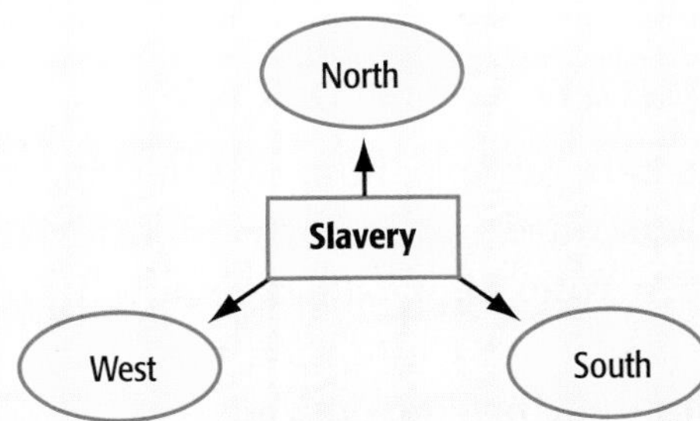

3. **Finding the Main Idea**
   a. How did new transportation systems affect the expansion and development of the nation?
   b. What caused the controversy surrounding the 1824 presidential election?

4. **Writing and Critical Thinking**
   Supporting a Point of View Imagine that you are Henry Clay. Write a letter to a friend in Missouri explaining your reasons for proposing the Missouri Compromise.
   Consider the following:
   - the balance of power between slave and free states in Congress
   - the prohibition of slavery in territory north of latitude 36°30'
   - the compromise's effect on national unity

Section 3

The Age of Jackson

Read to Discover

1. How was Jacksonian Democracy a sign of change in American politics?
2. How did tariff disputes lead to the nullification crisis, and how did President Jackson respond?
3. Why was President Jackson against a national bank, and how did his opposition affect the economy?

Define

- nominating conventions
- spoils system
- kitchen cabinet
- states' rights
- nullification crisis

Identify

- Andrew Jackson
- Democratic Party
- John C. Calhoun
- Martin Van Buren
- Tariff of Abominations
- Daniel Webster
- *McCulloch* v. *Maryland*
- Whig Party
- Panic of 1837
- William Henry Harrison

Why It Matters Today

Voting is the foundation of our democracy. Use CNNfyi.com or other **current events** sources to learn about a recent local, state, or federal election. Record your findings in your journal.

This small figure of a frog was meant to encourage voters to "Croak for the Jackson Wagon."

The Story Continues

John Quincy Adams once described himself as "a man of reserved, cold . . . and forbidding [threatening] manners." Many citizens viewed Adams as part of an old, upper-class culture—wealthy people out of touch with the country's needs. Political rallies of the 1820s showed that the people wanted a more lively leader. The wild gatherings held by Andrew Jackson's supporters amazed politicians. One writer noted that Jackson's appeal proved there "must be a new order of things."

Jacksonian Democracy

Western lawmakers began expanding voting rights in the 1790s. These changes spread eastward in the early 1800s. Many more Americans gained the right to vote. Many states removed property requirements for voting, allowing more white men to vote. Some political parties began holding **nominating conventions**. These were public meetings to select the party's presidential and vice presidential candidates.

Expanded voting rights and conventions let more people become active in politics. Historians began calling this democratic expansion Jacksonian Democracy after popular politician **Andrew Jackson**.

Not everyone gained greater political power, however. In 1820 women were not allowed to vote in any state. In addition, free African Americans had no voting rights in most states. The supporters of Andrew Jackson were mostly farmers, frontier settlers, and southern slaveholders. They believed their leader would defend the rights of the common people and the slave states.

Many of these Americans believed that a "corrupt bargain" between Henry Clay and John Qunicy Adams had stolen the 1824 election from Jackson. These people got together to make sure that Jackson would become the next president. They began to call themselves Democrats and formed the **Democratic Party**. Many people who backed President Adams began calling themselves National Republicans. In the presidential election of 1828, Adams ran as a National Republican, while Jackson ran as a Democrat. Jackson chose Senator **John C. Calhoun** of South Carolina as his vice presidential running mate.

✔ **Reading Check: Finding the Main Idea** What led to the creation of the Democratic Party?

Andrew Jackson

Andrew Jackson's nickname was Old Hickory. The name reflected his reputation for being extremely tough, like the hard wood of a hickory tree. He was born in 1767 in South Carolina. By the time he was 13 years old both his parents had died. Jackson moved to North Carolina, where he became a lawyer, and then to Tennessee. He earned respect as a military leader during the War of 1812 and later represented Tennessee in the U.S. Senate. In 1828 he won the presidency in a landslide.

Jackson believed in being a take-charge president. He vetoed more bills during his presidency than all the previous presidents combined. He also had a quick temper with people who disagreed with his views. He was popular with the common people, however. They saw him as a simple man who had gained great influence and respect through hard work. **Why was Andrew Jackson so popular?**

Jackson's Victory

The 1828 campaign focused a great deal on the candidates' personalities. Jackson's campaigners described him as a war hero. They said he had been born poor and rose to success through his own hard work. They contrasted this image with Adams, a Harvard-educated man whose father had been the second U.S. president. Some of Jackson's supporters also described Adams as being out of touch with everyday people. Even an ally of Adams said that he was as "cold as a lump of ice." In turn, Adams's supporters said Jackson was hot tempered, crude, and ill equipped to be president. Yet, when the election was over, Jackson and Calhoun had won with a record number of popular votes.

Jackson's supporters saw his victory as a win for the common people. One Kentucky newspaper editor described the feeling. "It was a proud day for the people. General Jackson is *their own* president." To show this, a crowd of Jackson voters celebrated his inauguration with a huge party on the White House lawn. The party caused a great deal of property damage. Some people feared that the mob at the White House was a sign of trouble. Margaret Bayard Smith recalled the inauguration party.

"What a scene did we witness! . . . a rabble, a mob, of boys, . . . women, children, scrambling, fighting, romping. . . . But it was the people's day, and the people's President, and the people would rule."

—Margaret Bayard Smith, quoted in *Eyewitness to America,* edited by David Colbert

Analyzing Primary Sources

Drawing Inferences and Conclusions How did this scene reflect Jacksonian Democracy?

Jackson rewarded some of his supporters with government jobs—a practice known as the **spoils system**. This term comes from the saying "to the victor belong the spoils [valued goods] of the enemy." However, Jackson changed few government positions, replacing less than one fifth of federal officeholders. Secretary of State **Martin Van Buren** was one of Jackson's strongest allies in his official cabinet. President Jackson also relied a great deal on an informal group of trusted advisers. This group was called the **kitchen cabinet** because its members sometimes met in the White House kitchen.

✔ **Reading Check:** **Analyzing Information** What effect did Jackson's election have on the government?

Conflict over Tariffs

One of the first challenges President Jackson faced was a growing regional conflict over tariffs. Northern manufacturers wanted high tariffs to protect their new industries from foreign competition, which came mostly from Great Britain. British companies could drive smaller American firms out of business by selling factory goods more cheaply than Americans could afford to make them. Protective tariffs blocked this practice.

However, the South had little industry to protect. The southern economy relied on agriculture, particularly cotton exports. Southerners imported most of their manufactured goods. High tariffs made these goods more expensive and also angered some of the South's European trading partners. Southerners thus wanted low tariffs. Westerners were divided on the tariff issue. Northern areas tended to support tariffs. For example, Kentucky wanted tariffs to protect its hemp industry, while further south, westerners tended to oppose tariffs.

In 1828, under strong pressure from northern manufacturers, Congress passed a tariff with very high rates. Angry southerners called the law the **Tariff of Abominations**. (An abomination is a hateful thing.) Some southern politicians saw the tariff as one way the federal government was abusing its power over the states.

✔ **Reading Check:** **Identifying Points of View** Why were the North, South, and West divided over the benefits of high tariffs?

The Nullification Crisis

Vice President John C. Calhoun, an experienced politician, helped lead opposition to the tariff. He wrote a statement in support of **states' rights**. People who favor states' rights believe that the federal government's authority is strictly limited by the Constitution. Calhoun's statement said that states had the right to nullify, or cancel, any federal law

Citizenship and You

Political Conventions

Before the 1830s U.S. presidential candidates were selected by members of Congress from each political party. In the election of 1832, however, the major parties began holding national conventions. There they chose their candidate for president. Each state held a convention to choose its delegates to the national meeting.

Many important changes have taken place over the years in party politics. For example, the number of delegates attending conventions has risen a great deal as the population has grown. In 1831 only 116 delegates attended the first convention. However, in 2000 the Democratic National Convention had 5,000 delegates. In addition, minorities, women, and young people have become an important influence on conventions. How have political nominating conventions changed over time?

George W. Bush at the 2000 Republican National Convention

they considered unconstitutional. The dispute between the state and federal governments became known as the **nullification crisis**. Calhoun warned that states had the right to rebel if their rights were violated. Senator **Daniel Webster** of Massachusetts disagreed. He vowed, "Liberty and Union, now and forever, one and inseparable!"

South Carolina tested the nullification theory after Congress passed a new tariff in 1832. The South Carolina state legislature passed a resolution declaring that the 1828 and 1832 tariffs were "null, void . . . [and not] binding upon this State, its officers or citizens." Calhoun resigned from the vice presidency in support of his home state. Some thought the federal government would use force to collect the tariff duties. South Carolina officials said the state would withdraw from the Union if this happened.

Jackson was strongly against nullification. "I consider, then, the power to annul [cancel] a law of the United States . . . incompatible with [contrary to] the existence of the Union," he said. Jackson said he would send U.S. troops into South Carolina to enforce federal laws. However, he did not have to take this step, because the two sides reached a compromise. Congress agreed to lower the tariffs little by little over several years. South Carolina's leaders agreed to enforce the tariff law. However, they still believed that nullification was legal.

✔ **Reading Check: Summarizing** What led to the nullification crisis, and why was it significant?

The Second Bank of the United States

President Jackson upheld federal authority in the nullification crisis. However, he did not always support greater federal power. For example, he was against the Second Bank of the United States, which Congress had founded in 1816. Many states had also opposed the Bank and had taken action against it. For example, several states, including Maryland, passed laws that taxed branches of the national bank. James McCulloch, cashier of the Bank's branch in Maryland, refused to pay this tax. The state took him to court, and the resulting case, ***McCulloch v. Maryland***, went all the way to the U.S. Supreme Court.

The Court, led by Chief Justice John Marshall, made two important rulings in the case. The Court supported the Bank's constitutionality. First, Marshall said that the elastic

Interpreting Political Cartoons

Jackson against the Bank *This political cartoon shows President Andrew Jackson, on the left, using his veto stick to fight against the Bank of the United States and its state branches.* ***Why do you think the artist portrayed the Bank as a monster with many heads?***

CONNECTING TO
MATH

Just the Facts

U.S. Debt from 1800 to 1840
(in thousands of dollars)

Year	Debt
1800	82,976
1805	82,312
1810	53,173
1815	99,834
1820	91,016
1825	83,788
1830	48,565
1835	38,000
1840	3,573

Using Mathematical Skills

1. What was the difference in the debt between 1800 and 1840?
2. Create a line graph that illustrates changes in the national debt between 1800 and 1840.
3. Imagine that you are a Democratic politician in 1836. Write a speech that summarizes the change in the national debt during Jackson's presidency.

clause of the Constitution allowed Congress to establish the Bank. This ruling was a broad interpretation of the implied powers of Congress. The Court also decided that federal law was superior to state law—an idea that challenged the principle of states' rights. This ruling meant that Maryland could not tax or interfere with the Bank.

This victory was not enough for Nicholas Biddle, the Bank's director, who decided to make the Bank a presidential issue. The Bank's charter was due to expire in 1836. Rather than wait, Biddle pushed for a bill to renew the Bank's charter in 1832. Jackson campaigned strongly for the defeat of this bill. "I will kill it," he promised. Jackson vetoed legislation to renew the charter. He then issued this strongly worded statement.

"It is to be regretted that the rich and powerful too often bend the acts of government to their selfish purposes. . . . By attempting to gratify their desires, we have in the results of our legislation arrayed [positioned] section against section, interest against interest."

—Andrew Jackson, quoted in *The Annals of America*

Congress could not gather the two-thirds majority needed to override Jackson's veto. Jackson also weakened the Bank's power by moving most of its funds to state banks, which his opponents called pet banks. In many cases, these state banks used the funds to offer credit to people buying land. While this practice helped promote expansion in the West, it also led to inflation.

In the summer of 1836, Jackson tried to slow this inflation. He did this by ordering Americans to use only gold or silver—instead of paper bank notes—to buy government-owned land. This policy did not help the national economy as Jackson had hoped. However, Jackson did improve the economy by lowering the national debt.

✔ **Reading Check: Contrasting** What positions did John Marshall and Andrew Jackson take on the Second Bank of the United States?

Van Buren's Presidency

Jackson was still very popular with voters in 1836 at the end of his second term. However, his actions had angered members of Congress, many of whom believed he had abused his presidential powers. In 1834 a group of Jackson opponents had formed the **Whig Party**. Many Whigs supported the idea of a weak president and a strong legislature. In 1836 the Whigs nominated four candidates to run for president against Martin Van Buren, the Democratic candidate and former vice president under Jackson. Despite this opposition, with strong support from Jackson, Van Buren won the election.

THE GRANGER COLLECTION, NEW YORK

Martin Van Buren became the new vice president when Andrew Jackson won re-election in 1832.

The people never liked Van Buren the way they had liked Jackson, however. Shortly after Van Buren took office, the country experienced a financial crisis. Called the **Panic of 1837**, this crisis led to a severe economic depression. The policies of the pet banks and Jackson's plan to curb inflation had helped lead to the panic. Nevertheless, Van Buren received the blame for it. The financial crisis hurt President Van Buren's re-election campaign in 1840. The Whigs ran **William Henry Harrison**, a general from the Battle of Tippecanoe, as their candidate. He and John Tyler, his running mate, ran under the popular campaign slogan "Tippecanoe and Tyler too."

The Whigs called Van Buren a friend of the rich and claimed Harrison was the friend of the common people. Harrison had actually been born to a wealthy family. However, the Whigs' emphasis on his war record and log-cabin roots made Harrison seem like a rugged man from the frontier, similar to Jackson. More than 75 percent of the eligible voters turned out for this election. Although the popular vote was close, Harrison won the electoral college in a landslide, gaining 234 electoral votes to Van Buren's 60. The Whigs had achieved their goal of winning the presidency.

THE GRANGER COLLECTION, NEW YORK

Interpreting the Visual Record

Log cabin *This 1840 campaign illustration supposedly shows the log cabin where William Henry Harrison grew up.* ***Why might showing Harrison in a setting like this have helped his popularity?***

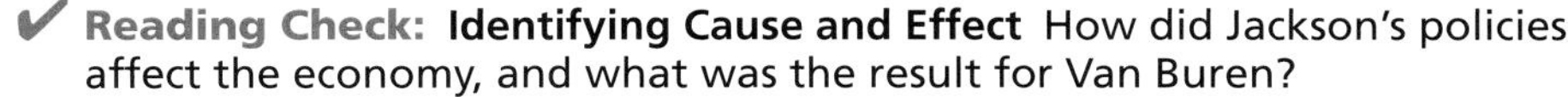

✔ **Reading Check: Identifying Cause and Effect** How did Jackson's policies affect the economy, and what was the result for Van Buren?

Section 3 Review

go.hrw.com Homework Practice Online
keyword: SC3 HP11

1. **Define** and explain:
   - nominating conventions
   - spoils system
   - kitchen cabinet
   - states' rights
   - nullification crisis
2. **Identify** and explain:
   - Andrew Jackson
   - Democratic Party
   - John C. Calhoun
   - Martin Van Buren
   - Tariff of Abominations
   - Daniel Webster
   - *McCulloch* v. *Maryland*
   - Whig Party
   - Panic of 1837
   - William Henry Harrison
3. **Summarizing** Copy the graphic organizer below. Use it to describe the main events of Jackson's presidency and the major changes in politics that took place during that time.

   Jackson Presidency

   Jacksonian Era

   Jacksonian Democracy
4. **Finding the Main Idea**
   a. What caused the nullification crisis, and how did President Jackson deal with this issue?
   b. Why did President Jackson veto the renewal of the Second Bank of the United States, and what effect did this have on the economy?
5. **Writing and Critical Thinking**
   Analyzing Information Imagine that you are a reporter covering the effect of Jackson's election. Write a newspaper article describing the rise of Jacksonian Democracy.
   Consider the following:
   - expansion of voting rights and nominating conventions
   - formation of the Democratic Party
   - Jackson's appeal to the common people

Section 4

Indian Removal

Read to Discover

1. Why did the federal and state governments begin an American Indian removal policy?
2. How did American Indians such as the Cherokee resist removal?
3. How were American Indians affected by the removal from their lands?

Identify

- Black Hawk
- Indian Removal Act
- Indian Territory
- Bureau of Indian Affairs
- Treaty of Dancing Rabbit Creek
- Sequoya
- John Ross
- *Worcester* v. *Georgia*
- Trail of Tears
- Osceola

Why it Matters Today

Many American Indians were forced to leave their homes to live on reservations. Use CNNfyi.com or other **current events** sources to identify a group of people being forced to leave their homeland today. Record your findings in your journal.

Black Hawk refused to leave his homeland.

The Story Continues

As American settlers moved west, American Indian leaders talked about the best way to deal with them. Keokuk, a Sauk leader from Illinois, wanted to compromise and avoid a war. Another Sauk leader named Black Hawk disagreed. He believed that U.S. officials had bribed Keokuk and other Indian leaders to gain their support. Black Hawk firmly resisted all attempts to take American Indian lands.

The Black Hawk War

In 1827 the federal government decided to end years of conflict between American Indians and U.S. settlers in Illinois. Officials ordered the removal of all Indians from the state. **Black Hawk** and his followers ignored the removal policy, rejecting the very idea of land ownership.

"My reason teaches me that land cannot be sold. The Great Spirit gave it to his children to live upon. So long as they occupy and cultivate it they have the right to the soil. Nothing can be sold but such things as can be carried away."

—Black Hawk, quoted in *Atlas of the North American Indian,* by Carl Waldman

When the Sauk returned from their winter hunt in 1830, they found that white settlers had moved into their village. But Black Hawk and his followers refused to be pushed out. Although his forces were flying a white flag, U.S. troops fired on them. Black Hawk then decided to fight. Indian groups began to raid American settlements and attack U.S. troops. However, by August 1832 the Sauk forces were running out of food and supplies. Black Hawk surrendered and gave up leadership of the Sauk. By 1850 the U.S. Army had removed the American Indians living within the old Northwest Territory.

✔ **Reading Check: Finding the Main Idea** What was the outcome of the Black Hawk War?

The Indian Removal Act

Indian removal was also an issue in the Southeast. American Indians had long lived in settlements stretching from Georgia to Mississippi. However, President Jackson and other political leaders wanted to open this land to settlement by American farmers. They said that Indians in the Southeast should move to lands in the West. Under pressure from Jackson, Congress passed the **Indian Removal Act** in 1830. This act authorized the removal of American Indians who lived east of the Mississippi River.

Congress then established **Indian Territory** as a new Indian homeland. This area contained most of what is now Oklahoma.

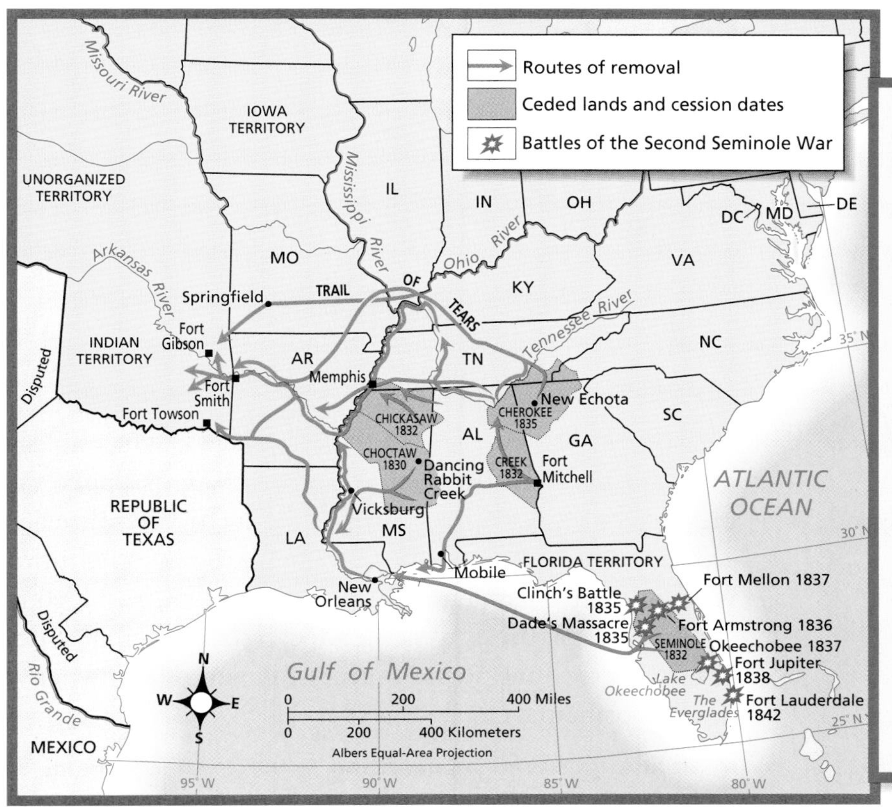

Indian Removal from the Southeast, 1830s

Interpreting Maps The Indian Removal Act of 1830 allowed the president to move American Indians in the Southeast to new lands west of the Mississippi River. American Indians were forced from their homes and marched hundreds of miles to the new Indian Territory.

Skills Assessment

1. **Locate** From what present-day state were the Cherokee removed?
2. **Analyzing Information** Which American Indian group traveled the greatest distance to Indian Territory?

Some supporters of this plan argued that it would protect American Indians. John C. Calhoun believed that removal would prevent more conflicts with American settlers. "One of the greatest evils to which they are subject is that incessant [constant] pressure of our population," he noted. Congress also approved the creation of the **Bureau of Indian Affairs** to oversee federal policy toward American Indians.

The Choctaw were the first American Indians sent to Indian Territory. After the Mississippi legislature abolished the government of the Choctaw, some Choctaw leaders signed the **Treaty of Dancing Rabbit Creek**. This treaty gave more than 7.5 million acres of their land to the state. The Choctaw journeyed from Mississippi to Indian Territory during the winter of 1831–32. The trip was disastrous. Federal officials in charge of the move did not provide enough food or supplies. As a result, about one fourth of the Choctaw died of cold, disease, and starvation. News of the U.S. treatment of the Choctaw caused other American Indians to resist removal. Some Creek decided to stay on their lands, located mainly in Alabama, but state officials ordered their forced removal. In 1836, federal troops led some 14,500 captured Creek, many in chains, to Indian Territory.

The Chickasaw, mostly from Mississippi, were moved west in the winter of 1837–38. They had been promised better supplies on their trip to Indian Territory. Yet, Chickasaw lives were also lost during removal.

✔ **Reading Check: Comparing** What was the Indian Removal Act, and how did it affect the Choctaw, Creek, and Chickasaw?

Interpreting the Visual Record

A new alphabet *Sequoya poses with the Cherokee alphabet he developed in the bottom image, while above him is a page from a Cherokee primer.* ***Why would the creation of an alphabet be important?***

THE GRANGER COLLECTION, NEW YORK

The Cherokee Nation

American Indians resisted removal in various ways. Many Cherokee believed that they could prevent conflicts with settlers by adopting the culture of white people. For example, in the early 1800s the Cherokee invited missionary societies to found schools in their towns. In these schools Cherokee children learned how to read and write English.

American Indians used complex spoken languages, but none had a written language. In the early 1800s a Cherokee named **Sequoya** developed a writing system that used 86 characters to represent Cherokee syllables. In 1828 the Cherokee began publishing a newspaper, the *Cherokee Phoenix*. This paper was printed in both English and Cherokee. The Cherokee also created a government inspired by the U.S. Constitution with an election system, a bicameral council, and a court system. All of these were headed by a principal chief. Voters elected **John Ross**, a successful plantation owner, as the first principal chief.

✔ **Reading Check: Summarizing** What contributions did Sequoya make to Cherokee culture?

The Trail of Tears

However, the adoption of white culture did not protect the Cherokee. After gold was discovered on Cherokee land in Georgia, their treaty rights were ignored. When the Cherokee refused to move, the Georgia militia began attacking Cherokee towns. In response, the tribe sued the state. The Cherokee said that they were an independent nation, and that the government of Georgia had no legal power within their territory.

In 1832 the Supreme Court, under the leadership of Chief Justice John Marshall, agreed. In ***Worcester* v. *Georgia*** the Court ruled that "[the Cherokee nation] is a distinct community, occupying its own territory, ... in which the laws of Georgia can have no force." The Court stated that only the federal government, not the states, had authority over the Cherokee.

The Supreme Court decision declared Georgia's actions illegal. However, when Georgia ignored the Court's ruling, President Jackson took no action. "John Marshall has made his decision; now let him enforce it," Jackson said. Most Americans accepted Jackson's position.

With President Jackson refusing to enforce the Supreme Court's decision, many Cherokee saw removal as unavoidable. Elias Boudinot, editor of the *Cherokee Phoenix*, wrote that he had no hope "that we will be reinstated in [given back] our rights." To silence further criticism, the Georgia militia destroyed the *Phoenix*'s printing press.

In the spring of 1838, U.S. troops began to remove all Cherokee to Indian Territory. A few were able to escape and hide in the mountains of North Carolina. After the Cherokee were removed, Georgia took their businesses, farms, and property. The Cherokee's 800-mile forced march, which lasted from 1838 to 1839, became known as the **Trail of Tears**. Almost one fourth of the 18,000 Cherokee on the march died.

✔ **Reading Check: Summarizing** What did John Marshall decide in *Worcester* v. *Georgia*, and how did Jackson's response affect the Cherokee?

Interpreting the Visual Record

The Trail of Tears *Disease and hunger were major causes of death for Cherokee on the Trail of Tears.* ***What does the way that people are dressed in this painting suggest about the harshness of the weather on the march?***

At the end of the Second Seminole War, several hundred Seminole remained carefully hidden in the Florida everglades.

The Second Seminole War

Unlike the Cherokee, the Seminole of Florida fought removal with armed resistance. In 1832 some Seminole leaders were forced to sign a treaty promising to leave Florida within three years. They also agreed that any Seminole of African ancestry would be considered a runaway slave. This condition worried the Seminole, because many escaped slaves had become accepted as family members of the Seminole.

The Seminole ignored the treaty and refused to leave Florida or sign a new removal agreement. A Seminole leader named **Osceola** called upon the Seminole to resist removal by force.

> **"When the Great Spirit tells me to go with the white man, I go, but he tells me not to go. I have a rifle, and I have some powder and some lead. I say, we must not leave our homes and lands."**
>
> —Osceola, quoted in *Native American Testimony,* edited by Peter Nabakov

Osceola's followers agreed, and the Second Seminole War began. At first, the Seminole won many battles against U.S. forces. Then in 1837, U.S. forces captured Osceola, who soon died in prison. The Seminole continued to fight against the United States. By 1842 the U.S. Army had captured and removed some 4,000 Seminole and killed hundreds of others. In the process, some 1,500 U.S. soldiers lost their lives. After spending millions of dollars, U.S. officials decided to give up the fight. The Seminole had resisted removal, and many live in Florida today.

✔ **Reading Check: Identifying Cause and Effect** Why did the Second Seminole War begin, and what was the result of the war?

Section 4 Review

go.hrw.com **Homework Practice Online**
keyword: SC3 HP11

1. **Identify** and explain:
   - Black Hawk
   - Indian Removal Act
   - Indian Territory
   - Bureau of Indian Affairs
   - Treaty of Dancing Rabbit Creek
   - Sequoya
   - John Ross
   - *Worcester* v. *Georgia*
   - Trail of Tears
   - Osceola

2. **Comparing and Contrasting** Copy the chart below. Use it to identify American Indian groups removed during this period and their responses to removal.

American Indian Group	Response to Removal

3. **Finding the Main Idea**
   a. Why did U.S. and state officials support an American Indian removal policy?
   b. How did the Cherokee use the courts to resist removal from their lands, and what were the results of their actions?

4. **Writing and Critical Thinking**
   Identifying Points of View Imagine that you are an American Indian forced to leave your home. Write a poem or song describing the effect of removal on American Indians in the East.
   Consider the following:
   - the American Indian policies of state and federal governments
   - the groups forced to leave and the conditions they faced

Section 5

American Culture

Read to Discover

1. Who were the favorite writers of the early 1800s, and what did they write about?
2. What was the focus of the Hudson River school?

Identify

- Washington Irving
- James Fenimore Cooper
- Catharine Maria Sedgwick
- Hudson River school
- Thomas Cole
- George Caleb Bingham

WHY IT MATTERS TODAY

Art and literature are important parts of a country's culture. Use CNNfyi.com and other **current events** sources to find an example of art or literature that reveals the culture of a country of your choice. Record your findings in your journal.

The Story Continues

In 1817 Virginia politician William Wirt published a popular biography of Revolutionary leader Patrick Henry. Wirt spent years researching his book. Yet he found that Henry was not as exciting as he had hoped. "The incidents of Mr. Henry's life are extremely monotonous [boring]," Wirt told a friend. "It is all speaking, speaking, speaking." To make his book more exciting, Wirt exaggerated certain events. Some critics accused him of rewriting history. Despite these complaints, Wirt's book helped make Patrick Henry a hero for a whole generation of Americans.

Patrick Henry was seen as a hero of the American Revolution.

American Tales

Many developments in American life led to the success of William Wirt's biography of Patrick Henry. For example, much of the public was interested in the Revolutionary era. Wirt represented a growing number of writers who wrote about the heroes of the Revolution. These writers inspired pride in the United States. Unlike Wirt, however, most of these writers used fictional characters to represent American ideals.

One of the first American writers to gain international fame was **Washington Irving**. Born in 1783, he was named after George

CONNECTING TO THE ARTS

The Legend of Sleepy Hollow The literature of the early 1800s often inspired artists. In his painting *The Headless Horseman Pursuing Ichabod Crane*, artist John Quidor captures one of the most frightening scenes in Washington Irving's story "The Legend of Sleepy Hollow." Here Crane, the local schoolmaster, flees a headless rider that he believes is an evil spirit. **How does the artist show the drama of this scene?**

Washington. Irving's writing often dealt with American history. He often wrote humorous stories, using a style of writing called satire. Through satire, Irving warned that Americans should learn from the past and be cautious about the future. He shared this idea in one of his best-known short stories, "Rip Van Winkle." Rip Van Winkle is a man who falls asleep during the time of the American Revolution. He wakes up 20 years later to a society he does not recognize. Irving published this and another well-known tale, "The Legend of Sleepy Hollow," in an 1819–20 collection.

Irving was one of the first American writers to gain respect in Europe. In fact, European writers helped shape his humorous style. Irving believed that the United States should not give up European traditions altogether. He said, "We are a young people . . . , and we must take our examples and models in a great degree, from the existing nations of Europe."

✔ **Reading Check: Finding the Main Idea** How did Washington Irving help make American writing more respected?

James Fenimore Cooper

In some of his most popular works, Irving combined European influences with American settings and characters. His work served as a bridge between European writing traditions and American writers exploring new styles. Perhaps the best known of these new writers was **James Fenimore Cooper**. Cooper was born to a wealthy New Jersey family in 1789. He never saw the American frontier, but stories about the West and the American Indians who lived there interested him. These topics became the focus of his best-known works.

In 1823 Cooper published *The Pioneers.* This novel was the first of five books that featured the heroic character Natty Bumppo. Together these books were called the Leatherstocking Tales. This series told of settling the western frontier. Cooper's hero, Bumppo, was a frontiersman who found truth in nature. Cooper's stories also included historical events. For example, *The Last of the Mohicans* takes place during the French and Indian War. By placing his fictional characters in the middle of a real historical event, Cooper popularized a type of writing called historical fiction.

Catharine Maria Sedgwick

Some critics, such as poet Russell Lowell, said that Cooper's characters were not interesting. They particularly criticized the women in his stories. Cooper's female characters seemed to have no purpose other than to be saved by the hero. Other authors of historical fiction, such as **Catharine Maria Sedgwick**, created more interesting heroines. In 1822 Sedgwick published her first novel, *A New England Tale.* This story describes the landscape and culture of New England life.

Another popular book by Sedgwick, *Hope Leslie*, was a historical novel set in Massachusetts in the 1600s. To make this 1827 novel realistic, Sedgwick did major research into the culture of the Mohawk who had lived in the area at the time. Some readers did not like Sedgwick's description of the Pilgrims. She included unpleasant parts of their lives, such as their superstitions and intolerance, in her novels. Sedgwick defended her work saying that it accurately showed both the strengths and weaknesses of early Americans in New England.

"These were the vices [bad habits] of their age. . . . They had a most generous and self-devoting zeal [energy] to the cause of liberty, so far as they understood it, but they were still in the thraldom [captivity] of . . . superstition."

—Catharine Maria Sedgwick, from *Life and Letters of Catharine M. Sedgwick,* edited by Mary E. Dewey

Sedgwick hoped that Americans could learn new ideas from reading about the lives of the Pilgrims.

Sedgwick was the most successful female author of her time, writing six books. Through her work, she also challenged commonly held ideas about women. For example, in *Married or Single?* Sedgwick, who never married, rejected the idea that all women had to marry. She hoped the novel would "lessen the stigma [disgrace] placed on the term, old maid."

✔ **Reading Check: Analyzing Information** How did American writers such as Cooper and Sedgwick describe the growth of a new cultural identity in the United States?

Catharine Maria Sedgwick hoped that her novels would teach people about America while entertaining them.

THE GRANGER COLLECTION, NEW YORK

THE GRANGER COLLECTION, NEW YORK

Thomas Cole painted The Notch in the White Mountains *in 1839.*

A New Style of Art

The writings of Irving and Cooper also inspired painters. These artists began to paint landscapes that showed the history of America and the beauty of the land. Earlier American painters, such as John Singleton Copley, were portrait painters. By the 1830s a group of artists called the **Hudson River school** emerged. These artists primarily painted landscapes. Their name came from the subject of many of their paintings—the Hudson River valley.

Thomas Cole was the leader of the group. He had moved to the United States from Britain in 1819 and soon recognized the unique qualities of the American landscape. As his work gained fame, he encouraged other American artists to show the beauty of nature. Observer William Bryant praised Cole's painting.

Analyzing Primary Sources

Identifying Points of View According to Bryant, why was Cole's painting uniquely American?

"[It] carried the eye over scenes of wild grandeur peculiar to our country, over our aerial mountain tops with their mighty growth of forests never touched by the axe, along the bank of streams never deformed by culture and into the depth of skies bright with the hues [colors] of our own climate."

—William Bryant, quoted in *Art and Life in America,* by Oliver W. Larkin

By the 1840s many American artists were combining rugged landscapes with scenes of frontier life. For example, **George Caleb Bingham** tried to show the ruggedness of the West. As the country grew, the new styles of art and literature helped form a new American national identity.

✔ **Reading Check: Finding the Main Idea** How did the style of American art change to reflect the American way of life in the early 1800s?

Section 5 Review

go.hrw.com **Homework Practice Online** keyword: SC3 HP11

1. **Identify** and explain:
   - Washington Irving
   - James Fenimore Cooper
   - Catharine Maria Sedgwick
   - Hudson River school
   - Thomas Cole
   - George Caleb Bingham

2. **Summarizing** Copy the graphic organizer below. Use it to identify the shared characteristics that made early American writers' and painters' work distinctly American.

3. **Finding the Main Idea**
   a. Who were some major early American authors, and what did they write about?
   b. What subjects did Thomas Cole and the other Hudson River school artists paint?

4. **Writing and Critical Thinking**
   Analyzing Information Imagine that you are an art student visiting America from Europe in the 1840s. Write a story to tell your classmates that describes how American culture reflects the American way of life.
   Consider the following:
   - the work of popular American writers
   - the work of popular American painters

CONNECTING TO

Literature

The Last of the Mohicans

James Fenimore Cooper

James Fenimore Cooper was the first major American novelist. His novels helped create the myth of the frontier and the American frontier hero. Natty Bumppo, also called Leatherstocking and Hawkeye, is the hero of the five novels called the Leatherstocking Tales. Chingachgook, a Mohican, is also an important character in the popular stories. Cooper did not have direct experience with American Indians or the frontier. He simply read books and listened to the stories his father told. Nevertheless, Cooper's novels brought the frontier to life for many readers. Cooper had a wide audience in the United States and Europe. His novels have remained popular since his death in 1851. The following excerpt is from The Last of the Mohicans, *set during the French and Indian War. In this passage Chingachgook tells Hawkeye about the Mohicans' recent history.*

"The first pale-faces who came among us spoke no English. They came in a large canoe, when my fathers had **buried the tomahawk**[1] with the redmen around them. Then, Hawkeye," he continued, betraying his deep emotion . . . : "then, Hawkeye, we were one people, we were happy. The salt lake gave us its fish, the wood its deer, and the air its birds. We took wives who bore us children; we worshipped the Great Spirit; and we kept the **Maquas**[2] beyond the sound of our songs of triumph! . . .

"The Dutch landed, and gave my people the **fire-water;**[3] they drank until the heavens and the earth seemed to meet, and they foolishly thought they had found the Great Spirit. Then they parted with their land. Foot by foot, they were driven back from the shores, until I, that am a chief and a **sagamore,**[4] have never seen the sun shine but through the trees, and have never visited the graves of my fathers. . . .

"Where are the blossoms of those summers!—fallen, one by one: so all of my family departed, each in his turn, to the land of spirits. I am on the hill-top, and most go down into the valley; and when Uncas follows in my footsteps, there will no longer be any of the blood of the sagamores, for my boy is the last of the Mohicans."

Understanding What You Read

1. Literature and History According to the story told by Chingachgook, what has happened to the Mohicans?
2. Literature and History What does Chingachgook mean by going down into the valley, and how is this significant for the Mohicans?
3. Literature and You Why do you think that Cooper chose to portray the decline of the Mohicans in this way?

[1]**buried the tomahawk:** made peace
[2]**Maquas:** their enemy
[3]**fire-water:** alcoholic beverages
[4]**sagamore:** a lesser chief of the Algonquian

Chapter 11 Review

The Chapter at a Glance

Examine the visual summary of the chapter below. Use the chapter's main ideas to create a five-section outline that you might give to a classmate to study.

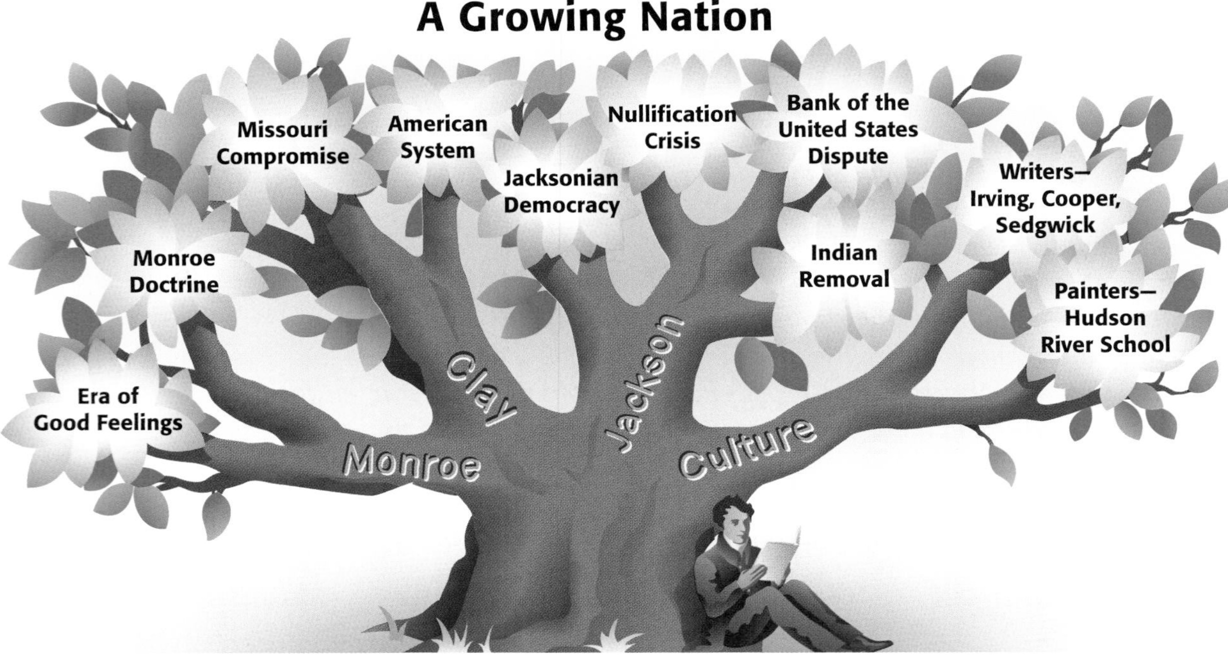

Identifying People and Ideas

Use the following terms or people in historically significant sentences.

1. Monroe Doctrine
2. Henry Clay
3. American System
4. Democratic Party
5. John C. Calhoun
6. nullification crisis
7. *McCulloch* v. *Maryland*
8. *Worcester* v. *Georgia*
9. Trail of Tears
10. Hudson River school

Understanding Main Ideas

Section 1 *(Pages 328–331)*

1. What effect did the revolutions in Latin America have on U.S. foreign policy, and what was the impact of the U.S. response?

Section 2 *(Pages 332–337)*

2. What led to the Missouri Compromise, and what did it achieve?

Section 3 *(Pages 338–343)*

3. How did the issue of protective tariffs divide northerners and southerners?
4. Why did President Jackson veto the rechartering of the Second Bank of the United States?

Section 4 *(Pages 344–348)*

5. How did American Indians resist removal to Indian Territory?

Section 5 *(Pages 349–352)*

6. What topics did early American authors write about?

You Be the Historian— Reviewing Themes

1. **Global Relations** How did the United States settle its border disputes with British Canada and Spanish Florida?
2. **Citizenship** How did U.S. political parties change between the elections of 1820 and 1828?
3. **Constitutional Heritage** What did Chief Justice John Marshall and the Supreme Court decide in *McCulloch* v. *Maryland* and *Worcester* v. *Georgia*, and how did these cases affect the power of state governments?

Thinking Critically

1. **Comparing** What was similar about the disputes that led to the Missouri Compromise and the nullification crisis?
2. **Contrasting** How did protective tariffs affect the economies of the North, the South, and the West?
3. **Analyzing Information** How did American culture develop in the 1820s?

Social Studies Skills Workshop

Interpreting Political Cartoons

Study the editorial cartoon of Andrew Jackson below. Then answer the questions that follow.

THE GRANGER COLLECTION, NEW YORK

1. Which of the following statements best describes the artist's attitude about Jackson?
   a. Jackson should be king.
   b. Jackson is a strong leader.
   c. Jackson has vetoed too many bills.
   d. Jackson is behaving more like a king than an elected leader.

2. Is the artist in favor of or opposed to Jackson's policies?

Analyzing Primary Sources

Read the following quote from Senator John C. Calhoun concerning tariffs and states' rights, then answer the questions that follow.

> **"The truth can no longer be disguised, that the peculiar domestick institutions of the Southern States [that is, slavery], and the consequent direction which that and her soil and climate have given to her industry, has placed them in regard to taxation . . . in opposite relation to [against] the majority of the Union; against the danger of which, if there be no protective power in the reserved rights of the states, they must in the end be forced to rebel."**

3. Why does Calhoun think that the South is opposed to the tariff that the other states support?
   a. The southern economy, based on agriculture and slavery, is very different from that of the North and other parts of the Union.
   b. Southern politicians believe that the tariff and other taxes like it are unconstitutional.
   c. The South fears that it might be attacked by other states in the Union.
   d. The true reasons why the South opposes the tariff are hidden.

4. Based on your knowledge of the period, do you think that President Jackson would have agreed or disagreed with Senator Calhoun's views?

Alternative Assessment

Building Your Portfolio

American History

Interdisciplinary Connection to Geography

Select a region of the country (either the South, the Northeast, or the Midwest). Then create a brochure that might be used to attract settlers or immigrants to that region in the 1830s. Your brochure should focus on the region's culture, economy, and historical points of interest.

internet connect

Internet Activity: go.hrw.com
keyword: SC3 CF11

Choose an activity about the New National Identity of America to:

- Learn about other wars of independence.
- Research the development of an American culture in art and literature.
- Create a newspaper about Andrew Jackson and the politics of the 1830s.

Social Studies Skills

WORKSHOP

Identifying Cause and Effect

Identifying and understanding cause-and-effect relationships is crucial to the study of history. To investigate why events happen and what else may have happened because of these events, historians often ask questions such as: What immediate activities may have triggered the event? What past activities may have led up to the event? Who was involved?

How to Identify Cause and Effect

1. **Look for clues.** Certain words and phrases are immediate clues. They reveal the existence of a cause-and-effect relationship in history. The following chart lists some examples of clue words and phrases.

Clue Words and Phrases

Cause	Effect
because	as a consequence
brought about	as a result of
gave rise to	depended on
inspired	originating from
led to	outcome
produced	proceeded from
provoked	resulting in
the reason	this led to

2. **Identify the relationship.** Read carefully to identify how historical events may be connected. Writers do not always state the link between cause and effect. Therefore, you must read very carefully. You may have to draw your own conclusions about the cause or the effect of an event.

3. **Check for complex connections.** Beyond the immediate cause and effect, check for other more complex connections. For example, an event might have multiple causes or effects. Effects may also be the causes of further events.

The following diagram presents an important cause-and-effect relationship involving the *Marbury* v. *Madison* Supreme Court case. In 1801 President John Adams appointed William Marbury as a federal judge. The new secretary of state, James Madison, refused to give Marbury his commission. This led Marbury to take his case to the Supreme Court. Chief Justice John Marshall decided that the Court did not have the power to force the government to give Marbury his commission. This ruling produced the principle of judicial review, which allows the Supreme Court to decide whether an act of Congress is constitutional.

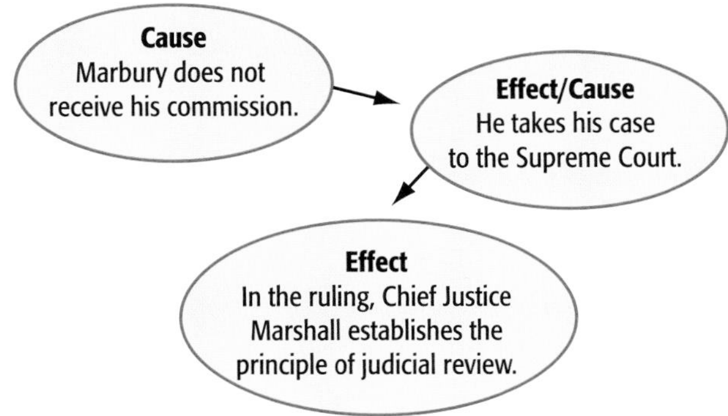

Practicing the Skills

1. Identify the clue words used in the example above.
2. Reread Chapter 11, Section 3, of your textbook, which discusses the causes of the War of 1812. Draw a diagram like the one above, showing the relationships between the important events leading up to the War of 1812.

History in Action

UNIT 4 SIMULATION

You Solve the Problem . . .

How Do You Encourage Westward Expansion during the Early 1800s?

Complete the following activity in small cooperative groups. It is 1803. Thomas Jefferson has purchased the Louisiana Territory from France. The United States has expanded to the Mississippi River. You are a member of a congressional subcommittee that will propose a plan to Congress to encourage westward expansion. Follow these steps to solve your problem.

1. Gather Information. Use your textbook and other resources to find information that might influence your plan of action for encouraging westward expansion. Be sure to use what you learned from the unit's Skills Workshop on Identifying Cause and Effect to help you find an effective solution to this problem. For example, you might consider why people choose to settle new lands and what effects their settlements may have. You may want to divide different parts of the research among group members.

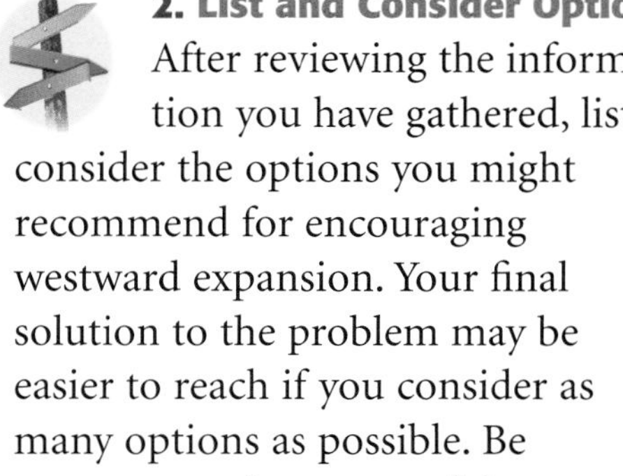

2. List and Consider Options. After reviewing the information you have gathered, list and consider the options you might recommend for encouraging westward expansion. Your final solution to the problem may be easier to reach if you consider as many options as possible. Be sure to record your possible options for your presentation.

3. Consider Advantages and Disadvantages. Now consider the advantages and disadvantages of taking each option. Ask yourselves questions like: "What are the main benefits of westward expansion for the nation and for individuals?" Once you have considered the advantages and disadvantages, record them as notes for your presentation.

4. Choose, Implement, and Evaluate a Solution. After considering the advantages and disadvantages, you should plan and create a presentation. Be sure to make your proposal very clear. You will need to support your proposed plans for encouraging westward expansion by including information you gathered and by explaining why you rejected other possible options or solutions. Your presentation needs to be visually appealing so that you can get Congress to support your proposal. When you are ready, decide which group members will make each part of the presentation, and then take your solution to Congress (the rest of the class). Good luck!

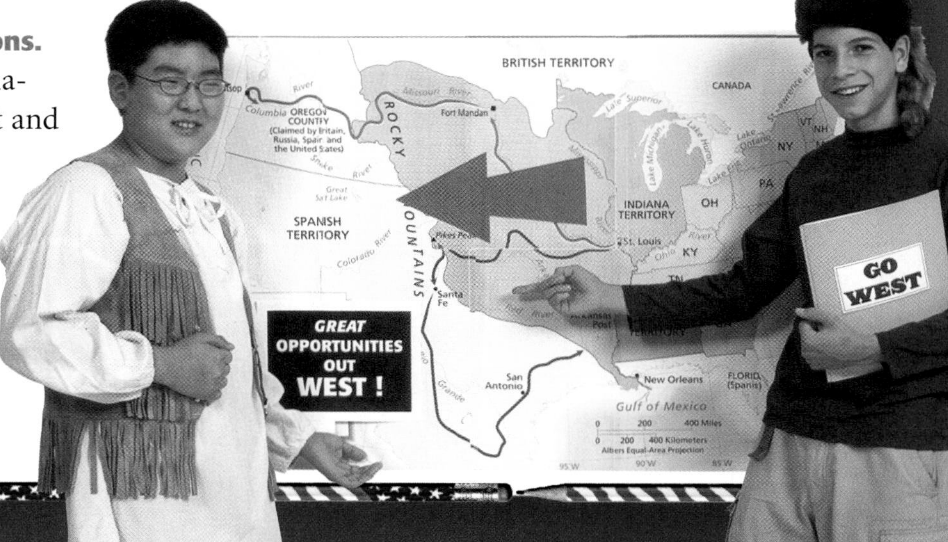

UNIT 5 A Changing Nation

(1790–1860)

Young People

IN HISTORY

Young Workers

By the mid-1800s teenage girls throughout New England were working and earning money of their own. These teenagers included girls in the city and in the country. Girls in rural areas usually worked out of their homes. They wove cloth, braided hats, or stitched together shoes. Girls in the cities often did needlework or found work as housekeepers or cooks.

In Fitzwilliam, New Hampshire, many young women made hats to be sold at the local store. They were usually not paid in money, but in store credit. Martha Alexander was 18 years old when she began making hats. Over a period of nearly four years, she braided 341 hats. Her store credit allowed her to buy teacups, saucers, and plates for her upcoming marriage.

Textile mills often employed young workers.

Other New England girls worked in textile mills. In Lowell, Massachusetts, about half of the young women working in the mills were between the ages of 15 and 19 when they first arrived. Despite the long hours, many girls enjoyed their work in the mills. It gave them independence and relieved the isolation of farm life. The girls used their hard-earned money in many ways. Many of them sent money home to help their families or saved it for their future. Some girls spent their money on clothes and recreation, such as plays and concerts.

Some teenagers found that life at the mills opened up a bright, new future for them. Lucy Larcom worked in the Lowell mills while she was a teenager and wrote about her experiences.

> **“And I was everyday making discoveries about life, and about myself. . . . I found that the crowd was made up of single human lives, not one of them wholly uninteresting, when separately known. . . . I defied the machinery to make me its slave. Its incessant discords [constant noise] could not drown the music of my thoughts. . . . I know that I was glad to be alive, and to be just where I was.”**

If You Were There *What sorts of jobs would you be interested in?*

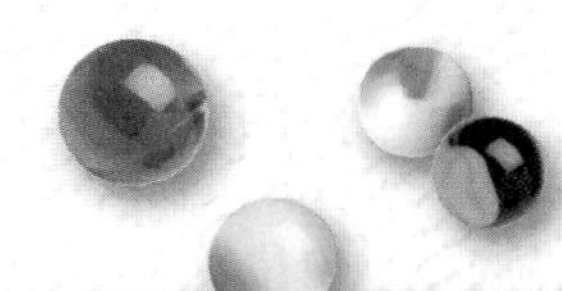

LEFT PAGE: *These workers from a shoe factory in Lynn, Massachusetts, went on strike in 1860.*

CHAPTER

12 The North and the South (1790–1860)

Eli Whitney's cotton gin had a simple design but made a tremendous impact on the southern economy.

Steamboats made river travel easier.

UNITED STATES

1793 Eli Whitney invents the cotton gin, which encourages southern farmers to grow more cotton.

1807 Robert Fulton's *Clermont* becomes the first commercially successful steamship.

1808 Congress bans the importation of slaves into the United States.

1824 *Gibbons* v. *Ogden*, a case dealing with the power of the federal government to regulate commerce, reaches the Supreme Court.

1790 | **1800** | **1810** | **1820**

1790 The first steam-powered mill opens in Great Britain.

1799 The Rosetta Stone, which makes possible the translation of Egyptian hieroglyphics, is discovered in Egypt.

1807 The British Parliament bans the slave trade in the British Empire.

1814 Sweden and Norway are united in the Treaty of Kiel.

1825 Nicholas I becomes ruler of Russia.

WORLD

THE GRANGER COLLECTION, NEW YORK

The manufacture of cloth was one of the first breakthroughs in the Industrial Revolution.

Build on What You Know

After gaining independence, the United States began a period of nation building. In the 1800s new ideas and inventions transformed the way people lived and worked in much of the United States. Both the North and the South went through significant changes. Industry grew dramatically in the North while agriculture became the economic focus of the South.

Railroads transported many of the goods that factories produced during the Industrial Revolution.

Slaves produced crafts, such as this quilt below showing stories from the Bible, that reflected their cultural and spiritual beliefs.

1830

1831 Nat Turner's Rebellion leads to fears of a slave revolt in the South.

1835 Alexis de Tocqueville publishes *Democracy in America*.

1837 Victoria is crowned queen of Great Britain.

1840

1844 Samuel Morse uses his invention, the telegraph, to send campaign news from Baltimore, Maryland, to Washington, D.C.

1846 Elias Howe patents his sewing machine.

1847 The British Factory Act limits the workday to 10 hours for women and children.

1850

1851 The Great Exhibition in London displays inventions from around the world.

1859 Construction of the Suez Canal begins in Egypt.

1860

1860 The South grows two thirds of all cotton in the United States.

Queen Victoria of Great Britain

If you were there . . .

Would you work in agriculture or industry?

You Be the Historian

What's Your Opinion? Do you **agree** or **disagree** with the following statements? Support your point of view in your journal.

- **Science, Technology & Society** Technological changes always improve society and social conditions.
- **Economics** Advances in transportation technology always affect a country's economy.
- **Geography** Geography determines a region's economic development.

Section 1

Revolutions in Industry

Read to Discover

1. How did the Industrial Revolution change the way people worked?
2. What types of factory systems did the New England textile industry use?
3. How did workers react to the changes brought about by the Industrial Revolution?

Define

- textiles
- technology
- mass production
- interchangeable parts
- trade unions
- strike

Identify

- Industrial Revolution
- Samuel Slater
- Eli Whitney
- Rhode Island system
- Francis Cabot Lowell
- Lowell system

Why it Matters Today

Each year inventors apply for patents and copyrights for their new inventions and products. Use CNNfyi.com or other **current events** sources to learn more about some of the different items that have been invented in recent years. Record your findings in your journal.

The Story Continues

In 1761 the British Society of Arts issued an advertisement asking for "the best invention of a machine that will spin six threads of wool . . . or cotton, at one time." The society also wanted only one person to work and attend the machine. The advertisement offered a cash reward for such an invention. No one had a good idea of how such a machine would work. But many inventors tried to create a device that would win the prize. The contest reflected a growing demand for new machinery to meet industrial needs.

In the 1700s, women like the ones in this picture worked to prepare wool for spinning.

The Industrial Revolution

During the 1700s most people in Europe and the United States lived and worked on farms, often making their own clothing and other basic necessities. In towns, a few skilled artisans—such as blacksmiths and shoemakers—crafted small numbers of manufactured goods by hand.

By the mid-1700s this way of producing goods began changing in Great Britain. As the population grew, more people wanted manufactured goods. Artisans could not meet this new demand, and people began looking for machines to provide faster and cheaper ways to manufacture goods. This process led to the **Industrial Revolution**, a period of extremely rapid growth in the use of machines in manufacturing and production.

The Industrial Revolution first affected the making of **textiles**, or cloth. Two British inventions—the spinning jenny and the water frame—increased the speed of thread production. The spinning jenny could be installed in a house, but the huge water frame required more space and a source of power. These needs led merchants to build large water-powered textile mills, or factories, filled with spinning machines.

At first, inventors in the United States did not have the knowledge to copy British **technology**—the tools and machinery used to produce goods. The British Parliament had made it illegal for skilled mechanics or machine plans to leave Britain. The British were trying to keep their country ahead of others in the Industrial Revolution. In September 1789, British mechanic **Samuel Slater** disguised himself as a farmer and sailed for New York. Slater had memorized the designs of textile mill machines and was confident he could build them in the United States.

"I flatter [praise] myself that I can give the greatest satisfaction, in making machinery, making good yarn . . . [as good] as any that is made in England."

—Samuel Slater, quoted in *The Ingenious Yankees,* by Joseph and Frances Gies

Analyzing Primary Sources

Drawing Inferences and Conclusions Why might Slater have wanted to make machines and yarn as good as those made in England?

Slater later formed a partnership with some New England businesspeople.

New England had many of the conditions that were needed to build a strong factory system—workers, investors, and rivers to supply power. By the early 1790s Slater was spinning cotton in his mill in Pawtucket, Rhode Island. Slater's success led other Americans to build textile mills.

✔ **Reading Check: Sequencing** List the events that led to the growth of industry in the United States in the order that they occurred.

Interpreting the Visual Record

Mills *The textile mill built by Samuel Slater used nearby waterfalls to turn waterwheels that powered the mill machinery.* ***How do you think a textile mill, like the one in the picture, might change a town?***

Interpreting the Visual Record

New opportunities *Some people left farm life to go to work in textile factories.* ***How would you describe the mix of workers shown in this picture?***

Mass Production

During the late 1700s, some businesspeople tried to use **mass production**—the making of large numbers of identical goods—to manufacture products. In 1798 inventor **Eli Whitney** approached the U.S. government with a plan to build about 10,000 muskets in two years. Whitney's new idea called for the use of **interchangeable parts**, a system in which each particular part of a product would be made exactly the same. Workers would be able to put together a musket by using any set of pieces, rather than making by hand a certain trigger to fit a certain handle. Although Whitney failed to complete his plan in two years, his idea later revolutionized many industries.

Despite Slater's and Whitney's efforts, American manufacturing grew slowly until the early 1800s. Then the Embargo of 1807 and the War of 1812 prevented Americans from buying British goods. American manufacturers were able to expand their factories and sell more goods. They also moved the nation away from its dependence on foreign producers. The Industrial Revolution was fully under way in the United States by the late 1830s.

As the Industrial Revolution progressed, more factory owners soon turned to steam power, which allowed them to build factories away from streams and waterfalls. Steady improvements in the design of machines also contributed to the growth of new factories. In the 1840s these improvements allowed gun makers to finally achieve Eli Whitney's dream of using interchangeable parts and mass production.

✔ **Reading Check: Summarizing** What factors led to the growth of factories in the United States?

This union banner was created by the New York chapter of the United Brotherhood of Carpenters and Joiners.

Factory Workers

Many people found factory work boring and repetitive, and owners tried several ways to solve their problem of attracting workers. Slater and his partners encouraged families to move to Pawtucket and work in the mill there. By hiring entire families and assigning simple jobs to children, he filled his labor needs at a low cost. Slater's approach became known as the **Rhode Island system**. New England businessman **Francis Cabot Lowell** built a water-powered loom that allowed workers to make thread and whole cloth under one roof, instead of just producing thread as Slater's mills did. He also hired young unmarried women from local farms. This practice became known as the **Lowell system**. Young women from across New England came to work at the Lowell mills and became known as the Lowell girls.

As factories became more common, workers began reacting to the changes, such as fast and dangerous machinery and long workdays, that occurred. In addition, artisans had to compete with cheaper, machine-made goods. Unable to make their products any faster, craftspeople wanted their employees to work longer hours for lower pay.

In the 1830s and 1840s, some skilled workers began forming **trade unions**—organizations of artisans in a particular trade—to improve working conditions. Union members sometimes staged a **strike**—the refusal to work until employers met their demands. Courts and police often supported companies against striking workers. The unions had some legal victories, but companies could often avoid labor laws by making workers sign special contracts agreeing to work longer hours. Union supporters continued to fight for work reforms during the 1800s.

✔ **Reading Check: Analyzing Information** How did the growth of factories change working conditions, and how did workers respond?

Section 1 Review

1 Define and explain:
- textiles
- technology
- mass production
- interchangeable parts
- trade unions
- strike

2 Identify and explain:
- Industrial Revolution
- Samuel Slater
- Eli Whitney
- Rhode Island system
- Francis Cabot Lowell
- Lowell system

3 Identifying Cause and Effect Copy the graphic organizer below. Use it to identify the causes of the Industrial Revolution and its effects on life in the United States.

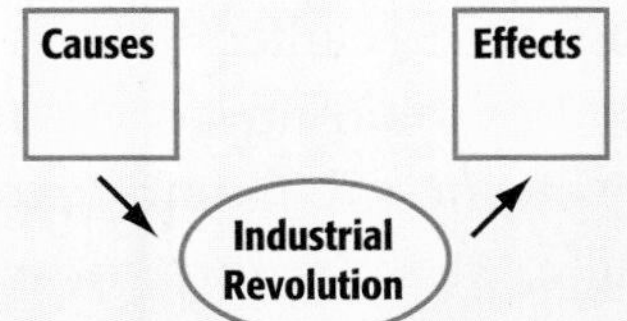

4 Finding the Main Idea

a. What were the two main systems used in the New England textile industry, and how were they different?

b. Why was New England an ideal place to build factories?

5 Writing and Critical Thinking

Identifying Points of View Imagine that you work in a textile mill. Write a speech explaining how you and your fellow workers plan to react to workplace changes.

Consider the following:
- factory hours
- factory safety
- role of trade unions

Section 2

New Technologies and Transportation

Read to Discover

1. How did the Transportation Revolution change life in the United States?
2. In what ways was the telegraph a useful invention?
3. How did technological advances affect both farmwork and life at home?

Define

- telegraph

Identify

- Transportation Revolution
- Robert Fulton
- *Clermont*
- *Gibbons* v. *Ogden*
- Samuel Morse
- Morse code
- John Deere
- Cyrus McCormick
- Isaac Singer

Why It Matters Today

Inventors continue to improve the forms of transportation we use. Use CNNfyi.com or other **current events** sources to learn how transportation is changing today. Record your findings in your journal.

The Story Continues

In 1806 inventor Robert Fulton returned to America from Europe. Neither the French nor the British wanted to give him money to build his steam-powered ships. Still, Fulton continued his work. In August 1807 he took his boat, which doubters called Fulton's Folly, out on the Hudson River. He traveled up the river, passing sailboats along the way. Instead of being a disaster, Fulton's Folly was a success. The steamboat was faster than the sailboats and did not rely on the wind for power. Fulton's boat revolutionized water transportation.

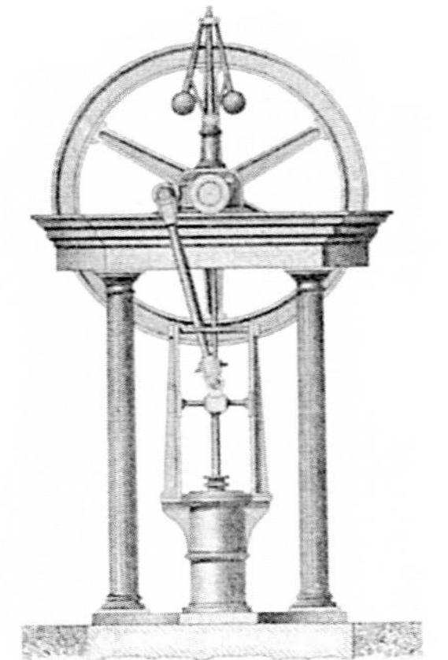

This picture shows an early design for a steam engine.

The Transportation Revolution

During the early 1800s the United States experienced a **Transportation Revolution**, a period of rapid improvement in the speed, ease, and cost of transportation. New inventions and a new energy source—steam—led to important changes. The first form of transportation affected by new technology was water travel. **Robert Fulton** successfully sent his steamboat—the ***Clermont***—up the Hudson River on August 9, 1807. News of the trip created an immediate demand for a steamboat ferry service. Within a few months Fulton and his partners had earned back all the money they had spent building the steamboat.

Steamboats, which were well suited to river travel, soon became a common sight on the Mississippi River. More than 500 of them were in use by 1840. The steamboat could move quickly against the current and did not rely on wind power. Steamboats cut the travel time between Pittsburgh and New Orleans from an average of five weeks to only two weeks. Steamboats also made it easier for eastern companies to ship their goods to western buyers.

What the steamboat did for water travel, the train did for land travel. Although steam-powered locomotives had appeared in Great Britain in the early 1800s, they did not become popular in the United States until the 1830s. American Peter Cooper built one of the earliest locomotives, which he named the *Tom Thumb*.

Railroad fever soon spread across the country. By 1840, U.S. railroad companies had laid about 2,800 miles of track, some 1,000 more miles

CONNECTING TO
SCIENCE AND TECHNOLOGY

The Age of Steam

Before the Industrial Revolution began, people used natural sources of energy to do work. These sources included animals, waterpower, and wind power. Steam power provided a new source of energy. The first efficient steam engines were built in the early 1700s in Europe. In the 1800s American Oliver Evans helped develop a smaller and more powerful steam engine. This engine was ideal for steamboats running on the Mississippi River or trains racing across the American countryside. Engineers continued to use and improve steam engines throughout the 1800s. How do you think steam engines changed the way people lived and worked?

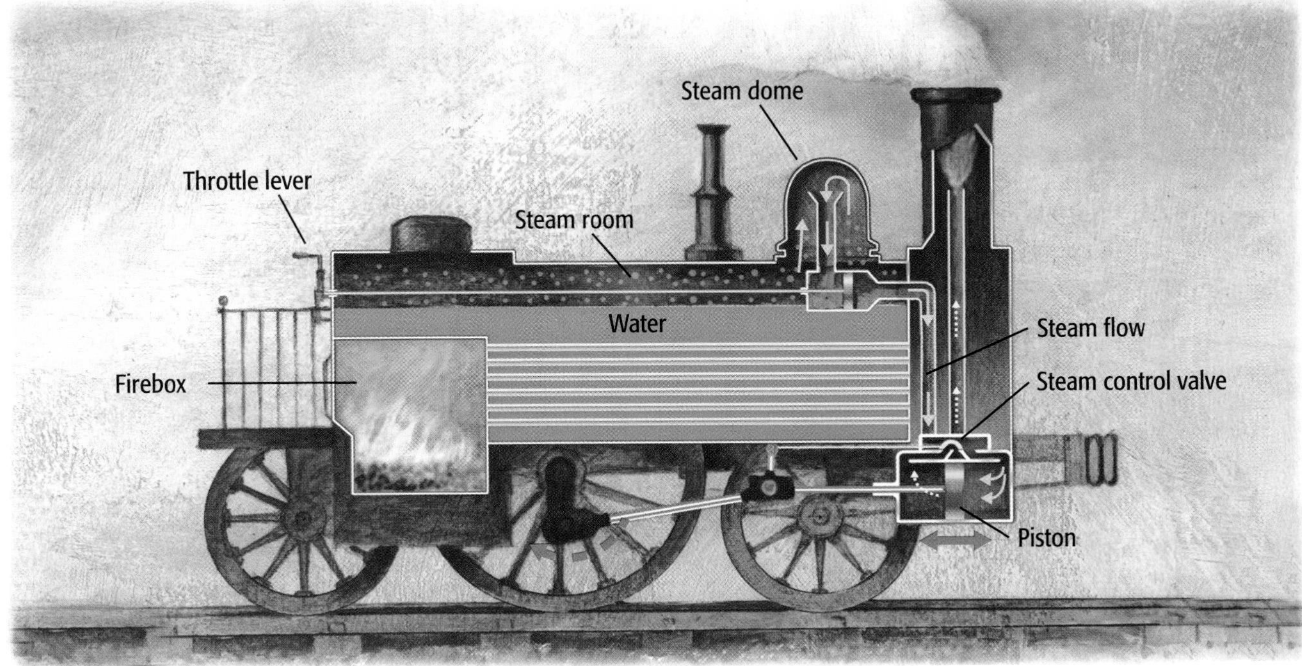

than existed in all of Europe. By 1860 there were about 30,000 miles of railroad track linking almost every major city in the eastern United States. Railroad companies became some of the most powerful businesses in the nation.

The railroad boom created new building and engineering challenges. Trains had to run up and down steep mountains, around tight curves, and over dangerous rivers. Architects designed tunnels and bridges, and engineers and mechanics built faster and more powerful locomotives. Trains were the fastest method of transportation available at the time, averaging about 20 miles per hour. In comparison, wagons traveled only about two miles per hour. Writer George Templeton Strong of New York City described the thrill of seeing a steam train pass by.

Analyzing Primary Sources

Drawing Inferences and Conclusions Why do you think Strong had such a dramatic reaction to seeing a train pass by?

> **"Whizzing and rattling and panting, with its fiery furnace gleaming in front, its chimney vomiting fiery smoke above, and its long train of cars rushing along behind like the body and tail of a gigantic dragon— . . . and all darting forward at the rate of twenty miles an hour. Whew!"**
>
> —George Templeton Strong, quoted in *The Market Revolution,* by Charles Sellers

✔ **Reading Check: Identifying Cause and Effect** What factors led to the Transportation Revolution, and how did this revolution affect the U.S. economy?

Just the Facts

The Railroad Boom, 1830–1860

Year	Miles of Railroad Operated
1830	23
1835	1,098
1840	2,818
1845	4,633
1850	9,021
1855	18,374
1860	30,626

Using Mathematical Skills

1. How much more track was in operation in 1840 than in 1830?
2. Create a line graph that illustrates changes in the total amount of railroad track operated from 1830 to 1860.
3. Imagine that you are a business leader in 1860. Using the figures above, prepare a speech to give to a group of investors. Explain why you think starting a new railroad company is or is not a good idea.

Gibbons v. Ogden

The growth of the steamboat shipping industry led to the first Supreme Court ruling on commerce between states. Thomas Gibbons held a federal license to operate a steamboat. He wanted to run his steamboats between New Jersey and New York. However, he did not have a license to travel in New York waters. New York had already given Aaron Ogden the monopoly on the steamboat business there. When Ogden sued Gibbons and won, Gibbons appealed his case.

The case of ***Gibbons* v. *Ogden*** reached the Supreme Court in 1824. The Supreme Court ruled that Gibbons had the right to operate in New York because his business crossed state lines. Chief Justice John Marshall explained that the federal law overruled the state law because the Constitution gave only Congress the power to regulate interstate commerce. Thus, Gibbons's federal license had priority over Ogden's state license.

Marshall's ruling reinforced the federal government's authority over the states. His ruling also expanded the legal definition of commerce. According to Marshall, commerce included navigation and communication that made trade possible. *Gibbons* v. *Ogden* was one of Marshall's most important decisions.

✔ **Reading Check: Summarizing** Explain the events surrounding *Gibbons* v. *Ogden* and how Marshall's ruling affected the power of the federal government.

Interpreting the Visual Record

Communications revolution *Several new inventions greatly increased the speed of communications in the 1800s.* ***What do you see in the picture that might have improved communications?***

Communication by Wire

The revolutions in industry and transportation created a need for faster ways to communicate. In 1832 **Samuel Morse** invented the **telegraph**—a device that sends and receives pulses of electrical current through a wire. Morse did not discover the principles behind the telegraph, but he successfully put them together in a usable machine. Telegraph operators communicated with Morse's invention by tapping a key to complete an electric circuit and thus send a signal to a distant receiver. The key allowed operators to control the length of each pulse. Different combinations of short and long pulses represented letters and numbers in a system known as **Morse code**. Skilled telegraph operators could send and receive many words per minute.

Several years passed before Morse connected two distant locations with telegraph wires. Finally, on May 24, 1844, Morse tested his machine in the Capitol Building in Washington. He asked a friend to write a message on a slip of paper. Morse then used his telegraph to send her message to Baltimore, Maryland—about 40 miles away. His associate in Baltimore quickly sent back the message, "What hath God wrought [made]?" An exchange that would have taken hours by train had taken only a minute by telegraph.

During the 1844 presidential campaign, Morse's telegraph became well known. Morse's associate in Baltimore sent news of events at the Democratic National Convention being held there to Morse in the Capitol Building in Washington. Almost immediately after the Democrats chose their presidential nominee, Morse received the news through the telegraph. When the Washington politicians learned the results, they responded, "Three cheers for the telegraph!"

Telegraph operators were soon sending and receiving information for the government, newspapers, businesses, and private citizens. Telegraph companies strung lines on poles alongside railroads across the country and opened offices in many train stations. Thousands more miles of telegraph were added every year in the 1850s. The first transcontinental line was finished in 1861.

✔ **Reading Check: Summarizing** How did the telegraph affect the movement of information?

Agricultural Improvements

With improvements in transportation and communication, trade goods, people, and information traveled from place to place with new speed and ease. As a result of these advances, businesses grew and settlement increased. More people living and working in new regions created an even greater demand for new technologies.

Improved transportation helped many more Americans move west to find land. At first, farmers who moved to the Midwest had difficulty plowing the rich thick soil. Their iron-bladed plows got stuck in the dirt and tough grass. To solve that problem, blacksmith **John Deere** designed a steel plow in 1837. The plow's steel blades could slice through the earth without getting stuck. By 1846 Deere was selling 1,000 plows a year. His business continued to prosper as more farmers moved west.

New advertisements helped sell farm machinery, such as the McCormick reaper shown below, to farmers.

Meanwhile, **Cyrus McCormick** was developing a new mechanical reaper that cut wheat more quickly. The *Times* of London described it as "a cross between a flying machine, a wheelbarrow, and an Astley chariot [a circus wagon]." The reaper made harvesting faster and easier. By the 1850s McCormick was using mass-production methods to build his reapers in a large steam-powered factory in Chicago. This factory was one of the first to use the new improvements in steam-engine technology for manufacturing. McCormick's business talents contributed to his great success. His company advertised, gave demonstrations, and provided a repair and spare-parts department. The company also allowed customers to buy on credit.

Together, Deere's plow and McCormick's reaper made it possible for midwestern farmers to plant and harvest huge fields of wheat. The process was both fast and cheap. In 1830 it took 20 hours to harvest an acre of wheat by hand. McCormick's reaper eventually reduced that time to an hour per acre and helped increase U.S. production of wheat. By 1860 more than 2 million U.S. farms were producing more than 170 million bushels of wheat a year and more than 800 million bushels of corn a year.

✔ **Reading Check: Analyzing Information** Why were inventions like the steel plow and the mechanical reaper successful?

Home Technology

Some inventions of the Industrial Revolution made work at home easier. Alexis de Tocqueville described what he saw as a particularly American desire. "The taste for physical gratifications [satisfactions] leads a democratic people . . . to be always making life more comfortable and convenient." The sewing machine was one invention that made life easier. In 1846 Elias Howe—a factory apprentice in Lowell, Massachusetts—patented the sewing machine. **Isaac Singer** improved the machine with a clever design and a simple way to run it. Singer worked very hard to promote his product, and by the 1850s Singer sewing machines became increasingly popular. Elegant sewing machines became symbols of wealth in some households. Many other women bought sewing machines to try to earn a living by sewing clothes at home for clothing companies.

By the late 1800s many American homes had sewing machines.

Other products were developed that helped meet people's everyday needs. In the 1830s iceboxes that cooled food with large blocks of ice became available, allowing families to store fresh food for longer periods. Iron cookstoves began replacing cooking fires and stone hearths. Companies also used mass-production methods to remake old inventions, such as the clock. As mass production lowered prices, more families were able to buy the improved products.

Some new household items depended on urban improvements. As more cities created public water systems, a few wealthy families installed indoor water pumps instead of using public pumps. Yet even in these homes, plumbing above the first floor was still rare. Other useful inventions introduced in the mid-1800s included matches and the safety pin. All of these items helped make life at home more convenient.

✔ **Reading Check: Comparing** How did technological advances affect farmwork and home life?

Section 2 Review

go.hrw.com Homework Practice Online keyword: SC3 HP12

1. **Define** and explain:
   - telegraph
2. **Identify** and explain:
   - Transportation Revolution
   - Robert Fulton
   - *Clermont*
   - *Gibbons* v. *Ogden*
   - Samuel Morse
   - Morse code
   - John Deere
   - Cyrus McCormick
   - Isaac Singer
3. **Summarizing** Copy the graphic organizer below. Use it to show how the Transportation Revolution changed people's lives during the early 1800s.

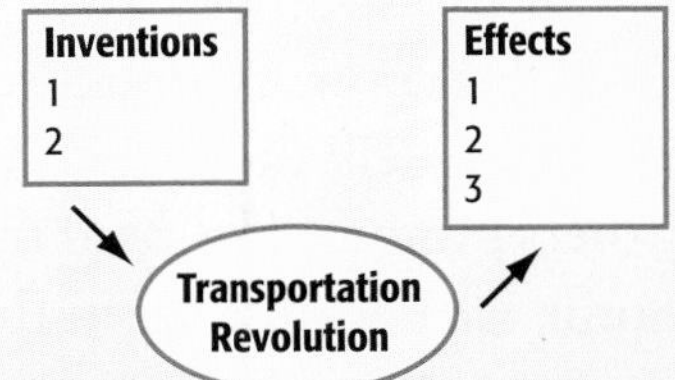

4. **Finding the Main Idea**
   a. Why was the telegraph a useful invention?
   b. How did improvements in machines for the farm and home affect people's lives?
5. **Writing and Critical Thinking:**
   Drawing Inferences and Conclusions Imagine that you are a reporter in 1870 looking back on your career. Write an article explaining how the telegraph changed the way that newspaper reporters worked and covered the news.
   Consider the following:
   - reporting before the telegraph
   - details about the invention of the telegraph
   - reporting with the use of the telegraph

Section 3

The South and King Cotton

Read to Discover

1. What effect did the cotton gin have on the South?
2. What was the state of manufacturing in the South?
3. What was life like for different groups of people in the South?

Define

- cotton gin
- cotton belt
- scientific agriculture
- planters
- yeomen

Identify

- Joseph R. Anderson
- Tredegar Iron Works

WHY IT MATTERS TODAY

After 1800 the southern economy came to depend more and more on the production of cotton. Use CNNfyi.com or other **current events** sources to find a region or a country whose economy today depends on one major product. Record your findings in your journal.

This fan was owned by a wealthy southerner.

The Story Continues

In 1758 Colonel George Washington returned from the French and Indian War to his home overlooking the Potomac River. He immediately started planting tobacco. Unfortunately, the stubborn soils of his Virginia estate did not allow him to grow the quality leaves produced by his neighbors. By 1762 Washington was discouraged. "I confess it [tobacco growing] to be an Art beyond my skill," he wrote in his diary.

Southern Agriculture

Other southern planters were more successful than Washington. Southern agriculture was based on three important products—tobacco, rice, and indigo. These crops were largely grown and harvested by slave labor and played a central role in the southern economy and culture. After the American Revolution, however, prices for tobacco, rice, and indigo dropped. When crop prices fell, the demand for and the price of slaves also went down. Farmers produced less and tried to grow other crops that needed less labor. Some farmers also freed their slaves. Soon, however, a new cash crop—cotton—transformed the southern economy and greatly increased the demand for slave labor.

Southern farmers had been growing small amounts of cotton since Jamestown was founded in 1607. Long-staple, or black-seed, cotton was the easiest to process. Workers could remove the seeds from its long fibers. But long-staple cotton grew well only in a few places in the South. Although short-staple, or green-seed, cotton grew well across the South, removing its seeds from its short fibers was very hard. A worker usually spent a day removing the seeds from just one pound of short-staple cotton. Cotton growers needed a machine to easily do this job.

In 1792 New England inventor Eli Whitney visited a Georgia plantation owned by his friend Catherine Greene. While there, he saw a machine that workers used to remove seeds from long-staple cotton. This machine did not work well on short-staple cotton because it tended to grind the seeds into the fibers. Challenged by this problem, Whitney began working on a solution. By spring 1793 Whitney had perfected a new machine for removing seeds from short-staple cotton. A simple device, the **cotton gin** used a hand-cranked cylinder to pull cotton fibers apart from the seeds. Whitney's gin breathed new life into the southern agricultural economy—and slavery.

✔ **Reading Check: Finding the Main Idea** Why did Eli Whitney invent the cotton gin? The short-staple cotton that grew best in the South had seeds that were difficult to remove from its short fibers.

Daily Life

King Cotton The cotton boom involved much more than growing and harvesting cotton. Harvested cotton had to be ginned, pressed into bales, and then shipped to market or to warehouses. Special agents helped do everything from marketing cotton to customers to insuring crops against loss or damage. Factories were built to produce items needed by cotton farmers, such as rope to bale cotton. As a result, cotton was part of the lives of many people beyond those who produced it. What were some of the different tasks required to produce and sell cotton?

Research on the ROM

Free Find:
Agriculture and Slavery
After reading about agriculture and slavery on the **Holt Researcher CD–ROM**, imagine that you are a farmer trying to get financial backing to produce a crop. Write a brief proposal explaining the crop you have chosen and why you think it will sell.

The Cotton Boom

Whitney's cotton gin caused southern farmers to switch from growing other, less profitable crops to cotton. Many moved west in search of new land suitable for planting cotton, taking their slaves with them. They generally settled in what became known as the **cotton belt**, an area from South Carolina to east Texas. Cotton had many advantages as a crop. It was easy to grow and transport. If stored correctly, it did not spoil. By crossbreeding, or combining, short-staple cotton with some Mexican varieties, agricultural scientists such as Dr. Rush Nutt produced stronger types of cotton.

Nutt was part of a larger movement throughout the South to apply **scientific agriculture**, or the use of scientific methods to improve crop production. Cotton had one disadvantage as a crop—it pulled large amounts of nutrients from the soil. Thus, cotton production left the land useless for growing crops after a few years. Some scientific agriculturists recommended crop rotation—periodically changing the types of crops grown on a particular piece of land. They also suggested more research to better understand soil chemistry.

The cotton boom and growth of the cotton belt made the institution of slavery stronger. Growing and harvesting cotton required many field hands. Most large growers chose to use slave labor in their search for profits. Planters also used many slaves on sugarcane plantations in Louisiana. Although Congress had outlawed the importation of slaves by 1808, the slave trade within the United States was still legal.

The cotton boom transformed the southern economy and made the South a major power in global trade. Great Britain was the region's main

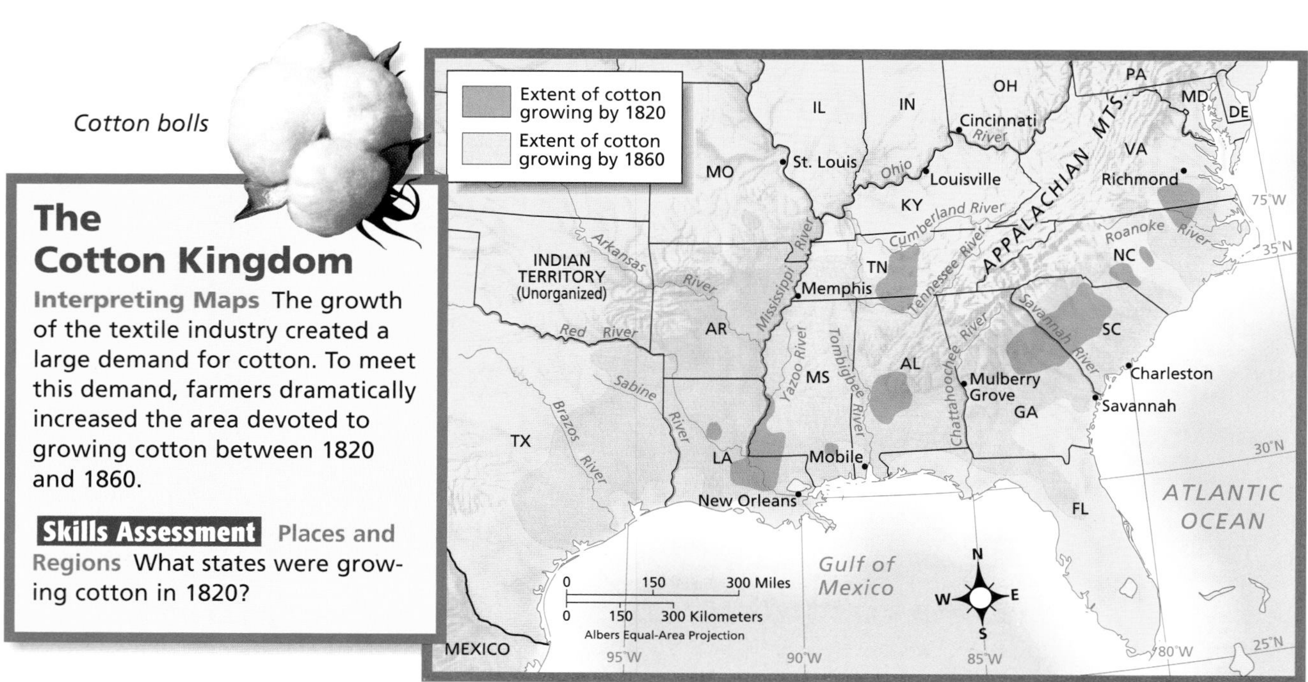

Cotton bolls

The Cotton Kingdom

Interpreting Maps The growth of the textile industry created a large demand for cotton. To meet this demand, farmers dramatically increased the area devoted to growing cotton between 1820 and 1860.

Skills Assessment **Places and Regions** What states were growing cotton in 1820?

foreign trading partner. Many other countries also bought cotton and other staple products from southern traders. This growing international, as well as domestic, trade led to the rise of major port cities such as Charleston, South Carolina; Savannah, Georgia; and New Orleans, Louisiana.

Most southern farmers got their products to market using the many navigable rivers in the region. Steamboats became common ways to ship goods on the Mississippi, Ohio, and smaller rivers. Overland trade and travel within the South remained difficult, however, and farmers who could not reach canals or usable rivers found it difficult to transport their crops to market.

The dominance of agriculture and cotton in the South also discouraged the growth of industry. Lumber and sugar-processing were some of the few southern industries that were mechanized in the mid-1800s. **Joseph R. Anderson** was one of the few southerners who worked to build southern industries. Anderson had worked as an army engineer, and in 1848 he became owner of the **Tredegar Iron Works** in Richmond, Virginia. Tredegar was the only large southern factory to make iron products. By 1860 Anderson had turned Tredegar into one of the nation's most productive iron works.

✔ **Reading Check: Identifying Cause and Effect** What factors led to the cotton boom in the South, and what was the result?

THE GRANGER COLLECTION, NEW YORK

Children of a wealthy plantation owner

Southern Society

Popular fiction of the early 1800s often made it seem that all white southerners had many slaves and lived on large plantations. However, the majority of white southerners did not hold slaves. During the first half of the 1800s, for example, just one third of all white southern families were slaveholders. Of this third, a much smaller percentage qualified as **planters**—large-scale farmers who held more than 20 slaves. Despite their small numbers, planters served as political leaders. Given their wealth, they also had a huge amount of economic power.

Male planters focused primarily on raising and selling crops and often left household management to their wives. The planter's wife oversaw her children's education and supervised the slaves who performed household duties.

Wealthy southern families often arranged their children's marriages for business or political reasons. Lucy Breckinridge, the daughter of a wealthy Virginia planter described her fear of an arranged marriage.

> **"A woman's life after she is married, unless there is an immense amount of love, is nothing but suffering and hard work. I never saw a wife and mother who could spend a day of unalloyed [pure] happiness and ease."**
>
> —Lucy Breckinridge, quoted in *Lucy Breckinridge of Grove Hill: The Journal of a Virginia Girl, 1862–1864,* edited by Mary D. Robertson

Analyzing Primary Sources

Identifying Points of View What was Lucy Breckinridge's view of married life?

Corn was the most common food crop grown in the South, and many yeomen grew it.

Breckinridge could not escape her family's wishes and entered into an arranged marriage. However, she died of typhoid fever soon after.

Most white southerners were **yeomen**, or owners of small farms. Yeoman families usually worked long days at many different tasks. Some yeomen held a few slaves but tended to work alongside them in the fields. Part of the South's population was also made up of very poor whites who often lived on land that could not be farmed. Many poor whites survived by hunting, fishing, raising small gardens, and doing odd jobs.

Most African Americans living in the South were enslaved. By 1860, however, there were more than 250,000 free African Americans in the area. Many were former slaves who had run away, been freed, or earned enough money to buy their freedom. Free African Americans who lived in rural areas worked as farmers or on plantations. Free African Americans in cities often worked a variety of jobs, mostly as skilled artisans. Some free African Americans, particularly those in the cities, formed loose social and economic ties. Churches often served as the center of their social lives.

Free African Americans faced constant discrimination from white southerners. Many governments passed laws limiting the rights of free African Americans to vote, travel freely, or hold certain types of jobs. In some places, laws forced free African Americans to have a white person represent them in their business dealings. To many white southerners, any and all free African Americans threatened the institution of slavery.

✔ **Reading Check: Summarizing** Describe the different groups of southern society.

Section 3 Review

go.hrw.com **Homework Practice Online**
keyword: SC3 HP12

1 Define and explain:
- cotton gin
- cotton belt
- scientific agriculture
- planters
- yeomen

2 Identify and explain:
- Joseph R. Anderson
- Tredegar Iron Works

3 Analyzing Information Copy the graphic organizer below. Use it to show how the cotton gin affected the South.

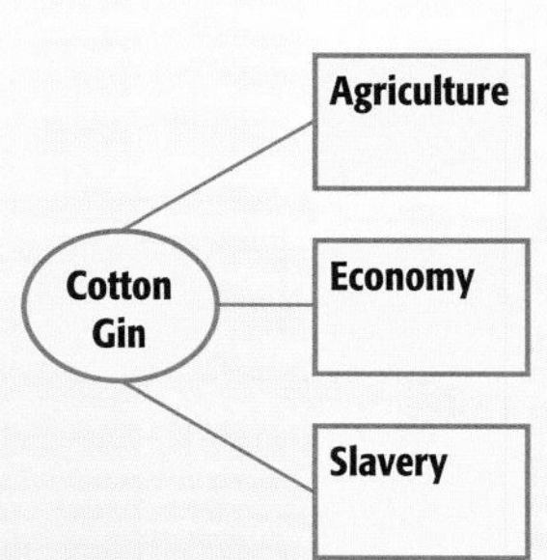

4 Finding the Main Idea

a. Describe manufacturing and industry in the South.

b. What were the different groups of people who made up southern society, and what were their lives like?

5 Writing and Critical Thinking

Summarizing Imagine that you are a novelist. Write a short story about the lives of free African Americans and the challenges they faced in the early 1800s.

Consider the following:
- how free African Americans earned their freedom
- how they earned a living
- the discrimination they faced

Section 4

The Slave System

Read to Discover

1. What were work and daily life like for most slaves?
2. How did slaves' family life, religion, and other aspects of their culture help them cope with the slave system?
3. How did enslaved African Americans challenge the slave system?

Define

- folktales
- spirituals

Identify

- Nat Turner
- Nat Turner's Rebellion

WHY IT MATTERS TODAY

Spirituals were one part of slave culture. Use CNNfyi.com or other **current events** sources to find out how art, literature, or music serves as part of a group's culture today. Record your findings in your journal.

The Story Continues

Harriet Jacobs was born into slavery in 1813 and worked for many years in a doctor's household. Determined that her children would not live as slaves, Jacobs ran away. "I had . . . a mother's love for my children," she explained. "I resolved that out of the darkness . . . a brighter dawn should rise for them." Jacobs knew that it would be hard to survive as a runaway slave, but she was hopeful. "My master had power and law on his side . . . ," Jacob noted. "I had a determined will."

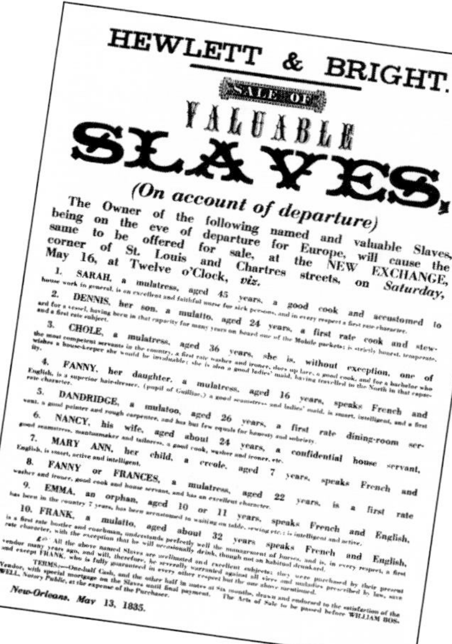

HEWLETT & BRIGHT.

SALE OF

VALUABLE

SLAVES,

(On account of departure)

The Owner of the following named and valuable Slaves, being on the eve of departure for Europe, will cause the same to be offered for sale, at the NEW EXCHANGE, corner of St. Louis and Chartres streets, on *Saturday*, May 16, at Twelve o'Clock, *viz.*

1. SARAH, a mulatress, aged 45 years, a good cook and accustomed to
2. DENNIS, her son, a mulatto, aged 24 years, a first rate cook and stew-
3. CHOLE, a mulatress, aged 36 years, she is, without exception, one of
4. FANNY, her daughter, a mulatress, aged 16 years, speaks French and
5. DANDRIDGE, a mulatoo, aged 26 years, a first rate dining-room ser-
6. NANCY, his wife, aged about 24 years, a confidential house servant,
7. MARY ANN, her child, a creole, aged 7 years, speaks French and
8. FANNY or FRANCES, a mulatress, aged 22 years, is a first rate
9. EMMA, an orphan, aged 10 or 11 years, speaks French and English,
10. FRANK, a mulatto, aged about 32 years speaks French and English,

New-Orleans, *May* 13, 1835.

This slave auction poster identifies and describes the people that the company planned to sell.

Slaves and Work

Although treatment of enslaved African Americans varied, most slaveholders tried to get slaves to work as much as they could. Enslaved people on small farms usually did many different jobs. On large plantations most slaves worked on specific jobs, with the majority working in the fields. Some larger plantations used men called overseers to make sure that slaves followed orders and also to carry out punishments. On many plantations a slave foreman called a driver also assisted in overseeing slaves.

Most plantation owners used the gang labor system. In this system all field hands worked on the same task at the same time, usually working from sunup to sundown. Former slave Harry McMillan had worked on a plantation in South Carolina. He recalled that the field hands usually did not even get a break to eat lunch. "You had to get your victuals [food] standing at your hoe," he remembered.

Men, women, and even children older than about 10 usually did the same work. Hardly anything, even sickness and poor weather, stopped the work. "The times I hated most was picking cotton when the frost was on the bolls [seed pods]," recalled former Louisiana slave Mary Reynolds. "My hands git sore and crack open and bleed."

Some slaves worked as butlers, cooks, or nurses in the planter's home. These slaves usually had better food and clothing than field hands. However, they often worked longer hours. They had to serve the planter's family 24 hours a day. House servants could also be sent to work in the fields.

On larger plantations, some slaves worked at skilled jobs such as blacksmithing or carpentry. Sometimes planters let these slaves hire out their services to other people. In this way, some skilled slaves earned enough money to buy their freedom. For example, William Ellison purchased his freedom by working for wages as a cotton gin maker. For several years he worked late at night and on Sundays. He bought his freedom with his earnings. Eventually, he was also able to buy the freedom of his wife and daughter.

✔ **Reading Check: Summarizing** What were some of the different types of work that slaves did on plantations?

Interpreting the Visual Record

Auction *Families of enslaved African Americans were often broken up at auctions and sold to slaveholders. Slaveholders used shackles like the ones shown here to punish slaves.* ***Why might an auction like this one frighten an enslaved person?***

Life under Slavery

Slaveholders treated slaves as property, not as people. Slaves were bought and sold to make a profit. Sometimes slave traders even kidnapped free African Americans and then sold them into slavery. For example, Solomon Northup was kidnapped in Washington, D.C. He spent 12 years as a slave, "shut out from the sweet light of liberty." He finally proved his identity and gained his release.

Slaves received poor clothing and shelter. They lived in cabins with dirt floors, leaky roofs, and few furnishings. Some slaves brightened their clothes by sewing on old scraps of cloth that had been thrown away. In this way, they individualized the clothing given to them by the planters. Likewise, many did what they could to improve the food they received. Some planters allowed slaves to plant their own vegetable gardens and raise chickens for eggs. If they had time, slaves might catch fish or pick berries. Some planters offered rewards to encourage slaves to obey. However, many slaveholders used punishment instead. Some slaveholders would severely punish one slave in front of others as a warning to them all. Harry McMillan recalled some of the punishments he saw.

"The punishments were whipping, putting you in the stocks [wooden frames to lock people in] and making you wear irons and a chain at work. Then they had a collar to put round your neck with two horns, like cows' horns, so that you could not lie down. . . . Sometimes they dug a hole like a well with a door on top. This they called a dungeon keeping you in it two or three weeks or a month, or sometimes till you died in there."

—Harry McMillan, quoted in *Major Problems in the History of the American South, Volume I,* edited by Paul D. Escott and David R. Goldfield

Many states also had strict slave codes that limited what slaves could do. Some laws kept slaves from traveling far from their homes. Teaching slaves to read or write was often illegal. Slaves thus did not have freedom of movement or the benefits of simple education.

✔ **Reading Check: Analyzing Information** How did slaveholders try to keep slaves under control?

That's Interesting!

The Road to Freedom Would you be willing to mail yourself to freedom? That is just what one enslaved man did. In the late 1840s, a slave named Henry Brown climbed into a special box. Brown's friend then nailed the box shut and shipped it to the North. Twenty-six hours later, the box arrived at the office of the antislavery committee in Philadelphia. Brown's creative escape earned him the name Henry "Box" Brown. In another creative escape, a fair-skinned female slave dressed in a man's clothes to pose as a plantation owner! Then she bandaged her jaw and put her arm in a sling. Her husband, also a slave, posed as her servant. Local authorities believed that the "plantation owner" and slave really were headed north to see a doctor. Not all slaves tried such clever escapes. Some simply followed the North Star.

Analyzing Primary Sources

Making Generalizations and Predictions What effect do you think the treatment Harry McMillan describes would have on slaves?

Slave Culture

Despite their difficult lives, slaves took some comfort in their community and culture. They worked hard to maintain strong ties to one another and to their heritage. The most important unit of slave communities was the family. Slaves feared being sold to another plantation and separated from their families more than physical punishment. Josiah Henson never forgot the day that he and his family were sold at a slave auction, a typical situation for many slaves. His mother begged the slaveholder who bought her to buy Josiah also. Then she would have at least one of her children

Interpreting the Visual Record

Funeral *Slaves often tried to practice their religious beliefs and ceremonies out of sight of slaveholders. Here a group of slaves conducts a funeral at night in the woods.* ***Why do you think slaves might have wanted privacy for a ceremony like this one?***

with her. The slaveholder refused, and Henson's family was separated. "I must have been then between five or six years old," he later recalled. "I seem to see and hear my poor weeping mother now."

Enslaved parents tried to ensure that their children never forgot their heritage. They passed down family histories as well as African customs and traditions by telling **folktales.** These oral stories often had a moral and were used to teach lessons about how to survive under slavery. Slaves used clever animal characters, such as Brer Rabbit, called tricksters to show how to survive by outsmarting slaveholders.

Free Find:
Nat Turner's Confession
After reading Nat Turner's Confession on the **Holt Researcher CD–ROM,** imagine that you are a journalist from the North. Write a brief article summarizing Nat Turner's views.

Religion also played an important part in slave culture. By the early 1800s many slaves were Protestant. White ministers often tried to use religion to control slaves. They preached that God wanted slaves to obey slaveholders. However, enslaved African Americans noted that the Bible views all people as equal in God's eyes. They came to believe that God would deliver them from the hardship of slavery. Much like the Hebrew slaves in ancient Egypt, slaves in the South had faith that they would someday live in freedom.

Some slaves sang **spirituals**, emotional Christian songs of sorrow that blended African and European traditions, to express their religious beliefs. For example, "The Heavenly Road" reflected slaves' belief in their equality before God.

Analyzing Primary Sources

Drawing Inferences and Conclusions What is implied by the spiritual's statement that a slave is "a child of God"?

"Come, my brother, if you never did pray,
I hope you may pray tonight;
For I really believe I'm a child of God
As I walk in the heavenly road."

—Anonymous, quoted in *Afro-American Religious History,* edited by Milton C. Sernett

Slaves blended aspects of traditional African religions with Christianity. They worshiped in secret, out of sight of slaveholders. Some historians have called slave religion the invisible institution.

✔ **Reading Check: Summarizing** What did slaves use to keep a sense of community among themselves?

Challenging Slavery

In other small ways slaves rebelled against the slave system on a daily basis to gain some control over their lives. Sometimes this meant working slower to protest long hours in the fields. Other times it meant running away to avoid an angry slaveholder. Some slaves tried to escape to southern cities or hide in African American communities. Although gaining freedom by escaping to the North was hard, thousands of enslaved people did succeed.

Although violent slave revolts were rare, planters lived in fear of them. In 1800 Gabriel Prosser planned a rebellion near Richmond, Virginia, and Denmark Vesey planned one in Charleston, South Carolina, in 1822. Both revolts were stopped before they could be carried out. Authorities executed most of those involved in planning the rebellions.

The most violent slave revolt in the United States occurred in 1831. **Nat Turner**, a slave from Virginia, believed that God had called on him to end slavery. **Nat Turner's Rebellion** began on an August night in 1831. Turner led a group of slaves in a plan to kill slaveholders and their families. First, they attacked the family that held Turner as a slave, and in a short time, they had killed almost 60 white people in the area.

More than 100 slaves were killed in the process of putting down the rebellion. Turner was caught within weeks and sentenced to hang. Before his trial, Turner confessed and expressed his belief that the revolt was justified and worth the loss of his own life. He was executed on November 11, 1831. Despite the resistance of enslaved people, slavery continued to expand throughout the South.

✔ **Reading Check: Identifying Cause and Effect** What caused Nat Turner's Rebellion, and what happened as a result?

BIOGRAPHY

Nat Turner

(1800–1831)

Nat Turner grew up believing he was called by God to do something important. As a child on a Virginia plantation, he gained a reputation among the other slaves for his religious beliefs and intelligence. Turner became a well-respected minister in the local slave community. In 1827 he even baptized a white overseer. When a solar eclipse took place in 1831, Turner interpreted it as a sign that the time had come to start a revolt. **What event led Nat Turner to believe that he should start a slave revolt?**

Section 4 Review

go.hrw.com Homework Practice Online
keyword: SC3 HP12

1. **Define** and explain:
   - folktales
   - spirituals
2. **Identify** and explain:
   - Nat Turner
   - Nat Turner's Rebellion
3. **Categorizing** Copy the graphic organizer below. Use it to describe life under slavery.

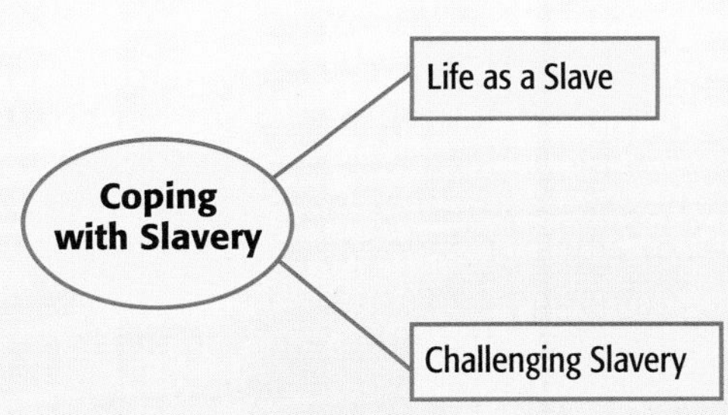

4. **Finding the Main Idea**
   a. What was a typical working day in the life of a slave like?
   b. How do you think Nat Turner's Rebellion affected the lives of southern slaves who did not take part in the revolt?
5. **Writing and Critical Thinking**
   Summarizing Imagine that you are a historian interviewing a former slave in the late 1800s. Write a half-page article on how enslaved people coped with the slave system.
   Consider the following:
   - the importance of family life
   - the role of religion in the lives of slaves
   - the functions of folktales and spirituals

Chapter 12 Review

The Chapter at a Glance

Examine the visual summary of the chapter below. Then prepare a fill-in-the-blanks chart that a classmate could use to test his or her knowledge of the chapter.

Industry and Agriculture

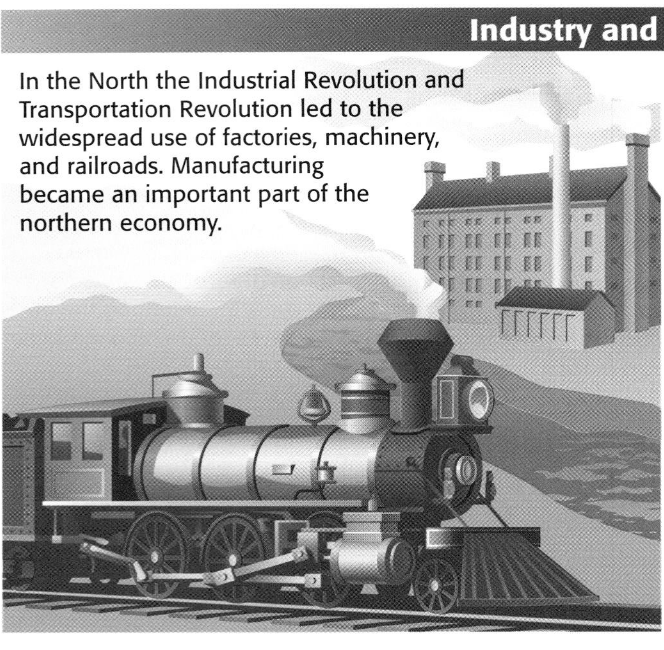

In the North the Industrial Revolution and Transportation Revolution led to the widespread use of factories, machinery, and railroads. Manufacturing became an important part of the northern economy.

In the South agriculture, particularly cotton production, was the key to the economy. Slaves performed much of the labor on large plantations, while yeoman farmers operated smaller farms.

Identifying People and Ideas

Use the following terms or people in historically significant sentences.

1. Industrial Revolution
2. textiles
3. Eli Whitney
4. Lowell system
5. Transportation Revolution
6. telegraph
7. Isaac Singer
8. cotton gin
9. planters
10. Nat Turner

Understanding Main Ideas

Section 1 *(Pages 362–365)*

1. How did the Industrial Revolution in the United States change people's lives in the Northeast?
2. Why did industrialization begin in New England?

Section 2 *(Pages 366–371)*

3. How did the steamboat and the railroad change transportation?

Section 3 *(Pages 372–376)*

4. What was the most important element of the economy in the South during the early 1800s?
5. How were planters and yeomen different?

Section 4 *(Pages 377–381)*

6. What was daily life and work like for slaves?

You Be the Historian— Reviewing Themes

1. **Science, Technology & Society** In what ways did new technology change the lives of both northerners and southerners?
2. **Economics** How did changes in transportation technology affect the economy?
3. **Geography** How did geography affect economic development in the North and in the South?

Thinking Critically

1. **Drawing Inferences and Conclusions** Create a chart listing what you think were the five most important inventions of the late 1700s and early 1800s. Briefly describe each invention and its effects on American life.
2. **Supporting a Point of View** Considering the fact that many laborers could earn better wages working in factories than on farms, do you think they were justified in their demands for reforms? Explain your answer.
3. **Comparing and Contrasting** What were the similarities and differences in the lives of free African Americans and slaves?

Social Studies Skills Workshop

Interpreting Charts

Study the chart below. Then use the information on the chart to help you answer the questions that follow.

Causes and Effects of the Industrial Revolution in America, 1790–1860

Long-Term Causes
- Industrial Revolution in Britain
- Transportation Revolution (canals, improved roads, railroads, steamboats)
- Introduction of steam power
- Growing cities
- Rise in immigration

Immediate Causes
- Technological innovations by individuals such as Samuel Slater and Eli Whitney in early 1800s
- War of 1812
- Founding of Lowell mills, 1822
- Tariffs on foreign manufactured goods

The First Industrial Revolution in America, 1790–1860

Effects
- Economic growth
- More manufactured goods produced at lower prices
- Factory jobs change working habits and conditions
- Women and children become wage-earners

1. Which of the following was not an immediate cause of the Industrial Revolution in America?
   a. the War of 1812
   b. the Lowell mills
   c. tariffs
   d. a rise in immigration

2. Based on your knowledge of the period, how do you think the long-term causes listed on the chart contributed to the first Industrial Revolution in the United States?

Analyzing Primary Sources

Read the following quotation by planter Bennet H. Barrow, and then answer the questions that follow.

> **"If I employ a laborer to perform a certain quantum [amount] of work per day, and I agree to pay him a certain amount for the performance of said work when he has accomplished it, I of course have no further claim on him for his time or services [when he is done]—but how different is it with a slave. . . . If I furnish my (slave) with every necessary of life, . . . am I not entitled to an exclusive right to his time?"**

3. Which of the following best describes Barrow's attitude toward slaves?
   a. A planter should treat slaves like parts of a machine and have control over all their time.
   b. Slavery is actually more expensive than paying people wages.
   c. Once they have finished their work, slaves should have free time to themselves.
   d. Plantations should make use of modern machinery as well as slaves.

4. According to his own words, how would Barrow expect to treat free workers whom he paid wages?

Alternative Assessment

Building Your Portfolio

Cooperative Learning

Complete the following activity in small groups. Each group should come up with an idea for a new invention that would make daily life easier. Draw a diagram or create a model of the proposed invention and create an advertisement for the invention that explains its benefits. Then share your invention idea with the class.

internet connect

Internet Activity: go.hrw.com
keyword: SC3 CF12

Choose an activity on the North and South to:
- Write a biography of Eli Whitney.
- Research the effect of *Gibbons* v. *Ogden* and other interstate commerce cases.
- Learn about Joseph R. Anderson and the Tredegar Iron Works.

Connecting to Geography

A Growing Economy

From 1790 to 1860, the economy of each region of the United States grew and developed in very different ways. The economies of the South and the West were based largely on farming. The economy of the North was increasingly focused on industry.

In some ways these differences worked together to help the nation grow. For example, the South provided some raw materials, such as cotton, to northern factories. The Midwest provided large supplies of food, which helped feed the growing population of northern cities.

American manufacturing grew in the late 1700s and early 1800s. This growth was made possible by the invention and development of new technologies. For example, new inventions improved textile manufacturing, and the use of waterpower was expanded. These developments increased the speed of production. By the 1830s, Americans were building railroad networks that moved goods rapidly and inexpensively to and from market.

The North

The North developed an industrial economy partly because of its geography and superior transportation system. Farmland in the North was not generally suited for large-scale agriculture. Industrial development was thus necessary for the region's economic growth.

Distribution of U.S. Manufacturing Establishments, 1860

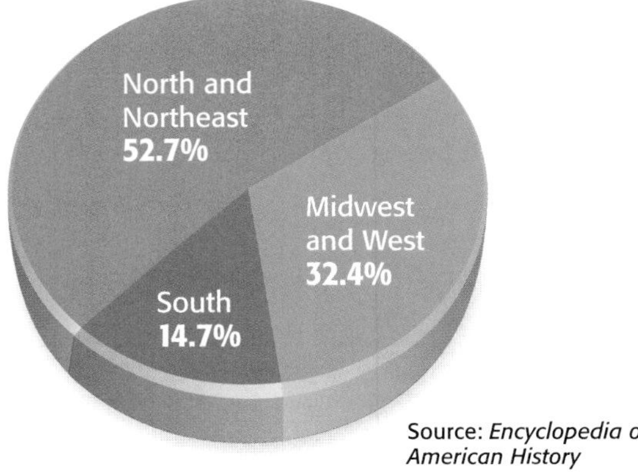

Source: *Encyclopedia of American History*

History Note 1

By 1860 only about one in seven U.S. factories and other manufacturing establishments were located in the South. As industry increased in the North, so did the region's urban population. Cities, particularly those in the Northeast and Midwest, grew larger as factories provided more and more jobs. In the South, which had fewer factories, urban growth was much slower.

Geography Skills

Interpreting Pie Graphs

1. What region had the largest percentage of the nation's manufacturing establishments in 1860?
2. **Comparing** How much greater was the percentage of manufacturing establishments in the Midwest and West than in the South in 1860?

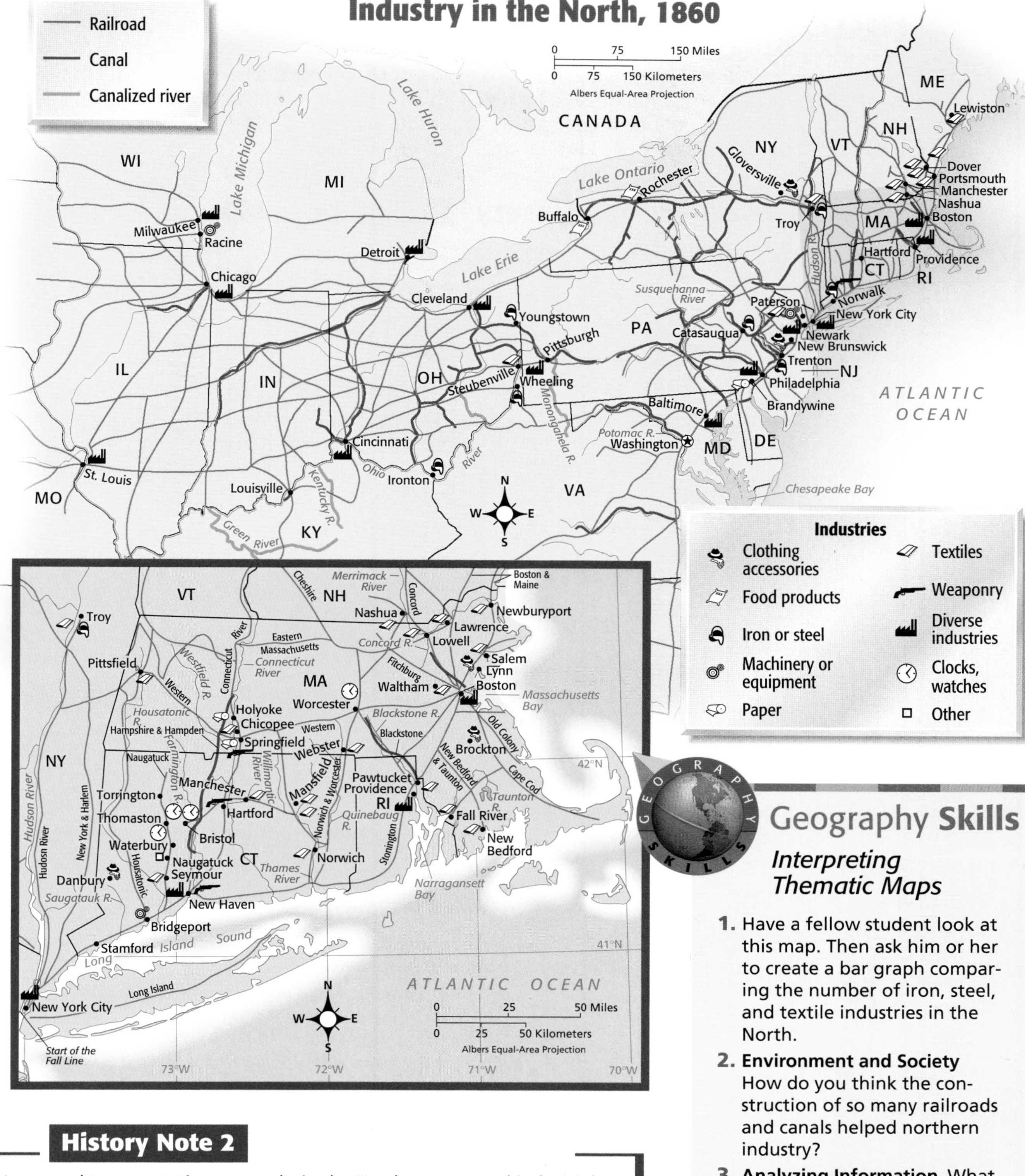

Geography Skills

Interpreting Thematic Maps

1. Have a fellow student look at this map. Then ask him or her to create a bar graph comparing the number of iron, steel, and textile industries in the North.
2. **Environment and Society** How do you think the construction of so many railroads and canals helped northern industry?
3. **Analyzing Information** What geographic features made New England more suitable for early industries?

History Note 2

Improved transportation networks in the North encouraged industrial expansion. Businesses shipped goods on rivers, the Great Lakes, and the growing networks of canals and railroads. The benefits of expanded transportation networks on industrial growth could be clearly seen in New England in the first half of the 1800s. Connecticut, Massachusetts, and Rhode Island provide good examples of this important relationship.

The South

While industry in the North grew, agriculture in the South boomed. The invention of the cotton gin in 1793 encouraged growth in southern cotton production. However, as that region's economy grew, so did disapproval in the North and the West of the South's use of slave labor.

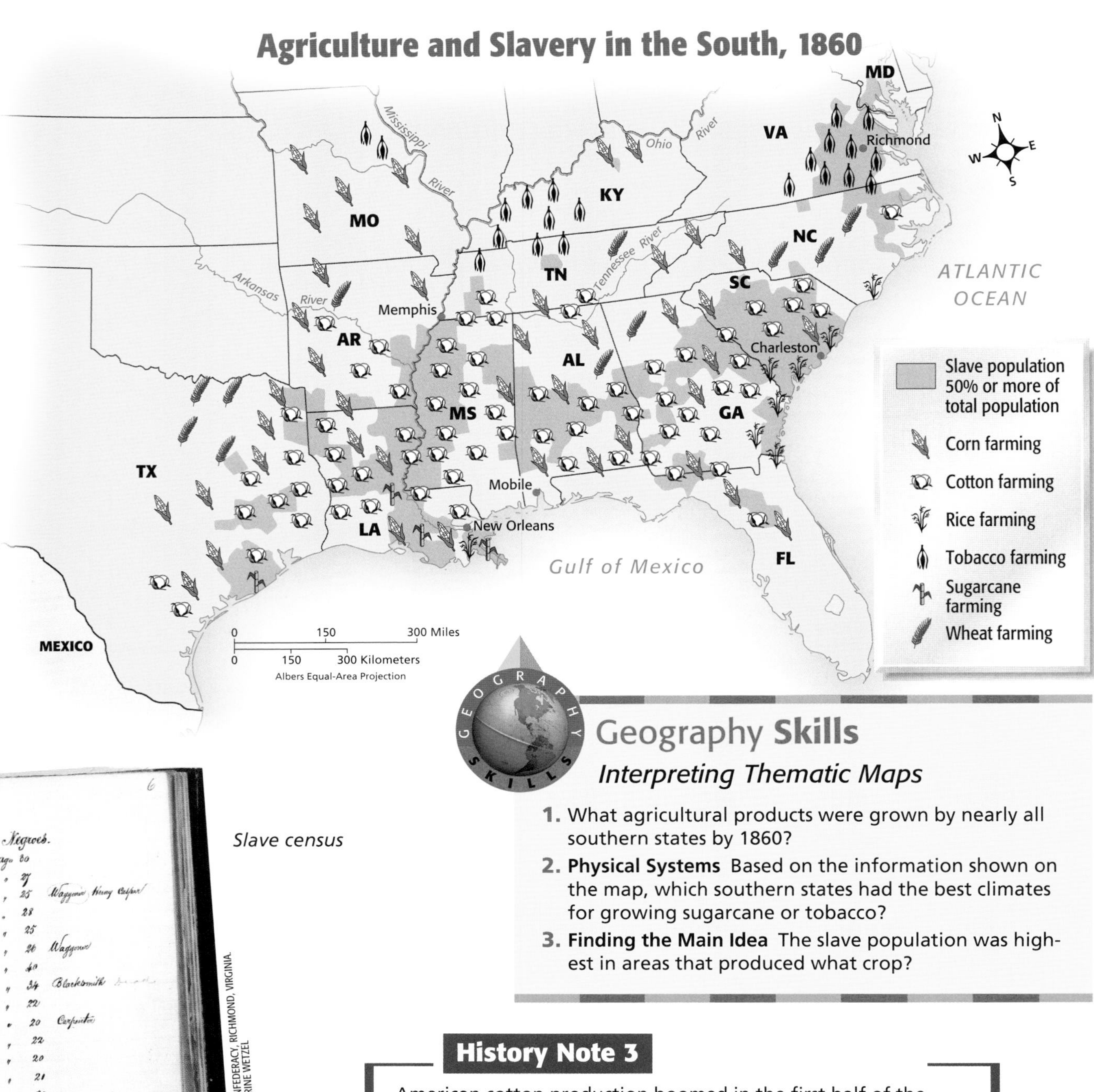

Geography Skills

Interpreting Thematic Maps

1. What agricultural products were grown by nearly all southern states by 1860?
2. **Physical Systems** Based on the information shown on the map, which southern states had the best climates for growing sugarcane or tobacco?
3. **Finding the Main Idea** The slave population was highest in areas that produced what crop?

Slave census

THE MUSEUM OF THE CONFEDERACY, RICHMOND, VIRGINIA. PHOTOGRAPHY BY KATHERINE WETZEL

History Note 3

American cotton production boomed in the first half of the 1800s. Cotton production was concentrated within a region called the cotton belt, which ran from South Carolina to eastern Texas. In 1860 the United States exported more than $190 million worth of cotton, most of it grown in the cotton belt.

U.S. Cotton and Tobacco Exports, 1790–1860

Cotton
Tobacco

1.7 billion lbs.

Exports (in millions of lbs.)

700
600
500
400
300
200
100
0

1790 1800 1810 1820 1830 1840 1850 1860

Year

Source: *Historical Statistics of the United States*

Geography Skills

Interpreting Bar Graphs

1. By what year had the amount of cotton exports overtaken the amount of tobacco exports?
2. **Summarizing** Show this bar graph to a classmate. Have this person write a paragraph describing the general trends in tobacco and cotton exports from 1790 to 1860.

History Note 4

Together Alabama, Georgia, Louisiana, and Mississippi produced about two thirds of the cotton in the United States in 1860. States that produced smaller amounts of cotton often produced larger amounts of other agricultural products. For example, in 1860 Virginia produced relatively little cotton. However, it produced nearly 30 percent of the nation's tobacco. South Carolina produced nearly two thirds of the nation's rice in that year.

Slaves returning from a hard day of laboring in the fields

CHAPTER

13 New Movements in America (1815–1850)

William Lloyd Garrison's antislavery banner announced, "I WILL BE HEARD."

Horace Mann fought for better salaries for teachers.

UNITED STATES

1817 Thomas Gallaudet founds a school for people who are hearing impaired.

1821 Emma Willard starts the Troy Female Seminary.

1831 William Lloyd Garrison begins publishing the abolitionist newspaper *The Liberator*.

1837 Horace Mann becomes the first secretary of education in Massachusetts.

1815 | 1820 | 1825 | 1830 | 1835

WORLD

1822 The American Colonization Society founds the city of Monrovia on Africa's west coast.

1829 French educator Louis Braille creates a system of writing that uses raised dots for people who are blind.

Slavery is banned in Mexico.

1834 A law abolishing slavery in the British Empire goes into effect.

Monrovia became the capital of the African nation Liberia.

Build on What You Know

The North and South developed very different economies during the early 1800s. Rising immigration led to population growth, especially in the North. As the country faced new challenges, social reform movements emerged in response. Many people joined groups to fight alcohol abuse, end slavery, or improve education.

Organizers of the Seneca Falls Convention based the Declaration of Sentiments in part on the Declaration of Independence.

During the mid-1800s, large numbers of German and Irish immigrants came to the United States.

1840 The World's Anti-Slavery Convention is held in London.

1845 A potato famine in Ireland causes more Irish to move to the United States.

1848 The first meeting for women's rights—the Seneca Falls Convention—is held in New York.

1850 Nathaniel Hawthorne publishes *The Scarlet Letter.*

1855 Boston lets African American children attend white schools.

1860 About 13 percent of the American population is foreign born.

1860 In England Florence Nightingale founds the first school for training nurses.

1840 | 1845 | 1850 | 1855 | 1860

In 1907 Florence Nightingale became the first woman to receive Britain's Order of Merit.

If you were there . . .
What social issues would you choose to work on?

You Be the Historian

What's Your Opinion? Do you **agree** or **disagree** with the following statements? Support your point of view in your journal.

- **Culture** People should try to improve the lives of the less fortunate.
- **Economics** Immigration makes a country's economy grow.
- **Citizenship** Citizens should try to change laws that they feel are unjust.

Section 1

America's Spiritual Awakening

Read to Discover

1. How did religion affect Americans during the Second Great Awakening?
2. What were the transcendentalists' views of American society?
3. What were some ideas of the romantic movement?

Define

- transcendentalism
- utopian communities

Identify

- Second Great Awakening
- Charles Grandison Finney
- Ralph Waldo Emerson
- Margaret Fuller
- Henry David Thoreau
- Thomas Cole
- Nathaniel Hawthorne
- Edgar Allan Poe
- Emily Dickinson
- Walt Whitman

Why it Matters Today

Art is a way to learn more about a culture or a community. Use CNNfyi.com or other **current events** sources to learn more about an American writer who is alive today. Record your findings in your journal.

The Story Continues

In her early teens, New Yorker Huldah Baldwin began thinking seriously about her spiritual life. When she became deathly ill, she asked relatives and friends to come to her bedside. She was concerned about the state of their souls. She pleaded with her family members as death grew near. "O live for him [God] that we may meet hereafter and enjoy a blessed eternity together." Such deep religious beliefs were increasingly common in the early 1800s in New York.

Traveling ministers were key to the success of the Second Great Awakening.

The Second Great Awakening

Beginning in the 1790s some Americans took part in a movement of Christian renewal called the **Second Great Awakening**. It swept through towns across upstate New York and through the frontier regions of Kentucky, Ohio, Tennessee, and South Carolina. By the 1820s and 1830s this new interest in religion had spread to New England, the Appalachians, and the South.

Charles Grandison Finney was one of the most important leaders of the Second Great Awakening. After experiencing a dramatic religious conversion in 1821, Finney left his career as a lawyer and began preaching. Speaking in a forceful and direct style, Finney challenged some traditional Protestant beliefs. He told congregations that each individual was responsible for his or her own salvation. He also believed that sin was avoidable. Finney held prayer meetings that would last for days. Many people converted to Christianity during these revivals. Finney told these converts to demonstrate their faith by doing good deeds.

In 1794 Richard Allen founded the Bethel African Methodist Episcopal Church in Philadelphia.

Finney's preaching angered some traditional ministers like Lyman Beecher of Boston. Beecher wanted to prevent Finney from holding revivals in the city. "You mean to carry a streak of fire to Boston. If you attempt it, as the Lord liveth, I'll meet you . . . and fight every inch of the way." However, the First Amendment guarantee of freedom of religion prevented local or state governments from passing laws banning the new religious practices. Ministers were thus free to spread their message of faith and salvation to whomever wished to listen.

As a result of their efforts, church membership across the country grew a great deal during the Second Great Awakening. Many of these new church members were women. African Americans were among those drawn to the new religious movement. Some became Baptist, Methodist, or Presbyterian ministers. The African Methodist Episcopal Church spread across the Middle Atlantic states. Although the movement had begun in the Northeast and on the frontier, the Second Great Awakening renewed Americans' religious faith throughout the country.

✔ **Reading Check: Finding the Main Idea** How did the Second Great Awakening affect Americans?

Daily Life

Revival Meetings Religious revivals swept the United States in the early 1800s. Some meetings drew up to 20,000 people at a time to huge outdoor camps. James Finley, who later became a Methodist preacher, described one revival as a "vast sea of human beings [that] seemed to be agitated as if by a storm." Preachers traveled from town to town, urging sinners to seek salvation. **How does this image portray the emotional qualities of a revival meeting?**

Interpreting the Visual Record

Utopian communities *Brook Farm, a utopian community in Massachusetts, attracted a number of famous writers.* ***What do you see in this picture that might attract people to live there?***

Transcendentalism and Utopian Communities

Some New England writers and thinkers found spiritual inspiration in **transcendentalism.** Transcendentalism was the belief that people could transcend, or rise above, the material things in life, such as money and personal belongings. Transcendentalists believed that people should depend on themselves instead of upon outside authority. Some important figures who believed in this philosophy were **Ralph Waldo Emerson**, **Margaret Fuller**, and **Henry David Thoreau**.

Emerson wrote an essay titled "Self-Reliance" in 1841. In this essay, he said that Americans depended too much on institutions and traditions. Emerson wanted people to follow their personal beliefs and use their own judgment. "What I must do is all that concerns me, not what the people think," he wrote. Fuller edited the transcendentalist publication *The Dial.* In 1845 she wrote a book called *Woman in the Nineteenth Century.* In it, she said that women had the right to choose their own paths in life. Some people saw her as a champion of women's rights.

Thoreau also believed in self-reliance and did not trust institutions. He expressed many of his ideas in *Walden, or Life in the Woods,* published in 1854. For two years, Thoreau lived alone in a small cabin in Massachusetts. He wrote about his experiences living near Walden Pond.

Analyzing Primary Sources

Drawing Inferences and Conclusions Why did Thoreau live in a cabin in the woods?

"I went to the woods because I wished to live deliberately [with a purpose], to front [experience] only the essential facts of life, and see if I could learn what it had to teach, and not, when I came to die, discover that I had not lived."

—Henry David Thoreau, *Walden*

In the 1840s some transcendentalists formed a community at Brook Farm, Massachusetts. Brook Farm did not last very long, however. It was one of many experiments with **utopian communities** that took place in America. These communities tried to form a perfect society on Earth. Some Americans founded utopian communities as places to practice their religious beliefs. In 1774 Ann Lee started a community of Shakers—so named because their bodies would often shake during worship. By the 1830s this group had about 6,000 members living in various communities. The Shakers did not believe in private ownership of property and lived a very plain lifestyle. The furniture they made reflected their simple approach to life.

Other utopian communities were based on social philosophies. Many groups wanted men and women to be equal. Mary Paul, a member of a group in Red Bank, New Jersey, explained this view. She said that in the community "both men and women have the *same pay* for the *same* work." Such utopian communities allowed people to pursue spiritual and cooperative lifestyles. However, only a few of these communities lasted very long. Most groups failed to get their members to work together well enough for the community to survive.

✔ **Reading Check: Identifying Points of View** How did transcendentalists believe people should live?

The American Romantics

Ideas about spirituality, the simple life, and nature also shaped painters and writers in the early 1800s. Some artists became part of the romantic movement, which began in Europe and drew upon the idea that each person brings a unique view to the world. Romantic artists such as **Thomas Cole** painted the American landscape. These images of nature and the wilderness contrasted with the large cities and the corruption that many Americans saw in Europe.

During this time the number of notable American authors grew. Many female authors, such as Ann Sophia Stephens, wrote historical fiction. These works became very popular during the mid-1800s. One of the best-known examples of romantic literature is *The Scarlet Letter*. This novel by New England writer **Nathaniel Hawthorne** describes Puritan life in the 1600s. Hawthorne's friend Herman Melville was a writer and a former sailor who wrote tales of the sea. *Moby-Dick* and *Billy Budd* are some of his more famous works.

Along with novels, American romantic authors also wrote many famous short stories and poems. **Edgar Allan Poe**, for example, is best known for his short stories and poetry. A verse from Poe's haunting poem, "The Raven," follows.

"Once upon a midnight dreary,[1]
while I pondered,[2] weak and weary,
Over many a quaint[3] and curious
volume of forgotten lore[4] —
While I nodded, nearly napping,
suddenly there came a tapping,
As of some one gently rapping,
rapping at my chamber door—
"Tis some visiter,' I muttered,
'tapping at my chamber door—
Only this and nothing more.'"

—Edgar Allan Poe, "The Raven," from *Anthology of American Literature*, edited by George McMichael

[1]**dreary:** gloomy [2]**pondered:** thought [3]**quaint:** odd [4]**lore:** legends

This illustration shows a scene from Edgar Allan Poe's poem "The Raven."

"This Is My Letter to the World"

Emily Dickinson

Born in 1830, Emily Dickinson led a quiet life in Amherst, Massachusetts. Her first published collection of poetry included the following selection.

This is my letter to the World
That never wrote to Me—
The simple News that Nature told—
With tender Majesty

Her Message is committed
To Hands I cannot see—
For love of Her—Sweet—countrymen
Judge tenderly—of Me.

Understanding What You Read
Literature and History What does Dickinson mean by her "Letter to the World"?

The United States produced several other gifted American poets during this period. These writers included **Emily Dickinson**, Henry Wadsworth Longfellow, John Greenleaf Whittier, and **Walt Whitman**. Only two of Dickinson's poems were published during her lifetime, both anonymously. After her death in 1886, her family discovered hundreds of her poems, some written on loose scraps of paper. Longfellow was the best-known poet of the mid-1800s. His long story-poems, such as *Hiawatha*, the *Courtship of Miles Standish*, and *Tales of a Wayside Inn* became favorites in many American households. Whittier spoke out against slavery in works such as *Poems Written during the Progress of the Abolition Question.*

Walt Whitman praised both American individualism and democracy in his simple, unrhymed poetry. His work *Leaves of Grass*, published in 1855, is noted for its distinct style. Whitman expressed his view of America's poetic gifts in the preface to *Leaves of Grass.* "Americans of all nations at any time upon the earth have probably the fullest poetical nature," he wrote. "The United States themselves are essentially the greatest poem."

✔ **Reading Check: Analyzing Information** What was the romantic movement, and who were some of the major American artists and writers of this movement?

Section 1 Review

1. **Define** and explain:
   - transcendentalism
   - utopian communities
2. **Identify** and explain:
   - Second Great Awakening
   - Charles Grandison Finney
   - Ralph Waldo Emerson
   - Margaret Fuller
   - Henry David Thoreau
   - Thomas Cole
   - Nathaniel Hawthorne
   - Edgar Allan Poe
   - Emily Dickinson
   - Walt Whitman
3. **Summarizing** Copy the graphic organizer below. Use it to identify the new ideas that emerged from religion, philosophy, art, and literature during the early 1800s.

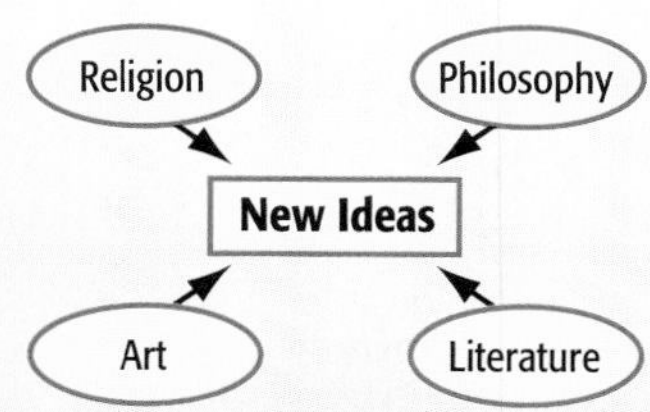

4. **Finding the Main Idea**
   a. What was the Second Great Awakening, and what effect did it have on religious life in America?
   b. How did the transcendentalists describe American society?
5. **Writing and Critical Thinking**
   Analyzing Information Imagine that you are an American poet in the early 1800s. Write a poem on a subject of your choice based on the style of the romantics.
   Consider the following:
   - the work of other romantic poets and writers
   - your personal perspective on life
   - an appeal to your readers' emotions

Section 2

Immigrants and Cities

Read to Discover

1. Why did so many Irish and German immigrants come to the United States in the 1840s and 1850s?
2. How did some Americans react to immigrants?
3. What caused U.S. cities to grow, and what benefits and problems did this growth create?

Define

- nativists
- middle class
- tenements

Identify

- Know-Nothing Party

WHY IT MATTERS TODAY

Many immigrants are still drawn to the United States today. Use CNNfyi.com or other **current events** sources to learn why people immigrate to the United States. Record your findings in your journal.

The Story Continues

Irish immigrants to the United States traveled in tightly packed sections of ships. They received little fresh air or light on their long journey. Dozens of immigrants suffered and died from fever and disease. In Herman Melville's story *Redburn*, a cabin boy describes one such journey in which fever had a terrible effect on the passengers. "By their own countrymen, they were torn from the clasp [embrace] of their wives . . . and with hurried rites [ceremonies], were dropped into the ocean." Of the millions of immigrants who left their homes in the mid-1800s, not all made it safely across the Atlantic.

Advertisements like this one encouraged people to immigrate to the United States.

Waves of Immigrants

In the mid-1800s large numbers of immigrants crossed the Atlantic Ocean to begin new lives in the United States. More than 4 million immigrants settled in the United States between 1840 and 1860, most of them from Europe. More than 3 million of these immigrants were German or Irish. Many immigrants were fleeing economic or political troubles in their native countries.

CONNECTING TO

MATH

Just the Facts

Some Occupations of Immigrants in New York, 1855

Occupation	Total Number of Workers	Foreign-Born Workers
Bakers	3,692	3,323
Blacksmiths	2,642	2,159
Leather workers	1,386	980
Jewelers	1,705	1,037
Carpenters	7,531	4,863
Clerks	13,929	5,921
Dressmakers/ seamstresses	9,819	6,606
Shoemakers/ tailors	19,354	18,600
Domestic servants	31,749	29,470
Merchants	6,299	1,705
Physicians	1,469	566

Using Mathematical Skills

1. Which occupation had the highest number of immigrant workers in 1855?
2. Create a bar graph that compares the total number of workers to the number of foreign-born workers.
3. Imagine that you are an immigrant. Write a letter to family members overseas, using the statistics in this chart to persuade them to immigrate to New York City.

Most immigrants from the British Isles during this period were Irish. In the mid-1840s potato blight, a disease that causes rot, left many families in Ireland with little food. Thomas Francis Meagher, an Irish leader, sadly commented, "One business survives! . . . That fortunate business . . . is the Irish coffin-maker's." More than 1 million Irish people died of starvation and disease. Even more fled to the United States. Most Irish immigrants were very poor. Many settled in towns and cities in Massachusetts, New Jersey, New York, and Pennsylvania. Those who did not live in cities commonly worked on building canals and railroads. Irish women often worked as domestic servants for wealthy families, laboring 16 hours or more a day. Irish men in the cities could usually find only unskilled work. As an 1849 Boston health committee reported, low wages forced most Irish immigrants to live in poor housing.

Nevertheless, some immigrants enjoyed a new feeling of equality. Patrick Dunny wrote home to his family about this situation.

"People that cuts a great dash [style] at home . . . think it strange [in the United States] for the humble class of people to get as much respect as themselves."

—Patrick Dunny, quoted in *Who Built America?,* by Bruce Levine et al.

Many Germans also came to the United States during this time. In 1848, numbers of German people had revolted against harsh rule. Some educated Germans came to the United States to escape persecution during this time. However, most of them came for economic reasons. Working-class Germans began to leave as well. These immigrants came in search of new economic opportunity and freedom from government control. While most Irish immigrants were Catholics, German immigrant groups included Protestants, Catholics, and Jews.

Many German immigrants arrived in the United States with money in hand. Germans were more likely than the Irish to become farmers and to live in rural areas. They moved particularly to midwestern states such as Michigan, Ohio, and Wisconsin where more land was available than in the eastern United States. German immigrants—like the Irish—often had to take low-paying jobs, despite their skills. The *Chicago Daily Tribune* declared that the German immigrant population was "fitted to do the cheap . . . labor of the country."

✔ **Reading Check: Comparing and Contrasting** What factors—both similar and different—led Irish and German people to immigrate to the United States in the mid-1800s?

The Nativist Response

Industrialization and the waves of people from Europe greatly changed the American labor force. The chance of getting farmland in the Midwest drew many immigrants to this area. Industrial jobs in the Northeast drew many immigrants who filled the need for cheap labor in many towns and cities. These new workers fueled the local economies, which led to the creation of new jobs for clerks, merchants, supervisors, and professional workers.

Yet many native-born citizens feared losing their jobs to immigrants who might work for lower wages. Many native-born Americans also felt threatened by the different cultures and religions of immigrant groups. Before Catholic immigrants arrived, most people living in the United States were Protestants. American Protestants did not always trust Catholic immigrants because of long-standing conflicts between Catholics and Protestants in Europe. Americans who held such views and who opposed immigration were called **nativists.**

In the 1840s and 1850s some of these people became politically active. One of their main goals was to try to stir up anti-immigrant feeling. An 1844 election flyer gave Americans a warning.

"Look at the . . . thieves and vagabonds [tramps], roaming about our streets . . . monopolizing [taking] the business which properly belongs to our own native and true-born citizens."

—Election flyer, quoted in *Who Built America?,* by Bruce Levine et al.

Analyzing Primary Sources

Identifying Bias Why might a reader think that the author of this quotation is a nativist?

In 1849, nativists founded a secret society that became a political organization known as the **Know-Nothing Party**. The party was so named because when asked questions by outsiders, its members usually answered, "I know nothing." The Know-Nothings wanted to keep Catholics and immigrants out of public office. They also wanted immigrants to have to live in the United States for at least 21 years before they could become citizens. Party politicians had some success, winning several state elections during the 1850s. They also controlled the Massachusetts legislature for a short time.

✔ **Reading Check: Analyzing Information** How did anti-Catholicism contribute to the views of nativists and the creation of the Know-Nothing Party?

A protest by a nativist group led to this riot in Philadelphia in 1844. Similar riots took place elsewhere in the country.

THE GRANGER COLLECTION, NEW YORK

Urban Growth

American cities in the Northeast began to grow rapidly in the mid-1800s.

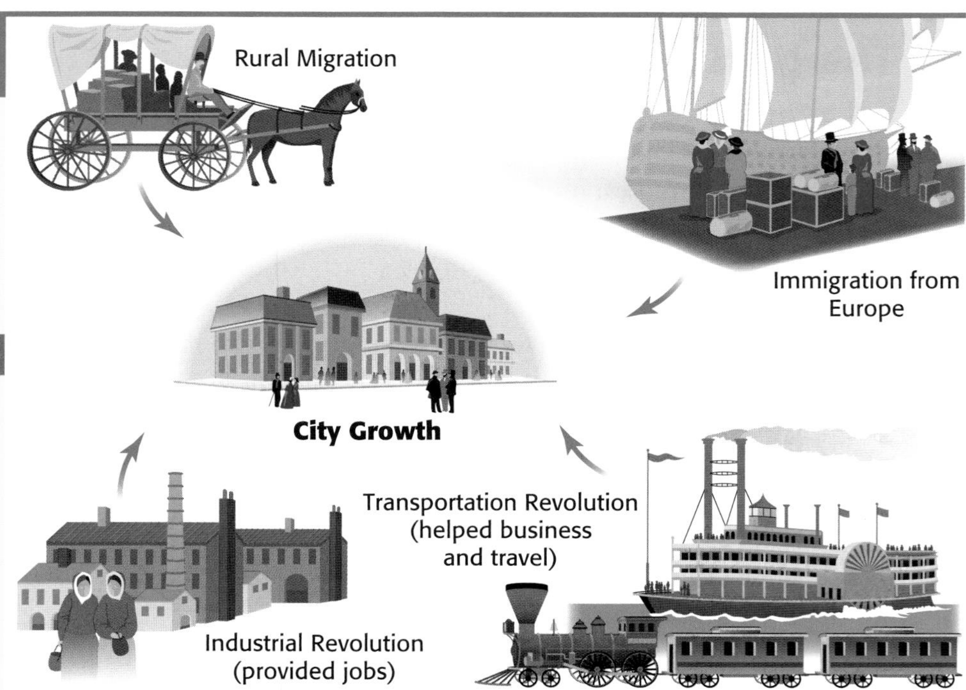

Visualizing History

1. **Geography** What factors contributed to the growth of American cities?
2. **Connecting to Today** How do you think these factors influence urban growth today?

The Growth of Cities

The Industrial Revolution led to the creation of many new jobs in U.S. cities. These city jobs drew immigrants as well as migrants from rural areas. The Transportation Revolution helped connect cities and made it easier for people to move to them. As a result of these two trends, U.S. cities grew rapidly during the mid-1800s. Cities in the northeastern and Middle Atlantic states grew the most. By the mid-1800s three quarters of the country's manufacturing jobs were in these areas.

The rise of industry and the growth of cities changed American life. Those who owned their own businesses or worked in skilled jobs benefited most from the changes. The families of these merchants, manufacturers, professionals, and master craftspeople made up a growing social class. This new **middle class** was a social and economic level between the wealthy and the poor.

In the growing cities, people found entertainment and an enriched cultural life. Many enjoyed visiting places such as libraries and clubs. In the early 1800s people also attended urban theaters. Favorite pastimes, such as bowling and playing cards, also provided recreation for urban residents.

Cities during this time were compact and crowded. Many people walked to work. Wagons carried goods down streets paved with stones, making a noisy, busy scene. One person noted that the professionals in New York City always had "a hurried walk."

✔ **Reading Check: Summarizing** How did the Industrial Revolution and the Transportation Revolution affect life in American cities?

That's Interesting!

Where are the police?
Can you imagine a city of more than 500,000 people without a permanent police force? Well, that's just what New York City was like before 1853. Before permanent forces were created, a volunteer night watch patrolled the city. During the daytime, an officer called a constable was on duty. He was paid a fee for each crime that he and his assistants helped stop. Private citizens were also asked to catch criminals. As cities grew larger, crime often grew out of hand. Many constables took bribes to ignore crimes. So the people of New York City created a paid police force.

Urban Problems

American cities in the early and mid-1800s faced many challenges as a result of their rapid growth. Because public and private transportation was limited, many city residents lived within a short distance of their workplaces. The crowded conditions meant that poor wage workers, members of the rising middle class, and the wealthy often lived near each other. Poor city dwellers often felt that they were treated unfairly by the rich—who in turn often accused the poor of being rude and violent. Disagreements between these social classes led to increasing conflict and sometimes even led to riots.

Other major problems in most large cities were the lack of safe housing and public services. Many people, particularly immigrants, could afford to live only in dirty, overcrowded buildings called **tenements.** Many cities did not have clean water, public health regulations, or clean ways to get rid of garbage and human waste. Diseases spread easily in these unhealthy conditions. In 1832 and 1849, for example, New York City suffered cholera epidemics that killed thousands of people.

Urban areas also became centers of criminal activity. Most cities—including New York City, Boston, and Philadelphia—had no permanent police force to fight crime. Instead, they used volunteer night watches, which offered little protection. Fire protection was often poor as well. Most cities were served by volunteer fire companies. Firefighters had to use hand pumps and buckets to put out fires. All of these conditions combined to make life difficult for many city residents.

During the 1800s poor city residents often lived in overcrowded tenement neighborhoods like this one.

✔ **Reading Check: Analyzing Information** What were some of the problems caused by urbanization?

Section 2 Review

go.hrw.com Homework Practice Online
keyword: SC3 HP13

1. **Define** and explain:
   - nativists
   - middle class
   - tenements

2. **Identify** and explain:
   - Know-Nothing Party

3. **Identifying Cause and Effect** Copy the graphic organizer below. Use it to identify the causes and effects of immigration and of urban growth.

Immigration	Urban Growth
Causes	Causes
↓	↓
Effects	Effects

4. **Finding the Main Idea**
   a. Why did many German and Irish people immigrate to the United States between 1840 and 1860?
   b. Why did nativists oppose immigration in the mid-1800s?

5. **Writing and Critical Thinking**
   Evaluating Imagine that you are visiting a northeastern American city in the mid-1800s. Create a postcard showing a city street scene. On the back of the card, write a short letter to a friend back home that describes the scene.
   Consider the following:
   - the benefits of city growth
   - the problems caused by city growth
   - immigration to cities

Section 3

Reforming Society

Read to Discover

1. How did reformers improve prisons in the early and mid-1800s?
2. Why did reformers start the temperance movement?
3. How did Americans' educational opportunities change during the early and mid-1800s?

Define

- temperance movement
- common-school movement

Identify

- Dorothea Dix
- Lyman Beecher
- Horace Mann
- Catharine Beecher
- Emma Willard
- Mary Lyon
- Samuel Gridley Howe
- Thomas Hopkins Gallaudet

WHY IT MATTERS TODAY

Many Americans today take part in reform efforts. Use CNNfyi.com or other **current events** sources to learn about current campaigns for efforts such as education reform. Record your findings in your journal.

Dorothea Dix helped improve the prison system in the United States.

The Story Continues

In 1841 Dorothea Dix visited a jail in Cambridge, Massachusetts, to teach a Sunday school class. What she saw there shocked her. Mentally ill women were jailed beside common criminals in dirty cells. Dix became angry at the conditions she found there and in other Massachusetts jails. As a result, she began to work to improve the care of mentally ill people across the country. She joined many other women reformers in the early and mid-1800s.

Prison Reform

The teachings of the Second Great Awakening had inspired many people to try to improve society. The growth of cities had caused social problems that many Americans wanted to correct. Often members of the growing middle class, particularly women, led these reform efforts. Many of these women did not work outside the home. Some hired domestic servants to help care for their households, which gave them more time to take part in reform groups.

Dorothea Dix was a middle-class reformer who helped change the prison system in the United States. After visiting prisons throughout

Massachusetts, Dix reported the terrible conditions. Mentally ill people were often jailed with criminals. Dix told the state legislature of her findings in this speech.

Dorothea Dix opposed the use of cages like this one to confine mentally ill people.

History Makers Speak

> **"I come to present the strong claims of suffering humanity . . . the miserable, the desolate [deserted], the outcast . . . to call your attention to the present state of insane persons confined within this Commonwealth, in cages, closets, cellars, stalls, pens! Chained, naked, beaten with rods, and lashed into obedience."**
>
> —Dorothea Dix, from *Memorial to the Legislature of Massachusetts*

In response, the government of Massachusetts created special, separate facilities for mentally ill people. The influence of Dix's work spread across the country. Eventually more than 100 state hospitals where mentally ill people received more professional care were built.

Other reformers protested the treatment of young offenders. Children who committed crimes such as begging or stealing were treated the same as adult criminals. Boston mayor Josiah Quincy asked that these young people be given different punishments than adults. In the 1820s several state and local governments founded reform schools for children who were once housed in prisons. In these schools children lived under strict rules. While living there, they received vocational training—learning useful skills through work.

Some reformers also tried to end the overcrowding and cruel conditions in prisons. Their efforts led to the creation of houses of correction. These institutions did not use punishment alone. Instead, they tried to change prisoners' behavior through education.

✔ **Reading Check: Summarizing** How did reformers try to change prisons in the early 1800s?

Reformers wanted to help prison inmates become productive citizens. These inmates are learning to make hats.

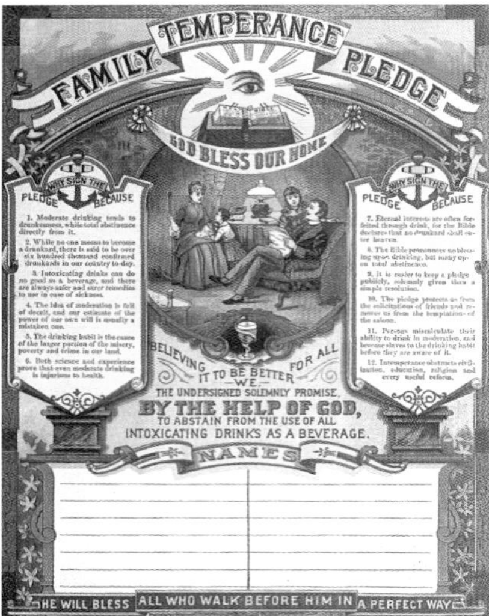

Interpreting the Visual Record

Temperance *Posters like this one urged people to stop drinking and thus help their families.* ***How do the scenes in this picture encourage people to give up drinking?***

Campaigning against Alcohol Abuse

A number of reformers also worked to prevent alcohol abuse. Many people believed that Americans were drinking liquor at an alarming rate in the early and mid-1800s. During the 1830s the average alcohol consumption per person was seven gallons a year. Abraham Lincoln recalled that in his youth liquor was an "angel of death." Many reformers believed alcohol abuse caused social problems such as family violence, poverty, and criminal behavior.

Americans' worries about the effects of alcohol led to the growth of a **temperance movement**. This social reform effort urged people to stop drinking hard liquor and limit drinking of beer and wine to small amounts. Various groups such as the American Temperance Society and the American Temperance Union helped spread this message. Minister **Lyman Beecher** spoke widely about the evils of alcohol. He said that people who drank alcohol were "neglecting the education of their families—and corrupting their morals."

Many people across the country were in favor of the temperance movement. However, some people believed that temperance alone would not fix social problems caused by alcohol abuse. People such as Neal Dow of Maine wanted to outlaw the sale of alcohol. Dow's efforts resulted in the Maine Law of 1846, which made selling alcohol illegal in the state. Banning the sale of alcohol became a major goal of reformers. By 1855 a dozen other states had passed laws like the one in Maine.

✔ Reading Check: **Finding the Main Idea** What were the goals of the temperance movement?

Education in America

Another problem facing America in the early 1800s was poor public education. As immigration increased, reformers argued that education would help Americans become good workers and citizens. Most families in the United States believed education was important. However, they did not expect their children to receive a great deal of formal schooling. Many children worked in factories or on farms to help support their families. Parents generally wanted their children to be able to read the Bible, write, and do simple math.

The availability of education varied a great deal throughout the United States. New England had the most schoolhouses, while the South and the West had the fewest. Most schoolteachers were untrained young men. They often taught for a short time before becoming farmers or practicing another trade. Teachers usually worked in small, poorly built schoolhouses, teaching students of many ages and abilities. As reformer Horace Mann wrote, students ranged from "infants just out of their cradles" to "men . . . enrolled in the militia."

PICTORIAL PRIMER

Mary reciting her Lesson.

Mary had learned to read and spell from the "Pictorial Primer" well. Could sew and knit a little too, and many other things could do, while her mother ever kind, would study to improve her mind, and in hymns of praise and love taught her to lift her heart above.

THE GRANGER COLLECTION, NEW YORK

N GALLERY OF AMERICAN ART, PHILLIPS ACADEMY

The textbooks most often used in public schools in the mid-1800s were the McGuffey's *Readers*. William Holmes McGuffey, an educator and Presbyterian minister, put together these textbooks. They were made up mostly of selections from British and American literature. McGuffey's *Readers* were used to teach students about moral and social values as well as literature and reading.

People from different backgrounds received very different educations in the United States. Rich people could send their children to private schools or hire private tutors. However, poor children could only attend public school. Girls could attend school, but parents kept them home more often than boys. The result was that fewer girls learned to read.

Interpreting the Visual Record

Early schools *Many children attended one-room schoolhouses in their local communities. Primers such as the one shown above were the most common textbooks.* ***How is the school shown here similar to or different from yours?***

The Common-School Movement

To teach children the necessary values and skills, reformers called for better schools. People in the **common-school movement** wanted all children educated in a common place, regardless of class or background. **Horace Mann** was the leading voice for education reform in the mid-1800s. He explained the idea of the common school.

> **"It is on this common platform that a general acquaintanceship [friendship] should be formed between the children of the same neighborhood. It is here that the affinities [bonds] of a common nature should unite them together."**
>
> —Horace Mann, quoted in *The Age of the Common School, 1830–1865,* by Frederick M. Binder

Analyzing Primary Sources

Supporting a Point of View Do you agree with Horace Mann's idea? Why or why not?

Mann became the first secretary of education for Massachusetts in 1837. The former lawyer and state legislator worked very hard—speaking, traveling, and writing—to help improve children's education. He doubled the state school budget and helped teachers earn better salaries. He also made the school year longer and founded the first school for teacher training.

ANDOVER, MA GIFT OF MAXIM KAROLIK, COURTESY, MUSEUM OF FINE ARTS BOSTON

Beyond grade school, classes for women were usually separated from classes for men.

Mann's ideas on education spread throughout the United States, and to Latin America and Europe as well. Mann won over many other educators by saying that "the common school, improved and energized, may become the most effective . . . of all the forces of civilization." Mann's work set the standard for education reform throughout the country.

✔ **Reading Check: Summarizing** Why did Horace Mann want to improve schools, and what did he accomplish?

Women's Education

The education reform movement also created greater opportunities for women. Before the 1820s few women in the United States could attend classes beyond grade school. **Catharine Beecher**, daughter of Lyman Beecher, grew up in a family committed to social reform. She became one of the most effective reformers of women's education in the early 1800s.

Catharine Beecher believed that women were better at teaching the moral lessons that made good citizens. "Let every woman become so . . . refined in intellect that her taste and judgment will be respected," she wrote. Beecher started an all-female academy in Hartford, Connecticut. She also wrote several important essays, including *On the Education of Female Teachers.*

In 1821 the citizens of Troy, New York, called on educator **Emma Willard** to found a college-level institution for women. Willard's Troy Female Seminary was the first school of its kind in the United States. At this school women studied many different subjects, ranging from mathematics to philosophy. Between 1821 and 1872, more than 12,000 women attended the school.

Several women's colleges opened in the 1830s. One of these colleges was Mount Holyoke Seminary in Massachusetts, founded by educator **Mary Lyon** in 1837. Lyon answered critics of her work by saying, "I am doing a great work, I cannot come down." In 1837 Oberlin College, located in Ohio, became the first co-educational college in the United States. This meant that both men and women were allowed to study there.

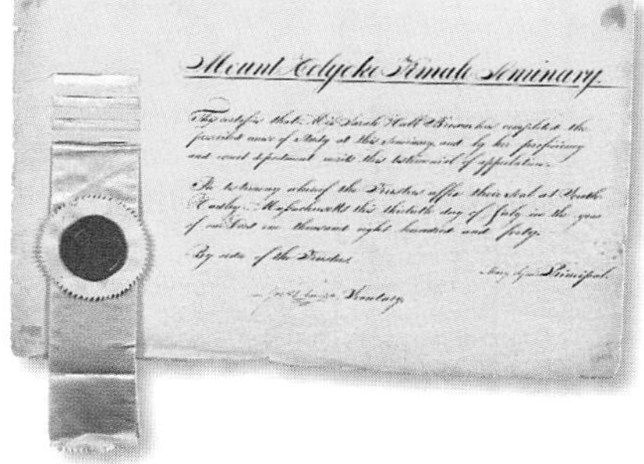

Mount Holyoke Seminary was one of the country's best schools for women.

African American Schools

Free African Americans also enjoyed some benefits of education reform. Although African Americans found more educational opportunities, they almost always went to separate schools from white students. The New York African Free School, which had opened in New York City in 1787, produced some notable scholars and leaders, such as Henry Highland Garnet.

The people of Philadelphia also supported the development of African American education. By 1800 the city had seven schools for black students. In 1820 Boston opened a separate elementary school for African American children. Also, in 1855 the city began allowing African Americans to attend white schools. However, James Thomas, a free African American in Tennessee, described the unequal education that many received in the 1830s.

> **"School was kept occasionally. It was regarded a great favor to have it allowed at any time. Each pupil or scholar paid one dollar per month. Often there was no school because there was no teacher."**
>
> —James Thomas, quoted in *From Slavery to Freedom*, by John Hope Franklin and Alfred A. Moss Jr.

Analyzing Primary Sources

Making Generalizations and Predictions How might citizens solve the problem with schooling that Thomas describes?

African Americans rarely attended college because only a few institutions of higher education would accept them. In 1835 Oberlin became the first to do so. Harvard later joined Oberlin in accepting African Americans. Black colleges also began to be founded in the 1840s. For example, in 1842 the Institute for Colored Youth and in 1849 Avery College were opened in Philadelphia.

As the examples above show, free African Americans did have some opportunities to attend school in the Midwest and the North. In the South, however, fewer free African Americans were able to obtain an education. Laws in the South prevented most slaves from receiving any education, in part due to southern whites' fears of potential slave rebellions.

✔ **Reading Check: Comparing** What educational challenges did women and African Americans face in the 1800s?

This typewriter produced raised dots representing the alphabet created by Louis Braille for visually impaired people.

Teaching People with Disabilities

Efforts to improve education also helped people with special needs. **Samuel Gridley Howe** worked to improve the education of visually impaired Americans. Howe also worked for education reform, prison reform, and care for mentally ill people. In 1831 Howe opened a school called the Perkins Institution in Massachusetts for people with visual impairments. He trained the school's workers to address the particular needs of the students. He also traveled to 17 other states to talk about teaching visually impaired people. Howe ran the Perkins Institution for 45 years. During this time he showed that people with visual impairments could lead economically and socially productive lives.

After graduating from Yale College, **Thomas Hopkins Gallaudet** worked to improve the education and lives of people who were hearing impaired. He went to Europe for two years to study ways to teach such students. In 1817, after he returned to the United States, Gallaudet founded the first free American school for people with hearing impairments in Hartford, Connecticut. He served as the school's principal until 1830. After he retired from the school, Gallaudet became a professor of philosophy of education at New York University. He called for special schools to train teachers and wrote textbooks for children and people with hearing impairments. Gallaudet University in Washington, D.C., was named in his honor. Thus, school reformers helped people in many parts of American society during the early and mid-1800s.

✔ **Reading Check: Summarizing** What kinds of schools were founded for people with disabilities?

Section 3 Review

go.hrw.com Homework Practice Online
keyword: SC3 HP13

1. **Define** and explain:
   - temperance movement
   - common-school movement

2. **Identify** and explain:
   - Dorothea Dix
   - Lyman Beecher
   - Horace Mann
   - Catharine Beecher
   - Emma Willard
   - Mary Lyon
   - Samuel Gridley Howe
   - Thomas Hopkins Gallaudet

3. **Categorizing** Copy the chart below. Use it to match reform leaders with their respective movements and the accomplishments of each movement.

Movement	Leaders	Accomplishments
Prison & Mental Health Reform		
Temperance		
Education		

4. **Finding the Main Idea**
   a. Describe the ways that reformers changed prisons and the treatment of the mentally ill.
   b. What did members of the temperance movement try to achieve?

5. **Writing and Critical Thinking**
   Summarizing Imagine that you are Horace Mann visiting a foreign country. Write a speech that describes the ways in which many more Americans gained the opportunity to receive an education in the early and mid-1800s.
   Consider the following:
   - education for women
   - education for African Americans
   - educating people with disabilities

Section 4

The Movement to End Slavery

Read to Discover

1. Why did some Americans become abolitionists?
2. How did abolitionists spread the movement's message?
3. Why were some Americans against abolition?

Define

- abolition
- emancipation

Identify

- Robert Finley
- American Colonization Society
- David Walker
- William Lloyd Garrison
- *The Liberator*
- American Anti-Slavery Society
- Angelina and Sarah Grimké
- Frederick Douglass
- Underground Railroad
- Harriet Tubman

Why It Matters Today

Citizens still organize to seek changes in laws. Use CNNfyi.com or other **current events** sources to learn more about a group trying to change a law. Record your findings in your journal.

The Story Continues

During the mid-1800s John Fairfield helped enslaved African Americans escape to freedom in the North. Fairfield traveled throughout the South under different disguises. Sometimes he posed as a slaveholder. Other times he dressed as a trader, or a peddler. Once he led 28 slaves to freedom by disguising them as part of a funeral procession. Most antislavery activists did not take such risks. However, they all helped a movement that grew much stronger in the mid-1800s.

Newspapers often published advertisements for the capture of runaway slaves.

Abolition

During the 1830s Americans who had been against slavery for years began to take organized action. They formed a movement to support **abolition**, or a complete end to slavery, in the United States. Some of these people wanted immediate **emancipation**. Through emancipation, all enslaved African Americans would be freed from slavery.

GLOBAL CONNECTIONS

British Abolitionists

Many American abolitionists looked to Great Britain for examples of how to fight slavery. Britain had outlawed the slave trade in 1807. In 1834 a law abolishing slavery in the British Empire went into effect. However, British antislavery work did not stop there. In 1840 the British and Foreign Anti-Slavery Society held the World's Anti-Slavery Convention in London. Convention members asked the British government to pressure other countries to end slavery as well. In the mid-1800s British warships began stopping slave ships in the Atlantic and Indian Oceans and freeing the slaves they found. **How did British abolitionists try to end slavery outside of Britain?**

Abolitionists were in the minority in the United States, but they were very vocal. They came from many different backgrounds and wanted to ban slavery for different reasons. The Quakers were among the first groups to challenge slavery on religious grounds. The Quakers had begun working for abolition during colonial times. Some ministers of the Second Great Awakening also believed that slavery was morally wrong. People such as Charles Grandison Finney and Theodore Weld moved many others to take up the cause of abolition. Other abolitionists pointed to the ideals of the Declaration of Independence. They reminded people that the American Revolution supported equality.

Abolitionists disagreed about what ending slavery should mean for African Americans. Some abolitionists thought that African Americans should be treated the same as white Americans. Many others, however, opposed full social and political equality for African Americans.

Some antislavery reformers wanted to send freed African Americans to Africa to start new colonies there. They thought that this would prevent conflicts between different races in the United States. Many Americans supported this view. J. C. Galloway of North Carolina described this idea. "It is impossible for us [whites] to be happy, if . . . they [freed African Americans] are to remain among us," he wrote.

In 1817 a minister named **Robert Finley** started the **American Colonization Society**. Five years later the society founded the colony of Liberia on the west coast of Africa. About 12,000 African Americans eventually settled in Liberia. However, many who were once in favor of colonization later turned against it. Some African Americans also opposed the colonization movement. **David Walker** was one such person. In an 1829 essay, *Appeal to the Colored Citizens of the World*, Walker explained why he was against colonization.

Analyzing Primary Sources

Identifying Points of View
Why was Walker against colonization?

"The greatest riches in all America have arisen from our blood and tears: And they [whites] will drive us from our property and homes, which we have earned with our blood."

—David Walker, quoted in *From Slavery to Freedom*, by John Hope Franklin and Alfred A. Moss Jr.

✔ **Reading Check: Contrasting** How did some abolitionists' goals differ?

This antislavery medallion was first used by an antislavery society in London.

Spreading the Abolitionist Message

Abolitionists found many ways to further their cause. Some abolitionists went on speaking tours or wrote newspaper articles and pamphlets. Editor Horace Greeley became a strong voice in the movement through the *New York Tribune*. Others, like John Greenleaf Whittier, spread the abolitionist message through their poetry and literature. **William Lloyd Garrison** published an abolitionist newspaper. This newspaper, ***The Liberator***, first appeared in 1831. Garrison became one of the most outspoken and controversial leaders of the movement. In 1833 Garrison helped found the **American Anti-Slavery Society**. This group wanted immediate emancipation and racial equality for African Americans. Garrison later became the group's president.

Both *The Liberator* and the Anti-Slavery Society relied on the support of free African Americans. Members of the society spread antislavery literature throughout the North and Midwest. They also sent petitions to Congress. In these petitions, they asked for an end to all federal support of slavery. Then in 1840 the American Anti-Slavery Society split. One group wanted immediate freedom for enslaved African Americans. This group also believed women should take part in the abolition movement on an equal basis with men. The other group wanted slower emancipation and a limited role for women.

Angelina and Sarah Grimké, two white southern women, became well-known antislavery activists of the 1830s. The sisters were members of a slaveholding family in South Carolina. They did not share their parents' support of slavery, however. Instead, they moved to Philadelphia and joined the abolition movement. Angelina Grimké tried to bring other white southern women to the cause. She wrote a pamphlet titled *Appeal to the Christian Women of the South* in 1836.

"I know you do not make the laws, but . . . if you really suppose you can do nothing to overthrow slavery, you are greatly mistaken. . . . Try to persuade your husband, father, brothers and sons that slavery is a crime against God and man."

—Angelina Grimké, quoted in *The Grimké Sisters from South Carolina,* edited by Gerda Lerner

Analyzing Primary Sources

Evaluating Sources How did Grimké believe women could help bring an end to slavery?

This essay was quite popular in the North. As a result, the Grimké sisters became the first women to speak before male and female audiences of the Anti-Slavery Society. The sisters gave lectures and formed dozens of female antislavery societies. In 1839 they wrote *American Slavery As It Is* with Angelina's husband, abolitionist leader Theodore Weld. This book was one of the most important antislavery writings of the time.

✔ **Reading Check: Finding the Main Idea** How did the members of the Anti-Slavery Society fight slavery?

William Lloyd Garrison's The Liberator *became one of the most widely read abolitionist newspapers in the North.*

Narrative of the Life of Frederick Douglass

In 1845 Frederick Douglass published the first of three autobiographies describing his life as a slave and his abolitionist efforts once he gained his freedom. In the following excerpt he explains the purpose of his autobiography.

> Sincerely and earnestly hoping that this little book may do something toward throwing light on the American slave system, and **hastening**[1] the glad day of deliverance to the millions of my **brethren**[2] in bonds—faithfully relying on the power of truth, love, and justice, for success in my humble efforts—and solemnly pledging myself anew to the sacred cause,—I **subscribe**[3] myself, Frederick Douglass.

[1]**hastening:** quickening
[2]**brethren:** brothers and sisters
[3]**subscribe:** pledge

Understanding What You Read
Literature and History Why did Frederick Douglass write his narrative?

African Americans Fight against Slavery

Many former slaves were very active in the antislavery movement. **Frederick Douglass**, who escaped from slavery at age 20, became one of the most important African American leaders of the 1800s. Douglass had secretly learned to read and write as a boy. In addition, his public-speaking skills greatly impressed the members of the Anti-Slavery Society. In 1841 they asked Douglass to give regular lectures. Speaking at a Fourth of July celebration in 1852, he captured the audience's attention with his powerful voice.

"The blessings in which you, this day, rejoice, are not enjoyed in common. . . . This Fourth of July is *yours*, not *mine*. You may rejoice, I must mourn."

—Frederick Douglass, quoted in *From Slavery to Freedom*, by John Hope Franklin and Alfred A. Moss Jr.

Douglass went on many speaking tours in the United States and Europe. He also published a pro-abolition newspaper called *North Star* and wrote several autobiographies.

African Americans such as Charles Remond and Sojourner Truth also helped the abolitionist cause. Truth became famous in the antislavery movement for her dramatic and fiery speeches. In 1842 Remond asked the Massachusetts legislature to end racial discrimination in the state. "It is JUSTICE I stand here to claim, and not FAVOR for either complexion [skin color]," he declared.

Other African Americans wrote slave narratives about their experiences. In 1861 abolitionists helped publish *Incidents in the Life of a Slave Girl* by Harriet Jacobs, one of the few slave narratives written by a woman. William Wells Brown wrote an antislavery play and an antislavery novel called *Clotel.* These writers and many other African Americans contributed significantly to the abolitionist cause.

The Underground Railroad

By the 1830s a loosely organized group had begun helping slaves escape from the South. Free African Americans, former slaves, and a few white abolitionists worked together to create the **Underground Railroad**. This network of people arranged transportation and hiding places for fugitives, or escaped slaves. Often wearing disguises, fugitives moved along the "railroad" at night, guided by the North Star. They stopped to rest during the day at various "stations." These stations were the homes of abolitionists known as conductors. The conductors hid the fugitives in barns, attics, and other secret locations. They would then send word to the next station farther north that they were on the way.

The most famous and daring conductor on the Underground Railroad was **Harriet Tubman**. When Tubman herself escaped in 1849, she left behind her husband, parents, sisters, and brothers. She returned to the South 19 times. Tubman successfully led her family and more than 300 other slaves to freedom. She never lost a fugitive. At one time the reward for Tubman's capture climbed to $40,000. Historians estimate that 40,000 slaves used the Underground Railroad to reach freedom between 1810 and 1850.

✔ **Reading Check: Analyzing Information** How did free African Americans and former slaves try to end slavery?

Harriet Tubman

The Underground Railroad

Interpreting Maps The Underground Railroad helped thousands of slaves escape to freedom.

Skills Assessment

1. **Places and Regions** Through which states might slaves pass if they were escaping from Alabama to Ohio?
2. **Analyzing Information** To what destinations besides the northern states did slaves escape?

Southern defenders of slavery used images like this one to argue that American slaves enjoyed a better life than British factory workers.

Opposition to Abolition

Many white northerners did not believe in equal treatment for African Americans. Newspaper editors and politicians often warned that freed slaves would move north and take jobs from white workers. Leaders of the abolitionist movement received threats. Some northerners joined violent mobs that attacked African Americans and burned antislavery literature.

The federal government also stood in the way of the abolitionist movement. Between 1836 and 1844 the U.S. House of Representatives used a Gag Rule to prevent discussion of the thousands of antislavery petitions it received. This rule effectively violated the First Amendment right of citizens to petition the government. But southern congressmen were against any debate about slavery, and many northern congressmen just wanted to avoid the issue.

Many white southerners thought slavery was a vital part of the South's economy and culture. White southerners also generally believed that outsiders had no business interfering with their way of life. After Nat Turner's Rebellion in 1831, open talk of the slavery question disappeared in the South. Abolitionists like the Grimké sisters chose to leave.

Some white southerners said slavery protected African Americans. Virginia lawyer George Fitzhugh said that freed slaves would "freeze or starve" in the North. Racism, fear, and the South's economic dependence on slavery made the idea of emancipation unpopular in the South.

✔ **Reading Check: Identifying Points of View** Why did some Americans oppose emancipation?

Section 4 Review

go.hrw.com Homework Practice Online
keyword: SC3 HP13

1. **Define** and explain:
   - abolition
   - emancipation

2. **Identify** and explain:
   - Robert Finley
   - American Colonization Society
   - David Walker
   - William Lloyd Garrison
   - *The Liberator*
   - American Anti-Slavery Society
   - Angelina and Sarah Grimké
   - Frederick Douglass
   - Underground Railroad
   - Harriet Tubman

3. **Analyzing Information** Copy the graphic organizer below. Use it to explain why some Americans joined the abolitionist movement and the methods they used to fight slavery.

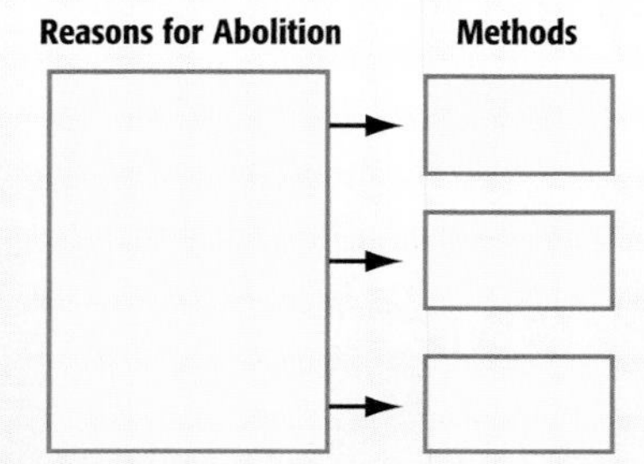

4. **Finding the Main Idea**
   a. For what reasons did many Americans in the North and the South oppose abolition?
   b. How might the issue of slavery lead to conflict as the United States expanded?

5. **Writing and Critical Thinking**
   Supporting a Point of View Imagine that you are a member of one of the antislavery societies in 1840. Create a poster announcing your group's next meeting.
   Consider the following:
   - the goals of the abolitionist movement
   - why Americans should become active in the movement
   - ways or methods to persuade other Americans to join the cause

Section 5

Women's Rights

Read to Discover

1. How did the abolitionist movement affect the women's rights movement?
2. What were some goals of the women's rights movement?
3. What was the purpose of the Seneca Falls Convention, and why was it significant?

Identify

- Elizabeth Cady Stanton
- Lucretia Mott
- Seneca Falls Convention
- Declaration of Sentiments
- Lucy Stone
- Susan B. Anthony

WHY IT MATTERS TODAY

The women's rights movement is still active in the United States today. Use CNNfyi.com or other **current events** sources to learn about the important roles women play in America today. These roles include positions in business, government, and society in general. Record your findings in your journal.

The Story Continues

In February 1838 Angelina Grimké nervously prepared to speak before the Massachusetts legislature. "I never was so near fainting under the tremendous pressure of feeling," she wrote her future husband. "My heart almost died within me." Grimké planned to present antislavery petitions to the 1,500 people gathered. However, she felt a great responsibility. She was the first woman to speak before a legislature in the United States. As she spoke, Grimké bravely addressed both the issue of abolition and the question of women's rights.

THE GRANGER COLLECTION, NEW YORK

Angelina Grimké was one of the first women to speak on behalf of the American Anti-Slavery Society.

The Influence of Abolition

Many female abolitionists, such as the Grimké sisters and Sojourner Truth, later became part of the women's rights movement of the mid-1800s. These women found that they had to defend their right to speak in public, particularly when a woman addressed both men and women. For example, members of the press, the clergy, and even some male abolitionists criticized the Grimké sisters for speaking in public. These critics believed that women should not give public speeches, and they did not want women to leave their traditional female roles. However, the Grimkés had a different view. They told their critics that women had a moral duty to lead the antislavery movement.

In 1838 Sarah Grimké published a pamphlet arguing for equal rights for women. She titled the essay "Letters on the Equality of the Sexes and the Condition of Women."

Analyzing Primary Sources

Identifying Points of View Using your own words, explain how Sarah Grimké wants women to be treated.

"I ask no favors for my sex. . . . All I ask our brethren [brothers] is, that they will take their feet from off our necks, and permit us to stand upright on that ground which God designed us to occupy."

—Sarah Grimké, quoted in *The Grimké Sisters from South Carolina,* edited by Gerda Lerner

Sarah Grimké also argued for equal educational opportunities. She pointed out laws that negatively affected women and called for equal pay for equal work.

Sojourner Truth was another powerful speaker for both abolition and women's rights. Writer Harriet Beecher Stowe said that she had never spoken "with anyone who had more . . . personal presence than this woman." Truth stood six feet tall and was a confident speaker. She often recalled her experiences as a slave. In 1851 she gave a speech at a women's rights convention. In her speech, she challenged the audience members not to think of women as the "weaker sex."

"That man over there says that women need to be helped into carriages and lifted over ditches, and to have the best place everywhere. Nobody ever helps me into carriages or over mud puddles, or gives me any best place. . . . Look at me! I have ploughed and planted and . . . no man could head [outwork] me. And ain't I a woman?"

—Sojourner Truth, quoted in *A History of Women in America,* by Carol Hymowitz and Michaele Weissman

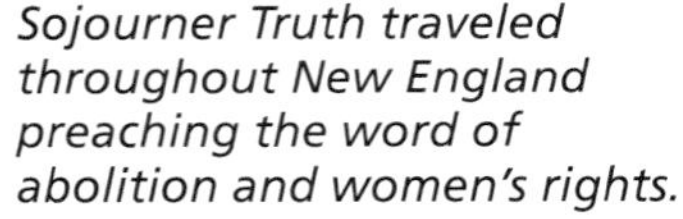
Sojourner Truth traveled throughout New England preaching the word of abolition and women's rights.

Truth and other supporters of the women's rights movement were determined to be heard.

✔ **Reading Check: Identifying Cause and Effect** Why did some people oppose women's efforts in the abolitionist movement, and how did this opposition affect the women's rights movement?

Women's Rights

Publications about women's rights first appeared in the United States shortly after the American Revolution. However, women's concerns did not become a national movement for many more years. This change took place when women took part in reform and abolition efforts. Other social changes also led to the rise of the movement. Women took advantage of better educational opportunities. They also learned how to organize more effectively by working together in reform groups. Some men also took part in the struggle for women's rights. Many activists were upset that women could not vote. In addition, married women in many states had little or no control over their own property.

Many people, both men and women, did not agree with some of the goals of the women's rights movement. Many women believed that they did not need any new rights. They said that women were not unequal to men, only different. Some critics believed that women should not try to work for social changes in public. In other words, they should work for change at home from within their families. "Let her not look away from her own little family circle for the means of producing moral and social reforms," wrote T. S. Arthur. His advice appeared in a popular women's magazine called *The Lady at Home.*

Some people also thought that women did not have the physical or mental strength to survive without men's protection. Such people believed that a woman needed to be under a man's authority. They also believed that her husband should control her property. Despite this strong opposition, women still pursued their goal of greater rights.

✔ **Reading Check: Summarizing** Why were some people against the goals of the women's movement?

The Seneca Falls Convention

In 1840 **Elizabeth Cady Stanton** attended the World's Anti-Slavery Convention in London, England, while on her honeymoon. Stanton had to watch the meeting separately from her husband, however, because women could not participate. Women in attendance had to sit in a separate gallery of the convention hall, hidden from the men's view by a curtain. In protest, William Lloyd Garrison sat with them, refusing to join a proceeding that did not allow women's equal participation.

This treatment of women abolitionists angered Stanton and her new friend, **Lucretia Mott**. Stanton later wrote that they "resolved to hold a convention as soon as we returned home." Mott and Stanton planned to "form a society to advance the rights of women." Eight years passed, however, before Stanton and Mott sent out a notice announcing the **Seneca Falls Convention**. The meeting, which began on July 19, 1848, in Seneca Falls, New York, launched an organized women's rights movement. This convention was the first public meeting about women's rights to be held in the United States.

To present their case, the convention organizers wrote a **Declaration of Sentiments** based on the language of the Declaration of Independence. The document detailed their beliefs about social injustice toward women. Some 100 people signed the Declaration of Sentiments.

Some 240 people attended the Seneca Falls Convention, including some men such as Frederick Douglass. Most of these reformers also worked in the temperance or antislavery movements. In addition,

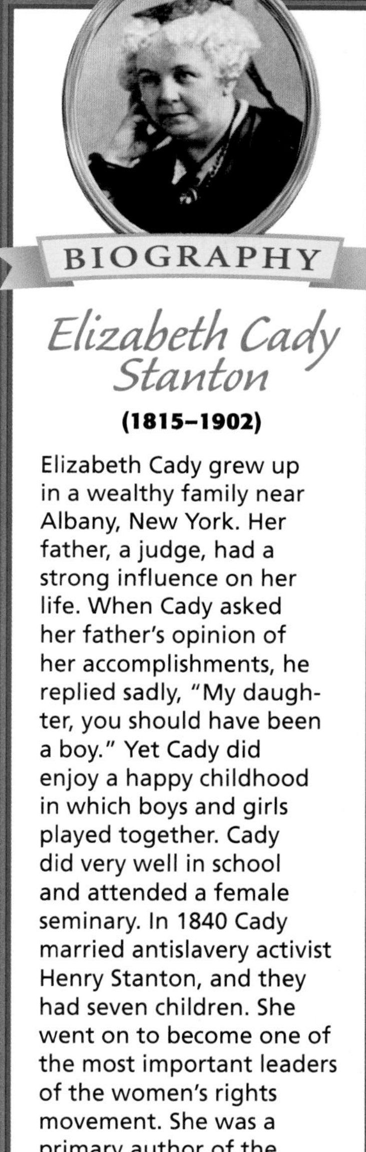

BIOGRAPHY

Elizabeth Cady Stanton

(1815–1902)

Elizabeth Cady grew up in a wealthy family near Albany, New York. Her father, a judge, had a strong influence on her life. When Cady asked her father's opinion of her accomplishments, he replied sadly, "My daughter, you should have been a boy." Yet Cady did enjoy a happy childhood in which boys and girls played together. Cady did very well in school and attended a female seminary. In 1840 Cady married antislavery activist Henry Stanton, and they had seven children. She went on to become one of the most important leaders of the women's rights movement. She was a primary author of the Declaration of Sentiments. **What was significant about Stanton's childhood?**

several women who worked in nearby factories participated in the convention as well. For example, 19-year-old Charlotte Woodward signed the Declaration of Sentiments because she was tired of making gloves for low wages. Woodward earned pennies that she then had to turn over to her father.

Women had spoken out for their rights earlier. However, the Seneca Falls Convention marked the first time that women in the United States organized as a group to promote their rights.

✔ **Reading Check: Finding the Main Idea** Why was the Seneca Falls Convention important?

Historical Document

1848 Seneca Falls Declaration of Sentiments

THE GRANGER COLLECTION, NEW YORK

A woman speaking before the Seneca Falls Convention

On July 19 and 20, 1848, people gathered in Seneca Falls, New York, to discuss women's rights. Elizabeth Cady Stanton and Lucretia Mott had organized the event. They also helped write the Declaration of Sentiments. Signed by some 100 people, this document helped shape the future of the women's rights movement.

We hold these truths to be **self-evident**:[1] that all men and women are created equal; that they are **endowed**[2] by their Creator with certain **inalienable**[3] rights; that among these are life, liberty, and the pursuit of happiness. . . .

The history of mankind is a history of repeated injuries and **usurpations**[4] on the part of man toward woman, having in direct object the establishment of an absolute **tyranny**[5] over her. To prove this, let facts be submitted to a **candid**[6] world.

He has never permitted her to exercise her inalienable right to . . . [the vote]. . . .

He has taken from her all right in property, even to the wages she earns. . . .

He has **monopolized**[7] nearly all the profitable employments, and from those she is permitted to follow, she receives but a scanty **remuneration**.[8] He closes against her all the avenues to wealth and distinction which he considers most honorable to himself. . . .

He has denied her the **facilities**[9] for obtaining a thorough education, all colleges being closed against her. . . .

He has endeavored, in every way that he could, to destroy her confidence in her own powers, to lessen her self-respect, and to make her willing to lead a dependent and **abject**[10] life. . . .

Resolved, That woman is man's equal—was intended to be so by the Creator, and the highest good of the race demands that she should be recognized as such.

---

[1]**self-evident:** obvious
[2]**endowed:** provided
[3]**inalienable:** permanent
[4]**usurpations:** seizures
[5]**tyranny:** unjust rule
[6]**candid:** fair
[7]**monopolized:** taken control of
[8]**remuneration:** payment
[9]**facilities:** means
[10]**abject:** hopeless

Analyzing Primary Sources

1. What are some of the injustices that the declaration describes?
2. How is the Declaration of Sentiments modeled after the Declaration of Independence?
3. Are the rights demanded in the declaration granted to women in the United States today? Explain your answer.

The Continuing Struggle

Although women's rights activists encountered many difficulties, they continued working together after the Seneca Falls Convention. **Lucy Stone** and Susan B. Anthony, along with Elizabeth Cady Stanton, became the most important leaders. Lucy Stone was a well-known member of the Anti-Slavery Society. She soon took on the cause of women's rights as well. During the early years of the women's rights movement, Stone became known as a gifted speaker.

Susan B. Anthony brought strong organizational skills to the women's rights movement. Anthony was largely responsible for turning the fight for women's rights into a political movement. As a single woman who supported herself, women's economic struggles were of particular importance to her. Anthony argued that women and men should receive equal pay for equal work and that women should be allowed to enter traditionally male professions such as law.

In 1979 Susan B. Anthony became the first American woman to be depicted on U.S. currency.

Anthony led a campaign to change laws regarding women's property rights. She wrote in her diary that no woman could be free without "a purse of her own." Anthony organized a network to cover every area of New York State. She collected more than 6,000 signatures to petition for a new property rights law. In 1860 New York finally gave married women ownership of their wages and property. Other states in the Northeast and Midwest followed with similar laws. Other major reforms, such as the right to vote, were not achieved at this time. However, more American women than ever before became actively involved in efforts to attain equal rights.

✔ **Reading Check: Comparing** What were some of the contributions of women's rights leaders Lucy Stone and Susan B. Anthony?

Section 5 Review

go.hrw.com **Homework Practice Online**
keyword: SC3 HP13

1. **Identify** and explain:
   - Elizabeth Cady Stanton
   - Lucretia Mott
   - Seneca Falls Convention
   - Declaration of Sentiments
   - Lucy Stone
   - Susan B. Anthony

2. **Summarizing** Copy the graphic organizer below. Use it to explain how the women's rights movement grew out of the abolitionist movement.

   Abolitionist Movement → [ ] → Women's Rights Movement

3. **Finding the Main Idea**
   a. What were the main goals of the women's rights movement?
   b. Why did Elizabeth Cady Stanton and Lucretia Mott organize the Seneca Falls Convention, and what did it achieve?

4. **Writing and Critical Thinking**
   Supporting a Point of View Imagine that you are a women's rights activist in the mid-1800s. Write an editorial responding to criticism of the women's rights movement.
   Consider the following:
   - women speaking in public
   - women's traditional roles in society
   - husbands' control of their wives' property

Chapter 13 Review

The Chapter at a Glance

Examine the visual summary of the chapter below. Then create a set of flash cards listing the key leaders of each reform movement on one side of the card and one key accomplishment on the other side. Use the flash cards to review the chapter material with a classmate.

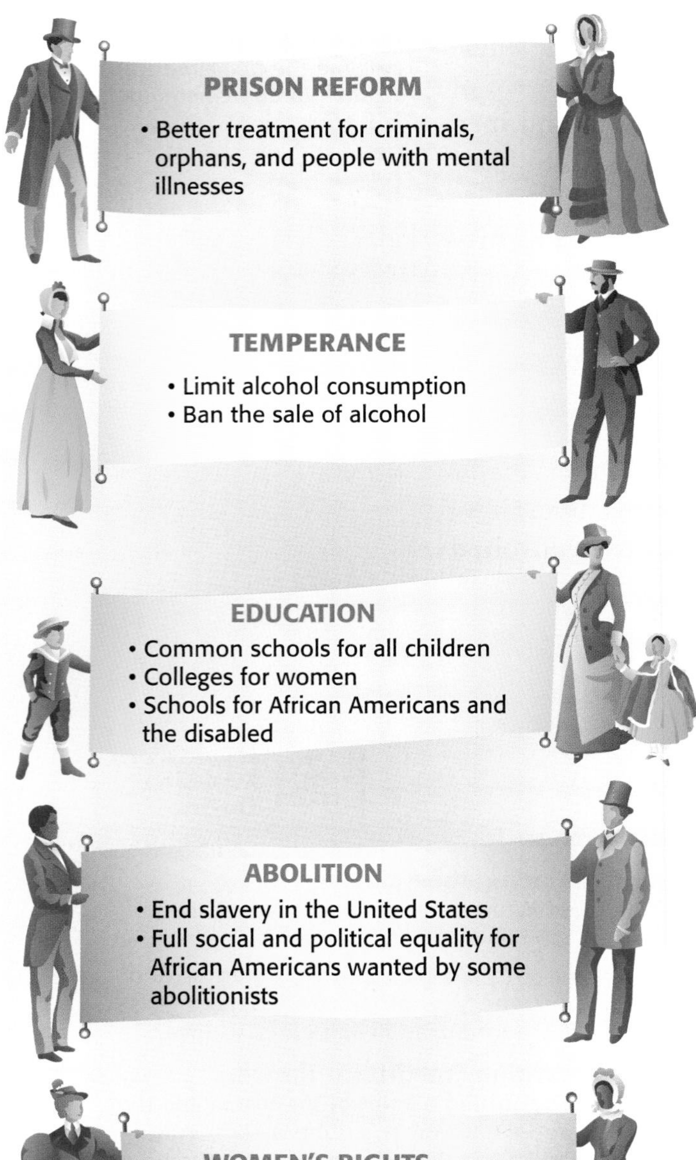

Identifying People and Ideas

Use the following terms or people in historically significant sentences.

1. Second Great Awakening
2. Henry David Thoreau
3. nativists
4. tenements
5. Horace Mann
6. abolition
7. Angelina Grimké
8. Frederick Douglass
9. Elizabeth Cady Stanton
10. Seneca Falls Convention

Understanding Main Ideas

Section 1 *(Pages 390–394)*

1. What did the transcendentalists and members of utopian communities believe?
2. Who were some of the most important artists and authors of the romantic movement?

Section 2 *(Pages 395–399)*

3. What caused the increase in immigration to the United States during the mid-1800s?

Section 3 *(Pages 400–406)*

4. What social issues did reformers address in the early to mid-1800s?

Section 4 *(Pages 407–412)*

5. Why did people join the abolitionist movement, and what were their goals?

Section 5 *(Pages 413–417)*

6. What were the major goals of the women's rights movement?

You Be the Historian— Reviewing Themes

1. **Culture** How did the Second Great Awakening affect the reform movements of the mid-1800s?
2. **Economics** How did U.S. immigration between 1840 and 1860 affect the economy?
3. **Citizenship** Choose three of the following people and explain how they worked to end slavery: Robert Finley, David Walker, William Lloyd Garrison, Angelina and Sarah Grimké, Frederick Douglass, and Harriet Tubman.

Thinking Critically

1. **Analyzing Information** How did cities change in the mid-1800s, and what caused these changes?
2. **Identifying Points of View** Why did nativists want to restrict immigration to the United States?
3. **Drawing Inferences and Conclusions** How did the freedoms protected by the First Amendment aid the Second Great Awakening and social reform movements?

Social Studies Skills Workshop

Interpreting Graphs

Study the graph below. Then use the information on the graph to help you answer the questions that follow.

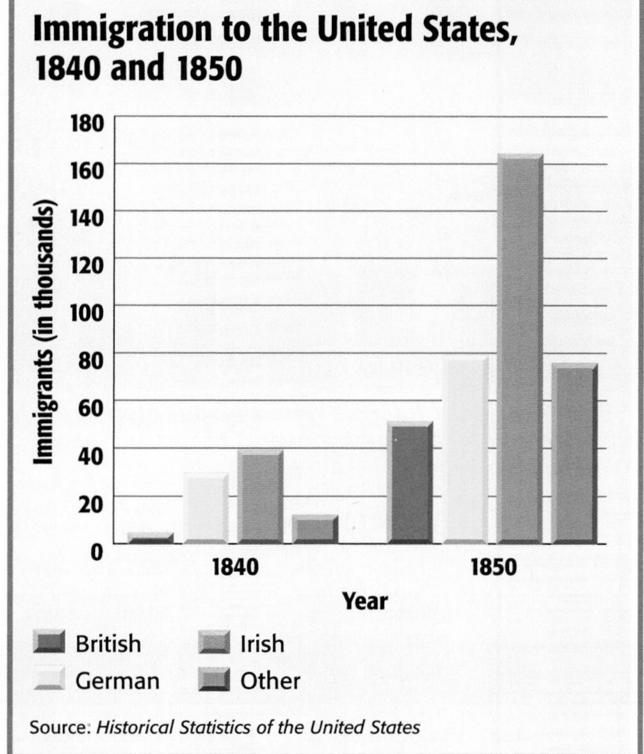

Source: *Historical Statistics of the United States*

1. Based on your knowledge of the period, what events could have led to the increase in the number of German and Irish immigrants to the United States between 1840 and 1850?

2. Which of the following statements was not true for 1850?
   a. The Irish were the largest group of immigrants to the United States.
   b. The number of German immigrants rose greatly from 1840.
   c. There were fewer immigrants from Britain than in 1840.
   d. There were nearly 80,000 immigrants from "Other" countries in 1850.

Analyzing Primary Sources

Read the following quote by abolitionist William Lloyd Garrison, then answer the questions that follow.

> **"I will be as harsh as truth, and as uncompromising as justice. On this subject, I do not wish to think, to speak, or write, with moderation. . . . I am in earnest—I will not equivocate [lie]—I will not excuse—I will not retreat a single inch—AND I WILL BE HEARD."**

3. What is the best interpretation for what Garrison means by, "I will be as harsh as truth, and as uncompromising as justice"?
   a. He will treat everyone equally.
   b. He will be truthful and fair in what he writes about slavery.
   c. He will pursue abolition no matter how long it takes or whom he offends.
   d. He will punish slaveholders for their crimes.

4. Based on your knowledge of the period, why do you think Garrison felt he needed to state his determination so forcefully?

5. Whom do you think Garrison was addressing when he made the statement above?

Alternative Assessment

Building Your Portfolio

American History

Linking to Community

As a group, select an issue that you think is important to your community today. Plan a campaign to educate the public about this issue. Assign each group member one of the following roles—artist, speechwriter, or presenter. The artists should design a poster explaining the issue. The speechwriters should write a script for a speech about the issue. Finally, the presenters should formally deliver the speech and artwork to the class.

internet connect

go.hrw.com

Internet Activity: go.hrw.com
keyword: SC3 CF13

Access the Internet through the HRW Go site to learn about the Astor Place riot of 1849 and how the riot reflected developments in drama and urban society in the 1800s. Then imagine that radio had been invented during this time and conduct a radio broadcast with one of the actors or witnesses of the riot. Include direct references to your research in our broadcast.

CHAPTER

14 Westward Expansion and War (1790–1860)

Moses Austin played an important role in encouraging American settlers to move to Texas.

By the 1810s fur trappers were already entering the Rocky Mountains region in search of furs and new trading partners.

UNITED STATES

1821 Moses Austin becomes the first American to receive a contract to bring settlers to Texas.

1825 Fur trappers in the Far West hold their first large trade meeting.

1835 The Texas Revolution against Mexico begins.

1790 **1810** **1820** **1830**

1792 British naval officer George Vancouver explores the northwest coast of North America.

1821 Mexico wins its independence from Spain.

1827 The United States and Great Britain agree to continue joint occupation of Oregon Country.

1830 Mexico makes it illegal to bring slaves into Texas.

WORLD

This mural celebrates the efforts of Father José María Morelos y Pavón to help win independence for Mexico.

Build on What You Know

After winning the war for independence, the U.S. government began acquiring more territories. Eager American settlers and traders continued to migrate westward. Many Americans believed it was their country's destiny to extend to the Pacific Coast. While this idea helped the United States gain more land, it also led to tensions with other nations.

John Gast's 1879 painting shows the spirit of manifest destiny leading settlers westward across the continent.

Wooden rockers like this one were used for mining gold.

1836 Mexican troops defeat Texan forces at the Alamo in San Antonio on March 6. The independent Republic of Texas is born on March 2.

1837 Reformers in Canada rebel against the government.

1840

1841 Britain takes control of the Chinese island of Hong Kong.

1845 John O'Sullivan coins the phrase *manifest destiny*, which is used to promote westward expansion.

1848 Gold is discovered in California on January 24.

The Treaty of Guadalupe Hidalgo is signed on February 2, ending the Mexican War.

1850

1851 A huge gold rush takes place in the colony of Victoria in Australia.

1852 The South African Republic is created.

1853 The United States buys part of what is now Arizona and New Mexico from Mexico in the Gadsden Purchase.

1858 Great Britain assumes formal control of India.

1860

1860 The Mormon population of Utah reaches about 40,000.

This Chinese punch bowl depicts European trading centers in China.

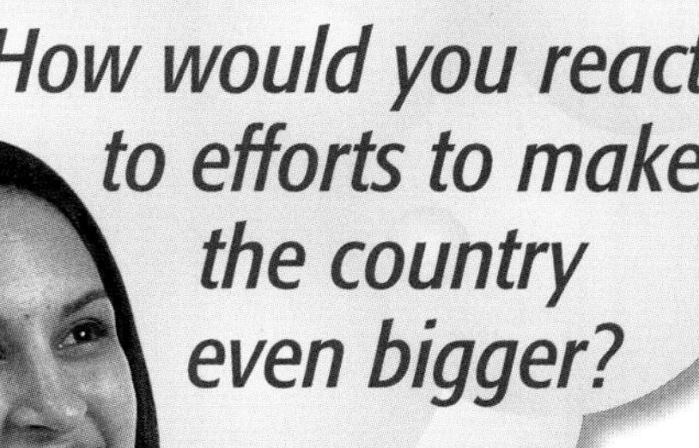

You Be the Historian

What's Your Opinion? Do you **agree** or **disagree** with the following statements? Support your point of view in your journal.

- **Culture** Cultural differences usually lead one region to declare independence from the rest of a country.
- **Global Relations** Nations only grow through conquest.
- **Geography** Settlers moving to new areas always change the environment instead of adapting to it.

Section 1

Texas Wins Its Independence

Read to Discover

1. Why did Mexico rebel against Spain?
2. What issues caused tension between American settlers in Texas and the Mexican government?
3. What events led Texas to become an independent country?

Define

- *empresarios*
- annex

Identify

- Father Miguel Hidalgo y Costilla
- Tejanos
- Stephen F. Austin
- Antonio López de Santa Anna
- William Travis
- Jim Bowie
- Alamo
- Battle of Goliad
- Sam Houston
- Battle of San Jacinto
- Republic of Texas

WHY IT MATTERS TODAY

Throughout the world many groups are struggling for political independence. Use CNNfyi.com or other **current events** sources to find out about one of these groups. Record your findings in your journal.

The Story Continues

In early September 1810 the bad news reached Miguel Hidalgo y Costilla (ee-DAHL-goh ee kaws-TEE-yah), a Mexican Catholic priest. Spanish officials knew that he had been plotting against them. On September 16 Hidalgo gathered his supporters in the town of Dolores. There he shouted the Grito de Dolores (Cry of Dolores): "Long live our Lady of Guadalupe [a Mexican saint], down with bad government, death to the Spaniards!"

Father Miguel Hidalgo y Costilla's Grito de Dolores *helped inspire the Mexican war for independence.*

The Mexican War for Independence

Father Miguel Hidalgo y Costilla and his followers hoped that independence would improve conditions for many poor American Indians and mestizos in New Spain. In addition, Hidalgo wanted to abolish slavery and end unfair taxes on Indians. About 80,000 Indians and mestizos joined Hidalgo's revolt against Spanish rule. In 1811, however, the Spanish defeated these untrained soldiers and executed Father Hidalgo. Fighting between the Spanish and various rebels continued for 10 years.

Finally, a revolutionary army led by officer Agustín de Iturbide (ee-toor-BEE-day) defeated the Spanish and declared Mexico an independent nation. The Mexican Constitution of 1824 made Mexico a republic. In addition to present-day Mexico, the new nation included what is now Arizona, California, Nevada, New Mexico, Texas, and Utah. It also contains parts of Colorado, Kansas, Oklahoma, and Wyoming.

✔ **Reading Check: Sequencing** List the events leading up to Mexico's independence in the order that they occurred.

Ethnic Traditions

In Texas a wide range of cultures influences everything from food to holidays. Holiday celebrations like Diez y Seis de Septiembre are among many Texas traditions celebrated by people of Mexican descent. Diez y Seis celebrates the September 16, 1810, beginning of the war for Mexican independence.

Thousands of European immigrants moved to Texas in the 1840s, bringing their customs with them. A modern annual festival in New Braunfels features traditional German music and dancing.

Every year the Institute of Texan Cultures in San Antonio hosts the Folklife Festival. Texans from 70 counties representing different backgrounds participate. **How do Texans currently honor their ethnic traditions?**

Texas children participating in a German festival

Anglos in Texas

With Mexican independence, Texas became part of the province of Coahuila (koh-ah-WEE-lah) y Texas. At that time, few people lived in Texas. In the late 1700s Comanche and Apache attacks had forced many **Tejanos**, the settlers of Spanish descent living in what is now southern Texas, to leave the region. Mexican officials feared new attacks from American Indians and even considered Great Britain and the United States possible enemies. The Tejanos, who were few in number, would be unable to defend themselves or the region.

To attract new residents, the Mexican government made contracts with ***empresarios***, agents who received large land grants in return for bringing families to Texas. Mexico required these new settlers to follow certain rules—to become Mexican citizens, be loyal to the Catholic Church, and obey Mexican laws.

Moses Austin, an American living in Missouri, became one of the first *empresarios*, but he died before he could bring any American settlers to Texas. His son, **Stephen F. Austin**, did establish a colony on the lower Colorado River in 1821. By 1834 more than 20,000 Americans—mostly from southern states—had moved to Texas. The promise of cheap or free land attracted most of these settlers.

Problems between the new settlers and the Mexican government soon developed. Americans in Texas often ignored Mexican laws, instead acting as if they were still living on U.S. soil. By 1830, Americans in Texas greatly outnumbered Tejanos. The Mexican government feared that these new settlers might take Texas from Mexico. As one Mexican warned the minister of war and navy, "Either the [Mexican] government occupies Texas *now*, or it is lost forever." The Mexican government began to restrict American immigration, enforced the ban on slavery, and sent more soldiers to Texas. However, many U.S. settlers moved to Texas illegally and felt little loyalty to Mexico.

✔ **Reading Check: Identifying Cause and Effect** Why did Mexico begin using *empresarios* in Texas, and what conflicts arose between U.S. settlers and the Mexican government?

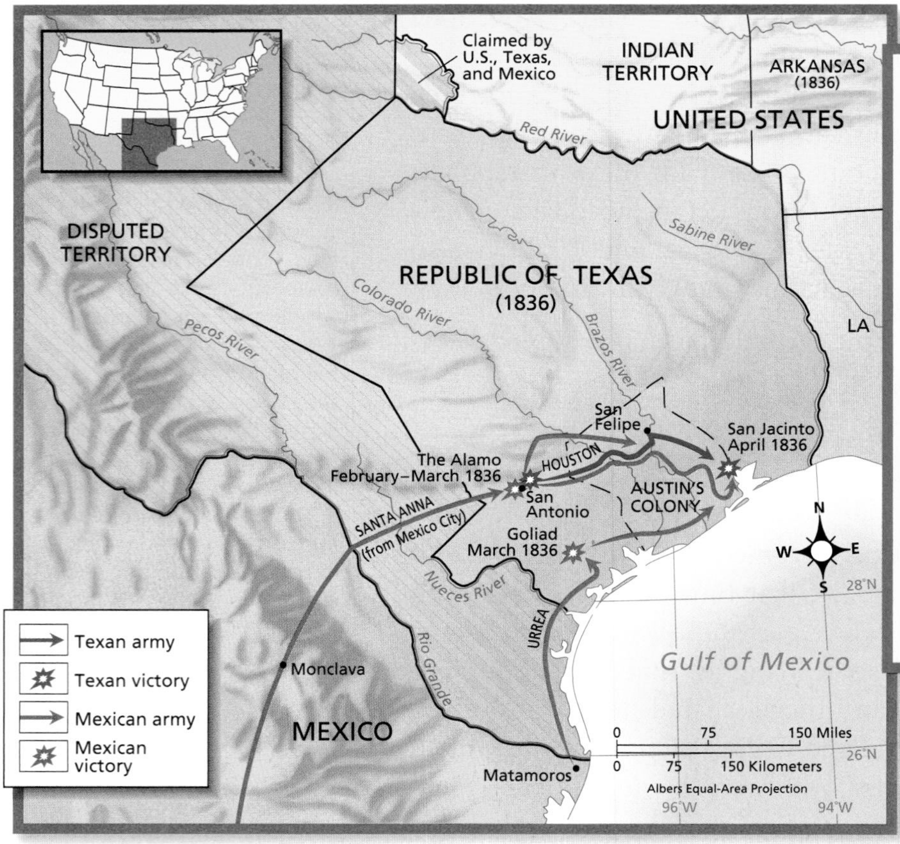

The Texas War for Independence

Interpreting Maps After defeats at Goliad and the Alamo, Texans rallied behind their leader, Sam Houston, and won a decisive victory at San Jacinto.

Skills Assessment

1. **The World in Spatial Terms** What battle took place within the boundaries of Austin's Colony?
2. **Drawing Inferences and Conclusions** In terms of geography, what advantage did the Texans have over the Mexican forces?

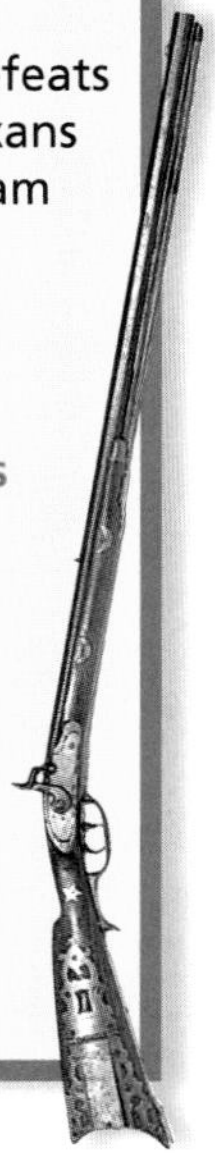

The Texas Revolution Begins

In 1833 Austin went to Mexico City to ask for more self-government for Texans. While there, he wrote to a government official in San Antonio to encourage Texans to organize a separate state government. Outraged Mexican officials threw Austin in jail and kept him there for a year and a half. Upon his release, Austin encouraged all Texans to take up arms against the Mexican government.

Analyzing Primary Sources

Drawing Inferences and Conclusions How is Austin trying to gain support for a war with Mexico?

"War is our only resource [option]. There is no other remedy. We must defend our rights, ourselves, and our country by force of arms."

—Stephen F. Austin, quoted in *Lone Star,* by T. R. Fehrenbach

The first battle of the Texas Revolution took place in Gonzales in October 1835. A group of Texans defeated a Mexican cavalry unit that was trying to retrieve a cannon from the town. One month later another group of Texans formed a temporary government. Their goal was to gain more independence and to resist the rule of Mexican leader General **Antonio López de Santa Anna**.

Elected president of Mexico in 1833, Santa Anna had quickly suspended Mexico's republican constitution. Many Texans believed this action violated their rights, and they hoped to restore the constitution. For his part, Santa Anna was determined to end the rebellion swiftly.

The Alamo and San Jacinto

Texan volunteers quickly captured the towns of Goliad and San Antonio. In San Antonio a group of Texans led by **William Travis** and **Jim Bowie** occupied the **Alamo**, an old Spanish mission. Outraged by Mexico's defeats, Santa Anna marched his army toward San Antonio. He arrived with about 1,800 soldiers on February 23, 1836. Volunteers had come to the Alamo's defense, including Jaun Seguín, who escaped before the battle, and frontiersman Davy Crockett, who did not. About 189 Texan soldiers defended the Alamo. Travis addressed an appeal for further assistance to the "People of Texas and All Americans in the World."

"I shall never surrender or retreat. If this call is neglected I am determined to sustain myself as long as possible and die like a soldier who never forgets what is due his honor and that of his country. VICTORY OR DEATH."

—William Travis, quoted in *Documents of Texas History,* edited by Ernest Wallace and David M. Vigness

Before dawn on March 6, 1836, Santa Anna's troops attacked the Alamo. The Mexicans quickly overwhelmed the Texans, killing Travis, Bowie, and the other defenders. Santa Anna spared the lives of the few women and children.

Meanwhile, delegates from throughout Texas met and declared independence from Mexico on March 2, 1836. In addition, the delegates wrote a constitution for Texas. The Texas Declaration of Independence and its Constitution were modeled on those of the United States. The Texas Constitution, however, granted land to every family in Texas and specifically legalized slavery.

The war continued, with Texan forces suffering another defeat in the **Battle of Goliad**. Santa Anna charged almost all of the 400 Texan soldiers captured in the battle with treason and had them executed. Texan commander **Sam Houston** then led an attack at San Antonio against Mexican troops under Santa Anna. The Texans overran the Mexican camp on April 21, 1836, shouting "Remember the Alamo! Remember Goliad!" During the brief **Battle of San Jacinto**, Houston's forces won an overwhelming victory. The Texans captured Santa Anna and forced him to sign a treaty recognizing Texas independence and ending the war. However, the Mexican congress refused to ratify the treaty.

✔ **Reading Check: Summarizing** What were the major battles of the Texas Revolution, and what were their outcomes?

BIOGRAPHY

Juan Seguín

(1806–1890)

Born to an important San Antonio family in 1806, Juan Seguín became a well-known Tejano politician. Seguín led a troop of Tejano cavalry in the victory at San Jacinto.

After the war, Seguín served in the Texas Senate and later became mayor of San Antonio. In 1842 Seguín moved his family to Mexico because of rising tensions between Anglos and Tejanos. **What role did Seguín play in the winning of Texas independence?**

The outnumbered defenders at the Alamo fought bravely but could not hold off the Mexican troops.

Interpreting the Visual Record

San Jacinto *After the Battle of San Jacinto, the wounded Texan leader Sam Houston (lying under the tree) accepted the surrender of Mexican general Santa Anna.* ***What does the Texans' clothing suggest about the organization of their army?***

The Texas Republic

The new town of Houston became the capital of the infant **Republic of Texas**. Voters elected Sam Houston, former governor of Tennessee, as president. The new nation was known as the Lone Star Republic because its flag had just one star.

The majority of Texans hoped that the United States would **annex**, or take control of, Texas. The U.S. Congress also wanted to annex Texas. However, U.S. president Andrew Jackson worried that because Texas supported slavery, admitting it to the Union would upset the balance between free states and slave states. Jackson also feared that annexing Texas might anger Mexican officials, who refused to acknowledge the independence of Texas.

In 1837 Jackson decided to recognize Texas independence, but not to annex it. Conflicts between Texas and Mexico continued. Mexican and Texan troops still fought on occasion. However, tens of thousands of Americans flocked to Texas in the next 10 years.

✔ Reading Check: **Identifying Points of View** What did President Jackson think might happen if the United States annexed Texas?

Section 1 Review

go.hrw.com Homework Practice Online
keyword: SC3 HP14

1. **Define** and explain:
   - *empresarios*
   - annex
2. **Identify** and explain:
   - Miguel Hidalgo y Costilla
   - Tejanos
   - Stephen F. Austin
   - Antonio López de Santa Anna
   - William Travis
   - Jim Bowie
   - Alamo
   - Battle of Goliad
   - Sam Houston
   - Battle of San Jacinto
   - Republic of Texas
3. **Sequencing** Copy the graphic organizer below. Use it to explain how Texas gained its independence from Mexico.

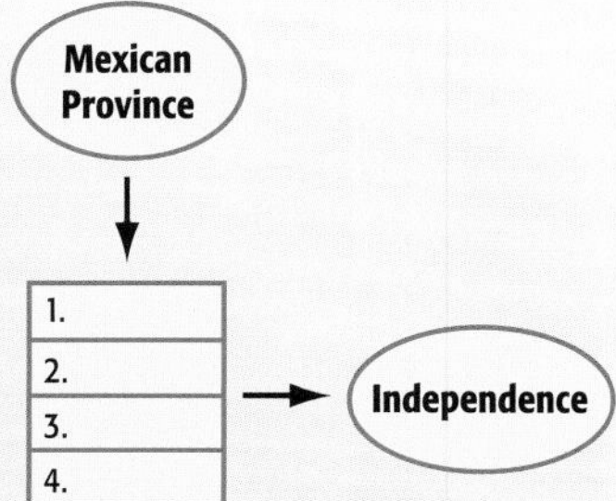

4. **Finding the Main Idea**
   a. What caused the Mexican war for independence?
   b. Why did tensions arise between American settlers in Texas and the Mexican government?
5. **Writing and Critical Thinking**
   Supporting a Point of View Imagine that you are a Texan under Sam Houston's command. You want to inspire your fellow soldiers before the Battle of San Jacinto. Write a song that will inspire the troops.
   Consider the following:
   - the causes of the Texas Revolution
   - the events at the Alamo and at Goliad
   - the future if Mexico is defeated

Section 2

The Far West

Read to Discover

1. Why did Americans live and settle in Oregon Country?
2. What was life like on the Oregon Trail?
3. Why did people use the California Trail and the Santa Fe Trail?

Define

- mountain men
- rendezvous

Identify

- Marcus and Narcissa Whitman
- Oregon Trail
- California Trail
- Donner party
- Sutter's Fort
- Californios
- Santa Fe Trail

Why It Matters Today

In the 1800s, Oregon was known as a place of opportunity for new life for Americans and immigrants. Use CNNfyi.com or other **current events** sources to find out why Oregon is in the news today. Record your findings in your journal.

The Story Continues

Fur trapper Manuel Lisa was one of the earliest explorers of the Rocky Mountains. Lisa once wrote to the famous explorer William Clark. "I go a great distance while some are considering whether they will start today or tomorrow." In 1807 Lisa led an expedition up the Missouri River. The explorers braved dangerous river rapids and freezing weather. In the winter, he established a trading post near what is now Omaha, Nebraska. Lisa's accomplishment helped blaze the westward trail for future generations.

To survive in isolated and dangerous conditions, many mountain men adopted American Indian customs.

Oregon Country

Most of the first non-Indians who traveled to the Rockies and beyond were fur traders and trappers known as **mountain men**. Manuel Lisa, Jim Bridger, and Jedediah Smith were well-known mountain men. They supported themselves by selling furs to merchants from the eastern states and Europe. Beginning in the 1820s, mountain men met at the **rendezvous** about once a year. At this event, mountain men and American Indian trappers would sell their furs to agents from fur companies.

Research on the ROM

Free Find:
Oregon
After reading about Oregon on the **Holt Researcher CD–ROM**, create a line graph showing the increase in the population of Oregon after it became a U.S. territory.

In 1811 John Jacob Astor founded Astoria at the mouth of the Columbia River. This fur-trading post was one of the earliest U.S. settlements in Oregon Country. American Indian peoples such as the Flathead, the Nez Percé, the Cayuse, and the Shoshone lived there. Great Britain, Russia, Spain, and the United States all claimed ownership of this land. Spain and Russia eventually gave up their claims. In 1827 the United States and Britain extended an 1818 treaty that allowed shared control of Oregon Country. Both nations wanted to maintain access to the Columbia River and its surrounding land without starting a war.

Very few British or Canadian settlers moved into the area. However, a growing number of Americans began making the difficult journey across the Great Plains and through the Rockies. Missionaries such as **Marcus and Narcissa Whitman** were among the first settlers. The Whitmans established a mission near what is now Walla Walla, Washington, in 1836. While the Whitmans failed to convince many Cayuse to give up their traditional way of life, their mission became a stopping point for newly arriving settlers.

The Whitmans' efforts ended in tragedy. Settlers stopping at the mission brought diseases that led to an epidemic, killing many Cayuse children. In anger, a group of Cayuse attacked the mission and killed the Whitmans and at least ten others. Their deaths did not slow the stream of pioneers coming to Oregon Country, however. Stories of good farmland and economic problems back east, such as the Panic of 1837, encouraged thousands of people to head west. In 1843 one midwestern newspaper reported that "the Oregon fever is raging in almost every part of the Union."

As more settlers came, the era of the mountain men was ending. Declining demand and overtrapping made the fur trade less profitable by the 1840s. Some of the former trappers began serving as guides.

✔ **Reading Check: Analyzing Information** What were some of the reasons Americans traveled to Oregon Country?

The Whitmans' mission, Waiilatpu, was a welcomed sight for many pioneers heading to Oregon Country. Narcissa Whitman was one of the first white women known to have crossed North America.

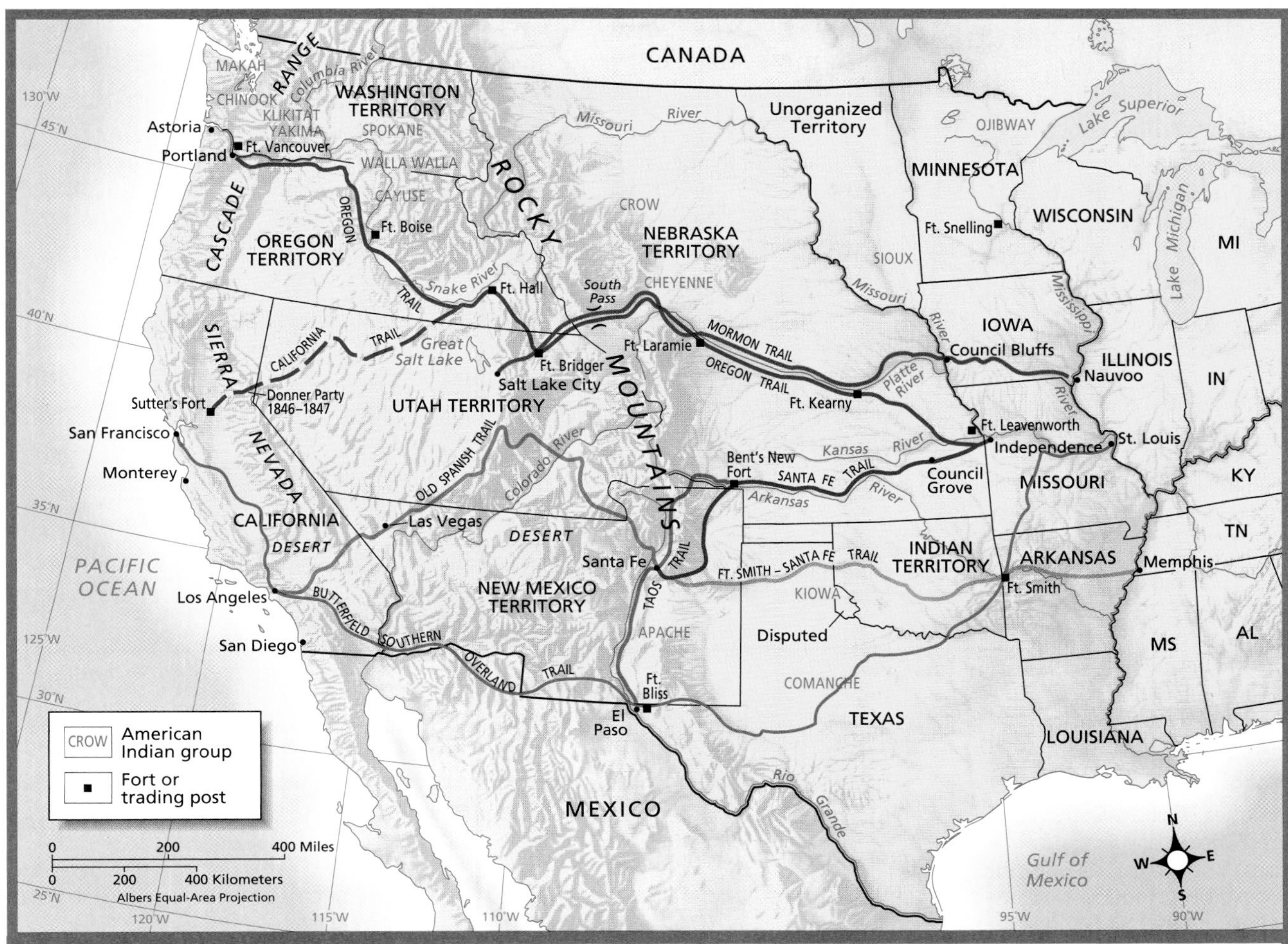

Major Overland Routes to the West by 1860

Interpreting Maps The rough terrain and lack of a constant water supply made many of the overland routes extremely dangerous.

Skills Assessment **Places and Regions** What trails led between Fort Laramie and Fort Bridger? What pass allowed settlers to cut through the Rocky Mountains?

A pioneer wagon

The Oregon Trail

Many settlers moving west followed the **Oregon Trail**. This trail began in Independence, Missouri, and stretched more than 2,000 miles across the northern Great Plains and the Rocky Mountains. The pioneers' journey usually began in late spring, once the rainy season ended. A family of four needed about $600 to buy the supplies necessary for the six- to eight-month trip.

Families formed wagon trains ranging in size from 10 to several dozen wagons to make the journey. Shortages of food, supplies, and water were a constant problem for many migrants. Pioneers also faced rough weather and natural barriers, such as rivers and mountains, as well as confusion over the best route to take. Lucy Hall Bennett was

13 years old when her family set out on the Oregon Trail. She described her family's struggles.

Analyzing Primary Sources

Making Generalizations and Predictions How do you think settlers reacted to such challenges?

"The road we took had been traveled by the Hudson Bay Fur traders, and while it might have been alright for pack horses, it was certainly not adapted to [made for] immigrants traveling by ox train. The water was [so] bad . . . you could hardly drink it. There was little grass and before long our cattle all had sore feet from traveling over the hard sharp rocks. . . . Several of our party died."

—Lucy Hall Bennett, quoted in *Women's Diaries of the Westward Journey,* by Lillian Schlissel

At the end of each day's journey, much work remained to be done, including unpacking, cooking, washing, hunting, and tending livestock. American Indians often acted as guides. By 1845 about 5,000 settlers had occupied the Willamette River valley in Oregon.

✔ **Reading Check: Finding the Main Idea** What obstacles did pioneers face on the Oregon Trail?

Other Trails West

Where the Oregon Trail split in what is now Idaho, a few settlers took the southern branch to California. Travelers on this **California Trail** had to cross a mountain range called the Sierra Nevada before the first snows made the journey almost impossible.

The **Donner party**, a group of families following the California Trail, began its journey west in the spring of 1846. Hoping to find a shortcut through the mountains, George Donner's group left the main trail and got lost. Their wagons were trapped by heavy winter snows. A rescue party finally found the group in February 1847. Of the original 87 members of the party, nearly half had died.

CONNECTING TO THE ARTS

George Catlin Artists like George Catlin brought images of the West to the rest of the country. Catlin is best known for his paintings of American Indians. From 1830 to 1836 he traveled throughout the western Great Plains. He painted portraits and important events such as buffalo hunts and religious ceremonies. In the East, thousands of people viewed Catlin's paintings. Today, his many paintings provide a valuable record of American Indian culture. **Why do you think Catlin's paintings were so popular with Americans in the East?**

In 1839 Swiss immigrant John Sutter started **Sutter's Fort**, a colony near the Sacramento River. Sutter's Fort soon became a popular destination for U.S. emigrants. But few Americans actually stayed in Mexican California. The population there included American Indians, Mexicans, and a small number of former Spanish colonists and their descendants, called **Californios**. American merchants in California were more interested in trading manufactured goods for hides, tallow (animal fat used for soap and candles), and gold dust than in settling the region.

A similar situation existed in the Southwest. For example, American merchants started the **Santa Fe Trail**, which ran from Independence, Missouri, to what is now Santa Fe, New Mexico. Unlike other routes, the Santa Fe Trail did not serve as a major migration route. It appealed mainly to profit-seeking traders who were willing to take the risks involved in crossing the desert and mountains.

✔ **Reading Check: Contrasting** What were the similarities and differences between the Santa Fe and California Trails?

Interpreting the Visual Record

Sutter's Fort *Mexican officials wanted to limit American settlement in California, but they allowed Sutter's Fort to become an important trading post for American immigrants to the region.* ***Why might a settlement like this one have appealed to weary travelers?***

Section 2 Review

go.hrw.com Homework Practice Online
keyword: SC3 HP14

1. **Define** and explain:
   - mountain men
   - rendezvous

2. **Identify** and explain:
   - Marcus and Narcissa Whitman
   - Oregon Trail
   - California Trail
   - Donner party
   - Sutter's Fort
   - Californios
   - Santa Fe Trail

3. **Comparing and Contrasting** Copy the table below. Use it to identify the locations of the major western trails and why people used them.

Trail	Location	Used for
California		
Oregon		
Sante Fe		

4. **Finding the Main Idea**
   a. What attracted Americans to Oregon Country?
   b. What difficulties did settlers face on the Oregon Trail?

5. **Writing and Critical Thinking**
   Analyzing Information Imagine that you and your family are pioneers who are considering moving west. Do you think that moving to Oregon would be worth the difficulties of the journey? Write a one-page essay to explain your answer.
   Consider the following:
   - the reasons people moved west
   - the dangers of the trail
   - the climate and environment of Oregon

Section 3

The Mexican War

Read to Discover

1. In what ways did belief in manifest destiny lead Americans to expand the borders of the United States?
2. How did the Mexican War progress?
3. What were the terms of the treaty that ended the war with Mexico?

Define

- manifest destiny

Identify

- John Tyler
- James K. Polk
- Zachary Taylor
- Henry David Thoreau
- Bear Flag Revolt
- Winfield Scott
- Treaty of Guadalupe Hidalgo
- Mexican Cession
- Gadsden Purchase

Why It Matters Today

Nations and groups still go to war with one another today. Use CNNfyi.com or other **current events** sources to learn about an armed conflict somewhere in the world today. Record your findings in your journal.

THE
UNITED STATES MAGAZINE,
AND
DEMOCRATIC REVIEW.

The Democratic Review *was one of several magazines that supported westward expansion.*

The Story Continues

By the 1840s, many Americans believed that the United States was meant to expand across the continent to the Pacific Ocean. John O'Sullivan, a New York editor, voiced this idea. "The American claim is by the right of our manifest destiny to overspread . . . the whole of the continent which Providence [God] has given us for the development of the great experiment of liberty. We are the nation of human progress, and who will, what can, set limits to our onward march?"

Manifest Destiny and Expansion

The view that the United States had a special mission to expand westward became known as **manifest destiny**. American Indians and people of Spanish descent had been living in the West for hundreds of years, but supporters of manifest destiny ignored that fact. They ignored it because manifest destiny included the belief that the spread of American democratic, economic, and religious values was good for the world as a whole.

The annexation of Texas became a major goal for supporters of manifest destiny and a critical issue in the presidential election of 1844. President **John Tyler** wanted to annex Texas, in part to increase the

Expanding Westward

Many Americans believed that the United States had a special destiny and was meant to expand across the continent.

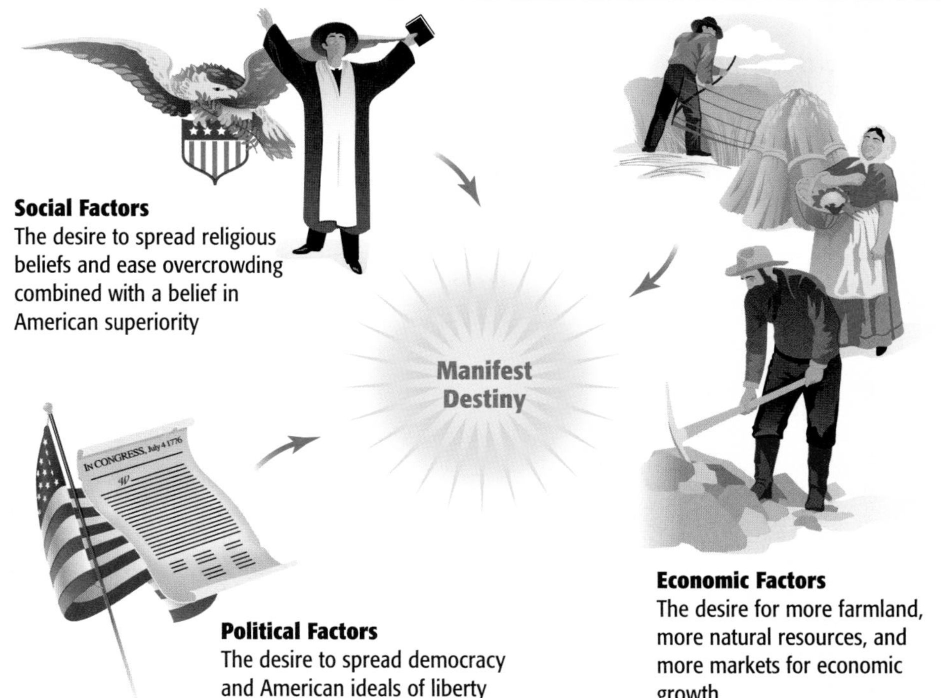

Visualizing History

1. **Culture** How do you think people of other cultures and nations viewed the idea of manifest destiny?
2. **Connecting to Today** What special purpose in the world do you think the United States has today?

number of slave states in the Union. Tyler's own Whig Party rejected this goal and nominated Senator Henry Clay, whose views on annexation were not entirely clear. The Democrats countered by choosing expansionist Governor **James K. Polk** of Tennessee as their candidate. Polk won a narrow victory, and in 1845 Congress voted to annex Texas to the United States.

Mexican officials, who considered Texas a rebel province, were outraged. They quickly cut off diplomatic relations with the United States. Polk inherited a boundary disagreement between Texas and Mexico. He sent General **Zachary Taylor** into the disputed border region between the Nueces River and the Rio Grande to protect U.S. interests. When Polk's efforts to buy California and New Mexico from the Mexican government failed, he ordered Taylor to move nearer the Rio Grande.

Mexican forces stationed across from Taylor demanded that he withdraw. When he refused, Mexican troops attacked a group of 63 U.S. soldiers, killing 11 and capturing the rest. Polk reacted with an angry message to Congress on May 11, 1846.

"Mexico has passed the boundary of the United States, has invaded our territory, and shed American blood upon the American soil. . . . The two nations are now at war."

—James K. Polk, from *Messages and Papers of the Presidents,* edited by James D. Richardson

Two days later, Congress declared war on Mexico.

✔ **Reading Check: Identifying Cause and Effect** What caused Mexico to cut off diplomatic relations with the United States, and what was the result?

Analyzing Primary Sources

Drawing Inferences and Conclusions In order for Polk's reasoning to be correct, what would have to be true of the U.S. border with Mexico?

Interpreting the Visual Record

The Mexican War *The cigar case below shows General Zachary Taylor leading his troops across the Rio Grande. The painting shows the Battle of Palo Alto, one of Taylor's early victories in the war.* ***Why do you think an artist would want to commemorate Taylor's crossing of the Rio Grande?***

War with Mexico

Most Americans supported the Mexican War, which they believed would spread democracy. American men volunteered to fight in record numbers. About 200,000 men—four times the number the U.S. government had requested—answered the call to enlist.

However, many Whigs thought the conflict was unjustified and unnecessary. Some people who opposed armed conflict in general and the expansion of slavery also disapproved of the war. Transcendentalist writer and antislavery advocate **Henry David Thoreau** went to jail rather than pay taxes to support the fight against Mexico. Fellow transcendentalist Ralph Waldo Emerson feared that the war would divide the country. "The United States will conquer Mexico, but it . . . will poison us."

While supporters and opponents of the war argued, the fighting itself was taking place. General Zachary Taylor's forces drove Mexican troops back into Mexico. Taylor then crossed the Rio Grande and occupied Matamoros. Farther west, General Stephen Kearny claimed the entire territory of New Mexico for the United States.

Kearny then began a long march to gain control of California. Kit Carson, an experienced explorer and army scout, guided Kearny's forces toward San Diego. In June 1846, before Kearny arrived, a small group of American settlers near Sutter's Fort in northern California revolted against Mexican rule. They declared California an independent republic and created a flag featuring a star and a grizzly bear. This flag gave the rebellion its name—the **Bear Flag Revolt**. The rebels were soon joined by John C. Frémont, a U.S. Army explorer.

Meanwhile, Kearny's army and the U.S. Navy joined the fighting. In August 1846, Commodore Robert Stockton declared that California belonged to the United States. Some Californios and Mexicans in California continued to resist until early 1847, when they surrendered.

✔ **Reading Check: Summarizing** How did the United States gain control of California during the Mexican War?

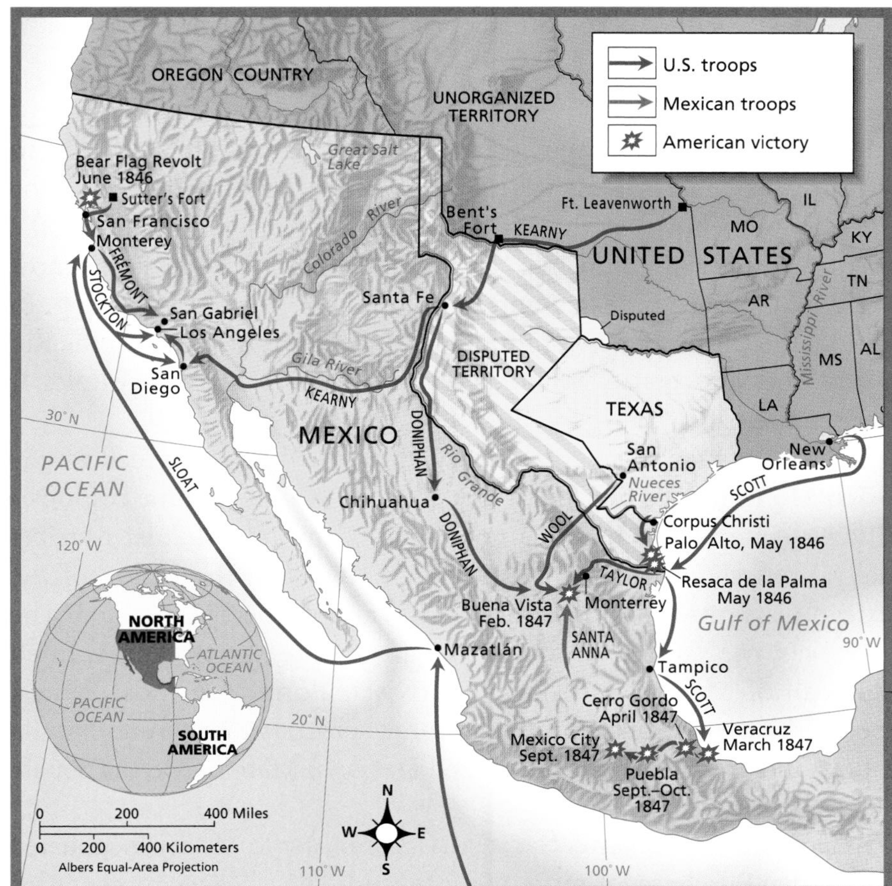

The Mexican War, 1846–1847

Interpreting Maps Within months of declaring war, U.S. forces had captured all the major cities and towns along the coast of California and controlled much of the territory north of Mexico City.

Skills Assessment

1. **Places and Regions** Which military commander led the U.S. forces from Santa Fe to Chihuahua?
2. **Summarizing** Who led U.S. forces into California?

California settlers raised this flag in 1846 to declare their independence from Mexico.

The War's End

U.S. forces continued to advance in Mexico. At Buena Vista, an overconfident General Santa Anna sent a note demanding surrender. A U.S. officer responded, "General Taylor never surrenders." Taylor's army won a stunning victory. Despite this success, Polk had come to believe that Taylor could not win the war. Polk also worried that Taylor, a Whig, was becoming popular enough to win the 1848 presidential election. As a result, Polk decided to give command to General **Winfield Scott** for a new invasion of Mexico farther south.

Scott soon launched a huge attack on the port city of Veracruz, the strongest fortress in Mexico. On March 29, 1847, after an 88-hour bombardment, Veracruz fell to U.S. forces.

Scott's troops then marched some 200 miles inland to the heart of Mexico. Santa Anna tried to stop the Americans along the way, but by August U.S. troops had reached the edge of Mexico City. After negotiations with the Mexican government failed, Scott ordered a massive assault on the city. On September 14, 1847, U.S. soldiers captured the Mexican capital.

✔ **Reading Check: Sequencing** List in proper sequence the major battles that brought an end to the Mexican war.

That's Interesting!

An Unpopular Peace Can you imagine being fired for negotiating a peace treaty? That's what happened to Nicholas Trist. President Polk had sent Trist, a State Department official, to help end the war with Mexico. Trist had little success for months, but he finally got his chance when Scott captured Mexico City. However, Polk had ordered Trist back to Washington to receive new instructions. Not wanting to lose his chance for a treaty, the diplomat ignored his orders. He stayed in Mexico and negotiated the Treaty of Guadalupe Hidalgo. When Polk first heard about the treaty, he was so angry that he fired Trist!

The Treaty of Guadalupe Hidalgo

The Mexican Cession

The fighting ended after Scott took Mexico City. The **Treaty of Guadalupe Hidalgo** was signed in February 1848. By this agreement much of Mexico's northern territory was ceded, or turned over, to the United States. Known as the **Mexican Cession**, this land included the present-day states of California, Nevada, and Utah. It also included most of Arizona and New Mexico and parts of Colorado and Wyoming. In addition, the United States got the area claimed by Texas north of the Rio Grande. The Mexican Cession totaled more than 500,000 square miles. It increased the size of the United States by almost 25 percent.

In exchange for this vast territory, the United States agreed to pay Mexico $15 million. The United States also agreed to assume responsibility for American claims of more than $3 million against Mexico. Finally, the treaty provided that Mexicans living in the region of the Mexican Cession would have their rights and property protected. The treaty was the source of much debate. Some Americans wanted to take all of Mexico. Antislavery activists, along with most Whigs, opposed the treaty. Polk responded to their protests by arguing that the treaty would greatly benefit the United States. In March 1848 the Senate ratified the treaty.

In December 1853 James Gadsden, U.S. minister to Mexico, negotiated the **Gadsden Purchase** for more Mexican land. The U.S. government paid Mexico $10 million for the southern parts of what are now Arizona and New Mexico. The United States wanted the region for a transcontinental railroad route. With this purchase, the continental boundaries of the United States were fixed.

✔ Reading Check: **Finding the Main Idea** How did the American victory in the Mexican War affect the United States?

Section 3 Review

go.hrw.com Homework Practice Online
keyword: SC3 HP14

1. **Define**
   - manifest destiny

2. **Identify** and explain:
   - John Tyler
   - James K. Polk
   - Zachary Taylor
   - Henry David Thoreau
   - Bear Flag Revolt
   - Winfield Scott
   - Treaty of Guadalupe Hidalgo
   - Mexican Cession
   - Gadsden Purchase

3. **Summarizing** Copy the graphic organizer below. Use it to show the events related to the Mexican War that took place in each location listed.

Declaration of War
New Mexico:
California:
Buena Vista:
Veracruz:
Mexico City:
Treaty of Guadalupe Hidalgo

4. **Finding the Main Idea**
   a. How did Americans' belief in manifest destiny contribute to the expansion of the United States?
   b. What did each side gain in the Treaty of Guadalupe Hidalgo?

5. **Writing and Critical Thinking**
   Summarizing Imagine that you are a U.S. soldier in California during the Mexican War. Write a short report to your commanders describing how the United States gained control of California.
   Consider the following:
   - Polk's offer to buy California
   - the Bear Flag Revolt
   - actions by Kearny's and Stockton's forces

Section 4

The Growth of the West

Read to Discover

1. Why did people head west to California in 1849?
2. What was life like in gold-rush mining camps and towns?
3. How did the Mormons change the landscape of the West?

Define

- forty-niners
- prospect

Identify

- California Gold Rush
- Joseph Smith
- Mormons
- Brigham Young
- Mormon Trail

WHY IT MATTERS TODAY

Individuals, corporations, and nations still search for and use Earth's mineral wealth. Use CNNfyi.com or other **current events** sources to learn about discoveries of oil, precious metals, or other minerals in recent years. Record your findings in your journal.

The Story Continues

In 1849 journalist Bayard Taylor traveled west to report on the discovery of gold in California. He spent five months wandering around the mining camps and gold mines. The work of prospecting looked hard and unpleasant to him, until he saw the many nuggets dug up by one group of miners in a single day. "The gold was of the purest quality and most beautiful color," wrote Taylor. "I confess there was a sudden itching in my fingers to seize the heaviest crowbar and the biggest shovel." Stories like Taylor's led countless Americans to the California gold fields seeking their fortunes.

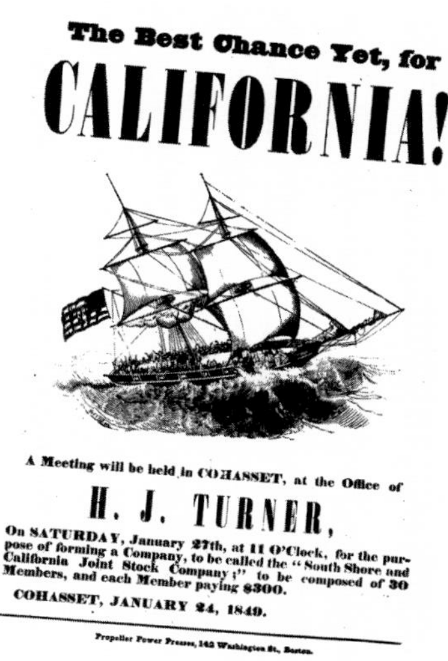

Advertisements like this one encouraged travelers to move to California.

The California Gold Rush

On January 24, 1848, a worker near Sutter's Mill made a surprising discovery. The worker later recalled, "My eye was caught with the glimpse of something shining in the bottom of the ditch. . . . I was certain it was gold." Sutter's other workers also found nuggets of gold, and stories of the discoveries spread quickly. In 1849 alone, nearly 80,000 gold-seekers, known as **forty-niners**, flocked to California in what is now known as the **California Gold Rush**. As an Iowa woman recalled, "At that time the 'gold fever' was contagious, and few, old or young, escaped the malady [illness]."

Interpreting the Visual Record

San Francisco *Most forty-niners arrived in San Francisco, which had a natural harbor and was close to the gold strikes. As a result, San Francisco's population jumped from about 800 in March 1848 to more than 25,000 by 1850.* ***What signs of increased American settlement do you see in the picture?***

Incredible stories of success inspired many forty-niners. One lucky miner pocketed two and a half pounds of gold after just 15 minutes of work. Generally, however, gold mining was a very difficult, time-consuming effort. Few forty-niners became rich. Most of them had no gold-mining experience when they came to **prospect**, or search for gold. Early miners frequently banded together to prospect for gold and share whatever they found. But competition led to arguments and even violence over claims.

Mining methods varied according to the time of year and the claim's location. The most popular method was placer mining. Placer miners put dirt in a pan or a rocker/cradle device. Then they ran water over the dirt to uncover any gold pieces. Sometimes they used a sluice box to wash gold nuggets out of the loose rock found along rivers and streams. Getting gold from hard rock was more difficult and expensive. To reach gold buried in the hills, miners had to dig shafts and tunnels. Mining companies usually worked these deposits. In 1852 California's gold production reached more than $81 million.

Mining camps sprang up wherever people gathered to search for gold. Most camps disappeared as quickly as claims died out. These camps had colorful names such as Skunk Gulch, Hangtown, Git-Up-and-Git, and Dry Diggings.

Some early miners tried to establish law and order in the camps, but others lived rowdy and dangerous lives. When William Perkins visited the Sonora mining camp in 1850, he remarked: "It is surprising how indifferent [uncaring] people become to the sight of violence and bloodshed in this country."

Most miners were young, unmarried men. Only about 5 percent of gold-rush immigrants were women or children. Wives made good money cooking meals, washing clothes, and operating boardinghouses. Catherine Haun recalled her first home in California.

Analyzing Primary Sources

Drawing Inferences and Conclusions What parts of Haun's recollection show the rapid growth and the character of her mining town?

"We were glad to settle down and go housekeeping in a shed that was built in a day of lumber purchased with the first fee. . . . For neighbors, we had a real live saloon. I never have received more respectful attention than I did from these neighbors."

—Catherine Haun, quoted in *Ordinary Americans,* edited by Linda R. Monk

Many people made a good living by selling food, clothing, and equipment to miners. Miners had to pay high prices for such goods because the gold in circulation caused severe inflation. A loaf of bread, for example, which cost 5 cents back east, sold for 50 to 75 cents in San Francisco.

✔ **Reading Check: Summarizing** Why did so many people move to California, and what types of work did they do there?

Effects of the Gold Rush

Although the vast majority of the forty-niners were Americans, gold fever lured miners from around the world. Chinese immigrants were known as *gam saan haak,* or "travelers to Gold Mountain." Most of them hoped to find great wealth and then return to China. Between 1849 and 1853, some 24,000 young Chinese men migrated to California. "From far and near we came and were pleased," wrote merchant Lai Chun-Chuen in 1855.

Many Americans did not welcome the Chinese immigrants, however. Chinese miners often suffered violent attacks in mining camps, yet the legal system offered them little protection. In addition, California placed a high monthly tax on all foreign miners in 1852. The U.S. government did not even allow Chinese immigrants to become citizens.

Despite such treatment, many Chinese continued to work in the gold mines. Others looked for different jobs or opened their own businesses. A California newspaper reported that Chinese people worked as "ploughmen, laundrymen, placer miners, woolen spinners and weavers, domestic servants, cigar makers, [and] shoemakers." Many Chinese opened laundries, which required little money to start and had steady business from mining camps.

Prospectors also went to California from Europe, Mexico, and South America. In 1849 alone, some 20,000 immigrants moved to California. Like most American gold-seekers, these new arrivals intended to return home after they had made their fortunes. However, even when they did not become rich overnight, many decided to stay. Some, such as German immigrant Levi Strauss, became successful business owners. Strauss sold dry goods to California miners and saw the need for durable work clothes. The pants he made from hard-wearing denim were a big success. They still bear his name—Levi's.

Before the discovery of gold, California's population had grown slowly. The arrival of the forty-niners changed everything. Almost overnight, gold mining, trade, and business growth transformed California's economy. Without the gold rush, California would probably have continued to grow slowly. However, after gold was discovered the population grew so quickly that California became a state just two years after the United States acquired it. Agriculture and industry flourished. After the gold rush faded, frontier society remained prosperous and became more stable. With luck and hard work, immigrants could build good lives for themselves in the West.

CONNECTING TO MATH

Just the Facts

Gold Production, 1847–1860

(in thousands of fine troy ounces)

Year	Amount	Year	Amount
1847	43	**1854**	2,902
1848	484	**1855**	2,661
1849	1,935	**1856**	2,661
1850	2,419	**1857**	2,661
1851	2,661	**1858**	2,419
1852	2,902	**1859**	2,419
1853	3,144	**1860**	2,225

Using Mathematical Skills

1. How much did gold production increase between 1848 and 1849? What do you think explains this increase?
2. Create a graph that shows the annual production of gold and silver for this period.
3. Imagine that you are an economic adviser to the president of the United States. Prepare a written report in which you discuss how increased gold production might affect prices, especially in California.

About 1,000 of the prospectors in California were African Americans.

Research on the ROM

Free Find:
California
After reading about California on the **Holt Researcher CD–ROM,** imagine that you work for the state tourism board. Create a short pamphlet describing California's natural resources.

Not everyone was pleased, however. One observer saw the problems that rapid population growth caused for many Mexicans, Californios, and American Indians.

> **"The Yankee regarded every man but a native American [meaning a white U.S. citizen] as an interloper [trespasser], who had no right to come to California and pick up the gold of 'free and enlightened citizens.'"**
>
> —W. Kelly, quoted in *The Other Californians,* by Robert F. Heizer and Alan F. Almquist

✔ **Reading Check: Identifying Cause and Effect** What caused California's population growth, and how did it affect California's position in the United States?

The Mormons

Like California, Utah also experienced a great deal of growth in the 1840s. The people who settled that area, however, came not for gold, but for religious freedom. In 1830 **Joseph Smith** had founded the Church of Jesus Christ of Latter-Day Saints in western New York. Smith said he had found a set of golden tablets with religious revelations in them. His translation of them became the Book of Mormon. The members of this church were known as **Mormons**, and their numbers grew rapidly. However, their beliefs and practices made Mormons targets of persecution. For example, some Mormon men practiced a form of polygamy in which a man has more than one wife at the same time.

During the early 1830s Smith and his converts left New York. Their first settlement in Ohio failed during the Panic of 1837, so they moved on to Missouri. There, Mormons were chased from their settlement by an angry mob. Their next settlement, at Nauvoo, Illinois, proved successful. The city grew, attracting some 20,000 Mormons. But in 1844 an anti-Mormon mob murdered Smith.

Interpreting the Visual Record

The Mormon Trail *Thousands of Mormons endured great hardships to move west to escape persecution.* ***What challenges does this illustration show the Mormon settlers facing on the trail?***

Following Smith's murder, **Brigham Young** became the head of the Mormon Church. He decided to move the Mormons west to what is now Utah, then in Mexican territory. An advance party arrived at the Great Salt Lake in July 1847. Erastus Snow, a Mormon follower, recalled Young's words: "This is the place whereon we will plant our feet." These pioneers began preparing the Great Salt Lake region for other Mormon immigrants.

Tens of thousands of Mormons traveled to Utah on a route called the **Mormon Trail**. Many pushed or pulled heavy handcarts across the rough ground. They were joined by converts from Great Britain and Scandinavia. Utah's Mormons numbered some 40,000 by 1860.

Joseph Smith did not live to see the successful community established by his followers in the West.

In their desert valley, the Mormons built their settlement at Salt Lake City. Carefully planned and prepared, the settlement had broad roads, gridlike street patterns, spacious lots, and surrounding farms. Soon after his arrival in 1847, Young had picked the site for the Mormons' Temple.

The Mormons set about turning the desert into their promised land. Because water was scarce, Mormons developed a strict water-use code. In the East, landowners could not change the flow or direction of rivers, or build dams. In the desert, however, dams and canals were needed to bring water to the fields. Under the Mormons' new water code, the first person to use the water had full rights to its use. However, the water had to be used for beneficial purposes such as farming, mining, or manufacturing. In disputes over water use, the good of the community outweighed individual interests. Young's new approach to water use helped the Mormons make the desert bloom with crops. The code also set an example for modern water-rights laws throughout the western United States.

✔ **Reading Check: Analyzing Information** How did the Mormons' water-use code reflect their sense of community?

Section 4 Review

go.hrw.com **Homework Practice Online**
keyword: SC3 HP14

1. **Define** and explain:
   - forty-niners
   - prospect
2. **Identify** and explain:
   - California Gold Rush
   - Joseph Smith
   - Mormons
   - Brigham Young
   - Mormon Trail
3. **Identifying Cause and Effect** Copy the graphic organizer below. Use it to show what caused inflation in California, and how inflation affected the economy of the area.

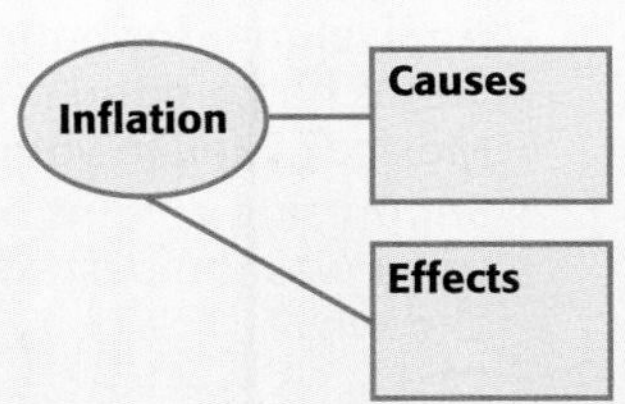

4. **Finding the Main Idea**
   a. Why did people move to California in 1849?
   b. What was life like in mining camps and towns?
5. **Writing and Critical Thinking**
   Analyzing Information Imagine that you are a reporter for an eastern newspaper. You have recently arrived at Salt Lake City to write a story on the ways that Mormon settlers have adapted to their environment.
   Consider the following:
   - the desert environment
   - the water-rights laws
   - the use of dams and canals

Chapter 14 Review

The Chapter at a Glance

Examine the visual summary of the chapter below. Use it to create a five-question quiz for a classmate on how Americans migrated to the West during the 1830s and 1840s.

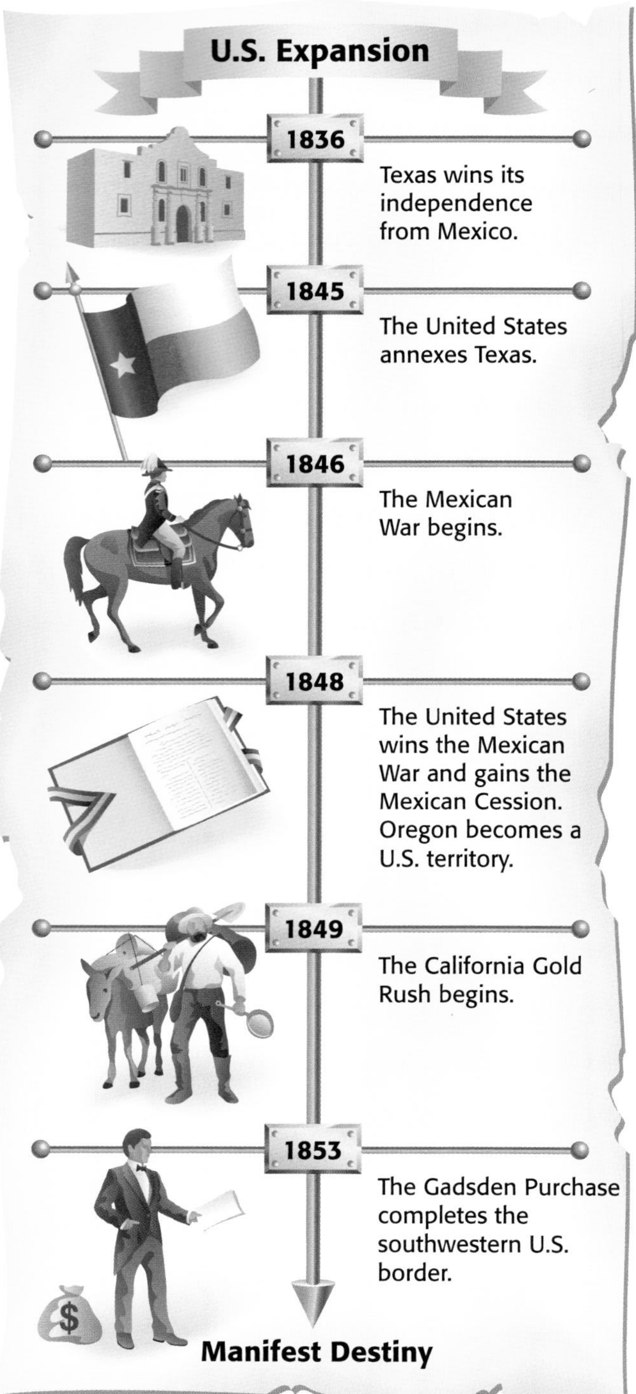

Identifying People and Ideas

Use the following terms or people in historically significant sentences:

1. Stephen F. Austin
2. Alamo
3. Sam Houston
4. Republic of Texas
5. Oregon Trail
6. manifest destiny
7. Treaty of Guadalupe Hidalgo
8. forty-niners
9. California Gold Rush
10. Mormons

Understanding Main Ideas

Section 1 *(Pages 422–426)*

1. Why did American Indians and mestizos revolt against Spanish rule in New Spain?
2. Why did Texans fight for independence from Mexico, and what was the outcome?

Section 2 *(Pages 427–431)*

3. What characteristics of the region attracted Americans to Oregon Country?
4. Describe the major western trails and the challenges they presented for travelers.

Section 3 *(Pages 432–436)*

5. How did Mexico respond to the U.S. annexation of Texas?

Section 4 *(Pages 437–441)*

6. How did the gold rush affect the population of California?
7. What reasons did Mormons have for moving west?

You Be the Historian— Reviewing Themes

1. **Culture** How did the idea of manifest destiny contribute to the growth of the West?
2. **Global Relations** How did the war with Mexico result in new U.S. territories?
3. **Geography** How did the Mormons improve the environment in Utah?

Thinking Critically

1. **Evaluating** What were some of the positive and negative effects of Americans' belief in manifest destiny?
2. **Analyzing Information** Do you think the United States had a good reason to declare war on Mexico? Explain your answer.
3. **Supporting a Point of View** Which trail do you think was the best route west during the 1800s, and why?

Social Studies Skills Workshop

Interpreting Maps

Study the map below. Then use the information on the map to help you answer the questions that follow.

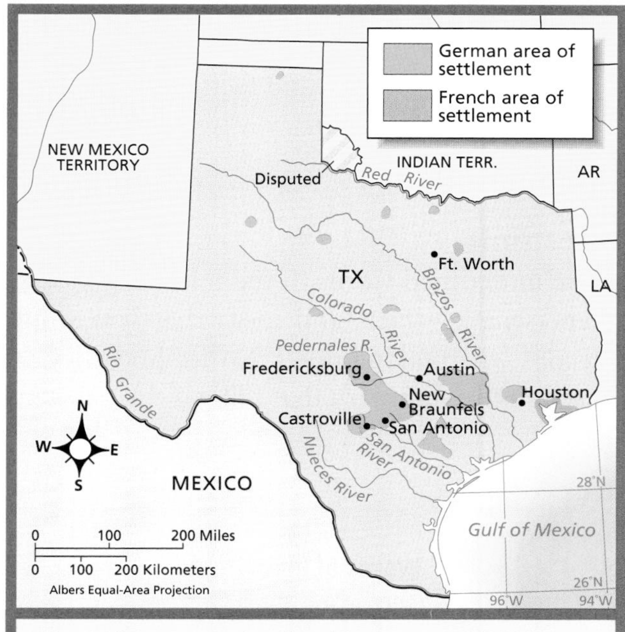

Settlements in Texas, 1850

1. What cities were located within the French area of settlement?
   a. Castroville
   b. Fort Worth
   c. Fort Worth and Houston
   d. Fredericksburg and New Braunfels
2. Based on your knowledge of the period and the information shown on the map, why do you think Texans moved the capital from Houston to Austin?

Analyzing Primary Sources

Read the following quotation by John O'Sullivan, which discusses the annexation of Texas, and then answer the questions that follow.

> **"It is time now for opposition to the annexation of Texas to cease [end], . . . even though it may perhaps be required of us as a necessary condition of the freedom of our institutions, that we must live on forever in a state of unpausing struggle and excitement upon some subject of party division or other. . . . It is time for the common duty of patriotism to the country to succeed; or . . . it is at least time for common sense to acquiesce [accept] with decent grace in the inevitable and the irrevocable."**

3. Which of the following statements best explains what the author is saying?
   a. With freedom comes responsibility.
   b. Americans should stop disagreeing about the future of Texas and accept that it has been annexed.
   c. American political parties spend too much time disagreeing about important issues.
   d. Patriotism is more important than any other responsibility that a U.S. citizen might have.
4. What does O'Sullivan mean when he says that political disagreements are "a necessary condition of the freedom of our institutions"?
   a. People will never get along.
   b. Americans are easily upset by U.S. political institutions.
   c. People in a democracy will disagree because they have the freedom to express their views.
   d. Political parties must exist in order to maintain a democracy.
5. Based on what you know about the period, who do you think O'Sullivan was addressing?

Alternative Assessment

Building Your Portfolio

American History

Interdisciplinary Connection to Economics

Complete the following activity in small groups. Imagine that you and your partners are planning to open a general store in a California mining camp. Create a poster showing the layout of your store and labeling the different items you will sell. Make a list of the five items you think will be the best sellers. Create advertisements to show your products and persuade people to buy them.

internet connect

Internet Activity: go.hrw.com
keyword: SC3 CF14

Choose an activity on Westward Expansion and War to:

- Research the events and leaders of the Texas Revolution.
- Create a scale model of a Spanish mission.
- Write a biography of James K. Polk.

Social Studies Skills

WORKSHOP

Study Skills

Taking notes and summarizing are key study skills. The following activities will help you develop and practice these skills.

Taking Notes

Taking notes helps you identify the main points of whatever you are studying, whether it is a book or a lecture. You should write your notes in your own words to help you understand them. Try to use the following steps when taking notes:

1. Identify the subject or main topic.
2. Identify the main ideas.
3. Note interesting and important details.
4. Identify key vocabulary terms.
5. Review your notes shortly after you write them.

Summarizing

Taking good notes can be very helpful when creating a summary—a brief statement of the important ideas in what you are studying. Summaries are a good tool to use when doing research for a report or presentation. The following strategies will help you write a summary:

- Write the summary in paragraph form, using as few words as possible without being inaccurate or too brief.
- Include key words and facts.
- Review your summary when you are finished.

Example

The underlined words in the following passage represent key facts and ideas that you would record when taking notes. Notice how they are used in the summary that follows the passage.

Waves of Immigrants

In the mid-1800s many immigrants crossed the Atlantic Ocean. More than 4 million immigrants from Europe settled in the United States between 1840 and 1860. More than 3 million of these immigrants arrived from Ireland and Germany. Many immigrants were fleeing from economic or political troubles in their native countries.

Summary More than 3 million Irish and German immigrants came to the United States between 1840 and 1860. Many immigrants came because of economic or political problems at home.

Practicing the Skills

1. Look at Chapter 15: Section 4, The Movement to End Slavery. Read the subsection titled The Underground Railroad. On your own paper, take notes by writing down the key words and phrases from each paragraph.
2. Now look at the notes that you have taken. Using only these notes and the strategies outlined above, write a short summary of the subsection. Show your summary to another student to see if he or she can understand the subject based on your summary.

History in Action

UNIT 5 SIMULATION

You Make the Decision . . .

What Should Immigrants Bring with Them to the United States?

Complete the following activity in small cooperative groups. It is the mid-1800s and America is the land of opportunity. Many people are coming to the United States from other countries to start new lives. Usually traveling in tightly packed sections of ships, immigrants are limited in what they can bring with them to America. Your community has asked you to serve on a committee to develop a flier that will identify for immigrants what items to bring with them to make the successful transition to life in the United States. Follow these steps to reach your decision.

1. Gather Information. Use your textbook and other resources to find information that might help you decide which items immigrants need to bring to America to start their new lives. Be sure to use what you learned from this unit's Skills Workshop on Summarizing and Taking Notes to help you record the information that you gather. You may want to divide different parts of the research among group members.

2. Identify Options. After reviewing the information you have gathered, consider the options for items to recommend. Your final decision may be easier to reach if you consider as many options as possible. Be sure to record your possible options for the preparation of your flier.

3. Predict Consequences. Now consider what might be the outcome if immigrants decide to bring or not to bring each of these items. Ask yourselves questions like: "Will the immigrants have enough room to bring these items on the ship?" Once you have predicted the consequences, record them as notes for the preparation of your flier.

4. Take Action to Implement Your Decision. After you have considered your options, you should plan and create your flier to present to the community board. Be sure to make your decision on which items immigrants should bring to the United States very clear. You will need to support your decisions by including information you gathered and by explaining why you rejected other options. Your flier needs to be visually appealing to the community board. When you are ready, decide which committee members will present each part of the flier, and then take your flier to the community board (the rest of the class). Good Luck!

UNIT 6

The Nation Breaks Apart

(1848–1877)

Young People

IN HISTORY

Young Soldiers

During the Civil War, 15-year-old Union soldier Thomas Galway described a fierce battle.

> **"Now we are close to the enemy. They rise up in the sunken lane and pour deadly fire into us. Our men drop. . . . We go forward on the run, heads downward as if under a pelting rain. . . . We are kneeling in the soft grass and I notice for a long time that almost every blade of grass is moving. For some time I supposed that this is caused by the merry crickets; and it is not until I made a remark to that effect to one of our boys near me and notice him laugh, that I know it is bullets that are falling thickly around us!"**

Young Union soldiers relax between battles.

Galway was one of the thousands of youths who fought in the Civil War.

Both the North and the South tried to keep boys out of their armies. However, many teenagers lied about their ages in order to join. Elisha Stockwell's father would not let his 15-year-old son enlist. So, Elisha told his parents that he was going to a dance in town. Instead, he joined the Union army. Although young Stockwell did not return home for two years, he thought of home often. One such time was during his first battle, kneeling on the ground in the middle of exploding shells. "I thought what a foolish boy I was to run away and get into such a mess as I was in."

Other boys joined the army as drummers. The beat of the drum was an important way to communicate orders to soldiers. Therefore, drummer boys often found themselves the target of enemy fire. Johnny Clem went from drummer boy to fighting soldier during the Battle of Shiloh. After his drum was shattered, 11-year-old Clem picked up a gun and began firing. Within two years, Clem was promoted to sergeant.

If You Were There *How would you view the war?*

LEFT PAGE: *Members of the 54th Massachusetts Infantry attack Confederate soldiers at Fort Wagner.*

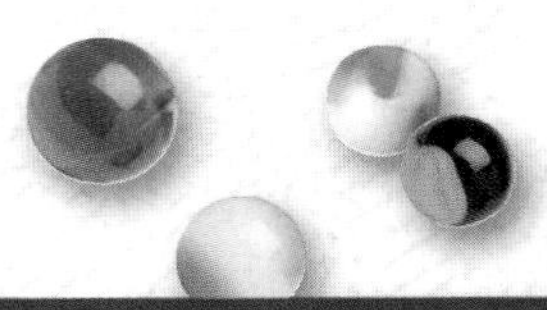

CHAPTER

15 A Divided Nation (1848–1860)

THE GRANGER COLLECTION, NEW YORK

Harriet Beecher Stowe was the daughter of Lyman Beecher, a prominent minister and reformer.

THE GRANGER COLLECTION, NEW YORK

Martin Van Buren and Charles F. Adams were the first presidential and vice presidential candidates of the Free-Soil Party.

UNITED STATES

1848 The Free-Soil Party is formed on August 9.

Zachary Taylor is elected president on November 7.

1850 On September 9 California enters the Union as a free state.

Congress passes the Fugitive Slave Act on September 18.

1852 Harriet Beecher Stowe publishes *Uncle Tom's Cabin*.

1853 Franklin Pierce is inaugurated as president.

1848 | **1850** | **1852** | **1854**

WORLD

1848 Revolutionary movements sweep across Europe.

1850 Hundreds of thousands of peasants and workers in China join the Taiping Rebellion against the Manchu dynasty.

1852 Louis-Napoléon declares himself Emperor Napoléon III of France.

1853 The Crimean War begins.

In 1848 German revolutionaries demanding a new republican government fought soldiers in the streets of Frankfurt.

Build on What You Know

After winning the Mexican War, the United States gained the Mexican Cession. Settlement of these lands renewed heated debate between northerners who opposed the expansion of slavery and southerners who supported it. Some southerners threatened to support secession if the government tried to block the westward expansion of slavery.

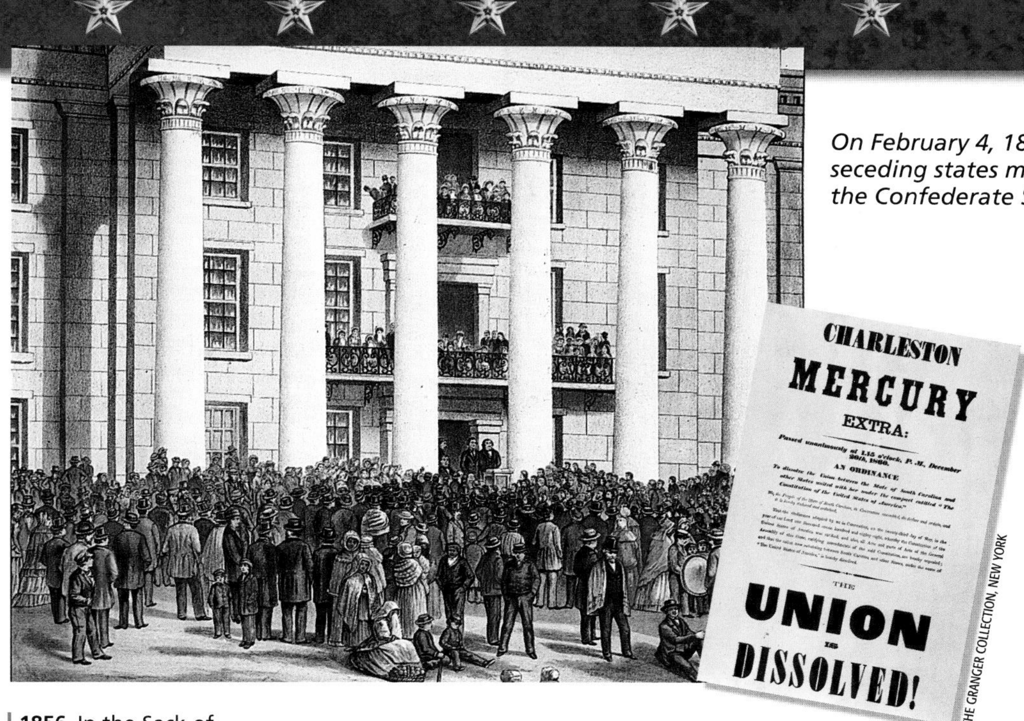
CHARLESTON

MERCURY

EXTRA:

Passed unanimously at 1.15 o'clock, P. M., December 20th, 1860.

AN ORDINANCE

To dissolve the Union between the State of South Carolina and other States united with her under the compact entitled "The Constitution of the United States of America."

THE

UNION

IS

DISSOLVED!

THE GRANGER COLLECTION, NEW YORK

On February 4, 1861, delegates from the seceding states met in Alabama to form the Confederate States of America.

The Charleston Mercury *issued a special broadside to announce the secession of South Carolina.*

1856 In the Sack of Lawrence, pro-slavery forces attack the town of Lawrence, Kansas, on May 21.

On May 24 abolitionist John Brown and his followers kill five pro-slavery settlers in the Pottawatomie Massacre.

1858 The Lincoln-Douglas debates begin in Illinois.

1859 John Brown takes control of the federal arsenal at Harpers Ferry, Virginia.

1860 Abraham Lincoln is elected president on November 6.

On December 20 South Carolina votes to secede from the United States.

1856 | **1858** | **1860** | **1862**

1856 British and French forces defeat Russia in the Crimean War.

1857 Indian soldiers in the British army begin the Sepoy Mutiny against British control of India.

You Be the Historian

What's Your Opinion? Do you **agree** or **disagree** with the following statements? Support your point of view in your journal.

- **Geography** Expansion often leads to conflict within a country.
- **Citizenship** The Supreme Court must protect all individuals' rights.
- **Constitutional Heritage** States should be able to legally leave the Union.

Section 1

The Debate over Slavery

Read to Discover

1. How did the outcome of the Mexican War affect the debate over the expansion of slavery?
2. What were the major provisions of the Compromise of 1850, and what reasons were given for supporting or opposing it?
3. Why was the Fugitive Slave Act controversial in the North?

Define

- sectionalism
- popular sovereignty

Identify

- Wilmot Proviso
- Free-Soil Party
- Henry Clay
- Daniel Webster
- Compromise of 1850
- Fugitive Slave Act
- Anthony Burns
- *Uncle Tom's Cabin*
- Harriet Beecher Stowe

Why It Matters Today

Congressional compromises are still an important part of the U.S. government. Use CNNfyi.com or other **current events** sources to learn about a recent issue that has led to compromise legislation in Congress. Record your findings in your journal.

The Story Continues

On August 8, 1846, the members of the U.S. House of Representatives slowly returned from dinner. They resumed their talk of the ongoing war with Mexico. It was one of the hottest nights of the summer. Ice water and fans were in heavy demand. As the representatives began to talk about the possible outcomes of the war, a congressman from Pennsylvania asked to speak. David Wilmot held the floor for 10 minutes—and changed the course of history.

This illustration shows the U.S. Capitol as it looked in the 1800s.

The Expansion of Slavery

Victory in the Mexican War in 1848 added more than 500,000 square miles to the United States and renewed the bitter debate over the expansion of slavery. The Missouri Compromise of 1820 had let Missouri enter the Union as a slave state. The Compromise divided the rest of the Louisiana Purchase into free and slave territory. Slavery was not allowed north of latitude 36°30'. President James K. Polk and others now wanted to run the 36°30' line to the Pacific coast, dividing the Mexican Cession into free and slave territory.

Some northerners wanted to prohibit slavery in all parts of the Mexican Cession. During the war, Representative David Wilmot had proposed a plan known as the **Wilmot Proviso**. It stated that "neither slavery nor involuntary servitude shall ever exist in any part of [the] territory." The House of Representatives, which had a northern majority, passed the proviso, but it died in the Senate, where the South had more power. Although the Wilmot Proviso never became law, the debate over the plan showed the growing **sectionalism** of the country. Sectionalism happens when people favor the interests of one region over the interests of the country as a whole.

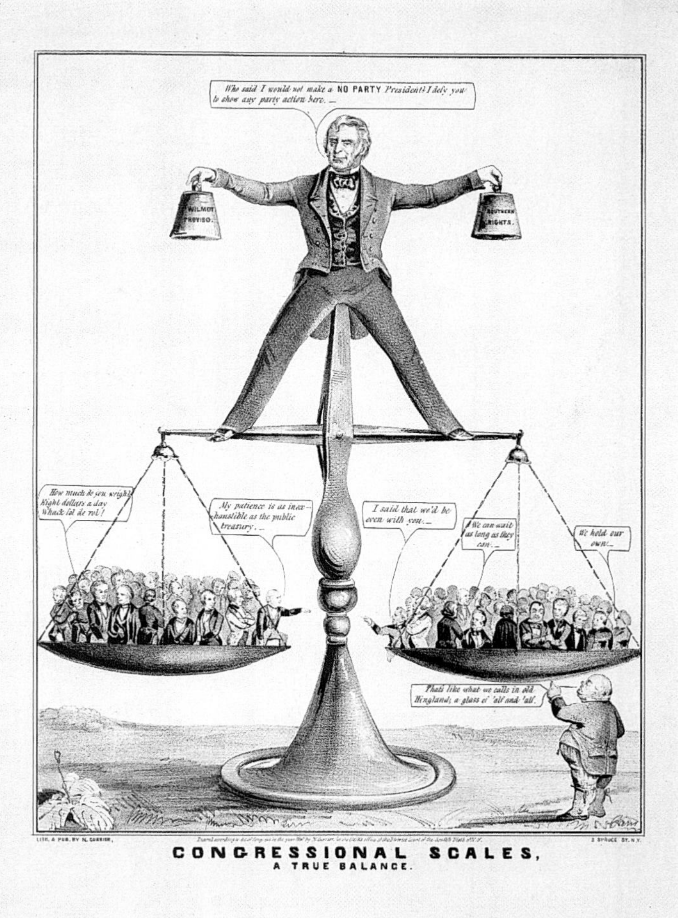

Interpreting Political Cartoons

Balancing act *The controversy over the Wilmot Proviso forced President Zachary Taylor to try to balance antislavery and pro-slavery interests.* ***How does the cartoonist show Taylor's efforts to preserve peace?***

Senator Lewis Cass of Michigan hoped to solve the conflict over slavery in new territories. He pushed for **popular sovereignty**, which would allow voters in a territory to decide whether they wanted to ban or allow slavery. They would make their choice by electing antislavery or pro-slavery representatives to their territorial legislatures. Based on the will of the majority, these legislatures then would pass laws either to ban or to allow slavery.

The debate over slavery in the Mexican Cession dominated the presidential campaign of 1848. However, neither the Democrats nor the Whigs took a clear position on slavery in the West. For this reason, thousands of antislavery northerners formed a new political party. In August 1848 in Buffalo, New York, they formed the **Free-Soil Party**. The Free-Soilers supported the Wilmot Proviso. They chose former president Martin Van Buren of New York as their candidate. The new party won 10 percent of the popular vote. This helped Whig candidate Zachary Taylor, a Mexican War hero, win a narrow victory over Democratic opponent Lewis Cass.

The California Gold Rush caused a population boom that allowed California to skip the territorial stage and apply directly for admission into the Union. This raised the issue of whether California would join as a free state or a slave state. Most Californians did not want slavery and hoped to enter the Union as a free state. However, doing so would upset the balance between free and slave states.

To many southerners such a step was unacceptable. "We are about permanently to destroy the balance of power between the sections," warned Senator Jefferson Davis of Mississippi. He and many other southerners declared that they would oppose the admission of California to the Union as a free state.

✔ **Reading Check: Contrasting** How were the Wilmot Proviso and the principle of popular sovereignty different?

"General Taylor Never Surrenders" is the motto of this 1848 Zachary Taylor campaign button.

The Compromise of 1850

Henry Clay had helped settle the Missouri crisis of 1819–20 and the nullification crisis of 1832–33. This senator from Kentucky, nicknamed "The Great Compromiser," now stepped forward with another plan. Clay's proposal had five main parts.

1. He urged Congress to let California enter the Union as a free state.
2. He called for the rest of the Mexican Cession to be organized as a federal territory. In this territory—already called New Mexico—popular sovereignty would decide the status of slavery.
3. He addressed a border dispute between Texas and New Mexico. He called on Texas to give up its claim to all land east of the upper Rio Grande. In exchange, the federal government would pay Texas's old debts. These debts remained from its days as an independent republic.
4. He called for an end to the slave trade—but not slavery—in the country's capital.
5. He called for a new, more effective fugitive slave law.

Almost immediately, Clay's plan came under fire. Senator William Seward of New York spoke for antislavery northerners. He demanded the admission of California "directly, without conditions, without qualifications, and without compromise." Senator John C. Calhoun of South Carolina spoke for many in the South. Near death, Calhoun was so weak that another senator had to read his speech. Calhoun argued that letting California enter as a free state would destroy the balance

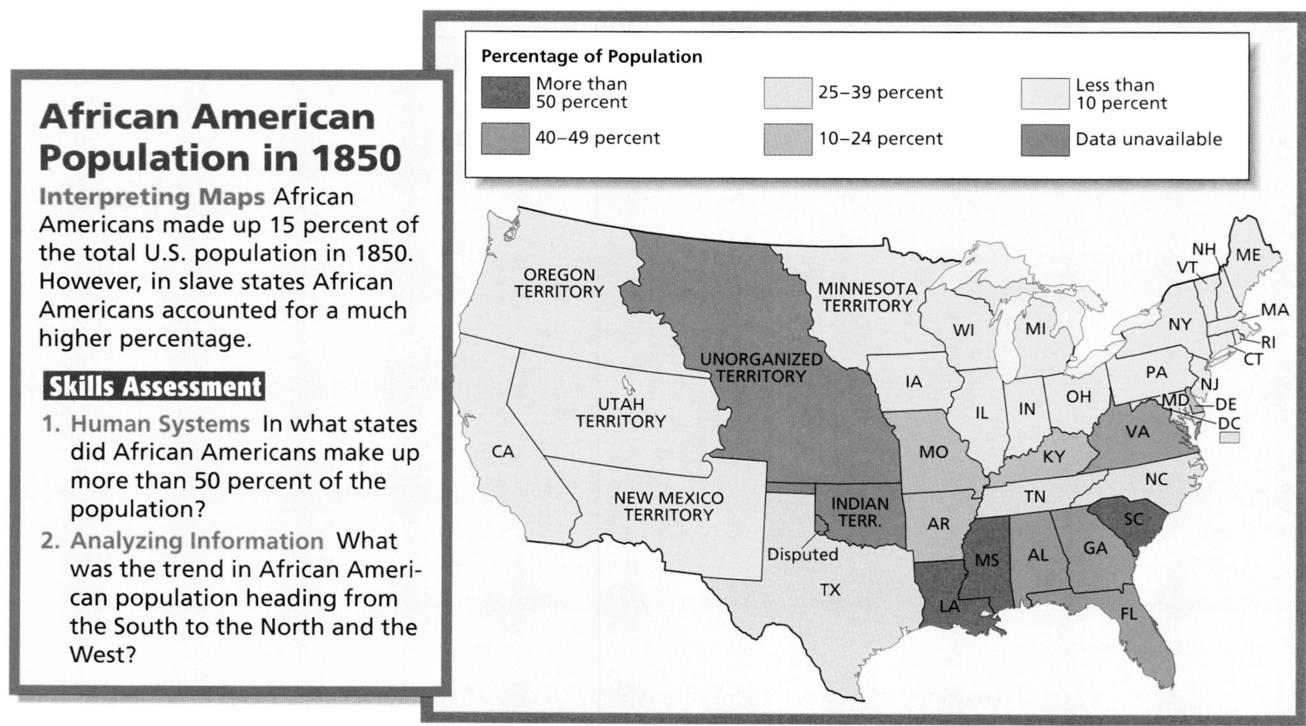

African American Population in 1850

Interpreting Maps African Americans made up 15 percent of the total U.S. population in 1850. However, in slave states African Americans accounted for a much higher percentage.

Skills Assessment

1. **Human Systems** In what states did African Americans make up more than 50 percent of the population?
2. **Analyzing Information** What was the trend in African American population heading from the South to the North and the West?

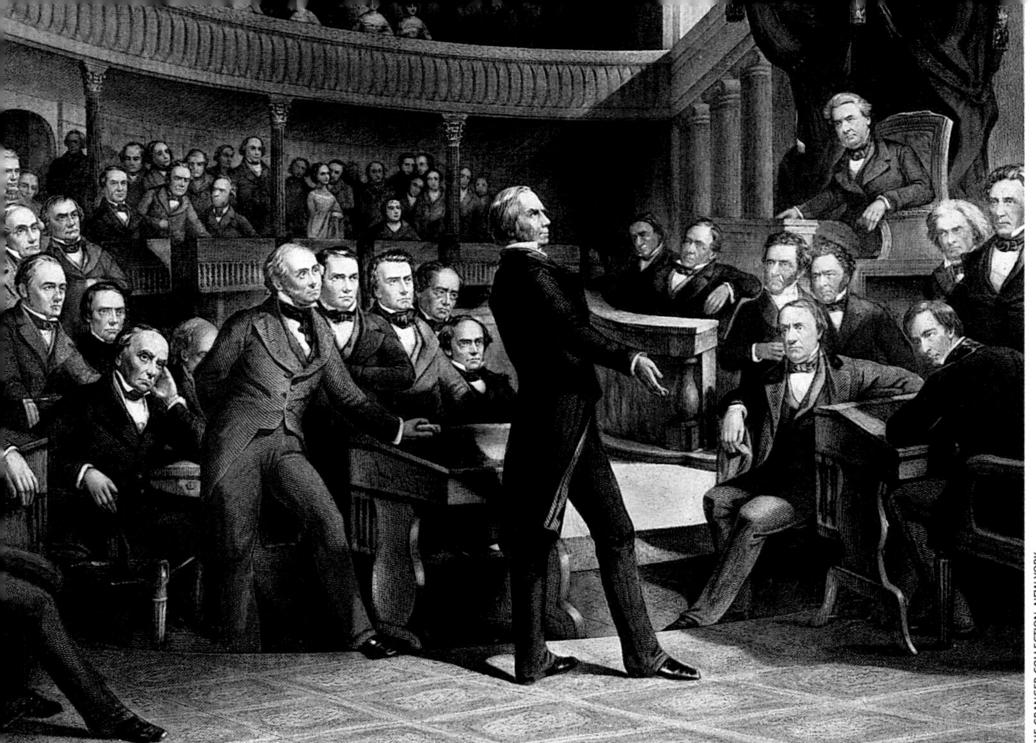

THE GRANGER COLLECTION, NEW YORK

Interpreting the Visual Record

Clay's compromise *In 1850 Senator Henry Clay once again urged Congress to compromise on the issue of slavery in the territories.* ***How does the image indicate that Clay was a central figure in the debates over slavery?***

between the two sections of the country. The slave states could not "remain in the Union consistently with their honor and their safety," he said. Calhoun asked that they be allowed "to separate and part in peace."

Others, such as Senator **Daniel Webster** of Massachusetts, were in favor of Clay's plan. Although Webster himself was opposed to the expansion of slavery, he argued that preserving the Union was more important than any regional differences.

> **"I wish to speak today, not as a Massachusetts man, nor as a Northern man, but as an American. . . . I speak today for the preservation of the Union. Hear me for my cause."**
>
> —Daniel Webster, quoted in *Battle Cry of Freedom*, by James M. McPherson

Analyzing Primary Sources

Drawing Inferences and Conclusions How did Senator Webster avoid sectionalism in his speech?

Webster criticized northern abolitionists and scolded southerners who spoke of breaking away from the Union. He also argued that fighting over slavery in the West was unnecessary. Because of the soil and climate in this region, he claimed, the kinds of crops for which slave labor was used would not grow.

The **Compromise of 1850** became law in September of that year. It accomplished most of what Clay had wanted. California entered the Union as a free state. The rest of the Mexican Cession was divided into two territories. In these territories—Utah and New Mexico—the status of slavery would be decided by popular sovereignty. Texas agreed to give up its land claims in New Mexico. In exchange, the federal government gave Texas the financial help it needed. Finally, the compromise outlawed the slave trade in the nation's capital and produced a new fugitive slave law that replaced the previous law of 1793.

✔ **Reading Check: Summarizing** How did the Compromise of 1850 attempt to resolve conflicts over the expansion of slavery?

Research on the ROM

Free Find:
John C. Calhoun
After reading about John C. Calhoun on the **Holt Researcher CD–ROM,** create a political profile of him. Be sure to give details of Calhoun's life and explain his positions on important political issues of the era.

BIOGRAPHY

Frederick Douglass

(1817–1895)

Frederick Douglass was born to an enslaved family in Maryland. At age 20, he escaped to freedom in the North. There he began speaking and writing for the abolition movement. In 1845 he published the *Narrative of the Life of Frederick Douglass*. The detail in this autobiography forced him to leave the country to avoid being arrested as a fugitive slave. He returned in 1847 and bought his freedom. He started an antislavery newspaper, which he named *North Star*. In the first issue, Douglass called on other former slaves to join his crusade for freedom. Why did Douglass have to leave the country?

The Fugitive Slave Act

One part of the Compromise of 1850 kept slavery very much on the minds of Americans. The **Fugitive Slave Act** made it a federal crime to help runaway slaves. The act even let officials arrest runaways in areas where slavery was illegal. Under the new law, slaveholders and their agents could take suspected fugitive slaves before U.S. commissioners. They would then try to prove ownership through documents or through the testimony of white witnesses. In contrast, the accused fugitives could not testify in their own defense. Commissioners who rejected a slaveholder's claim received $5 for their services. Those who returned a suspected fugitive to the slaveholder in the South received $10. Anyone who hid or otherwise helped a runaway slave faced six months in jail and a $1,000 fine.

In the 10 years after Congress passed this law, 343 fugitive slave cases came under the commissioners' review in the North. The accused fugitive was declared free in only 11 of these cases. Such numbers worried many African Americans living in the North—free individuals as well as former slaves. Thousands of African Americans went to Canada to escape potential prosecution under the Fugitive Slave Act.

The Fugitive Slave Act upset many northerners. They did not agree with the lack of a trial by jury. These northerners also disliked the higher fee given to commissioners who returned fugitives. This apparent bribe encouraged commissioners to send a suspected fugitive slave back to the South. As expected, abolitionists led the protests against the new law. One abolitionist said it was every citizen's duty to make sure that the new law was "resisted, disobeyed at all hazards." Martin R. Delany, a doctor and a leading African American abolitionist, spoke publicly to the mayor of Pittsburgh, Pennsylvania.

"If any man approaches that house in search of a slave—I care not who he may be . . . if he crosses the threshold of my door, and I do not lay him a lifeless corpse at my feet, I hope the grave may refuse my body a resting place, and righteous Heaven my spirit a home."

—Martin R. Delany, quoted in *The Negro Caravan,* edited by Sterling A. Brown, Arthur P. Davis, and Ulysses Lee

Analyzing Primary Sources

Identifying Points of View How did Delany react to the new fugitive slave law?

In general, northerners who resisted the Fugitive Slave Act did so without using violence. However, blood was spilled on several occasions. In 1854, for example, the case of **Anthony Burns** caught the nation's attention. Burns, a fugitive slave from Virginia, was arrested and jailed in Boston. A group of abolitionists in the city tried to rescue Burns by force. A deputy marshal was killed in the attempt, but Burns was eventually returned to slavery in Virginia.

✔ **Reading Check: Finding the Main Idea** How did many northerners respond to the Fugitive Slave Act?

Antislavery Literature

Abolitionists in the North used the stories of fugitive slaves such as Anthony Burns to help their cause. They also made use of slave narratives, which became popular around 1840. Among the best known were the narratives of Frederick Douglass and Sojourner Truth. Truth's narrative differed from most other slave narratives in two ways. First, its central character was a woman. Second, Truth had been a slave not in the South but in New York.

THE GRANGER COLLECTION, NEW YORK

THE GRANGER COLLECTION, NEW YORK

Abolitionists protested the arrest of suspected fugitive slaves, such as the capture shown above.

No other literary work, however, had the influence of ***Uncle Tom's Cabin***. This powerful antislavery novel was written by **Harriet Beecher Stowe**. Stowe was born into a religious family in Connecticut and moved to Ohio at the age of 21. There she met with fugitive slaves and learned about the cruelty of slavery. The passage of the Fugitive Slave Act of 1850 greatly angered Stowe, so she decided to write a book that would show northerners what slavery was really like.

Uncle Tom's Cabin was published in 1852. The main character is a kindly old slave named Tom, who is separated from his wife and sold. Tom becomes the slave of a cruel cotton planter in Louisiana. The novel sparked outrage in the South and gained praise in the North. Within 10 years, more than 2 million copies of *Uncle Tom's Cabin* were sold in the United States. The book's popularity caused one northerner to remark that Stowe had created "two millions of abolitionists."

✔ **Reading Check: Analyzing Information** How did literature help the antislavery movement?

Section 1 Review

go.hrw.com **Homework Practice Online**
keyword: SC3 HP15

1. **Define** and explain:
   - sectionalism
   - popular sovereignty
2. **Identify** and explain:
   - Wilmot Proviso
   - Free-Soil Party
   - Henry Clay
   - Daniel Webster
   - Compromise of 1850
   - Fugitive Slave Act
   - Anthony Burns
   - *Uncle Tom's Cabin*
   - Harriet Beecher Stowe
3. **Contrasting** Copy the diagram below. Use it to explain how the Compromise of 1850, Fugitive Slave Act, and antislavery literature related to the debate over the expansion of slavery.

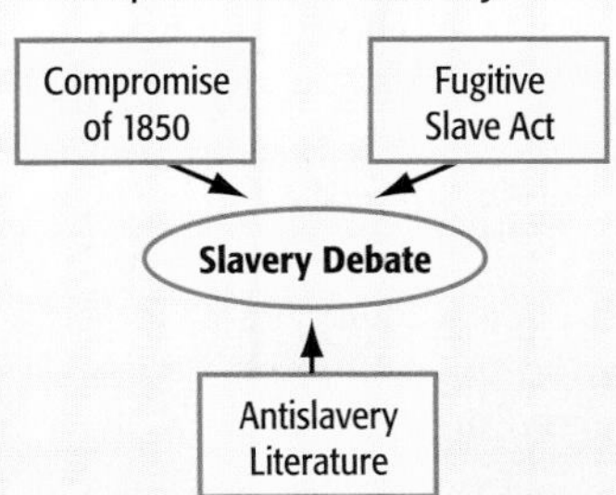

4. **Finding the Main Idea**
   a. How did U.S. territory change after the Mexican War ended, and how did this change renew the debate over slavery?
   b. What did the Compromise of 1850 propose? Why did Senator Daniel Webster support it, and why did Senator John C. Calhoun oppose it?
5. **Writing and Critical Thinking**
   Supporting a Point of View Imagine that you are a northerner who is opposed to the Fugitive Slave Act. Create a handbill that you would pass out at a town meeting to persuade members of your community to protest the law.
   Consider the following:
   - lack of trial by jury
   - "bribes" given to commissioners
   - examples of abolitionist protests

CONNECTING TO Literature

Uncle Tom's Cabin

Harriet Beecher Stowe

Like Mark Twain, Harriet Beecher Stowe was a local-color writer, concentrating on describing regional culture and language. Stowe wrote mostly about New England. However, she is best remembered for Uncle Tom's Cabin, *a powerful novel about slavery. In the following passage, Simon Legree is a northerner who has moved south and become a cruel slaveholder. He has ordered Sambo, a slave driver, to whip Tom. Legree wants to learn what Tom knows about the disappearance of two slaves. Tom, a slave, is one of the main characters of the novel. He has maintained his religious faith despite the brutality he has witnessed and experienced. The scene shows the consequences of slavery—both to the suffering slave and to the soul of the slaveholder. The criticism of slavery in the first and last paragraphs is the author's voice.*

Uncle Tom's Cabin *helped convince many Americans of the moral wrongs of slavery.*

Scenes of blood and cruelty are shocking to our ear and heart. What man has nerve to do, man has not nerve to hear. What brother-man and brother-Christian must suffer, cannot be told us, even in our secret chamber, it so **harrows up**[1] the soul! And yet, oh my country; these things are done under the shadow of thy laws! O, Christ! thy church sees them, almost in silence! . . . "He's most **gone**,[2] **Mas'r**,[3]" said Sambo, touched, in spite of himself, by the patience of his victim.

"Pay away, till he give up! Give it to him!—give it to him!" shouted Legree. "I'll take every drop of blood he has, unless he confesses!"

Tom opened his eyes, and looked upon his master. "Ye poor miserable crittur!" he said, "there ain't no more ye can do! I forgive ye, with all my soul!" and he fainted entirely away.

"I b'lieve, my soul, he's done for, finally," said Legree, stepping forward, to look at him. "Yes, he is! Well, his mouth's shut up, at last,—that's one comfort!"

Yes, Legree; but who shall shut up that voice in thy soul? that soul, **past repentance**,[4] past prayer, past hope, in whom the fire that never shall be quenched is already burning!

Understanding What You Read

1. **Literature and History** In the opening paragraph, whom does Stowe criticize for allowing slavery to occur?
2. **Literature and You** What do you think Stowe is asking of the reader?

[1]**harrows up:** frightens or shocks
[2]**gone:** dead
[3]**Mas'r:** master
[4]**past repentance:** beyond the ability to turn away from sin; past regret

Section 2

Trouble in Kansas

Read to Discover

1. How did different regions of the country react to the Kansas-Nebraska Act?
2. In what ways did people try to settle the conflict over slavery in Kansas?
3. What series of violent events showed growing division over slavery in the United States?

Identify

- Franklin Pierce
- Stephen Douglas
- Kansas-Nebraska Act
- Pottawatomie Massacre
- Charles Sumner
- Preston Brooks

Why It Matters Today

In the 1850s events in Kansas affected the entire nation. Use CNNfyi.com or other **current events** sources to learn about events in one part of the country that have affected the entire country. Record your findings in your journal.

The Story Continues

Franklin and Jane Pierce spent the morning taking a peaceful carriage ride just outside Boston, Massachusetts. On their way back to their hotel in the city, they saw a horseman racing toward them. When the rider reached the Pierces' carriage, he shouted the news. The Democratic convention in Baltimore, Maryland, had nominated Franklin Pierce for the presidency. The Pierces were stunned.

The Democratic Party nominated Franklin Pierce for president in 1852.

The Election of 1852

As the Democratic convention opened in 1852, there were four leading candidates for the presidential nomination. It soon became clear, however, that no one could win a majority of votes. After nearly 50 ballots, the frustrated delegates chose **Franklin Pierce**. Pierce was a little-known politician from New Hampshire. However, he and his party promised to honor the Compromise of 1850 and enforce the Fugitive Slave Act. Thus, many southerners saw Pierce "as reliable as Calhoun himself" on the slavery question.

The Whigs also held their convention in Baltimore in 1852. The divided party hoped to repeat earlier successes by nominating a well-known soldier for the presidency. They passed over Millard Fillmore, who had become president after Zachary Taylor's death. Instead, the Whigs chose Winfield Scott, a hero from the Mexican War. Although Scott was born in Virginia, many southerners did not trust him because he had not completely supported the Compromise of 1850.

The Democrats won the election by a large margin. Pierce won 27 of the 31 states. Even Scott's home state of Virginia voted for Pierce. Whig Representative Lewis Campbell of Ohio feared the worst after this painful defeat. "We are slayed," he cried. "The party is dead—dead—dead!"

✔ **Reading Check: Identifying Cause and Effect** Who won the 1852 presidential election, and how did the election affect the Whig Party?

The Kansas-Nebraska Act

Since entering Congress in the mid-1840s, **Stephen Douglas** had supported building a railroad to the Pacific. Douglas wanted a line running from Chicago, in his home state of Illinois. To build this railroad, however, the rest of the Louisiana Purchase had to be made into a federal territory. The Missouri Compromise banned slavery in this region, meaning that the land would eventually become free states.

Southerners in Congress did not support Douglas's plan. They wanted a line running from New Orleans across Texas. It would run through the already organized territory of New Mexico and into southern California. However, Douglas was determined to have the railroad start in Chicago. Thus, he asked a few key southern senators to support

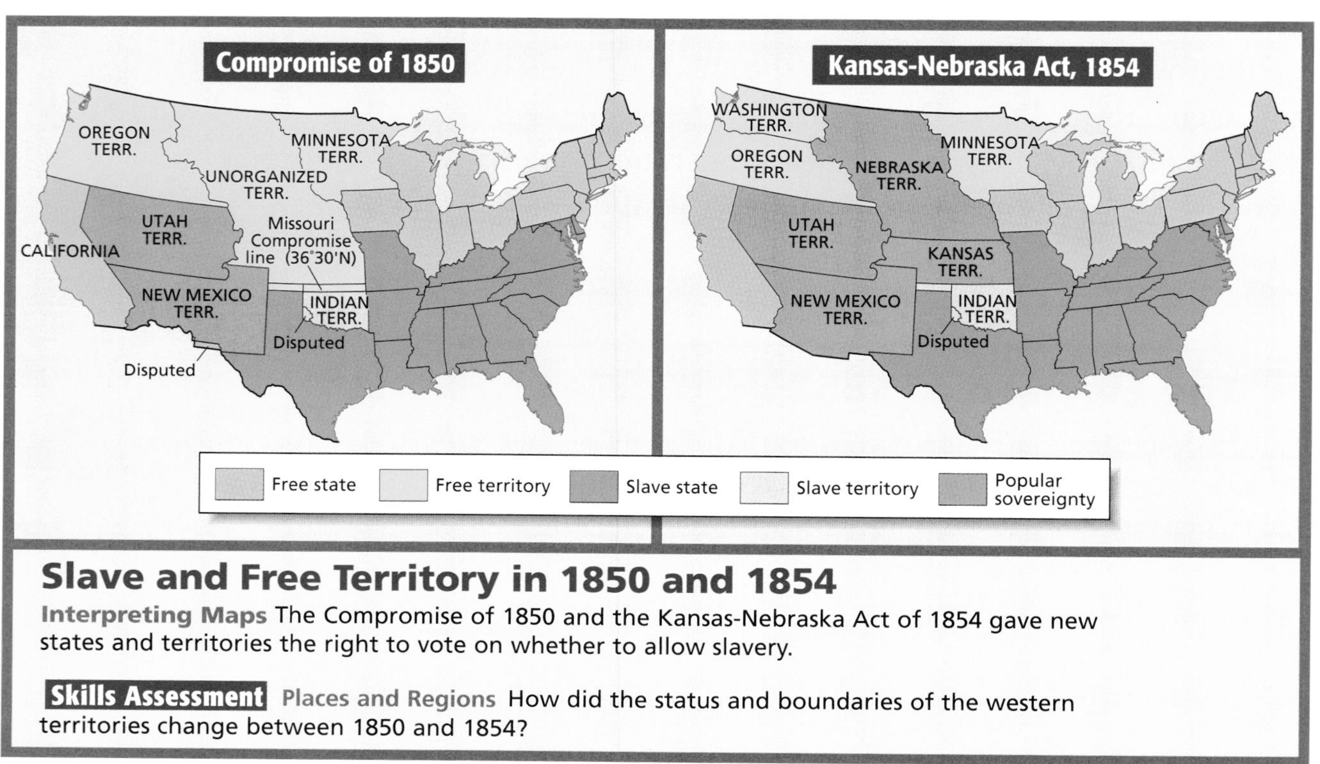

Slave and Free Territory in 1850 and 1854

Interpreting Maps The Compromise of 1850 and the Kansas-Nebraska Act of 1854 gave new states and territories the right to vote on whether to allow slavery.

Skills Assessment **Places and Regions** How did the status and boundaries of the western territories change between 1850 and 1854?

Comparing the Compromises

As disagreements over the expansion of slavery divided the nation, congressional leaders tried to find a compromise that would end sectional disagreements.

Missouri Compromise

No slavery in new states north of 36° 30′ line

Missouri joins the Union as a slave state

Maine joins the Union as a free state

Henry Clay

Compromise of 1850

California joins the Union as a free state

New Mexico and Utah Territories to use popular sovereignty to decide status of slavery

Stronger fugitive slave law passed

Slave trade ended in Washington, D.C.

Border dispute between New Mexico and Texas is resolved

Henry Clay

Daniel Webster

John C. Calhoun

Kansas-Nebraska Act

Kansas and Nebraska Territories are created

No more 36° 30′ boundary for slave states

Kansas and Nebraska Territories will use popular sovereignty

Stephen Douglas

Visualizing History

1. **Government** What are the main similarities and differences among the three compromises?
2. **Connecting to Today** Do you think compromise is still an important political tool today? Why or why not?

his plan. They said they would give up their plans for a southern railroad route. In return, they wanted the new territory west of Missouri opened up to slavery.

In January 1854 Douglas introduced what became the **Kansas-Nebraska Act**. This plan would divide the rest of the Louisiana Purchase into two territories—Kansas and Nebraska. In each territory, popular sovereignty would decide the question of slavery. Douglas's plan would remove the Missouri Compromise's restriction on slavery north of the 36°30' line.

Antislavery northerners were outraged. Some called the proposal a "gross violation of a sacred pledge." They thought it was part of a southern plot to turn free territory into a "dreary region . . . inhabited by masters and slaves." All across the North, citizens attended protest meetings and sent anti-Nebraska petitions to Congress. However, the measure carried strong southern support. Douglas and President Pierce also tried to get their fellow Democrats to vote for it. The measure passed the Senate in March and the House two months later. The president signed the act into law on May 30, 1854. Lost in the controversy was Douglas's proposed railroad to the Pacific. Congress would not approve the construction of such a railroad until 1862.

Advertisements like this 1855 poster encouraged settlers to buy land in Kansas.

✔ **Reading Check: Finding the Main Idea** Why were antislavery northerners angry about the Kansas-Nebraska Act?

THE GRANGER COLLECTION, NEW YORK

Antislavery activist Henry Ward Beecher helped raise money to send weapons to abolitionist settlers in Kansas.

"Bleeding Kansas"

Both northern and southern politicians saw that a contest had begun. As a result, antislavery and pro-slavery groups rushed to get people to Kansas. Senator William Seward of New York spoke on the issue.

History Makers Speak

> **"Gentlemen of the Slave States, since there is no escaping your challenge, I accept it in behalf of the cause of freedom. We will engage in competition for . . . Kansas, and God give victory to the side which is stronger in numbers as it is in right."**
>
> —William Henry Seward, quoted in *The Impending Crisis, 1848–1861,* by David M. Potter

Elections for the Kansas territorial legislature were held in March 1855. To ensure a pro-slavery victory, thousands of men crossed the border from Missouri, voted in Kansas, and then returned home. As a result, the territorial legislature, located at Lecompton, had a huge pro-slavery majority. The new legislature passed a series of strict pro-slavery laws. One law made it a crime to question anyone's right to hold slaves. Another law stated that anyone caught helping a fugitive slave could be punished by death. In protest, antislavery Kansans formed their own legislature 25 miles away in Topeka.

By early 1856 Kansas had two governments and an angry population divided into two armed camps. Many of the pro-slavery settlers had brought guns with them to the new territory. Meanwhile antislavery settlers had asked for shipments of weapons from their friends in the East. With both sides heavily armed, violence soon broke out. In May 1856 a pro-slavery grand jury charged the leaders of the antislavery government with treason. A posse of more than 700 men rode to Lawrence, where they destroyed buildings and printing presses.

Abolitionist John Brown decided that it was his duty to punish pro-slavery forces for the so-called Sack of Lawrence. He said it was time to

THE GRANGER COLLECTION, NEW YORK

Interpreting the Visual Record

The Sack of Lawrence *A pro-slavery force came to the town of Lawrence seeking to arrest antislavery leaders. When they could not find these people, they attacked the rest of the town, killing one man.* ***How does this image portray the violence of the pro-slavery settlers?***

"strike terror in the hearts of the pro-slavery people." Brown was a New Englander who moved to Kansas in 1855 with some of his sons. On the night of May 24, 1856, he led a group of seven men along Pottawatomie Creek in eastern Kansas. They killed five pro-slavery men in what became known as the **Pottawatomie Massacre**. Kansas collapsed into a state of civil war. About 200 people were killed in the months that followed. The events in "Bleeding Kansas" became front-page stories in many of the country's newspapers.

THE GRANGER COLLECTION, NEW YORK

Preston Brooks was fined $300 by a federal court for his attack on Charles Sumner, who was unable to return to the Senate until after a three-year absence.

Conflict also swept Congress, where Senator **Charles Sumner** of Massachusetts gave a speech called "The Crime Against Kansas." In it, he criticized pro-slavery efforts in Kansas and insulted Senator Andrew Pickens Butler of South Carolina. Representative **Preston Brooks**, a relative of Butler, was greatly upset. On May 22, 1856, Brooks approached Sumner in the Senate chamber and beat him unconscious with a walking cane. A newspaper editor in Virginia praised Brooks's actions.

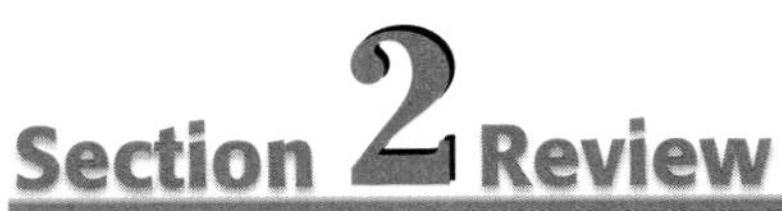

"We consider the act good in conception [thought], better in execution. . . . These vulgar [rude] abolitionists in the Senate . . . must be lashed into submission [surrender]. Sumner, in particular, ought to have nine-and-thirty [lashes] early every morning."

—*Richmond Enquirer*, June 2, 1856

Analyzing Primary Sources

Identifying Bias How can you tell that the speaker supports the spread of slavery?

Dozens of southerners sent Brooks new canes. In the North Sumner's beating outraged many people, who called the attacker Bully Brooks.

✔ **Reading Check: Comparing and Contrasting** How did northerners and southerners react to events involving Kansas?

Section 2 Review

go.hrw.com **Homework Practice Online**
keyword: SC3 HP15

1. **Identify** and explain:
   - Franklin Pierce
   - Stephen Douglas
   - Kansas-Nebraska Act
   - Pottawatomie Massacre
   - Charles Sumner
   - Preston Brooks

2. **Sequencing** Copy the graphic organizer below. Use it to describe the Kansas-Nebraska Act and the conflicts that followed in the order that they occurred.

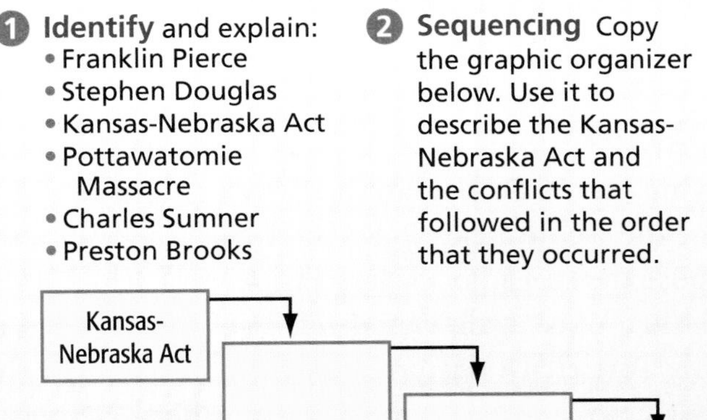

3. **Finding the Main Idea**
   a. What did northerners and southerners think of the Kansas-Nebraska Act?
   b. How did antislavery forces hope to prevent slavery in Kansas, and how did pro-slavery groups influence the Kansas territorial elections in 1855?

4. **Writing and Critical Thinking**
   Summarizing Imagine that you are a historian writing about the beating of Charles Sumner by Preston Brooks. Write a half-page essay describing the events leading up to the beating and the public's reactions.
   Consider the following:
   - reasons for the attack
   - northern reactions to the beating
   - southern reactions to the beating

Section 3

Political Divisions

Read to Discover

1. How did the Kansas-Nebraska Act affect U.S. political parties?
2. Why did Dred Scott sue for his freedom, and how did the Supreme Court rule on his case?
3. How did Abraham Lincoln and Stephen Douglas differ in their views on slavery?

Identify

- Republican Party
- James Buchanan
- John C. Frémont
- Dred Scott
- Roger B. Taney
- *Dred Scott* decision
- Abraham Lincoln
- Lincoln-Douglas debates
- Freeport Doctrine

Why It Matters Today

Supreme Court decisions have a major impact on life in the United States. Use CNNfyi.com or other **current events** sources to learn about how a recent Supreme Court decision will affect the whole country. Record your findings in your journal.

The Story Continues

On July 5, 1854, hundreds of people met at the town of Jackson, Michigan, to form a new political party. "We will . . . be known as Republicans," they declared in their platform. They promised to uphold the principles of republican government. They also said they would fight the spread of slavery "until the contest be terminated."

THE GRANGER COLLECTION, NEW YORK

This crowd has gathered to hear a speaker at the first Republican National Convention.

New Divisions

Political unrest led Whigs, some Democrats, Free-Soilers, and abolitionists to join and form the **Republican Party** in 1854. These different groups united to oppose the spread of slavery in the West. The Kansas-Nebraska Act of 1854 had once again raised this issue and divided the Democratic and Whig Parties. Under pressure from Senator Stephen Douglas and President Franklin Pierce, nearly 60 northern Democrats had voted for the Kansas-Nebraska bill. They suffered politically for their support, however. In the next congressional elections, only seven of the northern Democrats who voted for the bill kept their seats in the House of Representatives.

The Kansas-Nebraska Act was even more damaging to the Whigs. Every northern Whig voted against Douglas's bill. Most southern Whigs, however, voted for it.

The presidential election of 1856 showed just how divided the country was becoming. Some longtime Whigs and Democrats joined the Know-Nothing Party, which quickly fell apart over the slavery issue. Northern delegates left the convention hall when southerners refused to support the repeal of the Kansas-Nebraska Act. Many northerners later supported the Republican Party. Those Know-Nothings who remained behind chose former president Millard Fillmore as their presidential candidate.

The Democrats knew that they could not nominate anyone closely associated with the Kansas-Nebraska Act, which ruled out President Pierce and Senator Douglas. They chose **James Buchanan** of Pennsylvania instead. Buchanan had served roughly 20 years in Congress and as Polk's secretary of state for 4 years. Most importantly, he had not been involved in the Kansas-Nebraska controversy.

At their first presidential nominating convention, the Republicans chose **John C. Frémont** as their candidate. Frémont had little political experience, but his opposition to the spread of slavery appealed to Republicans. Although the Republicans also favored issues such as protective tariffs, they generally were seen as a "single-issue party." Their antislavery platform meant the Republicans had almost no supporters outside of the free states.

Some white southerners even said that they would not accept a Republican victory in the election. A politician from Georgia made a prediction: "The election of Frémont would be the end of the Union." On election day, Buchanan won 14 of the 15 slave states and 5 of the free states, the rest of which went to Frémont. Fillmore, meanwhile, won only one state—Maryland. Buchanan won the election.

✔ **Reading Check: Summarizing** How did the Kansas-Nebraska Act affect political parties in the 1856 election?

Watching Every Dime Would you remember to correct the error if you underpaid a bill by three cents? It was everyday policy for James Buchanan to follow such precision in his accounting. Throughout his life, he kept books in which he carefully recorded every penny that he earned or spent. While serving as ambassador to Great Britain, Buchanan recorded such daily details as how much he spent on pins and suspender buttons. One time during his presidency he realized he had underpaid by three cents for some food. Even though the merchant ignored the error, the president made sure the owner received his three pennies.

James Buchanan's inaugural parade stretched far down the streets of Washington, D.C.

Dred Scott argued that living on free soil had made him a free man.

The *Dred Scott* Decision

Just two days after Buchanan became president, the Supreme Court issued a ruling that threw the country back into crisis. This case involved **Dred Scott**, the slave of an army surgeon from St. Louis, Missouri. In the 1830s Scott had gone with the surgeon on tours of duty in Illinois and the northern part of the Louisiana Purchase. In 1846 Scott sued for his freedom after returning to Missouri. He argued that he had become free when he lived in free territory.

The case reached the U.S. Supreme Court in 1856. The justices—a majority of whom were from the South—had three key issues before them. First, the Court had to rule on whether Scott was a citizen of the United States. This ruling would determine if he was able to sue in federal court. Second, the Court had to decide if the time he had spent living on free soil made him free. Third, the Court had to decide whether the ban on slavery in parts of the Louisiana Purchase was constitutional. This last ruling would affect the Missouri Compromise.

The Chief Justice of the Supreme Court was **Roger B. Taney** (TAW-nee). Taney came from a slaveholding family in Maryland. He wrote the majority opinion in the ***Dred Scott* decision** in March 1857. Taney said the nation's founders believed that African Americans "had no rights which a white man was bound to respect." He therefore concluded that African Americans were not citizens under the U.S. Constitution. Thus, Dred Scott did not have the right to file suit in federal court.

Taney then said that living on free soil had not made Scott free. Thus, "his *status*, as free or slave, depended on the laws of Missouri." Finally, Taney said that the Missouri Compromise restriction on slavery north of 36°30' was unconstitutional. He used the Fifth Amendment as support. It said no one could "be deprived of life, liberty, or property without due process of law." Slaves were considered property, so Congress could not ban someone from taking slaves into a federal territory.

Most white southerners cheered the decision. It "covers every question regarding slavery and settles it in favor of the South," reported a Georgia newspaper. The ruling stunned many northerners. Republicans were particularly upset by the Court's ruling on the Missouri Compromise. Indeed, some northerners feared that the spread of slavery would not stop with the federal territories. Illinois lawyer **Abraham Lincoln** warned about the Court's future rulings.

Analyzing Primary Sources

Identifying Points of View What concerned Lincoln about the *Dred Scott* decision?

"We shall *lie down* pleasantly dreaming that the people of *Missouri* are on the verge of [close to] making their state *free*; and we shall *awake* to the *reality*, instead, that the *Supreme* Court has made *Illinois* a *slave* state."

—Abraham Lincoln, from *The Collected Works of Abraham Lincoln*, edited by Roy P. Basler

✔ **Reading Check: Summarizing** What were the three key issues in the Supreme Court's ruling on the *Dred Scott* case?

The Lincoln-Douglas Debates

At the time of the *Dred Scott* decision, few people outside of Illinois knew Abraham Lincoln. A native of Kentucky, he had moved to the Midwest in 1816. Lincoln became involved in politics, serving four terms in the Illinois legislature and one term in Congress. A longtime Whig, he joined the Republican Party in 1856. He supported the party's efforts to halt the spread of slavery.

In 1858 Illinois Republicans nominated Lincoln for a U.S. Senate seat. His opponent was Democrat Stephen Douglas, who had represented Illinois in the Senate since 1847. Douglas was well known for the Kansas-Nebraska Act, so Lincoln tried to take advantage of his opponent's fame. He challenged Douglas to a series of debates throughout the state.

Thousands of people attended the **Lincoln-Douglas debates**. In each of the seven debates, Lincoln stressed that the central issue in the campaign involved slavery and its future in the West. Lincoln said that the Democrats wanted to spread slavery across the continent. As a Republican, Lincoln believed that slavery was wrong. Lincoln added that "one of the methods of treating it as a wrong is to make provision [ensure] that *it shall grow no larger*." Lincoln also said that African Americans were "entitled to all the natural rights" listed in the Declaration of Independence. He specifically named "the right to life, liberty, and the pursuit of happiness."

Some voters asked Lincoln about his views on racial equality. He replied that African Americans were not necessarily the political or social equals of whites. However, "in the right to eat the bread . . . which his own hand earns, he [an African American] *is my equal and the equal of Judge Douglas*." Douglas insisted that Lincoln "thinks that the Negro is his brother. . . . Those of you who believe that the Negro is your equal . . . of course will vote for Mr. Lincoln." Douglas hoped that these statements would shock many voters and cost Lincoln votes.

Research on the ROM

Free Find:
Stephen Douglas
After reading about Stephen Douglas on the **Holt Researcher CD–ROM**, imagine that you are hosting one of the Lincoln-Douglas debates. Write a speech that introduces Stephen Douglas to the crowd of spectators.

Interpreting the Visual Record

Political debate *The Lincoln-Douglas debates established the reputation of Abraham Lincoln as a gifted public speaker. In this painting of the fourth debate in the series, Lincoln is standing to speak and Stephen Douglas is seated to Lincoln's right.* ***What is the mood of the politicians and audience members shown in this painting?***

Supporters of Stephen Douglas made this wooden campaign doll.

Douglas also criticized Lincoln for saying that the country could not remain "half slave and half free." He said that the Republicans wanted to make every state a free state. If this happened, he warned, it would only lead to "a dissolution [destruction] of the Union" and "warfare between the North and the South."

The second debate was held in the northern Illinois town of Freeport. At this meeting, Lincoln pointed out the difference between the Democrats' belief in popular sovereignty and the terms of the *Dred Scott* decision. He asked Douglas to explain how Congress could allow the citizens of a federal territory to ban slavery if Congress itself could not ban it. Douglas's response became known as the **Freeport Doctrine**. "It matters not" what the Supreme Court decides about slavery, responded Douglas.

"The people have the lawful means [way] to introduce it or exclude it [shut it out] as they please, for the reason that slavery cannot exist a day or an hour anywhere, unless it is supported by local police regulations."

—Stephen Douglas, quoted in *Stephen A. Douglas*, by Robert W. Johannsen

The Freeport Doctrine would put control of the slavery question back in the hands of American citizens. The doctrine helped Douglas win the Senate seat. However, Lincoln had made a strong showing in the debates. As a result, he became one of the important leaders of the new Republican Party.

✔ **Reading Check: Contrasting** How did Douglas oppose Lincoln's views on slavery and African Americans?

Section 3 Review

go.hrw.com Homework Practice Online
keyword: SC3 HP15

1. **Identify** and explain:
   - Republican Party
   - James Buchanan
   - John C. Frémont
   - Dred Scott
   - Roger B. Taney
   - *Dred Scott* decision
   - Abraham Lincoln
   - Lincoln-Douglas debates
   - Freeport Doctrine

2. **Analyzing Information** Copy the chart below. Use it to identify examples of deepening political divisions caused by the slavery issue.

Event	Results
Election of 1856	
Dred Scott decision	
Lincoln-Douglas debates	

3. **Finding the Main Idea**
   a. How did different political parties respond to the Kansas-Nebraska Act?
   b. What did Dred Scott claim made him free, and how did the Supreme Court rule in his case?

4. **Writing and Critical Thinking**
   Summarizing Imagine that you are an Illinois resident who attended the Lincoln-Douglas debates. Write a letter to a friend in another state explaining the candidates' views on the spread of slavery.
   Consider the following:
   - Lincoln's views on slavery and racial equality
   - Douglas's response to Lincoln
   - the Freeport Doctrine

Section 4

Secession

Read to Discover

1. How did Americans react to John Brown's raid on Harpers Ferry?
2. What factors led to Lincoln's victory in the presidential election of 1860?
3. Why did some southern states decide to leave the Union?

Why It Matters Today

There is still diversity among the different regions of the United States. Use CNNfyi.com or other **current events** sources to identify issues or features that show these differences. Record your findings in your journal.

Define

- secession

Identify

- John Brown's raid
- John C. Breckinridge
- Constitutional Union Party
- John Bell
- John J. Crittenden
- Confederate States of America
- Jefferson Davis

The Story Continues

After the Pottawatomie Massacre, John Brown was a hunted man. He left Kansas and eventually returned to New England. There Brown was frustrated that most abolitionists wanted to end slavery without using violence. "Talk! talk! talk!" he said with disgust after attending a meeting of the New England Anti-Slavery Society. "That will never free the slaves. What is needed is action—action."

John Brown believed that violence was the only way to end slavery.

The Raid on Harpers Ferry

In 1858 John Brown worked to start a slave uprising. He wanted to attack the federal arsenal, or military storehouse, in Virginia and seize the weapons stored there. He then planned to arm the slaves in the surrounding area. Brown was prepared to take hostages or kill any white southerners who stood in the way. He urged his fellow abolitionists to give him enough money to recruit, train, and supply a small army. However, after nearly two years of preparation, Brown's band had about 20 men, including three of his sons and himself.

On the night of October 16, 1859, **John Brown's raid** began. Brown and his men entered Harpers Ferry, Virginia. The town lay next to the Potomac River, about 55 miles northwest of Washington, D.C. Brown

GLOBAL CONNECTIONS

Reactions to John Brown's Raid

News of the raid on Harpers Ferry raised strong emotions across the Atlantic, particularly in Great Britain. British politician William Edward Forster expressed his views. "Whatever John Brown may have done toward freeing the slaves . . . he has exposed the utter [complete] weakness of the slave system." Other Europeans also praised Brown and the abolitionist cause.

In early 1860 the French writer Victor Hugo made a prediction. He thought that Brown's execution would lead to the breakup of the United States. "Between the North and the South stands the gallows of Brown," Hugo wrote. "Union is no longer possible: such a crime cannot be shared." **Why might Victor Hugo have said that Brown's raid would lead to the breakup of the Union?**

first took over the federal arsenal. Then he sent several of his men into the countryside to get slaves to come to Harpers Ferry.

Brown hoped enslaved African Americans would join him. None did. They most likely knew they would be severely punished if they were caught taking part in an uprising. Instead, white southerners from Harpers Ferry and the surrounding area armed themselves and attacked Brown. Eight of his men and three local men were killed in the exchange of gunfire. Brown and some of his followers retreated to the safety of a firehouse.

Federal troops arrived in Harpers Ferry on the night of October 17. The following morning Colonel Robert E. Lee ordered a squad of marines to storm the firehouse. In a matter of seconds, the marines killed two more of Brown's men. They captured the rest—including Brown.

Judging John Brown

Brown was quickly charged and convicted of treason, murder, and conspiracy to stir up slave rebellion. Some of the men who took part in the raid received death sentences. On the way to his execution, John Copeland—a fugitive slave—defended his actions. "If I am dying for freedom, I could not die for a better cause—I had rather die than be a slave!" On November 2, convinced that he also would be sentenced to death by the state of Virginia. Brown delivered a memorable speech.

"It is unjust that I should suffer such a penalty. . . . I believe that to have interfered . . . in behalf of His [God's] despised [hated] poor, is no wrong, but right. Now, if it is deemed [thought] necessary that I should forfeit [give up] my life for the furtherance of the ends of justice, and mingle [mix] my blood . . . with the blood of millions in this slave country whose rights are disregarded by wicked, cruel, and unjust enactments, I say, let it be done."

—John Brown, quoted in *John Brown, 1800–1859,* by Oswald Garrison Villard

As expected, the judge ordered Brown to be hanged. The sentence was carried out a month later, on December 2, 1859.

Many people in the North mourned the death of John Brown. Novelist Louisa May Alcott referred to him as "Saint John the Just." Not everyone who opposed slavery supported Brown's actions, however. Abraham Lincoln said Brown "agreed with us in thinking slavery wrong." He continued, "That cannot excuse violence, bloodshed, and treason." Most southern whites—including slaveholders and non-slaveholders—felt threatened. White southerners worried that a "John Brown the Second" might attack another southern target. One South Carolina newspaper wrote about these fears. "We are convinced the safety of the South lies only outside the present Union." Another journal from the same state was more blunt: "The sooner we get out of the Union, the better."

✔ **Reading Check: Summarizing** How did northerners differ in their reactions to John Brown's raid and execution?

John Brown, shown here kissing an African American child, was led to his execution on December 2, 1859.

THE METROPOLITAN MUSEUM OF ART

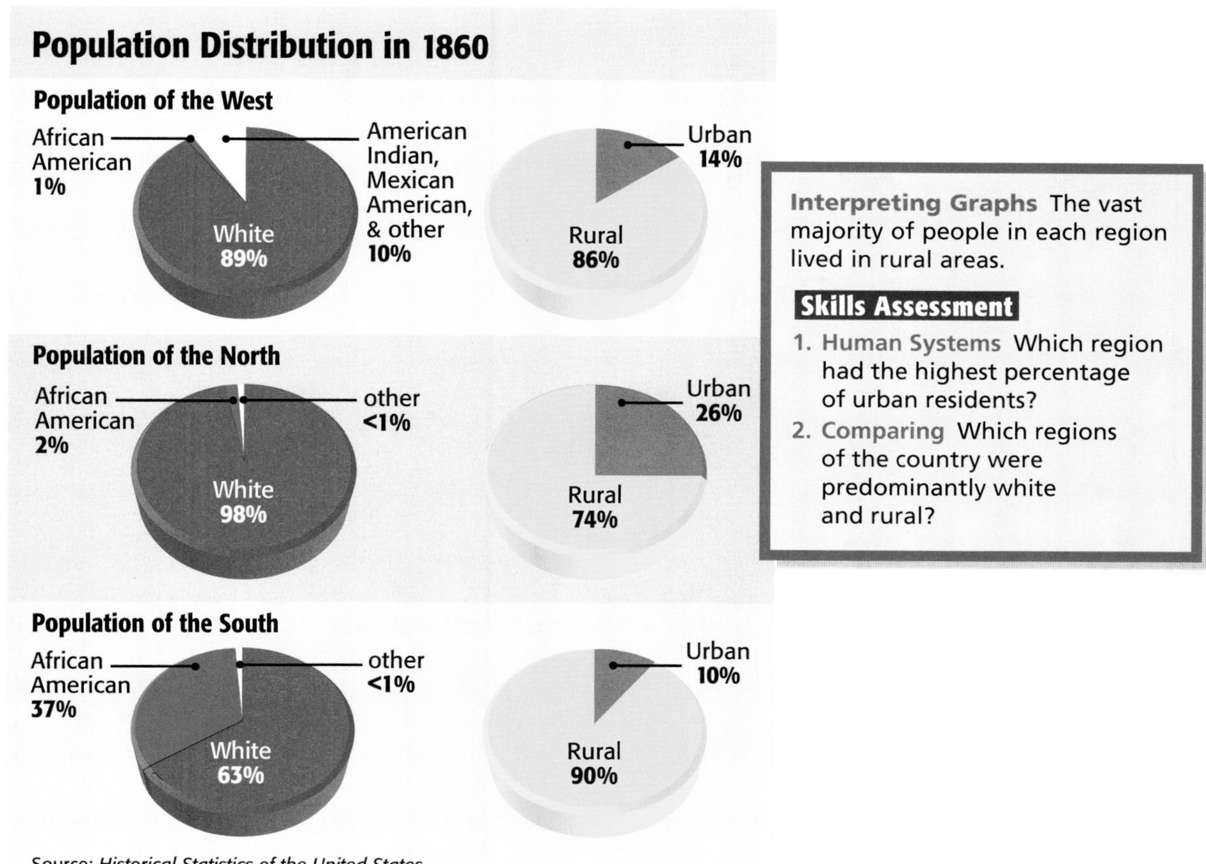

Interpreting Graphs The vast majority of people in each region lived in rural areas.

Skills Assessment

1. **Human Systems** Which region had the highest percentage of urban residents?
2. **Comparing** Which regions of the country were predominantly white and rural?

The Election of 1860

In this mood of distrust, Americans prepared for another presidential election. The Democrats were the first party to meet to nominate a presidential candidate in 1860. They met in Charleston, South Carolina, in late April. Yet the northern and southern members of the party could not agree on a candidate. When they could not agree, the party split in two. The Democrats met again six weeks later in Baltimore. Northern Democrats chose Senator Stephen Douglas. Southern Democrats backed the current vice president, **John C. Breckinridge** of Kentucky. Breckinridge strongly supported slavery in the territories. He did not believe, however, that a Republican victory in the election would give states the right to break up the Union.

Meanwhile, in early May some northerners and southerners—many of them former Whigs—decided to form a new political party. Called the **Constitutional Union Party**, its platform was simple. It recognized "no political principles other than the Constitution of the country, the Union of the states, and the enforcement of the laws." Members of this new party also met in Baltimore, Maryland. They selected **John Bell** of Tennessee as their presidential candidate. Bell was a slaveholder, but he had been against the Kansas-Nebraska Act in 1854.

THE GRANGER COLLECTION, NEW YORK

Daily Life

Political parties Crowds gathered at the 1860 Republican National Convention, the second time the Republicans had fielded a presidential candidate. The 1850s had seen the rise and fall of several political parties as Americans struggled to address the slavery issue. The Free-Soil, Know-Nothing, and Whig Parties had all collapsed or been greatly weakened during this period. Shortly before the Republican convention met, yet another political party—the Constitutional Union Party—had formed. Voters thus faced many choices but seemingly few solutions to the divisions that plagued the nation. **Why do you think women would have attended the Republican convention although they did not yet have the right to vote?**

In mid-May the Republicans held their convention in Chicago. Senator William Seward of New York was the leading candidate. However, many Republicans worried that his strong antislavery views made him a poor choice. Thus, Abraham Lincoln won the nomination on the third ballot. Lincoln was a moderate who was against the spread of slavery. He said, however, that he would not try to abolish slavery where it already existed.

The four-man election contest was really a pair of two-man contests. Lincoln challenged Douglas for the North's electoral votes. Bell and Breckinridge competed for those of the South. Douglas, Bell, and Breckinridge each knew he might not win the election. However, they hoped to win enough votes to prevent Lincoln from winning in the electoral college. Such an outcome would send the election to the House of Representatives.

In this they failed. Lincoln won the race. Although he gained less than 40 percent of the overall popular vote, he won 180 of the 183 electoral votes in the free states. Breckinridge and Bell split the electoral votes of slave states, with the exception of Missouri. Douglas had the second-highest number of overall popular votes. However, he won only one state—Missouri—outright. He finished with just 12 electoral votes. The election results angered many southerners. Lincoln did not carry a single southern state, yet he would be the next president. This election was a strong reminder of how the South was losing its political power on the national level.

✔ **Reading Check: Finding the Main Idea** How did Lincoln and the Republican Party win the presidential election of 1860?

 Breaking with the Union

Many southern whites believed that once in power, Lincoln would move to abolish slavery in the South. They feared this action would destroy the South's economy and society. Lincoln insisted he would not change slavery in the southern states. He had said, however, that slavery had to end at some point in the future. That was enough to greatly concern many southerners. A man in Mississippi urged white southerners to act quickly to protect their interests. "Let us rally . . . before the enemy can make good his promise to overwhelm us."

Just four days after Lincoln's election, South Carolina's legislature called for a special convention. There delegates met to consider the question of **secession**, the act of formally withdrawing from the Union. The convention opened in Charleston on December 17, 1860. After three days of speeches, all of the delegates voted to secede. They wanted to dissolve "the union now subsisting [existing] between South Carolina and other States."

The Constitution does not directly address the issue of secession. Therefore, southerners who wanted to secede believed that there was no constitutional barrier to a state leaving the Union. They pointed out that each of the original states had voluntarily joined the Union. Each of these states had held a special state convention to ratify the Constitution. Surely, southerners reasoned, states could also leave the Union by the same process.

This banner supports Republican candidates Abraham Lincoln and Hannibal Hamlin.

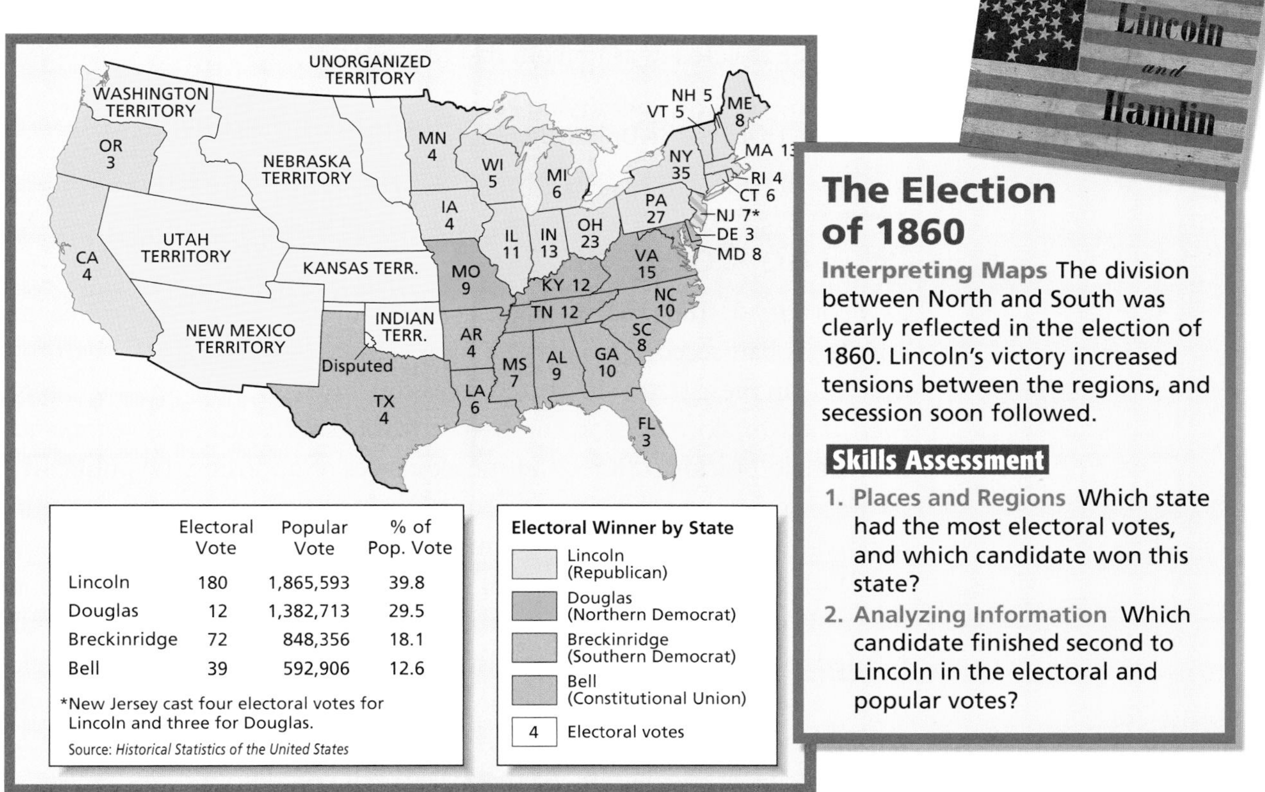

	Electoral Vote	Popular Vote	% of Pop. Vote
Lincoln	180	1,865,593	39.8
Douglas	12	1,382,713	29.5
Breckinridge	72	848,356	18.1
Bell	39	592,906	12.6

*New Jersey cast four electoral votes for Lincoln and three for Douglas.

Source: *Historical Statistics of the United States*

The Election of 1860

Interpreting Maps The division between North and South was clearly reflected in the election of 1860. Lincoln's victory increased tensions between the regions, and secession soon followed.

Skills Assessment

1. **Places and Regions** Which state had the most electoral votes, and which candidate won this state?
2. **Analyzing Information** Which candidate finished second to Lincoln in the electoral and popular votes?

CONNECTING TO

MATH

Just the Facts

Slave and Free States in Congress

Number of Representatives

Year	Slave states	Free states
1820	90	113
1830	99	125
1840	88	114
1850	89	118
1860	84	123

Source: *Historical Statistics of the United States*

Using Mathematical Skills

1. What was the largest gap between representatives of free and slave states?
2. Create a line graph that illustrates the statistics in the chart above. Label the *x*-axis "Number of Representatives," and label the *y*-axis "Year."
3. Imagine that you are a southern politician in 1860. Write a speech describing the trend that has taken place in the House between 1820 and 1860 and what it means to southern politics.

Critics of secession flatly rejected this idea. President Buchanan said that the Union was not "a mere voluntary association of States, to be dissolved at pleasure by any one of the contracting parties." President-elect Abraham Lincoln agreed. He said, "No State, upon its own mere motion, can lawfully get out of the Union." Lincoln added, 'They can only do so against [the] law, and by revolution."

While South Carolina representatives were meeting, Congress reviewed a plan to preserve the Union. Senator **John J. Crittenden** of Kentucky proposed a series of constitutional amendments to satisfy the South. One would extend the line created by the Missouri Compromise to the Pacific coast. It would allow slavery in all territories "now held, or hereafter acquired" south of this line. Another would use federal money to pay slaveholders who could not recover their fugitive slaves in the North. Crittenden hoped his plan would address the chief fears of slaveholders. He also hoped that the country would avoid secession and a civil war.

President-elect Lincoln did not agree with this plan. To express his views, he sent many letters to Republicans in the Senate. In these letters he asked Congress to vote against Crittenden's plan. "Entertain [consider] no proposition for a compromise in regard to the extension of slavery," Lincoln wrote. "The tug has to come and better now than later." A Senate committee voted on the Crittenden Compromise. Every Republican on the committee rejected it, as Lincoln had requested.

✔ **Reading Check: Identifying Points of View** Why did South Carolina decide to leave the Union, and how did politicians react?

The Confederate States of America

By February 1, 1861, Mississippi, Florida, Alabama, Georgia, Louisiana, and Texas had seceded from the Union. Their actions did not mean that everyone in these states supported secession, however. Some public figures even tried to slow or stop the march toward secession. However, such individuals quickly suffered the consequences of opposing the public will. In Texas, for example, Governor Sam Houston was removed from office for standing in the way of secession.

On February 4, delegates from six of the seven seceding states met in the town of Montgomery, Alabama. They established a new nation—the **Confederate States of America**, also known as the Confederacy. The delegates passed their new constitution on February 8. The document closely resembled the U.S. Constitution in many ways. However, the constitution of the Confederacy guaranteed that its citizens could hold slaves.

Jefferson Davis of Mississippi was elected president of the Confederate States of America. Alexander H. Stephens of Georgia became vice president. Davis was a graduate of West Point and a veteran of the Mexican War. He had been secretary of war under President Pierce and had served in the Senate until Mississippi left the Union. Davis had opposed secession as late as 1860, although he believed that states had the right to secede. But his loyalty to the South outweighed his hopes for peace. With his military background, Davis hoped to be appointed general in command of Mississippi's troops. He did not seek the presidency of the Confederacy. He greeted the news of his election with silence. Davis's wife, Varina, wrote about his reaction.

As an officer during the Mexican War, Jefferson Davis had led U.S. forces to victory in the Battle of Buena Vista.

> **"He looked so grieved that I feared some evil had befallen [happened to] our family. After a few minutes' painful silence he told me [what the telegram contained], as a man might speak of a sentence of death."**
>
> —Varina Davis, *Jefferson Davis: A Memoir*

Davis was a highly intelligent and hardworking politician. He also was very loyal to his friends. However, he tended to involve himself in details that would have been better left to his staff. Furthermore, his devotion to his friends often clouded his judgment. These personal qualities would increase the difficulty of the challenges he would face as president of the Confederacy.

✔ **Reading Check: Summarizing** What did the seceding states do in 1860 and 1861 after leaving the Union?

Section 4 Review

go.hrw.com Homework Practice Online
keyword: SC3 HP15

1. **Define** and explain:
   - secession

2. **Identify** and explain:
   - John Brown's raid
   - John C. Breckinridge
   - Constitutional Union Party
   - John Bell
   - John J. Crittenden
   - Confederate States of America
   - Jefferson Davis

3. **Summarizing** Copy the graphic organizer below. Use it to identify the causes of the secession of southern states in 1860 and 1861.

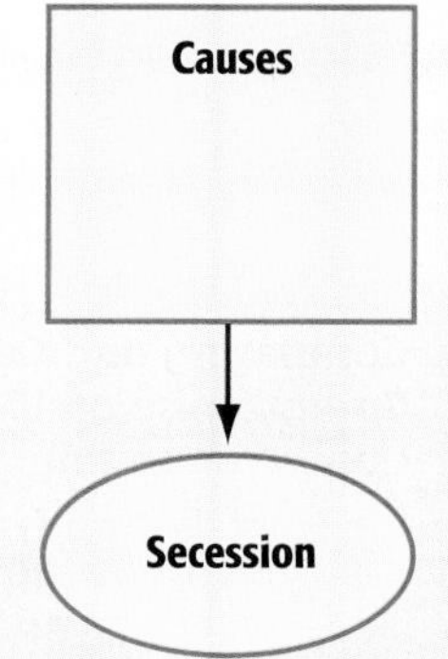

4. **Finding the Main Idea**
   a. Describe the northern and southern reactions to John Brown's raid on Harpers Ferry.
   b. How did the four-way race for president help Lincoln win the election of 1860?

5. **Writing and Critical Thinking**
   Supporting a Point of View Imagine that you are a foreign ambassador witnessing the conflicts over slavery in the United States. Write a speech for your home country that responds to South Carolina's secession from the Union.
   Consider the following:
   - reasons for secession
   - whether or not the Constitution mentions secession
   - your support for or opposition to South Carolina's secession

Chapter 15 Review

The Chapter at a Glance

Examine the visual summary of the chapter below. Make notes about each topic listed in the image. Then use the notes to create a simple board game to be played with a partner. Each player must explain the topics he or she lands on to continue proceeding along the "pathway to secession."

Identifying People and Ideas

Use the following terms or people in historically significant sentences.

1. sectionalism
2. Free-Soil Party
3. Daniel Webster
4. Stephen Douglas
5. Republican Party
6. Dred Scott
7. John Brown's raid
8. secession
9. Confederate States of America
10. Jefferson Davis

Understanding Main Ideas

Section 1 *(Pages 450–455)*

1. What were the parts of the Compromise of 1850?
2. How did the Fugitive Slave Act affect free and enslaved African Americans?

Section 2 *(Pages 457–461)*

3. How did pro-slavery and antislavery forces oppose each other in Kansas?

Section 3 *(Pages 462–466)*

4. Why was the Republican Party created, and what goals did it promote?

Section 4 *(Pages 467–473)*

5. How did each of the four presidential candidates in 1860 view the slavery issue?
6. What led many of the southern states to leave the Union?

You Be the Historian—Reviewing Themes

1. **Geography** Why did the Mexican Cession renew tensions about slavery between northern and southern states?
2. **Citizenship** How did the *Dred Scott* decision affect African Americans, and what was the response to the decision?
3. **Constitutional Heritage** What legal argument did South Carolina's officials use to justify secession?

Thinking Critically

1. **Summarizing** What roles did the politicians John C. Calhoun, Henry Clay, and Daniel Webster play in the compromise efforts prior to the Civil War?
2. **Comparing and Contrasting** How were the Compromise of 1850 and the Missouri Compromise similar, and how were they different?
3. **Analyzing Information** How did both congressional conflicts and efforts to compromise contribute to greater divisions within the United States?

Interpreting Maps

Study the map below. Then use the information on the map to help you answer the following questions.

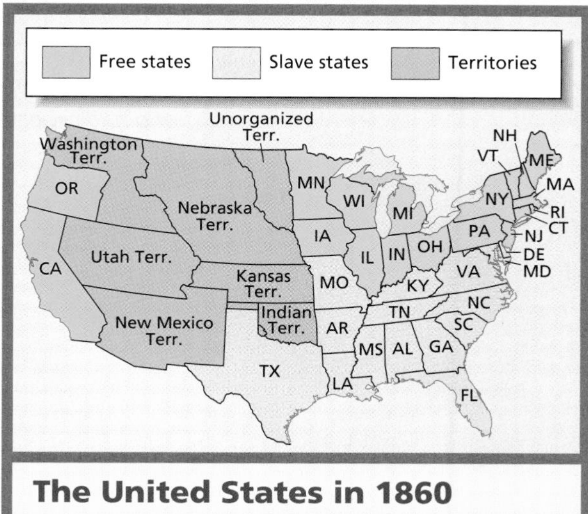

The United States in 1860

1. How many slave states and free states were there in 1860?
   a. 13 slave states, 20 free states
   b. 15 slave states, 16 free states
   c. 14 slave states, 18 free states
   d. 15 slave states, 18 free states
2. What would the total number of senators have been for the slave states and for the free states in 1860?
   a. 30 and 36
   b. 28 and 36
   c. 30 and 34
   d. 30 and 32
3. Based on the map and your knowledge of the period, where do you think southern politicians hoped to add additional slave states to the Union?

Analzying Primary Sources

Read the following quote by a reader of Harriet Beecher Stowe's *Uncle Tom's Cabin* and answer the questions that follow.

> **"My Dear Mrs. Stowe,—I sat up last night until long after one o'clock, reading and finishing "Uncle Tom's Cabin." I *could not* leave it any more than I could have left a dying child. . . . I thought I was a thoroughgoing abolitionist before, but your book has awakened so strong a feeling of indignation and of compassion that I seem never to have had *any* feeling on this subject till now. But what can we do? Alas! Alas! what *can* we do?"**

4. Which of the following statements best describes the letter writer's feelings about *Uncle Tom's Cabin*?
   a. The criticism of slavery offended her greatly and made her angry.
   b. The book made her want to do even more to try to abolish slavery.
   c. The book changed her mind about slavery, which had not bothered her before.
   d. The book does not matter because nobody can do anything about slavery.
5. Based on your knowledge of the period, why would such reactions to *Uncle Tom's Cabin* have been important to the relationship between the North and the South?

Alternative Assessment

Building Your Portfolio

American History

Cooperative Learning

As a group, prepare a chart showing the political parties that were formed from 1848 to 1860. The chart should include information on the year the party was formed (and ended, if applicable), the party's platform, presidential candidates, and region of strongest support. Add appropriate images to your chart and write a paragraph to explain the importance of third parties in political elections.

internet connect

Internet Activity: go.hrw.com
keyword: SC3 CF15

Choose a topic on the Divided Nation to:

- Understand the causes and effects of the European revolutions of 1848.
- Create a newspaper on John Brown and resistance movements against slavery.
- Research Supreme Court decisions regarding slavery.

CHAPTER

16 The Civil War

(1861–1865)

THE GRANGER COLLECTION, NEW YORK

The fierce fighting at the First Battle of Bull Run surprised many Americans who had expected the war to be over swiftly.

UNITED STATES

1861 Confederate guns open fire on Fort Sumter in South Carolina on April 12.

1861 Confederate forces win the first battle of the Civil War on July 21 at Bull Run Creek in Virginia.

1862 The *Monitor* fights the *Virginia* on March 9.

1862 On December 13 General Robert E. Lee wins a major victory at Fredericksburg, Virginia.

1863 The Emancipation Proclamation goes into effect on January 1.

1861 | **1862** | **1863**

1861 On March 17 nationalist leader Giuseppe Garibaldi declares Victor Emmanuel II king of Italy.

1862 Jean-Henri Dunant of Switzerland proposes the creation of the International Red Cross.

WORLD

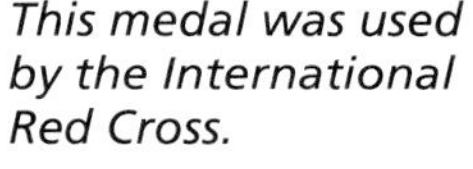

This medal was used by the International Red Cross.

Together, Giuseppe Garibaldi and Victor Emmanuel II helped unify Italy.

Build on What You Know

In the 1850s the North and the South were strongly divided over the issue of slavery. The election of Republican Abraham Lincoln as president in 1860 led 11 southern states to leave the Union. When the North refused to accept this secession, the opposing views of each side soon led to a terrible civil war between North and South.

When Lee surrendered to Grant, the Union commander agreed to treat the defeated Confederate troops with dignity.

This sword belonged to Robert E. Lee.

1863 Union forces capture Vicksburg, Mississippi, on July 4. That same day, General Lee's forces retreat after losing the Battle of Gettysburg in Pennsylvania.

1863 On November 19 President Lincoln delivers the Gettysburg Address.

1864 Union general William Techumseh Sherman takes Atlanta on September 2.

1865 General Lee surrenders to General Grant at Appomattox Courthouse on April 9.

1864

1865

1863 On June 7, French forces capture Mexico City.

1864 The Taiping Rebellion in China ends after the capture of Nanjing in July.

If you were there . . .
Would you support or oppose secession?

You Be the Historian

Themes Journal

What's Your Opinion? Do you **agree** or **disagree** with the following statements? Support your point of view in your journal.

- **Science, Technology & Society** New technology always makes wars easier to win.
- **Economics** Wars are bad for a nation's economy.
- **Citizenship** All citizens have a duty to support their government during a war.

Section 1

The War Begins

Read to Discover

1. What led to the bombardment of Fort Sumter, and why was this event important?
2. Which side of the conflict did Arkansas and the Upper South join, and why?
3. Why did both the North and the South want to claim the border states?
4. What strategies did each side follow at the beginning of the war?

Define

- border states
- cotton diplomacy

Identify

- Fort Sumter
- Abraham Lincoln
- Elizabeth Blackwell
- Winfield Scott

Why It Matters Today

Many countries around the world are currently experiencing civil wars. Use CNNfyi.com or other **current events** sources to find out about some of these places. Record your findings in your journal.

The Spirit of '61 was used as a symbol of Union pride on recruiting posters.

The Story Continues

When Abraham Lincoln took office, seven states had already left the Union. He wanted to keep more southern states from seceding. Lincoln gave his inaugural address on March 4, 1861. He pledged that he would not try to end slavery in the South. He also promised the South that the federal "government will not assail [attack] you. You can have no conflict without being yourselves the aggressors." At the same time, however, Lincoln spoke of his intention to preserve the Union.

Lincoln Faces a Crisis

The South did not respond to these calls for unity. Confederate officials were already taking over many federal mints, arms storehouses, and forts. One important federal post was **Fort Sumter**, located near Charleston, South Carolina. The fort controlled the entrance to Charleston Harbor. By early March 1861 the federal troops at Fort Sumter were running low on supplies. Instead of ordering the troops to surrender, President **Abraham Lincoln** decided to resupply them.

LINCOLN'S FIRST INAUGURAL ADDRESS

In the following excerpt from Abraham Lincoln's first inaugural address, he discusses the disagreements that led to the nation's greatest crisis.

I hold that, in contemplation of universal law, and of the Constitution, the Union of these States is **perpetual.**[1] . . .

It follows from these views that no State, upon its own mere **motion,**[2] can lawfully get out of the Union, —that ***resolves***[3] and ***ordinances***[4] to that effect are legally void; and that acts of violence, within any State or States, against the authority of the United States, are **insurrectionary**[5] or revolutionary, according to circumstances.

I therefore consider that, in view of the Constitution and the laws, the Union is unbroken. . . . I trust this will not be regarded as a menace, but only as the declared purpose of the Union that it *will* constitutionally defend, and maintain itself. In doing this there needs to be no bloodshed or violence; and there shall be none, unless it be forced upon the national authority. . . .

One section of our country believes that slavery is *right*, and ought to be extended, while the other believes it is *wrong*, and ought not to be extended. This is the only **substantial**[6] dispute. . . .

My countrymen, one and all, think calmly and *well*, upon this whole subject. . . . In *your* hands, my dissatisfied fellow countrymen, and not in *mine*, is the momentous issue of civil war.

Analyzing Primary Sources

1. According to Lincoln, what do the Constitution of the United States and the laws of the government say about the Union?
2. What does Lincoln say is the main dispute between the states?

[1]**perpetual:** everlasting
[2]**motion:** action
[3]**resolves:** resolutions
[4]**ordinances:** laws
[5]**insurrectionary:** rebellious
[6]**substantial:** important

Before the supply ships arrived, however, South Carolina demanded that the Union troops leave the fort. The fort's commander, Major Robert Anderson, refused to do so. He told the southerners, "Gentlemen, I will await your fire."

Before sunrise on April 12, 1861, Confederate guns opened fire on Fort Sumter. The Civil War had begun. A witness wrote that the first shots brought "every man, woman, and child in the city of Charleston from their beds." The fort withstood 34 hours of Confederate bombardment. Then Anderson had no choice but to surrender.

April 12, 1861
The Confederacy attacks Fort Sumter, starting the Civil War.

The attack on Fort Sumter outraged the North. Lincoln declared that the South was in rebellion and asked the state governors to provide 75,000 militiamen to help put down the revolt. Mary Boykin Chesnut, whose husband became a Confederate general, wrote about the events in her diary.

"I did not know that one could live in such days of excitement. . . . Everybody tells you half of something, and then rushes off . . . to hear the last news."

—Mary Boykin Chesnut, *Mary Chesnut's Civil War*, edited by C. Vann Woodward

Analyzing Primary Sources

Drawing Inferences and Conclusions How do Chesnut and the people around her regard the start of the Civil War?

✔ **Reading Check: Drawing Inferences and Conclusions** How do you think states' rights issues contributed to the attack on Fort Sumter?

The Union and Confederacy in 1861

Interpreting Maps After the 1860 election many slave states left the Union to form the Confederacy.

Skills Assessment

1. **Places and Regions** What states made up the Confederacy, and what states made up the Union?
2. **Analyzing Information** How was the state of Maryland strategically important to the Union in relationship to Washington, D.C.?

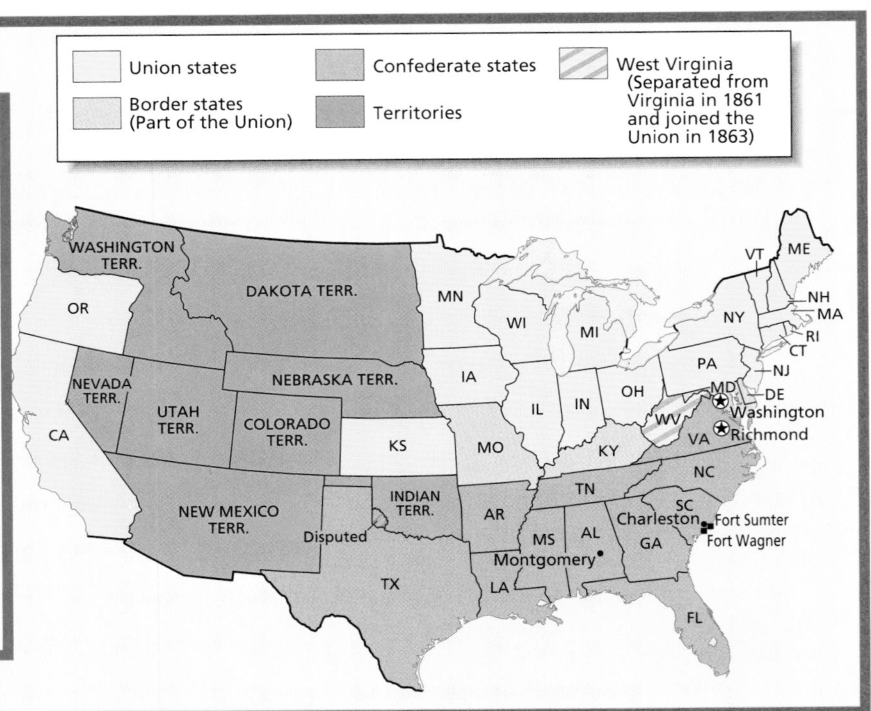

Choosing Sides

Democratic senator Stephen Douglas supported Lincoln's call for troops. He declared, "Every man must be for the United States or against it." The free northern states were solidly in the Union. Meanwhile, slave states that had not joined the Confederacy had to choose sides. The states of the Upper South—North Carolina, Tennessee, and Virginia—all joined the Confederacy soon after Lincoln's request for troops. So did Arkansas. "The South must go with the South," wrote a North Carolinian. The Upper South provided the Confederacy with soldiers and industrial resources. Richmond, Virginia, became the Confederacy's capital.

Four slave states—Delaware, Kentucky, Maryland, and Missouri—bordered the North. The position of these **border states** made them important to both the North and the South. Kentucky and Missouri controlled key stretches of the Ohio and Mississippi Rivers. The federal capital of Washington, D.C., was located within Maryland.

Slaveholders in Delaware supported secession, but they were few in number. In Kentucky, Missouri, and Maryland, however, people were deeply divided. Troops from Kentucky and Missouri served with each side in the war. There were riots against Union soldiers in Maryland. However, these three states eventually voted against secession. Lincoln sent federal troops into Maryland and into western Virginia, whose population was mostly loyal to the Union. People in the region set up their own state government. The new state of West Virginia joined the Union in 1863.

✔ **Reading Check: Comparing and Contrasting** Identify the similarities and differences between the Upper South and the border states.

The Union printed recruitment posters such as this one to encourage volunteers for the war effort.

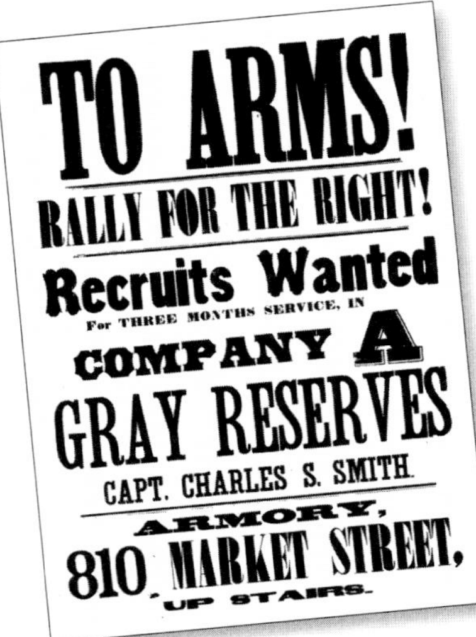

The Volunteer Spirit

Neither side was prepared for war. Therefore, both sides depended on volunteers. At the start of the war, the Union army had only 16,000 troops. Thousands of volunteers quickly joined the army. One Union recruit from the Midwest explained why he signed up.

"[It is] a duty I owe to my country and to my children to do what I can to preserve this government as I shudder to think what is ahead for them if this government should be overthrown."

—Union soldier, quoted in *Battle at Bull Run,* by William C. Davis

Virginian Thomas Webber also defended his way of life. He wanted to fight "against the invading foe [enemy] who now pollute the sacred soil of my beloved native state." Many southern volunteers shared his view. Early in the war, Union soldiers asked one southerner why he was fighting. He replied, "I'm fighting because you're down here."

In the border states, members of the same family often joined opposing sides in the war. The president's Kentucky-born wife, Mary Todd Lincoln, had four brothers who fought for the Confederacy. Disagreements over the war deeply divided many friends and families.

Civilians on both sides also helped the war effort. They raised money, provided aid for soldiers and their families, and ran emergency hospitals. Dr. **Elizabeth Blackwell**, the first woman to earn a medical license, helped convince President Lincoln to form the U.S. Sanitary Commission in June 1861. The Sanitary, as it was known, had tens of thousands of volunteers. They sent bandages, medicines, and food to Union army camps and hospitals. Staff and volunteers also worked to keep the Union troops healthy.

✔ **Reading Check: Analyzing Information** How did civilians help the war effort in both the North and the South?

THE GRANGER COLLECTION, NEW YORK

Abraham Lincoln

Abraham Lincoln was born on February 12, 1809, in Kentucky. He entered politics in 1834, serving four terms in the state legislature of Illinois and one in the U.S. House of Representatives. He helped spread the message of the new Republican Party in the 1850s and was elected president in 1860. Lincoln was a strong leader during the Civil War. With the Emancipation Proclamation, he began the process of freeing the slaves.

Today Lincoln is one of four presidents whose image is carved into the monument at Mount Rushmore, South Dakota. President's Day, a federal holiday, is held on the third Monday of every February near his birthday. **What were some of Lincoln's major accomplishments as a political leader?**

Many Confederate soldiers came from rural areas to fight for the South.

THE MUSEUM OF THE CONFEDERACY, RICHMOND, VIRGINIA PHOTOGRAPHY BY KATHERINE WETZEL

The North versus the South

At the beginning of the war, the North had several key advantages over the South. The much larger population of the North provided more soldiers. The North had most of the nation's factories and more shipyards. It also had a better network of railways, which allowed for more efficient transportation. Finally, the Union was able to raise more money to spend on the war.

The Confederacy also had advantages. The South's military tradition provided it with many skilled officers. In addition, the South needed only to defend itself until the North grew tired of the war. In contrast, the North had to defeat southern forces and occupy large areas of enemy territory.

Both the Union and the Confederacy based their military strategies on their strengths. Union general **Winfield Scott** developed the Union's

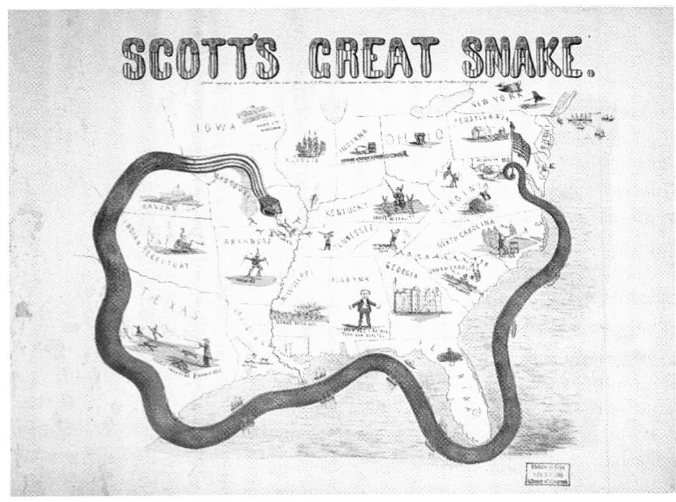

Interpreting Political Cartoons

Scott's Great Snake *This cartoon shows Union general Winfield Scott's plan to blockade the Confederacy as a giant snake wrapped around the southern coastline.* ***Why do you think the artist chose to represent the blockade plan as a snake squeezing the Confederacy?***

basic two-part strategy. He wanted to destroy the South's economy through a naval blockade of southern seaports. Scott also wanted to gain control of the Mississippi River to divide the Confederacy and cut its communications. Scott believed that this strategy would defeat the Confederacy "with less bloodshed than by any other plan." However, it would take time to succeed. Many northern leaders also called for a direct attack on Richmond, the Confederate capital.

The Confederacy's early strategy was to defend its territory and to wear down the Union's will to fight. Its offensive plan focused on taking Washington, D.C. Confederate president Jefferson Davis played a major role in the war. A demanding leader, Davis became so involved in war planning that he went through six secretaries of war in four years.

Davis and other Confederate leaders also tried to win foreign allies through **cotton diplomacy**. Cotton diplomacy was based on the southern belief that the British government would support them because cotton was important to Great Britain's textile industry. The British, however, had a large supply of cotton stockpiled when the war began. They were also able to get cotton from India and Egypt.

The strategies of the North and the South led to a war that was fought on land and at sea. As leaders made their plans, soldiers on both sides prepared to fight.

✔ **Reading Check: Supporting a Point of View** Which side do you think was best prepared for victory? Explain your answer.

Section 1 Review

go.hrw.com Homework Practice Online
keyword: SC3 HP16

1. **Define** and explain:
   - border states
   - cotton diplomacy
2. **Identify** and explain:
   - Fort Sumter
   - Abraham Lincoln
   - Elizabeth Blackwell
   - Winfield Scott
3. **Summarizing** Copy the chart below. Use it to identify key characteristics of the North and the South at the start of the Civil War.

	The North	The South
Slave states that joined		
Advantages		
Disadvantages		
Strategies		

4. **Finding the Main Idea**
   a. Why did the Confederates attack Fort Sumter, and what happened as a result?
   b. What did Arkansas, North Carolina, Tennessee, and Virginia decide about the Confederacy, and why did they make this decision?
5. **Writing and Critical Thinking**
   Analyzing Information Imagine that you are an adviser to President Lincoln. Write a plan that describes how the Union can keep the border states from seceding.
   Consider the following:
   - possible military actions
   - the loyalty of the states' citizens

Section 2

The War in the East

Read to Discover

1. What battles did the Confederates win in Virginia, and why were they important?
2. What stopped the northward advance of the Confederate army?
3. What was the significance of the *Monitor* and the *Virginia*?

WHY IT MATTERS TODAY

During the Civil War, powerful new types of warships were developed. Use CNNfyi.com or other **current events** sources to find out about the types of ships used by the U.S. Navy today. Record your findings in your journal.

Define

- ironclad

Identify

- Thomas "Stonewall" Jackson
- First Battle of Bull Run
- George B. McClellan
- Robert E. Lee
- Seven Days' Battles
- Second Battle of Bull Run
- Battle of Antietam

The Story Continues

After the fall of Fort Sumter, northerners demanded bold action. The Confederate Congress was supposed to meet in Richmond on July 20, 1861. Union troops gathered in Washington during the early summer. A northern newspaper headline urged, "Forward to Richmond! Forward to Richmond! The Rebel Congress Must Not Be Allowed to Meet There." President Lincoln decided to listen to public opinion. He ordered an attack on the Confederate capital.

This drum was used by the Union army.

Two Armies Meet

The first major clash of Union and Confederate armies took place in July 1861. President Lincoln had General Irvin McDowell lead about 35,000 troops from Washington toward Richmond. The soldiers were barely trained. McDowell complained that they "stopped every moment to pick blackberries or get water; they would not keep in the ranks."

The two armies met about 30 miles outside of Washington, near Manassas Junction, Virginia. Some 35,000 Confederates were lined along Bull Run Creek. At first the Union troops drove the left side of the

Confederate line back. However, a unit led by General **Thomas "Stonewall" Jackson** held firmly in place. Jackson's example inspired the other Confederate troops. "There is Jackson standing like a stone wall!" one southern officer cried out. "Rally behind the Virginians!" General "Stonewall" Jackson ordered his troops against the northern line. They charged forward, letting out the terrifying rebel yell.

Northern journalist Charles Coffin saw the battle. He described the confusion and shock of the fighting.

Analyzing Primary Sources

Drawing Inferences and Conclusions Based on Coffin's observation, what do you think the soldiers had expected war to be like?

"There is smoke, dust, wild talking, shouting; hissings, howlings, explosions. It is a new, strange, unanticipated [surprising] experience to the soldiers of both armies, far different from what they thought it would be."

—Charles Coffin, quoted in *Voices of the Civil War,* by Richard Wheeler

Fresh southern troops soon arrived, driving the Union army back. Soon the northerners were retreating to Washington. The Confederates might have captured the Union capital if they had not been so tired and disorganized. In the **First Battle of Bull Run**, the Confederacy broke the Union's hopes of winning the war quickly and easily.

✔ **Reading Check: Analyzing Information** Why did the Confederates win the First Battle of Bull Run?

Civil War photographs such as this one showed civilians the horrors of the battlefield.

The War in the East, 1861–1862

Interpreting Maps One Union objective was to capture the Confederate capital of Richmond.

Skills Assessment

1. **Human Systems** What battle took place in Maryland, and what was the outcome?
2. **Summarizing** What two battles took place within 25 miles of each other?

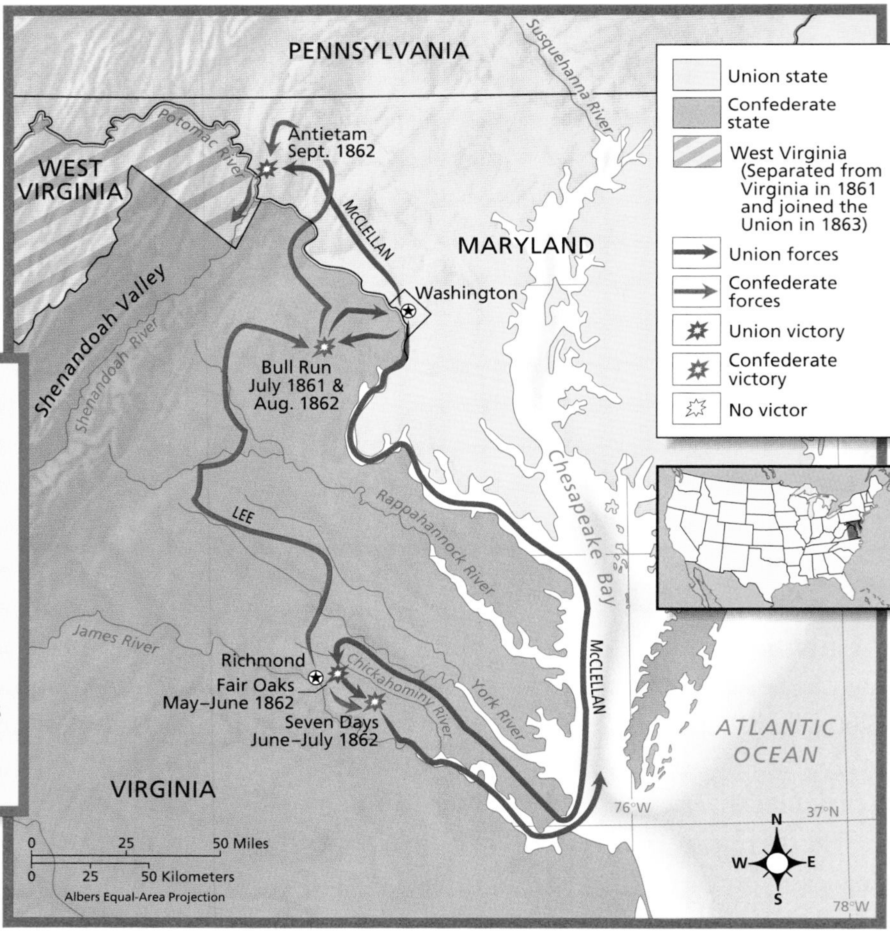

More Battles in Virginia

Lincoln still wanted to capture Richmond. He sent his new commander, General **George B. McClellan**, back into Virginia. By early April 1862 McClellan and a huge force were camped near Yorktown, Virginia, southeast of Richmond. McClellan did not attack, however, because he thought his troops were outnumbered. This gave the Confederates time to strengthen Richmond's defenses. In early May, McClellan finally took Yorktown. The Union army forced the southern troops to retreat. At the end of the month, the two armies fought again near Richmond.

President Jefferson Davis put General **Robert E. Lee** in charge of the Confederate army in Virginia in June 1862. Lee was one of the most talented officers on either side. A graduate of the U.S. Military Academy at West Point, he had served in the Mexican War. Later, Lee was an engineer for the Army Corps of Engineers. He had also led the federal troops that captured John Brown at Harpers Ferry. Lincoln had even asked Lee in 1861 to command the Union forces. Although Lee was against slavery and secession, he was loyal to the South. As he told a northern friend, "I cannot raise my hand against my birthplace, my home, my children." When Virginia left the Union, Lee resigned from the U.S. Army and returned home.

During the summer of 1862, General Lee strengthened his positions. Then he began attacking, hoping to push McClellan's army away from Richmond. After scouting Union positions, Lee attacked on June 26, 1862. During the next week, the two armies fought five separate times. This fighting became known as the **Seven Days' Battles**. Confederate general D. H. Hill described one failed attack. "It was not war—it was murder." The Confederates suffered more than 20,000 casualties, and the Union suffered nearly 16,000. However, Lee forced McClellan to retreat from the area around Richmond.

Next, Lincoln ordered General John Pope to advance directly on Richmond from Washington. Pope told his soldiers, "Let us look before us and not behind. Success and glory are in the advance." To stop the Union forces, Lee sent Jackson's troops around Pope's right side. Then Lee's main force fell upon the Union's left side. This battle became known as the **Second Battle of Bull Run**. Caught off guard, Pope's army fell apart. By the end of August 1862, Lee had pushed most of the Union forces out of Virginia. He then decided to take the war into the North.

✔ **Reading Check: Summarizing** How did Lee's forces drive the Union army from Virginia?

General Robert E. Lee was widely respected in both the North and the South for his leadership and daring strategies.

The Battle of Antietam

Confederate leaders hoped a victory on northern soil might break the Union's spirit and convince European powers to aid the South. On September 4, 1862, some 40,000 Confederate soldiers entered Maryland. Union soldiers, however, found a copy of Lee's battle plan, which General McClellan used to plan a counterattack. On September 17, 1862, the armies met along Antietam Creek in Maryland. The **Battle of Antietam** lasted for hours. By the end of the day, the Union had suffered more than 12,000 casualties, and the Confederates more than 13,000. Antietam was the bloodiest single-day battle of the war, but the Union won a key victory.

Antietam cost Lee many of his troops and stopped his northward advance. However, McClellan allowed Lee to retreat to Virginia. Two months later, tired of McClellan's delays, Lincoln took the command in the East away from him.

✔ **Reading Check:** **Finding the Main Idea** How did the Battle of Antietam help the Union?

CONNECTING TO
SCIENCE AND TECHNOLOGY

Photography and the Civil War

In 1862 Mathew Brady shocked the people of New York with his photographs from the Battle of Antietam. Brady and other photographers followed the Union army to record events with their cameras. The early cameras were bulky and hard to set up quickly. They could only be used to take pictures of still objects. As a result, the photographs of the Civil War were mostly portraits of soldiers and scenes of camp life. Brady's pictures of battlefields were taken only after the fighting had stopped. **Why did Brady not show images of battle?**

The War at Sea

While the two armies fought for control of the land, the Union controlled the sea. The North had most of the U.S. Navy's small fleet and enough industry to build more ships. The Union navy blockaded the South, cutting off southern trade and hurting the economy. The blockade was hard to maintain because the Union navy had to patrol thousands of miles of coastline from Virginia to Texas. The South used small, fast ships called blockade runners to outrun the larger Union warships and reach trading ports. These ships, however, could not make up for the South's loss of trade.

The Confederacy turned to a new type of warship, the **ironclad**, which was heavily armored with iron. The Confederates had turned a captured Union ship into an ironclad, renamed the *Virginia*. One Union sailor described it as "a huge half-submerged crocodile." In early March 1862 the ironclad sailed north into Hampton Roads, Virginia. Union ships guarded access to this important waterway. Before nightfall, the *Virginia* easily sank two of the Union's wooden warships while suffering only minor damage.

However, the Union navy had already built its own ironclad. The *Monitor* had unusual new features such as a revolving gun turret. Although small, the *Monitor* carried powerful guns and had thick plating. When the *Virginia* returned to Hampton Roads on March 9, 1862, the *Monitor* was waiting. After several hours of fighting neither ship was seriously damaged, but the *Monitor* forced the *Virginia* to withdraw. This success saved the Union fleet and kept the blockade going.

✔ **Reading Check: Identifying Cause and Effect** Why did the Confederates send the *Virginia* to sea in 1862, and what was the result?

Interpreting the Visual Record

Ironclads *The duel of the* Virginia *and the* Monitor *was the first naval battle between ironclad ships.* ***What features of these ships do you think made them more effective in combat?***

Section 2 Review

go.hrw.com Homework Practice Online keyword: SC3 HP16

1. **Define** and explain:
   - ironclad
2. **Identify** and explain:
   - Thomas "Stonewall" Jackson
   - First Battle of Bull Run
   - George B. McClellan
   - Robert E. Lee
   - Seven Days' Battles
   - Second Battle of Bull Run
   - Battle of Antietam
3. **Summarizing** Copy the graphic organizer below. Use it to identify the battles of the Civil War that took place in 1861 and 1862, which side won each, and their significance.

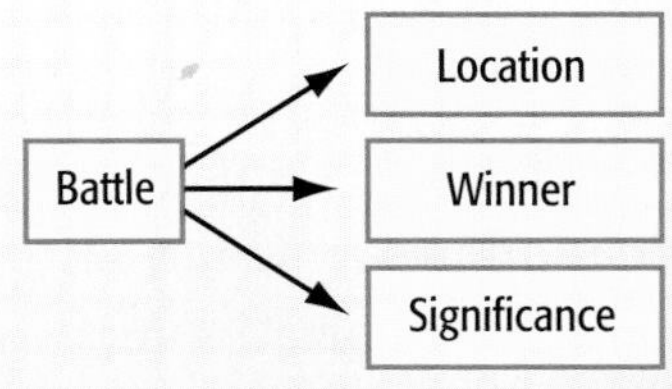

4. **Finding the Main Idea**
   a. Of the Confederate victories in Virginia, which do you think was the most important? Explain your answer.
   b. Why was the victory of the *Monitor* over the *Virginia* in 1862 important?
5. **Writing and Critical Thinking**
   Identifying Points of View Imagine that you are a war correspondent. Write an imaginary interview with Robert E. Lee.
   Consider the following:
   - why Lee is fighting for the South
   - Lee's training and experience
   - the South's strategy

Section 3

The War in the West

Read to Discover

1. What was General Ulysses S. Grant's strategy for the Union army in the West?
2. Why was the fall of Vicksburg, Mississippi, important?
3. What fighting took place in the Far West?

Identify

- Ulysses S. Grant
- Battle of Shiloh
- David Farragut
- John C. Pemberton
- Siege of Vicksburg
- Battle of Pea Ridge

Why It Matters Today

The brave actions of the soldiers and civilians who participated in the Civil War are remembered today. Use CNNfyi.com or other **current events** sources to find out about different ways that soldiers are honored. Record your findings in your journal.

Heavy mortars like this one were used to lob artillery shells onto forts.

The Story Continues

In February 1862 General Ulysses S. Grant led Union forces into Tennessee. Grant hoped to capture two important forts—Fort Henry and Fort Donelson. With help from Union gunboats, Grant took Fort Henry on February 6. He then attacked Fort Donelson six days later. The Confederate commander of Fort Donelson asked to discuss surrender terms. Grant replied, "No terms except an unconditional and immediate surrender can be accepted." The Confederate officer had no choice. Grant got his surrender and the fort.

Western Strategy

Union strategy in the West focused on controlling the Mississippi River. This strategy would allow the North to cut the eastern states of the Confederacy off from important sources of food production in the western states of Arkansas, Louisiana, and Texas. From bases on the Mississippi, the Union army would also be able to attack the South's communication and transportation network.

Ulysses S. Grant was the most important figure in the war in the West. A graduate of West Point, Grant had served in the Mexican War.

He later resigned from the army. When the Civil War broke out, Grant quickly volunteered to serve with the Union army. By September 1861, Lincoln had made him a general. Grant's strength in battle set him apart. *"I can't spare this man,"* Lincoln said of Grant. *"He fights."*

By late February 1862, Union forces had captured Nashville. They controlled Kentucky and much of Tennessee. By the spring the Union controlled key stretches of the Tennessee and Cumberland Rivers, as well as some important southern railroads. General Grant advanced south along the Tennessee River toward Mississippi. Following orders, he halted just north of the border. There, near a creek and a church named Shiloh, he waited for additional Union troops.

On April 6, 1862, the Confederates began the **Battle of Shiloh**. Catching Grant by surprise, they pushed his army back. Grant ordered his troops to hold their ground, whatever the cost. During the night, more Union soldiers arrived. On April 7, Grant began a counterattack. By evening's end, the Confederates were in retreat, and the Union had won greater control of the Mississippi River valley. The Battle of Shiloh was one of the first major battles of the war. Teenage Union soldier John Cockerill looked out in shock at the dead soldiers on the battlefield. "The blue and gray were mingled [mixed] together . . . as though they had bled to death while trying to aid each other," he wrote.

Ulysses S. Grant was working as a businessman when the Civil War broke out.

✔ **Reading Check: Analyzing Information** What role did the Battle of Shiloh play in Grant's western strategy?

Fighting for the Mississippi River

General Grant and other Union commanders wanted to capture key southern positions along the Mississippi River. The Union navy would first try to take the port of New Orleans, the largest city in the South. The Union could then send forces up the Mississippi to join Grant's army advancing from the north. However, two forts guarded the approach to New Orleans from the Gulf of Mexico.

The capture of New Orleans fell to Flag Officer **David Farragut**. He was a daring Union naval leader from Tennessee who had refused to serve in the Confederacy. Unable to destroy the forts guarding New Orleans, Farragut decided to sail boldly past them. Before dawn on April 24, 1862, Farragut ordered his warships to advance through a hail of Confederate fire. His ships arrived in New Orleans the next day, and the city surrendered on April 29. Farragut then sailed farther up the Mississippi River. Next he took Baton Rouge, Louisiana, and Natchez, Mississippi. After that, only the strong defenses at Vicksburg, Mississippi, stood in his way.

The southern defenders of Vicksburg had an important advantage—the city's high bluffs overlooking the river. These bluffs allowed the Confederates under General **John C. Pemberton** to cover the area with heavy guns. Previous attempts to take Vicksburg by land and sea had failed.

That's Interesting!

Cave Homes Would you believe that during the Siege of Vicksburg people lived in underground caves? It's true! To protect themselves from the Union cannons, many people moved into caves dug into the hillsides. Caves for a single family usually had one or two rooms. Some large caves could hold as many as 200 people. People furnished their caves with carpets, rocking chairs, and mirrors. They also built shelves into the walls to hold books, candles, flowers, and water jugs.

The War in the West, 1862–1863

Interpreting Maps After the Union victories at Murfreesboro and Chattanooga, the Union was in position to divide the Upper and Lower South.

Skills Assessment

1. **Human Systems** In which western state did the most battles take place?
2. **Analyzing Information** What Confederate victory took place in the West?

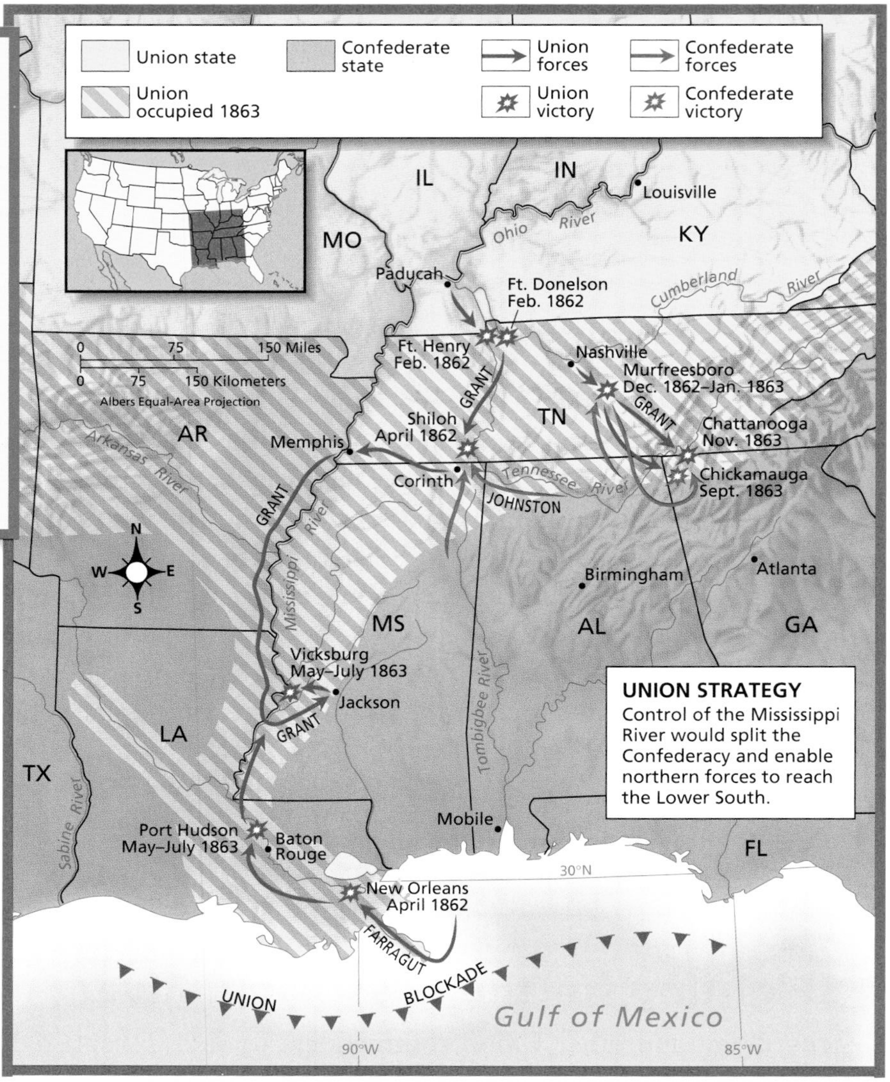

July 4, 1863

General Grant's troops capture Vicksburg.

In the spring of 1863 General Grant blocked southern forces from aiding Vicksburg. He then surrounded the city with his troops. The **Siege of Vicksburg** lasted about six weeks. As supplies ran out, the residents and soldiers inside the city survived by eating horses, dogs, and rats. "We are utterly [completely] cut off from the world, surrounded by a circle of fire," wrote one woman. "People do nothing but eat what they can get, sleep when they can and dodge the shells." In late June a group of Confederate soldiers sent General Pemberton a warning letter.

Analyzing Primary Sources

Supporting a Point of View What reason do the soldiers give Pemberton for thinking that surrender is necessary?

> **"The army is now ripe for mutiny [rebellion], unless it can be fed. If you can't feed us, you'd better surrender us, horrible as the idea is."**
>
> —Confederate soldiers at Vicksburg, quoted in *The Civil War,* by Geoffrey C. Ward

There was no real hope of relief. Pemberton surrendered Vicksburg on July 4, 1863, giving the Union control of the Mississippi River.

✔ **Reading Check: Summarizing** What events led to the Union gaining control of the Mississippi River in 1863?

The Far West

Fighting also took place in Arkansas and Missouri, along the Texas coast, and in New Mexico. Little or no fighting occurred in California, which was strongly pro-Union. In August 1861, Confederate forces from Texas marched into New Mexico. Union forces advancing from Colorado defeated the Confederates at Glorieta Pass, near Santa Fe, New Mexico. The Union victory ended Confederate hopes of controlling the Southwest.

Much of the fighting in the West involved the struggle for control of the Mississippi River. Neither side had many troops to spare for the fighting in the Far West.

The Confederates also tried to take Missouri. Union forces turned the Confederates back in their attempt to seize the federal arsenal at St. Louis in the summer of 1861. In March 1862, Union forces and pro-Confederate Missourians met at the **Battle of Pea Ridge** in northwestern Arkansas. Some American Indians, mainly Cherokee, fought on the side of the Confederates. They hoped that Confederate leaders would give the Indian nations greater independence than the Union had. In addition, slavery was legal in Indian Territory, and some American Indians who were slaveholders supported the Confederacy. Despite being outnumbered, the Union forces won the Battle of Pea Ridge. This victory gave the Union the upper hand in Missouri, but its hold was far from complete. Pro-Confederate units remained active in the region throughout the war. They attacked Union forts and raided towns in Missouri and Kansas forcing Union commanders to keep valuable troops stationed in the area.

✔ **Reading Check: Summarizing** What was the significance of the Battle of Pea Ridge, and what fighting took place afterward?

Section 3 Review

go.hrw.com Homework Practice Online
keyword: SC3 HP16

1. **Identify** and explain:
   - Ulysses S. Grant
   - Battle of Shiloh
   - David Farragut
   - John C. Pemberton
   - Siege of Vicksburg
   - Battle of Pea Ridge

2. **Identifying Cause and Effect** Copy the graphic organizer below. Use it to identify causes and effects of the listed battles.

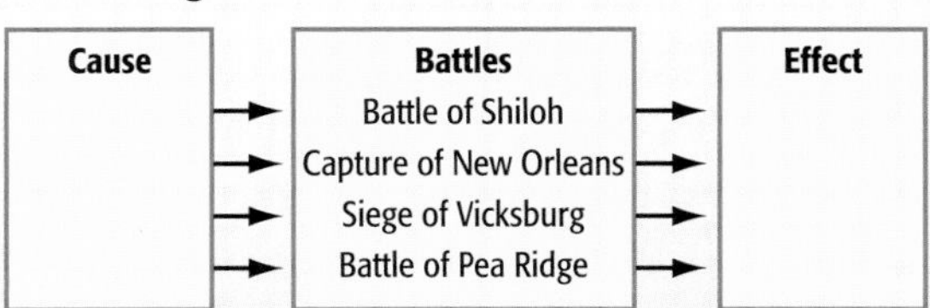

3. **Finding the Main Idea**
   a. How did General Grant plan to win the war in the West?
   b. Describe the battles that Confederate and Union forces fought in the Far West.

4. **Writing and Critical Thinking**
   Evaluating Imagine that you are a soldier fighting with the Confederacy at Vicksburg. Write a poem describing the siege and what you think the effect of the battle will be.
   Consider the following:
   - the hardships faced by the people in the city
   - why the results of the battle are important

Section 4

Life during the War

Read to Discover

1. How did different groups in the North react to Abraham Lincoln's Emancipation Proclamation?
2. How did African Americans and women contribute to the war effort?
3. How did northerners and southerners respond to the new draft laws?

Define

- contrabands
- *habeas corpus*

Identify

- Emancipation Proclamation
- 54th Massachusetts Infantry
- Copperheads
- Clara Barton

WHY IT MATTERS TODAY

During the Civil War, President Lincoln faced opposition from many Democrats in Congress. Use CNNfyi.com or other **current events** sources to find out about a current conflict between the president and members of the opposing party in Congress. Record your findings in your journal.

The Story Continues

In July 1862 President Lincoln met privately with members of his cabinet, including William H. Seward, to discuss freeing the slaves in the South—a topic of great concern to him. Lincoln felt that slavery strengthened and supported the South. "We must free the slaves or be ourselves subdued [defeated]," he explained. Lincoln's cabinet members told him to wait for a better time to put his plan into action.

Secretary of State William H. Seward was a key member of Lincoln's cabinet.

Freeing the Slaves

President Lincoln supported freeing slaves if it would help the North win the war. Many people in the North wanted to end slavery for other reasons. Some wished to punish southern slaveholders for their role in causing the war. Others argued that continuing slavery would lead to future conflict between the North and the South.

Lincoln faced two problems concerning emancipation, or the freeing of the slaves. First, he feared that northern prejudice against African Americans might weaken support for the war if emancipation became a Union goal. He was also afraid that some northerners would

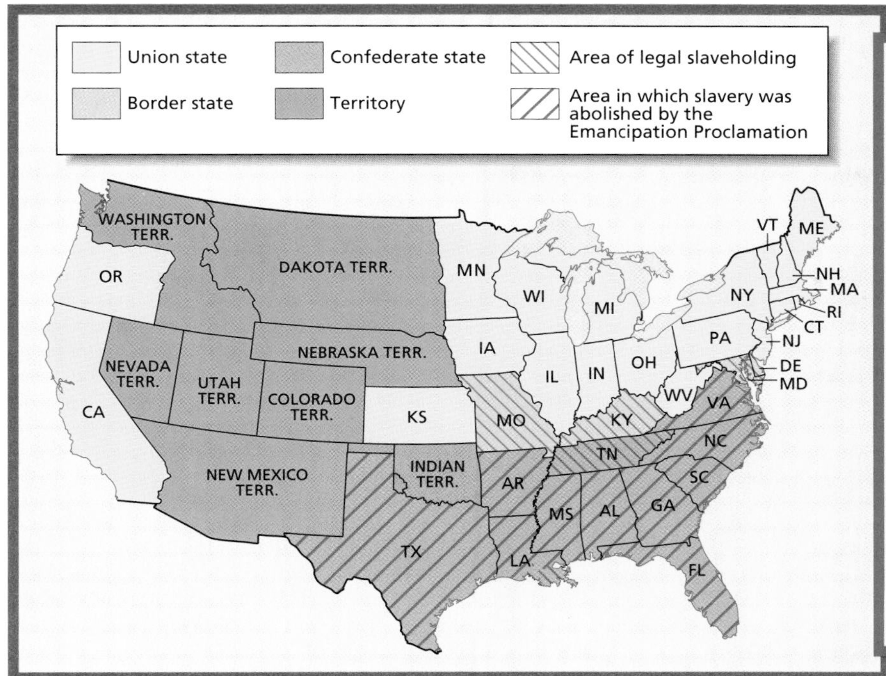

Emancipation in 1863

Interpreting Maps The Emancipation Proclamation freed slaves in states that were in rebellion against the Union. The Proclamation did not, however, free slaves in Union states or in areas occupied by Union troops.

Skills Assessment

1. **Places and Regions** In which states were slaves granted freedom by the Emancipation Proclamation?
2. **Summarizing** What was the location of most of the states where slaveholding remained legal?

consider slaves to be property that southerners had the right to keep. In addition, the Constitution did not give the president the power to end slavery in the United States.

Lincoln decided to issue a military order freeing slaves only in areas controlled by the Confederacy. Lincoln felt that his authority to end slavery did not apply to the loyal, slaveholding border states. He also did not want to anger citizens in these states.

President Lincoln waited for a northern victory in the East before announcing his plans. The Battle of Antietam was the victory he needed. On September 22, 1862, Lincoln called for all slaves in Confederate-controlled areas to be freed. This **Emancipation Proclamation** went into effect on January 1, 1863. News of the order encouraged southern slaves to escape when they heard that Union troops were nearby. This loss of slave labor hurt the southern economy and the Confederate war effort. Many African Americans and northerners praised the Emancipation Proclamation. Abolitionist Frederick Douglass called January 1, 1863, "the great day which is to determine the destiny [fate] not only of the American Republic, but that of the American Continent." There was also popular support for the Proclamation in Great Britain and France.

Many northern Democrats, however, opposed the Emancipation Proclamation. They wanted only to restore the Union, not to end slavery. A few abolitionists, on the other hand, argued that Lincoln had not gone far enough. William Lloyd Garrison complained that the president had left "slavery, as a system . . . , still to exist in all the so-called loyal Slave States."

✔ **Reading Check: Contrasting** In what different ways did people in the North view the Emancipation Proclamation?

GLOBAL CONNECTIONS

Reactions to Emancipation

Abraham Lincoln's Emancipation Proclamation drew the attention of many people in Europe. Some workers from Manchester, England, wrote to the president. "We joyfully honor you . . . [for] your belief in the words of your great founders: 'All men are created free and equal.'" A British noble praised the Union's high moral purpose in the Civil War. Giuseppe Garibaldi, an Italian leader, hailed Lincoln as "the heir of the aspirations [dreams] of . . . [abolitionist] John Brown." **How did some Europeans react to the Emancipation Proclamation?**

Daily Life

African American soldiers Frederick Douglass encouraged African Americans to fight in the Union army, calling it their "golden opportunity." Many men responded to the call. Despite making up only 2 percent of the North's population, African Americans made up nearly 10 percent of the Union army by the end of the war. Although they faced discrimination, many soldiers celebrated the opportunity to fight for freedom. **What reasons do you think African Americans would have had for joining the Union army cause despite facing discrimination?**

African Americans and the War

The question of whether to permit African Americans to serve in the military also troubled many northern leaders. The Union navy had already been accepting African American volunteers. Since the war began, abolitionists had called for the Union army to recruit African Americans as well. Frederick Douglass stated that military service would help African Americans earn equal rights.

> **"Once let the black man get upon his person the brass letters, U.S.; . . . and a musket on his shoulder and bullets in his pocket, and there is no power on earth which can deny that he has earned the right to citizenship."**
>
> —Frederick Douglass, quoted in *Battle Cry of Freedom*, by James McPherson

Analyzing Primary Sources

Identifying Points of View According to Douglass, what will serving as soldiers accomplish for African Americans?

Northern leaders also saw a practical reason to enlist African Americans—the Union needed soldiers. Congress allowed the army to sign up African American volunteers as laborers in July 1862. The War Department also gave **contrabands**, or escaped slaves, the right to join the Union army in South Carolina. Free African Americans in Louisiana and Kansas also formed units in the Union army.

By the spring of 1863, African American units were fighting in the field with the Union army. They took part in a Union attack on Port Hudson, Louisiana, in May 1863. The **54th Massachusetts Infantry** consisted mostly of free African Americans. In July 1863 this regiment played a key role in the attack on South Carolina's Fort Wagner. Lewis Douglass, Frederick Douglass's son, fought in the battle. "My regiment [unit] has established its reputation as a fighting regiment—not a man flinched," he proudly wrote later. The 54th became the most famous African American unit of the war.

About 180,000 African Americans served with the Union army during the war. Despite discrimination, African American soldiers fought bravely. For most of the war, African Americans received less pay than white soldiers. They were usually led by white officers. They also faced greater danger from Confederate troops, who often killed African American prisoners of war or sold them into slavery. In 1864 President Lincoln suggested rewarding African American soldiers in Louisiana by giving them the right to vote. He also wrote a letter praising the contributions of African Americans to the military effort.

"Abandon all the posts now possessed by black men, surrender all these advantages to the enemy, and we would be compelled [forced] to abandon the war in three weeks."

—Abraham Lincoln, quoted in *Battle Cry of Freedom*, by James McPherson

Analyzing Primary Sources

Identifying Points of View How does Lincoln view African American soldiers?

✔ **Reading Check: Finding the Main Idea** Why did African Americans serve in the Union army despite the problems they faced?

Problems in the North

The issue of ending slavery added to the problems already brewing in the North. Northerners were growing upset by the length of the war and the increasing number of casualties. A group of northern Democrats led by Clement L. Vallandigham of Ohio began to speak out against the war. War supporters compared these Democrats to a poisonous type of snake, calling them **Copperheads**. Many Copperheads were midwesterners who sympathized with the South, objected to abolition, and wanted the war to end. Vallandigham asked what the war had gained and then said, "Let the dead at Fredericksburg and Vicksburg answer."

Lincoln believed the Copperheads threatened the war effort. To stop them, he suspended the right of ***habeas corpus***—the constitutional

THE GRANGER COLLECTION, NEW YORK

Interpreting Political Cartoons

The Copperheads *In this cartoon, northern Democrats who called for peace are shown as deadly copperhead snakes threatening the Union.* ***Why do you think the artist chose to depict these politicians in this way?***

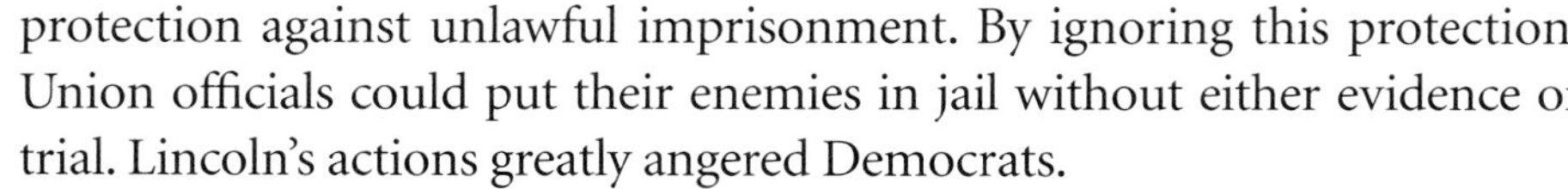

protection against unlawful imprisonment. By ignoring this protection, Union officials could put their enemies in jail without either evidence or trial. Lincoln's actions greatly angered Democrats.

More debate arose in March 1863 when Congress passed a law allowing men to be drafted into military service. Critics noted that dishonesty in the draft was common. Wealthy people could legally buy their way out of military service. The Copperheads complained that it was unfair to force unwilling white men to fight for the freedom of southern slaves.

Other critics shared this belief. In July 1863, riots targeting African Americans and draft officials broke out in New York City. Many of the rioters were poor immigrants afraid of losing their jobs to freed African Americans. Rioters damaged a great deal of property and killed more than 100 people before Union troops could stop the violence.

✔ **Reading Check: Identifying Cause and Effect** Why were people unhappy with Lincoln's war policies, and how did Lincoln attempt to deal with them?

Research on the ROM

Free Find:
Mary Boykin Chesnut
After reading about Mary Boykin Chesnut on the **Holt Researcher CD–ROM,** imagine that you are writing an entry in her journal. Describe the situation faced by the Confederacy during a particular period of the Civil War.

 Southern Struggles

The South also faced many challenges. The North's naval blockade took a heavy toll on southerners. Soldiers did not have enough supplies. "Every day we grow weaker. . . . Already they [Confederate soldiers] begin to cry out for more ammunition, and already the blockade is beginning to shut it all out," wrote Mary Boykin Chesnut. The value of Confederate money fell as southern exports dropped. The price of food, clothing, and medicine shot up as supplies ran low. Basic items such as bread cost more than most people could afford.

Southerner Mary Boykin Chesnut kept an extensive journal describing her experiences during the Civil War.

The severe shortages caused unrest in the South. In the spring of 1863, food riots took place in several southern cities, including Richmond. Southern officials ordered local newspapers not to mention these riots. Confederate president Jefferson Davis feared that the news would embarrass the South and encourage the North to keep fighting.

The government of the Confederacy faced problems because its officials disagreed on many issues. There was also controversy among southerners over their new draft law, approved by Davis in 1862 despite much criticism. One problem was that the southern draft did not apply to men who held many slaves. This rule angered poor southerners, who generally held few, if any, slaves. Confederate private Sam Watkins wrote that the draft law "raised the howl of 'rich man's war, poor man's fight.'" The draft was very unpopular in rural areas such as western North Carolina. Hatred of the draft and some pro-Union feeling in this region led to protests. Some southerners even took up arms against Confederate officials.

✔ **Reading Check: Comparing** What problems did both northerners and southerners have with the new draft laws, and how did they show their feelings?

Life on the Home Front

Interpreting the Visual Record

Camp life *Civil War soldiers on both sides often brought their families to camp with them.* ***What do you think some of the advantages and disadvantages of soldiers having their families with them might be?***

In both the North and the South, the war effort involved people at all levels of society. People too young or too old for military service worked in factories, on farms, and in other areas. Southern women also ran farms and plantations after their husbands and sons went to war.

Women played an important role in providing medical care for soldiers. Dorothea Dix headed more than 3,000 women who served as paid nurses in the Union army. **Clara Barton** worked as a volunteer, organizing the collection of medicine and supplies for delivery to Union troops on the battlefield. Barton often remained at field hospitals to comfort the wounded. Her work formed the basis for what would become the American Red Cross. Women in the South also cared for sick and wounded soldiers. For example, Sally Louisa Tompkins established a hospital in Richmond.

The efforts of these women volunteers were very important. Soldiers faced great dangers in daily life as well as in battles. For every day of fighting, soldiers spent weeks living in uncomfortable and unhealthy camps. They faced bad weather, disease, and unsafe food. About twice as many Civil War soldiers died of disease than died in combat.

Military prisoners also suffered greatly during the Civil War. The worst conditions were at Andersonville, in southwestern Georgia. Thousands of Union soldiers were held there with no shelter and little food. Following her visit to the prison, southerner Eliza Andrews was told that "at one time the prisoners died at the rate of a hundred and fifty a day."

✔ **Reading Check: Analyzing Information** How did southern and northern women affect the war efforts?

Section 4 Review

go.hrw.com Homework Practice Online
keyword: SC3 HP16

1. **Define** and explain:
   - contrabands
   - *habeas corpus*

2. **Identify** and explain:
   - Emancipation Proclamation
   - 54th Massachusetts Infantry
   - Copperheads
   - Clara Barton

3. **Categorizing** Copy the graphic organizer below. Use it to list the ways that people in different parts of society contributed to or reacted to the war.

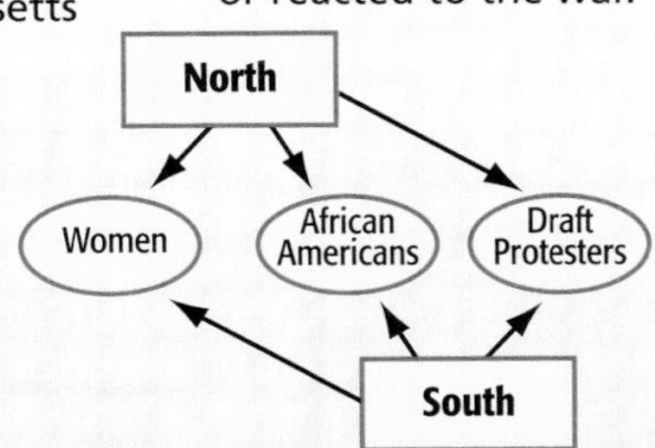

4. **Finding the Main Idea**
   a. Describe how each of the following groups reacted to the Emancipation Proclamation: African Americans, abolitionists, and Copperheads.
   b. What actions did Lincoln take that angered Democrats in the North?

5. **Writing and Critical Thinking**
   Summarizing Imagine that you are a foreign journalist reporting on the war in the North and the South. Write a half-page newspaper article about life on the home front.
   Consider the following:
   - responses to new draft laws
   - the contributions of African Americans
   - the contributions of women

Section 5

The Tide of the War Turns

Read to Discover

1. Why was the Battle of Gettysburg important?
2. What campaigns were launched in Virginia and the Lower South?
3. How and when did the war finally end?

Define

- total war

Identify

- Battle of Gettysburg
- George G. Meade
- George Pickett
- Pickett's Charge
- Gettysburg Address
- Wilderness Campaign
- William Tecumseh Sherman
- Appomattox Courthouse

Why it Matters Today

Many people participate in reenactments of Civil War battles or visit national parks located on Civil War battle sites. Use CNNfyi.com or other **current events** sources to find out about either a historical reenactment taking place today or a historical national park. Record your findings in your journal.

The Story Continues

General Stonewall Jackson was shot during the Battle of Chancellorsville.

In May 1863 General Lee's troops defeated a larger Union force near the town of Chancellorsville, Virginia. The fighting was heavy. While riding at the front lines, Lee's trusted general Stonewall Jackson was accidentally shot by his own troops. Doctors cut off Jackson's left arm in an effort to save his life. Still, his condition grew worse. When Lee found out that Jackson was hurt, he told an aide, "Tell him to . . . come back to me as soon as he can. He has lost his left arm, but I have lost my right." Jackson died just a few days after the battle ended.

The Battle of Gettysburg

In addition to the stunning victory at Chancellorsville, the Confederates also triumphed at Fredericksburg, Virginia. These successes encouraged General Lee to launch another offensive into Union territory. As before, his goals were to break the North's will to fight and to capture much-needed supplies for his army. Lee hoped that another victory would turn the tide of war in the Confederacy's favor.

Interpreting the Visual Record

Pickett's Charge *Confederate general George Pickett led thousands of troops in a costly charge against Union defenses.* ***How does this image show the violence of the Civil War?***

In mid-June 1863 Lee cut across northern Maryland into southern Pennsylvania. Lee's forces gathered near a small town called Gettysburg. Lee was unaware that Union soldiers were just northwest of the town. When a Confederate raiding party went to Gettysburg for supplies, the troops came under fire. This event triggered the **Battle of Gettysburg**. Some 75,000 Confederate soldiers faced about 90,000 Union troops.

The battle began on July 1, 1863. The Confederates pushed the Union line back to Cemetery Ridge, just south of the town. The Confederate forces occupied nearby Seminary Ridge. On July 2 Lee ordered an attack on the left side of the Union line. The bold charge of Union colonel Joshua Chamberlain's troops at Little Round Top, however, helped turn back the Confederates. Then General **George G. Meade** placed more soldiers on the Union line.

Lee planned to rush the center of the Union line. This task fell to three divisions of Confederate soldiers. General **George Pickett** commanded the largest unit. In the late afternoon, about 14,000 men took part in **Pickett's Charge** up Cemetery Ridge. The attack was a disaster. Confederate lieutenant G. W. Finley was part of the charge. "Men were falling all around us, and cannon and muskets were raining death upon us," he wrote. Fewer than half of Pickett's troops reached the top of the ridge. All those who reached the Union wall were captured or killed. Only about 6,500 men returned to the Confederate rear. Lee ordered Pickett to organize his division for a possible counterattack. "General Lee, I *have* no division now," Pickett replied. "The battle was now over," wrote Union lieutenant Jesse Young, "but nobody knew it."

✔ **Reading Check: Identifying Cause and Effect** What led to the Battle of Gettysburg, and what was its outcome?

A Turning Point

July 4, 1863
Union troops win the Battle of Gettysburg.

Rain slowed Meade's troops, allowing Lee to retreat from Gettysburg on July 4 and return to Virginia. Nonetheless, Gettysburg was a turning point in the war. Lee's troops would never again launch an attack onto northern soil. The Union victory at Gettysburg took place on the same day as General Grant's capture of Vicksburg in Mississippi. These critical victories made northerners believe that the Confederacy could be defeated. The Union triumph at Gettysburg, however, had come at a high price. Union casualties numbered more than 23,000. The Confederacy suffered more than 28,000 casualties.

President Lincoln expressed the Union's new sense of confidence and commitment. He delivered the **Gettysburg Address** on November 19, 1863. This short, moving speech is one of the most famous in American history. Lincoln spoke of the importance of liberty, equality, and democratic ideals. He reminded listeners that the war was being fought to protect these cherished principles. Lincoln dedicated himself and the rest of the North to winning the war and preserving the Union. He knew that a difficult road still lay ahead.

✔ **Reading Check: Drawing Inferences and Conclusions** Why do you think Lincoln talked about liberty, equality, democratic ideals, and unity in the Gettysburg Address?

This painting shows Robert E. Lee with some of his generals at his side in 1863.

Interpreting the Visual Record

Battles *During the Civil War, soldiers on each side were often ordered to charge well-defended positions, leading to very high casualties.* ***Whose perspective is the artist trying to portray? Explain your answer.***

Grant's Drive to Richmond

Lincoln was impressed with General Grant's successes at Vicksburg and in the West. He brought Grant to the East and gave him command of the Union army. In early 1864 Grant forced Lee to fight a series of battles in Virginia that stretched Confederate soldiers and supplies to their limits.

From May through June, the opposing armies fought a series of battles in northern and central Virginia. Union troops launched the **Wilderness Campaign** with about 100,000 men against 70,000 Confederates. The first battle took place in early May about 50 miles northwest of Richmond. Grant then ordered General Meade southeast to Spotsylvania. There the fighting raged for 10 days. Over the next month, Union soldiers pressed the Confederate troops back to just north of Richmond. The Battle of Cold Harbor took place from June 1 to June 3, only 10 miles northeast of Richmond. It was Grant's worst defeat of the campaign. During one brief assault some 7,000 Union troops were killed or wounded. The battle ended Grant's plans to advance on the Confederate capital.

Union forces suffered incredible losses in the Wilderness Campaign, with twice as many casualties as their Confederate opponents. Even so, Grant continued his aggressive strategy. He knew he would be getting additional soldiers, but that Lee was running low on troops. Grant slowly but surely pressed forward. He told another officer, "I propose to fight it out along this line if it takes all summer."

After Cold Harbor, Grant moved south of Richmond. He had hoped to take the key railroad junction at Petersburg, Virginia. Lee's army, however, formed a solid defense. Grant called off his attack and prepared to lay siege to Petersburg. Grant was winning the war, but he had not captured Richmond. This failure was discouraging for Lincoln.

✔ **Reading Check: Analyzing Information** Why was Grant's 1864 campaign in Virginia successful despite the huge casualties?

That's Interesting!

A Desperate Plan Did you know that near the end of the war the Confederacy considered having slaves serve in its army? It's true! As the South lost thousands of soldiers, some leaders suggested that slaves should serve in the army. They would then be freed after the war was over. Lee was in favor of this plan. Another general, however, was upset at the thought of drafting African Americans. He wrote, "If slaves will make good soldiers, our whole theory of slavery is wrong." In early 1865 the Confederate president Jefferson Davis had signed a "Negro Soldier Law." The war ended, however, before this law had much effect on Confederate forces.

Interpreting the Visual Record

Total war *General William Tecumseh Sherman, shown above, led his Union troops on a destructive March to the Sea.* ***What evidence of Sherman's total-war strategy can you identify in the scene shown above?***

Sherman Strikes the South

Lincoln needed a victory to help him win re-election in 1864. The bold campaign of General **William Tecumseh Sherman** provided this key victory. Sherman carried out the Union plan to destroy southern railroads and industries. In the spring of 1864, Sherman marched south from Tennessee with 100,000 troops. His goal was to take Atlanta, Georgia. From May through August, Sherman's army moved steadily through the Appalachian Mountains toward Atlanta. Several times, Sherman avoided defenses set up by Confederate general Joseph Johnston.

In July Sherman was within sight of Atlanta. His troops drove back Confederate forces trying to protect the city. The Confederate troops retreated as Sherman held Atlanta under siege. Atlanta fell to Sherman on September 2, 1864. Much of the city was destroyed by artillery and fire. Sherman ordered the residents who still remained to leave. The loss of Atlanta cost the South an important railroad link and center of industry. The victory also showed northerners that progress was being made in defeating the South. This success helped convince Union voters to re-elect Lincoln in a landslide.

Shortly after the election, General Sherman began his next attack. His goal was the port city of Savannah, Georgia. In mid-November 1864 Sherman left Atlanta with a force of about 60,000 men. He said he would "make Georgia howl!"

On his March to the Sea, Sherman waged **total war**—destroying both civilian and military resources. Sherman felt that total war would ruin the South's economy and its ability to fight. He ordered his troops to destroy railways, bridges, crops, livestock, and other resources. They burned plantations and freed slaves. Sherman's army reached Savannah on December 10, 1864. They left behind them a wide path of destruction more than 250 miles long. Sherman believed his tactics would hasten the end of the war.

✔ **Reading Check: Sequencing** List the key events in Sherman's march through the South in 1864 in their proper sequence.

The South Surrenders

In early April Sherman closed in on the last Confederate defenders in North Carolina. Grant finally broke through the Confederate defenses at Petersburg. On April 2 Lee was forced to retreat from Richmond. As Union troops poured into the Confederate capital, the final days of the war began.

By the second week of April 1865, Grant had surrounded Lee's army and demanded its surrender. Lee hoped to join the remaining Confederates in North Carolina, but Grant cut off his escape just west of Richmond. Trapped in the small town of **Appomattox Courthouse**, Lee concluded that the situation was hopeless.

The Union and Confederate leaders met on Palm Sunday, April 9, 1865. There Lee signed the surrender documents, ending the long bloody war. Grant later wrote that he found the scene at Appomattox Courthouse more tragic than joyful.

General Robert E. Lee signs the surrender documents. "There is nothing left for me to do but go and see General Grant," Lee had said. "I would rather die a thousand deaths."

"I felt . . . sad and depressed at the downfall of a foe [enemy] who had fought so long and valiantly [bravely], and had suffered so much for a cause, though that cause was, I believe, one of the worst for which a people ever fought."

—Ulysses S. Grant, *Personal Memoirs*

April 9, 1865

General Lee surrenders to General Grant at Appomattox Courthouse.

The Civil War had deep and lasting effects. Almost 620,000 Americans lost their lives in the four years of fighting. It was the most costly conflict in American history. Bitterness over the war would linger in both the North and the South for many years as the nation tried to heal its wounds and rebuild.

✔ **Reading Check: Finding the Main Idea** Why did Lee surrender?

Section 5 Review

go.hrw.com **Homework Practice Online**
keyword: SC3 HP16

1. **Define** and explain:
   - total war
2. **Identify** and explain:
   - Battle of Gettysburg
   - George G. Meade
   - George Pickett
   - Pickett's Charge
   - Gettysburg Address
   - Wilderness Campaign
   - William Tecumseh Sherman
   - Appomattox Courthouse
3. **Sequencing** Copy the graphic organizer below. Use it to fill in and explain the events that led to the end of the Civil War.

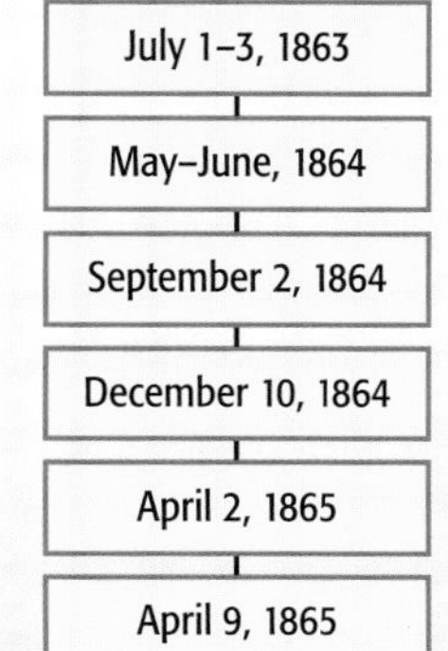

4. **Finding the Main Idea**
   a. How might the war have been different if Confederate forces had won the Battle of Gettysburg in 1863?
   b. How did the Union win the war in the East and in the South?
5. **Writing and Critical Thinking**
   Evaluating Imagine that you are either a northern or southern soldier present at Appomattox Courthouse. Write an account of General Lee's surrender.
   Consider the following:
   - the campaign against Richmond
   - the relations between northerners and southerners

1863

THE EMANCIPATION PROCLAMATION

A poster celebrating the Emancipation Proclamation

When the Union army won the Battle of Antietam, President Lincoln felt that the timing was right for a bold move. In late September 1862 he issued a preliminary Emancipation Proclamation. On January 1, 1863, the following official Proclamation went into effect.

A Proclamation by the President of the United States of America

Whereas on the twenty-second day of September, A.D. 1862, a proclamation was issued by the President of the United States, containing, among other things, the following, **to wit**:[1]

"That on the first day of January, A.D. 1863, all persons held as slaves within any state or designated part of a state, the people whereof shall then be in rebellion against the United States, shall be then, **thenceforward,**[2] and forever free; and the executive government of the United States, including the military and naval authority thereof, will recognize and maintain the freedom of such persons and will do no act or acts to **repress**[3] such persons or any of them, in any efforts they may make for their actual freedom.

"That the Executive will on the 1st day of January aforesaid, by proclamation, **designate**[4] the states and parts of states, if any, in which the people thereof, . . . shall then be in rebellion against the United States; and the fact that any state or the people thereof shall on that day be in good faith represented in the Congress of the United States by members chosen thereto at elections wherein a majority of the qualified voters of such states shall have participated shall, in the absence of strong **countervailing**[5] testimony, be **deemed conclusive**[6] evidence that such state and the people thereof are not then in rebellion against the United States."

Now, therefore, I, Abraham Lincoln, President of the United States, by virtue of the power in me **vested**[7] as Commander-in-Chief of the Army and Navy of the United States in time of actual armed rebellion against the authority and government of the United States, and as a fit and necessary war measure for suppressing said rebellion, do, on this first day of January, A.D. 1863, and in **accordance**[8] with my purpose so to do, publicly proclaimed for the full period of one hundred days from the first day above mentioned, order and designate as the states and parts of states wherein the people thereof, . . . are in this day in rebellion against the United States. . . .

And I hereby **enjoin upon**[9] the people so declared to be free to **abstain**[10] from all violence, unless in necessary self-defense; and I recommend to them that, in all cases when allowed, they labor faithfully for reasonable wages.

And I further declare and make known that such persons of suitable condition will be received into the armed service of the United States to **garrison**[11] forts, positions, stations, and other places, and to man vessels of all sorts in said service.

And upon this act, sincerely believed to be an act of justice, warranted by the Constitution upon military necessity, I **invoke**[12] the considerate judgment of mankind and the gracious favor of Almighty God.

Analyzing Primary Sources

1. What authority did Lincoln claim allowed him to issue the Emancipation Proclamation?
2. Why do you think Lincoln did not free all slaves?

[1]**to wit:** namely
[2]**thenceforward:** afterward
[3]**repress:** keep down
[4]**designate:** name
[5]**countervailing:** opposing
[6]**deemed conclusive:** considered certain
[7]**vested:** given
[8]**accordance:** agreement
[9]**enjoin upon:** order
[10]**abstain:** hold back
[11]**garrison:** defend
[12]**invoke:** call upon

1863

Abraham Lincoln's Gettysburg Address

On November 19, 1863, Abraham Lincoln addressed a crowd gathered to dedicate a cemetery at the Gettysburg battlefield. His short speech reminded Americans of the ideals on which the Republic was founded.

Lincoln gives the Gettysburg Address.

Four score and seven years ago our fathers brought forth on this continent, a new nation, **conceived**[1] in Liberty, and dedicated to the **proposition**[2] that all men are created equal.

Now we are engaged in a great civil war, testing whether that nation, or any nation so conceived and so dedicated, can long endure. We are met on a great battlefield of that war. We have come to dedicate a portion of that field, as a final resting place for those who here gave their lives that that nation might live. It is altogether fitting and proper that we should do this.

But, in a larger sense, we can not dedicate—we can not **consecrate**[3]—we can not **hallow**[4]—this ground. The brave men, living and dead, who struggled here, have consecrated it, far above our poor power to add or **detract**.[5] The world will little note nor long remember what we say here, but it can never forget what they did here. It is for us the living, rather, to be dedicated here to the unfinished work which they who fought here have thus far so nobly advanced. It is rather for us to be here dedicated to the great task remaining before us—that from these honored dead we take increased devotion to that cause for which they gave the last full measure of devotion—that we here highly **resolve**[6] that these dead shall not have died in vain—that this nation, under God, shall have a new birth of freedom—and that government of the people, by the people, for the people shall not perish from the earth.

Analyzing Primary Sources

1. For what cause does Lincoln say the soldiers at Gettysburg died?
2. How does Lincoln value liberty, equality, and democracy?

[1]**conceived:** created
[2]**proposition:** idea
[3]**consecrate:** set apart
[4]**hallow:** make holy
[5]**detract:** take away from
[6]**resolve:** decide

Chapter 16 Review

The Chapter at a Glance

Examine the visual summary of the chapter below. Work with a classmate to create a time line that shows the key events of the war.

Identifying People and Ideas

Use the following terms or people in historically significant sentences.

1. Fort Sumter
2. border states
3. First Battle of Bull Run
4. Robert E. Lee
5. Ulysses S. Grant
6. Siege of Vicksburg
7. Emancipation Proclamation
8. *habeas corpus*
9. Battle of Gettysburg
10. Appomattox Courthouse

Understanding Main Ideas

Section 1 *(Pages 478–482)*

1. What advantages and disadvantages did the North and the South each have at the beginning of the Civil War?

Section 2 *(Pages 483–487)*

2. How did the First Battle of Bull Run in 1861 change many northerners' ideas about the war?
3. How did the South attempt to avoid the naval blockade?

Section 3 *(Pages 488–491)*

4. How did the Siege of Vicksburg help the Union gain control of the Mississippi River?

Section 4 *(Pages 492–497)*

5. How did African Americans help the war effort?

Section 5 *(Pages 498–503)*

6. What campaigns did Grant plan in Virginia and the Lower South?
7. How did the war end in 1865?

You Be the Historian—Reviewing Themes

1. **Science, Technology & Society** How did ironclads reflect the changes that new technology brought to the war?
2. **Economics** What effect did the war have on the South's economy?
3. **Citizenship** How did northerners and southerners oppose the war, and how did the Union and Confederate governments respond?

Thinking Critically

1. **Supporting a Point of View** Which key 1863 battle—Vicksburg or Gettysburg—do you think was the most important turning point in the war? Explain your answer.
2. **Comparing and Contrasting** In what ways were the beliefs of, and challenges faced by, Presidents Lincoln and Davis similar and different?
3. **Summarizing** What ideas about equality, government, liberty, and union did Lincoln present in his first inaugural address and the Gettysburg Address?

Social Studies Skills Workshop

Interpreting Graphs

Study the graph below. Then use the information on the graph to help you answer the following questions.

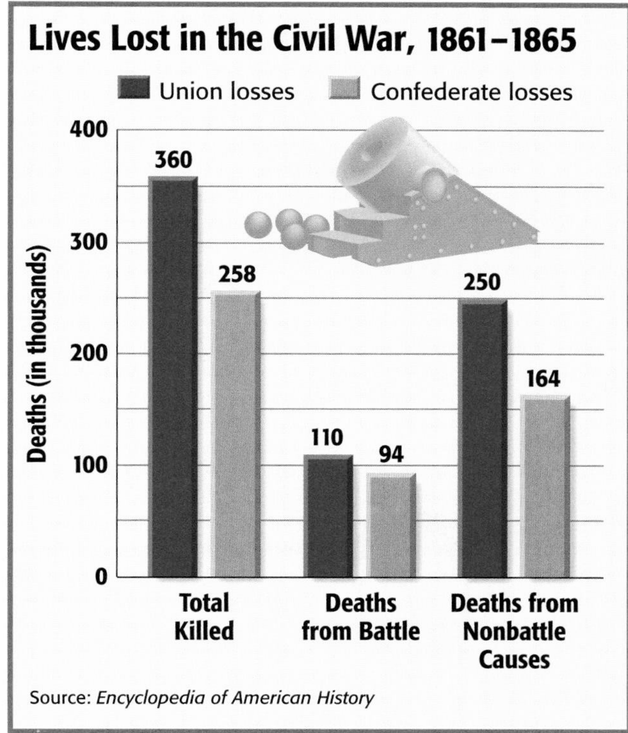

Source: *Encyclopedia of American History*

1. About how many soldiers in total were killed during the war?
   a. 418,000
   b. 618,000
   c. 102,000
   d. more than 1 million
2. About what percentage of the total deaths from battle were Union soldiers?
   a. about 66 percent
   b. about 30 percent
   c. about 54 percent
   d. 50 percent
3. Based on your knowledge of the period, why do you think the number of deaths from nonbattle causes was higher than the number of deaths caused by battles?

Analyzing Primary Sources

Read the following excerpt about the Fugitive Slave Act from Abraham Lincoln's first inaugural address, then answer the questions that follow.

> **"Again, in any law upon this subject, ought not all the safeguards of liberty known in civilized and humane jurisprudence to be introduced, so that a free man be not, in any case, surrendered as a slave? And might it not be well, at the same time, to provide by a law for the enforcement of that clause in the Constitution which guarranties that 'The citizens of each State shall be entitled to all previleges and immunities of citizens in the several States?'"**

4. Which of the following statements best describes Lincoln's view of liberty?
   a. No matter what their race, no free person should ever be treated like a slave.
   b. Different laws on freedom should apply to people in different states.
   c. Slavery is wrong and should be abolished.
   d. The current Fugitive Slave Act is fair.
5. How do you think Lincoln views the government's role in preserving the equality of all citizens?

Alternative Assessment

Building Your Portfolio

Cooperative Learning

Organize the class into small groups. Each group will write part of a chapter for a textbook on the consequences of the Civil War. Choose one of the following topics: the roles of women during the war, the lives of soldiers, or the war's effect on former slaves and free African Americans. Each group should conduct research and then write its section. Be sure to create images, maps, or charts as needed to place in your group's section.

internet connect

Internet Activity: go.hrw.com
keyword: SC3 CF16

Choose a topic about the Civil War to:

- View photographs and write a poem describing the life of a soldier in the war.
- Research Civil War authors.
- Create a 3-D model of the battlefield at Gettysburg and then pose and answer questions with a partner about the events of the battle.

Connecting to Geography

Theaters of War

Geography played an important role in the development of military strategies during the Civil War. The Confederacy occupied a large stretch of land from the Atlantic Ocean to west Texas. To achieve military victory, Union leaders had to capture key parts of this large region. Union leaders planned to gain control of key river routes, railroads, and seaports. The Union wanted to stop the movement of Confederate troops and supplies across the South, as well as Confederate trade with Europe.

Confederate armies did not have to invade the North to win the war. Their hope was to make the war so costly for the Union that the North would ask for peace.

Resources and Strategies

The North entered the war with many advantages over the South. The North had more people, industry, and money.

Farm Values by Region, 1860 and 1870

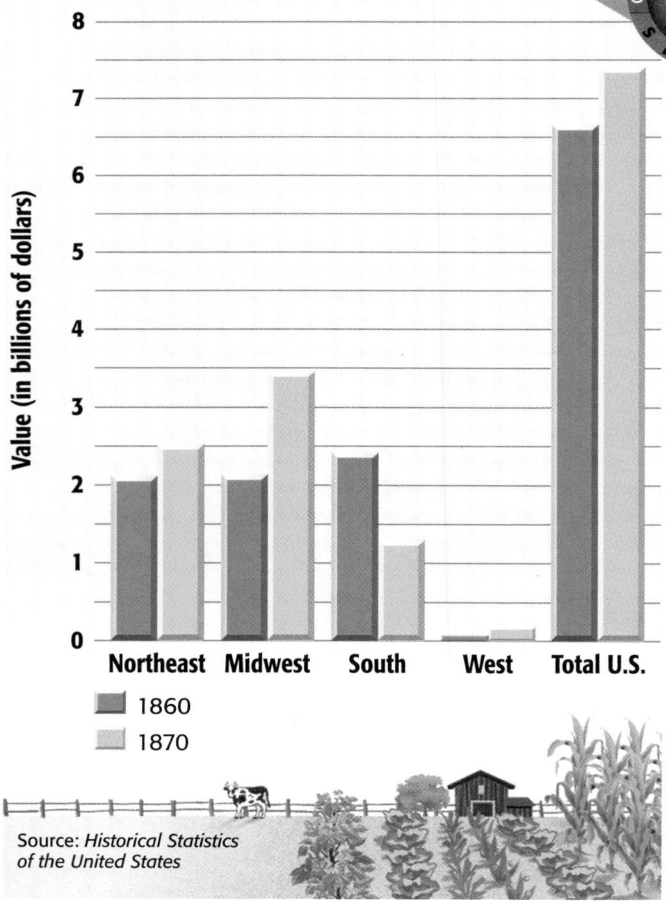

Value (in billions of dollars)

8
7
6
5
4
3
2
1
0

Northeast Midwest South West Total U.S.

1860
1870

Source: *Historical Statistics of the United States*

Geography Skills

Interpreting Bar Graphs

1. Which region's farms had the highest total value in 1860? in 1870?
2. **Analyzing Information** Where did farms have the greatest growth in value from 1860 to 1870?

Cotton plants

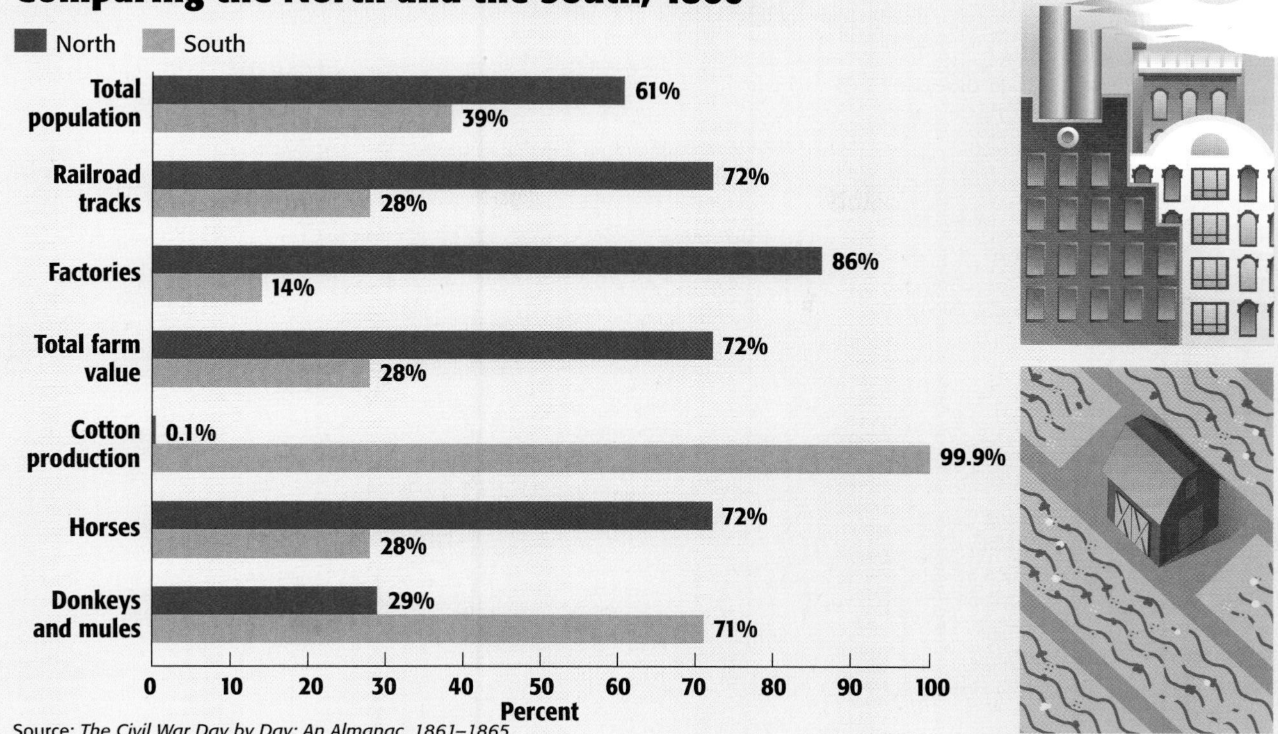

Source: *The Civil War Day by Day: An Almanac, 1861–1865*

Geography **Skills**

Interpreting Bar Graphs

1. What percentage of the nation's population lived in the North at the beginning of the war?
2. **Human Systems** What resources did the Union have more of than the Confederacy? What resources did the Confederacy have more of than the Union?
3. **Making Generalizations and Predictions** How do you think the resource advantages enjoyed by the Union affected the outcome of the Civil War?

History Note 1

One of the North's major advantages was its greater population, which allowed Union generals to put more soldiers in the field. In late 1862, an estimated 300,000 Confederate soldiers faced nearly 700,000 Union soldiers. By the end of the war, the Union had about 1 million troops. Confederate soldiers probably numbered fewer than 160,000.

History Note 2

The Union also had a great advantage in communications. The North controlled far more miles of telegraph line than the South. The telegraph made Union supply and reinforcement easier because field commanders could communicate quickly with officials in Washington. The South's expansion and repair of telegraph lines were hurt by a shortage of equipment and operators.

A telegraph key

Theaters of War

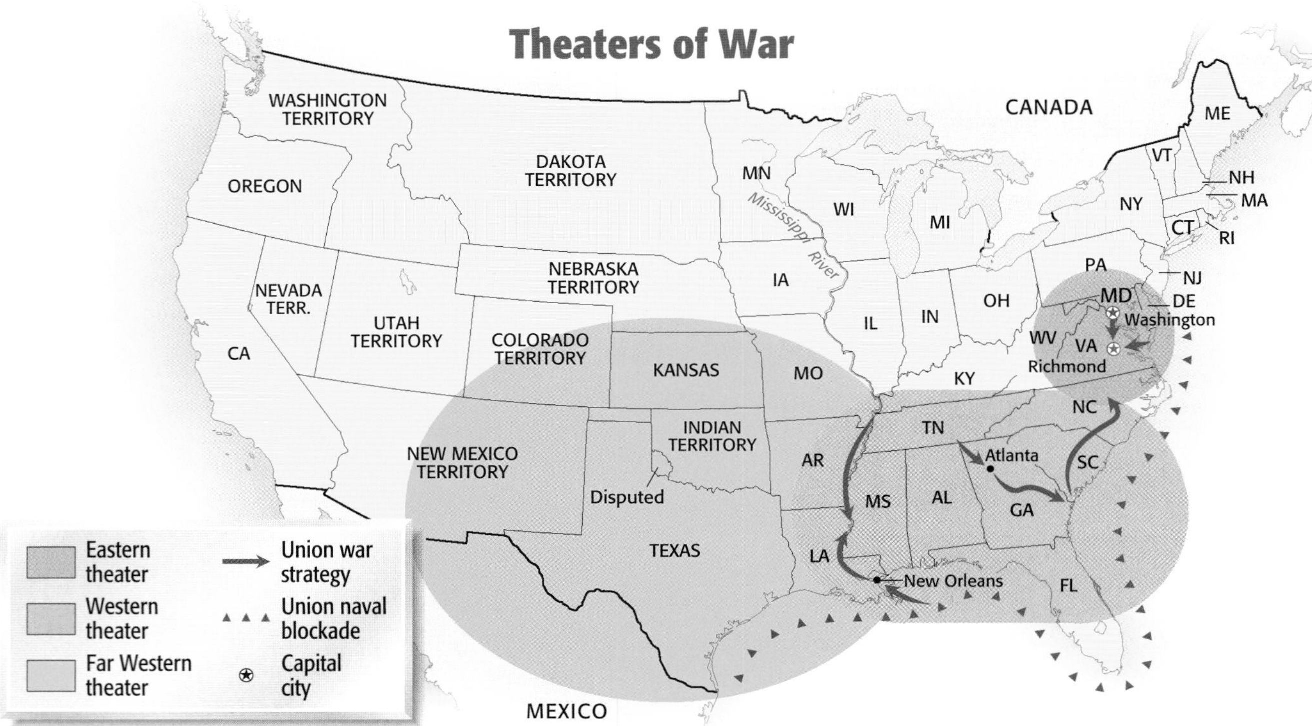

Geography **Skills**

Interpreting Thematic Maps

1. In what theater were the capitals of the Union and the Confederacy located?
2. What geographic feature of the Confederacy made the Union blockade difficult?
3. **The Uses of Geography** What river was a key to the Union strategy in the western theater? Why would controlling this river have been important?
4. **Drawing Inferences and Conclusions** Based on the map, why do you think the Union and the Confederacy concentrated little effort on the Far Western theater?

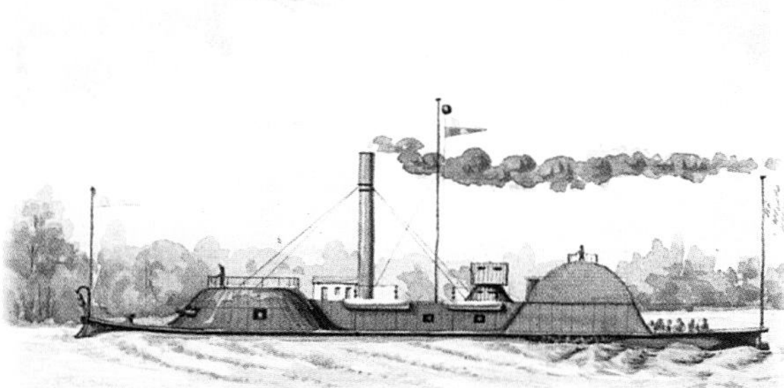

Union gunboat

History Note 3

Both the Union and the Confederacy concentrated their efforts in the eastern and western theaters of war. Battles took place on a smaller scale in the less-populated far western theater. For example, in 1862 a Confederate force of about 3,000 troops invaded the New Mexico Territory. They were eventually turned back. Part of the Union strategy when the war began was to split the Confederacy. Union commanders planned to cut off Arkansas, Louisiana, and Texas by taking control of the Mississippi River.

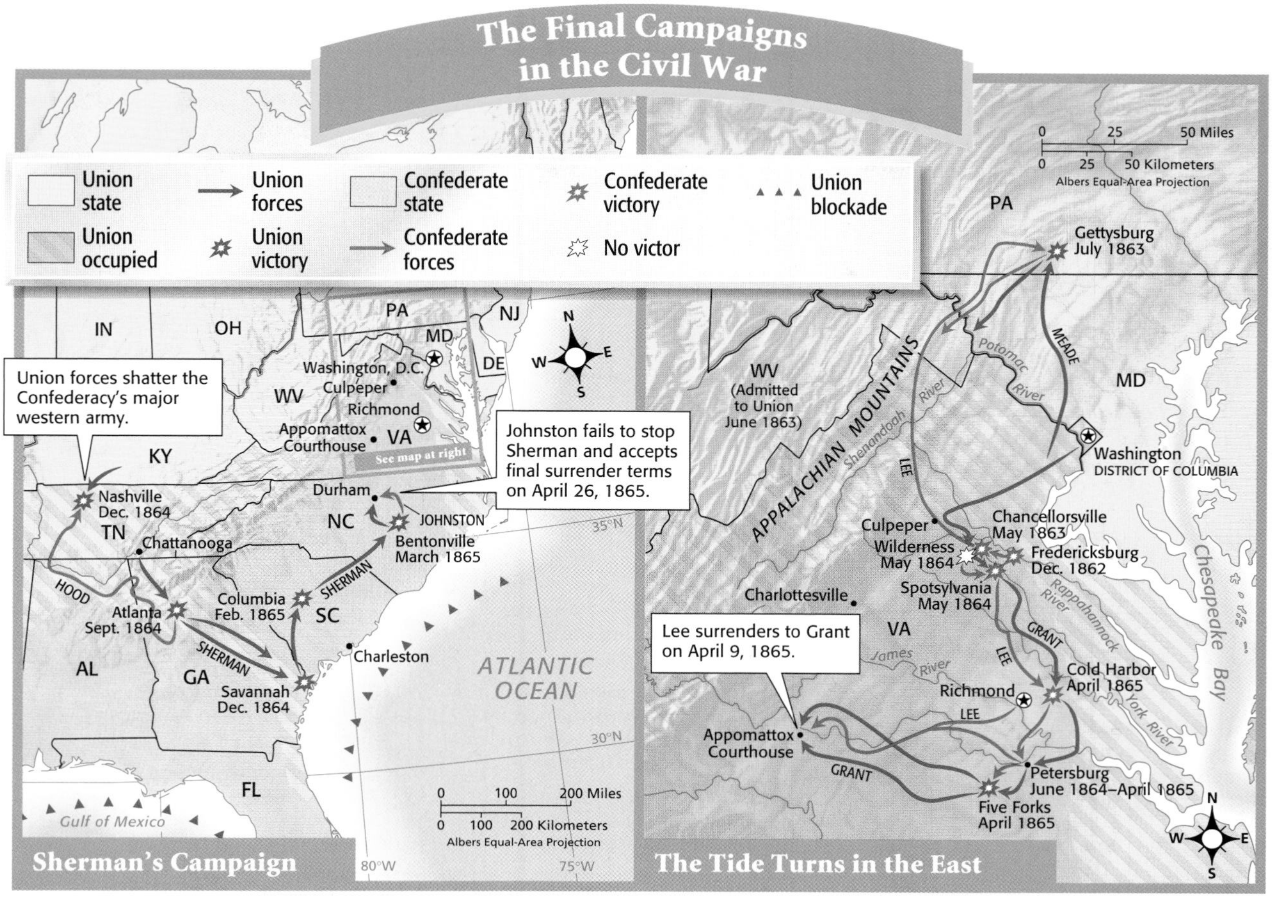

The Final Campaigns in the Civil War

Union state
Union forces
Confederate state
Confederate victory
Union blockade
Union occupied
Union victory
Confederate forces
No victor

Sherman's Campaign

IN
OH
PA
NJ
MD
DE
Washington, D.C.
Culpeper
Richmond
WV
Appomattox Courthouse
VA
See map at right
KY
Union forces shatter the Confederacy's major western army.
Johnston fails to stop Sherman and accepts final surrender terms on April 26, 1865.
Durham
NC
JOHNSTON
Bentonville March 1865
Nashville Dec. 1864
TN
Chattanooga
HOOD
Atlanta Sept. 1864
Columbia Feb. 1865
SHERMAN
SC
Charleston
AL
GA
SHERMAN
Savannah Dec. 1864
ATLANTIC OCEAN
FL
Gulf of Mexico
35°N
30°N
80°W
75°W
0 100 200 Miles
0 100 200 Kilometers
Albers Equal-Area Projection

The Tide Turns in the East

0 25 50 Miles
0 25 50 Kilometers
Albers Equal-Area Projection
PA
Gettysburg July 1863
MEADE
Potomac River
MD
WV (Admitted to Union June 1863)
APPALACHIAN MOUNTAINS
Shenandoah River
LEE
Washington
DISTRICT OF COLUMBIA
Culpeper
Chancellorsville May 1863
Wilderness May 1864
Fredericksburg Dec. 1862
Spotsylvania May 1864
Charlottesville
Rappahannock River
Chesapeake Bay
VA
GRANT
Lee surrenders to Grant on April 9, 1865.
James River
LEE
Richmond
Cold Harbor April 1865
York River
LEE
Appomattox Courthouse
GRANT
Petersburg June 1864–April 1865
Five Forks April 1865

Geography **Skills**

Interpreting Thematic Maps

1. Where did Sherman's army go after taking Savannah?
2. **Locate** Identify and list in the order that they occurred the battles fought during Sherman's campaign.
3. **Drawing Inferences and Conclusions** Why did so many eastern battles occur between the James and Potomac Rivers?

History Note 4

Most of the major battles near the end of the war took place in Virginia or the Lower South. Union commanders hoped to cut off Virginia from the Lower South. To do so, General William Techumseh Sherman led an army from Tennessee through Georgia to the Atlantic coast. Union leaders then planned to defeat Robert E. Lee's army and capture the Confederate capital of Richmond, Virginia.

Richmond, Virginia, after the war

CHAPTER

17 Reconstruction (1865–1877)

The race riots in New Orleans led to the deaths of 34 African Americans.

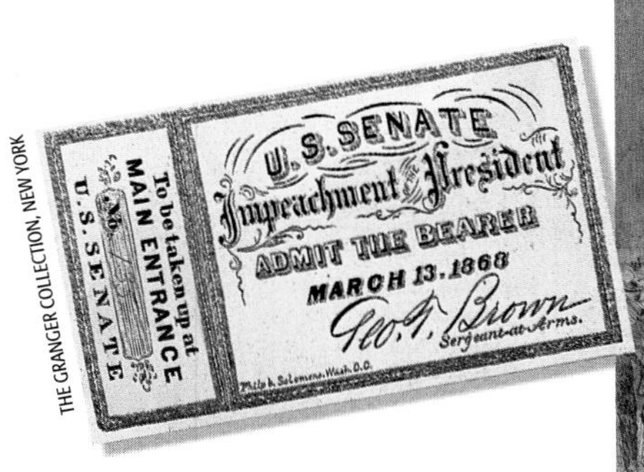

THE GRANGER COLLECTION, NEW YORK

This ticket allowed a spectator to observe President Andrew Johnson's impeachment trial.

UNITED STATES

1865 The Thirteenth Amendment is ratified, abolishing slavery.

1866 Race riots break out in New Orleans.

1867 Congress passes the first federal Reconstruction Act.

1868 President Andrew Johnson is impeached on February 24.

On July 28 the Fourteenth Amendment is ratified by the states, granting African Americans citizenship.

On November 3 Union general Ulysses S. Grant is elected president.

1870 On February 25, Hiram Revels becomes the first African American in the U.S. Senate.

The Fifteenth Amendment is ratified on March 30, giving African Americans the right to vote.

1865 | 1866 | 1867 | 1868 | 1869 | 1870 | 1871

WORLD

1868 The Meiji dynasty returns to power in Japan.

1869 The Suez Canal opens, linking the Mediterranean and Red Seas.

1870 France and the German state of Prussia go to war against each other.

1871 France loses the Franco-Prussian War.

This image shows the opening-day procession of ships through the Suez Canal.

Build on What You Know

The Civil War left two major issues unresolved. First, the federal government had to decide the conditions by which the defeated southern states could rejoin the Union. Second, it had to define the rights of African Americans freed by the Emancipation Proclamation. As southerners tried to rebuild their lives, the nation attempted to heal its wounds.

This poster—which includes images of African American preachers, soldiers, and students—celebrated the passage of the Fifteenth Amendment.

1872 The General Amnesty Act of 1872 restores voting rights to most former Confederate officials.

1873 Spain becomes a republic.

1874 Republicans lose their majority in the House of Representatives.

1874 The Spanish republic collapses, and the monarchy is restored.

1875 Congress passes the Civil Rights Act of 1875.

1876 Queen Victoria of Great Britain becomes empress of India.

1877 The Compromise of 1877 ends Reconstruction.

1872 1873 1874 1875 1876 1877

If you were there . . .

How would you try to reunite the nation?

You Be the Historian

What's Your Opinion? Do you **agree** or **disagree** with the following statements? Support your point of view in your journal.

- **Constitutional Heritage** Amending the Constitution is necessary to keep up with changes in government and society.
- **Government** New governments are necessary to rebuild a nation after a civil war.
- **Culture** Political changes bring about new forms of cultural expression.

Section 1

Rebuilding the South

Read to Discover

1. What effect did the end of the Civil War have on African Americans in the South?
2. How did President Lincoln, Congress, and President Johnson differ in their views on Reconstruction?

Define

- amnesty

Identify

- Reconstruction
- Ten Percent Plan
- Wade-Davis Bill
- Thirteenth Amendment
- Freedmen's Bureau
- John Wilkes Booth
- Andrew Johnson

WHY IT MATTERS TODAY

Nations today continue to rebuild after wars or natural disasters. Use CNNfyi.com or other **current events** sources to find a modern country or region that is rebuilding after a destructive event or period. Record your findings in your journal.

The Story Continues

Much of Richmond, Virginia, burned in the last days of the war.

When the Civil War ended, much of the South lay in ruins. Union troops had destroyed many major southern cities and railroads, wrecking trade and commerce. In the countryside, farms had suffered a similar fate. Harvests of corn, cotton, rice, and other important crops were well below normal prewar levels. In South Carolina, Mary Boykin Chesnut wrote in her diary about another problem faced by southerners in many communities—isolation. "We are shut in here. . . . All RR's [railroads] destroyed—bridges gone. We are cut off from the world."

Planning Reconstruction

After the South's surrender, tired southern soldiers returned home to find that the world they had left behind was gone. Because of high food prices and widespread crop failures, many southerners faced starvation. The Confederate money most southerners held was now worthless. Banks failed and merchants went bankrupt because people could not repay their debts. Former Confederate general Braxton Bragg found that "*all, all* was lost, except my debts."

The U.S. government faced the question of how to deal with the defeated southern states. **Reconstruction** was the process of reuniting the nation and rebuilding the southern states without slavery. It lasted from 1865 to 1877.

President Lincoln wanted to reunite the nation as quickly and painlessly as possible. He had proposed a plan for readmitting the southern states even before the war ended. Lincoln wanted to offer southerners **amnesty**, or an official pardon, for all illegal acts supporting the rebellion. To receive amnesty, southerners had to swear an oath of loyalty to the United States and accept a ban on slavery. Once 10 percent of voters in a state made these pledges, they could form a new government. The state then could be readmitted to the Union. Louisiana quickly elected a new state legislature under this **Ten Percent Plan**. Other southern states that had been occupied by Union troops followed Louisiana back into the Union.

Some politicians pointed out that Congress had the power to admit new states. They argued that Congress, not the president, should control the southern states' return to the Union. Also, many Republican members of Congress simply disagreed with Lincoln's Ten Percent Plan. Two Republicans—Senator Benjamin Wade and Representative Henry Davis—had an alternative to Lincoln's plan. Under the **Wade-Davis Bill**, a state had to meet two conditions before it could rejoin the Union.

Historical Document

1865

Lincoln's Second Inaugural Address

On March 4, 1865, President Lincoln laid out his approach to Reconstruction in his second inaugural address. As this excerpt shows, Lincoln hoped to peacefully reunite the nation and its people.

"On the occasion corresponding to this four years ago, all thoughts were anxiously directed to an **impending**[1] civil war. . . . One eighth of the whole population were colored slaves, not **distributed**[2] generally over the Union, but localized in the southern part of it. These slaves **constituted**[3] a peculiar and powerful interest. All knew that this interest was somehow the cause of the war. To strengthen, **perpetuate**,[4] and extend this interest was the object for which the **insurgents**[5] would **rend**[6] the Union even by war, while the Government claimed no right to do more than to restrict the territorial enlargement of it. . . . With **malice**[7] toward none; with charity for all; with firmness in the right, as God gives us to see the right, let us strive on to finish the work we are in, to bind up the nation's wounds, to care for him who shall have borne the battle, and for his widow, and his orphan—to do all which may achieve and cherish a just, and a lasting peace."

[1]**impending:** coming
[2]**distributed:** spread
[3]**constituted:** formed
[4]**perpetuate:** continue
[5]**insurgents:** rebels
[6]**rend:** tear apart
[7]**malice:** hatred

Analyzing Primary Sources

1. What does Lincoln believe the spread of slavery was doing to the Union, and how does he believe the government had to respond?
2. How do you think Lincoln views the issue of freeing the slaves?
3. How does Lincoln's speech promote union and equal treatment?

First, it had to ban slavery. Second, a majority of adult males in the state had to take the loyalty oath. However, only southerners who swore that they had never supported the Confederacy could vote or hold office. Because of this rule, the Wade-Davis Bill made it much harder for southern states to rejoin the Union than did Lincoln's plan. President Lincoln refused to sign this bill into law. He thought that few southern states would agree to meet its requirements.

✔ **Reading Check: Contrasting** How did Lincoln's Ten Percent Plan and the Wade-Davis Bill treat southerners differently?

The Thirteenth Amendment

Many African American families bought family records like this one after the war.

One issue Republicans agreed on was abolishing slavery. The Emancipation Proclamation had freed slaves only in the Confederate states that had not been occupied by Union forces. Slavery continued in the border states. In addition, many people feared that the federal courts might someday declare the Emancipation Proclamation unconstitutional.

On January 31, 1865, at Lincoln's urging, Congress proposed the **Thirteenth Amendment** to the Constitution. It made slavery illegal throughout the United States. The amendment was ratified and took effect on December 18, 1865. When abolitionist William Lloyd Garrison heard the news, he declared that his work was now finished. He called for

Aid for Freedpeople

Interpreting Maps In order to help African Americans, the Freedmen's Bureau and several private aid societies distributed food and clothing, set up hospitals, and operated schools.

Skills Assessment

1. **Places and Regions** According to the map, which states had major private aid projects?
2. **Drawing Inferences and Conclusions** Why do you think that most private aid societies had their headquarters in northern states?

the American Anti-Slavery Society to break up. Not all abolitionists agreed, however. Frederick Douglass insisted that "slavery is not abolished until the black man has the ballot [vote]."

Interpreting the Visual Record

New schools *This school for freedpeople was established in Vicksburg, Mississippi.* ***What does this image reveal about the ages of students in these early schools?***

Freedom did bring many changes to the lives of former slaves. Many couples held ceremonies to legalize marriages that had not been recognized under slavery. Many people searched for relatives who had been sold away from their families years earlier.

Some former slaves began to test their new freedom of movement. A South Carolina woman explained this need. "I must go, if I stay here I'll never know I'm free." Freedom to travel was just the first step on a long road toward equal rights and a new way of life. Adults took new last names. They insisted on being called Mr. or Mrs., rather than by their first name or by nicknames.

Across the South, freedpeople also demanded the same economic and political rights as white citizens. Henry Adams, a former slave, argued that "if I cannot do like a white man I am not free." Many former slaves wanted their own land to farm. Near the end of the Civil War, General William Tecumseh Sherman issued an order setting aside coastal lands in South Carolina, Georgia, and Florida for former slaves. However, the federal government soon returned these lands to the original owners. Many former slaves remained unsure about their future. They did not know where they would live, what kind of work they would do, and what rights they had.

✔ **Reading Check:** **Summarizing** What did the Thirteenth Amendment achieve, and how did this change the lives of enslaved African Americans?

The Freedmen's Bureau

In 1865 Congress established the **Freedmen's Bureau**. Its purpose was to provide relief for all poor people—black and white—in the South. Under Oliver O. Howard, the Bureau distributed food to the poor and supervised labor contracts between freedpeople and their employers. The Bureau also assisted African American war veterans.

In addition, the Freedmen's Bureau helped promote education in the South. Laws against educating slaves had kept most of them from learning to read or write. The Bureau and other groups established schools and provided books and teachers. Some former slaves also organized their own education efforts. African Americans opened schools in abandoned buildings. Some white southerners, however, burned down schools and attacked teachers and students. But by 1869, more than 3,000 schools had been established. More than 150,000 students attended these schools. The Freedmen's Bureau helped establish several colleges for African Americans, including Howard University in Washington, D.C., and Fisk University in Nashville, Tennessee. Students quickly filled the new classrooms, and working adults attended classes in the evening.

✔ **Reading Check: Analyzing Information** How did the Freedmen's Bureau help to provide educational reform in the South?

LINKING PAST to PRESENT

Historically Black Colleges and Universities

After the Civil War, colleges for African Americans were established in the South. These schools, now known as historically black colleges and universities, offered traditional education, training, and teaching degrees. At one time, laws in many states prohibited African Americans from attending white schools. Today, however, many students choose historically black colleges and universities for their emphasis on African American identity and history. According to United Negro College Fund president William H. Gray III, students receive valuable support from the faculty, administration, and fellow students. **What do historically black colleges and universities provide their students?**

African American students studying art

A New President

On the evening of April 14, 1865, President Lincoln and his wife attended a performance of *Our American Cousin* at Ford's Theatre in Washington. During the play, **John Wilkes Booth** sneaked into the president's theater box and shot him. Booth was a southerner who opposed Lincoln's policies. Lincoln was rushed to a boardinghouse across the street, where he died at about 7:30 the next morning. Across the North people were stunned and saddened by the news of Lincoln's death. His body was sent home to Springfield, Illinois, for burial. Vice President **Andrew Johnson** was sworn into office that morning. Reconstruction was now his responsibility.

Republicans liked President Johnson because he seemed to favor a tougher approach to Reconstruction than Lincoln had. Johnson's plan for bringing southern states back into the Union was similar to Lincoln's plan. Johnson gave amnesty to all southerners who took an oath of loyalty and who agreed to support the abolition of slavery. However, wealthy southerners and former Confederate officials would need a presidential pardon to qualify for amnesty. In the end, this restriction was not as harsh as it might seem. Johnson shocked Republicans by eventually pardoning more than 7,000 people.

✔ **Reading Check: Finding the Main Idea** How did Lincoln's assassination affect the nation?

President Johnson's Reconstruction Plan

Lincoln's funeral procession was witnessed by thousands of mourners.

Johnson's plan for Reconstruction established a system for setting up new southern state governments. First, he appointed a temporary governor for each state. Then southerners who had taken the loyalty oath elected delegates to a convention that would revise their state's constitution. Next, voters elected new state officials and representatives to the U.S. Congress. Each new state government was required to declare that secession was illegal. It also had to refuse to pay Confederate debts. No state could rejoin the Union until it had met these requirements. Governments already set up under Lincoln's Ten Percent Plan—in Arkansas, Louisiana, Tennessee, and Virginia—were allowed to remain in place.

By the end of 1865 all the southern states except Texas had created new governments. Johnson approved them all and declared that the United States was restored. Newly elected representatives soon came to Washington, D.C., from each reconstructed southern state. But Congress refused to allow them to take their seats in the House and Senate.

Republicans complained that many of the new southern representatives had been military officers and political leaders of the Confederacy. For example, Alexander H. Stephens, the newly elected U.S. senator from Georgia, had been the vice president of the Confederacy. Many Republicans did not believe that people like Stephens were truly loyal to the United States. Congress therefore refused to readmit the reconstructed southern states into the Union. Clearly, the nation was still divided over who should control Reconstruction and what direction it should take.

✔ **Reading Check: Summarizing** What steps did Johnson require southern states to take in order to be readmitted into the Union?

Section 1 Review

keyword: SC3 HP17

1. **Define** and explain:
   amnesty

2. **Identify** and explain:
   - Reconstruction
   - Ten Percent Plan
   - Wade-Davis Bill
   - Thirteenth Amendment
   - Freedmen's Bureau
   - John Wilkes Booth
   - Andrew Johnson

3. **Comparing and Contrasting** Copy the graphic organizer below. Use it to describe the three plans for Reconstruction that were developed over time.

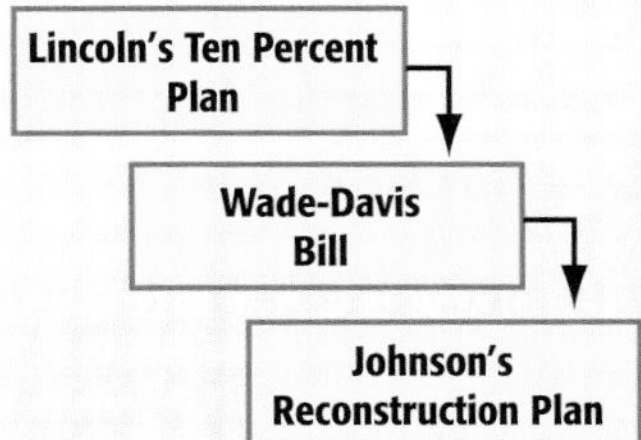

4. **Finding the Main Idea**
   a. How did life in the South begin to change for African Americans after the Civil War?
   b. What effect did Lincoln's assassination have on Reconstruction?

5. **Writing and Critical Thinking**
   Summarizing Imagine that you are a southern newspaper editor in 1865. Write a brief editorial that describes the condition of the South after the Civil War.
   Consider the following:
   - the economic condition of the South
   - the political situation of the ex-Confederate states
   - the effect of the Thirteenth Amendment

Section 2

The Fight over Reconstruction

Read to Discover

1. How did Black Codes restrict African Americans' freedoms?
2. Why did Radical Republicans try to impeach President Johnson?
3. How did Republicans try to protect the civil rights of African Americans?

Identify

- Black Codes
- Radical Republicans
- Thaddeus Stevens
- Civil Rights Act of 1866
- Fourteenth Amendment
- Reconstruction Acts
- Fifteenth Amendment

Why it Matters Today

In the 1860s the Radical Republicans used their control of Congress to pass major laws. Use CNNfyi.com or other **current events** sources to identify which political party controls each house of Congress today and one piece of legislation that party is trying to pass. Record your findings in your journal.

A federal soldier protects an African American man from violence.

The Story Continues

To test his newfound freedom, in 1865 Henry Adams left the plantation where he had been a slave. A group of white men stopped Adams on the road, demanding to know who owned him. When Adams replied that he was a free man, the strangers beat him. Such violent attacks were not unusual in the South in the years following the Civil War. Many white southerners opposed and feared African Americans' freedom. This resentment also affected local authorities and state governments.

The Black Codes

In 1866 Congress continued to debate the rules for restoring the Union. Meanwhile, new state legislatures approved by President Johnson had already begun passing laws to deny African Americans' civil rights. "This is a white man's government, and intended for white men only," declared Governor Benjamin F. Perry of South Carolina. Soon every southern state passed **Black Codes**—laws that greatly limited the freedom of African Americans.

Under the Black Codes, white southerners could arrest unemployed African Americans and auction their labor to the highest bidder.

Black Codes required African Americans to sign work contracts. This arrangement created working conditions similar to those experienced under slavery. In most southern states, any African American who could not prove he or she had a job could be arrested. Their punishment might be one year of forced labor without pay. African Americans were also prevented from owning guns. In addition, African Americans were not allowed to rent property in cities.

The Black Codes alarmed African Americans. As one Civil War veteran asked, "If you call this Freedom, what do you call Slavery?" African Americans organized to oppose the codes. One group sent a petition to officials in South Carolina.

History Makers Speak

"We simply ask . . . that the same laws which govern *white men* shall govern *black men*; that we have the right of trial by a jury of our peers; that schools be established for the education of *colored children* as well as white . . . that, in short, we be dealt with as others are—in equity [equality] and justice."

—Petition by an African American convention, quoted in *There Is a River: The Black Struggle for Freedom in America*, by Vincent Harding

Analyzing Primary Sources

Identifying Points of View What rights did these African Americans want?

Such calls for equality had little effect on the new state governments, however.

✔ **Reading Check: Finding the Main Idea** How were southern African Americans treated after the Civil War, and why did they receive this treatment?

 The Radical Republicans

The Black Codes angered many Republicans who felt the South was returning to its old ways. Most Republicans were moderates who wanted the South to have loyal state governments. They also believed that African Americans should have rights as citizens. Most moderates hoped that the national government would not have to force the South to follow federal laws.

Radical Republicans wanted the southern states to change much more than they already had before they could return to the Union. Like the moderates, they thought the Black Codes were cruel and unjust. Radicals, however, wanted the federal government to be much more involved in Reconstruction. They feared that too many southern leaders

Thaddeus Stevens was one of the most vocal Radical Republicans in Congress.

Andrew Johnson

Andrew Johnson had a long political career before becoming president. Born to a poor family in North Carolina, Johnson became a tailor's apprentice. Unhappy with this arrangement, the young Johnson ran away to Tennessee and started his own tailoring business. Eventually, he became a prosperous landowner and entered politics. However, he never forgot his humble beginnings and often criticized wealthy southern planters. Johnson served as governor of Tennessee and later as a U.S. senator from that state. When Tennessee seceded, Johnson remained loyal to the Union. The Republicans selected Johnson as Lincoln's running mate in the presidential campaign of 1864. They hoped that he would appeal to voters in the border states. He had been vice president for less than six weeks when Lincoln was assassinated. What parts of Andrew Johnson's experience prepared him for the presidency?

were still loyal to the former Confederacy. **Thaddeus Stevens** of Pennsylvania and Charles Sumner of Massachusetts were the leaders of the Radical Republicans.

A harsh critic of President Johnson, Stevens was known for his honesty and sharp tongue. He wanted economic and political justice for both African Americans and poor white southerners.

> **"Have not loyal blacks quite as good a right to choose rulers and make laws as rebel whites? Every man, no matter what his race or color . . . has an equal right to justice, honesty, and fair play with every other man; and the law should secure him those rights."**
>
> —Thaddeus Stevens, quoted in *Sources of the American Republic*

Sumner had been a strong opponent of slavery before the Civil War. He continued to argue for African Americans' civil rights, which included the right to vote and the right to fair treatment under the law. Both Stevens and Sumner felt that President Johnson's Reconstruction plan was a failure. Although the Radicals did not control Congress, they gained support among moderates when President Johnson ignored criticism of the Black Codes. "The same national authority that destroyed slavery must see that this other pretension [racial inequality] is not permitted to survive," said Sumner.

✔ Reading Check: **Comparing and Contrasting** How were Radical Republicans and moderate Republicans similar and different?

Johnson versus Congress

In early 1866 Congress proposed a bill to give the Freedmen's Bureau more powers. The law would allow the Freedmen's Bureau to use military courts to try people accused of violating African Americans' rights. The bill's supporters hoped that these courts would be fairer than local courts in the South. To the surprise of many members of Congress, Johnson vetoed the bill. He insisted that Congress could not pass any new laws until the southern states were represented in Congress. Johnson also argued that the Freedmen's Bureau was unconstitutional. He believed that African Americans did not need any special assistance.

Republicans responded with the **Civil Rights Act of 1866**. This act provided African Americans with the same legal rights as white Americans. President Johnson once again used his veto power. He argued that the law would give too much power to the federal government. He also rejected the principle of equal rights for African Americans. The president insisted that they did not understand "the nature and character of our institutions." Congress, however, overrode Johnson's veto.

✔ Reading Check: **Identifying Points of View** What Congressional laws did Johnson veto, and why?

The Fourteenth Amendment

Republicans feared the Civil Rights Act might be overturned. To protect civil rights laws from hostile presidents, courts, or future legislators, Republicans proposed a constitutional amendment in the summer of 1866. The **Fourteenth Amendment** included the following provisions.

1. It defined all people born or naturalized within the United States, except American Indians, as U.S. citizens.
2. It guaranteed to citizens the equal protection of the laws.
3. It said that states could not "deprive any person of life, liberty, or property, without due process of law."
4. It banned many former Confederate officials from holding state or federal offices.
5. It made state laws subject to review by federal courts.
6. It gave Congress the power to pass any laws needed to enforce any part of the amendment.

President Johnson and most Democrats opposed the Fourteenth Amendment. As a result, civil rights for African Americans became a key issue in the 1866 congressional elections. Republican candidates asked Americans to support civil rights by voting for the Republican Party. Johnson traveled around the country defending his Reconstruction plan, but his tour was of little help to Democratic Party candidates.

Two major riots in the South also hurt Johnson's campaign. On May 1, 1866, a dispute in Memphis, Tennessee, took place between local police and black Union soldiers. The dispute turned into a three-day wave of violence against African Americans. By the time the riots ended, 46 African Americans were dead. About three months later, another riot took place in New Orleans when African Americans attempted to hold a peaceful political demonstration. This time 34 African Americans and three white Republicans were killed. Federal troops had to restore order.

✔ **Reading Check: Summarizing** What issue did the Fourteenth Amendment address, and how did it affect the congressional elections of 1866?

Research on the ROM

Free Find:
Civil Rights Act of 1866
After reading about the Civil Rights Act of 1866 on the **Holt Researcher CD–ROM**, create an illustrated diagram that shows what rights former slaves had before and after Congress passed the act.

Interpreting the Visual Record

Johnson's tour *President Andrew Johnson often got into arguments with audience members during his speaking tour in 1866. When someone cried out, "Hang Jeff Davis!" Johnson replied angrily, "Why not hang Thad Stevens?"* ***What does this image tell you about how Johnson traveled on his tour?***

Congress Takes Charge

The 1866 elections gave the Republican Party a commanding two-thirds majority in both the House and the Senate. This majority gave the Republicans the power to override any presidential veto. In addition, the Republicans became united as the moderates joined with the Radicals. Together they called for a new form of Reconstruction.

In March 1867 Congress passed the first of several **Reconstruction Acts**. These laws divided the South into five districts, with a U.S. military commander in control of each district. The military would remain in the South until the southern states rejoined the Union. To be readmitted, a state had to write a new state constitution supporting the Fourteenth Amendment. Finally, the state had to give African American men the right to vote.

President Johnson disagreed strongly with the Reconstruction Acts. He argued that African Americans did not deserve the same treatment as white people. The Reconstruction Acts, he said, used "powers not granted to the federal government or any one of its branches." Republicans knew

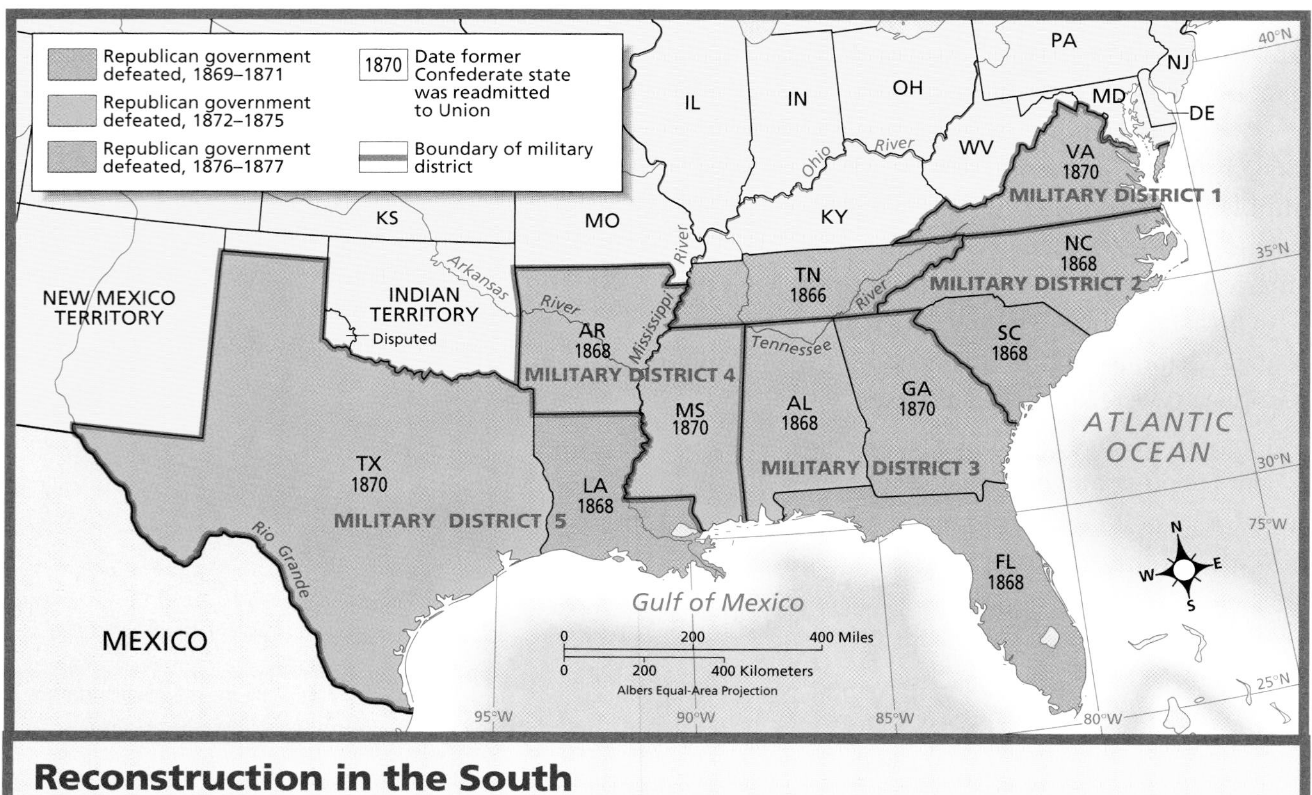

Reconstruction in the South

Interpreting Maps The Reconstruction Acts established military districts in the South that would be removed when the southern states drafted new state constitutions and adopted the Fourteenth Amendment.

Skills Assessment **Locate** During Reconstruction, which former Confederate state was not part of a military district?

that Johnson did not support their Reconstruction policies, so they passed a law to limit his power. This law prevented the president from removing cabinet officials without the U.S. Senate's approval. Johnson quickly broke the law by firing Edwin Stanton, the secretary of war.

The House of Representatives responded by voting to impeach the president. Impeachment is the process used by a legislative body to bring charges of wrongdoing against a public official. This was the first time in U.S. history that a president had been impeached. The next step, under Article I of the Constitution, was a trial in the Senate. If a two-thirds majority of the senators found Johnson guilty, he would be removed from office.

THE GRANGER COLLECTION, NEW YORK

President Andrew Johnson's impeachment trial in the Senate attracted many onlookers.

Although Johnson was unpopular with Republicans, some of them believed he was being judged unfairly. Others did not trust the president *pro tempore* of the Senate, Benjamin Wade, who would become president if Johnson were removed from office. By a single vote, Senate Republicans failed to convict Johnson. Even so, the trial broke his power.

✔ **Reading Check: Analyzing Information** What was the purpose of the Reconstruction Acts, and how did they affect the South?

The Election of 1868

The Democratic Party did not nominate Johnson for another term in 1868. Instead, the Democrats chose former New York governor Horatio Seymour as their presidential candidate. The Republicans selected Ulysses S. Grant. As a war hero, Grant appealed to many northern voters. He had no political experience but supported the congressional Reconstruction plan. He ran under the slogan "Let Us Have Peace."

Shortly after Grant was nominated, Congress readmitted seven southern states—Alabama, Arkansas, Florida, Georgia, Louisiana, North Carolina, and South Carolina. (Tennessee already had been readmitted in 1866.) Under the terms of readmission, these seven states approved the Fourteenth Amendment. They also agreed to let African American men have the vote. However, white southerners used violence to keep African Americans away from the polls during the presidential election.

Despite such tactics, hundreds of thousands of African Americans voted for Grant and the "party of Lincoln." The *New Orleans Tribune* reported that many former slaves "see clearly enough that the Republican party [is] their political life boat." African American votes helped Grant win a narrow victory.

✔ **Reading Check: Analyzing Information** What voters did Grant appeal to in the presidential election of 1868?

That's Interesting!

A Good Show Can you imagine a trial becoming a social event? That's just what happened when Andrew Johnson was impeached. People had to have tickets to attend the trial, and only 1,000 were printed. William H. Crook, President Johnson's bodyguard, described the scene. "Everyone who by any possible means could get a ticket . . . [showed] it early that morning at the Capitol. The floor and galleries were crowded." Washingtonians attended in their finest clothes and hoped for a good show. However, they were soon disappointed. Few were interested in the long speeches, and President Johnson did not even appear at his trial.

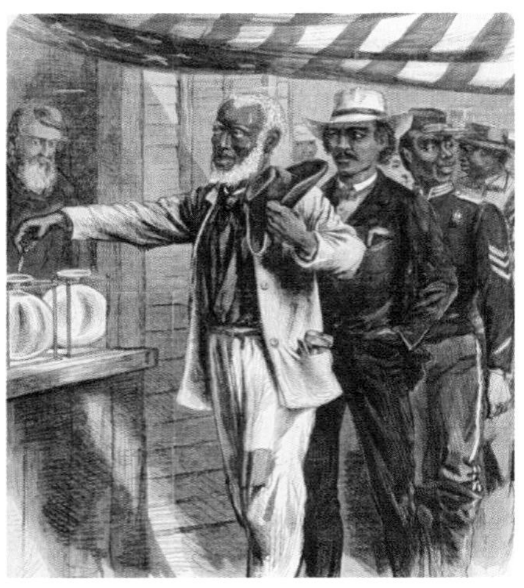

Interpreting the Visual Record

Gaining the vote *This illustration shows African Americans voting after the passage of the Fifteenth Amendment.* ***What types of individuals are shown in the voting line?***

The Fifteenth Amendment

Congressional Republicans wanted to protect their Reconstruction plan from any major changes. They believed that most African American voters would support Republican policies. In addition, some Radical Republicans argued that it was not fair that many northern states had laws that prevented African Americans from voting. After all, every southern state was now required to grant suffrage to African American men under the Republican plan.

These were some of the reasons why Congress proposed the **Fifteenth Amendment** in 1869. The amendment gave African American men throughout the United States the right to vote. Abolitionist William Lloyd Garrison praised "this wonderful, quiet, sudden transformation of four millions of human beings from . . . the auction block to the ballot-box." The amendment went into effect in 1870, and it was one of the last important Reconstruction measures passed at the federal level.

The Fifteenth Amendment did not please every reformer, however. Writer and editor Henry Adams commented that the Fifteenth Amendment was "more remarkable for what it does not than for what it does contain." For example, the act did not guarantee African Americans the right to hold public office. It also did not extend the right to vote to all Americans. This particularly upset women's rights activists, many of whom believed it was unfair to grant African American men the vote while still denying suffrage to all American women. Many women's rights activists opposed the amendment for this reason.

✔ **Reading Check: Finding the Main Idea** What did the Fifteenth Amendment achieve?

Section 2 Review

go.hrw.com Homework Practice Online
keyword: SC3 HP17

1. **Identify** and explain:
   - Black Codes
   - Radical Republicans
   - Thaddeus Stevens
   - Civil Rights Act of 1866
   - Fourteenth Amendment
   - Reconstruction Acts
   - Fifteenth Amendment

2. **Sequencing** Copy the time line below. Use it to list, in order, the reform legislation Congress proposed or passed as part of Reconstruction. Include the significance of each law or amendment.

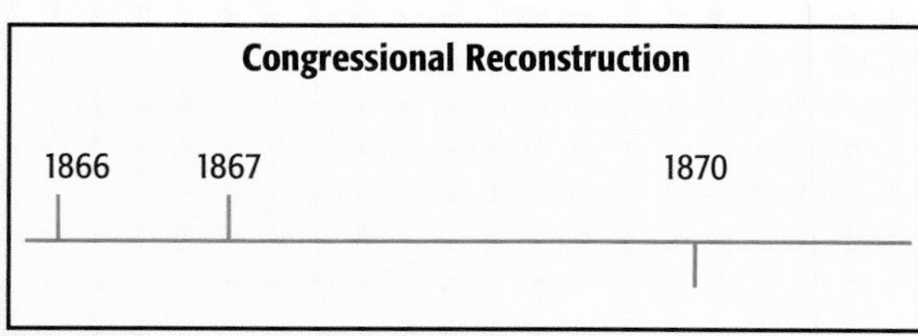

3. **Finding the Main Idea**
   a. In what ways did the Black Codes restrict the freedom of African Americans?
   b. Why did Radical Republicans want to remove President Johnson from office?

4. **Writing and Critical Thinking**
   Identifying Points of View Imagine that you are a member of the Republican Party. Write a slogan that might have been used by the Republican Party to appeal to voters in either the 1866 congressional elections or the 1868 presidential election.
   Consider the following:
   - how the party tried to protect the rights of African Americans
   - new amendments and congressional laws
   - differences between moderate and Radical Republicans

Section 3

Reconstruction in the South

Read to Discover

1. What reforms did Reconstruction governments carry out?
2. What factors led to the end of Reconstruction?
3. How did southern laws and governments change after Reconstruction ended?

Define

- carpetbaggers
- scalawags
- poll tax
- segregation

Identify

- Hiram Revels
- Blanche K. Bruce
- Ku Klux Klan
- General Amnesty Act of 1872
- Panic of 1873
- Civil Rights Act of 1875
- Compromise of 1877
- Redeemers
- Jim Crow laws
- *Plessy* v. *Ferguson*

Why It Matters Today

During Reconstruction, there were many Republican governments in the South. As Reconstruction ended, Democrats gained power. Use CNNfyi.com or other **current events** sources to learn which political party is leading a southern state today. Record your findings in your journal.

The Story Continues

Governments elected with the support of African American voters took control of most southern states. Planter Henry William Ravenel expressed concerns about the future in his daily journal. "The experiment [Reconstruction] is now to be tried. . . . It produces a financial, political, and social revolution [in] the South." Ravenel worried about how the actions of the new governments would affect southern society.

Henry William Ravenel hoped that Reconstruction would be successful.

Reconstruction Governments

The Republican Party controlled most southern governments, partly because the Fourteenth Amendment banned many former Confederates, who were Democrats, from holding office. Most of the Republican officeholders were unpopular with the majority of white southerners.

Some northern-born Republicans had moved south after the war. Many white southerners called these Republicans **carpetbaggers.** Supposedly the northerners carried all their possessions in bags made from

This is an example of the type of carpetbag from which the nickname carpetbaggers developed.

carpeting. Many southerners resented these northerners, believing that they had moved south to profit from Reconstruction. Some of the newcomers wanted to help former slaves. Others hoped to make money while rebuilding the southern economy.

Southern Democrats cared even less for white southern Republicans. They referred to them as **scalawags**, or "mean fellows." Democrats believed that these southerners had betrayed the South by voting for the Republican Party. Many southern Republicans were small farmers who had supported the Union during the war. Others, like Mississippi governor James Alcorn, were former members of the Whig Party. They preferred to become Republicans rather than join the Democrats.

African Americans were the largest group of southern Republican voters. During Reconstruction, more than 600 African Americans were elected as representatives to state legislatures. Of these politicians, 16 were elected to Congress. Other African Americans held important state offices such as lieutenant governor, treasurer, and secretary of state. Many more held local offices in counties throughout the southern states. Apart from their regular duties, African American politicians helped enforce laws that white officials ignored. In Georgia, for example, Justice of the Peace Tunis Campbell protected African Americans from attack by angry whites. One African American called Campbell "the champion of their rights and the bearer of their burden."

African American politicians came from many different backgrounds. **Hiram Revels** was born free in North Carolina and went to college in Illinois. He became a Methodist minister and served as a chaplain in the Union army. In 1870 Revels became the first African American in the U.S. Senate. He took over the seat previously held by Jefferson Davis in Mississippi. Unlike Revels, **Blanche K. Bruce** grew up in slavery in Virginia. He became an important Republican in Mississippi and served one term as a U.S. senator.

Reconstruction governments provided money for many new programs and organizations. They helped to establish some of the first state-funded public school systems in the South. They also built new hospitals, prisons, and orphanages and passed laws prohibiting discrimination against African Americans. Southern states under Republican control spent large amounts of money. They aided the construction or repair of railroads, bridges, and public buildings. These improvements were intended to help the southern economy recover from the war. To get the money for these projects, the Reconstruction governments raised taxes and issued bonds.

Interpreting the Visual Record

Representatives *The first African American members of Congress included, from left to right, Hiram Revels, Benjamin Turner, Robert DeLarge, Josiah Walls, Jefferson Long, Joseph Rainey, and Robert Elliott.* ***What was significant about the election of these politicians?***

THE GRANGER COLLECTION, NEW YORK

✔ **Reading Check: Summarizing** What reforms did Reconstruction state governments carry out?

Opposition to Reconstruction

Despite these efforts to rebuild the South, most white southerners opposed Reconstruction. Democrats claimed that the Reconstruction governments were corrupt and illegal. They also disliked having federal soldiers stationed in their states. Many white southerners disapproved of African American officeholders.

In 1866 a group of white southerners in Tennessee created the **Ku Klux Klan**. This secret society opposed civil rights, particularly suffrage, for African Americans. Klan members wore robes and disguises to hide their identities. The Klan used violence and terror against African Americans, white Republican voters, and public officials. The Klan's membership grew rapidly as it spread throughout the South. In response, Congress passed laws that made it a federal crime to interfere with elections or to deny citizens equal protection under the law. Within a few years the Klan was no longer an organized threat, but violence against African Americans and Republicans continued throughout the 1870s.

✔ **Reading Check: Finding the Main Idea** What was the purpose of the Ku Klux Klan?

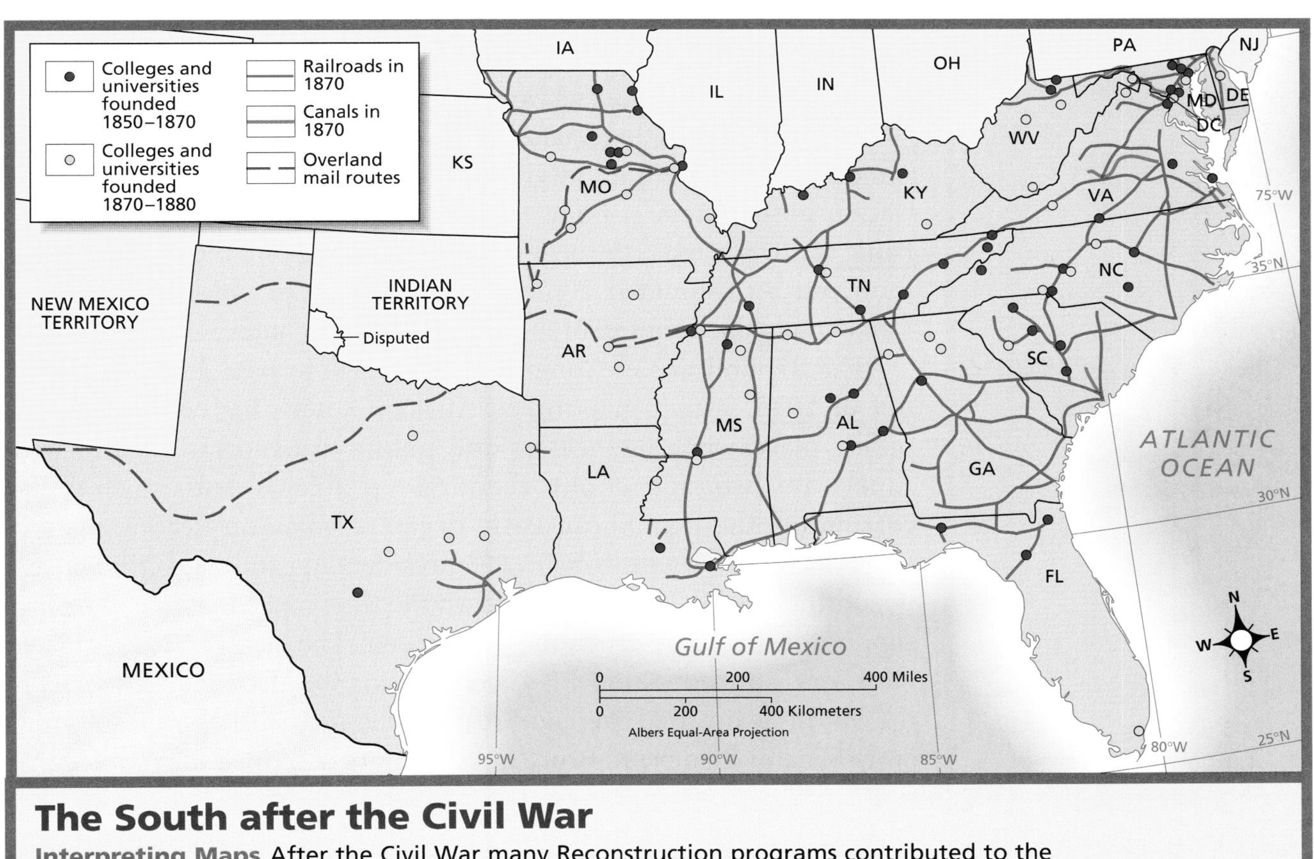

The South after the Civil War

Interpreting Maps After the Civil War many Reconstruction programs contributed to the rapid growth in transportation and education in the South.

Skills Assessment **Places and Regions** How many colleges and universities were founded in Alabama from 1850 to 1870?

Interpreting the Visual Record

Disputed votes *A special Election Commission heard testimony on disputed returns from the presidential election of 1876.* ***Why do you think so many people gathered to watch these proceedings?***

The End of Reconstruction

The violence of the Ku Klux Klan was not the only challenge to Reconstruction. The **General Amnesty Act of 1872** allowed former Confederates, except those who had held high ranks, to hold public office. Many of these former Confederates were soon elected to southern governments. Most were Democrats who opposed Reconstruction.

The Republican Party also began losing its power in the North. Although President Grant was re-elected in 1872, scandals in his administration upset voters. A poor economy also hurt the Republicans. The **Panic of 1873** marked the beginning of a severe economic downturn that soon put an estimated 2 million people out of work. In 1874 the Democrats gained control of the House of Representatives.

The Republicans in Congress did manage to pass the **Civil Rights Act of 1875**, which guaranteed African Americans equal rights in public places such as theaters and public transportation. But with Americans worried about economic problems and government corruption, the Republican Party began to abandon Reconstruction. Republicans selected for their 1876 presidential candidate Ohio governor Rutherford B. Hayes. He believed the time had come to end federal support of the Reconstruction governments. The Democrats nominated New York governor Samuel J. Tilden. During the election, Democrats in the South again used violence at the polls to keep Republican voters away. Senator Blanche K. Bruce of Mississippi described the problem.

Analyzing Primary Sources

Summarizing How did Democrats act to ensure that Republicans were defeated at the polls?

> **"In many parts of the State corrupt and violent influences were brought to bear [used] . . . changing the number of votes cast; . . . threats and violence were practiced directly upon the masses of voters . . . to deter [prevent] them from [voting]."**
>
> —Blanche K. Bruce, quoted in *Crossing the Danger Water,* edited by Deirdre Mullane

The election between Hayes and Tilden was very close. Tilden appeared to have won. Republicans, however, challenged the electoral votes in Oregon and three southern states. A special Election Commission of 10 members of Congress and five Supreme Court justices settled the issue. The commission narrowly decided to give all the disputed votes to Hayes, who thus won the election by one electoral vote. In the **Compromise of 1877**, the Democrats agreed to accept Hayes's victory. In return, they wanted all remaining federal troops removed from the South. They also asked for funding for internal improvements in the South and the appointment of a southern Democrat to the president's cabinet. Shortly after he took office in 1877, President Hayes removed the last of the federal troops from the South.

✔ **Reading Check: Sequencing** What issues led up to the Compromise of 1877, and how did it affect Reconstruction?

Interpreting Political Cartoons

Compromise of 1877 *Some saw the Compromise of 1877 as the only way to avoid violence in the South after the disputed election results.* ***Why do you think the artist chose to show a hand grasping at a pistol?***

Jim Crow and *Plessy* v. *Ferguson*

Gradually, Democrats regained control of state governments in the South. These Democrats were called **Redeemers**. They came from a variety of backgrounds. Texas governor Richard Coke, like many other Redeemers, was a former officer in the Confederate army. Some Redeemers came from business backgrounds. In general, Redeemers wanted to reduce the size of state government and limit the rights of African Americans. They lowered state budgets and got rid of social programs. The Redeemers cut property taxes and reduced public funding for schools.

Redeemers set up the **poll tax** in an effort to deny the vote to African Americans. The poll tax was a special tax people had to pay before they could vote. Some states also targeted African American voters by requiring them to pass a literacy test. A so-called grandfather clause written into law affected men whose fathers or grandfathers could vote before 1867. In those cases, a voter did not have to pay a poll tax or pass a literacy test. As a result, almost every white man could escape the voting restrictions, while few black men could.

Redeemer governments also introduced legal **segregation**, the forced separation of whites and African Americans in public places. **Jim Crow laws**—laws that required segregation—were common in southern states in the 1880s. African Americans had to stay in different hotels than whites. They had to sit in separate theater sections and ride in separate railcars. One white southerner described the segregated areas that African Americans were forced to use as "the most uncomfortable, uncleanest, and unsafest place[s]."

African Americans challenged Jim Crow laws in court. In 1883, however, the U.S. Supreme Court ruled that the Civil Rights Act of 1875 was unconstitutional. The Court also ruled that the Fourteenth

This African American man is being ordered to leave a whites-only railroad car.

Research on the ROM

Free Find:
Plessy* v. *Ferguson
After reading about *Plessy* v. *Ferguson* on the **Holt Researcher CD–ROM**, imagine that you are a newspaper reporter working at the time of the Supreme Court decision. Write a newspaper article about the case and the Court's decision.

Amendment applied only to the actions of state governments. This ruling allowed private individuals and businesses to practice segregation.

In 1896 the U.S. Supreme Court returned to the issue of segregation in the case ***Plessy* v. *Ferguson***. Homer Plessy, an African American, had purchased a ticket on a Louisiana train. When he refused to leave the whites-only section of the train car, he was arrested. Louisiana's Jim Crow laws did not allow African Americans to ride in cars with whites. Plessy's lawyers argued that the law violated his right to equal treatment under the Fourteenth Amendment.

The Court ruled that segregation was allowed if "separate-but-equal" facilities were provided for African Americans. Among the justices, only John Marshall Harlan disagreed with the Court's decision. He explained his disagreement in a dissenting opinion.

Analyzing Primary Sources

Identifying Points of View What does it mean to say that the Constitution is "color-blind"?

> **"In the eye of the law, there is in this country no superior, dominant [controlling], ruling class of citizens. . . . Our Constitution is color-blind, and neither knows nor tolerates classes among citizens. In respect of civil rights, all citizens are equal before the law."**
>
> —John Marshall Harlan, quoted in *American Issues*

Despite Harlan's view, segregation became widespread across the country. African Americans were forced to use separate public schools, libraries, and parks. When they existed, these facilities were usually of poorer quality than those created for whites. In practice, these so-called separate-but-equal facilities were separate and unequal.

✔ **Reading Check: Making Generalizations and Predictions** Why might the *Plessy* v. *Ferguson* decision make it hard to establish racial equality?

Section 3 Review

keyword: SC3 HP17

1. **Define** and explain:
   - carpetbaggers
   - scalawags
   - poll tax
   - segregation
2. **Identify** and explain:
   - Hiram Revels
   - Blanche K. Bruce
   - Ku Klux Klan
   - General Amnesty Act of 1872
   - Panic of 1873
   - Civil Rights Act of 1875
   - Compromise of 1877
   - Redeemers
   - Jim Crow laws
   - *Plessy* v. *Ferguson*
3. **Evaluating** Copy the graphic organizer below. Use it to identify the factors leading to the end of Reconstruction.

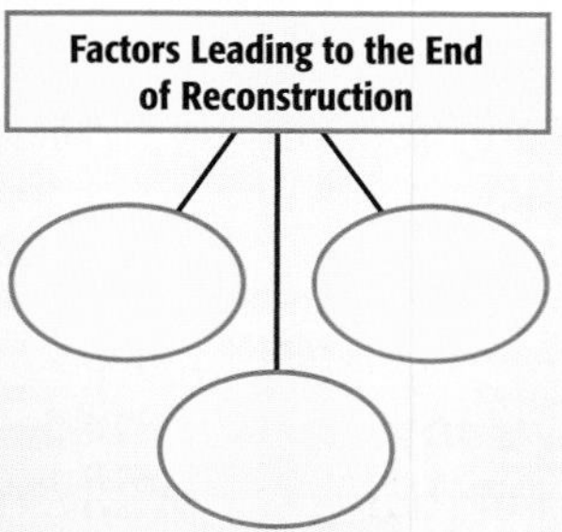

4. **Finding the Main Idea**
   a. What reforms took place under the Reconstruction state governments?
   b. Describe laws passed by the new southern state governments after Reconstruction ended.
5. **Writing and Critical Thinking**
   Supporting a Point of View Imagine that you are a Republican who opposes the *Plessy* v. *Ferguson* ruling. Write a letter to a friend in the North that expresses your views on the ruling.
   Consider the following:
   - the Fourteenth Amendment
   - the actions of Redeemer governments in the South
   - Jim Crow laws

Section 4

The New South

Read to Discover

1. How did southern agriculture change after the Civil War?
2. Why did some business leaders hope to create a "New South"?
3. What were some popular forms of southern culture during and after Reconstruction?

Define

- sharecropping

Identify

- Henry W. Grady
- Mary Noailles Murfree
- Joel Chandler Harris
- Charles W. Chesnutt

WHY IT MATTERS TODAY

Many large corporations today try to diversify, or produce a variety of goods and services, rather than relying on one product. Use CNNfyi.com or other **current events** sources to find a modern company that makes many different products. Record your findings in your journal.

The Story Continues

After farming for years, Charley White and his wife, Lucille, had saved enough money to buy their own farm in Texas. White later reflected on the purchase. "The house wasn't much more than a shack." But that it belonged to them made all the difference. "It just set us on fire. We didn't seem to get half as tired, or if we did we didn't notice it." Lucille White told her husband that "even the rocks look pretty." For many African American farmers, however, owning their own farms remained just a dream.

METROPOLITAN MUSEUM OF ART

Sharecroppers and other poor farmers often planted gardens to help provide food for their families.

Sharecropping

Few African Americans in the South could afford to buy or even rent farms. Moving west also was costly. Many African Americans, therefore, remained on plantations. Others tried to make a living in the cities.

African Americans who stayed on plantations often became part of a system known as **sharecropping**, or sharing the crop. Landowners provided the land, tools, and supplies, while sharecroppers provided the labor. At harvest time the sharecropper often had to give most of the

The Sharecropping Cycle

The sharecropping system trapped many black and white farmers in a cycle of poverty.

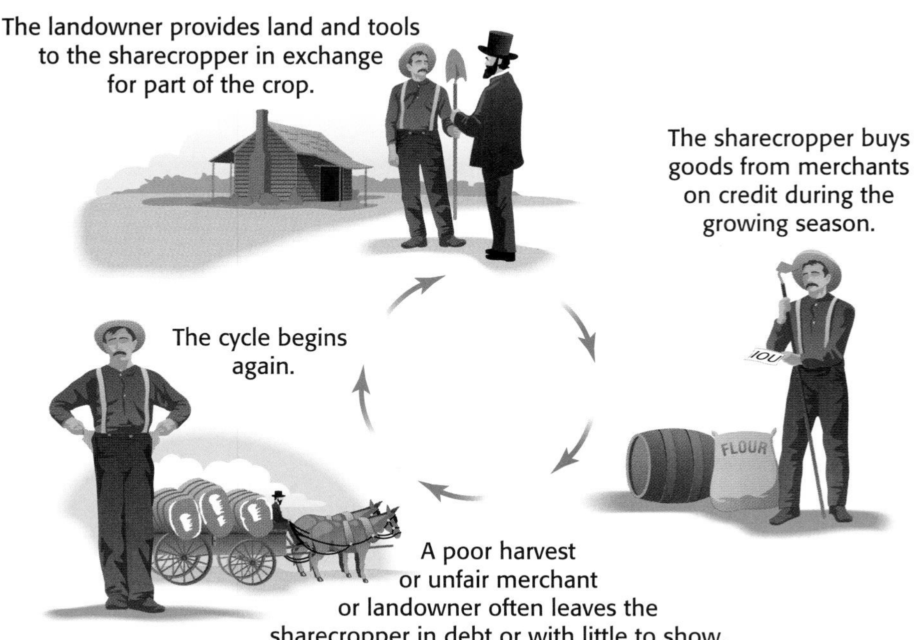

Visualizing History

1. **Economics** What economic disadvantages did sharecroppers face?
2. **Connecting to Today** What policies or programs might help poor farmers today?

crop to the owner. Whatever remained belonged to the sharecropper. Many sharecroppers hoped to save enough money from selling their share of the crops to one day be able to buy a farm. Unfortunately, only a few ever achieved this dream.

Most sharecroppers instead lived in a cycle of debt. When they needed food, clothing, or supplies, most families had to buy goods on credit because they had little cash. When sharecroppers sold their crops, they hoped to pay off these debts. However, bad weather, poor harvests, or low crop prices often made this impossible. Merchants sometimes cheated sharecroppers by charging them for items they did not buy. Some landowners also cheated sharecroppers by taking more than their fair share of the crops. Abolitionist Frederick Douglass complained about this poor treatment of sharecroppers.

Analyzing Primary Sources
Identifying Points of View According to Douglass, how did merchants keep sharecroppers in debt?

> **"The merchant puts him [the sharecropper] off with his poorest commodities [goods] at highest prices, and can say to him take these or nothing. . . . By this means the laborer is brought into debt, and hence is kept always in the power of the landowner."**
>
> —Frederick Douglass, quoted in *Enduring Voices*

As a result of such practices, most sharecroppers found themselves ever deeper in debt. They owed more at the end of the harvest than they had when they planted their crops.

Most sharecroppers grew cotton, one of the South's most important cash crops. When too many farmers planted cotton, however, the supply became too great. As a result, the price per bale dropped. One man wrote his father about a drop in the price of cotton. "It nearly ruined us. . . . But getting ready to plant cotton again."

Many farmers understood the drawbacks of planting cotton. However, they felt too much pressure from banks or landlords to change their ways. "Cotton raising has grown to be a necessity more than a choice," a farmer in Alabama said. A southern farmer explained why so many sharecroppers depended on cotton.

"Cotton is the thing to get credit on in this country. . . . You can always sell cotton. You leave home with a wagon load of cotton and you will go home that night with money in your pocket; you load up your wagon with wheat or corn . . . and I doubt some days whether you could sell it."

—Anonymous farmer, quoted in *The Promise of the New South*, by Edward L. Ayers

 **Reading Check: Finding the Main Idea** How did the sharecropping system limit the economic freedom of southern farmers?

Southern Industry

The southern economy suffered through cycles of good and bad years as cotton prices went up and down. Some business leaders hoped industry would strengthen the southern economy. They wanted to create a "New South." **Henry W. Grady**, an Atlanta newspaper editor, was a leader of the New South movement. Grady and his supporters wanted to take advantage of the South's resources. With its cotton production and cheap and abundant labor, the South could build textile mills and other factories.

The most successful industrial development in the South involved textile production. Businesspeople built textile mills in many small towns to produce cotton fabric. Hundreds of people from rural areas came to work in the mills. However, few cotton mills hired African Americans.

Work in the cotton mills appealed to farm families who had trouble making ends meet. As one mill worker explained, "It was a necessity to move and get a job, rather than depend on the farm." Recruiters sent out by the mills promised good wages and steady work. Entire families often worked in the same mill. Mills employed large numbers of women and children. Many children started working at about the age of 12. Women did most of the spinning and were valued workers. However, few women had the opportunity to advance within the company.

Mill work was often unpleasant. One unhappy worker described it as "the same thing over and over again. . . . The more you do, the more they want done." Workers often labored 12 hours a day, six days a week. Cotton dust and lint filled the air. This unhealthy air caused asthma and an illness known as brown-lung disease. Fast-moving machinery caused injuries and even some deaths. Despite the long hours and dangerous working conditions, wages were low. But mill work did offer an alternative to farming.

Reading Check: Comparing and Contrasting How was work in the cotton mills similar to and different from sharecropping?

CONNECTING TO MATH

Just the Facts

Cotton Production and Price

Year	Bales produced	Price per pound
1876	4,474,000	9.71¢
1877	4,773,000	8.53¢
1878	5,074,000	8.16¢
1879	5,756,000	10.28¢
1880	6,606,000	9.83¢
1881	5,456,000	10.66¢
1882	6,949,000	9.12¢
1883	5,713,000	9.13¢
1884	5,682,000	9.19¢
1885	6,576,000	8.39¢

Using Mathematical Skills

1. In how many of the years shown on the chart did the price of cotton go up?
2. Use these figures to create two line graphs, one showing cotton production from 1876 to 1885 and the other showing cotton prices during the same period.
3. What happened to cotton production each time the price rose to over 10 cents a pound? Why do you think this was the case?

A young African American girl working in the cotton fields

Southern Literature

The New South movement sought to modernize the South. Many southerners looked to the arts to keep their longstanding traditions alive, however. Southern literature gained national popularity in the late 1800s. Part of the reason for this was that many southern stories involved people and places in the South that seemed exciting and even exotic to northerners.

Mark Twain wrote many stories about the South, including *The Adventures of Tom Sawyer.* He was considered to be the most famous writer about the South at the end of Reconstruction. **Mary Noailles Murfree** wrote popular short stories and novels about the mountain people of eastern Tennessee. George Washington Cable wrote novels about the African American community in New Orleans. Cable used his writing to protest racial prejudice in the South. **Joel Chandler Harris** wrote short stories about fictional plantation life. His main character was a slave named Uncle Remus, who taught lessons by reciting folktales. Harris based his work on stories he was first told by enslaved African Americans.

Many white southern writers set their stories in a pre–Civil War South full of beautiful plantations and happy slaves. **Charles W. Chesnutt**, an African American, did not share this romantic image. Born in Ohio but raised in North Carolina, his plantation stories showed the greed and cruelty of slaveholders. Many of his short stories are collected in a book called *The Conjure Woman.*

✔ **Reading Check: Analyzing Information** What were the most common topics of southern literature in the late 1800s?

CONNECTING TO THE ARTS

The Fisk Jubilee Singers
During Reconstruction, students from Fisk University in Nashville, Tennessee, formed the Fisk Jubilee Singers. They traveled widely, touring the North in 1871 and 1872. They later performed in Europe. As they brought African American music, such as spirituals, to a wider audience, they made Fisk University famous. They also raised enough money to help the university build its first permanent building. Other African American colleges, such as Hampton Institute in Virginia, formed similar singing groups. As a result, the popularity of spirituals increased. **What is notable about the Fisk Jubilee Singers?**

JUBILEE SINGERS, COURTESY OF FISK UNIVERSITY

Southern Music

Southern music also grew in popularity after the Civil War. Some of the musical instruments popular in the South were the fiddle, the banjo, and the guitar. Fiddle players provided the music for square dancing, a favorite pastime.

One of the most important types of songs in the South was the spiritual. Spirituals were based on Christian hymns and African music sung in the days of slavery. The lead singer often called out a verse that the rest of the singers would repeat. Sometimes the lead singer might change the words slightly to reflect current events. The lyrics usually described the sorrows of slavery and the hope for freedom. One of the best-known spirituals was "Swing Low, Sweet Chariot." It expressed a longing for the promised land, where African Americans would be free from slavery.

Dancing parties were a common pastime in many parts of the South.

**"Swing low, sweet chariot,
Comin' for to carry me home,
Swing low, sweet chariot,
Comin' for to carry me home,
I look'd over Jordan, an' what did I see,
Comin' for to carry me home,
A band of angels comin' after me,
Comin' for to carry me home,
If you get-a there befo' I do,
Tell all my friends I'm comin' too."**

—From *Crossing the Danger Water,* edited by Deirdre Mullane

Analyzing Primary Sources

Drawing Inferences and Conclusions What does "home" represent in "Swing Low, Sweet Chariot"?

✔ **Reading Check: Making Generalizations and Predictions** How might the universal themes of spirituals have helped them become popular in the late 1800s?

Section 4 Review

go.hrw.com Homework Practice Online
keyword: SC3 HP17

1. **Define** and explain:
   - sharecropping

2. **Identify** and explain:
   - Henry W. Grady
   - Mary Noailles Murfree
   - Joel Chandler Harris
   - Charles W. Chesnutt

3. **Summarizing** Copy the graphic organizer below. Use it to show the main characteristics of the southern economy after the Civil War.

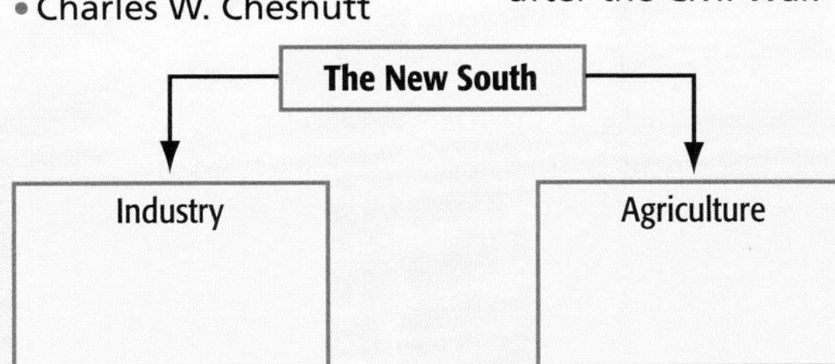

4. **Finding the Main Idea**
   a. How did the sharecropping system work, and what were its drawbacks for southern farmers?
   b. Why did some business leaders want to develop southern industry?

5. **Writing and Critical Thinking**
   Evaluating Imagine that you are a northern newspaper reporter in the South after the Civil War. Write a story that explains to northern readers how southern literature and music express the views of African Americans about life in the South.
   Consider the following:
   - the writings of African American southerners
   - the importance of spirituals
   - the lyrics to "Swing Low, Sweet Chariot"

Chapter 17 Review

The Chapter at a Glance

Examine the visual summary of the chapter below. Use it to write a five-question quiz for a classmate.

Reuniting the Nation

The Thirteenth, Fourteenth, and Fifteenth Amendments are ratified, ending slavery, granting equal protection to all citizens, and giving African Americans the vote. Other civil rights laws are also passed.

The Reconstruction Acts divide the South into military districts and install new governments. The changes lead to conflict between African Americans and white southerners and Republicans and Democrats.

The Compromise of 1877 ends Reconstruction. Legal segregation is upheld in the South by Jim Crow laws and by the Supreme Court ruling in *Plessy* v. *Ferguson*.

Identifying People and Ideas

Use the following terms or people in historically significant sentences.

1. Thirteenth Amendment
2. Freedmen's Bureau
3. Andrew Johnson
4. Black Codes
5. Fourteenth Amendment
6. Fifteenth Amendment
7. Hiram Revels
8. Compromise of 1877
9. *Plessy* v. *Ferguson*
10. sharecropping

Understanding Main Ideas

Section 1 *(Pages 514–519)*

1. How did the Reconstruction plans of Lincoln, the Radical Republicans, and Johnson differ?

Section 2 *(Pages 520–526)*

2. List the major parts of Congress's plan for Reconstruction.
3. Why did the Radical Republicans impeach President Johnson?

Section 3 *(Pages 527–532)*

4. How did Reconstruction state governments try to change and help rebuild the South?
5. What events helped bring about the end of Reconstruction?

Section 4 *(Pages 533–537)*

6. How did African American literature and music contrast with the romantic image of the South painted by many white southern writers?

You Be the Historian— Reviewing Themes

1. **Constitutional Heritage** How did the Thirteenth, Fourteenth, and Fifteenth Amendments protect the rights of African Americans?
2. **Government** How did Reconstruction affect governments in the South?
3. **Culture** What contributions did African Americans make to southern society, government, and culture after the Civil War?

Thinking Critically

1. **Analyzing Information** What economic problems did the South face during Reconstruction?
2. **Drawing Inferences and Conclusions** How do you think Abraham Lincoln would have viewed Reconstruction had he lived to see it?
3. **Evaluating** Do you think that Reconstruction was a success or a failure? Explain your answer, considering the perspectives of all groups involved.

Social Studies Skills Workshop

Interpreting Political Cartoons

Study the political cartoon of Reconstruction below. Then answer the questions that follow.

THE "STRONG" GOVERNMENT 1869–1877.

THE GRANGER COLLECTION, NEW YORK

1. Which of the following best describes the message that the artist is trying to present?
   a. Poor people in the South are forced to work on behalf of the rich.
   b. The South is being unfairly punished by the harsh military rule of the federal government.
   c. Military forces have taken control of President Grant and the federal government.
   d. The South is helping carry the burdens of the rest of the nation.
2. Based on your knowledge of the period and the imagery in this cartoon, do you think the artist would have been pleased by the Compromise of 1877? Explain your answer.
3. Based on your knowledge of the period, what do you think the carpetbag in the cartoon is supposed to represent?
   a. the military power of the federal government
   b. the corrupt politics of Grant's administration
   c. northern Republicans who have moved south to take part in Reconstruction
   d. the desire of southerners to move away from the Reconstruction South

Analyzing Primary Sources

Read the following excerpt from a southern African American newspaper in 1866, then answer the questions that follow.

> **"The future looks dark, and we predict, that we are entering upon the greatest political contest that has ever agitated the people of the country—a contest, in which, we of the South must be for the most part spectators [observers]; not indifferent [unconcerned] spectators, for it is about us that the political battle is fought. The issue is fairly joined [begun]."**

4. Which of the following statements best describes the viewpoint of the author?
   a. Reconstruction will unite the country peacefully and smoothly.
   b. Reconstruction will divide the nation, and the South can do little to control it.
   c. Few people in the South care one way or the other about Reconstruction.
   d. Southerners will play a major role in determining Reconstruction policies.
5. Based on your knowledge of the period, do you think these predictions were accurate? Explain your answer.

Alternative Assessment

Building Your Portfolio

American History

Interdisciplinary Connection to the Arts

Write a poem or song describing how an African American who was set free at the end of the Civil War might have felt. If you create a poem, find an image to illustrate it. If you write a song, select a musical style in which you want it to be performed.

internet connect

Internet Activity: go.hrw.com
keyword: SC3 CF17

Access the Internet through the HRW Go site to locate and use primary and secondary sources to acquire information on the differing points of view of Reconstruction. Then assume the point of view of someone living during the time and create a newspaper that reflects the historical context of Reconstruction and the frame of reference which influenced its participants.

Social Studies Skills

WORKSHOP

Distinguishing Fact from Opinion and Identifying Bias

Historical sources may contain both facts and opinions. Sources such as diaries, letters, and speeches usually express personal views. The ability to distinguish facts from opinions is very important. It allows you to judge the accuracy of an argument or a historical account.

When reading historical sources, try to identify a writer's bias—prejudices or strong feelings. Many famous historical people had strong opinions that appear in their writings and speeches. Remember that just because a person is famous does not mean that you must agree with his or her opinions.

How to Distinguish Fact from Opinion

1. **Identify the facts.** Ask yourself: Can the statement be proven? Determine whether the idea can be checked for accuracy in a source such as an almanac or encyclopedia. If so, the statement probably concerns a matter of fact. If not, it probably contains an opinion.
2. **Identify the opinions.** Look for clues that indicate a statement of opinion. These clues include phrases such as "I think" and "I believe," comparative words like *greatest* and *more important,* and value-filled words like *extremely* and *ridiculous.* All of these words imply a judgment and, thus, an opinion.

How to Identify Bias

1. **Evaluate the information presented.** What are the sources of information? How reliable are they? Why might a historical figure have supported one view over another? Be sure to distinguish between provable facts and someone's opinions.
2. **Make your own judgment.** Remember that many of the historical documents you read are created by people who have their own opinions and points of view. It is up to you to read each document critically and to draw your own conclusions.

Practicing the Skills

Read the excerpt below, in which a southern newspaper editor defends Representative Preston Brooks's beating of Senator Charles Sumner. Then answer the questions that follow.

> **"We consider the act good in conception [thought], better in execution. . . . These vulgar abolitionists . . . must be lashed into submission. Sumner, in particular, ought to have nine-and-thirty [lashes] early every morning."**

1. Is this excerpt an example of a fact or an opinion? Which words let you know?
2. What bias, if any, does the author express? If you found bias, how did you identify it?

History in Action

UNIT 6 SIMULATION

You Make the Decision . . .

Should Your Border State Support the Union or the Confederacy?

Complete the following activity in small cooperative groups. It is April 12, 1861. The Confederates have opened fire on Fort Sumter. You live in one of the four border states in which slavery is legal—Delaware, Kentucky, Maryland, or Missouri. The people in your state have strong feelings for both sides in the conflict. Your state legislature has asked a special committee to make a recommendation about which side your state should support—the Union or the Confederacy. Follow these steps to reach your decision.

1. Gather Information. Use your textbook and other resources to find information that might help you decide whether to support the North or the South in this conflict. Be sure to use what you learned from this unit's Skills Workshop on Distinguishing Fact from Opinion and Identifying Bias to help you make an informed decision. You may want to divide different parts of the research among group members.

2. Identify Options. After reviewing the information you have gathered, identify the options you might consider for which side to support in the Civil War. Your final solution to the problem may be easier to reach if you consider as many options as possible. Be sure to record your possible options for your presentation.

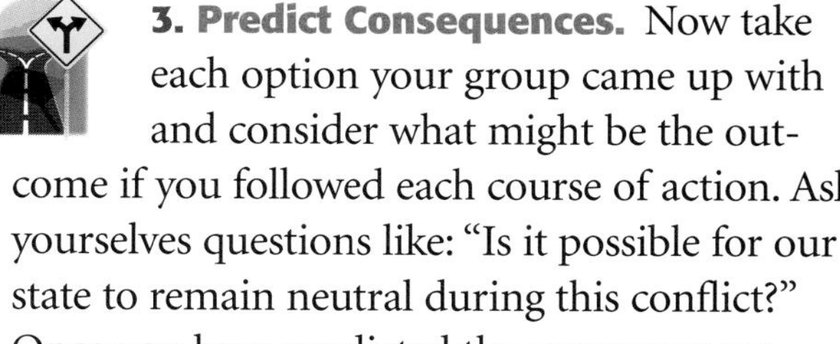

3. Predict Consequences. Now take each option your group came up with and consider what might be the outcome if you followed each course of action. Ask yourselves questions like: "Is it possible for our state to remain neutral during this conflict?" Once you have predicted the consequences, record them as notes for your presentation.

4. Take Action to Implement Your Decision. After you have considered your options, you should plan and create your presentation. Be sure to make your decision on whether to support the North or the South very clear. You will need to support your committee's recommendation by including information you gathered and by explaining why you rejected other options. Your presentation needs to be visually appealing to gain the support of the state legislature. When you are ready, decide which group members will make each part of the presentation, and then take your decision to the state legislature (the rest of the class). Good luck!

UNIT 7

A Growing America

(1850–1920)

CHAPTER 18 **The West** (1850–1890)

CHAPTER 19 **An Industrial and Urban Nation** (1876–1900)

CHAPTER 20 **The Spirit of Reform** (1868–1920)

Young People

IN HISTORY

Young Cowhands

Cowhands herded Texas longhorn cattle northward across the Great Plains to be sold in Kansas railroad towns. A cattle drive of this distance required working long hours in all kinds of weather. Sometimes cowhands would run into problems with cattle thieves known as rustlers. The greatest danger, however, was a stampede.

Many cowhands began working cattle when they were children. A rancher paid young Cliff Newland 50 cents a day to haul supplies to cattle drivers 75 miles away. From this job, Newland turned to wrangling—the work of herding and caring for livestock. To help him learn to stay in the saddle while training horses, Newland's father tied him onto the seat. By age 13, Newland had already been on three cattle drives and had a job training young horses.

Not all the young cowhands were boys. At age 13, Agnes Morley and her younger brother traveled across 130 miles of harsh New Mexico landscape to sell some cattle.

Many cowhands left home to work the cattle drives while they were still children. E. C. Abbott, also known as "Teddy Blue," went on his first cattle drive when he was 11 years old. He recalled his trip up the Western Trail in 1879.

Many young cowhands like this female broncobuster gained recognition for their unique skills.

"That trip up the trail in '79 was my second, but in a way it was the first that counted, because I was only a button [youngster] the other time. I wasn't nineteen years old when I come up the trail with the Olive herd, but don't let that fool you. I was a man in my own estimation and a man in fact."

Teddy Blue recalled a story he had once heard about a schoolteacher. She wanted a Texas cowhand to tell her about life on the trail. She asked, "Oh, Mister So-and-So, didn't the boys used to have a lot of fun riding their ponies?" He replied, "Madam, there wasn't any boys or ponies. They was all horses and men."

If You Were There ***Would the life of a cowhand be appealing to you?***

LEFT PAGE: *In many western families, like this one, all family members had to work hard.*

CHAPTER

18 The West

(1850–1890)

Fort Laramie was a fur-trading post built in 1834.

This stamp shows a rider with the Pony Express.

UNITED STATES

1851 The Treaty of Fort Laramie is signed.

1860 The Pony Express begins delivering mail between the East and West.

1862 Congress passes the Homestead Act.

1869 The first transcontinental railroad is completed.

1874 Gold is discovered in the Black Hills of the Dakota Territory.

1850 | 1855 | 1860 | 1865 | 1870

WORLD

1855 Paris holds a world's fair.

1864 French scientist Louis Pasteur invents the process of pasteurization.

Cans like this one were used to store meat.

People flocked to the 1855 World's Fair in Paris, shown below.

Build on What You Know

After the Civil War, the U.S. population grew rapidly. Settlements spread throughout the West. A flood of miners, ranchers, and farmers transformed the western landscape and adapted to their new environment. Often, however, these new settlers came into conflict with American Indians already living in the region.

This painting shows cowboys herding cattle.

Golden spike that joined the Central Pacific and Union Pacific Railroads

1875

1876 The Sioux defeat the U.S. Army in the Battle of the Little Bighorn.

1879 Thousands of African Americans migrate from the South to Kansas.

1880

1880 Australian merchants send meat to Great Britain for the first time by using refrigerated ships.

1883 The Orient Express makes its first run from Paris to Istanbul.

1885

1886 Ranchers lose most of their cattle during a severe winter.

1888 Brazil abolishes slavery.

1889 President Benjamin Harrison opens the Oklahoma District to settlers.

1890

1890 The Massacre at Wounded Knee occurs.

The Orient Express traveled across southeastern Europe.

If you were there . . .

What kind of work would you do in the West, and why?

You Be the Historian

What's Your Opinion? Do you **agree** or **disagree** with the following statements? Support your point of view in your journal.

- **Economics** The federal government should promote economic development in underdeveloped regions.
- **Culture** Cultural conflict will result when two different groups come into contact.
- **Geography** People will endure harsh environmental conditions in order to have new opportunities.

Section 1

The Wars for the West

Read to Discover

1. What animals did the Plains Indians use, and why were they important?
2. What caused conflicts between American Indians and American settlers in the West, and what were the results of these conflicts?
3. How did the reservation system and the Dawes Act affect American Indians?

Define

- reservations

Identify

- Treaty of Fort Laramie
- Crazy Horse
- Treaty of Medicine Lodge
- George Armstrong Custer
- Sitting Bull
- Battle of the Little Bighorn
- Ghost Dance
- Massacre at Wounded Knee
- Geronimo
- Sarah Winnemucca
- Dawes General Allotment Act

WHY IT MATTERS TODAY

Many American Indians continue to live on reservations. Use CNNfyi.com or other **current events** sources to find out about American Indians living on reservations today. Record your findings in your journal.

THE GRANGER COLLECTION, NEW YORK

The Cheyenne used shields like this one in battle.

The Story Continues

Like many Sioux before him, Standing Bear was eager for his first buffalo hunt. "Watch the buffalo closely. . . . They are very quick and powerful," warned his father. When he got close to the buffalo herd, Standing Bear recalled, "I realized how small I was." He brought down a buffalo and rode proudly back to camp to give his mother the animal's skin. Buffalo hunts were important to American Indians' ways of life on the Great Plains.

The Plains Indians

The Great Plains lie roughly between the 98th meridian and the Rocky Mountains. They stretch north into Canada and south into Texas. Despite their sometimes harsh conditions, the region was home to the Plains Indians. Groups such as the Apache and the Comanche lived in Texas and what is now Oklahoma. The Cheyenne and the Arapaho lived in different parts of the central Plains. The Pawnee lived in Nebraska. To the north were the Sioux, who spread from Minnesota to Montana.

For survival, Plains Indians depended on two animals—the horse and the buffalo. The Spanish brought horses to America in the 1500s. Plains Indians learned to ride horses and used them to follow the buffalo herds. They used the buffalo for food, shelter, and tools. The Plains Indians prospered and by 1850 some 75,000 American Indians were living on the Plains.

Miners and settlers began crossing the Great Plains in the mid-1800s. To protect these travelers, U.S. officials sent agents to negotiate treaties with the Plains Indians. The first major agreement was the **Treaty of Fort Laramie**, signed with northern Plains nations in Wyoming in 1851. Two years later, several southern Plains nations signed a treaty at Fort Atkinson in Nebraska. These treaties accepted Indian claims to much of the Great Plains. They also allowed Americans to build forts and roads and to travel across Indian homelands. The U.S. government promised to pay for any damages to Indian lands.

Sioux moccasins

✔ **Reading Check: Analyzing Information** What compromise did the United States and American Indians reach to allow miners and settlers to cross Indian lands?

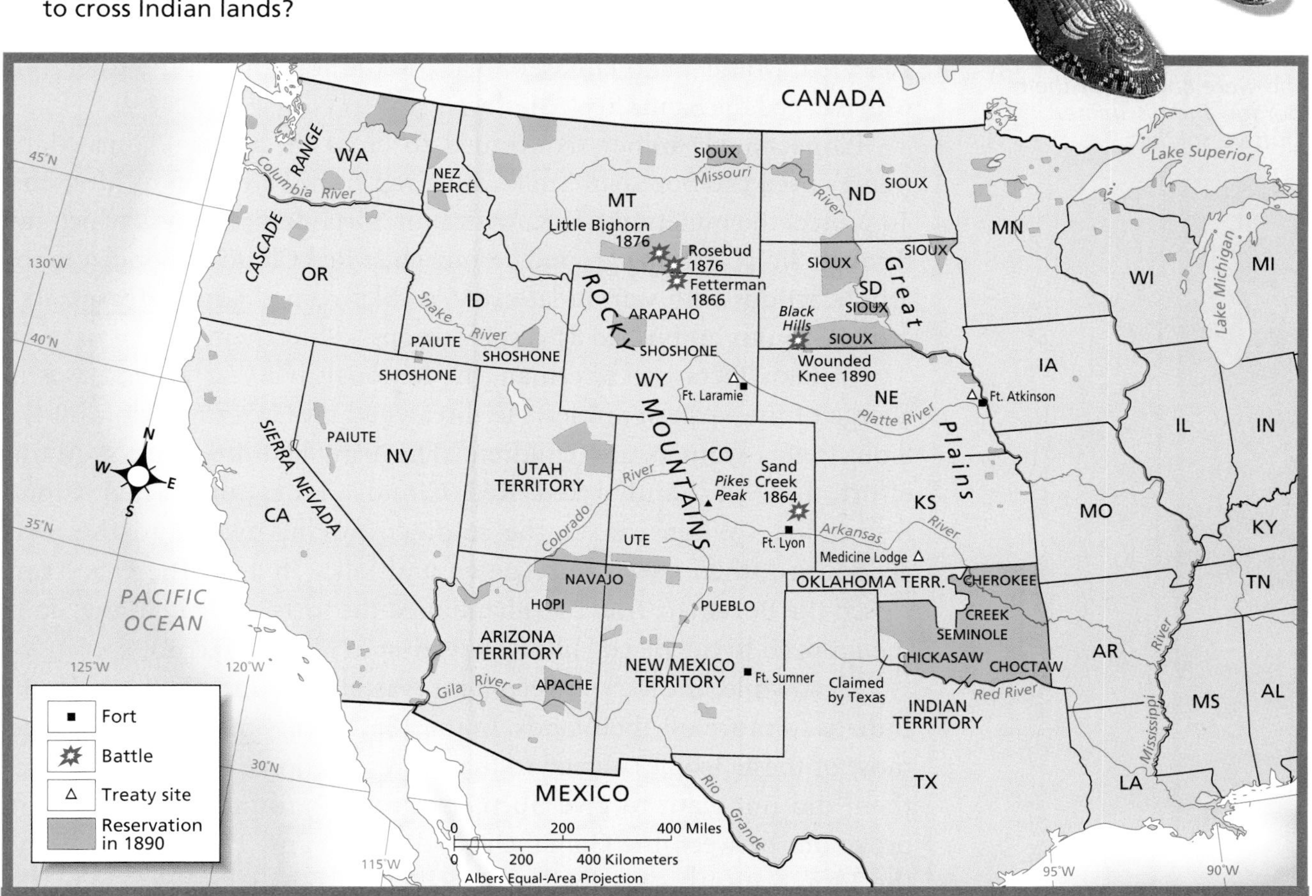

Indian Reservations and Battles to 1890

Interpreting Maps As more and more settlers moved to the West, American Indians were forced to accept treaties that placed them on reservations.

Skills Assessment **Human Systems** Which present-day state contained the most reservation lands?

THE GRANGER COLLECTION, NEW YORK

Several African American cavalry regiments served in the western U.S. Army. American Indians nicknamed these African American troops, who were known for their courage and discipline, "buffalo soldiers."

War on the Plains

The treaties did not keep the peace for long. Gold was discovered in what is now Colorado in 1858. The news brought thousands of miners to the West, where they soon clashed with the Cheyenne and the Arapaho. In 1861 the U.S. government negotiated a new treaty with these Indians. The treaty created **reservations**, areas of federal land set aside for American Indians. The government expected Indians to stay on the reservations, which made hunting buffalo almost impossible.

Many American Indians refused to live on reservations. Some continued to fight, while others shared the view of Cheyenne chief Black Kettle. "It is not my intention or wish to fight the whites," he declared. He did not get his wish. In November 1864, U.S. Army troops attacked Black Kettle's camp on Sand Creek in southeastern Colorado. The soldiers killed about 200 men, women, and children. Black Kettle was among the Cheyenne who escaped the Sand Creek Massacre.

Pioneers and miners continued to cross the Great Plains. Many miners used the Bozeman Trail, which ran from Wyoming to Montana. To protect the miners, the U.S. Army built forts along the trail, which ran through Sioux hunting grounds. Sioux chief Red Cloud responded to the army's actions with war. In late 1866 a chief named **Crazy Horse** and a group of Sioux ambushed 81 cavalry troops, killing them all.

William Tecumseh Sherman, the famous Civil War general, was in charge of the western armies. He threatened the "extermination [of the Sioux] men, women, and children." The army had little success in this effort, however, and asked Red Cloud to negotiate. Red Cloud responded, "When we see the soldiers moving away and the forts abandoned, then I will come down and talk." In 1868 the U.S. Army closed the Bozeman Trail and abandoned the forts along it. Many Sioux then moved to the Black Hills Reservation in Dakota Territory.

Meanwhile, the U.S. government was also asking southern Plains Indians to move off their lands. In the 1867 **Treaty of Medicine Lodge**, most of these peoples agreed to live on reservations. However, many of them did not want to give up their hunting grounds. Fighting soon broke out between the Comanche and the Texans. The U.S. Army and the Texas Rangers were unable to defeat the Comanche forces in battle. So U.S. forces cut off the Comanche's access to food. The Comanche could not survive under these conditions. In 1875 Quanah Parker, the last of the Comanche war leaders, surrendered.

✔ **Reading Check: Summarizing** What was the federal policy toward Plains Indians in the 1860s and 1870s?

 The U.S. War with the Sioux

As fighting on the southern Plains ended, new trouble was starting to the north. In 1874 Lieutenant Colonel **George Armstrong Custer**'s soldiers found gold in the Black Hills of the Dakota Territory. The U.S. government responded by insisting that the Sioux sell their reservation land in the Black Hills. **Sitting Bull**, a Sioux leader, protested these new demands.

> **"What treaty that the whites have kept has the red man broken? Not one. What treaty that the white man ever made with us have they kept? Not one."**
>
> —Sitting Bull, quoted in *Touch the Earth,* by T. C. McLuhan

Analyzing Primary Sources

Identifying Points of View Why did Sitting Bull not trust the U.S. government?

Other Sioux leaders listened to Sitting Bull and refused to give up the Black Hills. Fighting soon broke out between the U.S. Army and the Sioux.

Custer, a Civil War veteran, was in command of the U.S. Army 7th Cavalry. On June 25, 1876, his scouts found a Sioux camp along the Little Bighorn River in Montana. Leading 264 of his soldiers, Custer raced ahead without waiting for any backup forces. The Battle of the Little Bighorn followed. Sioux forces, led by Crazy Horse and Sitting Bull, surrounded Custer and his troops. Sitting Bull's cousin Pte-San-Waste-Win described the fighting. "The soldiers fired many shots, but the Sioux shot straight and the soldiers fell dead. When we came to the hill . . . Long Hair [Custer] lay dead among the rest." Newspapers called the battle "Custer's Last Stand."

The **Battle of the Little Bighorn** was the worst defeat the U.S. Army had suffered in the West. It was also the Sioux's last major victory. In late 1877 Crazy Horse was killed in prison after surrendering to the U.S. Army.

Interpreting the Visual Record

The Battle of the Little Bighorn *The 7th Cavalry suffered a devastating defeat at the hands of Sioux forces at the Battle of the Little Bighorn.* ***What advantages does the illustration show each side having?***

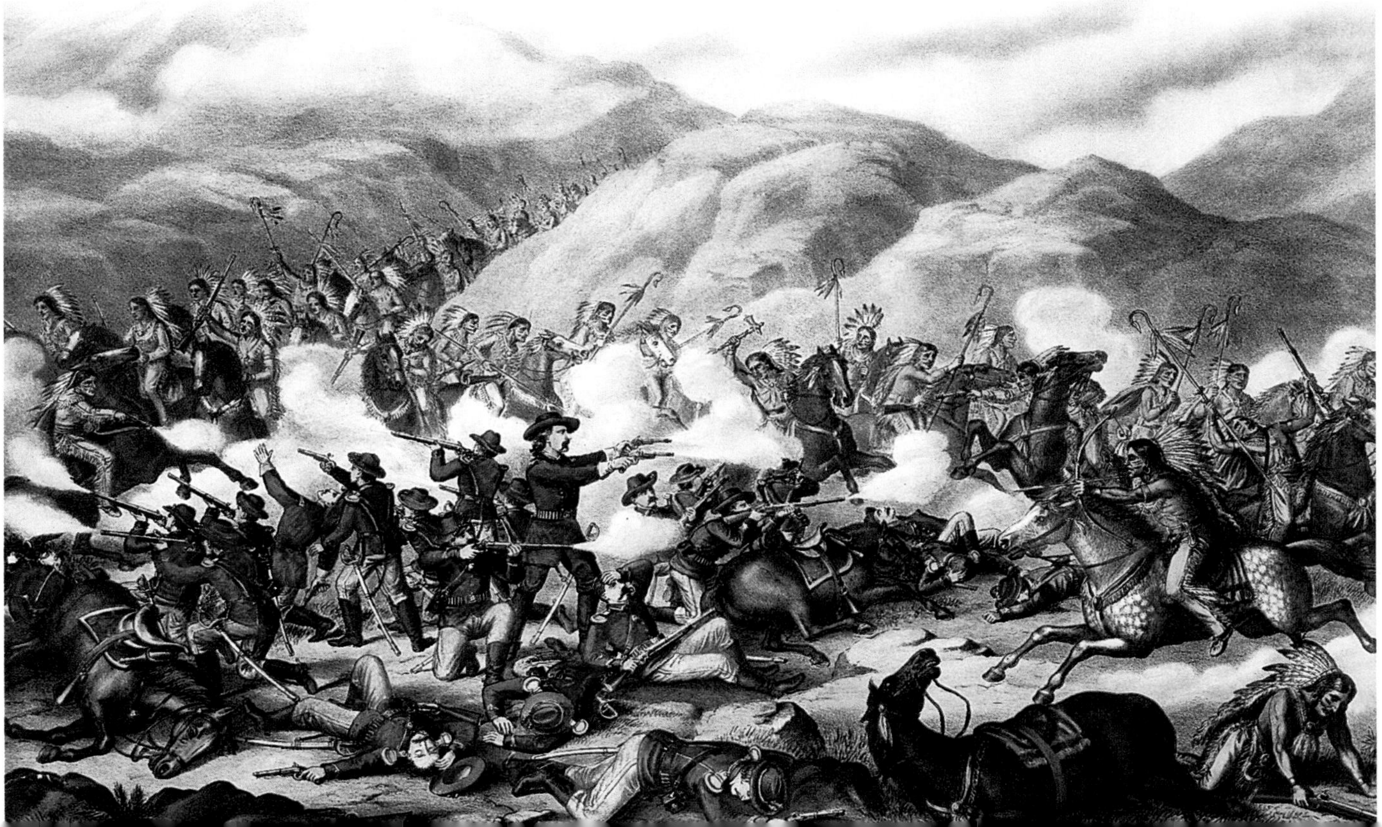

"I Will Fight No More Forever"

Chief Joseph

Chief Joseph led the Nez Percé from 1871 to 1877. He gave the following speech to the U.S. Army officers who took him prisoner on October 5, 1877. Chief Joseph died in 1904.

Tell General Howard I know his heart. What he told me before, I have in my heart. I am tired of fighting. Our chiefs are killed. . . . The old men are all dead. It is the young men who say yes and no. **He who led on the young men**[1] is dead. It is cold and we have no blankets. The little children are freezing to death. My people, some of them, have run away to the hills, and have no blankets, no food; no one knows where they are—perhaps freezing to death. I want to have time to look for my children and see how many I can find. Maybe I shall find them among the dead. Hear me, my chiefs. I am tired; my heart is sick and sad. From where the sun now stands I will fight no more forever.

[1]**He who led on the young men:** Joseph's brother, Alokut

Understanding What You Read

Literature and History Why has Chief Joseph chosen to "fight no more forever"?

Sitting Bull fled to Canada with a few of his followers. With two of their most important leaders gone, the northern Plains Indians soon surrendered.

In 1881 Sitting Bull and his Sioux followers returned from Canada. They had run out of food during the hard winter. "I wish it to be remembered," Sitting Bull said, "that I was the last man of my tribe to surrender my rifle." He joined most of the Sioux on Standing Rock Reservation in Dakota Territory.

Wovoka, a Paiute Indian, began a religious movement known as the **Ghost Dance**. He predicted the arrival of a paradise for American Indians. Indians who performed the dance believed that it would lead to a new life free from suffering. In this paradise, the buffalo herds would return, and the settlers would disappear. When the Ghost Dance spread across the Plains, U.S. officials feared it would lead to a Sioux uprising. While following orders to arrest Sitting Bull, reservation police killed the Sioux leader in 1890. In response, many Sioux left the reservations. Later that year, the U.S. Army found a camp of Sioux near Wounded Knee Creek in South Dakota. When the two groups faced one another, a shot rang out. The U.S. troops began firing and killed about 150 Indians. Known as the **Massacre at Wounded Knee**, this attack was the last major event of more than 25 years of war on the Great Plains.

Ghost Dance shirt

✔ **Reading Check: Sequencing** List the conflicts between the Great Plains Indians and U.S. forces in the order that they occurred.

Indians in the Southwest and Far West

Far from the Great Plains, other American Indians resisted being moved to reservations. The Navajo lived in what became Arizona and New Mexico. In 1863 when the U.S. government ordered them to settle on a reservation, the Navajo refused. In response, Kit Carson, a former scout, led U.S. troops in raids on the Navajo's fields, homes, and livestock.

When the Navajo ran out of food and shelter, they started surrendering to the U.S. Army. In 1864 the army led Navajo captives on the Long Walk. This 300-mile march took the Navajo across the desert to a reservation at Bosque Redondo, New Mexico. Along the way, hundreds of Navajo died. At Bosque Redondo the Navajo suffered harsh conditions. In 1868 they negotiated for a new reservation located in Arizona and New Mexico.

The U.S. government had promised to let the peaceful Nez Percé keep their homelands in northeastern Oregon. Within a few years, however, settlers asked the government to remove them. The government ordered the Nez Percé to a reservation in what is now Idaho. Nez Percé leader Chief Joseph reluctantly agreed to move. Before leaving, a few angry Nez Percé killed some local settlers. Fearing that U.S. forces would fight back, the Nez Percé fled. The U.S. Army chased this band of about 700 Indians across what are now Idaho, Wyoming, and Montana. Although outnumbered, the band defeated or avoided the army for weeks before trying to escape to Canada. Less than 40 miles from the border, U.S. troops overtook and surrounded the Nez Percé. Chief Joseph surrendered on October 5, 1877. The U.S. government sent the Nez Percé to a reservation in what is now Oklahoma.

By the 1880s most American Indians had stopped fighting. The Apache of the Southwest, however, continued to battle the U.S. Army. The Apache were raiders, known for their ability to survive in the desert. In the 1870s the U.S. Army gathered some Apache on a reservation in San Carlos, Arizona. One Apache called the reservation "nothing but cactus, rattlesnakes, heat, rocks, and insects."

A Chiricahua Apache named **Geronimo** and his small band of raiders left the reservation and avoided capture until 1884. The following year Geronimo escaped again. When the U.S. Army caught him, he broke free once more on the way to the reservation. "I feared treachery [dishonesty]," he said. This time the army sent 5,000 soldiers and 500 Apache scouts to capture Geronimo and 24 of his followers. Finally, in September 1886, he surrendered, ending the Apache armed resistance. The U.S. government sent Geronimo and many Chiricahua Apache to Florida as prisoners of war.

✔ **Reading Check: Identifying Cause and Effect** What led to some of the conflicts that took place between American settlers and American Indians in the 1800s, and what were the results of these conflicts?

Policy and Protest

By the 1870s many American Indian peoples were living on reservations. Indian leaders spoke out against the reservation system. They complained that government agents stole food and money meant for Indians. In addition, reservation land was usually not useful for farming or buffalo hunting. As a result, many Indians were starving.

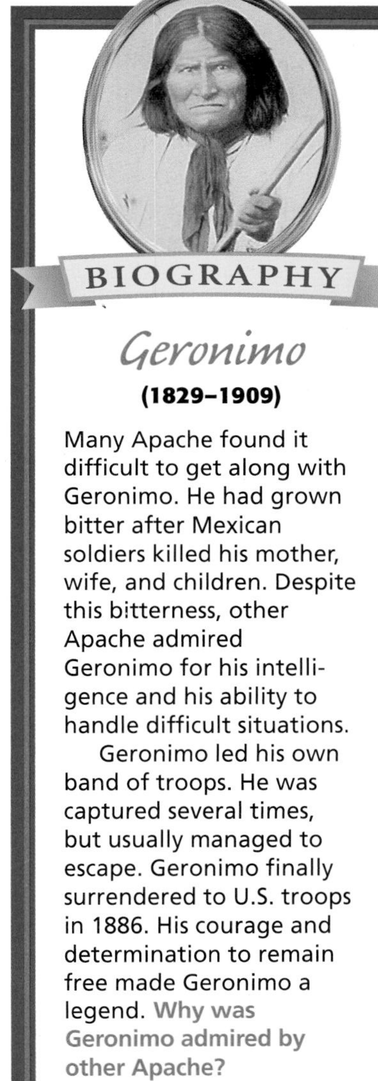

BIOGRAPHY

Geronimo

(1829–1909)

Many Apache found it difficult to get along with Geronimo. He had grown bitter after Mexican soldiers killed his mother, wife, and children. Despite this bitterness, other Apache admired Geronimo for his intelligence and his ability to handle difficult situations.

Geronimo led his own band of troops. He was captured several times, but usually managed to escape. Geronimo finally surrendered to U.S. troops in 1886. His courage and determination to remain free made Geronimo a legend. **Why was Geronimo admired by other Apache?**

Sarah Winnemucca went to Washington, D.C., to ask for reforms for American Indians.

In the late 1870s a Paiute Indian named **Sarah Winnemucca** became one of the first American Indians to call for reforms. She gave lectures on the problems of the reservation system and eventually pleaded her case in Washington, D.C. After listening to her, "many people were moved to tears," according to one spectator. Writer Helen Hunt Jackson also pushed for reform. In 1881 she published *A Century of Dishonor*. This book criticized the federal government's treatment of Indians. Jackson wrote that "it makes little difference where one opens the record of the history of the Indians; every page and every year has its dark stain." The popularity of her writings helped spread the reform message.

Many reformers believed that American Indians would be better off if they adopted the ways of white people. The **Dawes General Allotment Act**, passed by Congress in 1887, reflected this view. It tried to lessen the traditional influences on Indian society by making land ownership private rather than shared. Reservation lands were to be divided into 160-acre plots for families and 80 acres for single adults. The act also promised U.S. citizenship to American Indians.

After breaking up reservation land, the government sold the acreage that remained. As a result, Indians lost much of the land that they occupied before the Dawes Act. Reformers had hoped the Dawes Act would help American Indians. Instead, it resulted in the loss of about two thirds of their land. As enforced, the Dawes Act also did not lead to citizenship for many American Indians. Overall, the new policy failed to improve Indians' lives.

✔ **Reading Check: Drawing Inferences and Conclusions** How did reformers who fought for American Indian rights influence Indians' lives?

Section 1 Review

go.hrw.com **Homework Practice Online**
keyword: SC3 HP18

1. **Define** and explain:
   - reservations

2. **Identify** and explain:
   - Treaty of Fort Laramie
   - Crazy Horse
   - Treaty of Medicine Lodge
   - George Armstrong Custer
   - Sitting Bull
   - Battle of the Little Bighorn
   - Ghost Dance
   - Massacre at Wounded Knee
   - Geronimo
   - Sarah Winnemucca
   - Dawes General Allotment Act

3. **Identifying Cause and Effect** Copy the graphic organizer below. Use it to list the causes and effects of conflicts between the United States and American Indians in the West.

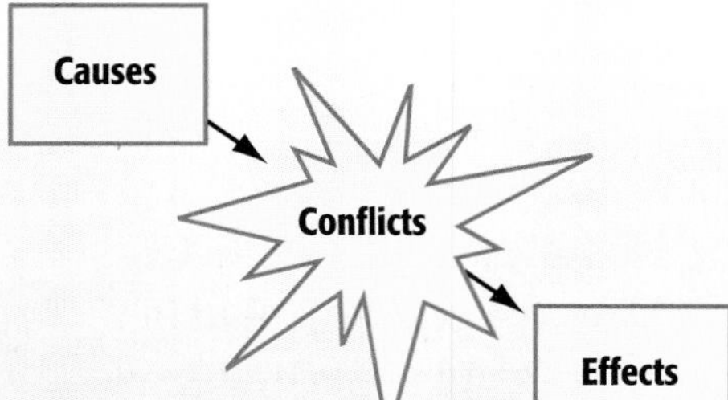

4. **Finding the Main Idea**
   a. Why were the horse and the buffalo important to the lives of Plains Indians?
   b. Why do you think the Ghost Dance was important to American Indians on the Great Plains?

5. **Writing and Critical Thinking**
   Comparing and Contrasting Imagine that you are an American Indian who has been affected by the Dawes Act. Write a letter to a member of Congress describing how your life has changed.
   Consider the following:
   - life on reservations
   - the positive and negative aspects of land ownership
   - the value of citizenship

Section 2

Miners and Railroads

Read to Discover

1. What were some of the challenges of mining in the West?
2. What obstacles did the builders of the transcontinental railroad face?
3. How did the transcontinental railroad affect the settlement and development of the West?

Define

- bonanza
- boomtowns
- transcontinental railroad

Identify

- Comstock Lode
- Pony Express
- Pacific Railway Acts
- Leland Stanford

WHY IT MATTERS TODAY

Railroads are still an important means of transportation in the United States. Use CNNfyi.com or other **current events** sources to learn about the role of railroads in the U.S. transportation system today. Record your findings in your journal.

The Story Continues

In 1858 gold was discovered in Colorado. After traveling west to see the new mine, *New York Tribune* editor Horace Greeley announced that the "discovery is . . . the richest and greatest [gold mine] in America." Thousands of prospectors raced west to the mining region around Pikes Peak. Many labeled their wagons "Pikes Peak or Bust." Most of them soon learned that Greeley had been fooled about the richness of the strike. The early prospectors had started the rush by filling part of the mine with extra gold.

The dream of finding pieces of gold ore like this one drew miners to the West.

The Mining Booms

The following year miners found gold and silver in western Nevada. The strike became known as the **Comstock Lode**, named after miner Henry Comstock. This time the wealth was real. The Comstock Lode was a **bonanza**— a large deposit of precious ore. Over the next 20 years, the Comstock Lode produced over $500 million worth of gold and silver. It took expensive equipment to remove the silver and gold trapped within the quartz rock. Large companies bought up claims from miners who

THE GRANGER COLLECTION, NEW YORK

Interpreting the Visual Record

Prospectors *This image shows prospectors at the entrance of a mineshaft.* ***What challenges do you think these miners faced?***

could not afford such equipment. As a result, mining became a big business in the West, dominated by corporations.

As companies dug bigger and deeper mines, the work became more dangerous. Miners had to use unsafe equipment such as wall-less elevator platforms. Many of the poorly lit tunnels had so little oxygen that candles would not burn. Dust from drilling also caused serious lung problems. Unexpected explosions killed or injured many miners. When there were cave-ins or floods from underground springs, miners were sometimes killed or trapped below ground. The threat of fire in the mines was also a great concern. In deeper tunnels, temperatures sometimes rose above 130° F. With all these hazards, mining was probably the most dangerous job in the country. In the West, worries about safety and pay led miners to form several labor unions in the 1860s.

Some miners came from the eastern United States. Others emigrated from Europe, Central and South America, Australia, and Asia. Some Mexican immigrants and Mexican Americans were skilled in assaying, or testing, the contents of valuable ore. Despite their skill, they were often denied the better-paying mining jobs. Chinese immigrants faced similar job discrimination.

✔ **Reading Check: Summarizing** How did mining affect the western economy, and what were its risks?

Mining Towns

Mining booms also produced **boomtowns.** These towns were communities that sprang up when a mine opened. They often disappeared just as quickly when the mine closed down. Most boomtowns had general stores, saloons, and boardinghouses. However, they were also dangerous places that lacked basic law and order. In his autobiographical work *Roughing It,* Mark Twain described Virginia City during its boom years.

Analyzing Primary Sources

Supporting a Point of View Judging from Twain's description, would you have chosen to live in a boomtown? Why or why not?

"[It] had grown to be the 'livest' town . . . that America had ever produced. The sidewalks swarmed with people. . . . The streets themselves were just as crowded. . . . Money-getting schemes . . . were . . . in every brain."

—Mark Twain, *Roughing It*

There were few women or families in most boomtowns. In 1860, for example, there were more than 75 men to each woman in Virginia City. Most women who lived in mining towns faced lives of hard work and few friends. "I was never so lonely and homesick in all my life," wrote one young woman. Women contributed to the local economy by washing, cooking, making clothes, and chopping wood. They also raised families, taught in schools, and wrote for local newspapers. Their work helped turn some mining camps into successful permanent towns.

✔ Reading Check: **Finding the Main Idea** Why were boomtowns created, and what was life like there?

The Railroads of India

As the United States was completing the world's first transcontinental railroad, Great Britain was building a huge railroad system in India to transport goods to and from remote regions. Between 1859 and 1869, Indian workers laid more than 5,000 miles of track. Workers had to build 81 bridges and 38 tunnels just to get through one mountain range. By 1900 the Indian rail network was the second largest in Asia after Russia's. The railroad carried mail, freight, and passengers. **What benefits did the railroad system in India have in common with the transcontinental railroad in the United States?**

Linking East and West

As more Americans began moving west, the need to send goods and information between the East and West increased. In 1860 the **Pony Express** was formed to meet this need. This company used a system of messengers on horseback to carry mail between relay stations on a route about 2,000 miles long. Telegraph lines, which sent messages faster, soon put the Pony Express out of business, however.

Americans thought of other ways to improve communication and travel across the United States. Some Americans wanted to build a **transcontinental railroad** to connect the East to the West. As a result, the federal government passed the **Pacific Railway Acts** of 1862 and 1864. These acts gave railroad companies loans and large land grants, which could be sold to pay for construction costs. Congress had granted tens of millions of acres of public land to railroad companies. In exchange, the government asked the railroads to carry U.S. mail and troops at lower rates. The railway acts inspired many companies to begin laying tracks.

✔ Reading Check: **Analyzing Information** What innovations helped link the East and the West?

Railroad building in the West involved overcoming many physical obstacles and dangers. Here Chinese workers celebrate the completion of a tunnel in the Sierra Nevada.

Interpreting the Visual Record

Celebration *The Central Pacific and Union Pacific connected their tracks at Promontory in Utah Territory.* ***Why would the completion of the transcontinental railroad have been a cause for celebration?***

The Great Race

Two companies, the Central Pacific and the Union Pacific, led the race to complete the transcontinental railroad. In February 1863 the Central Pacific began building east from Sacramento, California. At the end of the year, the Union Pacific started building west from Omaha, Nebraska.

The Union Pacific hired thousands of railroad workers, including Irish immigrants and Civil War veterans. The Central Pacific hired many Chinese immigrants. The railroad's part-owner **Leland Stanford** praised these Chinese workers, but he paid them less than white laborers. Chinese crews were also given the most dangerous tasks and longer hours. However, Chinese workers could earn much more money working for the Central Pacific than in China.

This advertisement for the Union Pacific Railroad praised the speed and comfort of railroad travel to the West.

Railroad companies faced many geographic challenges. The Central Pacific workers struggled to cross the Sierra Nevada range in California. Large amounts of explosives were used to blast a way through the mountains. In the winter of 1866, snowdrifts more than 60 feet high trapped and killed many workers. Meanwhile, the Union Pacific's workers faced harsh weather on the Great Plains.

For both lines, providing food and supplies for their workers was vital. To feed their workers, the railroad companies often relied on local resources. Professional hunters such as William "Buffalo Bill" Cody shot thousands of buffalo to feed workers for the Union Pacific.

Congress required the two railroads to connect at Promontory, Utah. On May 10, 1869, workers and reporters watched the two lines finally meet. In a dramatic ceremony, a golden spike was used to connect the railroad tie joining the two tracks. The transcontinental railroad had united the East and the West.

✔ **Reading Check: Summarizing** What difficulties did the builders of the transcontinental railroad face?

The Effects of the Railroads

The transcontinental railroad increased both economic and population growth in the West. Railroad companies provided better transportation for people and goods. They also sold land to settlers, encouraging people to move west. In addition, railroads saved time. The Union Pacific advertised that a trip from Omaha, Nebraska, to San Francisco, California, would take four days. By wagon the trip took about a month.

In addition, the new railroads helped businesses. Western timber and mining companies shipped wood and metals east by railroad. In exchange, eastern factories shipped manufactured goods to the West.

Population of Omaha

Year	Population
1860	1,833
1900	102,555

Sources: Bureau of the Census; U.S. Department of Commerce

Interpreting Graphs In 1863 the Union Pacific Railroad laid its tracks through the city of Omaha, Nebraska, causing the population to soar.

Skills Assessment **Analyzing Information** How much did Omaha's population increase between 1860 and 1900?

Railroad companies encouraged investors to put their money into the railroad business, which they did—sometimes unwisely. Railroad speculation and the collapse of railroad owner Jay Cooke's banking firm helped start the Panic of 1873. A depression soon followed. By the 1880s many of the smaller western railroads were deep in debt. Despite such setbacks, Americans remained interested in railroad investments. In 1865 only about 35,000 miles of railroad track existed, but by 1890 about 199,000 miles were in operation. Railroads had become the biggest industry in the United States.

✔ **Reading Check:** **Finding the Main Idea** How did the railroad affect the settlement and development of the West?

Section 2 Review

go.hrw.com Homework Practice Online
keyword: SC3 HP18

1. **Define** and explain:
   - bonanza
   - boomtowns
   - transcontinental railroad

2. **Identify** and explain:
   - Comstock Lode
   - Pony Express
   - Pacific Railway Acts
   - Leland Stanford

3. **Comparing** Copy the graphic organizer below. Use it to compare how mining and railroads led to the settlement and development of the West.

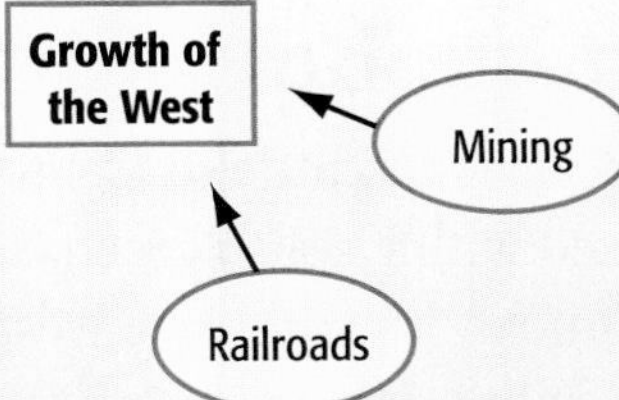

4. **Finding the Main Idea**
   a. Where did miners come from, and why was their job one of the most dangerous in the West?
   b. What were some of the difficulties faced in building a transcontinental railroad?

5. **Writing and Critical Thinking**
   Summarizing Imagine that you are a railroad worker. Write a short song that might have been sung in your community after the connection of the Union Pacific and the Central Pacific Railroads.
   Consider the following:
   - the challenges of building the railroad
   - how the railroad will change life in the West
   - improved communication between family members

Section 3

The Cattle Kingdom

Read to Discover

1. What led to the cattle boom?
2. What was life like for cowboys?
3. What caused the decline of the Cattle Kingdom?

Why It Matters Today

Cattle ranching continues to be important to the economy of many western states. Use CNNfyi.com or other **current events** sources to learn about cattle ranching today. Record your findings in your journal.

Define

- Texas longhorn
- open range
- range rights
- vaqueros
- roundup
- cattle drive
- range wars

Identify

- Joseph McCoy
- Cattle Kingdom
- Elizabeth Collins
- Nat Love
- Chisholm Trail

The Story Continues

The Texas longhorn was well suited to living on the Plains.

In the mid-1800s Texas ranchers began gathering huge herds of wild cattle. One rancher described how ranchers let their herds roam. "Cattle are permitted to range . . . over a large surface of country, thirty, forty, and even fifty miles in extent [size]." Keeping track of these roaming cattle required great skill. The ranch hands who did this work faced many hardships. However, one rancher believed that ranch hands liked their work. "The young men that follow this 'Cow-Boy' life . . . generally become attached to it," he wrote. These cowboys and ranchers helped start the cattle-ranching industry in the West.

The Cattle Boom

Spanish settlers brought their cattle to California and Texas in the 1700s. These cattle later mixed with English breeds to create the **Texas longhorn**. This breed spread quickly throughout western Texas. Longhorn cattle were lean and tough, with horns up to five feet across. Many butchers said the longhorn had too little meat. They called it "8 pounds of hamburger on 800 pounds of bone and horn." Nonetheless, settlers preferred to raise longhorns. Because the animals needed very little water and could survive harsh weather, they were more suitable for the environment.

Following the Civil War, the demand for beef increased in the East. The expanding economy and growing population created the higher demand. A steer worth $3 to $6 in Texas could be sold for $38 in Kansas. In New York it could be sold for $80. Nobody drove the longhorns to eastern markets, however. In addition to the problem of distance, people feared the western cattle would infect eastern farm animals with a disease called Texas fever.

In 1867 businessman **Joseph McCoy** had an idea. He decided "to establish a market whereat the southern . . . [rancher] and the northern buyer would meet." McCoy built pens for cattle in the small town of Abilene, Kansas. The Kansas Pacific Railroad line went through Abilene. As a result, cattle could be shipped by rail from there. Soon many Texas ranchers were making the trip north to sell their herds of cattle.

Around the same time, cattle ranching began to expand onto the Great Plains. The tough longhorns did well on the Plains. Ranchers began taking their cattle north to Colorado, Wyoming, Nebraska, and Montana. They built many ranches in the region stretching from Texas north to Canada. Eventually, this area became known as the **Cattle Kingdom**. Throughout the area, ranchers grazed their huge herds on public land called the **open range**. This land had once been occupied by Plains Indians and buffalo herds.

✔ **Reading Check: Finding the Main Idea** What factors led to the cattle boom?

Daily Life

Cattle Towns Long cattle drives ended at a town located along a railroad. In these towns, brokers bought cattle to ship east on railroad cars. Early cattle towns consisted of little more than a general store, a hotel or boardinghouse, a railroad depot, and a stockyard. Towns that drew enough business grew larger. They bustled with activity from spring to fall when the long drives took place. Prosperous cattle towns attracted businesspeople, doctors, lawyers, and their families. Once families arrived, the cattle towns built schools, hired teachers, and established police forces to maintain order. **How did the railroad contribute to the growth of western towns and businesses?**

The Ranches

One person who saw the profits to be made in ranching was **Elizabeth Collins**. She and her husband had had trouble mining gold, so they decided "to discontinue the business of mining and engage in that of cattle raising." She moved to the Teton Valley in Montana and started ranching. She was so successful that she earned the name Cattle Queen of Montana.

Elizabeth Collins became a successful cattle rancher in Montana.

Collins was just one of many ranchers who became wealthy during the cattle boom. Charles Goodnight started the first ranch in the Texas Panhandle. It was more than 250 miles from any town or railroad.

Speculators in the East and in Europe invested money in ranches the same way that they did in railroads. Some of the resulting ranches were huge. For example, the XIT Ranch covered more than 3 million acres. Few ranchers owned this much land, however. Instead, they concentrated on buying the **range rights**, or water rights, to ponds and rivers. Buying the range rights let them use the scarce water as well as the land around it. In this way, ranchers could cut out their competition by stopping farmers and other ranchers from using the water.

Because of the remote locations of many ranches, some ranchers served as the local authorities. Joseph McCoy described the view of a cattle rancher. He saw himself as "an independent sovereign [ruler] . . . capable of conducting his affairs in his own way." Mary Jaques, who lived on a Texas ranch for two years, noted ranchers' many different skills.

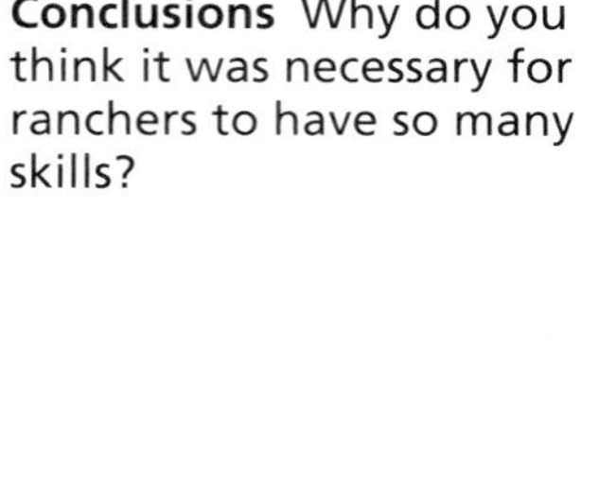

Analyzing Primary Sources

Drawing Inferences and Conclusions Why do you think it was necessary for ranchers to have so many skills?

"The ideal ranchman must be butcher, baker, carpenter, . . . blacksmith, plain cook, milker. . . . It is a fact that each of these trades will have to be practiced to some extent sooner or later."

—Mary Jaques, *Texan Ranch Life: With Three Months through Mexico in a "Prairie Schooner"*

✔ **Reading Check: Analyzing Information** How did ranchers influence western life?

The Cowboys

The workers who took care of ranchers' cattle were known as cowhands or cowboys. Cowboys borrowed many of their techniques from Mexican **vaqueros** (vah-KER-ohs), ranch hands who cared for cattle and horses. From the vaqueros came the western saddle, the lariat—a rope used for lassoing cattle—and the leather chaps cowboys wore over their pants for protection against the thorny brush. The cowboys borrowed the vaqueros' broad felt hat. However, they changed it into the familiar high-peaked cowboy hat. Cowboys also adopted the bandanna, a cloth that covered the face to protect it from dust. Sometimes it served as a handkerchief or bandage as well. Many cowboys were Mexican Americans or African Americans, like **Nat Love**, who wrote an autobiography about his life as a cowboy. Although most cowhands were men, some women worked alongside cowboys.

Nat Love

Cowboys borrowed many types of clothes, equipment, and cattle-driving methods from the vaqueros.

Gathering the cattle together was known as a **roundup**. During spring roundups, cowboys branded young calves and horses with a ranch's unique mark to prevent thieves from selling stolen horses and cattle.

Cowboys faced the danger of cattle thieves, bad weather, and unpredictable livestock. Although they worked hard, wages were low, and few were able to make enough money to start their own ranches. Despite these factors, many cowboys like Nat Love enjoyed their days on the range.

Interpreting the Visual Record

Cattle drives *Towns like Dodge City could be suddenly filled with cowboys driving the longhorns to market.* ***What does the image suggest about how cattle drives affected a town?***

Cattle Drives and Cattle Towns

One of the cowboy's most important and dangerous duties was the **cattle drive**. On these long journeys, cowboys herded cattle to the market or to the northern Plains for grazing. These trips usually lasted several months and covered hundreds of miles. The **Chisholm Trail** was one of the earliest and most popular routes for cattle drives. It was blazed, or marked, by Texas cowboy Jesse Chisholm in the late 1860s. This trail ran from San Antonio, Texas, to the cattle town of Abilene, Kansas. Charles Goodnight blazed a trail leading from Texas to New Mexico Territory, which became known as the Goodnight-Loving Trail. One of the most heavily used routes, the Western Trail, headed north from San Antonio to Dodge City, Kansas.

Cowboys herded their cattle through harsh country. They lived for months with "no tents or shelter of any sort other than [their] blankets," as cowboy James H. Cook recalled. The cattle could be difficult to handle, and they might stampede during storms. Then cowboys would have to track down the strays and round them up again. At night, cowboys had to stand watch over the cattle herds. Most cowboys were happy to reach the end of a cattle drive.

A large cattle town such as Dodge City or Abilene usually lay at the end of the trail. Small businesses sprang up as more cowboys passed through these towns. Some of these businesses were owned or operated by women. For example, Malinda Jenkins became a successful businesswoman who ran several boardinghouses.

Boardinghouses, hotels, saloons, and restaurants depended on tired cowboys spending money when they were in town. Cowboys spent their pay on food, hot baths, and comfortable beds after weeks on the trail. At times, rowdy cowboys could make life in cattle towns rough and violent. There were rarely shoot-outs in the streets, but disorderly behavior was common. Law officials such as Wyatt Earp became famous for keeping the peace in cattle towns.

✔ **Reading Check: Analyzing Information** How did the railroad affect the location and development of cattle trails and cattle towns?

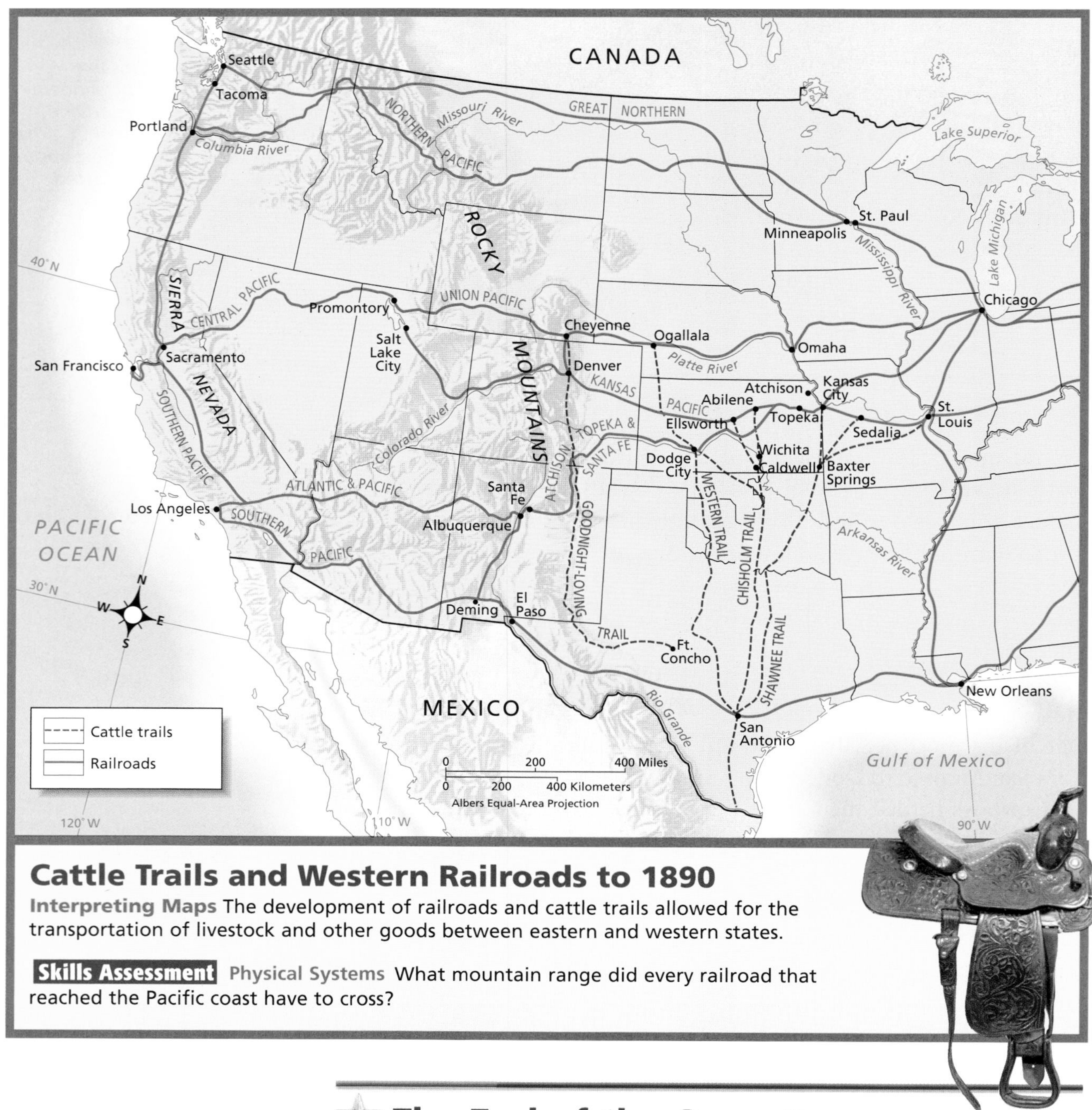

Cattle Trails and Western Railroads to 1890

Interpreting Maps The development of railroads and cattle trails allowed for the transportation of livestock and other goods between eastern and western states.

Skills Assessment **Physical Systems** What mountain range did every railroad that reached the Pacific coast have to cross?

The End of the Open Range

In the early 1880s the introduction of the refrigerator railroad car made it possible to carry meat from packing plants to eastern cities. As the national demand for beef grew, cities such as Chicago, Illinois, became famous for their meatpacking plants.

While the cattle business boomed, ranchers faced more competition for use of the open range. Farmers began to buy range land on the Great Plains where cattle had once grazed. Smaller ranchers also began competing with the large ranchers for land. Then in 1874 Joseph Glidden patented barbed wire, which allowed westerners to fence off large areas of land at a low cost.

As barbed wire came into wider use, large ranchers moved quickly to fence in the open range and valuable water sources, keeping out farmers and smaller ranchers. Some farmers and small ranchers cut the fences and moved onto the land or stole cattle in response. This competition led to **range wars** between large ranchers, small ranchers, and farmers. Large ranchers often won these battles, but few could let their cattle roam free on public land.

Cattle ranchers also fought with sheep owners. As the number of sheep grew even greater in the 1880s, so did the competition for grasslands. Sheep chewed the grass down so far that there was nothing left for the cattle. Despite threats and violence against them, sheep ranchers still usually did well in the West.

By the 1880s some 7.5 million cattle roamed the Great Plains. With the U.S. economy in a depression, cattle prices dropped in 1885. To improve prices, ranchers began to bring eastern cattle to the western range. These cattle produced more beef than the Texas longhorns but were not well adapted to the conditions on the Plains.

In 1885 and 1886 disaster struck the Cattle Kingdom. The huge cattle herds on the Plains had eaten much of the prairie grass that ranchers depended on for feed. Unusually severe winters in both years made the ranching situation even worse. Thousands of cattle died, and most ranchers lost at least 30 percent of their herds. Many ranchers were ruined financially. Cattle towns were also hit hard. While cattle ranching continued, it became more costly. Ranchers were forced to buy winter feed for their cattle and to reduce the size of their herds. Low prices, harsh weather, and greater competition for grazing land brought an end to the reign of the Cattle Kingdom.

✔ **Reading Check: Finding the Main Idea** Why did the Cattle Kingdom come to an end?

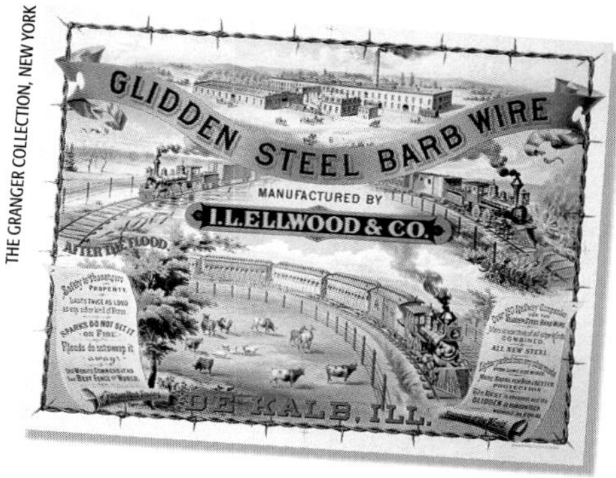

THE GRANGER COLLECTION, NEW YORK

Before Joseph Glidden invented barbed wire, westerners had not built fences because traditional fencing materials, such as stone and lumber, were scarce in the Great Plains.

Section 3 Review

go.hrw.com **Homework Practice Online** keyword: SC3 HP18

1. **Define** and explain:
   - Texas longhorn
   - open range
   - range rights
   - vaqueros
   - roundup
   - cattle drive
   - range wars

2. **Identify** and explain:
   - Joseph McCoy
   - Cattle Kingdom
   - Elizabeth Collins
   - Nat Love
   - Chisholm Trail

3. **Analyzing Information** Copy the graphic organizer below. Use it to describe the factors that caused the boom and then the bust of the Cattle Kingdom.

Boom	Bust
1.	1.
2.	2.
3.	3.

4. **Finding the Main Idea**
   a. What was cowboy life like?
   b. In what ways did the cattle boom show the benefits of free enterprise in the West?

5. **Writing and Critical Thinking**
   Summarizing Imagine that you are a cowboy during the late 1800s. Write a diary entry explaining what your daily life is like.
   Consider the following:
   - salary
   - work on ranches and cattle drives
   - freedom on the open range

Section 4

Farming the Great Plains

Read to Discover

1. What groups settled the Great Plains, and what were their reasons for moving there?
2. How did the environment of the Great Plains affect settlers' farming methods?
3. What was life on the Great Plains like for settlers, and how did they adapt to the conditions?

Define

- sodbusters
- dry farming

Identify

- Homestead Act
- Morrill Act
- Exodusters
- Cyrus McCormick

Why It Matters Today

Farming is still central to the economy of the Great Plains states, as well as much of the world. Use CNNfyi.com or other **current events** sources to learn about new farming methods being developed today. Record your findings in your journal.

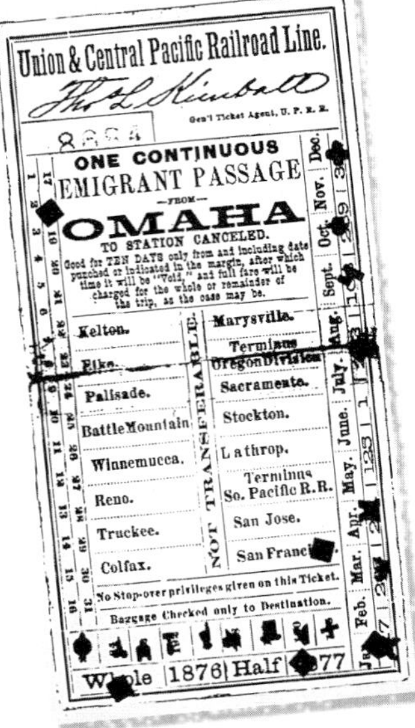

A pioneer's rail ticket

The Story Continues

In 1879 Scottish writer Robert Louis Stevenson took the transcontinental railroad across the United States. Most of the other passengers were settlers moving to the West. When a passenger began to play the song "Home Sweet Home," all conversation stopped. "The faces began to lengthen," noted Stevenson. Then "an elderly, hard-looking man . . . [asked] the performer [to] stop. 'I've heard about enough of that,' he [said]. 'Give us something about the good country we're going to.'" The passengers agreed, and the performer began to play music for dancing. Despite being homesick, most settlers hoped to build a better life in the West.

New Lands for Settlement

In 1862 Congress passed two important land-grant acts that helped open the West to settlers. The **Homestead Act** gave government-owned land to small farmers. Any adult who was a U.S. citizen or planned to become one could receive 160 acres of land. In exchange, homesteaders paid a small registration fee. They also promised to live on the land for five years. The **Morrill Act** granted more than 17 million acres of federal land to the states. The act required each state to sell this land and use the money to build colleges, such as Texas A&M, to teach agriculture and engineering.

The federal government also offered land in what is now Oklahoma. Some of this land had belonged to Creek and Seminole Indians. In April 1889, officials opened these lands to homesteaders. Within a month of the government's announcement, more than 50,000 people rushed to Oklahoma to stake their claims. In all, the settlers claimed more than 11 million acres of former Indian land in the Oklahoma land rush.

Interpreting the Visual Record

Westward expansion *The thousands of settlers who moved west formed many new communities.* ***How does this picture show settlers modifying their physical environment?***

✔ **Reading Check: Contrasting** List the different land acts that the federal government passed, and explain how they were different.

Settling the Plains

People from all over the country chose to move west. Settlers who had already moved to the Great Plains often chose to move again after a few years. All of these settlers hoped to find success on the Plains, often by starting their own farms. Many farming families moved from areas where farmland was becoming too scarce or expensive, such as New England. Others were the descendants of earlier pioneers to the Midwest. To encourage the presence of families and settlements in the West, the Homestead Act granted land to unmarried women.

The promise of land also drew a large group of Southern African Americans west. These settlers became known as **Exodusters** because of their exodus, or mass departure, from the South. Many Exodusters were sharecroppers such as John Solomon Lewis. He explained his reasons for moving his family.

"I one day said to the man I rented [land] from: 'It's no use, I works hard and raises big crops and you sells it and keeps the money, and brings me more and more in debt, so I will go somewhere else.'"

—John Solomon Lewis, quoted in *Exodusters: Black Migration to Kansas after Reconstruction,* by Nell Irvin Painter

Soon black communities such as Nicodemus, Kansas, developed. They drew many African Americans west by land advertisements. Exodusters wanted more economic opportunity as well as equal rights that they were being denied in the South after Reconstruction.

Free Find:
Homestead Act
After reading about the Homestead Act on the **Holt Researcher CD–ROM**, create a newspaper ad that advertises the land available through this act.

Many African American families, such as the Shores family shown here, moved to the Great Plains.

Western homesteads also were attractive to immigrants. Like Americans, they could get land grants under the Homestead Act if they planned to become citizens and promised to stay on the land for five years. Norwegian, Swedish, Danish, German, and Czech immigrants looking for economic opportunity formed many small communities on the Great Plains. Usually, a relative made the journey to America first. Then this person wrote letters home telling other family members to come. In addition, a number of Mennonites, members of a Protestant religious group, moved to the Great Plains from Russia. They were among the first to begin large-scale farming in the region.

✔ **Reading Check: Summarizing** Who moved to the Great Plains, and why did they choose to move there?

Farming on the Plains

The inexpensive land of the Great Plains drew settlers. Yet the Plains had many unique challenges. Plains settlers found a mostly flat landscape covered with grass. Settlers also encountered extreme seasons. In the winter, temperatures on the northern Plains could fall to –40° F. Hot summer temperatures in the southern Plains could reach 110° F. The climate of the Plains was much drier than in the East. Settlers also faced the threat of blizzards and tornadoes. All of these factors meant that farmers could not raise the same crops that they had grown in the East.

Farmers survived the challenges of the Great Plains by developing new farming equipment and methods. The root-filled sod, or dirt, of the Plains was so tough that it actually broke the plows of many farmers. Manufacturer John Deere's deep steel plow broke through the tough sod and enabled farmers to plant crops. This hard work of breaking up the sod earned farmers on the Plains the nickname **sodbusters**.

In the 1890s farmers on the western Plains began to learn a new method called **dry farming**. This method shifted the focus from water-dependent crops such as corn to hardier crops like a type of red wheat introduced by Mennonite farmers to the Plains. In addition, farmers left part of their fields unplanted each year to preserve water in the soil. Even on the eastern Plains, which got more rain, farmers found that the soil needed special care. These dry-farming methods helped farmers make it through drought years.

By the 1880s mechanical farming was becoming increasingly common. **Cyrus McCormick** made his fortune designing, building, and

That's Interesting!

Attack of the Grasshoppers
Can you imagine the fields of the Great Plains covered in grasshoppers four inches deep? Well, that's exactly what happened in the summer of 1874. The grasshoppers appeared without warning. Within a few minutes, swarms had blocked out the Sun. These bugs liked to eat plants the best, but they didn't stop there. They ate curtains, old boots, and even straw hats. One settler said that he saw grasshoppers eating the wool off of a live sheep! One couple managed to save enough wheat for seed by swinging a clothesline in the air when the grasshoppers attacked. Other people were not so lucky.

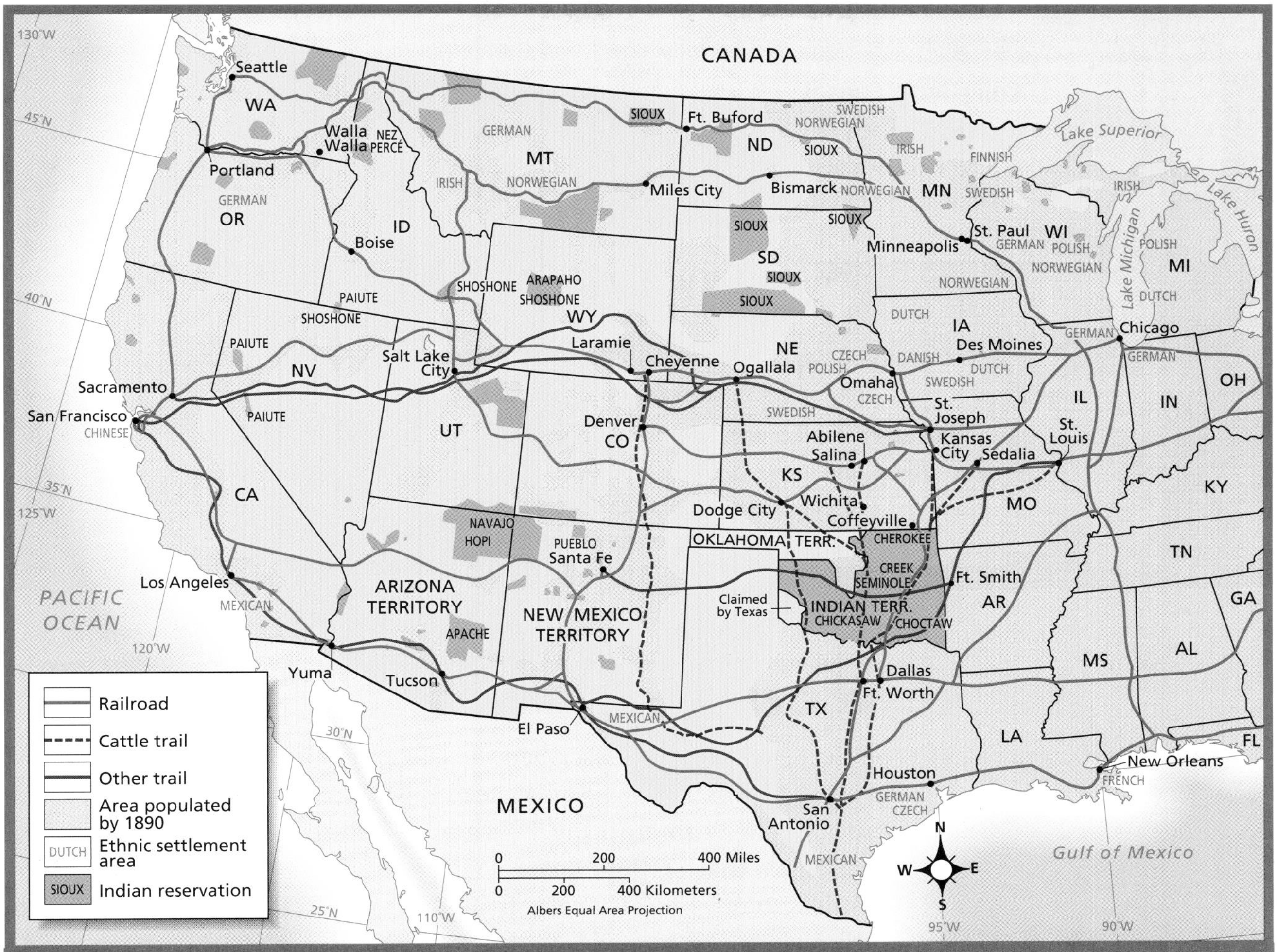

Railroad
Cattle trail
Other trail
Area populated by 1890
DUTCH Ethnic settlement area
SIOUX Indian reservation

0 200 400 Miles
0 200 400 Kilometers
Albers Equal Area Projection

Populating the West

Interpreting Maps By 1890, settlements stretched across the western United States, which was experiencing rapid population growth.

Skills Assessment **Human Systems** What man-made features typically correspond with the populated areas on the map?

A poster intending to persuade people to move west

selling farm equipment. Horse-drawn machines such as McCormick reapers collected wheat stalks. Threshing machines separated the grain from the husk. By using machinery, farmers could harvest large fields more quickly and with fewer workers. Wealthy farmers could afford the land and machinery needed to create huge farms that employed hundreds of workers. Once they harvested their crops, farmers shipped the grain east by train. Some of it was then shipped to customers overseas. As farming technology improved, the Great Plains became known as the breadbasket of the world because of the grain that the region's farms produced.

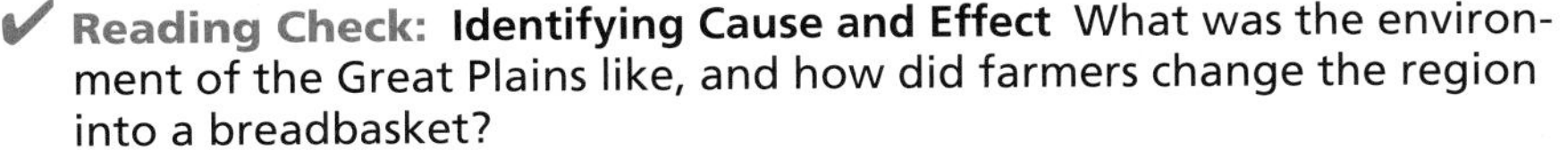

✔ **Reading Check: Identifying Cause and Effect** What was the environment of the Great Plains like, and how did farmers change the region into a breadbasket?

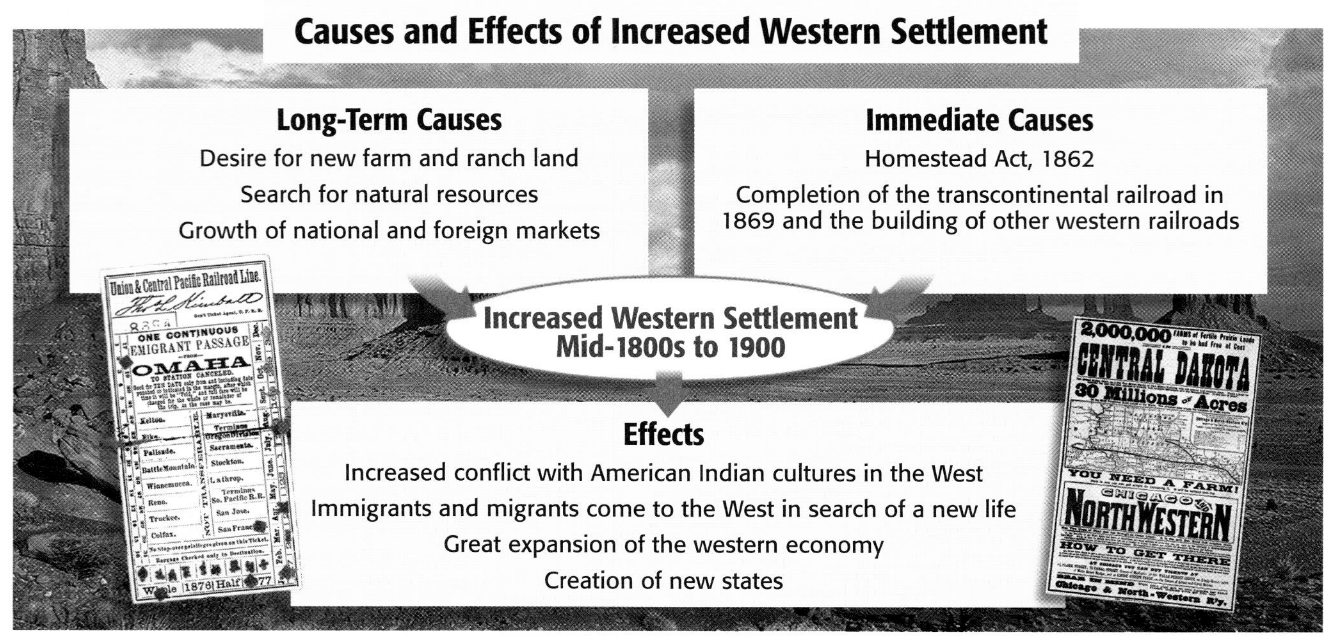

Daily Life on the Plains

Settler Gro Svendsen described the challenges of Plains life. "When one begins to farm, it takes a great deal to get started—especially when one must begin with nothing." Building a house was one of the first challenges that settlers faced. With very little wood available, many families built houses from bricks of sod cut out of the ground. Although cheap to build, these sod homes were often very small and uncomfortable. Pioneer May Avery explained a few of the common problems. "The roof leaked something awful [and inside] we killed a snake or two . . . and several centipedes." For all their faults, however, the small homes did provide necessary shelter.

Once a home was built, daily chores kept pioneer families busy. For example, settlers had to make and mend their own clothes. They had no washing machines, so washing clothes was a big chore that filled the entire day. Pioneers usually made their wash soap from lye, a liquid made from wood ashes and animal fat. One pioneer woman listed 11 washday chores. She started with "build fire in back yard to heat kettle of rain water." The list ended with "brew cup of tea, set and rest and rock a spell and count blessings." Women prepared meals and often grew vegetables. They also raised chickens or made butter to earn money for the family.

Farming families raised livestock and worked hard in the fields, plowing and planting. Pioneers often had to build most of their farm buildings and repair their machinery. Children helped with many tasks around the farms. Farm families were often large, and everyone had chores.

✔ **Reading Check: Categorizing** What different types of work did Great Plains farmers do?

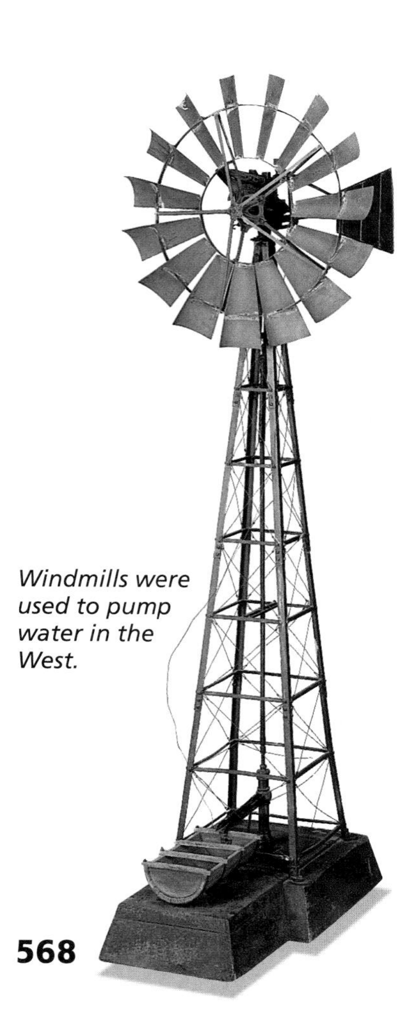

Windmills were used to pump water in the West.

This group of pioneer students posed with their teacher in October 1893.

Communities on the Great Plains

Communities were an important part of life on the Plains. Many early settlers found life on their remote farms to be extremely difficult. Esther Clark explained her mother's life as a pioneer. "It took [courage] to live twenty-four hours at a time, month in and out, on the lonely and lovely prairie." Farmers formed communities so that they could assist one another in times of need.

One of the first things that many pioneer communities did was establish a local church and a school. Churches offered a place for pioneer families to meet. Even small communities made efforts to get schools started. Many towns raised money by putting on plays or dinners. In many cases, townspeople even helped build the schools and ran them themselves. One woman recalled proudly, "They [the school board] and the pupils and I built that school house with our own hands."

Pioneer schools were usually small one-room buildings. A stove in the middle of the room provided heat, while the sunlight gave reading light. In these schools, children of all ages learned together in one class. Few children had schoolbooks. Many children went to school only part of the year because they had to help with farm work. Most teachers in these pioneer schools were young women who made little money. Frontier families worked very hard to provide communities for themselves and for their children. Through these efforts, more people found the West an appealing place to live and raise a family.

✔ **Reading Check: Summarizing** What roles did communities play in life on the Great Plains?

Section 4 Review

go.hrw.com **Homework Practice Online**
keyword: SC3 HP18

1. **Define** and explain:
   - sodbusters
   - dry farming
2. **Identify** and explain:
   - Homestead Act
   - Morrill Act
   - Exodusters
   - Cyrus McCormick
3. **Categorizing** Copy the graphic organizer below. Use it to identify the groups that settled on the Great Plains and what made them choose to move there.

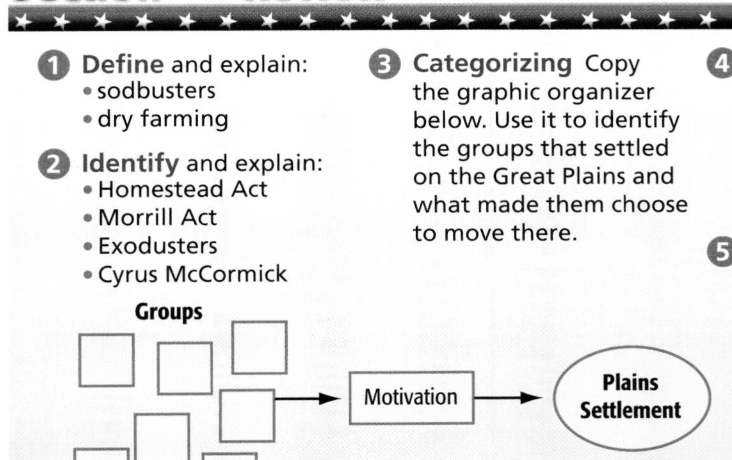

4. **Finding the Main Idea**
   a. How did the environment of the Plains affect farming methods, and how did settlers cope with these conditions?
   b. What was life on the Great Plains like, and how did pioneers adapt to this life?
5. **Writing and Critical Thinking**
   Supporting a Point of View Imagine that you are a pioneer on the Plains in the late 1800s. Write a newspaper advertisement encouraging other people to settle the region.
   Consider the following:
   - availability of land and economic opportunity
   - technological and scientific advances that have made Plains farming easier
   - growth of churches and schools

Chapter 18 Review

The Chapter at a Glance

Examine the visual summary of the chapter below. Use it to create a chart listing five major events discussed in this chapter. Then give your list to a classmate and ask him or her to write the results or descriptions of these events.

As settlers moved to the West, they came into conflict with American Indians. As the last armed Indian resistance was being defeated, the U.S. government moved many tribes to reservations.

The completion of the transcontinental railroad in 1869 opened the West to more settlement. Gold and silver strikes also drew people hoping to get rich.

The railroads helped make the rise of the Cattle Kingdom possible. Cowboys drove huge herds of cattle from ranches to railway stations to be shipped to the East.

Farmers settled the Great Plains in large numbers. They overcame many hardships to make the Plains the breadbasket of America.

Identifying People and Ideas

Use the following terms or people in historically significant sentences.

1. reservations
2. George Armstrong Custer
3. Sitting Bull
4. Comstock Lode
5. Pacific Railway Acts
6. Joseph McCoy
7. Elizabeth Collins
8. Chisholm Trail
9. Homestead Act
10. Exodusters

Understanding Main Ideas

Section 1 *(Pages 546–552)*

1. What caused some of the conflicts between the United States and American Indians, and what were the results of these conflicts?
2. How did reformers change the U.S. government's Indian policy in the late 1800s?

Section 2 *(Pages 553–557)*

3. What factors made mining in the West such a dangerous job?
4. What effect did the transcontinental railroad have on western settlement?

Section 3 *(Pages 558–563)*

5. Why was there a cattle boom in the 1870s?

Section 4 *(Pages 564–569)*

6. Why did many immigrants move to the West?
7. How did settlers use new scientific methods and technology to farm on the Great Plains?

You Be the Historian— Reviewing Themes

1. **Economics** What factors led to the expansion of the economy in the West in the late 1800s?
2. **Culture** How did U.S. settlement of the West affect American Indians?
3. **Geography** In what ways did the environment of the Great Plains affect the crops that farmers planted and the farming methods they used?

Thinking Critically

1. **Summarizing** What types of economic and social contributions did women make in the West?
2. **Evaluating** List two positive and two negative results of economic development in the West.
3. **Analyzing Information** What were some of the different ways in which immigrant groups interacted with and changed the environment of the West?

Social Studies Skills Workshop

Interpreting Graphs

Study the graph below. Then use the information on the graph to help you answer the questions that follow.

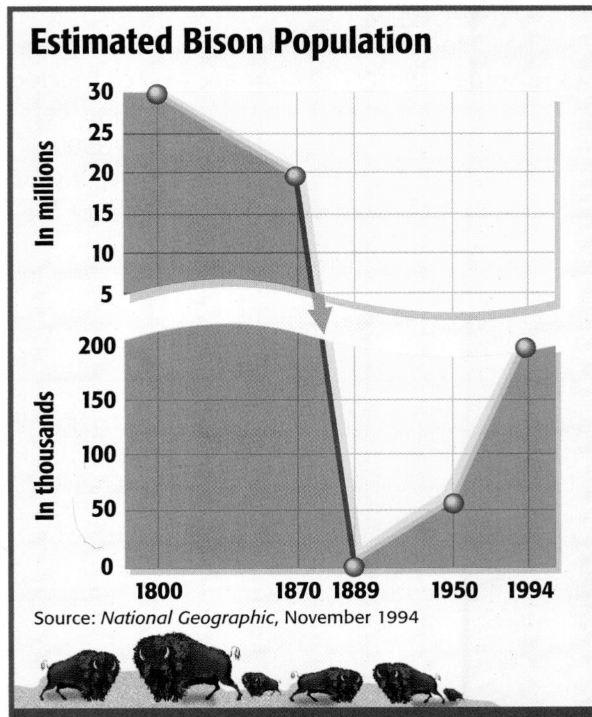

Source: *National Geographic*, November 1994

1. How many buffalo (bison) were there in the United States in 1800?
   a. 30
   b. 50 million
   c. 75 million
   d. 30 million
2. How many buffalo were there in the United States in 1889?
3. Based on your knowledge of the period and of current events, what factors do you think might have accounted for the increase in the buffalo population since 1889?

Analyzing Primary Sources

Read the following quotation about cattle drives from an American cowboy song, then answer the questions.

> **"It's whooping and yelling and driving the dogies;**
> **Oh how I wish you would go on;**
> **It's whooping and punching and go on little dogies,**
> **For you know Wyoming will be your new home.**
>
> **Some boys go up the trail for pleasure**
> **But that's where you get it most awfully wrong;**
> **For you haven't any idea of the trouble they give us**
> **While we go driving them along."**

4. Which of the following statements best describes the author's point of view?
   a. A cowboy's life is easy.
   b. Some people mistakenly believe that a cowboy's life is easy.
   c. More people should become cowboys.
   d. Cowboys do not get enough respect.
5. Based on the material that you have read about cattle drives, what problems on the trail might have led to the creation of this song? Give specific examples.
6. What do you think the lines, "It's whooping and yelling and driving the dogies" tells about cattle drives?

Alternative Assessment

Building Your Portfolio

Linking to Community

Mining, ranching, and farming continue to be important to the U.S. economy. Identify a person from your community who works in one of these fields. Then make a list of questions to use while interviewing this person. Conduct an interview to find out what his or her job is like today. When you finish the interview, share your results with the class.

internet connect

Internet Activity: go.hrw.com
keyword: SC3 CF18

Choose a topic on the West to:

- Learn the facts and mythology surrounding the Pony Express.
- Research Geronimo and other American Indian leaders and write biographies of their lives.
- Analyze the myths and realities of the West and the ways in which it shaped the United States.

The Economy of the West

In the last half of the 1800s, great numbers of settlers followed the trails of earlier pioneers to the West. People moved west for new economic opportunities in farming, mining, and ranching.

Prospectors and miners came to California during the gold rush of 1849. Many of these settlers continued pursuing the dream of striking it rich. Cattle drives brought the ranching industry from Texas to the northern Great Plains. Growing numbers of farmers also came to the Plains to plant fields of wheat and corn.

Railroads helped bring many of these settlers west. The railroads also connected farmers, miners, and ranchers to markets in the rest of the United States. By 1890 so many people had settled in the West that the U.S. Census Bureau reported that the frontier had officially closed.

Western Mining

A mining boom in the late 1800s brought thousands of prospectors to the West. Successful strikes in western mining contributed to a huge increase in the amount of gold and silver produced in the United States.

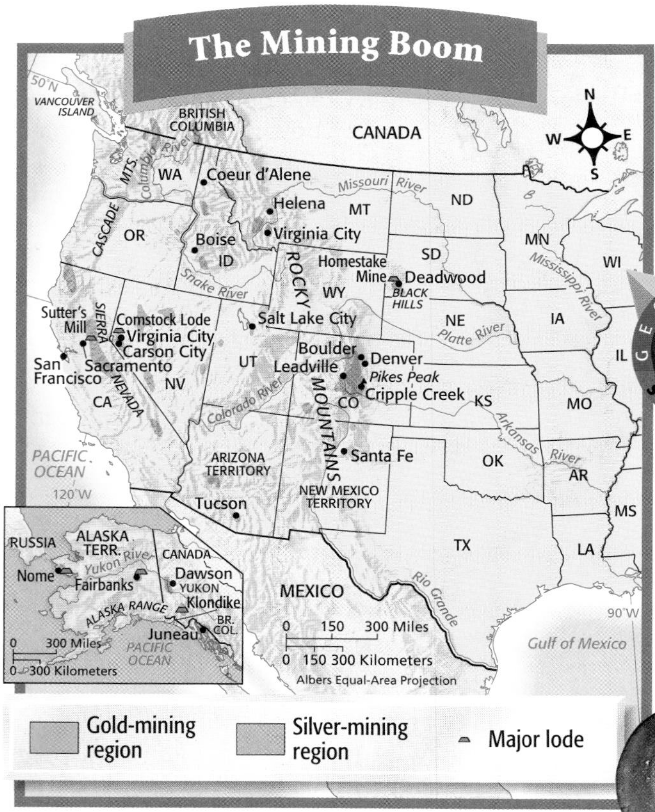

The Mining Boom

Gold-mining region | Silver-mining region | Major lode

0 150 300 Miles
0 150 300 Kilometers
Albers Equal-Area Projection

Geography Skills

Interpreting Thematic Maps

1. What types of mines surrounded Deadwood and Carson City?
2. **Environment and Society** What U.S. cities developed near gold-mining regions in the West?
3. **Comparing** In what type of terrain did most of the gold and silver strikes take place?

Mining tools

History Note 1

Individual prospectors found many of the richest gold and silver deposits in the West. Some prospectors became wealthy from their discoveries. However, the majority of the gold and silver produced was mined by corporations. Most of the profits from western mining were made by investors. They provided the money for heavy steam-powered machinery and equipment used in the mines.

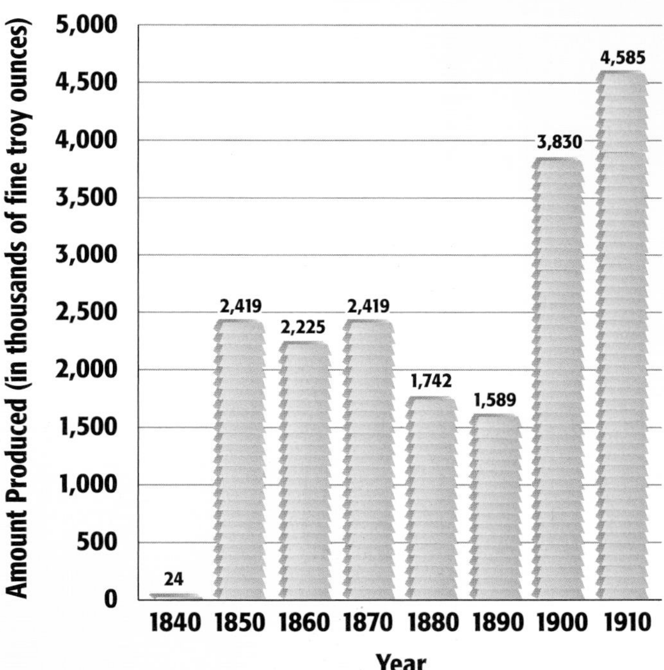

Source: *Historical Statistics of the United States*

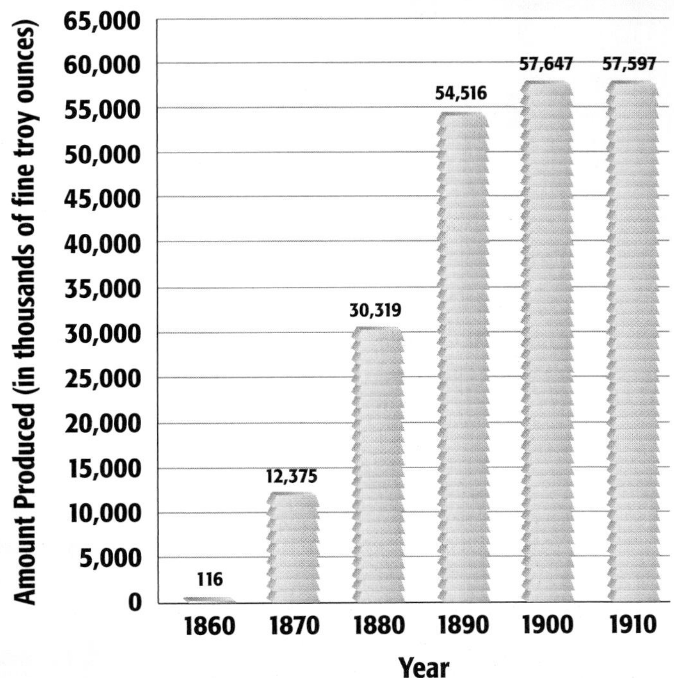

Source: *Historical Statistics of the United States*

Geography **Skills**

Interpreting Bar Graphs

1. In what year shown on the graph was gold production the highest in the United States? Silver production?
2. Combine the information on these two bar graphs for the year 1860 into a pie graph comparing the amount of gold and silver produced that year.
3. **Drawing Inferences and Conclusions** What discovery would account for the dramatic increase in U.S. gold production between 1840 and 1850?

History Note 2

Gold and silver have been made into coins since ancient times. These precious metals continue to be used as currency and to create jewelry and art. In addition, gold and silver are used in electronics and manufacturing. Most gold and silver mined in the United States today still comes from western states.

The Changing West

In the 1860s the U.S. government passed laws to encourage western settlement. The Homestead Act sold government-owned western lands at very low cost. The Pacific Railway Acts encouraged railroad construction. The acts gave railroad companies land for every mile of track they laid. By 1900 a network of railroad lines crossed the mountains and farmlands of the West.

The West around 1870

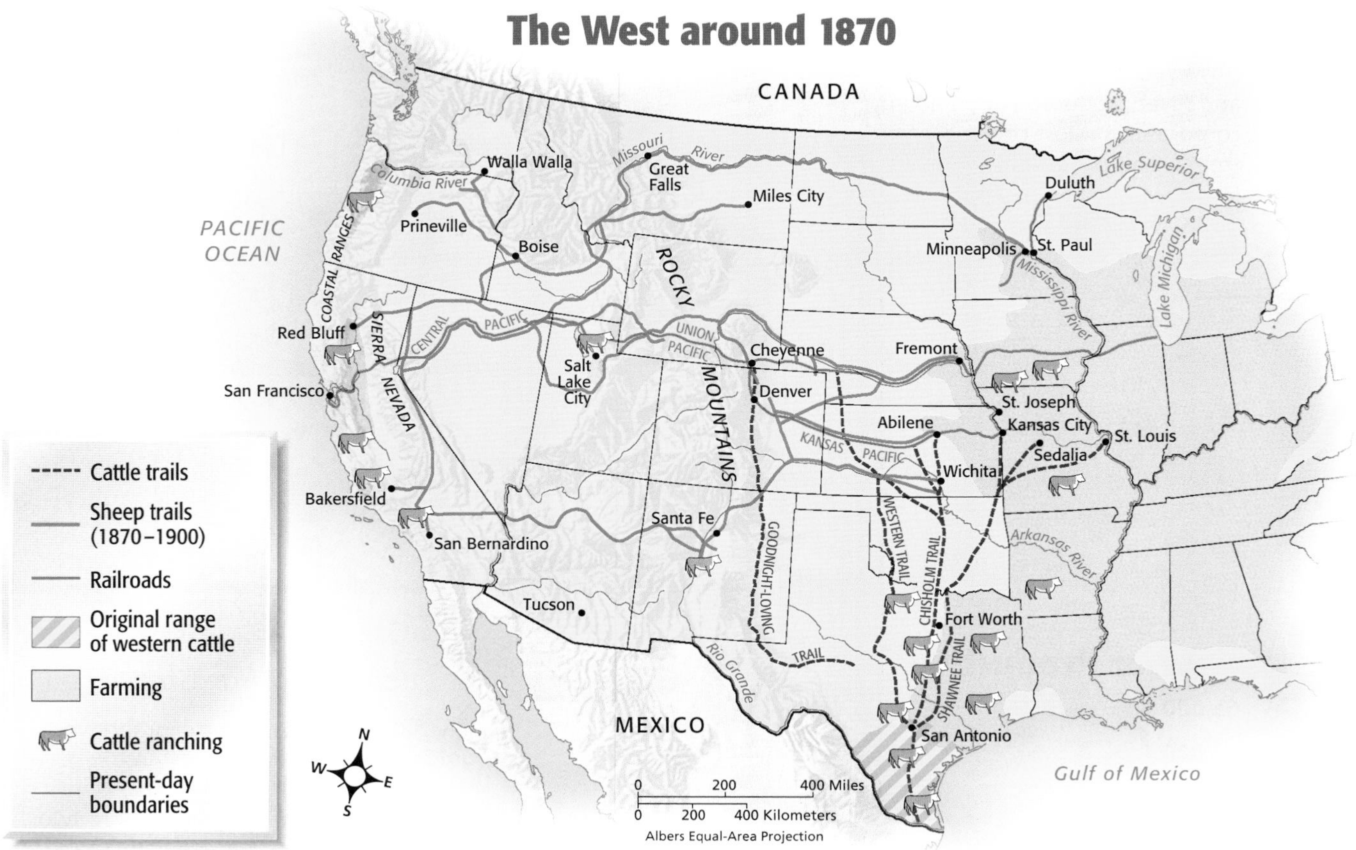

- ----- Cattle trails
- Sheep trails (1870–1900)
- Railroads
- Original range of western cattle
- Farming
- Cattle ranching
- Present-day boundaries

0 200 400 Miles
0 200 400 Kilometers
Albers Equal-Area Projection

History Note 3

Many of our images of the West are of cowboys and cattle drives. However, sheepherders also moved millions of sheep along a network of western trails. These experienced sheepherders were often immigrants from places like France, Mexico, and Spain. They helped move large western herds that sometimes numbered more than 10,000 sheep. One of the first great sheep drives in the West provided food for miners during the California Gold Rush.

Geography Skills

Interpreting Thematic Maps

1. What directions did cattle trails run? What about sheep trails?
2. **Human Systems** What areas of the West were focused on farming by around 1870? What regions were focused on ranching?
3. **Drawing Inferences and Conclusions** Why do you think cattle trails ended at towns along railroad lines?

The West around 1900

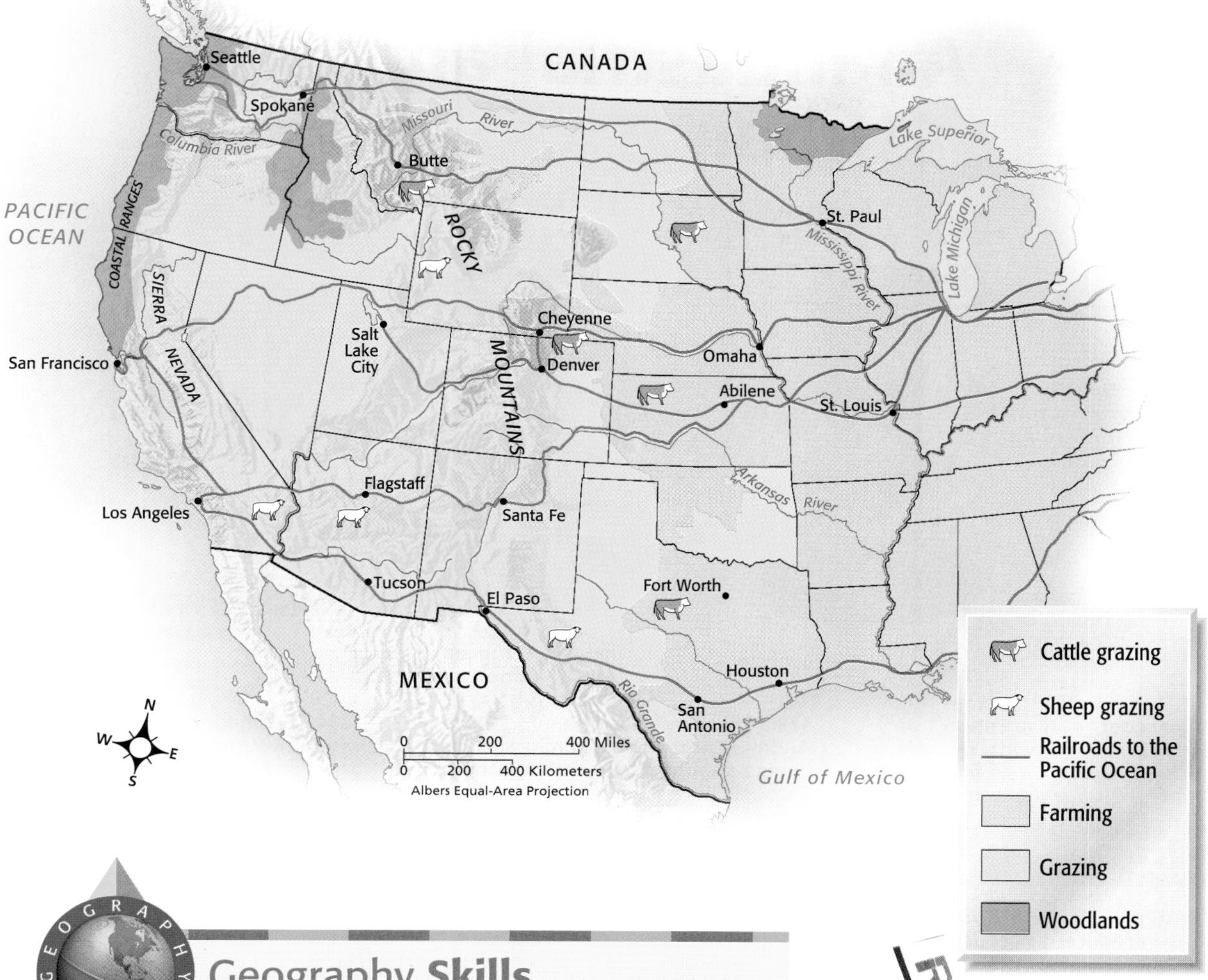

CANADA
Seattle
Spokane
Missouri River
Columbia River
Butte
PACIFIC OCEAN
COASTAL RANGES
ROCKY MOUNTAINS
St. Paul
Lake Superior
Lake Michigan
Mississippi River
SIERRA NEVADA
Salt Lake City
Cheyenne
Denver
Omaha
San Francisco
Abilene
St. Louis
Arkansas River
Flagstaff
Los Angeles
Santa Fe
Tucson
El Paso
Fort Worth
Houston
MEXICO
Rio Grande
San Antonio
Gulf of Mexico
N W E S
0 200 400 Miles
0 200 400 Kilometers
Albers Equal-Area Projection

Cattle grazing
Sheep grazing
Railroads to the Pacific Ocean
Farming
Grazing
Woodlands

GEOGRAPHY SKILLS

Geography **Skills**

Interpreting Thematic Maps

1. By 1900 what West Coast cities were linked by railroads to the eastern United States?
2. **Physical Systems** Based on the map, what parts of the western environment were most suited to grazing? What areas were suitable for farming?
3. **Comparing** Compare the map above to the one on page 676. Into what regions of the West had farming expanded between 1870 and 1900?

History Note 4

The construction of railroads in the West contributed much to the settlement of the region. It also helped the industrialization of the U.S. economy. In 1880 there were more than 93,000 miles of steel track in the United States. By 1900 there were almost 259,000 more miles. Much of the new mileage was located in the rapidly growing West.

CHAPTER

19 An Industrial and Urban Nation

(1876–1900)

An early version of Alexander Graham Bell's telephone

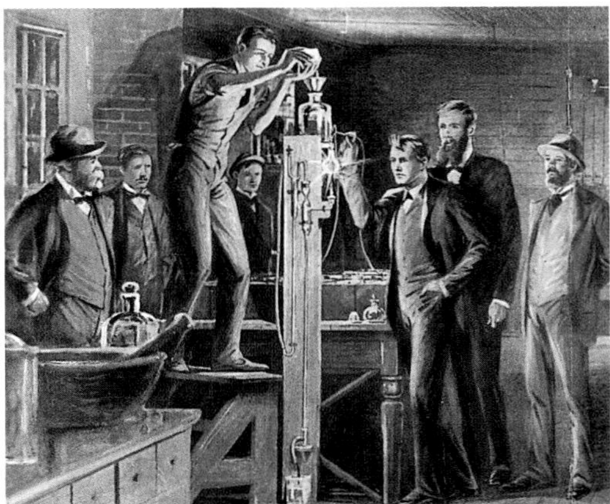

Thomas Edison's team of inventors at Menlo Park, New Jersey, works on creating a lightbulb.

UNITED STATES

1876 Alexander Graham Bell patents the telephone.

1879 Thomas Alva Edison invents the first lightbulb.

1880 Philanthropist Andrew Carnegie begins creating the Carnegie libraries.

1882 Congress passes the Chinese Exclusion Act, banning Chinese immigrants from entering the United States for 10 years.

1884 Telephone wires are strung between New York and Boston.

1886 More than 70 police officers are injured or killed during the Haymarket Riot.

1876 | 1878 | 1880 | 1882 | 1884 | 1886

1876 British inventors introduce the high-wheel bicycle to the United States at the Centennial Exhibition.

1878 Electric streetlights are introduced in London.

1880 The public is granted full admission to the British Museum.

1884 The first subway opens in London.

1885 The Canadian Pacific Railway is finished.

WORLD

High-wheel bicycles were difficult and often dangerous to ride.

Build on What You Know

Even as many settlers were heading west to start new lives, the Second Industrial Revolution was bringing great changes to the nation. New industries boomed, and immigrants seeking a better life came to the United States in record numbers. Workers and farmers also sought to improve their lives using political influence.

New York City became home to thousands of European immigrants to the United States.

An immigrant passport

1888 Benjamin Harrison is elected president.

1889 The Eiffel Tower is built in Paris.

1890 Congress passes the Sherman Antitrust Act, which makes monopolies illegal.

1890 Japan holds its first general election.

1892 The federal government opens the Ellis Island station in New York Harbor to receive immigrants to the United States.

1894 Rudolph Diesel invents the diesel engine.

1896 William McKinley is elected president.

1896 The first modern Olympics are held in Athens, Greece.

1897 Eugene V. Debs helps form the Social Democratic Party.

1898 French scientists Pierre and Marie Curie discover radium.

1888 | 1890 | 1892 | 1894 | 1896 | 1898

Marie Curie won a Nobel Prize for her research.

If you were there . . .
Would you seek your fortune in the country or in the city?

You Be the Historian

What's Your Opinion? Do you **agree** or **disagree** with the following statements? Support your point of view in your journal.

- **Science, Technology & Society** New forms of technology always boost a country's economy.
- **Government** The government should keep careful control over economic and industrial growth.
- **Citizenship** Private citizens cannot shape the way the national economy develops and changes.

Section 1

The Second Industrial Revolution

Read to Discover

1. What developments occurred in the steel, oil, and electric-power industries during the Second Industrial Revolution?
2. What changes occurred in the way that businesses were organized?
3. Why did some Americans oppose monopolies, and what actions did they take against them?

Define

- patents
- free enterprise
- entrepreneurs
- corporations
- vertical integration
- horizontal integration
- trust

Identify

- Second Industrial Revolution
- Bessemer process
- Orville and Wilbur Wright
- Thomas Alva Edison
- Andrew Carnegie
- John D. Rockefeller
- Sherman Antitrust Act

Why It Matters Today

Entrepreneurs continue to start new businesses today. Many of these companies ask for funding from outside sources. Use CNNfyi.com or other **current events** sources to learn about organizations that offer financial backing and other opportunities for entrepreneurs. Record your findings in your journal.

The Corliss steam engine weighed some 700 tons and stood about 40 feet high. Many people were awed by its size and power.

The Story Continues

The most popular exhibit at the 1876 Centennial Exhibition in Philadelphia was the huge Corliss steam engine, which helped power the equipment in Machinery Hall. Millions of people came to see what author William Dean Howells called "an athlete of steel and iron." For many, the Corliss engine symbolized the ever-improving future that modern machines seemed to promise.

An Age of Steel

Technological advances, such as the Corliss steam engine, were important to the **Second Industrial Revolution**. The Second Industrial Revolution was a period of rapid growth in U.S. manufacturing in the late 1800s. By the mid-1890s, the United States had become the industrial leader of the world.

Some of the most important advances in technology took place in the steel industry. Steel is iron that has been made stronger by heating it and adding other metals. Skilled workers once made steel in small batches, but the process was difficult and expensive. In the 1850s Henry Bessemer found a quick, cheap way to make steel by blasting hot air through melted iron to quickly remove waste material. Before Bessemer developed this method, it took a day or more to turn several tons of iron into steel. The **Bessemer process** took only 10 to 20 minutes.

Using the Bessemer process, U.S. steel production rose from 77,000 tons in 1870 to more than 1 million tons in 1879. At first the need for steel rails for railroads fueled this growth. However, steel mills were also soon making parts for tall buildings and bridges. As mills made more steel, steel prices dropped. People could afford to use steel for items such as nails, wire, and pipes.

Railroad companies took advantage of lower construction costs to build thousands of miles of new steel track. Railroad mileage increased from some 30,000 miles in 1860 to 193,000 miles by 1900. These stronger, longer-lasting rails could carry heavier loads. A network of rail lines soon carried heavy cargo across the nation.

New technology also made railroad travel safer. Inventor George Westinghouse's improved air brakes made travel on these heavier, faster trains safer. Passenger service also improved. George Pullman designed elegant passenger and sleeping cars that made long-distance trips more comfortable. Cornelius Vanderbilt and other railroad owners began buying smaller companies to form larger companies. This process improved efficiency and made rail travel faster. In 1860 it had taken two days and 17 line changes to go from New York City to Chicago. By 1870 the trip took one day and did not require changing trains.

Daily Life

Railroads Improvements in safety and comfort made railroad travel more appealing to Americans. Railroads also became faster and more efficient, helping businesses run more smoothly. Railroads thus helped drive the economy while connecting the nation. This image shows the Illinois Central Railroad connecting rural people to the rest of the world in the 1800s. **What do the various images in the cartoon represent?**

CONNECTING TO

SCIENCE AND TECHNOLOGY

The Wizard of Menlo Park

In 1876 Thomas Alva Edison built himself a new laboratory in Menlo Park, New Jersey. His plan was to create an "invention factory" where he and his team of skilled specialists would create all sorts of useful technologies. The idea proved to be a great success. In fewer than six years at Menlo Park, Edison patented more than 400 devices or processes, including the phonograph and the electric lightbulb. Such achievements gained Edison the nickname The Wizard of Menlo Park. What was the purpose of the laboratory at Menlo Park?

An early model of an electric lightbulb

The railroads had a major impact on the development of the country's economy. Manufacturers and farmers could get their products to market faster. Cities where major rail lines crossed, such as Chicago and Kansas City, grew rapidly. Railroads also spurred western growth by offering free tickets to settlers. As rail travel and shipping increased, railroads and their related industries employed more and more people.

✔ **Reading Check: Identifying Cause and Effect** How did steel processing change in the 1850s, and what effects did this change have on the population and economy of the United States?

New Sources of Power

Another important technological breakthrough in the late 1800s was the use of petroleum, or oil, as a power source. In the 1850s Dr. Benjamin Silliman Jr. discovered how to change crude, or unprocessed, oil into a fuel called kerosene. Kerosene could be used for cooking, heating, and home lighting. Suddenly the demand for oil increased. In 1859 Edwin L. Drake proved that it was possible to pump crude oil from the ground. Oil became a big business. States such as Ohio, Pennsylvania, and West Virginia began producing millions of barrels of oil a year.

In the late 1800s people found another use for oil—powering machinery. In 1876 German engineer Nikolaus A. Otto invented an engine powered by gasoline, another fuel made from oil. In 1893 Charles and J. Frank Duryea used a gasoline engine to build the first practical motorcar in the United States. By the early 1900s American manufacturers were building thousands of cars. Most of these early cars were too expensive for anyone but the wealthy to afford.

New engine technology also helped make another transportation breakthrough possible—flight. **Orville and Wilbur Wright** were bicycle makers. Fascinated by the possibility of flying, the brothers built a lightweight airplane with a small gas-powered engine. In Kitty Hawk, North Carolina, Orville Wright made the first piloted flight in a gas-powered plane on December 17, 1903. The Wright brothers patented their airplane in 1906.

Electricity became another source of power during the Second Industrial Revolution. Inventors such as **Thomas Alva Edison** investigated the practical uses of electricity, as he explained.

Analyzing Primary Sources

Identifying Points of View
Why did Edison not consider himself a pure scientist?

"I do not regard myself as a pure scientist, as so many persons have insisted that I am. I do not search for the laws of nature . . . for the purpose of learning truth. I am only a professional inventor."

—Thomas Edison, quoted in *American Made,* by Harold C. Livesay

Edison went on to be awarded more than 1,000 **patents**. A patent is an exclusive right to make or sell an invention. This right encourages inventors to develop new technologies.

In 1878, after viewing an experimental electric light source, Edison announced that he would soon invent a practical electric light. By the end of 1879 Edison and his team of inventors had created the electric lightbulb. Edison began supplying electricity to some buildings in New York City in September 1882. In the late 1880s Edison and George Westinghouse competed to provide communities with electric power. As a result, electric use spread rapidly, and electricity soon lit homes and businesses across the country. Streetcars in cities also ran on electrical power.

Electricity also played a part in communications advances. By 1861, telegraph wires connected the East and West Coasts. Five years later, a cable was laid on the floor of the Atlantic Ocean to connect the United States and Great Britain. Alexander Graham Bell invented the "talking telegraph," or telephone, in 1876. By the mid-1890s major cities such as Boston, Chicago, and New York were linked by telephone lines. The number of telephones in U.S. homes and businesses increased rapidly.

✔ **Reading Check: Comparing** What new sources of power became available in the late 1800s, and how were they used?

Free Enterprise and Big Business

As the U.S. economy grew during the Second Industrial Revolution, the federal government favored **free enterprise**, a term that means the government usually does not interfere with business. In the late 1800s this policy continued in the form of laissez-faire capitalism, with little government regulation of the market economy. Laissez-faire means "allow to do" in French. However, the government took some actions to help business. Protective tariffs aided manufacturers and land grants helped railroad companies. As a result, **entrepreneurs**—people who start new businesses—had a lot of freedom and many opportunities.

Many entrepreneurs formed their businesses as **corporations**. Corporations are formed by selling shares of ownership, called stock, to a number of individuals known as stockholders. Stockholders in a corporation typically get a share of company profits, based on how much stock they own. Corporations must be approved and chartered by state governments. Although the stockholders actually own the corporation, they do not run its day-to-day operations. Instead, they elect a board of directors. The board then chooses the main leaders of the corporation.

Corporations provide several important advantages over earlier ways of organizing companies. Unlike business partners or members of joint-stock companies, the stockholders in a corporation are not personally responsible for the debts of the business. As a result, if a corporation fails, the stockholders lose only the money that they invested. Stockholders are also usually free to sell their shares to whomever they want, whenever they want. These benefits encouraged investment. By 1900 more than 100 million shares a year were being traded on the New York Stock Exchange.

That's Interesting!

Why "Wall Street"? Did you know that the New York Stock Exchange (NYSE) began in 1792 as a group of stockbrokers meeting to trade stocks under a buttonwood tree? It's true! The tree has long since vanished, but it is believed to have stood somewhere near what is now 11 Wall Street, the current location of the NYSE. And by the way, Wall Street was named for the boundary stockade, or wall, that Dutch colonists built in 1653 for protection from English colonists and American Indians.

A stock certificate

BIOGRAPHY

Andrew Carnegie

(1835–1919)

Andrew Carnegie was born in Scotland. He immigrated to Pennsylvania at age 12. Carnegie constantly impressed his employers because he worked hard and learned quickly. One employer loaned Carnegie $600 to make his first investment in a company. He soon became wealthy by making wise investment and business choices. Unlike many other successful businesspeople of his era, Carnegie still lived very simply. He did not believe in showing off wealth. After retiring, Carnegie devoted his time to charitable efforts. In what ways was Andrew Carnegie different from other successful businesspeople of his time?

Business Leaders

Entrepreneurs and business leaders were some of the most widely respected members of American society in the late 1800s. Many Americans looked up to these self-made, wealthy individuals. Political leaders often praised prosperous businessmen as examples of American hard work, talent, and success.

Andrew Carnegie was one of the most admired business leaders of the late 1800s. While working for the Pennsylvania Railroad as a young man, Carnegie borrowed money and invested it in iron mills and bridge-building businesses. His investments did so well that Carnegie left the railroad company in 1865. "I was no longer merely an official working for others . . . ," he wrote, "but a full-fledged business man."

In 1873 Carnegie focused his efforts on steel production. He expanded his business by buying out his competitors when steel prices were low. Carnegie never held a monopoly on steel production in the United States. However, by 1901 Carnegie's mills were producing more steel than all of Great Britain's steel mills combined. He used a method called **vertical integration**—owning the businesses involved in each step of a manufacturing process. To lower his production costs, Carnegie bought the iron ore mines, the coal fields, and the railroads needed to supply and support his steel mills.

Another powerful businessman, **John D. Rockefeller**, started out as a bookkeeper. By age 21 he was a partner in a wholesale business, and he soon decided to start an oil-refining company. By 1870 Rockefeller's Standard Oil Company was the country's largest oil refiner. Like Carnegie, Rockefeller used vertical integration to improve production and profits. Standard Oil made its own barrels and controlled most of the pipelines, tank cars, and storage buildings it used. Many railroads offered lower rates to Standard Oil to attract its valuable shipping business. At times Rockefeller even got railroads to agree not to provide service to his competitors.

Rockefeller's company also used **horizontal integration**—owning all the businesses in a certain field. By 1880 he controlled some 90 percent of the oil-refining businesses in the United States. This level of control gave Rockefeller's companies a monopoly on the American oil-refining industry. Rockefeller used consolidation to cut his costs. He also formed a **trust**—a grouping together of a number of companies under one board of directors. To earn higher profits, trusts often tried to get rid of competition in their industry and to control production. These practices resulted in higher prices for buyers. Rockefeller explained, "The day of combination [trusts] is here to stay. Individualism has gone, never to return."

✔ **Reading Check: Summarizing** Describe the economic situation in the United States during the late 1800s.

Vertical and Horizontal Integration

Business methods such as horizontal and vertical integration helped corporations make huge profits.

Vertical Integration
Companies owned by U.S. Steel

Steel Mills

Railroads and Ships

Coal Mines

Iron Mines

Horizontal Integration
Competitors bought by Standard Oil Company

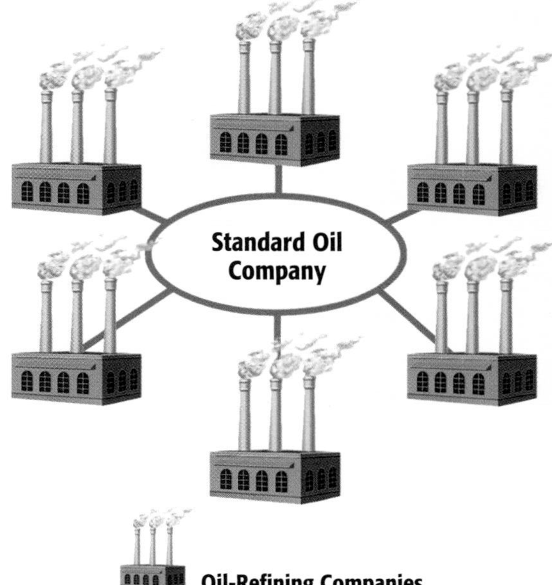

Oil-Refining Companies

Visualizing History

1. **Economics** Why would horizontal or vertical integration help a company?
2. **Connecting to Today** Would such business practices be allowed today? Explain your answer.

Social Darwinism and Philanthropy

Many people who favored free enterprise also believed in social Darwinism. This view of society was based loosely on scientist Charles Darwin's theory of natural selection. Darwin thought that species evolved by adapting to their environments over long periods of time. Social Darwinists said that "survival of the fittest" also determined who would succeed in human society. Sociologist Herbert Spencer even argued that government regulation of businesses hurt the "natural" economic order.

Many business leaders agreed. John D. Rockefeller declared, "The growth of large business is merely a survival of the fittest." Some wealthy business leaders argued that it was the poor person's responsibility to work hard for a better life. However, others claimed that the wealthy had a duty to aid the poor. These leaders practiced philanthropy—giving money to the needy. For example, during his lifetime Andrew Carnegie donated more than $350 million to charity. By the late 1800s, charities had received millions of dollars from philanthropists.

✔ **Reading Check: Analyzing Information** Did all business leaders become philanthropists? Explain your answer.

Interpreting Political Cartoons

Powerful trusts Some cartoonists portrayed trusts as oversized bullies taking advantage of consumers. ***What actions are the trusts taking in this cartoon?***

The Antitrust Movement

Critics of big business said that unfair business practices were responsible for the successes of many large companies. For example, big corporations often used their size and power to eliminate competition by driving smaller competitors out of business. Some trusts also gained monopolies on certain products or services. Members of the trust would then agree to match one another's prices on goods to avoid competition.

Many citizens and small-business owners wanted the government to control monopolies and trusts. People who favored trusts responded that trusts were more efficient and gave the consumer dependable products and services. One newspaper editor declared that "the right to cooperate is as unquestionable as the right to compete."

Many in Congress were sympathetic to the interests of big business. However, they could not ignore the voters' concerns. As Senator John Sherman explained, "You must heed [pay attention to] their appeal [request]. . . . Society is now disturbed by forces never felt before." In July 1890 Congress passed the **Sherman Antitrust Act**, which outlawed monopolies and trusts that restrained trade. However, the act did not clearly define what a trust was in legal terms. The antitrust laws were thus difficult to enforce, and corporations and trusts continued to grow in power.

✔ **Reading Check: Sequencing** How did antitrust feelings lead to the Sherman Antitrust Act?

Section 1 Review

go.hrw.com Homework Practice Online
keyword: SC3 HP19

1. **Define** and explain:
   - patents
   - free enterprise
   - entrepreneurs
   - corporations
   - vertical integration
   - horizontal integration
   - trust
2. **Identify** and explain:
   - Second Industrial Revolution
   - Bessemer process
   - Orville and Wilbur Wright
   - Thomas Alva Edison
   - Andrew Carnegie
   - John D. Rockefeller
   - Sherman Antitrust Act
3. **Summarizing** Copy the chart below. Use it to list the developments that took place in the steel, oil, and electric-power industries during the Second Industrial Revolution.

Industry	Developments
steel	
oil	
electricity	

4. **Finding the Main Idea**
   a. What are vertical integration and horizontal integration, and how did business leaders use these methods to organize their corporations?
   b. Why did some people oppose business monopolies, and what did these people do to control them?
5. **Writing and Critical Thinking**
   Supporting a Point of View Imagine that you are an editor of a magazine in the 1880s. Write a short editorial explaining what you think the key business innovation of the time is and why.
   Consider the following:
   - uses of steel, oil, and electricity
   - free enterprise and entrepreneurs
   - vertical and horizontal integration, monopolies, and trusts

Section 2

Industrial Workers

Read to Discover

1. How did the Second Industrial Revolution affect American workers?
2. Why did workers form labor unions, and how were they organized?
3. How did major labor strikes affect workers?

Define

- collective bargaining
- anarchists

Identify

- Frederick W. Taylor
- Knights of Labor
- Terence V. Powderly
- Mary Harris Jones
- American Federation of Labor
- Samuel Gompers
- Haymarket Riot
- Homestead strike
- Pullman strike

WHY IT MATTERS TODAY

Workers around the world use unions to fight for their rights. Use CNNfyi.com or other **current events** sources to learn about labor unions in another country. Record your findings in your journal.

The Story Continues

At the beginning of the Second Industrial Revolution, skilled workers called puddlers turned hot liquid iron into steel. Puddlers' skills made them valuable employees. However, as new technologies were developed, puddlers found themselves being replaced by machines. Like many other skilled workers, puddlers began searching for ways to increase their bargaining power with employers.

Attention Workingmen!

GREAT

MASS-MEETING

TO-NIGHT, at 7.30 o'clock,

AT THE

HAYMARKET, Randolph St, Bet. Desplaines and Halsted.

Good Speakers will be present to denounce the latest atrocious act of the police, the shooting of our fellow-workmen yesterday afternoon.

Workingmen Arm Yourselves and Appear in Full Force!

THE EXECUTIVE COMMITTEE

Achtung, Arbeiter!

Große

Massen-Versammlung

Heute Abend, ½8 Uhr, auf dem

Heumarkt, Randolph-Straße, zwischen Desplaines. u. Halsted-Str.

Gute Redner werden den neuesten Schurkenstreich der Polizei, indem sie gestern Nachmittag unsere Brüder erschoß, geißeln.

Arbeiter, bewaffnet Euch und erscheint massenhaft!

Das Executiv-Comite.

This announcement for a union meeting was written in both English and German.

The New Workplace

During the Second Industrial Revolution, machines run by unskilled workers took the places of many skilled craftspeople. These low-paid workers needed little training and could easily be replaced. As a result, untrained workers feared that complaining about pay or working conditions would cost them their jobs.

As machines became more widely used in industry, factories moved toward specialization. Specialization is having workers perform a single step in the production process again and again. This approach lowered costs and raised production. Such results encouraged managers to seek even more efficient production methods.

Interpreting the Visual Record

Knights of Labor The Knights of Labor was one of the few unions to accept African Americans. Here union member Frank J. Farrell (left) is shown introducing union president Terence V. Powderly (center). ***How might accepting members of different races be beneficial to the union?***

In the early 1880s **Frederick W. Taylor**, an engineer with a steel company, worked to find ways to increase production and lower costs. In 1911 he published *The Principles of Scientific Management* and established efficiency studies as a basic part of American industry. Taylor's idea of scientific management defined workers more as parts of the production process than as people. This approach led many factory managers to ignore unhealthy working conditions. More workers got hurt as they used more machines and were pushed to work faster. Companies rarely took responsibility for work-related injuries. As conditions grew worse, workers looked for ways to bring about change.

✔ **Reading Check: Identifying Cause and Effect** Why did companies begin to use scientific management, and how did it affect workers?

Labor Unions

To improve working conditions, workers formed labor unions. Union leaders tried to win better wages and labor conditions for all workers in a factory or industry. When workers acted collectively, or together, they had a much greater chance of winning labor disputes with employers. This method is called **collective bargaining**. Most employers opposed collective bargaining. One company president said, "I shall never give in. I would rather go out of business."

Founded by Uriah Stephens, the **Knights of Labor** was a union originally set up like a secret society. During an economic downturn in the early 1870s, the union built a network of local groups. Stephens said the goal of the Knights was to "include men and women of every creed and color." In 1879 **Terence V. Powderly** became the leader of the Knights. He ended the organization's secrecy, making it the first truly national labor union in the United States. Under Powderly's leadership, the Knights worked for improvements for workers. The union's goals included an eight-hour workday, equal pay for equal work for men and women, and an end to child labor. It also wanted the government to regulate trusts. Unlike most unions at the time, the Knights had both skilled and unskilled workers.

Many women joined the Knights of Labor and took active roles in it. Union organizer **Mary Harris Jones** was called Mother Jones by the workers whose rights she fought to protect. She organized many strikes among workers, such as one group of poorly paid Virginia miners whose lives were very difficult. Jones described their living conditions.

Free Find:
Mother Jones
After reading about Mary Harris Jones on the **Holt Researcher CD–ROM**, write a short speech she might have given to workers that draws upon her life experiences.

“In some of these [company] camps the miners are forced to pay as much as $9 a barrel for sugar, 18 cents a pound for fat pork, and $8 to $10 a month rent for a company shack, the roof of which is so poor that when it rains the bed is moved from place to place in the attempt to find a dry spot. Many a miner works his whole life and never handles a cent of money.”

—Mary Harris Jones, *The Speeches and Writings of Mother Jones*

Analyzing Primary Sources

Drawing Inferences and Conclusions Why do you think some miners never got to handle any money?

The **American Federation of Labor** (AFL), led by **Samuel Gompers**, took a different approach. Unlike the Knights, the AFL organized individual national unions such as the mineworkers' and the steelworkers' unions. In addition, the AFL limited its membership to skilled workers. This practice gave the union great bargaining power but left out most workers. Gompers said that the AFL tried to “accomplish the best results in improving the conditions of the working people . . . today and tomorrow.” The AFL tried to get better wages, hours, and working conditions for its members. By 1890 the AFL had more members than the Knights did.

✔ **Reading Check: Summarizing** How were the national unions organized?

The Haymarket Riot

By 1886, other unions were gaining strength as well. In May, thousands of union members in Chicago went on strike for an eight-hour workday. Two strikers were killed in a fight with police. The next night workers met at Haymarket Square to protest the killings. When police came to break up the crowd, someone threw a dynamite bomb. Seven officers and one civilian were killed, and some 60 other officers were wounded. The police responded by firing into the crowd. Several people were killed, and about 100 others were injured. The terrible event became known as the **Haymarket Riot**.

An investigation led to the arrest and conviction of eight **anarchists**—people who oppose all forms of government—on charges of conspiracy. One of them had a Knights of Labor membership card. Powderly and the other Knights' leaders never supported the strike or the Haymarket protest. However, several local chapters of the Knights had. Public opinion soon linked the Knights to the Haymarket Riot and its violence. News of the incident caused the membership in the Knights to fall quickly.

✔ **Reading Check: Identifying Cause and Effect** What led to the Haymarket Riot, and how did it affect labor unions?

Interpreting the Visual Record

A deadly riot The bombing at Haymarket Square stunned both police and demonstrators and caused many injuries and deaths. ***How does this scene depict the violence and confusion of the riot?***

The Homestead and Pullman Strikes

Unions continued to use strikes to try to improve working conditions. However, business owners sometimes pushed unions into striking in the hope of getting government support to break up a union. One such conflict happened at one of Andrew Carnegie's steel plants.

Workers had always gotten along well with managers at the Carnegie Steel Company in Homestead, Pennsylvania. This situation changed in 1889 when Henry Frick became company chairman. In 1892, union members protested Frick's plan to add new machinery that would replace workers. When an agreement could not be reached, Frick set out to break the union and cut costs. He announced that the company would try to work out labor contracts with individual workers, not the union.

On June 29 the **Homestead strike** began. Frick locked workers out of the plant. He refused to bargain with the union or allow union members back to work. The workers responded by seizing control of the town of Homestead. Frick then hired private detectives from the Pinkerton agency to break the power of the union by force.

On July 6, the Pinkerton detectives tried to enter the steelworks. Gunfire broke out and nine workers and seven detectives died as a result of the battle that followed. After a long standoff, the outnumbered and

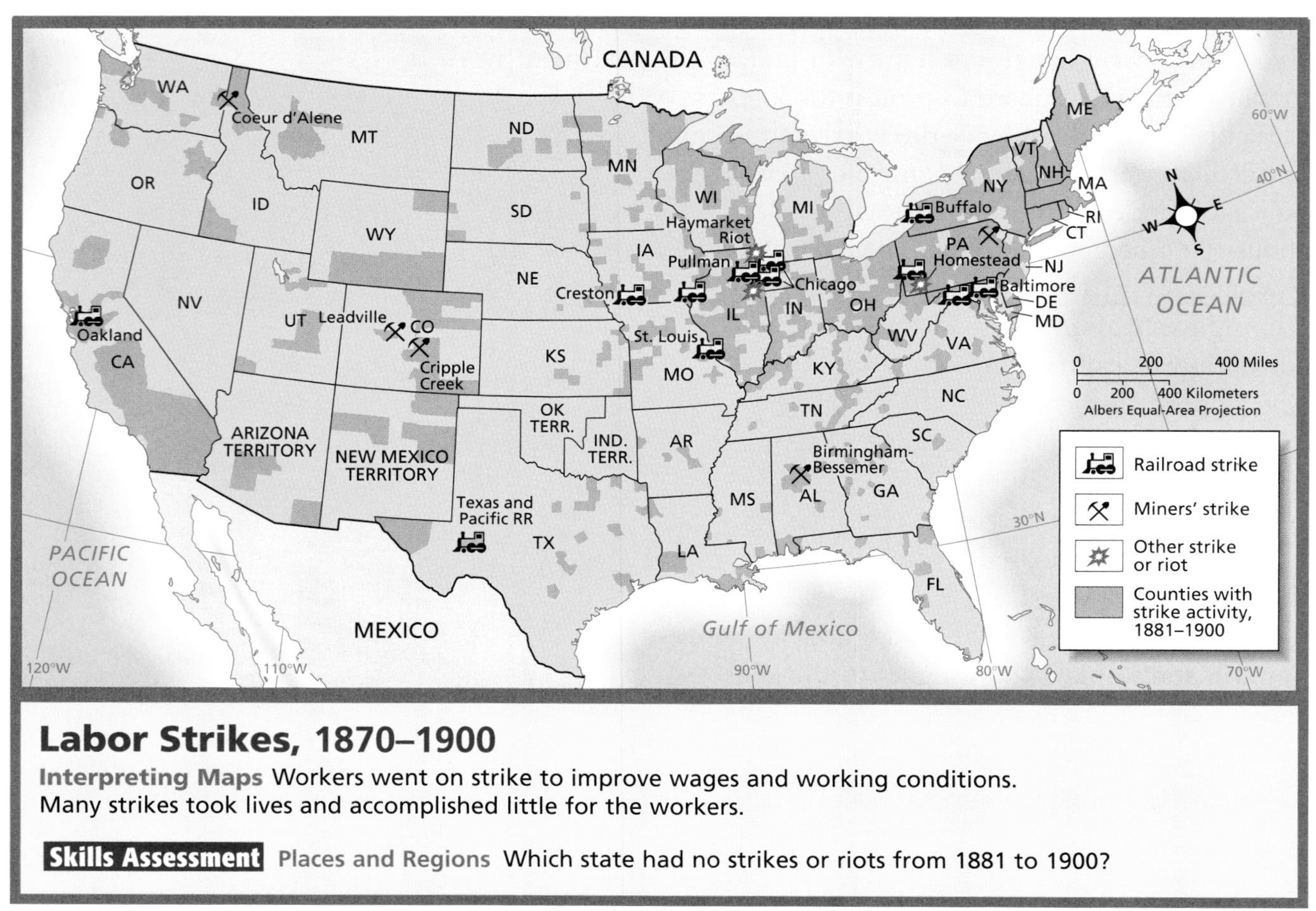

Labor Strikes, 1870–1900

Interpreting Maps Workers went on strike to improve wages and working conditions. Many strikes took lives and accomplished little for the workers.

Skills Assessment **Places and Regions** Which state had no strikes or riots from 1881 to 1900?

trapped detectives surrendered. They were then marched through the streets and insulted by crowds. Pennsylvania's governor called out the state militia to restore order. The strike continued for four more months. However, the union was eventually defeated. Frick sent a message to Carnegie, "Our victory is now complete."

Another major strike took place at George Pullman's Palace Car Company. Most of the company's workers lived in the company town of Pullman, Illinois. These workers had to pay higher rents and utility costs than people in nearby towns.

During the economic depression that began in 1893, Pullman laid off about half of the company's workers. He then cut the wages of those who were left. In May 1894, workers protesting the wage cuts began the **Pullman strike**. Support for the strike quickly spread throughout the railroad industry. The American Railway Union, headed by Eugene V. Debs, refused to work on trains carrying Pullman cars. By July, this strike had stopped traffic on most midwestern rail lines.

The majority of trains in the United States carried Pullman cars. The strike against George Pullman's company thus proved crippling for railroad traffic.

Railroad officials then ordered the Pullman cars to be attached to U.S. mail cars. Workers who stopped Pullman cars could then be charged with the federal crime of interfering with the U.S. mail. The federal government backed the railroad companies in this move. Despite the protest of Illinois's governor, President Grover Cleveland sent federal troops to Chicago.

The U.S. attorney general then used the Sherman Antitrust Act to stop the strikers. He obtained a court order stating that the strike was interfering with interstate trade. Debs was arrested for violating the court order. Government support for big business and defeats like that suffered in the Pullman strike set the labor movement back for several years.

✔ **Reading Check: Evaluating** What were the effects of early major strikes on workers and companies?

Section 2 Review

go.hrw.com **Homework Practice Online**
keyword: SC3 HP19

1. **Define** and explain:
   - collective bargaining
   - anarchists

2. **Identify** and explain:
   - Frederick W. Taylor
   - Knights of Labor
   - Terence V. Powderly
   - Mary Harris Jones
   - American Federation of Labor
   - Samuel Gompers
   - Haymarket Riot
   - Homestead strike
   - Pullman strike

3. **Analyzing Information** Copy the diagram below. Use it to show the effects that the Second Industrial Revolution had on businesses, workers, and the labor movement.

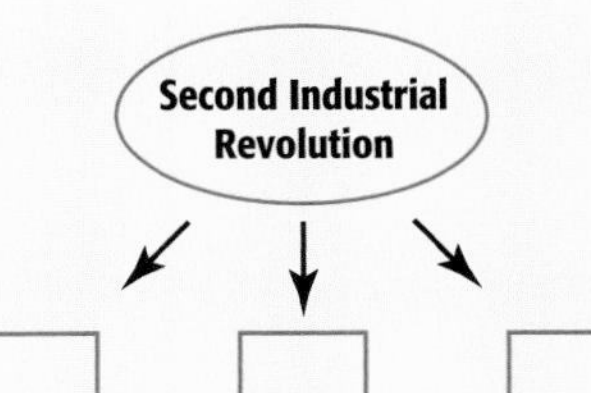

4. **Finding the Main Idea**
   a. Why were the Knights of Labor and the American Federation of Labor formed, and how did they operate?
   b. How did the major strikes of the late 1800s affect American workers?

5. **Writing and Critical Thinking**
   Analyzing Information Imagine that you are a newspaper journalist during the Haymarket Riot. Write a short article describing the events and outcome of the riot.
   Consider the following:
   - events that took place during the riot
   - connection to the Knights of Labor
   - public reaction to the riot

Section 3

Immigrants and the Cities

Read to Discover

1. Why did immigrants come to the United States, and what countries did they emigrate from during the late 1800s?
2. How did some Americans try to limit immigration?
3. How did city residents try to deal with the challenges of urban life?

Define

- old immigrants
- new immigrants
- steerage
- benevolent societies
- suburbs
- settlement houses

Identify

- Chinese Exclusion Act
- Immigration Restriction League
- Hull House
- Jane Addams
- Ellen Gates Starr

WHY IT MATTERS TODAY

People still immigrate to the United States today. Use CNNfyi.com or other **current events** sources to learn about today's immigration trends. Record your findings in your journal.

Asian immigrants in the United States in the 1800s

The Story Continues

Lee Chew lived in China. He was a poor peasant working on his father's farm with little hope of ever owning his own land. When a man from his village "returned with unlimited wealth, which he had obtained in the country of the American wizards," Lee decided to leave China. Like millions of other immigrants to the United States, he left behind everything and everyone he knew. He traveled to a strange new land, carrying little but his dream of success.

Increased Immigration

During the late 1800s immigrants like Lee continued to come to the United States by the millions. However, immigration patterns began to change. Immigrants who had come to the United States before the 1880s were mostly from Britain, Germany, Ireland, and Scandinavia. Most were Protestants, except for the Irish and some Germans who were Catholic. Many of them spoke English. These people, often called **old immigrants**, frequently settled outside cities and became farmers.

During the 1880s the number of immigrants to the United States increased dramatically. Many of these so-called **new immigrants** came from southern and eastern Europe. The jobs created by the Second Industrial Revolution attracted many people.

Other groups, including Armenians and Jews, were escaping political and religious persecution. New immigrants brought cultural practices with them that were unfamiliar to many native-born Americans. They also held diverse religious beliefs, such as Eastern Orthodox Christianity, Roman Catholicism, and Judaism.

Immigrants usually faced a difficult journey to America. Most of them bought the cheapest tickets available. They traveled in **steerage**, an area below deck on a ship's lower levels near where the steering mechanisms for the ship were located. In these cramped conditions, passengers often experienced overcrowding and seasickness. Some passengers even died from disease.

When immigrants reached the United States, they had to go first to immigration processing centers. In 1890 the federal government began assuming control of these immigration centers. One of the largest centers opened in 1892 on Ellis Island in New York Harbor. At these centers, officials interviewed immigrants to decide whether to let them enter the country. Officials also conducted physical examinations, deporting any person who carried a disease such as tuberculosis.

Ellis Island became so well known that songs were written about it.

✔ **Reading Check: Contrasting** How did immigration patterns change in the late 1800s?

Immigrant Life

Immigrants drawn to the United States by stories of wealth and quick success often found that the reality was more difficult. One girl described her adjustment to her new home.

> **"[I dreamed] of the golden stairs leading to the top of the American palace where father was supposed to live. [I] went 'home' to . . . an ugly old tenement in the heart of the Lower East Side. There were stairs to climb but they were not golden."**
>
> —Miriam Shomer Zunser, *Yesterday: A Memoir of a Russian Jewish Family*

Most immigrants settled in cities, where unskilled industrial jobs were plentiful but low paying. With little money or knowledge of English, these unskilled jobs were the only work most immigrants could get at first. Entire families often worked to survive. Despite such challenges, many immigrants found opportunities in the United States that they never had at home.

Many immigrants worked hard to build communities by moving into neighborhoods with others who shared their nationality. There they could hear their native languages, eat familiar foods, and keep their customs. Some immigrant communities formed **benevolent societies**, which offered help in cases of death, sickness, and unemployment. At that time, there were few national government agencies to provide such aid.

That's Interesting!

The People's Statue The Statue of Liberty was a gift from France to the United States. To make the trip to America the huge 151-foot-tall statue had to be separated into 350 pieces. For four months after reaching its new home, the statue stayed in pieces. There were parts of the statue throughout New York. The torch lay in Madison Square. Visitors even climbed inside it! Some people wanted to keep the statue in pieces. Others, such as publisher Joseph Pulitzer, set about raising funds to build the pedestal on which the statue would be built. Pulitzer asked his readers to give any money they could. Although many people donated less than a dollar, the funds were raised. The statue was put back together and raised again in 1886.

Immigrant families such as this one often worked together in sweatshops making clothing.

Many immigrant groups published newspapers in their own languages. They also founded schools, clubs, and places of worship to preserve their beliefs and customs. New immigrants also eagerly embraced American culture. They wanted their children to learn English and adopt American customs. While immigrants' lives were often difficult, they were usually able to build a better future for their families.

✔ **Reading Check: Summarizing** What steps did new immigrants take to help themselves and others?

Opposition to Immigration

Anti-immigrant feelings grew along with the increase in immigration in the late 1800s. People opposed to immigration believed that the new immigrants' poverty and lack of education would harm American society. Nativism—the favoring of native-born residents over the foreign-born—had started in the 1840s and 1850s with opposition to Irish Catholic newcomers. Many nativists held racial and religious prejudices against immigrants from Asia and southern and eastern Europe in particular.

Some labor unions also opposed immigration. They feared that immigrants willing to work for low wages would take jobs away from union members. Some business leaders favored immigration because the supply of new low-wage workers kept labor costs down. One businessman described the benefits of immigration. "Their home countries have borne [paid] the expense of rearing them . . . and then America . . . reaps whatever profits there are" from their work.

In some places nativists rioted violently against immigrants. Other nativists called for laws to stop or limit immigration. In 1882 Congress passed the **Chinese Exclusion Act**. This law banned Chinese people from coming to the United States for 10 years. The law marked the first time people of a specific nationality were banned from entering the country. Congress later extended the ban into the 1900s.

To further decrease the flow of immigrants, nativists formed the **Immigration Restriction League** in 1894. The league wanted all immigrants to prove that they could read and write in some language before being allowed into the country. Congress passed a law requiring a literacy test for immigrants in 1897. However, President Cleveland vetoed the bill, calling it "narrow, and un-American."

Despite opposition, the new immigrants played a key role in industrial growth in the late 1800s. They did much of the low-paying work on U.S. buildings, highways, and railroads that drove rapid growth.

✔ **Reading Check: Analyzing Information** Why did nativists oppose immigration, and what steps did they take against it?

Research on the ROM

Free Find:
Immigrant Voices
After reading the selection of immigrant stories on the **Holt Researcher CD–ROM**, write your own story about what you might have experienced as an immigrant coming to the United States.

 The Growth of Urban Communities

During the late 1800s immigrants and native-born Americans moved to cities in record numbers. In 1850 only six cities in the United States had populations greater than 100,000. By 1900 there were more than 35 such cities. In midwestern cities, in particular, the population grew rapidly during those years. Chicago's population, for example, rose from 30,000 in 1850 to 1.7 million in 1900. By 1900 about 40 percent of Americans lived in urban areas. This percentage continued to climb in the early 1900s.

Some city residents were businesspeople and skilled workers. But many more were poor laborers. Farming troubles drove large numbers of people to the cities looking for work. Author Henry Blake Fuller said Chicago's new residents had "come for the common avowed object [declared goal] of making money."

City residents often started organizations to improve their communities and bring their neighborhoods together. For example, African American religious groups organized and aided urban communities. African American ministers often served as both political and spiritual leaders in black neighborhoods. One report from a Baptist group described the ministers as "a class of men who . . . have won the confidence, love, and respect of their people."

✔ **Reading Check: Finding the Main Idea** Why did cities grow so quickly in the late 1800s, and how did people respond to the problems that resulted from this growth?

Interpreting the Visual Record

Urban crowding *Cities such as Chicago grew rapidly in the late 1800s, thanks to immigration, migration, and industrial development.* ***What aspects of this scene show the size of the city?***

CONNECTING TO THE ARTS

Central Park In 1857 Frederick Law Olmsted was appointed superintendent of New York City's Central Park, the first major public park in the United States. Olmsted wanted the park to be a place where city-dwellers could relax surrounded by nature. The park's design contained many trees and several bodies of water. In addition, Central Park offered activities such as horseback riding, ice-skating, boating, and baseball. Central Park proved to be very popular, drawing an average of 30,000 visitors a day for a total of 10 million in 1871. It remains a popular destination today for New York City's residents as well as its tourists. **Why do you think Central Park is so popular?**

Urban Changes and Problems

Organizations such as churches and social groups helped make life easier for many city residents. New technologies also brought improvements to urban centers. Engineers built taller buildings by using steel-beam frames for support. Elisha Otis's steam-powered elevators carried people up and down the floors of these so-called skyscrapers. Small local stores gave way to department stores, which offered a wider variety of goods in one place.

Cities sometimes grew too fast. Overcrowding and lack of sanitation resulted, leading to disease and poor health. Poor people, who often lived in run-down housing, suffered the most, as Jacob Riis described.

"Nine lived in two rooms, one about ten feet square that served as parlor, bedroom, and eating room, the other a small hall room made into a kitchen. The rent was . . . more than a week's wages for the husband."

—Jacob Riis, *How the Other Half Lives*

Analyzing Primary Sources

Drawing Inferences and Conclusions What do you think was difficult about the living conditions described?

Many cities began building parks to preserve green spaces for recreation. Cities also offered libraries, museums, theaters, and the best schools and hospitals. However, some people wanted private space. Many middle-class Americans chose to live in quieter areas where they could own homes. They moved to **suburbs**—neighborhoods outside of downtown areas. Mass transit networks of streetcars, subways, and commuter trains made living in the suburbs and working in the cities possible.

✔ **Reading Check: Summarizing** What developments eased the problems that arose from the rapid growth of cities?

Settlement Houses

Few government programs existed to help the urban poor in the late 1800s. However, many private aid organizations assisted poor people. In addition, **settlement houses**—neighborhood centers in poor areas staffed by professionals and volunteers—offered education, recreation, and social activities.

Settlement houses began in Great Britain and then became common in the United States. Janie Porter Barrett established an African American settlement house in Hampton, Virginia. The most famous settlement house was Chicago's **Hull House**, founded by **Jane Addams** and **Ellen Gates Starr** in 1889. Like many upper-class women of their era, they had received a college education. However, they found few job opportunities open to them. Addams wanted to help the poor. To reach this goal, she and Starr opened Hull House in a run-down building in a poor Chicago neighborhood. The work at Hull House focused most on the needs of families, especially immigrant families. Hull House served as a model for other settlement houses.

Addams and her staff took part in a variety of activities. They started the first kindergarten and public playground in Chicago. They also taught classes in English and U.S. government to help immigrants become citizens. In addition, the staff worked for reform of child-labor laws and the adoption of an eight-hour workday for women. Many of the women involved in running Hull House later became active in a variety of national reform movements.

✔ **Reading Check: Drawing Inferences and Conclusions** How might working at Hull House have prepared women to seek national reform?

Jane Addams, who remained active in reform movements her entire life, won the Nobel Peace Prize in 1931.

Free Find:
Jane Addams
After reading about Jane Addams on the **Holt Researcher CD–ROM**, create a list of community services you would provide if you worked in a settlement house.

Section 3 Review

go.hrw.com Homework Practice Online
keyword: SC3 HP19

1. **Define** and explain:
   - old immigrants
   - new immigrants
   - steerage
   - benevolent societies
   - suburbs
   - settlement houses

2. **Identify** and explain:
   - Chinese Exclusion Act
   - Immigration Restriction League
   - Hull House
   - Jane Addams
   - Ellen Gates Starr

3. **Summarizing** Copy the diagram below. Use it to show how city residents organized to deal with the challenges of urban life.

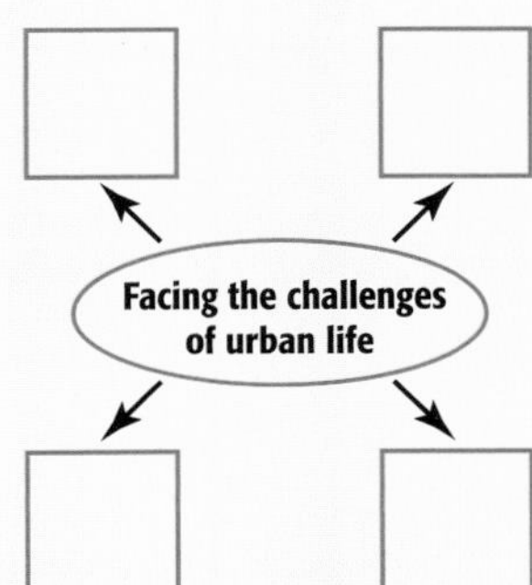

4. **Finding the Main Idea**
   a. What led immigrants to come to the United States, and what regions did they come from in the late 1800s?
   b. What were the nativists' attitudes toward new immigrants, and what actions arose from their bias?

5. **Writing and Critical Thinking**
   Supporting a Point of View Imagine that you are an immigrant to the United States in 1885. Write a letter to your family back home, telling them about your good and bad experiences. Try to persuade them to join you.
   Consider the following:
   - the journey to the United States
   - adjusting to a new country
   - support systems

Section 4

Populism

Read to Discover

1. What effects did industrialization have on farmers, and what actions did farmers take to bring about change?
2. Why did farmers want changes in the money supply?
3. What were the political and economic goals of the National Grange and the Populist Party?

WHY IT MATTERS TODAY

The United States has been off the gold standard since 1971. The Federal Reserve, founded in 1913, currently maintains the stability of the country's monetary system. Use CNNfyi.com or other **current events** sources to learn how "The Fed" works. Record your findings in your journal.

Define

- free coinage
- gold standard

Identify

- Oliver Hudson Kelley
- National Grange
- Interstate Commerce Act
- Interstate Commerce Commission
- William Jennings Bryan
- Benjamin Harrison
- Sherman Silver Purchase Act
- Farmers' Alliances
- Populist Party
- James B. Weaver

The Story Continues

Many farm families faced hard times in the late 1800s.

In the late 1800s many farmers blamed their economic hardships on the railroads. Frank Norris's 1901 novel *The Octopus* offers the farmers' point of view. In the story, high railroad rates threaten to leave Farmer Dyke with no profit from his harvest. He had borrowed money to raise his crops. Unless he pays it back, the bank will foreclose. Dyke realizes that "not only would the Railroad devour every morsel of his profits, but also it would take from him his home."

Rural Unrest and the National Grange

From 1860 to 1900 the U.S. population more than doubled. During this same time, the number of farms tripled. Many farmers borrowed money to buy land and machinery. With new machines, farmers in 1900 could produce a bushel of wheat almost 20 times faster than in 1830. However, the combination of more farms and greater productivity led to overproduction, which in turn led to lower prices for crops. Many farmers responded by increasing crop production, causing even lower prices.

Agricultural Regions, 1900

Interpreting Maps The diverse climates and soils of the United States enabled farmers to grow a wide variety of crops.

Skills Assessment **Human Systems** What types of agricultural products did people raise along the western coast of the United States?

Corn was a major American crop.

As their incomes decreased, many farmers found it more difficult to pay their bills, which the cost of new machinery had often increased. Farmers who could not make their mortgage payments lost their farms and homes due to bank foreclosures. Many of these hard-hit families became tenant farmers, while others could not even afford to rent land and thus became farm workers. By 1880 one fourth of all farms were rented by tenants, and the number kept growing.

Many farmers blamed businesspeople—wholesalers, brokers, grain buyers, and particularly railroad owners—for profiting at their expense. An editor of a North Carolina farm journal expressed this view.

"There is something radically wrong. . . . The railroads have never been so prosperous. . . . The banks have never done a better . . . business. . . . Manufacturing enterprises have never made more money. . . . Towns and cities flourish and 'boom,' . . . and yet agriculture languishes [declines]."

—Leonidas Polk, quoted in *The Shaping of Modern America, 1877–1916,* by Vincent P. DeSantis

Analyzing Primary Sources

Drawing Inferences and Conclusions What does Polk seem to say about the way that railroads, banks, and manufacturers deal with farmers?

As economic conditions for farmers grew worse, they began to organize associations as workers had done. In 1866 government official

The Grangers formed farm cooperatives to overcome lower crop prices and the cost of maintaining expensive new farm machinery such as this tractor.

Oliver Hudson Kelley toured the South for the U.S. Department of Agriculture. Kelley saw firsthand how the country's farmers suffered. After that tour, Kelley and several government clerks founded the National Grange of the Patrons of Husbandry in 1867. The **National Grange** was a social and educational organization dedicated to improving farmers' lives. Membership grew rapidly as local chapters were quickly started.

Granges formed organizations called cooperatives to buy goods in bulk, or large quantities, at lower prices. Farmers also formed cooperative groups to sell their crops at higher prices. Unfortunately, these cooperatives were often run by people who were not experienced in business. In addition, banks, merchants, and railroads often united to work against these cooperatives. As a result, most of the cooperatives did poorly.

✔ **Reading Check: Finding the Main Idea** How did new agricultural technologies affect farmers?

Fighting the Railroads

The National Grange soon changed its focus from economics to politics. Members campaigned for political candidates who supported farmers' interests. The Grange also called for laws to regulate rates for the use of railroads and grain elevators. In a few states, the Grange backed laws regulating railroads, which benefited farmers when shipping their crops.

The issue of railroad regulation by individual states came before the U.S. Supreme Court in 1877. The Court ruled in *Munn* v. *Illinois* that state governments could regulate the railroads and other businesses that affect the public interest. However, the Supreme Court modified this position in 1886. In *Wabash* v. *Illinois,* the Court said that state governments could not regulate traffic that crossed state boundaries. Only the federal government could regulate interstate traffic.

In February 1887 Congress passed the **Interstate Commerce Act**, which provided some consistent national regulations on trade between states. It also created the **Interstate Commerce Commission** (ICC) to ensure that railroads charged fair rates and did not favor big shippers. However, the commission lacked the power to enforce its regulations. In addition, the courts gave the agency little help when it appealed to them for assistance.

✔ **Reading Check: Analyzing Information** How did the government regulate railroads, and how successful were these efforts?

The Free Silver Debate

Railroad rates were not the only concern that farmers faced. Their problems usually involved money issues, such as credit, debt, and low crop prices. Many farmers thought that help would come only from national legislation that would affect the money supply.

Since 1792 the United States had allowed **free coinage**, meaning that both gold and silver were made into coins. Paper money was worth a specific amount of gold or silver. The Coinage Act of 1873 placed the United States on a strict **gold standard**, under which only gold could back U.S. currency. Tied to the gold standard, the money supply tended to grow more slowly than the country's population. This situation led to deflation—a drop in the money supply combined with falling prices.

Farmers favored coining silver to create inflation—an increase in the money supply and a rise in prices. They hoped that rising crop prices would then increase their income. During the late 1870s many farmers began backing political candidates who wanted free silver coinage. One such politician was **William Jennings Bryan** of Nebraska. In 1878 Congress passed the Bland-Allison Act, allowing limited silver coinage.

A new political party, the Greenback Party, favored inflating the money supply with paper dollars not backed by gold or silver. However, the two major parties largely ignored the money issue in the 1880 and 1884 presidential elections. In 1880 Republican James A. Garfield won the presidency over Democrat Winfield Scott Hancock in a close election. In 1884 Democrat Grover Cleveland defeated Republican James G. Blaine in another close contest. The Republicans finally made continued coinage of silver an issue in the 1888 elections. President Cleveland lost his bid for re-election that year to Republican **Benjamin Harrison**. After the election, the Republican-controlled Congress passed the **Sherman Silver Purchase Act.** The act increased the amount of silver the government bought for coinage, but the money supply did not increase enough to satisfy silver supporters.

✔ **Reading Check: Finding the Main Idea** Why did farmers want free coinage of silver?

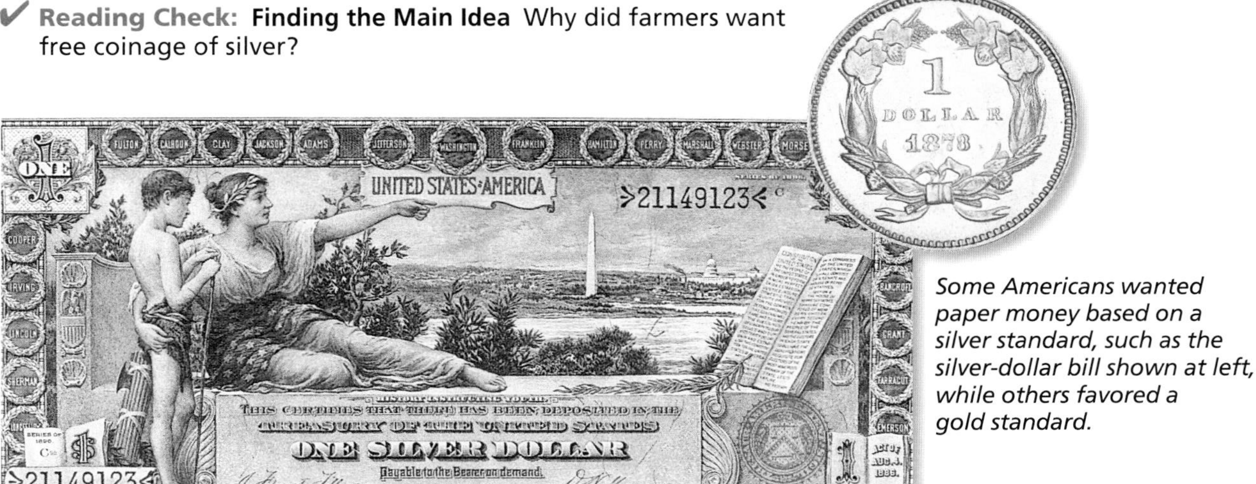

Some Americans wanted paper money based on a silver standard, such as the silver-dollar bill shown at left, while others favored a gold standard.

Mary Elizabeth Lease published her views on populism in an influential book, The Problem of Civilization Solved.

The Populist Party

Many farmers formed their own political organizations to increase their power. These groups became known as the **Farmers' Alliances**. The Texas alliance started in 1877 and quickly grew to become the Grand State Alliance in 1879. Membership soared. The Colored Farmers' Alliance had more than 1 million members of its own. The Farmers' Alliances were more politically active than the Grange had been. They focused their efforts on getting legislation passed to help farmers by regulating railroads and lowering interest rates.

In the 1890 elections, the Alliances were a strong political force. Alliance-backed candidates won the governorships of Texas and Georgia. In addition, many candidates for Congress who had expressed support for the Alliances were elected to office. At a conference in Cincinnati, Ohio, in 1891, Alliance leaders met with labor and reform organizations. At a convention in St. Louis in February 1892, they formed a new national political party, the People's Party. This organization, better known as the **Populist Party**, was the high point of farmers' political activity.

The Populist Party held its first national convention in 1892. The group adopted a platform of far-reaching reforms. The Populists' goal was to end the power that big business had over government. Populist speaker Mary Elizabeth Lease called for greater democracy and a voice in the government for all Americans. The Populist platform called for government ownership of railroads and telephone and telegraph systems. It also backed the "free and unlimited coinage of silver." To win votes from laborers, the Populists supported the eight-hour workday and immigration restrictions.

In the 1892 presidential election Democrat Grover Cleveland beat Republican Benjamin Harrison. The chief issue of the campaign was the Republicans' support for high tariffs. **James B. Weaver**, the Populist candidate, won about 8.5 percent of the total popular vote.

✔ **Reading Check: Analyzing Information** Why did farmers and laborers form the Populist Party?

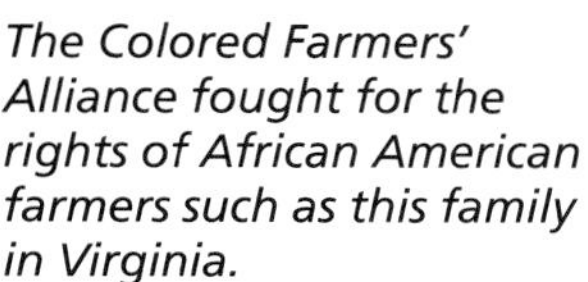
The Colored Farmers' Alliance fought for the rights of African American farmers such as this family in Virginia.

The Election of 1896

The Panic of 1893 led more people to join the Populists in calling for economic reforms. The depression had many causes, but some Americans blamed the money system. Many people sold their investments in exchange for gold, which in turn caused a shortage in U.S. gold reserves.

In 1896 the Republicans nominated William McKinley for president. McKinley was firmly against free coinage of silver. Many Democrats saw this opposition as an opportunity to win Populist and some Republican votes. At the Democratic Party's national convention, their nominee, William Jennings Bryan, swept the crowd with an emotional speech. He said, "You shall not press down upon the brow of labor this crown of thorns. You shall not crucify mankind upon this cross of gold!"

The Democrats had put the Populists in a difficult position by adopting their strongest issue. The Populists had to decide between running their own candidate and thus splitting the silver vote, or supporting Bryan. Supporting Bryan might put them in danger of being absorbed by the Democrats. The Populists decided to nominate Bryan, but they chose their own vice president.

The Democrats won the South and the West. However, the Republicans won the election. The heavily populated Midwest and Northeast provided strong Republican support. The party's well-financed campaign had convinced many workers that free coinage would cause unemployment to rise. This election marked the end of the Populist Party, and organized political action by farmers declined.

Interpreting Political Cartoons

"Cross of Gold" Judge *magazine published this cartoon on its cover after William Jennings Bryan gave his famous "Cross of Gold" speech.* ***Do you think the cartoon is intended to support or make fun of Bryan's speech? Explain your answer.***

✔ **Reading Check: Finding the Main Idea** Why did McKinley's victory in 1896 mark the end of the Populist Party?

Section 4 Review

1. **Define** and explain:
   - free coinage
   - gold standard
2. **Identify** and explain:
   - Oliver Hudson Kelley
   - National Grange
   - Interstate Commerce Act
   - Interstate Commerce Commission
   - William Jennings Bryan
   - Benjamin Harrison
   - Sherman Silver Purchase Act
   - Farmers' Alliances
   - Populist Party
   - James B. Weaver
3. **Identifying Cause and Effect** Copy the graphic organizer below. Use it to identify in order the problems that farmers faced as a result of industrialization, how they responded, and the eventual outcome of their actions.

   Problems → Responses → Results

4. **Finding the Main Idea**
   a. What problems did farmers face during the late 1800s?
   b. Why did many farmers support the free coinage of silver?
5. **Writing and Critical Thinking**
   Evaluating Imagine that you are a member of the Populist Party. Write a journal entry explaining the goals of the Populist Party and why it did not win the 1896 presidential election.
   Consider the following:
   - the depression of 1893
   - Democratic adoption of free-coinage issue
   - well-funded Republican campaign

Chapter 19 Review

The Chapter at a Glance

Examine the visual summary of the chapter below. Create a five-question, fill-in-the-blank quiz covering the chapter's main ideas that you might give to a classmate.

Inventions and Big Business

- Bessemer process
- Lightbulb
- Telephone
- Automobile
- Airplane
- Growth of corporations
- Rise of stock markets
- Carnegie and Rockefeller
- Sherman Antitrust Act

Immigration

- New immigrants from eastern and southern Europe
- Nativism
- Benevolent societies
- Chinese Exclusion Act

Labor Movement

- Knights of Labor
- American Federation of Labor
- Haymarket Riot
- Homestead strike
- Pullman strike

Populism

- National Grange
- Free coinage of silver
- Farmers' Alliances
- Populist Party

Identifying People and Ideas

Use the following terms or people in historically significant sentences.

1. Bessemer process
2. Thomas Alva Edison
3. free enterprise
4. Andrew Carnegie
5. Terence V. Powderly
6. Pullman strike
7. benevolent societies
8. suburbs
9. Jane Addams
10. gold standard

Understanding Main Ideas

Section 1 *(Pages 578–584)*

1. Explain the methods of vertical and horizontal integration used by business leaders to organize their corporations.
2. Why did some people oppose trusts, and what actions did they take?

Section 2 *(Pages 585–589)*

3. How did the Second Industrial Revolution affect workers?
4. What was the overall outcome of the major labor strikes in the late 1800s?

Section 3 *(Pages 590–595)*

5. Where did immigrants to the United States in the late 1800s come from, and why did they come?

Section 4 *(Pages 596–601)*

6. What problems did farmers face in the late 1800s, and how did they respond?

You Be the Historian— Reviewing Themes

1. **Science, Technology & Society** How did technological breakthroughs help bring about the Second Industrial Revolution?
2. **Government** What actions did government take to assist and control big business?
3. **Citizenship** Why was the Populist Party formed?

Thinking Critically

1. **Analyzing Information** Why do you think old immigrants were able to become a part of American society more quickly than new immigrants?
2. **Comparing and Contrasting** How was the Knights of Labor different from and similar to the American Federation of Labor?
3. **Evaluating** Although the Populist Party lost the presidential election of 1892, several reforms listed in the party's platform were later put into effect. Which reform do you think was the most important? Explain your answer.

Social Studies Skills Workshop

Interpreting Charts

Study the charts below. Then use the information on the charts to answer the questions that follow.

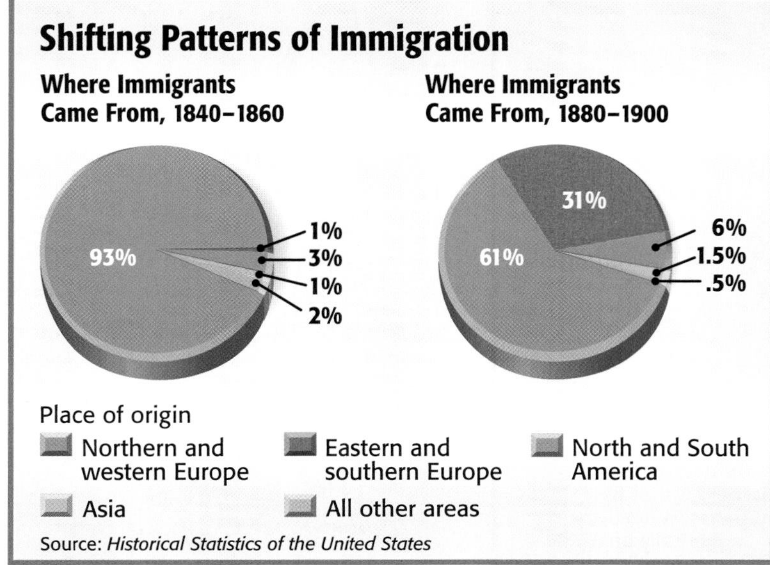

Source: *Historical Statistics of the United States*

1. What regions had the smallest percentage of immigrants to the United States from 1840 to 1860?
   a. North and South America
   b. Asia and eastern and southern Europe
   c. northern and western Europe
   d. Asia and Africa

2. What regions showed the greatest percentage increase in immigration to the United States between 1840 and 1860 and 1880 and 1900?

3. Based on your knowledge of the period, how do you think the changes in immigration shown on these charts affected the United States?

Analyzing Primary Sources

Read the following quotation by Mary Elizabeth Lease, who supported the Farmer' Alliances, then answer the questions that follow.

> **"The great common people of this country are slaves, and monopoly is the master. . . . The politicians said we suffered from overproduction. Overproduction, when 10,000 little children, so statistics tell us, starve to death every year in the United States. . . . We will stand by our homes and stay by our fireside by force if necessary, and we will not pay our debts to the loan-shark companies until the government pays its debt to us."**

4. Which of the following statements best describes Lease's point of view?
   a. The government owes farmers money and should pay them back immediately.
   b. Farmers would be more powerful if they united and formed a monopoly.
   c. The fact that American children starve to death proves that American farmers are not producing too much food.
   d. The loan sharks are treating farmers unfairly and driving them out of business.

5. Based on what you know about farming in the late 1800s, how might Lease suggest that farmers try to improve their situation?

Alternative Assessment

Building Your Portfolio

Linking to Community

Many immigrant communities established during the 1800s still thrive in U.S. cities today. Use the library and local historical societies to research an immigrant community today. Create a tourist brochure to attract visitors to that community. Your brochure should include some historical information about the community as well as descriptions and images of current attractions.

internet connect

Internet Activity: go.hrw.com
keyword: SC3 CF19

Choose a topic on the Industrial and Urban Nation to:

- Write a report on the effect of technology on daily life.
- Research the lives of steelworkers.
- Write a biography of Mother Jones and her work in the organized labor movement.

CHAPTER

20 The Spirit of Reform

(1868–1920)

This "Tammany Bank" reflects the political corruption of the 1870s. Place a coin in the politician's hand, and he puts it in his pocket.

Corrupt officials are shown weighing down President Grant's administration.

UNITED STATES

1868 Ulysses S. Grant is elected president.

1872 The Crédit Mobilier scandal reveals corruption in Grant's administration.

1873 The first public kindergarten in the United States opens in St. Louis, Missouri.

1881 President Garfield is shot by Charles Guiteau, a mentally unstable federal-job seeker, and later dies from the wounds.

1865 **1870** **1875** **1880** **1885** **1890**

1871 The British Parliament makes labor unions legal.

1873 Slave markets and the exporting of slaves are abolished on the African island of Zanzibar.

1888 Brazil officially outlaws slavery.

1894 Alfred Dreyfus is arrested on questionable treason charges, leading to political upheaval in France.

WORLD

French army captain Alfred Dreyfus had his sword broken as part of a ceremony intended to humiliate him.

Build on What You Know

After the Civil War ended, increased immigration caused American cities to grow. As cities grew, however, new problems arose. Reformers swung into action in areas such as city government, politics, public schools, and the workplace. African Americans, American Indians, immigrants, and women also called for reforms.

Theodore Roosevelt hit the campaign trail for the Progressive Party in 1912.

Booker T. Washington established the Tuskegee Institute in Alabama.

1895 Booker T. Washington gives his Atlanta Compromise speech, which calls for economic independence for African Americans.

1901 The first Nobel Prizes are awarded.

1901 President William McKinley is killed and Vice President Theodore Roosevelt becomes president.

1903 Emmeline Pankhurst forms the Women's Social and Political Union to fight for women's suffrage in Great Britain.

1905 The Industrial Workers of the World labor union is founded.

1911 The Triangle Shirtwaist Fire leads to calls for building-safety reforms.

1912 The British luxury liner *Titanic* sinks after hitting an iceberg during its first voyage.

1912 Theodore Roosevelt runs for president as the candidate of the Progressive Party but loses to Democrat Woodrow Wilson.

1913 Norway gives women the right to vote.

1916 Montana representative Jeannette Rankin is the first woman elected to Congress.

1917 Mexico adopts a new constitution.

1920 The Nineteenth Amendment, which gives women the vote, is ratified.

1895 1900 1905 1910 1915 1920

The Nobel Prize bears the image of Swedish inventor Alfred Nobel, who created a fund for the awards.

If you were there . . .

Which reform would you support?

You Be the Historian

What's Your Opinion? Do you **agree** or **disagree** with the following statements? Support your point of view in your journal.

- **Citizenship** Citizens should accept the government they have.
- **Constitutional Heritage** The rights of workers can only be determined by the Supreme Court.
- **Economics** The government should not regulate the economy.

Section 1

The Gilded Age

Read to Discover

1. In what ways did bosses control city politics?
2. How did scandals affect national politics during the Gilded Age?
3. How did the appointment of federal officials change during the late 1800s?

Define

- political machines
- bosses
- mugwumps

Identify

- William Marcy Tweed
- Rutherford B. Hayes
- James A. Garfield
- Chester A. Arthur
- Grover Cleveland
- Benjamin Harrison
- William McKinley
- Pendleton Civil Service Act

Why It Matters Today

Politicians today still try to solve problems by passing new laws. Use CNNfyi.com or other **current events** sources to learn about a problem that the U.S. government is trying to solve today. Record your findings in your journal.

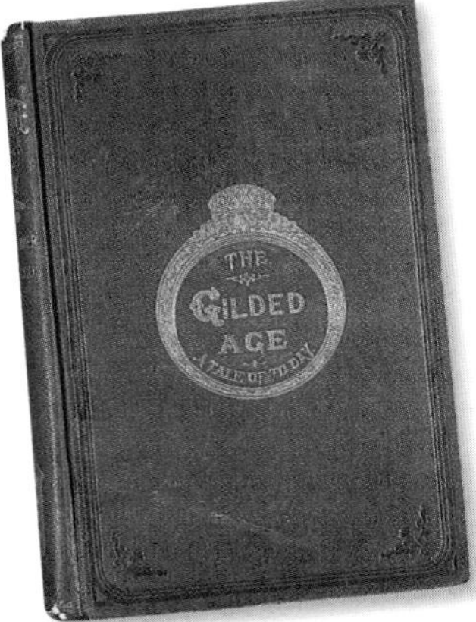

In the best-selling novel The Gilded Age, *Mark Twain argued that the United States lived by the motto "Get rich; dishonestly if we can, honestly if we must."*

The Story Continues

In 1873 Mark Twain and Charles Dudley Warner published the best-selling novel *The Gilded Age.* Twain believed that American society looked golden from a distance but was merely gilded, or coated with cheap gold paint. According to Twain, despite its positive outward appearance, society was ugly and corrupt on the inside.

Corruption in Politics

Politics at all levels experienced corruption during the Gilded Age. Powerful organizations called **political machines** influenced city and county politics. These groups used both legal and illegal means to get candidates elected to public office. For example, members of a political machine often printed election ballots listing only candidates from their party. They sometimes paid people for votes. If bribing voters did not work, the political machines might hire the people who counted the votes. Through such actions, a political party could control local government. During the late 1880s, Tammany Hall, the Democratic political machine in New York City, became widely known throughout the country for its power and corruption.

Political machines were run by powerful leaders known as **bosses.** The boss traded favors for votes. For example, a boss might need a certain number of votes to elect a candidate to office. In exchange for the votes he received, the boss might offer city jobs, order neighborhood improvements, or allow an illegal business to continue to operate.

The bosses drew much of their support from immigrants, who relied on them for jobs and social mobility. After winning city elections in 1888, Tammany Hall members rewarded supporters with some 12,000 jobs. Many jobs went to Irish immigrants. Some politicians saw nothing wrong with machines that exchanged money and jobs for working-class votes. However, once in power, bosses might use their control of the government to get rich. For example, Tammany Hall boss **William Marcy Tweed** may have stolen as much as $200 million from the city treasury. He was later convicted, however, and died in jail.

Corruption was also common in the federal government at this time. Many people saw the administration of Republican Ulysses S. Grant—who was elected president in 1868 and re-elected in 1872—as corrupt. During Grant's second term, for example, several government revenue officials were jailed for their part in the "Whiskey Ring." These officials took bribes from whiskey distillers who wanted to avoid paying taxes.

In 1872 the *New York Sun* printed a story about corruption in the U.S. Congress. The owners of the Union Pacific Railroad had started a construction company called Crédit Mobilier of America. The owners gave or sold shares in Crédit Mobilier to members of Congress. In return, these congressmembers approved large federal land grants to Crédit Mobilier. Scandals like these led many Americans to question the honesty of national leaders.

✔ **Reading Check: Comparing** How was political corruption at the city level like corruption at the federal level of government during the Gilded Age?

Interpreting Political Cartoons

The Tweed Ring *Cartoonist Thomas Nast portrayed the political and business associates of Boss Tweed as crooks trying to blame each other for gaining money in questionable ways.* ***Why do you think Nast chose to show the Tammany Hall politicians standing in a circle?***

Republican reformers, known as mugwumps, supported Democratic presidential candidate Grover Cleveland instead of Republican James Blaine in the 1884 election.

Gilded Age Presidents

During the 1876 presidential campaign, Democrats called for government reform. Their candidate, Samuel J. Tilden, promised to run an honest administration. The Republicans chose **Rutherford B. Hayes**, a Civil War hero they believed to be honest. Hayes promised to reform the civil service. In the disputed election that followed, a special electoral commission chose Hayes over Tilden by one vote.

Republicans won another close presidential race in 1880 when **James A. Garfield** and his vice president, **Chester A. Arthur**, were elected. On July 2, 1881, Charles Guiteau, an angry and mentally unstable federal-job seeker, confronted President Garfield at a Washington railroad station. He shouted, "Arthur [is] President now," and shot Garfield twice. The president died from his wounds in September, and Arthur became president.

In the 1884 election, Republicans chose James G. Blaine instead of another reform candidate. Many Republican reformers linked Blaine with corruption and did not want to back him. These Republican reformers came to be known as **mugwumps** (the Algonquian word for "big chiefs"). The dissatisfied mugwumps left the Republican Party and supported Democratic nominee **Grover Cleveland**. Unlike Blaine, Cleveland was known for his honesty. In a presidential race full of personal attacks, American voters chose Cleveland over Blaine. As president, Cleveland hired and fired government workers based on their merit, not on their party ties.

Four years later Cleveland again won the popular vote. This time, however, he lost the electoral vote to Republican **Benjamin Harrison**. Harrison supported passage of the Sherman Antitrust Act, which regulated monopolies. In addition, Harrison's support helped in the passage of a pension act and passage of the McKinley Tariff. However, Cleveland remained popular, and in 1892 crowds sang their support for him.

Analyzing Primary Sources

Drawing Inferences and Conclusions What did the crowds supporting Cleveland think would happen if he were elected?

"Grover, Grover, four more years of Grover—
Out they go and in we come and we'll be in the clover."

—Grover Cleveland supporters, quoted in *The Gilded Age*, by Mark Wahlgren Summers

Cleveland won the presidential election of 1892, but the country's economy entered a depression. Cleveland angered many fellow Democrats by opposing free coinage of silver and supporting a gold standard. In 1896 the Democrats chose William Jennings Bryan to run for president. He lost the election to Republican **William McKinley**. Practical and friendly, McKinley worked well with Congress and was re-elected in 1900.

✔ **Reading Check: Sequencing** List the winners of presidential elections between 1876 and 1900 in the order that the elections took place.

Civil Service Reform

A fellow official congratulates Senator George Pendleton on his plan for civil service reform.

Reacting to the corruption of the Gilded Age, many Americans called for changes in the civil service, or government jobs. Both major parties took advantage of the so-called spoils system when in power. Under the spoils system, government jobs were given to loyal party supporters, even if they were not qualified. Every time a new party took power, it fired many government employees to replace them with party members. Henry Adams, author and grandson of former president John Quincy Adams, remarked on this custom in 1870. "All my friends have been or are on the point of being driven out of the government."

Reformers wanted those seeking government jobs to take examinations. It was believed that such a system would reward merit rather than political connections. Reformers believed that an examination system would help prevent people who were unfit or corrupt from getting government jobs. Some Americans also believed that the spoils system was to blame for President Garfield's assassination. The *Nation*, a weekly newspaper, noted that "the crime seems to have acted on public opinion . . . like a spark on a powder-magazine [gunpowder storage]."

After Garfield was killed, President Chester A. Arthur addressed problems caused by the spoils system by supporting the **Pendleton Civil Service Act**. This law, passed in 1883, set up a merit system controlled by the Civil Service Commission. At first, the act affected only about 14,000 of 130,000 federal jobs. The act has since been expanded so that more than 90 percent of government jobs are covered by the Civil Service Commission.

✔ **Reading Check: Finding the Main Idea** How did the Pendleton Civil Service Act reform government?

Section 1 Review

go.hrw.com Homework Practice Online
keyword: SC3 HP20

1. **Define** and explain:
   - political machines
   - bosses
   - mugwumps
2. **Identify** and explain:
   - William Marcy Tweed
   - Rutherford B. Hayes
   - James A. Garfield
   - Chester A. Arthur
   - Grover Cleveland
   - Benjamin Harrison
   - William McKinley
   - Pendleton Civil Service Act
3. **Categorizing** Copy the graphic organizer below. Use it to identify the impact of government corruption at the local and federal levels during the Gilded Age, and the results of this corruption.

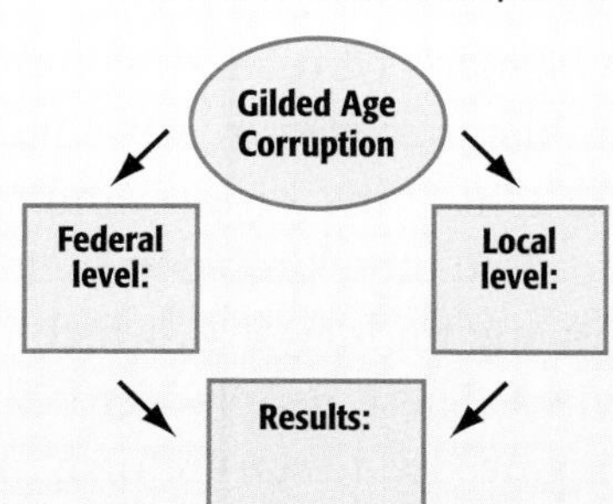

4. **Finding the Main Idea**
   a. How did bosses and political machines control city governments?
   b. What led to civil service reform, and how did the reform affect the appointment of federal officials?
5. **Writing and Critical Thinking**
   Supporting a Point of View Imagine that you are a political adviser to President Arthur in 1883. Prepare a memorandum urging the president either to sign or veto the recently passed Pendleton Civil Service Act.
   Consider the following:
   - examples of political corruption in the Gilded Age
   - the assassination of President Garfield
   - the terms of the Pendleton Civil Service Act

Section 2

The Progressive Movement

Read to Discover

1. What roles did middle-class reformers and muckrakers play in the progressive movement?
2. How did progressives change government?
3. How did progressives address the country's social problems?

Why It Matters Today

Reformers still seek to change the world today. Use CNNfyi.com or other **current events** sources to find out about one reform campaign going on in the United States. Record your findings in your journal.

Define

- progressives
- muckrakers
- direct primary
- recall
- initiative
- referendum

Identify

- Ida Tarbell
- Seventeenth Amendment
- Robert M. La Follette
- Wisconsin Idea
- John Dewey
- Joseph McCormack

Hull House, a settlement house in Chicago, gained a national reputation for its social work.

The Story Continues

One cold snowy morning in late December 1891, Florence Kelley and her three children arrived on the front steps of Hull House in Chicago. When she knocked on the door, Jane Addams answered. "We were welcomed as though we had been invited," Kelley later wrote. At Hull House, Kelley not only found refuge but also joined the growing movement for reform. She went on to become one of the country's leading social reformers.

The Progressive Movement

In the late 1800s reformers, who became known as **progressives**, began working to solve problems caused by rapid industrial and urban growth. Many progressives fought crime, disease, and poverty by trying to change the conditions that caused these problems. A large number of progressives were part of the growing middle class, which included professionals and small-business owners. These people were educated and often had the free time and training needed to start reform movements. Some working-class and wealthy Americans also worked for reforms.

Progressives did not always agree on which social problems were the most important. Even when they did agree, they might disagree on how to solve these problems. As a result, progressives worked for reforms in several areas. Some wanted health and education programs in poor neighborhoods as well as government reforms, while others fought for better working conditions. Many progressives did agree, however, that to reach these goals the federal government needed to step in. These progressives wanted the government and the public to solve social problems together.

Journalists moved progressives to action by writing about corruption in business and politics. Many journalists hoped their articles would lead to greater public awareness of problems. Eventually, reforms might follow. These journalists were soon nicknamed **muckrakers** because they "raked up" and exposed the muck, or filth, of society. Some muckrakers became well known for articles about the unfair business practices that accompanied the rise of corporations. **Ida Tarbell** wrote articles attacking John D. Rockefeller's Standard Oil Company.

"Very often people who admit the facts, who are willing to see that Mr. Rockefeller has employed force and fraud to secure his ends, justify him by declaring, 'It's business'. That is, 'it's business' has come to be a legitimate [acceptable] excuse for hard dealing, sly tricks, [and] special privileges."

—Ida Tarbell, *The History of the Standard Oil Company*

Analyzing Primary Sources

Identifying Points of View
What is Tarbell's opinion of Rockefeller's defenders?

Muckrakers also wrote about child labor, racial discrimination, and slum housing. Their articles angered many politicians and business leaders, but they helped unite progressives. Muckrakers influenced voters to question corrupt practices, and politicians to call for reforms.

✔ **Reading Check: Comparing and Contrasting** How were progressives and muckrakers alike, and how were they different?

 Expanding Democracy

Worries about political corruption caused some progressives to work to change state and local governments and reduce the power of political machines. In many places, reformers replaced multiple ballots that political parties distributed with government-prepared ballots listing all candidates. Under pressure from reformers, many states adopted secret ballots that gave every voter a private vote.

Reformers also tried to give voters more power. For example, they fought for the **direct primary**. The direct primary let voters choose candidates for public office instead of allowing party leaders to select them. Progressives also favored the **Seventeenth Amendment**. Passed in 1913, the amendment allowed Americans to vote directly for U.S. senators. In the past, senators had been selected by state legislatures.

Ida Tarbell wrote many muckraking articles for McClure's Magazine.

Other reform measures allowed voters to call for action on political issues. Some states and cities created a procedure known as the **recall.** This process allows voters to sign a petition asking for a special vote. The purpose is to recall, or remove, an elected official before the end of his or her term. If enough voters sign the petition, the vote takes place. If the majority votes to recall the official, then he or she is removed from office.

Progressives also pushed for reforms to give voters a direct voice in new legislation. The **initiative** allows voters to propose a new law by getting signatures on a petition. If enough people sign the petition, the proposed law is voted on at the next election. The **referendum** allows voters to approve or disapprove a law that has already been proposed or passed by state or local governments. This procedure gives voters a chance to overrule laws with which they disagree.

✔ Reading Check: **Summarizing** What types of reforms did progressives favor to change the ways that people took part in the political process?

Reforming City and State Governments

In addition to increasing political participation, progressives worked to change the structure of local government. Businesspeople and professionals wanted to make government more efficient and responsive to citizens' needs. Some reformers wanted city government to be run more like a business. Several cities changed to a council-manager system where voters elect a city council, which then chooses a professional manager to run the city. Progressives also started the commission form of government. Under this system, a group of elected leaders run city government. Each official runs a major city agency, such as housing, sanitation, or transportation. These new forms of government were most popular in small to medium-sized cities.

State governments faced some of the same problems as cities. City bosses and other corrupt urban officials were often part of a statewide political machine. Progressive Republican **Robert M. La Follette** took on the power of the party bosses in Wisconsin. La Follette favored the direct primary, tax reform, and new state commissions that relied on professionals to manage social problems.

La Follette failed to win his party's nomination for governor in 1896 and in 1898. He finally won the governor's race in 1900. As governor, La Follette developed the **Wisconsin Idea**, a program of reforms. The program set out to reduce the influence of political machines and to make state government more efficient in meeting the people's needs. This idea became a model for progressive reformers in other states.

Progressive leader Robert M. La Follette served as governor of Wisconsin from 1900 to 1906 and as U.S. senator from 1906 to 1925.

✔ Reading Check: **Analyzing Information** What reforms did progressives back to reduce the power of political machines and make governments more responsive to the needs of the people?

City Planning

Many native-born Americans and immigrants moved to U.S. cities looking for work. As cities grew, many people crowded into tenements, or poorly built, overcrowded apartments. The tenement owners often failed to make needed repairs to improve living conditions. As a result, thousands of poor families lived in dirty and dangerous buildings. Progressive Lawrence Veiller described the way tenement living hurt children and society.

"A child living its early years in dark rooms, without sunlight or fresh air, does not grow up to be a normal, healthy person. . . . It is not of such material that strong nations are made."

—Lawrence Veiller, quoted in *Readings in American History,* edited by Robert C. Cotner et al.

Analyzing Primary sources
Identifying Points of View According to Veiller, what happens to children who grow up in poor living conditions?

Progressives called on state and local governments to address these problems. Veiller helped get the New York State Tenement House Act passed in 1901. This act made it illegal to build poorly lit and airless tenements. The law also required new buildings to have better ventilation, running water, and toilets. New York's law became a model for housing reform in other states. Many progressives also started settlement houses like Jane Addams's Hull House in Chicago. These organizations worked to improve education, housing, and sanitation in immigrant and poor communities.

Urban reforms led to new professions such as city planning and civil engineering. City planners worked with local officials to control city growth. They passed zoning laws, created building-safety codes, and developed public parks. Civil engineers planned street-paving and bridge-building projects. Sanitation engineers tried to solve the problems of water supply, waste disposal, and pollution. Where these problems were attacked, death rates dropped dramatically. Many of these improvements gave urban Americans some of the best public services in the world.

✔ **Reading Check: Identifying Cause and Effect** What led to the rise of new professions such as city planning and civil engineering, and how did they change life in urban America?

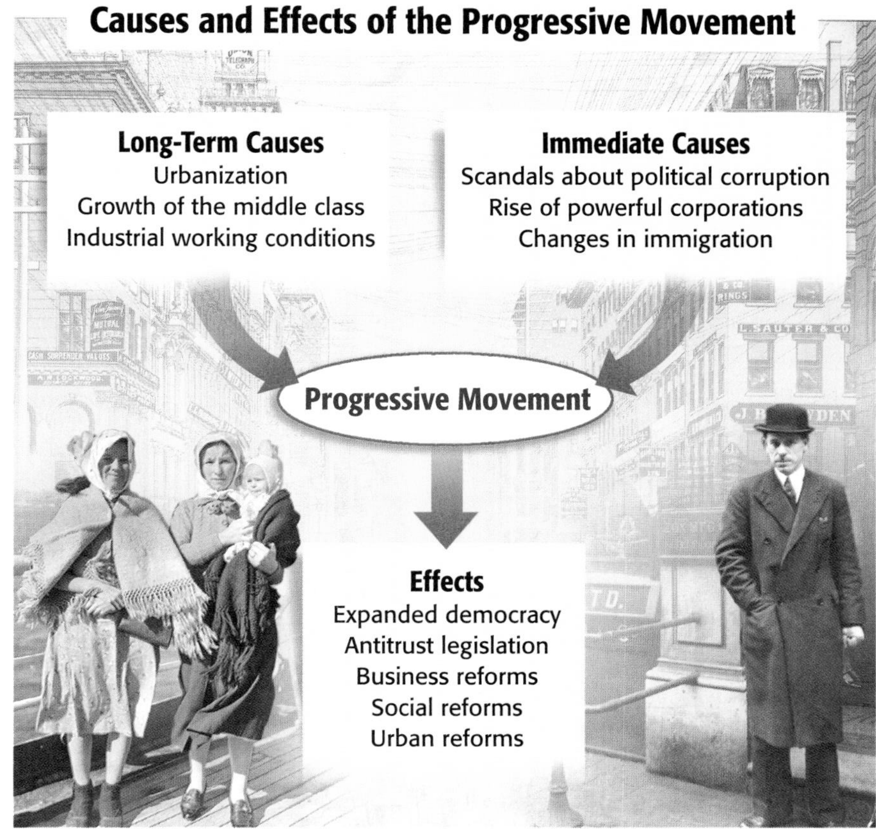

That's Interesting!

Learning to Play Did you know that the progressive movement led to some of the first playgrounds in the United States? It's true! In the early 1900s some progressives noticed that many urban children played in parking lots and other vacant areas. As a result, they formed the Playground Association of America (PAA) in 1906. The PAA built playgrounds with safe equipment in U.S. cities. The group even published a magazine called *Playground*. The PAA later merged with other playground groups to form the National Recreation and Park Association (NRPA). The NRPA continues to support park and recreation efforts today.

Social Reforms

Progressives also worked to improve education. School enrollment increased greatly in the late 1800s as states passed laws requiring children to attend school. Reformers pushed for new public high schools with courses in citizenship, health, and job training. Many progressives also opened kindergartens to teach basic social skills to poor children between the ages of three and seven. In 1873 reformer Susan Blow opened the first American public kindergarten in St. Louis, Missouri. By 1898, more than 4,000 kindergartens had opened in the United States. **John Dewey** was an important philosopher and educator who changed American education. His goal was to help children learn critical-thinking skills to aid them in everyday life. Dewey wanted children to learn problem-solving skills, not just to memorize their lessons. His teaching methods became the model for progressive education across the country.

Progressives also tried to improve the education of medical professionals. In the late 1800s the United States had few well-trained and professionally organized doctors. Researchers knew the causes of diseases such as malaria, pneumonia, tuberculosis, and yellow fever. However, there were few medical organizations to help spread this knowledge. Under the leadership of **Joseph McCormack**, the American Medical Association (AMA) was reorganized in 1901. The AMA brought local medical organizations together and supported laws protecting public health. The group's work showed how progressives could unite professionals to help improve society.

✔ **Reading Check: Summarizing** What educational reforms did progressives favor?

Section 2 Review

go.hrw.com Homework Practice Online
keyword: SC3 HP20

1. **Define** and explain:
   - progressives
   - muckrakers
   - direct primary
   - recall
   - initiative
   - referendum

2. **Identify** and explain:
   - Ida Tarbell
   - Seventeenth Amendment
   - Robert M. La Follette
   - Wisconsin Idea
   - John Dewey
   - Joseph McCormack

3. **Categorizing** Copy the diagram below. Use it to identify ways that progressives supported each type of reform.

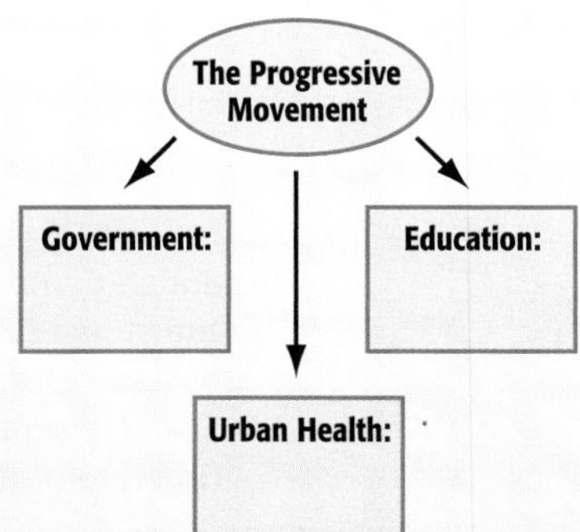

4. **Finding the Main Idea**
   a. What contributions did middle-class reformers and muckrakers make to the progressive movement?
   b. What caused progressives to fight corruption in local and state governments, and what effects did their efforts have?

5. **Writing and Critical Thinking**
   Analyzing Information Imagine that you are a muckraker for *McClure's Magazine*. Write a short article explaining how progressives have addressed social and political problems in U.S. cities in the early 1900s.
   Consider the following:
   - urban problems
   - the work of other muckrakers
   - new professions related to urban planning

Section 3

Reforming the Workplace

Read to Discover

1. What laws did progressives want to pass to protect workers?
2. How did the courts react to labor legislation?
3. How did labor organize to help improve working conditions?

Define

- socialism

Identify

- Florence Kelley
- Triangle Shirtwaist Fire
- Industrial Workers of the World
- William "Big Bill" Haywood

WHY IT MATTERS TODAY

Women still seek full equality around the world today. Use CNNfyi.com or other **current events** sources to find out about a situation or country in which women face inequality. Record your findings in your journal.

The Story Continues

Sadie Frowne was 15 years old. She worked in a garment factory in Brooklyn, New York. Every day at 7:00 A.M. she sat down at her machine. "The machines go like mad all day, because the faster you work the more money you get," she explained. "Sometimes in my haste I get my finger caught and the needle goes right through it." One of the progressives' main goals was to establish better working conditions for people like Sadie.

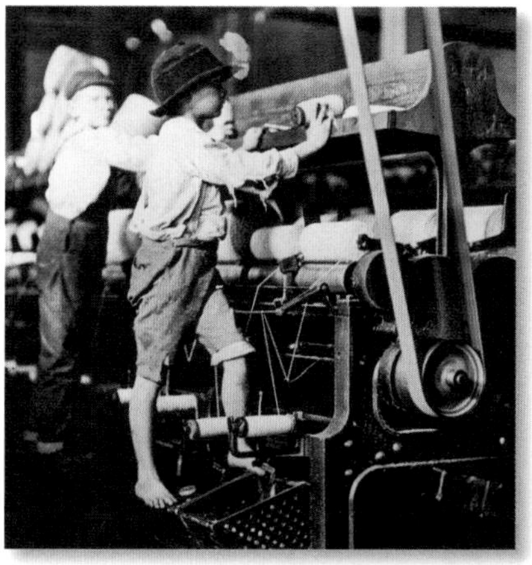

Many children, such as these young textile workers, labored in potentially dangerous jobs.

Child Labor Reform

Low wages for unskilled workers in the late 1800s meant that a growing number of children had to work to help support their families. Boys and some girls sold newspapers or shined shoes on the streets. Girls often cooked and cleaned for boarders staying with their families. Some girls worked at home, sewing garments with their mothers.

In addition, more than 1.75 million children, age 15 and under, worked in mines, mills, and factories by 1900. One wealthy reformer, Marie Van Vorst, posed as a poor woman so that she could investigate child labor conditions. She saw children as young as five years old working in a South Carolina textile mill.

Daily Life

Child factory workers In the early 1900s, many children labored in textile factories. Among their tasks was the responsibility of watching the bobbins, or cylinders that held thread. When the thread broke, children had to quickly tie the two ends together. Other children replaced bobbins that were full of thread with empty ones. Such jobs forced children to stand all day and risk injury by climbing on equipment. One little girl earned 4 cents for every 36 buttons she sewed. Many of the children who worked in factories did not go to school. One reformer noted that children who did attend school often fell asleep in class because they had been up late working. **How does the image show the difficult working conditions that these children faced?**

As more progressives learned about child labor, they began to take action. **Florence Kelley**, who had raised her three children at Chicago's Hull House, led the progressive fight against child labor. Kelley's plan was to "investigate, educate, legislate, and enforce." She was also a board member of the National Consumers' League, a group that spoke out on labor issues involving women and children. Kelley started about 60 local consumer leagues throughout the United States. The National Child Labor Committee worked for laws against child labor in many states. Congress passed federal child labor laws in 1916 and 1919. The Supreme Court, however, ruled that they were unconstitutional. A later attempt to pass a constitutional amendment limiting child labor failed.

✔ **Reading Check: Finding the Main Idea** How did reformers try to improve child labor conditions?

Safety in the Workplace

Child labor reform was only part of the progressive effort to help workers. Many progressives worked with labor unions to fight for the eight-hour workday. The National Consumers' League favored legislation for higher wages and fewer working hours. As a result, many states passed minimum-wage laws and maximum-hour laws for women.

Tragic accidents in the workplace led reformers to call for laws protecting workers from dangerous conditions. In 1900 some 35,000 people were killed by industrial accidents. About 500,000 others were hurt. One shocking incident took place in 1911 at the Triangle Shirtwaist Company in New York City. As some 500 workers, most of whom were immigrant women, prepared to leave the clothing factory, a fire broke out. They tried to escape through exit doors of the 10-story building but found the doors locked. By the time firefighters brought the **Triangle Shirtwaist Fire** under control, 146 workers had died. At a memorial service for the fire victims, union leader Rose Schneiderman called for action.

"This is not the first time girls have been burned alive in the city. Each week I must learn of the untimely death of one of my sister workers. . . . The life of men and women is so cheap and property is so sacred. . . . It is up to the working people to save themselves."

—Rose Schneiderman, *All for One*

Analyzing Primary Sources

Identifying Points of View Why does Schneiderman say that life had become so cheap?

Incidents such as the Triangle Shirtwaist Fire led to laws that improved factory safety standards and working conditions.

Labor leaders and progressives also fought for laws to pay workers injured on the job. In 1902, Maryland became the first state to adopt a workers' compensation law. But because workplace laws were not strictly enforced, working conditions remained poor in many places.

✔ **Reading Check: Summarizing** What types of laws did progressives and labor leaders support in order to improve working conditions?

The Courts and the Workplace

Some business leaders opposed workforce regulations, arguing that the government should not interfere with the economy. State and federal courts often upheld this view and ruled against progressive reform laws. Courts ruled that the Fourteenth Amendment protected businesses against laws that would take their property without due process of law.

In 1898 the Supreme Court ruled that states could limit workers' hours in dangerous jobs. The state of New York later passed a law that limited bakers to a 10-hour workday because of the unhealthy working conditions. But a bakery owner, Joseph Lochner, challenged the law. He claimed that this law interfered with his right to run his business. The case made its way to the Supreme Court. In *Lochner* v. *New York* the Supreme Court ruled that states could not restrict the rights of employers and workers to sign any type of labor agreement that they wished. The Court ruled that the New York law was unconstitutional. According to the Court, workers should be free to accept any conditions of employment that business owners required—even if that meant working 14 to 16 hours a day.

The Supreme Court did uphold some laws limiting the working hours of women and children. In *Muller* v. *Oregon* (1908) the Court upheld laws limiting women's working hours. According to the Court, the differences between women and men made the health and safety of women a matter of public interest. The Court then ruled that these differences meant laws regulating working conditions for women were constitutional. For the progressives, this was a key decision. It was the first case successfully argued from social evidence rather than precedent, or prior legal principle. Progressives continued to work to extend legal protections in the workplace to men.

✔ **Reading Check: Analyzing Information** How did the Supreme Court address labor laws in the late 1800s and early 1900s?

Worker Reforms

Like American laborers, European workers also formed unions. The labor movement was strongest in Great Britain, where there were about 4 million union members in 1913. As their standard of living dropped during the early 1900s, British workers staged several protests. Transportation strikes paralyzed the country in 1911.

In the early 1900s, British workers won retirement pensions and miners gained an eight-hour workday. In 1911 Parliament passed the British National Insurance Act, which gave some workers unemployment insurance. **What gains did British workers make?**

This pamphlet contained labor songs for members of the Industrial Workers of the World.

Labor Organizations

Unions fought for better working conditions and higher pay by bargaining with employers. Union membership rose from more than 800,000 in 1900 to about 5 million in 1920. Because most unions discouraged women from joining, some female workers formed their own unions. Reformers started the national Women's Trade Union League in 1903.

The American Federation of Labor (AFL) remained one of the most powerful labor unions, organizing workers in skilled trades. The goals of the AFL were better working conditions, higher pay, and union recognition. AFL president Samuel Gompers and others like him favored the economic system called capitalism. In this system, privately owned businesses run most industries, and competition determines prices and wages.

More radical unions claimed that capitalism itself was unfair. They supported **socialism**—an economic system in which the government owns and operates a country's means of production. Socialists hoped that the government would be more responsive to workers' needs. Some socialists and union leaders started the **Industrial Workers of the World** (IWW) in 1905. The IWW brought together many workers who were not welcome in the AFL. The union took in African Americans, immigrants, migrant workers, unskilled laborers, and women.

Led by **William "Big Bill" Haywood**, the IWW's goal was to organize all workers into one large union that eventually would try to overthrow capitalism. The IWW organized strikes across the country, but business leaders and many other Americans were alarmed by the IWW. Arrests of union leaders, government investigations, and political opposition weakened the IWW, and by 1920 the union had almost disappeared.

✔ **Reading Check: Comparing and Contrasting** How were the goals of the AFL and the IWW similar, and how were they different?

Section 3 Review

go.hrw.com Homework Practice Online
keyword: SC3 HP20

1 Define and explain:
- socialism

2 Identify and explain:
- Florence Kelley
- Triangle Shirtwaist Fire
- Industrial Workers of the World
- William "Big Bill" Haywood

3 Analyzing Information Copy the diagram below. Use it to identify how progressives tried to reform child labor, working conditions, and women's labor.

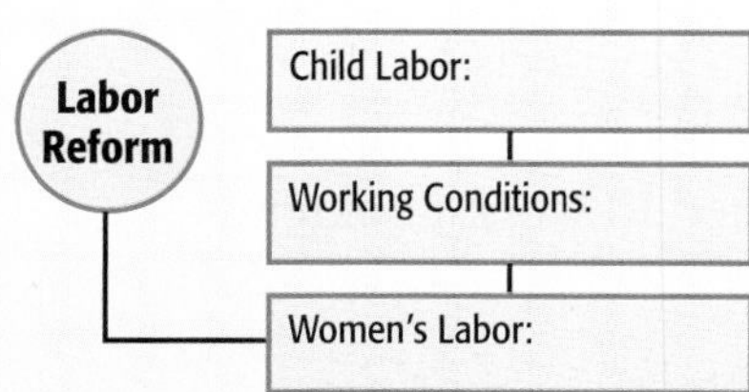

4 Finding the Main Idea

a. What working conditions led unions and progressives to call for laws to protect laborers?

b. What were the major goals of most unions?

5 Writing and Critical Thinking

Summarizing Imagine that you are a news reporter covering the Supreme Court in the early 1900s. Write a feature article about cases in which the Court has made rulings about laws involving workers' hours.

Consider the following:
- working conditions for women and children
- the case of *Lochner* v. *New York*
- the case of *Muller* v. *Oregon*

Section 4

The Rights of Women and Minorities

Read to Discover

1. Why did many women participate in the progressive movement, and what were their goals?
2. How did African American leaders try to improve conditions for African Americans?
3. What groups did not benefit from the progressive movement?

Identify

- Woman's Christian Temperance Union
- Frances Willard
- Eighteenth Amendment
- National American Woman Suffrage Association
- Carrie Chapman Catt
- Alice Paul
- National Woman's Party
- Nineteenth Amendment
- Booker T. Washington
- Atlanta Compromise
- Ida B. Wells
- W. E. B. Du Bois
- National Association for the Advancement of Colored People

Why it Matters Today

Women are much more active in political life than they were before gaining the right to vote. Use CNNfyi.com or other **current events** sources to find out about the number of women who voted in recent elections and the number elected to office. Record your findings in your journal.

The Story Continues

During the summer of 1910, a campaign tour for women's right to vote stopped in Warren, Illinois. Tour participants told the local crowd that greeted them that their state representative had opposed the woman suffrage bill. The crowd brought the representative forward. They demanded to know if he would support the bill the next time. "It looks as if I would have to," he responded. To the delight of the crowd, he shouted, "I can't fight against a woman's campaign. I'm for you."

This women's suffrage supporter marched in front of the White House.

Progressive Women

New educational opportunities drew more women into the progressive movement. In the late 1800s, women began attending colleges like Smith, Vassar, and Wellesley in record numbers. Their goal was "to develop as fully as may be the powers of womanhood," said Sophia Smith, founder of Smith College. New state universities also began to admit women. Educators like Professor Edward Clarke of Harvard Medical School opposed the admission of women, however. In 1872, Clarke argued that the physical and mental strain of too much thinking would harm a woman's health.

Despite such views, women seized the opportunities to improve their educations. In 1870 only some 20 percent of college students were women. By 1910 that number had doubled. However, many female graduates found few jobs open to them. Jane Addams explained that she could "not understand this apparent waste of herself, this elaborate [complex] preparation, if no work is provided for her." Many female graduates did enter fields such as teaching, social work, and library management. Yet they found it much harder to enter professions such as law and medicine, which were dominated by men. Denied such careers, women found that they could play active roles in reform movements. Women's clubs campaigned for dozens of causes, including child welfare, political reform, temperance, and women's suffrage.

✔ **Reading Check: Finding the Main Idea** What problem did college-trained women face after graduation?

The Temperance Movement

Progressive women played a vital role in the temperance movement. Since the 1840s temperance reformers had blamed alcohol for many of society's problems. By the 1870s the movement had spread to hundreds of small towns. More than 1,000 saloons were forced to shut down by these reformers. Some temperance activists followed the example of Carry Nation. In the 1890s Nation would storm into saloons with an ax, chopping bars and smashing liquor bottles and glasses.

In 1874, reformers formed the **Woman's Christian Temperance Union** (WCTU). Women from many different backgrounds united in the fight against alcohol abuse. **Frances Willard** served as president of the organization from 1879 to 1898. Under her leadership, the WCTU started 10,000 local branches that represented every state, territory, and major city in the United States. As a result of such pressure, many state and local governments passed laws restricting the sale of alcohol. Temperance efforts eventually led to the passage of the **Eighteenth Amendment** in 1919. This amendment outlawed the production and sale of alcoholic beverages in the United States.

✔ **Reading Check: Identifying Cause and Effect** Why did the WCTU fight for prohibition, and what effects did their crusade have?

Interpreting Political Cartoons

Carry Nation *Cartoons often showed temperance leader Carry Nation as a warrior attacking alcohol.* ***How does this cartoon illustrate women's role in the temperance movement?***

Historical Document

Susan B. Anthony

Women's Right to the Suffrage

Susan B. Anthony

After women's rights activist Susan B. Anthony was arrested for voting, she defended herself before a U.S. district court in New York in 1873. The following is an excerpt from a speech she gave to her supporters.

"Friends and fellow citizens: I stand before you to-night under indictment for the alleged crime [accusation] of having voted at the last presidential election, without having a lawful right to vote. It shall be my work this evening to prove to you that in thus voting, I not only committed no crime, but, instead, simply exercised my citizen's rights, guaranteed to me and all United States citizens by the National Constitution. . . . It was we, the people, not we, the white male citizens; nor yet we, the male citizens; but we, the whole people, who formed the Union. And we formed it, not to give the blessings of liberty, but to secure them; not to the half of ourselves and the half of our posterity, but to the whole people—women as well as men."

Analyzing Primary Sources

1. What crime was Susan B. Anthony accused of committing?
2. Why does Anthony believe that women should have the vote?

Women's Suffrage

The WCTU also started to fight for women's suffrage, but this movement had many opponents. Some people worried about what women might do if they had the vote. Political bosses were troubled by the anticorruption efforts of women. Many businesspeople believed that women voters would support child labor laws and minimum-wage laws. Some people simply believed that women belonged in the home, not in politics.

Elizabeth Cady Stanton and Susan B. Anthony began the **National American Woman Suffrage Association** (NAWSA) in 1890 to help get the vote for women. That same year, women gained the right to vote in Wyoming. Colorado, Idaho, and Utah followed in the 1890s.

Carrie Chapman Catt had fought successfully for women's suffrage in the West. After becoming president of the NAWSA in 1900, Catt mobilized more than 1 million volunteers. She argued that female voters were needed to help bring about progressive reforms. Catt insisted that women should have a voice in creating the laws that affected them.

However, some women believed that the efforts of the NAWSA did not go far enough. In 1913 NAWSA member **Alice Paul** left the organization and founded what would become the **National Woman's Party** (NWP). The NWP used parades, public demonstrations, and more controversial methods to draw attention to its cause. The party used hunger strikes,

Interpreting the Visual Record

Suffrage marchers *These women are marching in a suffragette parade in New York City in 1912.* ***How do you think the public would react to such a parade?***

pickets, and various forms of civil disobedience to build support. Paul and other NWP leaders were jailed several times for their actions.

The efforts of the NAWSA and the NWP helped lead to success. In 1919, 26 state legislatures asked Congress to pass a women's suffrage amendment. In 1920 the **Nineteenth Amendment** gave the vote to women in the United States.

✔ **Reading Check: Comparing and Contrasting** How were the NAWSA and the NWP alike, and how were they different?

African Americans Fight for Change

White progressive reformers often ignored issues such as discrimination and segregation. Some African American leaders like **Booker T. Washington** tried to improve the conditions of African Americans. Born into slavery, Washington became a respected educator while in his twenties. In 1881 he founded the Tuskegee Institute in Alabama for African Americans. He encouraged African Americans to improve their own educational and economic well-being rather than fight discrimination and segregation. Washington explained his philosophy in his **Atlanta Compromise** speech of 1895.

Analyzing Primary Sources

Drawing Inferences and Conclusions What social relationship between African Americans and whites does Washington seem to support?

"In all things that are purely social we [whites and African Americans] can be as separate as the fingers, yet one as the hand in all things essential to mutual [shared] progress."

—Booker T. Washington, Atlanta Compromise speech

Other African Americans, such as journalist **Ida B. Wells**, (later Wells-Barnett) were more outspoken about discrimination. Editorials in her Memphis newspaper, *Free Speech*, drew attention to the mob lynching, or violent killing, of black men. Her work gained her many enemies. Eventually, she had to move to the North because of death threats. In 1895 she published *Red Record*, which reported lynching statistics for a three-year period. Wells-Barnett later helped start an international crusade against lynching.

W. E. B. Du Bois also took a direct approach to fighting racial injustice. Born in Massachusetts, Du Bois attended Fisk University. He later went on to earn a doctoral degree from Harvard. Du Bois disagreed with Washington's focus on job training and downplaying of liberal arts education. Du Bois publicized cases of racial prejudice and wrote dozens of articles and speeches.

In 1905 Du Bois and other African Americans who wanted faster change met at Niagara Falls, Canada. Calling themselves the Niagara Movement, the group called for economic and educational equality, as well as an end to segregation and discrimination. The movement's Declaration of Principles said that "to ignore, overlook, or apologize for these wrongs is to prove ourselves unworthy of freedom."

Du Bois and other reformers founded the **National Association for the Advancement of Colored People** (NAACP) in 1909. Among the new organization's members were many well-known progressives such as Jane Addams and John Dewey. Du Bois acted as the director of publications and research and edited the NAACP journal, *The Crisis*. Opposing Washington's views, the NAACP worked to bring racial inequality to the attention of white Americans. The organization also attacked racial discrimination through the court system. In 1915 the NAACP won the important case of *Guinn* v. *United States*, which outlawed the grandfather clause. This type of law had been widely used in the South to keep African Americans from voting. It imposed qualifications on voters, unless the voters' grandfathers had been allowed to vote.

Another important organization, the National Urban League, was formed in 1911. This organization aided many African Americans moving from the South to northern cities. It helped them find jobs and housing and get used to life in the city.

✔ **Reading Check: Comparing and Contrasting** How were the views of Washington like and unlike those of Du Bois?

Free Find:
Booker T. Washington and W. E. B. Du Bois
After reading about Booker T. Washington and W. E. B. Du Bois on the **Holt Researcher CD–ROM**, imagine that you are hosting the two leaders on a talk show. Write a short transcript of a conversation that the two leaders might have.

W. E. B. Du Bois wrote many influential essays on race relations.

The Limits of Progressive Reform

The progressive movement left behind members of other minority groups. In the 1890s the American Indian population in the United States had declined to less than 250,000, its lowest point ever. To deal with poverty among American Indians, the Society of American Indians was started in 1911. Society members wanted Indians to obey the Dawes Act and adopt the ways of white society. The Society believed this would help solve the problems of poverty and unemployment, but most of its members did not understand the views of American Indians who lived

Interpreting the Visual Record

Immigrant communities *As Chinese immigrants arrived in the United States, they established communities, like this one in San Francisco, to maintain their culture.* ***How do you think immigrant communities changed the makeup of U.S. cities?***

on the reservations. Many of these American Indians wanted to preserve their traditional culture. They thought the breakup of reservations under the Dawes Act would bring an end to their way of life. Despite their poverty, some 2,000 Cherokee by 1912 had refused to accept lands granted to them by the government. Other Indians wanted to slow down the allotment process and allow people to stay on reservations. Eventually, new laws let Indians stay on reservations if they wanted to.

Some immigrant groups were also ignored by white progressives. Many Chinese immigrants who came to the United States to mine gold and build railroads had hard lives. Chinese immigration slowed sharply because of the Chinese Exclusion Act of 1882, which prohibited Chinese people from immigrating to the United States for 10 years. Congress later extended the ban, attempting to make immigration from China permanently illegal. Chinese immigrants also faced violence as well as discrimination. Anti-Chinese riots took place in several western states and territories during the late 1800s. As a result, many Chinese Americans formed their own communities in cities such as San Francisco.

While Chinese immigration dropped, Mexican immigration rose between 1901 and 1930. During this time, immigrants could move fairly easily across the U.S. borders with Mexico and Canada. Most Mexican immigrants moved to areas that had once been part of Mexico. Immigrants then invited their family and friends to move to the United States. Although Mexican immigrants were a key part of the Southwest economy, they faced discrimination and harsh labor conditions.

✔ **Reading Check:** **Summarizing** What groups received few benefits from the efforts of progressive reformers?

Section 4 Review

go.hrw.com **Homework Practice Online**
keyword: SC3 HP20

1. **Identify** and explain:
   - Woman's Christian Temperance Union
   - Frances Willard
   - Eighteenth Amendment
   - National American Woman Suffrage Association
   - Carrie Chapman Catt
   - Alice Paul
   - National Woman's Party
   - Nineteenth Amendment
   - Booker T. Washington
   - Atlanta Compromise
   - Ida B. Wells
   - W. E. B. Du Bois
   - National Association for the Advancement of Colored People

2. **Sequencing** Copy the graphic organizer below. Use it to list the events that led to the passage of the Nineteenth Amendment in the order that they occurred.

   Nineteenth Amendment

3. **Finding the Main Idea**
   a. What caused women to join the progressive movement, and what did they hope to achieve?
   b. What groups in the United States were not helped by progressive reformers?

4. **Writing and Critical Thinking**
   Analyzing Information Imagine that you are a muckraking magazine writer. Write an article that compares and contrasts the ways African Americans and women tried to reach their goals during the Progressive Era.
   Consider the following:
   - discrimination against African Americans and women
   - the similarities and differences between Booker T. Washington and W. E. B. Du Bois
   - the similarities and differences between the NAWSA and the NWP

Section 5

The Progressive Presidents

Read to Discover

1. What were the major points of President Roosevelt's progressive policy?
2. Why did progressives turn against President Taft?
3. What reforms did Woodrow Wilson accomplish during his presidency?

Define

- arbitration
- conservation

Identify

- Theodore Roosevelt
- Pure Food and Drug Act
- William Howard Taft
- Bull Moose Party
- Woodrow Wilson
- Underwood Tariff Act
- Sixteenth Amendment
- Federal Reserve Act
- Clayton Antitrust Act
- Federal Trade Commission
- Louis Brandeis

Why It Matters Today

The relationship between government and business is still changing. Use CNNfyi.com or other **current events** sources to find out one way in which government tries to control business today. Record your findings in your journal.

The Story Continues

On the tour following his second inauguration in 1901, President William McKinley was met by friendly people eager to shake his hand. As McKinley greeted a crowd in Buffalo, New York, however, anarchist Leon Czolgosz pulled out a pistol and shot the president at point-blank range. As he lay mortally wounded, the president whispered, "My wife, be careful how you tell her—oh be careful!" Just eight days later, McKinley was dead.

President William McKinley was assassinated in 1901.

President Theodore Roosevelt

After the assassination of McKinley in 1901, Vice President **Theodore Roosevelt** took office. Most Gilded Age presidents had seen themselves as administrators. However Roosevelt believed the president should be an active leader. He believed the interests of businesspeople, laborers, and consumers should be balanced for the public good. Roosevelt used this policy—known as the Square Deal—in the coal miners' strike in 1902. The strike lasted several months, causing coal shortages and rising coal prices. The country was in danger of having no heating fuel for the winter. Roosevelt declared that the coal shortages had "become a matter of vital concern to the whole nation." Roosevelt threatened to take over the mines unless managers agreed to **arbitration**, a formal process to settle disputes, with the strikers. Unlike previous presidents, Roosevelt helped labor to bargain with management. In 1903 he gave a promise.

Analyzing Primary Sources

Drawing Inferences and Conclusions What does Roosevelt mean by the word *square*?

"The labor unions shall have a square deal, and the corporations shall have a square deal, and in addition all private citizens shall have a square deal."

—President Theodore Roosevelt, quoted in *The Presidency of Theodore Roosevelt,* by Lewis L. Gould

Roosevelt used the Square Deal as a slogan in his successful presidential campaign in 1904.

President Roosevelt made regulating trusts the top goal of his first administration. He thought there were "good" trusts, which helped society, and "bad" trusts, which hurt the public. Roosevelt took on the Northern Securities Company, a big railroad trust in the Northwest. In 1904 the Supreme Court found that the Northern Securities Company had violated the Sherman Antitrust Act. The Court's ruling sent a warning to large corporations. The public was pleased, and Roosevelt gained a public reputation as a trustbuster. Business leaders, on the other hand, were outraged. They feared growing government interference in the country's economy and thus in their businesses.

In some cases, public pressure forced President Roosevelt to seek reform. Muckrakers helped build popular support for a larger government role in addressing problems. The American Medical Association also called for better food standards and proper labeling. Yet Congress would not pass reforms. Then Upton Sinclair's account of the meat-processing industry in his 1906 novel, *The Jungle*, shocked the public. Roosevelt responded by opening an investigation.

Roosevelt persuaded Congress to pass the **Pure Food and Drug Act** in 1906. The new law stopped the manufacture, sale, or transportation of mislabeled or contaminated food and drugs sold in interstate commerce. Congress also passed the Meat Inspection Act, which required inspections of meatpacking plants. Finally, Roosevelt got Congress to regulate railroad shipping rates. The public supported this expansion of federal regulatory powers. Roosevelt's activism set a standard for later progressive presidents.

Because of his love of the outdoors, Roosevelt became the first president to strongly favor **conservation,** or protection of nature and its resources. There were two different points of view among supporters of conservation. Preservationists believed that nature should be preserved because of its beauty. Many preservationists, such as John Muir, wanted to protect the remaining ancient forests of the West from logging. Other members of the conservation movement were known as conservationists.

Theodore Roosevelt

Theodore Roosevelt was born into a wealthy family in New York City in 1858. Despite his privileged upbringing, Roosevelt believed that his success came as a result of his hard work.

As a boy, he suffered from severe asthma and poor eyesight. At the age of 11, however, he began improving his health through exercise and outdoor activities. His asthma got better, and he became a strong and confident young man.

Reporter Lincoln Steffens once wrote about Roosevelt, "He took joy in everything he did, in hunting, camping, in ranching, in politics, in reforming the police or the civil service." **What qualities made Roosevelt a strong leader?**

These people wanted to save the natural resources of the United States. For example, Chief Forester Gifford Pinchot (PIN-shoh) valued forests because they produced the materials needed to build "prosperous homes."

By 1870, tens of millions of acres of federal land had been sold or given to private mining, logging, and railroad companies. These companies were against efforts to conserve federal land. Yet, while Roosevelt was in office, the forest service gained control of nearly 150 million acres of public land. Roosevelt doubled the number of national parks, created 16 national monuments, and started 51 wildlife refuges.

✔ **Reading Check: Analyzing Information** What reforms did President Roosevelt introduce when he was in office?

Taft Angers the Progressives

Theodore Roosevelt hoped that his secretary of war, **William Howard Taft**, would succeed him as president in 1908. Like Roosevelt, Taft opposed socialism and favored business regulation. With Roosevelt's help, Taft beat William Jennings Bryan in the election of 1908. However, despite their friendship, Roosevelt and Taft held different ideas about how a president should act. Taft thought Roosevelt had claimed more power than the executive branch was constitutionally allowed. Therefore, Taft chose to move more cautiously toward reform and regulation, which upset many progressives. Although he started twice as many antitrust suits as Roosevelt had, this was not enough to please progressives like Bryan and Robert M. La Follette, who wanted to destroy the trusts entirely. Taft angered progressives further when he signed the Payne-Aldrich Tariff of 1909. Although the Payne-Aldrich Tariff did reduce some rates, it raised others. The result was that tariffs were not reduced as much as many progressives wanted.

Taft's battle with Roosevelt's close friend and ally Gifford Pinchot also proved politically costly. In 1909 Pinchot accused Secretary of the Interior Richard Ballinger of hurting conservation efforts by leasing public lands to big business. Taft decided to fire Pinchot, which upset conservationists and many other progressives, including Roosevelt. Taft actually transferred more land into government reserves than Roosevelt had. However, he could not win back progressive support.

✔ **Reading Check: Summarizing** What actions did Taft take that angered Roosevelt and other progressives?

Interpreting Political Cartoons

Trustbusting *Roosevelt responds to public concerns by trying to break up trusts.* ***What roles are Roosevelt and the trusts assigned in this 1904 cartoon entitled "Jack the Giant Killer"?***

Research on the ROM

Free Find:
Pure Food and Drug Act
After reading about the Pure Food and Drug Act on the **Holt Researcher CD–ROM**, write a short essay that explains the role of this law in protecting public health.

That's Interesting!

The First Automobile at the White House Did you know that William Howard Taft was the first president to keep a car at the White House? It's true! In fact, Taft had four cars. When the Roosevelts left the White House in their horse-drawn carriage on inauguration day, the rest of the White House carriages were put in storage. An exception was made for Mrs. Jaffray, the White House housekeeper. She was afraid of cars and preferred to do her errands by carriage. The Taft family loved taking afternoon automobile rides.

The Election of 1912

Roosevelt was among the many progressives who believed that Taft was not running the government effectively. Explaining that "the bulk of the people wanted a given job done, and . . . wanted me to do that job," Roosevelt decided to run for president again. When he lost the Republican nomination to Taft, Roosevelt and his followers formed the Progressive Party. The party was nicknamed the **Bull Moose Party** after Roosevelt said he was "as strong as a bull moose." The party's platform was based on Roosevelt's progressive plan, the New Nationalism, which he proposed in August 1910. Roosevelt's plan called for more active regulation, increased social welfare measures, and a stronger executive.

The Democratic Party chose **Woodrow Wilson**. Born in Virginia, Wilson earned a doctoral degree in history, became a professor, and served as president of Princeton University. In 1910 he was elected governor of New Jersey. Wilson based his presidential campaign on a program called the New Freedom, which called for government action against monopolies as well as lower tariffs.

Wilson, Roosevelt, Taft, and Eugene V. Debs, the candidate of the Socialist Party, all were reformers in some fashion. Taft, however, represented more conservative views. All of the candidates disagreed on specific reforms and on how to achieve them. The split between Taft and Roosevelt divided the Republican Party and the Republican vote. Although no one received a majority of the popular vote, Wilson won the electoral vote by a wide margin and became the next president.

✔ **Reading Check: Summarizing** In 1912 who were the four candidates for the presidency, and what parties did each represent?

Interpreting Political Cartoons

Taft's presidency *Many Americans thought that President Taft struggled with issues that Theodore Roosevelt had handled with ease.* ***Whom do you think the man looking in the window represents, and what do you think he is doing?***

Woodrow Wilson's Reforms

In his inaugural address, Wilson spoke of the terrible social conditions under which many working-class Americans lived.

"We have been proud of our industrial achievements, but we have not hitherto [yet] stopped thoughtfully enough to count the human cost, . . . the fearful physical and spiritual cost to the men and women and children upon whom the . . . burden of it all has fallen."

—Woodrow Wilson, First Inaugural Address

Analyzing Primary Sources

Making Generalizations and Predictions What policy would you expect Wilson to follow during his presidency?

Reform legislation was Wilson's top goal, and he pushed for two measures soon after taking office: tariff revision and banking reform. Wilson backed the **Underwood Tariff Act** of 1913, which brought the lowest tariff rates in many years. The act also introduced a version of the modern income tax on personal earnings. This new tax on earnings was made possible when the **Sixteenth Amendment** was ratified in February 1913. This amendment allows the federal government to impose direct taxes on people's incomes.

President Wilson knew that banking reform would be much more difficult to pass than the tariff legislation. Some legislators favored a centralized banking system, while others wanted a decentralized system. The result was a compromise called the **Federal Reserve Act**. Passed in December 1913, the act created a national banking system called the Federal Reserve. This system is made up of 12 regional Federal Reserve

A button and bull moose pendant from Roosevelt's 1912 presidential campaign

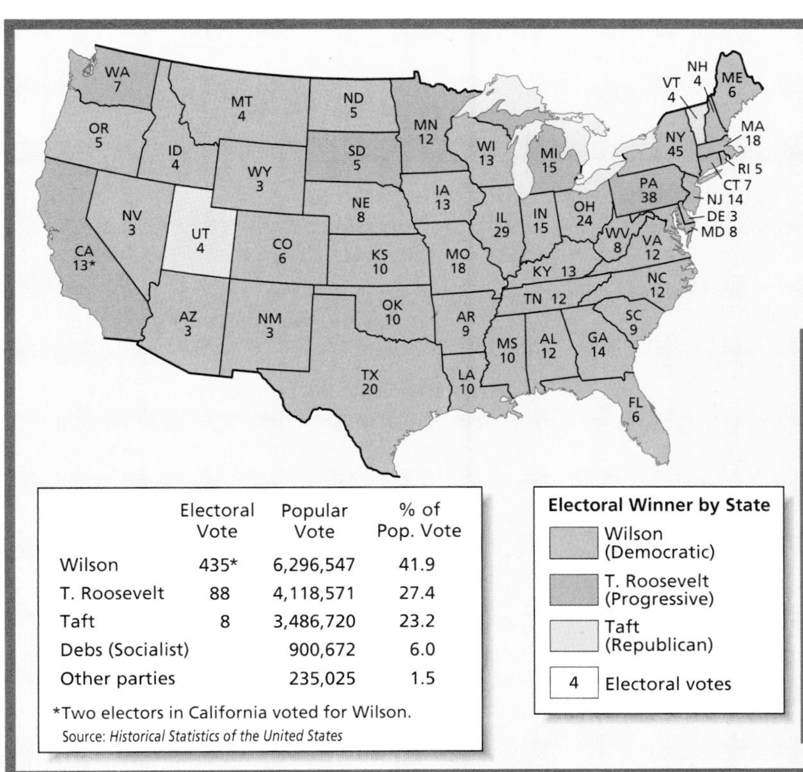

	Electoral Vote	Popular Vote	% of Pop. Vote
Wilson	435*	6,296,547	41.9
T. Roosevelt	88	4,118,571	27.4
Taft	8	3,486,720	23.2
Debs (Socialist)		900,672	6.0
Other parties		235,025	1.5

*Two electors in California voted for Wilson.

Source: *Historical Statistics of the United States*

The Election of 1912

Interpreting Maps Wilson's strength was in the South. Although he won the electoral vote by a landslide, the only states outside the former Confederacy where he won at least half the popular votes were Kentucky, Maryland, and Oklahoma.

Skills Assessment

Places and Regions Which state split its electoral vote?

This 1913 cartoon depicts President Wilson's antitrust legislation as a fence protecting small businesses.

banks as well as many privately owned banks. An independent decision-making board oversees the Federal Reserve. This new banking system enabled the government to try to prevent sudden changes between boom and bust in the economy. Wilson also pushed for laws to regulate big business. The **Clayton Antitrust Act** of 1914 strengthened earlier federal laws against monopolies. The new **Federal Trade Commission**, created in 1914, had the power to stop unfair trade practices by investigating corporations and issuing restraining orders.

As Wilson ran for re-election in 1916, he began to give more attention to farmers, businesspeople, and workers. He appointed **Louis Brandeis**, a progressive lawyer with a reputation for helping people, to the Supreme Court. Brandeis was the first Jewish Supreme Court justice. Wilson also helped pass the Keating-Owen Child Labor Act. In addition, he backed a law providing workers' compensation for federal employees. He also supported the Adamson Act, which limited the workday for railroad workers to eight hours. Wilson's actions helped him win a higher percentage of the vote in the 1916 election.

President Wilson showed great skill and determination in guiding his reform programs through Congress. He told a friend in 1913 that legislators followed his lead because "I do know how to put my mind at the service of others for the accomplishment of a common purpose."

✔ **Reading Check: Summarizing** What major reforms were carried out under President Wilson?

Section 5 Review

go.hrw.com Homework Practice Online keyword: SC3 HP20

1. **Define** and explain:
   - arbitration
   - conservation
2. **Identify** and explain:
   - Theodore Roosevelt
   - Pure Food and Drug Act
   - William Howard Taft
   - Bull Moose Party
   - Woodrow Wilson
   - Underwood Tariff Act
   - Sixteenth Amendment
   - Federal Reserve Act
   - Clayton Antitrust Act
   - Federal Trade Commission
   - Louis Brandeis
3. **Identifying Cause and Effect** Copy the graphic organizer below. Use it to show what caused Roosevelt and other progressives to turn against Taft and the effects this change had on the Republican Party in 1912.

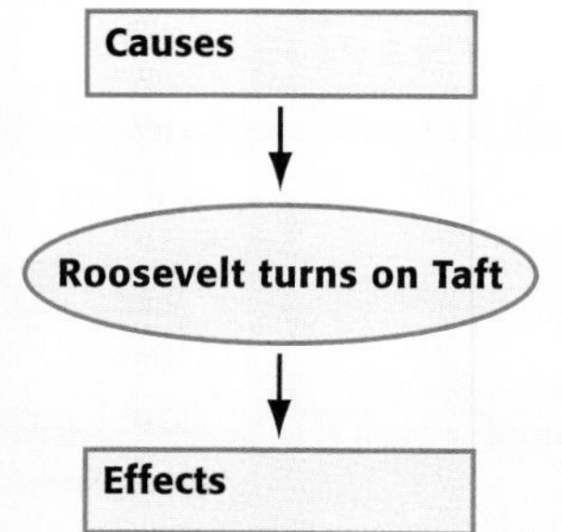

4. **Finding the Main Idea**
   a. What progressive actions did President Roosevelt take against large corporations and railroads?
   b. What reforms did President Wilson guide through Congress?
5. **Writing and Critical Thinking**
   Analyzing Information Imagine that you are a political adviser working for Theodore Roosevelt during the 1912 presidential campaign. Prepare a brochure that explains to the people why they should vote for Roosevelt, instead of the other candidates.
   Consider the following:
   - Roosevelt's record as president from 1901 to 1909
   - Roosevelt's conflict with Taft and the Republican Party
   - Roosevelt's New Nationalism program

Connecting to Literature

The Jungle

Upton Sinclair

Upton Sinclair wrote The Jungle *to create sympathy for immigrants, who lived and worked under difficult conditions. Readers were shocked by his descriptions of the unsanitary practices in the meatpacking industry. Sinclair later said about Americans' reaction, "I aimed at the public's heart, and by accident I hit it in the stomach." In the following excerpt from* The Jungle, *Jurgis Rudkus describes conditions at a Chicago meatpacking plant.*

Meat sales dropped after The Jungle *was published.*

The family had a first-hand knowledge of the great majority of Packingtown swindles. For it was the custom, as they found, whenever meat was so spoiled that it could not be used for anything else, either to can it or else to chop it up into sausage. With what had been told them by Jonas, who had worked in the **pickle**[1] rooms, they could now study the whole of the spoiled-meat industry on the inside, and read a new and grim meaning into that old Packingtown jest—that they use everything of the pig except the squeal.

Jonas had told them how the meat that was taken out of pickle would often be found sour, and how they would rub it up with soda to take away the smell, and sell it to be eaten on free-lunch counters; also of all the miracles of chemistry which they performed, giving to any sort of meat, fresh or salted, whole or chopped, any color and any flavor and any odor they chose. . . .

It was only when the whole ham was spoiled that it came into the department of Elzbieta. . . . Mixed with half a ton of other meat, no odor that ever was in a ham could make any difference. There was never the least attention paid to what was cut up for sausage; there would come all the way back from Europe old sausage that had been rejected. . . . There would be meat that had tumbled out on the floor, in the dirt and sawdust, where the workers had tramped and spit uncounted billions of . . . germs. There would be meat stored in great piles in rooms; and the water from leaky roofs would drip over it, and thousands of rats would race about on it. . . . These rats were nuisances, and the packers would put poisoned bread out for them, they would die, and then rats, bread, and meat would go into the **hoppers**[2] together. This is no fairy story and no joke.

---

[1]**pickle:** vinegar solution

[2]**hoppers:** containers for the temporary storage of material

Understanding What You Read

1. **Literature and History** Why do you think the descriptions in *The Jungle* led to new health laws? Use examples from the excerpt to support your answer.
2. **Literature and You** Conduct research to find out how consumers today can tell that their meats are safe to eat.

Chapter 20 Review

The Chapter at a Glance

Examine the visual summary of the chapter below. Create an outline of the major parts of the chapter, and compare your outline to a classmate's.

Progressive Reforms

Gilded Age
Political machines contributed to widespread political corruption, leading to civil service reform.

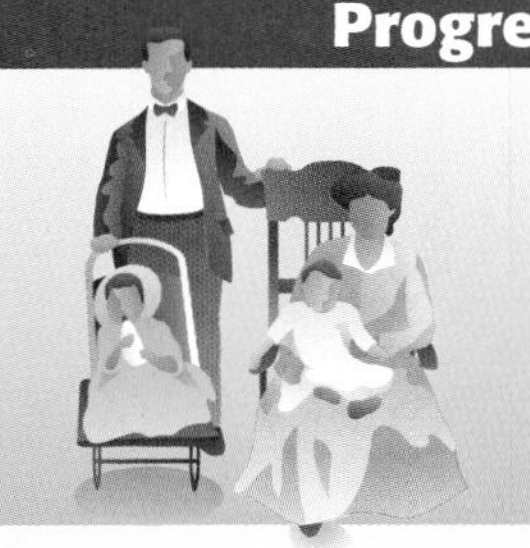

Progressive Era
Progressives supported democratic reforms such as the initiative, recall, and referendum. They also tried to improve government efficiency and workplace safety and worked to end child labor.

Progressive Presidents
Presidents Theodore Roosevelt, William Howard Taft, and Woodrow Wilson regulated trusts. Progressive presidents also concentrated on banking reform and conservation and called for new laws regulating food and drugs.

Women's and Minorities' Rights
Women's rights groups won the right to vote for women and addressed other social issues. Organizations such as the NAACP fought for fairer treatment for minorities.

Identifying People and Ideas

Use the following terms or people in historically significant sentences.

1. political machines
2. John Dewey
3. Industrial Workers of the World
4. Frances Willard
5. Carrie Chapman Catt
6. Nineteenth Amendment
7. Booker T. Washington
8. Atlanta Compromise
9. Theodore Roosevelt
10. Underwood Tariff Act

Understanding Main Ideas

Section 1 *(Pages 606–609)*

1. How did bosses use political machines to control local and city governments?

Section 2 *(Pages 610–614)*

2. Why did progressives want to reform local and state governments, and what did they achieve?

Section 3 *(Pages 615–618)*

3. What were working conditions like for children and other factory workers in the late 1800s, and what changes did reformers try to make?

Section 4 *(Pages 619–624)*

4. What caused some women to form the Woman's Christian Temperance Union?

Section 5 *(Pages 625–630)*

5. What was President Roosevelt's attitude toward trusts?
6. What reforms did President Wilson pass during his presidency?

You Be the Historian— Reviewing Themes

1. **Citizenship** Why did women form the National American Woman Suffrage Association?
2. **Constitutional Heritage** What was the significance of the Supreme Court's ruling in *Lochner* v. *New York*, and how did its decision in *Muller* v. *Oregon* partially reverse the earlier ruling?
3. **Economics** What role did Roosevelt believe government should play in the economy?

Thinking Critically

1. **Comparing and Contrasting** How were progressives and earlier reformers alike and different?
2. **Evaluating** Which of the progressive presidents do you think was most successful in reforming American society? Explain your answer.
3. **Identifying Cause and Effect** What led to the growth of the conservation movement, and what effects did it have on natural resources in the United States?

Social Studies Skills Workshop

Interpreting Graphs

Study the graphs below. Then use the information on the graphs to help you answer the questions that follow.

1. About how long was the average workday, and about how much was the average hourly wage in 1900?
   a. 15 hours per day and 10 cents per hour
   b. 10 hours per day and 15 cents per hour
   c. 8 hours per day and 20 cents per hour
   d. 9.5 hours per day and 20 cents per hour
2. What was the general trend in the length of the workday and the hourly wage between 1900 and 1910?

Analyzing Primary Sources

Read the following quotation by reformer Jacob Riis, from his book *How the Other Half Lives*. Then answer the following questions.

> **"Suppose we look into [a tenement on] Cherry Street. Be a little careful, please! The hall is dark and you might stumble. . . . A flight of stairs. You can feel your way, if you cannot see it. . . . all the fresh air that ever enters these stairs comes from the hall door. . . . Here is a door. Listen! That short hacking cough, that tiny, helpless wail—what do they mean? . . . Oh! a sadly familiar story—before the day is at an end. The child is dying with measles. With half a chance it might have lived; but it had none. That dark bedroom killed it."**

3. Which of the following best expresses Riis's view of tenement conditions?
   a. Landlords should lower tenement rents to help people with families.
   b. The lack of light and air is unhealthy, particularly for children.
   c. Mostly poor people live in tenements.
   d. There should be better medical care for people living in tenements.
4. Why do you think Riis uses the language he does to describe the tenement?
   a. He could not see things very clearly on his visit.
   b. He wants to create sympathy by helping the reader feel what the conditions are really like.
   c. He was frightened while in the tenement.
   d. He wants to reassure people that the tenements are not that bad.
5. Based on your knowledge of this period, how do you think people might have responded to Riis's description of tenement life?

Alternative Assessment

Building Your Portfolio

American History

Cooperative Learning

Complete the following activity in small groups. If muckrakers were investigating problems in American society today, what do you think would be the top five problems they would address? Find newspaper and magazine articles and images related to these topics. Use this information to create a bulletin board display titled Important Issues Today.

internet connect

Internet Activity: go.hrw.com
keyword: SC3 CF20

Choose an activity on the Spirit of Reform to:

- Learn about the role of the Tammany Hall political machine in the lives of citizens of New York City.
- Write a report on city planning in the early 1900s.
- Learn how the Federal Reserve system works today.

Social Studies Skills

WORKSHOP

Writing and Revising a Paragraph

A paragraph is a group of sentences that express an idea. Paragraphs almost always have a *main idea*, the big picture in the paragraph. The *topic sentence* states the main idea of the paragraph. You may find it at the beginning of the paragraph, in the middle, or even at the end. *Supporting sentences* give details that explain or prove the main idea.

How to Write a Paragraph

Always keep your purpose for writing in mind as you write your paragraph. That purpose might be to evaluate, to persuade, or to inform. Each different purpose for writing requires its own form, tone, and content.

Most writing assignments will have specific directions about what and how to write. The guidelines outlined below can help you plan and improve your writing.

1. **Identify your purpose in writing.** Read the directions carefully to identify the intended goal of the assignment.
2. **Collect information.** Think and plan before you begin writing your paragraph. Do research if necessary. Your paragraph will be more effective if you have plenty of details that can be used.
3. **Create unity and coherence.** A paragraph has *unity* when all of the sentences support, or tell something about, the main idea. A paragraph has *coherence* when readers can tell how and why ideas are connected.
4. **Use good sentence structure.** All of your sentences should begin with a capital letter and end with a period, a question mark, or an exclamation point. Avoid *sentence fragments* and *run-on sentences.*

Example:

Good: *Sofia's favorite dance is the merengue.*
Sentence Fragment: *The dance, which Sofia learned from her parents.*
Run-On Sentence: *Sofia's favorite dance is the merengue, she learned it from her parents.*

How to Revise a Paragraph

Revising is an important part of good writing. The guidelines below will help you edit your writing to improve its style and content. These guidelines will also help you edit the work of others, commonly referred to as peer editing.

1. **Evaluate the main idea.** The paragraph should express a single main idea or set of related ideas, with details for support. Make sure that the sentences in the paragraph support its topic sentence.
2. **Reorganize if needed.** Reorganize the draft as needed to make the ideas clearer and easier to follow.
3. **Rewrite.** Improve sentences by adding appropriate adjectives and adverbs. Check for proper spelling, grammar, and punctuation. Prepare a neat, clean final version.

Practicing the Skills

1. Follow the steps above to write a paragraph on one of the following: immigrants, reformers, or the West.
2. Peer edit the paragraph written by one of your classmates.

History in Action

UNIT 7 SIMULATION

You Solve the Problem . . .

How Can the Progressives Reform American Politics?

Complete the following activity in small cooperative groups. The year is 1900. Your city is going to be hosting a large conference of progressives from all around the country. Your group will be giving a presentation to these men and women on reforming the political process in the United States to make it more democratic. Follow these steps to solve your problem.

1. Gather Information Use your textbook and other resources to find information that might influence the arguments you will make in your presentation. Be sure to use what you learned from this unit's Skills Workshop on Writing and Revising a Pararaph to help you to effectively prepare your solution to this problem. You may want to divide up different parts of the research among group members.

2. List and Consider Options Based on the information you have gathered, list and consider the options you might recommend for making the American political process more democratic. Your final solution to the problem may be easier to reach if you consider as many options as possible. Be sure to record your possible options to help you prepare your presentation.

3. Consider Advantages and Disadvantages Now consider the advantages and disadvantages of taking each option. Ask yourselves questions like: "How will this reform help more people participate in the political process?" Once you have considered the advantages and disadvantages, record them as notes for use in your presentation.

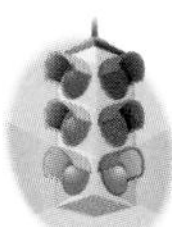

4. Choose, Implement, and Evaluate a Solution After considering the advantages and disadvantages, you should plan and create your presentation. Be sure to make your proposal very clear. You will need to support your plan for reforming American politics by including information you gathered and by explaining why you rejected other options. Your presentation needs to be visually appealing to gain the interest of others attending the conference. When you are ready, decide who in your group will make which part of the presentation and take your solution to the other progressives at the convention (the rest of the class). Good luck!

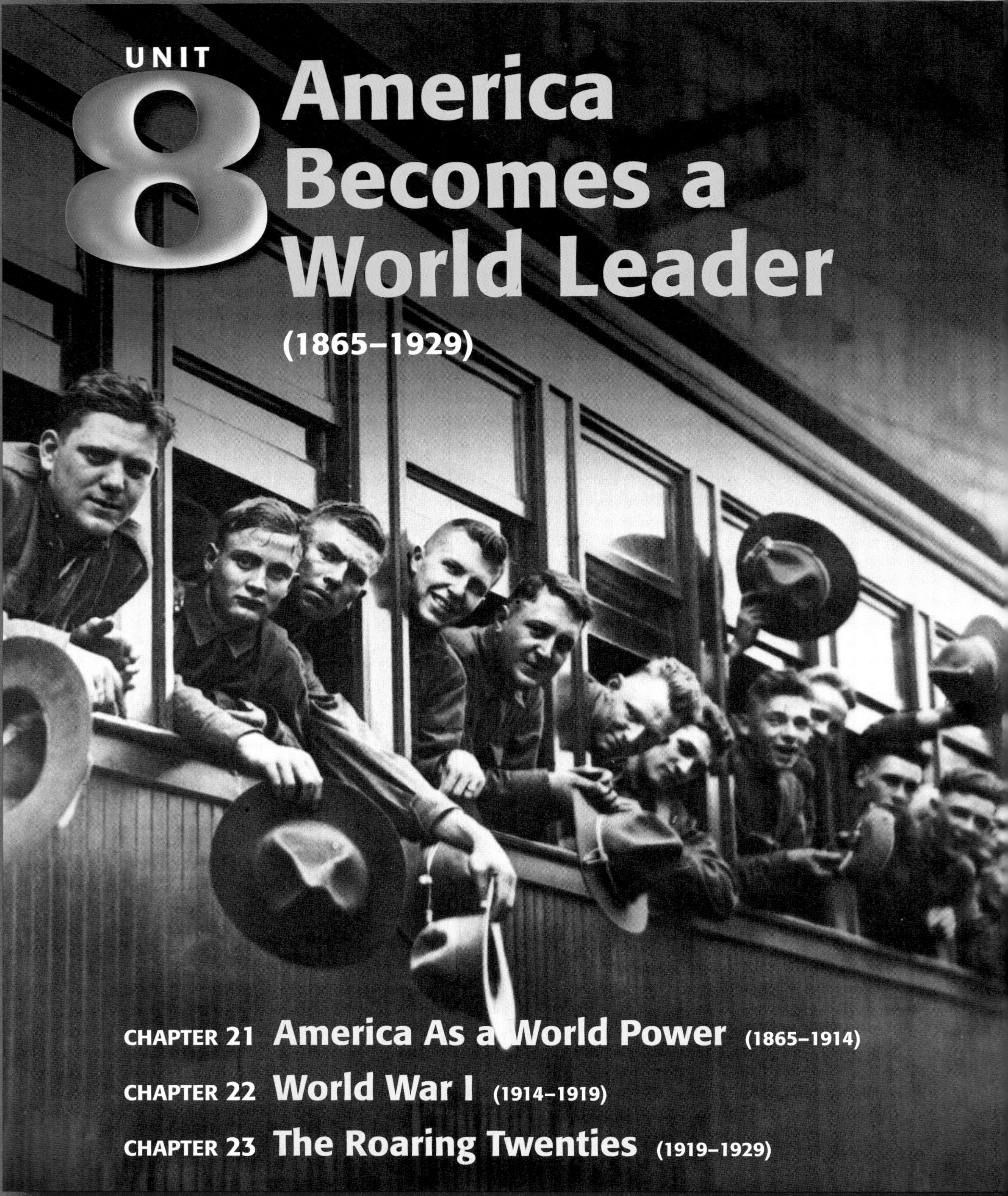

UNIT

8 America Becomes a World Leader

(1865–1929)

Young People

IN HISTORY

Young War Supporters

Young people across the United States supported the nation's fight in World War I. These boys and girls performed essential services and helped the Allies win.

When they joined their troops, Boy and Girl Scouts were required to take an oath to serve their country. Scouts fulfilled their duty with enthusiasm and dedication during the war years. Under the slogan "Every Scout to Save a Soldier," they sold almost half a billion dollars in Liberty Bonds and War Saving Stamps.

Some young people donated their own money for the war effort. Sunday school pupils in Cleveland, Ohio, each gave a dime toward the cost of a new warship. Victory Boys and Victory Girls also pledged up to $10 per child toward the war effort. They worked at odd jobs to earn money. These jobs included raising and selling guinea pigs, gathering nuts, and polishing shoes.

The U.S. government created posters to encourage young people to join in the war effort.

Other young people also volunteered their labor. Girls joined knitting parties to make scarves and gloves for soldiers. Boys on vacation from school signed up with the U.S. Boy's Working Reserve "agricultural army" to help farmers grow food for soldiers overseas. One writer credited the Reserve workers "with saving the sugar-beet crop in Michigan, the apple crop in Georgia, [and] the berry crop in Oregon."

Some young people even left school to help boost agricultural production. The New York legislature, for example, proposed to allow 12-year-olds to stay out of school seven months out of the year to work on farms. After the war, however, the government urged these young people to return to school. One poster read:

> **"Boys and Girls**
> **The School Is Your Training Camp**
> **Uncle Sam Says**
> **ENLIST TODAY."**

Young war supporters often found that their work offered unexpected benefits. One teen who served as a machine operator earned $3.50 a day—more than five times what he could have earned before the war. Other young adults got the chance to travel. And all had the satisfaction of serving their country.

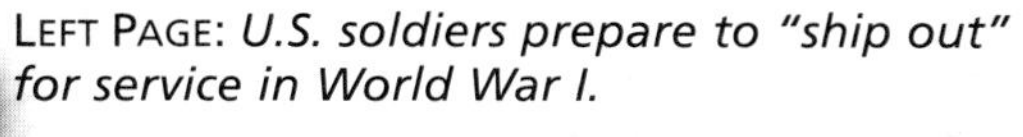

If You Were There *How would you have aided the war effort?*

LEFT PAGE: *U.S. soldiers prepare to "ship out" for service in World War I.*

CHAPTER

21 America as a World Power (1865–1914)

This eagle represents the United States stretching its wings across the Pacific.

Alaska's beautiful scenery and natural resources made it a valuable addition to the United States.

UNITED STATES

1867 The United States buys Alaska.

1887 Planters in Hawaii force King Kalakaua to sign a new constitution reducing his power.

1890 Congress passes the McKinley Tariff, which gives a subsidy to U.S. sugar producers.

1865 | **1870** | **1875** | **1880** | **1885** | **1890**

WORLD

1868 Japan begins a period of modernization known as the Meiji Restoration.

1881 A French company begins building a canal across the Isthmus of Panama.

1885 The Indian National Congress is formed in British-controlled India.

1894 China and Japan fight a war for control of Korea.

An international army storms into Beijing to free foreign diplomats trapped by the Boxer Rebellion in China.

Build on What You Know

While progressive reformers tried to solve political and social problems that went with the nation's rapid growth, the United States also began to expand overseas and play a greater role in world affairs. The Spanish-American War and the Mexican Revolution made Americans think about what role the United States should play in the politics of neighboring countries.

The Rough Riders and the 9th and 10th Cavalries fight to help secure the town of Santiago de Cuba during the Spanish-American War.

1895 Cuba revolts against Spain.

1898 The United States wins the Spanish-American War, gaining the Philippine Islands and Puerto Rico.

1900 The Boxer Rebellion occurs in China.

1903 Panama declares itself an independent nation.

1904 President Theodore Roosevelt presents his corollary to the Monroe Doctrine.

Construction of the Panama Canal begins.

1904 The Russo-Japanese War begins.

1910 The Mexican Revolution begins.

1914 The Panama Canal opens.

1895 | 1900 | 1905 | 1910 | 1915

José Martí was a leader in the struggle for Cuban independence.

If you were there . . .

Would you favor U.S. expansion overseas?

You Be the Historian

What's Your Opinion? Do you **agree** or **disagree** with the following statements? Support your point of view in your journal.

- **Geography** Distant lands have little value as colonies or territories.
- **Economics** A country's economic issues always affect its foreign policy.
- **Global Relations** A powerful nation should take part in the political affairs of its neighbors.

Section 1

The United States Gains Overseas Territories

Read to Discover

1. Why did some people favor expansion over isolationism?
2. What events led to the U.S. annexation of Hawaii?
3. What was the goal of U.S. foreign policy in Japan and China?

Define

- imperialism
- isolationism
- subsidy
- spheres of influence

Identify

- William H. Seward
- McKinley Tariff
- Liliuokalani
- Matthew Perry
- Open Door Policy
- Boxer Rebellion

WHY IT MATTERS TODAY

The United States still has military bases overseas. Use CNNfyi.com or other **current events** sources to find information about one U.S. military base located overseas. Record your findings in your journal.

In this cartoon, nations fight over a woman who symbolizes Samoa. In 1899 the United States and Germany agreed to divide Samoa between them.

The Story Continues

On March 16, 1889, one British, three German, and three U.S. warships prepared to fight for control of Samoa. Before any fighting could begin, however, a sudden storm blew in and destroyed all the ships except the British vessel. The storm prevented a battle that day, but it did not end Western countries' race to expand around the world.

Imperialism and Expansion

Europeans were willing to risk war in such far-off places as Samoa because they wanted to build naval bases and protect shipping routes in the Pacific. This effort was part of **imperialism**—the practice of building an empire by founding colonies or conquering other nations. Between 1870 and 1914, powerful Western nations built large colonial empires. They took control of most of Africa and much of Southeast Asia.

Several forces drove this wave of imperialism. Countries wanted raw materials—such as copper, rubber, and tin—to help their industrial growth. At the same time, businesspeople needed new markets to sell their goods. Many people also saw colonies as a source of power and national pride.

In 1867 the lure of land and resources encouraged Secretary of State **William H. Seward** to arrange the purchase of Alaska from Russia. At $7.2 million, the cost was less than two cents per acre. People laughed at the purchase, calling it "Seward's Folly" and the "Alaskan Icebox." However, Alaska added some 600,000 square miles to the United States and had valuable natural resources such as furs, minerals, and timber.

The United States did not begin expanding overseas until the late 1800s. Previously, Americans had followed a policy of **isolationism**—avoiding involvement in the affairs of other countries. Long before, President George Washington had warned Americans "to steer clear of permanent alliances" with other countries—particularly those in Europe. U.S. leaders had tried to follow this advice by staying out of overseas conflicts.

Not everyone favored isolationism. Some Americans thought the United States needed to expand to keep the country's economy strong. Alfred Thayer Mahan, in *The Influence of Sea Power upon History,* wrote that the United States needed a strong navy. Published in 1890, Mahan's book argued that the navy could protect U.S. economic interests abroad. This economic growth would in turn increase American military power. Senator Henry Cabot Lodge repeated Mahan's call for economic expansion through naval power.

Analyzing Primary Sources

Drawing Inferences and Conclusions What does Lodge mean when he says that "commerce follows the flag"?

"Commerce follows the flag, and we should build up a navy strong enough to give protection to Americans in every quarter of the globe."

—Henry Cabot Lodge, quoted in *The Annals of America*

✔ **Reading Check: Contrasting** How do imperialism and isolationism differ?

Interpreting the Visual Record

A mighty fleet *A modern navy helped the United States compete against other global powers.* ***How might such a fleet help the United States expand overseas?***

BIOGRAPHY

Queen Liliuokalani

(1838–1917)

Liliuokalani was born in Honolulu and was educated by American missionaries. In 1887 she toured the United States. Liliuokalani became queen of Hawaii in 1891. After the revolt that ended her short reign, she worked to reclaim her throne. In her autobiography, *Hawaii's Story by Hawaii's Queen*, she questioned whether overseas expansion was a proper goal for the United States. Throughout her life, Liliuokalani remained a symbol of Hawaiian pride and history. What contact did Liliuokalani have with the United States?

Free Find:
Liliuokalani
After reading about Liliuokalani on the **Holt Researcher CD–ROM**, write a song that honors her efforts on behalf of the Hawaiian people.

Hawaii

Another Pacific island nation—Hawaii—also interested imperial powers. The Hawaiian Islands had a tropical climate and fertile soil. The Hawaiian people had first contact with Europeans in 1778 when British explorer Captain James Cook arrived. Trading and whaling ships in the Pacific then began stopping in Hawaii for supplies. Later, American missionaries came to convert the Hawaiians to Christianity. These missionaries opened businesses and raised crops such as sugarcane. Some missionary families became rich sugar planters.

By the 1840s most shops and shipyards in Hawaii were owned by Americans. Sugar had become a leading export of the Hawaiian economy. An 1875 treaty allowed Hawaiian sugar to be shipped duty-free to the United States. In return, Hawaii agreed not to give territory or special privileges to any other country.

Hawaiian sugar production boomed, and the power of the planters grew. In 1887 they forced King Kalakaua (kah-LAH-KAH-ooh-ah) to sign a new constitution. This constitution granted more political power to the Hawaiian parliament, which the planters controlled. Many Hawaiians worried that foreigners were becoming too powerful.

Hawaiian sugar planters suffered a major economic setback in 1890 when Congress passed the **McKinley Tariff**. This law allowed all countries to ship sugar duty-free to the United States. However, the tariff also gave U.S. sugar producers a **subsidy**, or bonus payment by the government, of two cents per pound. The prices of Hawaiian sugar dropped, and the islands' economy collapsed.

In 1893 Queen **Liliuokalani** (li-lee-uh-woh-kuh-LAHN-ee) presented a new constitution that returned power to the monarchy. In response, the planters revolted. John L. Stevens, U.S. minister to Hawaii, called 150 U.S. Marines ashore to support the revolt. The rebellion succeeded without a shot being fired. The planters then formed a new government with lawyer Sanford B. Dole serving as president. Acting without authority from the U.S. State Department, Stevens recognized, or formally acknowledged, the new government. He declared Hawaii to be under U.S. control on February 1, 1893. "The Hawaiian pear is now fully ripe," wrote Stevens, "and this is the golden hour for the United States to pluck it."

President Grover Cleveland, who had met Hawaii's Queen Liliuokalani when she was a princess, disapproved of the revolt and refused to annex Hawaii. However, he took little effective action to help restore the monarchy. The islands remained an independent republic until July 7, 1898, when Congress annexed them. Hawaii became a U.S. territory in 1900 and the 50th state in 1959.

✔ **Reading Check: Finding the Main Idea** What effects did the McKinley Tariff have on Hawaii?

The Opening of Japan

By the mid-1800s some European powers had formed strong trade ties with much of East Asia. But the island nation of Japan had isolated itself from the rest of the world for hundreds of years. Japan's leaders had also banned travel to other countries.

The United States wanted to open Japan's trade before Europeans got there. President Millard Fillmore sent Commodore **Matthew Perry** to secure "friendship, commerce, a supply of coal and provisions." On July 8, 1853, a crowd of astonished Japanese watched a fleet of four U.S. warships enter Edo (now called Tokyo) Harbor. Perry delivered a letter to the Japanese government from President Fillmore suggesting peaceful trade ties. Perry returned to Japan in February 1854 with seven warships. He brought gifts showing some of the technological benefits the United States could offer. This effort—and the presence of American military power—persuaded Japanese leaders to sign a treaty opening trade with the United States. In 1856 Townsend Harris arrived in Japan as the first U.S. consul general, or chief diplomat. Despite some opposition in Japan, he negotiated a trade treaty in 1858.

Japanese leaders who believed their country needed to industrialize wanted trade with the United States. In 1868, those favoring industrialization came to power in Japan, beginning a time of modernization known as the Meiji (MAY-jee) Restoration. During the next 40 years, Japanese leaders invested heavily in industry and in making the country's military stronger. The government sent Japanese students to Western schools to study science, technology, and Western government. One such student explained his goal.

> **"The final purpose of all my work was to create in Japan a civilized nation as well equipped in the arts of war and peace as those of the Western world."**
>
> —Yukichi Fukuzawa, *The Autobiography of Yukichi Fukuzawa*

By the 1890s, Japan was becoming a major imperial power. Japan invaded China in 1894. After defeating China's military, Japan gained the same trade privileges in China as European countries enjoyed, in addition to winning new territory. In 1904, Japan and Russia went to war. President Theodore Roosevelt helped negotiate a peace treaty to end the war a year later. The Japanese had won the respect they desired. Japan gained Korea, a lease on Port Arthur in China, and other rights. In just 50 years, Japan had changed from an isolated nonindustrial country to a major world power. Hilary Herbert, U.S. secretary of the navy, said, "Japan has leaped, almost at one bound, to a place among the great nations of the earth."

✔ **Reading Check: Sequencing** List the steps Japan took after the arrival of Matthew Perry to become a world power.

Japan and Hawaii

In the 1860s the first Japanese immigrants began arriving in Hawaii. By 1923 they made up almost 43 percent of the population. Many Japanese went to work on the islands' sugar plantations. Workers had a difficult life raising and harvesting the sugarcane.

Many Japanese immigrants remained in Hawaii after their work contracts ended. Today people of Japanese descent make up about one fourth of Hawaii's population. They live on all the major islands and work in all types of fields, including education, government, and law. **How have Japanese immigrants contributed to Hawaiian society?**

Foreign Powers in China

Economic interests drew the United States not only to Hawaii and Japan but also to China. There the United States and many European nations engaged in profitable trade. After Japan defeated China in 1895, other countries quickly took further advantage of China's weakness. These nations seized **spheres of influence**—areas where foreign nations could control trade and natural resources. Many nations joined in what was called "the carving up of the Chinese melon." Germany took control of a harbor in Shandong Province in November 1897. Other nations did likewise. France and Japan occupied land in China's southern provinces, Russia moved into northern China, and Great Britain took over territory on the coast opposite Hong Kong Island. The United States, however, lacked the naval power to establish its own sphere of influence.

Fearing that the United States would be closed out of Chinese markets, U.S. Secretary of State John Hay announced the **Open Door Policy**. Hay sent a series of notes to Japan and some European countries in 1899. The main argument of the Open Door Policy was that all nations should have equal access to trade in China. When the European powers and Japan neither accepted nor rejected the policy, Hay announced that it had been accepted.

Within China there was strong resentment of the power and control held by foreign nations. In 1900 this antiforeign hostility grew until it erupted in the **Boxer Rebellion**. The Boxers were Chinese nationalists who were members of a group called the Fists of Righteous Harmony. Boxers got their name from foreigners who called the group this

Asian goods such as this decorated fan became popular trade items in the United States in the late 1800s.

PEABODY ESSEX MUSEUM, SALEM, MASSACHUSETTS

U.S. Territories in the Pacific

Interpreting Maps Between 1867 and 1900 Alaska and many Pacific islands, including Hawaii, became U.S. territories.

Skills Assessment

1. **Places and Regions** What U.S. territory was located below the equator?
2. **Analyzing Information** In what year did the United States acquire the most territories?

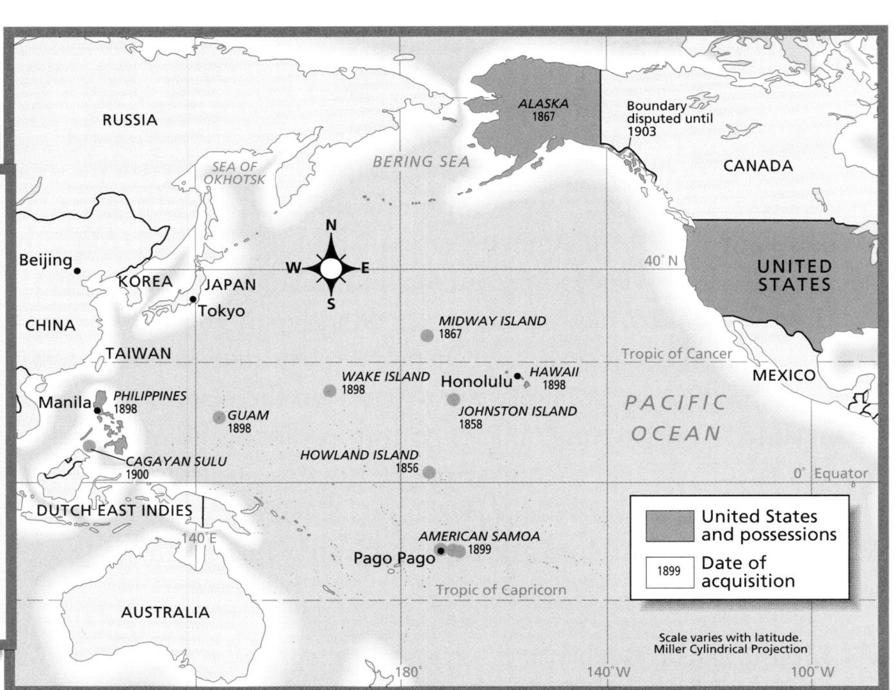

because of the boxing rituals that the members practiced. The Boxers were angered by foreign involvement in China's affairs and by the Chinese government's poor management. They were also frustrated by the hunger and homelessness caused by a series of natural disasters. In June the Boxers took to the streets of Beijing, China's capital, and laid siege to the walled settlement in which foreigners lived. They killed more than 200 people during the attack. Seeing that the attack was doomed, the Chinese government did not support the Boxers.

Boxers attack the foreigners' compound in Beijing.

For two months the siege continued as military forces that included U.S. Marines fought their way from the port of Tianjin to Beijing. The Boxers were soon defeated, and China was forced to accept a harsh settlement. The Chinese had to make a $333 million cash payment to foreign governments, $25 million of which went to the United States.

Secretary of State Hay then sent another Open Door note to Japan and the European nations. He restated the U.S. position that all nations should have equal access to Chinese markets. Hay wanted to prevent any European colonization of China that would limit U.S. influence. The Open Door Policy remained in effect long after the Boxer Rebellion.

✔ **Reading Check: Identifying Cause and Effect** What factors led to the Boxer Rebellion in China, and what was the result?

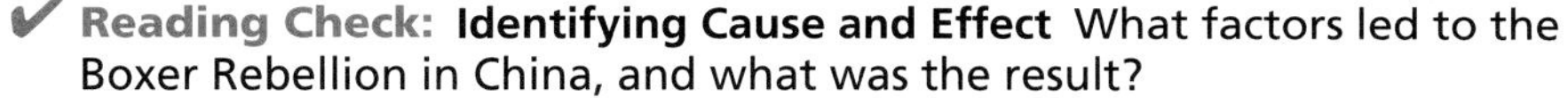

Section 1 Review

Homework Practice Online
keyword: SC3 HP21

1 **Define** and explain:
- imperialism
- isolationism
- subsidy
- spheres of influence

2 **Identify** and explain:
- William H. Seward
- McKinley Tariff
- Liliuokalani
- Matthew Perry
- Open Door Policy
- Boxer Rebellion

3 **Summarizing** Copy the graphic organizer below. Use it to describe the territories in the Pacific acquired by the United States and to show U.S. influence.

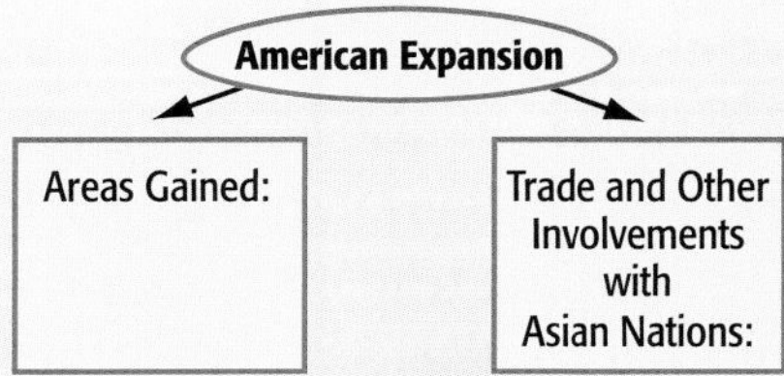

4 **Finding the Main Idea**
a. What arguments did supporters of American expansionism make in the 1890s?
b. How did Hawaii become a U.S. territory?

5 **Writing and Critical Thinking**
Supporting a Point of View Imagine that you are a member of Congress around 1900. Write a short speech that you might give to Congress about U.S. policy toward China and Japan. You may either support or oppose U.S. policy.
Consider the following:
- reasons the United States should expand
- China's attitude toward foreign nations
- Japan's attitude toward foreign nations

Section 2

The Spanish-American War

Read to Discover

1. How did the press affect U.S. involvement in the conflict between Spain and Cuba?
2. What enabled the United States to win the war against Spain?
3. How did the Spanish-American War affect the Philippines, Cuba, and Puerto Rico?

Define

- yellow journalism

Identify

- Joseph Pulitzer
- William Randolph Hearst
- Teller Amendment
- Emilio Aguinaldo
- Anti-Imperialist League
- Platt Amendment

WHY IT MATTERS TODAY

America's relations with Cuba have changed significantly since the Spanish-American War. Use CNNfyi.com or other **current events** sources to find out about one aspect of the relationship between the United States and Cuba today. Record your findings in your journal.

THE GRANGER COLLECTION, NEW YORK

President McKinley was sympathetic to the cause of Cuba's rebels.

The Story Continues

In 1895, Cubans revolted against Spanish colonial rule. In response, the Spanish army gathered several hundred thousand Cubans into *reconcentrados,* or reconcentration camps. Some 200,000 Cubans died in the camps because of poor food and sanitation. Such harsh measures led many Americans to support the Cuban rebels in their struggle for independence from Spain.

The Road to War

Many Americans believed Cuba's battle with Spain resembled America's Revolutionary War. The Cuban conflict was widely reported, even exaggerated, in the American press, further increasing American support for the Cubans.

The *New York World,* published by **Joseph Pulitzer**, was very critical of the Spanish, as was **William Randolph Hearst's** *New York Journal.* In their competition for more readers, both men printed sensational, often exaggerated stories. This exaggeration of news stories in order to sell newspapers became known as **yellow journalism**.

Pulitzer was first to engage in yellow journalism, but Hearst quickly responded and proved better at it. To sell papers and to get support for U.S. military action in Cuba, Hearst hired artist and illustrator Frederic Remington to provide pictures of conditions on the island. Remington supposedly sent Hearst a telegram from Cuba that read, "Everything is quiet. There is no trouble here. There will be no war." Hearst is said to have answered, "You furnish [provide] the pictures and I'll furnish the war."

Interpreting the Visual Record

Manila Bay *On May 1, 1898, Commodore George Dewey's fleet destroyed Spain's Pacific fleet in a decisive battle.* ***How does this image represent the success of the U.S. ships?***

Despite growing public support for military action, President Grover Cleveland remained strongly opposed to U.S. involvement in Cuba. However, in 1896, William McKinley, a supporter of Cuban independence, was elected president.

On January 25, 1898, the U.S. battleship *Maine* arrived in Havana Harbor to protect U.S. citizens and economic interests. On February 9 Hearst published a letter written by the Spanish minister to the United States that called President McKinley a weak leader. The letter outraged many Americans and embarrassed the Spanish government. Six days after Hearst published the letter, 260 American sailors were killed when the *Maine* exploded. Although the cause of the explosion was unclear, many Americans immediately blamed Spain.

Congress approved $50 million that McKinley requested to prepare for war. Spain offered to negotiate but would not consider Cuban independence. Congress then passed a resolution on April 20 declaring the island independent and giving Spain three days to leave the island. Attached to the resolution was the **Teller Amendment**, which stated that the United States had no interest in taking control of Cuba. In response to the U.S. declaration that Spain had to leave Cuba, the Spanish government declared war on the United States on April 24. The next day Congress passed and McKinley signed a declaration of war against Spain.

April 25, 1898

The United States declares war on Spain.

✔ **Reading Check: Sequencing** List the events in order that resulted in the Spanish-American War.

War with Spain

While attention was focused on Cuba, the U.S. Navy won a quick and spectacular victory nearly halfway around the world. Commodore George Dewey led the American Asiatic squadron at Hong Kong. When the war began, Dewey set out to attack the Spanish Philippines. On May 1 Dewey's ships boldly sailed into Manila Bay and destroyed Spain's Pacific fleet. While the Spanish lost 381 lives, none of Dewey's men were killed.

Research on the ROM

Free Find:
William Randolph Hearst
After reading about William Randolph Hearst on the **Holt Researcher CD–ROM**, create a front page for a newspaper with current news stories that reflect Hearst's style of journalism.

That's Interesting!

Cuban Baseball Did you know that baseball played a part in the Cuban struggle for independence? It's true! Cubans had been playing professional baseball since 1878. They learned the game from American college students and from sailors. One of the founders of Cuban baseball, Emilio Sabourín, was also a supporter of Cuban independence. He gave money to Cuban patriot José Martí to support a revolution against Spain. After the war, baseball remained hugely popular in Cuba, and many American baseball players and teams toured Cuba to play against the local stars.

Dewey had defeated the Spanish, but he lacked the forces necessary to occupy the islands. He decided to wait, and reinforcements eventually arrived. On August 13, U.S. troops helped take control of the Philippine capital, Manila. They were joined by Filipino rebels led by **Emilio Aguinaldo** (ahg-ee-NAHL-doh).

Training and supplying thousands of volunteer troops took longer than getting the navy under way. When the war began, only about 28,000 soldiers were serving in the U.S. Army. The army was unprepared to train and supply the 280,000 marines, sailors, and soldiers who would eventually see active duty. The army was at first unprepared to train and support them. There were shortages of bullets and rifles. Soldiers received warm woolen uniforms to wear in the tropical heat. Once in Cuba, many soldiers were struck by yellow fever and other deadly diseases. Of the few thousand members of the U.S. forces who died during the war, only a small percentage died in battle. The rest died from disease, food poisoning, and other causes unrelated to fighting.

The most colorful group of soldiers in the war was the First Volunteer Cavalry, or the Rough Riders. Organized by Lieutenant Colonel Theodore Roosevelt and led by General Leonard Wood, the volunteers came from many walks of life. Newspaper accounts of Roosevelt's charm and the Rough Riders' heroism earned the group the admiration of the American public. Many other U.S. soldiers also served bravely. Four privates of the African American 10th Cavalry received the Congressional Medal of Honor for their actions.

The U.S. Navy trapped the Spanish Caribbean fleet in the harbor of Santiago de Cuba in June 1898. U.S. troops landed on Cuba and moved to capture the hills around the Spanish forces. At the village of El Caney on

Interpreting the Visual Record

The Rough Riders *The diverse members of the Rough Riders included American Indians, college athletes, cowboys, and miners. Together, their heroic actions gained national attention.* ***How does this painting depict the dangers faced by the Rough Riders and their heroism?***

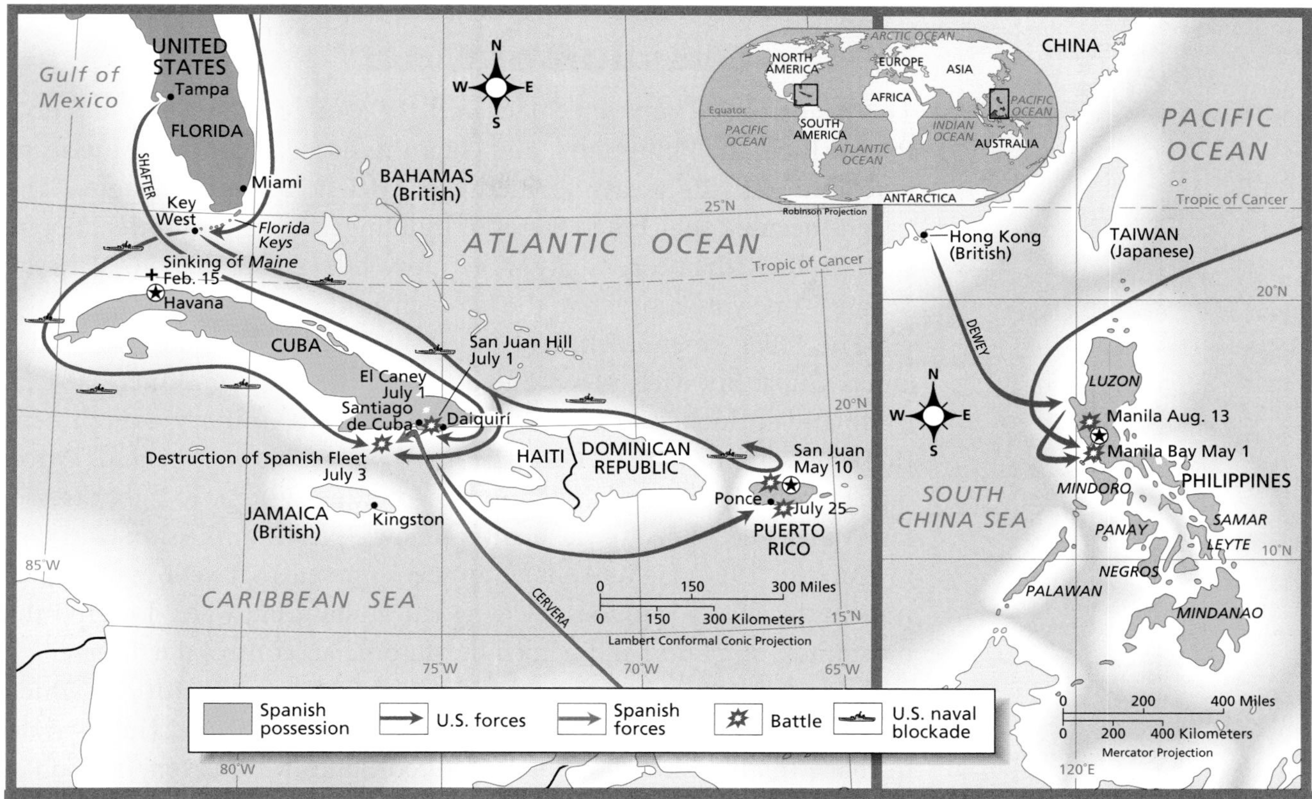

The Spanish-American War in 1898

Interpreting Maps A strong U.S. Navy won a victory at Manila Bay in the Philippines, destroyed the Spanish fleet near Cuba, and aided in the invasion of other Spanish territories.

Skills Assessment **Places and Regions** Near what Cuban cities did the Battle of San Juan Hill take place?

A postage stamp commemorating the Rough Riders

July 1, some 7,000 U.S. soldiers overwhelmed about 600 Spanish defenders. The main U.S. force under General Hamilton Hawkins then attacked and captured San Juan Hill. The Rough Riders and the African American 9th and 10th Cavalries captured nearby Kettle Hill. A journalist on the scene described their charge.

"It was a miracle of self-sacrifice, a triumph of bulldog courage. . . . The fire of the Spanish riflemen . . . doubled and trebled [tripled] in fierceness, the crests of the hills crackled and burst in amazed roars and rippled with waves of tiny flame. But the blue line [of U.S. soldiers] crept steadily up and on."

—Richard Harding Davis, quoted in *The American Reader,* edited by Paul M. Angle

Analyzing Primary Sources

Identifying Bias Do you think this reporter supported the war? Explain your answer.

On July 3 the Spanish fleet tried to break through the U.S. blockade. Every Spanish ship was destroyed in the battle, with 474 Spaniards killed and 1,750 others captured. U.S. forces suffered only two casualties. Santiago surrendered on July 17. U.S. troops soon captured Puerto Rico as well. Spain asked for peace and signed a cease-fire on August 12, 1898.

✔ **Reading Check: Summarizing** How did the Spanish-American War progress for the United States in the Philippines, Cuba, and Puerto Rico?

CONNECTING TO
MATH

Just the Facts

U.S. Trade with Cuba

Year	Imports from Cuba*	Exports to Cuba*
1890	54	13
1891	62	12
1892	78	18
1893	79	24
1894	76	20
1895	53	13
1896	40	8
1897	18	8
1898	15	10
1899	25	19
1900	31	26

*in millions of dollars

Source: *Historical Statistics of the United States*

Using Mathematical Skills

1. In what year shown on the chart did the United States have the most exports to Cuba? the least?
2. Imagine that you are a member of the presidential cabinet. Use these figures to create a bar graph comparing exports to and imports from Cuba from 1890 to 1900.
3. Then write a memo explaining whether you think the value of U.S. trade with Cuba was a factor in leading the United States into war with Spain.

The Question of Cuba

The peace treaty between Spain and the United States placed Cuba, Puerto Rico, the Philippines, and Guam under U.S. control. Americans who opposed the treaty formed the **Anti-Imperialist League**. The League accused the United States of building a colonial empire. Despite such protests, the peace treaty was approved by a vote of 57 to 27 in the Senate—one vote more than the two-thirds majority needed.

The Teller Amendment had stated that the United States would not annex Cuba. But McKinley wanted to create stability and increase U.S. trade and influence in the area, so he set up a military government there. He appointed General Leonard Wood governor, and Wood quickly began building schools and a sanitation system. To fight disease, Dr. Walter Reed, head of the army's Yellow Fever Commission, was sent to Cuba in 1900. He and his volunteers proved that yellow fever was transmitted by mosquitoes. Getting rid of standing water lowered the mosquito population and helped health officials control the disease.

Wood also oversaw the drafting of a Cuban constitution, which included the **Platt Amendment**. This amendment limited Cuba's right to make treaties and allowed the United States to intervene in Cuban affairs. The amendment also required Cuba to sell or lease land to the United States for naval stations. Cuban leaders protested.

> **"[This was like] handing over the keys to our house so that they [the Americans] can enter it at any time, whenever the desire seizes them, day or night, whether with good or evil design [intentions]."**
>
> —A committee report on the Constitutional Convention, quoted in *The Twentieth Century: A People's History,* by Howard Zinn

The Cubans reluctantly accepted the Platt Amendment, and U.S. troops withdrew. The amendment remained in force until 1934.

✔ **Reading Check: Evaluating** How did the Platt Amendment restrict Cuba's freedom?

New U.S. Lands

Spain had surrendered the Philippines in return for a $20 million payment from the United States. Many Americans wondered why their country wanted the islands. Some believed that it would be wrong to annex the islands without the consent of the Filipinos. Other people agreed with President McKinley, who said that the United States would benefit from the islands' naval and commercial value. He also argued that annexing the islands would keep Europeans from seizing them.

Filipino rebels had helped U.S. forces capture Manila. Now they expected to gain their independence. When the United States decided to keep the islands, the rebels began a guerrilla war against U.S. forces. Some 70,000 U.S. soldiers fought in the Philippines. Hundreds of thousands of Filipinos died before the conflict ended more than three years later, in 1902. The Philippine Government Act, passed in 1902 by the U.S. Congress, allowed Filipinos some governing control. The act provided that the Philippines would be ruled by an appointed governor and a two-house legislature. The lower house was to be elected. In 1946 the United States granted full independence to the Philippines.

After the United States acquired Puerto Rico, the government built many new schools.

Like Cubans and Filipinos, Puerto Ricans had hoped for independence after the war. Instead, the U.S. government made Puerto Rico a territory. On April 12, 1900, the Foraker Act established a civil government headed by a governor and including a two-house legislature.

A debate about the citizenship of the people in the new territories soon arose. Residents of Puerto Rico were considered citizens of the island but not of the United States. In 1916 the Jones Act granted Puerto Ricans U.S. citizenship and made both houses of the Puerto Rican legislature elective. However, another 30 years passed before Puerto Ricans could elect their own governor. In 1952 Puerto Rico became a U.S. commonwealth. This unique status means that the island has its own constitution and elected officials. As with the 50 states, Puerto Rico can change its constitution as long as it does not conflict with the U.S. Constitution.

✔ **Reading Check: Comparing and Contrasting** How was U.S. treatment of the Philippines similar to and different from its treatment of Puerto Rico?

Section 2 Review

go.hrw.com Homework Practice Online
keyword: SC3 HP21

1. **Define** and explain:
   - yellow journalism

2. **Identify** and explain:
   - Joseph Pulitzer
   - William Randolph Hearst
   - Teller Amendment
   - Emilio Aguinaldo
   - Anti-Imperialist League
   - Platt Amendment

3. **Identifying Cause and Effect** Copy the graphic organizer below. Use it to identify four causes of the Spanish-American War and areas that came under U.S. control as a result.

Spanish-American War

Causes	Areas
1.	1.
2.	2.
3.	3.
4.	4.

4. **Finding the Main Idea**
   a. Why did Pulitzer and Hearst use yellow journalism, and what effect did it have on public opinion about Cuba?
   b. How did the Spanish-American War change Cuba, the Philippines, and Puerto Rico?

5. **Writing and Critical Thinking**
   Analyzing Information Imagine that you are a soldier during the Spanish-American War. Write a journal entry describing how the United States was able to win the war.
   Consider the following:
   - Spanish forces in the Caribbean
   - problems of training and supply
   - battles between Spanish forces and U.S. troops

CONNECTING TO Literature

The War Dispatches of Stephen Crane

Most readers know of Stephen Crane for his novel The Red Badge of Courage. *He also worked as a journalist during the Spanish-American War, publishing many gripping war reports. While in his twenties, Crane was already so popular that his editors made a point of putting his name in their front-page headlines to attract more readers. The following war dispatch, "Night Attacks on the Marines and a Brave Rescue," describing fighting between U.S. Marines and Spanish soldiers, appeared in the* New York World *on July 16, 1898.*

THE GRANGER COLLECTION, NEW YORK

Stephen Crane

Guantanamo, July 4. —
Once upon a time there was a great deal of fighting between the marines and the **guerrillas**[1] here, and during that space things occurred.

The night attacks were heart-breaking affairs, from which the men emerged in the morning exhausted to a final degree, like people who had been swimming for miles. From colonel to smallest trumpeter went a great thrill when the dawn broke slowly in the eastern sky, and the weary band quite cheerfully ate breakfast. . . . Afterward the men slept, sunk upon the ground in an **abandon**[2] that was almost a **stupor**.[3]

Lieut. Neville, with his **picket**[4] of about twenty men, was entirely cut off from camp one night, and another night Neville's picket and the picket of Lieut. Shaw were cut off, fighting hard in the **thickets**[5] for their lives. At the break of day the **beleaguered**[6] camp could hear still the rifles of their lost pickets.

The problem of rescue added anxiety to the already tremendous anxiety of the fine old colonel. . . . the guerrillas were still **lurking**[7] in the near woods, and it was unsafe enough in camp without venturing into the bush.

Volunteers from Company C were called for, and these seventeen privates volunteered: Boniface, Conway, Fitzgerald, Heilner, Harmson, Hemerle, Lewin, Mann, Mills, Monahan, Nolan, O'Donnell, Ryan, Riddle, Sinclair, Sullivan, W.A., and Smith, J.H.

They went out under Lieut. Lucas. They arrived in Neville's vicinity just as he and his men, together with Shaw and his men, were being finally surrounded at close range. Lucas and his seventeen men broke through the guerrillas and saved the pickets, and the whole body then fell back to Crest Hill. That is all there is to it.

Understanding What You Read

1. **Literature and History** What effect do you think this war dispatch had on readers in the United States?
2. **Literature and You** Would you have volunteered with the other soldiers to help in the rescue of the pickets that were cut off from camp? Why or why not?

[1] **guerrillas:** in this instance, Spanish soldiers
[2] **abandon:** physical exhaustion
[3] **stupor:** daze
[4] **picket:** detached body of soldiers serving as guards
[5] **thickets:** thick growth of bushes or trees
[6] **beleaguered:** surrounded
[7] **lurking:** sneaking, or waiting quietly

Section 3

The United States and Latin America

Read to Discover

1. What steps did the United States take to build a canal across Panama?
2. How did U.S. involvement in Latin America change under President Theodore Roosevelt?
3. How did Presidents Taft and Wilson enforce the Monroe Doctrine?

Why It Matters Today

Businesses in the United States continue to have economic interests in other countries. Use CNNfyi.com or other **current events** sources to find out something about U.S. businesses that have manufacturing plants or major offices in other nations. Record your findings in your journal.

Define

- dollar diplomacy

Identify

- John Hay
- Hay-Herrán Treaty
- Philippe Bunau-Varilla
- Hay–Bunau-Varilla Treaty
- Panama Canal
- Roosevelt Corollary

The Story Continues

When the Spanish-American War began in 1898, the U.S. battleship *Oregon* was stationed at Puget Sound in Washington State. After receiving orders, the *Oregon* set out at top speed on a 12,000-mile voyage. It traveled around the southern tip of South America to join the fighting near Cuba. Newspapers charted the *Oregon*'s daily progress while the American public "breathlessly pushed her along." The trip lasted from March 19 to May 24—67 days!

The U.S. battleship Oregon *took more than two months to join the fighting in the Caribbean.*

The Panama Canal

The *Oregon* barely arrived in time to take part in the major battles around Cuba because travel around the southern tip of South America took weeks. This delay concerned many people. In the late 1800s some U.S. leaders began to explore ways to dig a canal across the narrow neck of Central America. Such a canal would link the Atlantic and Pacific

Oceans and cut 8,000 miles off the voyage. It would also allow the U.S. Navy to link the Atlantic and Pacific naval fleets quickly.

In 1850 the United States and Great Britain had signed the Clayton-Bulwer Treaty. This agreement called for the two countries to jointly build and maintain a canal. Despite the treaty, they never built a canal. In 1881 France began work on a canal in Central America. After spending nearly $300 million and losing some 20,000 lives, the company became financially ruined in 1887. Less than one third of the planned 51-mile canal had been dug.

This poster celebrates the growing strength of the U.S. Navy under President Roosevelt.

No one was a stronger supporter of a Central American canal than Theodore Roosevelt. Roosevelt had become president after the assassination of William McKinley in 1901. Influenced by the ideas of Alfred Thayer Mahan, Roosevelt believed that a canal was important to U.S. naval power, security, and strength. Earlier, Roosevelt had written to Mahan, "I believe we should build the [Central American] canal at once." Secretary of State **John Hay** negotiated the Hay-Pauncefote Treaty with Britain in 1901. The British gave up their interest in a Central American canal. In return, the United States agreed to keep the canal open to all vessels at all times.

Hay then began negotiations with Colombia, because the Isthmus of Panama was part of that country. Hay and the Colombian minister Thomas Herrán soon reached an agreement. The United States would pay $10 million plus $250,000 a year for a 99-year lease on a strip of land across the isthmus. The U.S. Senate approved the **Hay-Herrán Treaty** in 1903. However, the Colombian senate, hoping for better terms, rejected the treaty. President Roosevelt refused to pay more to Colombia. He considered other ways of gaining the Isthmus of Panama, such as seizing it by force.

Philippe Bunau-Varilla, chief engineer of the French Canal Company, offered an alternative plan. He met with Hay and Roosevelt and told them of a possible revolt in the Colombian province of Panama. Bunau-Varilla knew about the effort because he was organizing the plot. Bunau-Varilla left the meeting believing that the United States would not oppose or might even support the Panamanian revolt.

On November 2, 1903, a U.S. warship arrived in Colón, Panama. The next day a revolt began. Colombian forces tried to stop the rebellion but could not get to Panama. Dense jungles blocked land routes, and the U.S. warship blocked travel in the Atlantic Ocean. Panama then declared itself an independent country. The United States recognized the new nation on November 6. On November 13, Bunau-Varilla arrived in the United States as Panama's new foreign minister. Five days later he signed the **Hay–Bunau-Varilla Treaty**. This agreement closely resembled the Hay-Herrán Treaty. One exception was that the canal zone was widened to 10 miles.

✔ **Reading Check: Making Generalizations and Predictions** Do you think the United States would have given up its goal of building a canal if Panama had not gained independence? Explain your answer.

That's Interesting!

A Visit to Panama Did you know that the first president to leave the United States while in office was Theodore Roosevelt? It's true! No president from George Washington through William McKinley had done that, despite all the foreign policy decisions and despite the major treaties that had been signed. When Roosevelt left the country in 1906, it wasn't because of politics. He wanted to see firsthand the construction of the Panama Canal. A famous picture of Roosevelt's trip shows the president sitting at the controls of a huge steam shovel. It almost seems as if Roosevelt is digging the canal himself!

Building the Canal

Building the canal proved to be very difficult. The first obstacle to overcome was tropical disease. The canal route ran through jungles and swamps filled with mosquitoes, many of which carried malaria and yellow fever. Dr. William C. Gorgas, who had helped Dr. Walter Reed in Cuba, organized a successful effort to rid the canal route of disease-carrying mosquitoes. If Gorgas had not been successful, the canal's construction would have taken much longer. It also would have cost much more in terms of both lives and money.

Even with the reduced risk of disease, the work was very dangerous. The high mountain range of central Panama created a major obstacle. Much of the canal had to be blasted out of solid rock. Engineers directed workers to use dozens of steam shovels to cut a narrow, eight-mile-long channel through the mountains.

CONNECTING TO SCIENCE AND TECHNOLOGY

The Panama Canal

Completed in 1914, the Panama Canal remains one of the greatest engineering accomplishments in the world. To travel from the Atlantic to the Pacific Ocean, a ship enters the Panama Canal near the town of Colón. The ship travels through the Gatun Locks, where the water level, and therefore the ship, is raised 85 feet. Then the ship travels down a long channel in Gatun Lake until it passes through the Gaillard Cut in the mountains. There the vessel is lowered 31 feet. The ship eventually descends to sea level by another series of locks, after which it follows another channel out into the ocean. The entire Panama Canal is about 51 miles long. A typical trip takes about nine hours. The canal reduces the distance a ship has to travel from one coast of the United States to the other by about 8,000 miles. **How do ships travel through the Panama Canal?**

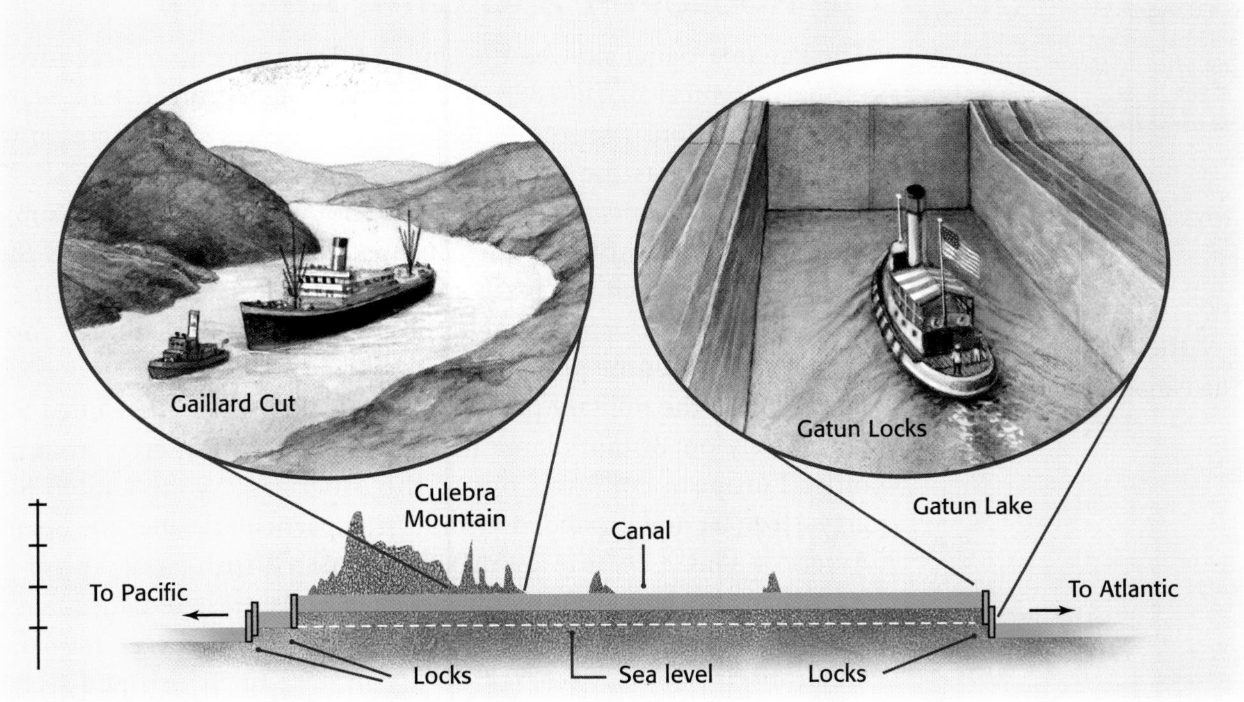

THE GRANGER COLLECTION, NEW YORK

Daily Life

Digging the Canal Excavating the huge amounts of rock necessary to build the Panama Canal was extremely dangerous, requiring workers to handle powerful explosives. Workers sometimes died when their shovels struck the caps of unexploded charges. On one occasion, a bolt of lightning struck a 12-ton explosive charge, killing seven workers. Landslides were also a danger. **What about this image shows the scale of the effort needed to build the canal?**

Some 6,000 lives were lost building the **Panama Canal**, which was finally opened to traffic on August 15, 1914. The cost was $375 million on top of the nearly $300 million spent in the failed French effort. In the end, however, the world had its "highway between the oceans."

✔ **Reading Check: Finding the Main Idea** Why did construction of the canal cost so many lives?

Roosevelt and Latin America

The Panama Canal allowed the United States to become more involved in Latin America. In 1823 President James Monroe had warned European nations not to interfere in the Western Hemisphere. In what became known as the Monroe Doctrine, he outlined his views. "The American continents . . . are henceforth not to be considered as subjects for future colonization by any European powers." The United States would view any such actions as a threat to its security.

August 15, 1914
The Panama Canal opens.

The Monroe Doctrine had become a major principle of U.S. foreign policy. When Monroe presented the doctrine, however, the United States did not have the military power to enforce it. Instead, the United States had to rely on Britain's large navy. Britain had an interest in keeping other European countries out of the Americas. As the United States grew stronger and expanded its influence, particularly after the Spanish-American War, it became less dependent upon British naval power.

During the late 1800s many European investors had made loans to a number of Latin American countries. Venezuela, under the rule of dictator Cipriano Castro, fell deeply in debt to British and German investors. In 1902 the Venezuelan government refused to repay these debts or to have the claims settled by a neutral third party.

European leaders wanted to act but were worried about the Monroe Doctrine. In 1901, however, President Roosevelt had stated that the United States did "not guarantee any State against punishment if it misconducts itself." The European countries interpreted this to mean that they could collect their debts—by force if necessary. Britain and Germany sent ships to blockade Venezuela. Castro then asked Roosevelt to propose having the matter settled by a third party, which the Europeans accepted.

Interpreting Political Cartoons

Roosevelt's big stick *In this cartoon President Roosevelt carries a big stick and leads a string of gunboats through the Caribbean Sea.* ***Why do you think the artist chose to portray Roosevelt wading through the Caribbean?***

A similar situation arose in the Caribbean country of the Dominican Republic in 1904. Again, European countries considered using force to collect debts. This time Roosevelt worried that foreign forces might not leave once they had collected their debts. The presence of European forces in the Caribbean would violate the Monroe Doctrine. Furthermore, their presence could threaten U.S. power in the region and control of the Panama Canal.

But what if the United States kept European creditors from collecting debts owed them? Roosevelt knew that U.S. officials would then have to force debtor nations to repay their loans. In December 1904 the president explained his thinking in what became known as the **Roosevelt Corollary** to the Monroe Doctrine.

"Chronic wrongdoing . . . may in America, as elsewhere, ultimately require intervention [involvement] by some civilized nation, and in the Western Hemisphere the adherence [observance] of the United States to the Monroe Doctrine may force the United States, however reluctantly [unwillingly], in flagrant [extreme] cases of such wrongdoing . . . to the exercise of an international police power."

—Theodore Roosevelt, quoted in *A Diplomatic History of the American People,* by Thomas A. Bailey

Analyzing Primary Sources

Identifying Points of View How did Roosevelt view the other nations of the Western Hemisphere?

This new role of the United States as the "police officer" of the Western Hemisphere suited Roosevelt's style. In 1900 he had said, "I have always been fond of the West African proverb: 'Speak softly and carry a big stick, you will go far.'" Roosevelt actively enforced the corollary throughout the rest of his presidency.

✔ **Reading Check: Finding the Main Idea** What responsibility did the United States take on as a result of the Roosevelt Corollary?

Taft and Wilson

When William Taft became president in 1909, he also acted to protect U.S. interests in Latin America. However, instead of Roosevelt's "big stick," Taft used a policy known as **dollar diplomacy**. Taft tried to influence Latin American governments through economic, not military, intervention. He wanted to encourage stability in Latin America by expanding American business interests there.

Analyzing Primary Sources

Identifying Points of View According to Taft, how would dollar diplomacy help the United States control Latin America?

"[Dollar diplomacy] has been characterized as substituting dollars for bullets. It is . . . directed to the increase of American trade . . . [and] the substitution of arbitration [negotiation] and reason for war in the settlement of international disputes."

—William Howard Taft, quoted in *The Annals of America*

Taft tried to replace European investments in Latin America with U.S. investments. For example, in June 1911 the United States agreed to help obtain private loans from American banks to pay Nicaragua's national debt. In return, Nicaraguan leaders would allow U.S. troops in Nicaragua. The United States also signed a similar agreement with Honduras. Although the U.S. Senate rejected both agreements, the Taft administration followed the treaty terms anyway. In July, Nicaragua failed to repay a large loan from British investors. American bankers gave Nicaragua a $1.5 billion loan in exchange for control of the

U.S. Foreign Policy

Following the example of James Monroe, the progressive presidents each developed their own diplomatic policy toward Latin America.

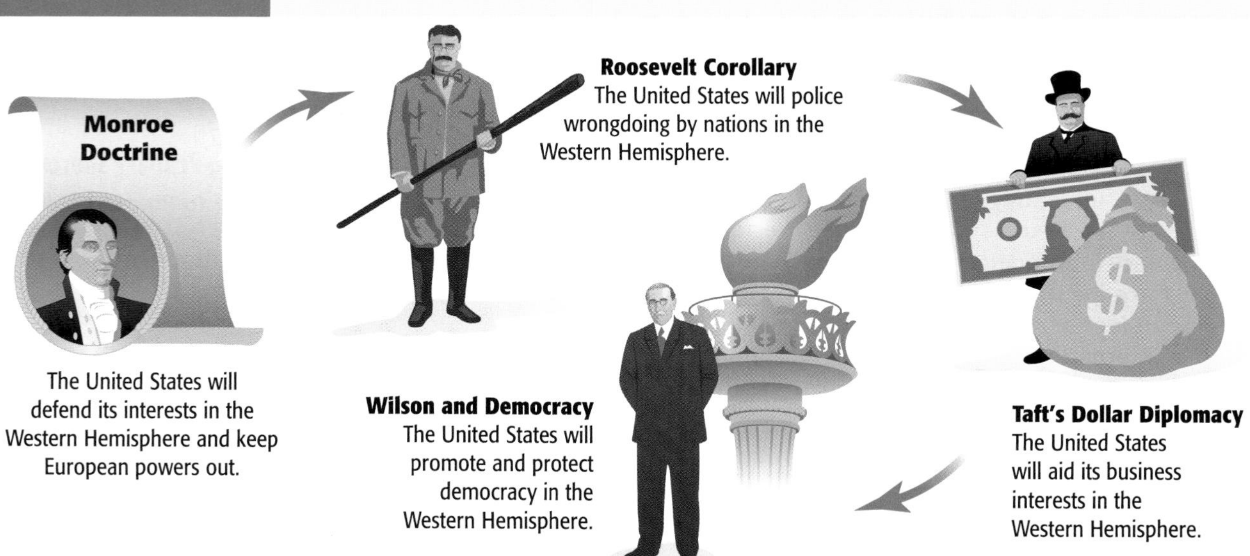

Visualizing History

1. **Government** Compare and contrast the main goal of each president's foreign policy.
2. **Connecting to Today** How would you characterize current U.S. relations with Latin America?

National Bank of Nicaragua and the national railway. Local anger over this agreement soon led to a revolt in Nicaragua. Taft sent in U.S. Marines to protect American interests. The marines remained until 1925, returned the next year, and finally left in 1933.

When President Woodrow Wilson took office in 1913, he rejected Taft's dollar diplomacy. Wilson did not like the role of big business in foreign affairs. Instead, he believed the United States had a moral obligation to promote democracy in Latin America. He wanted to protect U.S. interests in the area by backing democratic government.

Wilson often opposed imperialism. Yet he sent more troops into Latin America than any president before him. For example, the Caribbean country of Haiti had long suffered economic and political problems. In 1915 another revolt took place in Haiti. Previously, Germany and France had sent troops to Haiti for short times to protect their interests. Wilson feared that those countries might try to take control of Haiti during the unrest. To keep this from taking place, U.S. Marines landed in Haiti on July 29, 1915, and quickly restored peace.

These U.S. Marines were among the many that President Wilson sent to restore order in Haiti.

Similar events took place in the Dominican Republic. The customs policies set up by Roosevelt in 1905 had brought a stable government to this country. In 1911, however, the Dominican president was killed, and troubles returned. By threatening to withhold customs revenue, Secretary of State Philander Knox forced the Dominicans to accept a U.S.-backed government. Fearing more political unrest, President Wilson declared martial law on the island and set up a government run by the U.S. Navy in 1916. Wilson, like Roosevelt and Taft, would not allow unrest in Latin America to threaten U.S. interests there.

✔ **Reading Check: Contrasting** How were the foreign policies of Roosevelt, Taft, and Wilson different?

Section 3 Review

go.hrw.com Homework Practice Online
keyword: SC3 HP21

1. **Define** and explain:
   - dollar diplomacy

2. **Identify** and explain:
   - John Hay
   - Hay-Herrán Treaty
   - Philippe Bunau-Varilla
   - Hay–Bunau-Varilla Treaty
   - Panama Canal
   - Roosevelt Corollary

3. **Sequencing** Copy the diagram below. Use it to identify the four treaties signed by the United States to gain land and build the Panama Canal.

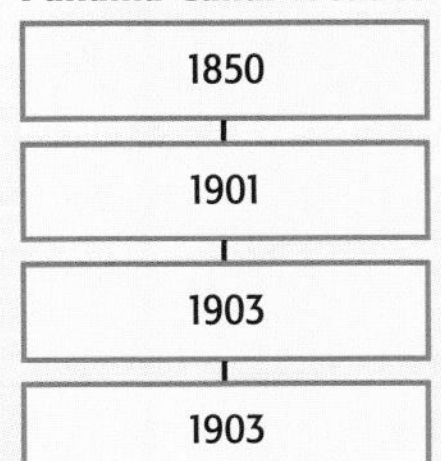

4. **Finding the Main Idea**
   a. How did Roosevelt change U.S. policy in the Western Hemisphere?
   b. In what ways did Presidents Taft and Wilson differ from Roosevelt in their handling of the Monroe Doctrine?

5. **Writing and Critical Thinking**
   Summarizing Imagine that you are a worker helping to build the Panama Canal. Write a letter home to your family, describing the difficulties you have encountered during your time in Panama.
   Consider the following:
   - the geography
   - new technology
   - disease

Section 4

The United States and Mexico

Read to Discover

1. Why did the Mexican people revolt against their government in 1910?
2. What caused Mexican immigration to the United States to increase in the early 1900s?
3. Why did President Woodrow Wilson intervene in the Mexican Revolution?

Identify

- Porfirio Díaz
- Francisco Madero
- Mexican Revolution
- Victoriano Huerta
- Venustiano Carranza
- Francisco "Pancho" Villa
- Emiliano Zapata
- ABC Powers
- John J. Pershing

Why It Matters Today

Relations between the United States and Mexico continue to change. Use CNNfyi.com or other **current events** sources to find out about current economic, political, or social issues involving these two countries. Record your findings in your journal.

THE GRANGER COLLECTION, NEW YORK

Porfirio Díaz refused to resign and allow free elections.

The Story Continues

In 1910 Mexico celebrated the 100th anniversary of the Grito de Dolores, Father Miguel Hidalgo y Costilla's call for revolution against Spain. Mexican president Porfirio Díaz treated international guests to entertainment and fine food. They toasted Mexico's independence, but little did Díaz realize that he would soon face a revolution against his own rule.

The Mexican Revolution

Porfirio Díaz was president of Mexico from 1877 to 1880 and 1884 to 1911, a total of 30 years. During his rule he eagerly welcomed foreign investment. The United States became the biggest investor in Mexico. By 1913, Americans had invested more than $1 billion in Mexican land, mining, oil, railways, and manufacturing. More than 50,000 U.S. citizens lived and worked in Mexico. Díaz ruled the Mexican people harshly. He imprisoned his opponents and rewarded his supporters. Most of Mexico's 15 million people were landless and poor.

Interpreting the Visual Record

The revolutionaries *Followers of Emiliano Zapata, known as* zapatistas, *march in August 1914.* ***What does the photograph reveal about the forces that fought in the Mexican Revolution?***

Many Mexicans found a new leader in democratic reformer **Francisco Madero**, who began the **Mexican Revolution** in 1910. Madero gained support throughout Mexico, violently forcing Díaz to resign in May. The Taft administration wanted a stable government in Mexico and quickly recognized the Madero administration.

The revolution to end the Díaz dictatorship caused a civil war. Many Mexicans came to the United States to escape the violence and to avoid political persecution. These immigrants came from all levels of Mexican society. Many hoped to find industrial jobs in the United States. Between 1905 and 1909, 28,000 Mexicans came to the United States. Between 1910 and 1915, that number rose to more than 100,000. Many Mexican citizens fled to South Texas, and cities such as San Antonio became important refugee centers.

However, the struggle for power continued. In February 1913 General **Victoriano Huerta** took power and had Madero killed. The violence angered President-elect Woodrow Wilson. Once in office, Wilson refused to recognize the Huerta government.

A revolt led by **Venustiano Carranza** against Huerta began to gain support in Mexico. Wilson wanted the two sides to stop fighting and agree to hold a free election. If they agreed, Wilson said he would help the newly elected Mexican government obtain loans from U.S. banks. However, Wilson said that Huerta could not be a candidate. Not surprisingly, Huerta refused Wilson's urging.

Wilson then lifted U.S. restrictions against selling arms to Mexico so that weapons could be supplied to the forces opposing Huerta. Wilson also stationed U.S. warships in the Gulf of Mexico to block any foreign aid to Huerta. In addition to Carranza, two other major revolutionaries led movements to overthrow Huerta. **Francisco "Pancho" Villa** led rebels in the north, and **Emiliano Zapata** led rebels in the south. Like Carranza, both Villa and Zapata had supported Madero against Díaz. Both were heroes to Mexico's poor.

Carranza, Villa, and Zapata had a common goal in hoping to overthrow Huerta. However, they were not close allies.

✔ **Reading Check: Identifying Cause and Effect** What caused the Mexican Revolution, and what were its immediate effects on Mexico?

Pancho Villa (left) and Emiliano Zapata (right) led revolutionaries against Victoriano Huerta's government.

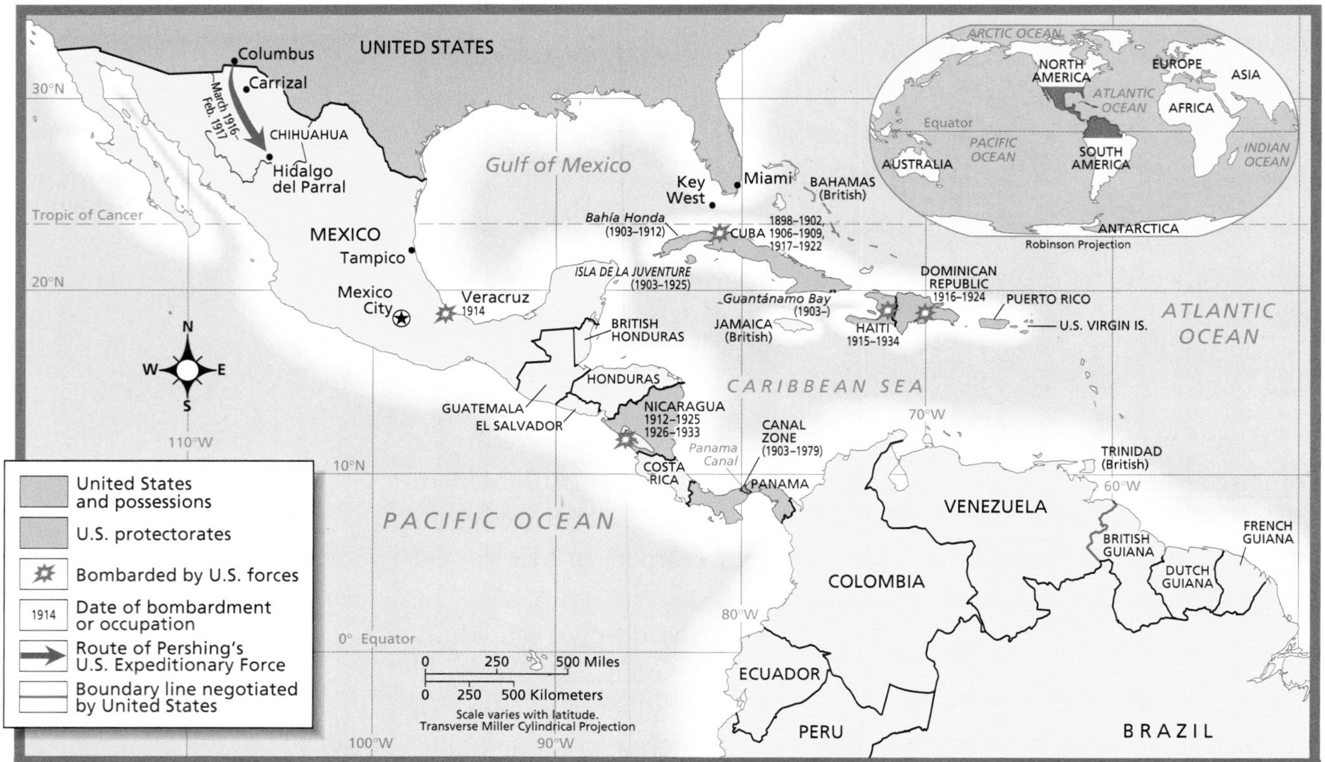

United States and possessions

U.S. protectorates

Bombarded by U.S. forces

1914 Date of bombardment or occupation

Route of Pershing's U.S. Expeditionary Force

Boundary line negotiated by United States

U.S. Interests in Latin America

Interpreting Maps The policy of the United States in Latin America was to protect U.S. interests and keep European countries out of the region.

Skills Assessment **Places and Regions** What countries were U.S. protectorates?

Wilson's Reaction

A number of American business leaders feared they would lose investments in Mexico. They wanted Huerta out of office, by force if necessary. President Wilson, however, refused to intervene, despite added pressure from Congress and the press. He explained his reasoning.

Analyzing Primary Sources

Identifying Points of View Why does Wilson have to remind himself that he does not have vested interests in Mexico?

"I have to pause and remind myself that I am President of the United States and not of a small group of Americans with vested interests [investments] in Mexico."

—Woodrow Wilson, quoted in *A Diplomatic History of the American People*, by Thomas A. Bailey

Wilson adopted a policy of "watchful waiting" toward the unrest in Mexico. At the same time, he looked for a chance to act against Huerta.

In 1914 Wilson finally found a reason to act. In April, a group of U.S. sailors from the cruiser *Dolphin* landed in a restricted area of Tampico, Mexico. They were arrested but were soon released with an apology. However, Huerta refused the commander of the *Dolphin*'s demands for severe punishment of the responsible Mexican officer and for a 21-gun salute to the American flag. With tensions running high, Wilson learned that a German ship carrying a large supply of arms was headed to the port of Veracruz. To keep the weapons from Huerta, Wilson ordered the U.S. Navy to seize Veracruz. In late April 1914, U.S. forces captured the city.

The quick assault on Veracruz united Mexicans against the United States, and the two countries stood on the edge of war. Then the **ABC Powers**, Argentina, Brazil, and Chile, offered to negotiate the dispute. Wilson accepted the proposed settlement, but Huerta and Carranza did not. In July, fighting in Mexico forced Huerta to flee. In August 1914, Carranza and his forces took Mexico City and set up a new government a year later. The United States recognized Carranza as president of Mexico in October 1915, and U.S. troops withdrew from Veracruz six months later.

THE GRANGER COLLECTION, NEW YORK

General John J. "Black Jack" Pershing led the failed effort to capture Pancho Villa.

Although Huerta was no longer in power, Pancho Villa and Emiliano Zapata continued their revolts. Villa hoped to destroy the Carranza government and to win the support of the Mexican people by attacking the United States. In January, Villa and his troops stopped a train at Santa Ysabel, Mexico, killing 18 American mining engineers on board. On March 9, 1916, Villa and his troops attacked Columbus, New Mexico, burning the town and killing 17 U.S. citizens.

In response, President Wilson sent General **John J. Pershing** and 15,000 soldiers into Mexico. Pershing's forces chased Villa more than 300 miles but failed to capture him. Wilson eventually agreed to recall the troops. In 1917 Carranza approved a new constitution to bring orderly rule to Mexico. However, in 1920 the forces of Álvaro Obregón, a trusted aide to Carranza, revolted and killed the Mexican leader. After 1920 peace gradually returned to Mexico.

✔ **Reading Check: Summarizing** How did Wilson respond to events in Mexico?

Section 4 Review

go.hrw.com **Homework Practice Online**
keyword: SC3 HP21

1. **Identify** and explain:
   - Porfirio Díaz
   - Francisco Madero
   - Mexican Revolution
   - Victoriano Huerta
   - Venustiano Carranza
   - Francisco "Pancho" Villa
   - Emiliano Zapata
   - ABC Powers
   - John J. Pershing

2. **Identifying Cause and Effect** Copy the graphic organizer below. Use it to identify the causes of the Mexican Revolution of 1910 and its effects on Mexico and the United States.

3. **Finding the Main Idea**
   a. Why did President Wilson become involved in Mexican affairs?
   b. Why did Mexican immigration to the United States increase during and after the Mexican Revolution?

4. **Writing and Critical Thinking**
   Evaluating Imagine that you are a Mexican journalist in 1920. Write an article describing the role Pancho Villa played in the Mexican Revolution.
   Consider the following:
   - political unrest in Mexico
   - involvement in the Mexican Revolution
   - Villa's actions against the United States

Chapter 21 Review

The Chapter at a Glance

Examine the visual summary of the chapter below. Use the visual summary to write five multiple-choice questions to ask a classmate about when, where, and why the United States intervened in foreign affairs.

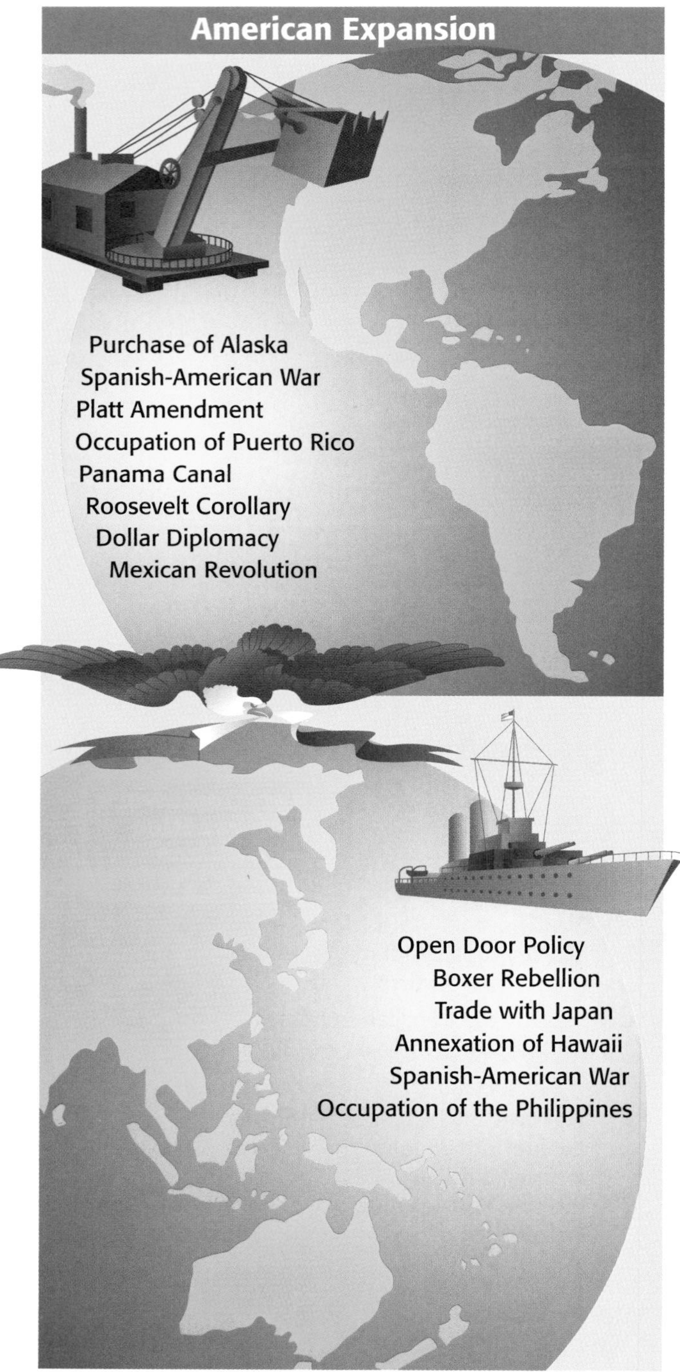

Identifying People and Ideas

Use the following terms or people in historically significant sentences.

1. imperialism
2. Liliuokalani
3. Boxer Rebellion
4. Teller Amendment
5. Panama Canal
6. Roosevelt Corollary
7. dollar diplomacy
8. Francisco "Pancho" Villa
9. ABC Powers
10. John J. Pershing

Understanding Main Ideas

Section 1 *(Pages 640–645)*

1. Why did the United States propose the Open Door Policy, and how was it received?

Section 2 *(Pages 646–651)*

2. How did the press help spark U.S. involvement in the conflict in Cuba?
3. How did the outcome of the Spanish-American War affect the United States, Spain, and Cuba?

Section 3 *(Pages 653–659)*

4. Explain the steps that the United States took to build and control the Panama Canal.
5. What policies did Roosevelt, Taft, and Wilson use to expand U.S. power in the Western Hemisphere?

Section 4 *(Pages 660–663)*

6. What were the causes of the Mexican Revolution, and what effects did the Mexican Revolution have on Mexico and the United States?

You Be the Historian— Reviewing Themes

1. **Geography** Why did the United States want to control certain Pacific islands?
2. **Economics** How did U.S. business interests affect U.S. foreign policy in Asia and Latin America?
3. **Global Relations** Why did the United States support Cuba against Spain?

Thinking Critically

1. **Evaluating** Do you think the Spanish-American War helped or hurt the people of Cuba, the Philippines, and Puerto Rico? Explain your answer.
2. **Identifying Cause and Effect** Why did the United States build the Panama Canal, and what effect did this have on U.S. foreign policies in the Western Hemisphere?
3. **Supporting a Point of View** Which president's foreign policy in Latin America do you think was most effective? Explain your answer.

Interpreting Political Cartoons

Study the political cartoon shown below. Then answer the following questions.

PATIENT WAITERS ARE NO LOSERS.

UNCLE SAM.—I ain't in a hurry;—it 'll drop into my basket when it gets ripe!

THE GRANGER COLLECTION, NEW YORK

1. Which of the following answers best describes what the pieces of fruit on the tree and in the basket represent?
   a. nations with which the United States is at war
   b. foreign allies of the United States
   c. territories that the United States claims or wants to claim
   d. overseas colonies of the United States

2. Based on the political cartoon, do you think the artist was in favor of imperialism or isolationism? Explain your answer.

Analyzing Primary Sources

Read the following statement by President William McKinley and answer the questions that follow.

> **"We have the right as conquerors to hold the Philippines. . . . This policy may be characterized as unjust to Spain; but it is the result of the fortunes of war. All nations recognize that the conqueror may dictate the terms of peace. . . . The Philippines are a foothold for us in the Far East. Their possession gives us standing and influence. It gives us also valuable trade both in exports and imports."**

3. Which of the following statements best explains McKinley's view on why the United States should keep the Philippines?
   a. Holding the Philippines will gain the United States respect and valuable trade in Asia.
   b. Spain should be punished for losing the war.
   c. Under international law the United States is required to keep the Philippines.
   d. Keeping the Philippines will pay for the U.S. war expenses.

4. What justification does McKinley give for keeping the Philippines?
   a. The United States won the war.
   b. The Philippines have asked for U.S. control.
   c. The Philippines are not ready for independence.
   d. Spain no longer wants the Philippines.

5. Do you think that most Americans would agree with McKinley's statement? Explain your answer.

Alternative Assessment

American History

Building Your Portfolio

Interdisciplinary Connection to Science

Use the library and the HRW Web site to research the construction of the Panama Canal. Then create a poster in which you outline the steps in the canal's construction. Your display should include illustrations, graphics, and at least 10 statistics about the canal.

internet connect

Internet Activity: go.hrw.com
keyword: SC3 CF21

Choose a topic on America as a World Power to:

- Research Stephen Crane's life and career as a novelist and journalist.
- Create a public service advertisement on the effort to stop yellow fever.
- Create a brochure on the Panama Canal.

CHAPTER

22 World War I
(1914–1919)

The Los Angeles Times

SATURDAY MORNING, MAY 8, 1915

In Three Parts—24 Pages.

Liberty Under Law—Equal Rights—True Industrial Freedom

PRICE 2½ CENTS

OVER A THOUSAND LIVES PROBABLY LOST WHEN THE GERMANS SANK THE LUSITANIA.

SUSPEND JUDGMENT, SAYS PRESIDENT WILSON.

Executive Faces Necessity of Making Good War Zone Protest to Germany.

United States Authorities will Make a Thorough Inquiry into the Number of Americans Lost on the Lusitania and will Include in Whatever Representations are Made Some Other Grievances.

Two Views of Ship that Was.

FIVE TO SIX HUNDRED SURVIVORS LANDED ALONG THE IRISH COAST.

Two Torpedoes Fired, Without a Note of Warning, into the Steel Sides of the Huge Cunarder.

Passengers at Luncheon, Confident that the Swift Atlantic Liner Could Elude Any War Craft Afloat, Taken Completely by Surprise — England's Fastest Merchant Vessel Submerged in Fifteen Minutes.

[BY ATLANTIC CABLE AND A. P.]

QUEENSTOWN, May 8, 4:24 a.m.—Survivors of the Lusitania who have arrived here estimate that only about 650 of those aboard the steamer were saved and only a small proportion of those rescued were saloon passengers.

LONDON, May 8.—Only a few of the first-class passengers on board the Lusitania, sunk today by a German submarine, were saved. Most of them remained on board, thinking the great ship would stay afloat. Trawlers arriving at Queenstown have about one hundred bodies on board.

WASHINGTON, May 8.—A dispatch to the State Department early today from American Consul Frost at Queenstown stated that the total number of survivors of the Lusitania was about 700. The Consul's dispatch gave a partial list of American survivors, but did not say definitely whether any Americans had been lost.

LONDON, May 8, 5:58 a.m.—Signals have been received at Queenstown that an armed trawler believed to be the Heron and two fishing trawlers are bringing in 100 more bodies. The Cunard line agent states that the total number of persons aboard the Lusitania was 2160.

LONDON, May 8, 4:42 a.m.—The Times' Queenstown correspondent says that some of the survivors who have arrived there report that Alfred Vanderbilt was drowned. Inquiry failed to develop any trace of Charles Frohman, who is believed lost.

THE GRANGER COLLECTION, NEW YORK

Many Americans were outraged when they learned that Germany had sunk the Lusitania.

THE GRANGER COLLECTION, NEW YORK

This 1917 U.S. Army Air Service recruiting poster asks Americans to join the fight in Europe.

UNITED STATES

1915 A German submarine sinks the British passenger liner *Lusitania*, killing some 1,200 people, including 128 Americans.

1916 Woodrow Wilson is re-elected president in November.

1914 | **1915** | **1916**

1914 A Serb nationalist assassinates Austrian Archduke Franz Ferdinand on June 28.

World War I begins after Austria-Hungary declares war on Serbia on July 28.

1916 Tanks are used in war for the first time at the Battle of the Somme.

WORLD

Tanks were first used in World War I.

Soldiers used gas masks to protect themselves from poison gas.

Build on What You Know

After victory in the Spanish-American War, the United States stood ready to take a greater role in international affairs. When World War I began in Europe, however, many Americans opposed getting involved. Eventually, the United States joined the Allied Powers in the war and contributed to their victory in Europe.

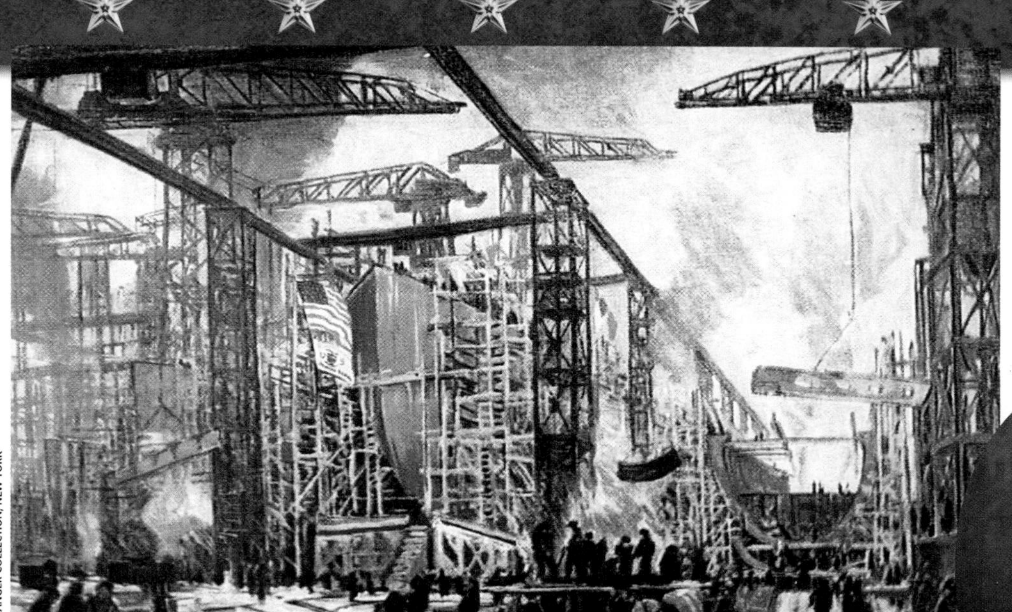
THE GRANGER COLLECTION, NEW YORK

American propaganda, such as this poster from the United States Shipping Board, helped encourage support for the war.

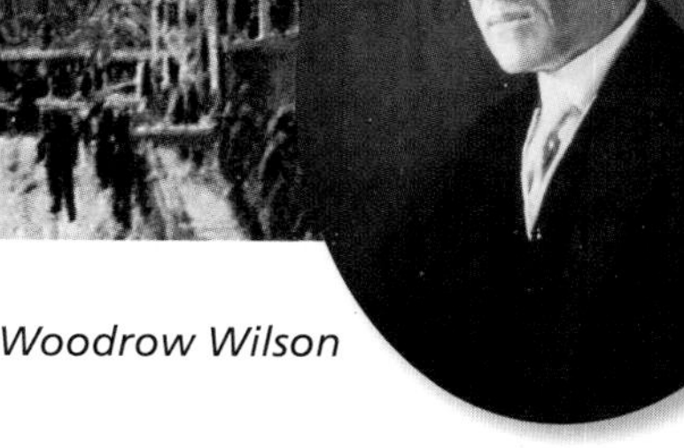

Woodrow Wilson

1917 On March 1, U.S. newspapers publish the Zimmermann Note, which helps draw the United States into World War I.

The U.S. Congress declares war on Germany on April 6.

1918 President Wilson announces the Fourteen Points to negotiate peace after World War I.

1919 In March the U.S. Senate rejects the Treaty of Versailles, the peace treaty resolving World War I.

1917 | **1918** | **1919**

1917 The Bolshevik Revolution sweeps Russia creating a communist government.

1918 In July the Allied Powers stop Germany's last major offensive.

Germany agrees to an armistice on November 11, ending World War I.

1919 Leaders of the Allied and Central Powers sign the Treaty of Versailles.

This poster shows the flags of many of the Allied Powers.

If you were there . . .

Would you support U.S. involvement in World War I?

You Be the Historian

What's Your Opinion? Do you **agree** or **disagree** with the following statements? Support your point of view in your journal.

- **Citizenship** To be successful in a war effort, a government must gain support from its citizens.
- **Global Relations** International alliances always cause conflicts.
- **Science, Technology & Society** Advances in weaponry make wars shorter.

Section 1

The Road to War

Read to Discover

1. What were the main causes of World War I?
2. How did most of Europe become involved in the war?
3. Where did the early fighting in the war take place, and what were the results?

Why It Matters Today

Nationalism and militarism still exist in the world. Use CNNfyi.com or other **current events** sources to find out about a country in which nationalism or militarism is common. Record your findings in your journal.

Define

- nationalism
- militarism
- balance of power
- mobilize

Identify

- Triple Alliance
- Triple Entente
- Franz Ferdinand
- Nicholas II
- Central Powers
- Allied Powers
- Wilhelm II
- First Battle of the Marne

World War I artillery

The Story Continues

In the early 1900s Europe seemed to be at peace. There had not been a major war in the region since 1871. Yet political tensions were building, and most nations continued to strengthen their armed forces. In 1888 German chancellor Otto von Bismarck had introduced a bill to the German parliament that added 750,000 soldiers to the German army. In his address he declared, "We no longer ask for love, either from France or Russia. We run after nobody. We Germans fear God and nothing else on earth!" Before long, such aggressive attitudes would lead to war on the European continent.

Causes of War

During the 1800s Europe had been swept by a rise in **nationalism**—the belief that a specific nation, language, or culture is superior to all others. Nationalism led a number of German states to join together in 1871 to form the German Empire. In contrast, nationalism tended to divide the Austro-Hungarian Empire, also called Austria-Hungary. This empire included people of many nationalities and language groups. One of these groups, the Slavs, wanted to create a nation of their own. Serbia was already an independent Slavic state on the Balkan Peninsula. The Serbs encouraged Slavs in Austria-Hungary to break free and join them in creating an independent, united Slavic empire in the Balkans. Russia, which was itself largely Slavic, supported Serbia's goal.

Austro-Hungarian leaders saw the Slavic independence movement as a threat to the unity of the empire. One Austrian official predicted that Slavic nationalism was "one of the powerful national movements which can neither be ignored nor kept down." The growing tensions in the Balkans made them seem a likely place for a major European war to erupt.

Imperialism also led to greater tensions as countries competed to build overseas empires. By the late 1800s Great Britain was the world's greatest imperial power. France, Germany, Italy, and Russia were building their own empires. These countries also struggled over territory in Europe. France, for example, wanted to take back Alsace-Lorraine (al-SAS-law-RAYN), a border region that it had lost in a war with Germany in 1871.

Interpreting Political Cartoons

The boiling point *This 1912 British cartoon shows European leaders trying to keep a lid on trouble in the Balkans.* ***What does this cartoon suggest about international cooperation?***

As relations grew more uncertain, countries began building up their armed forces to prepare for war. This policy, along with the strong influence of military values on a society, is known as **militarism**. European nations built larger militaries than ever before. Germany created the most powerful army in Europe and a navy to rival that of Britain.

In the late 1800s European countries began to form alliances. They did so to try to create a **balance of power**—a situation in which the strength of rival alliances is nearly equal. Most European leaders believed that no country would start a war if it lacked a real advantage in military strength. In 1879 Germany allied with Austria-Hungary. Three years later, Italy joined the union, making it the **Triple Alliance**. As allies, Austria-Hungary, Germany, and Italy pledged to support one another in case of attack.

Worried by Germany's growing power, France formed a military alliance with Russia in 1892. Britain feared Germany's growing naval force and signed an entente, or understanding, with France. In 1907 Russia and Britain reached a similar agreement. The so-called **Triple Entente** thus united Britain, France, and Russia.

The Triple Alliance and the Triple Entente created an unsteady and complicated balance of power in Europe. Many people, like German general Helmuth von Moltke, felt that "a European war is bound to come sooner or later."

✔ **Reading Check: Summarizing** What factors increased military and political tensions in Europe?

THE GRANGER COLLECTION, NEW YORK

Felix Schwarmstadt's painting captures the 1914 assassination of Archduke Franz Ferdinand and his wife, Sophie.

The Spark

In the Balkan Peninsula, relations between Austria-Hungary and Slavic nationalists grew increasingly hostile. People began referring to the Balkans as a "powder keg" that might explode at any moment. In 1908 Austria-Hungary annexed the independent province of Bosnia and Herzegovina. This annexation angered Slavic nationalists who wanted the region allied with Serbia.

On June 28, 1914, Archduke **Franz Ferdinand** visited Sarajevo, the capital of Bosnia and Herzegovina, with his wife, Sophie. The archduke was the heir to the throne of Austria-Hungary. As the visitors rode through the streets, Gavrilo Princip, a 19-year-old Serb nationalist stepped out from the crowd. He quickly shot the archduke and his wife, killing them both. The archduke's assassination lit the fuse on the "powder keg" of Europe. The president of France gave the following advice to an Austro-Hungarian official.

"With a little good will, this Serbian business is easy to settle. But it can just as easily become acute [severe]. Serbia has some very warm friends in the Russian people. And Russia has an ally, France."

—President Raymond Poincaré, quoted in *America Enters the World,* by Page Smith

Austro-Hungarian leaders ignored his advice. On July 28, 1914, Austria-Hungary declared war on Serbia. The next day, Austria-Hungary began shelling the Serbian city of Belgrade. An earlier promise of support required Russia to defend Serbia. At first, however, Russian czar **Nicholas II** hesitated to **mobilize**, or prepare his military for war. His foreign minister described the czar's hesitation.

Analyzing Primary Sources

Identifying Points of View
What do you think Czar Nicholas II's biggest concern is about defending Serbia?

"The Tsar was silent. Then he said to me, in a voice full of deep feeling: 'This would mean sending hundreds of thousands of Russian people to their death. How can one help hesitating to take such a step?'"

—Serge Sayonov, quoted in *Imperial Russia,* edited by Basil Dmytryshyn

The czar eventually decided to come to Serbia's defense. Russia's mobilization led other countries to fulfill their own alliance promises. In support of Austria-Hungary, Germany declared war on Russia on August 1, and on France, Russia's ally, two days later. German troops invaded Belgium on August 3 to move westward to attack France. Britain, which had pledged to defend Belgian neutrality, then declared war on Germany. On August 5 Austria-Hungary declared war on Russia. The Great War—which later generations would know as World War I—had begun.

✔ **Reading Check: Analyzing Information** Why did many European nations get involved in the conflict?

Europe Goes to War

GREAT BRITAIN DECLARES WAR ON GERMANY.

The Daily Mirror

DECLARATION OF WAR BY GREAT BRITAIN AFTER UNSATISFACTORY REPLY TO YESTERDAY'S ULTIMATUM.

Britain's declaration of war against Germany was front-page news.

The alliance of Austria-Hungary and Germany became known as the **Central Powers**. Bulgaria and the Ottoman Empire later joined the Central Powers. Britain, France, and Russia fought together as the **Allied Powers**, or the Allies. Although previously allied with Austria-Hungary and Germany, Italy joined the Allies in 1915. Eventually, 30 nations would fight in World War I.

Many Europeans expected the war to last no more than six months. Kaiser **Wilhelm II** was sure Germany would achieve a fast victory. Germany hoped to quickly defeat France before Russia had a chance to fully mobilize its army. The Schlieffen Plan, as Germany's military strategy was known, called for a fast attack on France followed by an attack on Russia. German troops would have to strike at France through Belgium for the plan to work.

The Belgians fiercely resisted the German army, giving France and Britain valuable time to mobilize their troops. Yet by September 3, 1914, the Germans were 25 miles from Paris, the French capital. In the **First Battle of the Marne**, French troops launched a daring counterattack against Germany. The French rushed to stop the enemy along the Marne River east of Paris. After a few days of fighting, the Germans retreated.

Fighting between the armies continued as French and German troops faced each other across the western front. This battle line extended from Switzerland to the North Sea. Russia fought the Central Powers along the eastern front, which stretched from the Black Sea to the Baltic Sea. By mid-September 1914 the Central and Allied Powers both realized that the war would not be a short one.

✔ **Reading Check: Identifying Cause and Effect** Why did Germany invade Belgium and France, and how did the early fighting change attitudes about the war?

Section 1 Review

1. **Define** and explain:
   - nationalism
   - militarism
   - balance of power
   - mobilize

2. **Identify** and explain:
   - Triple Alliance
   - Triple Entente
   - Franz Ferdinand
   - Nicholas II
   - Central Powers
   - Allied Powers
   - Wilhelm II
   - First Battle of the Marne

3. **Categorizing** Copy the chart below. Use it to identify the long-term and immediate causes of World War I.

Causes of World War I

Long Term	Immediate

4. **Finding the Main Idea**
   a. Why did other European countries become involved in the conflict between Austria-Hungary and Serbia?
   b. Describe the early fighting in the war.

5. **Writing and Critical Thinking**
   Analyzing Information Imagine that you are a German army officer in September 1914. Write a memo to the kaiser explaining the outcome of the Schlieffen Plan.
   Consider the following:
   - the main points of the plan
   - Belgian resistance
   - the outcome of the First Battle of the Marne

Section 2

Wilson and Neutrality

Read to Discover

1. How did trench warfare and new weapons affect the fighting in World War I?
2. How did the United States try to remain neutral during the war?
3. What events led the United States to enter the war?

Define

- trench warfare
- no-man's-land
- stalemate

Identify

- U-boats
- *Lusitania*
- *Sussex* pledge
- Arthur Zimmermann
- Zimmermann Note

Why It Matters Today

Americans continue to debate whether the United States should become involved in conflicts elsewhere in the world. Use CNNfyi.com or other **current events** sources to study a recent U.S. decision to play a role in an international conflict. Record your findings in your journal.

The Story Continues

This painting shows a group of Allied soldiers eating lunch.

The day's fighting seemed over. Two Allied officers sat on a hill in southwestern Belgium. As they looked out over fields and villages, a dog barked at some sheep, and a girl sang as she walked by. Soldiers laughed as they cooked their evening meal. As darkness fell, one officer remembered, "without a moment's warning, . . . we saw the whole horizon burst into flame." The Germans had begun to bombard the area. The officers were stunned and soon concluded that World War I had "a merciless, ruthless aspect [part] that we had not realized till then."

A New Kind of War

New war strategies—along with new weapons—made the Great War a conflict unlike any other. After the First Battle of the Marne, the Germans dug in and prepared to hold their ground. Both the French and German armies soon turned to **trench warfare**. Using this strategy, armies fought from the protection of deep ditches to defend their positions. Two massive systems of opposing trenches stretched for 400 miles across the

western front. Trenches ranged from simple holes to complex networks with rooms for sleeping and eating.

The trenches were typically cold, wet, and dirty. A reporter described a common effect of these conditions.

"Men standing in slime for days and nights in field boots . . . lost all sense of feeling in their feet. These feet of theirs, so cold and wet, began to swell, and then go 'dead' and then suddenly to burn as though touched by red hot pokers."

—Philip Gibbs, *Realities of War*

In the trench environment disease spread rapidly. The area between opposing trenches was called **no-man's-land.** Much of the fighting took place in this area, which varied in width from about 200 to 1,000 yards.

In the trenches, soldiers set up groups of machine guns that fired 400 to 600 rounds of ammunition per minute. In addition, huge guns launched artillery shells. Some shells contained poison gas, such as chlorine gas or mustard gas. Poison gas destroyed soldiers' lungs, killing them slowly. Gas masks could provide protection. However, soldiers had to either wear masks all the time or slip them on in seconds.

The armies also introduced new war machines. Airplanes, submarines, and tanks were all used in World War I. Armies used airplanes to gather information, shoot down enemy planes, and fire on trenches. Germany's fleet of **U-boats**, or submarines, was the world's largest and most advanced, causing heavy losses to Allied shipping. British and French forces developed armored tanks to support infantry attacks on trenches. Early tanks were very tough and could cause heavy damage but were also slow and hard to maneuver in muddy conditions.

✔ **Reading Check: Summarizing** How did trench warfare and new weaponry affect the fighting in World War I?

Daily Life

Trench Warfare Life in the trenches along the western front varied a great deal. In quieter areas, troops suffered from boredom. In areas that saw more fighting, soldiers faced danger and anxiety. During the night, troops often completed construction and repair work. These jobs might include laying cable or barbed wire. Most attacks began in the early morning. At daybreak, soldiers on both sides usually waited with their rifles loaded. If there was no enemy attack, they would eat breakfast and prepare for a day of listening to mortar fire. **What challenges did soldiers face in the trenches?**

Research on the ROM

Free Find:
Trench Warfare
After reading about trench warfare on the **Holt Researcher CD–ROM**, imagine that you are a soldier fighting on the western front. Write a letter home describing your experiences.

A Military Deadlock

By late 1914 the war on the western front had become a **stalemate**, a situation in which neither side can win a clear victory. During 1915 much of the fighting took place in eastern Europe. In February 1916 the Germans attacked France again. They decided to try to capture the French city of Verdun, near the southern end of the trench line. In response, French general Philippe Pétain (pay-tan) vowed: "They shall not pass." After initial success, the German advance stalled outside the city. The battle for Verdun continued for 10 months, making it the longest battle of the war. When it was over, France still held the city.

In July, while fighting raged at Verdun, Allied forces began to attack the Germans along the Somme River in northeastern France. Almost 20,000 Allied troops were killed in the first day of the battle. After months of fighting, the Allied soldiers had forced the Germans to retreat only a few miles. Allied and German forces both suffered terrible losses at the Somme and Verdun. The death total reached almost 1 million. An average of more than 138 soldiers died every hour.

CONNECTING TO

SCIENCE AND TECHNOLOGY

The Airplane in World War I

The Wright brothers built the first successful powered airplane in 1903. When World War I began, the Allied and Central Powers used airplanes mostly for scouting. Pilots flew high over the battlefield to take pictures of enemy troops and equipment. The pictures provided valuable information for military commanders. As the war went on, the armies of both sides installed machine guns on fighter planes and shot down enemy scouts. Engineers improved fighter planes' speed and ability to maneuver. In addition, both the Allies and the Central Powers built large bombers and developed planes that could take off from ships. Thousands of planes were built during the war. **How were airplanes used in World War I?**

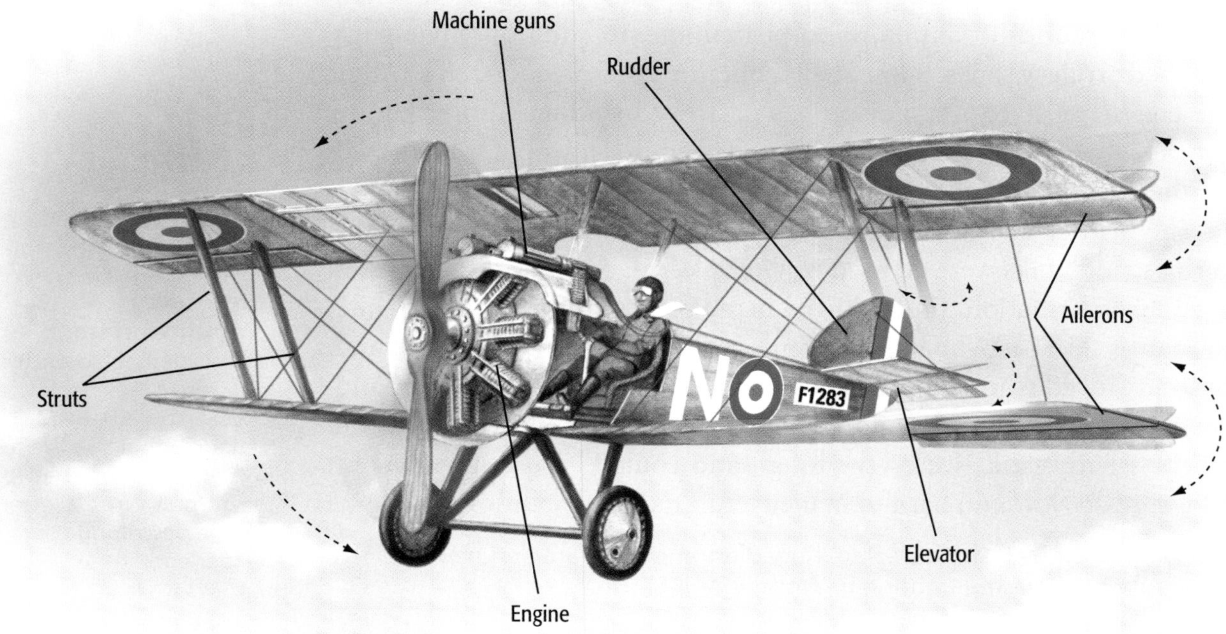

World War I, 1914–1917

Interpreting Maps World War I saw few large-scale troop movements on the western front, with soldiers often fighting for many months in the same location.

Skills Assessment **Human Systems** What battles took place along the western front trench lines?

The stalemate on land made the battles in the North Sea and the Atlantic Ocean even more important. Each side depended on war materials shipped by sea. Britain used its large navy to cut off the shipment of much-needed supplies to Germany. The German navy responded by sending its submarine fleet out to sink ships carrying supplies for the Allies.

✔ **Reading Check:** **Finding the Main Idea** Where did some of the World War I fighting take place in 1915 and 1916?

Wilson Campaigns for Peace

Shortly after the war began in Europe, President Woodrow Wilson announced that the United States would remain neutral. This decision reflected the traditional U.S. policy of isolationism. Most Americans saw the war as a European conflict. The popularity of one American song—"I Didn't Raise My Boy to Be a Soldier"—showed the antiwar views of

Woodrow Wilson

To many people, President Woodrow Wilson seemed cold and distant. In private, however, Wilson could be warm and lively. He was well educated, the first president to have a Ph.D. As a college professor and later the president of Princeton University, Wilson was respected for his writings on government and political science. He brought his knowledge and personal ideals to his administration, helping push through many reforms.

Wilson was also heavily involved in foreign policy. Although he had wanted to avoid joining the war in Europe, he worked hard to mobilize the U.S. war effort. Wilson also played a major role in the peace negotiations that followed the war. However, his efforts were limited by a severe stroke that he suffered on October 2, 1919. **How did Wilson's educational background affect his presidency?**

many people. Not wanting to become involved in the fighting did not keep Americans from choosing sides in the conflict. Most Americans supported the Allies because of long-standing ties with either Britain or France. However, millions of Americans had emigrated from the countries of the Central Powers, and people tended to sympathize with their homelands.

Official U.S. neutrality did not stop American merchants from trading with the warring European nations. U.S. ships carried most of the supplies, including war materials, to the Allies. By April 1917, American banks had invested $2.6 billion in European war bonds. However, only $27 million was spent on German bonds.

During the war, Germany often broke the rules of neutrality in the Atlantic. These rules required warships to stop and search merchant vessels rather than simply destroy them on sight. The Germans knew their submarines were defenseless above water, however, so they often attacked without warning.

In May 1915 a U-boat sank the British passenger liner ***Lusitania*** off the coast of Ireland. The attack killed nearly 1,200 people, including 128 Americans. The American public was outraged. President Wilson called the attack "a violation not only of international law but of the fundamental decencies of civilization." The German government argued that the *Lusitania* had been carrying war materials. The Germans added that Americans had been warned not to travel through the war zone.

Less than a year later, a U-boat sank the French passenger ship *Sussex*. After this attack, Wilson threatened to end diplomatic relations with Germany. Germany then issued the ***Sussex* pledge**, which included a promise not to sink merchant vessels "without warning and without saving human lives."

As President Wilson campaigned for re-election during the fall of 1916, he continued to work for peace. Wilson's opponent was Republican Charles Evans Hughes, a Supreme Court justice and former governor of New York. Hughes criticized Wilson for not strongly defending American rights in Europe. The race between Wilson and Hughes was very close. Many Americans opposed Wilson's foreign policy. Other voters were not sure Wilson could keep the United States out of the war. In the end, however, the belief that Wilson would avoid a war helped him win re-election in November 1916.

Once re-elected, Wilson began work on a settlement to end the war. In a speech to the Senate on January 22, 1917, Wilson proposed "peace without victory." He called on the Allied and Central Powers to declare peace without either side winning. Wilson's speech angered the Allies, particularly the British. The Allies blamed the Central Powers for the war and wanted them to pay for wartime destruction. At the very least, the Allies demanded a German admission of guilt.

✔ **Reading Check: Supporting a Point of View** Do you think the United States was truly neutral in 1914–1916? Support your answer.

Congress Declares War

All hopes for peace soon ended. The Germans broke the *Sussex* pledge and began unrestricted submarine warfare again on February 1, 1917. President Wilson quickly cut off diplomatic relations with Germany and ordered U.S. merchant ships to be fitted with guns. Tensions rose when American newspapers printed a secret German telegram in March. In it, German foreign secretary **Arthur Zimmermann** proposed an alliance between Germany and Mexico against the United States. He told the German minister in Mexico that Germany would help Mexico "reconquer the lost territory in New Mexico, Texas, and Arizona." The telegram, known as the **Zimmermann Note**, outraged the American public.

Submarine attacks with results like the sinking of the Lusitania *were a major cause of American outrage toward Germany.*

In early April, Wilson responded to the new threats by asking Congress to declare war on Germany. He said that "the world must be made safe for democracy."

"We shall fight for the things which we have always carried nearest our hearts, for democracy . . . [and to] bring peace and safety to all nations and make the world itself at last free."

—Woodrow Wilson, quoted in *America Enters the World,* by Page Smith

Analyzing Primary Sources
Identifying Points of View What does Wilson say the United States is fighting for?

Congress approved President Wilson's request. On April 6, 1917, the United States declared war on Germany.

✔ **Reading Check: Sequencing** What events, in their proper sequence, resulted in the United States entering World War I?

Section 2 Review

go.hrw.com **Homework Practice Online** keyword: SC3 HP22

1. **Define** and explain:
   - trench warfare
   - no-man's-land
   - stalemate
2. **Identify** and explain:
   - U-boats
   - *Lusitania*
   - *Sussex* pledge
   - Arthur Zimmermann
   - Zimmermann Note
3. **Analyzing Information** Copy the graphic organizer below. Use it to explain why the United States decided to declare war on Germany in 1917.

   Causes → War

4. **Finding the Main Idea**
   a. What effects did trench warfare and new weapons have on the fighting in World War I?
   b. What steps did President Wilson take to preserve U.S. neutrality and end the war?
5. **Writing and Critical Thinking**
   Identifying Points of View Imagine that you are an American journalist. Write a short editorial describing the *Lusitania* incident.
   Consider the following:
   - how the American public reacted
   - why Germany believed such attacks were necessary

Section 3

Americans Prepare for War

Read to Discover

1. How did the U.S. government prepare citizens and the military for war?
2. What contributions did women and African Americans make to the war effort?
3. How did the war affect industry and labor?

Identify

- Committee on Public Information
- George Creel
- Espionage Act of 1917
- Sedition Act of 1918
- Selective Service Act
- Liberty bonds
- War Industries Board
- Bernard Baruch
- National War Labor Board

Why It Matters Today

Today's U.S. military must still maintain its preparedness for war. Use CNNfyi.com or other **current events** sources to find out how the military recruits and keeps members. Record your findings in your journal.

The Story Continues

Political groups like the Socialist Party questioned the reasons for the U.S. entry into World War I.

Shortly after Congress declared war, Major Palmer E. Pierce appeared before the Senate Finance Committee. Pierce answered questions from the committee about how the War Department planned to spend the $3 billion it had requested. He explained that the money would go for "clothing, cots, camps, food, pay. . . . And we may have to have an army in France." The chairman of the Senate committee exclaimed, "Good Lord! You're not going to send soldiers over there, are you?" Although most Americans supported the declaration of war, few were ready to risk the lives of U.S. troops.

Rallying the Public

One week after Congress declared war on Germany, President Wilson created a new agency—the **Committee on Public Information** (CPI), to help raise public support for the war effort. **George Creel**, the head of the CPI, began a nationwide publicity campaign. Creel used rallies, parades, posters, and pamphlets to persuade Americans to support the war effort. The committee recruited movie stars to entertain troops.

Hollywood made movies like *The Kaiser: The Beast of Berlin.* Some 75,000 speakers, called "four-minute men," gave short patriotic speeches in churches, movie theaters, and schools. They explained why the United States should take part in the Great War.

At the same time, the government limited some freedoms. The **Espionage Act of 1917** and the **Sedition Act of 1918** outlawed actions against the U.S. government. The Espionage Act punished people for aiding the enemy or refusing military duty. The Sedition Act made it illegal for Americans to speak disloyally about the U.S. government, Constitution, or flag. More than 1,000 opponents of the war were jailed under these laws. Some Americans also considered religious groups that believed in peace to be disloyal. In addition, German Americans faced harassment and charges of disloyalty because of strong anti-German feelings.

✔ **Reading Check: Contrasting** How did the government build support for the war and punish those who opposed it?

Interpreting the Visual Record

Rallying support *Movie stars such as Douglas Fairbanks, Mary Pickford, and Charlie Chaplin helped sell Liberty bonds.* ***How do you think these movie stars were able to increase public support for the war?***

Mobilizing for War

When the war began, the U.S. Army and National Guard had some 750,000 men. This number was not enough to help the Allies, even with thousands of men enlisting. On May 18, 1917, Congress passed the **Selective Service Act**. This act required men between the ages of 21 and 30 to register to be drafted into the armed forces. Almost 3 million men who served during the war were draftees. Some Americans saw the draft as a violation of civil liberties. Others, such as Quakers, refused to fight because of their religious beliefs. Many of these men served in noncombat roles.

At first the government limited African American soldiers to noncombat roles, bringing protests from the National Association for the Advancement of Colored People (NAACP). In response, the military formed some African American combat units and an officer-training camp for African Americans. However, the majority of the more than 370,000 African Americans who served in the military did so in segregated units commanded by white officers. Once in Europe, most African American troops fought alongside the French army. U.S. officials worried that conflict might erupt if white and black soldiers fought together in the U.S. Army.

At the same time, African Americans at home faced ongoing discrimination and violence. On July 28, 1917, some 15,000 African Americans marched in silence down New York City's Fifth Avenue. They carried signs and passed out *Why We March* leaflets containing their message.

History Makers Speak

"We march because we are thoroughly opposed to Jim Crow cars, segregation, discrimination, and disfranchisement [denial of voting rights], lynching, and the host of evils that are forced on us. We march because we want our children to live in a better land."

—Anonymous, quoted in *Eyewitness: The Negro in American History,* by William Loren Katz

Analyzing Primary Sources

Identifying Points of View Why did African Americans march?

Women joined the war effort by serving as ambulance drivers, often transporting wounded soldiers directly from the front lines to hospitals.

Women in Wartime

Some American women also aided the war effort. About 25,000 female volunteers served in France, working as interpreters, nurses, and typists. The "Hello Girls" of the U.S. Army Signal Corps handled military telephone service, including translating calls and sending battle orders. None of the women in the military received a pension for their service.

Although officially not allowed in combat, many female nurses and ambulance drivers worked at the front lines.

"We had our first air-raid work last night. I was the night-driver on duty. . . . Some bombs fell very near just as I got to the [evacuation hospital]. . . . I had just stopped . . . when shrapnel [metal fragments] whizzed past my head and there was a tremendous crash close beside. . . . Then an ambulance call came and I tore off"

—Mrs. Guy Napier-Martin, quoted in *The Overseas War Record of the Winsor School*

Many other women volunteered for the Red Cross and worked at home and abroad. Women also filled important industrial jobs and clerical positions. Some 1 million women filled positions in the U.S. labor force.

Some women, including social reformer Jane Addams, opposed America's entry into the war and worked for peace. Jeannette Rankin of Montana, the first woman elected to the U.S. Congress, cast one of the few votes against President Wilson's war resolution. She stated, "I want to stand by my country but I cannot vote for war."

✔ **Reading Check:** **Comparing and Contrasting** How did African Americans and women contribute to the war effort?

That's Interesting!

War without Weapons
Did you know that early in World War I military airplanes were not armed? It's true! The fragile aircraft used in 1914 could not carry weapons. These planes struggled in strong winds and were often brought down by bad weather. Still, airplanes were quite important to the war effort. Planes were eventually equipped with machine guns and were used to bomb enemy positions. By 1918 Great Britain, France, and Germany each fielded several thousand aircraft.

Organizing for the War

In addition to raising troops, the government needed to raise money and supplies. To do so, it expanded its role in the economy. Congress raised income taxes and started a tax on business profits. Most importantly, the government issued war bonds, called **Liberty bonds**. Money from the sale of these bonds provided loans to the Allies, allowing them to buy food and war supplies. The U.S. government raised more than $20 billion by selling Liberty bonds.

President Wilson also created the **War Industries Board** (WIB) to oversee the production and distribution of goods made by the country's war industries. **Bernard Baruch**, head of the WIB, explained the agency's role. "No steel, copper, cement, rubber, or other basic materials could be used without our [WIB] approval."

The passage of the Lever Food and Fuel Control Act of 1917 gave the federal government the power to set price and production controls over food and fuel. Herbert Hoover led the new Food Administration, created to increase food supplies for the troops. The Food Administration's slogan was "Food Can Win the War." He got farmers to grow more food by promising high prices for crops. Production and prices increased greatly. Hoover also urged Americans to eat less by calling for "meatless Mondays" and "wheatless Wednesdays." He asked people to plant vegetables at home in "victory gardens."

The effort to supply the troops proved helpful to most workers in the United States. Three conditions combined to produce higher wages and better conditions for labor.

1. The Allied need for American products.
2. The labor shortage as men joined armed forces.
3. The decline in immigrant workers.

The entry of many women into the industrial workforce was not enough to fill all the empty positions.

THE GRANGER COLLECTION, NEW YORK

THE GRANGER COLLECTION, NEW YORK

U.S. propaganda posters encouraged Americans to work hard and make sacrifices to help win the war.

New and remaining workers took advantage of the labor shortage by demanding higher wages and better working conditions. Union membership grew during the war. More than 4 million workers went on strike in 1919, the highest proportion of the workforce to strike either before or since the war.

In April 1918 President Wilson created the **National War Labor Board**. This board worked to settle disputes between workers and management and to prevent strikes. The board was sympathetic to workers and supported their right to collective bargaining. It also outlined both minimum-wage and maximum-hour standards in the workplace.

✔ **Reading Check: Analyzing Information** How did the war affect industry and labor?

Section 3 Review

go.hrw.com Homework Practice Online
keyword: SC3 HP22

1 Identify and explain:
- Committee on Public Information
- George Creel
- Espionage Act of 1917
- Sedition Act of 1918
- Selective Service Act
- Liberty bonds
- War Industries Board
- Bernard Baruch
- National War Labor Board

2 Summarizing Copy the graphic organizer below. Use it to identify the changes made by the U.S. government to prepare to fight in World War I.

3 Finding the Main Idea

a. How did women and African Americans contribute to the war effort?

b. What changes did the war create for industry and labor?

4 Writing and Critical Thinking

Supporting a Point of View Imagine that you are the head of the Committee on Public Information. Create a poster to encourage Americans to support the war effort.

Consider the following:
- popular American views of the enemy
- the importance of buying Liberty bonds
- the importance of volunteering

Section 4

Americans "Over There"

Read to Discover

1. How did the Bolshevik Revolution affect World War I?
2. How did the entry of the United States affect the war?
3. Why did Germany finally agree to an armistice?

Define

- armistice

Identify

- American Expeditionary Force
- Communists
- Treaty of Brest-Litovsk
- Second Battle of the Marne

Why it Matters Today

Russia continues to play a significant role in international politics. Use CNNfyi.com or other **current events** sources to find out about Russian economics, politics, or society today. Record your findings in your journal.

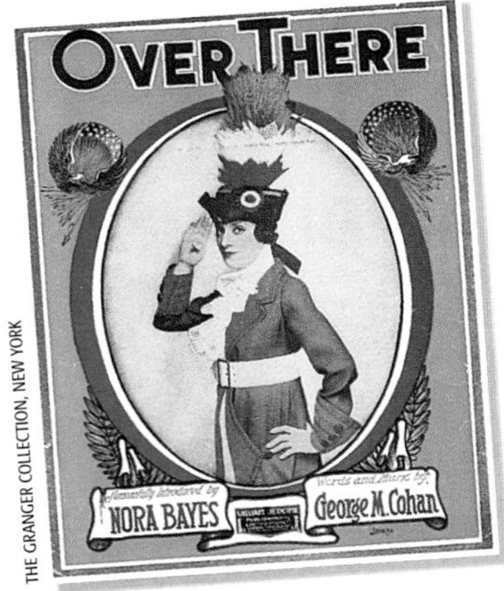

THE GRANGER COLLECTION, NEW YORK

George M. Cohan's song "Over There" celebrated the arrival of U.S. forces in Europe.

The Story Continues

In June 1917 the first U.S. forces arrived in France. In Boulogne the French Republican Guard band greeted the soldiers with "The Star-Spangled Banner." They followed with the French national anthem, "La Marseillaise" (mahr-se-yays). The sidewalks overflowed with people welcoming the troops. An American journalist traveling with the soldiers described the scene. "From the crowded balconies and windows overlooking the route, women and children tossed down showers of flowers and bits of colored paper. . . . Occasionally there came from the crowds a good old genuine American whoop-em-up yell."

The Americans Arrive

When the first U.S. troops arrived, the Allies were in bad shape. German troops occupied Belgium and part of France. The German navy was destroying Allied ships at an alarming rate. Russia was barely able to hold the Germans back. General John J. Pershing commanded the **American Expeditionary Force** (AEF). The AEF included a large force of volunteers and draftees as well as soldiers from the regular army and the National Guard. Pershing worked hard to train his troops for trench warfare.

Meanwhile, the Allies suffered a major blow when the Bolshevik Revolution took place in Russia in November 1917. The Bolsheviks took control of Russia's government. They were **Communists**—people who seek the equal distribution of wealth and an end to all forms of private property. The new government, led by Vladimir I. Lenin, faced famine and civil war. Russia thus withdrew from the fighting in December. In March 1918 Russia signed the **Treaty of Brest-Litovsk**, a peace agreement with the Central Powers.

✔ Reading Check: **Finding the Main Idea** What effect did the Communist takeover of Russia have on the war?

Research on the ROM

Free Find:
John Pershing
After reading about General John Pershing on the **Holt Researcher CD–ROM**, imagine that you are introducing General Pershing at a banquet being held in his honor. Write a short speech describing his accomplishments.

The Final Battles

With Russia out of the conflict and most U.S. troops not yet ready to fight, Germany saw its last chance to win the war. In the spring of 1918 Germany launched a series of major attacks on the western front. During these weeks, the first U.S. troops suffered the cruel realities of war.

On March 21 the Germans attacked along the Somme River in northern France. Two days later, German artillery bombarded Paris from about 75 miles away. But after pushing some 40 miles into Allied lines, the advance stalled as German troops advanced farther and faster than their supplies. The attack cost the German army 250,000 casualties. Allied losses were slightly lower. On April 9 the German army began a second offensive against the British line in northwestern France, near Belgium. Urged to "fight on to the end," the British stopped the Germans. In 20 days of combat, there were 110,000 casualties on the two sides.

CONNECTING TO THE ARTS

John Philip Sousa

John Philip Sousa

John Philip Sousa was born in 1854 in Washington, D.C. He earned a place in the world of music by writing more marches than anyone else in history. Sousa wrote more than 135 military marches, including "Semper Fidelis" and "The Stars and Stripes Forever." His marches were hugely popular and still inspire strong feelings of patriotism.

During World War I, Sousa joined the U.S. Naval Reserve at the age of 62 to organize its band units. He toured with a navy band of more than 300 sailors. In addition to entertaining the troops, Sousa's band also assisted in the Liberty Loan and Red Cross drives. Sousa wrote many marches during the war, including "The Chantyman's March" and "Sabre and Spurs." In 1918, when anti-German feelings were running high, the American Relief Legion asked Sousa to write a wedding march. Some Americans wanted to replace the often-used music of German composers. Sousa's "Wedding March" was performed at many wedding ceremonies held during World War I.

Understanding What You Read
The Arts and History Why do you think Sousa's music was so popular?

The Western Front in 1918

Interpreting Maps In 1918, after Russia withdrew from the war, Germany used its eastern forces to push into France.

Skills Assessment

1. **The World in Spatial Terms** What was the farthest distance the German forces had to retreat to reach the armistice line?
2. **Analyzing Information** How close did the Germans get to reaching Paris by June 1918?

Allied Powers
Central Powers
Neutral countries
Central Powers forces
German advance (Summer 1918)
Allied Powers forces
Allied victory
Armistice line, Nov. 11, 1918

Tins used by soldiers to store food and condiments

World War I soldiers carried all their necessary equipment on their backs, making for a heavy load.

Allies on the Attack

Farther south, German forces were threatening to break through the thin French line and march toward Paris. Then two divisions of the American Expeditionary Force joined the French to strike back. U.S. troops stopped the German advance at the town of Château-Thierry (shah-toh-tye-REE), within 50 miles of Paris. The Allies then gradually pushed back another German offensive at Belleau Wood, a forest in northern France.

By the beginning of July 1918, some 1 million U.S. troops and military personnel were stationed in France. In mid-July the Germans launched their last, desperate offensive. At the **Second Battle of the Marne**, both sides suffered heavy casualties. However, the German losses destroyed their ability to attack again.

The Allies counterattacked in September. In the first mainly American assault, U.S. forces defeated the Germans at Saint-Mihiel, near the border of France and Germany. By November 1918 General Pershing's troops had broken through enemy lines. The Allies continued to advance toward the railway at Sedan on the Belgian border, which was the main supply line for German forces. Other Allied forces also advanced.

✔ **Reading Check: Sequencing** List the final battles of the war in their proper sequence.

Armistice

The French government rewarded these African American soldiers with the Croix de Guerre (right) for their bravery during the war.

By the fall of 1918, food riots and strikes were taking place in Germany and other countries of the Central Powers. Some German soldiers deserted and others were captured by Allied forces. Faced with these conditions, members of the Central Powers began to surrender. In early November the Allies reached a peace agreement with Austria-Hungary.

Germany soon agreed to a cease-fire. As part of the agreement, Kaiser Wilhelm II abandoned the German throne and fled to the Netherlands. Germany became a republic. The Allied Powers demanded that Germany leave all occupied territory. German aircraft, heavy artillery, tanks, and U-boats were to be surrendered. Germany was also required to accept the occupation of some German territory by Allied troops. On the 11th hour of the 11th day of the 11th month of 1918, the **armistice**, or truce, officially ended the war. An Allied soldier described the troops' reaction to the news.

> **"There came a second of expectant silence, and then a curious rippling sound. . . . It was the sound of men cheering from the Vosges [a French mountain range] to the sea."**
>
> —John Buchan, *The King's Grace*

November 11, 1918
The armistice officially ends World War I.

However, the terrible tragedy of the war limited the celebration.

✔ **Reading Check: Summarizing** What conditions led Germany to sign the armistice?

Section 4 Review

go.hrw.com Homework Practice Online
keyword: SC3 HP22

1. **Define** and explain:
   - armistice

2. **Identify** and explain:
   - American Expeditionary Force
   - Communists
   - Treaty of Brest-Litovsk
   - Second Battle of the Marne

3. **Sequencing** Copy the graphic organizer below. Use it to explain, in the order that they occurred, the events that led to the end of the war after the United States joined the fighting.

4. **Finding the Main Idea**
   a. Why did Russia withdraw from the war, and how did this affect the Allies?
   b. Do you think the Allies would have won the war if the United States had not joined them? Explain your answer.

5. **Writing and Critical Thinking**
   Evaluating Imagine that you are a reporter for an American newspaper who has been assigned to cover the western front in 1918. Write a one- or two-paragraph story analyzing the reasons Germany agreed to an armistice.
   Consider the following:
   - the condition of the German and Allied troops in the final battles
   - conditions in Germany
   - the surrender of other Central Powers

Section 5

Establishing Peace

Read to Discover

1. What were the human and economic costs of World War I?
2. What were the terms of the Treaty of Versailles?
3. How did the U.S. government respond to the Treaty of Versailles?

Define

- self-determination
- reparations

Identify

- Fourteen Points
- League of Nations
- Treaty of Versailles

WHY IT MATTERS TODAY

International agreement on peace treaties is often difficult to achieve. Use CNNfyi.com or other **current events** sources to study recent attempts to make peace agreements between countries in conflict. Record your findings in your journal.

The Story Continues

When news of the armistice reached the United States, Americans celebrated with great enthusiasm. U.S. cities and industries were untouched by the destruction of the war. But World War I had left much of Europe in ruins. A British visitor described the war's impact on the French countryside. "For mile after mile nothing was left. No building was habitable." Millions of people found their lives and homelands wrecked by the terrible conflict.

Two women sweep this marine off his feet after the armistice.

Europe after the War

World War I carried a heavy human cost. The Allies lost more than 5 million soldiers on the battlefield. More than 112,000 U.S. troops died, more than half of them from influenza, a viral infection. The Central Powers lost about 3.4 million soldiers. More than 20 million soldiers on both sides were wounded. Millions of civilians were also killed during the four years of fighting.

The economies of the countries of Europe were ruined. Estimates of the damage caused by the war were difficult to make because of the scale of the destruction. In 1920 the Carnegie Endowment for International

Peace declared that the total cost of the war had exceeded $330 billion. Industry and agriculture were nearly wiped out in Belgium, France, Russia, and other parts of Europe.

France and Britain owed American banks billions of dollars borrowed during the war. Germany also faced heavy debts and severe food shortages. Many people feared that these economic troubles would allow the communist revolution in Russia to spread to other countries.

✔ **Reading Check: Finding the Main Idea** How did the war affect economic and social life in Europe?

Interpreting the Visual Record

Disarmament *These members of the Disarmament Conference of the League of Nations are struggling with the problems of enforcing the peace.* ***What challenges do you think these people face during the conference?***

Wilson's Fourteen Points

While Americans welcomed the armistice, President Wilson tried to make a lasting peace. Even before the United States entered the war, Wilson had been preparing for its end. On January 8, 1918, Wilson outlined a plan for postwar Europe and proposed a system to avoid future wars. This plan was called the **Fourteen Points** because it set forth 14 basic ideals. (See pages 348–49.) The president believed that the peace terms should not be so harsh on the Central Powers that the settlement would provoke another war.

Most of the Fourteen Points dealt with the future of specific nations and regions. Some points called for the freedom of ships on the seas, smaller armies and navies, and lower tariffs. Wilson asked for fair settlement of colonial demands for independence and an end to secret agreements between nations. Wilson stressed the right of people to decide their own political status—the right of **self-determination.** Wilson's last point called for the creation of the **League of Nations**. The League would be a congress of nations formed to settle international disputes and maintain peace and collective security.

Other Allied leaders, however, disagreed. An American journalist wrote that these leaders wanted "a new world domination with themselves and ourselves [Americans] dominating; what they decidedly do not want is a democratic peace." France and Britain wanted to punish Germany and make sure that it would never again be a world power. As one reporter wrote, Britain and France wanted Germany to "pay, pay, pay." Many Americans agreed. However, a Montana rancher who had three sons in the army in France wanted the government to do more. "Take steps to see that there shall never be another tragedy like this," he wrote in a letter to Wilson's cabinet. "Fix the matter so that neither Germany nor any other nation can ruin the world."

✔ **Reading Check: Identifying Cause and Effect** Why did Wilson propose the Fourteen Points, and what measures did they include?

LINKING PAST to PRESENT

The League of Nations and the United Nations

Countries formed the League of Nations after World War I to maintain international peace. After World War II, countries formed the United Nations (UN) for similar reasons. The League of Nations failed partly because the United States was not a member. The United States has been a member of the UN since its creation in 1945.

During the UN's early years of existence, fear of a U.S.-Soviet confrontation limited its use of force to resolve conflicts. In recent years, however, increased international cooperation has strengthened the UN. The number of ongoing peacekeeping missions conducted by the UN increased from 5 in 1988 to 15 in 2001. The UN also runs many humanitarian programs, including aid to refugees and to developing countries as well as famine relief. **What does the United Nations do today?**

The Paris Peace Conference

President Wilson arrived in Europe on December 13, 1918. He ignored protests from Republican critics that no American president had ever gone to Europe before. Some supporters also worried about the amount of time he would spend overseas during the negotiations. Wilson believed it was "now my duty to play my full part in making good what [our soldiers] offered their lives to obtain." He was ready to persuade the Allies to adopt a peace plan based on his Fourteen Points. Leaders of the Allied nations attended the peace conference at the palace of Versailles (ver-SY) outside Paris. The new leaders of Russia refused to attend, and no representatives of the Central Powers were invited. President Woodrow Wilson of the United States, British prime minister David Lloyd George, and French premier Georges Clemenceau (kle-mahn-soh) attended the conference. Together with Italian prime minister Vittorio Orlando, these "Big Four" dominated the peace conference.

Wilson and the European leaders clashed, however. Wilson favored his ideals of peace and democracy as set forth in the Fourteen Points. The three European leaders wanted to reward the Allies and punish the former Central Powers. Lloyd George's main concern was keeping the British Empire together and protecting its interests. Clemenceau wanted to punish Germany so severely that it could never again harm France. Orlando wanted Italy to receive land it had been promised when it entered the war on the Allied side.

The other national leaders also wanted Germany to accept the blame and pay the Allied Powers for the full cost of the war. Wilson was forced to compromise. He agreed that Germany should pay **reparations**—payments for damages and expenses caused by the war. The amount was eventually set at $33 billion. The president also agreed that Germany must return the border region of Alsace-Lorraine to France, giving France some of the defensive security that it desired. Also, the Allies would gain control of a region in western Germany.

The final peace settlement of World War I, the **Treaty of Versailles**, did include some of the Fourteen Points. The treaty partially used the right of national self-determination. Some countries won the right to decide their own political situation, rather than have an outside imperial power decide it. Some new countries were formed and old ones were restored. Czechoslovakia and Yugoslavia were created and Poland was re-established. Estonia, Finland, Latvia, and Lithuania became free nations. The Central Powers were also forced to surrender control of their colonies to the Allies.

A system of mandates gave the League of Nations control over the former colonies of the Central Powers. Under this system, the League placed each of the colonies into one of several categories. Some areas, particularly the German colonies in the Pacific, were given to

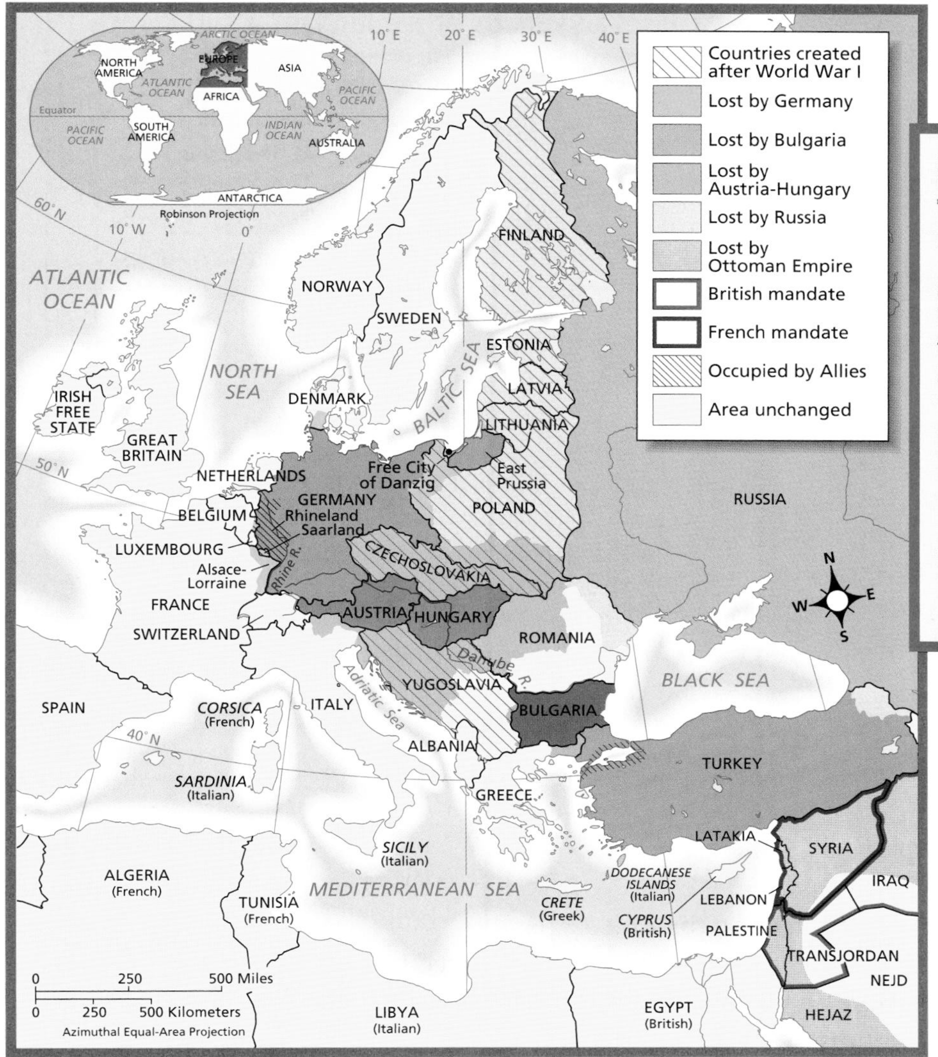

Europe after the Treaty of Versailles, 1919–1920

Interpreting Maps World War I led to the collapse of empires and to the formation of several new European countries.

Skills Assessment

1. **Places and Regions** How many new European countries were formed after World War I?
2. **Summarizing** What countries had regions occupied by the Allies after the war?

Woodrow Wilson's efforts were key to the creation of the League of Nations.

Allied countries to control. Other former colonies were placed under the temporary control of Allied nations until they were ready for independence. For example, Britain and France were granted mandates to administer several states in the Middle East.

Although the treaty did not include everything that Wilson wanted, he believed that the League of Nations could resolve any problems the treaty itself created or that it had failed to solve. When Wilson addressed the members of the peace conference on February 14, 1919, he stated that the war had in fact done some good.

> **"Some very beautiful things have come out of it. Wrong has been defeated, but the rest of the world has been more conscious than it was before of the majesty of right."**
>
> —Woodrow Wilson, quoted in *America Enters the World,* by Page Smith

Analyzing Primary Sources

Supporting a Point of View
Do you agree or disagree with Wilson that some good had come out of the war? Explain your answer.

All that remained was to convince the U.S. Senate to approve the treaty, but Wilson was not prepared for the opposition he met there.

✔ **Reading Check: Summarizing** What did the Treaty of Versailles call for?

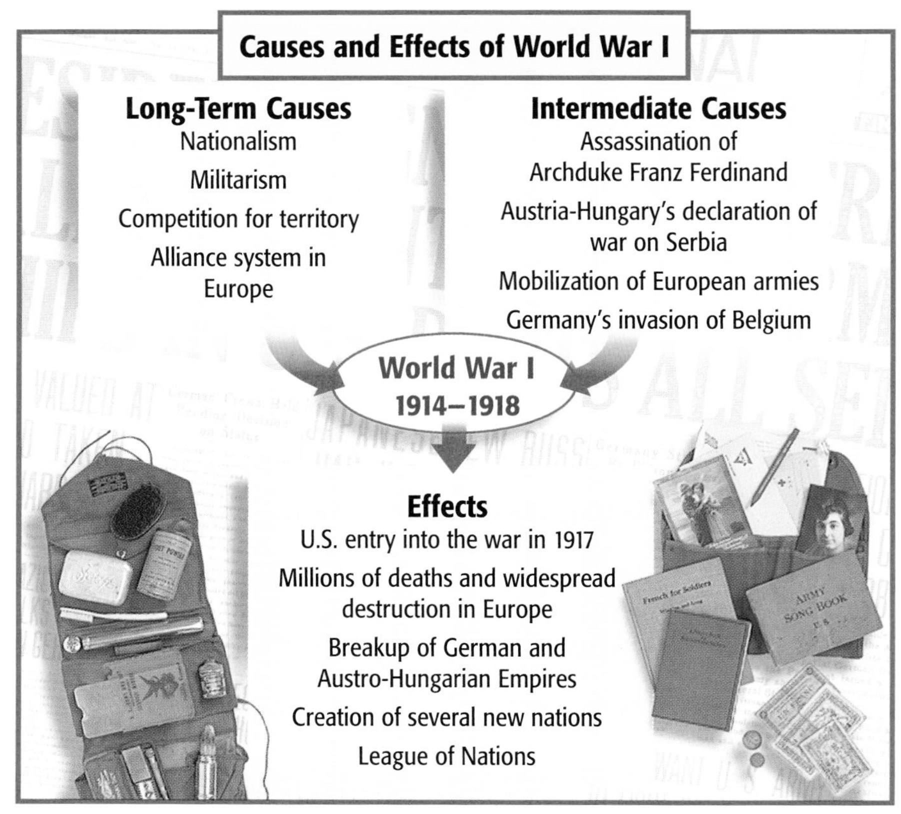

The League of Nations

For President Wilson, the most important of the treaty's terms was the creation of the League of Nations. In his view, the League of Nations would include representatives from democratic countries. It would promote peace by working cooperatively to settle disputes and to reduce armaments. The League would include a council, an assembly, and a permanent administrative staff.

Each member state would be represented in the assembly and would have one vote. The council would also include five permanent members—Great Britain, France, Italy, Japan, and the United States. Eventually, all independent countries would be allowed to join. However, the former Central Powers could not be members in the beginning.

Member nations would present disagreements to the Permanent Court of International Justice, or World Court. If a member nation did not obey the court's judgment, the League could impose penalties on that nation. Penalties included banning trade or even the use of military force.

Peace without a Treaty

President Wilson was surprised that Congress did not share his enthusiasm for the Treaty of Versailles or the League of Nations. Republican senator Henry Cabot Lodge, argued, "No peace that satisfied Germany in any degree can ever satisfy us."

The Foreign Relations Committee, led by Senator Henry Cabot Lodge, demanded changes to the Treaty of Versailles.

To get the two-thirds majority necessary for Senate approval of the treaty, Wilson needed Republican support. Although most Democratic senators supported the treaty, many Republican senators disagreed with certain parts of it and demanded changes. Wilson, who expected the treaty to pass, stubbornly refused to compromise.

Most of the Republicans worried about the collective security clause of the League of Nations. Collective security—the promise to defend other countries if they are attacked—would involve the United States more closely in European affairs. The Republicans were strongly isolationist and suspicious of European countries' motives.

Wilson took his cause to the American public by going on an extended speaking tour and urging Americans to pressure the Senate Republicans to pass the treaty. However, he suffered a stroke in October 1919. Although Wilson survived, he never fully recovered.

In November, Senator Lodge presented the treaty for Senate consideration with a list of 14 changes, or reservations. He wanted to limit U.S. military involvement in the League. Otherwise, his reservations did not change the treaty greatly. However, Wilson pressured Democrats to vote against any compromise. After several earlier votes failed to approve the treaty, the Senate defeated the measure for the last time in March 1920.

Wilson's refusal to compromise cost him his goal of U.S. membership in the League of Nations. In the end, the United States signed separate peace treaties with Austria, Germany, and Hungary. Without the United States in the League of Nations, its ability to protect world peace seemed uncertain.

✔ **Reading Check: Analyzing Information** Why did some Americans oppose membership in the League of Nations?

Section 5 Review

keyword: SC3 HP22

1. **Define** and explain:
   - self-determination
   - reparations

2. **Identify** and explain:
   - Fourteen Points
   - League of Nations
   - Treaty of Versailles

3. **Identifying Cause and Effect** Copy the graphic organizer below. Use it to explain the reasons many senators opposed the Treaty of Versailles and what the results were.

   Senate Opposition → **Results**

4. **Finding the Main Idea**
   a. How did the war affect the people and the economies of the countries involved?
   b. What were the conditions and requirements of the Treaty of Versailles?

5. **Writing and Critical Thinking**
   Supporting a Point of View Imagine that you are a senator debating the Treaty of Versailles. Write a speech explaining your position for or against the treaty.
   Consider the following:
   - punishing Germany for the destruction of World War I
   - preventing a similar war in the future
   - the constitutionality of the League of Nations

The Fourteen Points

President Wilson announced his specific proposals for a postwar peace in an address to Congress on January 8, 1918. His proposal became known as the Fourteen Points. An excerpt from the Fourteen Points appears below.

President Wilson hoped his efforts would lead to greater international cooperation and world peace.

Gentlemen of the Congress:

It will be our wish and purpose that the processes of peace, when they are begun, shall be absolutely open and that they shall involve and permit henceforth no secret understandings of any kind. . . . The program of the world's peace, therefore, is our program; and that program, the only possible program, as we see it, is this:

I. Open **covenants**[1] of peace, openly arrived at, after which there shall be no private international understandings of any kind but **diplomacy**[2] shall proceed always frankly and in the public view.

II. Absolute freedom of navigation upon the seas, outside territorial waters, alike in peace and in war, except as the seas may be closed in whole or in part by international action for the enforcement of international covenants.

III. The removal, so far as possible, of all economic barriers and the establishment of an equality of trade conditions among all the nations consenting to the peace and associating themselves for its maintenance.

IV. **Adequate**[3] guarantees given and taken that national **armaments**[4] will be reduced to the lowest point consistent with domestic safety.

V. A free, open-minded, and absolutely **impartial**[5] adjustment of all colonial claims, based upon a strict **observance**[6] of the principle that in determining all such questions of **sovereignty**[7] the interests of the populations concerned must have equal weight with the **equitable**[8] claims of the government whose title is to be determined.

VI. The evacuation of all Russian territory and such a settlement of all questions affecting Russia as will secure the best and freest cooperation of the other nations of the world in obtaining for her an . . . opportunity for the independent determination of her own political development and national policy and assure her of a sincere welcome into the society of free nations under institutions of her own choosing; and, more than a welcome, assistance also of every kind that she may need and may herself desire.

VII. Belgium, the whole world will agree, must be evacuated and restored, without any attempt to limit the **sovereignty**[9] which she enjoys in common with all other free nations. No other single act will serve as this will serve to restore confidence among the nations in the laws which they have themselves set and determined for the government of their relations with one another. Without this healing act the whole structure and **validity**[10] of international law is forever **impaired.**[11]

VIII. All French territory should be freed and the invaded portions restored, and the wrong done to France by Prussia in 1871 in the matter of Alsace-Lorraine, which has unsettled the peace of the world for nearly fifty years,

[1]**covenants:** agreements
[2]**diplomacy:** negotiations
[3]**adequate:** enough
[4]**armaments:** military equipment
[5]**impartial:** fair
[6]**observance:** following
[7]**sovereignty:** who should rule
[8]**equitable:** just
[9]**sovereignty:** self-rule
[10]**validity:** authority
[11]**impaired:** damaged
[12]**readjustment:** correction to

should be righted, in order that peace may once more be made secure in the interest of all.

IX. A **readjustment**[12] of the frontiers of Italy should be effected along clearly recognizable lines of nationality.

X. The peoples of Austria-Hungary, whose place among the nations we wish to see safeguarded and assured, should be **accorded**[13] the freest opportunity of **autonomous**[14] development.

XI. Rumania, Serbia, and Montenegro should be evacuated; occupied territories restored; Serbia accorded free and secure access to the sea; and the relations of the several Balkan states to one another determined by friendly **counsel**[15] along historically established lines of allegiance and nationality; and international guarantees of the political and economic independence and territorial **integrity**[16] of the several Balkan states should be entered into.

XII. The Turkish portions of the present Ottoman Empire should be assured a secure sovereignty, but the other nationalities which are now under Turkish rule should be assured an **undoubted**[17] security of life and an absolutely **unmolested**[18] opportunity of autonomous development, and the Dardanelles should be permanently opened as a free passage to the ships and commerce of all nations under international guarantees.

XIII. An independent Polish state should be **erected**[19] which should include the territories inhabited by **indisputably**[20] Polish populations, which should be assured a free and secure access to the sea, and whose political and economic independence and territorial integrity should be guaranteed by international covenant.

XIV. A general association of nations must be formed under specific covenants for the purpose of **affording**[21] mutual guarantees of political independence and territorial integrity to great and small states alike.

The Big Four; seated from left to right: Italian prime minister Vittorio Orlando, British prime minister David Lloyd George, French premier Georges Clemenceau, and U.S. president Woodrow Wilson

Analyzing Primary Sources

1. What freedoms does President Wilson want to guarantee?
2. What countries does President Wilson want to be created or restored?
3. Do you think the Fourteen Points were fair to all the countries involved? Explain your answer.

[13]**accorded:** given
[14]**autonomous:** independent
[15]**counsel:** agreement
[16]**integrity:** completeness
[17]**undoubted:** beyond dispute
[18]**unmolested:** unquestioned
[19]**erected:** created
[20]**indisputably:** without question
[21]**affording:** providing

Chapter 22 Review

The Chapter at a Glance

Examine the visual summary of the chapter below. Then create three lists explaining the reasons the United States entered World War I, how it prepared for the war, and how the war ended.

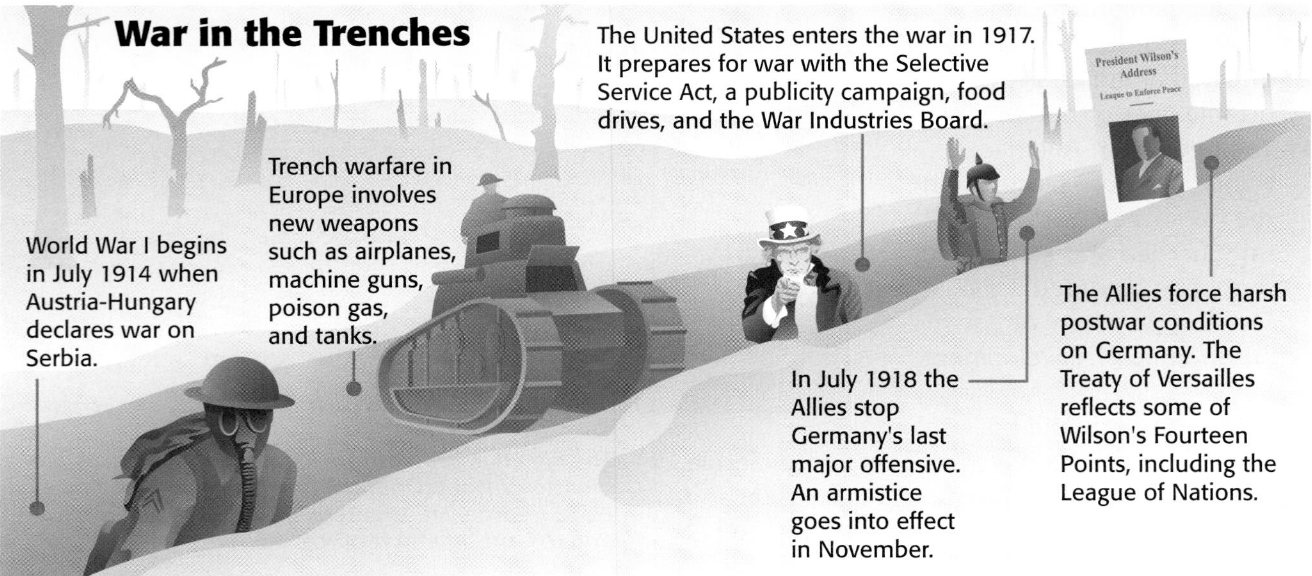

Identifying People and Ideas

Use the following terms or people in historically significant sentences.

1. nationalism
2. Allied Powers
3. stalemate
4. *Sussex* pledge
5. George Creel
6. National War Labor Board
7. American Expeditionary Force
8. Second Battle of the Marne
9. reparations
10. Treaty of Versailles

Understanding Main Ideas

Section 1 *(Pages 668–671)*

1. What conditions and events led to the outbreak of World War I?

Section 2 *(Pages 672–677)*

2. Why did President Wilson try to keep the United States out of World War I?

Section 3 *(Pages 678–681)*

3. How did the war affect African Americans and women?
4. How did Americans at home contribute to the war effort?

Section 4 *(Pages 682–685)*

5. How did U.S. forces help the Allies win the war?

Section 5 *(Pages 686–691)*

6. How did the Treaty of Versailles reflect Wilson's Fourteen Points?
7. How and why did American opinions differ on U.S. participation in the League of Nations?

You Be the Historian— Reviewing Themes

1. **Citizenship** How did the United States attempt to increase support for World War I at home?
2. **Global Relations** How did the assassination of Archduke Franz Ferdinand start a world war?
3. **Science, Technology & Society** Explain how the airplane and the machine gun changed fighting in World War I.

Thinking Critically

1. **Analyzing Information** How did nationalism and imperialism contribute to tensions in Europe before World War I?
2. **Evaluating** Which one of the Fourteen Points described in the chapter do you think is the most important? Explain your answer.
3. **Supporting a Point of View** Do you think that Germany should have been held totally responsible for the cost of World War I? Explain your answer.

Social Studies Skills Workshop

Interpreting Maps

Study the map below. Then use the information on the map to help you answer the questions that follow.

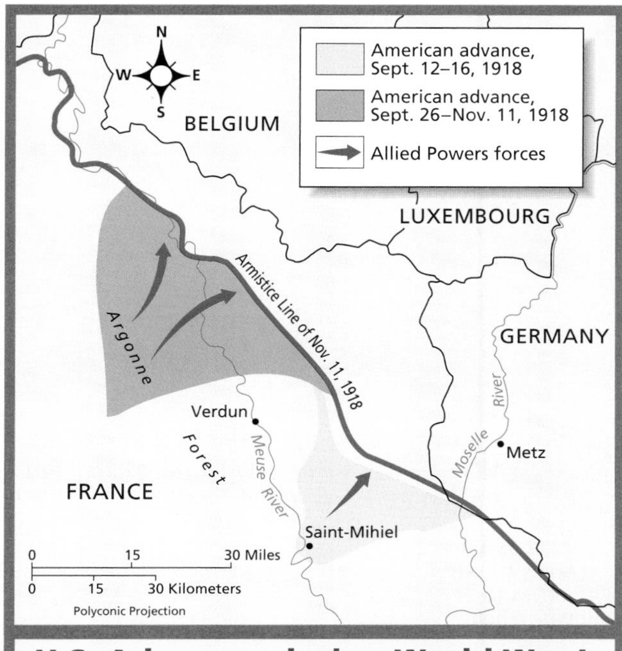

U.S. Advances during World War I, Sept.–Nov. 1918

1. Which of the following statements correctly describes the U.S. advances from September to November 1918?
   a. Neither U.S. advance reached the armistice line.
   b. Both advances crossed the Moselle River.
   c. The advance ending in November covered more territory.
   d. The advance from Saint-Mihiel crossed the armistice line first.
2. Based on the map and your knowledge of the period, how might a reporter on the western front have described and compared these advances?

Analyzing Primary Sources

Read the following quotation by John Maynard Keynes describing the French countryside after the war, then answer the questions.

> **"The horror and desolation of war was made visible to the sight on an extraordinary scale. . . . The completeness of the destruction was evident. For mile after mile nothing was left. No building was habitable and no field fit for the plow. . . . One devastated area was exactly like another—a heap of rubble, a morass [an overwhelming mass] of shell-holes, and a tangle of wire. . . ."**

3. Which of the following statements best describes Keynes's point of view?
   a. He is shocked by the level of destruction caused by the war.
   b. He is impressed by the military power of the Allies.
   c. He is relieved that the war mainly damaged cities.
   d. none of the above
4. Based on this quotation and your knowledge of the period, how do you think Europe's economy was affected by the war?
5. What would you have suggested that the United States do to help Europe recover from the war?

Alternative Assessment

Building Your Portfolio

Interdisciplinary Connection to Art

Create three posters to promote the war effort on the home front. You might develop posters for recruiting, for the war effort in the United States, or for agencies such as the Food Administration. Write a paragraph explaining each poster. Then explain how each poster would have helped the war effort.

internet connect

Internet Activity: go.hrw.com
keyword: SC3 CF22

Choose a topic on World War I to:

- Understand how the weaknesses of the Versailles Treaty led to future conflict.
- Create a propaganda poster supporting either the Allied Powers or the Central Powers.
- Write a biography of Woodrow Wilson.

CHAPTER

23 The Roaring Twenties (1919–1929)

Louis Armstrong was one of the most famous trumpeters and singers of the Jazz Age.

Howard Thain's painting The Great White Way — New York *captured the excitement of New York City in the 1920s.*

UNITED STATES

1919 A deadly race riot breaks out in Chicago, Illinois.

1920 The first radio broadcasting station, KDKA in Pittsburgh, goes on the air.

1921 President Harding signs the Emergency Quota Act, limiting immigration.

1922 Jazz pioneer Louis Armstrong moves to Chicago, which helps his musical career take off.

1924 Calvin Coolidge is elected president.

1919 1920 1921 1922 1923 1924

1919 The League of Nations is formed.

1920 Terence McSwiney, lord mayor of Cork, goes on a hunger strike in a London prison to try to change British policy in Ireland.

1921 Congress declares World War I ended. Treaties are signed with Germany, Austria, and Hungary.

1922 The tomb of Tutankhamen is uncovered by British archaeologists near Luxor, Egypt.

1923 Adolf Hitler tries to overthrow the Weimar Republic in Germany.

1924 Joseph Stalin becomes leader of the Communist Party in Russia.

WORLD

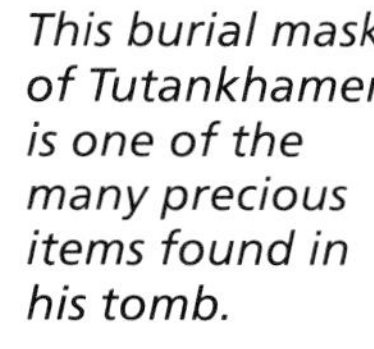

This burial mask of Tutankhamen is one of the many precious items found in his tomb.

Build on What You Know

After the end of World War I, the United States suffered a brief economic downturn before business and industry began growing rapidly. Many Americans took advantage of these good times, enjoying new forms of entertainment and art. However, American society remained divided over issues such as alcohol use and the treatment of minorities.

THE GRANGER COLLECTION, NEW YORK

Charles Lindbergh posed for this photograph just before his historic flight across the Atlantic Ocean.

As this *Life* magazine cover shows, some young women adopted new fashions and roles during the 1920s.

THE GRANGER COLLECTION, NEW YORK

1925 Science teacher John Scopes is brought to trial in Tennessee for teaching Darwin's theory of evolution.

1926 Georgia O'Keeffe paints *Black Iris*.

1927 In May Charles Lindbergh finishes the first solo transatlantic flight.

The Jazz Singer, the first movie with singing and spoken dialogue, is released in October.

1929 The Museum of Modern Art opens in New York City.

1925 | **1926** | **1927** | **1928** | **1929**

1925 U.S. troops withdraw from Nicaragua, only to return again in 1926.

1926 Hirohito becomes emperor of Japan.

1927 "Black Friday" takes place in Germany, and the economic system collapses.

1929 The first exhibition by Spanish painter Salvador Dali opens in Paris.

Emperor Hirohito of Japan

If you were there . . .
How would you describe Americans in the 1920s?

You Be the Historian

Themes Journal

What's Your Opinion? Do you **agree** or **disagree** with the following statements? Support your point of view in your journal.

- **Economics** The end of a war is always good for a country's economy.
- **Science, Technology & Society** New technology always improves the environment of the workplace.
- **Culture** The experiences of a particular group affect the culture of an entire country.

Section 1

The Transition to Peace

Read to Discover

1. How did the 1920s bring greater independence to many American women?
2. How did the end of World War I affect American workers?
3. What types of social problems did the United States face after World War I?

Define

- flappers
- xenophobia

Identify

- Communists
- Red Scare
- Palmer raids
- Nicola Sacco
- Bartolomeo Vanzetti
- American Civil Liberties Union
- Great Migration

WHY IT MATTERS TODAY

Women continue to make great strides in the political arena. Use CNNfyi.com or other **current events** sources to find out about the positions women hold at different levels of government. Record your findings in your journal.

Many Americans spent their leisure time listening to records played on phonographs such as this one.

The Story Continues

One afternoon in February 1919, teenager Bernard Katz and his friends walked up New York City's Fifth Avenue. Suddenly they saw a parade. The parade celebrated the return of the 369th U.S. Infantry, a heavily decorated African American unit. Katz and his friends got caught up in the joy of the moment and joined the parade. Soon the nation would have to stop celebrating, however. The end of the war had brought with it many difficult challenges.

A Changing Society

For many Americans the 1920s brought greater independence. In 1920 more than half the nation's population lived in urban areas that offered new economic and cultural opportunities. In addition, more Americans were attending high school and college. Some young people enjoyed their new freedom by attending parties and dances, listening to popular music, and driving fast cars.

Women in particular experienced more social, economic, and political freedom. Many more women went to college, and the number of working women rose by 2 million during the 1920s. The Nineteenth

Amendment, which was passed in August 1920, gave women the right to vote in all elections. Soon voters elected more women to public office. By 1928, 145 women were serving in state legislatures, and 2 had been elected to the U.S. House of Representatives.

Some young women—known as **flappers**—used their freedom to challenge traditional dress and behavior. A historian of the time described a typical flapper.

> **"[She is] breezy, slangy, and informal in manner; slim and boyish in form; covered with silk and fur . . . with carmined [reddened] cheeks and lips, plucked eyebrows, and close-fitting . . . hair. . . . She cared little for approval or disapproval."**
>
> —Preston W. Slosson, *The Great Crusade and After, 1914–1928*

The presence of flappers and female politicians showed that social traditions were changing dramatically for some women in the 1920s.

✔ **Reading Check: Finding the Main Idea** What changes did women's roles undergo in the 1920s?

The Peacetime Economy

A return to peacetime brought new economic troubles. Some 4.5 million soldiers returned home after the war to find that their old jobs had been filled by others. To make room for these returning veterans, many women were forced to give up their jobs. Just as veterans began looking for work, the government canceled its huge contracts for war materials. As a result, businesses slowed production and laid off workers. Soon the demand for goods exceeded supply, and prices rose rapidly. As prices and unemployment rose, wages fell or stayed about the same, causing a severe recession.

In January 1919, members of the Metal Workers Union in Seattle, Washington, walked off the job, demanding higher pay and shorter

GLOBAL CONNECTIONS

The Influenza Epidemic

Americans faced more than just economic challenges at the end of World War I. The global epidemic of 1918–19 was one of the deadliest outbreaks of disease in recorded history. U.S. soldiers carried influenza, or flu, to Europe during World War I. The disease was soon spread around the world.

The flu was very contagious, and its symptoms, such as terrible fever and headache, developed rapidly. A young nurse recalled, "We'd be working with someone one day, . . . and the next day they were gone [dead]." The epidemic killed more than half a million people in the United States, more than 10 times the number of Americans killed in battle during World War I. Worldwide at least 20 million people died from the flu. **Why was the flu so deadly?**

Interpreting the Visual Record

The Seattle strike *During the Seattle general strike, union leaders set up community kitchens and milk stations to feed the strikers and their families.* ***How might such community support help strikers get their labor demands met?***

hours. On February 6 some 60,000 workers throughout the city joined the strike. The strikers tried to keep order on the streets and provide food to strikers and their families. Some reporters blamed the strike on **Communists** and anarchists. Communists are people who want the government to own all property. Anarchists, on the other hand, want to get rid of all government. Seattle mayor Ole Hanson gave his explanation of why the strike took place.

Analyzing Primary Sources
Identifying Points of View What was Hanson's opinion of the Seattle strike?

> **"[The Seattle strike] was an attempted revolution . . . for the overthrow of the industrial system. . . . True, there were no flashing guns, no bombs, no killings. Revolution . . . doesn't need violence. . . . The . . . strike is of itself the weapon of revolution, . . . it puts the government out of operation."**
>
> —Ole Hanson, quoted in *A People's History of the United States,* by Howard Zinn

Hanson called in the state militia to keep order, but no violence took place. Within five days, the strikers had returned to work with none of their demands met.

In September two other major strikes occurred. In one strike, Boston police officers walked off the job, demanding the right to form a union. Governor Calvin Coolidge rejected their right to strike, and an entirely new police force was hired. Then the steel industry was rocked by a huge protest that began in Pennsylvania. Soon some 365,000 steelworkers—more than half the industry's workforce—were on strike. They demanded higher pay, an eight-hour workday, and a six-day workweek. Their efforts nearly shut down the steel industry. But mill owners brought in strike-breakers and used violence against strikers, forcing the union to call off the strike in January 1920. The failed efforts were a serious blow to unions.

✔ **Reading Check: Identifying Cause and Effect** Why did many workers go on strike after World War I, and what did these strikes accomplish?

Interpreting Political Cartoons

Red Scare *This cartoon showing a foreign anarchist appeared in the* Philadelphia Inquirer *in 1919.* ***Why do you think the cartoon shows the anarchist crawling under the American flag?***

Fear and Violence

The strikes and riots of 1919 scared some Americans. They worried that a communist revolution like the one in Russia might take place in the United States. In 1919 and 1920 these fears led to a **Red Scare**, a widespread fear of political radicals, particularly Communists, who were called Reds.

Public concern grew after several bombings in 1919 were aimed at business and government leaders. One bomb damaged the house of Attorney General A. Mitchell Palmer, who then ordered raids on suspected radical organizations, often without warrants. The largest of these so-called **Palmer raids** took place in January 1920. There was little evidence against many of those arrested, yet hundreds of immigrants were eventually deported. These civil rights violations began to upset the public. When a revolution did not occur, the Red Scare began to fade.

Many African Americans had to seek safe areas of the city during the Chicago race riots of 1919.

Xenophobia—the fear and hatred of foreigners—played a large part in the Red Scare. This fear greatly influenced the trial of two Italian immigrants. On May 5, 1920, police authorities arrested **Nicola Sacco** and **Bartolomeo Vanzetti**. The two men were charged with robbing a Massachusetts shoe factory and murdering the payroll clerk and guard. Some people insisted that both men were innocent and were being punished because they were anarchists. The state did not have solid evidence, and many people considered the trial unfair. However, the two were convicted and sentenced to death. Thousands of people protested. Joining these protests was the new **American Civil Liberties Union** (ACLU), a civil rights organization. Despite these efforts, Sacco and Vanzetti were executed on August 23, 1927.

Many African Americans faced racial violence in the 1920s. During World War I, hundreds of thousands of southern African Americans had begun relocating to the northern United States—a movement known as the **Great Migration**. As African Americans continued to move north, many whites feared competition for housing and jobs. These tensions led to urban race riots. One of the worst riots took place in July 1919 in Chicago. A young African American man swimming in Lake Michigan accidentally drifted into the white area. People on shore threw rocks at him, and he drowned. Fighting broke out between whites and African Americans at the beach and quickly spread through the city. By the time the riots ended a week later, 38 people had died, and more than 500 had been injured. By the end of the year, some 25 race riots had taken place across the nation.

✔ **Reading Check: Analyzing Information** What contributed to social fears after World War I?

Section 1 Review

go.hrw.com **Homework Practice Online**
keyword: SC3 HP23

1. **Define** and explain:
   - flappers
   - xenophobia

2. **Identify** and explain:
   - Communists
   - Red Scare
   - Palmer raids
   - Nicola Sacco
   - Bartolomeo Vanzetti
   - American Civil Liberties Union
   - Great Migration

3. **Summarizing** Copy the graphic organizer below. Use it to explain how the 1920s brought greater independence to many women.

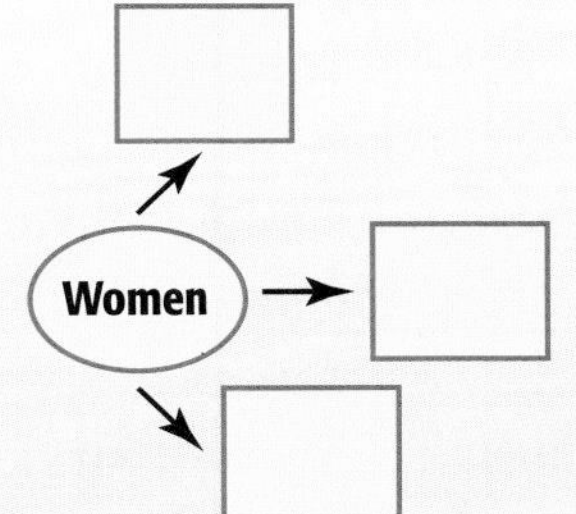

4. **Finding the Main Idea**
   a. What changes did the post–World War I years bring for workers?
   b. What social issues concerned Americans following World War I?

5. **Writing and Critical Thinking**
   Supporting a Point of View Imagine that you are an antiunion politician in the early 1920s. Write a newspaper editorial to encourage workers to refuse to join a strike.
   Consider the following:
   - the post–World War I economy
   - the results of the strikes of 1919 and 1920
   - the fear of Communists

Section 2

Returning to Normalcy

Read to Discover

1. What political problems did the Harding administration face?
2. How did Presidents Harding and Coolidge work to strengthen the U.S. economy?
3. What were the goals of Republican foreign policy during the 1920s?

Define

- disarmament

Identify

- Warren G. Harding
- Calvin Coolidge
- Herbert Hoover
- Ohio Gang
- Albert Fall
- Teapot Dome scandal
- Washington Conference
- Kellogg-Briand Pact

Why It Matters Today

Many world leaders still try to achieve world peace and disarmament. Use CNNfyi.com or other **current events** sources to learn about the peace efforts of a group or individual. Record your findings in your journal.

The Story Continues

As the presidential election of 1920 drew near, many people began looking for someone to bring better times. In May, Warren G. Harding, a U.S. senator from Ohio, summed up the country's mood. Speaking to an audience in Boston, Harding said that "America's present need is not heroics but . . . normalcy." Few people really knew what he meant by "normalcy." However, after years of war followed by economic and social problems, Americans liked the sound of the word.

Warren G. Harding's main strengths were his party loyalty and his ability to make political allies.

The Harding Years

In the 1920 election the Democrats chose Ohio governor James M. Cox to run for president. They also chose as his running mate Franklin D. Roosevelt. The Democratic campaign focused on passing the Treaty of Versailles and joining the League of Nations. The Republicans chose Senator **Warren G. Harding** of Ohio to run for president and Massachusetts governor **Calvin Coolidge** as his running mate. Harding ran on a pro-business platform. Most Americans wanted to avoid more involvement in European affairs. This viewpoint helped Harding win a landslide victory with about 60 percent of the popular vote. Some 900,000 voters supported Socialist candidate Eugene V. Debs, who was still in prison for violating the Espionage Act.

Although popular with voters, Harding was not a particularly gifted leader. He did, however, put some talented leaders in his cabinet. Charles Dawes, who once had been in charge of the country's currency under President McKinley, became director of the Bureau of the Budget. Secretary of State Charles Evans Hughes was a former governor of New York and former associate justice of the Supreme Court. Secretary of Commerce **Herbert Hoover** was a wealthy mining engineer. Hoover had organized wartime relief for millions of Belgians. For secretary of the treasury, Harding chose Andrew Mellon, one of the nation's richest men.

The Harding administration focused on strengthening the U.S. economy. Harding believed that government should promote business growth but otherwise leave the economy alone. Mellon proposed many tax cuts, several of which were passed by Congress. These tax cuts commonly benefited businesses and wealthy Americans. The public was generally pleased as business boomed and the postwar recession came to an end. The country soon entered a period of rapid economic growth as both unemployment and prices went down.

That's Interesting!

Let the People Come to Him For most of his 1920 presidential campaign, Harding's advisers kept him home in Marion, Ohio. Capitalizing on trends of the time, his strategists brought the public to him. A major-league baseball game was booked in Marion so Harding could toss the opening game ball. Broadway and Hollywood stars led parades through the Ohio town. Groups of people even came to hear Harding speak from his front porch. Ads, articles, and radio broadcasts further helped his success. In this way, Harding visited Americans' homes without ever leaving his.

Scandals

The trust that President Harding put in others did not always lead to good results. A series of scandals rocked his administration. Many of the men involved were the president's longtime friends from Ohio, who became known as the **Ohio Gang**. Harding once complained, "I have no trouble with my enemies. . . . But my . . . friends . . . keep me walking the floor nights."

Harding died suddenly of a heart attack on August 2, 1923, before the scandals came to light. Vice President Calvin Coolidge became president. An investigation soon showed that Charles Forbes, head of the Veterans' Bureau, had taken bribes in exchange for awarding government contracts for the construction of hospitals. He also sold medical supplies meant for injured World War I veterans. Forbes was fined $10,000 and sentenced to two years in prison.

The biggest scandal involved Secretary of the Interior **Albert Fall**. Fall had transferred control of two federal oil reserves—one at Teapot Dome, Wyoming—from the navy to the Department of the Interior. He then leased the reserves to two oil companies. In return, Fall and a relative received cattle and gifts, or "loans," worth some $385,000. The **Teapot Dome scandal** led to Fall's conviction. He was sentenced to a year in jail and fined $100,000. Eventually, four members of Harding's administration resigned as a result of corruption charges.

✔ **Reading Check: Contrasting** What were the major successes and failures of the Harding administration?

Interpreting Political Cartoons

Political scandal *The Teapot Dome scandal was a major embarrassment for the Republican Party.* ***Why do you think the artist chose an elephant in the shape of a teapot to represent the Republicans?***

Calvin Coolidge was known for his honesty and to many people he stood for old-fashioned values.

Coolidge as President

Calvin Coolidge quickly fired the people involved in the Harding scandals, keeping the Democrats from using the events to win votes. In 1924 Coolidge ran for president on a stronger pro-business platform than Harding had. Some progressive Republicans broke away to choose Senator Robert La Follette of Wisconsin as their Progressive Party candidate. The Democrats were deeply divided between urban and rural interests and chose lawyer John W. Davis, who was not well known to the public. Coolidge won a landslide victory that November.

Coolidge declared that "the business of America is business." He reduced government spending, and Secretary of the Treasury Mellon kept his tax-cutting program. The Republican-controlled Congress raised tariffs on foreign goods to increase their prices and to prevent competition with domestic goods. Coolidge believed that the best government was one that seldom interfered in daily life. For four years, Coolidge limited government activity, and the economy boomed.

✔ **Reading Check: Comparing** How were Coolidge's domestic policies similar to those of Harding?

Republican Foreign Policy

Coolidge also followed Republican policy in keeping the country out of world affairs. The United States, however, did become involved in some international issues. During World War I, European allies had borrowed billions of dollars from the United States. To pay back their loans, they needed to trade with the United States to earn money. The United States thus increased its trade with Europe, despite higher tariffs.

Hoping to prevent another world war, the United States followed a policy of **disarmament**—limits on military weapons. To further this goal, in November 1921 the United States invited the world's major nations to the **Washington Conference**. At the Conference, Secretary of State Charles Evans Hughes proposed limiting the total naval strength of the world's most powerful nations. The conference did result in treaties that limited the size of the world's major navies.

In 1928 the United States and 14 other countries also signed the **Kellogg-Briand Pact**, which outlawed war. Most countries eventually signed the agreement. Their leaders could not decide how to enforce the treaty, however. As one U.S. senator remarked, the treaty would be "as effective to keep down war as a carpet would be to smother an earthquake."

President Calvin Coolidge and Secretary of State Frank B. Kellogg hoped that the Kellogg-Briand Pact would keep the United States out of war.

✔ **Reading Check: Sequencing** List the major accomplishments that took place in foreign policy from 1920 to 1928 in their proper order.

The Election of 1928

Because Americans were pleased about the treaties and the booming economy, Republicans believed they would easily win the 1928 presidential election. They nominated Secretary of Commerce Herbert Hoover. Hoover based his campaign platform on promises of more prosperity.

This truck showed short films of Herbert Hoover to audiences during his presidential campaign.

> **"We in America today are nearer to the final triumph over poverty than ever before in the history of any land. We shall soon . . . be in sight of the day when poverty will be banished from [thrown out of] this nation."**
>
> —Herbert Hoover, quoted in *Who Built America?*, edited by Joshua Freeman et al.

Analyzing Primary Sources

Identifying Points of View What does Hoover believe is important to American voters?

Hoover's campaign slogan was "A chicken for every pot and a car in every garage."

The Democrats chose Alfred E. Smith, governor of New York, to run for president. Because Smith was a Roman Catholic, many Protestants feared that he would follow the orders of church officials rather than lead the nation independently. Smith was also seen as representing urban interests, which helped him win votes in large cities but hurt his support in rural areas.

In the end, Hoover received 444 electoral votes to Smith's 87. To many Americans, it seemed that the good times would never end.

✔ **Reading Check: Analyzing Information** What were some of the key issues in the 1928 presidential election, and how did they affect the outcome?

Section 2 Review

keyword: SC3 HP23

1. **Define** and explain:
   - disarmament
2. **Identify** and explain:
   - Warren G. Harding
   - Calvin Coolidge
   - Herbert Hoover
   - Ohio Gang
   - Albert Fall
   - Teapot Dome scandal
   - Washington Conference
   - Kellogg-Briand Pact
3. **Comparing and Contrasting** Copy the diagram below. Use it to explain the economic policies of Harding's and Coolidge's administrations.

   Harding | BOTH | Coolidge

4. **Finding the Main Idea**
   a. What scandals occurred as a result of President Harding's administration?
   b. Why did the Republicans have the advantage in the presidential elections of the 1920s?
5. **Writing and Critical Thinking**
   Supporting a Point of View Imagine that you are an adviser to President Coolidge. Write a memo describing the Republican foreign-policy goals of the 1920s and whether you agree with them.
   Consider the following:
   - trade with Europe
   - the Washington Conference
   - the Kellogg-Briand Pact

Section 3

A Changing Population

Read to Discover

1. What was the goal of prohibition, and why was it eventually ended?
2. How did differing religious views affect American society?
3. What challenges did foreigners and minorities face from the United States during the 1920s?

Why It Matters Today

Many people from other countries still settle in the United States today. Use CNNfyi.com or other **current events** sources to learn about the contributions of immigrant groups. Record your findings in your journal.

Define

- speakeasies
- bootleggers

Identify

- Twenty-first Amendment
- Fundamentalism
- Scopes trial
- Clarence Darrow
- Emergency Quota Act
- National Origins Act
- Marcus Garvey
- Universal Negro Improvement Association

This illustration shows temperance supporters celebrating the passage of prohibition.

The Story Continues

One cold winter night Isadore "Izzy" Einstein and Moe Smith stood out on the sidewalk. Einstein, dressed in light clothing, started shivering after a while and even turned blue. Smith then pounded on the door of a nearby secret bar. He shouted, "Give this man a drink! He's been frostbitten." The surprised owner opened the door and served them a drink. Unfortunately for the owner, Einstein and Smith were undercover government agents who arrested the owner for selling alcohol illegally. Often wearing outrageous disguises, Einstein and Smith made more than 4,000 arrests in five years.

Prohibition

On January 16, 1920, the Eighteenth Amendment went into effect, establishing national prohibition. The amendment banned the sale, manufacture, and transportation of alcoholic beverages. Although supporters of prohibition thought most people agreed with the law, making people follow prohibition proved difficult. In cities and towns across the United States, more than 500,000 people were arrested for violating prohibition.

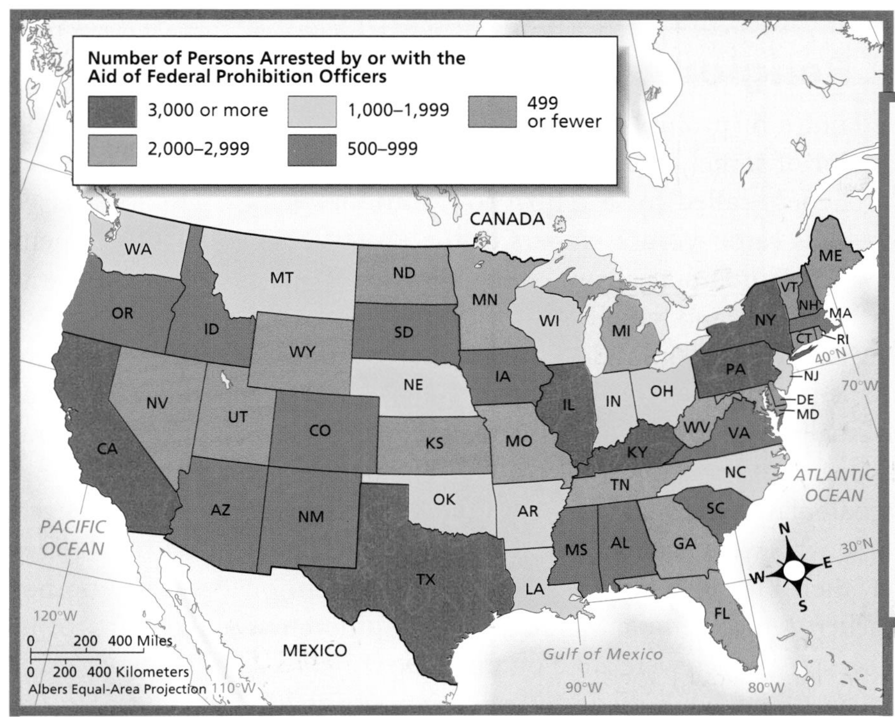

Arrests under Prohibition, 1929

Interpreting Maps Bootleggers smuggled illegal alcohol into the United States from Mexico and Canada.

Skills Assessment

1. **Places and Regions** In which states along the U.S.-Mexico border were the most prohibition arrests made?
2. **Summarizing** What states had the fewest prohibition arrests?

Some speakeasies were so successful they printed their own business cards.

Some people made illegal liquor from industrial alcohol meant for legal products, such as perfume and paint. These people helped supply liquor to **speakeasies**—secret illegal clubs that served alcohol. The name speakeasy came from the need for customers to keep quiet about the clubs. Speakeasies also got liquor from **bootleggers**, a name that described how smugglers used to hide bottles of alcohol in their boots. The federal government tried to close down the speakeasies and stop the bootleggers, but it met with limited success.

Prohibition shifted millions of dollars from legal businesses to criminal organizations, and crime became big business. In 1925 gangster Al "Scarface" Capone took control of Chicago's bootlegging business. By 1927 he was earning about $60 million a year. Capone defended his criminal activities.

"I make my money by supplying a public demand. If I break the law, my customers, who number hundreds of the best people in Chicago, are as guilty as I am. Everybody calls me a racketeer [criminal]. I call myself a businessman."

—Al Capone, quoted in *1919: America's Loss of Innocence*, by Eliot Asinof

Analyzing Primary Sources

Drawing Inferences and Conclusions What does Capone's statement tell you about society in Chicago during the prohibition years?

Capone's career in crime ended in 1931, when he was sent to jail for not paying taxes.

In addition to being difficult to enforce, prohibition proved unpopular with many otherwise law-abiding Americans. A movement calling for the repeal of the Eighteenth Amendment grew in strength. In early December 1933, the **Twenty-first Amendment** ended national prohibition.

✔ **Reading Check: Summarizing** What problems arose because of prohibition?

Religious Beliefs

The failure of prohibition worried many religious leaders, as did the behavior of some young people. During the 1920s many ministers and churchgoers called for a return to traditional values. The loudest of these calls came from members of the Protestant religious movement known as **Fundamentalism**. Fundamentalism taught that the Bible was free from error and literally true.

Many people who did not trust modern industry and science were attracted to this movement. Fundamentalism was strongest in rural areas and small towns, but it also attracted followers in large cities where rural residents had moved to find work. Billy Sunday, a former professional baseball player, drew large crowds to his revival meetings. He challenged people who were against prohibition. "I will fight them till hell freezes over, then I'll buy a pair of skates and fight 'em on the ice." Another preacher, Aimee Semple McPherson, used an orchestra and a chorus in her services, which were aired on the radio.

Charles Darwin's theory of evolution worried Fundamentalists. He held that humans had evolved, or developed, from simpler forms of life over millions of years. His theory states that species evolve over time by adapting to their environment. Many people believed that his theory contradicted the biblical account of creation.

Interpreting Political Cartoons

The Scopes trial *The ape standing between opposing attorneys William Jennings Bryan (left) and Clarence Darrow (right) represents Darwin's theory of evolution.* ***Why do you think the cartoonist chose an ape to indicate evolution?***

In 1925 a Tennessee law made it illegal to teach any theory other than creationism. Later that year, John Scopes, a high school science teacher in Dayton, Tennessee, was arrested for teaching evolution. Scopes was brought to trial in July 1925. Newspaper, magazine, and radio reporters from the United States and abroad covered the **Scopes trial**. Preachers held meetings in tents on the edge of town, and vendors sold soda, hot dogs, fans, and Bibles.

Clarence Darrow, a famous criminal defense attorney, and the American Civil Liberties Union defended Scopes. Three-time presidential candidate William Jennings Bryan led the prosecution. He also took the stand as an expert on the Bible. The crowd watching Bryan was so large that officials moved the trial outdoors. While on the stand, Bryan seemed to accept that some parts of the Bible might be open to interpretation. Despite Darrow's efforts, Scopes was convicted and fined $100. In 1927 the Tennessee Supreme Court overturned his conviction. People still remained divided over evolution and religious views, however.

✔ **Reading Check: Identifying Cause and Effect** Why did Fundamentalism grow, and how did it affect American society?

Nativism

Immigration laws also caused conflicts. Before World War I, immigration to the United States had nearly stopped, but it rose rapidly after the war ended. More than 800,000 immigrants arrived in 1921 alone. Soon a wave of nativism—strong anti-immigrant feelings—swept the country. Nativists saw immigrants as a threat to the nation's future. Many voters agreed with Alabama senator James Thomas Heflin, who said that immigrants "fill places that belong to the loyal wage-earning citizens of America."

On May 19, 1921, President Harding signed the **Emergency Quota Act**. The law set total immigration at 357,000 people a year. It also limited the number of immigrants from any country to 3 percent of each nationality's 1910 U.S. census population. However, the act did not limit immigration from countries in the Western Hemisphere. In May 1924 Congress passed the **National Origins Act**, which further reduced immigration but favored northern European immigrants. It also completely stopped Japanese immigration.

Some of the loudest voices against immigration came from the Ku Klux Klan, which had formed again in Georgia in 1915. The new Klan was hostile toward Catholics, Jews, and foreigners, in addition to African Americans. It used cross-burnings, beatings, and murders to scare its victims. At its peak in the mid-1920s, the Klan had perhaps as many as 5 million members, including women and children. It became a powerful political force in states from Oregon to Maine. After Indiana Klan leader David Stephenson was found guilty of murder in 1925, he revealed the Klan's secrets. His reports, along with the news that Klan leaders were getting rich on membership fees, weakened the Klan's influence.

✔ **Reading Check: Analyzing Information** How did events in the 1920s show some Americans' fears of people of different cultures and races?

Interpreting the Visual Record

Nativist views *Anti-immigrant sentiment led to the publishing of songs like this one, which encouraged restrictions on immigration to the United States.* ***What do you think the "Gates" in the song title are referring to?***

Minority Rights

Many African Americans and other minorities worked together to protect their rights and fight racial hatred. African American leaders urged black people to take pride in their culture and to become economically independent. These leaders became known as black nationalists. **Marcus Garvey** was an important black nationalist. Born in Jamaica, he founded the **Universal Negro Improvement Association** (UNIA) in 1914. This group wanted to end imperialism in Africa and discrimination in the United States. Two years later, Garvey moved to New York City, where he started a UNIA chapter. In his speeches, Garvey encouraged African Americans to learn about their heritage. "You must fall back on the intelligence of others who came before you and have left their records behind."

Free Find:
Marcus Garvey
After reading about Marcus Garvey and black nationalism on the **Holt Researcher CD–ROM**, create a script for a scene from a movie about Garvey's back-to-Africa movement.

A delegation of Pueblo Indians traveled to Washington, D.C., in 1923 to protest the mistreatment of their people and threats to their lands.

Garvey started a number of businesses to offer economic opportunities for African Americans. However, he was arrested in connection with his business activities and served two years in jail. Despite his difficulties and limited success in fighting discrimination, Garvey influenced millions of people around the world. As the *Amsterdam News,* a New York newspaper, wrote, Garvey "made black people proud of their race. In a world where black is despised he taught them that black is beautiful."

Like African Americans, American Indians organized for their rights. Thousands of American Indians had served in the U.S. armed forces during World War I, even though many were not U.S. citizens. Indian leaders pointed to these patriotic acts and demanded citizenship. In response, Congress passed the Indian Citizenship Act in June 1924. This law gave all American Indians the legal and voting rights of U.S. citizens. During the 1920s Indians also successfully stopped the federal government from taking away some of their remaining lands.

Many Mexicans and Mexican Americans moved to U.S. cities to fill jobs during World War I. Immigration restrictions did not apply to Mexico, and during the 1920s about half a million Mexicans moved to the United States. Some looked for factory work in northern cities such as Chicago, Detroit, and Pittsburgh. Most chose to settle in the Southwest where they found work on farms. Like other immigrants, Mexican immigrants usually received low wages and faced discrimination in employment and housing.

✔ **Reading Check: Summarizing** How did African Americans, American Indians, and Mexican Americans work to improve their lives?

Section 3 Review

go.hrw.com Homework Practice Online
keyword: SC3 HP23

1. **Define** and explain:
   - speakeasies
   - bootleggers
2. **Identify** and explain:
   - Twenty-first Amendment
   - Fundamentalism
   - Scopes trial
   - Clarence Darrow
   - Emergency Quota Act
   - National Origins Act
   - Marcus Garvey
   - Universal Negro Improvement Association
3. **Analyzing Information** Copy the chart below. Use it to show the challenges that foreigners and minorities faced in the United States in the 1920s.

	Challenges
Foreigners	
Minorities	

4. **Finding the Main Idea**
   a. What did prohibition hope to accomplish, and how was it unsuccessful?
   b. What new religious beliefs did some Americans come to hold, and how did these affect society?
5. **Writing and Critical Thinking**
   Summarizing Imagine that you are a newspaper reporter in the 1920s. Write an article about the efforts that members of different racial groups made in order to improve their lives.
   Consider the following:
   - immigration quotas
   - the efforts of African Americans, American Indians, and Mexican Americans

Section 4

Boom Times

Read to Discover

1. What was the growth of the automobile industry in the United States like?
2. What were important elements of the 1920s economy?
3. What workers struggled during the 1920s?

Define

- assembly line
- installment plans

Identify

- Henry Ford
- Model T

Why It Matters Today

Changing market demands continue to cause new industries to develop and old ones to decline. Use CNNfyi.com or other **current events** sources to learn about industries that are on the rise or on the fall. Record your findings in your journal.

The Story Continues

Engineer and inventor Henry Ford founded the Ford Motor Company in 1903. His goal was to develop a car made "of the best materials, . . . after [using] the simplest design." Ford confidently predicted that he could build a vehicle "so low in price that no man making a good salary will be unable to buy one." In 1908 he achieved his goal with the Model T, helping change American industry and society.

Nicknamed the Tin Lizzie by owners, the Model T could be driven on almost any surface—an important consideration because most roads in the 1920s were unpaved.

The Rise of the Automobile

Henry Ford and his engineers designed the **Model T** to be durable, reliable, and easy to repair. The car was not fancy, and for many years came only in black. By 1921 Ford was selling more than 1 million cars a year.

Ford's goal was "to make one automobile just like another." To accomplish this goal, Ford equipped his plant with an **assembly line**, a system of chains, slides, and conveyor belts. Parts and partly assembled cars moved along the assembly line from one group of workers to another. This production method cut the time needed to put together a Model T from 12.5 hours to less than 2 hours. Lower production costs helped reduce the price of a Model T from about $850 in 1908 to about $290 in 1927.

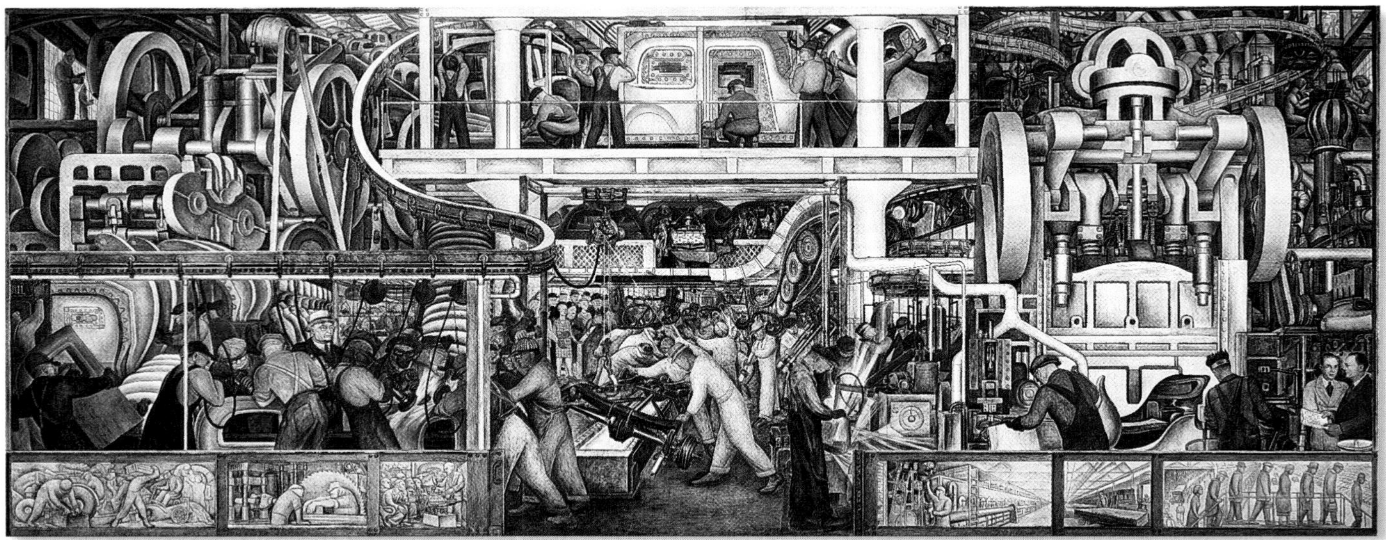

Interpreting the Visual Record

Industry *Mexican artist Diego Rivera based this mural on one of Ford's automobile plants.* ***How does this mural show the energy of the assembly line?***

Ford offered his employees an eight-hour workday and wages of $5 per day. Both of these incentives were excellent for the time. Ford also hired African Americans as well as people with disabilities.

However, working for Ford had drawbacks as well. Laboring on the assembly line was fast-paced yet dull, as one worker explained.

Analyzing Primary Sources

Identifying Points of View Why does this worker feel that assembly-line work is stressful?

"The weight of a tack . . . is insignificant, but if you have to drive eight tacks in every Ford cushion . . . and you continue to do this for four years, you are going to break under the strain."

—Anonymous assembly-line worker, quoted in *Who Built America?*, edited by Joshua Freeman et al.

Ford also used a private police force to check up on his workers' activities after hours.

As more people bought automobiles, the American economy was transformed. By 1929 the auto industry employed some 375,000 workers and had created jobs in related industries. Millions of Americans produced steel for auto bodies and rubber for tires, as well as auto paint, glass, and machine tools. Cars required gasoline and oil, leading to explosive growth in the petroleum industry. As the number of automobile accidents increased, drivers also needed insurance companies and repair shops.

The construction industry benefited from the need for new roads. Two early motorists described the roads between New York City and Buffalo as "nothing but muddy ditches." Soon federal, state, and local governments were spending millions of dollars to build bridges, tunnels, and highways. New businesses, such as service stations and restaurants, began appearing beside the roads. Many of these businesses served the growing number of Americans taking driving vacations. *Motor Car* magazine explained the appeal of this new pastime. "You are your master, the road is ahead. . . . Your freedom is complete."

Research on the ROM

Free Find:
Henry Ford
After reading about Henry Ford on the **Holt Researcher CD–ROM**, create a chart that shows how Ford's business strategies both benefited and created hardships for the average American worker.

✔ **Reading Check: Identifying Cause and Effect** What led to the growth of the automobile industry, and how did the automobile industry change the U.S. economy?

Business Booms

Mass production methods soon spread beyond automobile manufacturing to other industries. These improvements lowered the prices of many goods in the 1920s. Between 1921 and 1929 U.S. manufacturing nearly doubled, giving Americans many new products to enjoy. Much of the growth came in the electrical appliances industry. By 1930 some 85 percent of all Americans who lived in towns or cities had electricity, which was used to run newly purchased washing machines, vacuum cleaners, and refrigerators.

Many consumers bought these labor-saving devices through **installment plans.** These programs let customers buy goods by making a small down payment followed by additional monthly payments with interest. The new system let people buy goods that had once been out of their reach.

The new products led to a huge boom in advertising. Magazines and newspapers carried ads urging people to buy, and radios aired a steady stream of commercials. These ads often led people to buy new goods, even when they did not have enough money. An ad for car tires summed up how people spent money in the 1920s when it encouraged consumers to "Ride Now, Pay Later."

✔ **Reading Check: Finding the Main Idea** How did advertising affect consumer spending?

Struggling Industries

Despite the prosperity of the 1920s, several large U.S. industries faced major challenges.

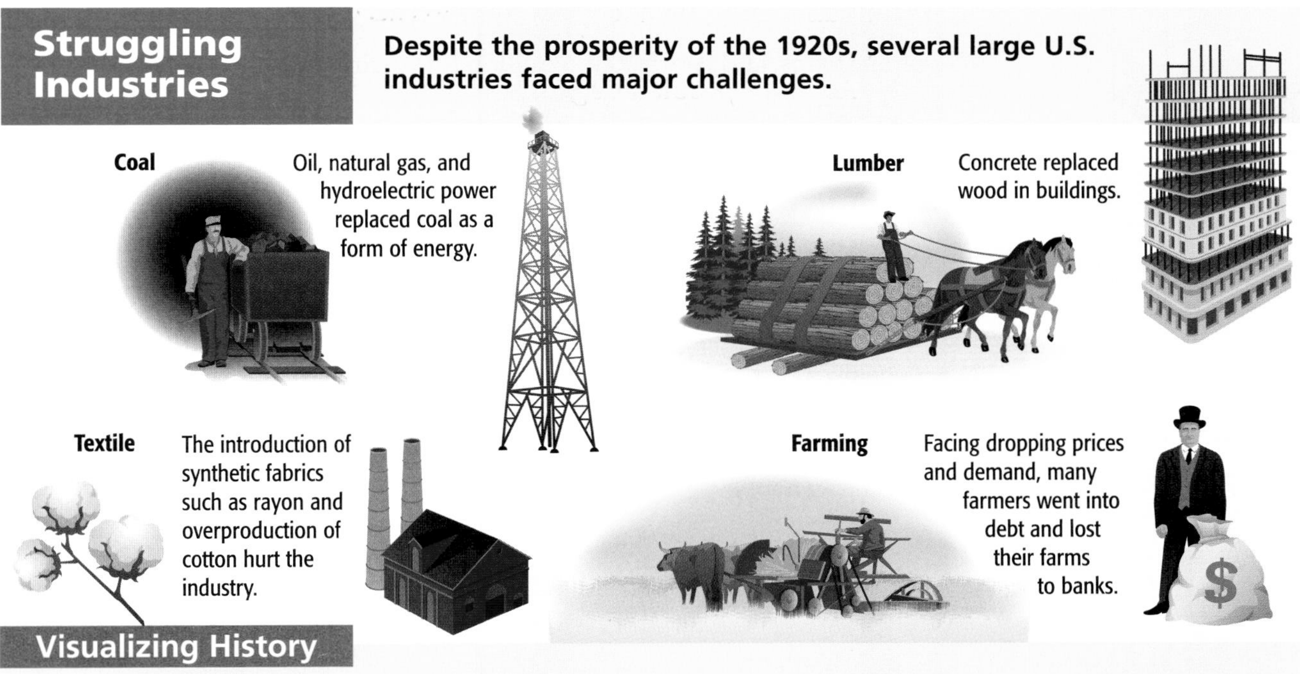

Visualizing History

1. **Economics** What problems caused these industries to struggle?
2. **Connecting to Today** What major U.S. industries are facing difficult challenges today?

The drop in agricultural prices following World War I meant hard times for many farm families.

The Limits of Prosperity

Despite the economic boom, some laborers and industries suffered during the 1920s. Skilled workers at successful corporations often received good pay and benefits. However, unskilled workers in smaller industries generally received poor pay and few benefits. Many of these people worked in "sick," or economically depressed, industries. For example, the growth in the use of synthetic, or artificial, fabrics hurt the textile industry. Workers suffered because synthetics required less labor to produce than did traditional materials.

Organized labor lost government support after World War I. The violent strikes of 1919 also had led to strong antiunion feelings across the United States. During the 1920s union membership dropped, from more than 5 million in 1920 to 3.6 million just three years later. Business leaders also started an open-shop campaign called the American Plan. In an open shop, union membership was not required and was sometimes even forbidden. Unions fought unsuccessfully against the American Plan. Such antiunion efforts were supported by President Harding's administration. The courts also often struck down laws that helped workers and upheld those that enabled companies to ban unions.

The postwar years also brought hardships to farmers. Keeping the Allies supplied during World War I had led to high demand and high prices for agricultural goods. In response, many farmers grew more crops, often buying land and equipment on credit. The war's end brought a steep drop in prices. For example, Nebraska corn dropped from $1.22 to 41 cents a bushel in just one year. Soon, many farmers could not repay their loans, and nearly half a million lost their land.

✔ **Reading Check: Summarizing** What workers did not benefit from the 1920s economic boom, and why?

Section 4 Review

go.hrw.com Homework Practice Online
keyword: SC3 HP23

1. **Define** and explain:
   - assembly line
   - installment plans
2. **Identify** and explain:
   - Henry Ford
   - Model T
3. **Summarizing** Copy the graphic organizer below. Use it to describe the growth of the automobile industry and how it changed American society.

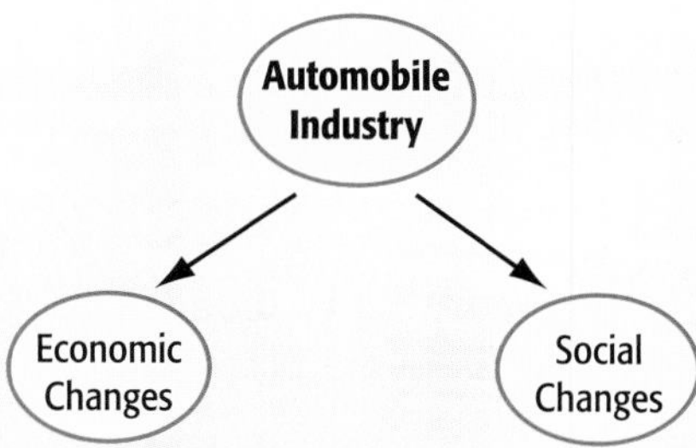

4. **Finding the Main Idea**
   a. What contributed to the economic boom of the 1920s?
   b. Why did some workers not share in the prosperity of the 1920s?
5. **Writing and Critical Thinking**
   Contrasting Imagine that you are an American who has just bought a new Ford car. Write a letter to a friend in another country telling that person how life in the United States has changed because of the booming car industry.
   Consider the following:
   - consumer spending habits
   - new industries
   - American lifestyles

Section 5

The Jazz Age

Read to Discover

1. How did mass media contribute to the new national culture of the 1920s?
2. What types of people became heroes of the 1920s, and how did many Americans treat them?
3. What developments occurred in music, literature, and other arts during the Jazz Age?

Define

- fads
- nickelodeons
- talkie
- expatriates

Identify

- Charles Lindbergh
- Jazz Age
- Harlem Renaissance
- Lost Generation

Why It Matters Today

Americans of all ages often follow the newest fads. Use CNNfyi.com or other **current events** sources to find out about some of the most recent fads. Record your findings in your journal.

The Story Continues

One day in 1927 Alvin "Shipwreck" Kelly climbed onto a flagpole and did not come down. Day after day, he perched on top of the pole. Kelly had food and drink hauled up to him in a bucket. At night he slept only briefly, fearing he would fall to his death. He took a five minute nap every hour. After 23 days and seven hours on his flagpole, Kelly finally climbed down. He had achieved his goal. Kelly was the new world-record holder in flagpole sitting. Some hotels actually hired him to attract business by sitting on flagpoles.

Alvin "Shipwreck" Kelly made $29,000 in 1929 for sitting on flagpoles.

A National Culture

Shipwreck Kelly's stunt showed the popularity of **fads** during the 1920s. Fads are interests that many people follow with great excitement for a short time. Other fads included marathon dancing and mah-jongg, a Chinese game played with tiles. The mass media—newspapers, magazines, movies, and radio—greatly helped the development and spread of fads. In the 1920s these old and new forms of information and entertainment linked the country in a truly national culture.

BIOGRAPHY

Mary Pickford

(1893–1979)

Mary Pickford first appeared on stage at the age of five and quickly rose to stardom. By 1916 Pickford was earning $10,000 a week. Movies such as *Poor Little Rich Girl* and *Rebecca of Sunnybrook Farm* established her as "America's Sweetheart."

Although fans wanted her to play familiar, girlish roles, Pickford, was determined to find new challenges. With fellow Hollywood legends D. W. Griffith, Charlie Chaplin, and Douglas Fairbanks she helped form the independent film distribution company United Artists in 1919. **Why do you think Pickford helped found United Artists?**

In 1920 WWJ in Detroit became the first radio station to air regular programs. Other stations soon followed. On November 2, 1920, KDKA in Pittsburgh broadcast the results of that year's presidential election. Just one year later, stations announced the plays at the 1921 World Series. In 1926 the first network, National Broadcasting Company (NBC), was created, followed by the Columbia Broadcasting System (CBS). By gathering stations together, these networks reached huge numbers of listeners. Soon they were broadcasting radio shows coast-to-coast to a growing audience. By 1929, more than 10 million households owned radios.

Radio broadcasts educated many Americans. A woman working at home in rural Idaho, for example, could hear the daily news from New York City. One man remembered how the new technology amazed him. "[We] could pull unseen voices out of the air and into the living room from all over the world." Businesspeople also loved radio because it let them capture listeners' attention and advertise products.

When Americans went out for entertainment, movies were a popular choice. Thomas Alva Edison and others had invented motion pictures, or "movies," in the late 1800s. Some early theaters were called **nickelodeons** because admission usually cost five cents. In the 1920s millions of Americans went to the movies. Young people copied movie stars' clothes, hairstyles, and ways of walking and talking. When heartthrob Rudolph Valentino died in 1926, tens of thousands of women lined up outside the funeral home. Other movie stars of this period included Douglas Fairbanks, Charlie Chaplin, and Mary Pickford.

In 1927, movies became even more exciting with the release of *The Jazz Singer*. This film was the first full-length feature **talkie**—a movie with sound or dialogue. One Mississippi theater owner remembered it as "just about the most wonderful thing I had ever seen in my life." By 1928 there were some 20,000 movie theaters across the country.

✔ **Reading Check: Analyzing Information** How did mass media affect American culture in the 1920s?

A Search for Heroes

Movie stars were not the only famous people of the 1920s. As organized sports became more popular, Americans also made celebrities out of star athletes. Perhaps the greatest athlete of all was Jim Thorpe, an American Indian of Sauk and Fox descent. Thorpe won several gold medals at the 1912 Olympics and later played professional baseball and football. Tennis star Helen Wills and champion swimmer Gertrude Ederle also became sports heroes. Wills won more than 30 tennis championships during her career. Ederle won a gold medal and two bronze medals at the 1924 Olympics. Two years later she broke the world record when she swam the English Channel in under 15 hours.

Team sports were popular as well. Thousands of fans packed stadiums to see college football games. One of the greatest players was halfback Harold "Red" Grange of the University of Illinois. Fans also flocked to see professional baseball players, particularly George Herman "Babe" Ruth. In 1927 Ruth hit 60 home runs for the New York Yankees—a record that stood for 34 years. African Americans were not allowed to play in the major leagues. In response, Andrew "Rube" Foster formed the Negro National League. African American stars such as Leroy Robert "Satchel" Paige and James T. "Cool Papa" Bell were eventually elected to the Baseball Hall of Fame.

Pilots also became famous during the 1920s. Many veteran World War I pilots flew stunt flights and earned money by giving rides. Pilot **Charles Lindbergh** was perhaps the biggest hero of the 1920s. On May 20, 1927, Lindbergh loaded his plane with sandwiches, personal papers, and fuel and took off from Long Island, New York. Less than 34 hours later he completed the first nonstop solo flight across the Atlantic Ocean. About 100,000 people welcomed Lindbergh as he landed the *Spirit of St. Louis* in Paris. Lindbergh later recalled his arrival.

"I opened the door, and started to put my foot down onto ground. But dozens of hands took hold of me—my legs, my arms, my body. . . . I found myself lying . . . up on top of the crowd, in the center of an ocean of heads that extended as far out into the darkness as I could see."

—Charles Lindbergh, *The Spirit of St. Louis*

Other pilots soon followed Lindbergh. In 1932 Amelia Earhart became the first woman to fly solo across the Atlantic.

✔ **Reading Check: Summarizing** Who were some of the major celebrities of the 1920s?

That's Interesting!

Dance 'Til You Drop How far would you go to win a dance contest? Would you believe that one couple danced in three different states to avoid having their contest ended? Well, believe it! Alma Cummings, a 32-year-old dance teacher, helped start the dance marathon craze in 1923.

Some people did not approve of these dance marathons, however. In 1923 a group of dancers learned that local police planned to end their contest. The contestants danced their way into a van, which carried them, still dancing, to a ferry. When the contest finally ended, the winning couple had danced for 69 hours in three states, four moving vans, and one ferry.

Blues and Jazz

During the 1920s ragtime, blues, and jazz music were very popular. African American musician Scott Joplin had written the first popular ragtime tune, "Maple Leaf Rag," in 1899. Blues developed in the rural Mississippi Delta region of the South and expressed the difficulties that African Americans faced during and after slavery. Jazz came from southern cities such as New Orleans and blended many influences, including African American spirituals, European harmonies, and West African rhythms. As African Americans moved north, they carried these musical styles with them.

W. C. Handy is known as the Father of the Blues. However, Bessie Smith, Empress of the Blues, was possibly the most successful blues artist of the 1920s. Jazz singer and trumpeter Louis (LOO-ee) Armstrong said that Smith had a "certain something in her voice that no other blues singer could get. She had music in her soul." Other famous blues singers included Mamie Smith, Memphis Minnie, and Gertrude "Ma" Rainey.

In 1920 Babe Ruth hit more home runs in one season than all of the other players in the American League combined.

Many jazz musicians moved from the South to Chicago during the 1920s. Armstrong and his band, the Hot Five, recorded classics such as "Willie the Weeper" and "Jazz Lips." Armstrong also invented new ways of performing, such as stepping out from the group to play a solo. Some of these techniques are still used today. Edward "Duke" Ellington began appearing at jazz clubs in New York City in 1927. He composed jazz classics such as "Black and Tan Fantasy" and "Take the A Train." His unique sound came from a skillful blend of the many instruments in his big band. Jazz became so popular that the 1920s are often called the **Jazz Age**.

✔ **Reading Check: Comparing** What did blues and jazz have in common?

Literature and the Arts

Jazz was only one of many art forms that bloomed in the 1920s. The Great Migration made the New York City neighborhood of Harlem the country's largest African American community. The **Harlem Renaissance**—an important period of African American artistic growth—took its name from the neighborhood, although many Harlem Renaissance artists did not live there. Poet Countee Cullen, writer Zora Neale Hurston, and singer-actor Paul Robeson were all important Harlem Renaissance artists.

Literature played a key role in the Harlem Renaissance. In 1920 writer W. E. B. Du Bois called for "a renaissance of American Negro literature." As editor of *The Crisis*, Du Bois published the works of many young African American writers, such as Langston Hughes and Claude McKay. Much of this literature showed the struggles of African American life.

Harlem Renaissance writers were not alone in examining American society. Other writers of the 1920s were disgusted by the destruction caused by World War I. Ernest Hemingway called the war "the most

CONNECTING TO THE ARTS

Georgia O'Keeffe

Georgia O'Keeffe was born in Wisconsin in 1887. She studied art in Chicago and New York City. While teaching in Texas, she first sketched the western landscapes that became a key part of her art. O'Keeffe often painted single flowers in great detail. "Most people in the city rush around so, they have no time to look at a flower," O'Keeffe said. After becoming a successful artist, O'Keeffe spent time in Taos, New Mexico. There she again painted desert images—bleached bones, old churches, and storms sweeping in over the mountains. **Why do you think Georgia O'Keeffe used the desert as a subject for many of her paintings?**

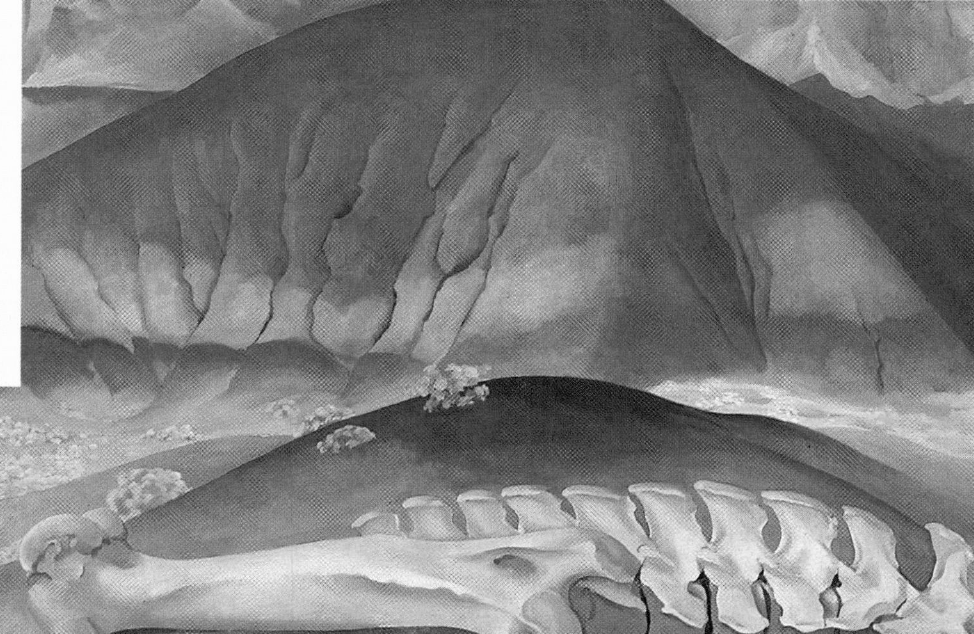

colossal [huge], murderous, mismanaged butchery that had ever taken place on earth." Author Gertrude Stein named the writers who spoke against postwar American society the **Lost Generation**. These well-known authors included Sherwood Anderson and John Dos Passos, and poets e. e. cummings, Edna St. Vincent Millay, and Wallace Stevens. Novelist F. Scott Fitzgerald described the sadness and glamour of the Jazz Age in *The Great Gatsby*.

"All night the saxophones wailed the . . . *Beale Street Blues* while a hundred pairs of golden and silver slippers shuffled the shining dust. . . . Fresh faces drifted here and there like rose petals blown by the sad horns around the floor."

—F. Scott Fitzgerald, *The Great Gatsby*

Analyzing Primary Sources

Drawing Inferences and Conclusions What mood does Fitzgerald create in this paragraph?

Some Lost Generation writers moved to Europe and became **expatriates**—people who leave their native country to live elsewhere. Hemingway's novel about expatriates in Paris, *The Sun Also Rises*, became a best-seller.

Visual arts and architecture also boomed. Many painters created images of workers, factories, and technology. Edward Hopper focused on the loneliness of modern city life. Artists such as George Bellows, Georgia O'Keeffe, and Charles Sheeler also contributed to new painting styles, while Alfred Stieglitz and Ansel Adams were well-known photographers. Architects often used a "modernistic" style that later became known as art deco. Art deco included numerous vertical and zigzag design elements. Its clean simple shapes sometimes looked like the lines of machines. These new styles of architecture and art showed both the spirit of the times and hopes for the future.

The Chrysler Building is an example of art deco design.

✔ **Reading Check: Analyzing Information** How did developments in literature, arts, and architecture reflect the period?

Section 5 Review

go.hrw.com **Homework Practice Online** keyword: SC3 HP23

1. **Define** and explain:
   - fads
   - nickelodeons
   - talkie
   - expatriates

2. **Identify** and explain:
   - Charles Lindbergh
   - Jazz Age
   - Harlem Renaissance
   - Lost Generation

3. **Categorizing** Copy the chart below. Use it to show new artistic developments of the Jazz Age.

Visual Arts	
Architecture	
Music	
Literature	

4. **Finding the Main Idea**
   a. How did developments in media change American culture?
   b. How did Americans pick their celebrities and respond to them?

5. **Writing and Critical Thinking**
   Summarizing Imagine that you are a historian who is writing a book about the arts of the 1920s and how they reflected the issues and interests of American society. Write a brief essay explaining what you would propose to say in your book.
   Consider the following:
   - the Harlem Renaissance
   - the Lost Generation
   - the visual arts and architecture

Chapter 23 Review

The Chapter at a Glance

Examine the following visual summary of the chapter. Then use it to write five true-or-false statements about life in the 1920s. Give your statements to a classmate to complete.

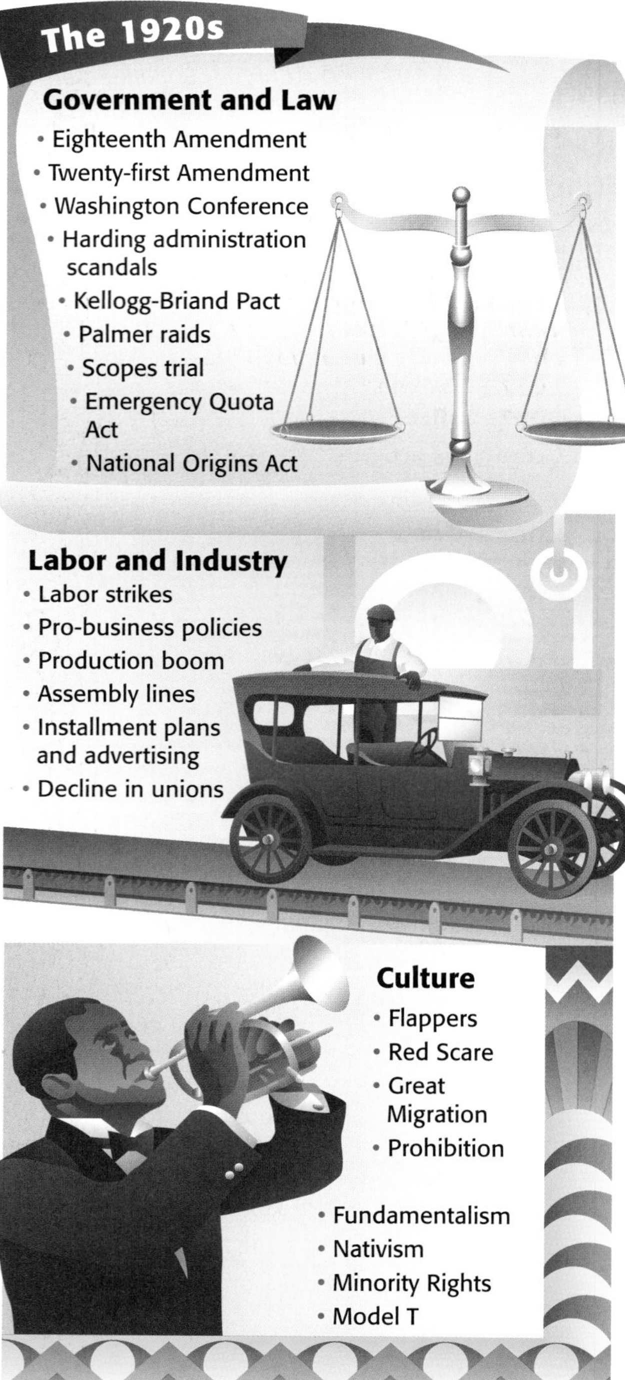

Identifying People and Ideas

Use the following terms or people in historically significant sentences.

1. American Civil Liberties Union
2. Great Migration
3. Calvin Coolidge
4. Washington Conference
5. speakeasies
6. Marcus Garvey
7. assembly line
8. installment plans
9. Charles Lindbergh
10. Harlem Renaissance

Understanding Main Ideas

Section 1 *(Pages 698–701)*

1. What social problems faced the United States after World War I?

Section 2 *(Pages 702–705)*

2. What actions did Presidents Harding and Coolidge take to strengthen the U.S. economy?

Section 3 *(Pages 706–710)*

3. What was the goal of prohibition, and why was prohibition eventually ended?
4. How did minorities try to improve their lives during the 1920s?

Section 4 *(Pages 711–714)*

5. How did the growth of the automobile industry affect the U.S. economy and society?

Section 5 *(Pages 715–719)*

6. What new forms of entertainment and artistic movements became popular in the 1920s?

You Be the Historian— Reviewing Themes

1. **Economics** What difficulties did the U.S. economy face after the end of World War I?
2. **Science, Technology & Society** How did the development of new manufacturing techniques change the way some Americans worked?
3. **Culture** How did African Americans contribute to the cultural changes in the United States during the 1920s?

Thinking Critically

1. **Categorizing** What types of social changes did women experience in the 1920s?
2. **Summarizing** What were the goals of Republican foreign policy during the 1920s?
3. **Supporting a Point of View** What do you think was the most important contribution to economic growth in the 1920s? Explain your answer.

Social Studies Skills Workshop

Interpreting Political Cartoons

Look at the following political cartoon created after the end of World War I and answer the questions that follow.

1. Which of the following statements best reflects the message of this political cartoon?
   a. Europe took a long time to recover from the Napoleonic Wars.
   b. Problems in the American government caused the Civil War.
   c. World War I differed from previous wars because it brought destruction to the whole world.
   d. World War I had the worst effect on the United States.

2. Based on your knowledge of Harding's and Coolidge's foreign policy and the cartoon, how do you think they would have responded to this cartoon?

Analyzing Primary Sources

Read the following quotation by Dud Lee, who tried to make a living as a farmer in the 1920s. Then answer the questions that follow.

> **"We replanted the entire 330 acres as fast as we could. Dad had to borrow money to buy the cottonseed. . . . Soon the stalks loaded up with squares and blooms, promising a bumper [unusually large] crop after all. Dad was really happy. Despite all his troubles, this time he was going to make it. But then the dang armyworms came in by the billions and started eating the crop. We worked day and night spraying arsenic [poison] on the cotton to try to kill the armyworms. But the poison wasn't very effective. We finally harvested about twenty bales of poor quality cotton, which wasn't nearly enough to get Dad out of debt."**

3. What challenges kept Lee and his family from earning enough money from their crops?
   a. They could not plant the crops fast enough.
   b. The quality of the cotton was too poor to sell for a good price.
   c. Cotton prices were too low.
   d. Armyworms destroyed the crop, and there was not enough to pay off the debt.

4. Based on your knowledge, what other circumstances would have made it difficult for Lee and his father to get out of debt by selling crops?

Alternative Assessment

Building Your Portfolio

American History

Building Your Portfolio

Cooperative Learning Complete the following activity in small groups. Imagine that you and your group are in charge of running a radio station in the 1920s. As a group, decide what programs you will have and create a detailed outline. Include any celebrities who might appear on your show, events that you might report on, and music that you might play. Then write a script for the different radio shows.

internet connect

Internet Activity: go.hrw.com
keyword: SC3 CF23

Choose an activity on the Roaring Twenties to:

- Explore cultural changes of the Jazz Age.
- Write a biography of a baseball player of the 1920s.
- Research the trial of Sacco and Vanzetti.

Connecting to Geography

American Migrations, 1865–1930

The United States became increasingly industrialized from 1865 to 1930. Some of today's major U.S. cities, such as Chicago, Detroit, and St. Louis, grew rapidly during this time.

Many Americans moved from rural areas, hoping to find industrial jobs in large towns and cities. For example, many African Americans began moving from the South to northern cities in the 1890s.

Immigration also added to the urban population. Millions of immigrants came from all across Europe, many settling in cities in the Northeast and Midwest. Large numbers of immigrants also arrived from Mexico. Most Mexican immigrants settled in rural areas in the Southwest. Many Mexican Americans later moved to cities, particularly in Texas and California. Gradually, all these different migrations transformed U.S. cities.

Farms to Cities

In 1880 more than two and a half times as many people lived in rural areas than in cities. By 1930 the United States had become a mostly urban nation. Many people moved to cities to find work.

Population Shift: Rural to Urban, 1880–1930

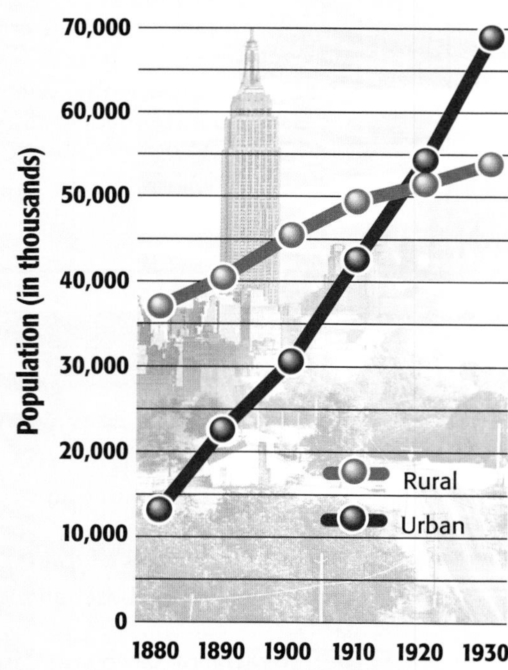

Source: *Historical Statistics of the United States*

Geography Skills

Interpreting Line Graphs

1. In what census year did the urban population of the United States become larger than the rural population?
2. **Human Systems** In what decade did the rural population experience the least growth? In what decade did the urban population experience the most growth?
3. **Making Generalizations and Predictions** What do you think the graph would show if it continued on to the present?

Mexican American Population in 1930

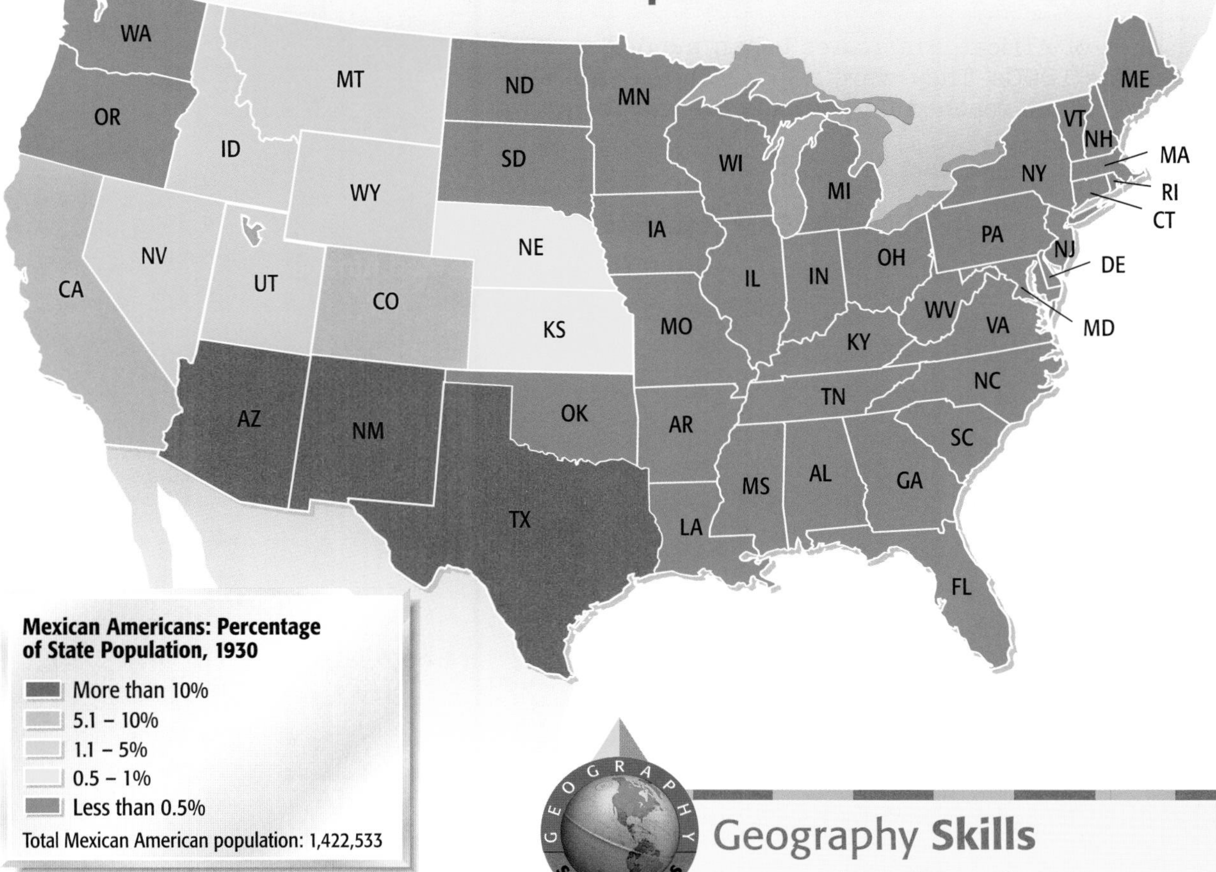

Mexican Americans: Percentage of State Population, 1930

- More than 10%
- 5.1 – 10%
- 1.1 – 5%
- 0.5 – 1%
- Less than 0.5%

Total Mexican American population: 1,422,533

Geography Skills

Interpreting Thematic Maps

1. **The Uses of Geography** In which states did the highest percentage of Mexican Americans live? Why do you think this was the case?
2. **Analyzing Information** In 1930 how many states had a Mexican American population that was less than 0.5 percent of the total state population?

History Note 1

In the early 1900s large numbers of Mexican immigrants began arriving in the United States. Between 1920 and 1930, nearly 500,000 Mexican immigrants settled in the United States. Most of these immigrants started out in rural areas in the West and Southwest. By the 1930s, however, many Mexican Americans had migrated to large cities in search of higher-paying industrial jobs. These cities included Chicago, Los Angeles, and San Antonio.

In 1937 this family of Mexican American migrant workers from Texas picked sugar beets in Minnesota.

The Great Migration

Thousands of African Americans began moving from the rural South to northern cities in the 1890s. They were seeking better jobs. This movement, known as the Great Migration, reached its peak during World War I and the 1920s.

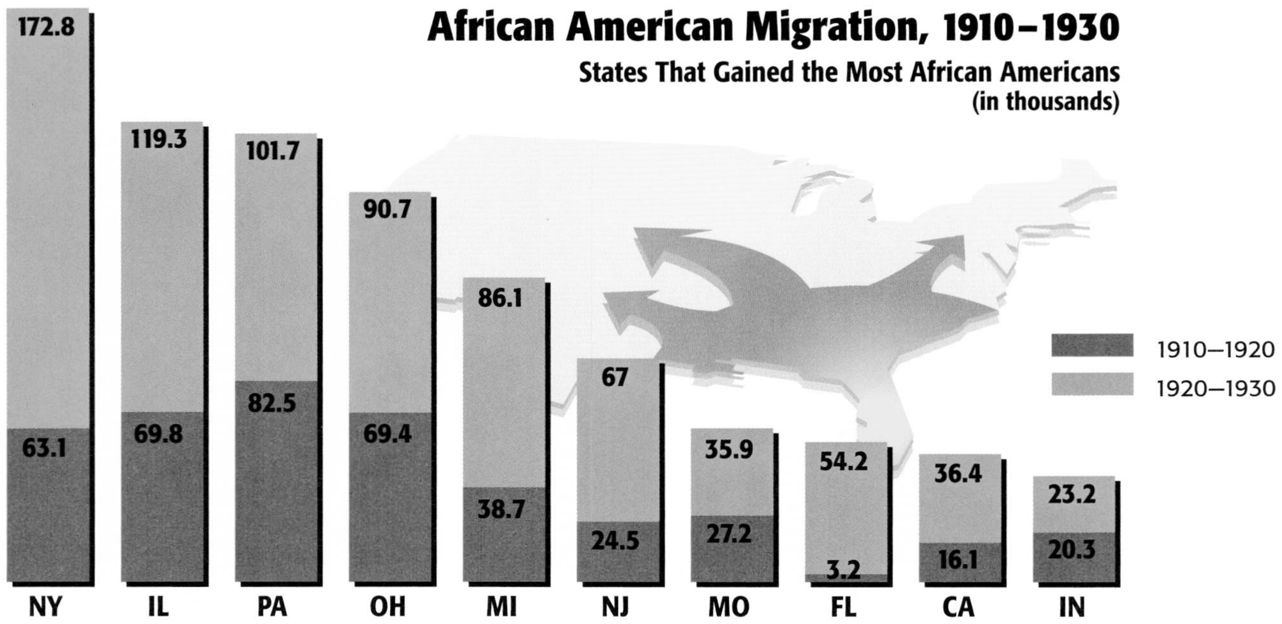

Geography Skills

Interpreting Bar Graphs

1. Which state listed had the smallest increase in its African American population between 1910 and 1920?
2. **Human Systems** Which states' African American population increased by more than 100,000 between 1910 and 1930? By more than 200,000?
3. **Summarizing** Use the information presented on this bar graph to create a map of the United States showing the states whose African American population grew the most by 1930.

History Note 2

Although the Great Migration began in the 1890s, more than 80 percent of African Americans still lived in the South as late as 1910. Beginning in 1910, however, even more African Americans began moving to northern and western cities. The Great Migration changed the nation's population dramatically. In 1930 Chicago, Detroit, and New York had African American populations three times greater than they had in 1910. Today about half of all African Americans live outside the South.

History Note 3

During the 1930s many African Americans had hoped to find better opportunities in the North. However, during the Great Depression northern cities experienced high unemployment and poverty. The National Association for the Advancement of Colored People fought to ensure equal treatment for African Americans during these hard times.

In 1912 this African American family moved to Chicago from the rural South.

Discrimination Against African Americans in 1930

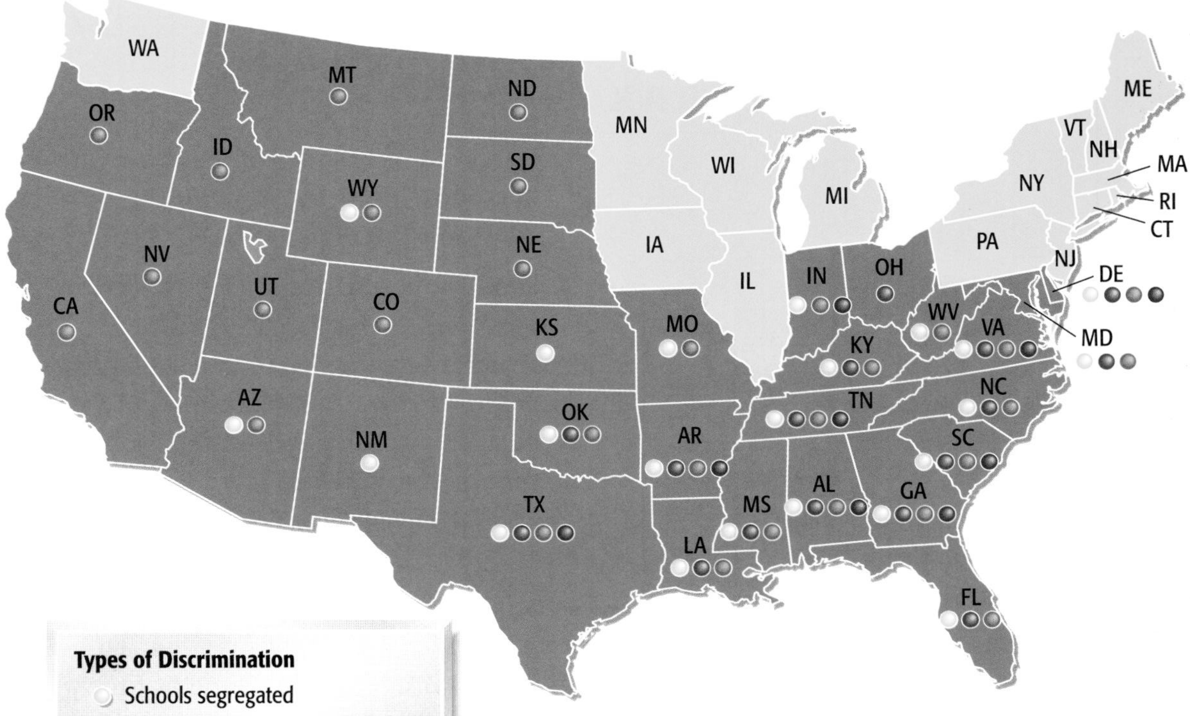

Geography **Skills**

Interpreting Thematic Maps

1. In which states did African Americans face the most discriminatory legislation?
2. **Places and Regions** Which geographic region of the United States had the fewest discriminatory laws? Which region had the most discriminatory laws?
3. **Finding the Main Idea** What was the most common form of legal discrimination?

New city residents

Social Studies Skills

WORKSHOP

Reading Skills

One of the biggest challenges you face in learning history is understanding what you read. By using appropriate Reading Skills, you will be able to understand more of what you read. Two important Reading Skills are Finding the Main Idea and Sequencing Information. The following activities will help you develop and practice these skills.

Finding the Main Idea

The main idea statement summarizes the most important point of a reading section. The main idea of a reading section is usually supported by sentences that provide details. Listed below are guidelines that will help you find the main idea of any reading assignment.

1. **Preview the material.** Read the title, introduction, and any other study clues that the assignment provides. These will often point to the main ideas being covered.
2. **Keep questions in mind.** Read the study questions that accompany the text. If the assignment does not provide study questions, create your own. Keeping these questions in mind as you read will help you focus your reading.
3. **See how ideas are arranged.** Pay attention to the headings, subheadings, and opening paragraphs. Major ideas are often introduced in such material.
4. **Look for conclusions.** As you read, try to separate sentences that supply details from sentences that make general statements. Often a string of sentences providing detailed information leads to a conclusion that expresses a main idea.

Sequencing Information

Sequencing involves trying to determine the order in which certain events occurred. Specific dates and words related to time or time periods can provide clues for use in determining the proper sequence of certain events. For example, suppose you were asked to explain how World War I started in Europe. You might come up with a series of ideas that you place in the following sequence:

Austria-Hungary annexed the Balkan provinces against their will.

↓

A Serb nationalist assassinated the Archduke of Austria-Hungary.

↓

Austria-Hungary declared war on Serbia.

↓

Austria-Hungary's allies joined the fighting.

Practicing the Skills

1. In Chapter 22, World War I, read the section entitled Establishing Peace. Read the subsections The League of Nations and Peace without a Treaty. Write four sentences that summarize the material in these subsections. Then condense your sentences into a single sentence that states the main ideas of these subsections.
2. Brainstorm some important events that took place during World War I. Then place these events in their proper sequence from first to last.

History in Action

UNIT 8 SIMULATION

You Solve the Problem . . .

Should the United States join the fighting in World War I?

Complete the following activity in small cooperative groups. It is early 1917, and the members of Congress are about to begin a debate on whether the United States should join the fighting in Europe on the side of the Allies. You are part of a special joint congressional committee that will recommend a course of action to Congress. Follow these steps to reach your decision.

1. Gather Information. Use your textbook and other resources to find information that might help you decide whether the United States should join the Allies in World War I. Be sure to use what you learned from this unit's Skills Workshop on Reading Skills, such as Finding the Main Idea and Sequencing Information, to help you make an informed decision. You may want to divide up different parts of the research among group members.

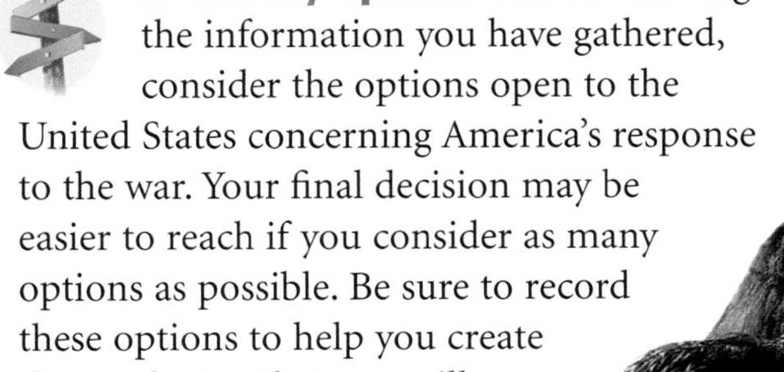

2. Identify Options. After reviewing the information you have gathered, consider the options open to the United States concerning America's response to the war. Your final decision may be easier to reach if you consider as many options as possible. Be sure to record these options to help you create the resolution that you will present to Congress.

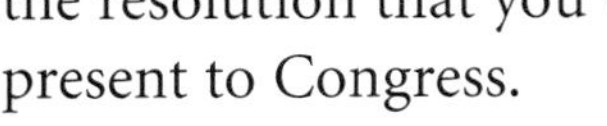

3. Predict Consequences. Now take each option you and your associates came up with and consider what might be the outcome if France followed this course of action. Ask yourselves questions like: "How will this choice benefit the United States?" Once you have predicted the consequences, record them as notes for your resolution.

4. Take Action to Implement. Once you have considered your options, you should plan and create your resolution to present to Congress. Be sure to make your decision on whether the United States should join the Allies in World War I very clear. You will need to support your decision by including information you gathered and by explaining why you rejected other options. Your presentation needs to be visually appealing to gain the interest of other members of Congress. When you are ready, decide who in your group will make which part of the presentation and take your resolution to the members of Congress (the rest of the class). Good luck!

UNIT 9 A World in Crisis (1929–1945)

CHAPTER 24 The Great Depression (1929–1939)

CHAPTER 25 World War II (1938–1945)

Young People

IN HISTORY

Young Relief Workers

When the Great Depression hit, it placed a significant burden on young Americans. Economic hardship forced many young people to drop out of school or college to look for work. However, jobs were scarce. By May 1935 more than 1 million Americans between the ages of 16 and 24 years were unemployed.

In June 1935 President Franklin D. Roosevelt created the National Youth Administration (NYA), a special division of the Works Progress Administration. The NYA was one of many relief programs designed to help young people. It offered part-time jobs for young Americans still in school. For those no longer in school, the NYA provided jobs and work training.

High school students in campus work programs often received jobs in or around their schools. They earned only about $6 a month, but the pay made a huge difference to the 1.5 million students enrolled in the program. The money allowed students to stay in school. These teenagers used the money to pay for their own schoolbooks, supplies, and bus fare. Other young people took part in out-of-school programs. Boys on the Onondaga Indian Reservation in New York built a summer camp for children. Other young workers painted buildings, maintained city parks, performed carpentry tasks, and much more.

The NYA provided new opportunities for all of its participants. Rural teenagers, for example, learned industrial skills. The NYA also attempted to integrate teenagers of different races. One boy recalled the program's meaning in his life:

The Civilian Conservation Corps was one of many relief programs. It provided jobs for young men 17 to 24 years old.

"Maybe you don't know what it's like to come home and have everyone looking at you, and you know they're thinking . . . 'He didn't find a job.' . . . It gets terrible. You just don't want to come home. . . . I tell you, the first time I walked in the front door with my paycheck, I was somebody!"

If You Were There *What type of relief work would you do?*

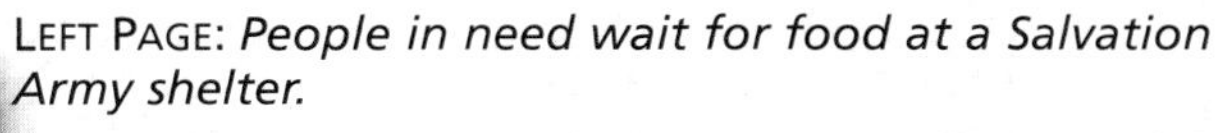

LEFT PAGE: *People in need wait for food at a Salvation Army shelter.*

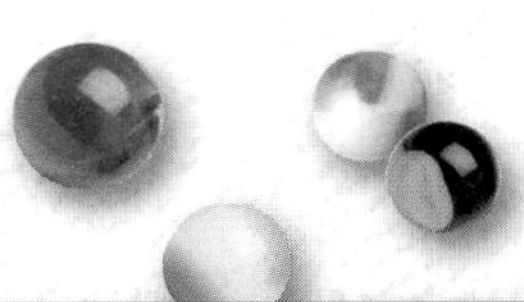

CHAPTER

24 The Great Depression (1929–1939)

STAGE BROADWAY SCREEN

VARIETY

PRICE 25¢

NEW YORK, WEDNESDAY, OCTOBER 30, 1929

WALL ST. LAYS AN EGG

Going Dumb Is Deadly to Hostess In Her Serious Dance Hall Profesh

DROP IN STOCKS ROPES SHOWMEN

Kidding Kissers in Talkers Burns Up Fans of Screen's Best Lovers

THE GRANGER COLLECTION, NEW YORK

The stock market crash on Wall Street made front-page news across the nation.

The Great Depression left thousands of Americans unemployed and homeless.

UNITED STATES

1929 The stock market crashes on October 29, leading to the Great Depression.

1930 The Smoot-Hawley Tariff raises taxes on imports.

1932 Franklin D. Roosevelt is elected president.

1933 Roosevelt takes office in March, and during the first Hundred Days his administration creates many new relief agencies.

1934 The Indian Reorganization Act is passed, returning some lands to American Indian groups.

1929 | 1930 | 1931 | 1932 | 1933 | 1934

WORLD

1930 An economic depression hits countries in Europe and South America.

1931 Japan invades Manchuria.

1932 Twenty-five percent of the German workforce is unemployed.

1933 In January Adolf Hitler becomes chancellor of Germany.

The United States formally recognizes the Soviet Union in November.

1934 Mao Zedong leads Chinese Communists on the Long March into northern China.

These Spanish loyalists are marching from Madrid to fight a rebel army in the Spanish Civil War.

Build on What You Know

American society went through great social change in the 1920s. Many Americans enjoyed more prosperity than ever before, while some groups struggled to improve their living conditions. The 1920s ended with the shock of the stock market crash and the start of the Great Depression. Many Americans looked to their government for help.

Soup kitchens were a common means of providing some relief to hungry, out-of-work Americans.

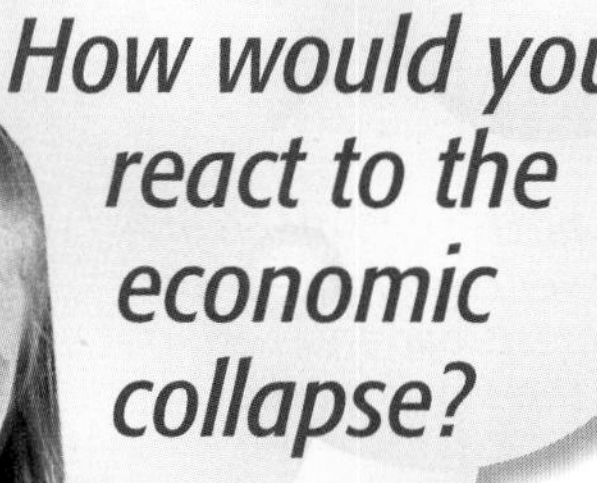

New Deal policies helped labor unions such as the CIO.

1935 The Second New Deal begins in January.

In August Congress passes the Social Security Act, which helps older people, those with disabilities, children, and job seekers.

1936 In November President Roosevelt defeats Alfred Landon to win re-election.

Autoworkers at a General Motors plant in Flint, Michigan, begin a sit-down strike in December.

1937 Roosevelt tries unsuccessfully to increase the number of Supreme Court justices.

1938 The unemployment rate jumps as the U.S. economy continues to decline.

1939 Partly as a result of European orders for arms and war equipment, the U.S. economy begins to recover and then to boom.

1935 **1936** **1937** **1938** **1939**

1935 Great Britain grants India a constitution.

1936 The Spanish Civil War begins.

1937 The German airship *Hindenburg* explodes, killing 36 people.

1938 Great Britain, France, Germany, and Italy sign the Munich Pact.

1939 World War II begins in Europe.

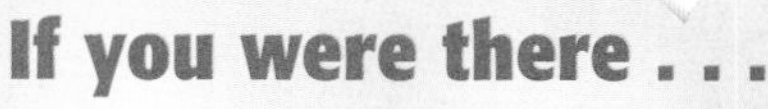

If you were there . . .

How would you react to the economic collapse?

You Be the Historian

What's Your Opinion? Do you **agree** or **disagree** with the following statements? Support your point of view in your journal.

- **Economics** Economic problems can always be predicted and planned for.
- **Constitutional Heritage** A president who controls the courts and the legislature has too much power.
- **Global Relations** Economic problems in one nation will always hurt the world economy.

Section 1

The End of Prosperity

Read to Discover

1. What was the stock market like before the crash?
2. What were the major causes of the Great Depression, and how did it weaken the U.S. economy?
3. How did economic hard times affect Americans?

Define

- bull market
- bear market
- buying on margin
- speculation
- business cycle

Identify

- Great Depression
- Bonus Army
- Herbert Hoover

Why It Matters Today

Americans continue to invest heavily in the stock market today. Use CNNfyi.com or other **current events** sources to find out how the stock market is performing today. Record your findings in your journal.

A March 1929 magazine cover highlighted the widespread interest in the stock market.

The Story Continues

American businesses boomed during the 1920s. Both production and employment were high and on the rise. More Americans than ever before owned houses and cars. Each week about 80 million Americans went to the movies. At his March 1929 inauguration, President Herbert Hoover said, "I have no fears for the future of our country. It is bright with hope."

The Stock Market Crash

Further proof of a healthy economy was the rise in stock prices in the late 1920s. Many Americans, from homemakers to business executives, bought and sold stocks. The rising demand for stocks led to a **bull market**, or a continuing rise in stock market prices. Many experts thought that a **bear market**, or a continuing drop in stock prices, was unlikely. General Motors executive John J. Raskob wrote an article titled "Everyone Ought to Be Rich."

Many people who invested in the stock market were **buying on margin**—buying stocks on credit with a loan from a broker. Brokers, in turn, had borrowed this money from banks. This activity is called **speculation**—putting money in a high-risk investment with the hope of making a profit. Speculators gambled that no matter how much they had paid for a stock, someone else would pay more.

The stock market reached a high point in September 1929. On October 23, however, it dropped sharply. On October 24, which became known as Black Thursday, thousands of frightened investors tried to sell their stocks before prices fell any lower. By noon the market had lost $9 billion in value. After a brief recovery, the stock market collapsed completely on October 29—Black Tuesday. In just one day the market lost a full year's profits. One journalist recalled the public response to the event.

October 29, 1929
The stock market crashes.

History Makers Speak

"The wires to other cities were jammed with frantic orders to sell [stock]. So were the cables, radio, and telephones to Europe and the rest of the world. Buyers were few, sometimes wholly absent. . . . This was real panic. . . . When the closing bell rang, the great bull market was dead and buried."

—Jonathan Norton Leonard, *Three Years Down*

Analyzing Primary Sources

Drawing Inferences and Conclusions What does the description tell you about how people responded to the news of the market's collapse?

Many speculators who had bought on margin lost everything. They were forced to pay their brokers with savings or by selling their china, clothing, and jewelry to get cash. Even Americans who had never invested in the market soon felt the effects of the Great Crash. The nation became locked in a downward economic spiral known as the **Great Depression**.

✔ **Reading Check: Summarizing** Describe the rise and fall of the stock market in the late 1920s.

The Economy Collapses

The crash hurt banks in two main ways. First, banks and small investors suffered great losses from their stock investments. Second, banks had encouraged their customers to buy stocks, even when the investments were very risky. After the crash many of these customers could not repay their bank loans. Such problems caused some banks to close.

BROOKLYN DAILY EAGLE

WALL ST. IN PANIC AS STOCKS CRASH

Attempt Made to Kill Italy's Crown Prince

Hollywood Fire Destroys Films Worth Millions

High Duty Group Gave $700,000 to Coolidge Drive

Interpreting the Visual Record

The Crash *The stock market collapse led to financial panic.* ***Why is this man selling his car so cheaply?***

When news of the first bank closings spread, millions of people panicked. Their deposits were not insured, as deposits are now. Americans rushed to withdraw their money before more banks failed. However, because banks generally do not keep enough money on hand to cover all deposits, many literally "ran out of money" and shut their doors. The banking crisis continued. In 1931 alone, some 2,294 banks closed their doors. Millions of Americans lost their life savings.

The banking crisis soon caused a business crisis. Bank closures left many businesses without corporate savings and operating accounts. Lacking money to stay in business, some closed down entirely. Other businesses canceled plans to build new factories or expand existing ones. Industries slowed production and cut their workforces. In 1930 more than 26,000 businesses failed.

Businesses tried to encourage consumers to buy goods and stimulate growth.

✔ **Reading Check: Analyzing Information** How did the stock market crash affect banks and businesses?

The Causes

The Great Depression occurred so quickly that most Americans were left wondering what had happened. Traditionally, when production exceeds consumption and surpluses pile up, manufacturers cut production and lay off workers. This pattern causes a recession, and some businesses fail. However, consumers eventually buy up surpluses and companies increase production and rehire workers, leading to prosperity. This economic pattern is known as the **business cycle**.

The Typical Business Cycle

Prosperity
Recession
Recovery
No Growth
Depression
Economic Growth
Time

Interpreting Graphs At first, most Americans thought the stock market crash had caused only a temporary recession.

Skills Assessment **Drawing Inferences and Conclusions** What do you think a graph of the business cycle during the Great Depression would look like?

Before 1929 the economy had followed the business cycle, recovering more or less on its own. The Great Depression was much longer and much more severe than past downturns, however. Historians and economists still disagree about its exact causes. However, most agree that both overproduction and global trade problems helped cause the Great Depression.

The 1920s were years of high business productivity. Between 1919 and 1929 productivity rose 43 percent. Farmers' production levels also increased. As long as demand stayed high, rising productivity caused growing profits. But many markets in the late 1920s stopped expanding. Most of the people who could afford luxury items had already bought them.

An unequal distribution of wealth in the United States made the problem worse. In 1929 only 1 percent of the U.S. population owned about one third of all personal wealth. At the same time, about 60 percent of all American families earned less than $2,000 a year. Most Americans could not afford to buy many products. This situation left businesses with larger surpluses than usual.

At the same time, international trade declined significantly, further reducing the market for American goods. Europeans still recovering from World War I could not afford American products. As a result, concerned that American goods were not selling well in Europe, U.S. lawmakers set high tariffs, or taxes on imported goods. These tariffs made it difficult for European nations to sell their goods in the United States. Without these crucial sales, Europeans had less money to purchase American surpluses.

✔ **Reading Check: Summarizing** Identify the two main factors leading to the Great Depression.

Research on the ROM

Free Find:
Herbert Hoover
After reading about the presidency of Herbert Hoover on the **Holt Researcher CD–ROM**, outline the policies and programs that Hoover developed to assist the economy during the Great Depression.

The Depression Hits Home

The Great Depression hit Americans very hard, and unemployment skyrocketed. Many people struggled just to feed and house themselves. Some turned to theft. As one man explained, "People that didn't wanna steal had to steal. . . . they were honest people, but they stole to survive." Even the lucky people with jobs saw their wages and hours drop.

State and local governments and private charities raised money to help poor and unemployed Americans. Soup kitchens, breadlines, and shelters sprang up across the country. The need, however, was far greater than the available resources. Many people became angry with the lack of help from the federal government.

In May 1932 these frustrations led a small group of unemployed World War I veterans to protest. They traveled to Washington, D.C., from all over the country demanding payment of their government war bonuses. Soon these veterans became known as the **Bonus Army**.

President **Herbert Hoover** saw the Bonus Army as a dangerous mob and ordered federal troops to restore order. The troops drove the veterans from their camps with bayonets and tear gas. Most Americans were angry at the government's treatment of these people who had once risked their lives for their country. The incident led many to criticize President Hoover.

✔ **Reading Check: Supporting a Point of View** How do you think Hoover should have dealt with the Bonus Army?

Interpreting the Visual Record

Hoovervilles *As homelessness increased, people built camps of shacks in vacant lots or on the outskirts of cities.* ***How do the camp buildings contrast with the rest of the neighborhood?***

Many people blamed President Hoover for not bringing the depression to a quick end.

President Hoover Fights Back

The rising suffering and unrest concerned President Hoover. However, he felt that the government should not support the people. Instead, he believed that relief and recovery should come largely through voluntary cooperation rather than federal efforts.

Despite this belief, Hoover did approve some federal relief programs such as the Reconstruction Finance Corporation (RFC). The RFC lent money to railroads, banks, and other key businesses to keep them running. Hoping to create jobs, he asked the RFC to lend up to $1.5 billion to the states for public works in 1932.

Hoover's efforts were not enough to end the depression. Overall, he failed to recognize how serious the depression was. In March 1930 he told Americans, "We have now passed the worst and with continued unity of effort we shall rapidly recover." However, the economic situation only grew worse. As the depression deepened, many people began insisting that the federal government should play a greater role in fixing the economy. One New Jersey resident wrote to President Hoover in 1930.

Analyzing Primary Sources

Drawing Inferences and Conclusions What does the author believe President Hoover values least of all?

"Our children have Schoolless days and Shoeless days. . . . Why does Every Thing have Exceptional Value. Except the Human being—why are we reduced to poverty and starving and anxiety and Sorrow. . . . Why not End the Depression have you not a Heart[?]"

—Anonymous letter to President Hoover, quoted in *Down and Out in the Great Depression*, edited by Robert S. McElvaine

✔ **Reading Check: Identifying Points of View** Why was Hoover reluctant to provide government aid to people?

Section 1 Review

1. **Define** and explain:
   - bull market
   - bear market
   - buying on margin
   - speculation
   - business cycle
2. **Identify** and explain:
   - Great Depression
   - Bonus Army
   - Herbert Hoover
3. **Identifying Cause and Effect** Copy the graphic organizer below. Use it to show the major causes of the Great Depression and how each cause weakened the U.S. economy.

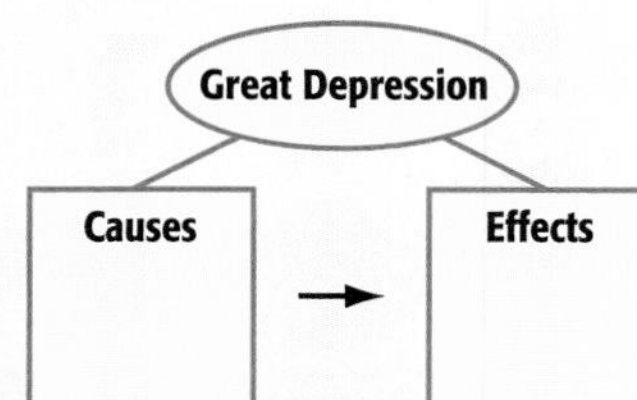

4. **Finding the Main Idea**
   a. What were the characteristics of the stock market before the crash?
   b. How did Americans' lives change during the Great Depression?
5. **Writing and Critical Thinking**
   Summarizing Imagine that you are an unemployed worker in 1930. Write a letter to President Hoover describing your troubles and telling him what you think should be done to end the depression.
   Consider the following:
   - bank failure
   - access to basic necessities
   - government assistance and programs

Section 2

Roosevelt's New Deal

Read to Discover

1. How did President Roosevelt and Congress try to help Americans during the Hundred Days?
2. How did the New Deal help Americans suffering from the depression?
3. Why did some people criticize the New Deal?

Define

- fireside chats
- sit-down strike

Identify

- Brain Trust
- New Deal
- Harry L. Hopkins
- Tennessee Valley Authority
- National Industrial Recovery Act
- Huey Long
- Works Progress Administration
- Social Security Act
- Frances Perkins
- National Labor Relations Act
- Congress of Industrial Organizations

WHY IT MATTERS TODAY

Many New Deal agencies still exist. Use CNNfyi.com or other **current events** sources to find out about one federal agency created during the New Deal that continues to operate today. Record your findings in your journal.

The Story Continues

As Hoover's popularity fell, Democrats felt certain that they could win the election. They chose Franklin D. Roosevelt (FDR), the governor of New York, as their candidate. Usually candidates did not attend their party's nominating convention. However, FDR immediately flew to Chicago to accept his nomination. There, he offered new hope to the country. "I pledge you, I pledge myself, to a new deal for the American people."

This magazine cover showed a cheerful Roosevelt riding to his inauguration next to a sullen Hoover.

 The Election of 1932

Roosevelt won a landslide victory in the November election. Additionally, the Democrats won majorities in both houses of Congress. President-elect Roosevelt began working before his inauguration, with Hoover still in the White House. During his campaign, Roosevelt had brought experts together for advice on policies and programs. Most members of this so-called **Brain Trust** were college professors, labor leaders, lawyers, and

Franklin D. Roosevelt

Franklin D. Roosevelt was born into a wealthy New York family. Roosevelt served in the New York legislature and as assistant secretary of the navy. In 1920 he was the Democratic vice presidential candidate. Although he was popular and intelligent, Roosevelt was not considered a strong leader.

His life changed dramatically in 1921 when he suffered an attack of polio. This disease left him paralyzed in both legs. He learned to move again with the help of leg braces, though he often used a wheelchair. He re-entered politics and enjoyed great success. Roosevelt's private battle with polio made him more compassionate. It also gave him the strength to lead the nation during the depression crisis. **What event changed Roosevelt's life?**

social workers. As Roosevelt and his Brain Trust worked day and night, Americans hoped their new leaders could end the depression.

On the day of his inauguration, Roosevelt told the American people "the only thing we have to fear is fear itself." Roosevelt called a special session of Congress, which became known as the Hundred Days. During the Hundred Days, Congress passed many programs to battle the depression. Together, these programs became known as the **New Deal**. The federal government paid for many of these New Deal programs by raising taxes or by spending more money than it took in.

✔ **Reading Check:** **Drawing Inferences and Conclusions** Why do you think a Democratic Congress helped FDR accomplish his programs?

New Deal Programs

The New Deal's first goal was to restore the nation's confidence in its banks. On March 6, 1933, Roosevelt called for a "bank holiday" and ordered all banks to close temporarily. Three days later Congress passed the Emergency Banking Act. Under this law the government planned to inspect each bank's finances and then allow healthy banks to reopen.

Little more than a week after his inauguration, Roosevelt began giving his **fireside chats**—radio addresses to the American people. In a March 12 chat he declared that "it is safer to keep your money in a reopened bank than under the mattress." Banks began reopening the next day. By the end of March, people had deposited nearly $1 billion in American banks. Congress also created the Federal Deposit Insurance Corporation (FDIC) to protect bank accounts. During the depression, the FDIC insured deposits up to $5,000 per account.

With banks working again, Roosevelt turned his attention to the unemployed. By 1933 one fourth of all American wage earners were jobless. Many others had only temporary or part-time work. Even full-time employees had a hard time buying the basic necessities. In May 1933 Congress created the Federal Emergency Relief Administration (FERA), granting states money to give to those in need.

However, most Americans wanted jobs, not charity. Therefore, the president put the head of FERA, **Harry L. Hopkins**, in charge of the Civil Works Administration (CWA). CWA employees built airports, roads, and sewers. Another jobs program, the Civilian Conservation Corps (CCC), hired 18- to 25-year-old men from families on relief. These CCC recruits lived in U.S. Army camps while fighting forest fires, improving national parks, and planting trees.

One New Deal program, the **Tennessee Valley Authority** (TVA), was planned to help one of the poorest and least-developed parts of the country. The TVA built dams along the Tennessee River, providing flood control and hydroelectric power. Thousands of rural families received electricity in their homes for the first time.

During the Hundred Days, Congress also helped farmers by passing the Agricultural Adjustment Act (AAA) to lower production and raise prices. The AAA paid farmers to cut production of certain crops. However, the Supreme Court ruled that the way the AAA raised money was unconstitutional. Roosevelt also created the Farm Credit Administration (FCA). In its first 18 months the FCA refinanced more than 20 percent of all farm mortgages. The agency helped farmers keep their farms and also saved many rural banks from closing.

Roosevelt then turned to the problem of economic recovery and growth. He proposed the **National Industrial Recovery Act** (NIRA), which would suspend antitrust laws and stop unfair competition. In a fireside chat Roosevelt explained the idea behind the NIRA.

"If all employers in each competitive group agree to pay their workers the same wages . . . and require the same hours . . . then higher wages and shorter hours will hurt no employer. Moreover, such action is better for the employer than unemployment and low wages, because it makes more buyers for his product."

—Franklin D. Roosevelt, quoted in *The Public Papers and Addresses of Franklin D. Roosevelt*

For example, the NIRA created the National Recovery Administration (NRA) to help companies in the same business create codes of fair competition to prevent further business failures.

✔ **Reading Check: Summarizing** Describe how President Roosevelt's New Deal addressed four key areas of need.

Analyzing Primary Sources

Making Generalizations and Predictions What would be the effect if all employers paid the same wages and required the same hours?

New Deal Critics

Soon after the Hundred Days ended, two main groups of critics began attacking the New Deal. One group believed the New Deal went too far in expanding the size and power of the federal government. Others in this group said that the cost of New Deal programs would bankrupt the country.

A second group of critics thought the New Deal did not go far enough in helping the needy and promoting social reform. Father Charles E. Coughlin, a Catholic priest in Detroit, wanted America's wealth and natural resources nationalized. Louisiana senator **Huey Long** also called for a more equal distribution of wealth. During the depression, Long proposed a Share-Our-Wealth plan. This plan called for every family to receive a guaranteed income of $2,500 a year, funded by higher taxes on the wealthy. He promised that his plan would give every family "enough [money] for a home, an automobile, a radio, and the ordinary conveniences." Long's dream of running for president ended when he was assassinated in 1935.

✔ **Reading Check: Contrasting** Explain the different criticisms of the New Deal.

CONNECTING TO MATH

Just the Facts

Percentage of Labor Force Unemployed

Year	Percentage
1933	24.9
1934	21.7
1935	20.1
1936	16.9
1937	14.3
1938	19.0
1939	17.2

Using Mathematical Skills

1. What year showed the highest percentage of unemployment?
2. Use these figures to create a line graph showing the change in unemployment during the depression.
3. Imagine that you are a member of Congress. Use these figures to write a speech arguing either for or against the effectiveness of New Deal work programs.

The Second New Deal

In the 1934 midterm elections, the Democrats strengthened their control of Congress. This sign of public support led President Roosevelt to propose new programs. Comparing the depression to an illness, he said that this Second New Deal sought "not only cure of the symptoms but also removal of their cause."

In 1935 Roosevelt created the **Works Progress Administration** (WPA) to put Americans to work. Before the WPA ended in 1943, millions of its workers built hospitals, parks, roads, and schools. WPA workers also cared for small children, surveyed historical sites, and offered other services. The National Youth Administration (NYA) was another WPA program. It gave part-time work to high school-age youth and college students. These jobs helped many students stay in school instead of dropping out to search for work.

Roosevelt also wanted to help those Americans who, as he said, were "unable . . . to maintain themselves independently . . . through no fault of their own." In August 1935 Congress passed the **Social Security Act** to help older people, those with disabilities, children, and job seekers.

The Social Security program had three main parts. First, it set up a pension system for retired workers age 65 and older. Second, it gave the unemployed short-term cash benefits while they looked for work. Third, the Social Security administration offered payments to women with dependent children as well as to people with disabilities. It did not cover all workers, however. Many people, particularly agricultural and domestic workers, did not get benefits.

✔ **Reading Check: Finding the Main Idea** What Second New Deal programs offered aid and benefits to American workers?

CONNECTING TO THE ARTS

The Federal Arts Project Under the direction of the WPA, the Federal Arts Project sponsored artists around the nation. When asked why he was spending money to support artists, Harry L. Hopkins, director of the WPA, replied, "They've got to eat just like other people." During the Great Depression, WPA artists painted many murals celebrating the achievements of American workers in many different industries. This mural inside Coit Tower in San Francisco shows the accomplishments of California agriculture. **How does this image try to provide a positive message during the hard times of the depression?**

New Deal Labor Programs

President Roosevelt chose **Frances Perkins** as his secretary of labor in 1933. She was the first female cabinet member in American history. In May 1935 Roosevelt and Perkins received a serious blow when the Supreme Court declared the NIRA unconstitutional.

The same year Congress passed the **National Labor Relations Act** (NLRA). The NLRA protected unions and upheld their right to collective bargaining—negotiations between unions and owners. As a means of enforcement, the NLRA created the National Labor Relations Board. The board oversaw union elections and helped settle disputes between workers and employers. Largely because of the NLRA, labor became a powerful force in politics during the depression. Backed by a growing number of members, unions campaigned for pro-labor candidates and lobbied Congress for pro-labor legislation. The new, stronger labor movement benefited the Democrats the most.

At the start of the depression, many skilled workers had belonged to craft-based unions associated with the American Federation of Labor (AFL). In 1938 several former AFL leaders founded the **Congress of Industrial Organizations** (CIO). The CIO wanted to organize both skilled and unskilled workers in major industries into individual unions. The CIO also welcomed African Americans, immigrants, and women as union members.

Union efforts to improve working conditions led to a number of major strikes during the depression. Workers created the **sit-down strike**, in which they stayed in the factories but refused to work. Strikers hoped that the sit-down strike would keep owners from replacing them with new employees. Major sit-down strikes took place at the Goodyear Tire Factory in Akron, Ohio, and at General Motors plants in Flint, Michigan, during the Great Depression.

✔ **Reading Check: Summarizing** How did New Deal legislation affect labor?

The Election of 1936

As the presidential election of 1936 drew near, Republicans still criticized the New Deal. However, they offered few new options. The Republicans nominated Alfred M. Landon, the governor of Kansas, as their candidate for president. President Roosevelt fought back against the Republicans, saying that they had given Americans "nine crazy years at the [stock market] ticker and three long years in the breadlines."

Still, some Democrats worried about losing the election. The Republicans had strong backing from the business community and other groups. In addition, a few major issues, such as labor unrest, the ongoing depression, and Supreme Court opposition to parts of the New

Social Security

Congress passed the Social Security Act in 1935. Critics, however, complained that it ignored large segments of the population who needed assistance. Since then, lawmakers have made many changes to expand the act. By the late 1990s, Social Security programs covered 95 percent of the nation's workers. The Social Security old-age pension program has proved to be expensive. By 1989 it accounted for one fourth of the federal budget. As the nation's population ages, many Americans worry that Social Security funds will run out. Congress has considered several ways to help protect Social Security funds. For example, Congress has increased the number of workers paying Social Security taxes and the amount of those taxes. In addition, Congress has gradually increased the retirement age from 65 to 67. **How has the Social Security program expanded since 1935?**

Select New Deal Programs

FIRST NEW DEAL, 1933–1934	PROVISIONS
Emergency Banking Act	Gave the executive branch the right to regulate banks
Farm Credit Administration (FCA)	Refinanced loans to keep farmers from losing their land
Civilian Conservation Corps (CCC)	Employed young men on public-works projects
Federal Emergency Relief Administration (FERA)	Provided relief to the needy
Agricultural Adjustment Act (AAA) of 1933	Paid farmers to grow fewer crops; later declared unconstitutional
Tennessee Valley Authority (TVA)	Built dams and power plants in the Tennessee Valley region
Home Owners Loan Corporation (HOLC)	Lent money to home owners to refinance their mortgages
Federal Deposit Insurance Corporation (FDIC)	Insured deposits in individual bank accounts
National Recovery Administration (NRA)	Regulated industry and raised wages and prices
Public Works Administration (PWA)	Set up public-works projects to increase employment
Civil Works Administration (CWA)	Provided federal jobs to the unemployed
Securities and Exchange Commission (SEC)	Regulated the securities market
Federal Housing Administration (FHA)	Insured bank loans for building and repairing homes
SECOND NEW DEAL, 1935–1938	**PROVISIONS**
Works Progress Administration (WPA)	Created jobs in public works, research, and the arts
Rural Electrification Administration (REA)	Provided electricity to rural areas lacking public utilities
National Youth Administration (NYA)	Provided job training and part-time jobs to students
National Labor Relations Act (NLRA)	Recognized labor's right to bargain collectively
Social Security Act	Provided unemployment benefits and retirement pensions
Farm Security Administration (FSA)	Provided loans to help tenant farmers buy land
Agricultural Adjustment Act (AAA) of 1938	Paid farmers to voluntarily limit crop production
Fair Labor Standards Act	Established a minimum wage and a 40-hour workweek

Public support for programs such as the WPA helped Roosevelt win reelection in 1936.

Deal, hurt Roosevelt's reputation. However, a majority of Americans still favored Roosevelt. Roosevelt won an even bigger victory than in 1932, with 523 electoral votes to Landon's 8.

Like many New Deal critics, some Supreme Court justices worried that President Roosevelt was taking more power than the Constitution allowed. During Roosevelt's first term, they had ruled several New Deal programs unconstitutional. After he was re-elected, Roosevelt tried to avoid more rulings like that one. In February 1937 Roosevelt asked Congress to pass the Judicial Procedures Reform Act. This act would have allowed the president to appoint a new justice, up to a total of six, for every justice who did not resign after turning 70 years old.

Roosevelt's critics said he was "court packing," or filling the Court with his own judges. Even his allies worried that his plan would upset the checks and balances of the federal government. Congress denied the request. However, the Supreme Court did not rule against any other New Deal legislation. Roosevelt later appointed new justices who favored his programs to replace justices who retired.

✔ **Reading Check: Analyzing Information** Why was Roosevelt able to win over the American people, yet not the Supreme Court?

Evaluating the New Deal

The New Deal changed almost every aspect of American life and greatly expanded the role of the federal government. Similarly, Roosevelt expanded the role of the president.

Did the New Deal actually end the Great Depression? Many critics feel that it never led to full economic recovery. They point out that the United States suffered another small depression in 1937–38. In addition, some critics blame the New Deal for promoting deficit spending, in which the government spends more than it takes in as income.

Interpreting Political Cartoons

New cures *This political cartoon pokes fun at Roosevelt's willingness to try any solution to the problems caused by the depression.* ***What do the bottles in the cartoon represent?***

New Deal supporters believe that it saved the United States from economic and political collapse. They argue that its expansion of government was necessary during a time of crisis. They also believe that New Deal programs helped keep future depressions from happening. Some of these—such as the Federal Deposit Insurance Corporation and Social Security—still exist today.

✔ **Reading Check: Contrasting** How do opinions about the outcomes of the New Deal differ?

Section 2 Review

go.hrw.com Homework Practice Online
keyword: SC3 HP24

1. **Define** and explain:
   - fireside chats
   - sit-down strike

2. **Identify** and explain:
   - Brain Trust
   - New Deal
   - Harry L. Hopkins
   - Tennessee Valley Authority
   - National Industrial Recovery Act
   - Huey Long
   - Works Progress Administration
   - Social Security Act
   - Frances Perkins
   - National Labor Relations Act
   - Congress of Industrial Organizations

3. **Categorizing** Copy the graphic organizer below. Use it to show how President Roosevelt and Congress fought the depression during the Hundred Days.

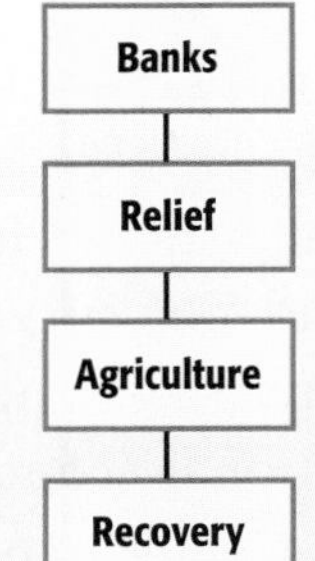

4. **Finding the Main Idea**
   a. How did Americans benefit from the New Deal?
   b. What were the major criticisms of the New Deal?

5. **Writing and Critical Thinking**
   Supporting a Point of View Imagine that you are a New Deal supporter. Pick the New Deal program you think was most important. Prepare an argument in support of your choice for a debate with a critic of the New Deal. Explain the reasons for your choice.
   Consider the following:
   - weakened economy
   - personal suffering
   - role of government

Section 3

Americans Face Hard Times

Read to Discover

1. What effect did the Great Depression have on families and farmers?
2. How did farmers try to survive the depression?
3. How did government programs help support the arts during the depression?

Identify

- Dust Bowl
- Eleanor Roosevelt
- Marian Anderson
- John Steinbeck
- Dorothea Lange
- Margaret Mitchell
- Woody Guthrie
- Will Rogers

Why it Matters Today

The U.S. government continues to support programs to aid people in need. Use CNNfyi.com or other **current events** sources to investigate federal programs designed to help families and children. Record your findings in your journal.

During the depression, many American families had to live in whatever makeshift shelters they could create.

The Story Continues

In the difficult days of the fall of 1931, after her husband lost his job, Freda Stallings gave birth to her third child. The Stallings family did everything humanly possible to take care of their family. Freda's husband, Odie, walked miles looking for work. Freda and Odie often kept their baby warm by sleeping with him. One morning, after a cold night, they woke to find him dead. With no money for a coffin, they buried him in a cardboard box.

Family Life

The Great Depression took a heavy toll on American families. Like Freda and Odie Stallings, many families lacked the money for basic necessities such as clothing, food, and shelter. In the difficult struggle to make ends meet, some families did not survive. Divorce rates rose during the depression, and both marriage and birth rates fell. Men and women often found their traditional economic roles changing, depending on which spouse had work. Unable to find work nearby, some men left their families and traveled the country in search of jobs. Some never returned.

Even children felt the harsh realities of the Great Depression. To help their families, children often had to drop out of school and go to work. Others ran away from home and tried to support themselves. One boy wrote this diary entry about his struggle to survive in 1932.

> **"Slept in paper box. Bummed swell breakfast. . . . Rode freight to Roessvile. Small burg, but got dinner. . . . Rode to Sidell. . . . Hit homes for meals and turned down. Had to buy supper 20 cents. Raining."**
>
> —Blink, quoted in *The Great Depression,* by T. H. Watkins

Analyzing Primary Sources

Drawing Inferences and Conclusions How can you tell that the Great Depression has affected this boy?

In many cases, however, the struggle brought out the strengths of family and community. One New York resident recalled that "the safety net at that time was the big families. Even though you were unemployed, there was always somebody working, and the families somehow managed to hold together."

✔ **Reading Check: Summarizing** What was life like for families in the depression?

Farmers in the Depression

Even before the depression, farmers faced the problems of low prices and overproduction. The crash made things even worse. As prices bottomed out, many farmers could not sell their crops at all. It cost more to grow and ship their products than people would pay for them. Without income, farmers could not repay their house and land loans.

Banks would then take over ownership of the farms by a process known as foreclosing. Frustrated farmers often fought back. For instance, when banks held auctions to sell farms and belongings, many people would not bid market prices. With no other offers, the banks had to accept the lower bids. The buyers usually gave the items back to their neighbors.

Interpreting the Visual Record

Lobbying for agriculture *Groups such as the Southern Tenant Farmers Union fought to protect the rights of African American and white farmers and sharecroppers.* ***What conditions during the Great Depression might have caused people from different backgrounds to work together?***

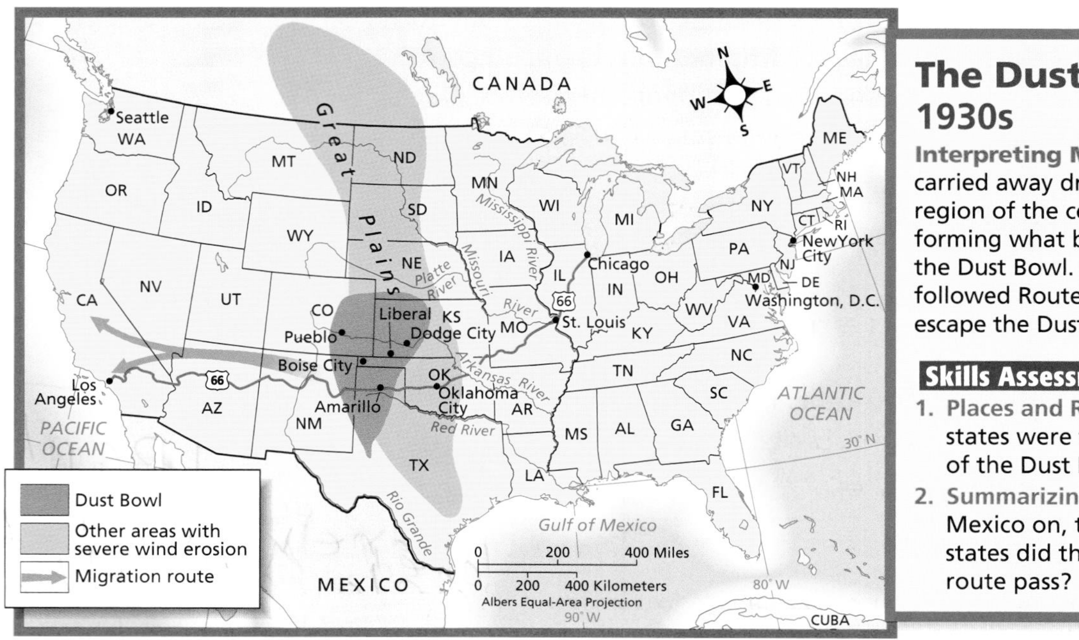

The Dust Bowl, 1930s

Interpreting Maps Strong winds carried away dry topsoil in a vast region of the central United States, forming what became known as the Dust Bowl. Many farmers followed Route 66 west to escape the Dust Bowl.

Skills Assessment

1. **Places and Regions** In what states were the main effects of the Dust Bowl located?
2. **Summarizing** From New Mexico on, through which states did the typical migration route pass?

The Resettlement Administration was a New Deal program that helped farmers who had lost their land find new places to live.

During the mid-1930s the situation grew even worse. A severe drought struck the Great Plains—the region from North Texas up to North Dakota. Farmers there usually overworked their land and did little to prevent soil erosion. Soon heavy winds began sweeping away the dried-out topsoil. These dust storms turned parts of the Great Plains into the so-called **Dust Bowl**, destroying farm life in the area. One woman from Kansas recalled how the dust seemed to cover everything. "Our hair was gray and stiff and we ground dirt between our teeth." A dust storm could rage from one hour to more than three days.

✔ **Reading Check: Identifying Cause and Effect** How did farmers' practices help cause the Dust Bowl, and what was the result?

Working Hard to Survive

The Great Depression hit minorities very hard. In order to reserve jobs for Americans, the government deported many Mexican-born farmworkers and their families. Some of the workers' children were American-born, and therefore were U.S. citizens, but they were deported as well.

African Americans, who also faced discrimination, were often the last to be hired and the first to be fired. They also usually received lower wages than white workers. NIRA codes protected this kind of inequality. African Americans also faced segregation in some government work programs. New Deal agencies sometimes gave less help to African Americans than to whites. Despite the discrimination and segregation, New Deal programs still helped hundreds of thousands of African Americans. Most African Americans backed President Roosevelt and the New Deal. They simply believed that things would be worse under the Republicans.

Roosevelt asked for advice from African American leaders on matters ranging from economics to education. He appointed so many African Americans to his administration that they became known as the Black Cabinet. This group included Mary McLeod Bethune and Robert C. Weaver.

First Lady **Eleanor Roosevelt** also fought for minority rights. In early 1939, members of the patriotic organization Daughters of the American Revolution (DAR) refused to let **Marian Anderson**, a world-famous African American singer, use their hall for a concert. Eleanor Roosevelt, a DAR member, quit the group. With her support, Anderson performed for 75,000 people at the Lincoln Memorial in the spring of 1939.

✔ **Reading Check: Finding the Main Idea** What was the depression like for African Americans?

Interpreting the Visual Record

Documenting the depression *Dorothea Lange's* Migrant Mother *became a well-known symbol of the depression.* ***What mood is expressed in this photograph?***

Arts and Literature

Unemployment hit actors, dancers, and other artists very hard during the depression. Roosevelt's administration created programs to help them, such as the WPA's Federal Writers' Project (FWP). The writers hired by the Federal Writers' Project created many valuable resources. These included state travel guides, oral histories, and American folklore collections. In April 1939 former FWP employee **John Steinbeck** published *The Grapes of Wrath*—the best-known novel of the depression.

The Federal Theater Project, the Federal Music Project, and the Federal Arts Project were among the new programs. Many Americans heard their first orchestra or saw their first play because of these programs. The Federal Arts Project hired artists to create posters for other agencies and murals for public buildings. The Farm Security Administration (FSA) used art to give Americans a close look at the effects of the depression. **Dorothea Lange** and other FSA photographers recorded rural life.

Many painters during the depression were inspired by local customs and folk themes. A group of these artists, including Thomas Hart Benton and Grant Wood, became known as the regionalists. Jacob Lawrence was a well-known artist who painted famous African Americans. Anna "Grandma" Moses painted images of what she called "old-timey" farm life.

Some novels offered an escape from the depression. *Gone With the Wind*, the best-selling novel by **Margaret Mitchell**, let readers leave their own troubles behind. Readers followed the adventures of Scarlett O'Hara, a once wealthy woman raised on a southern plantation. In the novel, Scarlett tries to rebuild her family's fortune after the Civil War and Reconstruction. Many readers could relate to her drive to triumph over hard times.

✔ **Reading Check: Summarizing** Identify and describe some major works of art and literature of the 1930s.

That's Interesting!

The Book that Almost Wasn't
Did you know that Margaret Mitchell almost did not give her book *Gone With the Wind* to a publisher? It's true! She had finished most of the book by 1929. However, she lacked confidence in her work. "I know good writing, and I don't think mine good," she once said. Mitchell finally decided to give the book to an agent in 1935. The novel was enormously successful, selling as many as 50,000 copies in one day. Mitchell also won the Pulitzer Prize for her work. She later sold the movie rights for $50,000—a large sum of money at the time.

Big band leaders such as Duke Ellington (shown here with members of his band), Count Basie, and Benny Goodman helped swing music sweep the nation.

Popular Entertainment

Many Americans used music to lift their spirits. Jazz remained popular during the Great Depression. Millions of Americans enjoyed dancing to the fast rhythms of a new jazz style called swing. Americans also drew inspiration and comfort from another traditional form of African American music—gospel. The vocal styles and religious messages of gospel became very popular during the 1930s. Mahalia Jackson was one of the most popular gospel singers.

Folk music, particularly the work of singer and songwriter **Woody Guthrie**, also touched Americans. Guthrie's songs were tales of loss and struggle. One song had the line, "All along your green valley I'll work till I die"—a grim reality for some Americans.

Radio shows also offered low-cost entertainment. Popular shows included *Little Orphan Annie*, *The Lone Ranger*, and *The Shadow*. Humorist **Will Rogers** had a popular radio show during the early days of the depression.

Many people escaped the depression through movies. Some of these films were serious, such as Pare Lorentz's documentaries on the Dust Bowl and the Tennessee Valley region. However, most movies were produced strictly to entertain. Historical costume dramas, cartoons, comedies, and musicals were all popular. Movies, along with music and radio shows, helped Americans live through the Great Depression.

✔ **Reading Check: Analyzing Information** How did Americans use entertainment to escape their worries during the depression?

Section 3 Review

go.hrw.com Homework Practice Online keyword: SC3 HP24

1. **Identify** and explain:
   - Dust Bowl
   - Eleanor Roosevelt
   - Marian Anderson
   - John Steinbeck
   - Dorothea Lange
   - Margaret Mitchell
   - Woody Guthrie
   - Will Rogers

2. **Summarizing** Copy the graphic organizer below. Use it to identify the effects of the Great Depression on families and farmers.

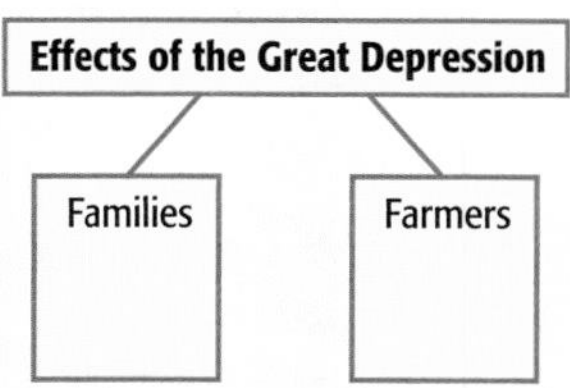

3. **Finding the Main Idea**
   a. How did farmers try to cope with the problems that they faced during the depression?
   b. How did New Deal programs support the arts?

4. **Writing and Critical Thinking**
   Identifying Cause and Effect Imagine that you are a present-day farmer whose family has been on the Great Plains for years. You have been asked to visit a local high school to talk about the Dust Bowl. Prepare a brief report on the Dust Bowl. Create a diagram showing the factors that created it and the effects it had. Assess the possibility of it occurring today.

   Consider the following:
   - environmental factors
   - farming practices
   - foreclosures

CONNECTING TO

Literature

For writing The Grapes of Wrath, *John Steinbeck won a Pulitzer Prize. The novel describes the hardships and suffering some Americans experienced during the 1930s.*

The Grapes of Wrath

John Steinbeck

John Steinbeck's The Grapes of Wrath *was published in 1939. The novel describes the Joad family's struggle during the Great Depression. After losing their farm in Oklahoma, the Joads travel to California. They find hard, miserable work as migrant farm laborers. In the following excerpt, the Joads prepare to leave their own farm.*

Now they were ready. Granma . . . saying, "What's all this? What you doin' now, so early?" But she was dressed and agreeable. And Ruthie and Winfield were awake, but quiet with the pressure of tiredness and still half dreaming. . . . And the movement of the family stopped. They stood about, **reluctant**[1] to make the first active move to go. They were afraid, now that the time had come—afraid in the same way Grampa was afraid.

And Tom shook himself free of the **numbness**[2]. . . . "We got to get goin." And the others came out of their numbness and moved toward the truck.

"Come on," Tom said. "Let's get Grampa on." Pa and Uncle John and Tom and Al went into the kitchen where Grampa slept. . . . They took him under the elbows and lifted him to his feet, and he grumbled and cursed thickly. . . . Out the door they boosted him, and when they came to the truck Tom and Al climbed up, . . . hooked their hands under his arms and lifted him gently up, and laid him on top of the load.

They got into the cab, and then the rest swarmed up on top of the load. Connie and Rose of Sharon, Pa and Uncle John, Ruthie and Winfield, Tom and the preacher. Noah stood on the ground, looking up at the great load of them sitting on top of the truck. . . . Noah said, "How about the dogs, Pa?"

"I forgot the dogs," Pa said. He whistled shrilly, and one bouncing dog ran in, but only one. Noah caught him and threw him up on the top, where he sat **rigid**[3] and shivering at the height. "Got to leave the other two," Pa called. "Muley, will you look after 'em some? See they don't starve?"

"Yeah," said Muley. "I'll like to have a couple dogs. Yeah! I'll take 'em."

"Take them chickens, too," Pa said.

Al got into the driver's seat. The starter whirred and caught. . . . And then the loose roar of the six cylinders and a blue smoke behind. "So long, Muley," Al called.

And the family called, "Good-by, Muley."

---

[1]**reluctant:** unwilling
[2]**numbness:** dullness or shock
[3]**rigid:** stiff

Understanding What You Read

1. **Literature and History** How does John Steinbeck's *The Grapes of Wrath* reflect the everyday experiences of some people during the depression?
2. **Literature and You** How would you feel if you were faced with the Joads' situation?

Section 4

The Rise of Totalitarianism

Read to Discover

1. How did President Roosevelt deal with Latin America?
2. In what ways did different dictators take power in Latin America and Europe during the Great Depression?
3. What were the areas that Italy, Germany, and Japan took over in the 1930s?

Define

- totalitarianism
- fascism

Identify

- Good Neighbor policy
- Benito Mussolini
- Blackshirts
- Adolf Hitler
- Nazis
- Axis Powers
- *Kristallnacht*

Why It Matters Today

The U.S. relationship with Latin America remains important to American economic and security interests. Use CNNfyi.com or other **current events** sources to identify a recent political or economic tie or event that involved both the United States and one or more Latin American countries. Record your findings in your journal.

The Story Continues

The Great Depression touched the entire world. In the tiny Central American country of El Salvador, for example, the economy depended heavily on a single crop—coffee. Coffee prices fell so low that for most growers, harvesting the beans was not worth the effort. One person wrote that "the country became permeated [filled] with the sick-sweet smell of rotting coffee fruits." In this and other hard-hit countries, economic disaster led to political unrest and even to revolt.

Coffee was an important cash crop for some developing countries.

Latin America

During the 1930s President Roosevelt often used economic influence rather than military force in Latin America. This policy, along with more trade and cultural exchanges, helped improve U.S. ties with Latin America.

Roosevelt's Latin American policy was to make the United States a "good neighbor—the neighbor who . . . respects the rights of others." As part of his **Good Neighbor policy**, Roosevelt canceled the Platt Amendment, which the United States had used to intervene in Cuban affairs. He also gave up the U.S. government's right to intervene in Panama and withdrew marines who had been stationed in Haiti since 1915.

The United States still had a great deal of economic and political influence in Latin America. The region was hard hit by the depression. Describing El Salvador, a U.S. diplomat noted a problem shared by many Latin American countries.

"There is practically no middle class between the very rich and the poor. Roughly 90 percent of the wealth of the country is held by about one-half of one percent of the population. . . . The [rest of the] population has practically nothing."

—Major A. R. Harris, quoted in *The Good Neighbor,* by George Black

Analyzing Primary Sources

Making Generalizations and Predictions What problems do you think this extreme difference in wealth might cause?

In the 1920s these conditions led to a civil war in Nicaragua that continued despite U.S. intervention. President Hoover withdrew the last U.S. troops from Nicaragua in 1933. In 1937 General Anastasio Somoza took power and ruled as a dictator. Dictators also took over in Cuba, El Salvador, and Guatemala during the 1930s.

In Mexico, President Lázaro Cárdenas put the oil industry under government control in 1938. British and American oil companies operating in Mexico protested, but the United States did not intervene. Eventually Mexico agreed to pay the oil companies for their property.

✔ **Reading Check: Summarizing** How did the U.S. relationship with Latin America change in the 1930s?

Empires in Europe and Asia

Harsh new governments also came to power in Europe. European economies still recovering from World War I were devastated by the global depression. In response, nations such as Italy and Germany moved toward **totalitarianism**, a political system in which the government controls every aspect of citizens' lives.

Italy had been on the winning side in World War I but had gained little land. The country also suffered economic difficulties after the war. Frustrated with these problems, Italians sought strong leadership. They found it in former journalist and soldier **Benito Mussolini**.

In 1922 Mussolini and his followers, called **Blackshirts** after their uniform color, marched on Rome and took over the city. Soon after, Mussolini established a government based on the political theory of **fascism**. In fascism, a single person leads the "state"—or government—which is seen as more important than individuals.

In October 1935 Mussolini conquered the African country of Ethiopia and made it a colony. Favoring isolationism, the United States stayed out of the conflict.

Germany was even harder hit by the terms and reparations required by the Treaty of Versailles. When the global depression caused Germany's

The Italian king granted Mussolini, shown here giving a speech, "temporary" dictatorial powers in 1922. Mussolini kept these powers for more than 20 years.

Interpreting the Visual Record

The Third Reich *The Nazis used large, elaborate parades to encourage feelings of national pride and gain support for their plans.* ***How does this photograph suggest the military emphasis of the Nazi government?***

economy to collapse, World War I veteran and politician **Adolf Hitler** began to gain a following. In his book *Mein Kampf (My Struggle)*, Hitler blamed Communists, intellectuals, and particularly Jews for Germany's defeat in World War I and for its later problems. He also described his plans for Germany's rise to regional and global power.

In 1932 members of Hitler's National Socialist Party, or **Nazis**, won 37 percent of the vote in national elections. The next year Hitler became the German Chancellor. Soon he took dictatorial power and formed the Third Reich, a hostile new German empire. Violating the Treaty of Versailles, Hitler rebuilt the army and moved to occupy the Rhineland. In 1936 Germany and Italy formed a military alliance called the **Axis Powers.**

The Nazis banned Jews and non-Nazis from government positions, deprived Jews of their citizenship, and destroyed or seized their property. In September 1935 the government assigned Jews a lower class of citizenship. On November 9, 1938, Nazis went on a rampage called ***Kristallnacht***, or the "night of broken glass." That night, throughout Germany and Austria, 91 Jews were killed, and hundreds more were seriously injured. Some 7,500 Jewish businesses were demolished, and some 200 synagogues were damaged. Nazi persecution of Jews rose after *Kristallnacht.*

Japan also used military force to solve its economic problems. The country's military leaders wanted to seize new territories to gain control of additional natural resources and lower Japan's reliance on foreign imports. In 1931 Japan invaded Manchuria in northern China. Though the League of Nations and the United States formally condemned the invasion, no one wanted to fight a war to undo it. Japan also began a huge naval buildup, directly violating its pledge at the Washington Conference in the early 1920s. By 1937 Japan occupied much of northern China. In the late 1930s the United States spoke out against Japan's aggression. However, most Americans feared another world war and opposed using force to stop Japan.

✔ **Reading Check: Summarizing** What Japanese actions led to growing global tensions, and how?

On December 12, 1937, Japanese planes sank the U.S. gunboat Panay. *President Roosevelt demanded and received an apology and payment for damages. War was avoided for the moment.*

2 CENTS Chicago Daily Tribune FINAL

JAPANESE SINK U. S. GUNBOAT

Convicts Defy Governor; Kill Guard

1 DEAD, 18 MISSING, 54 SAVED AS BOMBS WRECK SHIP AIDING NANKING YANKS

Roosevelt's Response

President Roosevelt faced a difficult situation when confronting the expansion of Germany, Italy, and Japan. He opposed military aggression but wanted to avoid war. Thus Roosevelt tried to maintain a balance between stopping aggression and keeping the United States at peace. This approach met with only limited success.

Most Americans favored a foreign policy of isolationism. Few wanted to risk repeating the horrors of World War I. Some Americans, such as Quakers and Mennonites, were pacifists who opposed war for any reason. Others argued that the Axis Powers did not truly pose a great danger to national security or world peace. In the late 1930s Congress even passed four Neutrality Acts intended to keep the United States out of international conflicts. These acts prevented the U.S. government from shipping arms to nations at war or to groups involved in civil wars.

Some Americans wanted to stop the expansion of Germany, Italy, and Japan. They feared that a slow response would only encourage these nations to take more land. By 1937 even Roosevelt was concerned. "The epidemic of world lawlessness is spreading," he warned. The threat of war seemed increasingly real.

Interpreting Political Cartoons

The threat of war *Military aggression by nations such as Japan greatly concerned U.S. politicians.* ***What agreements are the Japanese shown destroying in this cartoon?***

✔ **Reading Check: Supporting a Point of View** What do you think was the key cause of the rising global conflict? Why?

Section 4 Review

go.hrw.com Homework Practice Online
keyword: SC3 HP24

1. **Define** and explain:
   - totalitarianism
   - fascism
2. **Identify** and explain:
   - Good Neighbor policy
   - Benito Mussolini
   - Blackshirts
   - Adolf Hitler
   - Nazis
   - Axis Powers
   - *Kristallnacht*
3. **Analyzing Information** Copy the graphic organizer below. Use it to show how different dictators gained power during the 1930s.

Ruler	Region	How They Came to Power

4. **Finding the Main Idea**
   a. What was President Roosevelt's Latin American policy?
   b. Which areas did Italy, Germany, and Japan seize during the 1930s?
5. **Writing and Critical Thinking**
   Supporting a Point of View Imagine that you are a government adviser in Italy or Germany in the early 1930s. Write a letter advising your superior to establish an alliance with your former enemy. (Italy and Germany had fought on opposite sides in World War I.)
   Consider the following:
   - postwar grievances
   - economic conditions
   - political similarities

Chapter 24 Review

The Chapter at a Glance

Examine the visual summary of the chapter below. Create a five-question multiple-choice quiz covering the chapter's main ideas that you might give to a classmate.

Hard Times

The Crash of 1929 marked an economic collapse. Millions of people were unemployed. Events such as the Dust Bowl made life even harder for struggling farmers.

New Deal

President Roosevelt's administration began the New Deal, a series of federal relief efforts. Congress passed relief measures such as the Agricultural Adjustment Acts and the Federal Emergency Relief Administration.

Trouble Abroad

Economic troubles in nations such as Germany, Italy, and Japan aided the rise of military dictatorships that threatened world peace.

Identifying People and Ideas

Use the following terms or people in historically significant sentences.

1. bull market
2. Bonus Army
3. New Deal
4. fireside chats
5. Social Security Act
6. Frances Perkins
7. Dust Bowl
8. totalitarianism
9. fascism
10. *Kristallnacht*

Understanding Main Ideas

Section 1 *(Pages 732–736)*

1. Describe the state of the stock market prior to the crash.

Section 2 *(Pages 737–743)*

2. What New Deal programs did lawmakers create during the Hundred Days?
3. How did Americans benefit from the New Deal?

Section 3 *(Pages 744–748)*

4. What were the effects of the depression on farmers, and how did they cope?
5. In what ways did the government support the arts during the depression?

Section 4 *(Pages 750–753)*

6. What factors helped dictators gain power in Latin America and Europe?

You Be the Historian—Reviewing Themes

1. **Economics** What were the major causes of the Great Depression?
2. **Constitutional Heritage** How did Roosevelt's presidency affect the balance of power among the three branches of government?
3. **Global Relations** How did economic troubles in the United States affect other nations?

Thinking Critically

1. **Contrasting** What were the differences between President Hoover's and President Roosevelt's efforts to fight the depression?
2. **Analyzing Information** Why did African Americans support the New Deal, even though some of its programs discriminated against them?
3. **Supporting a Point of View** Do you think that the New Deal was successful? Explain your answer.

Interpreting Charts

Study the chart below. Then use the information on the chart to answer the questions that follow.

The Crash

Company	High Price Sept. 3, 1929	Low Price Nov. 13, 1929
American Telephone and Telegraph	304	197 1/4
General Electric	396 1/4	168 1/8
General Motors	72 3/4	36
Montgomery Ward	137 7/8	49 1/4
U.S. Steel	261 3/4	150
Woolworth	100 3/8	52 1/4

Source: Frederick Lewis Allen, *Only Yesterday*

1. Which of the following stocks lost the most points between September 3 and November 13, 1929?
   a. American Telephone and Telegraph
   b. General Electric
   c. General Motors
   d. U.S. Steel
2. Based on this chart and your knowledge of the time period, how do you think the losses by these companies would affect the national economy?

Analyzing Primary Sources

Read the following quotation by Clara Hancox, who was 11 years old when the Great Depression began, and then answer the questions that follow.

> **"My father walked the streets every day. . . . My mother went to work, and I even worked, playing the piano for dancing class on Saturday mornings for fifty cents an hour. My mother would find a few pennies and we would go to the greengrocer and wait until he threw out the stuff that was beginning to rot. We could pick out the best rotted potato and greens and carrots that were already soft. Then we would go to the butcher and beg [for] a marrow bone. And then with the few pennies we would buy a box of barley, and we'd have soup to last us for three or four days. I remember she would say to me sometimes, 'You go out and do it. I'm ashamed.'"**

3. Which of the following statements best describes the feelings of Clara's mother about the lifestyle they had to lead?
   a. She was proud of the family's resourcefulness in providing for its members.
   b. She was angry at the government for not providing greater relief.
   c. She was sometimes ashamed by the family's need to beg for food.
   d. She was optimistic that good times would soon come.
4. Based on your knowledge of the period, do you think the experience of Clara's family was typical or unusual during the Great Depression? Explain your answer.

Alternative Assessment

Building Your Portfolio

Cooperative Learning

Complete the following activity in small groups. Imagine that you and your classmates are advisers to FDR during the Great Depression. You have discovered that farmers cannot afford to ship their crops to market. People in cities need food but cannot afford to buy it. Propose a New Deal program that will meet the needs of each group. You might also create posters and brochures to advertise your New Deal program.

internet connect

Internet Activity: go.hrw.com
keyword: SC3 CF24

Choose an activity on the Great Depression to:

- Learn about the WPA and create a mural.
- Learn about Social Security and the Second New Deal.
- Research conditions during the depression and write a journal entry taking the point of view of people affected by it.

Connecting to Geography

The Global Depression

Although it began in the United States, the Great Depression soon became a global economic disaster. The economies of many nations were badly shaken. Industrial and agricultural production fell, and millions of people lost their jobs. Many people lost their entire savings.

As the depression deepened, the economies of many countries kept shrinking. Unemployment rates skyrocketed. In the United States, more than 20 percent of the labor force was out of work by 1932. Some other nations suffered even higher unemployment. The average amount of money people earned was cut nearly in half.

In the United States and many other countries, governments increased spending to help the unemployed and the poor. Yet the depression did not end until the onset of World War II, when wartime production increased employment.

A World in Crisis

In many countries the saw their gross national product (GNP) fell dramatically during the depression. GNP is the total value of all goods and services produced by a country in one year. To make matters worse, unemployment rates soared.

Decline in Gross National Product, 1929–1932

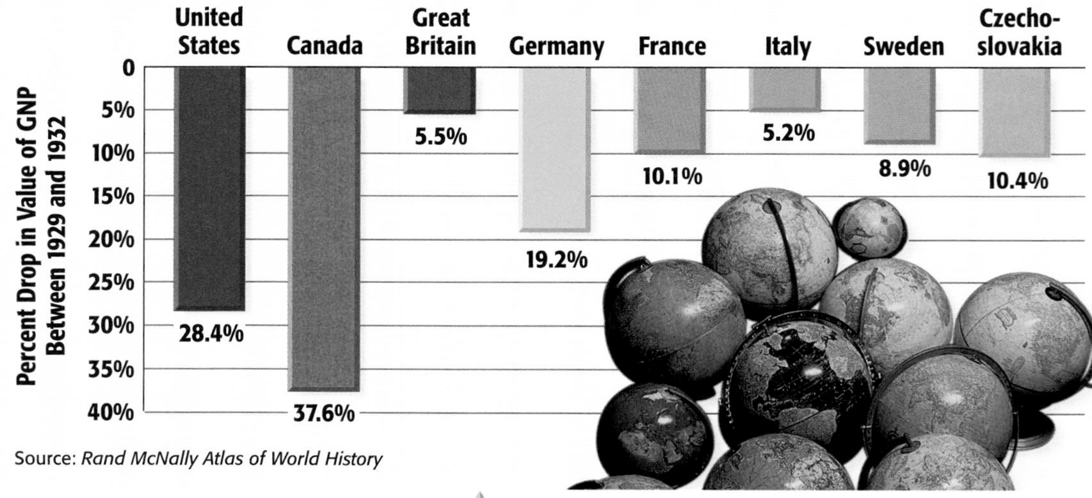

Source: *Rand McNally Atlas of World History*

Geography **Skills**

Interpreting Bar Graphs

1. **Human Systems** How much did the U.S. GNP fall between 1929 and 1932?
2. **Contrasting** Which country's GNP fell the most between 1929 and 1932? Which country's GNP fell the least?

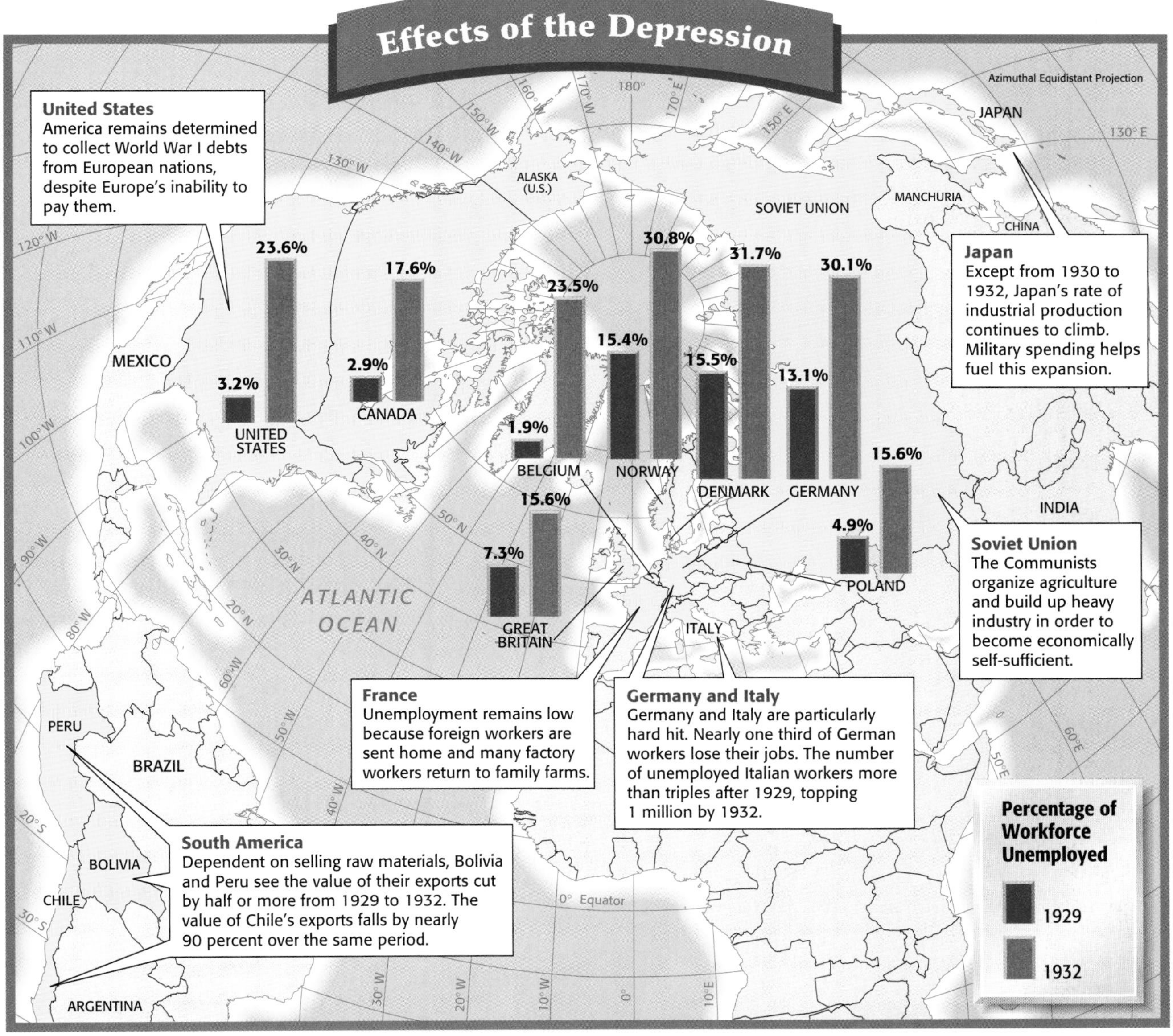

Effects of the Depression

Azimuthal Equidistant Projection

United States
America remains determined to collect World War I debts from European nations, despite Europe's inability to pay them.

Japan
Except from 1930 to 1932, Japan's rate of industrial production continues to climb. Military spending helps fuel this expansion.

Soviet Union
The Communists organize agriculture and build up heavy industry in order to become economically self-sufficient.

France
Unemployment remains low because foreign workers are sent home and many factory workers return to family farms.

Germany and Italy
Germany and Italy are particularly hard hit. Nearly one third of German workers lose their jobs. The number of unemployed Italian workers more than triples after 1929, topping 1 million by 1932.

South America
Dependent on selling raw materials, Bolivia and Peru see the value of their exports cut by half or more from 1929 to 1932. The value of Chile's exports falls by nearly 90 percent over the same period.

Percentage of Workforce Unemployed

Country	1929	1932
UNITED STATES	3.2%	23.6%
CANADA	2.9%	17.6%
BELGIUM	1.9%	23.5%
NORWAY	15.4%	30.8%
DENMARK	15.5%	31.7%
GERMANY	13.1%	30.1%
POLAND	4.9%	15.6%
GREAT BRITAIN	7.3%	15.6%

ALASKA (U.S.) · SOVIET UNION · JAPAN · MANCHURIA · CHINA · INDIA · MEXICO · ITALY · ATLANTIC OCEAN · PERU · BRAZIL · BOLIVIA · CHILE · ARGENTINA · 0° Equator

Geography Skills

Interpreting Thematic Maps

1. How were some South American nations affected by the depression?
2. Which country had the greatest increase in unemployment from 1929 to 1932?
3. **Places and Regions** By 1932, what three countries had more than 30 percent of their workforce unemployed?
4. **Evaluating** How did France and Japan avoid some of the problems of the global depression?

While traveling around Britain in search of work, this man lived in this mobile home he built.

The Depression in the United States

In addition to increasing unemployment and lowering GNP, the depression left people with less money to purchase goods. Increased government spending helped the economy recover, but it could not relieve all of the country's economic problems.

Average Income per Person, 1929–1939

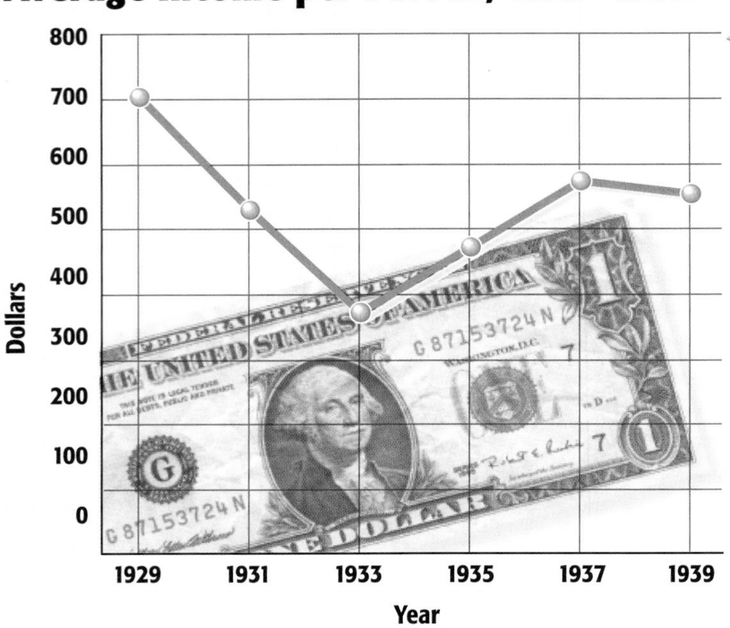

Source: *Datapedia of the United States, 1790–2000: America Year by Year*

Geography Skills
Interpreting Line Graphs

1. In which year shown on this graph was the average income per person highest? Lowest?
2. **Analyzing Information** What happened to the average income per person between 1935 and 1939?

History Note 1

How much Americans earned largely depended on where they lived. Workers in the Lower South, for example, generally earned far less than the national average in 1929. The average Mississippian earned only about $216 in 1940. This amount was about one third of the national average of $593 a year. The average worker in Alabama, Arkansas, and South Carolina earned about $300 or less in 1940.

Some unemployed workers earned money selling apples on street corners.

History Note 2

About 1.5 million Americans were out of work in 1929. That number grew rapidly to about 12 million in 1932. Nearly 10 million Americans were still out of work when World War II broke out in Europe in 1939. During World War II, millions of American civilians found jobs in factories and plants producing war goods.

Growth in Federal Spending, 1928–1940

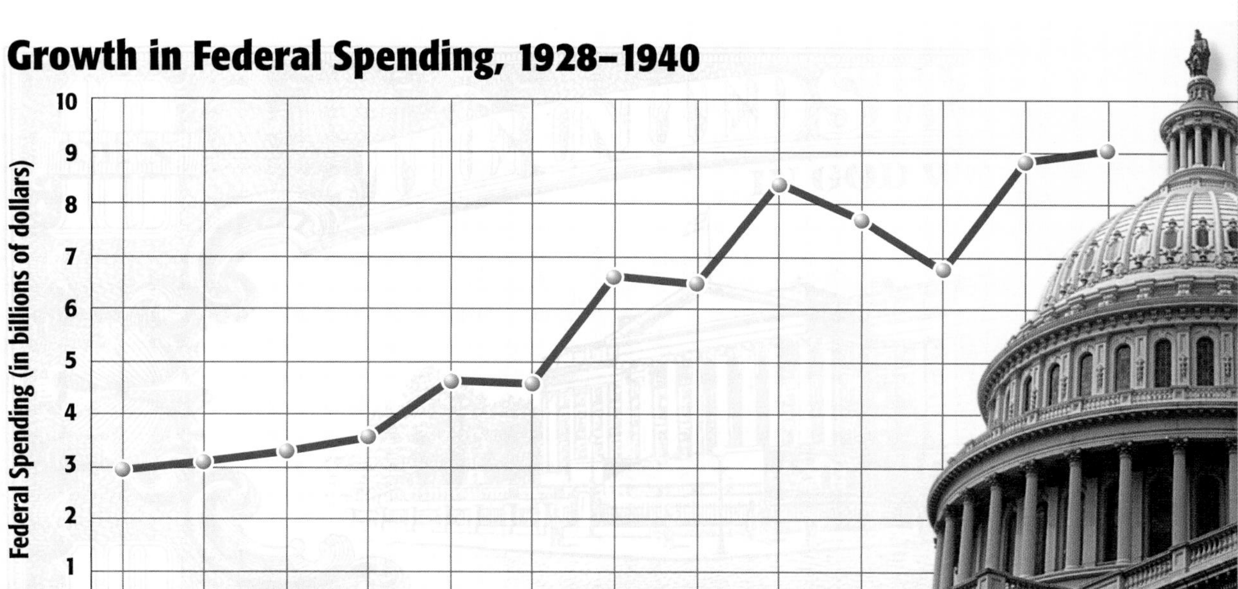

Source: *Historical Statistics of the United States*

Geography **Skills**

Interpreting Line Graphs

1. About how much more did the U.S. government spend in 1940 than it did in 1929?
2. What happened to U.S. government spending in 1937, 1938, and 1939?
3. **Drawing Inferences and Conclusions** Look at the Average Income per Person graph on page 758. Write a brief report describing the relationship between federal spending and average income from 1935 to 1939.

History Note 3

Under President Franklin D. Roosevelt's New Deal programs, the federal government gradually spent more money each year to pull the country out of the depression. The unemployment rate did drop—from 25 percent in 1933 to some 14 percent in 1937—but not as much as was necessary to pull the nation out of the depression. The economy weakened again in 1937 and 938, causing unemployment to rise and contributing to still higher federal spending.

The depression left many Americans struggling to find enough to eat.

CHAPTER

25 World War II

(1938–1945)

The USS Shaw *explodes in Pearl Harbor after being bombed by Japanese planes.*

The character Rosie the Riveter became a symbol of female workers' contributions to the war effort.

UNITED STATES

1941 Congress passes the Lend-Lease Act in March.

On December 7, Japanese planes bomb Pearl Harbor. Congress declares war the next day.

1938	1939	1940	1941

WORLD

1939 Germany and the Soviet Union sign a nonaggression pact on August 23.

On September 1 Germany invades Poland and starts World War II.

1940 Winston Churchill is elected prime minister of Great Britain on May 10.

On June 10 Italy declares war on France and Britain.

In August German planes begin bombing London.

1941 German troops invade the Soviet Union.

Russian and German soldiers fight among destroyed buildings in the Battle of Stalingrad.

Build on What You Know

During the 1930s, the United States and much of the world struggled with problems caused by a deep economic depression. Many Americans faced hard times. In Europe and Asia, new dictatorships rose to power and began to expand their territories. As conflict overseas continued, the United States prepared for war.

More than 155,000 Allied troops landed in France during the D-Day invasion on June 6, 1944.

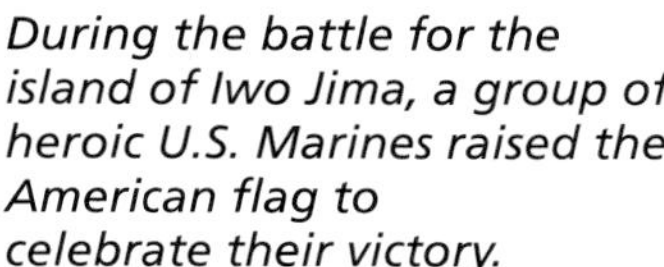

During the battle for the island of Iwo Jima, a group of heroic U.S. Marines raised the American flag to celebrate their victory.

1942 In March the U.S. government begins moving Japanese Americans to internment camps.

In May U.S. forces in the Philippines surrender to the Japanese.

In June U.S. planes sink four Japanese aircraft carriers in the Battle of Midway.

1943 The musical *Oklahoma!* opens in March and is a huge hit.

In June the zoot-suit riots take place in Los Angeles.

1944 On June 6, Allied troops storm German defenses on the beaches of Normandy, France.

In October U.S. forces defeat a Japanese fleet in the Battle of Leyte Gulf, the largest naval battle in history.

1945 A U.S. warplane drops an atomic bomb on Hiroshima, Japan, on August 6. On August 9 a second atomic bomb is dropped on Nagasaki, Japan.

1942 **1943** **1944** **1945**

1942 British general Bernard Montgomery defeats German general Erwin Rommel at the Battle of El Alamein in Egypt.

1943 In January the German invasion of the Soviet Union is finally turned back at Stalingrad.

Italy surrenders to the Allies in September, but German forces occupy the country and continue fighting.

1944 On July 1, delegates from 44 nations meet at Bretton Woods, New Hampshire, to establish an international agreement on banking, exchange rates, and trade.

1945 Germany surrenders to the Allies on May 7.

Japan formally surrenders to the Allies on September 2.

If you were there . . .

Would you support getting involved in a war while the nation faces a depression?

You Be the Historian

What's Your Opinion? Do you **agree** or **disagree** with the following statements? Support your point of view in your journal.

- **Citizenship** Involvement in a foreign war changes the way a government treats its citizens.
- **Economics** Fighting a war always hurts a nation's economy.
- **Global Relations** Conflicts between nations never affect neutral parties.

Section 1

World War II Begins

Read to Discover

1. What parts of Europe did Germany control by mid-1940?
2. How did President Roosevelt aid Great Britain while preserving U.S. neutrality?
3. What events led to the conflict between the United States and Japan?

Define

- appeasement
- nonaggression pact

Identify

- Munich Conference
- Winston Churchill
- Allied Powers
- Blitzkrieg
- Maginot Line
- Battle of Britain
- Lend-Lease Act
- Battle of the Atlantic
- Atlantic Charter

Why It Matters Today

Although most nations try to solve their problems without going to war, disagreements between countries still arise. Use CNNfyi.com or other **current events** sources to find out about an international conflict in the world today. Record your findings in your journal.

A German tank

The Story Continues

On the night of August 31, 1939, German troops disguised as Polish soldiers attacked a German radio station located on the Polish border. Their mission was to stage an incident that the German government could use to justify an invasion of Poland. Within hours, German forces began streaming across the Polish border in response to this "attack."

Hitler's War Machine

Adolf Hitler had long dreamed of revenge for Germany's defeat in World War I. In 1936 he stationed German troops in the Rhineland, thereby violating the Treaty of Versailles. Two years later, Hitler forced Austria to unite with Germany. Still concerned with their own economic problems during the Great Depression, many countries ignored Hitler's actions. But in 1938 Hitler called for Czechoslovakia to turn over the Sudetenland (soo-DAYT-uhn-land)—an area with many ethnic Germans—to Germany. When the Czechs refused the demand, Hitler threatened war.

At the **Munich Conference** in September 1938, France and Great Britain gave the Sudetenland to Germany. British politician **Winston Churchill** was outraged by this act of **appeasement**—giving in to an aggressor to keep peace. He said, "The government had to choose between shame and war. They have chosen shame and they will get war." Churchill was right. Hitler took the rest of Czechoslovakia in March 1939. He then demanded that Poland return the city of Danzig (what is now Gdańsk), which had been part of Germany until World War I.

✔ **Reading Check: Drawing Inferences and Conclusions** Why did Churchill think that appeasement would lead Britain into war against Germany?

Research on the ROM

Free Find:
Winston Churchill
After reading about Winston Churchill on the **Holt Researcher CD–ROM**, create a sketch of a memorial to honor Churchill's inspiring leadership during World War II.

The Fighting Begins

Great Britain and France responded to Hitler's demands by pledging to defend Poland. Hitler secretly negotiated a **nonaggression pact** with Soviet leader Joseph Stalin in August 1939. The Soviet Union and Germany agreed not to attack one another and to divide Poland between them. Germany invaded Poland on September 1, 1939. World War II had begun. Two days later, Britain and France—known as the **Allied Powers**—declared war against Germany.

German forces attacked Poland in a **Blitzkrieg**, a new kind of "lightning war." The Blitzkrieg concentrated airplanes and tanks in strategic areas to break through enemy lines. German troops stormed across the Polish border from the west, and soon afterward the Soviets invaded from the east. By the end of the month, the two armies occupied Poland.

Meanwhile, Britain and France began to mobilize their armed forces. The French gathered their troops behind the **Maginot Line**, a fortified line of defenses along its border with Germany. In April 1940, German troops occupied Denmark and invaded Norway. In May, Germany took Belgium, Luxembourg, and the Netherlands. This allowed German troops to bypass the Maginot Line and invade France from the northeast. Belgian, British, and French soldiers were trapped at the French port of Dunkirk and had to escape to Britain.

Interpreting the Visual Record

Dunkirk *Hundreds of ships, including many privately owned boats, helped rescue some 330,000 Allied soldiers from the French port of Dunkirk between May 26 and June 4, 1940.* ***How does this image show the scale and the danger of the rescue effort?***

Interpreting the Visual Record

The blitz *In August 1940 the Luftwaffe began bombing London. These raids, which continued into the spring of 1941, destroyed much of the city. However, St. Paul's Cathedral, shown in the background, survived.* ***How might such attacks challenge a nation's willingness to continue fighting?***

Hitler's forces advanced on the French capital, Paris, in June 1940. At the same time, Italy joined Germany and declared war on the Allied Powers. Together, Italy and Germany were known as the Axis Powers. On June 22, France surrendered to Germany. In central France, a German-controlled French government was established in the city of Vichy. Based in London, French general Charles de Gaulle (gohl) formed a Free French army that fought alongside other Allied troops.

With France defeated, Hitler prepared to invade Britain. But Germany first needed to defeat the British Royal Air Force (RAF). In July 1940 the Luftwaffe—the German air force—began to attack RAF airfields and aircraft. For months the two sides fought for control of the skies in the **Battle of Britain**. With the help of a new invention called radar, which detected enemy aircraft, the RAF won. Hitler canceled his invasion plans in mid-September. Winston Churchill, now British prime minister, expressed his nation's gratitude to the RAF pilots. "Never in the field of human conflict was so much owed by so many to so few."

✔ **Reading Check: Finding the Main Idea** Who won the Battle of Britain, and why was it important?

U.S. Neutrality

Although most Americans opposed Hitler, they did not want to fight in a European war. Some Americans, like Charles Lindbergh, favored isolationism. However, in 1939 Congress approved the "cash-and-carry" system to let the Allies buy U.S. war supplies. The Allies had to pay cash for the weapons and carry them back to Europe on their own ships. Roosevelt also sent 50 U.S. destroyers to Great Britain in exchange for 99-year leases on several British naval bases in the Caribbean.

As the war continued in Europe, Franklin D. Roosevelt decided to break with tradition and run for a third term as president in 1940. The Republicans chose lawyer Wendell Willkie to run against him. Most Americans chose to stick with the leader they knew, and Roosevelt won an easy victory. He had promised during the election campaign that "your boys are not going to be sent into any foreign wars." Even so, Roosevelt knew that a German victory would be a disaster for America.

Analyzing Primary Sources

Drawing Inferences and Conclusions What role did Franklin Roosevelt think the United States should play in the war?

"[I]t is no exaggeration to say that all of us in the Americas would be living at the point of a gun. . . . We must be the great arsenal [arms supplier] of democracy."

—President Roosevelt, quoted in *The Reluctant Belligerent,* by Robert A. Divine

Roosevelt again asked Congress to increase U.S. aid to the Allies. In March 1941 Congress passed the **Lend-Lease Act**. This law allowed the president to loan $7 billion worth of weapons and supplies to Britain. In June, Hitler broke the nonaggression pact and invaded the Soviet Union. Roosevelt then gave Lend-Lease aid to the Soviets.

As U.S. aid to Great Britain increased, Germany tried to cut Britain off from the United States completely. This plan resulted in a long fight to control the ocean trade routes, called the **Battle of the Atlantic**. German U-boats sank many Allied cargo ships. In response, the Allies organized their cargo ships into convoys, or protective groups. The U.S. Navy began escorting the convoys toward Europe as far as Iceland.

In August, Roosevelt and Prime Minister Winston Churchill signed the **Atlantic Charter**, in which they agreed to work for peace after the war ended. Just a month later, a German U-boat fired on a U.S. destroyer. When Roosevelt ordered U.S. forces to "shoot on sight" any threatening submarines, war with Germany seemed certain.

✔ **Reading Check: Identifying Cause and Effect** Why did the U.S. Navy escort ships across the Atlantic, and how did this affect U.S.-German relations?

World War II in Europe, 1939–1941

Interpreting Maps Within two years of unleashing its Blitzkrieg in 1939, Germany controlled most of Europe and North Africa.

Skills Assessment **Places and Regions** What European countries remained free from Axis control?

The USS Arizona *memorial at Pearl Harbor stands above the sunken remains of the U.S. battleship. American leaders vowed to avenge the deadly surprise attack.*

Conflict with Japan

Like Germany and Italy, Japan wanted to expand. The Japanese had conquered much of China during the 1930s. Japan officially joined the Axis Powers in 1940, and in 1941 the Japanese seized French Indochina. President Roosevelt froze Japanese funds in the United States and blocked the sale of oil to Japan. U.S. officials also demanded that Japanese troops leave China and French Indochina. These actions angered Japanese leaders.

On December 7, 1941, Japanese planes launched a surprise attack on U.S. forces at Pearl Harbor. One sailor aboard the huge battleship USS *Oklahoma* remembered the attack.

> **"Suddenly the ship lurched! . . . As she rolled over, I was . . . buffeted [knocked] and tossed about. Then the dark waters closed over me as the ship came to rest upside down on the bottom of the harbor."**
>
> —Stephen Bower Young, quoted in *Eyewitness to World War II*, edited by Stephen W. Sears

The Japanese sank or damaged all of the U.S. battleships at Pearl Harbor. That same day, Japan attacked U.S. military bases in the Philippines and on Guam, Midway, and Wake Island.

The attack on Pearl Harbor shocked many Americans. The next day Roosevelt asked Congress to declare war on Japan. He called December 7 "a date which will live in infamy [disgrace]." Germany, an ally of Japan, then declared war on the United States.

✔ **Reading Check: Drawing Inferences and Conclusions** What did Japan hope to accomplish by its attack on Pearl Harbor?

Section 1 Review

go.hrw.com Homework Practice Online
keyword: SC3 HP25

1. **Define** and explain:
   - appeasement
   - nonaggression pact
2. **Identify** and explain:
   - Munich Conference
   - Winston Churchill
   - Allied Powers
   - Blitzkrieg
   - Maginot Line
   - Battle of Britain
   - Lend-Lease Act
   - Battle of the Atlantic
   - Atlantic Charter
3. **Sequencing** Copy the graphic organizer below. Use it to list the major events on the road to war between Japan and the United States in the order that they occurred.

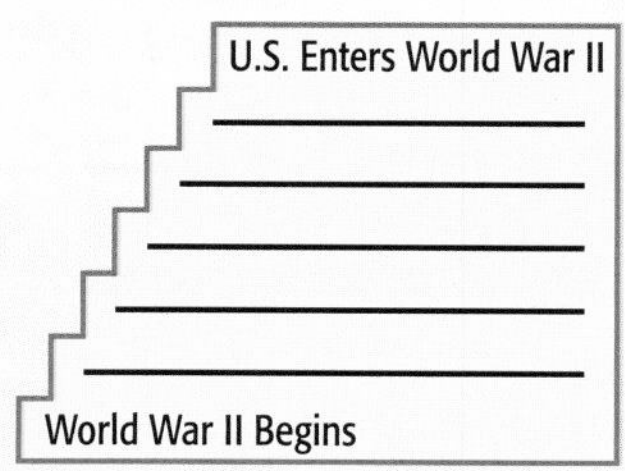

4. **Finding the Main Idea**
   a. How did the United States aid the Allies without sending troops to fight?
   b. What areas in Europe had Germany come to control by the middle of 1940?
5. **Writing and Critical Thinking**
   Evaluating Imagine that you are a historian writing a book on World War II. Write an outline for a chapter that argues for or against the idea that World War II could have been prevented if Britain and France had refused Hitler's demands at the Munich Conference.
   Consider the following:
   - Hitler's desire for revenge
   - Hitler's violations of the Treaty of Versailles
   - the military condition of Britain and France, and the economic problems of the United States

Section 2

Mobilizing for War

Read to Discover

1. How did the United States prepare for World War II?
2. How did women and minorities participate in the war effort, and what effects did World War II have on civilian women and minorities?
3. Why did the U.S. government intern Japanese Americans during the war?

Define

- braceros
- zoot-suit riots
- internment

Identify

- Selective Training and Service Act
- War Production Board
- A. Philip Randolph
- Fair Employment Practices Committee

Why It Matters Today

Fair treatment of workers continues to be a major concern in the United States. Use CNNfyi.com or other **current events** sources to research a government agency that deals with issues of fairness in the workplace. Record your findings in your journal.

The Story Continues

After the United States entered World War II, the government called on Americans to support the war. Many Americans flew flags outside their homes, but patriotism was not enough. The war required everyone to make sacrifices. Civilians were asked to limit their use of canned foods, gasoline, and tires. These and other items were rationed, or restricted because they were needed to supply the troops.

The U.S. government issued ration stamps to citizens for various goods during the war.

Building an Army

The U.S. government had to recruit millions of soldiers for World War II. In 1940 Congress passed the **Selective Training and Service Act**, which started the first peacetime draft in U.S. history. At first, only men between the ages of 21 and 35 had to register. Later, men aged 18 to 45 were included. People with jobs that were an important part of the war effort were excused from the draft. Local draft boards also granted deferments, or postponements of service, for medical or religious reasons.

Some 15 million Americans served in the military. One million African Americans and some 300,000 Mexican Americans formed part

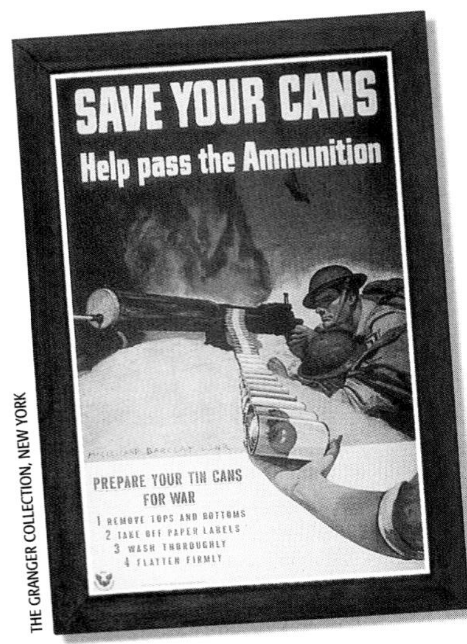

The government encouraged Americans to recycle scrap metal in order to help provide needed materials for weapons and war supplies.

of this group. African American troops faced discrimination in the armed forces and generally served in segregated units. As the war went on, however, they were given more opportunities to serve in infantry, tank, and air force units.

✔ **Reading Check: Finding the Main Idea** What was the purpose of the Selective Training and Service Act of 1940?

The Wartime Economy

The United States was still suffering from the Great Depression when World War II began. However, the economy began to recover as the country mobilized for war. Production boomed as American factories turned out large numbers of guns, jeeps, tanks, and ammunition for the Allies.

Incomes rose, and unemployment nearly vanished. Many Americans, including some rural residents, moved to the North and Midwest to take high-paying factory jobs. Others took shipyard jobs along the West Coast. Even so, agricultural production remained high. U.S. farmers managed to feed European allies as well as Americans.

To prepare the nation for war, the government began to increase its control over the economy. The **War Production Board** (WPB) supervised the conversion of factories to wartime production. For example, the WPB banned the production of cars in 1942 so that automotive plants could focus on making military vehicles and equipment. The Office of War Mobilization (OWM) later replaced the WPB.

To collect necessary supplies such as rubber and metal, the government organized scrap drives. The government also began rationing, or

Helping on the Home Front

During the war Americans found many ways to contribute to the war effort at home.

Women and minority workers

Scrap drives

Winning the War

Wartime rationing

Ration Books

BUY BONDS

War bonds

Visualizing History

1. **Economics** Why would the activities suggested here have been important to the war effort?
2. **Connecting to Today** In what ways do people in your community help each other in a time of crisis?

controlling the amounts of goods available for use. People needed special ration coupons to buy goods such as coffee, gasoline, meat, and shoes. Larger families received more coupons than smaller ones. Rationing was unpopular but did help save key supplies for the war.

Officials knew that Americans had to endure hardships, shortages, and worse—the loss of loved ones. As a result, the government worked hard to keep morale high. The Office of War Information (OWI) kept the public and the press aware of government policies. However, the government limited military reports, such as information about troop movements and casualties. The government also warned Americans about possible German and Japanese spies in the United States. Slogans like "A slip of the lip may sink a ship" became common.

To pay for the war effort, the government drastically increased taxes. For the first time, middle- and lower-income Americans had to pay income taxes. These tax increases only paid 40 percent of the war expenses, however. The government borrowed the difference, mostly by selling war bonds to the public. Movie stars, such as Betty Grable and Loretta Young, encouraged people to buy bonds. Americans bought billions of dollars' worth of bonds to support the war effort.

✔ **Reading Check: Analyzing Information** What wartime developments showed that the U.S. economy was recovering?

That's Interesting!

Fly Girls Did you know that the first time women flew for the U.S. military was during World War II? It's true! From 1942 through 1944, more than 1,000 members of the Women Airforce Service Pilots (WASPs) were trained to fly aircraft across the country. They also tested planes, trained male pilots, and even towed targets for antiaircraft practice. Thirty-eight WASPs died while serving their country. When the WASPs were disbanded in late 1944, General Hap Arnold praised their efforts. "When we needed you, you came through." Despite their contributions, 30 years passed before women were allowed to fly for the military again.

Women and the War Effort

When the United States entered the war, there were many new jobs and not enough workers. The government urged women to fill these new positions. As men left for war, women replaced them in factories and business offices. One female worker recalled her job at Rohr Aircraft.

> **"I was an eager learner, and I soon became an outstanding riveter. At Rohr I worked riveting the boom doors on P-38s [fighter planes]. . . . The war really created opportunities for women. It was the first time we got a chance to show that we could do a lot of things that only men had done before."**
>
> —Winona Espinosa, quoted in *The Homefront,* by Mark Jonathan Harris, Franklin D. Mitchell, and Steven J. Schechter

Although they did the same work as men, women often faced discrimination and received less pay.

Some 300,000 women worked in the armed forces. They served in the Women's Auxiliary Army Corps (WAAC) and the Women Airforce Service Pilots (WASPs). Women's military jobs ranged from helping run military communications systems to flying planes from factories to military units. Army and navy nurses served in combat areas.

✔ **Reading Check: Identifying Cause and Effect** What caused more women to enter the workforce during World War II, and what were the results of this change?

Interpreting the Visual Record

Female workers *The efforts of female workers such as these airplane builders were vital to America's wartime industries.* ***Why would work like that shown below have been important to the war effort?***

Opportunities and Obstacles

The mobilization for war brought new opportunities to minorities. However, as they entered new jobs these groups still sometimes faced unfair treatment. Many African Americans migrated from the South to cities in the North to join the industrial labor force. Once there, they often received less pay than white workers in similar jobs.

To protest this kind of treatment, African American labor leader **A. Philip Randolph** planned a march on Washington, D.C. When President Roosevelt issued an executive order forbidding racial discrimination in defense industries, Randolph agreed to cancel the march. The order created the **Fair Employment Practices Committee** (FEPC) to prevent discrimination in war industries and government jobs. African Americans gained new opportunities in some defense companies, earning better pay than before.

Many Mexican Americans moved to the West Coast and the Midwest to take advantage of wartime job opportunities. To meet a labor shortage in the Southwest, the federal government allowed Mexican workers called **braceros** to enter the United States beginning in 1942. Some 200,000 braceros became a key part of the agricultural economy in the West and the Southwest.

Although they supported the war effort, Mexican Americans still faced discrimination. For example, many young Mexican American men of the time wore zoot suits—outfits with oversized jackets, wide-brimmed hats, and baggy pants that fit tightly at the ankles. In June 1943, groups of sailors in Los Angeles attacked Mexican Americans wearing zoot suits. For several days, mobs roamed the city assaulting Mexican Americans in the so-called **zoot-suit riots**. Riots against Mexican Americans broke out in seven other cities as well.

✔ **Reading Check: Comparing** How was the experience of African Americans similar to the experience of Mexican Americans during the war?

Interpreting the Visual Record

The Tuskegee Airmen *These men are signing up to join the 99th Pursuit Squadron, whose members were nicknamed the Tuskegee Airmen after their training base in Alabama. Formed in 1941, the unit was the first in the U.S. Army Air Corps to allow African Americans to enlist. It served with distinction during the war.* ***Why might this air unit have been a source of pride to African Americans during the war?***

Japanese American Internment

Americans' anger over the Pearl Harbor attack led to widespread discrimination against Japanese Americans. In 1941, more than 125,000 people of Japanese descent lived in the United States, mostly on the West Coast. Some of these immigrants were Issei, or born in Japan. More of them were Nisei, or full citizens who had been born in the United States.

After Pearl Harbor, many Americans questioned the loyalty of Issei and Nisei. Fearing the possibility of spying or sabotage, the U.S. government began a process of **internment** in 1942. Under this system, the government forcibly relocated and imprisoned Japanese Americans. Most Japanese Americans were moved to remote camps and kept under guard. Most of the camps were located in the western United States. One Japanese American woman recalled her experience.

"I remember that sad morning when we realized suddenly that we wouldn't be free. . . . Suddenly you realized that human beings were being put behind fences just like on the farm where we had horses and pigs in corrals."

—Mary Tsukamoto, quoted in *And Justice for All*, edited by John Tateishi

Despite the internment policy, many Japanese Americans volunteered for military service. Many Nisei served in the 442nd Regimental Combat Team. This unit fought in Europe and won many medals for bravery. Other Japanese Americans served as interpreters and translators with military intelligence units in the Pacific campaign.

✔ **Reading Check: Finding the Main Idea** What led to the internment of Japanese Americans, and how did that process affect them?

These Japanese American women are standing outside the barber shop at the internment center in Malheur County, Oregon.

Analyzing Primary Sources

Identifying Points of View What was the reaction of Japanese Americans like this woman to the knowledge that they were to be interned?

Section 2 Review

go.hrw.com **Homework Practice Online** keyword: SC3 HP25

1. **Define** and explain:
   - braceros
   - zoot-suit riots
   - internment
2. **Identify** and explain:
   - Selective Training and Service Act
   - War Production Board
   - A. Philip Randolph
   - Fair Employment Practices Committee
3. **Summarizing** Copy the graphic organizer below. Use it to show how women took part in the war effort.

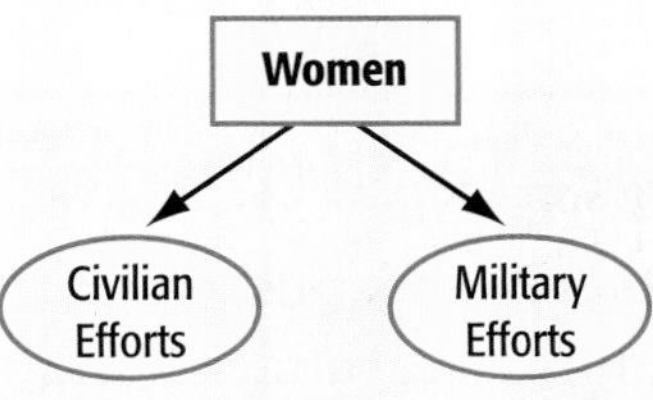

4. **Finding the Main Idea**
   a. How did the war affect African Americans and Mexican Americans?
   b. How did the U.S. government treat Japanese Americans during the war?
5. **Writing and Critical Thinking**
   Supporting a Point of View Imagine that you are an adviser to President Roosevelt as the United States enters World War II. Prepare a memorandum to the president advising him on how the United States should mobilize its resources to fight the war.
   Consider the following:
   - the need for weapons, ammunition, and other vital supplies
   - the costs of fighting the war
   - workforce needs in military and defense-related industries

Section 3

The War in North Africa and Europe

Read to Discover

1. Why was the Allies' North Africa campaign so important?
2. What were the major turning points of the war in Europe?
3. How did the Allies drive the Germans out of France?

Identify

- Erwin Rommel
- Bernard Montgomery
- Battle of El Alamein
- Dwight D. Eisenhower
- Battle of Stalingrad
- George C. Marshall
- D-Day
- Omar Bradley
- George S. Patton
- Battle of the Bulge

WHY IT MATTERS TODAY

Many veterans of World War II have vivid memories of the battles they fought and the war they won. Use CNNfyi.com or other **current events** sources to find out how veterans or veterans' organizations commemorate past military service today. Record your findings in your journal.

The Story Continues

Winston Churchill became Britain's prime minister in 1940 and led his nation throughout the war.

During the difficult early days of the war, British prime minister Winston Churchill's words inspired his nation. He declared, "We shall defend our Island, whatever the cost may be." Despite Germany's tremendous early successes and the hardships faced by the British people, Churchill remained determined. Churchill said, "We shall fight on the beaches, . . . we shall fight in the fields and in the streets . . . ; we shall never surrender."

A Desperate Situation

In late 1941 the Axis Powers pushed the Allies nearly to the breaking point. German submarine attacks strained Great Britain's North Atlantic supply lines. Axis forces occupied Greece and Yugoslavia and were advancing in North Africa and the Soviet Union.

Roosevelt and Churchill met in Washington, D.C., two weeks after the attack on Pearl Harbor. They agreed that a full attack on Japan would have to wait. Instead, they decided to concentrate on defeating

Germany first. The two leaders also discussed a possible attack on Axis forces in North Africa. In January 1942 China and the Soviet Union agreed to help defeat the Axis Powers. They also agreed not to make a separate peace with any Axis state.

In 1942 the war in the Atlantic began looking more hopeful. The Allies introduced new sonar technology, which helped locate and track German submarines. New long-range bombers also gave some protection to ships far out at sea. While Allied naval forces fought for control of the Atlantic, air forces tried to destroy Germany's economic resources. From Britain, Allied bombers struck factories, military centers, and railroads. They also hit German cities. To improve the accuracy and effectiveness of their raids, U.S. bombers flew their missions in broad daylight. As a result, bomber crews had greater success but suffered very high casualties.

✔ **Reading Check: Summarizing** What did Roosevelt and Churchill agree would be the main strategy of the Allies?

North Africa and Italy

In September 1940, Italian forces in Libya attacked Egypt. They hoped to capture the Suez Canal, a vital Allied supply route. The British resisted, however, and drove back the Italians. Hitler then sent the German Afrika Korps, led by General **Erwin Rommel**, to the region. For the next two years, Rommel fought the Allies in a back-and-forth battle over some 1,500 miles. A master of warfare and surprise attacks, Rommel soon gained the nickname the Desert Fox. By the summer of 1942, he seemed ready to take Egypt. However, a shortage of troops and supplies slowed Rommel's offensive. In November, British forces under General **Bernard Montgomery** stopped Rommel's advance in the **Battle of El Alamein**. About the same time, British and American forces, led by U.S. general **Dwight D. Eisenhower**, landed west of Egypt in French North Africa. Eisenhower was a master at organization and planning. Soon his forces pushed back the Germans. Then the British and American troops trapped Rommel's retreating Afrika Korps between them. After a series of hard battles in early 1943, the Afrika Korps surrendered.

Having driven the Axis troops from North Africa, the Allies could invade Italy, which Churchill called the enemy's "soft underbelly." In July 1943, Allied forces landed on the island of Sicily. After taking the island, they began landing troops on the Italian mainland in September. As the Allies advanced, the Italian government overthrew dictator Benito Mussolini in order to make peace. Hitler was still determined to stop the Allies in Italy. He stepped in to save Mussolini, and German troops took control of Italy. Fighting fiercely, they slowed the Allied advance.

In January 1944 the Allies tried to take the Germans by surprise. A force landed behind German lines at the seaport of Anzio. Failing to

BIOGRAPHY

Daniel Inouye

(1924–)

Daniel Inouye was born in Hawaii in 1924. He volunteered for military service after finishing high school in 1942 and served in the famous 442nd Regimental Combat Team. While in Italy, the 442nd captured Mount Folgorito with a heroic effort. While climbing the cliffs, some men fell down the rocks, but they kept from crying out so the Germans would not hear them coming. In a later battle with the Germans, Inouye was wounded and later lost his right arm. After the war Inouye studied law and entered politics. He eventually became a U.S. representative and later a senator. **How do you think Inouye's wartime experiences affected his later life?**

GLOBAL CONNECTIONS

The Eastern Front

Before the Allies tried to retake western Europe, a fierce battle had raged along the 4,000-mile eastern front. The fighting between German and Soviet soldiers was brutal. German troops blockaded Leningrad (what is now St. Petersburg) for some 900 days. About 1 million people died, many from exposure to extreme cold and starvation. But the Russians eventually drove back the Germans.

The Allied victory on the eastern front came at a great price. About 10 million Soviet soldiers and some 10 million civilians lost their lives. **What was the cost of victory on the eastern front?**

A Soviet poster encouraging people to support the war effort

break through German defenses, they were trapped at Anzio for four months. Other Allied forces fought their way up the Italian Peninsula. Eventually, they joined with Allied troops at Anzio and went on to capture Rome, Italy's capital, in June 1944. In April 1945, Italian resistance fighters captured and killed Mussolini. In early May the Allies finally drove the Germans out of Italy.

✔ **Reading Check: Drawing Inferences and Conclusions** Why did Hitler want to defeat the Allies in Italy?

Turning Points

In early 1943 the Allies had begun the final push to defeat the Axis Powers. Victories during the winter of 1942–43 brought the Allies closer to their goal. After their initial invasion in June 1941, Axis forces had advanced deep into the Soviet Union. In September 1942 a German army entered the city of Stalingrad and began fighting for the city. The main battle, the **Battle of Stalingrad**, was a fierce struggle. Soldiers fought for each city block. In November more Soviet troops arrived and surrounded the German army. One German soldier described the scene.

"The men in field grey just slouched on, . . . filthy and . . . louse-ridden [covered with lice], their weary shoulders sagging. . . . Skin now loose-stretched over bone, so utter [complete] was the exhaustion, so utter the starvation. . . . And whenever any individual could do no more, when even the . . . fear of death ceased to have meaning, . . . the debilitated [weakened] body . . . came to a standstill."

—Benno Zieser, *In Their Shallow Graves,* translated by Alec Brown

In late January 1943, with supplies running very low, the remaining German troops in Stalingrad surrendered. The Axis Powers had lost some 200,000 soldiers in the fighting.

Six months later, the Soviets dealt another great blow to the Germans. They defeated the Germans in a huge tank battle near the Soviet city of Kursk. The Soviet victories at Stalingrad and Kursk marked a turning point in the war. Hitler's attempt to conquer the Soviet Union had failed. Axis troops retreated westward toward Germany.

Roosevelt's top military adviser, General **George C. Marshall**, supported an Allied invasion of German-occupied France. General Eisenhower was put in charge of planning the invasion, called Operation Overlord. His plan called for a massive landing on the beaches of Normandy, in northwestern France. To fool the Germans about the exact location of the attack, the Allies made several fake landings in other places. On the morning of June 6, 1944, known as **D-Day**, Allied soldiers finally landed in Normandy. Hundreds of warships off the coast tried to protect them by providing a cover of artillery fire. D-Day was the largest sea-and-land invasion in history.

The Allies faced fierce German resistance on the beaches of Normandy. One U.S. officer on the scene reported what it was like.

"[The assault units] were disorganized, had suffered heavy casualties and were handicapped by losses of valuable equipment. . . . They were pinned down along the beach by intense enemy fire. . . . Personnel and equipment were being piled ashore . . . where congested [crowded] groups afforded good targets for the enemy."

—Anonymous, quoted in *The Struggle for Europe,* by Chester Wilmot

Analyzing Primary Sources

Identifying Points of View According to the officer, what handicaps did the invading troops face on D-Day?

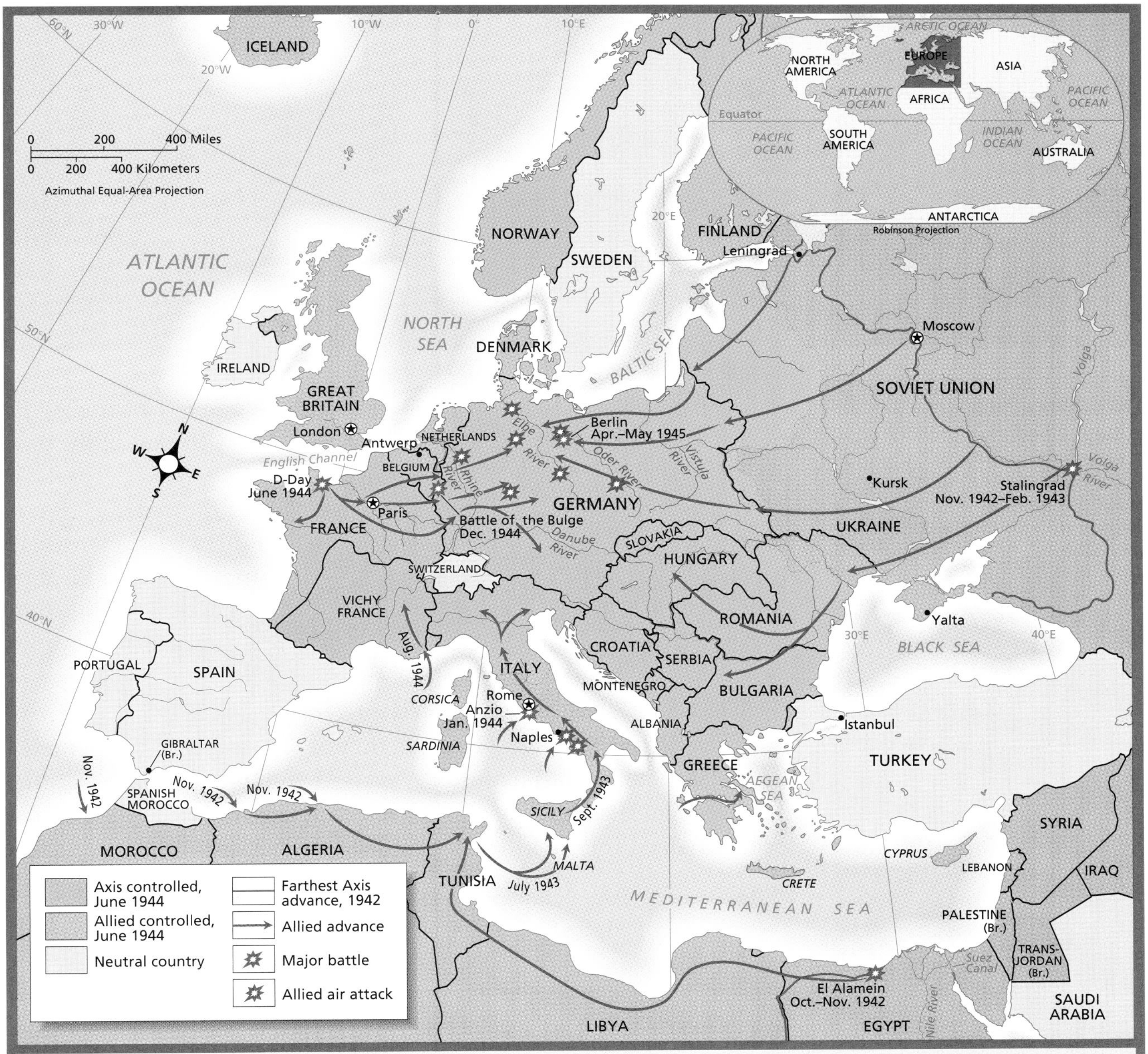

World War II in Europe, 1942–1945

Interpreting Maps By 1942 the Axis Powers controlled most of Europe, but Allied forces soon launched counterattacks.

Skills Assessment **Places and Regions** Which European countries remained neutral?

Interpreting the Visual Record

D-Day *Allied troops watch as fellow soldiers attempt to land on the beaches of Normandy during the D-Day invasion.* ***Where do you see battles taking place?***

The determined Allies continued their assault despite terrible losses. By the end of D-Day, they had gained a foothold and landed more than 155,000 troops in France.

Hundreds of thousands more Allied troops followed the D-Day forces during the summer. U.S. general **Omar Bradley** led the breakout from the beaches and into occupied France. Tank forces under General **George S. Patton** then broke through German lines in July. Meanwhile, new Allied forces landed in southern France and began to advance northward. The liberation of France was at last in sight.

As the Allies advanced, French citizens rose up against German forces in Paris. On August 24 a small unit of Free French troops entered the city. The next morning, Bradley arrived with his 12th Army Group. One historian later described the group's arrival, "All Paris surged out to meet the Allied columns" and welcome their liberators.

✔ **Reading Check: Comparing and Contrasting** How was the D-Day invasion similar to and different from the Battle of Stalingrad?

Research on the ROM

Free Find:
D-Day
After reading about the D-Day invasion on the **Holt Researcher CD–ROM**, create a drawing of the invasion site that shows the obstacles the Allied troops faced.

The Battle of the Bulge

After freeing Paris, the Allies began to push through Belgium and France toward Germany itself. Although defeat seemed certain, Hitler refused to surrender. In December 1944 he made a desperate attempt to split the advancing Allied armies. The Germans launched an offensive in the Ardennes (ahr-DEN), a forest region defended by just a few U.S.

Interpreting the Visual Record

Liberation of Paris *Victorious Allied troops move under Paris's Arc de Triomphe after recapturing the French capital from the Germans.* ***What sort of reception do the Allied troops appear to be receiving?***

divisions. Hitler hoped to recapture Antwerp, Belgium, the Allies' major supply port.

On December 16 some 25 divisions of the German army attacked in the heavy snow. They almost broke the Allied lines. Surprised, outnumbered, and without air support, the Americans fought bravely in the **Battle of the Bulge**. U.S. losses were heavy—some 77,000 casualties—but the Americans slowed the German counterattack. As more Allied troops arrived, the German offensive stalled, then turned into a general retreat. The Battle of the Bulge lasted into early January and ended Germany's ability to wage offensive war.

As 1945 began, the Soviet armies were pushing toward Berlin, Germany's capital, from the east. U.S. and British troops were preparing to cross the Rhine into Germany from the west.

✔ **Reading Check: Analyzing Information** Why was the Battle of the Bulge important?

Section 3 Review

go.hrw.com **Homework Practice Online**
keyword: SB3 HP16

1. **Identify** and explain:
   - Erwin Rommel
   - Bernard Montgomery
   - Battle of El Alamein
   - Dwight D. Eisenhower
   - Battle of Stalingrad
   - George C. Marshall
   - D-Day
   - Omar Bradley
   - George S. Patton
   - Battle of the Bulge

2. **Summarizing** Copy the graphic organizer below. Use it to identify the major turning points in the Allied war against Axis Powers in Europe.

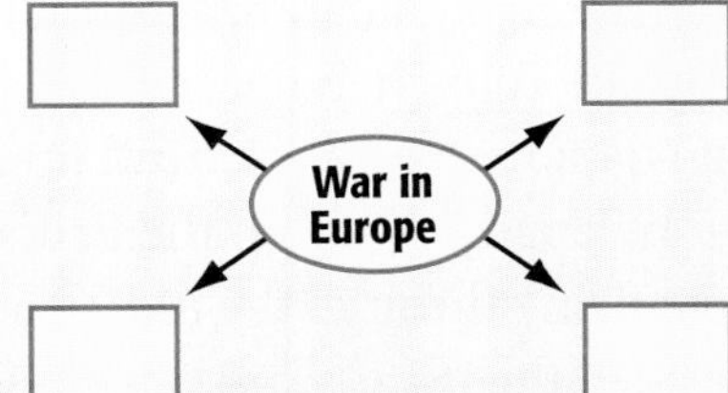

3. **Finding the Main Idea**
   a. Why was the North Africa campaign important to the Allies?
   b. How were the Allies able to push the Germans out of France?

4. **Writing and Critical Thinking**
   Summarizing Imagine that you are a war correspondent in early 1945. Write a magazine article that describes current conditions during the Allied offensive against German forces in eastern and western Europe.
   Consider the following:
   - turning points in the Soviet Union
   - turning points in western Europe

Section 4

War in the Pacific

Read to Discover

1. Where did the Japanese attack after they bombed Pearl Harbor?
2. What three battles were the major turning points in the war in the Pacific?
3. How did the Allies advance toward Japan?

Define

- island-hopping
- kamikaze

Identify

- Hideki Tōjō
- Douglas MacArthur
- Bataan Death March
- Chester Nimitz
- Battle of the Coral Sea
- Battle of Midway
- Battle of Leyte Gulf

WHY IT MATTERS TODAY

Relations between the United States and Japan changed greatly after the end of World War II. Use CNNfyi.com or other **current events** sources to find out about some aspect of trade relations between Japan and the United States today. Record your findings in your journal.

U.S. soldiers often had little protection as they tried to retake Japanese-controlled islands during fighting in the Pacific.

The Story Continues

On November 20, 1943, U.S. Marines swarmed into the lagoon of Tarawa, one of the Gilbert Islands in the Pacific Ocean. The marines waded ashore in chest-deep water, coming under a hail of Japanese machine-gun fire. "The water seemed never clear of . . . men," one witness recalled. "They kept falling, falling, falling . . . singly, in groups, and in rows." Yet the marines pressed on. Three days and some 3,000 casualties later, they had taken the island. Tarawa was just one of many difficult Allied landings in the Pacific.

Japan Advances across the Pacific

In 1931, years before Tarawa, Japan had conquered Manchuria in China. Under General **Hideki Tōjō** (hee-dek-ee toh-joh), Japan continued its policy of expansion. Japanese troops spread throughout East Asia and the Pacific. By early 1942 Japan had taken the British colonies of Hong Kong and Singapore. Advancing through the independent country of Thailand, Japanese forces invaded the British colony of Burma. They then took control of the oil-rich Dutch East Indies (now called Indonesia).

At the same time, the Japanese expected a U.S. counterattack in the Pacific. After Pearl Harbor, Japanese forces tried to press their advantage, moving quickly to grab U.S. territories in the Pacific. Japan captured Guam and Wake Island, both U.S. territories since 1898. Japanese forces then landed on the U.S.-owned Aleutian Islands of Kiska and Attu, near mainland Alaska. Japan also invaded the Philippines, another U.S. possession.

Under General **Douglas MacArthur**, U.S. and Filipino forces made their stand against the Japanese invasion. When the capital, Manila, fell quickly to the Japanese, MacArthur's troops retreated across Manila Bay to the Bataan Peninsula. In March 1942, President Roosevelt ordered MacArthur to go to Australia. "I shall return," the general vowed before making his escape.

Weak and hungry, U.S. and Filipino units remaining on the Bataan Peninsula and Corregidor surrendered soon afterward. The Japanese then marched more than 70,000 Americans and Filipinos—many of whom were sick and wounded—to prison camps. The Japanese treated the prisoners harshly during their 65-mile forced march up the peninsula. No one knows just how many deaths took place on the **Bataan Death March**. However, historians estimate that between 400 and 1,000 Americans and possibly as many as 10,000 Filipinos died.

✔ **Reading Check: Summarizing** Into what areas did Japan expand to strengthen its position in the Pacific and Asia?

Halting Japan's Advance

In early 1942 the Japanese seemed unstoppable. They appeared to be ready to strike at Australia, Hawaii, and India. Americans even feared a Japanese invasion of the West Coast of the United States. During 1942, however, Allied forces began to turn the tide of the war against Japan.

To stop Japan's advance, the Allies had to defeat the Japanese navy. Admiral **Chester Nimitz**, commander of the U.S. Navy in the Pacific, had an important, top secret advantage against the Japanese. Navy experts had cracked the Japanese naval code and could therefore read secret Japanese messages. As a result, Nimitz knew that the Japanese planned to capture Port Moresby, New Guinea.

Nimitz moved to cut the Japanese forces off. In early May 1942, he sent an Allied fleet to attack the Japanese invasion force. The fleet met the Japanese northeast of Australia in the **Battle of the Coral Sea**. U.S. planes sank one Japanese carrier and damaged another. The U.S. Navy suffered losses as well. Japanese planes sank the aircraft carrier *Lexington* and damaged the *Yorktown*. Despite their losses, the Allies had turned back the Japanese advance for the first time.

Interpreting the Visual Record

Code talkers *The Navajo Code Talkers were a group of marine radio specialists in the Pacific theater. They used a special code based on the Navajo language to quickly and accurately send messages that the Japanese were never able to crack.* ***Why would having an unbreakable code have helped the marines during the war?***

Interpreting the Visual Record

Midway *The U.S. victory in the Battle of Midway was a major blow to the Japanese navy.* ***What does this painting tell you about the type of fighting that took place during the battle?***

Just weeks after victory in the Coral Sea, Nimitz learned about another Japanese plan. Japanese forces hoped to seize the Midway Islands, located northwest of Hawaii. Nimitz ordered U.S. carriers to intercept the Japanese fleet. The **Battle of Midway**, which took place between June 3 and 6, was a battle of carrier-based airplanes. Japanese and U.S. warplanes fought in the air, trying to sink each other's aircraft carriers. When the battle was over, the U.S. Navy had crippled the Japanese navy by sinking four of its carriers, while losing only one of its own. An officer on the Japanese carrier *Akagi* described his ship's fate.

Analyzing Primary Sources

Identifying Points of View How did the Japanese officer's viewpoint change when he saw the Allied planes?

"Within five minutes all her planes would be launched. Five minutes! Who would have dreamed that the tide of battle would shift completely in that brief interval of time? . . . The first Zero fighter [Japanese warplane] gathered speed and whizzed off the deck. At that instant a lookout screamed, 'Hell-divers!' I looked up to see three black enemy planes plummeting [diving] toward our ship. . . . Bombs! Down they came straight toward me!"

—Mitsuo Fuchida, *Midway: The Battle That Doomed Japan*

After its defeat at Midway, the Japanese navy was on the defensive for the rest of the war. The U.S. Navy had finally stopped the advance of Japanese forces in the Pacific. The Allies then began to put the pressure on Japan. They turned their efforts toward Guadalcanal, one of the Solomon Islands in the southwest Pacific. Japanese troops were building an airstrip there. From Guadalcanal, Japanese forces could threaten the important sea link between Australia and the United States. In August 1942 the United States began landing marines on the island. The fight for Guadalcanal took place on land, at sea, and in the air. For months neither side could gain a clear advantage. Finally, the Allies won control of the island in early 1943.

✔ **Reading Check: Analyzing Information** How did the Allies put Japan on the defensive in 1942 and 1943?

Taking the Offensive

After Guadalcanal, Allied commanders began to develop plans to attack Japan itself. Japanese forces in the Pacific were still strong. In Asia, they controlled China and were continuing to advance through Burma toward India. The Allies planned to conquer one Pacific island after another, landing only on the most important islands. Gradually, they would move closer to Japan while isolating Japanese troops on bypassed islands. This strategy, called **island-hopping**, would help the Allies gain new bases. From these bases, the Allies could bomb and later invade Japan. U.S. leaders used the strategy quite effectively. The U.S. Navy's Construction Battalions, known as Seabees, played an important role in the campaign. They built airstrips, naval bases, and roads to keep the Allied forces on the move.

The island-hopping campaign began in late 1943. Forces under General MacArthur battled the Japanese on New Guinea in November. Other troops launched a series of attacks on the Gilbert, Bonin, Mariana, Marshall, and Volcano Islands. U.S. forces captured the islands of Saipan and Tinian in the Marianas. From these bases, U.S. planes began bombing the main islands of Japan. U.S. submarines were attacking Japanese cargo ships, cutting off the flow of raw materials to Japan.

With New Guinea under Allied control, General MacArthur planned to take back the Philippines. The Japanese navy gathered to block the Allied invasion force in October 1944. The two sides met in the **Battle of Leyte Gulf**—the largest naval battle in history. Both sides took heavy losses from airplane raids and artillery fire. In the end, however, the Allies won, greatly reducing the strength of the Japanese fleet.

Daily Life

Island war Massive landing craft, like these in Philippine waters, delivered U.S. troops to enemy beaches. The landing craft used in World War II transported tanks, troops, and supplies to battle sites. Troops in isolated locations might pass several weeks with no outside help and relied on landing craft stocked with ammunition, food, fresh water, and equipment to keep them supplied. Other landing craft were converted into hospital ships. Soldiers being transported on landing crafts faced crowded living conditions and hours of boredom. However, soldiers always had to remain alert because enemy gunfire or a submarine attack were always threats. **Why might life on a World War II landing craft be difficult?**

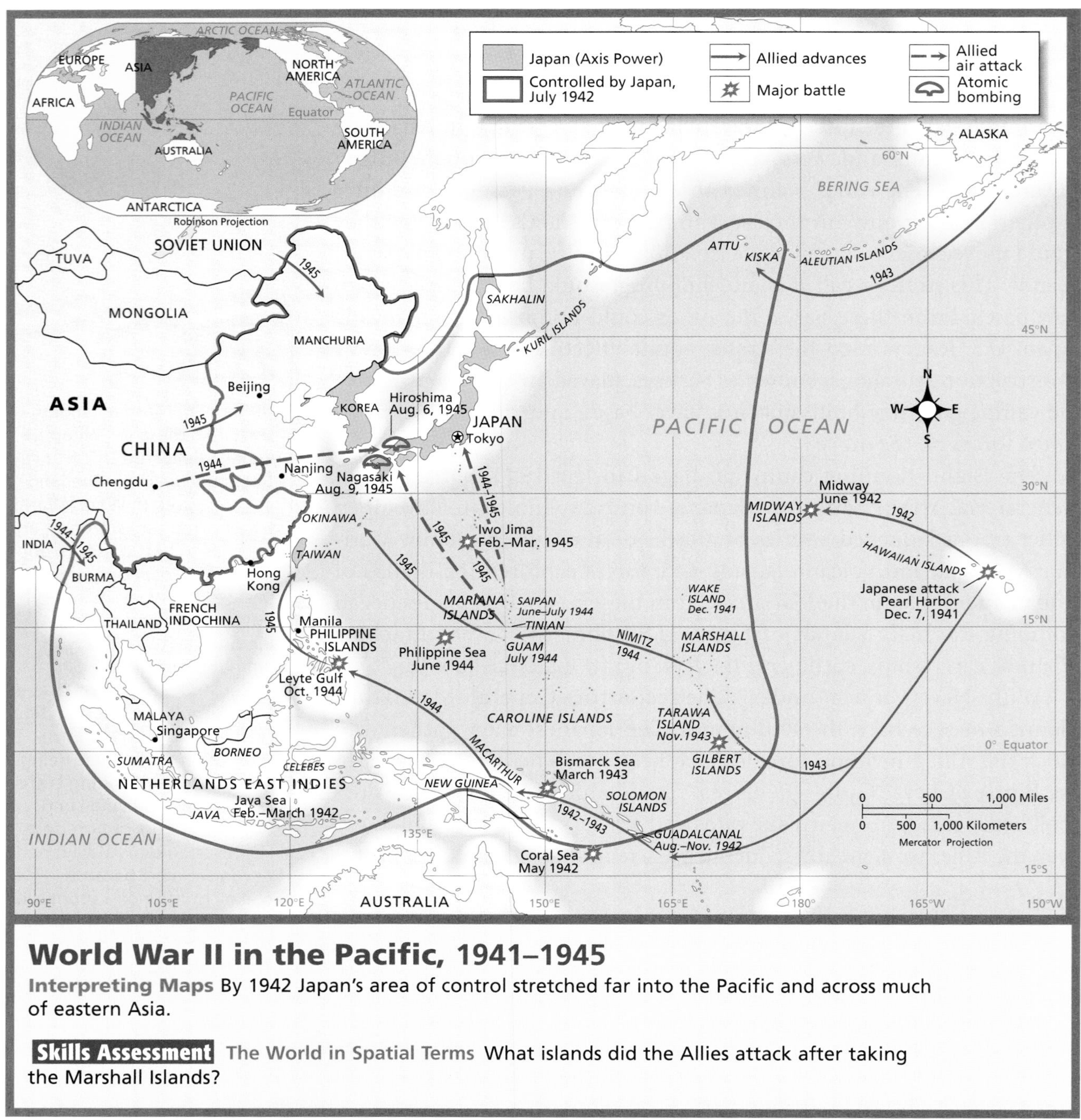

World War II in the Pacific, 1941–1945

Interpreting Maps By 1942 Japan's area of control stretched far into the Pacific and across much of eastern Asia.

Skills Assessment **The World in Spatial Terms** What islands did the Allies attack after taking the Marshall Islands?

Shortly after the battle, MacArthur waded ashore on Leyte. He had kept his promise to return to the Philippines. Aided by Filipino guerrillas, Allied forces began the advance toward Manila. In January 1945, Allied troops landed on the main island of Luzon. On March 3 they captured Manila. However, the Japanese put up fierce resistance. Summer came before the main towns, roads, and airfields in the Philippines were in Allied hands.

✔ **Reading Check: Finding the Main Idea** How did the strategy of island-hopping reduce the effectiveness of Japanese troops?

Closer to Japan

By spring 1945 the war against Japan had entered its final phase. U.S. bombers hit targets in Japan during massive nighttime raids. These attacks caused great damage. A raid on Tokyo in March 1945 destroyed about one fourth of the Japanese capital. The Allies also bombed other major Japanese cities into ruins and killed tens of thousands of Japanese. Despite great destruction and loss of life, Japan still refused to surrender. As Allied forces got closer to Japan, they faced some of the fiercest fighting of World War II. For example, several thousand Americans and most of the 22,000 Japanese defenders died in the February 1945 battle for Iwo Jima (ee-woh jee-mah).

In the battle for Okinawa, which lasted from April through June 1945, the Japanese airforce used a deadly tactic involving crashing piloted planes into Allied ships. Many of these **kamikaze** planes found their targets off the island of Okinawa. They caused heavy damage to Allied ships and killed nearly 5,000 Allied sailors.

Despite the kamikaze attacks, the Allies stuck to their goal—the complete defeat of Japan. The losses during nearly three months of fighting on Okinawa were staggering. More than 110,000 Japanese troops—almost the entire force on Okinawa—died. The Allies suffered some 12,000 dead and about 37,000 wounded. With the fall of Okinawa, Allied leaders looked to attack Japan itself for final victory.

Kamikaze attacks were responsible for damaging hundreds of warships and sinking 34.

✔ **Reading Check: Making Generalizations and Predictions** What would you expect to happen if the Allies actually invaded Japan?

Section 4 Review

go.hrw.com Homework Practice Online
keyword: SC3 HP25

1. **Define** and explain:
   - island-hopping
   - kamikaze

2. **Identify** and explain:
   - Hideki Tōjō
   - Douglas MacArthur
   - Bataan Death March
   - Chester Nimitz
   - Battle of the Coral Sea
   - Battle of Midway
   - Battle of Leyte Gulf

3. **Evaluating** Copy the graphic organizer below. Use it to identify the three major battles that were turning points in the Pacific war and to explain why they were so critical.

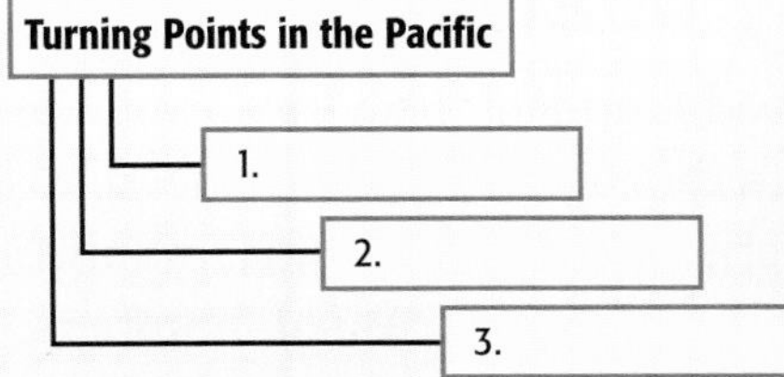

4. **Finding the Main Idea**
   a. What areas did Japan conquer after bombing Pearl Harbor, and why did the Japanese want to control these areas?
   b. What was the island-hopping strategy, and how did the Allies use it to help win the war against Japan?

5. **Writing and Critical Thinking**
   Identifying Points of View Imagine that you are a sailor on a U.S. warship in the Pacific during World War II. Write a letter home describing a kamikaze attack.
   Consider the following:
   - the increasingly fierce Japanese resistance
   - the goal of the kamikaze pilots
   - the effectiveness of kamikaze attacks

Section 5

Final Victory and Consequences

Read to Discover

1. How did the Allies force Germany and Japan to surrender?
2. What were the human and economic costs of World War II?
3. What events led to the Holocaust?

Define

- atomic bomb
- genocide

Identify

- Harry S Truman
- Manhattan Project
- Holocaust

WHY IT MATTERS TODAY

World War II caused massive destruction to much of Asia and Europe. Use CNNfyi.com or other **current events** sources to find out how one of the countries heavily damaged during the war is doing today. Record your findings in your journal.

Victory medal from World War II

The Story Continues

Toward the end of the war, the Allies mounted bombing raids against the Axis Powers. In long flights over the Pacific Ocean, U.S. bombers battled Japanese fighter planes. Then they dropped tons of explosives on enemy positions. One crew member described an attack on a Japanese airstrip. The "black puffs of ack-ack [antiaircraft fire] surround us, and some of the stuff hits. . . . The plane lurches and reels." The bomber survived. Yet that one mission lasted nine hours and covered more than 1,500 miles. The Allies would fight many more such battles before their final victory.

Victory in Europe

The Allies bombed Germany heavily during the final months of World War II. From both the east and the west the Allies launched bombing raids against major German cities. Berlin, Hamburg, and Leipzig were greatly damaged. In February 1945, Allied bombers destroyed the historic German city of Dresden. These bombing raids were intended to destroy Germany's ability to make weapons but also killed many civilians.

During the early months of 1945, the Allies pushed the Germans back. U.S. and British troops raced toward the Rhine River to enter Germany from the west. The Allies needed to move fast. They wanted to capture bridges across the Rhine before the Germans destroyed them. Some Allied leaders, particularly Winston Churchill, had other worries. They wanted the noncommunist Allies to occupy as much of Germany as possible. Churchill thought it was important to keep the territory out of Soviet hands.

By mid-March 1945, British and U.S. forces had crossed the Rhine and were advancing east toward Berlin. Meanwhile, the Soviets pushed west toward the city. With his enemies closing in, Hitler retreated to his underground bunker, or shelter, in Berlin. On April 30 Hitler committed suicide. Just days later, on May 7, German authorities surrendered unconditionally to the Allies. The next day—May 8, 1945—was declared V-E (Victory in Europe) Day. It marked the official end of World War II in Europe. For Americans, the joy was mixed with sorrow. Only weeks before, on April 12, President Roosevelt had died of a stroke. Vice President **Harry S Truman** took over as the new president.

✔ **Reading Check:** **Summarizing** How did the Allies force Germany to surrender?

Victory in the Pacific

As Germany surrendered, the Allies also neared victory in the Pacific. However, Allied leaders feared that the final invasion of Japan would result in great loss of life.

Since 1942 Allied scientists had been working on what became an alternative to invading Japan. The scientists worked to develop an **atomic bomb**, a weapon that produced great destructive power by splitting atoms. Known as the **Manhattan Project**, this huge effort to develop an atomic bomb employed more than 600,000 people. World-class scientists, worried that Germany would build an atomic bomb first, worked at a top-secret facility in Los Alamos, New Mexico. Plants in Hanford, Washington, and Oak Ridge, Tennessee, produced the radioactive materials needed to build the bomb. In the end, the project cost some $2 billion.

On July 16, 1945, scientists exploded the world's first atomic bomb in the desert near Alamogordo, New Mexico. The bomb's destructive power went beyond all expectations. The explosion disintegrated the steel tower that held the bomb. For 800 yards in all directions, the desert sand melted into glass.

President Truman called the atomic bomb "the most terrible thing ever discovered" but never doubted whether it should be used. The invasion of Japan, Truman thought, would cost much more in human lives than using the atomic bomb. When the Allies did not get an uncon-

CONNECTING TO SCIENCE AND TECHNOLOGY

Antibiotics

Infected wounds killed some 15 percent of all soldiers who died in World War II. Even a scratch from barbed wire could kill a soldier in days if it became infected. By the end of World War II, such deaths were rare among Allied troops, thanks to a new drug called penicillin. British scientist Alexander Fleming discovered the penicillin mold by accident in 1928. Penicillin was the first antibiotic ever discovered. Antibiotics prevent bacteria from growing, and in some cases, kill them. This allows the body's immune system to fight against disease and infection caused by bacteria.

It took researchers years to refine the mold into a useful drug. By 1944 there was enough penicillin to treat thousands of wounded soldiers. After the war, doctors used penicillin to treat different diseases and infections throughout the world. Today penicillin and other antibiotics are widely available and commonly prescribed by doctors. The drug that was such a lifesaver during the war is still saving lives. **Why was penicillin important during World War II?**

ditional surrender from Japan, Truman gave the order to use the bomb. On August 6, 1945, the B-29 bomber *Enola Gay* flew over the Japanese city of Hiroshima and dropped the first atomic bomb used in warfare. One survivor recalled the destruction.

Analyzing Primary Sources

Making Generalizations and Predictions What do you think the speaker might have done next?

"When I saw a very strong light, a flash, I put my arms over my face unconsciously. Almost instantly I felt my face was inflating. . . . I saw people looking for water and they died soon after they drank it. . . . The whole city was destroyed and burning. There was no place to go."

—Michiko Yamaoka, quoted in "Voices of A-Bomb Survivors: A-Bomb WWW Project"

In almost an instant, the atomic blast killed between 70,000 and 80,000 people. Thousands more died later from serious burns and radiation poisoning.

Stunned, Japanese leaders still did not surrender. Then, on August 9, U.S. forces dropped a second atomic bomb on the city of Nagasaki. A few days later, on August 15, 1945, Japan surrendered. Japan's emperor, Hirohito, still led the country, but his powers were greatly reduced.

✔ **Reading Check: Identifying Cause and Effect** What led President Truman to order the use of atomic weapons, and what effects did they have on the war?

 The Costs of the War

With Japan's surrender, World War II finally ended after nearly six years of destruction. Some 50 million people had died—more than half of them civilians. Millions more were injured or left suffering from disease or lack of food. China, Poland, and the Soviet Union were hit very hard. Both Germany and Japan lost many people as well.

Interpreting the Visual Record

Hiroshima *The atomic bomb dropped on Hiroshima destroyed everything within 1.2 miles of the spot where it exploded. This watch, found in the ruins, stopped at the exact moment of the explosion—8:15 A.M.* ***How does this photograph show the destructive power of the atomic bomb?***

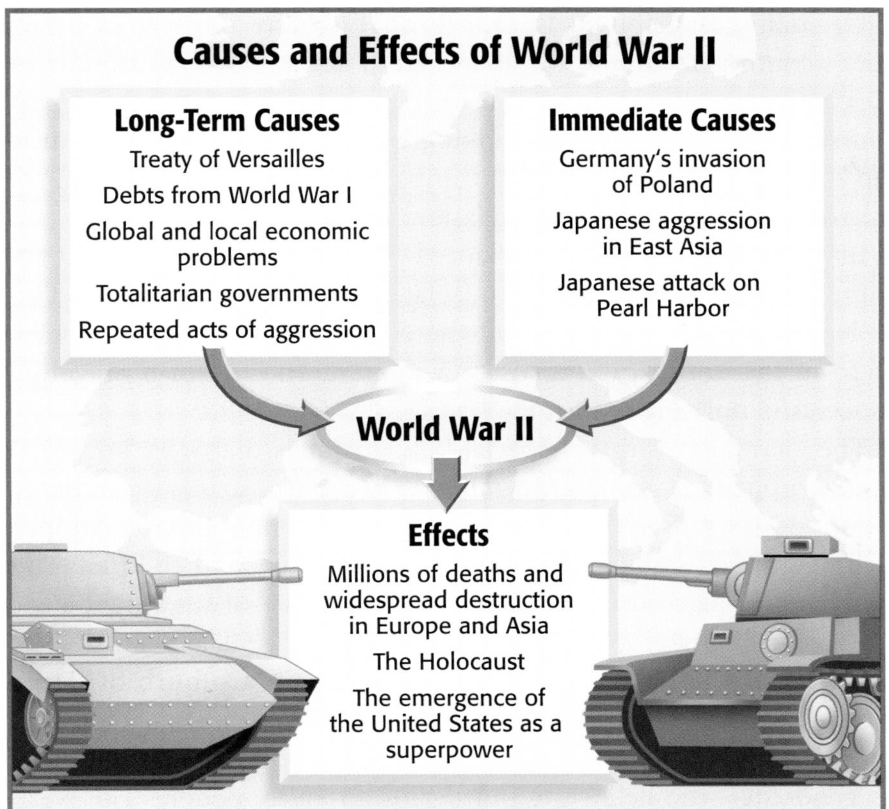

In Europe, as in Asia, the war ruined national economies. Food production, industry, and transportation networks were destroyed in many areas. Millions of people found themselves homeless, lacking even the basic necessities of food, fuel, shelter, and water. From London to Warsaw to Leningrad, large cities lay in ruins. Much of the world's great art and architecture was lost forever.

The war had not been fought on American soil. As a result, the United States escaped the physical destruction that Europe and Asia suffered. Therefore, the U.S. economy emerged from the war more powerful than ever. Much of the cost of the rebuilding efforts after the war would fall to the United States.

✔ **Reading Check: Summarizing** What were the costs of World War II?

The Holocaust

One of the most horrifying aspects of World War II was the **Holocaust**—the attempt by Hitler and the Nazis to murder the Jews of Europe. Soon after taking power in Germany in 1933, the Nazis had written new laws for German Jews. They were stripped of their civil rights, jobs, and property. The Nazis encouraged German Jews to leave the country. Many Jews who remained were imprisoned in concentration camps, such as Dachau (DAH-kow) near Munich.

German expansion in Europe brought many more Jews under Hitler's control. Thousands of Jews lived in France, the Low Countries, and eastern Europe. Millions more lived in Poland and the Soviet Union. Hitler and other high-ranking Nazis thought it impractical to keep these Jews in concentration camps. The Nazis looked instead for ways to eliminate the Jewish population.

In Poland the Germans uprooted Jews from their homes in the countryside and forced them into isolated urban areas known as ghettos. However, some Jews resisted the Nazis. In the spring of 1943, a ghetto in the Polish capital, Warsaw, became the site of a brave but unsuccessful uprising against the Nazis.

The Germans also used special killing squads that were known as Einsatzgruppen (YN-sahts-groo-puhn). Their purpose was to round up and shoot Jews. For three days in 1941, German Einsatzgruppen machine-gunned some 33,000 Jewish men, women, and children. This massacre took place at Babi Yar near the Soviet city of Kiev. By the end of 1941, the Einsatzgruppen troops had killed some 600,000 Jews.

In January 1942, senior Nazi officials met in a suburb of Berlin called Wannsee. At the Wannsee Conference these leaders agreed on a "final solution to the Jewish question." For the Nazis this "final solution" was **genocide**—the deliberate murder of an entire people. The Nazis planned to kill the Jews in specially built death camps across Europe. These camps were equipped with gas chambers designed to kill great numbers of people. The camps also had special furnaces to burn the remains of the dead.

By mid-1942 the Nazis had begun to ship Jews from German-occupied Europe to the camps in Austria, Germany, and Poland. People were packed shoulder-to-shoulder in railroad boxcars. Nazi officers sorted the arriving Jews by age, sex, and health, often tearing families apart. Camp officers sent physically fit Jews to work as slave laborers in camp factories. The Nazis sent many other prisoners directly to gas chambers for immediate

Interpreting the Visual Record

Failed resistance in Warsaw *Jews in this Warsaw ghetto surrendered to Nazi soldiers after an unsuccessful uprising.* ***What does this image tell you about the conditions in which many Jews lived under Nazi rule?***

execution. These victims were most often women and children, the elderly, the sick, and the weak.

Moritz Vegh, age 13, was sent from his home in the former Czechoslovakia to Auschwitz, the most notorious of all death camps. He recalled his terrifying arrival.

"When we got off the cattle truck, they ordered, 'Men, right; women, left.' . . . I went with my father. My little sister, Esther, she went with my mother. Esther was only eleven. She was holding my mother's hand. When they made a selection of the women, Esther clung to my mother. My mother wouldn't give her up. . . . They went straight to the gas chamber."

—Moritz Vegh, quoted in *The Boys: Triumph over Adversity,* by Martin Gilbert

Interpreting the Visual Record

The Holocaust *Prisoners at this concentration camp in Evensee, Austria, were liberated by U.S. troops in 1945.* ***How does the appearance of these prisoners show the harsh conditions of the concentration camps?***

The Nazis made Moritz and others work as slaves at Auschwitz for the rest of the war. When the Allies liberated the concentration camps in April 1945, many of the survivors were too weak or sick to move.

As the Allies freed the camps, the full horror of the Holocaust became clear. Some 6 million Jews had been killed or had died in the camps. This number equaled about two thirds of all Jews living in Europe before the war. The Nazis had also sent hundreds of thousands of other people to be killed in the camps. Gypsies, Slavs, political and religious radicals, and others were among the victims. The Holocaust is a chilling reminder of the brutal and inhumane nature of Nazi beliefs and of the terrible cost of Nazi aggression.

✔ **Reading Check: Identifying Cause and Effect** What led to the Holocaust, and what effect did it have on the Jewish population of Europe?

Section 5 Review

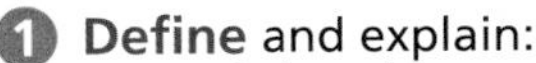

go.hrw.com **Homework Practice Online**
keyword: SC3 HP25

1. **Define** and explain:
   - atomic bomb
   - genocide

2. **Identify** and explain:
   - Harry S Truman
   - Manhattan Project
   - Holocaust

3. **Summarizing** Copy the graphic organizer below. Use it to identify five events that led to the Holocaust.

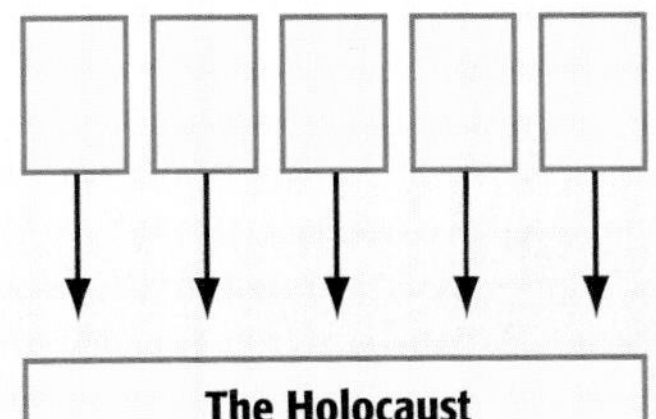

4. **Finding the Main Idea**
   a. How did the Allies eventually force both Germany and Japan to surrender?
   b. What were the consequences of World War II in both human and economic terms?

5. **Writing and Critical Thinking**
   Supporting a Point of View Imagine that you are one of the U.S. soldiers who helped defeat Germany. Write a journal entry describing your feelings on V-E Day.
   Consider the following:
   - the costs of fighting and winning the war
   - the liberation of Jews from death camps
   - the fear of German territory falling into communist hands

Chapter 25 Review

The Chapter at a Glance

Examine the visual summary of the chapter below. Use it to create a five-question matching quiz on the turning points of World War II. Give the quiz to a classmate and check that the items are correctly matched.

The World at War

Asia

- Pearl Harbor
- Coral Sea
- Midway
- Island-hopping campaign
- Leyte Gulf
- Capture of Okinawa
- Hiroshima and Nagasaki

United States

- Wartime rationing
- Women industrial workers
- Japanese American internment

Europe and North Africa

- Invasion of Poland
- The Holocaust
- El Alamein
- Stalingrad
- D-Day
- Liberation of Paris
- Battle of the Bulge
- V-E Day

Identifying People and Ideas

Use the following terms or people in historically significant sentences.

1. appeasement
2. Winston Churchill
3. internment
4. Dwight D. Eisenhower
5. Omar Bradley
6. Battle of the Bulge
7. Bataan Death March
8. Battle of Midway
9. Manhattan Project
10. Holocaust

Understanding Main Ideas

Section 1 *(Pages 762–766)*

1. How did the United States remain neutral during the early part of World War II while still helping the Allies?

Section 2 *(Pages 767–771)*

2. How did World War II affect women and minorities in the United States?

Section 3 *(Pages 772–777)*

3. What were the turning points of World War II in Europe?

Section 4 *(Pages 778–783)*

4. Why were the Battle of the Coral Sea, the Battle of Midway, and the Battle of Leyte Gulf important?

Section 5 *(Pages 784–789)*

5. What was the Holocaust, who was responsible for it, and how did it affect the Jewish population of Europe?

You Be the Historian—Reviewing Themes

1. **Citizenship** How did the war affect the rights of Nisei?
2. **Economics** How did mobilizing for war change the U.S. economy?
3. **Global Relations** Why did President Franklin D. Roosevelt feel that the United States needed to serve as "the arsenal of democracy" for the world and become involved in World War II?

Thinking Critically

1. **Contrasting** How did Allied strategy differ in Europe and the Pacific?
2. **Evaluating** What do you think were the greatest challenges that U.S. soldiers faced while fighting in World War II? Explain your answer.
3. **Drawing Inferences and Conclusions** Why might fighting a war in different places at the same time be difficult?

Social Studies Skills Workshop

Interpreting Maps

Study the map of the Bataan Death March below. Then use the information on the map to help you answer the questions that follow.

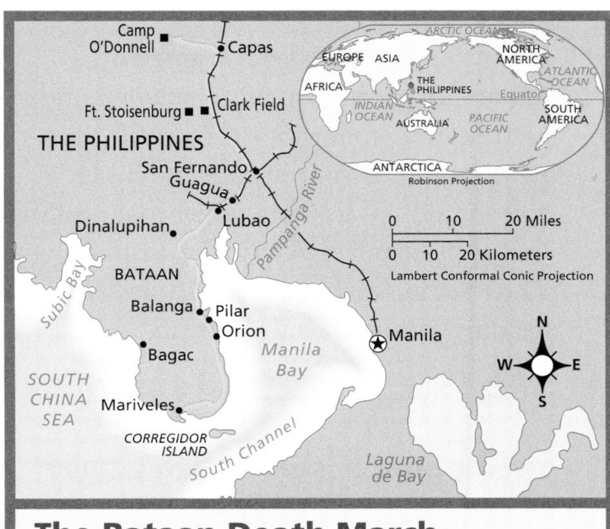

The Bataan Death March

1. How far did the prisoners march from Mariveles to San Fernando?
   a. 100 miles
   b. about 60 miles
   c. about 600 miles
   d. about 80 miles
2. What was the final destination of the prisoners sent on the Bataan Death March?
3. Based on the information shown on the map and your knowledge of the period, why do you think the Japanese chose to march the Allied prisoners inland?

Analyzing Primary Sources

Read the following quote by platoon sergeant Buck Eversole, who described his troops fighting in World War II. Then answer the questions that follow.

> **"It gets so it kinda gets you, seein' these new kids come up. . . . Some of them have just got fuzz on their faces, and don't know what it's all about, and they're scared to death. No matter what, some of them are bound to get killed. . . . I know it ain't my fault that they get killed. . . . And I do the best I can for them, but I've got so I feel like it's me killin' 'em instead of a German. I've got so I feel like a murderer. I hate to look at them when the new ones come in."**

4. Which of the following statements best describes the speaker's feelings?
   a. He thinks the U.S. government needs to recruit more soldiers.
   b. He disagrees with U.S. military strategy.
   c. He feels responsible for the lives of the young men in his platoon.
   d. He wants the United States to win the war.
5. Why does the sergeant hate to look at new recruits?
   a. Because he thinks they are stupid.
   b. Because he knows some of them will die in the war.
   c. Because he wants only experienced soldiers.
   d. Because he does not think more troops are needed.
6. When interpreting a primary source, historians examine the historical context in which it was written. What events in the United States might have inspired young men to serve in the military?

Alternative Assessment

Building Your Portfolio

American History

Linking to Community
Americans have served in the military during times of both peace and war. Write a report that summarizes the experience of a person in your community who served in the armed forces. Contact local veterans' groups such as the American Legion or Veterans of Foreign Wars to find a person who served in the armed forces. Ask him or her to explain what the experience was like.

internet connect

Internet Activity: go.hrw.com
keyword: SC3 CF25

Choose an activity on World War II to:

- Create a display on U.S. neutrality early in the war.
- Learn about Navajo Code Talkers and code breaking.
- Learn about Norman Rockwell's *Four Freedoms* posters.

Social Studies Skills

WORKSHOP

Creating a Database

A database is a collection of information that is organized so that you can find the facts you need efficiently. This organization can take many forms, depending upon your resources and needs. For example, a database can be presented in the form of a chart or a table. It could even be a collection of computer files that you can search to find specific information on a topic.

By gathering and organizing the necessary facts, you can create your own database on a research topic. The following guidelines will help you create a database addressing almost any subject.

1. **Gather information.** Use the library, your textbook, or other current events sources to find information on the appropriate topic. Make sure that the data you collect covers the correct time period for your research. You should also record the source of your information so that you can include it in your database.
2. **Create a framework to organize the data.** Give your database a clear title so that others will be able to identify its topic easily. Use headings to identify the types of data that your database includes, such as dates, locations, or quantities.
3. **Enter the data into your framework.** Make sure the information included under each heading follows a consistent format. For example, if your heading is STATES, you should not list data under that heading that applies only to a city. If your heading is YEARS, then each date you list under that heading should include the year.

Sample Database

Twenty Most Populous States, 2000*

State	Population	Rank
Arizona	5,140,683	20
California	33,930,798	1
Florida	16,028,890	3
Georgia	8,206,975	10
Illinois	12,439,042	5
Indiana	6,090,782	14
Maryland	5,307,886	19
Massachusetts	6,355,568	13
Michigan	9,955,829	8
Missouri	5,606,260	17
New Jersey	8,424,354	9
New York	19,004,973	4
Ohio	11,374,540	7
Pennsylvania	12,300,670	6
Tennessee	5,700,037	16
Texas	20,903,994	2
Virginia	7,100,702	12
Washington	5,908,684	15
Wisconsin	5,371,210	18

**Based on Census 2000 figures*

Practicing the Skills

Use the library, your textbook, or other resources to find information on the U.S. economy during the Great Depression. This could include information on national employment, inflation rates, government expenditures, or trade with foreign countries. Use this information to create a database that clearly displays the facts and figures about the economy that you have found.

History in Action

UNIT 5 SIMULATION

You Make the Decision . . .

How can the government help end the Great Depression?

Complete the following activity in small cooperative groups. It is 1932. Franklin D. Roosevelt has just defeated Herbert Hoover in the presidential election. Roosevelt won the race with a campaign promise to give Americans a New Deal—federal government programs to help cope with the effects of the Great Depression. Millions of Americans are in need of work, food, clothing, and shelter. You are members of Roosevelt's staff. Prepare a proposal for the president to send to Congress that outlines your recommendations for government programs.

1. Gather Information Use your textbook and other resources to find information that might help you decide what programs would benefit people during this economic crisis. Be sure to use what you learned from this unit's Skills Workshop on Taking Notes and Summarizing to help you reach an informed decision. You may want to divide up different parts of the research among group members.

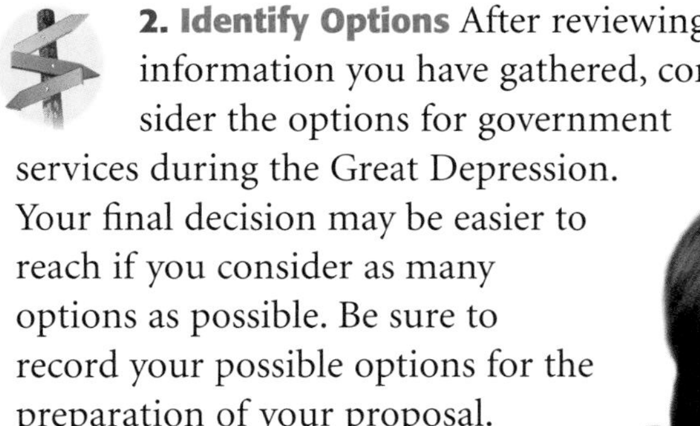

2. Identify Options After reviewing the information you have gathered, consider the options for government services during the Great Depression. Your final decision may be easier to reach if you consider as many options as possible. Be sure to record your possible options for the preparation of your proposal.

3. Predict Consequences Now take each option you and your associates came up with and consider what might be the outcome if Congress followed this course of action. Ask yourselves questions like: "How will this program help people without making them dependent on government assistance?" "How will the government fund this program?" Once you have predicted the possible consequences of each option, record the predictions as notes for the preparation of your proposal.

4. Take Action to Implement Once you have considered your options, you should plan and create the president's proposal to Congress. Be sure to make very clear your decision on what government programs should be created. You will need to support your decision by including the information that you gathered and by explaining why you rejected other options. Your proposal to Congress needs to be visually appealing. When you are ready, decide which staff members will make which part of the presentation and take your proposal to Congress (the rest of the class). Good luck!

UNIT 10 Postwar America

(1945–1975)

Young People

IN HISTORY

Young Musicians

When he was just 14 years old, Buddy Holly saw what his future held. A friend played a Fats Domino record for him, and suddenly Holly knew: he wanted to be a rock 'n' roll star. However, he had doubts about whether he could succeed. In 1953, after just a few years of practice, Holly and a friend won regular spots on a weekly radio show in their hometown of Lubbock, Texas. "You're destined to be a star," a manager at the radio station told Holly.

The manager's prediction came true. In 1957 Buddy Holly and the Crickets topped the charts with the hit single "That'll Be the Day." Later that year, after Holly performed on The *Ed Sullivan Show*, the host asked him about his rapid rise to stardom. Holly admitted, "Well, we've had a few rough times, I guess you'd say, but we've been real lucky, getting it this quick."

Holly was just one of many young musicians who became famous in the late 1950s. Following the great success of Elvis Presley—a huge star by the age of 19—many young people took up instruments and started bands. Excited teenagers crowded concert halls to listen to these new singing sensations.

The Everly Brothers perform with Sam Cooke (center) on Shindig, *a popular television show.*

One popular road show was called "America's Greatest Teenage Performing Stars." That tour included the Everly Brothers—Don and Phil. This duo started in show business at a young age. They made radio appearances on the *Everly Family Show* when they were just eight and six. In 1955 the teenage brothers headed to Nashville to write songs for a country music publisher. Two years later they had their first number one hit with "Bye Bye Love."

Some other young stars of the 1950s included Ritchie Valens as well as Frankie Lymon and the Teenagers. Valens died at age 17 in a plane crash that also killed Buddy Holly. Young musicians such as "Little" Stevie Wonder and the Jackson Five continued to top the charts throughout the 1960s and 1970s.

If You Were There *What style of music would you listen to?*

LEFT PAGE: *Teenagers at a dance*

CHAPTER

26 The Cold War Begins (1945–1955)

German children gather to watch a U.S. relief plane bringing supplies to West Berlin.

These veterans are enrolling in Austin College in Sherman, Texas.

UNITED STATES

1945 Franklin D. Roosevelt dies on April 12, and Harry S Truman becomes president.

1946 Some 400,000 members of the United Mine Workers go on strike.

1947 President Truman announces the Truman Doctrine.

1948 Truman wins an upset victory over Thomas Dewey in the presidential election.

1949 The North Atlantic Treaty Organization (NATO) is created.

1945 | 1946 | 1947 | 1948 | 1949

1945 In February the leaders of Great Britain, the Soviet Union, and the United States meet at the Yalta Conference.

Trials of Nazi war criminals begin in Nuremberg, Germany, in November.

1946 The United States and other member nations attend the first session of the United Nations in January.

In August Communist guerrillas attempt to overthrow the government of Greece.

1947 The independent nations of India and Pakistan are created.

1948 The Jewish state of Israel is founded in May.

The Soviet Union blockades the city of West Berlin in June. U.S. and British planes respond with the Berlin Airlift.

1949 Chinese Communists defeat the Nationalists and establish the People's Republic of China.

The national flag of Israel

WORLD

Winston Churchill, Franklin D. Roosevelt, and Joseph Stalin (seated left to right) met at Yalta.

Build on What You Know

During World War II the United States and the Soviet Union had been allies. Soon after the war ended, however, this relationship changed as communism spread throughout Eastern Europe. The United States and the Soviet Union became locked in a struggle for world power. American fears of communism grew, affecting foreign policy and life at home.

The development of the hydrogen bomb contributed to the arms race between the United States and the Soviet Union.

The Rosenberg spy case shocked and worried the nation.

1950 In February, Senator Joseph McCarthy claims that Communists are working in the U.S. State Department.

U.S. and UN troops go to the aid of South Korea on June 27.

1951 President Truman removes General Douglas MacArthur from command of U.S. troops in Korea.

1952 World War II General Dwight D. Eisenhower is elected president.

1953 Julius and Ethel Rosenberg are executed for stealing U.S. nuclear secrets.

1954 The Army-McCarthy hearings are televised to the American public.

1950 1951 1952 1953 1954 1955

1950 Communist North Korea invades South Korea.

1953 A cease-fire ends the Korean War.

1955 The Warsaw Pact, an alliance between the Soviet Union and Eastern European nations, is created.

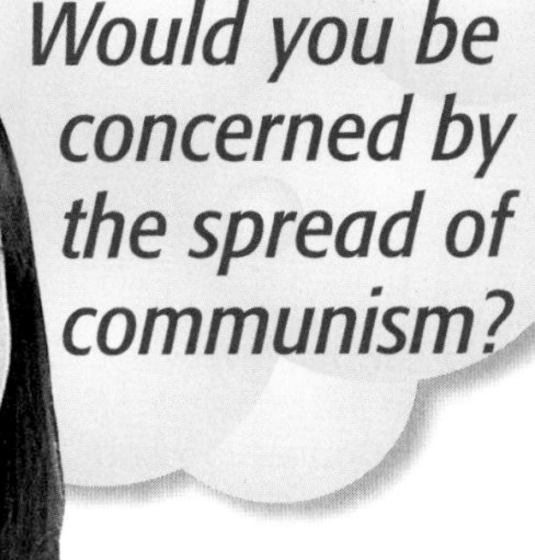

You Be the Historian

What's Your Opinion? Do you **agree** or **disagree** with the following statements? Support your point of view in your journal.

- **Economics** Sending economic aid to another country leads to political stability throughout the world.
- **Global Relations** Nations with political differences cannot be allies.
- **Citizenship** Fears of international conflict can affect civil rights at home.

Section 1

The Roots of the Cold War

Read to Discover

1. What steps did the Allies take to prevent another world war?
2. What were the major events in the Cold War between the United States and the Soviet Union from 1945 to 1950?
3. What were the major U.S. foreign-policy strategies following World War II?

Define

- containment

Identify

- Yalta Conference
- Harry S Truman
- Potsdam Conference
- United Nations
- Nuremberg Trials
- Cold War
- Truman Doctrine
- George C. Marshall
- Marshall Plan
- Berlin Airlift
- North Atlantic Treaty Organization
- Warsaw Pact

Why It Matters Today

The United Nations still plays an active role in world affairs. Use CNNfyi.com or other **current events** sources to find out about world conflicts in which the UN has recently been involved. Record your findings in your journal.

The New York Times.

PRESIDENT ROOSEVELT IS DEAD; TRUMAN TO CONTINUE POLICIES; 9TH CROSSES ELBE, NEARS BERLI

As president, Franklin Delano Roosevelt had led the United States through the Great Depression and most of World War II.

The Story Continues

At 5:47 P.M. on April 12, 1945, newscasters announced that President Franklin D. Roosevelt had died. Numb with shock, Americans faced the awful news. The man who had led the United States through the Great Depression and most of World War II was gone. The next day Vice President Harry S Truman spoke to reporters. "When they told me . . . I felt like the moon, the stars, and all the planets had fallen on me." After just 82 days as second in command, Truman had to fill the great man's shoes.

Yalta and Potsdam

As World War II wound down, world leaders began discussing their plans for the postwar world. The "Big Three" world leaders were Franklin D. Roosevelt of the United States, Winston Churchill of Great Britain, and Joseph Stalin of the Soviet Union. In February 1945 they met in the town of Yalta in the Soviet Union. During the **Yalta Conference**, the Big Three worked out an agreement that would shape international affairs for years to come. The Yalta accord strongly supported the creation of a world peacekeeping organization. It also called for free elections and democratic governments in the nations being freed from Axis control.

Stalin did not honor many of the agreements he made at Yalta. For example, he opposed democracy in Poland. He had a pro-communist government set up there to help guard the Soviet Union from future German aggression.

In July 1945, just months after President Roosevelt's death, President **Harry S Truman** met with Churchill and Stalin in Potsdam, Germany. At the **Potsdam Conference**, the three leaders agreed to divide Germany into four zones of occupation. Great Britain, France, the United States, and the Soviet Union would each control one zone. The German capital of Berlin, within the Soviet zone, was also divided into four zones.

The World after War

After seeing the wartime damage in Europe, Truman and other political leaders looked for ways to prevent future wars. British, Chinese, Soviet, and U.S. representatives had met in Washington, D.C., in 1944. They drafted a plan for the **United Nations** (UN)—an international organization that would work for world peace. In 1945, representatives from 50 nations came together in San Francisco to write the UN charter.

In another effort to promote world peace, the Allies held war crimes trials. The International Military Tribunal tried high-ranking Nazi leaders. The trials began in late 1945 in Nuremberg, Germany—where huge Nazi rallies had been held. In his opening speech at the **Nuremberg Trials**, the chief American attorney stressed the importance of the event.

History Makers Speak

"The wrongs which we seek to condemn [criticize] and punish have been so calculated [planned], so malignant [harmful] and devastating, that civilization cannot tolerate [accept] their being ignored because it cannot survive their being repeated."

—Robert Jackson, quoted in *The Holocaust: A History of Courage and Resistance*, by Bea Stadtler

Analyzing Primary Sources

Identifying Points of View According to the speaker, why is it important that the Nuremberg Trials take place?

These Nazi officials, including the head of Hitler's secret police, were the first of many charged with war crimes.

The court found 19 Nazi leaders guilty and sentenced 12 of them to death. The court also tried and convicted many lower-ranking officials.

The International Military Tribunal for the Far East held similar war crimes trials in Japan. The tribunal convicted and executed Hideki Tōjō and six other Japanese leaders. The court also convicted some 4,200 other Japanese as war criminals of a lesser degree. Of these, 720 were executed.

The Nuremberg Trials also exposed the horrors of the Holocaust and caused more people to favor the creation of a Jewish homeland—Israel. Great Britain had occupied Palestine since World War I. In November 1947 the UN General Assembly ordered that Palestine be divided into two states—one Arab and one Jewish. Britain soon pulled its troops out. On May 14, 1948, David Ben-Gurion, Israel's first prime minister, announced the establishment of the independent Jewish state of Israel.

The United States immediately recognized Israel. In response to Israel's declaration of independence, the armies of the neighboring Arab states attacked. Israeli forces not only drove back the attackers, they also advanced to occupy Arab territory. After a bitter fight, the two sides agreed to peace in 1949. Jews had a homeland, but perhaps as many as 1 million Palestinian Arabs became refugees.

✔ **Reading Check: Summarizing** How did the Allies try to prevent future wars?

American Military Bases Abroad

During the Cold War, the United States wanted to keep the Soviet Union from spreading its influence. American leaders were particularly worried about the Soviet threat to West Germany. Therefore, the United States built many army command headquarters, airfields, and smaller bases in West Germany. The United States also built bases in other Western European nations, as well as in Japan, South Korea, and the Philippines. To protect its interests in the Persian Gulf, the United States built bases in Bahrain and Saudi Arabia.

After the Cold War ended, the Department of Defense decided that there was less need for overseas bases. The United States has since closed or reduced the size of many overseas bases, notably in Europe. **Why and when were most U.S. overseas military bases established?**

Allies Become Enemies

During World War II the United States and the Soviet Union had worked together to fight Germany. With Germany defeated, the two rivals returned to the unfriendly relationship that they had had before the war. The conflicts between the two countries arose from their very different economic and political ideas—U.S. capitalism and democracy versus Soviet communism. The United States saw itself as a beacon of freedom for the world. The Soviet Union, on the other hand, hoped to spread communism around the world.

The immediate postwar conflict between the United States and the Soviet Union focused on Germany. The Western Allies wanted a united, demilitarized, and independent Germany. The Soviets feared a united Germany and created a buffer of communist "satellite states" in Eastern Europe. Despite the Yalta agreement on free elections, the governments of these countries were under Soviet control.

"An Iron Curtain has descended across the [European] Continent," remarked Winston Churchill. British and U.S. leaders feared that the Soviets would soon dominate the rest of Europe. In April 1947 presidential adviser Bernard Baruch explained the U.S.-Soviet relationship. "Let us not be deceived—we are today in the midst of a cold war." Over time, many people used the term **Cold War** to describe the two countries' competition for world power.

In August 1946, communist rebels in Greece threatened to take control of the British-backed government. In February 1947, British leaders told President Truman that they could no longer afford to help the Greek government fight the Communists. President Truman became very worried about the spread of communism in Europe. If Greece fell to communism, he thought, so might Turkey, Greece's neighbor. In March 1947 President Truman asked Congress for $400 million in aid for Greece and Turkey. He also stated that the United States would use economic aid to help foreign countries fight communism. This policy became known as the **Truman Doctrine**. Congress passed Truman's aid package to Greece and Turkey. This aid helped the Greek army to defeat the rebels. However, the U.S. intervention greatly angered Soviet leaders.

✔ **Reading Check: Analyzing Information** What were some of the major issues that marked the beginning of the Cold War?

Interpreting Political Cartoons

Iron Curtain *This cartoon shows the nation of Czechoslovakia being crushed by the Soviets' Iron Curtain.* ***What do you think the extinguished torch in the cartoon represents?***

The Marshall Plan

Despite the Truman Doctrine, U.S. officials continued to worry about European affairs. U.S. Army General **George C. Marshall** became Truman's secretary of state in 1947. Marshall believed that European countries that were rebuilding had far greater needs than they could afford to fulfill. He saw the situation as a danger to both world peace and the U.S. economy, which depended on trade with Europe.

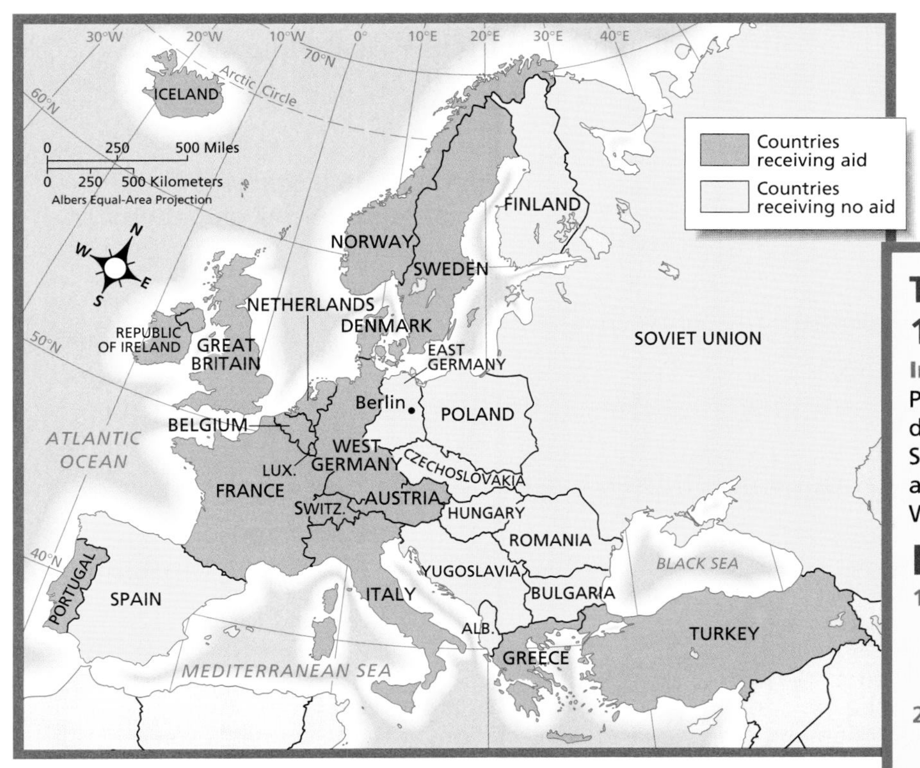

The Marshall Plan, 1948–1951

Interpreting Maps The Marshall Plan lasted from 1948 until 1951, during which time the United States sent about $13 billion in aid to countries recovering from World War II.

Skills Assessment

1. **Places and Regions** Which nation in Western Europe did not receive aid under the Marshall Plan?
2. **Analyzing Information** What was the easternmost country to receive aid?

Tons of goods sent through the Marshall Plan greatly aided Europe's recovery after the war.

Marshall called on European leaders to create long-range plans for economic recovery. He said that the United States would offer "friendly aid" to help European countries rebuild. Congress approved aid money for this program, known as the **Marshall Plan**. Between 1948 and 1951, the United States gave or loaned more than $13 billion to Western European countries. Although the United States also offered economic aid to the Soviet Union, the Soviets refused. They stopped their Eastern European satellites from accepting any U.S. aid as well.

✔ **Reading Check: Identifying Cause and Effect** Why did the United States want to help Europe after World War II, and what was the result?

Containment

At the beginning of the Cold War, the United States started a new foreign policy to stop the spread of communism. This policy was known as **containment**—the effort to prevent the Soviet Union from expanding into strategically important areas. In the late 1940s a crisis in occupied Germany tested containment. In 1948 the Western powers joined their occupied areas of Berlin into one—West Berlin. Because it had been invaded many times by Germany, the Soviet Union feared a strong West German state. On June 24, 1948, the Soviets suddenly blocked all rail and highway traffic between western Germany and Berlin.

This Soviet move threatened to become a communist takeover. Deprived of essential supplies, West Berlin was left with only 36 days' worth of food. To solve the crisis without direct military confrontation, U.S. officials decided to fly supplies into West Berlin. On June 26, U.S.

Causes of the Cold War

Although allies during World War II, the United States and the Soviet Union were soon locked in a competition for global power.

Military
The United States and the Soviet Union were the only two military superpowers left at the end of World War II.

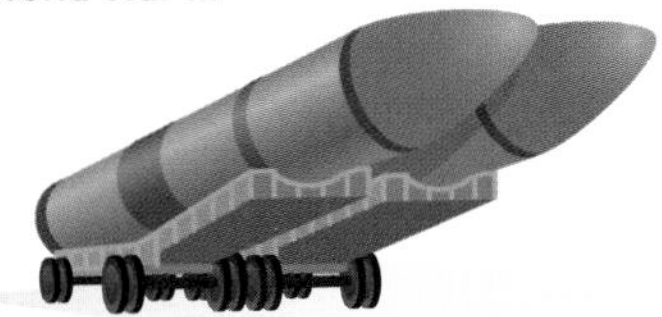

Political
The United States supported democracy, while the Soviet Union practiced totalitarianism.

Economic
The United States supported capitalism and free enterprise, while the Soviet Union supported communism and a state-controlled economy.

Visualizing History

1. **Global Relations** What were the major differences between the Soviet Union and the United States?
2. **Connecting to Today** What is the current status of relations with the former Soviet Union?

and British planes began the **Berlin Airlift**. This operation brought food and supplies to the more than 2 million people in the western part of the city. On September 9, 1948, the mayor of West Berlin reminded the world of the issues at stake.

> **"We cannot be bartered [traded], we cannot be negotiated, we cannot be sold. . . . People of the world, look upon this city! You cannot, you must not, forsake [abandon] us!"**
>
> —Ernst Reuter, quoted in *Telegraf,* September 9, 1948

The airlift lasted until the Soviet Union lifted its blockade on May 12, 1949. That same year, Germany was divided into two nations. West Germany became the Federal Republic of Germany, and East Germany became the German Democratic Republic.

In April 1949 the United States and nine Western European nations formed the **North Atlantic Treaty Organization** (NATO). Canada and Iceland also became members. Member nations pledged to defend one another if they were attacked. In 1955 the Soviet Union responded to NATO by creating its own military alliance, the **Warsaw Pact**. This group included the Soviet Union and its Eastern European satellite nations.

In August 1949 the Soviet Union shocked the United States by exploding its own atomic bomb. The Cold War soon grew more intense. The United States quadrupled its defense spending, and President Truman approved the development of more powerful nuclear weapons. Just a few years after the end of World War II, the Cold War between the United States and Soviet Union was spreading around the world.

This NATO badge bears a Latin inscription meaning "Vigilance is the price of liberty."

✔ **Reading Check: Finding the Main Idea** What foreign policy strategy did the United States follow after World War II, and how was it tested in Berlin?

Section 1 Review

1. **Define** and explain:
   - containment
2. **Identify** and explain:
   - Yalta Conference
   - Harry S Truman
   - Potsdam Conference
   - United Nations
   - Nuremberg Trials
   - Cold War
   - Truman Doctrine
   - George C. Marshall
   - Marshall Plan
   - Berlin Airlift
   - North Atlantic Treaty Organization
   - Warsaw Pact
3. **Summarizing** Copy the graphic organizer below. Use it to explain the actions of the United States and the Soviet Union in the Cold War during the five years after World War II.

   United States → Cold War 1945–50 ← Soviet Union

4. **Finding the Main Idea**
   a. How did the Allies try to preserve world peace?
   b. How did the United States attempt to stop Soviet expansion and strengthen Western Europe through its foreign policy after World War II?
5. **Writing and Critical Thinking**
   Analyzing Information Imagine that you are a Jew who survived the Holocaust. Write a short article for an Israeli newspaper that expresses your reaction to the Nuremberg Trials.
   Consider the following:
   - the Allies' reasons for holding the trials
   - the effect of the trials on public awareness of crimes against Jews
   - the outcome of the trials

Section 2

The Truman Era

Read to Discover

1. What steps did the U.S. government take to help returning veterans?
2. What problems took place in the workforce during the 1940s?
3. What problems did Truman face in the 1948 presidential election, and why did he win?

Identify

- GI Bill of Rights
- United Mine Workers
- John Lewis
- Taft-Hartley Act
- Dixiecrats
- Fair Deal

Why it Matters Today

Close elections continue to be a part of American political life. Use CNNfyi.com or other **current events** sources to find out about a closely decided federal or state election that has recently taken place. Record your findings in your journal.

Like Chesterfield Smith, millions of veterans went back to school.

The Story Continues

Chesterfield Smith entered the University of Florida in 1935. By 1940 he had completed only three and a half years of school. "I chose the easy life in college," Smith explained. Then World War II came, and Smith served in France. In 1946 he returned home and quickly finished college. Smith's wife described the change. "Something happened to Chesterfield's attitude in the war, I don't know just what, he was a serious man when he returned." Smith was one of many Americans who became serious about the future after the war.

Returning to Peace

After World War II the United States faced the challenge of returning to a peacetime economy. Truman worried that ending defense contracts might cause a recession, as had happened after World War I. Yet he believed that the United States needed a strong economy to compete in the Cold War.

More than 15 million Americans had served in the armed forces. Most of them needed jobs when they left the service. To create these jobs, the government encouraged millions of women who had taken part in the wartime economy to stop working. Many women were unhappy about this loss of income and independence. One woman complained about the pressure to leave her job.

> **"They say a woman doesn't belong behind a factory machine or in any business organization. But . . . who will give my family the help they have been getting from me? No one has thought to ask me whether or not I need my job."**
>
> —Mary Smith, quoted in *Born for Liberty,* by Sarah M. Evans

Analyzing Primary Sources
Identifying Points of View How does this speaker feel about the postwar labor situation?

Although government officials feared that millions of Americans would be unemployed, the economy continued to grow. New laws such as the Servicemen's Readjustment Act, also called the **GI Bill of Rights**, helped veterans. Passed in 1944, the GI Bill offered generous benefits such as affordable home and business loans. It also provided financial aid to attend colleges and technical schools. Veteran Guy Owen earned his graduate degree and became a professor. "The GI Bill, I can't emphasize enough, really saved me," he recalled. "[It] took me . . . to places . . . where I had different experiences from what I would have ever seen." Millions of veterans took advantage of such aid.

✔ **Reading Check: Analyzing Information** How did the GI Bill of Rights help veterans?

Labor Unrest

Despite President Truman's efforts, there were some postwar economic troubles. With the end of rationing and fixed controls on prices, consumers rushed to buy goods. As a result, prices skyrocketed. Between 1945 and 1947, food prices rose by more than one third. The inflation rate in 1946 was more than 18 percent.

Daily Life

Labor unrest After World War II ended, the lives of some workers became very difficult. Many people lost their jobs to returning veterans. Workers who kept their jobs found that their wages did not keep up with rising food costs. At one point, the cost of meat rose so high that some markets began selling cheaper horsemeat to desperate customers. Many workers responded to such conditions by going on strike for higher pay. What do these strikers' signs call for?

Harry S Truman

Harry S Truman was born in May 1884 in Lamar, Missouri. From an early age he was a good student. "I don't know anybody in the world [who] ever read as much or as constantly as he did," a friend remembered. Truman also studied human nature, a skill that helped him in his political career.

During World War I Truman felt a duty to serve his country. Several personal factors, such as his age and poor eyesight, would have allowed him to avoid military service. He joined nonetheless, saying it was "a job somebody had to do." After serving in a command position, Truman returned to Missouri where he began his political career. He became a U.S. senator in 1935. Ten years later he became vice president. **Why did Truman join the military during World War I?**

As inflation soared, unions went on strike for higher pay. Around 4.5 million workers across the country took part in nearly 5,000 strikes in 1946. In April some 400,000 members of the **United Mine Workers** (UMW) walked off their jobs. When President Truman could not work out a settlement between management and labor, he placed the coal mines under government control. Then, in November, UMW president **John Lewis** called a second strike. This time Truman pledged to "fight to the finish." A federal judge ordered Lewis to stand trial for contempt, or disobeying an official order. "You can't dig coal with bayonets," replied Lewis. After receiving a $3 million fine, however, Lewis finally called an end to the strike.

Republicans in Congress wanted to weaken the power of labor unions. They were particularly worried about closed shops—workplaces in which job applicants must join a union before being hired. In 1947 Ohio senator Robert Taft led the drive to pass the **Taft-Hartley Act**. This act made closed shops illegal and required union leaders to swear they were not Communists. It also gave the president the power to prevent strikes. The president could get a court order forcing striking unions to call off their strikes for an 80-day "cooling off" period. Truman thought that the Taft-Hartley Act placed too many limits on unions. He vetoed the bill, but Congress overrode his veto.

✔ **Reading Check: Identifying Cause and Effect** Why did the UMW members go on strike, and how did the U.S. government respond?

The 1948 Election

The labor unrest caused many Americans to question Truman's ability to serve as president. These worries helped the Republican Party. In 1946 the Republicans had gained control of Congress for the first time in 18 years. After this victory, they began to believe they could win the White House in 1948. In 1948 the Republicans nominated New York governor Thomas Dewey for president. Dewey chose California governor Earl Warren to run for vice president. Meanwhile, even leaders of the Democratic Party did not think that Truman could win re-election. Many Democrats joined a "dump Truman" movement that tried to replace him with another candidate. At the 1948 national convention, however, Truman was able to win the party's nomination.

Some southern Democrats who were upset with Truman's position on civil rights walked out of the convention. Many of them joined the new States' Rights Party, whose members were called **Dixiecrats**. The Dixiecrats backed racial segregation and the limiting of African American voting rights. They nominated South Carolina governor J. Strom Thurmond for president. A second group of Democrats disliked Truman's position on labor strikes. They joined a new Progressive Party to support former vice president Henry Wallace for president.

One of President Truman's supporters made this model donkey for him.

Truman campaigned with great energy. He traveled more than 30,000 miles by train and delivered hundreds of speeches. He attacked Congress as "do-nothing" and "good-for-nothing." Yet public opinion polls predicted a huge victory for Dewey. Truman's victory surprised almost everyone but himself.

Truman's victory had several explanations. He had won union support with his veto of the Taft-Hartley Act. He had won African American support with his position on civil rights. In addition, many Wallace supporters switched to Truman when it looked as if Dewey would win. Perhaps the best explanation for Truman's victory came from the postwar economy. As one suburban voter explained, "I own a nice house. I have a new car. . . . Why change?"

Interpreting the Visual Record

Surprise winner *Some newspapers were so confident of Dewey's victory that they printed papers for the day after the election with the wrong headlines.* ***Why do you think Truman is smiling as he poses with this newspaper?***

Truman was certain that Americans supported his policies. He suggested a series of reform programs that became known as the **Fair Deal**. The Fair Deal was intended to provide full employment, a higher minimum wage, and a national health insurance plan. Truman also called for more affordable housing, greater Social Security benefits, and aid for farmers. Congress approved some Fair Deal reforms, such as expanding Social Security and raising the minimum wage. However, Congress rejected some civil rights laws, federal aid to education, and the national health insurance program. But other acts did provide billions of dollars for domestic improvements and the GI Bill of Rights. This government spending helped to keep the postwar boom going.

✔ **Reading Check: Summarizing** What were the major presidential election issues in 1948, and how did they affect the election's outcome?

Section 2 Review

go.hrw.com **Homework Practice Online** keyword: SC3 HP26

1. **Identify** and explain:
   - GI Bill of Rights
   - United Mine Workers
   - John Lewis
   - Taft-Hartley Act
   - Dixiecrats
   - Fair Deal

2. **Contrasting** Copy the chart below. Use it to show successes and failures in postwar American society.

	Successes	Failures
Economy		
Society		
Fair Deal		

3. **Finding the Main Idea**

   a. What assistance did returning U.S. veterans receive from their government?

   b. Why did so many workers go on strike during the 1940s, and what effect did this have on governmental policy?

4. **Writing and Critical Thinking**

   Identifying Cause and Effect Imagine that you are an American voter in 1948. Write a letter to a friend in another country describing the progress and outcome of the presidential election.

   Consider the following:
   - the problems arising at the Democratic Convention
   - the Truman campaign
   - why people supported Truman in his victory

Section 3

The War in Korea

Read to Discover

1. How did communism affect Asia after World War II?
2. What were the main events of the Korean War, and how did the war end?
3. How did the Korean War affect the 1952 presidential election?

Identify

- Mao Zedong
- Long March
- 38th parallel
- Douglas MacArthur
- Adlai Stevenson
- Dwight D. Eisenhower

Why It Matters Today

North Korea and South Korea remain divided today, but in recent years have looked for ways to have a closer relationship. Use CNNfyi.com or other **current events** sources to learn about what the current relationship between the two countries is like today. Record your findings in your journal.

The Imperial Palace in Beijing

The Story Continues

In January 1949, Chinese Communists took control of the capital city of Beijing. It was a major victory in their civil war with the ruling Nationalist Party. In Congress, John F. Kennedy called the Communists' success a "failure of our foreign policy in the Far East." He feared that nothing would keep "the onrushing tide of Communism from engulfing all of Asia." Many Americans agreed that Asia was now a major front in the Cold War.

The Cold War in Asia

China's monarchy fell in 1912, causing great political unrest. During the 1920s the Chinese Nationalist Party and the Chinese Communists began a bitter civil war. In 1934 some 100,000 Communists fled from a Nationalist army attack. **Mao Zedong** (MOW DZUH-DOOHNG) led the Communists' escape. The Communists' months-long, 6,000-mile retreat to northwestern China became known as the **Long March**. Over time, the Communists gained control of northern China.

During the mid-1930s the Nationalists joined with the Communists to defeat the invading Japanese. The two sides continued to cooperate throughout World War II. After this war, however, the civil war resumed. Although the Nationalist government was corrupt, the U.S. government preferred it to communism. Despite U.S. support for the Nationalists, the Communists won the Civil War in 1949. They forced their enemies to flee to the island of Taiwan and founded the People's Republic of China on the mainland.

Made up primarily of U.S. troops, UN forces scaled Korea's mountainous landscape to fight Communist forces. Many U.S. soldiers received the Korean service medal, shown here.

The postwar period also brought new governments to Japan and Korea. After World War II, U.S. forces occupied Japan and began rebuilding the country's ruined economy. Military leaders also created a U.S.-style constitution. The constitution placed more power in the hands of the Japanese people and gave women the right to vote.

Japan had controlled Korea from 1910 until the end of World War II. After the war, the Allies divided Korea between U.S. and Soviet troops. Each country created a government in its part of Korea that was friendly to the country that was occupying it. The pro-Soviet Democratic People's Republic of Korea controlled the northern half of the peninsula. The U.S.-backed Republic of Korea controlled the south. When U.S. and Soviet troops pulled out in 1949, both the North and South Korean governments claimed the entire country.

✔ **Reading Check:** **Analyzing Information** What successes did Communists experience in postwar Asia?

The Korean War

When the Soviets withdrew from Korea in 1949, they left behind a well-equipped and well-trained army. On June 25, 1950, North Korean forces quickly advanced across the **38th parallel**, the line of latitude that divided the two Koreas. The UN Security Council immediately called for a cease-fire. However, the North Koreans continued the invasion.

On June 27 the UN called on its members to support South Korea. President Truman announced that he had ordered United States air and sea forces to assist the Korean troops. General **Douglas MacArthur** flew to Korea and reported that South Korea needed ground troops immediately. MacArthur was named commander of the UN forces, which consisted largely of U.S. and South Korean troops.

Research on the ROM

Free Find:
Douglas MacArthur
After reading about General Douglas MacArthur on the **Holt Researcher CD–ROM**, write a short essay examining why his military experiences might have led him to develop such an aggressive strategy in Korea.

June 27, 1950
The United States agrees to intervene in the Korean War.

By September the North Korean army had driven UN forces to the very tip of the peninsula. UN forces occupied a small area near the port city of Pusan. For six weeks, fierce fighting raged along the Pusan front. Though the situation seemed hopeless at times, military leaders had a daring plan to turn the tide of the war—a surprise attack behind enemy lines. On September 15, UN forces streamed onto shore near the port city of Inch'ŏn. Then they attacked the North Korean forces from behind. Just over a month later, MacArthur's forces captured P'yŏngyang (pyuhng-yang), North Korea's capital. Later, they reached the Yalu River, the border between China and North Korea. MacArthur boasted, "[I'll] have the boys home by Christmas."

Then, quite unexpectedly, hundreds of thousands of Chinese troops crossed the border to help the North Koreans. The Chinese drove the UN forces back below the 38th parallel. A platoon leader in the 24th Infantry described one of these difficult battles.

"I was trying to . . . figure out how to attack the hill when suddenly three shells landed directly in front of me. . . . The explosions were near enough to knock out the entire group of eight or nine men. . . . The medics could scarcely keep up with the men who had been hit. . . . When we reached the top of the hill, the enemy had cut and run, and we collapsed on the ground, not bothering to dig in."

—Lyle Rishell, *With a Black Platoon in Combat: A Year in Korea*

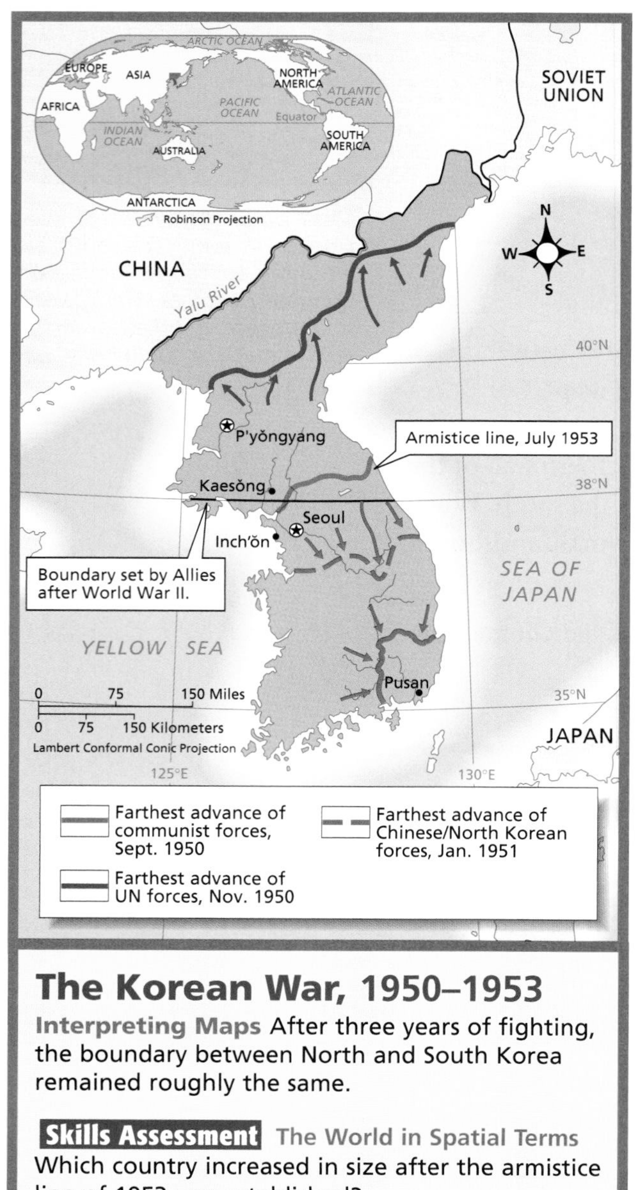

The Korean War, 1950–1953

Interpreting Maps After three years of fighting, the boundary between North and South Korea remained roughly the same.

Skills Assessment **The World in Spatial Terms** Which country increased in size after the armistice line of 1953 was established?

Truman did not want the war to expand beyond Korea. Despite knowing Truman's position, General MacArthur called for air strikes on Chinese cities and a ground attack on the Chinese coast. When Truman refused, MacArthur criticized the president openly. Truman then removed MacArthur as commander on April 11, 1951. Truman's decision was unpopular with many Americans. MacArthur returned home to parades and celebrations. Soon after, UN forces pushed the Chinese and North Koreans back across the 38th parallel, where fighting settled into a standstill.

By the spring of 1951, it seemed clear that neither side in Korea was going to win on the battlefield. Peace negotiations began in July 1951, but little progress was made. As the negotiations and the war dragged on, the American public grew more frustrated.

✔ **Reading Check: Sequencing** List the events of the Korean War in the order that they took place.

The End of the War

The Korean War became the major issue in the presidential election of 1952. Knowing that many voters blamed him for the war, President Truman did not seek re-election. The Democrats nominated Illinois governor **Adlai Stevenson** for president. Stevenson was intelligent but he seemed out of touch with the "real world" to many voters. Hoping to win the White House for the first time since 1928, the Republicans nominated General **Dwight D. Eisenhower**. Ike, as he was often called, probably won the race when he pledged to end the Korean War.

> **"The first task of a new administration will be to . . . bring the Korean War to an early and honorable end. . . . For this task a wholly new administration is necessary. . . . The old administration cannot be expected to repair what it failed to prevent."**
>
> —Dwight D. Eisenhower, quoted in the *New York Times,* October 25, 1952

Interpreting the Visual Record

Eisenhower *During the 1952 campaign, Eisenhower attracted crowds of supporters.* ***What signs of Eisenhower's popularity can you see in this picture?***

Eisenhower won the election easily with 55 percent of the vote.

Despite Eisenhower's efforts, the peace talks remained stalled. He even hinted that the United States might use atomic weapons if the conflict did not end. On July 27, 1953, the two sides signed a cease-fire.

After three years of fighting, Korea remained divided roughly along the 38th parallel. U.S. forces alone had suffered some 155,000 casualties. North Korean and Chinese military casualties totaled more than 1.5 million. Tense relations continued between the two Koreas, and U.S. forces have remained stationed along the border ever since.

✔ Reading Check: **Summarizing** How did the Korean War end?

Section 3 Review

go.hrw.com **Homework Practice Online**
keyword: SC3 HP26

1. **Identify** and explain:
   - Mao Zedong
   - Long March
   - 38th parallel
   - Douglas MacArthur
   - Adlai Stevenson
   - Dwight D. Eisenhower

2. **Analyzing Information** Copy the diagram below. Use it to show how communism affected Asia after World War II. Identify the new governments that came to power and note those that were communist.

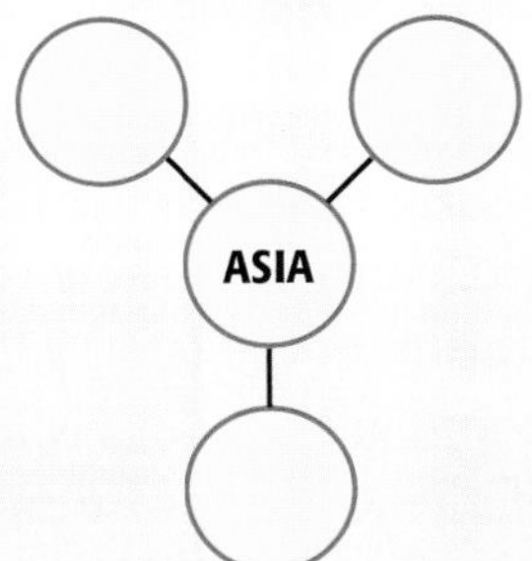

3. **Finding the Main Idea**
   a. Why did the United States become involved in the Korean War, and what were the major events in the war?
   b. How was the 1952 presidential election influenced by the Korean War, and how did the election's outcome affect the end of the war?

4. **Writing and Critical Thinking**
   Supporting a Point of View Imagine that you are a U.S. soldier who has been stationed in South Korea since the start of the Korean War. Write a letter to a family member arguing for or against President Truman's removal of General Douglas MacArthur.
   Consider the following:
   - the main events of the war
   - MacArthur's military successes
   - MacArthur's public criticism of Truman

Section 4

Cold War Fears

Read to Discover

1. What caused the new Red Scare?
2. What role did Senator Joseph McCarthy play in the new Red Scare?
3. How did post–World War II popular culture reflect Cold War fears?

Define

- blacklisting

Identify

- House Un-American Activities Committee
- Internal Security Act
- Whittaker Chambers
- Alger Hiss
- Julius and Ethel Rosenberg
- Joseph McCarthy
- McCarthyism
- Edward R. Murrow
- Army-McCarthy hearings

WHY IT MATTERS TODAY

As during the Red Scare, current movies often reflect the concerns of many Americans. Use CNNfyi.com or other **current events** sources to find out how television, books, or movies address important social issues today. Record your findings in your journal.

Paul Robeson was just one of many entertainers investigated as a result of fears such as this magazine's claim that Communists controlled the American media.

The Story Continues

In the 1940s, African American actor and singer Paul Robeson found his career threatened by accusations that he was a communist. Because Robeson favored a close U.S.-Soviet relationship, in 1950 the State Department took away his passport. When asked why he did not leave the United States, Robeson replied, "My father was a slave, and my people died to build this country. No . . . people will drive me from it." Many other artists faced similar difficulties due to their political beliefs.

A New Red Scare

The Cold War created strong fears of Communists and communism in the United States, leading to a new Red Scare. The first Red Scare had begun just after World War I and the communist revolution in Russia. The new Red Scare started in the late 1930s and reached its full strength during the late 1940s and early 1950s. Many Americans were concerned about the growth of the U.S. Communist Party. The Soviet Union's expanded control over Eastern Europe also worried Americans. The

Communist successes in China and involvement in the Korean War further increased anticommunist feeling in the United States.

In May 1938 Congress had established the **House Un-American Activities Committee** (HUAC). This committee looked into disloyalty and harmful foreign influences in the United States. In 1947 HUAC began a series of widely publicized hearings to prove that Communists were working in the State Department and in Hollywood. The committee often ignored citizens' rights. One writer called before the committee charged that HUAC "conducted an illegal and indecent [rude] trial of American citizens." HUAC investigations of the motion picture industry found no widespread communist activities. Yet executives in film, radio, television, and theater began **blacklisting**, or refusing to hire, suspected Communists. The most famous of those blacklisted were the so-called Hollywood Ten, a group of writers who would not cooperate with HUAC.

During the Red Scare even popular culture began to reflect many Americans' fear of communism. Magazines published articles like "Communists Are After Your Child." Between 1948 and 1954 Hollywood produced more than 40 anticommunist films. Science fiction movies often combined fears about new forms of technology with the fear of communism.

✔ **Reading Check: Identifying Cause and Effect** What led to the new Red Scare, and how did it affect some Americans?

The Crucible

Arthur Miller

A courtroom scene from a film version of The Crucible

In his 1953 play, *The Crucible*, author Arthur Miller compared McCarthyism to the Salem witch trials of 1692. In the following excerpt John Proctor, a man accused of witchcraft, refuses to identify other witches for Deputy Governor Danforth.

DANFORTH: Mr. Proctor, a score of people have already testified they saw this woman with the Devil.

PROCTOR: Then it is proved. Why must I say it?

DANFORTH: Why "must" you say it! Why, you should rejoice to say it if your soul is truly purged of any love for Hell! . . . Look you, sir. I think you mistake your duty here. It matters nothing what she thought—she is convicted. . . . Your soul alone is the issue here, Mister, and you will prove its whiteness or you cannot live in a Christian country. Will you tell me now what persons **conspired**[1] with you in the Devil's company? *Proctor is silent.* To your knowledge was Rebecca Nurse ever—

PROCTOR: I speak my own sins; I cannot judge another. *Crying out, with hatred:* I have no tongue for it.

Understanding What You Read

1. **Literature and History** Which elements of this excerpt reflect colonial times? Which reflect the 1950s?
2. **Literature and You** What would you do if you were in Proctor's situation?

[1] **conspired:** planned

That's Interesting!

The Pumpkin Papers
Would you hide top-secret government documents in a pumpkin? Well, Whittaker Chambers did. After Chambers accused Alger Hiss of being a communist spy, Hiss sued for libel. To prove his claims, Chambers decided to produce secret government microfilm Hiss had given him years earlier. Chambers revealed that he had concealed it in a hollowed-out pumpkin on his Maryland farm! The microfilm, nicknamed the "pumpkin papers," brought even more interest to the already spectacular spy case.

Spies in Government

After World War II, many Republicans said President Truman had allowed Communists to sneak into the government. In response, Truman created the Loyalty Review Board in March 1947 to investigate the background of thousands of federal workers. The board reviews did not find any Communists. However, some people lost their jobs because of "reasonable grounds" to suspect their loyalty. Other organizations, such as the Federal Bureau of Investigation (FBI) and Justice Department, soon started their own loyalty oaths and investigations. State and local governments, schools, and universities were among these organizations. Thousands of people lost their jobs because they were suspected of sympathizing or agreeing with communism.

In 1950 Congress passed the **Internal Security Act**. This law forced organizations thought to be communist to register with the government. The law also gave the government the right to arrest people suspected of treasonous activities during times of national emergency.

In the late 1940s, dramatic spy cases made Cold War fears worse. In 1948 journalist **Whittaker Chambers** confessed that he had spied for the Soviets. Testifying before HUAC, Chambers accused **Alger Hiss**, a former State Department official, of being a Soviet spy. Hiss denied the charges. Chambers later produced secret papers that he said Hiss had passed to the Soviet Union. Hiss insisted he was innocent. Nevertheless, he was tried, found guilty of perjury, and sentenced to five years in prison.

The spy cases went on into the 1950s. In 1951 **Julius and Ethel Rosenberg** were convicted of passing secret atomic weapons information to the Soviet Union. People around the world protested, claiming that the Rosenbergs were innocent victims of the Red Scare. Despite this support, they were executed in June 1953 for spying.

✔ **Reading Check: Summarizing** How did the government try to identify spies, and who became the most famous spies?

McCarthyism

More than anyone else, Senator **Joseph McCarthy** helped stir up Cold War fears. McCarthy, a Republican from Wisconsin, began a campaign to find Communists in the U.S. government. McCarthy blamed the spread of communism on government leaders involved in making foreign policy.

Analyzing Primary Sources
Identifying Bias Why do you think McCarthy made dramatic accusations such as this?

"The State Department . . . is thoroughly infested with Communists. I have in my hand fifty-seven cases of individuals who would appear to be either card-carrying members or certainly loyal to the Communist Party, but who nevertheless are still helping to shape our foreign policy."

—Joseph McCarthy, quoted in *The Annals of America, Vol. 17*

McCarthy's charges shocked many people, and members of Congress challenged him to make public the names on his list. He finally offered one name. When an early investigation called McCarthy's charges "a fraud and a hoax," he simply made up more charges. His method of making accusations without offering proof became known as **McCarthyism**.

Few Americans challenged McCarthy. Others were afraid of being labeled "soft on communism" themselves. In addition, many Americans wanted an explanation for the spread of communism in Eastern Europe and Asia, and McCarthy gave them one.

A few people did attempt to stop Senator McCarthy. Journalist **Edward R. Murrow** tried to expose McCarthy on the television show *See It Now.* Instead of being congratulated, Murrow received bundles of hate mail. However, in late 1953, the senator went too far when he claimed that there were Communists in the military. To investigate his charges, a group of senators decided to hold televised hearings on the matter. These **Army-McCarthy hearings** proved to be McCarthy's downfall. Over time, the army's attorney, Joseph Welch, won the other senators' favor with his polite charm. In desperation, McCarthy charged that Welch's law firm employed a former Communist. Senators were stunned by this statement, which had nothing to do with the hearings. Welch responded, "Have you left no sense of decency?" At this remark, the people watching the hearing applauded.

Viewers across the nation finally saw McCarthy for what he was—a bully. In 1954 the Senate voted 67 to 22 to condemn McCarthy. However, many people's careers and lives had been destroyed by McCarthy's lies. For these victims, it was a classic case of too little, too late.

Interpreting Political Cartoons

Red Scare *This political cartoon shows the damage that McCarthy's anticommunist campaign did to the reputation of the U.S. State Department.* ***Do you think this artist supported or opposed McCarthy's tactics?***

✔ **Reading Check: Finding the Main Idea** How did Joseph McCarthy contribute to the new Red Scare?

Section 4 Review

go.hrw.com Homework Practice Online
keyword: SC3 HP26

1. **Define** and explain:
   - blacklisting

2. **Identify** and explain:
   - House Un-American Activities Committee
   - Internal Security Act
   - Whittaker Chambers
   - Alger Hiss
   - Julius and Ethel Rosenberg
   - Joseph McCarthy
   - McCarthyism
   - Edward R. Murrow
   - Army-McCarthy hearings

3. **Summarizing** Copy the graphic organizer below. Use it to identify the factors that led to the new Red Scare.

   New Red Scare
   4.
   3.
   2.
   1.

4. **Finding the Main Idea**
   a. What methods did the U.S. government use to find spies in the postwar period?
   b. How were Cold War fears apparent in popular culture?

5. **Writing and Critical Thinking**
   Supporting a Point of View Imagine that you are a radio broadcaster who has observed Joseph McCarthy's rise to power. Write the script to a radio editorial describing McCarthy's role in the new Red Scare. Then state your opinion of his actions.
   Consider the following:
   - the reasons for the Red Scare
   - McCarthy's accusations without proof
   - the effect on citizens' rights and freedoms

Chapter 26 Review

The Chapter at a Glance

Examine the visual summary of the chapter below. Then use it to write a fill-in-the-blank quiz that you can give to a classmate.

Domestic Events

1944: The GI Bill of Rights is passed.
1946: The United Mine Workers go on strike.
1950s: The House Un-American Activities Committee (HUAC) investigates Communists.
1951: Julius and Ethel Rosenberg are convicted for spying.
1954: The Army-McCarthy hearings take place.

Foreign Events

1945: The Potsdam Conference is held. The United Nations is formed.
1947: The Truman Doctrine is announced.
1948–49: The Berlin Airlift takes place.
1949: The North Atlantic Treaty Organization is formed.
1950–53: The Korean War is fought.

Identifying People and Ideas

Use the following terms and people in historically significant sentences.

1. Yalta Conference
2. Nuremberg Trials
3. George C. Marshall
4. GI Bill of Rights
5. Fair Deal
6. Mao Zedong
7. 38th parallel
8. Dwight D. Eisenhower
9. blacklisting
10. McCarthyism

Understanding Main Ideas

Section 1 *(Pages 798–803)*

1. What steps did the Allies take to prevent another world war?
2. How did the United States fight the spread of Communism in Western Europe after World War II?

Section 2 *(Pages 804–807)*

3. What major events took place during the Truman administration?
4. What challenges did President Truman face in the 1948 election, and how did he win the election?

Section 3 *(Pages 808–811)*

5. What were the causes and outcomes of the Korean War?

Section 4 *(Pages 812–815)*

6. What led to a new Red Scare in the United States?

You Be the Historian—Reviewing Themes

1. **Economics** Why did George C. Marshall think that aiding the European economies would help prevent the spread of communism?
2. **Global Relations** What events led to the Cold War between the United States and the Soviet Union?
3. **Citizenship** How did the Cold War affect Americans' freedoms?

Thinking Critically

1. **Drawing Inferences and Conclusions** Why do you think the United States offered economic aid to the Soviet Union, and why do you think the Soviet Union refused?
2. **Finding the Main Idea** Why did Americans' Cold War fears center on communism, and how did these fears affect U.S. foreign policy?
3. **Analyzing Information** What was the status of the national economy in 1948, and how did that affect the presidential election?

Social Studies Skills Workshop

Interpreting Maps

Study the map below. Then use the information on the map to help you answer the questions that follow.

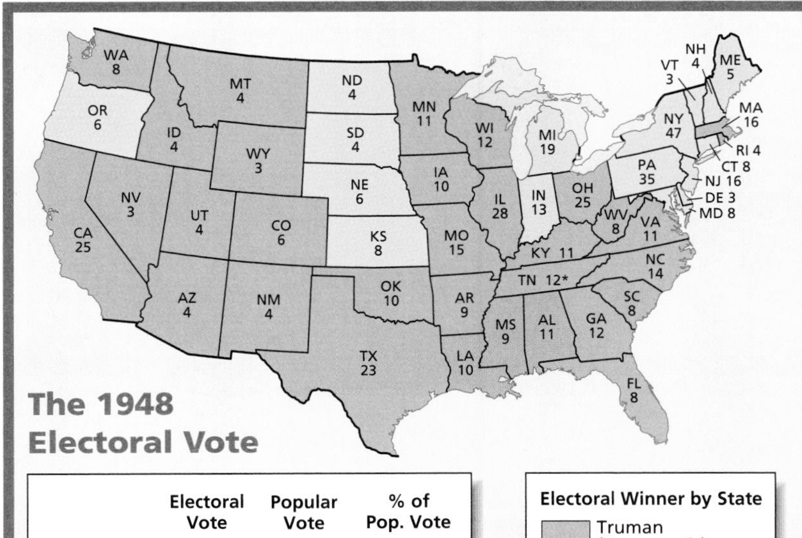

The 1948 Electoral Vote

	Electoral Vote	Popular Vote	% of Pop. Vote
Truman	303	24,179,345	49.6%
Dewey	189	21,991,291	45.1
Thurmond	39*	1,176,125	2.4
Other parties		1,443,653	2.9

*One elector in Tennessee voted for Thurmond.
Source: *Historical Statistics of the United States*

1. Which of the following statements is most accurate based on the information shown on the map?
   a. Truman had strong support in New England.
   b. Most western states voted for Dewey.
   c. If Dewey had won California, Ohio, and Texas, Truman would have lost the election.
   d. If Thurmond's supporters had voted for Dewey, then Dewey would have won the election.

2. Based on the map and your knowledge of the period, why do you think Strom Thurmond's support came from the South?

Analyzing Primary Sources

Read the following excerpt from a report by the Women's Advisory Committee (WAC). Then answer the questions that follow.

> **"Prospects for job security and other new job opportunities after the war are as important to women as to men. The American people therefore must demand consideration of the status of women in all postwar plans. . . . No society can boast of democratic ideals if it utilizes womanpower in a crisis and neglects it in peace."**

3. Which of the following statements best describes the views expressed by the WAC in this excerpt?
   a. It is unjust to take women's wartime jobs away in peacetime.
   b. The United States is not a democratic society.
   c. Women should keep their jobs during a crisis.
   d. Women should be appointed to postwar planning committees.
4. Based on your knowledge of the period, why do you think the WAC was so concerned about women losing their jobs?

Alternative Assessment

Building Your Portfolio

Interdisciplinary Connection to the Arts

The Korean War is often called the Forgotten War. Imagine that you have been chosen to design a memorial to the soldiers of the Korean War. Consider the causes, major battles, and results of the war, and decide what your memorial should look like. Create a sketch or a model of the memorial. Hold a ceremony to present the memorial to your class.

internet connect

Internet Activity: go.hrw.com
keyword: SC3 CF26

Choose an activity on the Cold War to:

- Write a biography of Harry S Truman.
- Examine the rise of Mao Zedong and Communists in China.
- Learn about the second Red Scare.

CHAPTER

27 Peace and Prosperity

(1945–1960)

Dwight D. Eisenhower was often met by cheering crowds during his presidential campaign.

Lucille Ball and Desi Arnaz made the I Love Lucy show an American favorite.

A 1950s jukebox

UNITED STATES

1946 President Harry S Truman appoints the Committee on Civil Rights.

1947 The National Security Act creates the Central Intelligence Agency (CIA).

1948 President Truman bans segregation in the military.

1950 The United States begins to work on the hydrogen bomb.

1951 The *I Love Lucy* show first appears on television.

1945 1947 1949 1951

WORLD

1948 The National Party gains control of the South African government and begins its policy of apartheid.

1951 Mohammad Mosaddeq becomes Iran's premier.

Dictator Joseph Stalin ruled the Soviet Union with an iron fist until his death in 1953.

Build on What You Know

The years following World War II were generally a time of peace and prosperity for the United States. Increased Cold War defense spending soon gave the economy a welcomed boost. Business boomed, and many Americans moved into the middle class. Other Americans, however, felt that these economic opportunities were passing them by.

Jonas Salk became famous around the world after he developed a vaccine for polio.

The movement of Americans to the suburbs became common in the 1950s.

1953 Soviet dictator Joseph Stalin dies.

1954 The Supreme Court declares segregation illegal in its *Brown* v. *Board of Education* ruling.

1955 The polio vaccine that Dr. Jonas Salk developed is released for use in the United States in April.

In December police arrest Rosa Parks in Montgomery, Alabama, for refusing to give up her seat on a bus to a white passenger.

1956 France, Great Britain, and Israel invade Egypt, setting off the Suez Crisis.

1957 In January President Eisenhower issues the Eisenhower Doctrine, which promises U.S. aid to any Middle Eastern country facing communist aggression.

Federal troops are sent to enforce desegregation at Central High School in Little Rock, Arkansas, in September.

1957 The Soviet Union launches *Sputnik*, the first artificial satellite.

1959 Alaska and Hawaii become the forty-ninth and fiftieth states of the Union.

1959 Soviet premier Nikita Khrushchev visits the United States.

1960 The Soviet Union shoots down a U.S. U-2 spy plane.

1953 | 1955 | 1957 | 1959

The launch of Sputnik *started a space race between the United States and the Soviet Union.*

If you were there . . .

How would you react to the Cold War?

You Be the Historian

What's Your Opinion? Do you **agree** or **disagree** with the following statements? Support your point of view in your journal.

- **Science, Technology & Society** New weapons change foreign policy.
- **Economics** Economic growth affects all citizens of a country the same way.
- **Constitutional Heritage** Courts are the best place for minority groups to protest.

Section 1

The Eisenhower Administration

Read to Discover

1. What domestic policies did President Eisenhower follow?
2. How did the existence of nuclear weapons influence U.S. foreign policy?
3. What methods did the United States use to fight communism abroad?

Define

- hydrogen bomb
- massive retaliation
- brinkmanship
- covert operations

Identify

- Dwight D. Eisenhower
- *Sputnik*
- National Aeronautics and Space Administration
- John Foster Dulles
- Central Intelligence Agency
- Nikita Khrushchev
- Suez Crisis

Why It Matters Today

The United States is still an important world power. Use CNNfyi.com or other **current events** sources to research U.S. involvement in international affairs. Record your findings in your journal.

General Dwight D. Eisenhower was a decorated war hero as well as a popular political leader.

The Story Continues

Sherman Adams, New Hampshire's governor, had a problem. He wanted to enter Dwight D. Eisenhower in the state's Republican presidential primary. However, he did not know if the quiet World War II general was a Republican. Adams asked the county clerk in Eisenhower's boyhood town. The clerk wrote back, "I don't think [Eisenhower] has any politics." Eisenhower, who was often called Ike, ran on his personal popularity with the American people. His approach helped win him the 1952 presidential election.

America under Eisenhower

When **Dwight D. Eisenhower** was elected president in 1952, he seemed like the ideal person to bring peace and prosperity. He was a Republican, but voters of both parties trusted the war hero's leadership and liked his middle-of-the-road policies. Eisenhower did take steps to prevent what he called the "creeping socialism" of some New Deal programs. For example, he gave states and private companies control over some federal lands and projects. Yet, despite pressure from some Republicans, Eisenhower refused to cut other New Deal programs. In fact, while Eisenhower was in office, Congress raised the minimum wage, expanded Social Security, and increased unemployment benefits.

During Eisenhower's presidency, personal incomes rose a great deal. By the mid-1950s nearly 60 percent of the population qualified as middle-class, earning between $3,000 and $7,000 a year. The new prosperity brought important changes. More Americans bought large appliances and suburban homes, took vacations, and sent their children to college. Some Americans saw huge growth in their incomes.

This widespread prosperity helped Eisenhower gain re-election in 1956. Not everyone shared in the prosperity, however. In 1960, more than 20 percent of all families earned less than $3,000 a year.

✔ **Reading Check: Summarizing** How did the economic boom of the 1950s affect American families?

That's Interesting!

A Secret Bomb Shelter for Congress Did you know that Congress had its own bomb shelter? It's true! In the late 1950s a secret bunker was designed to protect members of Congress in the event of nuclear war. The two-story, 112,544-square-foot facility was hidden under the Greenbrier Resort in West Virginia. Completed in 1962, it was kept ready to be occupied for more than 30 years! In 1993 an investigative reporter wrote a story revealing the top-secret facility. The bunker is now open to tourists.

The Nuclear Age

Despite the nation's new prosperity, Americans lived under the threat of nuclear war. In January 1950 President Truman had approved work on the **hydrogen bomb**, which was far more powerful than the atomic bombs dropped on Japan in 1945. The United States tested the first hydrogen bomb in November 1952 in the West Pacific. One person who watched the explosion later wrote an account of it.

History Makers Speak

"The fireball expanded to three miles in diameter. Observers, all evacuated to 40 miles or more away, saw millions of gallons of lagoon water turned to steam, appear as a giant bubble. When the steam had evaporated, they saw that the island of Elugelab where the bomb (or building) had been, had vanished. . . . In its place [was] a crater 1/2 mile deep and two miles wide."

—Leona Marshall Libby, quoted in *The Fifties,* by David Halberstam

Analyzing Primary Sources

Drawing Inferences and Conclusions What point was the observer making about the power of the hydrogen bomb?

Interpreting the Visual Record

The hydrogen bomb *The first test of the hydrogen bomb completely destroyed a small island in the West Pacific.* ***How do you think an image of such destruction might affect a nation's foreign policy?***

Less than a year later, the Soviet Union tested its own hydrogen bomb. The United States and the Soviet Union rapidly increased their nuclear stockpiles. The nuclear arms race frightened many Americans. Some people built underground bomb shelters. At school, children took part in "duck-and-cover" drills. Antinuclear groups argued that nuclear tests released radioactive particles that caused birth defects and disease.

Yet the arms race continued. In October 1957 the Soviet Union launched ***Sputnik***, the world's first artificial satellite. Many Americans worried that *Sputnik* gave the Soviets a big advantage in space. In 1958 the United States launched its first satellite. That same year, Congress created the **National Aeronautics and Space Administration** (NASA). The purpose of this new agency was to conduct important space research. Congress also provided much funding for math, science, and foreign language instruction.

✔ **Reading Check: Identifying Cause and Effect** What caused many Americans to fear a nuclear war, and how did some Americans react as a consequence?

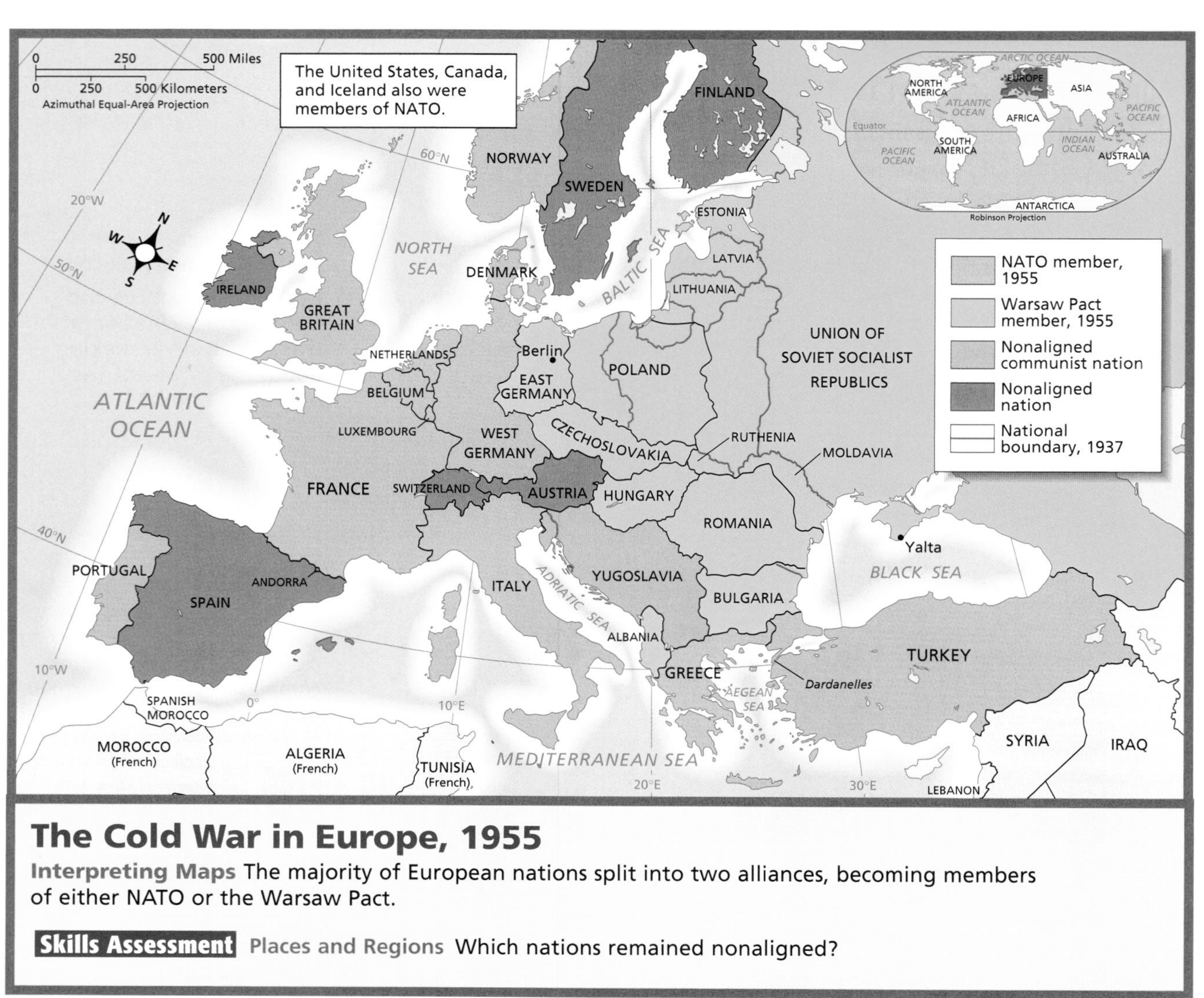

The Cold War in Europe, 1955

Interpreting Maps The majority of European nations split into two alliances, becoming members of either NATO or the Warsaw Pact.

Skills Assessment **Places and Regions** Which nations remained nonaligned?

Eisenhower's Foreign Policy

President Eisenhower and Secretary of State **John Foster Dulles** began a "New Look" in U.S. foreign policy. During the Truman years, the United States had tried to contain the spread of communism. Eisenhower, however, wanted the United States to actually "roll back" communism from certain areas. The New Look used a strategy known as **massive retaliation**, or the threat of using nuclear weapons, to stop communist aggression.

Few diplomats favored the use of nuclear weapons. However, officials like Dulles argued that the United States might have to come to the brink of, or come close to, war to stop communism. Dulles explained this idea, known as **brinkmanship**. "The ability to get to the verge [brink or edge] without getting into war is the necessary art."

Despite the tough talk, the United States did not openly threaten to use nuclear weapons. For example, in 1953 the Soviets crushed anti-communist protests in three East German cities. U.S. leaders did not want to become involved and risk a nuclear war.

President Eisenhower sometimes used **covert operations**, or secret actions, to help the United States during the Cold War. The **Central Intelligence Agency** (CIA) carried out these covert actions. Created by the National Security Act in 1947, the CIA grew powerful during Eisenhower's presidency.

The CIA's first important covert operation took place in the Middle Eastern country of Iran. In 1951 Mohammad Mosaddeq (MAWS-ad-dek) became premier of Iran. He soon became more powerful than the shah, Iran's ruler. The shah tended to side with the United States on Cold War issues. Mosaddeq nationalized, or placed under government control, Iran's oil industry. Because communism is based on government ownership and control of industry, U.S. diplomats feared that he was a communist. The move also angered the British government, which had held a very profitable monopoly on Iranian oil production. Great Britain and the United States created Operation Ajax, which overthrew Mosaddeq and returned the shah to power in 1953.

The CIA also intervened in the Central American country of Guatemala. In 1951 Colonel Jacobo Arbenz Guzmán became president of Guatemala and began land and labor reforms. He nationalized the property of the American-owned United Fruit Company. Secretary of State Dulles protested this action to the world court, arguing that Arbenz's programs were a turn toward "international communism." In 1954 the CIA hired an army to invade Guatemala and remove Arbenz from power. This army failed, but CIA pilots using Nicaraguan aircraft still intervened. These CIA actions led to an anticommunist military government taking Arbenz's place.

✔ **Reading Check: Summarizing** What was the goal of Eisenhower's foreign policy, and what methods did he use to achieve it?

CONNECTING TO MATH

Just the Facts

U.S. Cold War Defense Spending, 1945–1990

Year	National Defense in billions of dollars
1945	83
1950	13.7
1955	42.7
1960	48.1
1965	50.6
1970	81.7
1975	86.5
1980	134
1985	253
1990	299

Using Mathematical Skills

1. What years had the smallest and largest national defense budget?
2. Plot a line graph showing the national defense budget from 1945 to 1990.
3. Imagine that you are a presidential adviser. Use these figures to help you write a speech either against or in support of cuts in defense spending.

The Eisenhower Doctrine

After the Suez Crisis ended, President Eisenhower announced the Eisenhower Doctrine, in which he asked Congress for money to help Middle Eastern countries fight communism. Many in Congress disagreed with Eisenhower's plan. Secretary of State Dulles argued that the free countries of the Middle East would turn to communism if they did not receive U.S. aid.

Congress finally adopted a revised version of the Eisenhower Doctrine that committed armed forces to help countries in the Middle East resist aggression. **How might the location of the Middle East have made it important to the Soviet Union and the United States?**

Eisenhower (left) and Dulles (center) discuss foreign policy.

Cold War Crises

In 1953 Soviet premier Joseph Stalin died. He was replaced by Soviet leader **Nikita Khrushchev** (kroosh-CHAWF). Khrushchev soon shocked the communist world by announcing that Stalin had committed criminal acts against the Soviet people. He said that people should no longer follow Stalin's policies. Khrushchev later surprised U.S. leaders by stating that capitalism and communism could exist together peacefully in the world.

Khrushchev's announcement was a blow to the Stalinist governments in Eastern Europe. Citizens in many Soviet satellite nations hoped a new era was beginning. In Poland, for example, new leaders began to demand democratic reforms. A new Hungarian government called for Western-style democracy. Determined to crush the uprisings, the Soviet army invaded Hungary in November 1956. Hungarians fought back with stones, rifles, and homemade bombs. The United States publicly opposed the invasion but did not want a war with the Soviet Union, particularly not in Eastern Europe. No other nation intervened to aid Hungary, and the Soviets easily crushed the revolt.

Even as Soviet tanks were threatening to sweep aside the Hungarian rebels, U.S. leaders faced an even greater threat to world peace. In 1955 the United States agreed to help Egypt finance the Aswan High Dam, an irrigation project on the Nile River. U.S. officials hoped this aid would win Egypt's support in the Cold War. But Gamal Abdel Nasser, the Egyptian leader, put an end to those hopes. He bought arms from Soviet-controlled Czechoslovakia, invited Soviet technicians to enter Egypt, and recognized communist China. U.S. leaders felt betrayed by Nasser's friendly relations with communist governments and backed out of the Aswan Dam project.

In July 1956 Nasser declared that Egypt would pay for the dam instead by nationalizing the Suez Canal. He would then charge a toll to use this important waterway connecting the Mediterranean and Red Seas. Nasser's plan upset France, Great Britain, and Israel, all of which used the Suez Canal for trade. These three countries invaded the areas around the Suez Canal in November 1956.

The **Suez Crisis** raised the possibility of a third world war. The Soviets said they would "crush the aggressor"—the British, French, and Israeli forces in the area. The United States threatened to respond by sending in its own troops. The Soviet Union did not attack, however, and the United States later joined the Soviet Union in condemning the invasion. The brief cooperation between the United States and the Soviet Union shocked many observers. Others wondered if the alliance of Western democracies would last.

✔ **Reading Check: Analyzing Information** In what ways do you think the Soviet Union may have contributed to the uprisings in Hungary, which it put down with force in 1956?

The U-2 was an advanced spy plane that flew at very high altitudes.

A Thaw in the Cold War?

In the late 1950s there were a few signs of a thaw in the Cold War. For example, Vice President Richard M. Nixon visited the Soviet Union in 1959. Soviet leader Nikita Khrushchev then visited the United States. He and Eisenhower agreed to hold a superpower summit meeting in Paris, France, in 1960.

Before the two leaders could meet, however, U.S.-Soviet relations took a turn for the worse. On May 5, 1960, Khrushchev announced that the Soviets had shot down an American plane. U.S. officials announced that a weather plane was missing. Khrushchev then revealed that the pilot, Francis Gary Powers, had survived the crash. Powers admitted that he had been on a secret mission in a U-2 spy plane. Only then did Eisenhower admit that Powers's account was correct.

Because of the U-2 incident, the summit meeting was a disaster. Khrushchev shouted so loudly that a diplomat had to ask him to lower his voice. The thaw in the Cold War was over.

✔ **Reading Check: Finding the Main Idea** How did the U-2 incident affect Soviet attitudes toward the United States?

Section 1 Review

keyword: SC3 HP27

1. **Define** and explain:
   - hydrogen bomb
   - massive retaliation
   - brinkmanship
   - covert operations
2. **Identify** and explain:
   - Dwight D. Eisenhower
   - *Sputnik*
   - National Aeronautics and Space Administration
   - John Foster Dulles
   - Central Intelligence Agency
   - Nikita Khrushchev
   - Suez Crisis
3. **Analyzing Information** Copy the diagram below. Use it to identify the domestic policies that President Eisenhower followed.

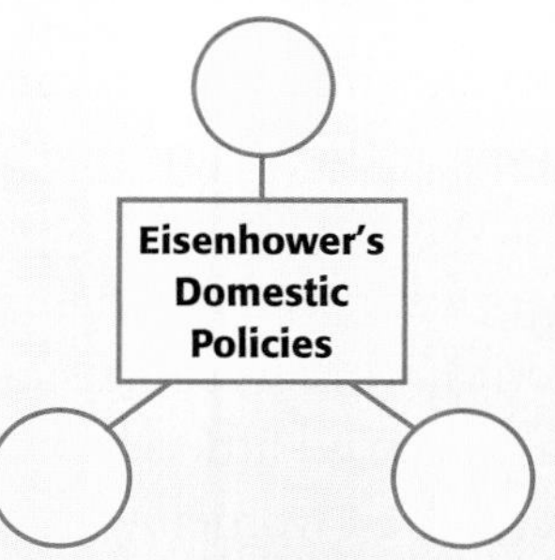

4. **Finding the Main Idea**
   a. How was Eisenhower's foreign policy influenced by the nuclear arms race?
   b. How did the United States attempt to fight communism around the world?
5. **Writing and Critical Thinking**
   Supporting a Point of View Imagine that you are a member of the State Department under John Foster Dulles. Write a memo to Secretary Dulles in which you argue for or against the idea of brinkmanship.
   Consider the following:
   - the end of America's nuclear monopoly
   - the goals of the New Look foreign policy
   - the expansion of Soviet influence in Central America, Eastern Europe, and the Middle East

Section 2

A Prosperous Nation

Read to Discover

1. How did changes in the workplace affect Americans?
2. Why did more Americans move to the South and the West during the 1950s?
3. What were the major complaints of social critics in the 1950s?

Define

- automation
- baby boom
- urban renewal
- beats
- silent generation

Identify

- Sunbelt
- Highway Act
- Levittown
- Lucille Ball
- J. D. Salinger
- Ralph Ellison
- James Baldwin
- Elvis Presley

Why It Matters Today

People in the suburbs and those in urban areas continue to face different challenges. Use CNNfyi.com or other **current events** sources to research the challenges experienced by people living in each area today. Record your findings in your journal.

Author Norman Vincent Peale promised to teach Americans how to live their lives with greater confidence and satisfaction.

The Story Continues

In the 1950s Reverend Norman Vincent Peale was a best-selling American author. In his book *The Power of Positive Thinking* Peale told Americans that "happiness is achievable. . . . Anyone who desires it . . . and applies the right formula may become a happy person." Peale's books were very influential in the 1950s, a time when many Americans were sure that they could gain wealth and happiness.

A Changing Workforce

The working environment and the workforce changed dramatically during the 1950s. **Automation**, or the use of machines in production, decreased the need for workers. While machines replaced many low-level workers, more middle managers were needed. These new managers, usually men, in turn needed more clerical workers as assistants. Women usually filled these positions. But clerical jobs paid little and offered little chance for advancement. Some people criticized women who worked outside the home. One career woman recalled the pressure from her family.

“The only person who approved of me in those days was my father. He had encouraged me to be an accountant and whatever I did was all right with him. But my mother thought I was terrible. She used to read newspaper clippings to me about the importance of mothers being home [with their children].”

—Gail Kaplan, quoted in A *History of Women in America*, by Carol Hymowitz and Michaele Weissman

Analyzing Primary Sources

Identifying Points of View What did this observer's mother want for her daughter?

As the American workplace and workforce changed, so did the influence of labor unions. Overall union membership declined. Few of the new managers or clerical workers joined labor unions. Evidence of union corruption and the Red Scare also contributed to declining union strength.

✔ **Reading Check: Analyzing Information** How did changes in the workplace affect the lives of men and women?

Suburban Life

In the 1950s many people moved to take new jobs and find a better life. The **Sunbelt** states of the South and the West—with their warmer climates and lower taxes—experienced the greatest growth of businesses and people. The Sunbelt population more than doubled in the 30 years after World War II.

Government efforts further increased mobility. In 1956 Congress passed the **Highway Act**, which provided money to create a national system of highways. This system greatly increased business and personal travel across the country. The highways also allowed many Americans to move to suburbs — smaller towns outside of cities — and to commute to work. By 1960 about one fourth of the entire U.S. population lived in the suburbs.

Interpreting the Visual Record

Suburban life *Magazines promoted an idealized image of suburban life that was full of modern conveniences like this TV dinner.* ***What appears to be idealized in this photograph?***

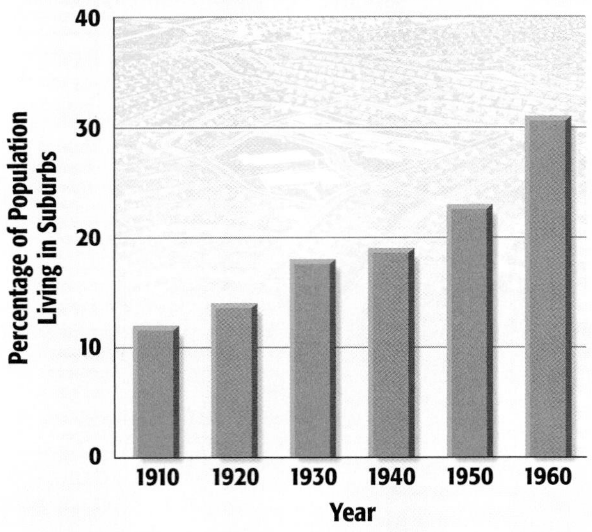

Developers rushed to build new suburban neighborhoods. On Long Island, New York, William Levitt created **Levittown**, a planned, mass-produced housing development. In Levittown and other suburbs, inexpensive homes looked much the same. They came with labor-saving devices such as washing machines and dryers, big rooms, and large lawns. Americans experiencing a **baby boom**—an increase in the number of babies born after World War II—welcomed these comforts.

Suburban life focused on families and children. Suburban children often took music and dance lessons, joined the Boy Scouts and Girl Scouts, and played sports. Many people thought of the ideal suburban woman as a full-time mother. Despite this image, some suburban mothers worked part-time. Their wages often paid for "extras" for the children, such as summer camps and music and dance lessons.

The growth of highways and suburbs made the daily commute by car a central part of many Americans' lives.

Neighbors often quietly competed to see who could buy the latest cars, clothes, and gadgets. This competition led some people to complain that the new consumer culture was wasteful. They wondered whether people really needed new cars every two years, or new kitchen appliances every three years. Other critics questioned whether material things could make people happy. One woman called suburban life "quite stale," despite her family's many possessions.

Some people disliked suburban life because they thought it helped lead to conformity, or sameness. Most suburban residents were white, middle-class Americans. Some suburban communities even excluded people who did not fit their mold—whether because of race, ethnicity, or religion.

Despite these criticisms, many residents felt they made good friends and enjoyed a high quality of life in their neighborhoods. They liked the strong social networks that suburban life provided during a time when many people were moving to new communities.

As more middle-class whites moved from the cities to the suburbs, they left behind many poor and nonwhite residents. Fewer tax dollars remained, leading to a decline in urban conditions and services. In 1949 the federal government started an **urban renewal** program to improve public services and housing. Large new housing projects replaced buildings in poor, run-down neighborhoods. However, some residents felt that the plain-looking, multilevel housing projects destroyed the culture and friendly feeling of neighborhoods. In response to these concerns, officials gradually changed the program to focus on restoring old buildings rather than tearing them down.

✔ **Reading Check: Contrasting** How was life in the suburbs different from life in the city?

The Golden Age of Television

The 1950s were television's golden years. In 1949 less than a million American households had a television set. By 1953 that number had grown to more than 20 million. These families shared the experience of watching the same program, whether a sports event or a news broadcast.

Lucille Ball, a famous television star of the 1950s, starred in a weekly series with her husband, Cuban American bandleader Desi Arnaz. Soon after the show began in 1951, *I Love Lucy* became the most popular show on television. Almost 30 percent of the country watched the 1953 episode in which Ball's character gave birth. In fact, more people tuned in to that show than watched Eisenhower's inauguration the next day. "It looks like Lucy's more popular than Ike [Eisenhower]," declared Arnaz. "I wonder if we could run her for President in [nineteen] fifty-six?"

Dramas, game shows, soap operas, and westerns were also popular. Many well-known television shows, such as Milton Berle's *Texaco Star Theatre*, were sponsored by a particular company. Companies hoped that television advertising and celebrity support would help sell their products.

CONNECTING TO

SCIENCE AND TECHNOLOGY

Television

Television developed from radio broadcasting technology. A video signal carries information about the shape, brightness, and color of the images being filmed. The television turns this signal into beams of electrons that activate phosphors. These phosphors then light up the television screen to create pictures.

TV sets typically show about 30 still images every second—a rate so fast that the viewer's eyes cannot see individual pictures. The brain interprets these images as a moving picture instead of a series of many still images. Today television signals are often carried by cables or broadcast from satellites. How do televisions work?

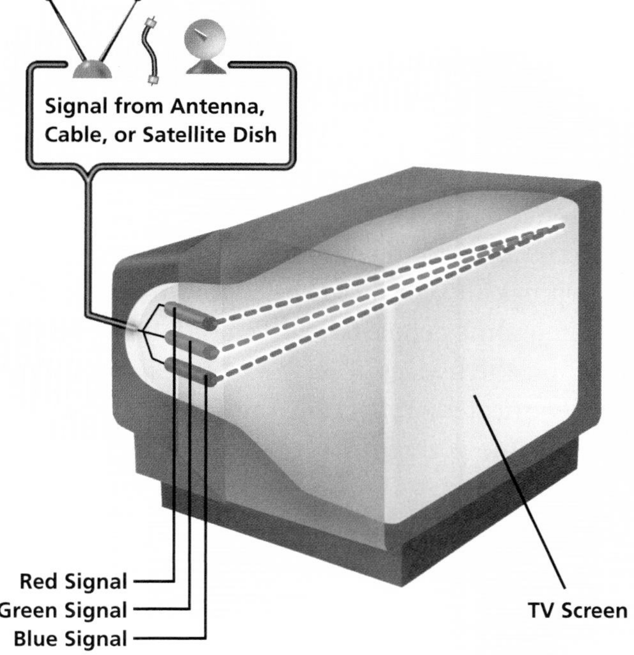

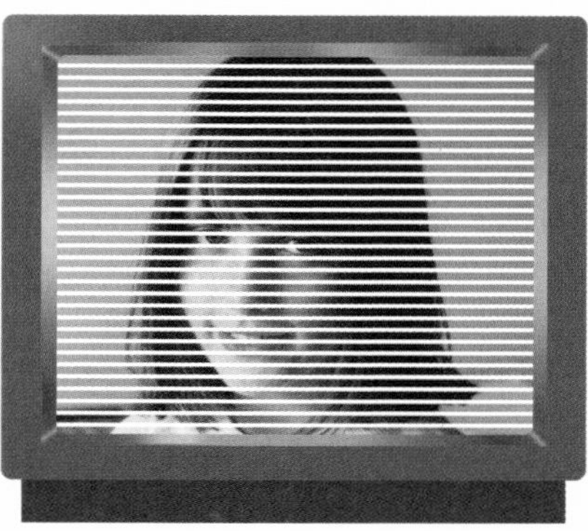

CONNECTING TO THE ARTS

Jackson Pollock Artist Paul Jackson Pollock was born in Cody, Wyoming, in 1912. He grew up in California and Arizona. About 1947 he began the work that would make his reputation—the so-called drip and splash paintings. He spread a huge piece of canvas across the floor and then stood over it, dripping different types and colors of paint onto the canvas. His paintings were wild combinations of color, shape, and texture. Pollock's drip and splash paintings became leading examples of a new movement in art called action painting. **What was original about Pollock's style of painting?**

Social Critics

Some artists, scholars, and writers criticized the materialism and conformity of American society. Several university professors said that American values, such as going against the crowd to defend a moral principle, were being destroyed. In *The Lonely Crowd*, writer David Riesman argues that the tendency to conform limited creativity and new ideas.

Other writers criticized society through their fiction and essays. **J. D. Salinger** wrote *The Catcher in the Rye* in 1951. In that novel, teenager Holden Caulfield, the book's main character, criticizes the "phoniness" of the adult world. In *Invisible Man*, **Ralph Ellison** explores the isolation and loneliness of African Americans. The novel's hero is an innocent youth who struggles to get ahead, but he finds that discrimination and powerful, selfish leaders, both African American and white, hold him back. **James Baldwin** also wrote about racism in his 1955 collection of essays *Notes of a Native Son*. "I love America . . . and, exactly for this reason, I insist on the right to criticize her," Baldwin wrote.

Younger writers called beatniks, or **beats**, also criticized American life through their unusual writings and rebellious behavior. In *On the Road*, author Jack Kerouac inspired some people to reject traditional society and set out on their own to find themselves. The work of beat authors was often rambling and disconnected, reflecting their rootless, carefree lifestyle. Yet they inspired some young people to question the rules of American society.

✔ **Reading Check: Analyzing Information** In what ways were popular media, like television, and the message of social critics different?

Young Americans

Social critics argued that young people suffered from the same problem as suburban residents and corporate workers—conformity and the deep desire to avoid conflict. This led some people to call teenagers and college students of this time the **silent generation.**

Some teenagers and college students rebelled quietly. They read *Mad* magazine and comic books that made fun of 1950s society. Others imitated the young rebels they saw in popular movies of the era. James Dean, who starred in three films before dying in a car wreck when he was 24, was a popular 1950s actor. In *Rebel Without a Cause*, Dean plays a troubled middle-class teen who feels like an outcast because he cannot live up to the expectations of his parents and those around him.

Rock star Elvis Presley sold hundreds of millions of records and starred in more than 30 movies.

Other young people rebelled through their choice in music. During the 1950s two important new styles of music—bebop and rock 'n' roll—became popular. Bebop, or bop, was an up-tempo form of jazz music that originated in the 1940s. Rock 'n' roll used new instruments like electric guitars and drew heavily from African American rhythm and blues. The biggest rock 'n' roll star of the 1950s was **Elvis Presley**.

Critics argued that rock 'n' roll contributed to juvenile delinquency. Other adults simply thought that it was bad music. They said it was too loud and filled with meaningless lyrics, such as "*do*-wop, *do*-wop." Still others worried that rock 'n' roll cut across racial lines. Teenagers who liked white artists such as Presley also liked African American artists such as Chuck Berry, Fats Domino, and Little Richard. Such fear of integration was also a major obstacle to civil rights efforts in the South.

✔ **Reading Check: Categorizing** What types of entertainment were popular with young Americans in the 1950s?

Section 2 Review

go.hrw.com **Homework Practice Online**
keyword: SC3 HP27

1. **Define** and explain:
   - automation
   - baby boom
   - urban renewal
   - beats
   - silent generation

2. **Identify** and explain:
   - Sunbelt
   - Highway Act
   - Levittown
   - Lucille Ball
   - J. D. Salinger
   - Ralph Ellison
   - James Baldwin
   - Elvis Presley

3. **Summarizing** Copy the graphic organizer below. Use it to identify criticisms of American society in the 1950s.

Major Criticisms of American Society in the 1950s	→	1.
		2.

4. **Finding the Main Idea**
   a. What was the impact of changes in the workplace during the 1950s?
   b. Why did the South and West benefit from the increasing mobility of the American population?

5. **Writing and Critical Thinking**
   Supporting a Point of View Imagine that you work for William Levitt. Prepare a pamphlet persuading people to move to your new suburb, Levittown II.
   Consider the following:
   - contrast between city and suburban life
   - rising incomes and goals of the middle class
   - the issue of conformity

Section 3

The Early Civil Rights Movement

Read to Discover

1. How did African American World War II veterans influence the early civil rights movement?
2. What were some of the main events in the struggle for school desegregation?
3. Why did the Montgomery Bus Boycott succeed?

Why It Matters Today

Many organizations around the world continue to struggle for civil rights. Use CNNfyi.com or other **current events** sources to learn about one of these organizations' latest activities. Record your findings in your journal.

Identify

- Committee on Civil Rights
- Thurgood Marshall
- *Brown* v. *Board of Education*
- Little Rock Nine
- Rosa Parks
- Montgomery Bus Boycott
- Montgomery Improvement Association
- Martin Luther King Jr.

This civil rights protester is picketing outside the 1948 Democratic National Convention.

The Story Continues

Many African American veterans came home from service in World War II filled with anger. Civil rights lawyer Constance Baker Motley explained the situation. "Black servicemen were overseas dying for this country," she said. Yet, "they would be coming home to a situation that said, in effect, You're a second-class citizen." James Hicks, an African American veteran, shared his feelings. "I paid my dues over there and I'm not going to take this anymore over here." Veterans like Hicks prepared to take up the next fight—this one against discrimination in the United States.

Segregation after World War II

Many returning African American veterans focused their efforts on voting discrimination. Fees, literacy tests, and threats of violence—particularly in the South—kept African Americans from voting or even registering to vote. Some politicians encouraged such discrimination when they ran for office.

The drive for African American voting rights brought intense conflict. As the violence grew, many African American leaders asked President Truman for help. In the summer of 1946, a group of civil rights activists protested outside the White House. Their signs called on Truman to "SPEAK, SPEAK, MR. PRESIDENT." That same summer nearly 15,000 protesters marched to the Lincoln Memorial to demand that the Ku Klux Klan be outlawed.

Interpreting the Visual Record

Segregation *Some states had separate public facilities for African Americans.* ***What signs of segregation are noticeable in the photograph?***

In December 1946 President Truman responded to this pressure. He created the **Committee on Civil Rights** to study racial discrimination and to suggest federal solutions to the problem. The committee's report, *To Secure These Rights*, noted that there was racial discrimination throughout the country. The report recommended new laws to protect all voters, including African Americans. The committee also supported desegregating the armed forces. Finally, the report called for establishing a permanent Fair Employment Practices Commission. Truman promised to support the committee's recommendations.

African American leaders became frustrated as months passed with little action by Truman or Congress. Finally, in July 1948 Truman ended segregation in the military. That same year he also banned racial discrimination in the hiring of federal employees.

✔ **Reading Check: Summarizing** What were the major recommendations of Truman's Committee on Civil Rights?

Brown v. *Board of Education*

The National Association for the Advancement of Colored People (NAACP) wanted to end racial segregation, particularly in schools. Many states kept separate schools for African American and white students. Public leaders often said that these schools were "separate but equal." However, African American schools usually received far less money and fewer supplies.

This NAACP button was worn by some Truman supporters who rallied behind the Democratic Party platform committee's proposal for a strong civil rights plank.

The NAACP legal defense team won a series of court cases that challenged the constitutionality of separate-but-equal schools. In 1938 the Supreme Court ruled that every state had to offer equal educational opportunities. This meant that states offering law schools and medical schools for whites had to provide such institutions for African Americans as well.

The NAACP then tried to show that separate schools did not provide African American students with equal educational opportunities. In 1946 an African American named Heman Sweatt applied to the law school at the University of Texas, which did not accept black students. Rather than admit Sweatt, school officials chose to create a separate African American law school. In 1950 the Supreme Court ruled in *Sweatt* v. *Painter* that the new school did not provide African Americans

Interpreting the Visual Record

Separate schools *Nearly 90 African American children crowded into this segregated kindergarten class.* ***How might these crowded conditions affect a child's education?***

with access to equal academic prestige, facilities, or instructors. The Court ordered the university to admit Sweatt to its law school.

In the 1950s the NAACP decided to focus its legal efforts on ending segregation in public schools. **Thurgood Marshall**, the NAACP attorney who had argued the *Sweatt* case, led the courtroom battles on this issue. A number of school segregation cases came together under the title of ***Brown* v. *Board of Education***. The title case involved Linda Brown, a seven-year-old from Topeka, Kansas. She lived very close to a school for white children. However, officials in the school district forced her to attend an African American school located across town. Linda's father sued the school board to allow Linda to go to the nearby white school.

The NAACP used studies by African American psychologist Kenneth Clark to support its case. Clark found that many segregated African American children felt they were less important than white children. "Segregation was, is, the way in which a society tells a group of human beings that they are inferior to other groups of human beings in the society," he explained.

In May 1954 the Supreme Court ruled in the Brown case that segregation in public schools was illegal.

Analyzing Primary Sources

Drawing Inferences and Conclusions According to the Supreme Court ruling, why should there not be segregation in public schools?

"To separate [African American students] from others of similar age and qualifications solely because of their race generates a feeling of inferiority as to their status in the community that may affect their hearts and minds in a way very unlikely ever to be undone. . . . In the field of public education the doctrine [belief] of 'separate but equal' has no place. Separate educational facilities are inherently [by their very nature] unequal."

—Earl Warren, quoted in *Eyes on the Prize,* by Juan Williams

The Court's decision overturned the 1896 *Plessy* v. *Ferguson* ruling that had established the "separate-but-equal" doctrine. In 1955 the Court made its ruling stronger, ordering public schools to desegregate "with all deliberate speed."

Public reaction to the *Sweatt* and *Brown* decisions was mixed. Some white leaders promised to follow the law. Others, like South Carolina governor James F. Byrnes, stated that desegregation "would mark the beginning of the end of civilization in the South as we have known it." Some white citizens vowed to close their local public schools and open private all-white academies. Most African Americans were pleased with the Supreme Court decisions. However, they wondered whether white leaders would really enforce desegregation laws.

✔ **Reading Check: Summarizing** What decision did the Supreme Court make in *Brown* v. *Board of Education* and why?

The Little Rock Nine

Despite the Court's order to desegregate schools "with all deliberate speed," only three school districts in the entire South began to desegregate in 1954. Other districts adopted gradual desegregation plans. The school board in Little Rock, Arkansas, decided to integrate one high school first. Then it would slowly work down to the elementary level. The school board selected nine outstanding African American students, known as the **Little Rock Nine**, to attend Central High School in 1957.

Although Little Rock was highly segregated, it had a reputation for being moderate. This gave some African American leaders the hope that opposition to integration would be limited. Yet many white residents tried to stop the integration plan. Arkansas governor Orval Faubus arranged for a group to appeal to a judge to halt integration. When that failed, he declared on television that state National Guard units would stop the Little Rock Nine from starting school. Faubus claimed that his actions would prevent violence.

Daisy Bates, the president of the Arkansas NAACP, arranged rides to the high school for the students on September 4. But Elizabeth Eckford, one of the Little Rock Nine, did not get the message. When Eckford went to school by herself, a mob met her. With the screaming crowd behind her, the soldiers would not allow her to enter. Alone and without protection, she faced a large mob of enraged protesters. She recalled, "Somebody started yelling, '*Lynch her! Lynch her!*'" Eckford ran to a nearby bus stop to escape, but the crowd followed. Finally, a white woman guided Eckford to safety.

This tense situation continued for several weeks as Faubus refused President Eisenhower's requests to follow the law. Finally, in late September, Eisenhower sent federal troops to enforce desegregation at

This antidiscrimination poster shows the growing interest in the early civil rights movement.

Interpreting the Visual Record

Starting school *Elizabeth Eckford tries to make her way into Little Rock's Central High School.* ***What dangers does Eckford face?***

BIOGRAPHY

Rosa Parks

(1913–)

Rosa Parks spent most of her early life in Montgomery, Alabama. Parks became involved with the local NAACP and served as the secretary of the Montgomery branch as well as its youth council adviser. In the summer of 1955, she attended a workshop on race relations at the Highlander Folk School in Tennessee. This integrated school taught people how to organize movements for social reform. Parks lost her seamstress job after her arrest for refusing to give up her seat on a Montgomery bus to a white passenger. She and her husband later moved to Detroit, Michigan, where she continued her civil rights work. **How might the race relations workshop have influenced Parks's actions on the Montgomery bus?**

Research on the ROM

Free Find:
Rosa Parks
After reading about Rosa Parks on the **Holt Researcher CD–ROM**, write a short essay explaining the significance of her contribution to the civil rights movement.

Central High. One of the Little Rock Nine, Melba Pattillo Beals, remembered her feelings when she attended classes.

> **"I went in not through the side doors, but up the front stairs, and there was a feeling of pride and hope that yes, this is the United States; yes, there is a reason I salute the flag; and it's going to be okay."**
>
> —Melba Pattillo Beals, quoted in *Voices of Freedom*

After the federal troops left, Eisenhower ordered the Arkansas National Guard units to protect the students.

Although the Little Rock Nine faced insults and abuse from white students, eight of them stayed. In May 1958 Ernest Green became the first African American student to graduate from Central High School. "When they called my name. . . . Nobody clapped," Green remembered. "But I figured they didn't have to . . . because after I got that diploma, that was it. I had accomplished what I had come there for."

Governor Faubus continued to fight integration. He even closed the Little Rock public schools during the 1958–59 school year. The schools finally reopened under court order in 1959 and began a process of slow integration.

✔ **Reading Check: Sequencing** List the steps to desegregation, from the decision of the school board to integrate Central High to the graduation of Ernest Green, in the order that they occurred.

The Montgomery Bus Boycott

In most southern cities all public facilities, including buses, were segregated. In Montgomery, Alabama, African American passengers had to enter through the front door of the bus to pay their fare. Then they got off the bus, walked to the back door, and boarded. African American passengers had to stay in the back. Only white passengers rode in the front of the buses. If the front section filled up, African American passengers had to give up their seats to white passengers.

The NAACP helped to plan a challenge to Montgomery's bus segregation system. On December 1, 1955, the ideal case arose. African American seamstress **Rosa Parks** refused to give up her seat to a white passenger. She was quickly arrested. Former NAACP leader E. D. Nixon used her case to challenge the bus segregation law. He then organized an African American boycott of the city bus system. This effort became known as the **Montgomery Bus Boycott**.

To coordinate their efforts, local leaders formed the **Montgomery Improvement Association** and chose 26-year-old Baptist minister **Martin Luther King Jr.** to lead the group. King was known as an inspiring speaker who could motivate listeners. Since he was new to town, members of the association thought that he might risk less by participating in the protest.

Almost all of the city's African Americans, and some sympathetic whites, supported the boycott. Their refusal to ride the buses eliminated about 70 percent of the system's regular passengers. African Americans set up a carpool system to replace the buses and pitched in to help pay the cost of gas. Jo Ann Robinson, who helped organize the boycotts, explained, "I think people were fed up, they had reached the point that they knew there was no return."

Martin Luther King Jr. with his wife, Coretta, and his family

The city refused to integrate its bus system, and the boycott lasted for months. Some white residents resorted to violence in their attempt to break the boycott. People who wanted to maintain segregation bombed the homes of King and Nixon. The boycott continued, however, and inspired similar protests in cities such as Birmingham, Alabama, and Tallahassee, Florida.

In November 1956 the Supreme Court ruled that Montgomery's segregated bus system was illegal. The victory brought Martin Luther King Jr. to the forefront of the civil rights movement and also energized the African American community. "We had won self-respect," Robinson remembered. "It . . . makes you feel that America is a great country and we're going to do more to make it greater."

✔ **Reading Check: Identifying Cause and Effect** What caused the Montgomery Bus Boycott, and what effect did it have on the civil rights of African Americans?

Section 3 Review

go.hrw.com **Homework Practice Online**
keyword: SC3 HP27

1. **Identify** and explain:
   - Committee on Civil Rights
   - Thurgood Marshall
   - *Brown* v. *Board of Education*
   - Little Rock Nine
   - Rosa Parks
   - Montgomery Bus Boycott
   - Montgomery Improvement Association
   - Martin Luther King Jr.

2. **Sequencing** Copy the graphic organizer below. Use it to identify the main events leading to the desegregation of schools.

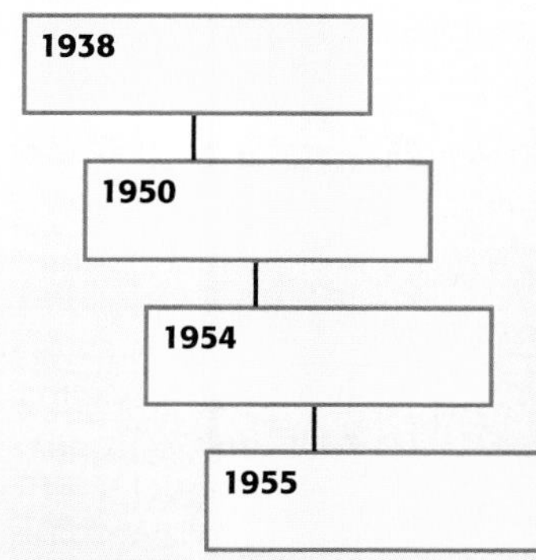

3. **Finding the Main Idea**
   a. What impact did African American World War II veterans have on the early civil rights movement?
   b. How did African Americans organize to desegregate the Montgomery bus system?

4. **Writing and Critical Thinking**
   Analyzing Information Imagine that you have played an important role in the Montgomery Bus Boycott. Civil rights supporters in another state have asked you to give a speech explaining why the Montgomery protest worked. Write a detailed outline of your speech.
   Consider the following:
   - the organization of the boycott
   - use of Rosa Parks's arrest to start a legal challenge
   - setting up a carpool system as an alternative to buses

Chapter 27 Review

The Chapter at a Glance

Examine the visual summary of the chapter below. Use it to write a short quiz with five true-or-false questions for a classmate that deal with major events that took place in the 1950s.

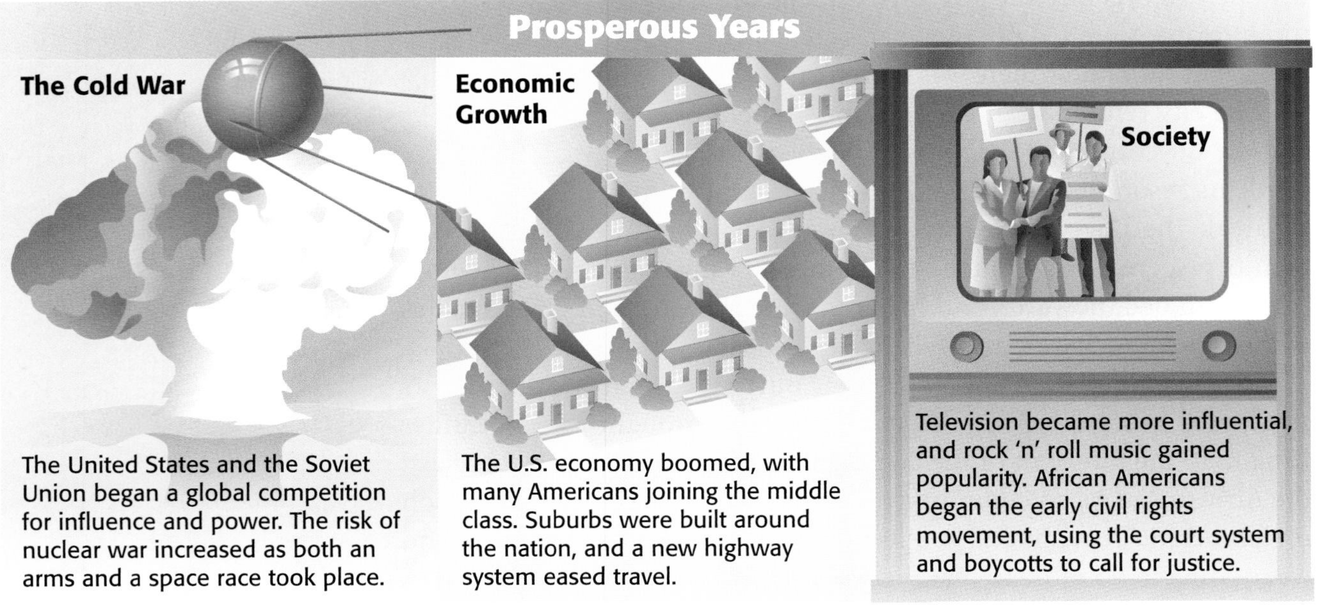

Identifying People and Ideas

Use the following terms or people in historically significant sentences.

1. Dwight D. Eisenhower
2. *Sputnik*
3. John Foster Dulles
4. brinkmanship
5. Levittown
6. baby boom
7. Lucille Ball
8. Little Rock Nine
9. Rosa Parks
10. Montgomery Bus Boycott

Understanding Main Ideas

Section 1 *(Pages 820–825)*

1. What Cold War events took place in the 1950s?
2. How did the United States attempt to fight communism overseas?

Section 2 *(Pages 826–831)*

3. What business trends affected workers during the 1950s?
4. How did writers criticize American society during the 1950s?

Section 3 *(Pages 832–837)*

5. How did African American World War II veterans play an important role in the early civil rights movement?
6. List the key events in the effort to end segregation in schools.

You Be the Historian—Reviewing Themes

1. **Science, Technology & Society** How did nuclear weapons affect U.S. foreign policy and American society during the Cold War?
2. **Economics** How did economic prosperity following World War II affect the daily lives of many middle-class Americans?
3. **Constitutional Heritage** In what ways did important court decisions affect African Americans' civil rights during the early civil rights movement?

Thinking Critically

1. **Drawing Inferences and Conclusions** What economic factors helped to make the Montgomery Bus Boycott successful?
2. **Contrasting** How were the beats different from other writers who criticized society in the 1950s?
3. **Making Generalizations and Predictions** Do you think that U.S. efforts to halt the worldwide spread of communism in the 1950s were successful? Explain your answer.

Social Studies Skills Workshop

Interpreting Maps

Study the map below. Then use the information on the map to help you answer the questions that follow.

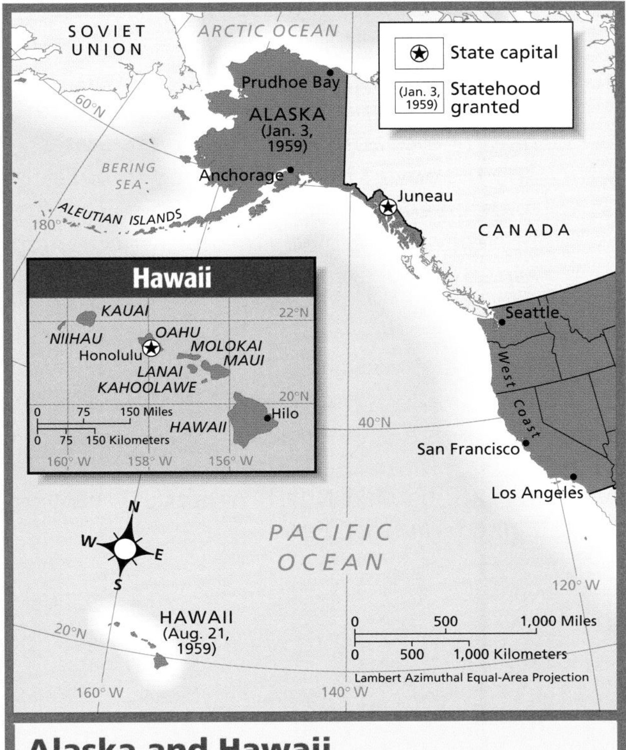

Alaska and Hawaii

1. Approximately how far is Hawaii from the West Coast of the United States?
   a. about 4,000 miles
   b. a little over 2,000 miles
   c. about 1,200 miles
   d. a little over 2,500 miles

2. Based on the map and your knowledge of the period, why do you think Alaska might have been strategically important during the Cold War?

Analyzing Primary Sources

Read the following quotation by President Dwight D. Eisenhower on the integration of the school system in Little Rock, Arkansas. Then answer the questions that follow.

> **"The overwhelming majority of our people in every section of the country are united in their respect for observance of the law—even in those cases where they may disagree with that law. . . . If resistance to the federal court orders ceases at once, the further presence of federal troops will be unnecessary, and the city of Little Rock will return to its normal habits of peace and order, and a blot upon the fair name and high honor of our nation in the world will be removed."**

3. Which of the following statements best describes Eisenhower's view of the Little Rock crisis?
   a. All citizens should personally support integration.
   b. Federal troops will not leave until all the lawbreakers are arrested.
   c. It is the responsibility of citizens to obey the law whether they agree with it or not.
   d. Little Rock will probably not recover from the crisis.

4. Based on your knowledge of the period, why do you think Eisenhower referred to the crisis as "a blot upon the fair name and high honor of our nation"?

5. Which do you think citizens are more likely to respond to: President Eisenhower's insistence that federal troops will stay in Little Rock, or his praise of the city's "normal habits of peace and order"? Explain your answer.

Alternative Assessment

Building Your Portfolio

American History

Linking to Community

Imagine that you are an architect in a local firm. Draw a plan for or build a model of a new neighborhood near where you live. Your plan should include designs for houses, streets, and community buildings that will fit in with the local architecture. Interview at least one person from your community to learn about the area's needs and include this information in your plan.

internet connect

Internet Activity: go.hrw.com
keyword: SC3 CF27

Choose an activity on Peace and Prosperity in the 1950s to:

- Use the Holt Grapher to create graphs and databases on defense spending.
- Create a newspaper on the Little Rock Nine.
- Create a poster on popular culture in the 1950s.

The Cold War

The end of World War II left much of Europe and parts of Asia in ruins. France and Great Britain, two traditional world powers, were greatly weakened. Much of Germany and Japan had been destroyed.

After the war only two great powers remained—the United States and the Soviet Union. For the next 45 years, the two superpowers were locked in a struggle known as the Cold War. The United States and the Soviet Union competed to establish alliances and spread their influence. They never openly went to war with each other. However, they supported opposing sides in many small wars and conflicts.

The superpower rivalry also created a new kind of arms race. The United States and the Soviet Union competed to build huge arsenals of nuclear weapons. This nuclear arms race was the most frightening aspect of the Cold War.

A World Divided

YOU ARE NOW LEAVING BRITISH SECTOR

By the end of the 1950s, much of the world was divided into two camps. Many countries were allied with either the United States or the Soviet Union. In Europe the U.S.-backed North Atlantic Treaty Organization (NATO) faced the Soviet-backed Warsaw Pact.

History Note 1

The United States offered economic aid under the Marshall Plan to the European countries weakened by World War II. The Soviet Union refused to participate. Instead, it set up its own plan for aiding its allies. This effort was called the Molotov Plan, after Soviet foreign minister Vyacheslav Molotov.

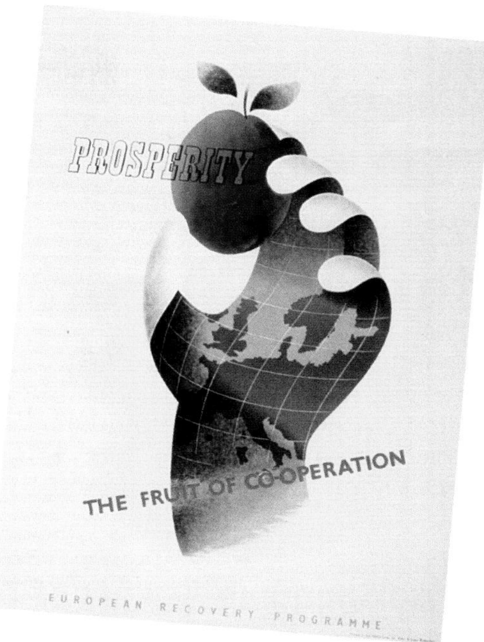

The Marshall Plan created new opportunities through economic aid.

Geography **Skills**

Interpreting Thematic Maps

1. Which non-NATO countries in Europe received aid under the Marshall Plan?
2. **Places and Regions** Which East Asian and Pacific countries were allies of the United States in 1960?
3. **Summarizing** Create a chart showing the nations that were members of NATO or the Warsaw Pact in 1960.

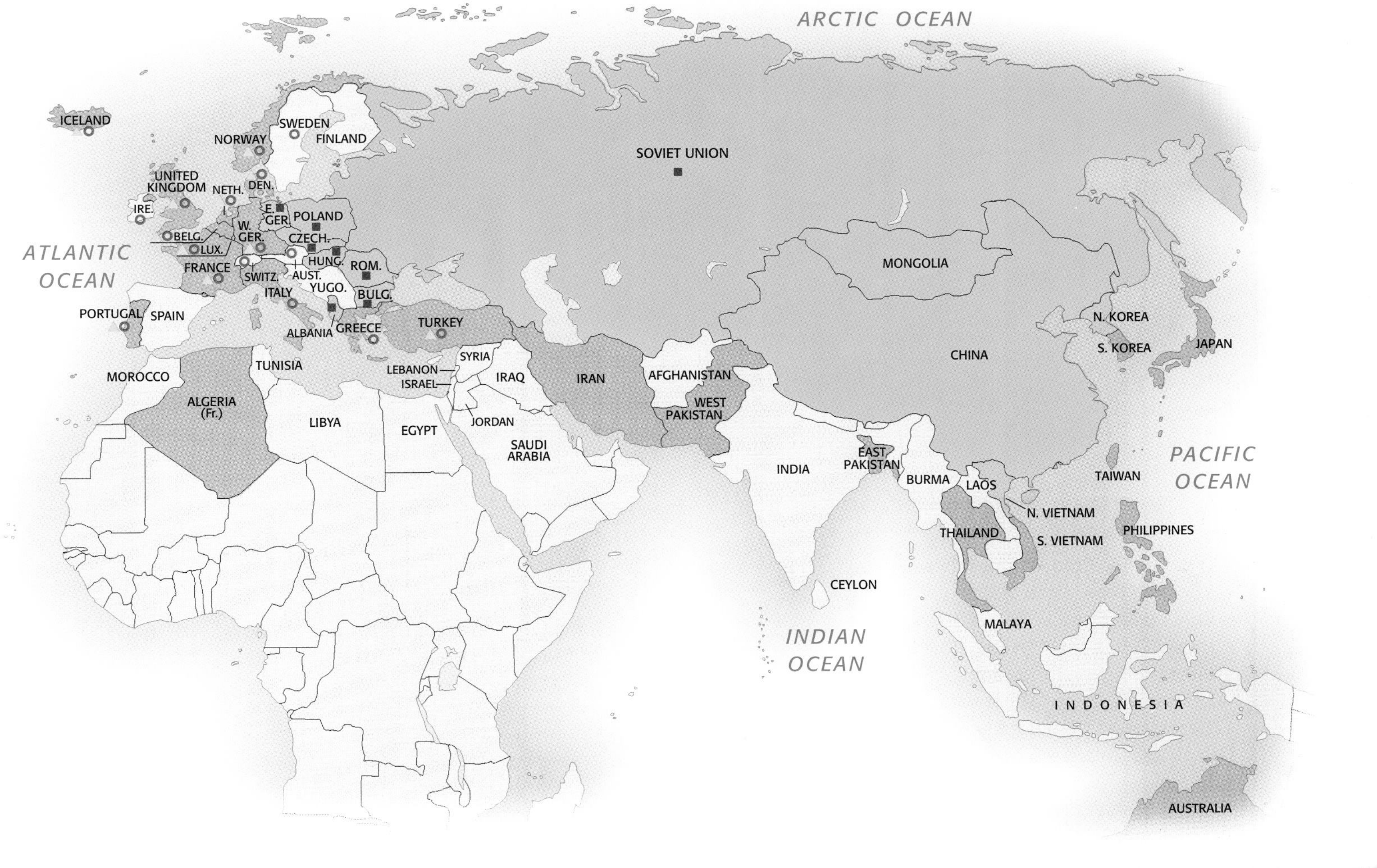

A U.S. Air Force B-52 bomber

Defending America

U.S. military spending fell greatly in the years just after World War II. However, after communist North Korea invaded South Korea in 1950, the United States increased its military spending. Over the next 40 years, the United States spent more than $4 trillion on defense. Much of this money was spent trying to contain communist expansion around the world.

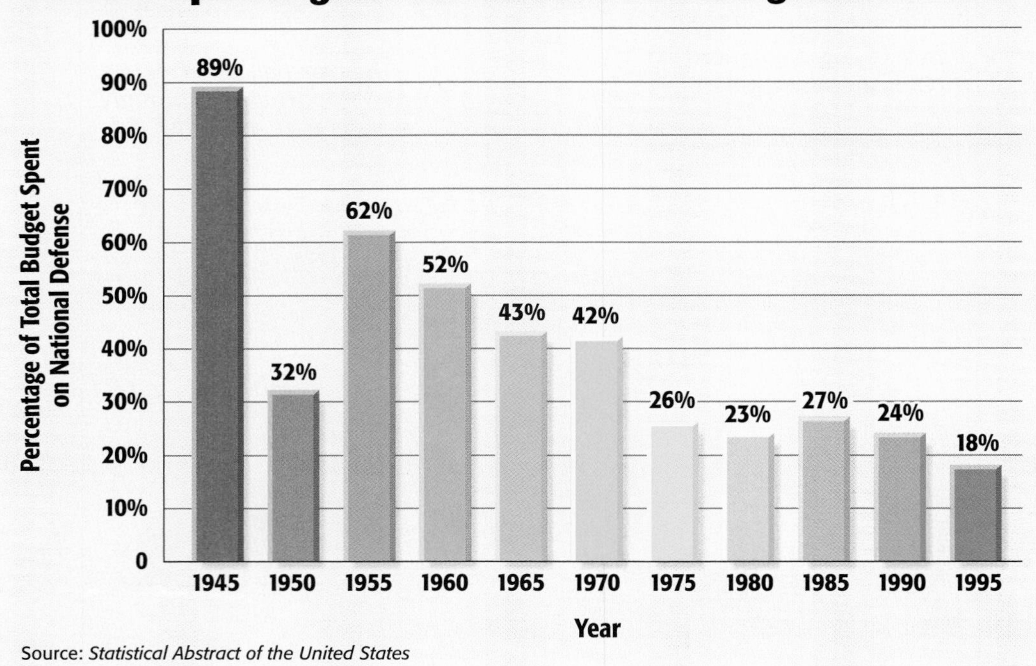

History Note 2

As part of its Cold War defense program, the United States built a huge nuclear stockpile. At first the United States and the Soviet Union relied mainly on long-range bombers to carry nuclear weapons. These planes were largely replaced by nuclear missiles by 1970.

Geography **Skills**

Interpreting Bar Graphs

1. In which two years did the United States spend the highest percentage of its national budget on defense?
2. How many percentage points did defense spending fall from 1970 to 1975?
3. **Analyzing Information** During what decades, or 10-year periods, shown on the graph did defense spending increase?

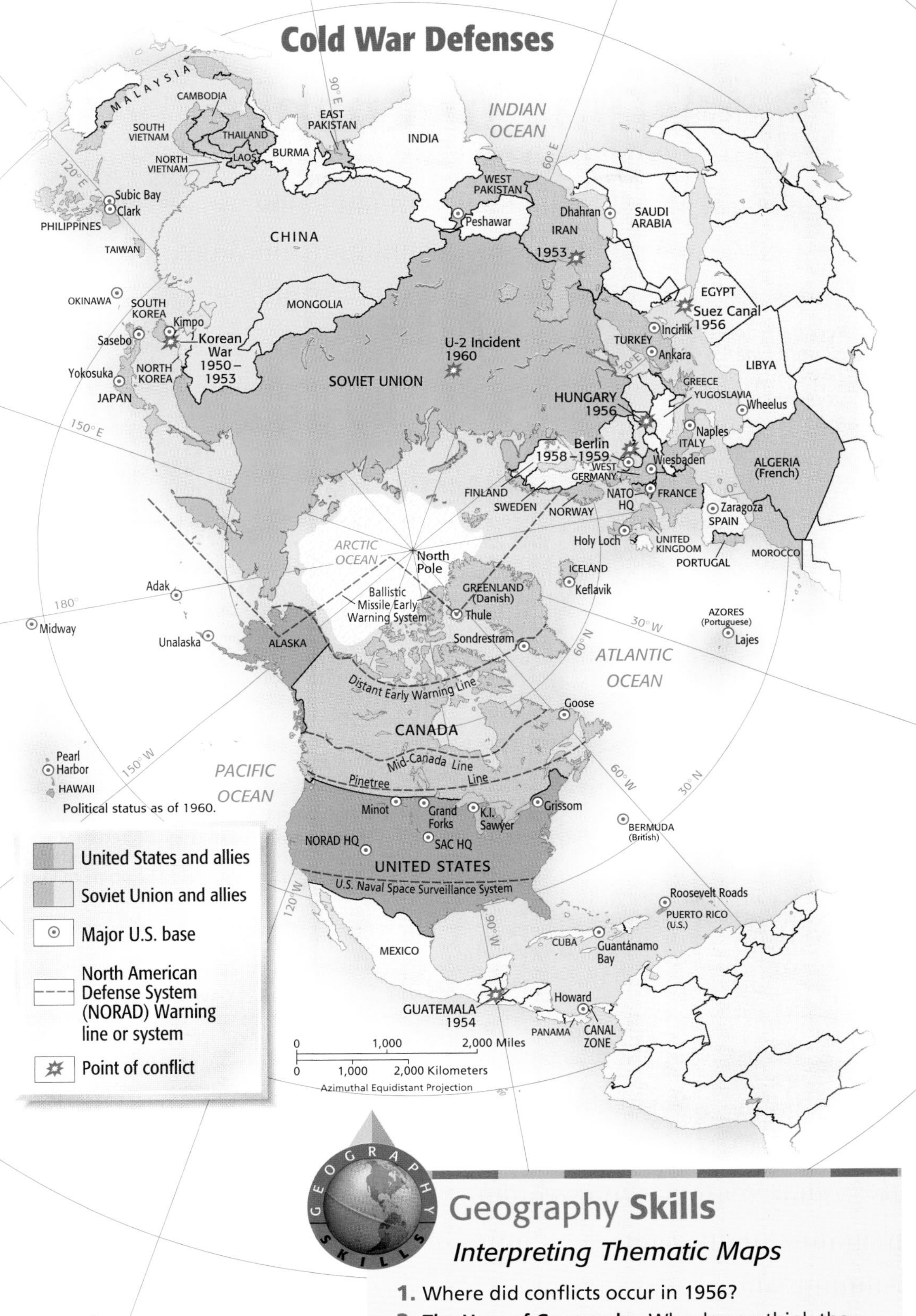

Missiles were a major part of Cold War defenses.

Geography Skills

Interpreting Thematic Maps

1. Where did conflicts occur in 1956?
2. **The Uses of Geography** Why do you think the United States located its early warning systems where it did?
3. **Summarizing** How many major military bases did the United States have in Western Europe?

CHAPTER

28 A Time of Change (1960–1975)

Protesters participated in a civil rights march in Selma, Alabama, to call for laws protecting African American voters.

After winning the presidency in 1960, John F. Kennedy called his inauguration "a celebration of freedom."

UNITED STATES

1960 In February students begin sit-ins in Greensboro, North Carolina, to protest segregation.

1962 President Kennedy demands that the Soviets remove missiles from Cuba during the Cuban missile crisis.

1963 President Kennedy is assassinated in Dallas, Texas, and vice president Lyndon B. Johnson becomes president.

1964 In July President Johnson signs the Civil Rights Act of 1964.

1966 Betty Friedan and other feminists found the National Organization for Women in October.

1960 | **1963** | **1966**

WORLD

1961 CIA-trained Cuban exiles fail to remove Castro from power at the Bay of Pigs in April.

On August 13 the Berlin Wall is built between East and West Berlin.

1963 President Kennedy and Premier Khrushchev sign the Limited Nuclear Test Ban Treaty.

1964 The Beatles, a British rock group, tour the United States, playing sold-out shows.

1966 Golda Meir becomes Israel's first female prime minister.

A Soviet nuclear missile on parade in Moscow

East German soldiers building the Berlin Wall

Build on What You Know

Not all Americans enjoyed the peace and prosperity of the 1950s. The 1960s brought social and political unrest to the country. The growing civil rights movement and its successes inspired other groups to demand their equal rights. Some Americans also questioned traditional values through protests, art, and music.

U.S. astronaut Neil Armstrong made history when he became the first person to walk on the Moon.

New laws provided disabled children with more educational opportunities.

1968 North Korea seizes the USS *Pueblo,* a U.S. Navy ship, and does not release the crew for nearly a year.

1969

1969 U.S. astronauts walk on the Moon in July.

An estimated 400,000 people attend the Woodstock Music and Art Fair in August.

1970 La Raza Unida Party is formed in January to fight for Hispanic rights.

1972

1973 Members of the American Indian Movement stage a protest against broken treaties at Wounded Knee in South Dakota.

1975

1975 The Education for All Handicapped Children Act is passed.

1975 The United Nations observes 1975 as International Women's Year.

Golda Meir served as Israel's minister of labor and foreign minister before becoming the nation's prime minister.

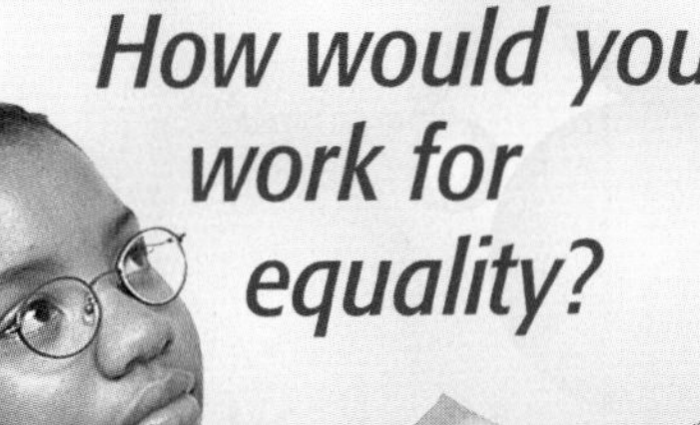

You Be the Historian

What's Your Opinion? Do you **agree** or **disagree** with the following statements? Support your point of view in your journal.

- **Global Relations** Powerful nations settle their differences with force.
- **Economics** Creating new educational possibilities for needy people always increases their economic opportunities.
- **Citizenship** People, rather than the government, should change society.

Section 1

The Kennedy Administration

Read to Discover

1. What proposals did Kennedy's New Frontier include?
2. What foreign-policy approaches did Kennedy support to fight communism?
3. What Cold War crises did Kennedy face, and how did he deal with them?

Identify

- John F. Kennedy
- Peace Corps
- New Frontier
- Fidel Castro
- Nikita Khrushchev
- Berlin Wall
- Cuban missile crisis
- Limited Nuclear Test Ban Treaty

WHY IT MATTERS TODAY

Some countries still have communist governments. Use CNNfyi.com or other **current events** sources to identify a country with a communist government today. Record your findings in your journal.

Campaign buttons for John F. Kennedy and Richard Nixon

The Story Continues

On the evening of September 26, 1960, American viewers saw the first-ever televised debate between presidential candidates. Most Americans saw John F. Kennedy as calm, confident, and relaxed in front of the cameras. Richard Nixon, his Republican opponent, seemed tense and sweaty, with a tight smile. One Kennedy adviser remembered his party's reaction. "As the moderator signed off, our small band erupted in cheers. . . . It was over! We had won! Not just the debate. We had won the election!"

Kennedy's Domestic Policies

At 43, **John F. Kennedy** became the youngest person ever elected president of the United States. As a Catholic, Kennedy had to overcome religious prejudice and convince voters that his political decisions would not be influenced by religious leaders. His message to the American people was one of hope. At his inauguration, President Kennedy called on Americans to look beyond their own needs and to help others.

John F. Kennedy arrives in Los Angeles for the 1960 Democratic National Convention.

Analyzing Primary Sources

Supporting a Point of View Would President Kennedy's speech have inspired you to become involved in public service? Explain your answer.

"And so, my fellow Americans—ask not what your country can do for you—ask what you can do for your country. My fellow citizens of the world—ask not what America will do for you, but what together we can do for the freedom of man."

—John F. Kennedy, quoted in *Annals of America, Vol. 18*

Young Americans responded to Kennedy's call to public service. Some joined the **Peace Corps**, a volunteer organization created by Kennedy in 1961 to carry out improvement projects in developing countries.

President Kennedy also announced a set of domestic reforms he called a **New Frontier**. To stimulate the economy, he recommended cutting taxes. At the same time, he wanted to increase spending on the poor, the military, and the space program. One goal of the New Frontier was to improve the economy. A slight economic decline in the late 1950s caused many Americans to worry that the prosperity of the postwar years had come to an end.

To lower inflation and reduce unemployment, Kennedy proposed voluntary wage-and-price controls for businesses. Addressing the steel industry, Kennedy asked union members to accept smaller raises and business owners not to raise prices. Steelworkers agreed, but U.S. Steel and other companies raised their prices. In response, Kennedy asked the Federal Trade Commission to investigate whether the steel industry had broken antitrust laws. U.S. Steel soon lowered its prices.

The New Frontier worried some members of Congress who feared a budget imbalance. Republicans and conservative southern Democrats, therefore, blocked much of the president's legislation. Kennedy's administration was able to raise the minimum wage and to increase spending for urban improvements, however.

✔ **Reading Check: Summarizing** What domestic proposals did President Kennedy make?

The Peace Corps

In March 1961 President Kennedy established the Peace Corps to "promote world peace and friendship." Since then, more than 150,000 Americans have served in more than 134 countries. In the early 1960s, Peace Corps volunteers were mostly young college graduates who served in Africa, Asia, and Latin America.

The Peace Corps now admits many retired people, and it serves countries in Eastern Europe and the former Soviet Union. Many Peace Corps volunteers find their experiences enriching. One volunteer explained: "I have come to appreciate . . . the freedoms we, as Americans, take for granted." **How has the Peace Corps changed over time?**

Kennedy Fights the Cold War

To fight communism, President Kennedy maintained a strong military and increased the number of nuclear weapons on hand. He also offered economic aid to needy countries in Africa, Asia, and Latin America.

The first of three major Cold War crises that President Kennedy had to deal with took place in Cuba. By 1960, revolutionary leader **Fidel Castro** had set up a communist dictatorship that had ties to the Soviet Union. In response, Kennedy approved a plan that the Eisenhower administration had developed to invade Cuba. In April 1961 about 1,500 Cuban exiles waded ashore at the Bay of Pigs in Cuba. After three days of fighting, about 1,200 of the invaders had been captured and the rest killed. Castro remained firmly in power.

A second crisis took place in Berlin, located in the heart of East Germany. For many East Berliners, democratic West Berlin stood for

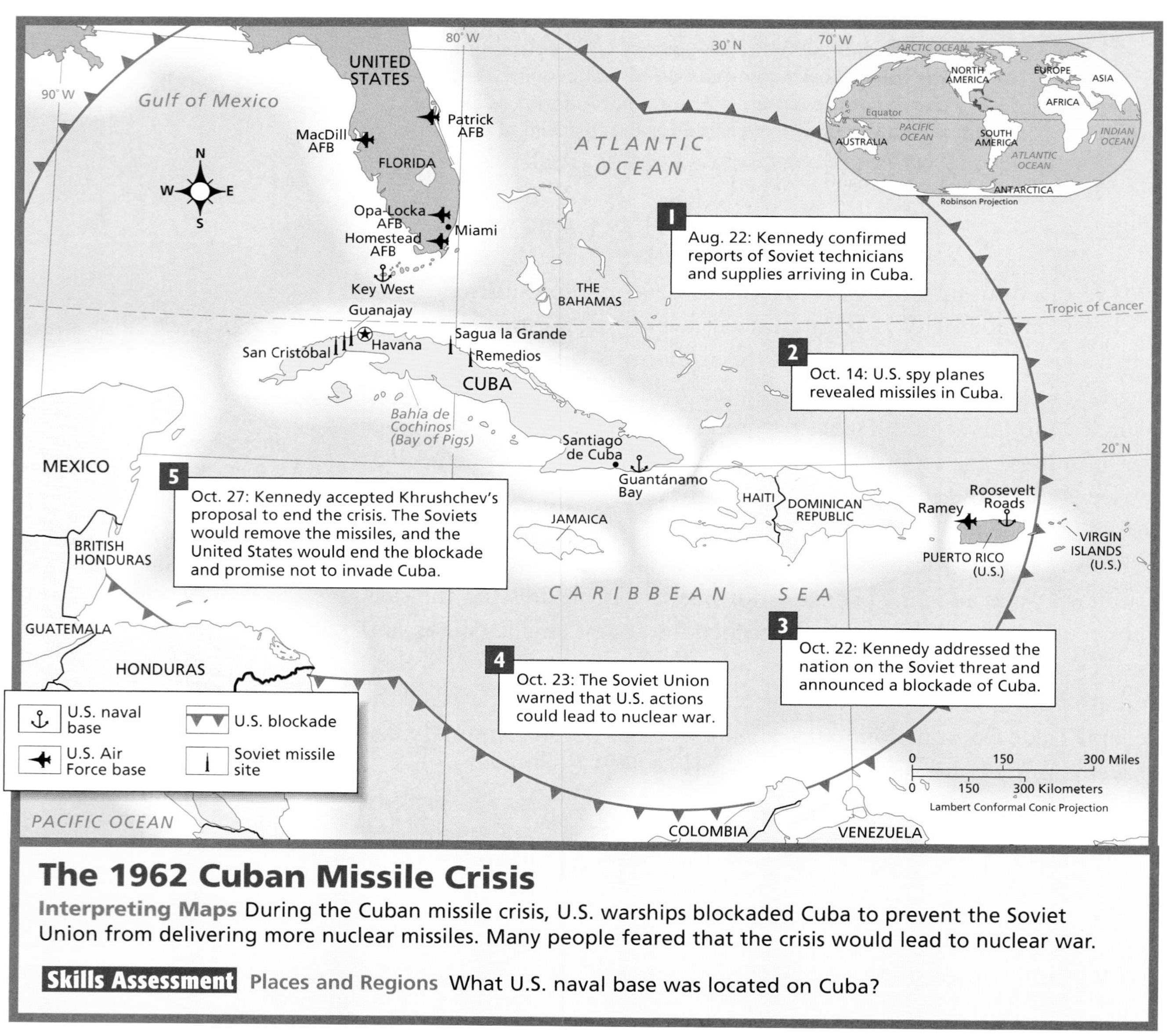

The 1962 Cuban Missile Crisis

Interpreting Maps During the Cuban missile crisis, U.S. warships blockaded Cuba to prevent the Soviet Union from delivering more nuclear missiles. Many people feared that the crisis would lead to nuclear war.

Skills Assessment **Places and Regions** What U.S. naval base was located on Cuba?

prosperity and freedom. By the summer of 1961, thousands of East Germans were leaving the country through East Berlin, greatly alarming Communist officials. Soviet leader **Nikita Khrushchev** demanded the removal of all foreign troops from West Berlin.

On the morning of August 13, 1961, Berliners woke to find workers building the **Berlin Wall** out of cement and barbed wire. The barrier, which separated East and West Berlin, was successful in stopping the escapes. President Kennedy responded to the "brutal border closing" by sending additional U.S. troops to the city. Neither Kennedy nor Khrushchev, however, was willing to go to war over Berlin.

Another Cold War crisis came in the fall of 1962. U.S. spy planes discovered that the Soviets were placing nuclear missiles in Cuba. Any missile launched from there could hit the United States within minutes. At a news conference on October 22, President Kennedy demanded that Khrushchev remove the missiles. The U.S. Navy was sent to Cuba to prevent the Soviets from bringing in more weapons. Two days later, armed Soviet ships approached the U.S. blockade. Attorney General Robert Kennedy, the president's younger brother, described the crisis as "the time of gravest [deepest] concern for the President." Soon word came that the Soviet ships had turned back. Many Americans gave Kennedy the credit.

The **Cuban missile crisis** encouraged Kennedy and Khrushchev to work to prevent conflicts that might lead to nuclear war. The Soviets agreed to remove missiles from Cuba in return for a U.S. promise not to invade Cuba. Kennedy also agreed to remove some missiles from Italy and Turkey. In 1963 the superpowers set up a telephone "hotline" so that the two leaders could talk to each other at a moment's notice. Kennedy and Khrushchev also signed the **Limited Nuclear Test Ban Treaty**, which ended the testing of new nuclear weapons aboveground.

Interpreting Political Cartoons

"Kennedy karate" *This cartoon shows President Kennedy responding forcefully to the Cuban missile crisis.* ***Do you think the artist approved of Kennedy's actions during the crisis? Explain your answer.***

✔ **Reading Check: Summarizing** Describe the three major Cold War crises of Kennedy's administration.

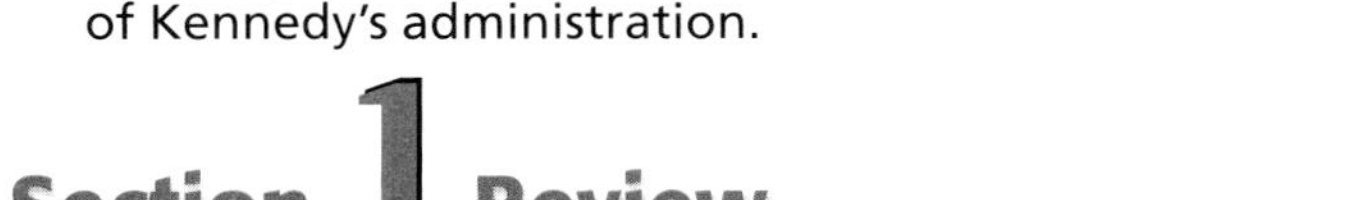

Section 1 Review

go.hrw.com Homework Practice Online
keyword: SC3 HP28

1 Identify and explain:
- John F. Kennedy
- Peace Corps
- New Frontier
- Fidel Castro
- Nikita Khrushchev
- Berlin Wall
- Cuban missile crisis
- Limited Nuclear Test Ban Treaty

2 Analyzing Information Copy the diagram below. Use it to explain the causes of the three major Cold War crises that President Kennedy faced and how he addressed them.

3 Finding the Main Idea

a. What was Kennedy's New Frontier, and which of its goals did his administration achieve?

b. How did Kennedy respond to the threat of communist expansion?

4 Writing and Critical Thinking

Evaluating Imagine that you are a foreign-policy adviser to President Kennedy. Write a memo telling Kennedy how effective you think his administration has been at fighting communism.

Consider the following:
- events in Cuba
- tensions in Berlin
- efforts to prevent future conflicts

Section 2

The Johnson Administration

Read to Discover

1. What effect did Kennedy's assassination have on the United States?
2. How did Johnson attempt to help poor Americans?
3. What scientific events and issues were important in the 1960s?

Identify

- Lyndon B. Johnson
- Warren Commission
- War on Poverty
- Great Society
- Medicare
- Medicaid
- Alan Shepard Jr.
- Neil Armstrong
- Edwin "Buzz" Aldrin
- Rachel Carson

Why It Matters Today

The security of the president of the United States is still an important challenge for the federal government. Use CNNfyi.com or other **current events** sources to learn about challenges that the Secret Service faces when protecting the president. Record your findings in your journal.

On his third birthday, John F. Kennedy Jr. saluted his father's coffin in the funeral procession.

The Story Continues

In November 1963 President Kennedy began a quick tour of Texas cities. On the morning of November 22 he worked on a speech he planned to deliver that day in Dallas. "We ask therefore that we may be worthy of our power and responsibility," he was to say. Kennedy never delivered that speech. To the nation's horror, by that afternoon, he had died from an assassin's bullet. That same day, Vice President Lyndon B. Johnson became the nation's president.

The Kennedy Assassination

On November 22, 1963, as President Kennedy's motorcade traveled through Dallas, shots rang out. Kennedy slumped forward, severely wounded, and died soon afterward. Vice President **Lyndon B. Johnson**, following in another car, was unharmed. Just two hours after Kennedy's assassination, Johnson took the presidential oath of office on board *Air Force One*, the presidential airplane. Kennedy's body was taken back to Washington, D.C.

Interpreting the Visual Record

Swearing in *Vice President Lyndon Johnson took the oath of office on* Air Force One *shortly after Kennedy's death. Standing next to Johnson (to his left) is Jacqueline Kennedy.* ***What does the mood of the participants gathered for the ceremony appear to be?***

The assassination shocked Americans. One Kennedy administration official remembered his reaction on hearing of the president's death.

History Makers Speak

> **"I was crying. It was unbelievable, stunning. An awful feeling of helplessness—nothing could be done. . . . John Kennedy was not the sixties. But he fueled the smoldering embers [fire], and, for a brief while, was the exemplar [prime example] who led others to discover their own strength and resurgent [renewed] energy."**
>
> —Richard N. Goodwin, *Remembering America*

Analyzing Primary Sources

Identifying Points of View How did the author believe Kennedy influenced the sixties?

People around the world were also saddened by Kennedy's death. More than 90 percent of American homes and millions of people worldwide watched Kennedy's funeral on television.

Within hours of the assassination, police arrested Soviet sympathizer and former U.S. Marine Lee Harvey Oswald. Two days later, as officials moved Oswald to another jail, nightclub owner Jack Ruby pushed his way through the crowd and killed Oswald. Oswald's death left many unanswered questions. To try to clear up the mystery of Kennedy's assassination, President Johnson chose a special commission headed by Chief Justice Earl Warren. The **Warren Commission**, as the group of investigators was called, spent months studying the evidence. The Warren Commission concluded that Oswald was the assassin and that he had acted alone. Not everyone agreed with that conclusion, however. There remains much controversy surrounding the Kennedy assassination to this day.

✔ **Reading Check: Summarizing** What did the Warren Commission conclude, and how did the public react to this news?

Lyndon B. Johnson

Lyndon B. Johnson was born in 1908 in central Texas. His father was a politician, and Johnson grew up with politics in his blood. Johnson became known as the wonder kid of Texas politics for his early accomplishments. In 1935 President Franklin D. Roosevelt made Johnson director of the Texas National Youth Administration (NYA), a New Deal program. He was the youngest state NYA director. Under his leadership the NYA built highways, parks, and playgrounds throughout Texas. Johnson won election to the House of Representatives in 1937 at age 29.

Johnson continued his rise into the Senate, on to the vice presidency, and then the presidency. A former colleague described Johnson's determined pace. "Lyndon behaves as if there were no tomorrow coming and he had to do everything today."

What did Johnson accomplish in his early political career?

Analyzing Primary Sources

Drawing Inferences and Conclusions What were Johnson's main goals in the Great Society?

Johnson in Office

President Johnson tried to comfort the nation and promised to work for the reforms of the New Frontier. Johnson differed from Kennedy in many ways, however. While Kennedy's family enjoyed wealth and power, Johnson grew up poor in rural Texas. Kennedy attended Harvard University, but Johnson worked his way through a local teacher's college. However, Johnson had more political experience than Kennedy did. As majority leader in the Senate, Johnson had learned what it took to win the votes of his fellow senators. One member of Congress recalled Johnson's forceful debating technique. "Lyndon got me by the lapels and put his face on top of mine and he talked and talked."

As President, Johnson was determined to pass the education and civil rights legislation that he and Kennedy had supported. He also made helping the poor "the highest priority." In 1964 Johnson launched the **War on Poverty**, a series of programs to help poor Americans. Johnson called for the creation of the Office of Economic Opportunity (OEO) to develop programs to help poor people earn money. The OEO started the Job Corps, a program to teach young adults basic job skills. In addition, it established Head Start, an educational program to prepare poor children for school. The OEO also created a domestic version of the Peace Corps—the Volunteers in Service to America (VISTA).

President Johnson's popularity soared because of his success in getting legislation passed. The Democrats nominated him as their candidate for president in 1964. Barry Goldwater ran as the Republican candidate. A conservative senator from Arizona, Goldwater wanted to reduce federal social programs and expand the U.S. military. Johnson won a landslide victory of 486 electoral votes to Goldwater's 52.

President Johnson saw his victory as a public vote of approval for his policies. He set out to expand his domestic reforms. Johnson called his new program for reform and for aid to poor Americans the **Great Society**. He described the program in a speech he gave in 1964.

"The Great Society rests on abundance [plenty] and liberty for all. It demands an end to poverty and racial injustice. . . . The Great Society is a place where every child can find knowledge to enrich [improve] his mind and to enlarge his talents."

—Lyndon B. Johnson, quoted in *Annals of America, Vol. 18*

Johnson saw his Great Society as an expansion of Roosevelt's New Deal of the 1930s. Some reforms focused on improving health care and education. The Great Society established **Medicare**, which includes people age 65 and older in a government health care plan, and **Medicaid**, which provides health insurance for people with low incomes. Another law gave more than $1 billion to local schools to help students with special needs. To help improve housing for low-income families, Congress created the Department of Housing and Urban Development (HUD). Former New Deal official Robert C. Weaver became HUD's secretary and the first African American member of a presidential cabinet.

President Johnson also shared Kennedy's views on communism. Like Presidents Eisenhower and Kennedy, President Johnson believed communism was a major threat to democracy and world peace. Fearing a communist takeover in the Dominican Republic, he sent U.S. Marines there in April 1965 to stop rioting. He also sent more U.S. troops to help defend South Vietnam from communist North Vietnam. (See Chapter 29, War in Vietnam, for more information.)

✔ **Reading Check: Comparing and Contrasting** How was the Great Society like the War on Poverty, and how was it different?

Research on the ROM

Free Find:
HUD
After reading about the Housing and Urban Development Act on the **Holt Researcher CD–ROM,** create an informational brochure that encourages Americans to participate in the program.

Science and Technology

Like President Kennedy, President Johnson saw the space race as a key part of the Cold War. After Soviet cosmonaut Yuri Gagarin orbited Earth in 1961, the Soviets appeared to be winning the space race. Kennedy pushed the newly created National Aeronautics and Space

CONNECTING TO SCIENCE AND TECHNOLOGY

The Apollo Program

The Apollo program was created to meet the long-range goal of landing an American on the Moon. Even with careful planning, the Apollo astronauts faced great danger. For example, only quick thinking and technical skill saved the crew of *Apollo 13* after an equipment malfunction in space. Despite its difficulties, the Apollo program was very successful. Altogether, there were eight missions to the Moon, six of which landed on the surface. The final Apollo mission took place in 1972. Today NASA uses robots for much of its space exploration. **How have U.S. space missions changed since the Apollo program was created?**

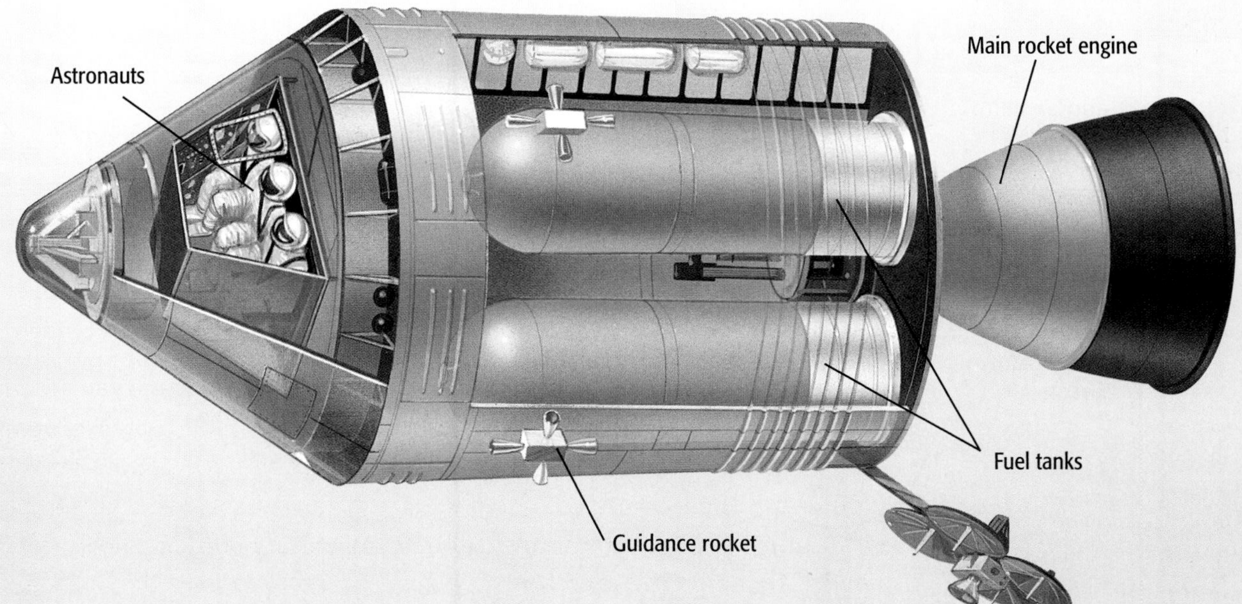

Biologist Rachel Carson, shown in the woods near her home, raised many people's awareness of the dangers of insecticides like DDT.

Administration (NASA) to catch up. He committed the nation to "landing a man on the moon and returning him safely to the earth" before the end of the 1960s. In May 1961 **Alan Shepard Jr.** became the first American launched into space. Then, in 1962, astronaut John Glenn became the first American to orbit Earth.

With President Johnson's support, NASA soon surpassed the achievements of the Soviets. On July 20, 1969, U.S. astronauts reached the Moon nearly six months ahead of Kennedy's target date. While their *Apollo 11* spacecraft orbited the Moon, **Neil Armstrong** and **Edwin "Buzz" Aldrin** piloted a landing vehicle toward the Moon's surface. Millions of people around the world watched on television as the craft touched down and Armstrong took the first steps on the Moon. He said, "That's one small step for [a] man, one giant leap for mankind."

The Apollo program led to new technologies that changed daily life. These "spin-offs" included improved building materials, computers, medical devices, and communications systems. Satellites became particularly important tools for sending telephone and television signals and for collecting weather data.

While NASA led efforts to explore space, scientists discovered new dangers on Earth. Biologist **Rachel Carson** studied a noticeable increase in the death rate of birds in Massachusetts. In her 1962 book *Silent Spring*, she concluded that DDT—a widely used insecticide, or insect poison—had caused the deaths. Additional studies helped prove her findings, and in 1972 the United States limited the use of DDT. The birds had eaten bugs that had been poisoned by leaves on trees sprayed with DDT.

✔ **Reading Check: Finding the Main Idea** What scientific achievements did the United States make in the 1960s?

Section 2 Review

go.hrw.com **Homework Practice Online**
keyword: SC3 HP28

1. **Identify** and explain:
   - Lyndon B. Johnson
   - Warren Commission
   - War on Poverty
   - Great Society
   - Medicare
   - Medicaid
   - Alan Shepard Jr.
   - Neil Armstrong
   - Edwin "Buzz" Aldrin
   - Rachel Carson

2. **Comparing and Contrasting** Copy the diagram below. Use it to compare and contrast Johnson's domestic programs in his first and second terms.

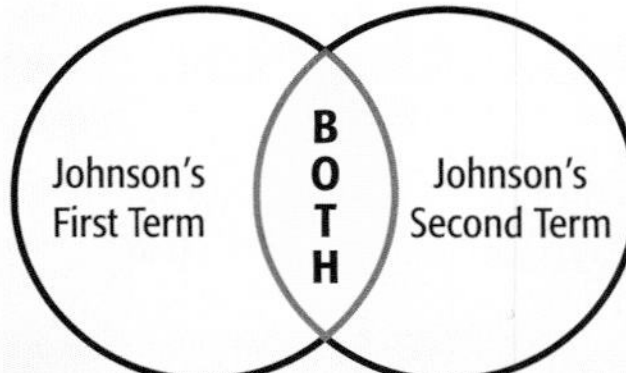

3. **Finding the Main Idea**
   a. How did Americans respond to Kennedy's assassination?
   b. What were the achievements and problems of U.S. engineers and scientists in the 1960s?

4. **Writing and Critical Thinking**
   Analyzing Information Imagine that you are a historian writing a book about President Lyndon Johnson's reforms to help poor Americans. Write an introduction to your book in which you describe what actions Johnson took.
   Consider the following:
   - the War on Poverty
   - the Great Society
   - the Office of Economic Opportunity

Section 3

The Civil Rights Movement

Read to Discover

1. What changes in southern society resulted from protest demonstrations?
2. What events led to the passage of the Civil Rights Act of 1964 and the Voting Rights Act of 1965?
3. How did the civil rights movement change in the late 1960s and early 1970s?

Why It Matters Today

Young people continue to be actively involved in reform movements. Use CNNfyi.com or other **current events** sources to research an area of reform that young people in the United States are involved in today. Record your findings in your journal.

Define

- sit-in
- nonviolent resistance

Identify

- Student Nonviolent Coordinating Committee
- Freedom Rides
- March on Washington
- Civil Rights Act of 1964
- Voting Rights Act of 1965
- Malcolm X
- Black Power

The Story Continues

On the afternoon of February 1, 1960, Joseph McNeil and Franklin McCain entered the Woolworth's department store in Greensboro, North Carolina. The two African American men sat down at the "whites-only" section of the lunch counter. The waitress refused to serve them, but they sat at the counter until the store closed for the day. They returned the next morning with about 20 more students.

Restaurants throughout the South segregated white and African American customers.

Peaceful Protests

The tactic used in Greensboro was known as a **sit-in**—a demonstration in which protesters sit down in a location and refuse to leave. The Greensboro group inspired other students to hold sit-ins at segregated stores. To achieve their goals, the sit-in protesters practiced **nonviolent resistance.** This strategy of peaceful protest rejected the use of violence, even for self-defense. Remaining nonviolent was not always easy. Crowds of angry white citizens often shouted insults, threw food, and even attacked protesters. One protester described her appearance after a sit-in that turned violent.

Analyzing Primary Sources

Drawing Inferences and Conclusions How can you tell that Moody was committed to the protest?

"[My hair] was stiff with dried mustard, ketchup and sugar. . . . I didn't have on any shoes because I had lost them when I was dragged across the floor at Woolworth's. My stockings were sticking to my legs from the [dried] mustard."

—Anne Moody, *Coming of Age in Mississippi*

Over time, Woolworth's and some other businesses in the South integrated. This success encouraged African American student leaders to form the **Student Nonviolent Coordinating Committee** (SNCC) in 1960 to organize civil rights demonstrations.

The leaders of SNCC soon had a chance to show their determination. In May 1961 the Congress of Racial Equality (CORE) began a series of **Freedom Rides** to protest segregation on buses and in southern bus stations. On these rides African American protesters used "whites-only" bus-station facilities and white protesters used "blacks-only" facilities. The first two buses of Freedom Riders were attacked in Alabama by angry white mobs. When CORE leaders called off the rides due to the danger, SNCC stepped in to continue the protests.

Attacks on the riders continued. Attorney General Robert Kennedy asked the riders to accept a "cooling-off period." Ride organizer James Farmer replied, "Please tell the attorney general that we have been cooling off for three hundred and fifty years." The attorney general sent a police escort, and the rides went on. On November 1, 1961, an Interstate Commerce Commission ban on bus and railroad segregation went into effect. The Freedom Riders had made an important contribution to desegregation.

African American and white civil rights activists worked together on protests such as the Freedom Rides.

The 1961 Freedom Rides

Interpreting Maps Civil rights workers stage Freedom Rides throughout the South to protest the region's segregated bus stations.

Skills Assessment

1. **The World in Spatial Terms** In which states did the Freedom Riders meet with violence?
2. **Analyzing Information** Which Freedom Ride route covered the greatest distance?

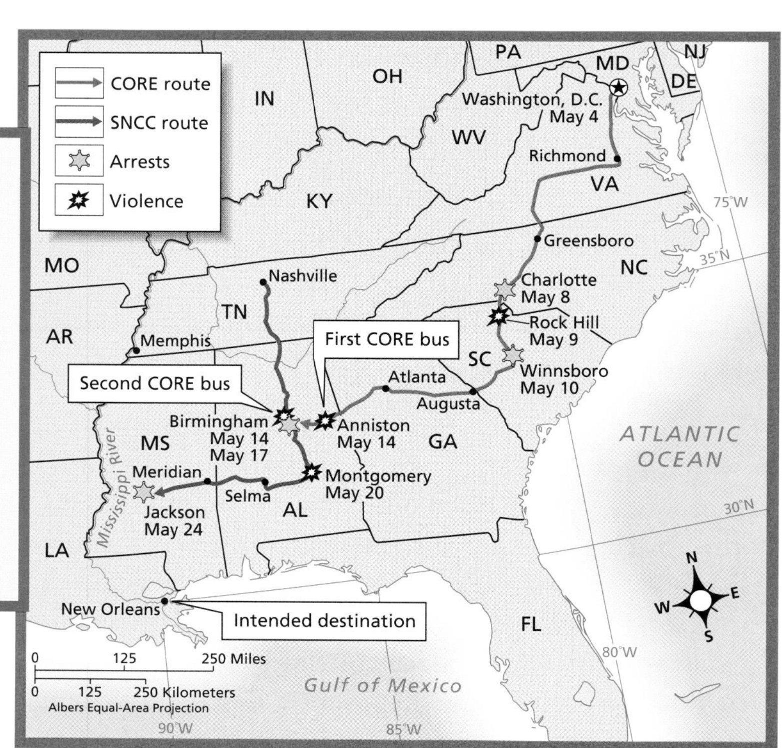

Working for Freedom

The fight for civil rights went on. In 1962 an African American named James Meredith arrived to take classes at the all-white University of Mississippi. Riots broke out, army troops restored order, and Meredith went on to graduate. In April 1963 Martin Luther King Jr., who led the Southern Christian Leadership Conference, organized a series of marches in Birmingham, Alabama. King was arrested and put in jail, where he wrote *Letter from Birmingham Jail*, explaining his faith in nonviolence.

In May, King and the Reverend Fred Shuttlesworth, a Birmingham civil rights leader, led more protests in the city. As 2,500 marchers walked through the streets, Police Commissioner Eugene "Bull" Connor ordered his officers to use their attack dogs against the marchers. Then the fire department turned water hoses on the protesters. When Americans turned on the news, they saw men and women—even children—being beaten, blasted with water, and attacked by dogs. Many people began to understand that the civil rights movement was a life-and-death struggle.

With public pressure rising, in June 1963 President Kennedy asked Congress for a sweeping new civil rights bill. African American leaders decided to hold a nationwide demonstration, called the **March on Washington**, in support of civil rights. On August 28 more than 250,000 people—African American and white—gathered near the Lincoln Memorial and listened to speakers. It was at this gathering that Martin Luther King Jr. gave his now famous "I Have a Dream" speech and filled the crowd with hope.

After the march, however, the hopeful mood disappeared in a wave of violence. In September a bomb exploded at an African American church in Birmingham and killed four girls. In November, Lee Harvey Oswald killed President Kennedy. However, Lyndon B. Johnson, Kennedy's successor, took up the cause of civil rights legislation. On July 2 Johnson signed the **Civil Rights Act of 1964**. This act banned segregation in public places, such as restaurants and transportation facilities. The law also prohibited discrimination by employers, unions, or universities with federal-government contracts on the basis of race, sex, religion, and national origin.

✔ **Reading Check: Drawing Inferences and Conclusions** How great was King's contribution to the passage of the Civil Rights Act of 1964?

Interpreting the Visual Record

Demonstrations *During the 1963 March on Washington, more than 250,000 people—both black and white—gathered to listen to speakers.* ***What kind of message do you think such a large gathering would send other Americans?***

Free Find:
Martin Luther King Jr.
After reading the biography of Martin Luther King Jr. on the **Holt Researcher CD–ROM**, create an annotated time line that shows the important events in his life.

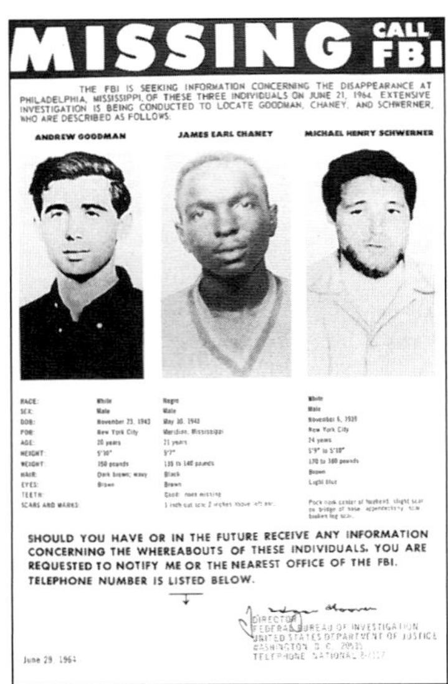

The search for the three missing Freedom Summer volunteers focused national attention on civil rights.

The Right to Vote

That same summer of 1964, hundreds of white college students traveled to Mississippi to help African Americans register to vote. African American activists had been working to protect voting rights in several southern states since the early 1960s. Unfair election rules, along with threats of job loss and violence, often kept many African Americans from voting. Many young civil rights workers faced violent attacks. On June 21, 1964, three Freedom Summer volunteers—James Chaney, an African American, and Andrew Goodman and Michael Schwerner, both white students—disappeared. In early August, searchers finally found the men shot to death.

The brutal murders drew national attention to the voter registration effort. As the Johnson administration prepared a bill to protect African American voters, King organized a voter registration march from Selma to Montgomery, Alabama, the state capital. Dozens of marchers were beaten and jailed. As the violence broke out, television news programs broadcast the bloody events. In August, President Johnson signed the **Voting Rights Act of 1965**. It gave the federal government the power to inspect voter registration procedures and to protect all citizens' voting rights. Within three years, more than half of all qualified African American voters in the South had registered to vote.

✔ **Reading Check: Supporting a Point of View** How successful were voter registration efforts in Mississippi? Explain your answer.

New Directions

Malcom X posed for this picture while visiting Egypt in 1964.

During the mid- to late 1960s, many younger reformers began to criticize the civil rights movement. Some wanted faster progress. Others rejected racial integration and nonviolence. As a result, some of these activists were drawn to **Malcolm X**, a leader of the Nation of Islam, a religious group that favored black separatism. Malcolm X argued that African Americans should work for social and economic independence rather than for racial integration. He also believed that African Americans had the right to protect themselves from violence.

"You're getting a new generation . . . and they're beginning to think with their own minds and see that you can't negotiate up on freedom nowadays. If something is yours by right, then fight for it or shut up. If you can't fight for it, then forget it."

—Malcolm X, *By Any Means Necessary*

Malcolm X eventually left the Nation of Islam and began to reconsider his views on integration. He did not have much time to share his views, however. In 1965, three members of the Nation of Islam killed Malcolm X as he was giving a speech in New York City.

Over time, increasing numbers of young activists came to support the **Black Power** movement. This was a social and political movement that called for greater African American power and independence. Like Malcolm X, some Black Power activists rejected integration as a final goal. Many also encouraged African Americans to take control of their own communities and futures.

Despite the efforts of activists, discrimination still affected many African Americans. In August 1965 a riot broke out in the Watts section of Los Angeles, killing 34 people and destroying the neighborhood. This event triggered many more riots in cities across the country. President Johnson appointed the Kerner Commission to investigate the violence. In 1968, the commission reported that anger over racism was a leading cause of the riots. The report also warned that "the nation is rapidly moving toward two increasingly separate Americas"—one white and wealthy, the other African American and poor.

That same year Martin Luther King Jr. announced plans for a march to begin the "Poor People's Campaign." First, however, he visited Memphis, Tennessee, to support striking garbage workers. On April 4, as King stood on his hotel balcony, a hidden gunman fired at him. King fell dead. About two months later, the police arrested ex-convict James Earl Ray for the murder. King's assassination horrified many people in the United States and around the world. Riots broke out in more than 100 cities nationwide. With King's death, part of the civil rights movement also seemed to die, but other leaders vowed to carry on the fight.

Leaders of the Black Power movement wanted to increase African American economic and political influence.

✔ **Reading Check: Contrasting** How did the civil rights movement of the late 1960s differ from the movement in the early 1960s?

Section 3 Review

go.hrw.com **Homework Practice Online**
keyword: SC3 HP28

1. **Define** and explain:
   - sit-in
   - nonviolent resistance
2. **Identify** and explain:
   - Student Nonviolent Coordinating Committee
   - Freedom Rides
   - March on Washington
   - Civil Rights Act of 1964
   - Voting Rights Act of 1965
   - Malcolm X
   - Black Power
3. **Sequencing** Copy the time line below. Use it to place in order what you think are the five most important events or pieces of legislation of the civil rights movement of the 1960s.

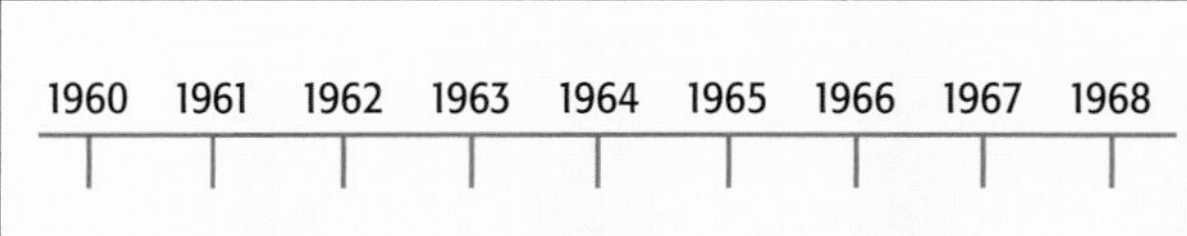

4. **Finding the Main Idea**
   a. How did protest demonstrations aid the civil rights movement?
   b. What efforts did civil rights activists take to help bring about the passage of the Civil Rights Act of 1964 and the Voting Rights Act of 1965?
5. **Writing and Critical Thinking**
   Supporting a Point of View Imagine that you are taking part in a debate on the different strategies of civil rights activists. Write an opening speech explaining how the civil rights movement changed during the late 1960s and early 1970s and whether it was more effective as a result.
   Consider the following:
   - long-term goals
   - ideas about nonviolence
   - successes and failures

1963

MARTIN LUTHER KING JR.'S "I HAVE A DREAM"

On August 28, 1963, more than 250,000 people participated in the March on Washington in support of civil rights. The demonstrators gathered near the Lincoln Memorial, where Martin Luther King Jr. delivered his "I Have a Dream" speech. His address is remembered as one of the most powerful and effective speeches of modern times. An excerpt appears here.

Five score[1] years ago, a great American, in whose symbolic shadow we stand, signed the Emancipation Proclamation. This momentous **decree**[2] came as a great **beacon**[3] light to millions of Negro slaves who had been **seared**[4] in the flames of withering injustice. It came as a joyous daybreak to end the long night of captivity.

But one hundred years later, we must face the tragic fact that the Negro is still not free. One hundred years later, the life of the Negro is still sadly crippled by the **manacles**[5] of segregation and the chains of discrimination. . . .

In a sense we have come to our nation's Capital to cash a check. When the architects of our republic wrote the magnificent words of the Constitution and the Declaration of Independence, they were signing a **promissory note**[6] to which every American was **to fall heir.**[7] This note was a promise that all men would be guaranteed the **unalienable**[8] rights of life, liberty, and the pursuit of happiness.

It is obvious today that America has **defaulted**[9] on this promissory note insofar as her citizens of color are concerned. Instead of honoring this sacred obligation, America has given the Negro people a bad check; a check which has come back marked "insufficient funds." But we refuse to believe that the bank of justice is bankrupt. . . .

But there is something that I must say to my people who stand on the warm **threshold**[10] which leads into the palace of justice. In the process of gaining our rightful place we must not be guilty of wrongful deeds. Let us not seek to satisfy our thirst for freedom by drinking from the cup of bitterness and hatred. We must forever conduct our struggle on the high plane of dignity and discipline. We must not allow our creative protest to **degenerate**[11] into physical violence. Again and again we must rise to the majestic heights of meeting physical force with soul force. . . .

I say to you today, my friends, that in spite of the difficulties and frustrations of the moment I still have a dream. It is a dream deeply rooted in the American dream.

I have a dream that one day this nation will rise up and live out the true meaning of its **creed:**[12] "We hold these truths to be self-evident; that all men are created equal."

I have a dream that one day on the red hills of Georgia the sons of former slaves and the sons of former slaveowners will be able to sit down together at the table of brotherhood.

I have a dream that one day even the state of Mississippi, a desert state sweltering with the heat of injustice and **oppression,**[13] will be transformed into an oasis of freedom and justice.

I have a dream that my four little children will one day live in a nation where they will not be judged by the color of their skin but by the content of their character.

I have a dream today.

I have a dream that one day the state of Alabama, whose governor's lips are presently dripping with the words of **interposition**[14] and **nullification,**[15] will be transformed into a situation where little black boys and black girls will be able to join hands with little white boys and white girls and walk together as sisters and brothers.

I have a dream today.

I have a dream that one day every valley shall be **exalted,**[16] every hill and mountain shall be made low, the rough places will be made plain, and the crooked places will be made straight, and the glory of the Lord shall be revealed, and all flesh shall see it together.

This is our hope. This is the faith with which I return to the South. With this faith we will be able to **hew**[17] out of the mountain of despair a stone of hope. With this faith we will be able to transform the jangling **discords**[18] of our nation into a beautiful symphony of brotherhood. . . .

This will be the day when all of God's children will be able to sing with new meaning, "My country 'tis of thee, sweet land of liberty, of thee I sing. Land where my fathers died, land of the Pilgrims' pride, from every mountainside, let freedom ring."

And if America is to be a great nation, this must become true. So let freedom ring from the **prodigious**[19] hilltops of New Hampshire. Let freedom ring from the mighty mountains of New York. Let freedom ring from the heightening Alleghenies of Pennsylvania!

Let freedom ring from the snowcapped Rockies of Colorado! Let freedom ring from the **curvaceous**[20] peaks of California! But not only that; let freedom ring from Stone Mountain of Georgia! Let freedom ring from Lookout Mountain of Tennessee!

Let freedom ring from every hill and molehill of Mississippi. From every mountainside, let freedom ring.

When we let freedom ring, when we let it ring from every village and every **hamlet,**[21] from every state and every city, we will be able to speed up that day when all of God's children, black men and white men, Jews and **Gentiles,**[22] Protestants and Catholics, will be able to join hands and sing in the words of the old Negro spiritual, "Free at last! Free at last! Thank God Almighty, we are free at last!"

Martin Luther King Jr. waves to the huge crowd gathered to support the civil rights movement during the March on Washington.

Understanding Primary Sources

1. What did Martin Luther King Jr. mean when he said that the United States had given African Americans a "bad check"?
2. What did King caution African Americans against in their fight for freedom?

[1] **five score:** 100
[2] **decree:** important order
[3] **beacon:** light of hope
[4] **seared:** burned
[5] **manacles:** handcuffs
[6] **promissory note:** note promising to pay
[7] **to fall heir:** to inherit
[8] **unalienable:** permanent
[9] **defaulted:** failed to pay
[10] **threshold:** entrance
[11] **degenerate:** fall
[12] **creed:** formal statement of beliefs
[13] **oppression:** persecution
[14] **interposition:** interference
[15] **nullification:** refusal
[16] **exalted:** raised
[17] **hew:** carve
[18] **discords:** lack of harmony
[19] **prodigious:** vast
[20] **curvaceous:** having curves
[21] **hamlet:** community
[22] **Gentiles:** non-Jews

Section 4

Rights for All

Read to Discover

1. What were the main successes of the Hispanic rights movement?
2. What did members of the women's movement seek?
3. What were the methods used by members of the American Indian Movement and the disability rights movement?

Identify

- César Chávez
- United Farm Workers
- Chicano movement
- Betty Friedan
- National Organization for Women
- Equal Rights Amendment
- American Indian Movement
- Disabled in Action

Why It Matters Today

Women continue today to comment on their roles in American life. Use CNNfyi.com or other **current events** sources to identify one feminist writer and his or her views on the status of women in the United States today. Record your findings in your journal.

The Story Continues

Like many other Americans, Félix Longoria served his country in World War II. After he was killed in action, his body was returned to his hometown in Texas for burial. The local funeral-home director refused to hold services in the chapel for him because he was a Mexican American. Texas senator Lyndon B. Johnson arranged for Longoria to be buried at Arlington National Cemetery in Virginia. He was laid to rest with full honors.

World War II veteran Félix Longoria

Hispanic Americans

Throughout the 1960s the Hispanic population of the United States was on the rise. It grew from about 4 million to more than 10 million by the end of the 1960s. Their growing population and the success of the African American civil rights movement encouraged many Hispanic Americans to begin a fight for their own rights.

Some Hispanic activists focused on economic opportunities. **César Chávez** formed a union in 1962 to improve pay and working conditions for migrant farmworkers, many of whom were Mexican and Mexican

American. Chávez's organization eventually became the **United Farm Workers** (UFW) union. In 1965 the union began a strike and boycott against California grape growers. Five years later the union won several of its demands, and Chávez became a nationally recognized Hispanic rights leader. Like Martin Luther King Jr., Chávez believed in nonviolent protest. He explained his beliefs to his supporters.

"Naturally, nonviolence takes time. But poverty has been with us since the beginning of time. We just have to work for improvement. I despise exploitation [unjust profit] and I want change, but I'm willing to pay the price in terms of time."

—César Chávez, quoted in *Cesar Chavez: Autobiography of La Causa,* by Jacques E. Levy

The UFW and activists like poet Rudolfo "Corky" Gonzales inspired younger Hispanic leaders to take action. Some activists fought discrimination by forming the **Chicano movement**. Chicano activists sought to increase Hispanic cultural pride and political power.

The Hispanic civil rights movement led to important new laws. The 1968 Elementary and Secondary Education Act addressed the needs of students who did not speak English. In some cases, the law allowed for federally funded bilingual programs. The Voting Rights Act of 1975 required areas with large immigrant populations to provide ballots in different languages.

✔ **Reading Check: Summarizing** What goals did Hispanic American reformers reach during the 1960s and 1970s?

The Women's Movement

Women also worked for their civil rights and equality during the 1960s. Esther Peterson, the director of the Women's Bureau in the Department of Labor, organized a study of inequality in the workplace. In 1963 the Commission on the Status of Women reported that women often received lower pay and fewer job opportunities than men. In response, Kennedy outlawed gender discrimination in civil service jobs. That same year, Congress passed the Equal Pay Act, which made many employers pay men and women the same wages for the same job. The Civil Rights Act of 1964 also outlawed discrimination based on sex as well as race.

In 1963 *The Feminine Mystique* by **Betty Friedan** began a national debate on the roles of women. Friedan described what she saw as the dissatisfaction of some homemakers.

"As she made the beds, shopped for groceries, matched slipcover material, ate peanut butter sandwiches with her children, chauffeured Cub Scouts and Brownies, lay beside her husband at night—she was afraid to ask even of herself the silent question—'Is this all?'"

—Betty Friedan, *The Feminine Mystique*

BIOGRAPHY

César Chávez

(1927–1993)

César Chávez was born in Arizona, but he lived in dozens of towns as his family moved in search of farmwork. His early experience led him to help form unions for migrant workers. Chávez viewed union work as a part of a larger fight for human rights—a goal he called *La Causa*, or "The Cause."

Chávez's patience and dedication to the cause of human rights inspired many people and won many supporters. He helped make migrant farmworkers' rights a national issue. Before his death in 1993, Chávez insisted, "It's not me who counts, it's the Movement." **How did Chávez's youth influence his tactics for *La Causa* later in his life?**

Analyzing Primary Sources

Drawing Inferences and Conclusions Why did Friedan think women were not happy as mothers and wives?

Interpreting Graphs Increasing numbers of women joined the workforce after 1950.

Skills Assessment **Analyzing Information** By about how much did the percentage of women in the workforce increase between 1950 and 1980?

Source: *Statistical Abstract of the United States*

NOW was both the name of the organization and when women wanted their rights.

The modern women's rights movement was born as more women questioned their roles. In 1966 Friedan and others formed the **National Organization for Women** (NOW). This group fought for women's rights in educational and job opportunities.

In 1972 Congress approved the **Equal Rights Amendment** (ERA), which was intended to prevent gender discrimination in any form. By mid-1973, 28 of the required 34 states had ratified the ERA. But opponents—including many women—felt that the ERA was too radical, and it failed to become law. Women's rights activists did achieve a victory with the passage of the Educational Amendments Act of 1972. Title IX of this act states that no college that receives federal aid can discriminate against women. This law opened up new educational opportunities for many women.

✔ **Reading Check: Identifying Cause and Effect** What led to the women's movement, and what were some of its results?

That's Interesting!

A Long-Lasting Experiment Did you know that a 30-year-old magazine began as a "one-shot" project? It's true! *Ms.*, a feminist magazine, first appeared as an insert in *New York* magazine in December 1971. But the 300,000 test copies sold out in just eight days. Within weeks, the editors had received 26,000 subscription orders and more than 20,000 letters from readers. When the first regular issue appeared in July 1972, it was simply labeled *Spring*. One news anchor even commented, "I'll give it six months before they run out of things to say." Despite the doubts of some people, the magazine sold very well.

Other Groups Fight for Equal Rights

American Indians and people with disabilities also called for greater rights. Some American Indian reformers worked through the National Congress of American Indians (NCAI) to help win passage of the Indian Civil Rights Act in 1968. This law sought to protect the constitutional rights of American Indians and their right to self-government on reservations.

Red Power spokespeople of the late 1960s said the NCAI moved too slowly. In 1968 activists established the **American Indian Movement** (AIM) to fight for the rights and properties guaranteed in earlier treaties. "We don't want civil rights in the white man's society—we want our own sovereign [self-governing] rights," one AIM leader explained. In

February 1973 AIM members took over a trading post and church at Wounded Knee, South Dakota—the site of the U.S. Army's 1890 massacre of Sioux Indians. After a 71-day standoff, a gun battle broke out. Two protesters died, and one federal marshal was seriously hurt. Although AIM's protests drew attention to the group's cause, its methods frightened away many potential supporters. AIM achieved few of its long-term goals.

In the 1960s people with disabilities also began to fight for the right of access—both to buildings and to better opportunities. Activists formed the group **Disabled in Action** (DIA) in 1970. The DIA brought together people with many different disabilities. As one member said, "Everybody who came out felt, We are beautiful, we are powerful, we are strong, we are important."

Interpreting the Visual Record

Protest *These American Indians in New Mexico are participating in a civil rights protest.* ***What do you think the message of the child's sign is?***

DIA protests drew public attention to problems facing people with many disabilities. The group also lobbied for some new laws. The Rehabilitation Act of 1973 outlawed discrimination by federal agencies against people with disabilities. The Education of All Handicapped Children Act of 1975 required public schools to provide a quality education to children with disabilities. DIA protests showed that people with disabilities were determined to be seen and heard.

✔ **Reading Check: Finding the Main Idea** What actions did the American Indian Movement and the Disabled in Action take, and what did each group hope to accomplish?

Section 4 Review

go.hrw.com Homework Practice Online
keyword: SC3 HP28

1. **Identify** and explain:
   - César Chávez
   - United Farm Workers
   - Chicano movement
   - Betty Friedan
   - National Organization for Women
   - Equal Rights Amendment
   - American Indian Movement
   - Disabled in Action

2. **Summarizing** Copy the chart below. Use it to explain how various groups attempted to fight for their rights in the 1960s and to show how successful these groups were.

	Issues	Actions	Results
Hispanic Americans			
Women			
American Indians			
People with Disabilities			

3. **Finding the Main Idea**
   a. Describe the progress of the Hispanic rights movement.
   b. How were the actions of the American Indian Movement and the Disabled in Action different?

4. **Writing and Critical Thinking**
   Analyzing Information Imagine that you are a founding member of the National Organization for Women. Write a speech to deliver at the first meeting in which you explain why the women's movement was formed and what it hopes to accomplish.
   Consider the following:
   - the report of the Commission on the Status of Women
   - the Equal Pay Act
   - Betty Friedan's book *The Feminine Mystique*

Section 5

American Society in the 1960s

Read to Discover

1. What issues concerned student protesters during the 1960s?
2. What were the counterculture movement and its members like?
3. How did art and music change in the 1960s?

Define

- generation gap
- counterculture
- hippies
- pop art

Identify

- Students for a Democratic Society
- Andy Warhol
- Beatles
- Motown Records
- Woodstock

WHY IT MATTERS TODAY

Popular culture still shapes American society. Use CNNfyi.com or other **currents events** sources to identify a type of popular culture that exists today. Record your findings in your journal.

Student protests occurred on many college campuses during the 1960s.

The Story Continues

In 1960 Mickey Flacks was a student at City College of New York. When a student demonstration was called on the college campus, she attended. To her amazement, hundreds of students also rushed to join in the protest. The high turnout for this event inspired Flacks and other activists like her. These students came away from the protest thinking that students could make a difference. They realized that the student body could bring about social reform, both at their college and across the country.

Youth Movements

Student protests took place across the country. The civil rights movement greatly inspired some members of **Students for a Democratic Society** (SDS). The SDS and other students held protests against racial discrimination, strict college rules, and the growing U.S. military presence in Vietnam. (See Chapter 29 for more information.) The student protests shocked many older Americans. For them, the students' actions showed a lack of respect for authority.

One cause of this social conflict was the emergence of a new generation of Americans. During the 1960s the first baby boomers—children born between the end of World War II and 1964—entered young adulthood. The number of people aged 15 through 24 rose almost 50 percent during the 1960s. In 1964 the first wave of the baby-boom generation entered college. Many American leaders were concerned about the attitudes of these young students. Columbia University president Grayson Kirk shared his fears.

> **"Our young people, in disturbing numbers, appear to reject all forms of authority. . . . I know of no other time in our history when the gap between the generations has been wider or more potentially dangerous."**
>
> — Grayson Kirk, quoted in *Up Against the Wall,* by Jerry L. Avorn

Analyzing Primary Sources

Drawing Inferences and Conclusions Why do you think Kirk believed the generation gap could be dangerous?

This **generation gap**, or division between older and younger people, grew as more young people rejected their parents' values and beliefs.

In the early 1960s much of society and culture seemed unchanged from the 1950s. The media celebrated white, middle-class suburban values and traditions. Some young people rejected the materialism of the larger society and chose to "drop out." They created a **counterculture**—a culture with values that ran counter to, or against, those of the main society. The counterculture stressed individual freedom, group sharing, and nonviolence. Members of the counterculture, some of whom called themselves **hippies**, tried different lifestyles. They often wore their hair long and dressed in unusual clothing. Hippies often dyed their own clothes in a process known as tie-dyeing. Many hippies also used drugs such as marijuana or LSD, sometimes leading to drug dependence and even death.

Some young leaders tried to bring together members of the student movement and the counterculture. Many student leaders believed, however, that the aims of the counterculture were too different from their own goals. Student activists wanted to challenge society in order to improve it. Hippies rejected that society and tried to form an alternative culture. Many students believed the counterculture abandoned its responsibility to society by encouraging unhealthy behavior, such as drug abuse.

Both youth movements challenged the way many Americans viewed their world. The movements also led to a greater acceptance in American society of differences in dress, music, and personal relationships.

✔ **Reading Check: Comparing and Contrasting** What were the goals of the student movement and the counterculture?

Hippies expressed their rejection of traditional values and customs with new ways of dressing and behaving.

CONNECTING TO THE ARTS

Andy Warhol After graduating from the Carnegie Institute of Technology in 1949, Andy Warhol worked as a commercial artist in New York City. Many of his commercial drawings were used in advertisements and greeting cards. In the late 1950s Warhol began to paint and create his own art. In the 1960s he exhibited his prints of Campbell's soup cans, a turning point in his career. Warhol's pop art used popular or common objects as subjects. He often reproduced brightly colored copies of familiar everyday objects and celebrities—even his own image as seen here. These images of mass culture led viewers to question both the seriousness of traditional art and American materialism in the 1960s. **Why do you think pop art was so popular in the 1960s?**

An Artistic Revolution

The art and music world reflected these new points of view. The **pop art** movement took its name from its use of popular, everyday images and objects. Pop artists believed that traditional art lacked humor and humanity. They challenged long-standing values of art and culture and tried to create new connections between art and life. **Andy Warhol** was the most famous pop artist. He created many paintings of Campbell's soup cans and of Marilyn Monroe's face. Art critics debated whether Warhol was criticizing or celebrating consumer culture. Although some critics saw little value in pop art, it forced people to discuss the question, "What is art?"

Musical styles also reflected the social changes of the era. British performers became popular in the United States. This "British Invasion" began with the **Beatles**, a foursome from Liverpool, England. Their 1964 U.S. tour sparked a wave of excitement among their fans, which reporters labeled "Beatlemania." One journalist, puzzled by the screams of teenage girls, concluded that "the Beatles themselves don't know how they do it."

The Beatles' popularity opened opportunities for other British musicians. The Moody Blues, the Rolling Stones, the Who, and many other bands toured the United States and sold millions of records. These successes made the growing generation gap more obvious because most older Americans could not understand the appeal of this music.

In 1959 African American businessperson Berry Gordy founded **Motown Records** in Detroit, Michigan. The following year the company produced the first of many gold records—records selling 500,000 copies. The "Motown sound" was soul music, which combined the strong beat of traditional rhythm and blues with smoother sounds. Many Motown performers were popular with both African American and white listeners. Aretha Franklin, Marvin Gaye, and the Temptations were among some of the most successful soul artists. Diana Ross and the Supremes and Stevie Wonder were also popular.

Aretha Franklin and Bob Dylan were among the most popular performers of the 1960s.

During this period folk musicians also gained in popularity while addressing political and social issues. Bob Dylan sang about the struggles of poor and powerless people to rise above their troubles. His "Blowin' in the Wind" urged people to fight against injustice.

In the 1960s, however, rock was the most popular form of American music. Electrically amplified instruments, particularly the guitar, became the driving sound. Jimi Hendrix added electronic distortions, called feedback, to his music. In his version of "The Star-Spangled Banner," Hendrix used his guitar to produce the screaming sound of the "rockets' red glare."

In August 1969 about 400,000 people came to upstate New York for the Woodstock Music and Art Fair. Despite rain, overcrowding, and a shortage of food, many fans considered this show the high point of the 1960s. **Woodstock** became a symbol of the counterculture's optimistic spirit. Singer Richie Havens described the scene as he saw it from the stage.

"I just saw color to the top of the hill and beyond. . . . The best sound that I have ever played on outdoors to date happened at Woodstock. As a matter of fact, they said they heard it ten miles away in every direction. . . . We not only did it for the crowd there, we did it for the whole countryside. . . . "

—Richie Havens, quoted in *Woodstock: The Oral History,* by Joel Makower

✔ **Reading Check: Categorizing** What new forms of music became popular in the 1960s, and which people and events were most influential in each form?

Section 5 Review

go.hrw.com Homework Practice Online
keyword: SC3 HP28

1. **Define** and explain:
   - generation gap
   - counterculture
   - hippies
   - pop art

2. **Identify** and explain:
   - Students for a Democratic Society
   - Andy Warhol
   - Beatles
   - Motown Records
   - Woodstock

3. **Categorizing** Copy the diagram below. Use it to show important people, events, and movements that led to changes in society during the 1960s.

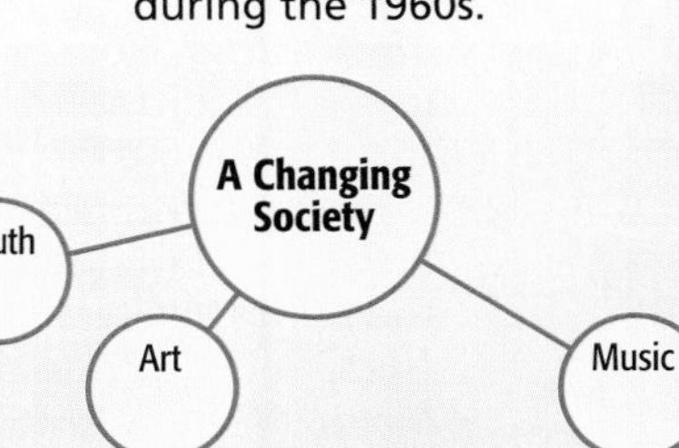

4. **Finding the Main Idea**
   a. What issues led to student demonstrations during the 1960s?
   b. How did art and music reflect social and cultural changes in the 1960s?

5. **Writing and Critical Thinking**
   Summarizing Imagine that you are a reporter who is covering the counterculture. Write an article for your hometown newspaper describing this movement.
   Consider the following:
   - the values of the counterculture
   - the actions of the counterculture
   - the behaviors of the counterculture

Chapter 28 Review

The Chapter at a Glance

Examine the visual summary of the chapter below. Then write a paragraph in which you list what you believe were the three most important events in the visual summary. Be sure to explain your answer. Compare your paragraph with a classmate's and see if you agree on the events.

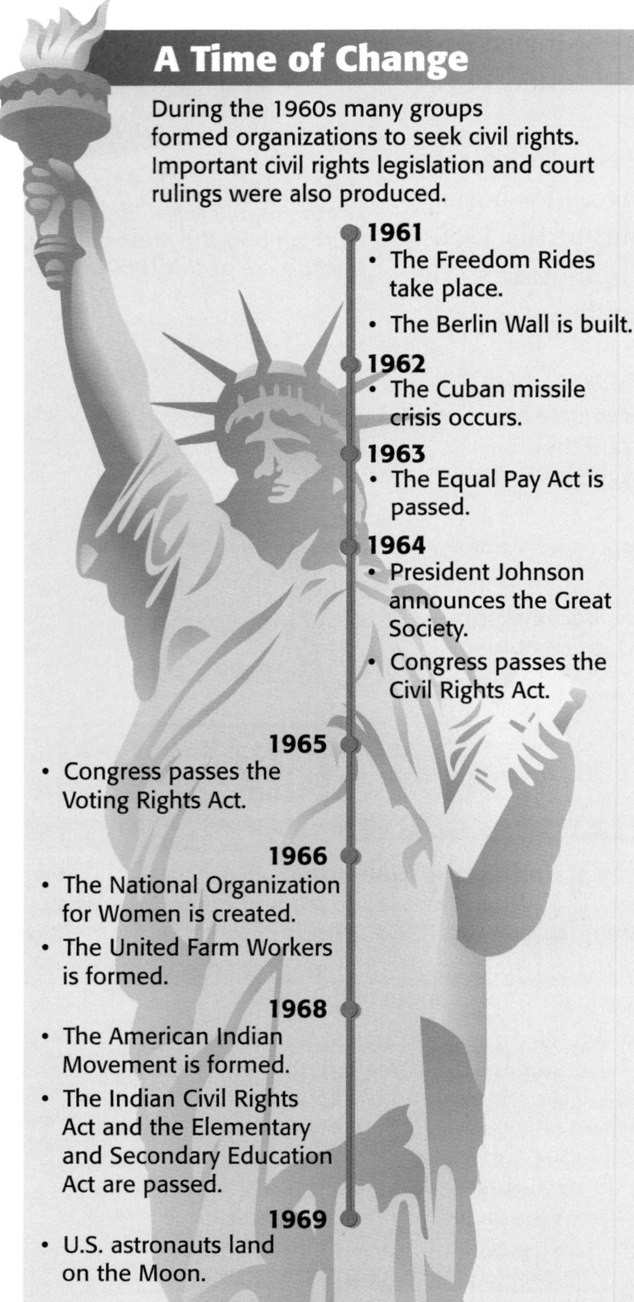

Identifying People and Ideas

Use the following terms or people in historically significant sentences.

1. Peace Corps
2. New Frontier
3. Lyndon B. Johnson
4. Great Society
5. nonviolent resistance
6. Black Power
7. United Farm Workers
8. Betty Friedan
9. hippies
10. pop art

Understanding Main Ideas

Section 1 *(846–849)*

1. What major Cold War crises took place during President Kennedy's administration, and how did he deal with them?

Section 2 *(Pages 850–854)*

2. How did President Johnson bring relief to poor Americans?

Section 3 *(Pages 855–859)*

3. What events in the 1960s helped bring about major new civil rights and voting laws?

Section 4 *(Pages 862–865)*

4. Which different groups fought for civil rights and economic opportunities during the 1960s, and why?

Section 5 *(Pages 866–869)*

5. How were members of the counterculture different from members of the student movement?
6. How did art and music change in the years following John F. Kennedy's election?

You Be the Historian— Reviewing Themes

1. **Global Relations** What did the United States and the Soviet Union do to try to avoid a nuclear war?
2. **Economics** List three new programs established during the 1960s to help Americans economically.
3. **Citizenship** How did African Americans work to change society in the 1960s, and what were the results?

Thinking Critically

1. **Contrasting** How were civil rights activists in the late 1960s different from civil rights activists in the early 1960s?
2. **Drawing Inferences and Conclusions** How might the Bay of Pigs invasion have helped bring about the Berlin Wall incident and the Cuban missile crisis?
3. **Making Generalizations and Predictions** How would you describe American youth in the 1960s?

Interpreting Political Cartoons

Study the political cartoon of John F. Kennedy below and answer the questions that follow.

1. What do the different tails on the cat represent?
   a. labor unions
   b. political parties
   c. steel companies
   d. civil rights groups
2. Based on your knowledge of the period, what do the jars on Kennedy's desk represent, and how are they different from the steel-price increase?

Analyzing Primary Sources

Read the following poem by Mexican American author Angela de Hoyos, and then answer the questions that follow.

> **"Brothers, today we drink**
> **the fresh milk of dawn**
> **—for once, not tasting**
> **of sourness.**
>
> **For once,**
> **the table is set**
> **with plates full of hope,**
> **and in our illiterate hands**
> **some kind fate has placed**
> **a promise of gold for tomorrow.**
>
> **Not that the hollows**
> **in your sad face of death**
> **will ever be filled**
> **—or the seedy, stale figure**
> **of the poor**
> **feel at ease in fine clothes—**
>
> **but today we eat**
> **to soothe a pain**
> **—a pain of alien-hungers**
> **Vallejo never knew."**

3. What do you think de Hoyos means by "a promise of gold for tomorrow?"
   a. The speaker in the poem hopes to find gold and strike it rich.
   b. There is hope that greater opportunities lie ahead for Mexican Americans.
   c. The government is beginning a new economic program.
   d. She is promising wealth to her friends.
4. How does this poem express issues in the Mexican American community?

Alternative Assessment

Building Your Portfolio

American History

Cooperative Learning
Imagine that you and your group are Peace Corps volunteers who are recruiting Americans to work on a specific project in a foreign country. Develop a recruitment program that offers information about what the project is, where it is, what it will accomplish, and what kinds of skills volunteers will need. Create a poster, a sign, and a recruiting brochure to advertise your program.

internet connect

Internet Activity: go.hrw.com
keyword: SC3 CF28

Choose a topic on a Time of Change to:

- Learn about pop art and new cultural movements in the United States.
- Write a profile of outstanding women in science, technology, or mathematics today.
- Create a pamphlet on the United Farm Workers.

CHAPTER 29 War in Vietnam (1945–1975)

Members of the Special Forces wore green berets such as this one to set them apart from other army units.

The 173rd Airborne Brigade is supported by helicopters during one of its operations.

UNITED STATES

1961 President Kennedy sends members of the Special Forces and more U.S. military advisers to Vietnam.

1965 The first U.S. combat troops arrive in Vietnam.

1945 **1955** **1959** **1963**

WORLD

1954 French forces lose to Vietnamese nationalists in May at the Battle of Dien Bien Phu.

In July Vietnam is divided into North Vietnam and South Vietnam.

1956 President Ngo Dinh Diem of South Vietnam refuses to let his nation take part in elections to reunify Vietnam.

1963 The United States, Soviet Union, and Great Britain sign a nuclear-test-ban treaty.

President Ngo Dinh Diem received U.S. support largely because of his strong anticommunist views.

French casualties were heavy during the battle at Dien Bien Phu.

Build on What You Know

After World War II, U.S. leaders worried about the spread of communism abroad. Determined to keep the Asian country of Vietnam from falling to communism, the United States sent thousands of troops there. As the fighting went on, however, the war in Vietnam began raising troubling questions for many Americans.

The Tet Offensive involved some of the hardest fighting of the war.

The Vietnam Veterans Memorial attracts thousands of visitors, including many veterans and their families.

1967

1968 In January communist forces attack throughout South Vietnam in the Tet Offensive.

1968 President Johnson withdraws from the presidential election.

1969 The British prime minister sends troops into Belfast, Northern Ireland, to stop rioting.

1971

1971 The Twenty-sixth Amendment is passed, lowering the voting age from 21 to 18.

1973 The Paris Peace Accords are signed on January 27, ending U.S. involvement in the Vietnam War.

On November 7, Congress passes the War Powers Act to restrict presidential powers in committing U.S. troops to armed conflicts.

1975

1975 Saigon, the capital of South Vietnam, falls to North Vietnamese forces.

If you were there . . .

Would you support U.S. involvement in the war in Vietnam?

You Be the Historian

What's Your Opinion? Do you **agree** or **disagree** with the following statements? Support your point of view in your journal.

- **Global Relations** A nation should become involved with foreign countries to encourage the growth of democracy.
- **Geography** Geography determines a country's chances of winning a war.
- **Government** New legislation can change the roles of the different branches of government.

Section 1

Early Conflicts in Vietnam

Read to Discover

1. What events led to the creation of North and South Vietnam?
2. Why did the U.S. government support South Vietnam?
3. How did some South Vietnamese who disliked Diem's government show their beliefs?

Define

- domino theory

Identify

- Ho Chi Minh
- Vietminh
- Geneva Accords
- Ngo Dinh Diem
- National Liberation Front
- Vietcong

Why It Matters Today

The United States still sends troops to areas around the world even when war has not been declared. Use CNNfyi.com or other **current events** sources to learn about places where U.S. troops have played an important role. Record your findings in your journal.

A Vietnamese villager transports a French colonist.

The Story Continues

In 1873 French explorer Francis Garnier encouraged the French to colonize Southeast Asia for trade and to bring Western culture to the people. However, one of Garnier's associates warned that colonization would be a mistake. "The extraordinary resistance [of the Vietnamese], sometimes violent, . . . is stronger now than at any time since the conquest," he warned. "We must open our eyes."

Vietnam Divides

For many years, France controlled Vietnam along with neighboring Laos and Cambodia as a colony called French Indochina. Vietnamese nationalist **Ho Chi Minh** helped fight French rule. Over time, Ho came to believe that the best way to fight colonial imperialism was through a communist revolution. During World War II, Japanese troops and local nationalists drove French soldiers out of Indochina. Ho then refused to accept Japanese rule. After Japan's surrender to the Allies, Ho declared Vietnam independent on September 2, 1945. But France insisted that Vietnam was still a French colony. Ho warned the French to leave Vietnam alone.

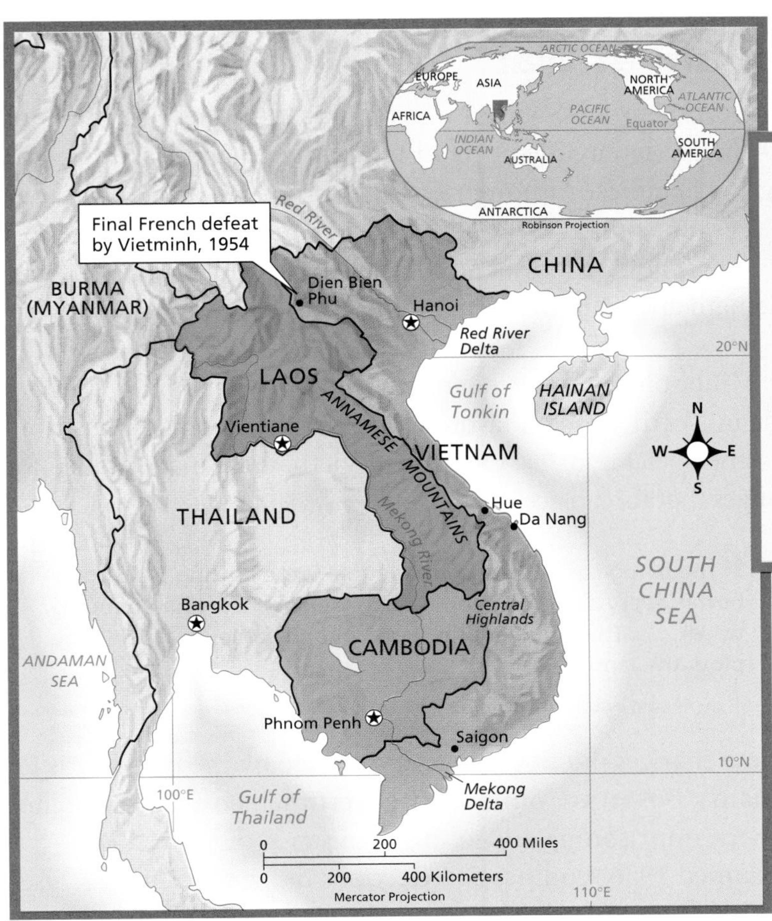

French Indochina

Interpreting Maps French Indochina consisted of Vietnam, Laos, and Cambodia. At the end of World War II, Vietnam sought its own independence.

Skills Assessment

1. **Places and Regions** What were the capitals of the three countries that made up French Indochina?
2. **Contrasting** What major geographic difference can you see between Laos and Vietnam?

A French Foreign Legion pin

The French ignored Ho's warnings and moved to retake Vietnam. President Eisenhower's administration aided France's efforts based on his belief in the **domino theory**. According to this theory, if Vietnam fell to the Communists—as China and North Korea had done—all of Southeast Asia would fall. "You have a row of dominoes set up," Eisenhower explained. "You knock over the first one, and . . . the last one . . . will go over very quickly."

The **Vietminh**, as the Vietnamese nationalist forces were known, fought the war mostly through hit-and-run guerrilla attacks and ambushes. In March 1954 they trapped some 13,000 French troops at the village of Dien Bien Phu (DYEN BYEN FOO), causing more than 7,000 French casualties. On May 7, 1954, the French surrendered.

The day after the Vietminh victory, an international conference in Geneva, Switzerland, addressed the future of Indochina. In July the delegates worked out the **Geneva Accords**, which temporarily divided Vietnam. North Vietnam was a communist state led by Ho Chi Minh. South Vietnam was a democracy led by **Ngo Dinh Diem** (NGOH DIN de-EM), an anticommunist. The Geneva Accords also called for free elections in July 1956 to reunite North and South Vietnam.

✔ **Reading Check: Contrasting** How were the governments of North Vietnam and South Vietnam different?

Born in Vietnam in 1890, Nguyen That Thanh later adopted the name Ho Chi Minh, which means "he who enlightens."

Vietnam at War

The new government in South Vietnam was dishonest and brutal. President Diem put family members in top positions and was aggressive in silencing his enemies. Although Diem was not a very good leader, many American policy makers believed he was the best alternative to a communist state. The Eisenhower administration began sending supplies to South Vietnam and training Diem's military forces during its last years in office.

Ho Chi Minh, on the other hand, enjoyed greater popular support. Many people in North Vietnam favored his government's land redistribution policies and social reforms. One North Vietnamese man recalled the positive changes that took place.

"The living conditions of the people were getting better and better every day. The people were well off. They had enough to eat. . . . They had land to work and buffaloes to help them plow the land."

—Anonymous, quoted in *The Vietnam Wars: 1945–1990,* by Marilyn B. Young

Analyzing Primary Sources

Drawing Inferences and Conclusions What do you think life was like in North Vietnam before Ho Chi Minh took over leadership of the government?

However, these changes did not help everyone. Ho blamed landlords for North Vietnam's poverty. Communist government officials searched out landowners, imprisoning and killing thousands of them.

As the planned 1956 reunification elections drew near, Diem refused to allow South Vietnam to take part. He feared that the northern communist government would win. U.S. officials backed his decision. Diem tried to stamp out support for the Vietminh by arresting thousands of South Vietnamese citizens. Many nationalists in South Vietnam joined the **National Liberation Front** (NLF), a group that fought Diem's government. The NLF largely depended on the **Vietcong**,

Interpreting the Visual Record

U.S. advisers *As Diem's government in South Vietnam faced increasing opposition, the United States sent more military advisers to train his army.* ***What type of training do these U.S. troops appear to be providing?***

communist guerrilla forces, as its army. North Vietnam supplied and funded the Vietcong as its soldiers began a civil war against Diem's government in the late 1950s.

As fighting between the Vietcong and Diem's Army of the Republic of Vietnam grew worse, President Eisenhower sent more aid and advisers to South Vietnam. By the end of 1960, some 900 U.S. military advisers were stationed in South Vietnam. When John F. Kennedy became president, he sent even more advisers. He also sent 400 Special Forces soldiers to Vietnam in May 1961. By the end of 1963, some 16,000 U.S. military personnel were serving there.

Buddhist monks held many nonviolent demonstrations against President Diem and his policies.

Despite U.S. help, Diem's government was losing power. Diem became even more unpopular when his soldiers fired on Buddhist demonstrators. Some Buddhist monks set themselves on fire in protest. Appearing on television and in newspapers, these shocking images helped turn Americans against Diem. Some of Diem's military leaders came to believe that his unpopularity hurt the war effort. In November 1963 a group of South Vietnamese generals took over the government and killed Diem. After the takeover, the political situation in South Vietnam grew worse.

✔ **Reading Check: Identifying Cause and Effect** Why was Diem's government in South Vietnam unpopular, and how did the citizens respond to it?

Section 1 Review

go.hrw.com Homework Practice Online
keyword: SC3 HP29

1. **Define** and explain:
   - domino theory
2. **Identify** and explain:
   - Ho Chi Minh
   - Vietminh
   - Geneva Accords
   - Ngo Dinh Diem
   - National Liberation Front
   - Vietcong
3. **Sequencing** Copy the time line below. Use it to explain important events in Vietnam's history following the end of World War II.

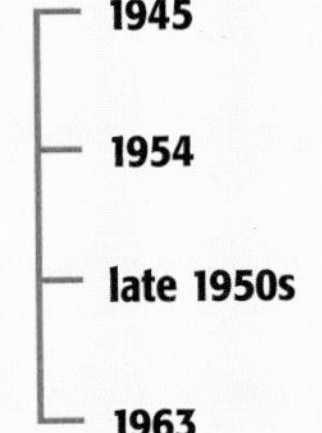

4. **Finding the Main Idea**
   a. What events in Vietnam ended in the creation of two separate countries?
   b. How were North Vietnam and South Vietnam different, and why did the United States support South Vietnam?
5. **Writing and Critical Thinking**
   Summarizing Imagine that you are a State Department official. Write a report for President Eisenhower explaining why many South Vietnamese dislike Diem's government and how they are expressing their disapproval.
   Consider the following:
   - Diem's methods of ruling and maintaining order
   - the influence and support of North Vietnam on resistance efforts
   - the nonviolent protests of Buddhist demonstrators

Section 2

The Escalation of the War

Read to Discover

1. What actions did President Johnson take to involve the United States more deeply in the war in Vietnam?
2. How did U.S. military leaders try to defeat the North Vietnamese?
3. How did the Vietnam War affect South Vietnamese civilians and American soldiers?

Why it Matters Today

Civilians who live in war-torn regions are often affected by the fighting. Use CNNfyi.com or other **current events** sources to identify a country or region that is suffering or has suffered under the violent conditions of war. Record your findings in your journal.

Define

- escalation
- search-and-destroy missions
- pacification

Identify

- Tonkin Gulf Resolution
- Operation Rolling Thunder
- Ho Chi Minh Trail
- William Westmoreland

Soon after taking office, President Johnson expanded the U.S. role in Vietnam.

The Story Continues

On November 24, 1963, the new president, Lyndon B. Johnson, met with his foreign-policy advisers to discuss Vietnam. One aide recalled Johnson's fear that the Communists would think that "with Kennedy dead [the Americans] have lost heart." Johnson increased military support for South Vietnam and insisted that a message go out to South Vietnam "that Lyndon Johnson intends to stand by [the United States's] word."

Johnson's Vietnam Policy

President Lyndon B. Johnson faced a complicated situation in Vietnam. After Diem's assassination, some of the new South Vietnamese leaders wanted to work out an agreement with the Communists. Johnson and his advisers, however, refused to accept the possibility of a communist South Vietnam.

On August 2, 1964, a U.S. navy vessel exchanged fire with North Vietnamese vessels in the Gulf of Tonkin off the North Vietnamese coast. U.S. ships later reported that the North Vietnamese had launched

The U.S. Air Force used long-range bombers such as this B-52 to drop huge numbers of explosives on targets in North and South Vietnam.

torpedoes at them. Although the ships were not damaged, Johnson called the reported attack an act of war. He ordered air strikes against bases in North Vietnam.

On August 7 Congress passed the **Tonkin Gulf Resolution**, which gave President Johnson the power "to take all necessary measures to repel any armed attack against the forces of the United States." With the authority granted by this resolution, President Johnson greatly increased U.S. military involvement in Vietnam. In March 1965 the first U.S. combat troops arrived in South Vietnam. That same month, Johnson ordered **Operation Rolling Thunder**—a series of air strikes meant to destroy war industries in North Vietnam. Johnson also saw the operation as a way to destroy the **Ho Chi Minh Trail**. This trail was a network of paths, small roads, and tunnels leading from North Vietnam through neighboring Laos and Cambodia and into South Vietnam. The Vietcong used the Ho Chi Minh Trail as their major supply route. Johnson and his advisers wanted to destroy North Vietnam's ability to supply the Vietcong. They believed that if they succeeded, the United States could win the war.

Thick jungle covered much of the trail and hid the movement of the supplies. To burn off the forests, U.S. airplanes dropped napalm, or jellied gasoline. The planes also released chemical poisons, such as Agent Orange, that killed vegetation and tree leaves. These chemicals caused environmental damage to the area and led to health problems for Vietnamese civilians and U.S. veterans.

The bombing raids lasted until late 1968. Before they ended, U.S. planes had dropped more than a million tons of explosives, much of it on South Vietnam. Operation Rolling Thunder killed many Vietnamese soldiers and civilians. However, the U.S. effort did not stop the Communists' ability to fight the war.

✔ **Reading Check: Summarizing** Describe Operation Rolling Thunder and how it affected the North Vietnamese Communist war effort.

That's Interesting!

Underground Tunnels Did you know that the Vietcong used underground tunnels as military bases? American soldiers were baffled when the Vietcong launched attacks and then seemed to disappear into thin air. The Vietcong were actually using hidden tunnels to escape detection and shield themselves from bombing raids. The tunnels were about two feet wide and five feet high and had thick roofs. These narrow passages connected rooms such as kitchens, hospitals, and storage areas. Many tunnel systems had several levels and were protected by deadly traps. Today, tourists in Vietnam can go on special tours to view these amazing tunnel systems.

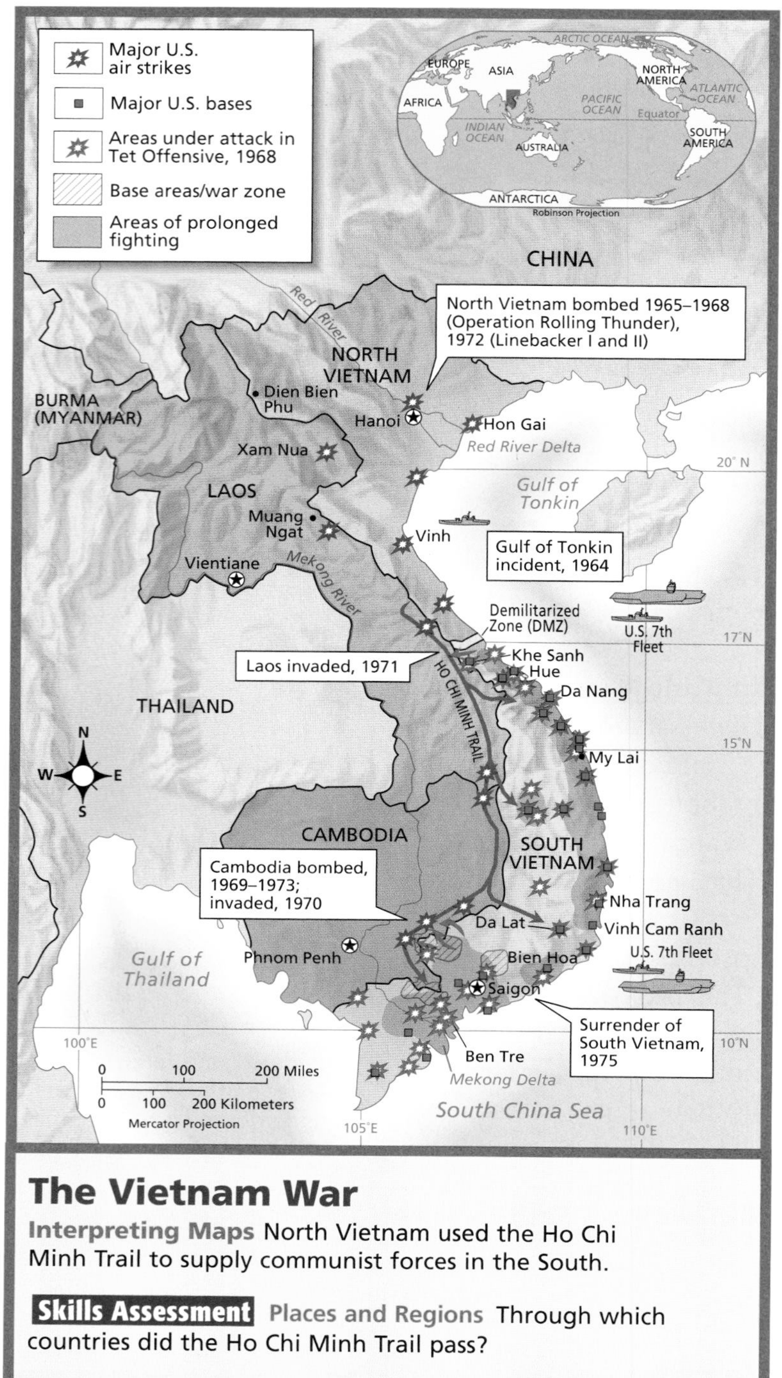

The Vietnam War

Interpreting Maps North Vietnam used the Ho Chi Minh Trail to supply communist forces in the South.

Skills Assessment **Places and Regions** Through which countries did the Ho Chi Minh Trail pass?

The Ground War

In the mid-1960s President Johnson sent more ground forces to Vietnam. Between 1965 and 1967 the number of U.S. soldiers grew rapidly as Johnson followed a policy of **escalation**, or increased U.S. involvement in the war. At the same time, North Vietnam also became more involved. North Vietnam sent more of its regular army units, the North Vietnamese Army (NVA), to fight alongside the Vietcong.

General **William Westmoreland**, who led the U.S. ground forces in Vietnam, developed a new fighting strategy. He sent U.S. patrols on **search-and-destroy missions.** U.S. patrols searched for enemy camps and supplies hidden in the jungle. Then the soldiers destroyed them with massive firepower and air raids. Because the United States had better military technology, officials believed there would be a quick American victory. One U.S. general said, "The solution in Vietnam is more bombs, more shells, more napalm." However, U.S. generals did not understand just how difficult it would be to defeat the North Vietnamese.

The Vietcong and the NVA had certain key advantages, which made up for their inferior firepower. They used effective guerrilla strategies and had a better knowledge of the local geography. Moving secretly, they set traps and land mines to kill and wound U.S. soldiers. The Vietcong and the NVA usually attacked quickly and by surprise. Marine Philip Caputo recalled the effects of this kind of fighting.

Analyzing Primary Sources

Identifying Bias What mistake does Caputo say U.S. soldiers first made about the Vietnamese?

"The discovery that the men we had scorned [disregarded] as peasant guerrillas were, in fact, a lethal [deadly], determined enemy . . . broke our early confidence."

—Philip Caputo, *A Rumor of War*

✔ **Reading Check: Contrasting** In what different ways did the Americans and the North Vietnamese use their advantages in the war?

No Safe Place

South Vietnamese villagers found themselves caught in the middle of the fighting. U.S. and South Vietnamese officials tried to win their support through a policy of **pacification.** Under this program, they set aside civilian areas guarded by government troops. Even in areas protected by soldiers, villagers were not safe, however. At night, while the government forces stayed in their camps, the Vietcong came out of hiding. They attacked or killed people they believed had helped the South Vietnamese government. South Vietnamese civilians had no safe place to go.

Many Vietnamese civilians also suffered at the hands of U.S. forces. Sometimes U.S. troops destroyed the villages and crops of innocent civilians, believing they belonged to the Vietcong. Soldier Kenneth Campbell recalled how an officer explained the destruction of two seemingly peaceful farming villages. According to Campbell, the officer "said they were probably feeding the NVA with rice anyway, so therefore they are the enemy." Such reasoning led to a larger number of deaths and injuries among civilians. It also made it harder for Americans to win local support or loyalty.

✔ **Reading Check: Analyzing Information** What types of problems did South Vietnamese civilians face during the war?

A Difficult War

Despite its size and power, the United States faced many challenges in the Vietnam War.

U.S. Military Advantages

The U.S. military had advanced weapons, many soldiers, and tremendous firepower to use against the enemy.

U.S. Military Disadvantages

The North Vietnamese and the Vietcong used the difficult terrain and aggressive guerrilla tactics to hide themselves and attack by surprise. U.S. soldiers often did not know who might be the enemy.

Visualizing History

1. **Science and Technology** How would the weapons shown have helped the United States during the war?
2. **Connecting to Today** What types of challenges do U.S. military forces face on their missions around the world today?

U.S. troops often used helicopters to reach jungle areas.

The Soldiers' Stories

The war in Vietnam greatly affected the more than 2 million U.S. soldiers who served in it. Many soldiers were very young. Their average age was 22, about four years younger than in previous wars. Most of the soldiers had been drafted into service. They were often from minority groups and poor families. On the other hand, college students—most of whom were white and from the middle and upper classes—could earn draft releases called deferments.

Many of the young men who served in Vietnam supported the war in the beginning. However, by mid-1967 more than 300 U.S. soldiers a week were dying in combat. As the war dragged on and the number of casualties rose, support for the war dropped. Some 10,000 women also served in the military during the war. One nurse recalled watching a soldier die.

Analyzing Primary Sources

Identifying Points of View How does this nurse seem to feel about her experience in Vietnam?

"When you are sitting there working on . . . a 19-year-old kid who's 10,000 miles from home, and you know that he's going to die before dawn . . . and you're the only one that he's got . . . well it [gets] into your soul."

—Dusty, quoted in *Shrapnel in the Heart,* by Laura Palmer

Like the nurse, many of those who served in Vietnam found that the experience left them forever changed.

✔ **Reading Check: Finding the Main Idea** How did many soldiers' beliefs about the war change over time?

Section 2 Review

go.hrw.com Homework Practice Online
keyword: SC3 HP29

1. **Define** and explain:
   - escalation
   - search-and-destroy missions
   - pacification
2. **Identify** and explain:
   - Tonkin Gulf Resolution
   - Operation Rolling Thunder
   - Ho Chi Minh Trail
   - William Westmoreland
3. **Identifying Cause and Effect** Copy the chart below. Use it to explain American policies and strategies during the war and their effects.

Event	Cause	Effect
Tonkin Gulf Resolution		
Operation Rolling Thunder		
escalation		
search-and-destroy missions		
pacification		

4. **Finding the Main Idea**
   a. How did President Johnson increase U.S. involvement in the Vietnam War?
   b. How did the lives of many South Vietnamese civilians change as a result of the war?
5. **Writing and Critical Thinking**
   Analyzing Information Imagine that you are a U.S. soldier stationed in Vietnam. Write a letter home describing your experiences in the war.
   Consider the following:
   - the strategies of the Vietcong and the NVA
   - the condition of South Vietnamese civilians
   - the progress of the war

Section 3

A Divided Nation

Read to Discover

1. How did doves protest U.S. involvement in the war?
2. How did the Tet Offensive change public opinion about the Vietnam War?
3. How did the Vietnam War affect American politics during the 1968 presidential election?

Define

- doves
- hawks

Identify

- Tet Offensive
- Eugene McCarthy
- Robert F. Kennedy
- Hubert Humphrey
- George Wallace
- Richard M. Nixon

Why It Matters Today

Television news programs, newspapers, and other media sources influence the way people see the world around them. Use CNNfyi.com or other **current events** sources to learn how the media shape Americans' views today. Record your findings in your journal.

The Story Continues

The women gathered at about 6:00 A.M. outside the military office, before the arrival of the new recruits for the Vietnam War. They marched with signs reading "I Support Draft Refusal," and some sat down in the street to block the recruits' buses. A police officer warned an older woman, "Missus, you don't want to get arrested." She answered, "I have to, my grandson's in Vietnam." As more American soldiers went off to fight—and to die—in Vietnam, the antiwar movement grew stronger.

As the fighting dragged on, more Americans began demanding an end to the war.

Divided Opinions

Journalists, particularly television reporters, played an important role in shaping public opinion about the war. Through television, Americans felt the violence of the war right in their own homes. The graphic images of war led many people to wonder if the war in Vietnam was worth the cost. Some journalists began to report their growing suspicions that the fighting was not going as well as the military claimed. Gradually, some people who had supported the Vietnam War began to call for the United States to get out of the conflict. These people were called **doves**—named after the birds that symbolize peace.

CONNECTING TO MATH

Just the Facts

U.S. Troops in Vietnam, 1966–1973

Year	Number U.S. Troops	U.S. Military of Personnel Killed in Action
1966	385,300	6,008
1967	485,600	9,377
1968	536,000	14,589
1969	475,200	9,414
1970	334,600	4,221
1971	156,800	1,381
1972	24,000	300
1973	50	—

Using Mathematical Skills

1. In what year were the most U.S. military personnel sent to Vietnam?
2. Create a bar graph showing how many military personnel in Vietnam, out of the total, were killed in action from 1966 to 1973.
3. Imagine that you are a member of Congress in 1974. Write a report to your colleagues explaining the significance of these statistics.

Arkansas senator J. William Fulbright became a leading dove. As the chairman of the Senate Foreign Relations Committee, Fulbright had strongly supported the Tonkin Gulf Resolution. But he later questioned whether U.S. troops should even be in Vietnam. "You don't want to negotiate," he accused a group of Johnson's advisers. Other doves, like Martin Luther King Jr., believed that the U.S. government spent money on the war that could better be used for important social programs.

President Johnson and most members of Congress said that defeating communism in Vietnam took priority over domestic reforms. These so-called **hawks** wanted more military spending to send new forces to Vietnam.

Many Americans did not agree with the hawks. College students often held protests to call for a change in U.S. war policy. Many of them had already taken part in the civil rights movements. The Students for a Democratic Society (SDS) became one of the most active antiwar groups. SDS protested the draft system and the companies that made weapons used in the war. In 1965, SDS led 20,000 protesters in a march on Washington, D.C. As the war continued, the student movement grew bolder and sometimes even grew violent. By the end of 1968, protests had taken place on almost 75 percent of the country's college campuses.

Many ordinary citizens also took part in antiwar protests. Charlotte Keyes helped organize a group called Women Strike for Peace. She described the different types of people in the antiwar movement.

"The peaceniks [war protesters] these days are legion [very large]—they are ninety years old and fifteen, heads of families and housewives with babies, students, (and) young people."

—Charlotte Keyes, "Suppose They Gave a War and No One Came," *McCall's*

✔ **Reading Check: Summarizing** Why and how did some Americans oppose the Vietnam War?

Interpreting the Visual Record

Reporting on the war *A team of television journalists interviews a group of U.S. soldiers in Vietnam.* ***How might interviews such as this one bring the war closer to the American public?***

Interpreting the Visual Record

The Tet Offensive *These U.S. military police are leading away one of the Vietcong guerrillas who attacked the U.S. embassy in Saigon during the Tet Offensive.* ***How do you think Americans might respond to this photograph?***

The Tet Offensive

Despite the growing antiwar movement, most Americans supported the Vietnam War until early 1968. In previous years, a cease-fire had halted all fighting during Tet—the Vietnamese New Year. On January 30, 1968, however, during Tet, North Vietnamese and Vietcong soldiers launched the **Tet Offensive**—a surprise attack on U.S. forces throughout southern Vietnam. The soldiers even invaded the U.S. Embassy in Saigon. In most places, the U.S. and South Vietnamese troops defeated most of the communist forces quickly. Still, the Tet Offensive shocked Americans and changed many people's opinions about the war. A short time earlier, General Westmoreland had said that the war would soon be over. There is "light at the end of the tunnel," he promised. The Tet Offensive, however, appeared to show the opposite—that communist forces still had the strength and the will to fight.

The Tet Offensive also convinced many Americans that officials were not telling the truth about the war. Several well-known journalists doubted leaders' claims of success. Television news anchor Walter Cronkite shared his views in February 1968. "To say that we are closer to victory today is to believe, in the face of the evidence, the optimists who have been wrong in the past."

Although there were already about 525,000 U.S. troops in Vietnam, General Westmoreland asked for 206,000 more soldiers. Many people questioned whether such an increase was necessary if the United States was really winning the war. President Johnson turned down Westmoreland's request.

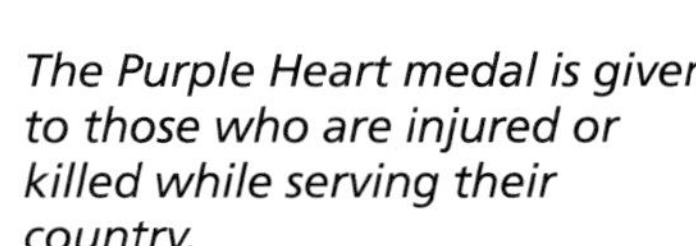

The Purple Heart medal is given to those who are injured or killed while serving their country.

✔ **Reading Check: Analyzing Information** What effect did the Tet Offensive have on the American public, and why?

Research on the ROM

Free Find:
Election of 1968
After reading about the election of 1968 on the **Holt Researcher CD–ROM**, create a bar graph that shows how many votes each candidate won.

The Democrats in 1968

As doubts about the war increased, President Johnson began losing public support. A new poll showed that only 33 percent of Americans believed that the United States was winning the war. About 49 percent said that the United States should never have gotten involved in Vietnam.

Johnson, who had won the presidency by a landslide in 1964, was expected to win the Democratic primaries easily. At first, his main opponent was **Eugene McCarthy**, a senator from Minnesota. McCarthy was a major antiwar critic. "The Democratic Party in 1964 promised 'no wider war,'" he reminded voters. "Yet the war is getting wider every month." In the New Hampshire primary, Johnson narrowly beat McCarthy. This result showed how unpopular Johnson and his Vietnam policies had become. Physically and emotionally exhausted, President Johnson stunned the nation by announcing on March 31 that he would drop out of the election.

Meanwhile, Senator **Robert F. Kennedy** of New York, the former U.S. attorney general, had entered the race for the Democratic nomination on March 16. He believed that the United States should do everything possible to bring a quick and peaceful end to the war.

Analyzing Primary Sources
Identifying Points of View How can you tell that Kennedy wanted a peaceful settlement to end the war?

"Unable to defeat our enemy or break his will—at least without a huge, long, and ever more costly effort—we must actively seek a peaceful settlement. . . . [that] will give the Vietcong and the National Liberation Front a chance to participate in the political life of the country. Not because we want them to, but because that is the only way in which this struggle can be settled."

—Robert F. Kennedy, "Vietnam—Illusion and Reality," *Chicago Sun-Times*

Kennedy's positions on civil rights reform, assistance to the poor, and the war drew him much support.

Johnson, however, backed another Democratic candidate—his vice president **Hubert Humphrey**. Many voters disliked Humphrey for his support of the war, and Kennedy began gaining ground. On June 5, 1968, Kennedy won the California primary, a major step before the Democratic National Convention in Chicago. That night a gunman named Sirhan Sirhan shot Kennedy.

After Robert Kennedy died, Humphrey was almost sure to win the Democratic nomination. However, the party remained bitterly divided. Many delegates at the Democratic National Convention wanted a candidate who was not tied to the war. Angry debates soon broke out inside the convention hall. In the streets outside the convention hall, hundreds of antiwar protesters marched, shouting, "Peace now! Peace now!" Police officers moved in to stop the protesters, using clubs and tear gas to break up the crowd. A riot broke out, with television cameras broadcasting live images of the events to a concerned nation.

✔ **Reading Check: Evaluating** How did the Vietnam War affect the 1968 Democratic presidential campaign?

Robert F. Kennedy was a popular political leader.

A Republican Victory

Humphrey won the Democratic nomination for president and chose Maine senator Edmund Muskie as his running mate. Conservative Alabama governor **George Wallace** entered the race as the candidate of the American Independent Party. Wallace wanted to overturn civil rights legislation as well as most federal social programs. The Republicans nominated former vice president **Richard M. Nixon**, who said that he could restore order to American society. Nixon also hinted that he had a "secret plan" for ending the Vietnam War.

Interpreting the Visual Record

Protests *More people, including returned veterans, protested the war as it escalated. Growing concern over the Vietnam War forced presidential candidates to address the issue in their campaigns.* ***How do you think these protests might affect the actions of government officials?***

Millions of Americans had been alarmed by the events at the Democratic National Convention. To these people, the riots showed the decline of law and order in society and politics. Many voters blamed the Democrats. However, the election of 1968 was still quite close. Nixon received only 43.4 percent of the popular vote, but won the presidency with 302 electoral votes. Humphrey received 42.7 percent of the popular vote and 191 electoral votes. Wallace won 45 electoral votes, all from southern states. As President-elect Nixon prepared to take office, Americans watched events in Vietnam closely.

✔ Reading Check: **Drawing Inferences and Conclusions** Why do you think Nixon won the 1968 election?

Section 3 Review

go.hrw.com Homework Practice Online
keyword: SC3 HP29

1. **Define** and explain:
   - doves
   - hawks

2. **Identify** and explain:
   - Tet Offensive
   - Eugene McCarthy
   - Robert F. Kennedy
   - Hubert Humphrey
   - George Wallace
   - Richard M. Nixon

3. **Contrasting** Copy the diagrams below. Use them to show the different views that Americans had of the Vietnam War.

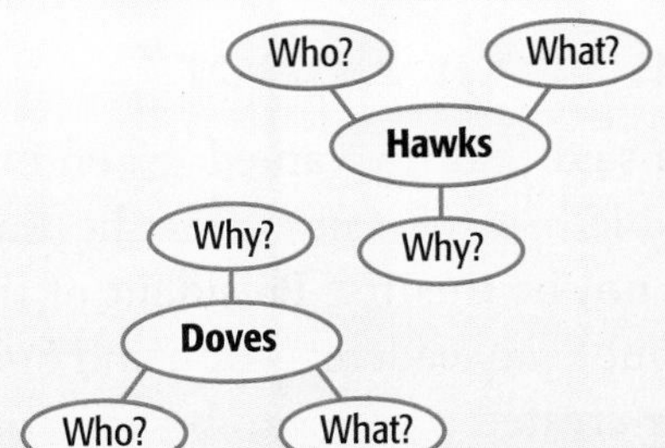

4. **Finding the Main Idea**
   a. What actions did doves take to try to change U.S. war policy?
   b. What effects did the Tet Offensive have on Americans' attitudes toward the war?

5. **Writing and Critical Thinking**
   Supporting a Point of View Imagine that you are a journalist reporting on the 1968 elections. Write an opinion piece sharing your thoughts on how the Vietnam War affected the presidential primaries and election.
   Consider the following:
   - Johnson's decision not to run for re-election
   - the Democratic National Convention
   - the appeal that Nixon had for voters

Section 4

The War under Nixon

Read to Discover

1. What policy for Vietnam did President Nixon follow when he first took office?
2. What were the final years of the Vietnam War like?
3. What effects did the war have on those countries that took part in it?

Why It Matters Today

Although the Vietnam War ended more than 25 years ago, many Americans and Vietnamese still remember the war very well. Use CNNfyi.com or other **current events** sources to identify ways Americans view the effects of the Vietnam War today. Record your findings in your journal.

Identify

- Henry Kissinger
- Vietnamization
- Khmer Rouge
- Twenty-sixth Amendment
- Paris Peace Accords
- MIAs
- War Powers Act
- Vietnam Veterans Memorial

U.S. combat troops arriving in Vietnam

The Story Continues

January 20, 1969, was the day of President Nixon's inauguration. That day, a top aide distributed a detailed questionnaire about Vietnam to high-level military and diplomatic personnel. One question indirectly asked was Could the United States win the war, even at that late date? One army general who took part in the study remembered the answer that came back. "Nobody believed the war could be won in the foreseeable [near] future." That answer left the new president with another pressing issue. How was he going to end the Vietnam War?

"Peace with Honor"

President Nixon said that he wanted to "end the war as quickly as was honorably possible." At the same time, he wanted to avoid appearing defeated. "I will not be the first President of the United States to lose a war," he told Republican leaders. Nixon and his national security adviser **Henry Kissinger** created a policy to bring about "peace with honor." In a process called **Vietnamization**, they would gradually turn over all of

Interpreting the Visual Record

Military secrets *U.S. troops hoped that North Vietnamese Army papers captured in Cambodia would reveal important military secrets.* ***How might intelligence-gathering operations like this one be valuable to the U.S. military?***

the fighting to the South Vietnamese army. The United States would continue to provide supplies and training to South Vietnam even as U.S. troops left the country. Nixon also believed that the threat of using nuclear weapons against the North Vietnamese might help end the war. He explained this view privately to an aide.

"I call it the madman theory. . . . I want the North Vietnamese to believe I've reached the point where I might do anything to stop the war. We'll just slip the word to them that, . . . 'Nixon is obsessed [crazed] about Communists. We can't restrain [control] him when he's angry—and he has his hand on the nuclear button,'—and Ho Chi Minh himself will be in Paris in two days begging for peace."

—Richard M. Nixon, quoted in *The Vietnam Wars, 1945–1990,* by Marilyn R. Young

However, Nixon and Kissinger misjudged the determination of the North Vietnamese and the Vietcong. Even though Ho Chi Minh died in September 1969, his followers promised to keep fighting to reunite Vietnam. New U.S. leaders refused to consider any peace agreement that did not include the immediate removal of all U.S. troops.

After he took office, President Nixon did begin withdrawing U.S. ground troops from Vietnam. But he also ordered bombing raids on Laos and Cambodia without telling Congress or the American public. Like President Johnson, Nixon wanted to cut off use of the Ho Chi Minh Trail. The North Vietnamese responded to the bombings by giving more support to the **Khmer Rouge** (kuh-MER ROOZH), the Cambodian communist army.

Nixon announced on April 30, 1970, that he would send U.S. troops to protect Cambodia's new, pro-U.S. government. When he announced the invasion of Cambodia, many Americans were outraged. Instead of working for peace, it looked as if Nixon was expanding the war.

✔ **Reading Check: Contrasting** What actions did President Nixon take to end the war, and what actions did he take to expand the war?

Richard M. Nixon

Richard Milhous Nixon was born in 1913 and grew up in and around Whittier, California. Even as a young man, Nixon showed various aspects of his adult personality. He was shy and socially awkward, but he pushed himself to meet people and win their support. His determination helped him to become a leader. At both Whittier College and Duke Law School, Nixon was elected student-body president. After practicing law and serving in World War II, he ran for Congress in 1946. Writer David Halberstam described Nixon's drive. "Once he started in politics, he could never stop: there would always be one more office to run for." **What events in Nixon's life demonstrated his interest in politics?**

Interpreting the Visual Record

Kent State *The killings of antiwar protesters by National Guardsmen at Kent State University in 1970 hardened many Americans' attitudes against the war.* ***Why do you think scenes like this one upset the American public?***

 New Protests

Students responded to President Nixon's announcement by demonstrating at hundreds of college campuses, including Ohio's Kent State University. After students attacked a military training building, the governor called in the National Guard. On May 4, 1970, students at Kent State started to demonstrate again. The National Guard troops tried to break up the protest with tear gas. As the students threw rocks at the soldiers, some of the guardsmen opened fire. When the smoke cleared, 4 students were dead and 9 others were hurt. The Kent State killings shocked the public, and antiwar activists held more protests. Nearly 20 years later, university officials dedicated markers in the parking lot where the four students were killed.

As the year went on, political and public opinion continued to turn against the war. In December 1970 Congress overturned the Tonkin Gulf Resolution. Public opinion grew even more divided when the *New York Times* published secret U.S. government documents obtained from Daniel Ellsberg, a former Pentagon official. The Pentagon Papers, as they were called, showed that U.S. officials had been lying about the progress of the Vietnam War for years. "It is a system that lies automatically from top to bottom," Ellsberg said.

After the Pentagon papers were published, some members of Congress wanted to cut off all funds for the Vietnam War. As the 1972 election drew near and as public opinion continued to turn against the war, President Nixon began to change his strategy. He ended the invasion of Cambodia and became more open to compromise. In 1972 Henry Kissinger began secret peace negotiations with North Vietnamese leaders.

✔ **Reading Check: Identifying Cause and Effect** Why did American public opinion continue to turn against the Vietnam War, and what effect did this have on political leaders?

The United States and Vietnam Today

After the war, the United States and Vietnam had a very unfriendly relationship for many years. Recently, however, the two countries have formed closer ties. The United States first lifted its trade ban on Vietnam in 1994. The United States opened a new embassy in Vietnam in 1997. Then in December 2000 President Bill Clinton made the first presidential visit to Vietnam in more than 30 years.

Vietnamese leaders have encouraged American businesses to open operations in Vietnam. Many well-known American goods are now available in Vietnam, and signs for American products can be seen in the streets of Vietnamese cities. **Give examples of the new relationship between Vietnam and the United States.**

The End of the War

The presidential election of 1972 offered voters a choice between two candidates with very different ideas about the war. Running against President Nixon was Senator George McGovern of South Dakota. A Democrat and a long-standing opponent of the war, McGovern promised that he would immediately pull all U.S. troops from Vietnam. "The doors of government will be opened, and that brutal war will be closed," he said.

In 1971 the **Twenty-sixth Amendment** had lowered the federal voting age from 21 to 18 years of age. Many Americans saw this change as fair because people of these ages were being drafted to serve in Vietnam. Some politicians expected this amendment to lead to a "youth rebellion" in the 1972 election.

McGovern won the support of the majority of younger voters. However, most older voters from both parties supported Nixon. Although most Americans were tired of the war, they feared continued disorder and protests. Nixon also promised to end the war soon if re-elected. The public re-elected Nixon by a huge margin—520 electoral votes compared to 17 for McGovern.

Ending the war proved difficult. Negotiations slowed after the election, and the United States began large-scale bombing of North Vietnam in December 1972. Finally, peace talks began again. On January 27, 1973, representatives of the National Liberation Front, North Vietnam, South Vietnam, and the United States signed a cease-fire and a series of peace agreements in Paris. Known as the **Paris Peace Accords**, the agreements called for the removal of all U.S. troops and the return of all American prisoners of war (POWs). The accords also set up a demilitarized buffer zone between North and South Vietnam to maintain peace between the troops on each side. Under the agreement, Communists in South Vietnam could take part in politics. Further decisions about unification of the country were put off until later.

Late in 1974, however, fighting broke out again between North and South Vietnam. The United States made it clear that it would not send troops back to South Vietnam. The following year large numbers of North Vietnamese troops invaded the South, where resistance collapsed rapidly. By the end of April 1975, the North Vietnamese had captured the southern capital, Saigon. Panic gripped the city, and many people fled. On July 2, 1976, the Socialist Republic of Vietnam was proclaimed. North and South Vietnam were officially unified under a communist government.

✔ **Reading Check:** **Sequencing** List the important events in the final years of the war in the order they occurred.

Interpreting the Visual Record

The fall of Saigon *South Vietnamese who had supported the United States rushed to the U.S. embassy in hopes of escaping before the Communists took over. U.S. helicopters carried many people to safety, but more were left behind.* ***How does this photograph indicate the urgency of the evacuation?***

CONNECTING TO

THE ARTS

The Vietnam Veterans Memorial In November 1982 the Vietnam Veterans Memorial opened in Washington, D.C., honoring the Americans who served in the Vietnam War. Designed by Maya Ying Lin, a 21-year-old Yale architecture student, the monument is a wall of black granite. The wall rises from the ground on one end and slopes back to the earth on the other end. The names of the more than 58,000 dead or missing Americans are listed according to the date that each died or disappeared. These names—the only words on the monument—force visitors to face the human costs of the war. The wall brings out strong emotions in visitors. Many people who visit the memorial leave behind keepsakes or military items. **Why do you think this memorial brings out such strong emotions for visitors?**

The Consequences of the War

The Vietnam War left long-lasting problems in Southeast Asia and the United States. Life was extremely difficult in Vietnam after the war. The death toll there was enormous. About 1 million North Vietnamese and Vietcong soldiers and about 185,000 South Vietnamese soldiers had died. Some 500,000 civilians also died, and almost 1 million Vietnamese children had become orphans. Cities and villages lay in ruins, while forests and farmlands lay bare. One Vietnamese newspaper editor described the damage. "The war lasted thirty years, but it will take another twenty years before we will be able to overcome the legacy [history] of the problems it has left."

Also in ruins, Laos and Cambodia fell to communist dictatorships in 1975. In Cambodia the Khmer Rouge Communists killed about 2 million people in a massive campaign to destroy supposed enemies of communism. Eventually, the Vietnamese and Cambodian Communists clashed. In 1979 Vietnam invaded Cambodia to drive out the Khmer Rouge. For many years afterward, Cambodia experienced ongoing conflict.

Between 1975 and 1985 more than 1.5 million Southeast Asians left the region. Many of them died while trying to escape. About half of the refugees came to the United States. Le Ly Hayslip was a former Vietcong supporter who immigrated to the United States and later became a successful businesswoman. In her memoirs she addressed the U.S. soldiers who had fought in the war. "Most of you did not know, or fully understand, the different wars my people were fighting when you got [to Vietnam]," Hayslip wrote.

The war also carried huge costs for the United States. Some 58,000 Americans died as a result of the war. About 2,500 remain **MIAs**. MIA stands for "missing in action." Many soldiers faced difficulties after the war. Instead of a warm welcome, many veterans faced insults from some Americans. While most veterans readjusted to civilian life, others suffered from depression and a condition known as post-traumatic stress disorder.

The Vietnam War also left the United States deeply divided. The discoveries of government dishonesty weakened Americans' trust in their leaders. In 1973 Congress passed the **War Powers Act** to prevent undeclared wars. The act required the president to get approval from Congress before sending U.S. troops to an armed struggle. President Nixon vetoed the measure, but Congress overrode the veto. Passage of the War Powers Act gave Congress greater responsibility in setting U.S. military policy.

On Veterans Day in 1982, officials dedicated the **Vietnam Veterans Memorial** to honor those who died in the war. Designed by Maya Ying Lin, the memorial is a black granite wall engraved with the names of the dead and the missing. Bruce Weigl explained why he and other veterans have visited the wall.

U.S. Air Force captain Ronald Bliss runs to meet his wife after spending seven years as a POW in Vietnam. Some Americans bought wristbands, like the one shown here, to remember POWs.

> **"We came to find the names of those we lost in the war, as if by tracing the letters cut into the granite we could find what was left of ourselves."**
>
> —Bruce Weigl, "Welcome Home," *The Nation*

Hundreds of people, some weeping, visit the memorial daily. Many leave flowers, personal mementos, or written messages. Others simply ponder what the memorial—with its dark silence—has to tell them.

✔ **Reading Check: Analyzing Information** How did the Vietnam War affect Vietnam and the United States?

Section 4 Review

go.hrw.com Homework Practice Online
keyword: SC3 HP29

1. **Identify** and explain:
   - Henry Kissinger
   - Vietnamization
   - Khmer Rouge
   - Twenty-sixth Amendment
   - Paris Peace Accords
   - MIAs
   - War Powers Act
   - Vietnam Veterans Memorial

2. **Comparing and Contrasting** Copy the diagram below. Use it to list the consequences of the Vietnam War, both in Vietnam and the United States.

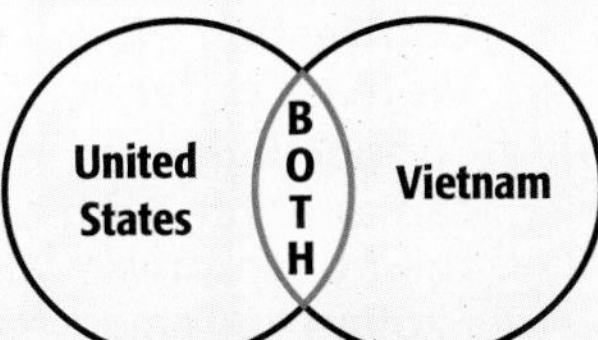

3. **Finding the Main Idea**
   a. How did President Nixon handle the conflict in Vietnam when he first became president?
   b. Why do you think the United States did not send troops back to South Vietnam in 1974 to protect it from invasion by North Vietnam?

4. **Writing and Critical Thinking**
   Summarizing Imagine that you are a South Vietnamese citizen in 1975. Write a journal entry describing the feelings you have had during the last years of the war.
   Consider the following:
   - the Paris Peace Accords
   - the North Vietnamese invasion
   - the takeover of the government by the Communists

Chapter 29 Review

The Chapter at a Glance

Examine the visual summary of the chapter below. Then write a paragraph explaining your opinion of which was the most important event in the Vietnam War. Compare your paragraph with a classmate's paragraph.

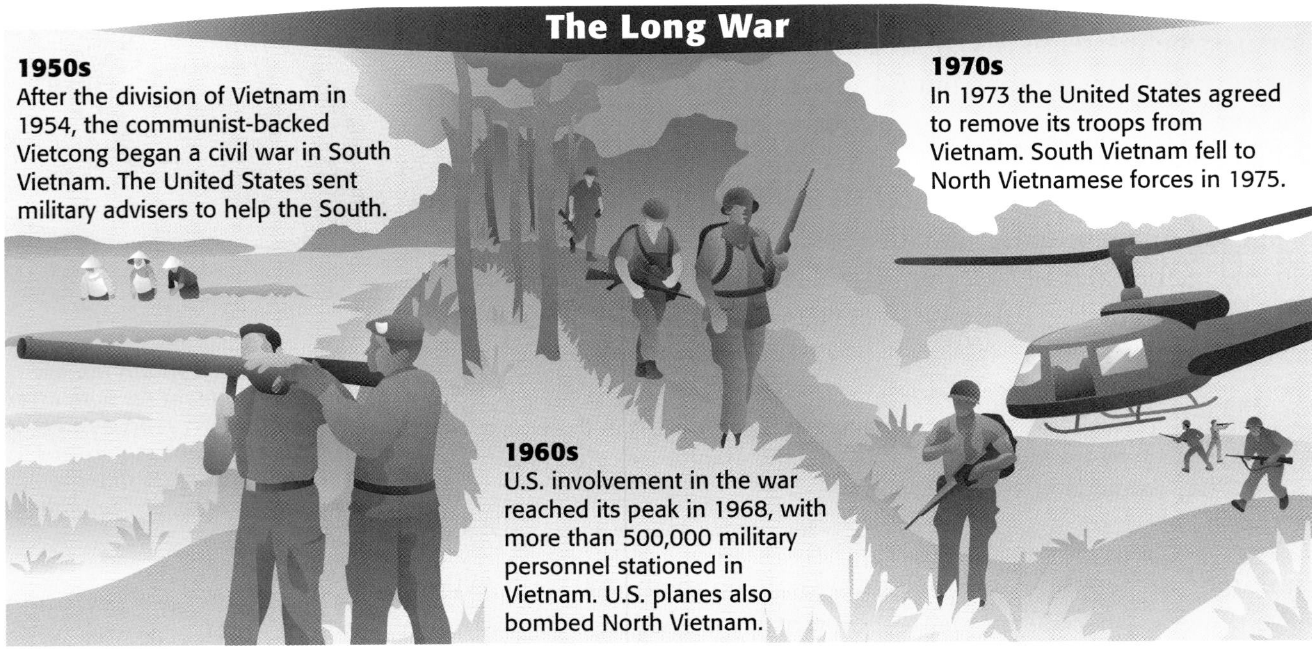

Identifying People and Ideas

Use the following terms or people in historically significant sentences.

1. domino theory
2. National Liberation Front
3. Tonkin Gulf Resolution
4. Ho Chi Minh Trail
5. William Westmoreland
6. pacification
7. Tet Offensive
8. Richard M. Nixon
9. Vietnamization
10. War Powers Act

Understanding Main Ideas

Section 1 *(Pages 874–877)*

1. What led to the establishment of South Vietnam and North Vietnam?

Section 2 *(Pages 878–882)*

2. How did President Johnson follow a policy of escalation in the Vietnam War?

Section 3 *(Pages 883–887)*

3. How did some doves try to change U.S. war policy?
4. How did news of the Tet Offensive change many Americans' attitudes toward the war?

Section 4 *(Pages 888–893)*

5. How did President Nixon end U.S. involvement in the Vietnam War?
6. How did the Vietnam War affect Americans and the Vietnamese?

You Be the Historian— Reviewing Themes

1. **Global Relations** Why did the United States fight in Vietnam?
2. **Geography** How did Vietnam's geography challenge the U.S. military effort there?
3. **Government** How did the Tonkin Gulf Resolution and the War Powers Act affect the relationship between the legislative and executive branches of the U.S. government?

Thinking Critically

1. **Contrasting** How were North and South Vietnam different?
2. **Supporting a Point of View** Do you think people can disagree with the policies and actions of their government and still be loyal citizens? Explain your answer.
3. **Drawing Inferences and Conclusions** Why did North Vietnam attack South Vietnam in 1975 despite the cease-fire?

Social Studies Skills Workshop

Interpreting Charts

Study the chart below. Then use the chart to answer the questions that follow.

1. Which of the following was not one of the effects of the Vietnam War?
   a. Vietnam was united as a communist nation.
   b. The Gulf of Tonkin incident occurred.
   c. U.S. veterans suffered ailments.
   d. Many Americans and Vietnamese were killed and injured.
2. How do you think the long-term causes of the war shaped the U.S. government's responses to the immediate causes of the war?

Analyzing Primary Sources

Read the following excerpt from the War Powers Act, and then answer the questions that follow.

> **"Whenever United States Armed Forces are introduced into hostilities [fighting] the President shall . . . report to the Congress . . . on the status [state] of such hostilities. . . . Within sixty calendar days after a report is submitted . . . the President shall terminate [end] any use of the . . . Armed Forces . . . unless the Congress (1) has declared war . . . (2) has extended by law such sixty-day period, or (3) is physically unable to meet as a result of an armed attack . . . ."**

3. How does the War Powers Act lessen the president's control of the military?
   a. It limits the president's power to send troops to fight and involves Congress in decisions about war.
   b. It limits the troops that the president can send.
   c. It requires the president to get the permission of Congress to send troops.
   d. It limits the president's authority to declare war.
4. Why do you think Congress passed this law?

Alternative Assessment

Building Your Portfolio

American History

Cooperative Learning

Complete the following activity in small groups. Imagine that you work in the map bureau of the State Department. A new U.S. diplomat to Southeast Asia has asked for a historical map of the region spanning the years 1954 to 1975. Create a detailed map for the diplomat. Make sure that your map explains important historical events in the region. As a group, present your map to the class.

internet connect

Internet Activity: go.hrw.com
keyword: SC3 HP29

Choose a topic on the War in Vietnam to:

- Create a map on the geographic features of Southeast Asia.
- Write a journal entry from the point of view of a soldier in the war.
- Create a pamphlet describing the war under Nixon.

Social Studies Skills

WORKSHOP

Using Primary and Secondary Sources

There are many sources of firsthand historical information. These sources include diaries, editorials, letters, and legal documents, such as wills and titles. All of these are *primary sources.* Newspaper reports are also considered primary sources. However, they are typically written after an event has taken place. The same is true for personal memoirs and autobiographies, which are usually written late in a person's life. The editorial cartoons, paintings, and photographs that make up history's visual record are also primary sources. Primary sources are valuable historical tools that allow a close-up look at the past.

Secondary sources are descriptions or interpretations of historical events written after the events have occurred by persons who did not take part in or witness the events. Biographies, encyclopedias, history books, and other reference works are examples of secondary sources. Writers of secondary sources have the advantage of knowing the long-range consequences of events. This knowledge helps shape their viewpoints.

Primary and secondary sources are both essential tools for historians. Primary sources contain information that cannot be found anywhere else. Secondary sources can cover broad topics and evaluate the events.

How to Study Primary and Secondary Sources

1. **Study the material carefully.** Consider the nature of the material. Is it verbal or visual? Is it based on firsthand information or on the accounts of others? Note the major ideas and supporting details.
2. **Consider the audience.** Ask yourself: For whom was this message originally meant? Whether a message was intended, for example, for the general public or for a specific private audience may have influenced its style or content.
3. **Check for bias.** Watch for certain words or phrases that signal a one-sided view of a person or event.
4. **When possible, compare sources.** Study more than one source on a topic if you can. Comparing sources gives you a more complete and balanced account.

Practicing the Skills

1. How are secondary sources different from primary sources?
2. What advantages do secondary sources have over primary sources?
3. Select a topic from Unit 10. Write a brief report on this topic, using one primary source and one secondary source. Explain why each source is considered a primary or a secondary source.

History in Action

UNIT 10 SIMULATION

You Solve the Problem . . .

How can the United States protect its national security in the postwar period?

Complete the following activity in small cooperative groups. It is the 1950s. Cold War tensions between the United States and the Soviet Union are on the rise. You are members of a special task force in the State Department. Your group is working to create a policy statement that outlines the U.S. government's plans for protecting national security. Your policy statement will be presented in the form of a brochure for approval by the president.

1. Gather Information Use your textbook and other resources to find information that might influence your plans for protecting U.S. national security after World War II. Be sure to use what you learned from this unit's Skills Workshop on Using Primary and Secondary Sources to help you find information to use in reaching a solution to this problem. You may want to divide up different parts of the research among group members.

2. List and Consider Options Based on the information you have gathered, list and consider the options you might recommend for protecting national security during the postwar years. Your final solution to the problem may be easier to reach if you consider as many options as possible. Be sure to record your possible options as notes for use in your policy statement.

3. Consider Advantages and Disadvantages Now examine each option that your group came up with and consider the advantages and disadvantages of taking each option. Ask yourselves questions like: "How does this action involve U.S. national interests?" Once you have considered the advantages and disadvantages, record them as notes for use in your policy statement.

4. Choose, Implement, and Evaluate a Solution After considering the advantages and disadvantages, you should plan and create your brochure. Be sure to make your proposal very clear. You will need to support your plan to protect U.S. national security by including information you gathered and by explaining why you rejected other options. Your presentation needs to be visually appealing. When you are ready, decide who in your group will make which part of the presentation and take your solution to the White House (the rest of the class). Good luck!

UNIT 11

Modern America

(1968–Present)

Young People

IN HISTORY

Young Volunteers

"I think everybody should volunteer," says high school student Beth Kungel. "You don't need to get paid to help somebody else. It's fun, and it makes you feel good." Many children and teenagers from across the country share Kungel's feelings. Through their volunteer work, these active young people have improved the world around them. They have saved animals, protected the environment, tutored classmates, fed the homeless, and built homes—among many other projects.

Young people have volunteered to protect the environment in different ways. Some young volunteers have raised money to buy and preserve acres of rain forest. Others have focused their efforts closer to home. Some junior high school students from the Chicago area took part in the Spring into Action campaign. The project cleaned up local parks, planted trees, and restored sports fields in the community. In 1998 the Rouge River Rescue Cleanup in Michigan received assistance from MTV. The cable music channel held a cleanup party for volunteers to encourage more young people to join the effort.

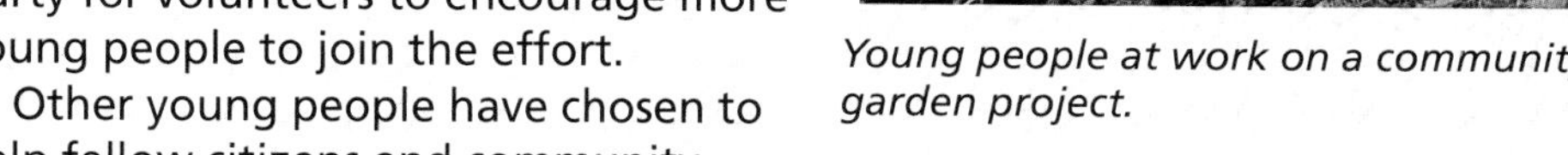

Young people at work on a community garden project.

Other young people have chosen to help fellow citizens and community members. Many have joined Habitat for Humanity, a nonprofit organization that relies on volunteers to build homes for people with low incomes. When asked why she chose to spend her vacations working for free, teenager Regan Beard answered, "Because it's awesome. It's definitely worth it. . . . We start with a concrete base and end with walls." America' s Promise is another nonprofit organization that provides many young people with volunteer opportunities in their own communities. Founded in 1997, the group promotes community service as a way for young Americans to grow as individuals and citizens.

If You Were There *How would you volunteer your time?*

LEFT PAGE: *Fireworks brighten the sky over the Statue of Liberty during a bicentennial celebration.*

CHAPTER

30 A Search for Order (1968–1980)

This cartoon dollar shows American concerns over inflation.

Many middle-class Americans voted for Richard Nixon because they believed that he would bring order back to the United States.

UNITED STATES

1968 Richard Nixon wins the presidency.

1969 President Nixon announces the first withdrawal of U.S. troops from Vietnam.

1970 Millions of Americans celebrate the first Earth Day, which reminds them to protect the environment.

1971 Nixon sets a 90-day freeze on salaries, prices, and rents to lower inflation.

1972 Nixon visits China.

1973 The Organization of Petroleum Exporting Countries (OPEC) bans the sale of oil to the United States and causes an energy crisis.

1974 Nixon resigns the presidency, and Gerald Ford becomes president.

1968 **1970** **1972** **1974**

1969 Soviet and Chinese forces clash in Manchuria, in northeastern China.

1970 Anwar Sadat becomes president of Egypt.

1972 Twelve European countries agree not to dump garbage into the Atlantic Ocean.

1973 Egypt and Syria attack Israel, beginning the Yom Kippur War.

1974 OPEC ends the oil embargo against the United States.

WORLD

After the Yom Kippur War started, the United Nations persuaded Arabs and Israelis to accept a cease-fire. However, many worried whether peace in the Middle East would last.

Build on What You Know

The 1960s were marked by political and social unrest. By the 1970s, however, many Americans wanted a return to stability. Instead, the 1970s brought a presidential scandal, an energy crisis, rising inflation, and environmental worries. Presidents Nixon, Ford, and then Carter each tried different solutions to resolve these issues.

Americans held parades across the nation to celebrate the bicentennial, or the 200th birthday of the United States.

A commemorative bicentennial patch

1975 The National Cancer Institute links cancer to pollution.

1975 U.S. *Apollo 18* spacecraft links up with the Soviet *Soyuz 19* in orbit around Earth.

1976 Americans celebrate the 200th birthday of the United States.

1976

1977 President Jimmy Carter makes human rights a top priority of U.S. foreign policy.

1977 Soviets arrest human rights activists in Czechoslovakia and other Soviet bloc countries.

1978

1978 The Camp David Accords are signed by the leaders of Egypt and Israel.

1979 A nuclear accident takes place at Three Mile Island, Pennsylvania.

1979 An Iranian mob takes hostages from the U.S. embassy in Tehran.

1980

1980 Ronald Reagan wins the presidency.

An artist's drawing shows the historic meeting of the U.S. Apollo 18 *(left) and the Soviet* Soyuz 19 *spacecraft (right).*

If you were there . . .

How would you deal with the nation's problems?

You Be the Historian

What's Your Opinion? Do you **agree** or **disagree** with the following statements? Support your point of view in your journal.

- **Economics** A country's economy depends upon the availability of energy sources.
- **Government** Impeachment is an effective way to address government scandals.
- **Global Relations** The president shapes U.S. foreign policy more than international events do.

Section 1

The Nixon Presidency

Read to Discover

1. How did President Nixon try to address the concerns of the Silent Majority?
2. What effects did the poor economy and the energy crisis have on Americans?
3. How did realpolitik affect U.S. relations with other countries?

Define

- southern strategy
- stagflation
- energy crisis
- realpolitik
- détente

Identify

- Richard M. Nixon
- Silent Majority
- New Federalism
- Organization of Petroleum Exporting Countries
- Henry Kissinger
- Leonid Brezhnev
- Strategic Arms Limitation Talks

Why It Matters Today

Presidential candidates and their political parties continue to focus on the concerns of select groups of voters. Use CNNfyi.com or other **current events** sources to learn about the issues that current political parties seek to address. Record your findings in your journal.

Demonstrators fill the streets of New York City to show their support for Nixon.

The Story Continues

Some 100,000 workers—most of them construction workers—jammed shoulder to shoulder on already crowded New York City streets. "All the way with the U.S.A.," they yelled, showing support for President Richard Nixon. Many of these workers considered themselves the backbone of the nation. They saw student protesters as dangerous and anti-American. A few days later, one worker gave the president a hard hat. The worker called it "a symbol, along with our great flag, for freedom and patriotism to our beloved country."

The Silent Majority

Many Americans voted for **Richard M. Nixon** in November 1968 because they disliked the changes taking place during the 1960s. President Nixon called these voters the **Silent Majority**—"the forgotten Americans, the non-shouters, the non-demonstrators." Nixon won their votes by promising to restore law and order. One Nixon supporter expressed the views of this group.

"I want my children to live and grow up in an America as I knew it, where we were proud to be citizens of this country. I'm . . . sick and tired of listening to all this nonsense about how awful America is."

—Barbara Baisley, quoted in *Time*

Analyzing Primary Sources

Drawing Inferences and Conclusions What does this person believe American attitudes were like in the past?

The Silent Majority blamed the federal government for high taxes and social unrest. In response, Nixon tried to reduce the size of the government. He also called antiwar protesters criminals and backed policies that increased the power of the police and the courts.

In addition, Nixon wanted to limit further civil rights legislation. He said, "The laws have caught up with our consciences." This idea was part of the Republicans' so-called **southern strategy**—an attempt to win the support of white southern Democrats and other opponents of civil rights reforms.

The U.S. Supreme Court blocked some of Nixon's efforts. For example, the Court supported busing programs to desegregate public schools, which Nixon opposed. In 1969 he replaced retiring Chief Justice Earl Warren with Warren E. Burger, a more conservative judge. Nixon went on to appoint three more conservative justices. After these changes, the Court began to reverse some of its earlier civil rights decisions.

✔ **Reading Check: Summarizing** What were the main goals of Nixon's domestic policy?

The Economy

One critical problem facing President Nixon was the U.S. economy. In the early 1970s **stagflation**, a period of high inflation and high unemployment, hurt the country. Several factors caused stagflation. The cost of social programs and the Vietnam War had raised the national debt. Paying the interest on this debt cost the federal government billions of dollars a year. These payments contributed to inflation. In addition, American manufacturers faced stronger foreign competition, causing some major industries to lay off workers in order to cut costs. Many Americans lost their jobs. Even those who kept working were hurt by rising prices caused by inflation. The buying power of the U.S. dollar fell by 30 percent from 1967 to 1974.

Nixon hoped the economy would correct itself. He believed the federal government should avoid interfering with businesses and state governments. Instead, he called for a system of revenue sharing called **New Federalism**. Under this system, the federal government would give grants to the states. Local leaders would then decide how to use this money. However, Nixon placed limits on wage and price increases when inflation hit 6 percent in 1971. These controls slowed inflation for a short time.

✔ **Reading Check: Identifying Cause and Effect** What caused stagflation, and how did Nixon respond to it?

That's Interesting!

Nixon and Elvis Did you know that President Nixon met Elvis Presley? It's true! On December 21, 1970, the "King of Rock 'n' Roll" hand-delivered a letter to the White House requesting a private meeting with the president. Presley was interested in being appointed as a "Federal Agent at Large" against drugs. Nixon did grant the meeting—but not the position—and 28 memorable photos were taken of the event. Before the meeting's end, the two exchanged gifts. Presley was given a badge, and the president received a World War II Colt 45 pistol.

The Energy Crisis

Scarce energy resources and rising oil prices also led to U.S. economic problems. By 1974 the United States was importing more than a third of its oil, much of which came from Middle Eastern countries. In 1960 Venezuela, Saudi Arabia, Iran, Iraq, and Kuwait—all oil-producing countries—formed the **Organization of Petroleum Exporting Countries** (OPEC). OPEC hoped to control oil production and sales to keep oil prices high. The group also used its power to influence international politics. Most OPEC members were Arab countries opposed to Israel, an ally of the United States. In October 1973 Egypt and Syria attacked Israel on Yom Kippur, a Jewish holy day. The United States sent military supplies to Israel during the Yom Kippur War. This act upset Egypt and Syria's OPEC allies.

OPEC declared an embargo, or a ban, on the sale of oil to the United States and some other countries. The oil embargo caused a worldwide **energy crisis** that was marked by high fuel prices and fuel shortages. Some schools and businesses had to shut down because they lacked fuel for heat and transportation. Nixon supported nuclear power research and construction of a pipeline to connect the Alaskan oil fields to the lower 48 states.

✔ **Reading Check: Sequencing** List the key events of the energy crisis in the order that they took place.

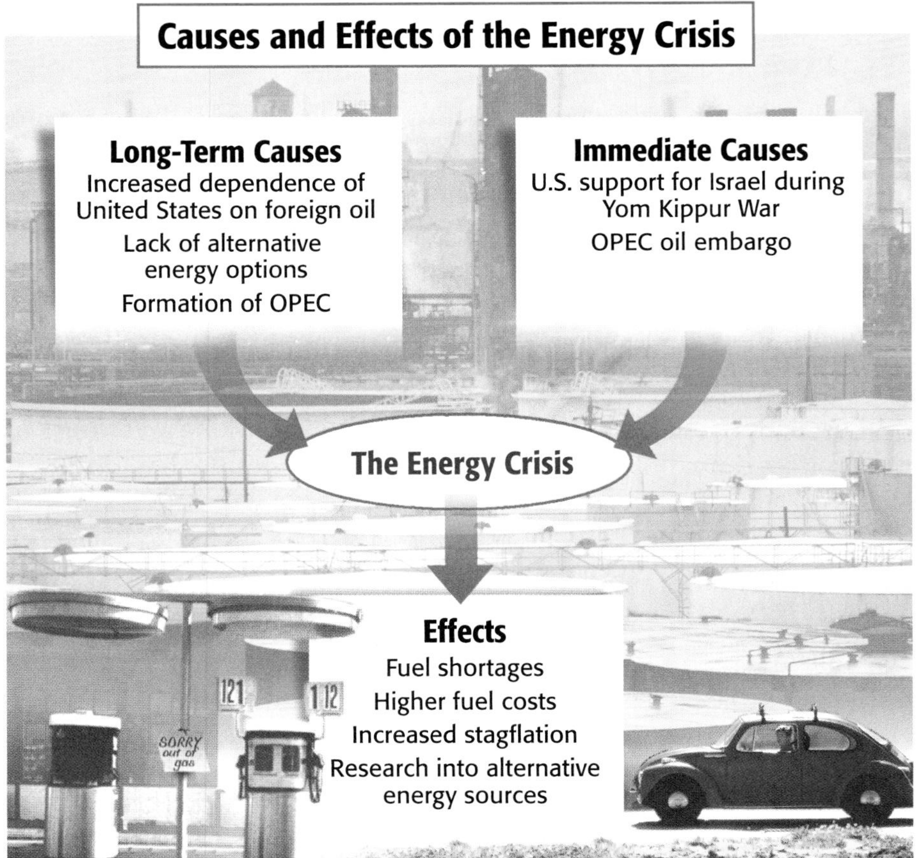

Interpreting the Visual Record

Nixon in China *President Nixon visited China with hopes for further dividing the communist world.* ***How might this photograph change some Americans' impression of relations between the United States and China?***

Foreign Policy

The energy crisis showed how complicated foreign policy had become. President Nixon had already begun working with advisers on a new approach to deal with such issues. **Henry Kissinger** served as Nixon's national security adviser during his first term and became secretary of state during Nixon's second term. He helped shape U.S. foreign policy.

Kissinger based his foreign policy on the idea of **realpolitik**, a German word that means "practical politics." This policy favored protecting U.S. interests over defending political or moral ideals overseas. For example, Kissinger believed that the United States should be willing to cooperate with nondemocratic countries in certain cases. Nixon agreed with most of Kissinger's policy views.

Some people complained that realpolitik led to U.S. support of dictators who violated human rights. In Latin America, for example, the United States gave military and economic aid to several harsh military dictatorships. These governments were strongly anticommunist and generally supported U.S. foreign-policy interests.

Realpolitik greatly affected U.S. relations with communist China. In 1949, communist rebels had defeated U.S.-backed Chinese Nationalists. Since then the United States had refused to officially recognize the government of communist China.

Many U.S. officials had long assumed that China and the Soviet Union were close allies. However, in early 1969 the two communist nations had argued over their shared border. This dispute almost caused a war. By 1970 China and the Soviet Union had become bitter rivals.

Hoping to widen the split between China and the Soviet Union, Nixon administration officials began secret talks with the Chinese. In February 1972 Nixon and his wife, Pat, visited China.

Henry Kissinger (center) played a key role in U.S. negotiations with foreign governments.

To keep the United States from forming an alliance with China, the Soviets showed more willingness to negotiate with the United States. In May 1972 Nixon became the first U.S. president to visit Moscow, meeting with Soviet leader **Leonid Brezhnev** (BREZH-nef). The two leaders focused their talks on the nuclear arms race. The buildup of nuclear weapons was getting expensive for both nations, and the risk of nuclear war worried many observers. To slow the arms buildup, the two leaders signed the **Strategic Arms Limitation Talks** (SALT) treaty. The SALT treaty limited the numbers and types of long-range nuclear missiles each country could have. The SALT treaty began a period of **détente** (day-TAHNT), or an easing of tensions, between the two countries. Détente also improved U.S.-Soviet economic relations. Trade between the two countries tripled in 1972. The opening of this new market pleased American farmers.

Although some people criticized Nixon for forming closer ties with communist governments, other Americans supported him.

Analyzing Primary Sources

Identifying Points of View Why did this American support Nixon's policy?

"I applaud [Nixon's] timely acceptance of the changing conditions in the world today. . . . If pragmatism [practicality] is indeed to be the byword [guiding principle] for U.S. policy, then all the better for the American people."

—Barbara Langsam, Letter to the editor, *Time*

✔ **Reading Check: Supporting a Point of View** What do you think was the most important element of President Nixon's foreign policy? Explain your answer.

Section 1 Review

go.hrw.com Homework Practice Online keyword: SC3 HP30

1. **Define** and explain:
   - southern strategy
   - stagflation
   - energy crisis
   - realpolitik
   - détente
2. **Identify** and explain:
   - Richard M. Nixon
   - Silent Majority
   - New Federalism
   - Organization of Petroleum Exporting Countries
   - Henry Kissinger
   - Leonid Brezhnev
   - Strategic Arms Limitation Talks
3. **Identifying Cause and Effect** Copy the graphic organizer below. Use it to show what caused the energy crisis and how it affected Americans.

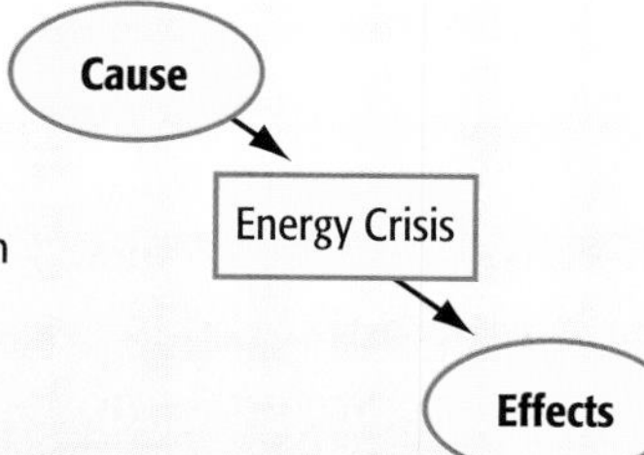

4. **Finding the Main Idea**
   a. How did President Nixon appeal to the Silent Majority?
   b. What effect did realpolitik have on U.S. foreign relations?
5. **Writing and Critical Thinking**
   Summarizing Imagine that you are an economist studying the effect of the poor economy on Americans during the Nixon years. Write an editorial about the problem.
   Consider the following:
   - stagflation
   - New Federalism
   - the energy crisis

Section 2

Watergate and Beyond

Read to Discover

1. How did the events of Watergate lead to President Nixon's resignation?
2. On what grounds did the House Judiciary Committee think Nixon should be impeached?
3. What challenges did President Ford face while in office?

Define

- executive privilege
- trade deficit

Identify

- Watergate
- Bob Woodward and Carl Bernstein
- Saturday Night Massacre
- Gerald Ford
- Barbara Jordan

WHY IT MATTERS TODAY

International trade remains an important issue for the American public. Use CNNfyi.com or other **current events** sources to learn about the trade deficit and the difference between the amount of exports and the amount of imports in the United States or another country. Record your findings in your journal.

The Story Continues

It was around 2:00 A.M. on June 17, 1972. A security guard was doing a routine check at the Watergate apartment and office complex in Washington, D.C. At first, everything seemed quiet. Then he saw that the doors to the Democratic National Committee headquarters were open. The guard called the police, who arrested five men. These men were no ordinary burglars—they had camera equipment, large amounts of cash, and secret electronic recording devices. Bob Woodward, a *Washington Post* reporter, was sure there was more to the story than simple burglary.

Reporters Bob Woodward (top) and Carl Bernstein (bottom) became famous for breaking the Watergate story.

The Beginning of a Scandal

The police learned that some of the Watergate burglars had ties to President Richard Nixon's office. One burglar worked for the Committee to Re-elect the President (CRP). The other burglars tied to the crime were former White House aides. The incident developed into **Watergate**, a political scandal named after the burglarized building.

President Nixon quickly said that nobody in his administration had taken part in the break-in, and the story had little effect on the presidential election of 1972. Nixon won a landslide victory over George McGovern, the Democratic senator from South Dakota. However, **Bob Woodward and Carl Bernstein**, two reporters for the *Washington Post*, continued to look into the break-in.

At first, people involved in the incident refused to talk. Then an unknown White House informant gave Woodward key inside information about Watergate. This news led Woodward and Bernstein to discover that the CRP had hidden illegal campaign contributions and spread false rumors about Democratic candidates. These "dirty tricks" had helped Nixon and other Republicans win the election. The reporters began publishing articles about these events in the *Washington Post*.

Evidence of a Watergate cover-up also began to build. Convicted Watergate burglar James McCord wrote a letter to Judge John J. Sirica. This letter became public in March 1973. In the letter, McCord said that he had been told to plead guilty and keep silent. McCord also stated that the five burglars who had been arrested were not the only ones involved.

✔ **Reading Check: Summarizing** What details were uncovered as the Watergate incident unfolded?

 The Investigation

Many members of Congress believed James McCord's claim of a cover-up. Some people even thought that President Nixon was part of the scandal. In February 1973 the Senate began its own investigation of the Watergate break-in.

Nixon tried to shift the blame to others in his administration. He forced H. R. Haldeman, his chief of staff, and John Ehrlichman, a chief adviser, to resign. He also fired White House attorney John Dean. Nixon agreed to Senate demands to appoint an independent special prosecutor to investigate the Watergate scandal. Harvard law professor Archibald Cox, known for his honesty and legal skill, became that investigator.

Nixon adviser John Ehrlichman testifies before the Senate.

North Carolina Senator Sam Ervin led the Senate Select Committee that investigated Watergate. Millions of Americans watched the Senate hearings on television. Accusations against the president and his closest advisers soon unfolded. The most damaging witness was former White House attorney John Dean. He said that Nixon had taken part in the cover-up. Another witness revealed that Nixon had recorded most of the conversations in his office. The Senate committee asked Nixon to turn over the tapes. Nixon refused based on **executive privilege**—the president's right to keep information secret to protect national security.

The tapes were the key to determining the truth of Dean's claims. Special Prosecutor Cox asked for a court order to get them, but President Nixon and his attorneys felt that Cox's request violated executive privilege. Cox responded, "There is no exception for the president. . . . Even the highest executive officials are subject to the rule of law." The federal judge in charge of the case ordered Nixon to hand over the tapes.

Nixon asked if he could submit summaries of the tapes rather than the originals, but Cox refused. On Saturday evening, October 20, 1973, Nixon ordered Attorney General Elliott Richardson to fire the special prosecutor to protect the national interest. Richardson chose to resign rather than fire Cox. "Mr. President," Richardson answered, "it would appear that we have a different assessment [view] of the national interest." The next-highest Justice Department official also resigned rather than fire the special prosecutor. Nixon then named Solicitor General Robert Bork acting attorney general. Bork fired Cox. The resignations and firing became known as the **Saturday Night Massacre**. Nixon's approval rating dropped to 22 percent in some polls, and many goverment officials began to talk about impeaching the president.

Interpreting the Visual Record

Conspiracy *As the Watergate investigations continued, Nixon claimed that his opponents were plotting against him.* ***Do you think that this cartoon supports or criticizes President Nixon? Explain your answer.***

Nixon had other problems as well. In October Vice President Spiro Agnew faced charges that he had failed to pay his taxes and that he had taken bribes as a public official. Agnew resigned just a few days before the Saturday Night Massacre and received a fine and probation for his crimes. Nixon selected a Michigan representative and House minority leader **Gerald Ford** as his new Vice President.

Nixon's Resignation

Following the Saturday Night Massacre, some members of Congress began the formal process of requesting President Nixon's impeachment. The president then handed over a few of the tapes. He provided a heavily edited transcript of other tapes. Investigators also learned that an 18-minute segment of one of the tapes had been erased.

The Impeachment Process

Grounds	Officials establish grounds for impeachment, which could include treason, bribery, and other offenses.
Phase 1	The House of Representatives announces articles of impeachment, thus formally accusing an official.
Phase 2	The Senate holds a trial for the accused, with a two-thirds vote needed for a conviction.
Penalty	A convicted official is removed from his or her post and cannot hold any public office in the future.

A ticket to President Andrew Johnson's 1868 impeachment trial in the Senate.

The Granger Collection, New York

Research on the ROM

Free Find:
Barbara Jordan
After reading about Barbara Jordan on the **Holt Researcher CD–ROM**, write a short play that illustrates her accomplishments and the obstacles she overcame.

The new special prosecutor, Leon Jaworski, demanded the release of 64 more tapes. In July 1974 the U.S. Supreme Court ordered the president to turn over all of the tapes that had been subpoenaed, or legally requested as evidence. This time Nixon obeyed the court order. Conversations on the tapes proved that Nixon had ordered the Watergate cover-up. The president had also lied to Congress and the American people about his involvement in Watergate.

The truth shocked many Americans who until then had believed the president. The evidence on the tapes moved Congress to act. The House Judiciary Committee soon asked the full House of Representatives to vote to impeach the president on three articles—abusing his authority, obstructing justice, and "violating the constitutional rights of citizens."

Texas congresswoman **Barbara Jordan** was a committee member. Like others, she believed that Nixon had violated his oath to uphold the nation's laws. Jordan explained why she favored Nixon's impeachment.

Analyzing Primary Sources

Drawing Inferences and Conclusions Why did Barbara Jordan believe that President Nixon should be impeached?

> **"My faith in the Constitution is whole, it is complete, it is total, and I am not going to sit here and be an idle spectator to the . . . destruction of the Constitution."**
>
> —Barbara Jordan, Speech before the House Judiciary Committee

After the tapes were released, Nixon had little support in Congress. If the House voted to impeach him, it was very possible that the Senate would find him guilty. It was not until former supporters began asking for his resignation that Nixon knew he was defeated. On August 8, 1974, Nixon became the first U.S. president to announce his resignation from office. In a shaky voice, he admitted only to "a few mistakes in judgment." The next day, Vice President Gerald Ford was the first person to be sworn in as president without being elected as either vice president or president.

The Watergate scandal hurt many Americans' faith in the government. "We [now] assume that politicians are without honor," wrote poet and journalist Adrienne Rich. Others disagreed, however. They believed that the hearings and Nixon's resignation showed that the government of the United States could beat corruption.

✔ **Reading Check: Identifying Cause and Effect** Why did Nixon resign, and what was the public's reaction?

Interpreting the Visual Record

Nixon's resignation *As President Nixon boarded a helicopter to leave the White House, the* Washington Post *announced his resignation.* ***Does Nixon's expression seem appropriate for the occasion? Explain your answer.***

The Washington Post

Nixon Resigns

Ford Assumes Presidency Today

The Ford Presidency

President Gerald Ford called Watergate a "long national nightmare" that was now over. Ford pardoned Richard Nixon. This pardon meant that Nixon would never face trial for any of the illegal activities that took place during his presidency. Many Americans felt relieved to finally move past Watergate. Others questioned why Nixon escaped punishment when other Watergate figures had gone to jail. As a result of the pardon, Ford's approval rating fell from more than 70 to less than 50 percent.

Ford also offered a conditional pardon to young men who had illegally avoided the draft during the Vietnam War. Under Ford's plan, these young men could avoid criminal charges by performing community service. Many veterans felt that the punishment was too light. However, antiwar activists thought it punished them unfairly for doing what they believed was morally right. Just 19 percent of those eligible for the pardon responded to the offer.

Ford faced another controversy in the mid-1970s. Congressional investigations revealed that both the CIA and the FBI had abused their power. The FBI, for example, had spied on radical groups without proper cause. Ford tried to reorganize and reform the agencies to restore Americans' faith in government.

The economy also presented Ford with a challenge. Within months of taking office, Ford said that the country was nearing a recession. Business had slowed because of high oil prices and continuing stagflation. The United States also had a growing **trade deficit**—a trade imbalance that happens when a country imports more goods than it exports. Many American automakers struggled to compete with popular imported cars such as the Volkswagen Beetle. The trade deficit made inflation and unemployment even worse. Ford believed that if the United States could control inflation, it could lower both prices and the trade deficit. To fight high prices, Ford began a voluntary campaign called Whip Inflation Now (WIN). He asked Americans to save their money and businesses to keep salaries and prices down. However, only 100,000 Americans joined a voluntary organization supporting the president's battle against inflation, and Congress rejected Ford's economic plan.

Ford also wanted to lower government spending to reduce inflation. However, the Democrat-controlled Congress wanted more spending to help poor and unemployed citizens. Because of this dispute, few laws were passed. Ford vetoed more than 30 Democrat-backed spending bills during his term. In 1975 the president and Congress agreed to expand unemployment benefits and to cut some taxes. Although the economy recovered slightly, inflation and unemployment remained high, and the trade deficit grew.

✔ **Reading Check: Finding the Main Idea** What challenges did Ford face while in office?

Interpreting the Visual Record

Inflation *Widespread price increases led President Ford to create his Whip Inflation Now program.* ***What do you think was the purpose of the button?***

President Ford reviews Chinese troops with Chinese Premier Deng Xiaoping.

Ford's Foreign Policy

In foreign affairs, President Ford tried to follow Nixon's policy of détente. He and Soviet leader Brezhnev agreed to limit underground nuclear testing. They also discussed a second SALT treaty to further limit nuclear arms. In addition, U.S. astronauts and Soviet cosmonauts performed a series of experiments together while in orbit in July 1975.

Despite such events, conservative politicians argued that U.S. cooperation with the Soviet Union would cause other NATO nations to lose trust in the United States. Some conservatives also believed that the Soviet Union might see détente as a sign of American weakness.

President Ford shared these fears and soon acted on them. In the spring of 1975, when communist Cambodians took over the American cargo ship *Mayaguez*, Ford authorized a military rescue. Forty-one Americans died in the failed attempt to rescue some 40 crewmembers. It was later discovered that the hostages had already been released.

As time went on, conservatives in Congress took a firm stand against communism and would not back any more deals with the Soviet Union. The Soviets also became less cooperative and further SALT talks stalled. By 1976 little remained of the cooperation between the Soviet Union and the United States.

✔ **Reading Check: Analyzing Information** What was the state of détente under President Ford? Explain your answer.

Section 2 Review

go.hrw.com Homework Practice Online
keyword: SC3 HP30

1. **Define** and explain:
   - executive privilege
   - trade deficit
2. **Identify** and explain:
   - Watergate
   - Bob Woodward and Carl Bernstein
   - Saturday Night Massacre
   - Gerald Ford
   - Barbara Jordan
3. **Sequencing** Copy the time line below. Use it to list the Watergate events through President Nixon's resignation in the order that they occurred.

   Summer 1972 | Summer 1973 | Summer 1974

4. **Finding the Main Idea**
   a. Why did the House Judiciary Committee conclude that Nixon's role in Watergate was a serious violation of the Constitution?
   b. How did President Ford address domestic and foreign challenges?
5. **Writing and Critical Thinking**
   Evaluating Imagine that you are a political activist in 1974. President Ford has just granted Nixon a full pardon. Create a leaflet explaining why you support or oppose Ford's action.
   Consider the following:
   - Saturday Night Massacre
   - Ford's desire to help the country move past Watergate

Section 3

The Carter Administration

Read to Discover

1. How was President Carter different from other politicians, and why did he lose public support?
2. How did Carter handle economic problems during his presidency?
3. What was Carter's approach to foreign policy, and how did he apply it?

Define

- apartheid
- sanctions

Identify

- Jimmy Carter
- Panama Canal treaties
- Anwar Sadat
- Menachem Begin
- Camp David Accords
- Ayatollah Khomeini
- Iran hostage crisis

Why It Matters Today

Humanitarian concerns continue to play a role in some foreign-policy decisions. Use CNNfyi.com or other **current events** sources to research issues being raised by humanitarian groups and others about a particular country in the world today. Record your findings in your journal.

The Story Continues

The morning of July 4, 1976, dawned clear and cool over New York Harbor. A steady wind filled the sails of 225 tall ships as they silently made their way past the Statue of Liberty. For a few days most Americans set aside their worries about the economy and foreign policy. Instead they celebrated the country's bicentennial, or 200th birthday. One person stated that the bicentennial had "become a way of clearing the American soul in a very positive way."

Many Americans gathered to see the bicentennial celebration in New York Harbor.

The Election of 1976

Democratic Party leaders hoped that the bicentennial would also mark a Democratic presidential victory. Democrats thought they had a good chance of winning the White House in 1976. Many Americans linked the Republicans to the Watergate scandal. In addition, a large number of voters were disappointed with the way President Gerald Ford had addressed economic and diplomatic issues. Other Americans were upset that he had pardoned former president Nixon.

Ford defeated former California governor Ronald Reagan in a tough battle for the Republican presidential nomination. After he won, he chose Kansas senator Bob Dole as his running mate. The Democrats wanted a candidate who was not linked to any political scandals. At first there was no clear front-runner. However, an unexpected candidate emerged during the primaries—a little-known former governor of Georgia named **Jimmy Carter**.

The two most important factors in Carter's life were his family and his religion. These personal values strongly shaped Carter's political career. Carter's religious faith played a key role in his political views. As a result, he thought that policy should be based on moral ideals such as equality and justice.

Carter's campaign focused more on his personal character than on his political platform. His background and straightforward approach impressed many people. "I will never lie to you," he told voters. He promised a "new era of honest, compassionate, responsive government." His words appealed to Americans still troubled by the Watergate incident. Carter narrowly beat Ford in the 1976 election. Strong support from African American and Hispanic voters helped him win.

As president, Carter wanted to show the nation a new spirit of openness in the White House. On Inauguration Day, he and his family walked down Pennsylvania Avenue instead of riding in a limousine. Carter also tried to make the presidency more personal. He had few politicians from Washington in his cabinet. He also reduced the size of the presidential staff. Early in his administration, the public seemed to like Carter's approach.

✔ **Reading Check: Drawing Inferences and Conclusions** Why do you think Carter's character helped him win this election?

Daily Life

Carter's Inauguration
Instead of wearing formal attire to his inauguration, President Jimmy Carter wore a business suit. His wife Rosalynn also chose a more low-key approach to the event. Instead of buying a new gown, as most first ladies did, she wore the dress that she had worn to her husband's past two inaugurations as Georgia's governor. After his inauguration, Carter became the first president to walk back to the White House from the Capitol. **How do you think Carter's actions might have changed the government?**

Domestic Challenges

President Carter faced two major problems at home—the economy and the energy crisis. Because the economy was still slow, Carter called for a tax cut and increases in government spending. He also tried to get management and organized labor to help out by holding down prices and wages. However, Carter achieved few of his domestic-policy goals. Inflation reached more than 13 percent in 1980, partly because of rising oil prices.

The energy crisis continued to hurt the economy. Oil prices remained high, and the United States still depended on foreign oil. Nuclear energy was not a popular alternative. Many Americans began to fear nuclear power after an accident occurred on Three Mile Island, Pennsylvania. In March 1979 the reactor core of a nuclear power plant located there overheated and nearly released deadly radiation into the air. The accident raised new questions about the safety of nuclear power.

Carter created a detailed energy policy and asked Americans to use less fuel. He found it difficult to win public support for energy conservation, however. Carter also supported the development of alternative energy sources such as natural gas. As an inexperienced political "outsider," Carter had trouble winning support in Congress. For example, Carter did not want Congress to make any changes to his complex energy plan. As a result, Congress approved only some of the plan. Although his own party controlled Congress, few of his proposals were passed. Carter's rigid style limited his ability to get things done.

✔ **Reading Check: Analyzing Information** What factors kept Carter from lowering inflation and solving the energy crisis?

The Changing Automobile

The energy crisis of the 1970s led car companies to make smaller, more fuel-efficient cars. Today automakers are using new technology to create cars that cause less pollution and use less fossil fuel. Electric cars run on powerful batteries instead of gasoline. Hybrid cars combine electric batteries with small gasoline engines that extend battery life. Hydrogen-powered cars use devices called fuel cells to turn hydrogen and oxygen into electricity.

These new car designs face a variety of problems, ranging from car size to cost. But they show that interest in energy-saving technologies remains strong in many nations. **What are some of the new cars being developed?**

A new hybrid car

Carter's Foreign Policy

President Carter rejected the policy of realpolitik. Instead, he said that "fairness, not force, should lie at the heart of our dealings with the nations of the world." Carter had harsh words for foreign governments that tortured or unlawfully jailed their citizens. He insisted that other governments protect citizens' human rights—the basic rights and freedoms owed to all human beings. Carter reduced U.S. aid to some former allies, such as Argentina and Ethiopia, for human-rights violations.

President Carter soon applied his new foreign-policy plan to U.S. relations with Latin America. Many Latin Americans resented past U.S. interference in their countries, such as the U.S.-built and controlled Panama Canal. In 1977 Carter signed the **Panama Canal treaties**, which gave control of the canal to Panama by the year 2000. Many Americans opposed the treaties because of the canal's strategic value. Nevertheless, the Senate approved them in 1978. Like Carter, the Senate hoped that the treaties would lead to closer ties with Latin America and reduce communist influence in the region.

Jimmy Carter

James Earl Carter Jr. was born in Plains, Georgia. After graduating from the U.S. Naval Academy, Carter was an engineer in the nuclear submarine program. After his father died, Carter returned to Georgia to help rebuild the family peanut warehouse. He became active in politics, and in 1970 he was elected governor of Georgia.

When Carter announced his decision to run for president in December 1974, few politicians thought he could win. However, by the time of the Democratic National Convention, Carter had won 18 state primaries. He then won the nomination for president. **How do you think Carter's early experiences prepared him for the presidency?**

President Carter also became involved in Middle Eastern diplomacy. In September 1978 he brought Egyptian president **Anwar Sadat** and Israeli prime minister **Menachem Begin** (BAY-gin) together for peace talks. The leaders met at Camp David, the U.S. presidential retreat. In two weeks of meetings they crafted a set of peace agreements known as the **Camp David Accords**. The accords marked the first time that an Arab country had formed peaceful ties with Israel. Many historians view the accords as Carter's greatest accomplishment.

In relations with Africa, Carter tried to encourage respect for human rights and win allies. He provided economic aid to developing countries struggling to establish economic independence after years of European colonial rule. He also tried to preserve U.S. trade interests in the region. In addition, Carter's administration addressed the issue of **apartheid**, the system of laws requiring racial segregation in South Africa. Andrew Young, the U.S. ambassador to the United Nations, was a strong critic of apartheid. Young called for **sanctions**, or economic penalties, to persuade South Africa to desegregate. The United States began applying sanctions against South Africa in 1985.

Carter was very critical of the Soviet government's many human-rights abuses. This criticism upset Soviet leaders. The situation became even more serious in 1979 when the Soviets invaded the Central Asian country of Afghanistan. Carter reacted to the invasion by postponing talks on SALT II—a new arms control treaty. He also placed an embargo on U.S. grain sales to the Soviet Union. Finally, Carter declared a U.S. boycott of the 1980 Summer Olympics in Moscow.

The Olympic boycott and the grain embargo upset many American athletes and farmers. Some Americans believed that beating the Soviets in competition was a better way to show U.S. strength than boycotting the games. Other Americans worried about the economic effects of the grain embargo. "[W]e shouldn't have to go broke being patriotic," said one Kansas farmer.

✔ **Reading Check: Summarizing** How did Carter apply "fairness, not force" in his foreign policy?

Anwar Sadat of Egypt (left) and Menachem Begin of Israel (right) signed the first peace treaty between Israel and an Arab nation.

Interpreting the Visual Record

Hostages *Iranian revolutionaries parade some of the U.S. hostages through the streets of Tehran.* ***How might this image create problems for the U.S. government?***

The Iran Hostage Crisis

Another crisis soon drew Americans' attention. In the 1950s the United States had helped bring the shah of Iran, Mohammad Reza Pahlavi (RAY-zah pah-LAHV-ee), to power. Over the next 20 years, the shah had supported U.S. interests in the region. In the late 1970s, however, Islamic fundamentalists began to challenge the shah's power. They called for a strict return to Islamic teachings and an end to cooperation with the United States.

By February 1979, followers of religious leader **Ayatollah Khomeini** (eye-uh-TOH-luh koh-MAY-nee) had overthrown the shah. They formed a fundamentalist dictatorship that was hostile to the United States. In October U.S. leaders allowed the shah into the United States for medical treatment. Angry Iranian revolutionaries staged massive protests. They also attacked the U.S. Embassy in Tehran, Iran's capital. On November 4 they seized American hostages, whom they abused and tortured. They let one hostage go free, but the rest were still held captive.

The **Iran hostage crisis** dragged on for months with no end in sight. Many horrified Americans believed that the hostage situation was proof of America's declining strength. In April 1980 a rescue attempt by the U.S. military went terribly wrong. Confusion and mechanical problems caused a rescue helicopter and a transport plane to collide in the desert. The rescuers never reached Tehran. One American explained how the failure caused many Americans to lose faith in Carter's leadership.

"America today needs a tough-talking and tough-acting leader. America's strength was built on national pride and morale [positive feeling], and both of these have dropped under the weight of the defeat in Vietnam, the scandal of Watergate, and the catastrophic [disastrous] policies of Jimmy Carter."

—Anonymous, quoted in *America in the Twentieth Century,* by James T. Patterson

Analyzing Primary Sources

Drawing Inferences and Conclusions What kind of leader do you think this speaker would support?

✔ **Reading Check: Finding the Main Idea** How did Carter respond to the hostage crisis, and how did public opinion of him change?

The Election of 1980

While President Carter prepared to run for re-election in 1980, his popularity was falling. Many people blamed him for the hostage crisis and the country's economic problems. He had also lost the support of many Democratic leaders in Congress. One southern Democratic senator said privately, "He hasn't a single friend up here [on Capitol Hill]."

Now it was the Republicans' turn to challenge an unpopular president. Republican Party leaders chose Ronald Reagan, the former governor of California, to run against Carter. During his campaign, Reagan claimed that the country needed new leadership.

Ronald Reagan's promise to make America strong again appealed to many voters.

"I will not stand by and watch this great country destroy itself under mediocre [average] leadership. . . . This is the greatest country in the world. We have the talent, we have the drive, we have the imagination. Now all we need is the leadership."

—Reagan advertisement, quoted in *It Seemed Like Nothing Happened,* by Peter Carroll

Analyzing Primary Sources

Identifying Points of View Why did Reagan feel his country needed new leadership?

In the November 1980 election Reagan defeated Carter in a landslide victory, 489 electoral votes to 49. Republicans also gained control of the Senate for the first time in 28 years. Despite his defeat, Carter's administration continued to negotiate for the release of the hostages. After 444 days in captivity, on January 20, 1981, the hostages were finally freed—just moments after Reagan was sworn in as president. When the hostages returned home five days later, people across the country welcomed them back with banners and parades.

✔ **Reading Check: Identifying Cause and Effect** What caused President Carter's popularity to decline, and what was the result?

Section 3 Review

go.hrw.com Homework Practice Online
keyword: SC3 HP30

1. **Define** and explain:
   - apartheid
   - sanctions

2. **Identify** and explain:
   - Jimmy Carter
   - Panama Canal treaties
   - Anwar Sadat
   - Menachem Begin
   - Camp David Accords
   - Ayatollah Khomeini
   - Iran hostage crisis

3. **Summarizing** Copy the table below. Use it to list the ideas that shaped Carter's foreign policy and how he applied them.

Ideas that shaped Carter's foreign policy	Ways Carter applied these ideas

4. **Finding the Main Idea**
   a. In what ways was President Carter unlike other politicians, and why did this affect his public support?
   b. What economic problems did the nation face during Carter's presidency, and how did he address them?

5. **Writing and Critical Thinking**
   Supporting a Point of View Imagine that you are an Olympic athlete in 1980. Write a letter to President Carter sharing your opinions on the boycott of the 1980 Summer Games in Moscow.
   Consider the following:
   - the invasion of Afghanistan
   - human-rights abuses
   - Carter's fairness and morality approach

Section 4

American Society in the 1970s

Read to Discover

1. How did the U.S. population change during the 1970s?
2. What environmental and health concerns drew Americans' attention, and how were they addressed?
3. In what ways did popular entertainment and computers change in the 1970s?

Why It Matters Today

Immigration and migration continue to change the face of the United States. Use CNNfyi.com or other **current events** sources to learn about current immigration and migration trends in the United States. Record your findings in your journal.

Identify

- Endangered Species Act
- Earth Day
- Environmental Protection Agency
- George Lucas
- Donna Summer

The Story Continues

Despite the problems the United States faced in the 1970s, America was still a land of opportunity for immigrants. Many immigrants were like Erasmo and Eloina Ortega, who emigrated from the Dominican Republic in the 1970s. Although their family had to work hard in the troubled U.S. economy, they were happy to be in the United States. "The political situation [in the Dominican Republic] was bad," recalled Eloina. "We're very glad that our children have a future that our country could never provide them."

A flag from the Dominican Republic

 Changing Immigration

The Ortegas were part of a changing pattern of immigration in the United States. Until the mid-1960s most immigrants came from Europe. By the 1970s, however, the majority of immigrants were coming from Latin America and Asia.

Immigrants from Latin America and Asia were often political refugees. For example, thousands of people, many of whom were educated professionals, left communist Cuba and came to the United States. These immigrants helped form a powerful Cuban American political movement in southern Florida. Some Asian immigrants were also refugees from communist countries, such as Vietnam.

Thousands of other immigrants came to the United States in search of economic opportunities. Mexican immigrants looking for jobs made up the majority of Latin American immigrants during the 1970s. Although the U.S. economy was struggling, many immigrants still found better jobs than they could in their homelands.

Immigrants also sought educational opportunities. A large number of Asians came to the United States to attend college and often stayed and worked in technical industries and other professions. Educated middle-class professionals also immigrated to the United States, sometimes with their families, to find new opportunities. Chinese immigrant Subi Lin Felipe recalled how her brother-in-law "brought in a sister and his wife, who brought over one of her brothers and me." Many immigrants shared the outlook of Korean Kim Ta Tai.

Analyzing Primary Sources

Identifying Points of View What does this person seem to love so much about America?

"The fascination of America . . . is to come to a free and abundant [plentiful] country, and breathe the air of freedom, and make plans for a new life."

—Kim Ta Tai, quoted in *Strangers from a Different Shore,* by Ronald Takaki

✔ **Reading Check: Contrasting** How were immigration patterns of the 1970s different from earlier years?

Growth in the Sunbelt

Thousands of immigrants settled in the Sunbelt states of the South and the West. Migrants from the Northeast and the Midwest also moved to the Sunbelt. By 1970 California had become the most populous state in the Union. The populations of other Sunbelt states such as Arizona and Florida also increased dramatically during the 1970s. By comparison, Midwestern and Northeastern populations grew slowly or even decreased.

Many people moved to the Sunbelt states to take new jobs in growing high-tech industries such as aerospace and electronics. Many companies got their start by filling federal defense contracts during the Cold War military buildup.

Many older Americans moved to the Sunbelt for its warm climate. They were part of a major change in the U.S. population. More Americans were living longer because health care had improved and the birthrate was dropping. More adults were waiting longer to have children and were having smaller families. As a result, the percentage of the U.S. population aged 65 and older grew rapidly. The expansion of Social Security benefits in the 1960s made retirement easier for many older Americans.

✔ **Reading Check: Summarizing** In what ways did the U.S. population change in the 1970s?

Interpreting the Visual Record

The Sunbelt *Many older Americans enjoyed active lifestyles in the warm climate of the Sunbelt.* ***Why might people prefer the Sunbelt?***

Interpreting the Visual Record

Earth Day *Many thousands of people have observed Earth Day since the first celebration was held in 1970.* ***How can this event help the environmental movement?***

Environmental and Health Issues

As the human population expanded across the nation, wildlife species were pushed into smaller habitats. In 1966 Congress passed one of the earliest environmental measures, the **Endangered Species Act**. This act protects animals threatened with extinction. The Department of the Interior maintains a list of species that are in danger. Federal law forbids hunting these species or destroying their natural habitats. Some activists have used the Endangered Species Act to stop building projects. However, critics claim that the law goes too far. These people agree that wildlife should be protected but feel that people need the jobs that new development brings. As the debate continues, some developers today are searching for ways to both protect the environment and make a profit.

Some Americans were also concerned about the effect of rapid growth on the environments of the Sunbelt and northwestern states. The worldwide energy crisis also led to growing concern about the use of natural resources. American activists tried to raise environmental awareness by sponsoring the first **Earth Day** on April 22, 1970.

> **"Earth Day is to remind each person of his [or her] . . . equal responsibility . . . to preserve and improve the Earth and the quality of life thereon."**
>
> —John McConnell, "Proposed Earth Day Resolution"

Analyzing Primary Sources

Identifying Points of View According to McConnell, who is responsible for protecting the environment?

Since then, people around the world have held similar events. Groups also offer tips about saving energy, picking up litter, and recycling.

Congress addressed concerns about the environment in the late 1960s and early 1970s by passing laws to improve air and water quality and to limit pollution. In 1970 Congress created the **Environmental Protection Agency** (EPA) to enforce these laws. Then in 1977 the federal government banned the use of chemicals that were believed to weaken Earth's atmospheric ozone layer. The ozone layer helps protect Earth's surface from excessive solar radiation.

The smiley face became a symbol of positive thinking in the 1970s.

Environmental concerns shaped the consumer activist movement of the 1970s. This movement showed that worries about public health could change business practices and safety regulations. Led by consumer advocate Ralph Nader, activists pushed for improved safety and environmental regulations for many consumer goods. These activities resulted in stricter rules for product safety and tougher pollution standards for automobiles.

Concern for public health also led to many changes in medical technology in the 1970s. Patented in 1972, the MRI machine could find tumors and other problems more accurately than X-ray machines. The following year, researchers created the CAT scanner. This device produces images called CAT scans that allow doctors to detect tumors in and injuries to the brain. Medical research indicated that people could lower their risk for certain diseases with exercise and a better diet. In addition, studies exposed the dangers of tobacco products, and antismoking campaigns encouraged Americans to give up smoking. These studies caused many Americans to live healthier lives in the 1970s. Jogging, dance, and other aerobic activities became popular. Scientists believe that better diet and exercise led to about a 20 percent drop in the death rate from heart disease between 1969 and 1977.

✔ **Reading Check: Summarizing** How were environmental and health concerns addressed in the 1970s?

Advances in Computers

Computer technology also changed during the 1970s. Computer designers began making wide use of the microchip, invented in 1958. A microchip is a tiny piece of silicon that contains many small electronic parts. Placing all of these parts on a single chip allowed computers to become smaller and faster. As computers did more and cost less, more people used them. The most powerful machines, known as "supercomputers," allowed for advanced scientific research. The military also used computers in many of its new defense and weapons systems. In addition, scientists created the first computer networks for military research. These networks allowed computer users in different places to share data.

For the first time the development of small personal computers became possible. In 1976 Steven Jobs and Stephen Wozniak founded the Apple computer company. Their first successful home computer had simple graphics and could run only a few programs. Despite these limitations, Apple had sold thousands of computers by 1980. Although computer designers made better models during the 1970s, the new machines still cost too much to be practical for most people.

The Apple II was the first fully assembled home computer.

✔ **Reading Check: Making Generalizations and Predictions** How do you think the changes in computer technology during the 1970s affected later innovations?

Popular Culture

Star Wars dazzled audiences with its images of alien worlds and earned more than $100 million during its opening release, a record at that time.

New technology had a major effect on moviemaking. The most successful film of the 1970s was **George Lucas**'s 1977 classic, *Star Wars*. Lucas used new filmmaking and sound-recording techniques to create amazing special effects that audiences loved. The success of *Star Wars* resulted in a new era of "blockbuster" films. These big-budget, special-effects movies were aimed at younger audiences.

Lucas said that he felt the story's "universal themes like friendship, loyalty, [and] morality [right and wrong]" appealed to young audiences. Director Steven Spielberg, who made blockbusters like *Close Encounters of the Third Kind*, praised this change.

Films became a valuable U.S. export. However, there were also risks involved for the movie studios. Big-budget films cost so much to make that if one failed it could ruin a studio. In addition, some viewers began to complain that blockbuster movie plots were too simple and violent.

Music also changed during the 1970s. Americans enjoyed dance-oriented musical styles, such as disco, at discotheques, or discos. Dances like "The Hustle" were popular, and musicians like the Bee Gees and **Donna Summer** made best-selling records. As with big-budget movies, the new music had its critics. Some argued that disco lyrics encouraged irresponsible behavior. Despite such criticisms, disco music remained popular with young fans in the 1970s.

✔ **Reading Check: Summarizing** Why did some people criticize popular forms of entertainment of the 1970s?

go.hrw.com Homework Practice Online
keyword: SC3 HP30

1. **Identify** and explain:
   - Endangered Species Act
   - Earth Day
   - Environmental Protection Agency
   - George Lucas
   - Donna Summer

2. **Analyzing Information** Copy the graphic organizer below. Use it to identify the environmental issues that concerned Americans in the 1970s and the ways that these concerns were addressed.

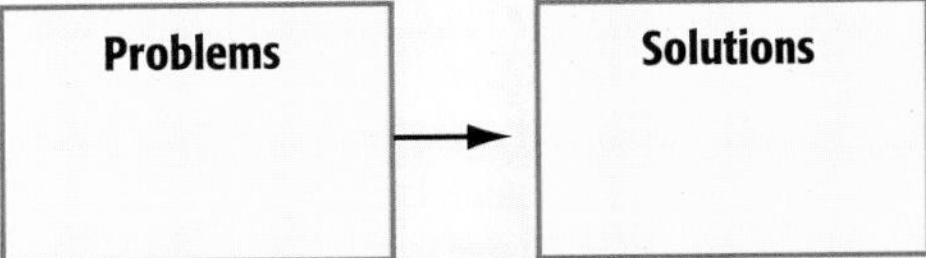

3. **Finding the Main Idea**
   a. How was the population of the United States affected by changes in immigration and migration during the 1970s?
   b. How did popular entertainment and computers change during the 1970s?

4. **Writing and Critical Thinking**
   Evaluating Imagine that you are a public health worker in the 1970s who is trying to raise public awareness of health issues. Create an informational brochure telling Americans about recent health concerns and how they are being addressed.
   Consider the following:
   - MRI machines and CAT scans
   - better exercise and diet
   - the results of medical improvements

Chapter 30 Review

The Chapter at a Glance

Examine the visual summary of the chapter below. Create a five-question multiple-choice quiz covering the chapter's main ideas that you might give to a classmate.

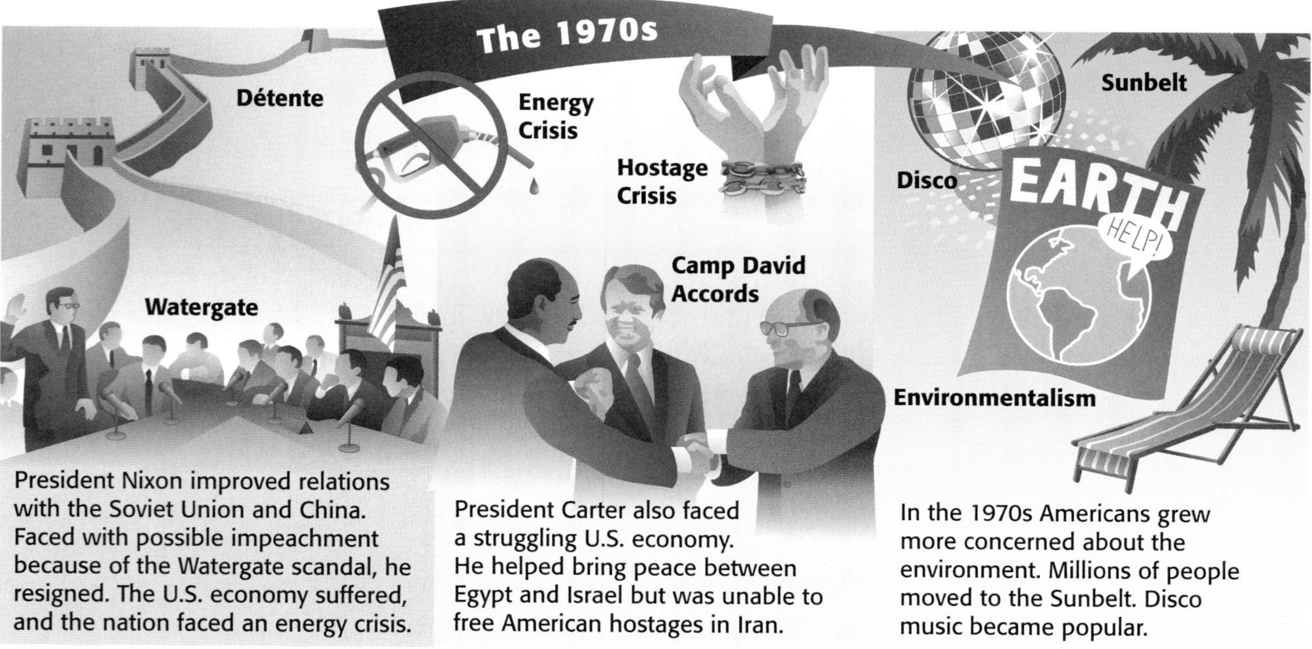

Identifying People and Ideas

Use the following terms or people in historically significant sentences.

1. Richard Nixon
2. stagflation
3. Strategic Arms Limitation Talks
4. Watergate
5. Barbara Jordan
6. Jimmy Carter
7. apartheid
8. Iran hostage crisis
9. Earth Day
10. Environmental Protection Agency

Understanding Main Ideas

Section 1 *(Pages 902–906)*

1. How did President Nixon try to address the concerns of the Silent Majority?
2. How did realpolitik affect U.S. foreign relations?

Section 2 *(Pages 907–912)*

3. What events led to the discovery of Nixon's role in Watergate?

Section 3 *(Pages 913–918)*

4. What made Jimmy Carter seem different than other politicians, and why did he lose public support?
5. Explain Carter's foreign-policy approach, and give examples of how he applied it.

Section 4 *(Pages 919–923)*

6. What environmental issues arose in the 1970s, and what actions did the federal government take to improve the situation?
7. In what ways did 1970s films and music change?

You Be the Historian—Reviewing Themes

1. **Economics** How did U.S. dependence on foreign oil affect the economy during the mid-1970s?
2. **Government** How did Watergate affect Americans' opinions of the presidency?
3. **Global Relations** How did Carter's foreign-policy approach differ from that of Nixon?

Thinking Critically

1. **Identifying Cause and Effect** Why did Nixon try to form closer ties with China, and how did this affect U.S. relations with the Soviet Union?
2. **Supporting a Point of View** Which do you think would have been better for the nation—pardoning President Nixon for Watergate or trying him in a court of law? Explain your answer.
3. **Analyzing Information** How did Presidents Nixon, Ford, and Carter try to improve economic conditions during the 1970s?

Social Studies Skills Workshop

Interpreting Political Cartoons

Study the political cartoon below. Then answer the questions that follow.

"You've got to admit we're getting Watergate behind us."

1. What is the cartoon's message?
   a. Watergate continued to trouble President Ford and the nation even after Nixon resigned.
   b. Nixon abused his powers as president.
   c. Ford was not prepared for the new responsibilities that he assumed as president.
   d. Nixon was a stronger leader than Ford.
2. Based on what you know about the 1970s, what is President Ford doing and why?

Analyzing Primary Sources

Read the following quotation by consumer advocate Ralph Nader, who lobbied for better consumer protection laws, and then answer the questions that follow.

> **"Air pollution alone is a devastating form of violence. It takes far more lives and maims far more victims each year than street crime, and destroys more property each year than all the bank robbers' hauls a thousand times over. According to government figures, bank robbers have gotten away with more than twenty million dollars a year in recent years . . . but the cost of air pollution alone in one recent year ran to more than sixteen billion dollars."**

3. Which of the following statements best describes the author's point of view?
   a. The government needs to crack down on crime.
   b. Bank robbers are responsible for America's economic problems.
   c. The health risks of air pollution are greater than the amount of money bank robbers steal.
   d. The government should not spend so much money enforcing environmental protection laws.
4. Why do you think Nader compares air pollution with bank robbers?
5. Based on what you know about the environmental movement of the 1970s, what federal actions indicated that U.S. government officials were working to protect the environment?

Alternative Assessment

Building Your Portfolio

American History

Linking to Community

Contact your City Hall and local Chamber of Commerce to locate information about activities planned for the next Earth Day in your community. Create a poster and leaflets that might be used for the event. On your poster, use art or photographs to show why environmental activities are important. In the leaflets, persuade people to work to preserve the environment and explain how to accomplish that goal.

internet connect

Internet Activity: go.hrw.com

keyword: SC3 CF30

Choose a topic on the 1970s to:

- Create a visual display on the Watergate scandal.
- Write a biography of Jimmy Carter.
- Create an annotated scrapbook on life in the 1970s.

CHAPTER

31 America Looks to the Future (1980–Present)

U.S. troops fighting in the Persian Gulf War wore camouflage to blend into the desert landscape of Kuwait and Saudi Arabia.

President Reagan and Soviet leader Mikhail Gorbachev met in Moscow in 1988.

UNITED STATES

1981 Ronald Reagan becomes president of the United States.

1987 The U.S. stock market crashes in October.

1988 George Bush is elected president.

1991 An international coalition led by the United States launches a ground attack in the Persian Gulf War.

1980 | **1982** | **1984** | **1986** | **1988** | **1990**

1981 Great Britain's Prince Charles weds Lady Diana Spencer in a ceremony viewed by an estimated 700 million people worldwide.

1986 The Chernobyl nuclear accident takes place in Ukraine, in the Soviet Union.

1989 Germans tear down the Berlin Wall.

1991 The Commonwealth of Independent States is formed, replacing the former Soviet Union.

WORLD

The marriage of Lady Diana and Prince Charles drew worldwide attention.

Germans celebrated their greater civil freedoms by tearing down the Berlin Wall.

Build on What You Know

During the 1970s the Watergate scandal and the Iran hostage crisis shook the faith of many Americans. When Ronald Reagan became president in 1981 he offered new hope and supported many conservative changes. However, he and his successor, George Bush, also faced many foreign and domestic challenges while in office.

President George W. Bush greets firefighters while touring the rubble of the World Trade Center after the September 11, 2001, attack.

The Sojourner *rover explored the surface of Mars and analyzed this rock to learn about the planet's soil.*

1992 Democrat Bill Clinton is elected president.

1993 The Senate passes the North American Free Trade Agreement.

1995 The Dayton peace accords are signed, bringing an end to the Bosnian war.

1997 The *Pathfinder* spacecraft lands on Mars.

2001 On September 11, terrorists attack the World Trade Center and the Pentagon.

1992 **1994** **1996** **1998** **2000**

1997 Pacific Rim countries suffer a steep economic recession.

1999 Eleven members of the European Union adopt a single currency, the euro.

2000 Hundreds of people are killed as fighting breaks out between Israelis and Palestinians.

Each of the 11 different versions of the euro has an image or symbol of the member nation that designed it.

If you were there . . .

What changes would you make in government policy?

You Be the Historian

Themes Journal

What's Your Opinion? Do you **agree** or **disagree** with the following statements? Support your point of view in your journal.

- **Economics** Economic conditions affect a country's political situation.
- **Global Relations** Domestic politics affect a nation's foreign relations.
- **Science, Technology & Society** Technological changes both solve and create problems.

Section 1

The Reagan Years

Read to Discover

1. How did President Reagan hope to balance the budget?
2. What were the major issues in foreign affairs during Reagan's presidency?
3. What political events took place in the Soviet Union during Reagan's presidency?

Define

- supply-side economics
- deficit
- perestroika
- glasnost

Identify

- Walter Mondale
- Geraldine Ferraro
- Sandinistas
- Contras
- Iran-Contra affair
- Mikhail Gorbachev
- Intermediate-Range Nuclear Forces Treaty

Why It Matters Today

Part of the federal government's job is to spend taxpayers' money wisely. Use CNNfyi.com or other **current events** sources to find out about the federal budget and issues involving the budget today. Record your findings in your journal.

Ronald Reagan posed for this photo at his ranch in Santa Barbara, California.

The Story Continues

During Ronald Reagan's first week as president, he was eager to explore his new home. In the White House, he flipped light switches and looked in closets. He even paid a sudden visit to the kitchen, startling the cooks. One morning the Marine Band played "Hail to the Chief" as he ate breakfast. Reagan loved the show but promised the musicians that he would not expect the performance every day. A Reagan aide explained that although the president was "impressed with the history of it all, . . . he's not overwhelmed." Reagan's obvious ease in his all-important position reassured many Americans.

Reagan in Office

When President Reagan came into office, he aimed to balance the budget, reduce regulations on business, and expand the military. He also wanted to cut taxes and reduce the size of the federal government. In his 1981 inaugural address, Reagan shared his views on the proper role of government.

"Government is not the solution to our problems; government is the problem. . . . It is not my intention to do away with government. It is, rather, to make it work—work with us, not over us."

—Ronald Reagan, First Inaugural Address

Reagan quickly put his new economic plan into place. His policies, which some called Reaganomics, were based on an idea called **supply-side economics**. According to this theory, the government could balance the budget by first cutting taxes. This would increase personal income and business profits. People would then save or invest this extra income, thus causing the economy to grow and creating new jobs. Over time this growth in business activity would create greater tax revenues, or money collected from taxes, which would help balance the budget.

Reagan's supply-side economic policies did lead to higher business profits and tax revenues. However, defense spending increased from $134 billion in 1980 to some $250 billion in 1985. In the end, defense and other federal spending grew faster than the new tax revenues and budget cuts. This caused a dramatic increase in the **deficit**—the amount by which a government's spending exceeds its tax revenues. The economy was starting to boom by 1983. However, some of Reagan's critics noted that not everyone was able to enjoy this new wealth. Unemployment increased to about 10 percent in 1982 and 1983. It was particularly high among African Americans and Hispanics.

To support Republican policies, Reagan appointed conservative judges to the Supreme Court. During Reagan's presidency, Sandra Day O'Connor, Antonin Scalia, and Anthony Kennedy joined the Court. These justices gave the Supreme Court a more conservative outlook.

The Republican Party nominated Reagan to run again in 1984. The Democrats chose **Walter Mondale**, Jimmy Carter's vice president, as their candidate. Mondale selected **Geraldine Ferraro**, a congressmember from New York, as his running mate. She became the first woman to run for vice president on a major-party ticket. Ferraro explained why her candidacy was important.

"By choosing an American woman to run for our nation's second-highest office, you send a powerful signal to all Americans. . . . We will place no limits on achievement. If we can do this, we can do *anything*."

—Geraldine Ferraro, *Ferraro: My Story*

Although Mondale said that Reagan's economic policies greatly favored the wealthy, voters gave the president credit for the economic good times. Reagan won in a landslide, capturing 525 electoral votes to Mondale's 13.

✔ **Reading Check: Summarizing** What steps did president Reagan take to improve the economy, and what were the results?

Ronald Reagan

Ronald Reagan was born in Tampico, Illinois, in 1911. He became a well-known actor, twice serving as president of the Screen Actors Guild. Reagan's experience as an actor would later help him in politics. He became a Republican in part because he believed the Democratic Party focused too much on social reform.

Reagan gained national political recognition in 1964, when he gave campaign speeches for Republican presidential candidate Barry Goldwater. Two years later, Reagan's combination of wit, positive thinking, and conservative politics helped him win election as governor of California. He told voters, "It is time we ended our obsession with what is wrong, and realized how much is right." He carried this message with him to the White House. **What was Reagan's background before becoming president?**

Analyzing Primary Sources

Drawing Inferences and Conclusions Why do you think that Ferraro believed her nomination would "send a powerful signal"?

Interpreting the Visual Record

Contras *Nicaraguan Contra rebels train for their military effort to overthrow the Sandinistas.* ***Why might U.S. military aid be particularly valuable to small groups such as this one?***

Reagan's Foreign Policy

President Reagan held strong anticommunist views and called for more defense spending and military intervention. For example, he sent U.S. Marines to Lebanon in 1982 as part of an international peacekeeping mission. After terrorist attacks against the U.S. Embassy and a marine headquarters in Lebanon resulted in the deaths of more than 300 people, Reagan pulled the marines out in February 1984. In October 1983 Reagan sent U.S. troops on a brief and successful mission to topple the pro-communist government of Grenada. This action was part of Reagan's strong anticommunist policy in Central America and around the world. He declared that the Cold War was a fight of "good versus evil, right against wrong."

In the early 1980s the United States again became involved in Central American politics. The country raising concerns this time was Nicaragua. Reagan believed the **Sandinistas**, the revolutionary political party that was in power, were Communists. He cut off all aid to Nicaragua and began backing anti-Sandinista rebels called **Contras**. Fearing a new war, Congress banned the U.S. government from sending military aid to the Contras.

In the mid-1980s issues surrounding Contra aid became a national controversy. In 1983, Iranian terrorists in Lebanon took some Americans hostage. Then, in secret dealings, they offered to free the hostages in return for U.S. weapons for Iran. Oliver North, a U.S. national security aide, arranged the secret deal. Such a trade of arms for hostages violated the U.S. policy against dealing with terrorists. North passed the profits from the sales to the Contras, violating Congress's ban on Contra aid.

In 1986 the **Iran-Contra affair**—the name given to the secret arms deal—became public. Afterward, President Reagan swore that the United States had not traded weapons for hostages. Nevertheless, Congress held hearings on the Iran-Contra affair. The investigation turned up no proof of illegal actions by the president.

✔ **Reading Check: Analyzing Information** What were the key issues surrounding the Iran-Contra affair?

Research on the ROM

Free Find:
Reagan on Communism
After reading Ronald Reagan's speech on communism on the **Holt Researcher CD–ROM**, write a letter to a member of Congress explaining why you agree or disagree with Reagan's view of communism.

U.S.-Soviet Relations

During his first term, President Reagan called the Soviet Union an "evil empire" and refused to hold any arms-limitation talks with the Soviets. In addition, Reagan expanded the U.S. defense budget and called for the development of the Strategic Defense Initiative (SDI). This proposed defense system would use space-based lasers to shoot down incoming missiles. Congress approved $26 billion to develop SDI, but scientists were unable to produce a working version.

In 1985 **Mikhail Gorbachev** became the new Soviet leader. Gorbachev knew that the Soviet Union was in deep economic trouble. He began a series of political and economic changes, known as **perestroika**, that sought to restructure the Soviet economy. He also started a policy of political openness and freedom of expression called **glasnost**. Gorbachev's reforms led to reduced Soviet defense spending and cuts in economic support for other communist nations. They also resulted in the first free elections held in the Soviet Union since the earliest days of the Soviet state.

These changes led to a softening of Reagan's hard-line stand in the Cold War, and he met with the Soviet leader in November 1985. He soon believed that Gorbachev was truly working to change the Soviet Union. In December 1987 the two leaders signed the **Intermediate-Range Nuclear Forces Treaty** (INF). The INF Treaty called for the elimination of all medium-range nuclear weapons from Europe. For the first time in almost 10 years, Cold War tensions between the United States and the Soviet Union were easing.

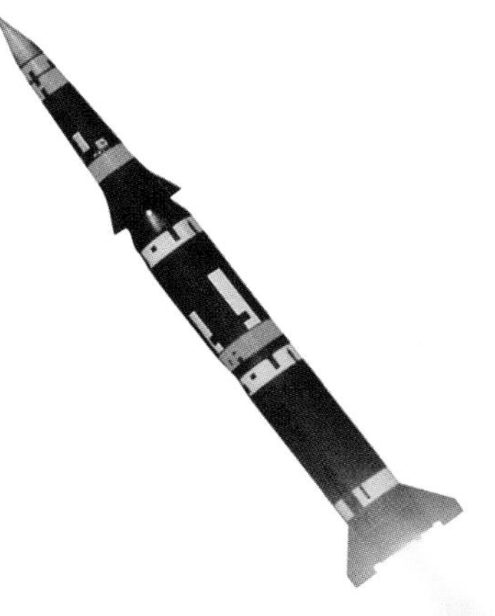

As a result of new U.S.-Soviet arms agreements, U.S. Pershing II missiles like this one were removed from Europe.

✔ **Reading Check: Finding the Main Idea** How did the Soviet Union change politically during Reagan's presidency?

1. **Define** and explain:
   - supply-side economics
   - deficit
   - perestroika
   - glasnost

2. **Identify** and explain:
   - Walter Mondale
   - Geraldine Ferraro
   - Sandinistas
   - Contras
   - Iran-Contra affair
   - Mikhail Gorbachev
   - Intermediate-Range Nuclear Forces Treaty

3. **Summarizing** Copy the graphic organizer below. Use it to explain the changes in domestic and foreign policies during President Reagan's administration.

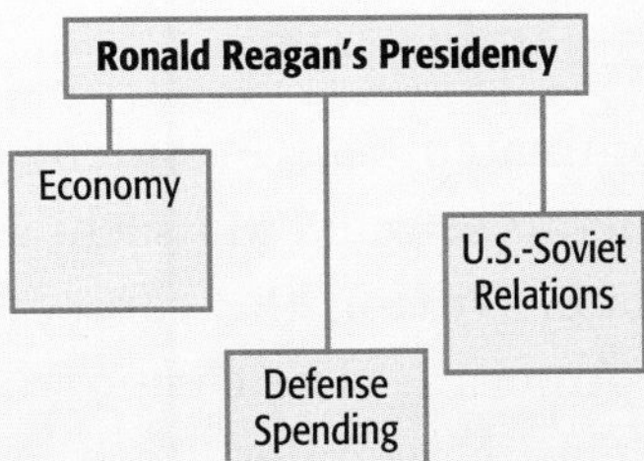

4. **Finding the Main Idea**
   a. What did President Reagan do to balance the budget and improve the economy?
   b. What political policies were introduced in the Soviet Union while Reagan was in office?

5. **Writing and Critical Thinking**
   Supporting a Point of View Imagine that you are a newspaper reporter. Write an editorial explaining whether you think President Reagan successfully addressed key foreign-policy issues.
   Consider the following:
   - Reagan's opposition to communism
   - U.S. policy to not negotiate with terrorists
   - U.S. law preventing aid to the Contras

Section 2

George Bush's Presidency

Read to Discover

1. What domestic issues did President Bush work on while he was in office?
2. What events led to the final breakup of the Soviet Union?
3. What caused the Persian Gulf War, and how did the conflict end?

Identify

- George Bush
- Michael Dukakis
- War on Drugs
- Americans with Disabilities Act
- Commonwealth of Independent States
- Saddam Hussein
- Operation Desert Storm
- Norman Schwarzkopf

Why It Matters Today

Every president introduces new policies and legislation. Use  or other **current events** sources to learn what new programs the current president is trying to introduce. Record your findings in your journal.

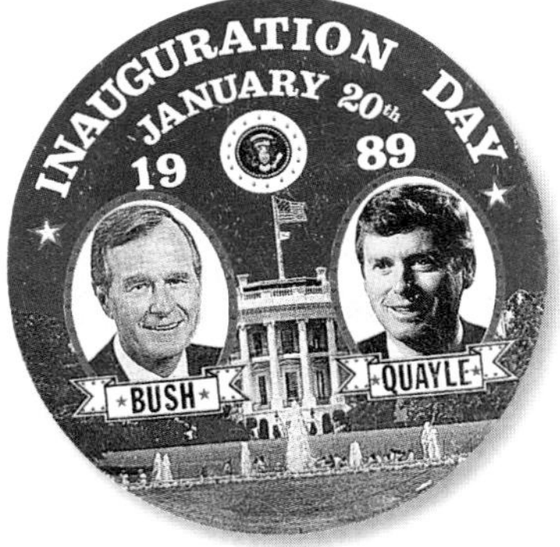

George Bush selected Indiana senator Dan Quayle as his running mate in the 1988 presidential campaign.

The Story Continues

By late May 1988, Republican candidate George Bush was far behind in presidential election polls. Over the Memorial Day weekend, Bush met with his campaign team to come up with a new campaign strategy. Bush's advisers told him to go on the offensive and to stress just a few themes. Bush focused on his patriotism, his tough position against crime, and his ability to continue the Reagan prosperity. During the rest of the campaign, Bush steadily repeated these messages over and over again. On election day, he won a stunning victory, taking 40 of 50 states.

Bush's Policies

Republicans nominated Vice President **George Bush** for president in 1988. The Democrats selected Massachusetts governor **Michael Dukakis** as their candidate. During the campaign, George Bush promised a "kinder, gentler America." The election battle itself, however, was bitter and hard-fought. In November, Bush won the race with 426 electoral votes to Dukakis's 111.

One of the first issues that President Bush faced was a savings-and-loan (S&L) crisis. During the Reagan administration, the government had lifted restrictions on the types of investments that S&Ls could make. As a result, many S&L owners made risky investments with their customers' savings. Some bank officials even committed fraud and used their clients' money to buy themselves mansions and yachts. In August 1989 President Bush authorized $166 billion to close or merge many S&Ls. This financial crisis and the need to balance the federal budget forced Bush to break his campaign promise not to raise taxes.

Soon after taking office, President Bush gave more support to the **War on Drugs**—an organized effort that had begun in the 1970s to end the trade and use of illegal drugs. Drug treatment and education efforts were part of Bush's War on Drugs, but he focused mostly on using law enforcement to end drug use. U.S. officials offered legal assistance and financial aid to help foreign countries arrest major drug smugglers. In December 1989 Bush authorized a military invasion of Panama to capture the country's dictator, Manuel Noriega. He was charged with drug smuggling and later convicted. A U.S. federal court sent him to prison in 1992.

In 1990 Bush signed an update of the Clean Air Act. Bush launched other domestic programs including the **Americans with Disabilities Act** (ADA), which he signed in 1990. The ADA guarantees people with disabilities equal access to public employment opportunities, places, and transportation.

✔ **Reading Check: Summarizing** What were George Bush's domestic programs during his presidency?

The Fall of the Berlin Wall

Encouraged by new freedoms in the Soviet Union, many East Germans began demanding similar rights. Protests pushed the East German government in 1989 to end its restrictions on crossing into the West. Thousands of people gathered for the opening of the gates. At midnight, they streamed into the western side. Celebrators began to dismantle the Berlin Wall piece by piece. Other people danced on top of the wall. Some chanted, "The Wall is gone, the Wall is gone."

The Berlin Wall was perhaps the most despised symbol of communist rule in Eastern Europe. One American explained the meaning of the wall's destruction. "It [removal of the wall] shows the indomitability [strength] of the human spirit." **How and why was the Berlin Wall torn down?**

The End of the Cold War

While Bush was in office, Soviet leader Mikhail Gorbachev continued to push for changes that moved his country toward democracy and weakened the Communist Party. During this period, Eastern European countries removed their Communist leaders from power. In November 1989 pro-democracy Germans began tearing down the Berlin Wall. One person described the historic moment.

> **"The city was overcome by a joyful madness in which astonishment mingled with unspeakable joy. . . . There were unforgettable scenes of rejoicing, with shouting, tears, applause, laughter and singing. . . . East Germans were welcomed with flowers. . . . The Wall was taken by storm by the crowds singing and dancing."**
>
> —Anonymous, quoted in *A Concrete Curtain: The Life and Death of the Berlin Wall*

West Germany and East Germany officially came together as one country in October 1990.

Interpreting the Visual Record

Russian crisis *Standing on top of a tank, Boris Yeltsin (center, holding papers) asks the Russian people to resist the military leaders who took Mikhail Gorbachev hostage.* ***Why do you think this scene would be inspiring to prodemocracy supporters in Russia?***

Gradually, some Soviet republics, such as Lithuania, Estonia, and Latvia, declared their independence. More Soviet republics then declared independence. As hard-line Communists watched their country begin to fall apart, several of them made one last try to stop the reforms. In August 1991 they took Gorbachev hostage and ordered troops and tanks into the streets of Moscow to put down protests. Instead, crowds of people filled the streets. Russian pro-democracy leader Boris Yeltsin, backed by some members of the military, told the people to stand strong and resist the troops. Many of the soldiers joined the crowd and promised to fight with them. The hard-line Communists knew they were defeated and called the troops back. Soon after, the Soviet Union broke apart. However, in December 1991 many of the former Soviet republics formed an alliance—the **Commonwealth of Independent States**.

✔ **Reading Check: Analyzing Information** What events brought about the end of the Soviet Union?

Conflict in the Persian Gulf

As the Soviet Union was breaking apart, problems were arising in the Middle East. **Saddam Hussein** (sah-DAHM hoo-SAYN), the leader of Iraq, had long claimed that neighboring Kuwait actually belonged to his country. In August 1990, Iraqi tanks and ground troops poured across the border into Kuwait.

The United Nations (UN) condemned the invasion, banned trade with the Iraqis, and demanded that they leave Kuwait. On August 7, U.S. troops began arriving in Saudi Arabia to protect the country. The next day President Bush explained why the United States was sending troops.

Analyzing Primary Sources

Drawing Inferences and Conclusions How is President Bush trying to win public support for his actions?

> **"In the life of a nation, we're called upon to define who we are and what we believe. Sometimes these choices are not easy. But today as President, I ask for your support in a decision I've made to stand up for what's right and condemn what's wrong."**
>
> —George Bush, speech given August 8, 1990

Troops from some 30 other countries eventually joined the U.S. forces in an international military coalition. The UN gave Iraq until January 15, 1991, to remove its troops from Kuwait. Bush warned Saddam Hussein, "A line has been drawn in the sand. . . . Withdraw from Kuwait unconditionally and immediately, or face the terrible consequences." Many Americans supported the president's tough stand. One journalist wrote, "Like all bullies [Saddam Hussein] will in the end be deterred [stopped] only by superior force."

When the Iraqis did not withdraw by the deadline, the coalition launched **Operation Desert Storm**. During this offensive, airplanes pounded Iraq for six weeks with bombs. The UN coalition was made up mostly of U.S. forces and was commanded by U.S. Army general **Norman Schwarzkopf** (SHAWAWRTS-kawf). On the night of February 23, the UN coalition launched a massive ground invasion. Within days, Iraq agreed to cease-fire conditions. The United States lost 148 soldiers, while Iraq lost up to 100,000 soldiers as well as many civilians.

More than 35,000 American women served in the Persian Gulf War. However, Congress did not let women take part in combat. They could not serve as fighter pilots or ground soldiers. After the Persian Gulf War, the debate over whether to expand the role of women in combat intensified. In November 1991 Congress voted to allow women to serve as combat pilots.

Hussein remained in power and relations with Iraq remained unstable. Yet for many Americans, victory in the Persian Gulf helped erase painful memories of the Vietnam War.

In the Persian Gulf War, female soldiers played many important roles but were not allowed into direct combat positions.

✔ **Reading Check: Identifying Cause and Effect** What led to Operation Desert Storm, and what was the result of the war?

Section 2 Review

go.hrw.com Homework Practice Online
keyword: SC3 HP31

1. **Identify** and explain:
   - George Bush
   - Michael Dukakis
   - War on Drugs
   - Americans with Disabilities Act
   - Commonwealth of Independent States
   - Saddam Hussein
   - Operation Desert Storm
   - Norman Schwarzkopf

2. **Analyzing Information** Copy the graphic organizer below. Use it to list the major events that took place during Bush's presidency and their effects.

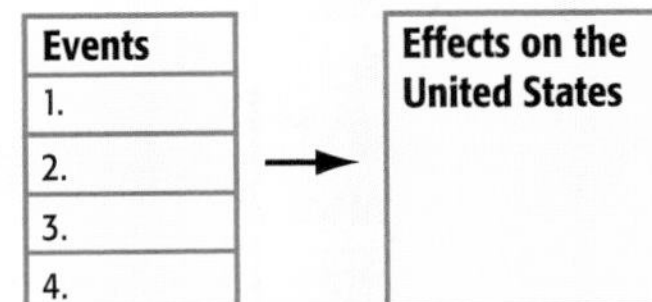

3. **Finding the Main Idea**
   a. What were some of the domestic policies that President Bush pursued?
   b. Why did the United States and other countries fight a war against Iraq, and what was its outcome?

4. **Writing and Critical Thinking**
   Summarizing Imagine that you are a historian giving a lecture on the Soviet Union. Write a three-paragraph essay that describes the factors that caused the final breakup of the Soviet Union.
   Consider the following:
   - causes of political change
   - events leading to the breakup
   - outcomes of political change

Section 3

The Clinton and Bush Administrations

Read to Discover

1. What domestic issues were important during Clinton's administration?
2. What economic changes affected the United States in the 1990s?
3. What were the issues in the 2000 election, and why was this election unusual?

Define

- terrorism

Identify

- Bill Clinton
- North American Free Trade Agreement
- Contract with America
- Bob Dole
- Al Gore
- George W. Bush

Why It Matters Today

The United States continues to play an active role in world affairs. Use CNNfyi.com or other **current events** sources to learn more about current U.S. foreign policy. Record your findings in your journal.

The Story Continues

Bill Clinton became the first Democratic president in 12 years.

By 1991 the United States was in a recession. During the 1992 presidential campaign, President George Bush faced strong challenges from Democratic candidate Bill Clinton and independent candidate Ross Perot. Perot, a billionaire business leader, argued that his lack of political experience would help him in office. All three contenders met in a nationally televised debate to discuss key election issues, such as the economy. The three-way race led to greater voter interest in the election.

The Clinton Years

The Republican Party nominated President Bush for re-election in 1992. **Bill Clinton**, governor of Arkansas, won the Democratic nomination and chose Tennessee senator Al Gore as his running mate. On Election Day, Clinton won with 370 electoral votes to Bush's 168. President Clinton promised in his inaugural address to bring an end to gridlock—the complete lack of movement or progress—in the government.

"We must invest more in our own people, in their jobs, in their future, and at the same time cut our massive debt. . . . We must do what America does best: offer more opportunity to all and demand responsibility from all."

—Bill Clinton, First Inaugural Address

Analyzing Primary Sources

Making Generalizations and Predictions Do you think President Clinton's plan for reform would be possible to achieve? Explain your answer.

Clinton persuaded Congress to pass the **North American Free Trade Agreement** (NAFTA), which took effect on January 1, 1994. NAFTA removed trade barriers between the United States, Canada, and Mexico, allowing for a freer flow of trade goods. However, Clinton failed to reform health care or provide universal medical coverage to all Americans, as he had hoped to do.

In 1994, as congressional elections approached, House minority whip Newt Gingrich of Georgia and others created a campaign pledge called the **Contract with America.** Many Republican candidates signed the contract, which promised a smaller government and a balanced budget. The contract also included tax reforms and term limits for members of Congress. Voters responded, and Republicans gained majorities in both houses of Congress for the first time in 42 years. By the end of 1995, five items in the contract had become law.

As the 1996 election drew near, Republicans chose Senator **Bob Dole** of Kansas to run for president. President Clinton ran on a platform of conservative ideas like welfare reform and tax cuts. Clinton won the election with 379 electoral votes to Dole's 159. During Clinton's second term he reached an agreement with Congress to balance the federal budget. The U.S. economy continued its longest period of growth in the country's history. This economic expansion led to a huge amount of extra money, or a surplus, in the government's budget. The surplus in 1999 alone totaled $99 billion.

While the economy boomed, questions about President Clinton's personal and official conduct arose. In 1998 an independent counsel's report charged that the president had conducted an improper relationship with a young White House intern and had lied about it under oath before a grand jury. Voting largely along party lines, the House of Representatives impeached Clinton. The Senate, however, found Clinton innocent of the charges. The scandal of the impeachment and his personal actions harmed his public image.

✔ **Reading Check: Categorizing** What were the domestic successes and failures of Clinton's presidency?

The Poetry of Maya Angelou

Many Americans saw the 1990s as a time of challenge and change. Poet Maya Angelou expressed her hopes for the future in a poem she read at President Clinton's inauguration in 1993.

Lift up your faces, you have a piercing need
For this bright morning dawning for you.
History, despite its wrenching pain,
Cannot be unlived, and if faced
With courage, need not be lived again.

Understanding What You Read

Literature and History What historical events do you think Angelou was referring to with the words "wrenching pain?"

Al Gore (left) selected Joe Lieberman (right) as his vice presidential running mate, making Lieberman the first Jewish candidate on a major party's presidential ticket.

The 2000 Presidential Election

With the economy in seemingly strong shape, the 2000 presidential election centered on issues such as tax reform and foreign policy. The United States was the world's only superpower following the collapse of the Soviet Union. Many Americans questioned what role U.S. troops should play in peacekeeping missions in regions such as the Balkans. The United States also faced the threat of **terrorism**—the use of violent attacks by individuals or small groups with political goals.

In 2000 the Democrats nominated Vice President **Al Gore** as their presidential candidate. Gore chose Senator Joe Lieberman of Connecticut to be his running mate. Gore and Lieberman promised to keep paying down the national debt and to use the government surplus for education and health care.

Republicans nominated **George W. Bush**, the governor of Texas and the son of former president George Bush, as their candidate for president. Bush chose former defense secretary Dick Cheney as his running mate. Bush said that he would use most of the government surplus for tax cuts. Both candidates promised that they would be cautious in assigning military forces abroad.

The presidential election of 2000 was unlike any before it. The vote was so close that several states could not declare a winner. Florida's 25 electoral votes became the key to the White House. The state's first results were so close that Florida law required recounts. After machine recounts revealed a narrow Bush lead, Gore requested manual recounts in four counties. The Bush campaign challenged these manual recounts in court. Both campaign teams began public relations efforts to gain support. Court challenges over manual recounts, ballot designs, and absentee ballots kept the country in suspense for five weeks. Eventually, the issue went to the Supreme Court. The Court ruled that hand recounts in several Florida counties were not valid. Florida's electoral votes went to Bush. As a result, he became the first president in more than 100 years to win the electoral vote but not the popular vote.

That's Interesting!

Election Drama Can you imagine not knowing whether you won or lost the presidency? Well, it happened to Al Gore and George W. Bush. On November 7, 2000, all the major networks announced that Gore had won Florida and the presidency. But by early next morning most networks had changed and were calling George W. Bush the president-elect. Gore called Bush to concede the election, but after further counting narrowed Bush's lead in Florida, Gore called again—to take back his concession! Not until the Supreme Court ruled on the Florida vote recount was Gore comfortable in conceding victory to Bush.

A New Presidency

George W. Bush had won a close election. In his inauguration speech, he called for Americans to help one another.

> "I ask you to seek a common good beyond your comfort; . . . I ask you to be citizens. Citizens, . . . not subjects. Responsible citizens, building communities of service and a nation of character."
>
> —George W. Bush, Inaugural Address

Interpreting the Visual Record

Inauguration day *George W. Bush's inaugural celebration was a blend of Washington and Texan styles.* ***Based on this photograph, what sort of tone do you think President Bush is trying to set in the White House?***

During his first weeks in office, President Bush sent an education reform package and a plan for tax cuts to Congress. He also appointed his cabinet, which included former general Colin Powell as the first African American secretary of state.

The newly seated Congress was almost equally divided between Republicans and Democrats. In the House of Representatives, the Republicans maintained a small majority. The Senate was split 50–50, with Vice President Cheney holding the tie-breaking vote. However, the balance of power shifted again when Jim Jeffords, a senator from Vermont, left the Republican Party to become an independent in 2001. With one less Republican in the Senate, the Democratic Party gained control of the Senate for the first time since 1994.

The near-deadlock in Congress forced each party to compromise on some of its issues. On June 7, 2001, President Bush did sign into law a $1.35 trillion tax-cut plan that included much of the tax relief that he had promised during his campaign.

✔ Reading Check: **Making Generalizations and Predictions** What steps do you think President Bush might take to unite all Americans?

Section 3 Review

go.hrw.com Homework Practice Online
keyword: SC3 HP31

1. **Define** and explain:
   - terrorism

2. **Identify** and explain:
   - Bill Clinton
   - North American Free Trade Agreement
   - Contract with America
   - Bob Dole
   - Al Gore
   - George W. Bush

3. **Categorizing** Copy the chart below. Use it to identify the major issues in Bill Clinton's presidency.

	Domestic	Foreign
Successes		
Challenges		

4. **Finding the Main Idea**
   a. During President Clinton's administration, what were some important domestic issues?
   b. What were the candidates' positions on the issues in the 2000 presidential election, and why was the outcome unusual?

5. **Writing and Critical Thinking**
   Analyzing Information Imagine that you are the editor an American business journal. Write an article that describes the condition of the U.S. economy during the Clinton administration?
   Consider the following:
   - economic growth
   - the federal budget
   - the government surplus

Section 4

American Culture and Society

Read to Discover

1. What concerns did people have about the environment in the 1990s?
2. What economic trends did the international community experience in the 1990s?
3. What scientific and technological developments took place during the 1980s and 1990s?

Define

- ozone layer
- global warming

Identify

- International Space Station
- European Union
- World Trade Organization
- Information Revolution
- Internet

WHY IT MATTERS TODAY

Many important issues face the world today. Use CNNfyi.com or other **current events** sources to learn more about an issue that you believe is critical to the world's future. Record your findings in your journal.

The Story Continues

Teenagers Maria Perez, Fabiola Tostado, and Nevada Dove spent hours studying test results, chemical analyses, and groundwater-safety studies. The girls were not preparing for a school test. These young activists were preparing to meet with local community leaders. They lobbied for the temporary closing of a middle school so that hazardous chemicals could be cleaned up at the site. "We're the new generation," Dove explained. "One day you're going to have to stand up . . . for something you believe in. Why not get an early start?"

Recycling is one of the many ways that students and communities are taking action to protect the environment.

Challenges for a New Millennium

During the 1990s, some countries worked together to solve environmental problems. One such challenge was the thinning of the **ozone layer.** This thin layer of gas in the upper atmosphere keeps harmful solar rays from reaching Earth's surface. Some scientists predicted that a thinning of the ozone layer would lead to more cases of skin cancer.

Daily Life

Young Environmentalists Youth are often among the most vocal and active members of the environmental-protection movement. Letter-writing campaigns, petitions, and volunteering for cleanup efforts are common tactics. Many teenagers use the Internet to become informed and involved in global environmental issues. Here a group of children pose in front of a mural at the 1992 Earth Summit in Rio de Janeiro. **How are students taking action to protect the environment?**

Another issue of concern was **global warming**. Some scientists warned that a greenhouse effect is trapping heat in the Earth's atmosphere, thus raising the planet's temperature. They blamed the burning of forests and fossil fuels for this climate change and warned that it could have dangerous results. In 2000 a United Nations report predicted Earth's average temperature could rise between 3 and 11 degrees during the next 100 years.

Space 2000 and Beyond

While some scientists studied Earth, others researched space. Space exploration took a new turn in 1981, when NASA launched its first space shuttle. The shuttle was a cost-saving reusable spacecraft. During the 1980s and 1990s, NASA flew nearly 100 space shuttle missions. In November 1998, John Glenn flew on a shuttle mission, becoming at age 77 the oldest space traveler.

In 1997 NASA's *Pathfinder* spacecraft landed on Mars. *Sojourner,* a small robotic car, emerged from the spacecraft and traveled over the planet collecting data for scientists on Earth.

After the Cold War ended, the United States and Russia decided to work together on the **International Space Station** (ISS). In November 2000, one U.S. astronaut and two Russian cosmonauts began a four-month stay in the new station. NASA hoped the event would mark the beginning of humans' permanent residence in space.

✔ **Reading Check: Categorizing** What challenges did scientists face regarding the environment and space in the 1990s and 2000s?

Global Trade 2000

The United States conducts billions of dollars worth of trade with foreign nations each year.

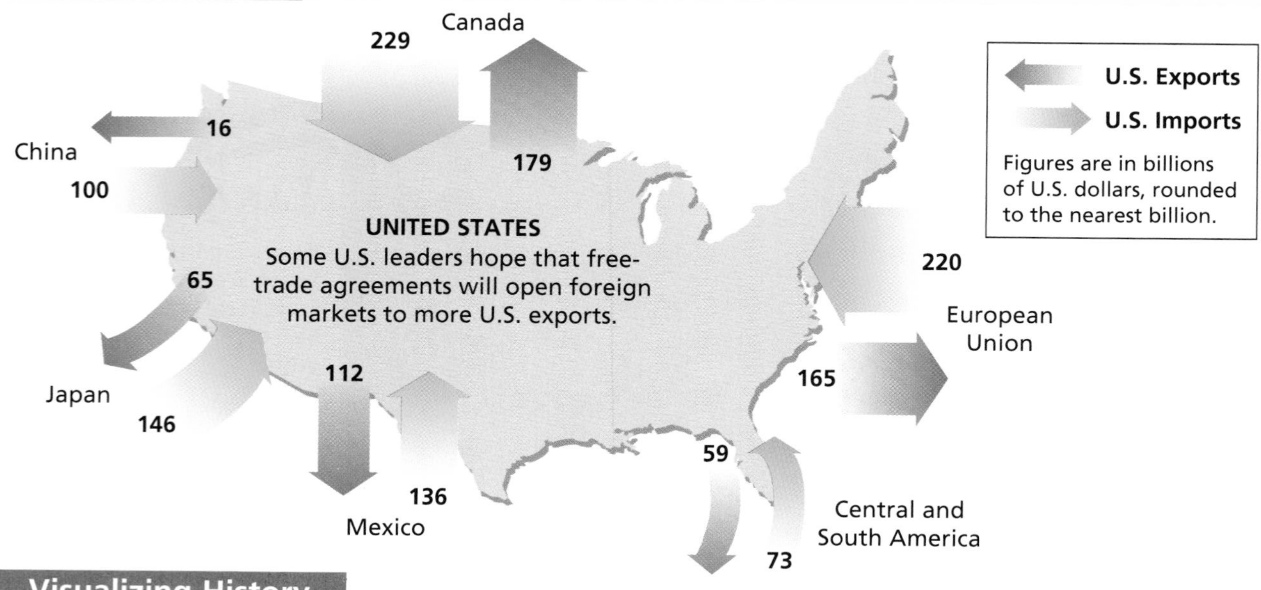

Visualizing History

1. **Economics** What was the total value of U.S. exports to and imports from the regions shown above?

2. **Connecting to Today** Why would it benefit the United States to export more than it imports?

 Economic Trends

During the 1990s, the United States recovered from a recession and experienced the longest period of economic growth in the nation's history. A major feature of the economy in the 1990s was the increase in international trade. The rise of multinational corporations—companies that do business in more than one country at a time—also shaped the world economy.

Some nations even joined together to increase their global economic power. In 1993, a total of 12 countries of Western Europe joined to form the **European Union** (EU). The EU joined member nations' economies into a single market with a common currency—the euro—and a common central bank.

As countries exported more goods, governments saw the need to form an organization that would set rules for international trade. In 1995, some 128 nations joined together in the **World Trade Organization** (WTO). The WTO supervises international trade. By November 30, 2000, the number of members in the WTO had risen to 140 countries. More than 30 more countries, including China, were in the process of negotiating membership. The WTO is just one organization through which countries work to keep the world economy strong. The United States still looks for new ways to support economic stability throughout the world.

The Information Revolution

Technology was an important factor contributing to the U.S. economic boom of the 1990s. In the 1990s, computers made it easier and faster for people to access and transfer information. This development was called the **Information Revolution**. Computers became necessary tools in business, education, and every activity that requires the organization and processing of information. In the 1980s, new technologies linked computers via networks so that they could communicate and transfer information to one another. Over time, different computer networks formed a worldwide link called the **Internet**. The development of the Internet allowed people anywhere in the world to communicate and share information with one another.

Use of the Internet grew remarkably during the late 1990s. Consumers spent an average of one hour per day online. Bill Gates, a leading figure in the computer industry, saw the growth of the Internet as a major step in the Information Revolution.

> **"We are watching something historic happen, and it will affect the world . . . the same way the scientific method, the invention of printing, and the arrival of the Industrial Age did."**
>
> —Bill Gates, *Newsweek*, November 1995

Internet expansion and the high-tech industry helped fuel the economic boom by providing jobs and economic growth. Some high-tech firms struggled in 2000, but technology remained a key part of the U.S. economy.

✔ **Reading Check: Finding the Main Idea** How have computers affected the way people share information?

CONNECTING TO SCIENCE AND TECHNOLOGY

The Internet

The Internet began as a 1960s Defense Department project. However, most people did not become familiar with this computer network until the creation of the World Wide Web in the 1990s.

The Web makes it easier to use the Internet to access information stored on computers around the world. Many people use the Internet to obtain documents stored on Web sites. For example, the Smithsonian Institution's Web site links to hundreds of related sites through its subject index. The Internet puts an amazing amount of information at people's fingertips. In what ways could you use the Internet for school?

Section 4 Review

go.hrw.com Homework Practice Online
keyword: SC3 HP31

1. **Define** and explain:
   - ozone layer
   - global warming
2. **Identify** and explain:
   - International Space Station
   - European Union
   - World Trade Organization
   - Information Revolution
   - Internet
3. **Summarizing** Copy the diagram below. Use it to identify the changes that took place in the United States between 1981 and 2000.

   United States 1981–2001
   - economy:
   - environment:
   - science & technology:
4. **Finding the Main Idea**
   a. how did the global economy change during the 1990s?
   b. What environmental issues have concerned people around the world?
5. **Writing and Critical Thinking**
   Supporting a Point of View Imagine that you are a teacher. Write a letter to a local newspaper to persuade the community to raise taxes to buy computers for your school.
   Consider the following:
   - how computers have affected the transfer of information
   - how computers have affected access to information
   - how computers will help students learn

Section 5

September 11, 2001: A Day That Changed the World

Read to Discover

1. How was the United States attacked on September 11, 2001, and how did Americans respond?
2. How did the events of September 11 affect the economy?
3. What immediate steps did U.S. leaders take to find those responsible and bring them to justice?

Identify

- World Trade Center
- Pentagon
- Rudolph Giuliani
- George W. Bush
- Tom Ridge
- Donald Rumsfeld
- Colin Powell

Why It Matters Today

The terrorist attacks of September 11, 2001, continue to affect American life and U.S. foreign policy. Use CNNfyi.com or other **current events** sources to learn about the latest issues and events stemming from this national tragedy.

As seen from New York Harbor, smoke, ash, and debris obscure downtown Manhattan after the terrorist attacks.

The Story Continues

On Tuesday morning, September 11, 2001, it was business as usual in the downtown financial district of New York City. In the World Trade Center complex, an estimated 10,000 employees were starting their workday. Most of them were within the Twin Towers that dominated the Manhattan skyline. On Fifth Avenue a group of pedestrians noticed a large airplane pass overhead. "We all thought it would be unusual for a plane to be flying so low over the city," recalled one man. Moments later they witnessed a terrible disaster unfold.

The Attack

At 8:48 A.M., an American Airlines passenger jet crashed into the north tower of the **World Trade Center**. The impact was devastating, as though a bomb had struck the 110-story building. Stunned men and women began evacuating the building as emergency crews rushed to the scene. Then at 9:03 A.M. a second plane slammed into the south tower and exploded.

Many Americans saw the second crash broadcast live on television and realized that this was not a tragic accident but a deliberate attack. It was also soon clear that New York was not the terrorists' only target. At approximately 9:40 A.M. a third plane hit the west side of the **Pentagon**. Located just outside Washington, D.C., the Pentagon is the headquarters of the U.S. military. The impact of the crash caused massive damage and started fires deep within the huge five-sided building.

At the World Trade Center complex, hundreds of rescue workers struggled to aid victims and firefighters tried to control the raging fires. Then, further disaster struck. Just before 10:00 A.M. the south tower suddenly collapsed, followed half an hour later by the fall of the north tower. The collapse of the massive buildings killed or trapped thousands of people still inside or near the towers, including hundreds of firefighters, police officers, and other rescuers.

A fourth plane was also hijacked and still in the air over southern Pennsylvania. Passengers aboard the plane made cell phone calls indicating that they had learned of the other attacks and decided to stop the terrorists on board from hitting their next target. Flight 93 crashed southeast of Pittsburgh at 10:10, between the times the World Trade Center's Twin Towers collapsed.

In downtown New York City, clouds of smoke, dust, and ash drifted through the streets. Meanwhile, emergency teams battling fires in the Pentagon were unable to search for survivors. All 265 passengers and crew aboard the four hijacked flights had been killed. Americans everywhere were shocked, wondering what was to come next.

✔ **Reading Check: Sequencing** In what order did the events on the morning of September 11, 2001, take place?

Firefighters raise an American flag over the rubble of the World Trade Center towers.

The Nation Responds

Government officials raced to increase rescue efforts and placed the U.S. military on full alert. The Federal Aviation Administration temporarily grounded air traffic nationwide and closed airports. Key government centers, such as the White House and the Capitol, were evacuated.

Firefighters and other rescue workers from across the nation came to New York. There they joined state and city emergency personnel searching the rubble for survivors. Their efforts were blocked by the intense heat from underground fires. New York hospitals mobilized hundreds of doctors but found, tragically, that there were relatively few survivors to treat. New York mayor **Rudolph Giuliani** said of the final death toll, "It will be more than we can bear." More than 5,500 people were killed by the attack on the World Trade Center. This number included more than 300 firefighters and many other rescue workers who were on the scene. At the Pentagon, 189 military and civilian personnel, including those on the hijacked plane, were killed.

GLOBAL CONNECTIONS

The World Reaches Out

The tragic events of September 11, 2001, drew sympathy and support from around the world. Citizens of more than 40 countries were among the missing. The European Union declared September 14 a day of mourning. British prime minister Tony Blair called the terrorist acts "an attack on the free and democratic world everywhere." The French newspaper *Le Monde* ran a headline saying, "WE ARE ALL AMERICANS." Russian and Chinese leaders gave their condolences. Even traditional opponents of the United States, such as Cuba and Iran, expressed their sympathy and regret. U.S. leaders gave thanks for these gestures and worked to form an active coalition against terrorism. **Why might global support be important to the United States?**

BIOGRAPHY

Rudolph Giuliani

(1944–)

As mayor of New York City, Rudy Giuliani played a key role during the early weeks of the crisis. Coordinating relief efforts, consoling victims, and calling for resolve and renewed confidence, he served as an important symbol of strength to the city and the nation as a whole. A national poll conducted following the attacks found a 95 percent approval rating for how the mayor performed his duties. **Why do you think Giuliani's popularity increased after the attacks?**

Congress swiftly approved a $40 billion relief package to fund emergency assistance and national security measures. The government also passed legislation that provided financial support to the families of victims. Democrats and Republicans displayed an unusual degree of cooperation in pushing through these measures.

Political leaders also tried to rally Americans' spirit on the day of the attack. Mayor Giuliani assured fellow New Yorkers, "We're going to rebuild and rebuild stronger." President **George W. Bush**, who had been in Florida visiting an elementary school, was moved to a safer location. From there, he gave a brief speech to the nation and told Americans that "we [the United States] will do whatever is necessary to protect America and Americans." Republican and Democratic members of Congress issued a joint declaration to the country from the Capitol steps. They said that the United States would not be intimidated by terrorism. The members then sang a chorus of "God Bless America."

Perhaps the greatest show of unity came from the American people themselves. Many were inspired to displays of charity and patriotism. Within two days Wal-Mart, the nation's largest retail chain, had sold its entire stock of half a million American flags. Charitable groups across the country moved swiftly to raise funds for relief efforts. Thousands of people went to Red Cross centers to donate blood.

People also came together in public to heal their wounds and show their strength. When professional sports leagues resumed their schedules, stadiums were filled with patriotic tributes and fans waving flags. Actor James Earl Jones drew cheers as he opened a mass prayer service held in New York City's Yankee Stadium.

> **"Our spirit is unbroken. In fact, it is stronger than ever. Today we reaffirm our faith in the essential dignity of every individual. What we share as Americans and as human beings is far greater than what divides us."**
>
> —James Earl Jones, prayer service, September 23, 2001

Analyzing Primary Sources

Drawing Inferences and Conclusions What do you think James Earl Jones means when he says what Americans share is greater than what divides them?

Religious leaders representing many faiths led prayers for the victims and called for unity as a nation. The Boys and Girls Choir of Harlem sang a stirring version of "We Shall Overcome."

✔ **Reading Check: Summarizing** In what ways did Americans first respond to the terrorist attacks?

The Investigation

Immediately after the attacks, the largest criminal investigation in U.S. history began. Within 48 hours the Federal Bureau of Investigation (FBI) placed more than 4,000 special agents on the case. The FBI soon released the names of 19 suspected hijackers from several nations in the Middle East. Investigators gathered evidence suggesting that each group of hijackers included trained pilots. Some of these men had been living and training in the United States for months. Even more crucial was the identity of those who had planned these acts of terror.

A prime suspect surfaced almost immediately—Osama bin Laden. This wealthy Saudi Arabian exile was already wanted for his suspected role in earlier terrorist attacks against U.S. forces overseas. A supporter of an extreme form of Islamic fundamentalism, bin Laden had publicly called for attacks on the United States. He claimed that the United States had corrupted and oppressed Muslims. Bin Laden's global terrorism network is known as al Qaeda, or "the Base." U.S. officials believe that it is one of the few terrorist groups with the resources and organizational structure to have carried out the attacks.

Experts also agreed that the attacks of September 11 likely involved the cooperation of more than one terrorist group. Investigators from a broad range of federal agencies began a global manhunt with assistance from other nations. Investigators sifted through debris at the crash sites to find physical evidence. They also attempted to track airline, telephone, credit card, and other financial records to trace terrorists' movements. The Bush administration pledged to release conclusive evidence about the attacks as soon as it was possible to do so.

✔ **Reading Check: Analyzing Information** What early conclusions did investigators draw about who carried out the attacks, and how did they investigate them?

Historical Document

President Bush's Address to the Nation

On September 20, 2001, President George W. Bush addressed the joint houses of Congress and the American people. The following is an excerpt from his speech.

Tonight we are a country awakened to danger and called to defend freedom. Our grief has turned to anger, and anger to resolution. . . .

Every nation, in every region, now has a decision to make. Either you are with us, or you are with the terrorists. From this day forward, any nation that continues to harbor or support terrorism will be regarded by the United States as a hostile regime. . . .

Great harm has been done to us. We have suffered great loss. And in our grief and anger we have found our mission and our moment. Freedom and fear are at war. The advance of human freedom . . . now depends on us. . . . We will not tire, . . . and we will not fail.

Analyzing Primary Sources

1. What did President Bush call on other nations to do?
2. How did the president say the United States would react to terrorist acts?

The Economic Impact

The terrorist strikes on the World Trade Center also had a high cost in economic terms. The costs related to the immediate physical damage were estimated at $25 billion. In addition, the New York Stock Exchange (NYSE) had to shut down operations for four days, the longest period of time since it closed at the beginning of World War I in 1914. When the NYSE reopened, it had one of the worst weeks in its history.

One area of particular concern was the airline industry. Major airlines were forced to shut down operations for days and faced greatly increased security expenses. In addition, many people were reluctant to fly. Major airlines took heavy financial losses and laid off thousands of workers. Tourism declined severely around the nation, and companies relying on supplies shipped by air continued to have shortages. The president and Congress rushed to pass a $15 billion bail-out package to help keep the nation's airlines operating.

One of the most difficult economic problems for the government to address was falling consumer confidence. Many Americans had been concerned about the economy before the terrorist attacks. The events of September 11 raised feelings of uncertainty and made many Americans believe the country was headed for a recession. Government officials responded by emphasizing that the long-term health of the economy was strong, even if difficult times lay ahead.

✔ **Reading Check: Finding the Main Idea** What immediate effects did the terrorist attacks have on the U.S. economy?

Interpreting the Visual Record

The stock market *Concerns about a potential war and poor economic indicators caused prices on the NASDAQ stock exchange to fall dramatically after the market reopened following the terrorist attacks. European and Asian stock markets also suffered heavy losses.* ***How does this photograph reflect that decline?***

A Call to Action

In a national address on September 20, President George W. Bush called the attacks on the World Trade Center and the Pentagon "an act of war." He promised that the United States would bring those responsible to justice and wage war on terrorism itself. President Bush emphasized that the efforts of the United States would be aimed not only against terrorist organizations but also against national governments that supported and protected terrorists.

In his speech the president singled out one government—the ruling Taliban of Afghanistan—as a key sponsor of terror. The Taliban emerged in the mid-1990s as a splinter group of fundamentalist Muslims. Many members had fought against the Soviets during their occupation of Afghanistan. The Taliban's leaders had developed ties to Osama bin Laden, whom they later sheltered. Bush demanded that the Taliban turn Osama bin Laden over to the U.S. government.

The campaign against terrorism involved defensive and offensive measures. President Bush appointed Pennsylvania governor **Tom Ridge** to head the Office of Homeland Security, a new cabinet-level position. This office was created to coordinate the domestic national security efforts of various government agencies. Key goals included improving airport security and protecting vital systems such as transportation and power networks from attack. Political leaders such as U.S. Attorney General John Ashcroft also called for expanded law-enforcement powers to combat terrorism. This led to debate over how best to protect Americans' civil liberties while increasing domestic security.

Administration officials, including Secretary of Defense **Donald Rumsfeld**, agreed that locating and striking at terrorists outside the United States would be a lengthy and difficult task.

The Bush administration sought to fight terrorism using economic, diplomatic, and military means. The president froze the assets of individuals, groups, and companies with suspected terrorist ties. Secretary of State **Colin Powell** led U.S. efforts to build an international coalition against terrorism and to isolate the Taliban regime.

The United States also began mobilizing military forces. Aircraft carrier groups and ground troops were assembled in preparation for possible attacks on terrorist targets. On October 7, the United States and Great Britain began air strikes against Afghanistan. The strikes targeted al Qaeda and Taliban training camps, air-defense systems, and airfields, as well as Kabul, the country's capital. President Bush explained that the Taliban regime had been warned to meet American demands to surrender Osama bin Laden.

This mother and her daughter joined many Americans who attended an interfaith memorial service for the victims of the September 11 attacks.

Meanwhile, as the military action continued, Americans and the military remained on alert for other possible terrorist actions. Several letters containing dried anthrax spores were sent to locations in Florida, New York City, and Washington, D.C., including Senator Tom Daschle's office. Some who handled these letters, including postal workers, became infected and died. Anthrax is a potentially deadly disease caused by spore-form bacterium. It was used in World War I as a means of biological warfare.

As U.S. leaders responded to the attacks, it was evident that a new era in global relations had begun. The events of September 11 had exposed both the vulnerability and the strength of the United States. Americans faced the uncertain future with hope and determination.

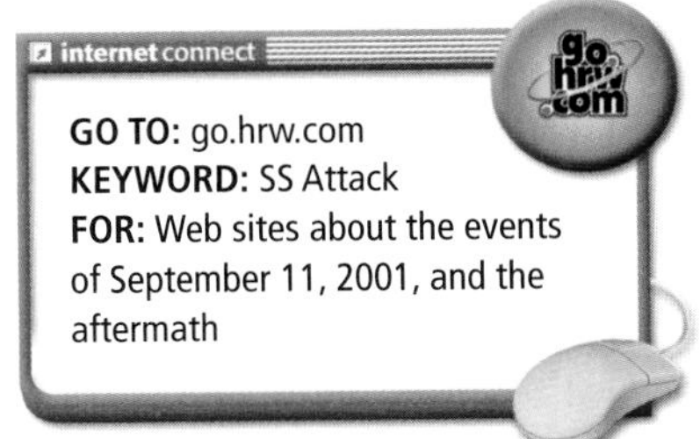

✔ **Reading Check: Summarizing** What early steps did U.S. leaders take to respond to the terrorist attacks on the United States?

Section 5 Review

go.hrw.com **Homework Practice Online**
keyword: SC3 HP31

1. **Identify** and explain:
   - World Trade Center
   - Pentagon
   - Rudolph Giuliani
   - George W. Bush
   - Tom Ridge
   - Donald Rumsfeld
   - Colin Powell

2. **Analyzing Information** Copy the graphic organizer below. Use it to explain some of the ways in which the government responded to protect Americans and bring terrorists to justice.

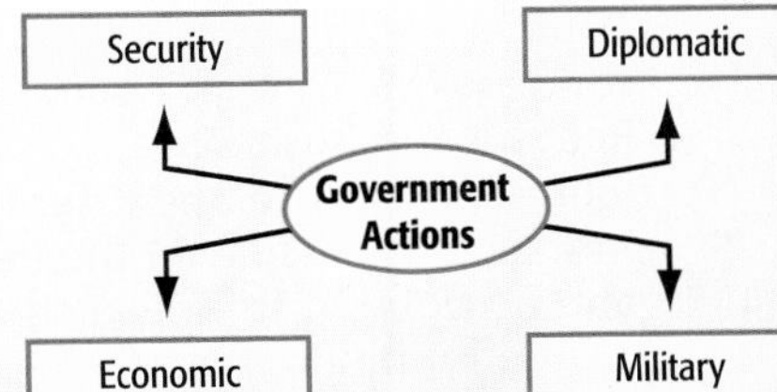

3. **Finding the Main Idea**
   a. Whom did investigators suspect of carrying out the terrorist attacks of September 11, 2001, and how did they pursue the investigation?
   b. How did the attacks affect the economy?

4. **Writing and Critical Thinking**
   Evaluating Imagine that you are first learning of the attacks on September 11, 2001, and want to help however you can. Write a paragraph describing possible actions you could take to assist those in need.
   Consider the following:
   - the efforts of relief agencies to help victims
   - the need for national unity
   - the importance of tolerance

Chapter 31 Review

The Chapter at a Glance

Examine the visual summary of the chapter below. Then write a five-question multiple-choice quiz that you can give to a classmate.

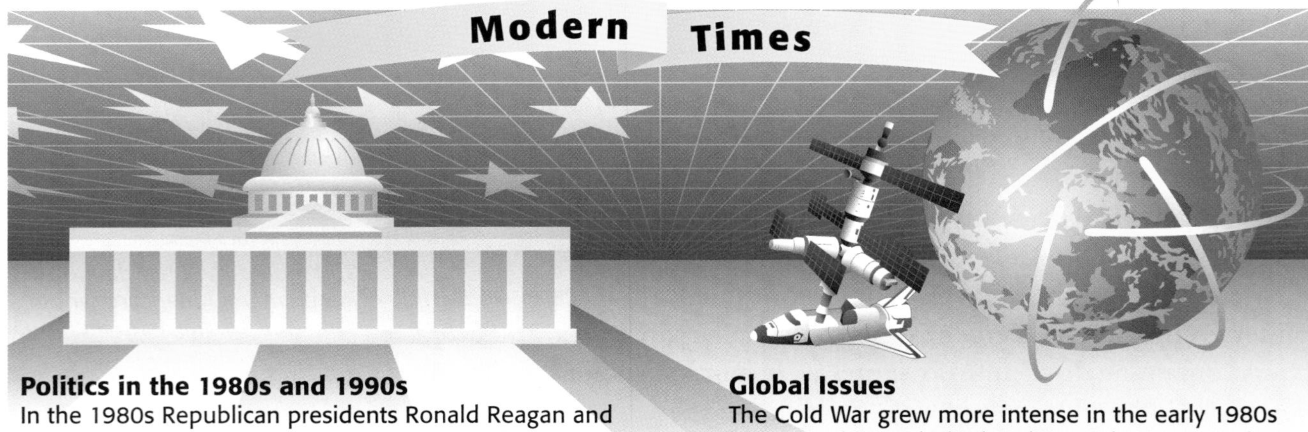

Politics in the 1980s and 1990s
In the 1980s Republican presidents Ronald Reagan and George Bush called for tax cuts and increased military spending. Democrat Bill Clinton served two terms in the 1990s. During his administration the government passed a balanced budget and the U.S. economy grew significantly. Republican George W. Bush won a close election in 2000.

Global Issues
The Cold War grew more intense in the early 1980s before ending with the breakup of the Soviet Union. In 1991 the United States and its allies were victorious in the Persian Gulf War. Free trade and use of the Internet expanded around the world.

Identifying People and Ideas

Use the following terms or people in historically significant sentences.

1. supply-side economics
2. Iran-Contra affair
3. Mikhail Gorbachev
4. War on Drugs
5. Commonwealth of Independent States
6. Saddam Hussein
7. Contract with America
8. terrorism
9. George W. Bush
10. Information Revolution

Understanding Main Ideas

Section 1 *(Pages 928–931)*

1. What economic policies did President Reagan support, and what were the results of this approach to the economy?

Section 2 *(Pages 932–935)*

2. What events and trends led to the breakup of the Soviet Union and the end of the Cold War?
3. How did the United States respond to Iraq's invasion of Kuwait, and what were the results?

Section 3 *(Pages 936–939)*

4. What laws and reforms did President Clinton support, and which of these programs or policies were successful?
5. Why were the 2000 congressional and presidential elections unusual?

Section 4 *(Pages 940–943)*

6. How did changes in technology affect Americans' lives in the 1990s?

Section 5 *(Pages 944–949)*

7. How did Americans resond after the terrorist attacks of September 11, 2001?

You Be the Historian—Reviewing Themes

1. **Economics** How did the U.S. economy affect the presidential elections of 1992 and 1996?
2. **Global Relations** What effect did the policies of perestroika and glasnost have on the Cold War?
3. **Science, Technology & Society** How did technologies that were developed or improved during the 1980s and 1990s affect society?

Thinking Critically

1. **Comparing and Contrasting** Compare and contrast U.S. foreign policy under Presidents Reagan and Bush.
2. **Identifying Cause and Effect** What role did female soldiers play in the Persian Gulf War, and how might this have changed some people's opinions about women's roles in the military?
3. **Evaluating** How did the actions of U.S. presidents contribute to the ending of the Cold War?

Social Studies Skills Workshop

Interpreting Political Cartoons

Look at the political cartoon below, which illustrates the effect of oil prices on the United States. Then use the cartoon to help you answer the questions that follow.

1. What is about to happen in the cartoon?
   a. The United States needs to export oil to address the problem of higher oil prices.
   b. Rising oil prices are about to collide with and seriously hurt the U.S. economy.
   c. Rising oil prices are about to cause train fares to increase rapidly.
   d. More Americans are using cars instead of trains for transportation.
2. Based on what you know about the 1990s, what do you think the president might suggest to keep oil prices low?

Analyzing Primary Sources

Read the following quotation by Justice Sandra Day O'Connor, the first woman ever to serve on the Supreme Court, then answer the questions that follow.

> **"Judges are supposed to be objective; they're supposed to study and look at the law and apply the law to the particular case in an objective way, not from any particular point of view. So does being a woman make a difference in what answer is given? I tend to think that probably at the end of the day, a wise old woman and a wise old man are going to reach the same answer."**

3. What point of view does Justice O'Connor express?
   a. Men make better judgments than women do on legal issues.
   b. Women make better judgments than men do on legal issues.
   c. Men and women make the same types of objective judgments on legal issues.
   d. Men and women come to different conclusions on legal issues in most cases.
4. What do you think led Justice O'Connor to make these observations?
5. What information does Justice O'Connor cite to help support her conclusion?
6. Do you agree or disagree with Justice O'Connor's statement? Explain your answer.

Alternative Assessment

Building Your Portfolio

American History

Linking to Community

Use newspapers or other sources at your local library to identify a business in your area that uses the Internet to buy or sell products. Contact a representative of this business and conduct an interview. Find out when the company started its online business and whether it has grown, fallen, or stayed the same during the past year. Write a report based on your interview describing the effect of the Internet on the business.

internet connect

Internet Activity: go.hrw.com
keyword: SC3 CF31

Choose an activity on America Looking to the Future to:

- Write a biography on Ronald Reagan.
- Research the presidency of Bill Clinton.
- Create a brochure on the fall of communism in the Soviet Union.

Connecting to Geography

The World's Energy

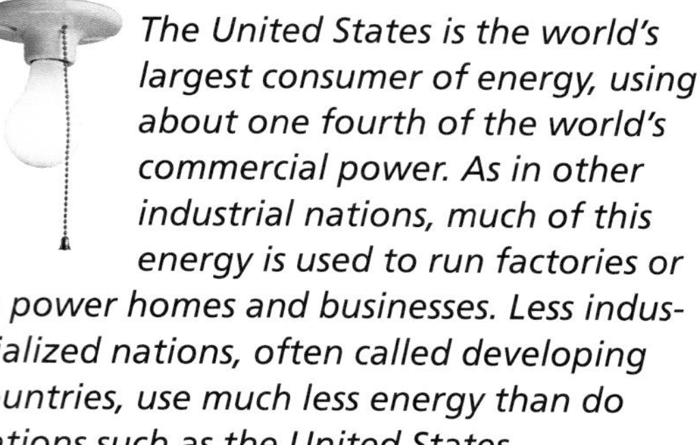

The United States is the world's largest consumer of energy, using about one fourth of the world's commercial power. As in other industrial nations, much of this energy is used to run factories or to power homes and businesses. Less industrialized nations, often called developing countries, use much less energy than do nations such as the United States.

Much of the world's energy resources consist of fossil fuels. Fossil fuels include oil, natural gas, and coal. Fossil fuels were formed from the remains of prehistoric plants and animals. These fuels are limited and cannot be replaced. Some people estimate that the world will eventually run out of these energy sources. Leaders from the United States and other nations are working to protect Earth's limited resources.

Energy Resources

Many wealthy countries, such as the United States and Canada, are among the biggest consumers and producers of energy.

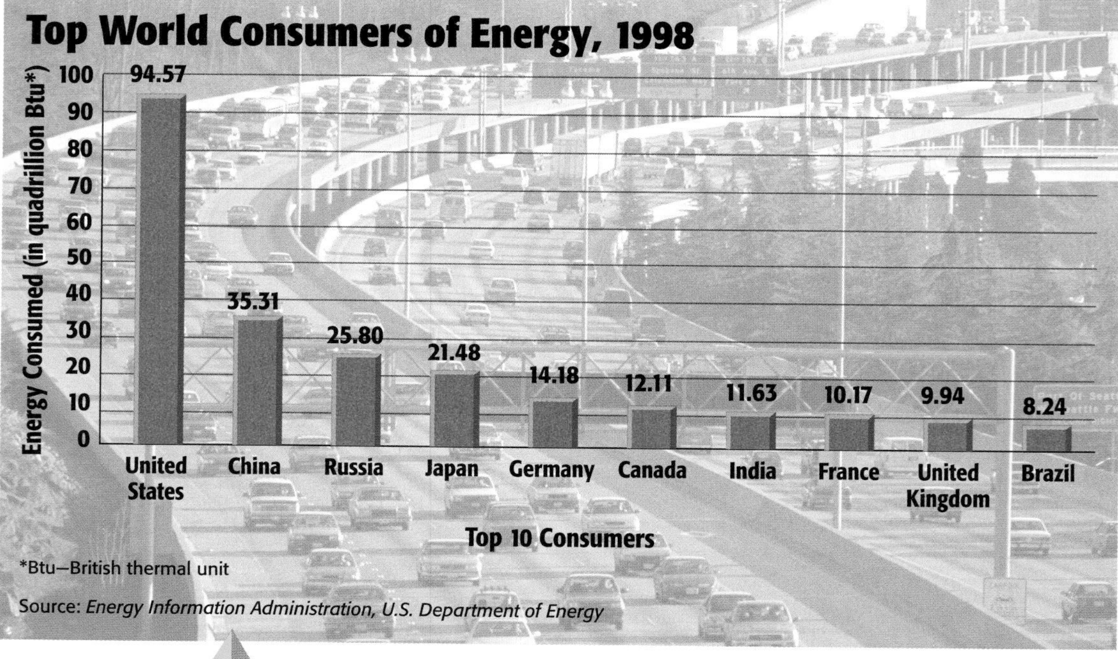

Geography Skills

Interpreting Bar Graphs

1. **The World in Spatial Terms** Use the world map on page A4 to check the location of the countries listed in this bar graph. On which continent is each country located?
2. **Analyzing Information** About how much energy did the United States consume compared to the second-largest energy consumer in 1998?

Leading Energy Producers, 1998

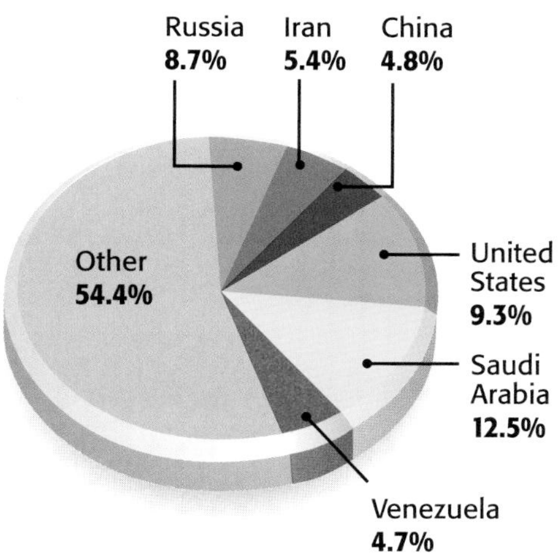

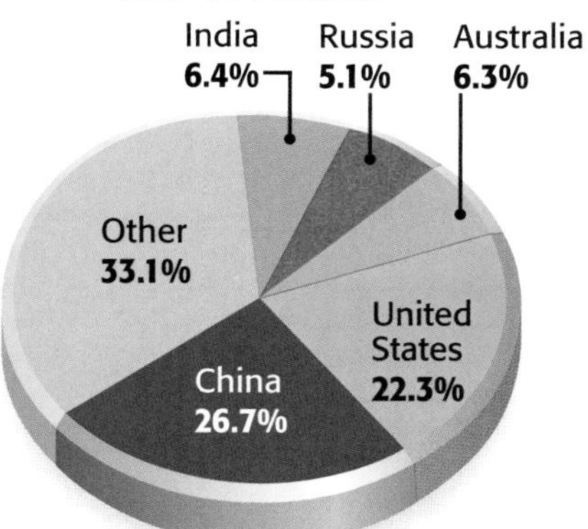

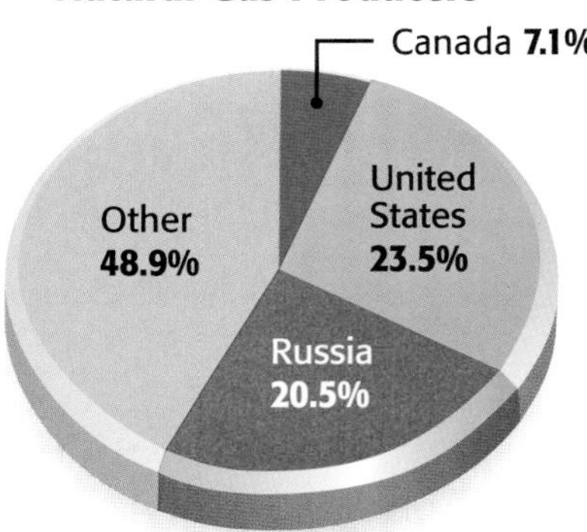

Source: Energy Information Administration
U.S. Department of Energy

Geography Skills

Interpreting Pie Graphs

1. What percentage of the world's coal was produced by China, Russia, and the United States combined?
2. **Environment and Society** The United States produces the smallest percentage of what energy source?
3. **Finding the Main Idea** What nation ranked in the top three in all areas of energy production?

Natural gas, oil, and coal provide most of the world's energy.

History Note 1

These pie graphs show the three major sources of energy—coal, natural gas, and oil—in the world today. These fossil fuels made up about 90 percent of the world's total commercial energy supply at the beginning of the 1990s.

Energy at Home

Most energy used in the United States is produced at home. However, the United States does buy large amounts of oil, as well as certain other fuels, from other countries. Imported fuel is important because U.S. oil consumption is so high.

Energy Sources in the United States

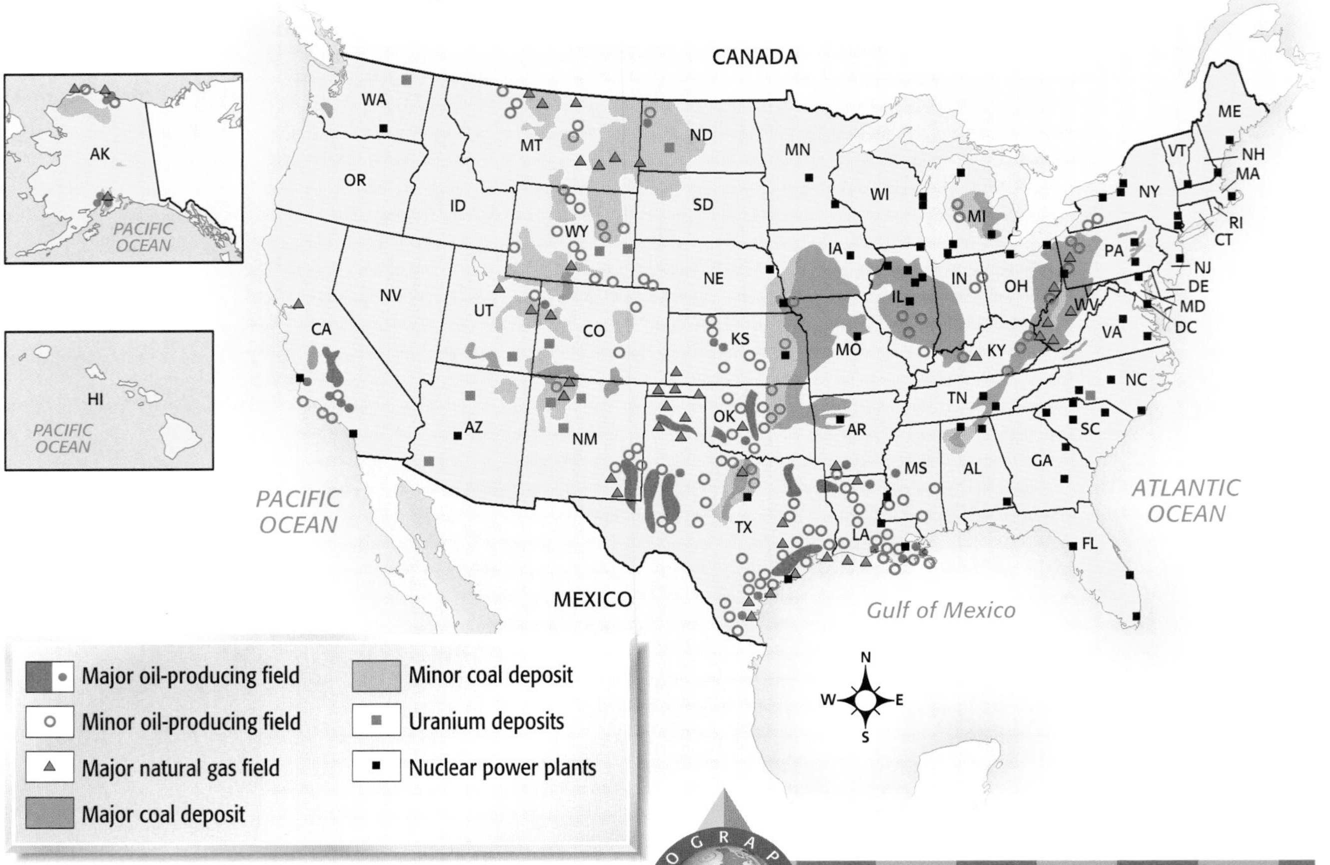

CANADA
MEXICO
PACIFIC OCEAN
ATLANTIC OCEAN
Gulf of Mexico

Major oil-producing field	Minor coal deposit
Minor oil-producing field	Uranium deposits
Major natural gas field	Nuclear power plants
Major coal deposit	

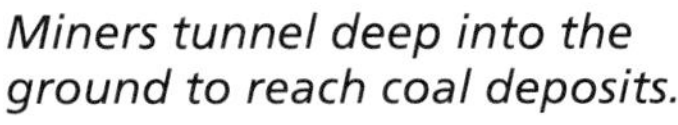

Miners tunnel deep into the ground to reach coal deposits.

Geography Skills
Interpreting Thematic Maps

1. **Physical Systems** What energy sources can be found off the coast in the Gulf of Mexico?
2. **Summarizing** Where are major coal deposits and major oil fields found?

History Note 2

About 80 percent of U.S. energy production in the mid-1990s came from fossil fuels. Nuclear power provided another 10 percent of the country's energy production. Coal has been the largest single source of U.S. energy production since the mid-1970s. Coal is also the country's largest energy-resource export.

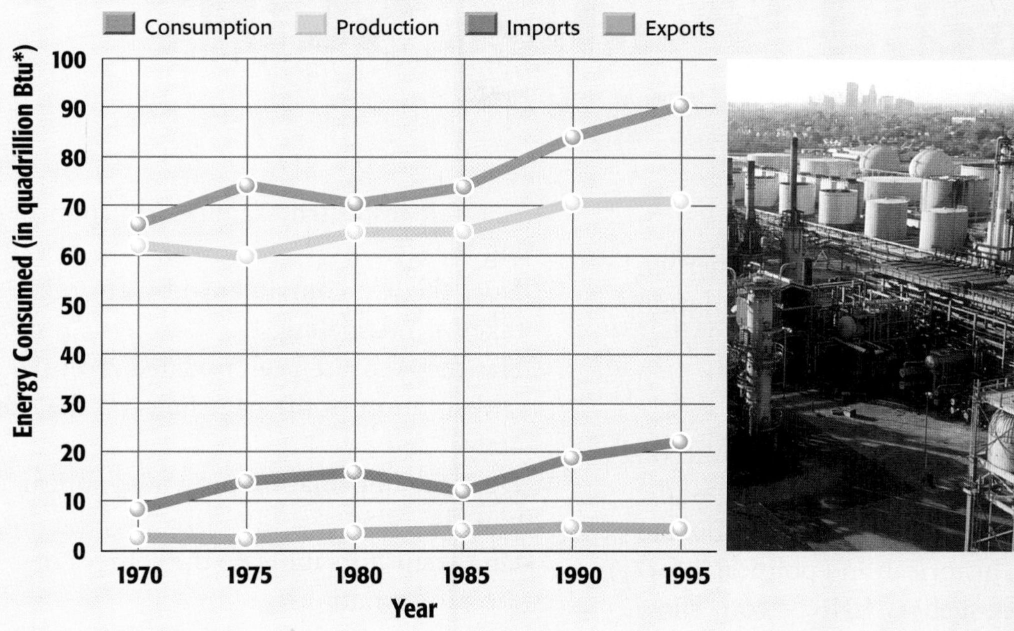

*Btu—British thermal unit

Source: Energy Information Administration, U.S. Department of Energy

Geography **Skills**

Interpreting Line Graphs

1. Use this graph to write a short quiz for a fellow student. Ask him or her to identify the peak years for U.S. energy consumption and production and the amount of energy consumed in those years.
2. **Human Systems** How much more energy did the United States import in 1990 than it exported in that year?
3. **Contrasting** During what five-year period shown on the graph did U.S. energy consumption decrease? During what period did U.S. energy consumption increase by the greatest amount?

History Note 3

Texas and California rank first and second among the 50 states in total energy consumption. However, Alaska consumes more energy per person than any other state. This is due in part to its long and extremely cold winters.

Derricks like this one pump oil from beneath Earth's surface.

Social Studies Skills

WORKSHOP

Using the Internet

There is a wealth of information on the Internet. However, it takes a careful approach to find accurate and useful information.

Finding a Web Site

There are many Web sites that concentrate on specific topics. Government sites such as the Library of Congress and the U.S. Census Bureau provide economic, historical, and political information. Other sites such as CNNfyi.com allow you to access up-to-the-minute news and information on domestic and world events.

If you are not sure which Web site might have the data you want, directories and search engines can help you search the Internet. Many Internet browsers include lists of such search tools. Whatever tool you use, reading its search tips can help you search more efficiently. For example, many search engines allow you to specify words or phrases that must or must not appear in the sites located. Most search tools provide a brief list. Examining these descriptions can help you decide if a particular site is appropriate before you even go there.

Evaluate the Content

Once you have found a Web site, you should determine whether the information it contains is reliable. Ask yourself the following questions:

- Is a well-respected organization sponsoring the site?
- Does the text contain any obvious mistakes or misspellings?
- Has the Web site been updated recently, and are most of the page links on the site active?
- Does the information presented appear biased?
- Do the authors indicate the sources of their information?

Be Careful There is a lot of inappropriate material on the Web, and you should exercise caution when visiting unfamiliar sites. It is also unwise to give out personal information if you are not on a well-respected site.

In addition, providing personal information to strangers that you encounter on the Web can be dangerous. Use common sense and the advice and assistance of parents and teachers when searching for information on the Web.

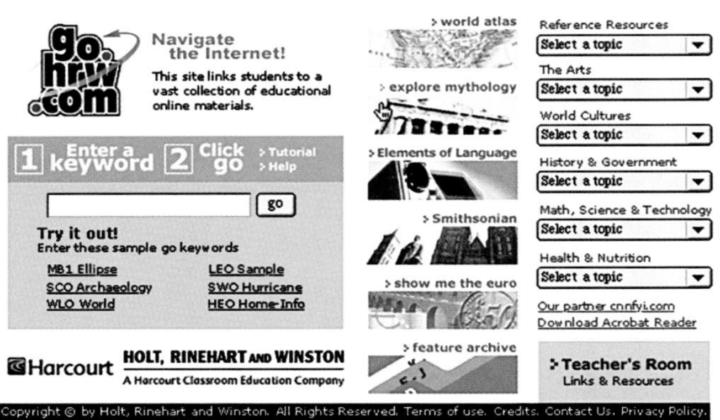

Practicing the Skills

Search the Internet through the HRW Go site to find information about a recent major political event in the domestic or foreign policy of the United States. Use this information to create a brief written or oral report that describes or discusses the event.

History in Action

UNIT 11 SIMULATION

You Solve the Problem . . .

How can you help meet the humanitarian needs of a global society?

Complete the following activity in small cooperative groups. You are the current U.S. representatives on a United Nations human welfare committee. Your committee is responsible for preparing an international plan to help address global humanitarian problems such as health, hunger, and poverty. You will be making a presentation of your plan in the form of a poster that summarizes your committee's findings and ideas.

1. Gather Information Use your textbook and other resources to find information that might influence how you would address worldwide humanitarian needs. Be sure to use what you learned in this unit's Skills Workshop on Using the Internet to help you find information to be used in reaching an effective solution to this problem. You may want to divide different parts of the research among group members.

2. List and Consider Options Based on the information you have gathered, list and consider the options you might recommend for meeting humanitarian needs around the world. Your final solution to the problem may be easier to reach if you consider as many options as possible. Be sure to record your possible options as notes for the preparation of your poster.

3. Consider Advantages and Disadvantages Now consider the advantages and disadvantages of taking each option. Ask yourselves questions like the following: What are the benefits and costs of ending world hunger? Once you have considered the advantages and disadvantages, record them as notes for the preparation of your poster.

4. Choose, Implement, and Evaluate a Solution After considering the advantages and disadvantages, you should plan and create your poster. Be sure to make your proposal very clear. You will need to support your plan to meet global humanitarian needs by including information you gathered and by explaining why you rejected other options. Your presentation needs to be visually appealing. When you are ready, decide who in your group will make which part of the presentation and take your solution to the United Nations General Assembly (the rest of the class). Good luck!

REFERENCE

The Statue of Liberty

Colonial pottery
Colonial Williamsburg Foundation

Advertisement for the Pony Express

Collection of the American Numismatic Society

U.S. coins celebrating Thomas Jefferson's inauguration

Presidents of the United States

The Official Portraits

1 George Washington
Born: 1732 **Died:** 1799
Years in Office: 1789–97
Political Party: None
Home State: Virginia
Vice President: John Adams

2 John Adams
Born: 1735 **Died:** 1826
Years in Office: 1797–1801
Political Party: Federalist
Home State: Massachusetts
Vice President: Thomas Jefferson

3 Thomas Jefferson
Born: 1743 **Died:** 1826
Years in Office: 1801–09
Political Party: Republican*
Home State: Virginia
Vice Presidents: Aaron Burr, George Clinton

4 James Madison
Born: 1751 **Died:** 1836
Years in Office: 1809–17
Political Party: Republican
Home State: Virginia
Vice Presidents: George Clinton, Elbridge Gerry

5 James Monroe
Born: 1758 **Died:** 1831
Years in Office: 1817–25
Political Party: Republican
Home State: Virginia
Vice President: Daniel D. Tompkins

6 John Quincy Adams
Born: 1767 **Died:** 1848
Years in Office: 1825–29
Political Party: Republican
Home State: Massachusetts
Vice President: John C. Calhoun

7 Andrew Jackson
Born: 1767 **Died:** 1845
Years in Office: 1829–37
Political Party: Democratic
Home State: Tennessee
Vice Presidents: John C. Calhoun, Martin Van Buren

* The Republican Party of the third through sixth presidents is not the party of Abraham Lincoln, which was founded in 1854.

8 Martin Van Buren
Born: 1782 **Died:** 1862
Years in Office: 1837–41
Political Party: Democratic
Home State: New York
Vice President: Richard M. Johnson

9 William Henry Harrison
Born: 1773 **Died:** 1841
Years in Office: 1841
Political Party: Whig
Home State: Ohio
Vice President: John Tyler

10 John Tyler
Born: 1790 **Died:** 1862
Years in Office: 1841–45
Political Party: Whig
Home State: Virginia
Vice President: None

11 James K. Polk
Born: 1795 **Died:** 1849
Years in Office: 1845–49
Political Party: Democratic
Home State: Tennessee
Vice President: George M. Dallas

12 Zachary Taylor
Born: 1784 **Died:** 1850
Years in Office: 1849–50
Political Party: Whig
Home State: Louisiana
Vice President: Millard Fillmore

13 Millard Fillmore
Born: 1800 **Died:** 1874
Years in Office: 1850–53
Political Party: Whig
Home State: New York
Vice President: None

14 Franklin Pierce
Born: 1804 **Died:** 1869
Years in Office: 1853–57
Political Party: Democratic
Home State: New Hampshire
Vice President: William R. King

15 James Buchanan
Born: 1791 **Died:** 1868
Years in Office: 1857–61
Political Party: Democratic
Home State: Pennsylvania
Vice President: John C. Breckinridge

16 Abraham Lincoln
Born: 1809 **Died:** 1865
Years in Office: 1861–65
Political Party: Republican
Home State: Illinois
Vice Presidents: Hannibal Hamlin, Andrew Johnson

17 Andrew Johnson
Born: 1808 **Died:** 1875
Years in Office: 1865–69
Political Party: Republican
Home State: Tennessee
Vice President: None

18 Ulysses S. Grant
Born: 1822 **Died:** 1885
Years in Office: 1869–77
Political Party: Republican
Home State: Illinois
Vice Presidents: Schuyler Colfax, Henry Wilson

19 Rutherford B. Hayes
Born: 1822 **Died:** 1893
Years in Office: 1877–81
Political Party: Republican
Home State: Ohio
Vice President: William A. Wheeler

20 James A. Garfield
Born: 1831 **Died:** 1881
Years in Office: 1881
Political Party: Republican
Home State: Ohio
Vice President: Chester A. Arthur

21 Chester A. Arthur
Born: 1829 **Died:** 1886
Years in Office: 1881–85
Political Party: Republican
Home State: New York
Vice President: None

22 Grover Cleveland
Born: 1837 **Died:** 1908
Years in Office: 1885–89
Political Party: Democratic
Home State: New York
Vice President: Thomas A. Hendricks

23 Benjamin Harrison
Born: 1833 **Died:** 1901
Years in Office: 1889–93
Political Party: Republican
Home State: Indiana
Vice President: Levi P. Morton

24 Grover Cleveland
Born: 1837 **Died:** 1908
Years in Office: 1893–97
Political Party: Democratic
Home State: New York
Vice President: Adlai E. Stevenson

25 William McKinley
Born: 1843 **Died:** 1901
Years in Office: 1897–1901
Political Party: Republican
Home State: Ohio
Vice Presidents: Garret A. Hobart, Theodore Roosevelt

26 THEODORE ROOSEVELT
Born: 1858 Died: 1919
Years in Office: 1901–09
Political Party: Republican
Home State: New York
Vice President: Charles W. Fairbanks

27 WILLIAM HOWARD TAFT
Born: 1857 Died: 1930
Years in Office: 1909–13
Political Party: Republican
Home State: Ohio
Vice President: James S. Sherman

28 WOODROW WILSON
Born: 1856 Died: 1924
Years in Office: 1913–21
Political Party: Democratic
Home State: New Jersey
Vice President: Thomas R. Marshall

29 WARREN G. HARDING
Born: 1865 Died: 1923
Years in Office: 1921–23
Political Party: Republican
Home State: Ohio
Vice President: Calvin Coolidge

30 CALVIN COOLIDGE
Born: 1872 Died: 1933
Years in Office: 1923–29
Political Party: Republican
Home State: Massachusetts
Vice President: Charles G. Dawes

31 HERBERT HOOVER
Born: 1874 Died: 1964
Years in Office: 1929–33
Political Party: Republican
Home State: California
Vice President: Charles Curtis

32 FRANKLIN D. ROOSEVELT
Born: 1882 Died: 1945
Years in Office: 1933–45
Political Party: Democratic
Home State: New York
Vice Presidents: John Nance Garner, Henry Wallace, Harry S Truman

33 HARRY S TRUMAN
Born: 1884 Died: 1972
Years in Office: 1945–53
Political Party: Democratic
Home State: Missouri
Vice President: Alben W. Barkley

34 DWIGHT D. EISENHOWER
Born: 1890 Died: 1969
Years in Office: 1953–61
Political Party: Republican
Home State: Kansas
Vice President: Richard M. Nixon

35 John F. Kennedy
Born: 1917 **Died:** 1963
Years in Office: 1961–63
Political Party: Democratic
Home State: Massachusetts
Vice President: Lyndon B. Johnson

36 Lyndon B. Johnson
Born: 1908 **Died:** 1973
Years in Office: 1963–69
Political Party: Democratic
Home State: Texas
Vice President: Hubert H. Humphrey

37 Richard M. Nixon
Born: 1913 **Died:** 1994
Years in Office: 1969–74
Political Party: Republican
Home State: California
Vice Presidents: Spiro T. Agnew, Gerald R. Ford

38 Gerald R. Ford
Born: 1913
Years in Office: 1974–77
Political Party: Republican
Home State: Michigan
Vice President: Nelson A. Rockefeller

39 Jimmy Carter
Born: 1924
Years in Office: 1977–81
Political Party: Democratic
Home State: Georgia
Vice President: Walter F. Mondale

40 Ronald Reagan
Born: 1911
Years in Office: 1981–89
Political Party: Republican
Home State: California
Vice President: George Bush

41 George Bush
Born: 1924
Years in Office: 1989–93
Political Party: Republican
Home State: Texas
Vice President: J. Danforth Quayle

42 Bill Clinton
Born: 1946
Years in Office: 1993–2001
Political Party: Democratic
Home State: Arkansas
Vice President: Albert Gore Jr.

43 George W. Bush
Born: 1946
Years in Office: 2001–
Political Party: Republican
Home State: Texas
Vice President: Richard B. Cheney

The American Flag

The American flag is a symbol of the nation. It is recognized instantly, whether as a big banner waving in the wind or a tiny emblem worn on a lapel. The flag is so important that it is a major theme of the national anthem, "The Star-Spangled Banner." One of the most popular names for the flag is the Stars and Stripes. It is also known as Old Glory.

THE MEANING OF THE FLAG

The American flag has 13 stripes—7 red and 6 white. In the upper-left corner of the flag is the union—50 white five-pointed stars against a blue background.

The 13 stripes stand for the original 13 American states, and the 50 stars represent the states of the nation today. According to the U.S. Department of State, the colors of the flag also are symbolic:

Red stands for courage.

White symbolizes purity.

Blue is the color of vigilance, perseverance, and justice.

DISPLAYING THE FLAG

It is customary not to display the American flag in bad weather. It is also customary for the flag to be displayed outdoors only from sunrise to sunset, except on certain occasions. In a few special places, however, the flag is always flown day and night. When flown at night, the flag should be illuminated.

Near a speaker's platform, the flag should occupy the place of honor at the speaker's right. When carried in a parade with other flags, the American flag should be on the marching right or in front at the center. When flying with the flags of the 50 states, the national flag must be at the center and the highest point. In a group of national flags, all should be of equal size and all should be flown from staffs, or flagpoles, of equal height.

The flag should never touch the ground or the floor. It should not be marked with any insignia, pictures, or words. Nor should it be used in any disrespectful way—as an advertising decoration, for instance. The flag should never be dipped to honor any person or thing.

SALUTING THE FLAG

The United States, like other countries, has a flag code, or rules for displaying and honoring the flag. For example, all those present should stand at attention facing the flag and salute it when it is being raised or lowered or when it is carried past them in a parade or procession. A man wearing a hat should take it off and hold it with his right hand over his heart. All women and hatless men should stand with their right hands over their hearts to show their respect for the flag. The flag should also receive these honors during the playing of the national anthem and the reciting of the Pledge of Allegiance.

THE PLEDGE OF ALLEGIANCE

The Pledge of Allegiance was written in 1892 by Massachusetts magazine (*Youth's Companion*) editor Francis Bellamy. (Congress added the words "under God" in 1954.)

I pledge allegiance to the flag of the United States of America and to the republic for which it stands, one nation under God, indivisible, with liberty and justice for all.

Civilians should say the Pledge of Allegiance with their right hands placed over their hearts. People in the armed forces give the military salute. By saying the Pledge of Allegiance, we promise loyalty ("pledge allegiance") to the United States and its ideals.

"THE STAR-SPANGLED BANNER"

"The Star-Spangled Banner" is the national anthem of the United States. It was written by Francis Scott Key during the War of 1812. While being detained by the British aboard a ship on September 13–14, 1814, Key watched the British bombardment of Fort McHenry at Baltimore. The attack lasted 25 hours. The smoke was so thick that Key could not tell who had won. When the air cleared, Key saw the American flag that was still flying over the fort. "The Star-Spangled Banner" is sung to music written by British composer John Stafford Smith. In 1931 Congress designated "The Star-Spangled Banner" as the national anthem.

I

Oh, say, can you see, by the dawn's early light,
What so proudly we hailed at the twilight's last gleaming,
Whose broad stripes and bright stars through the perilous fight,
O'er the ramparts we watched were so gallantly streaming?
And the rockets' red glare, the bombs bursting in air,
Gave proof through the night that our flag was still there.
Oh, say, does that star-spangled banner yet wave
O'er the land of the free, and the home of the brave?

II

On the shore, dimly seen through the mists of the deep,
Where the foe's haughty host in dread silence reposes,
What is that which the breeze, o'er the towering steep,
As it fitfully blows, half conceals, half discloses?
Now it catches the gleam of the morning's first beam,
In full glory reflected, now shines on the stream.
'Tis the star-spangled banner; oh, long may it wave
O'er the land of the free, and the home of the brave!

III

And where is that band who so vauntingly swore
That the havoc of war and the battle's confusion
A home and a country should leave us no more?
Their blood has washed out their foul footsteps' pollution.
No refuge could save the hireling and slave
From the terror of flight, or the gloom of the grave:
And the star-spangled banner in triumph doth wave
O'er the land of the free, and the home of the brave!

IV

Oh! thus be it ever when freemen shall stand
Between their loved homes and the war's desolation!
Blest with victory and peace, may the heaven-rescued land
Praise the Power that hath made and preserved us a nation!
Then conquer we must, for our cause it is just,
And this be our motto: "In God is our trust!"
And the star-spangled banner in triumph shall wave,
O'er the land of the free, and the home of the brave!

Sheet music to the national anthem

"AMERICA, THE BEAUTIFUL"

One of the most beloved songs celebrating our nation is "America, the Beautiful." Katharine Lee Bates first wrote the lyrics to the song in 1893 after visiting Colorado. The version of the song we know today is set to music by Samuel A. Ward. The first and last stanzas of "America, the Beautiful" are shown below.

O beautiful for spacious skies,
For amber waves of grain,
For purple mountain majesties
Above the fruited plain!
America! America!
God shed his grace on thee
And crown thy good with brotherhood
From sea to shining sea!

• •

O beautiful for patriot dream
That sees beyond the years
Thine alabaster cities gleam
Undimmed by human tears!
America! America!
God shed his grace on thee
And crown thy good with brotherhood
From sea to shining sea!

Facts About the States

STATE	YEAR OF STATEHOOD	2000 POPULATION	REPS. IN CONGRESS	AREA (SQ. MI.)	POPULATION DENSITY (SQ. MI.)	CAPITAL
Alabama	1819	4,461,130	7	51,705	86.3	Montgomery
Alaska	1959	628,933	1	591,004	1.1	Juneau
Arizona	1912	5,140,683	8	114,000	45.1	Phoenix
Arkansas	1836	2,679,733	4	53,187	50.4	Little Rock
California	1850	33,930,798	53	158,706	213.8	Sacramento
Colorado	1876	4,311,882	7	104,247	41.4	Denver
Connecticut	1788	3,409,535	5	5,018	679.5	Hartford
Delaware	1787	785,068	1	2,057	381.7	Dover
District of Columbia	–	572,059	–	69	8,290.7	–
Florida	1845	16,028,890	25	58,664	273.2	Tallahassee
Georgia	1788	8,206,975	13	58,910	139.3	Atlanta
Hawaii	1959	1,216,642	2	6,471	188.0	Honolulu
Idaho	1890	1,297,274	2	83,557	15.5	Boise
Illinois	1818	12,439,042	19	56,400	220.6	Springfield
Indiana	1816	6,090,782	9	36,291	167.8	Indianapolis
Iowa	1846	2,931,923	5	56,275	52.1	Des Moines
Kansas	1861	2,693,824	4	82,277	32.7	Topeka
Kentucky	1792	4,049,431	6	40,395	100.2	Frankfort
Louisiana	1812	4,480,271	7	48,523	92.3	Baton Rouge
Maine	1820	1,277,731	2	33,265	38.4	Augusta
Maryland	1788	5,307,886	8	10,460	507.4	Annapolis
Massachusetts	1788	6,355,568	10	8,284	767.2	Boston
Michigan	1837	9,955,829	15	58,527	170.1	Lansing
Minnesota	1858	4,925,670	8	84,068	58.6	St. Paul
Mississippi	1817	2,852,927	4	47,689	59.8	Jackson
Missouri	1821	5,606,260	9	69,697	80.4	Jefferson City
Montana	1889	905,316	1	147,046	6.2	Helena
Nebraska	1867	1,715,369	3	77,355	22.2	Lincoln
Nevada	1864	2,002,032	3	110,561	18.1	Carson City
New Hampshire	1788	1,238,415	2	9,279	133.5	Concord
New Jersey	1787	8,424,354	13	7,787	1,081.8	Trenton
New Mexico	1912	1,823,821	3	121,593	15.0	Santa Fe
New York	1788	19,004,973	29	49,576	383.4	Albany
North Carolina	1789	8,067,673	13	52,669	153.2	Raleigh
North Dakota	1889	643,756	1	70,655	9.1	Bismarck
Ohio	1803	11,374,540	18	41,222	275.9	Columbus
Oklahoma	1907	3,458,819	5	69,956	49.4	Oklahoma City
Oregon	1859	3,428,543	5	97,073	35.3	Salem
Pennsylvania	1787	12,300,670	19	45,333	271.3	Harrisburg
Rhode Island	1790	1,049,662	2	1,212	866.1	Providence
South Carolina	1788	4,025,061	6	31,113	129.4	Columbia
South Dakota	1889	756,874	1	77,116	9.8	Pierre
Tennessee	1796	5,700,037	9	42,144	135.3	Nashville
Texas	1845	20,903,994	32	266,807	78.3	Austin
Utah	1896	2,236,714	3	84,899	26.3	Salt Lake City
Vermont	1791	609,890	1	9,609	63.5	Montpelier
Virginia	1788	7,100,702	11	40,767	174.2	Richmond
Washington	1889	5,908,684	9	68,192	86.6	Olympia
West Virginia	1863	1,813,077	3	24,181	75.0	Charleston
Wisconsin	1848	5,371,210	8	56,154	95.7	Madison
Wyoming	1890	495,304	1	97,914	5.1	Cheyenne

Important Supreme Court Cases

MARBURY v. MADISON, 1 CRANCH (5 U.S.) 137 (1803)

Significance: **This ruling established the Supreme Court's power of judicial review, by which the Court decides whether laws passed by Congress are constitutional. This decision greatly increased the prestige of the Court and gave the judiciary branch a powerful check against the legislative and executive branches.**

Background: William Marbury and several others were commissioned as judges by Federalist president John Adams during his last days in office. This act angered the new Democratic-Republican president, Thomas Jefferson. Jefferson ordered his secretary of state, James Madison, not to deliver the commissions. Marbury took advantage of a section in the Judiciary Act of 1789 that allowed him to take his case directly to the Supreme Court. He sued Madison, demanding the commission and the judgeship.

Decision: This case was decided on February 24, 1803, by a vote of 5 to 0. Chief Justice John Marshall spoke for the Court, which decided against Marbury. The court ruled that although Marbury's commission had been unfairly withheld, he could not lawfully take his case to the Supreme Court without first trying it in a lower court. Marshall said that the section of the Judiciary Act that Marbury had used was actually unconstitutional, and that the Constitution must take priority over laws passed by Congress.

MCCULLOCH v. MARYLAND, 4 WHEAT. (17 U.S.) 316 (1819)

Significance: **This ruling established that Congress had the constitutional power to charter a national bank. The case also established the principle of national supremacy, which states that the Constitution and other laws of the federal government take priority over state laws. In addition, the ruling reinforced the loose construction interpretation of the Constitution favored by many Federalists.**

Background: In 1816 the federal government set up the Second Bank of the United States to stabilize the economy following the War of 1812. Many states were opposed to the competition provided by the new national bank. Some of these states passed heavy taxes on the Bank. The national bank refused to pay the taxes. This led the state of Maryland to sue James McCulloch, the cashier of the Baltimore, Maryland, branch of the national bank.

Decision: This case was decided on March 6, 1819, by a vote of 7 to 0. Chief Justice John Marshall spoke for the unanimous Court, which ruled that the national bank was constitutional because it helped the federal government carry out other powers granted to it by the Constitution. The Court declared that any attempt by the states to interfere with the duties of the federal government could not be permitted.

GIBBONS v. OGDEN, 9 WHEAT. (22 U.S.) 1 (1824)

Significance: **This ruling was the first case to deal with the clause of the Constitution that allows Congress to regulate interstate and foreign commerce. This case was important because it reinforced both the authority of the federal government over the states and the division of powers between the federal government and the state governments.**

Background: Steamboat operators who wanted to travel on New York waters had to obtain a state license. Thomas Gibbons had a federal license to travel along the coast, but not a state license for New York. He wanted the freedom to compete with state-licensed Aaron Ogden for steam travel between New Jersey and the New York island of Manhattan.

Decision: This case was decided on March 2, 1824, by a vote of 6 to 0. Chief Justice John Marshall spoke for the Court, which ruled in favor of Gibbons. The Court stated that the congressional statute (Gibbons's federal license) took priority over the state statute (Ogden's state-monopoly license). The ruling also defined commerce as more than simply the exchange of goods, broadening it to include the transportation of people and the use of new inventions (such as the steamboat).

WORCESTER v. *GEORGIA*, 6 PET. (31 U.S.) 515 (1832)

Significance: **This ruling made Georgia's removal of the Cherokee illegal. However, Georgia, with President Andrew Jackson's support, defied the Court's decision. By not enforcing the Court's ruling, Jackson violated his constitutional oath as president. As a result, the Cherokee and other American Indian tribes continued to be forced off of lands protected by treaties.**

Background: The state of Georgia wanted to remove Cherokee Indians from lands they held by treaty. Samuel Worcester, a missionary who worked with the Cherokee Nation, was arrested for failing to take an oath of allegiance to the state and to obey a Georgia militia order to leave the Cherokee's lands. Worcester sued, charging that Georgia had no legal authority on Cherokee lands.

Decision: This case was decided on March 3, 1832, by a vote of 5 to 1 in favor of Worcester. Chief Justice John Marshall spoke for the Supreme Court, which ruled that the Cherokee were an independent political community. The Court decided that only the federal government, not the state of Georgia, had authority over legal matters involving the Cherokee people.

SCOTT v. *SANDFORD*, 19 HOW. (60 U.S.) 393 (1857)

Significance: **This ruling denied enslaved African Americans U.S. citizenship and the right to sue in federal court. The decision also invalidated the Missouri Compromise, which had prevented slavery in territories north of the 36° 30' line of latitude. The ruling increased the controversy over the expansion of slavery in new states and territories.**

Background: John Emerson, an army doctor, took his slave Dred Scott with him to live in Illinois and then Wisconsin Territory, both of which had banned slavery. In 1842 the two moved to Missouri, a slave state. Four years later, Scott sued for his freedom according to a Missouri legal principle of "once free, always free." The principle meant that a slave was entitled to freedom if he or she had once lived in a free state or territory.

Decision: This case was decided March 6–7, 1857, by a vote of 7 to 2. Chief Justice Roger B. Taney spoke for the Court, which ruled that slaves did not have the right to sue in federal courts because they were considered property, not citizens. In addition, the Court ruled that Congress did not have the power to abolish slavery in territories because that power was not strictly defined in the Constitution. Furthermore, the Court overturned the once-free, always-free principle.

PLESSY v. *FERGUSON*, 163 U.S. 537 (1896)

Significance: **This case upheld the constitutionality of racial segregation by ruling that separate facilities for different races were legal as long as those facilities were equal to one another. This case provided a legal justification for racial segregation for nearly 60 years until it was overturned by *Brown* v. *Board of Education* in 1954.**

Background: An 1890 Louisiana law required that all railway companies in the state use "separate-but-equal" railcars for white and

African American passengers. A group of citizens in New Orleans banded together to challenge the law and chose Homer Plessy to test the law in 1892. Plessy took a seat in a whites-only coach, and when he refused to move, he was arrested. Plessy eventually sought review by the U.S. Supreme Court, claiming that the Louisiana law violated his Fourteenth Amendment right to equal protection.

Decision: This case was decided on May 18, 1896, by a vote of 7 to 1. Justice Henry Billings Brown spoke for the Court, which upheld the constitutionality of the Louisiana law that segregated railcars. Justice John M. Harlan dissented, arguing that the Constitution should not be interpreted in ways that recognize class or racial distinctions.

LOCHNER v. *NEW YORK*, 198 U.S. 45 (1905)

Significance: **This decision established the Supreme Court's role in overseeing state regulations. For more than 30 years *Lochner* was often used as a precedent in striking down state laws such as minimum-wage laws, child labor laws, and regulations placed on the banking and transportation industries.**

Background: In 1895 the state of New York passed a labor law limiting bakers to working no more than 10 hours per day or 60 hours per week. The purpose of the law was to protect the health of bakers, who worked in hot and damp conditions and breathed in large quantities of flour dust. In 1902 Joseph Lochner, the owner of a small bakery in New York, claimed that the state law violated his Fourteenth Amendment rights by unfairly depriving him of the liberty to make contracts with employees. This case went to the U.S. Supreme Court.

Decision: This case was decided on April 17, 1905, by a vote of 5 to 4 in favor of Lochner. The Supreme Court judged that the Fourteenth Amendment protected the right to sell and buy labor, and that any state law restricting that right was unconstitutional. The Court rejected the argument that the limited workday and workweek were necessary to protect the health of bakery workers.

MULLER v. *OREGON*, 208 U.S. 412 (1908)

Significance: **A landmark for cases involving social reform, this decision established the Court's recognition of social and economic conditions (in this case, women's health) as a factor in making laws.**

Background: In 1903 Oregon passed a law limiting workdays to 10 hours for female workers in laundries and factories. In 1905 Curt Muller's Grand Laundry was found guilty of breaking this law. Muller appealed, claiming that the state law violated his freedom of contract (the Supreme Court had upheld a similar claim that year in *Lochner* v. *New York*). When this case came to the Court, the National Consumers' League hired lawyer Louis D. Brandeis to present Oregon's argument. Brandeis argued that the Court had already defended the state's police power to protect its citizens' health, safety, and welfare.

Decision: This case was decided on February 24, 1908, by a vote of 9 to 0 upholding the Oregon law. The Court agreed that women's well-being was in the state's public interest and that the 10-hour law was a valid way to protect their well-being.

BROWN v. *BOARD OF EDUCATION*, 347 U.S. 483 (1954)

Significance: **This ruling reversed the Supreme Court's earlier position on segregation set by *Plessy* v. *Ferguson* (1896). The decision also inspired Congress and the federal courts to help carry out further civil rights reforms for African Americans.**

Background: Beginning in the 1930s, the National Association for the Advancement of Colored People (NAACP) began using the courts to challenge racial segregation in public education. In 1952 the NAACP took a number of school segregation cases to the Supreme Court. These included the Brown family's suit against the school board of Topeka, Kansas, over its "separate-but-equal" policy.

Decision: This case was decided on May 17, 1954, by a vote of 9 to 0. Chief Justice Earl Warren spoke for the unanimous Court, which ruled that segregation in public education created inequality. The Court held that racial segregation in public schools was by nature unequal, even if the school facilities were equal. The Court noted that such segregation created feelings of inferiority that could not be undone. Therefore, enforced separation of the races in public education is unconstitutional.

GIDEON v. WAINWRIGHT, 372 U.S. 335 (1963)

Significance: **This ruling was one of several key Supreme Court decisions establishing free legal help for those who cannot otherwise afford representation in court.**

Background: Clarence Earl Gideon was accused of robbery in Florida. Gideon could not afford a lawyer for his trial, and the judge refused to supply him with one for free. Gideon tried to defend himself and was found guilty. He eventually appealed to the U.S. Supreme Court, claiming that the lower court's denial of a court-appointed lawyer violated his Sixth and Fourteenth Amendment rights.

Decision: This case was decided on March 18, 1963, by a vote of 9 to 0 in favor of Gideon. The Court agreed that the Sixth Amendment (which protects a citizen's right to have a lawyer for his or her defense) applied to the states because it fell under the due process clause of the Fourteenth Amendment. Thus, the states are required to provide legal aid to those defendants in criminal cases who cannot afford to pay for legal representation.

MIRANDA v. ARIZONA, 384 U.S. 436 (1966)

Significance: **This decision ruled that an accused person's Fifth Amendment rights begin at the time of arrest. The ruling caused controversy because it made questioning suspects and collecting evidence more difficult for law enforcement officers.**

Background: In 1963 Ernesto Miranda was arrested in Arizona for a kidnapping. Miranda signed a confession and was later found guilty of the crime. The arresting police officers, however, admitted that they had not told Miranda of his right to talk with an attorney before his confession. Miranda appealed his conviction on the grounds that by not informing him of his legal rights the police had violated his Fifth Amendment right against self-incrimination.

Decision: This case was decided on June 13, 1966, by a vote of 5 to 4. Chief Justice Earl Warren spoke for the Court, which ruled in Miranda's favor. The Court decided that an accused person must be given four warnings after being taken into police custody: (1) the suspect has the right to remain silent, (2) anything the suspect says can and will be used against him or her, (3) the suspect has the right to consult with an attorney and to have an attorney present during questioning, and (4) if the suspect cannot afford a lawyer, one will be provided before questioning begins.

REED v. REED, 404 U.S. 71 (1971)

Significance: **This ruling was the first in a century of Fourteenth Amendment decisions to say that gender discrimination violated the equal protection clause. This case was later used to strike down other statutes that discriminated against women.**

Background: Cecil and Sally Reed were separated. When their son died without a will, the law gave preference to Cecil to be appointed the administrator of the son's estate. Sally sued Cecil for the right to administer the estate, challenging the gender preference in the law.

Decision: This case was decided on November 22, 1971, by a vote of 7 to 0. Chief Justice Warren Burger spoke for the unanimous Supreme Court. Although the Court had upheld laws based on gender preference in the past, in this case it reversed its position. The Court declared that gender discrimination violated the equal protection clause of the Fourteenth Amendment and therefore could not be the basis for a law.

Gazetteer

Africa Second-largest continent. Lies in both the Northern and the Southern Hemispheres. **A10**

Alabama (AL) State in the southern United States. Admitted as a state in 1819. Capital: Montgomery. (33°N 87°W) **A1**

Alaska (AK) U.S. state in northwestern North America. Purchased from Russia in 1867. Organized as a territory in 1912. Admitted as a state in 1959. Capital: Juneau. (64°N 150°W) **A1**

Albany Capital of New York State. (42°N 74°W) **A1**

Alsace-Lorraine Region between Belgium, France, Germany, and Switzerland. **675**

Andes Mountain range that extends along almost the entire western coast of South America. **A7**

Antarctica Continent that surrounds the South Pole. **A4**

Appalachian Mountains Mountain system in eastern North America that extends from Canada to central Alabama. **A2**

Arctic Ocean Ocean north of the Arctic Circle. **A4**

Argentina Republic located in the south-central and southern part of South America. Capital: Buenos Aires. (34°S 64°W) **A7**

Arizona (AZ) State in the southwestern United States. Organized as a territory in 1863. Admitted as a state in 1912. Capital: Phoenix. (34°N 113°W). **A1**

Arkansas (AR) State in the south-central United States. Admitted as a state in 1836. Capital: Little Rock. (35°N 93°W) **A1**

Asia Largest continent. Occupies the same landmass as Europe. **A9**

Atlanta Capital of Georgia. (33°N 84°W) **A1**

Atlantic Ocean Body of water separating North and South America from Europe and Africa. **A4**

Austin Capital of Texas. (30°N 98°W) **A1**

Australia Island, continent, and country located between the Indian and the Pacific Oceans. Capital: Canberra. (25°S 135°E) **A11**

Austria Republic in central Europe. Capital: Vienna. (48°N 16°E) **A8**

Austria-Hungary Monarchy in central Europe from 1867 to 1919. Consisted of Austria, Bohemia, Hungary, Monrovia, and parts of Poland, Romania, and the former Yugoslavia. **675**

Bahamas Country in the Atlantic Ocean consisting of hundreds of islands. Capital: Nassau. **A6**

Balkans Region that occupies the Balkan Peninsula; includes Albania, Bosnia and Herzegovina, Bulgaria, Croatia, Greece, Macedonia, Romania, Slovenia, Yugoslavia, and northwestern Turkey. **A8**

Baltic Sea Arm of the Atlantic Ocean in northern Europe. **A8**

Baltimore Maryland city northeast of Washington, D.C., on the Chesapeake Bay. (39°N 76°W) **A1**

Bataan Peninsula Peninsula in the western Philippines. (14°N 120°E) **791**

Belgium Kingdom in northwestern Europe. Capital: Brussels. (51°N 13°E) **A8**

Black Sea Sea between Europe and Asia. **A8**

Bosnia and Herzegovina Country in southeastern Europe annexed to Austria-Hungary in 1908; after World War I became part of the former Yugoslavia; declared independence in 1992. Capital: Sarajevo. (44°N 17°E) **A8**

Boston Capital of Massachusetts. (42°N 71°W) **A1**

Brazil Republic in eastern South America. Capital: Brasília. (9°S 53°W) **A7**

Bulgaria Republic in southeastern Europe. Capital: Sofia. (42°N 23°E) **A8**

California (CA) State in the western United States. Admitted as a state in 1850. Capital: Sacramento. (38°N 121°W) **A1**

Cambodia Republic in southeastern Asia. Capital: Phnom Penh. (11°N 105°E) **A9**

Canada Country in northern North America. Capital: Ottawa. (50°N 100°W) **A6**

Cape of Good Hope Southern tip of Africa. **A10**

Caribbean Sea Arm of the Atlantic Ocean between North and South America. **A4**

Central America The southern portion of North America, beginning south of Mexico. **A6**

Charleston Port city in southeastern South Carolina. Originally called Charles Town. (33°N 80°W) **A1**

Chesapeake Bay Inlet of the Atlantic Ocean in Virginia and Maryland. **67**

Chicago City in northeastern Illinois on Lake Michigan. Major port and large U.S. city. (42°N 88°W) **A1**

China Country in central and eastern Asia with the world's largest population. Capital: Beijing. (Official name: People's Republic of China) A9

Colombia Republic in northwestern South America. Capital: Bogotá. (3°N 72°W) **A7**

Colorado (CO) State in the west-central United States. Admitted as a state in 1876. Capital: Denver. (39°N 107°W) **A1**

Connecticut (CT) State in the northeastern United States. One of the original thirteen colonies. Admitted as a state in 1788. Capital: Hartford. (41°N 73°W) **A1**

Croatia Country in southeastern Europe; part of the former Yugoslavia until 1991. Capital: Zagreb. (45°N 15°E) **A8**

Cuba Country north of the Caribbean about 90 miles south of Florida. Capital: Havana. (22°N 79°W) **A6**

Czechoslovakia Former republic in central Europe made up of present-day Czech Republic and Slovakia. **821**

Czech Republic Country in central Europe. Capital: Prague. (50°N 14°E) **A8**

Dallas City in northeastern Texas. (32°N 96°W) **A1**

Delaware (DE) State in the eastern United States. One of the original thirteen colonies. Capital: Dover. (38°N 75°W) **A1**

Denmark Kingdom in northwestern Europe. Capital: Copenhagen. (56°N 10°E) **A8**

District of Columbia Federal district between Maryland and Virginia where the capital of the United States is located. (39°N 77°W) **A1**

Dominican Republic Country in the Caribbean Sea. Located on the eastern part of the island of Hispaniola. Capital: Santo Domingo. (19°N 70°W) **A6**

Egypt Country in northeastern Africa on the Mediterranean Sea. Capital: Cairo. (27°N 27°E) **A10**

El Paso City in western Texas. (32°N 106°W) **A1**

El Salvador Republic in Central America. Capital: San Salvador. (14°N 89°W) **A6**

England Country of the United Kingdom that makes up most of the southern part of the island of Great Britain. Capital: London. (51°N 1°W) **A8**

Estonia Country in northern Europe on the Baltic Sea. Capital: Tallinn. (55°N 23°F) **A8**

Ethiopia Country in eastern Africa. Capital: Addis Ababa. (7°N 38°E) **A10**

Europe Continent occupying the same landmass as Asia. **A8**

Finland Country in northeastern Europe. Capital: Helsinki. (62°N 26°E) **A8**

Florida (FL) State in the southeastern United States. Organized as a territory in 1822. Admitted as a state in 1845. Capital: Tallahassee. (30°N 84°W) **A1**

France Country in western Europe. Capital: Paris. (46°N 1°E) **A8**

Georgia (GA) State in the southeastern United States. Admitted as a state in 1788. One of the original thirteen colonies. Capital: Atlanta. (32°N 84°W) **A1**

Germany Country in central Europe. Capital: Berlin. (51°N 8°E) **A8**

Gettysburg Town in southern Pennsylvania. (40°N 77°W) **511**

Grand Canyon Enormous gorge in northwest Arizona. **A2**

Great Basin Region including Nevada and parts of California, Idaho, Oregon, Utah, and Wyoming that was home to some American Indian nations. **11**

Great Lakes Chain of lakes located in central North America that extends across the U.S.-Canada border. Includes Lake Superior, Lake Michigan, Lake Huron, Lake Erie, and Lake Ontario. **A2**

Great Plains Region of central North America that lies between the Mississippi River and the Rocky Mountains, stretching north into Canada and south into Texas. **A2**

Great Salt Lake Salty lake in northern Utah. **A2**

Greece Country in southeastern European on the Balkan Peninsula that includes many surrounding islands. Capital: Athens. (39°N 21°E) **A8**

Grenada Country in the Caribbean Sea made up of the island of Grenada and the southern Grenadines. Capital: St. George's. (12°N 61°W) **A6**

Guam Pacific island that became a U.S. territory after the Spanish-American War. Capital: Agana. (14°N 143°E) **A11**

Guatemala Republic in Central America. Capital: Guatemala City. (15°N 91°W) **A6**

Gulf of Mexico Gulf on the southeastern coast of North America; bordered by the United States, Mexico, and Cuba. **A6**

Haiti Country in the West Indies. Located on the western part of the island of Hispaniola. Capital: Port-au-Prince. (19°N 72°W) **A6**

Hawaii (HI) U.S. state in the central Pacific Ocean that is made up of the Hawaiian Islands. Organized as a territory in 1900. Admitted as a state in 1959. Capital: Honolulu. (20°N 157°W) **A1**

Hiroshima Japanese city bombed by a U.S. atomic weapon in August 1945. (34°N 132°F) **782**

Hispaniola Island that includes the countries of Haiti and the Dominican Republic. **41**

Honduras Republic in Central America. Capital: Tegucigalpa. (15°N 86°W) **A6**

Houston City in southeastern Texas. (30°N 95°W) **A1**

Hudson Bay Inland sea in east-central Canada. Explored by Henry Hudson in 1610. **49**

Hudson River River flowing from northeastern to southern New York. **A2**

Hungary Republic in central Europe. Capital: Budapest. (47°N 19°E) **A8**

Iceland Island republic located between the Arctic and North Atlantic Oceans. Capital: Reykjavik (65°N 18°W) **A8**

Idaho (ID) State in the northwestern United States. Admitted as a state in 1890. Capital: Boise. (44°N 115°W) **A1**

Illinois (IL) State in the north-central United States. Admitted as a state in 1818. Capital: Springfield. (40°N 90°W) **A1**

India Large republic in southern Asia. Capital: New Delhi. (28°N 77°E) **A9**

Indiana (IN) State in the north-central United States. Admitted as a state in 1816 Capital: Indianapolis. (40°N 86°W) **A1**

Indiana Territory Former territory created from the division of the Northwest Territory in 1800. It included Illinois, Indiana, Wisconsin, much of Michigan, and part of Minnesota. **304**

Indian Ocean Body of water east of Africa, south of Asia, west of Australia, and north of Antarctica. **A4**

Indian Territory Former territory in the south-central United States. Set aside in 1820 as a home for forcibly displaced American Indians. **345**

Iowa (IA) State in the north-central United States. Admitted as a state in 1846. Capital: Des Moines. (42°N 94°W) **A1**

Iran Country in southwestern Asia. Capital: Tehran. (31°N 53°E) **A9**

Iraq Country in southwestern Asia. Capital: Baghdad. (32°N 43°E) **A9**

Ireland Island in the British Isles. Divided into Northern Ireland (Capital: Belfast), which is part of Great Britain, and the independent Republic of Ireland (Capital: Dublin). (54°N 8°W) **A8**

Israel Country in Southwest Asia on the eastern Mediterranean coast. Capital: Jerusalem. (32°N 34°E) **A9**

Isthmus of Panama Thin landmass that links North America to South America and separates the Atlantic and Pacific Oceans. Forms the Republic of Panama. **A6**

Italy Country in southern Europe. Capital: Rome. (44°N 11 °E) **A8**

Jamaica Island-nation in the West Indies. Capital: Kingston. (18°N 78°W) **A6**

James River River in Virginia that flows into Chesapeake Bay. **67**

Jamestown First successful English colony in America. Established in eastern Virginia in 1607. 95

Japan Country in the western Pacific Ocean. Made up of a chain of islands. Capital: Tokyo. (37°N 134°E) **A9**

Jerusalem Capital of Israel. **A9**

Kansas (KS) State in the central United States. Organized as a territory in 1854. Admitted as a state in 1861. Capital: Topeka. (38°N 99°W) **A1**

Kentucky (KY) State in the east-central United States. Admitted as a state in 1792. Capital: Frankfort. (37°N 87°W) **A1**

Kuwait Country on the northeast Arabian Peninsula at the northern end of the Persian Gulf. Capital: Kuwait City. (29°N 48°E) **A9**

Lake Erie One of the Great Lakes, located in the United States and Canada. **A2**

Laos Country in southeastern Asia. Capital: Vientiane. (18°N 102°E) **A9**

Latvia Country in northern Europe on the Baltic Sea. Declared independent of the Soviet Union in 1991. Capital: Riga. (57° N 24°E) **A8**

Lebanon Country at the eastern end of the Mediterranean Sea. Capital: Beirut. (34°N 36°F) **A9**

Liberia Country on the west coast of Africa, founded in 1822 as a colony for freed American slaves. (6°N 10°W) **A10**

Lithuania Country in northern Europe on the Baltic Sea. Declared independence from the Soviet Union in 1990. Capital: Vilnius. (59°N 25°E) **A8**

London Capital of the United Kingdom. Located in England. (51°N 0°W) **A8**

Los Angeles Large city in southern California. (34°N 118°W) **A1**

Louisiana (LA) State in the southeastern United States carved out of the Louisiana Territory. Admitted as a state in 1812. Capital: Baton Rouge. (31°N 92°W) **A1**

Louisiana Territory Organized in 1805, extended from the Mississippi River to the Rocky Mountains and from the Gulf of Mexico to Canada, except for the Orleans Territory. **304**

Maine (ME) State in the northeastern United States. Admitted as a state in 1820. Capital: Augusta. (45°N 70°W) **A1**

Maryland (MD) State in the east-central United States. One of the original thirteen colonies. Admitted as a state in 1788. Capital: Annapolis. (39°N 76°W) **A1**

Massachusetts (MA) State in the northeastern United States. One of the original thirteen colonies. Admitted as a state in 1788. Capital: Boston. (42°N 72°W) **A1**

Mediterranean Sea Large sea bordered by southern Europe, Southwest Asia, and northern Africa. **A8**

Mexico Country in southern North America. Capital: Mexico City. (23°N 104°W) **A6**

Michigan (MI) State in the north-central United States. Admitted as a state in 1837. Capital: Lansing. (46°N 87°W) **A1**

Middle East Vast region made up of countries in south-western Asia and northeastern Africa. **A9**

Minnesota (MN) State in the north-central United States. Admitted as a state in 1858. Capital: St. Paul. (46°N 90°W) **A1**

Mississippi (MS) State in the southeastern United States. Admitted as a state in 1817. Capital: Jackson. (32°N 90°W) **A1**

Mississippi River River that flows from Minnesota south to the Gulf of Mexico. **A3**

Missouri (MO) State in the central United States. Admitted as a state in 1821. Capital: Jefferson City. (38°N 93°W) **A1**

Missouri River River that flows from southern Montana and joins the Mississippi River north of St. Louis, Missouri. **A3**

Montana (MT) State in the northwestern United States. Admitted as a state in 1889. Capital: Helena. (47° N 112° W) **A1**

Moscow Capital of Russia. (61°N 60°E) **A8**

Munich City in southern Germany. (48°N 11°E) **A8**

Nagasaki Second Japanese city bombed by a U.S. atomic weapon in August 1945. (32°N 130°E) **782**

Nebraska (NE) State in the central United States. Admitted as a state in 1867. Capital: Lincoln. (41°N 101°W) **A1**

Netherlands Country in northwestern Europe. Capital: Amsterdam. (52°N 5°E) **A8**

Nevada (NV) State in the western United States. Organized as a territory in 1861. Admitted as a state in 1864. Capital: Carson City. (39°N 117°W) **A1**

New England Northeastern section of the United States. Made up of Connecticut, Maine, Massachusetts, New Hampshire, Rhode Island, and Vermont. **78**

New France Former French territory in North America that included eastern Canada and the Mississippi Valley. **86**

New Hampshire (NH) State in the northeastern United States. One of the original thirteen colonies. Admitted as a state in 1788. Capital: Concord. (44°N 71°W) **A1**

New Jersey (NJ) State in the northeastern United States. One of the original thirteen colonies. Admitted as a state in 1787. Capital: Trenton. (40°N 75°W) **A1**

New Mexico (NM) State in the southwestern United States. Organized as a territory that included Arizona and part of Colorado in 1850. Admitted as a state in 1912. Capital: Santa Fe. (34°N 107°W) **A1**

New Orleans Port city in southeastern Louisiana. (30°N 90°W) **A1**

New Spain Vast area of North America controlled by Spain. It extended from Mexico to California and Florida and included some Caribbean islands and also the Philippines. **44**

New York (NY) State in the northeastern United States. One of the original thirteen colonies. Admitted as a state in 1788. Capital: Albany. (42°N 78°W) A1

New York City Largest city in the United States. (41°N 74°W) A1

Nicaragua Republic in Central America on the Caribbean Sea and the Pacific Ocean. Capital: Managua. (12°N 86°W) **A6**

Nile River River that flows through east and northeast Africa. **A10**

North America Continent in the northern Western Hemisphere. **A6**

North Carolina (NC) State in the southeastern United States. One of the original thirteen colonies. Admitted as a state in 1789. Capital: Raleigh. (35°N 81°W) **A1**

North Dakota (ND) State in the north-central United States. Organized as part of the Dakota Territory in 1861. Admitted as a state in 1889. Capital: Bismarck. (47°N 102°W) **A1**

North Korea Country in eastern Asia. Capital: P'yŏngyang. (40° N 102° W) **A9**

Northwest Territory Region of the north-central United States that extended from the Ohio and Mississippi Rivers to the Great Lakes. Later divided into what are now Illinois, Indiana, Michigan, Ohio, Wisconsin, and part of Minnesota. **189**

Norway Kingdom in northwestern Europe. Capital: Oslo. (62°N 10°E) **A8**

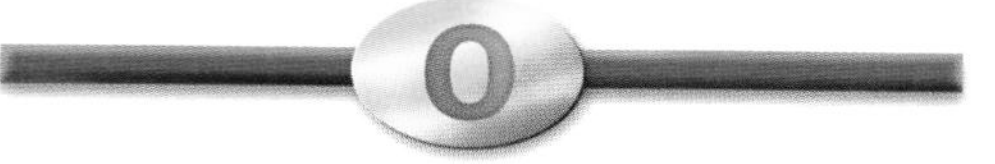

Ohio (OH) State in the north-central United States. Originally part of the Northwest Territory. Admitted as a state in 1803. Capital: Columbus. (40°N 83°W) **A1**

Ohio River River that flows through Pennsylvania, Ohio, Indiana, and Illinois and empties into the Mississippi. **A3**

Oklahoma (OK) State in the south-central United States. Organized as a territory in 1890. Admitted as a state in 1907. Capital: Oklahoma City. (36°N 98°W) **A1**

Oklahoma City Capital of Oklahoma. (35°N 98°W) **A1**

Oregon (OR) State in the northwestern United States. Admitted as a state in 1859. Capital: Salem. (43°N 122°W) **A1**

Pacific Ocean Body of water extending from the Arctic Circle to Antarctica and from western North and South America to Australia, the Malay Archipelago, and East Asia. **A4**

Panama Country in southern Central America that occupies the Isthmus of Panama. Location of the Panama Canal. Capital: Panama City. (8°N 81°W) **A6**

Pennsylvania (PA) State in the eastern United States. One of the original thirteen colonies. Admitted as a state in 1787. Capital: Harrisburg. (41°N 78°W) **A1**

Persian Gulf Arm of the Arabian Sea between the Arabian Peninsula and southwestern Iran in southwestern Asia. **A9**

Peru Country in western South America. Capital: Lima. (10°S 75°W) **A7**

Philadelphia City in southeastern Pennsylvania. Capital of the United States from 1790 to 1800. (40°N 75°W) **A1**

Philippines Country in the western Pacific Ocean. Made up of an archipelago of about 7,100 islands lying approximately 500 miles off the southeast coast of Asia. Capital: Manila. (14°N 125°E) **A9**

Pittsburgh City in southwestern Pennsylvania. (40°N 80°W) **A1**

Plymouth Site in Massachusetts where the Pilgrims first landed in North America in 1620. (42°N 71°W) **78**

Poland Country in central Europe on the Baltic Sea. Capital: Warsaw. (52°N 17°E) **A8**

Portugal Country in southwestern Europe on the western Iberian Peninsula. (38°N 8°W) **A8**

Potomac River River that flows through West Virginia, Virginia, and Maryland and empties into Chesapeake Bay. **A3**

Providence Capital of Rhode Island. (42°N 71°W) **78**

Puerto Rico Island east of Cuba and southeast of Florida. A U.S. territory acquired in the Spanish-American War. Capital: San Juan. (18°N 67°W) **A6**

Rhode Island (RI) State in the northeastern United States. One of the original thirteen colonies. Admitted as a state in 1790. Capital: Providence. (41°N 71°W) **A1**

Richmond Capital of Virginia. Capital of the Confederate States of America during the Civil War. (37°N 77°W) **484**

Rio Grande Spanish for Great River. Forms the border between Texas and Mexico. **340**

Rocky Mountains Mountain range in western North America that extends from Alaska south to Mexico. **A2**

Romania Republic in southeastern Europe. Capital: Bucharest. (46°N 25°E) **A8**

Rome Capital of Italy. (42°N 12°E) **A8**

Russia Vast country that extends from eastern Europe through northwestern Asia. Capital: Moscow. (61°N 60°E) **A9**

Sahara Vast desert in northern Africa. **26**

St. Lawrence River River in southeastern Canada. **A6**

Salt Lake City Capital of Utah. (41°N 112°W) **A1**

Samoa Group of volcanic islands in the southwestern-central Pacific Ocean. Divided into American Samoa and Western Samoa. (14°S 171°W) **A11**

San Diego City in southern California. Located on San Diego Bay, an inlet of the Pacific Ocean near the Mexican border. (33°N 117°W) A1

San Francisco City in western California on a peninsula between the Pacific Ocean and San Francisco Bay. (38°N 122°W) **A1**

Saratoga Site in eastern New York of a key battle of the Revolutionary War. **173**

Saudi Arabia Kingdom on the Arabian Peninsula in southwestern Asia. Capital: Riyadh. (22°N 46°E) **A9**

Scandinavia Region of northern Europe that includes Denmark, Norway, and Sweden. **A8**

Serbia Part of Yugoslavia, located in southeastern Europe. Capital: Belgrade. (45°N 20°E) **A8**

Sierra Nevada Mountain range in eastern California. **A2**

Slovakia Country in central Europe. Capital: Bratislava. (48°N 17°E) **A8**

Slovenia Country in southern Europe. Declared independence from Yugoslavia in 1991. Capital: Ljubljana. (46°N 15°F) **A8**

Somalia Country in eastern Africa. Capital: Mogadishu. (3°N 44°F) **A10**

South Africa Country in southern Africa. Pretoria is the administrative capital, Cape Town is the legislative capital, and Bloemfontein is the judicial capital. (30°S 26°E) **A10**

South America Continent in the southern Western Hemisphere. **A7**

South Carolina (SC) State in the southeastern United States. One of the original thirteen colonies. Admitted as a state in 1788. Capital: Columbia. (34°N 81°W) **A1**

South Dakota (SD) State in the north-central United States. Organized as part of the Dakota Territory in 1861. Admitted as a state in 1889. Capital: Pierre. (44°N 102°W) **A1**

South Korea Country in eastern Asia. Capital: Seoul. (40°N 127°F) **A9**

Spain Country in southwestern Europe that occupies most of the Iberian Peninsula. Includes the Balearic and Canary Islands. Capital: Madrid. (40°N 4°W) **A8**

Strait of Magellan Strait at the southern tip of South America that connects the southern Atlantic Ocean with the southern Pacific Ocean. **40**

Suez Canal International waterway in the Middle East that connects the Red Sea and the Mediterranean Sea. **A9**

Sweden Kingdom in northwestern Europe. Capital: Stockholm. (62°N 15°E) **A8**

Switzerland Country in central Europe. Capital: Bern. (47°N 7°E) **A8**

Syria Country in southwestern Asia on the eastern Mediterranean coast. Capital: Damascus. (35°N 37°E) **A9**

Taiwan Island-nation off the southeastern coast of China. Capital: Taipei. (23°N 121°F) **A9**

Tennessee (TN) State in the southeast-central United States. Admitted as a state in 1796. Capital: Nashville. (36°N 88°W) **A1**

Texas (TX) State in the south-central United States. Independent republic from 1836 to 1845. Admitted as a state in 1845. Capital: Austin. (31°N 101°W) **A1**

Turkey Country in southwestern Asia and southeastern Europe between the Mediterranean and the Black Seas. Capital: Ankara. (38°N 32°W) **A9**

United States of America Country in central North America. Capital: Washington, D.C. (38°N 110°W) **A1**

Utah (UT) State in the western United States. Admitted as a state in 1896. Capital: Salt Lake City. (39°N 112°W) **A1**

Valley Forge Site in southeastern Pennsylvania where General George Washington and his troops spent the harsh winter of 1777-78 during the Revolutionary War. **173**

Venezuela Country in northern South America on the Caribbean Sea. Capital: Caracas. (8°N 65°W) **A7**

Vermont (VT) State in the northeastern United States. Admitted as a state in 1791. Capital: Montpelier. (44°N 73°W) **A1**

Vicksburg City in western Mississippi on the bluffs above the Mississippi River. (32°N 91°W) **592**

Vietnam Country in southeastern Asia. Capital: Hanoi. (18°N 107°E) **A9**

Virginia (VA) State in the eastern United States. One of the original thirteen colonies. Admitted as a state in 1788. Capital: Richmond. (37°N 78°W) **A1**

Washington (WA) State in the northwestern United States. Bounded by British Columbia, Canada, to the north and by the Pacific Ocean to the west. Admitted as a state in 1889. Capital: Olympia. (47°N 121°W) **A1**

Washington, D.C. Capital of the United States. Located on the Potomac River between Virginia and Maryland. (39°N 77°W) **A1**

West Indies Islands between North and South America enclosing the Caribbean Sea. **A6**

West Virginia (WV) State in the east-central United States. Part of Virginia until the area refused to join the Confederacy in 1861. Admitted as a state in 1863. Capital: Charleston. (39°N 81°W) **A1**

Wisconsin (WI) State in the north-central United States. Became part of the Northwest Territory in 1787. Admitted as a state in 1848. Capital: Madison. (44°N 91°W) **A1**

Wyoming (WY) State in the western United States. Admitted as a state in 1890. Capital: Cheyenne. (43°N 108°W) **A1**

Yorktown Town in southeastern Virginia. Site of the last battle of the Revolutionary War. (37°N 76°W) **173**

Yugoslavia Country in southeastern Europe that was formed as the Kingdom of the Serbs, Croats, and Slovenes after the collapse of Austria-Hungary in 1918; renamed Yugoslavia in 1929. Capital: Belgrade. **A8**

Glossary

This Glossary contains terms you need to understand as you study American history. After each key term there is a brief definition or explanation of the meaning of the term as it is used in *Call to Freedom*. The page number refers to the page on which the term is introduced in the textbook.

Phonetic Respelling and Pronunciation Guide

Many of the key terms in this textbook have been respelled to help you pronounce them. The letter combinations used in the respelling throughout the narrative are explained in the following phonetic respelling and pronunciation guide. The guide is adapted from *Webster's Tenth New College Dictionary, Merriam-Webster's New Geographical Dictionary,* and *Merriam-Webster's New Biographical Dictionary.*

MARK	AS IN	RESPELLING	EXAMPLE
a	alphabet	a	*AL-fuh-bet
ā	Asia	ay	AY-zhuh
ä	cart, top	ah	KAHRT, TAHP
e	let, ten	e	LET, TEN
ē	even, leaf	ee	EE-vuhn, LEEF
i	it, tip, British	i	IT, TIP, BRIT-ish
ī	site, buy, Ohio	y	SYT, BY, oh-HY-oh
	iris	eye	EYE-ris
k	card	k	KAHRD
ō	over, rainbow	oh	OH-vuhr, RAYN-boh
u̇	book, wood	ooh	BOOHK, WOOHD
ȯ	all, orchid	aw	AWL, AWR-kid
ȯi	foil, coin	oy	FOYL, KOYN
au̇	out	ow	OWT
ə	cup, butter	uh	KUHP, BUHT-uhr
ü	rule, food	oo	ROOL, FOOD
yü	few	yoo	FYOO
zh	vision	zh	VIZH-uhn

*A syllable printed in small capital letters receives heavier emphasis than the other syllable(s) in a word.

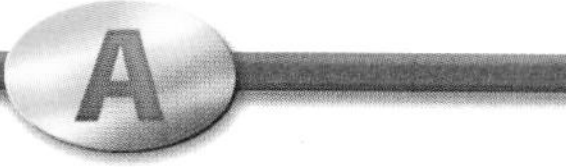

ABC Powers Argentina, Brazil, and Chile. 663

abolition An end to slavery. 407

Adams-Onís Treaty (1819) Agreement in which Spain gave up all of Florida to the United States. 330

Alamo Spanish mission in San Antonio, Texas, that was the site of a famous battle of the Texas Revolution in 1836; the Mexican army's victory resulted in the deaths of all the Texans defending the building. 425

Albany Plan of Union (1754) Plan written by Benjamin Franklin and other colonial delegates that called for the colonies to unite under a common governing body. 128

Alien and Sedition Acts (1798) Laws passed by a Federalist-dominated Congress aimed at protecting the government from treasonous ideas, actions, and people; used against Democratic-Republicans. 290

Allied Powers World War I alliance that included Britain, France, Russia, and later the United States; also the World War II alliance between Britain and France, and later the United States and other countries, that fought against the Axis Powers. 671, 763

amendments Official changes, corrections, or additions to a law or constitution. 210

American Anti-Slavery Society Group founded in 1833 by William Lloyd Garrison and others to work for immediate abolition and racial equality for African Americans. 409

American Civil Liberties Union (ACLU) Organization formed in 1920 to protect civil rights. 701

American Colonization Society Society organized in 1817 that established the colony of Liberia in West Africa as a home for free African Americans. 408

American Expeditionary Force (AEF) U.S. troops that served overseas in World War I. 682

American Federation of Labor (AFL) One of the first large labor unions in the United States; organized in the1880s by Samuel Gompers as an association of individual skilled craft unions. 587

American Indian Movement (AIM) Organization formed in 1968 to fight for the rights of American Indians. 864

Americans with Disabilities Act (ADA) (1990) Law that guarantees people with disabilities equal access to public accommodations, transportation, and employment opportunities. **933**

American System Henry Clay's plan for raising tariffs to pay for internal improvements such as better roads and canals. **334**

amnesty An official pardon issued by the government for an illegal act. **515**

anarchists People who want to abolish all forms of government. **587**

annex To take control of land and incorporate into a country, state, etc. **426**

Antifederalists People who opposed ratification of the Constitution. **206**

Anti-Imperialist League Group of Americans who opposed the creation of an American colonial empire. **650**

apartheid System of laws in South Africa that required racial segregation. **916**

appeasement The act of giving in to an aggressor to preserve peace. **763**

Appomattox Courthouse Virginia town where General Robert E. Lee was forced to surrender, thus ending the Civil War. **503**

apportionment The use of population to determine how many legislative representatives an area will have. **222**

apprentices People who learn skilled trades from a master craftsperson. **105**

arbitration Formal meetings to discuss and settle disagreements using a third party. **626**

archaeology Scientific study of the unwritten past. **5**

armistice A truce between warring groups or countries. **685**

Army-McCarthy hearings Televised hearings in the 1950s of the U.S. Senate's investigations into Senator Joseph McCarthy's charges that Communists were in the U.S. military. **815**

Articles of Confederation (1777) Document that created the first central government for the United States; was replaced by the Constitution in 1789. **189**

artifacts Remains of objects that have been made by humans. **5**

assembly line A system that moves parts and partly assembled products among factory workers to speed production. **711**

astrolabe A tool once used by navigators to determine a ship's position at sea by charting the position of the stars. **33**

Atlanta Compromise (1895) Speech given by Booker T. Washington stating that African Americans should focus on improving their education and economic situation instead of fighting discrimination and segregation. **622**

Atlantic Charter (1941) Pledge signed by U.S. president Franklin D. Roosevelt and British prime minister Winston Churchill to work for peace after World War II. **765**

atomic bomb A nuclear weapon that produced an explosion by splitting atoms; the United States dropped two atomic bombs on Japan during World War II. **785**

automation The use of machines in production. **826**

Axis powers Military alliance formed by Italy and Germany in 1936; later joined by Japan and other countries. Fought against the Allied powers in World War II. **752**

baby boom A significant increase in the number of children being born. **828**

backcountry Frontier region in Virginia and the Carolinas between coastal settlements and the Appalachian Mountains. **131**

Bacon's Rebellion (1676) Attack led by Nathaniel Bacon against American Indians and the colonial government in Virginia. **69**

balance of power A situation in which the strength of rival alliances or nations is nearly equal. **669**

balance of trade Relationship between what goods a country purchases from other countries and what goods it sells to other countries. **98**

Bank of the United States National bank chartered by Congress in 1791 to provide security for the U.S. economy. **277**

Bataan Death March (1942) Forced march of tens of thousands of American and Filipino prisoners during World War II up the Bataan Peninsula to internment camps. **779**

Battle of Antietam (1862) Union victory in the Civil War that marked the bloodiest single-day battle in U.S. military history. **486**

Battle of Britain (1940–41) Battle fought between British and German air forces for control of the skies over Great Britain. **764**

Battle of Brandywine Creek (1777) Revolutionary War battle in which British forces overwhelmed the Patriots in Pennsylvania. **172**

Battle of Bunker Hill (1775) Revolutionary War battle in Boston that demonstrated that the colonists could fight well against the British army. **156**

Battle of El Alamein (1942) British victory in World War II over Axis forces in North Africa. **773**

Battle of Fallen Timbers (1794) Battle between U.S. troops and an American Indian confederation resisting white settlement in the Northwest Territory. **284**

Battle of Gettysburg (1863) Union Civil War victory that turned the tide against the Confederates at Gettysburg, Pennsylvania; resulted in the loss of more than 50,000 soldiers. **499**

Battle of Goliad (1836) Mexican victory during the Texas Revolution in which Mexican leader Antonio López de Santa Anna ordered the execution of Texas soldiers after their surrender. **425**

Battle of Horseshoe Bend (1814) U.S. victory in the War of 1812 in which Andrew Jackson's troops forced Creek Indians to give up much of their land in the South. **317**

Battle of Lake Erie (1813) U.S. victory in the War of 1812, led by Oliver Hazard Perry; broke Britain's control of Lake Erie. **316**

Battle of Leyte Gulf (1944) World War II battle in the Philippines that was the largest naval battle in history. **781**

Battle of Midway (1942) World War II battle in which U.S. warplanes crippled Japan's navy. **780**

Battle of New Orleans (1815) Greatest U.S. victory in the War of 1812; actually took place two weeks after a peace treaty had been signed ending the war. **318**

Battle of Pea Ridge (1862) Civil War battle in which Confederate forces from Missouri, joined by some American Indians, were defeated in Northwestern Arkansas. **491**

Battle of Princeton (1777) Revolutionary War battle in which the Patriots drove back British forces in New Jersey. **171**

Battle of San Jacinto (1836) Final battle of the Texas Revolution; resulted in the defeat of the Mexican army and independence for Texas. **425**

Battle of Saratoga (1777) Revolutionary War battle in New York that resulted in a major defeat of British troops; marked the Patriots' greatest victory up to that point in the war. **172**

Battle of Shiloh (1862) Civil War battle in Tennessee in which the Union army gained greater control over the Mississippi River valley. **489**

Battle of Stalingrad (1942–43) Critical victory by the Soviet Union against German forces during World War II. **774**

Battle of the Atlantic Long-lasting World War II naval war to control Atlantic Ocean trade routes. **765**

Battle of the Bulge (1944–45) World War II battle in which Allied forces ended Germany's ability to wage an offensive war. **777**

Battle of the Coral Sea (1942) World War II battle in which the Allies first stopped the Japanese advance in the Pacific. **779**

Battle of the Little Bighorn (1876) "Custer's Last Stand"; battle between U.S. soldiers, led by George Armstrong Custer, and Sioux warriors, led by Crazy Horse and Sitting Bull; the worst defeat for the U.S. Army in the West. **549**

Battle of the Thames (1813) U.S. victory in the War of 1812, led by William Henry Harrison, that ended the Indian-British alliance in the Great Lakes. **316**

Battle of Tippecanoe (1811) U.S. victory over an Indian confederation that wanted to stop white settlement in the Northwest Territory; increased tensions between Great Britain and the United States. **311**

Battle of Trenton (1776) Revolutionary War battle in New Jersey in which Patriot forces captured more than 900 Hessian troops. **171**

Battle of Vincennes (1779) Revolutionary War battle in the West in which Patriots retook Vincennes, a mostly French town along the Wabash River, from the British. **178**

Battle of Yorktown (1781) Last major battle of the Revolutionary War; site of British general Charles Cornwallis's surrender to the Patriots in Virginia. **180**

Bear Flag Revolt (1846) Revolt against Mexico by American settlers in California who declared the territory an independent republic. **434**

bear market A stock market with declining stock prices. **732**

beats Young writers who criticized American life in the1950s; also called beatniks. **830**

benevolent societies Organizations that helped immigrants in cases of sickness, unemployment, and death. **591**

Berlin Airlift (1948) Joint effort by the United States and Britain to fly food and supplies into West Berlin after the Soviets blocked off all ground routes to the city. **803**

Berlin Wall Wall built in 1961 between East and West Berlin to stop East Berliners from crossing into the West. **849**

Bessemer process A method of faster, cheaper steel production developed in the 1850s. **579**

bicameral legislature A lawmaking body made up of two houses. **93**

Bill of Rights First 10 amendments to the Constitution; ratified in 1791. **211**

Black Codes Laws passed in the southern states during Reconstruction that greatly limited the freedom and rights of African Americans. **521**

blacklisting Refusing to hire a person; common action toward suspected Communists during the 1950s. **813**

Black Power Social and political movement in the 1960s that called for greater African American economic and political power. **859**

Blackshirts Group of Italians led by Benito Mussolini that gained power in the early 1920s. **751**

Blitzkrieg "Lightning war"; type of fast-moving warfare used by German forces against Poland in 1939. **763**

bonanza A large deposit of precious ore. **553**

bonds Certificates that represent money the government has borrowed from private citizens. **273**

Bonus Army Group of World War I veterans that marched on Washington, D.C., in 1932 to demand the immediate payment of their government war bonuses in cash. **735**

boomtowns Western communities that grew quickly because of the mining boom. **554**

bootleggers People who smuggled liquor into the United States from Canada and Mexico during prohibition. **707**

borderlands Region of Spanish America where few Europeans lived; included northern Mexico, Florida, and parts of present-day Arizona, California, New Mexico, and Texas. **46**

border states Delaware, Kentucky, Maryland, and Missouri; slave states that lay between the North and the South and did not join the Confederacy during the Civil War. **480**

bosses Corrupt political leaders who used bribery and favors to win votes and elections. **607**

Boston Massacre (1770) Incident in which British soldiers fired into a crowd of angry colonists, killing five people. **140**

Boston Tea Party (1773) Protest against the Tea Act in which a group of colonists boarded British tea ships and dumped some 340 chests of tea into Boston Harbor. **142**

Boxer Rebellion (1900) Revolt in which Chinese nationalists known as the Boxers attacked foreigners in order to end outside involvement in China's affairs; put down by U.S. Marines and other forces after two months. **644**

boycott To refuse to buy certain goods; method often used in protest movements. **137**

braceros Mexican workers authorized by the U.S. government to enter the United States during World War II. **770**

Brain Trust Group of expert policy advisers who worked with President Franklin D. Roosevelt in the 1930s to end the Great Depression. **737**

brinkmanship The Eisenhower administration's policy of being willing to go to the very brink of war to oppose communist expansion. **823**

Brown* v. *Board of Education (1954) Supreme Court ruling that declared that segregation in public schools is illegal; overturned the separate-but-equal doctrine established in 1896 case *Plessy* v. *Ferguson*. **834**

bull market A stock market with rising stock prices. **732**

Bull Moose Party Nickname for the Progressive Party, which was formed by Theodore Roosevelt and his supporters in 1912. **628**

Bureau of Indian Affairs Government agency created in the 1800s to oversee federal policy toward American Indians. **346**

business cycle Economic pattern in which business goes through periods of prosperity and depression. **734**

buying on margin Purchasing stocks on credit. **732**

cabinet Group made up of the heads of the executive departments that advises the U.S. president. **224**

California Gold Rush Migration of thousands of people to California in 1849 after gold was discovered there. **437**

California Trail The southern branch of the Oregon Trail, which crossed the Sierra Nevada and ended in California. **430**

Californios Spanish colonists in California. **431**

Camp David Accords (1978) Peace agreements between Israel and Egypt, negotiated by President Jimmy Carter. **916**

caravel A fast, maneuverable ship originally designed by the Portuguese. **33**

carpetbaggers Name given to northerners who moved to the South during Reconstruction. **527**

cash crops Agricultural products grown primarily to be sold for profits, not for personal use. **103**

casualties People who are killed, wounded, captured, or missing in a war. **129**

cattle drive Long journeys on which cowboys herded cattle to northern markets or better grazing lands. **561**

Cattle Kingdom Area of the Great Plains, stretching from Texas to Canada, on which many ranchers raised cattle in the late 1800s. **559**

Central Intelligence Agency (CIA) An organization established by the federal government in 1947 to conduct covert operations. **823**

Central Powers World War I alliance led by Austria-Hungary and Germany and later joined by Bulgaria and the Ottoman Empire. **771**

charter Official document that gives a person the right to establish a colony. **51**

checks and balances A system established by the Constitution that prevents any branch of government from becoming too powerful. **205**

Chicano movement Effort of young Hispanic activists to end discrimination and increase cultural pride. **863**

Chinese Exclusion Act (1882) Law prohibiting Chinese people from immigrating to the United States for a period of 10 years; was extended into the early 1900s. **592**

Chisholm Trail Trail from San Antonio, Texas, to Abilene, Kansas, established by Jesse Chisholm in 1867 for cattle drives. **561**

circumnavigate To sail completely around. **40**

Civil Rights Act of 1866 Law that gave African Americans legal rights equal to those of white Americans. **522**

Civil Rights Act of 1875 Law guaranteeing African Americans equal rights in public places such as theaters and public transportation. **530**

Civil Rights Act of 1964 Law banning segregation in public places and prohibiting employers, unions, and universities from discriminating on the basis of color, sex, religion, and national origin. **857**

Clayton Antitrust Act (1914) Act that strengthened federal laws against monopolies. **630**

Clermont First full-sized U.S. commercial steamboat; developed by Robert Fulton and tested in 1807. **366**

Cold War Global power struggle between the United States and the Soviet Union that lasted from 1945 to 1991. **800**

collective bargaining Process in which union leaders negotiate with factory owners on behalf of workers in a particular business or industry for better wages and working conditions. **586**

Columbian Exchange Transfer of plants, animals, and diseases between the Americas and Europe, Asia, and Africa. **41**

Committee on Civil Rights (1946) Committee appointed by President Harry S Truman to investigate racial discrimination and to suggest federal solutions to the problem. **833**

Committee on Public Information (CPI) Agency created by President Woodrow Wilson in 1917 to increase public support for World War I. **678**

Committees of Correspondence Committees created in Massachusetts in the 1760s to help towns and colonies share information about resisting the new British laws. **137**

common-school movement Social reform efforts begun in the mid-1800s that promoted the idea of having all children educated in a common place regardless of social class or background. **403**

Common Sense (1776) Pamphlet written by Thomas Paine that criticized monarchies and convinced many American colonists of the need to break away from Britain. **158**

Commonwealth of Independent States (CIS) An alliance formed by many of the former Soviet republics in December 1991. **934**

Communists People who seek the equal distribution of wealth and the end of all forms of private property. **683, 700**

Compromise of 1850 Henry Clay's proposed agreement that allowed California to enter the Union as a free state and divided the rest of the Mexican Cession into two territories where slavery would be decided by popular sovereignty; also settled land claims between Texas and New Mexico, abolished the slave trade in Washington, and produced a new Fugitive Slave Act. **453**

Compromise of 1877 Agreement to settle the disputed presidential election of 1876; Democrats agreed to accept Republican Rutherford B. Hayes as president in return for the removal of federal troops from the South. **531**

Comstock Lode Nevada gold and silver deposit discovered by Henry Comstock in 1859. **553**

concurrent powers Powers that are shared by the federal and state governments. **221**

Confederate States of America Nation formed by the southern states on February 4, 1861; also known as the Confederacy. **472**

Congress of Industrial Organizations (CIO) National labor group formed in 1938 that joined together many industrial unions. **741**

conquistadores Spanish soldiers and explorers who led military expeditions in the Americas and captured land for Spain. **42**

conservation Protection of nature and its resources. **626**

constitution A set of basic principles that determines the powers and duties of a government. **188**

Constitutional Convention (1787) Meeting in Philadelphia at which delegates from the states wrote the Constitution. **201**

Constitutional Union Party Political party formed in 1860 by a group of northerners and southerners who supported the Union, its laws, and the Constitution. **469**

containment U.S. foreign policy followed during the Cold War that sought to prevent the expansion of Soviet communism. **802**

Continental Army Army created by the Second Continental Congress in 1775 to defend the American colonies from Britain. **154**

contrabands Escaped or captured slaves taken in by the Union army during the Civil War. **494**

Contract with America Ten-point Republican reform plan created in the mid-1990s; proposals included a balanced budget amendment and tax reform. **937**

Contras A group of anti-Sandinista rebels in Nicaragua. **930**

Convention of 1818 Agreement between the United States and Great Britain that settled fishing rights and established new North American borders. **329**

Copperheads Northern Democrats who opposed abolition and sympathized with the South during the Civil War. **495**

corporations Companies that sell shares of ownership, called stocks, to investors in order to raise money. **581**

cotton belt Region stretching from Georgia to east Texas where most U.S. cotton was produced during the mid-1800s. **374**

cotton diplomacy Confederate efforts to use the importance of southern cotton to Britain's textile industry to persuade the British to support the Confederacy in the Civil War. **482**

cotton gin Device invented by Eli Whitney in 1793 to separate cotton plants' fibers from the seeds; revolutionized the cotton industry. **373**

Council of the Indies Group of royal officials established in 1524 that oversaw the government and enforced laws in Spanish America. **44**

counterculture An alternative culture with values that run counter to, or against, those in the main society. **867**

covenant Sacred agreement. **76**

covert operations Secret missions. **823**

creditors People who lend money. **197**

Crusades (1096–1221) Series of wars launched by European Christians to gain possession of the Holy Land. **25**

Cuban missile crisis (1962) Military crisis that almost led to nuclear war when U.S. naval ships blockaded Cuba until the Soviet Union agreed to remove its missiles from the island. **849**

culture Common values and traditions of a society, such as language, government, and family relationships. **6**

Cumberland Road First federal road project, construction of which began in 1815; ran from Cumberland, Maryland, to present-day Wheeling, West Virginia. **335**

Daughters of Liberty Women's groups that used boycotts and other measures to support the colonies' resistance to the British. **139**

Dawes General Allotment Act (1887) Legislation passed by Congress that split up Indian reservation lands among individual Indians and promised them citizenship. **552**

D-Day June 6, 1944; date of Allied invasion of France during World War II. **774**

debtors People who owe money. **197**

Declaration of Independence (1776) Statement of the Second Continental Congress that defined the colonists' rights, outlined their complaints against Great Britain, and declared the colonies' independence. **159**

Declaration of Sentiments (1848) Statement written and signed by women's rights supporters at the Seneca Falls Convention; detailed their complaints about social injustice against women. **415**

deficit The amount by which a government's borrowing and spending is greater than its income. **929**

delegated powers Powers that are specifically granted to the federal government by the Constitution. **220**

Democratic Party Political party formed by supporters of Andrew Jackson after the presidential election of 1824. **339**

Democratic-Republican Party Political party founded in the 1790s that sought to preserve the power of the state governments and promote agriculture. **288**

deport To send an immigrant back to his or her country of origin. **255**

depression A steep drop in economic activity combined with rising unemployment. **197**

détente Period in the 1970s of reduced hostility between the United States and the Soviet Union. **906**

direct primary Method of allowing voters to choose their own candidates for office. **611**

Disabled in Action (DIA) Group formed in 1970 to coordinate reform efforts for people with disabilities. **865**

disarmament The act of limiting military weapons. **704**

dissenters People who disagree with official religious or political opinions. **75**

Dixiecrats Members of the States' Rights Party; formed in the 1940s by southern Democrats who were upset with President Harry S Truman's support for civil rights. **806**

dollar diplomacy President William Howard Taft's policy of influencing Latin American governments through economic, not military, intervention. **658**

domestication Process of breeding plants and animals for use by humans. **6**

Dominion of New England Union of some northeastern American colonies created by King James II in 1686; lasted until 1689. **95**

domino theory Cold War belief that if one nation in Southeast Asia fell to communism, the rest of Southeast Asia would also fall. **875**

Donner party Group of western travelers who were stranded in the Sierra Nevada during the winter of 1846-47; only 40 of the party's 87 members survived. **430**

double jeopardy Illegal act of trying a person twice for the same crime. **251**

doves Americans who called for U.S. withdrawal from the Vietnam War. **883**

draft A system of required service in the armed forces. **257**

***Dred Scott* decision** (1857) U.S. Supreme Court ruling that declared African Americans were not U.S. citizens and that the Missouri Compromise's restriction on slavery was unconstitutional. **464**

dry farming Method of farming taught by Hardy Campbell to Plains farmers in the 1890s that allowed farmers to grow certain crops with less water. **566**

due process Fair application of the law. **251**

Dust Bowl Name given to parts of the Great Plains in the 1930s after a severe drought dried out the region. **746**

duties Taxes on imported goods. **99**

Earth Day Day celebrated annually on April 22 to increase environmental awareness; first celebrated in 1970. **921**

Eighteenth Amendment (1919) Constitutional amendment that outlawed the production, sale, and transportation of alcoholic beverages in the United States; repealed in 1933. **620**

elastic clause Article I, Section 8, of the Constitution that has been interpreted as giving Congress authority to stretch its delegated powers to address issues not otherwise specified in the document. **221**

electoral college Group selected from each of the states to cast votes in presidential elections. The number of each state's electors is equal to the number of its representatives and senators in Congress. The electors are expected to vote for the candidate chosen by popular vote in their states. **269**

emancipation Freedom from slavery. **407**

Emancipation Proclamation (1862) Order issued by President Abraham Lincoln freeing the slaves in areas rebelling against the Union; took effect January 1, 1863. **493**

embargo Banning of trade with a country. **309**

Embargo Act (1807) Law that prohibited American merchants from trading with other countries. **309**

Emergency Quota Act (1921) Law that limited the number of immigrants to the United States to 357,000 per year. **709**

eminent domain The government's power to take personal property to further the public good. **251**

empresarios Agents who were contracted by the Mexican republic to bring settlers to Texas in the early l800s. **423**

***encomienda* system** System in Spanish America that gave settlers the right to tax local Indians or to demand their labor in exchange for protecting them and teaching them skills. **44**

Endangered Species Act (1966) Legislation that protects animals threatened with extinction. **921**

energy crisis Situation in the 1970s marked by high fuel prices and fuel shortages. **904**

English Bill of Rights (1689) Shifted political power from the British monarchy to Parliament. **97**

Enlightenment Age of Reason; movement that began in Europe in the 1700s as people began examining the natural world, society, and government. **113**

entrepreneurs People who start new businesses. **581**

Environmental Protection Agency (EPA) Agency established by Congress in 1970 to enforce environmental laws. **921**

environments Climates and landscapes that surround living things. **6**

Equal Rights Amendment Proposed constitutional amendment that would guarantee women's rights by prohibiting discrimination based on sex; passed by Congress in 1972 but never ratified by enough states to become a constitutional amendment. **864**

Erie Canal Canal that ran from Albany to Buffalo, New York; completed in 1825. **335**

escalation President Lyndon B. Johnson's policy of increasing U.S. involvement in the Vietnam War. **880**

Espionage Act of 1917 Law punishing people for aiding the enemy or refusing military duty during World War I. **679**

European Union (EU) Group of 11 European nations that joined together in 1993 to form a single market with a common currency and a common bank in order to increase their global economic power. **942**

executive branch Division of the federal government that includes the president and the administrative departments; enforces the nation's laws. **204**

executive order Nonlegislative directive issued by the U.S. president in certain circumstances; an executive order has the force of congressional law. **223**

executive privilege Right of the president to keep information secret to protect national security. **908**

Exodusters A large group of southern African Americans who settled western lands in the late 1800s. **565**

expatriates People who leave their native country to live elsewhere. **719**

exports Items that a country sells to other countries. **98**

fads Interests followed for a short time with great enthusiasm. **715**

Fair Deal Series of reform programs proposed by President Harry S Truman. **807**

Fair Employment Practices Committee (FEPC) Committee created during World War I to prevent discrimination in war industries and government jobs. **770**

Farmers' Alliances Political groups formed by farmers in the late 1800s that worked to elect candidates favorable to farmers. **600**

fascism Political theory that calls for a strong government headed by one individual and in which the state is more important than the individual. **751**

federalism System of government in which power is distributed between a central authority and individual states. **204**

Federalist Papers Series of essays that defended the Constitution and tried to reassure Americans that the states would not be overpowered by the proposed national government. **208**

Federalist Party Political party created in the 1790s that wanted to strengthen the federal government and promote industry and trade. **288**

Federalists People who supported ratification of the Constitution. **207**

Federal Reserve Act (1913) Act that created a national banking system to help regulate the economy. **629**

Federal Trade Commission (FTC) (1914) Commission established to investigate and punish unfair trade practices. **630**

feudalism System of government that arose during the Middle Ages in which people gave their loyalty to a lord in exchange for land or protection. **19**

Fifteenth Amendment (1870) Constitutional amendment that gave African American men the right to vote. **526**

54th Massachusetts Infantry African American Civil War regiment that played a key role in the attack on Fort Wagner in South Carolina. **494**

fireside chats President Franklin D. Roosevelt's radio addresses to the American people. **738**

First Battle of Bull Run (1861) First major battle of the Civil War, resulting in a Confederate victory; showed that the Civil War would not be won easily. **484**

First Battle of the Marne (1914) World War I battle in which French forces stopped a German advance near Paris. **771**

First Continental Congress (1774) Meeting of colonial delegates in Philadelphia to decide how to respond to increased taxes and abuses of authority by the British government; delegates petitioned King George III, listing the freedoms they believed colonists should enjoy. **152**

flappers Young women in the 1920s who challenged social traditions with their dress and behavior. **699**

folktales Oral stories that often provide a moral lesson. **380**

Fort Sumter Federal outpost in Charleston, South Carolina, that was attacked by the Confederates in April 1861, sparking the Civil War. **478**

forty-niners Gold-seekers who moved to California during the gold rush. **437**

Fourteen Points (1918) President Woodrow Wilson's plan for organizing post World War I Europe and for avoiding future wars. **687**

Fourteenth Amendment (1866) Constitutional amendment that, among other provisions, gave full rights of citizenship to all people born or naturalized in the United States, except for American Indians. **523**

free coinage Type of monetary system in which both gold and silver were coined. **599**

Freedmen's Bureau Agency established by Congress in 1865 to help poor people throughout the South. **518**

Freedom Rides (1961) Bus trips through several southern states that civil rights workers used to challenge illegal bus segregation. **856**

free enterprise Economic system in which there is competition between businesses with little government control. **99, 581**

Freeport Doctrine (1858) Argument made by Stephen Douglas during the Lincoln-Douglas debates that popular sovereignty would determine whether a state or territory could permit slavery. **466**

Free-Soil Party Political party formed in 1848 by antislavery northerners who left the Whig and Democratic Parties because neither addressed the slavery issue. **451**

French Revolution French rebellion begun in 1789 in which the French people overthrew the monarchy and made their country a republic. **278**

Fugitive Slave Act (1850) Law that made it a crime to help runaway slaves; allowed for the arrest of escaped slaves in areas where slavery was illegal and required their return to slaveholders. **454**

Fundamentalism Protestant religious movement that teaches that the Bible is literally true. **708**

Fundamental Orders of Connecticut (1639) A written set of principles that made Connecticut's colonial government more democratic. **77**

Gadsden Purchase (1853) U.S. purchase of land from Mexico that included the southern parts of present-day Arizona and New Mexico. **436**

General Amnesty Act of 1872 Law repealing Section III of the Fourteenth Amendment, which forbade former Confederates from holding public office. **530**

generation gap Division between older and younger people. **867**

Geneva Accords (1954) Agreement that temporarily divided Vietnam into North and South Vietnam and called for free elections in 1956 to reunite the country. **875**

genocide Deliberate murder of an entire people. **788**

Gettysburg Address (1863) Speech given by Abraham Lincoln in which he praised the bravery of Union soldiers and renewed his commitment to winning the Civil War. **500**

Ghost Dance A religious movement among Plains Indians in the 1880s. **550**

Gibbons* v. *Ogden (1824) Supreme Court ruling that federal law has priority over equivalent state law; expanded definition of interstate commerce. **368**

GI Bill of Rights (1944) Servicemen's Readjustment Act, which offered veterans education benefits and loans for houses, farms, and businesses. **805**

glasnost Soviet policy established in the 1980s that promoted political openness and freedom of expression. **931**

global warming Potential environmental threat caused by the rising temperature on Earth from heat trapped in the planet's atmosphere. **941**

Glorious Revolution (1688) A revolt in England against Catholic king James II that led to his overthrow and put Protestants Mary and William of Orange on the throne. **96**

glyphs Symbols or images, often cut into a surface, that represent ideas. **6**

gold standard Type of monetary system in which currency is backed exclusively by gold. **599**

Good Neighbor policy President Franklin D. Roosevelt's foreign policy of promoting better relations with Latin America by using economic influence. **750**

Great Awakening A Christian movement that became widespread in the American colonies in the 1730s and 1740s. **109**

Great Compromise (1787) Agreement worked out at the Constitutional Convention establishing that a state's population would determine representation in the lower house of the legislature, while each state would have equal representation in the upper house of the legislature. **202**

Great Depression Serious, global economic decline that began with the crash of the U.S. stock market in 1929. **733**

Great Migration Mass migration of thousands of English people to the Americas that took place between 1630 and 1640. Also the mass migration of thousands of African Americans from the South to the northern United States during and after World War I. **76, 701**

Great Society Social reform programs established by President Lyndon B. Johnson. **852**

guerrilla warfare Type of fighting in which soldiers use swift hit-and-run attacks against the enemy, usually behind the battle lines. **179**

habeus corpus Constitutional protection against unlawful imprisonment. **495**

Harlem Renaissance Period of great African American artistic achievement in the 1920s; named for the Harlem neighborhood of New York City. **718**

Hartford Convention (1815) Meeting of Federalists at Hartford, Connecticut, to protest the War of 1812. **319**

hawks Americans who pushed for increased military spending and involvement in the Vietnam War. **884**

Hay-Bunau-Varilla Treaty (1903) Agreement between the United States and Panama that gave the United States a 99-year lease to build a canal on a 10-mile-wide strip of land across the Isthmus of Panama. **654**

Hay-Herrán Treaty (1903) Proposed agreement with Colombia to allow the United States to build a canal across the Isthmus of Panama. **654**

Haymarket Riot (1886) Incident in which a bomb exploded during a labor protest held in Haymarket Square in Chicago, leading to deaths and injuries. **587**

headright System set up by the London Company in 1618 that gave 50 acres of land to colonists who paid their own way to Virginia. **67**

Highway Act (1956) An act that provided money to create a national interstate highway system. **827**

hippies Members of the 1960s counterculture who experimented with different ways of living and behaving. **867**

Ho Chi Minh Trail A Vietcong supply network that led from North Vietnam, through Laos and Cambodia, to South Vietnam. **879**

Holocaust The Nazis killing of some 6 million Jews and about 3 million other people in World War II. **787**

Homestead Act (1862) Law passed by Congress to encourage settlement in the West by giving government-owned land to small farmers. **564**

Homestead strike (1892) Violent strike at Andrew Carnegie's Homestead steel factory in Pennsylvania. **588**

horizontal integration Ownership of all businesses in a particular field. **582**

House of Burgesses Colonial Virginia's elected assembly. **94**

House Un-American Activities Committee (HUAC) Congressional committee created in 1938 to investigate U.S. citizens accused of communist activities. **813**

Hudson River school Group of American artists in the mid-1800s whose pictures focused on the American landscape. **352**

Hull House Settlement house founded by Jane Addams and Ellen Gates Starr in Chicago in 1889. **595**

hunter-gatherers People who hunt animals and gather wild plants to provide for their needs. **5**

hydrogen bomb A type of nuclear bomb. **821**

igloos Houses that were built out of blocks of ice by the Inuit peoples in what is now Canada and Alaska. **12**

immigrants People who move to another country after leaving their homeland. **71**

Immigration Restriction League Organization formed in 1894 by nativists who wanted to reduce immigration. **592**

impeach To vote to bring charges against. **223**

imperialism The practice of building an empire by founding colonies or conquering other nations. **640**

imports Items that a country purchases from other countries. **98**

impressment British practice of forcing people, including U.S. citizens, to serve in the British army or navy; led to increasing tensions between Great Britain and the United States in the early 1800s. **309**

indentured servants Colonists who received free passage to North America in exchange for working without pay for a certain number of years. **68**

Indian Removal Act (1830) Congressional act that authorized the removal of American Indians who lived east of the Mississippi River. **345**

Indian Territory Area covering most of present-day Oklahoma to which most American Indians in the Southeast were forced to move in the 1830s. **345**

indict[†] To formally accuse. **251**

Industrial Revolution Period of rapid growth in the use of machines in manufacturing that began in the mid-1700s. **363**

Industrial Workers of the World (IWW) Socialist organization formed in 1905 to bring all workers into one large union. **618**

inflation Increased prices for goods and services combined with the reduced value of money. **48, 196**

Information Revolution Rapid growth in the availability and transfer of information that took place in the 1990s; made possible by the increased use of computers. **943**

initiative Law enabling voters to propose a new law by collecting signatures on a petition. **612**

installment plans Programs for purchasing goods in which the customer makes a small initial payment and then continues to make monthly payments with interest until the item is paid for. **713**

interchangeable parts Process developed by Eli Whitney in the 1790s that called for making each vital part of a machine exactly the same. **364**

Intermediate-Range Nuclear Forces Treaty (INF) (1987) Treaty signed by President Ronald Reagan and Soviet leader Mikhail Gorbachev that eliminated all medium range nuclear weapons from Europe. **931**

Internal Security Act (1950) Law requiring registration of suspected communist groups and granting the government the power to arrest anyone suspected of disloyalty during national emergencies. **814**

International Space Station A space station built jointly by the United States, Russia, and other nations after the end of the Cold War. **941**

Internet Worldwide system of computer networks. **943**

internment Forced relocation and imprisonment of people. **771**

interstate commerce Trade that is conducted between states. **196**

Interstate Commerce Act (1887) Law regulating trade between the states. **598**

Interstate Commerce Commission (ICC) (1887) Commission created by the Interstate Commerce Act to ensure that railroads charged fair rates. **598**

Intolerable Acts (1774) A set of laws passed by Parliament to punish the colonists for the Boston Tea Party and to tighten government control of the colonies. **143**

Iran-contra affair Name given to the 1986 scandal in which the U.S. government secretly sold weapons to Iran, using the profits to fund the contras in Nicaragua. **930**

Iran hostage crisis Situation that began in 1979 in which 53 Americans were taken hostage in the U.S. Embassy in Tehran, Iran, and were held for 444 days. **917**

ironclad Warship heavily armored with iron. **487**

Iroquois League A political confederation of five northeastern American Indian nations—the Seneca, Oneida, Mohawk, Cayuga, and Onondaga. **16**

Islam A faith that arose in the Middle East in the A.D. 600s under the guidance of Muhammad; it's holy book is the Qur'an. **23**

island-hopping World War II strategy of conquering only certain Pacific islands that were important to the Allied advance toward Japan. **781**

isolationism Policy of avoiding involvement in other nations' affairs. **641**

Jay's Treaty (1794) Agreement negotiated by John Jay to work out problems between Britain and the United States over the western frontier trade in the Caribbean, British seizure of U.S. ships, and debts owed to British merchants. **281**

Jazz Age A term for the 1920s; so called because of jazz music's popularity during the decade. **718**

Jim Crow laws Laws that enforced segregation in the southern states. **531**

John Brown's raid (1859) Incident in which abolitionist John Brown and 21 other men captured a federal arsenal in Harpers Ferry, Virginia, in hopes of starting a slave rebellion. **467**

judicial branch Division of the federal government that is made up of the national courts; interprets laws, punishes criminals, and settles disputes between states. **204**

judicial review The Supreme Court's power to declare acts of Congress unconstitutional. **301**

Judiciary Act of 1789 Legislation passed by Congress that created the federal court system. **271**

kamikaze World War II tactic used by Japanese pilots of crashing planes filled with explosives into Allied ships. **783**

Kansas-Nebraska Act (1854) Law that allowed voters in the Kansas and Nebraska territories to choose whether to allow slavery. **459**

kayaks One-person canoes almost completely enclosed by animal skins. **12**

Kellogg-Briand Pact (1928) Pact signed by the United States and 14 other nations that tried to outlaw war. **704**

Kentucky and Virginia Resolutions (1798–1799) Republican documents that argued the Alien and Sedition Acts were unconstitutional. **290**

Khmer Rouge Cambodian communist army. **889**

kitchen cabinet President Andrew Jackson's group of informal advisers; so called because they sometimes met in the White House kitchen. **340**

kivas Circular ceremonial rooms used for religious activities by Native American peoples of the American Southwest. **14**

Knights of Labor The first national labor union in the United States; organized in 1869 and included workers of different races, gender and skills. **586**

Know-Nothing Party Political organization founded in 1849 by nativists who supported measures making it difficult for foreigners to become citizens and to hold office. **397**

Kristallnacht "Night of broken glass"; November 9, 1938; night when Nazis killed or injured many Jews and destroyed many Jewish properties. **752**

Ku Klux Klan Secret society created by white southerners in 1866 that used terror and violence to keep African Americans from obtaining their civil rights. **529**

Land Ordinance of 1785 Legislation passed by Congress authorizing surveys and the division of public lands in the western region of the country. **190**

League of Nations International congress of nations formed in 1919 that was designed to settle disputes and maintain peace and collective security. **687**

legislative branch Division of the government that proposes bills and passes them into laws. **204**

Lend-Lease Act (1941) Law that allowed the United States to loan weapons and other war supplies to Britain and the Soviet Union. **764**

Levittown Early example of a preplanned and mass-produced housing development; created by William Levitt on Long Island in New York. **827**

Lewis and Clark expedition Expedition led by Meriwether Lewis and William Clark that began in 1804 to explore the lands bought from France by the United States in the Louisiana Purchase. **306**

libel A false statement, usually published, that damages a person's reputation. **94**

Liberator, The Antislavery newspaper first published by William Lloyd Garrison in 1831. **408**

Liberty bonds U.S. bonds sold during World War I to raise money for loans to the Allies. **680**

limited government A political principles which holds that government should be bound by laws that limit its power. **188**

Limited Nuclear Test Ban Treaty (1963) International agreement to ban above-ground testing of new nuclear weapons; signed by the United States and Soviet Union. **849**

Lincoln-Douglas debates Series of seven debates between Republican Abraham Lincoln and Democrat Stephen Douglas during the 1858 U.S. Senate campaign in Illinois. **465**

Line of Demarcation Boundary established by Pope Alexander VI in 1493 about 300 miles west and south of the Azores; gave unclaimed land west of the line to Spain, and east of the line to Portugal. **36**

Little Rock Nine African American students who first integrated Central High School in Little Rock, Arkansas, in 1957. **835**

longhouses Rectangular dwellings built by the Iroquois that were shared by several families. **16**

Long March (1934) Retreat of Chinese Communists to escape destruction by the Chinese Nationalist army. **808**

loose construction Way of interpreting the Constitution that allows the federal government to take actions that the Constitution does not specifically forbid it from taking. **276**

Lord Dunmore's Proclamation (1775) Statement issued by Virginia's royal governor promising freedom to any slave who fought for the British in the American Revolution. **167**

Lost Generation A group of U.S. writers who reacted to the death and destruction of World War I by criticizing postwar American society. **719**

Louisiana Purchase (1803) Purchase of French land between the Mississippi River and the Rocky Mountains that nearly doubled the size of the United States. **304**

Lowell system The use of water powered textile mills that employed young unmarried women in the 1800s. **365**

Loyalists Colonists who sided with Britain in the American Revolution. **160**

Lusitania British passenger liner sunk by a German U-boat in May 1915; the deaths of 128 Americans on board contributed to U.S. entry into World War I. **676**

Maginot Line Fortified line of defenses that France built along its border with Germany after World War I. **763**

Magna Carta (1215) Great Charter; agreed to by King John of England, it gave nobles and other individuals greater rights and made it clear that the nobility and monarchs must obey the law. **22**

maize Corn, the most important crop grown by Native Americans in North America and Mesoamerica. **6**

Manhattan Project Secret Allied project begun in 1942 to develop an atomic bomb. **785**

manifest destiny Belief shared by many Americans in the mid-1800s that the United States should expand across the continent to the Pacific Ocean. **432**

manors Large estates held by monarchs and nobles in the Middle Ages. **19**

Marbury* v. *Madison (1803) U.S. Supreme Court case that established the principle of judicial review. **300**

March on Washington A massive civil rights demonstration held on August 28, 1963, in Washington, D.C. **857**

Marshall Plan U.S. program of giving aid to Europe countries to help them rebuild their economies after World War II. **802**

Massacre at Wounded Knee (1890) U.S. Army's killing of approximately 150 Sioux at Wounded Knee Creek in South Dakota; ended U.S-Indian wars on the Plains. **550**

massive retaliation The strategy of threatening to use nuclear weapons in order to stop communist aggression. **823**

mass production Efficient production of large numbers of identical goods. **364**

Mayflower Compact (1620) Document written by the Pilgrims that established general guidelines for self government. **71**

McCarthyism Method of making vicious accusation without offering proof; named after Senator Joseph McCarthy. **815**

McCulloch* v. *Maryland (1819) U.S. Supreme Court case that declared the Second Bank of the United States was constitutional and that because it was a federal institution Maryland could not interfere with its operations. **341**

McKinley Tariff (1890) Law that allowed all countries ship sugar duty-free to the United States. **642**

Medicaid (1965) Federal health insurance program for people with low incomes. **852**

Medicare (1965) Federal health care program for people over the age of 65. **852**

mercantilism Practice of creating and maintaining wealth by carefully controlling trade. **98**

mercenaries Hired foreign soldiers. **167**

Mexican Cession (1848) Land that Mexico gave to the United States after the Mexican War through the Treaty of Guadalupe Hidalgo; included in what is now California, Nevada, and Utah; most of Arizona and New Mexico; and parts of Colorado, Texas, and Wyoming. **436**

Mexican Revolution Revolution begun in 1910 by Francisco Madero against Mexican dictator Porfirio Díaz. **661**

MIAs Soldiers who are missing in action. **892**

Middle Ages Period of European history that lasted from about A.D. 500 to 1500. **19**

middle class Social and economic level between the wealthy and the poor. **398**

Middle Passage Voyage that brought enslaved Africans across the Atlantic Ocean to North America and the West Indies. **101**

migration Movement of people from one region to another. **5**

militarism Policy of aggressive military preparedness combined with the influence of military institutions on a society. **669**

militia An army made up of civilians serving temporarily as soldiers. **126**

minutemen American colonial militia members who were supposed to be ready to fight at a minute's notice. **153**

missions Settlements established by priests in Spanish America to convert local Indians to Catholicism. **44**

Missouri Compromise (1820) Agreement proposed by Henry Clay that allowed Missouri to enter the Union as a slave state and Maine to enter as a free state; also outlawed slavery in any territories or states north of the 36°30′ line. **333**

mobilize Prepare a military force for war. **670**

Model T Car created by Henry Ford in 1908 that was priced low enough that many Americans could afford to buy it; also known as the Tin Lizzie. **711**

monopoly Sole economic control of a business or product. **32**

Monroe Doctrine (1823) President James Monroe's statement forbidding further colonization in the Americas and declaring that the United States would view any attempt by a foreign country to colonize the region as a hostile act. **331**

Montgomery Bus Boycott (1955–56) African American boycott of the city buses in Montgomery, Alabama, which led to the changing of discriminatory bus rules. **836**

Montgomery Improvement Association Organization formed by African Americans in Montgomery, Alabama, in 1956 to strengthen the bus boycott. **836**

Mormons Members of the Church of Jesus Christ of Latter-Day Saints. **440**

Mormon Trail Route by which Mormons traveled west to Utah. **441**

Morrill Act (1862) Federal law passed by Congress that gave land to western states to encourage them to build colleges. **565**

Morse code System developed by Samuel Morse's assistant that represented each letter of the alphabet by a certain combination of dots and dashes; used with the telegraph. **369**

Motown Records First major record label owned by an African American; founded by businessman Berry Gordy in 1959. **868**

mountain men Men hired by eastern companies to trap animals for fur in the Rocky Mountains and other western regions of the United States. **427**

muckrakers Journalists who wrote about corruption in business and politics in order to bring about reform. **611**

mugwumps Nickname given to Republican reformers during the 1884 presidential election; from the Algonquian word for "big chiefs." **608**

Munich Conference (1938) Meeting between British, French, and German leaders in which Germany was given control of the Sudetenland in exchange for German leader Adolf Hitler's promise to make no more claims on European territory. **763**

National Aeronautics and Space Administration (NASA) Agency established by Congress in 1958 to conduct space research. **822**

National American Woman Suffrage Association (NAWSA) Group formed in 1890 by Elizabeth Cady Stanton and Susan B. Anthony to win the vote for women. **621**

National Association for the Advancement of Colored People (NAACP) Group formed by W. E. B. Du Bois and others in 1909 to pursue the goals of economic, educational, and social equality for African Americans; inspired by the Niagara Movement. **623**

national debt Total amount of money owed by a country to its lenders. **273**

National Grange Social and educational organization founded in 1867 to gain more political representation for farmers and to improve their living standards. **598**

National Industrial Recovery Act (NIRA) (1933) Federal law intended to encourage economic growth by eliminating unfair competition among employers; declared unconstitutional in 1935. **739**

nationalism The belief that a specific nation, language, or culture is superior to others. **668**

National Labor Relations Act (NLRA) (1935) Federal law that made unions and collective bargaining legal. **741**

National Liberation Front (NLF) Organization formed to fight Ngo Dinh Diem's government in South Vietnam. **876**

National Organization for Women (NOW) Group formed in 1966 by Betty Friedan and other feminists to increase women's political power. **864**

National Origins Act (1924) Law reducing immigration to the United States and completely stopping Japanese immigration; set quotas favoring northern European immigrants. **709**

National War Labor Board Agency created by President Woodrow Wilson in 1918 to settle disputes between workers and management. **681**

National Woman's Party (NWP) Organization founded by Alice Paul in 1913 that used controversial methods to help women win the vote. **621**

nativists U.S. citizens who opposed immigration. **397**

Nat Turner's Rebellion (1831) Rebellion in which Nat Turner led a group of slaves in Virginia in an unsuccessful attempt to overthrow slavery. **381**

naturalized citizen A person born in another country who has been granted citizenship. **255**

Navigation Acts (1650–96) A series of English laws that required the American colonies to trade primarily with England; set duties on some goods. **99**

Nazis National Socialist Party; political group led by Adolf Hitler that rose to power in Germany during the 1930s. **752**

Neutrality Proclamation (1793) Statement made by President George Washington that the United States would not side with any of the nations at war in Europe following the French Revolution. **280**

New Deal President Franklin D. Roosevelt's programs for helping the U.S. economy during the Great Depression. **738**

New Federalism A system of revenue sharing proposed by President Richard Nixon under which the states would receive money to use as they saw fit. **903**

New Frontier A set of domestic and foreign-policy proposals announced by President John F. Kennedy in his 1961 inaugural address. **847**

new immigrants Immigrants who came to the United States during and after the 1880s; most were from southern and eastern Europe. **590**

New Jersey Plan Proposal to create a unicameral government with representation by state rather than by population; rejected at the Constitutional Convention. **202**

nickelodeons Early motion picture theaters; so called because admission was usually a nickel. **716**

Nineteenth Amendment (1920) Constitutional amendment that gave women the vote. **622**

no-man's-land Strip of land between the trenches of opposing armies along the western front during World War I. **673**

nominating conventions Meetings where a political party selects its presidential and vice presidential candidates; first held in the 1820s. **338**

nonaggression pact Agreement between nations not to attack each other. **763**

Non-Intercourse Act (1809) Law that replaced the Embargo Act and restored trade with all nations except Britain and France. **310**

nonviolent resistance Method of peaceful protest that rejects the use of violence even in self-defense. **855**

North American Free Trade Agreement (NAFTA) Trade agreement between the United States, Canada, and Mexico reached in the early 1990s. **937**

North Atlantic Treaty Organization (NATO) Military alliance formed in 1949 by the United States and 11 other countries to help defend each other in case of attack. **803**

Northwest Ordinance of 1787 Legislation passed by Congress to establish a political structure for the lands in the Northwest Territory and create a system for the admission of new states. **190**

Northwest Passage A nonexistent path through North America that early explorers searched for, which would allow ships to sail from the Atlantic to the Pacific Ocean. **49**

Northwest Territory Lands including present-day Illinois, Indiana, Michigan, Ohio, Wisconsin, and part of Minnesota; organized by the Northwest Ordinance of 1787. **190**

nullification crisis A dispute between South Carolina and the federal government in the late 1820s over the state's right to nullify, or cancel, an unpopular federal tariff. **341**

Nuremberg Trials (1945) War crimes trials of high-ranking Nazi officials held by the International Military Tribunal in Nuremberg, Germany. **799**

Ohio Gang Group of President Warren G. Harding's political friends from Ohio, many of whom were involved in a series of government scandals. **703**

old immigrants Immigrants who came to the United States before the 1880s; most were from northern Europe. **590**

Olive Branch Petition (1775) Peace request sent by the Second Continental Congress to Britain's King George III, who rejected it. **154**

Open Door Policy (1899) Declaration made by U.S. Secretary of State John Hay that all nations should have equal access to trade with China. **644**

open range Public land used by ranchers who were part of the Cattle Kingdom. **559**

Operation Desert Storm (1991) United Nations invasion led by the United States to make Iraq withdraw from Kuwait. **935**

Operation Rolling Thunder A series of air strikes launched by the United States during the Vietnam War to destroy North Vietnam's war industries. **879**

Oregon Trail A 2,000-mile trail stretching through the Great Plains from western Missouri to the Oregon Country. **429**

Organization of Petroleum Exporting Countries (OPEC) Alliance formed by major oil-producing nations in 1960 to control the production and sale of oil. **904**

ozone layer A thin layer of gas in the upper atmosphere that keeps harmful solar rays from reaching Earth's surface. **940**

pacification Policy followed by U.S. and South Vietnamese officials of trying to protect villagers by creating civilian areas guarded by government troops. **881**

Pacific Railway Acts (1862, 1864) Two laws passed by the federal government that gave loans and land grants to railroad companies to encourage them to build a transcontinental railroad. **555**

Paleo-Indians The first Americans who crossed from Asia into North America sometime between 10,000 and 3,800 B.C. **5**

Palmer raids (1920) Raids ordered by Attorney General A. Mitchell Palmer on suspected radical organizations. **700**

Panama Canal Canal built by the United States across the Isthmus of Panama to link the Atlantic and Pacific Oceans; opened in 1914. **656**

Panama Canal treaties (1977) Agreement made between U.S. and Panamanian leaders to transfer control of the Panama Canal to Panama by the year 2000. **915**

Panic of 1837 A financial crisis in the United States that led to an economic depression. **342**

Panic of 1873 A financial crisis in the United States that led to an economic depression and weakened the Republican Party. **530**

pardon Freedom from punishment. **223**

Paris Peace Accords (1973) Agreement made by leaders of the National Liberation Front, North Vietnam, South Vietnam, and the United States to end the Vietnam War. **891**

Parliament The British national legislature. **93**

patents Exclusive rights to manufacture or sell inventions. **580**

Patriots American colonists who fought for independence from Great Britain during the Revolutionary War. **160**

Peace Corps President John F. Kennedy's program that sends American volunteers to assist developing nations with improvement projects. **847**

Pendleton Civil Service Act (1883) Act that established a merit system for awarding federal jobs. **609**

Pentagon A huge building complex located in Arlington, Virginia, that houses the leadership of the U.S. military; named after its five-sided shape. **945**

perestroika Soviet policy established in the 1980s that initiated political and economic reforms. **931**

petition A formal request. **249**

Pickett's Charge (1863) Failed Confederate attack, led by General George Pickett, at the Battle of Gettysburg. **499**

Pilgrims Members of a Puritan Separatist sect that left England in the early 1600s to settle in the Americas. **71**

Pinckney's Treaty (1795) Agreement between the United States and Spain that changed Florida's border and made it easier for American ships to use the port of New Orleans. **282**

pioneers People who first settle an area. **131**

plantations Large farms that usually specialize in growing one kind of crop. **45**

planters Wealthy farmers with large plantations. **69, 375**

Platt Amendment (1902) Amendment to the Cuban constitution that gave the United States the right to become involved in Cuba's foreign and domestic affairs; was in effect until 1934. **650**

Plessy* v. *Ferguson (1896) U.S. Supreme Court case that established the separate-but-equal doctrine for public facilities. **532**

political action committees (PACs) Organizations that collect money to distribute to candidates who support the same issues as the contributors. **258**

political machines Political organizations that used legal and illegal methods to ensure that their candidates won elections. **606**

political parties Groups of people who organize to help elect government officials and influence government policies. **287**

poll tax A special tax that a person had to pay in order to vote. **531**

Pontiac's Rebellion (1763) Unsuccessful effort by Ottawa chief Pontiac and his allies to drive out British on the frontier. **133**

Pony Express A system of messengers that carried mail between relay stations on a route from St. Joseph, Missouri, to San Francisco, California, in 1860 and 1861. **555**

pop art Art movement that challenged the values of traditional art by using popular, commonplace images and objects. **868**

popular sovereignty The idea that political authority belongs to the people; principle that would allow voters in a particular territory to decide whether to ban or permit slavery. **204, 451**

Populist Party National political party formed in 1891 that supported free coinage of silver, labor reforms, immigration restrictions, and government ownership of railroads and the telegraph and telephone systems. **600**

potlatches Ceremonial events held by Indian peoples of the American Northwest at which hosts gave away most of their goods to gain respect. **12**

Potsdam Conference (1945) Meeting of U.S. president Harry S Truman, British prime minister Winston Churchill, and Soviet leader Joseph Stalin after Germany's surrender in World War II, at which they divided Germany into four zones of occupation. **799**

Pottawatomie Massacre (1856) Incident in which abolitionist John Brown and seven other men murdered pro-slavery Kansans. **461**

Powhatan Confederacy Powerful alliance of Algonquian Indians under the leadership of Wahunsonacock. **66**

precedent An action or decision that later serves as an example. **270**

presidios Spanish military bases located in the Americas. **44**

privateers Private ships authorized by a nation to attack its enemies. **280**

Privy Council Group of royal advisers who set policies for Britain's American colonies. **92**

Proclamation of 1763 British proclamation banning further colonial settlement west of the Appalachian Mountains and ordering colonists already living there to move their settlements. **134**

progressives Group of reformers who worked to improve social and political problems, beginning in the late 1800s. **610**

propaganda Stories and images designed to support a particular point of view. **140**

proprietors Owners. **82**

prospect To search for gold. **438**

protective tariff A tax on imported goods that raises the price of imports so people will buy domestic goods. **275**

Protestant Reformation Religious movement begun by Martin Luther and others in 1517 to reform the Catholic Church. **47**

Protestants Reformers who protested certain practices of the Catholic Church. **47**

pueblos Spanish towns in the Americas. **44**

Pullman Strike (1894) Railroad strike by workers at Pullman's Palace Car Company that stopped traffic on many railroad lines until federal courts ordered the workers to return to their jobs. **589**

Pure Food and Drug Act (1906) Legislation that prohibited the manufacture, sale, or transportation of mislabeled or contaminated food and drugs through interstate commerce. **626**

Puritans Protestants who wanted to reform the Church of England. **70**

Quakers Society of Friends; Protestant sect founded in the mid-1800s in England that believed salvation was available to all people. **85**

Radical Republicans Republican members of Congress who felt that southern states needed to make great social changes before they could be readmitted to the Union. **521**

range rights Rights to water on the Plains that smaller ranchers bought from larger ranchers. **560**

range wars Competition among large ranchers, small ranchers, and farmers on the Plains for the use of the open range. **563**

ratification Formal approval. **190**

realpolitik German word meaning "practical politics"; policy developed by Henry Kissinger and implemented by President Richard Nixon that put American interests, rather than political or moral ideals, first in foreign-policy decisions. **905**

recall Process that allows voters to recall, or remove, an elected official before the end of his or her term. **612**

Reconstruction (1865–77) Period following the Civil War during which the U.S. government worked to reunite the nation and to rebuild the southern states. **515**

Reconstruction Acts (1867–68) Laws that put the southern states under U.S. military control and required them to draft new constitutions upholding the Fourteenth Amendment. **524**

Redcoats British soldiers who fought against the colonists in the American Revolution; so called because of their bright red uniforms. **154**

Redeemers Group of southerners who helped return the Democrats to political power in the South during Reconstruction and tried to limit the civil rights of African Americans. **531**

Red Scare A wave of anticommunist fear that swept the United States after World War I. **700**

referendum Measure allowing citizens to vote on proposed laws. **612**

rendezvous Annual event held by mountain men to trade furs and socialize. **427**

reparations Payments for damages and expenses brought on by war. **688**

repeal To end or abolish. **138**

representative democracy A government that is led by officials who are chosen by the people. **220**

republicanism Support for a system of representative government known as a republic. **188**

Republican Party Political party formed in the 1850s to stop the spread of slavery in the West. **462**

Republic of Texas Independent nation of Texas, which lasted from 1836 until 1848, when Texas was annexed to the United States. **426**

reservations Federal lands set aside for American Indians. **548**

reserved powers Powers retained by the state governments or by citizens. **221**

revivals Public church gatherings at which ministers preach to a large number of people. **108**

Rhode Island System System developed by Samuel Slater in the mid-1800s, in which families were hired as textile workers. **365**

right of deposit Right to transfer goods at a destination without having to pay fees for the cargo. **281**

Roosevelt Corollary (1904) President Theodore Roosevelt's addition to the Monroe Doctrine; declared that the United States would police affairs in the Western Hemisphere to keep Europeans from intervening in the region. **657**

roundup Act of driving cattle together and collecting them into a herd. **560**

Rush-Bagot Agreement (1817) Agreement that limited naval power on the Great Lakes to the United States and British Canada. **328**

sanctions Economic penalties. **916**

Sandinistas Revolutionary political party in Nicaragua that overthrew a pro-American dictator in 1979. **930**

Santa Fe Trail A route running from Independence, Missouri, to Santa Fe in what is now New Mexico; used primarily by merchants. **431**

Saturday Night Massacre Name given to the series of events that included the firing of a special prosecutor investigating Watergate and the resignations of the U.S. attorney general and his next in command for refusing to fire the prosecutor. **909**

scalawags Name given to white southerners who supported Reconstruction for private gain; roughly defined as "mean fellows." **528**

scientific agriculture Use of scientific techniques to improve crop production. **374**

scientific method Observation of and experimentation with natural events in order to form theories that could predict other events or behaviors. **113**

Scientific Revolution Period of great learning that began in the 1600s as European scientists, mathematicians, and astronomers looked for explanations about how the universe worked. **112**

Scopes trial (1925) Trial of John T. Scopes, a high school science teacher who was arrested in Dayton, Tennessee, and tried for teaching Darwin's theory of evolution. **708**

sea dogs English sailors encouraged by Queen Elizabeth I to raid Spanish treasure ships in the late 1500s. **48**

search-and-destroy missions U.S. strategy in the Vietnam War in which U.S. patrols searched for hidden enemy camps and supplies and destroyed them with massive firepower and air raids. **880**

search warrant A judge's order authorizing the search of a person's home or property to look for evidence of a crime. **250**

secession Act of formally withdrawing from an organization, such as a country. **471**

Second Battle of Bull Run (1862) Civil War battle in which the Confederate army forced most of the Union army out of Virginia. **485**

Second Battle of the Marne (1918) Last offensive launched by the Germans during World War I. **684**

Second Continental Congress (1775) Meeting of colonial delegates in Philadelphia to decide how to react to fighting at Lexington and Concord. **154**

Second Great Awakening A period of religious evangelism that began in the 1790s and became widespread in the United States by the 1830s. **390**

Second Industrial Revolution A period of explosive growth in manufacturing and industry in the late 1800s. **578**

sect A religious group. **70**

sectionalism A devotion to the interests of one geographic region rather than those of the country as a whole. **451**

Sedition Act of 1918 Law passed during World War I that made it illegal for Americans to speak disloyally about the U.S. government, Constitution, or flag. **679**

segregation Forced separation of people of different races in public places. **531**

Selective Service Act (1917) Law that required men between the ages of 21 and 30 to register for the draft into the armed forces. **679**

Selective Training and Service Act (1940) First peacetime draft in U.S. history. **767**

self-determination Right of people to decide their own political status. **687**

Seneca Falls Convention (1848) First national women's rights convention at which the Declaration of Sentiments was written. **415**

separation of powers The division of governmental power into distinct areas with different branches of government exercising different powers; prevents one branch from becoming too powerful. **221**

Separatists Radical group of Puritans who wanted to cut all ties with the Church of England. **70**

settlement houses Neighborhood centers that arose in the late 1800s to offer education, recreation, and social activities to immigrants and poor people. **595**

Seven Days' Battles (1862) Series of Civil War battles in which Confederate army successes forced the Union army to retreat from near Richmond, Virginia, the Confederate capital. **485**

Seventeenth Amendment (1913) Constitutional amendment allowing American voters to directly elect U.S. senators. **611**

sharecropping System used on southern farms after the Civil War in which farmers worked land owned by someone else in return for a small portion of the crops. **533**

Shays' Rebellion (1786-87) Uprising of Massachusetts's farmers, led by Daniel Shays, to protest high taxes, heavy debt, and farm foreclosures. **198**

Sherman Antitrust Act (1890) Law that made it illegal to create monopolies or trusts that restrained trade. **584**

Sherman Silver Purchase Act (1890) Law that increased the amount of silver purchased by the U.S. government for coinage. **599**

siege Military blockade of a city or fort. **155**

Siege of Vicksburg (1863) Union army's six-week blockade of Vicksburg that led the city to surrender during the Civil War. **490**

silent generation Name given to teenagers and college students in the 1950s because many of them seemed to conform to social expectations without protest. **831**

Silent Majority President Richard Nixon's term for a large group of conservative voters who disliked the changes that took place in the 1960s. **902**

Silk Road Overland trade route that linked China with other Asian markets as far west as the Black Sea. **25**

sit-down strike Type of strike in which striking workers refuse to leave the factories so that owners cannot replace them. **741**

sit-in Demonstration in which protesters sit down in a location and refuse to leave. **855**

Sixteenth Amendment (1913) Constitutional amendment that allowed the federal government to pass direct taxes, such as an income tax. **629**

slave codes Laws passed in the colonies to control slaves. **104**

GLOSSARY

socialism Economic system in which the government or the workers own and operate the means of production. **618**

Social Security Act (1935) Legislation that created Social Security, which provides retirement pensions and unemployment insurance to American workers, as well as aid to older Americans and people with disabilities. **740**

societies Groups of people who share a common culture. **6**

sodbusters Name given to both the Plains farmers and the plows they used to break up the region's tough sod. **566**

Sons of Liberty Secret societies formed in the mid-1700s by colonists to protest new taxes and to frighten tax collectors. **137**

southern strategy The Republican Party's attempt to win the support of southern Democrats and others who opposed civil rights reform by limiting further civil rights legislation. **903**

Spanish Armada Large Spanish fleet defeated by England in 1588. **48**

speakeasies Secret, illegal clubs that served alcohol during prohibition. **707**

speculation The investing of money in a high-risk venture in hopes of making a profit. **732**

speculators Investors who buy items at low prices in hopes that their value will rise. **273**

spheres of influence Areas of a country, particularly in China during the late 1800s, where foreign nations control much of the trade and natural resources. **644**

spirituals Emotional Christian songs sung by slaves in the South that mixed African and European elements and usually expressed slaves' religious beliefs. **380**

spoils system Politicians' practice of giving government jobs to their supporters. **340**

Sputnik (1957) The world's first artificial satellite; launched by the Soviet Union. **822**

stagflation Economic situation characterized by both high inflation and high unemployment. **903**

stalemate Situation in which neither side of a conflict can win a decisive victory. **674**

Stamp Act (1765) Law passed by Parliament that raised tax money by requiring colonists to pay for an official stamp whenever they bought paper items such as newspapers, licenses, and legal documents. **137**

staple crops Crops that are continuously in demand. **106**

states' rights Belief that the federal government's power over the states is strictly limited. **340**

steerage Area in a ship's lower levels; many immigrants who came to the United States traveled in this less-expensive space. **591**

strait Narrow, winding sea passage. **39**

Strategic Arms Limitation Talks (SALT) (1972) Talks between U.S. president Richard Nixon and Soviet leader Leonid Brezhnev that led to a treaty limiting the numbers and types of long-range nuclear missiles each country could have. **906**

strict construction Way of interpreting the Constitution that allows the federal government to take only those actions the Constitution specifically says it can take. **276**

strike Refusal of workers to perform their jobs until employers meet their demands. **365**

Student Nonviolent Coordinating Committee (SNCC) Student organization formed in 1960 to coordinate civil rights demonstrations and provide training for protesters. **856**

Students for a Democratic Society (SDS) Student group that actively protested discrimination, strict college rules, and the growing U.S. presence in Vietnam. **866**

subsidy Bonus payment. **642**

suburbs Residential neighborhoods surrounding a city. **594**

Suez Crisis International crisis that began in 1956 when Britain, France, and Israel invaded the Suez Canal region in Egypt. **824**

suffrage Voting rights. **188**

Sugar Act (1764) Law passed by the British Parliament setting taxes on molasses and sugar imported by the colonies. **135**

Sunbelt States in the South and Southwest that attracted many new people and businesses in the 1950s because of low tax rates, a warm climate, and jobs. **827**

supply-side economics Economic theory that lowering taxes would boost the economy. **929**

***Sussex* pledge** (1916) Promise issued by German leaders during World War I not to sink merchant vessels without warning. **676**

Sutter's Fort Northern California colony founded by Swiss immigrant John Sutter in 1839 that became a popular destination for American immigrants. **431**

Taft-Hartley Act (1947) Law that gave the federal government greater authority to end strikes and required union leaders to take an oath stating that they were not Communists. **806**

talkie A movie with sound or dialogue. **716**

Tariff of Abominations (1828) Nickname given to a new tariff by southerners who opposed it. **340**

tariffs Taxes on imports or exports. **196**

Tea Act (1773) Law passed by Parliament allowing the British East India Company to sell its low-cost tea directly to the colonies, undermining colonial tea merchants; led to the Boston Tea Party. **141**

Teapot Dome scandal Scandal during President Warren G. Harding's administration involving Secretary of the Interior Albert Fall's illegal leasing of oil reserves in return for personal gifts and loans. **703**

technology Tools used to produce goods or to do work. **363**

Tejanos Spanish settlers who lived in what is now southern Texas. **423**

telegraph Machine invented by Samuel F. B. Morse in 1837 that uses pulses of electric current to send messages across long distances through wires. **369**

Teller Amendment (1898) Amendment to a U.S. resolution declaring that the United States did not intend to take over and annex an independent Cuba. **647**

temperance movement A social reform effort begun in the mid-1800s to encourage people to drink less alcohol. **402**

tenements Poorly built, overcrowded housing where many immigrants lived. **399**

Tennessee Valley Authority (TVA) (1933) New Deal program that built dams to provide hydroelectric power and flood control to the Tennessee River valley. **738**

Ten Percent Plan President Abraham Lincoln's plan for Reconstruction; once 10 percent of voters in a former Confederate state took a U.S. loyalty oath, they could form a new state government and be readmitted to the Union. **515**

terrorism Use of violent attacks by individuals or small groups to advance political goals. **938**

Tet Offensive (1968) Attack by North Vietnamese and Vietcong troops against South Vietnam during the Vietnam War; took place during Tet (the Vietnamese New Year) and demonstrated that the North Vietnamese were still militarily strong. **885**

Texas longhorn Hearty breed of cattle raised by ranchers throughout western Texas. **558**

textiles Cloth. **363**

Thirteenth Amendment (1865) Constitutional amendment that outlawed slavery. **516**

38th parallel Line of latitude that separates North Korea and South Korea. **809**

Three-Fifths Compromise (1787) Agreement worked out at the Constitutional Convention stating that three fifths of the slaves in each state should be counted as part of the state's population for determining representation in the lower house of Congress. **203**

Toleration Act of 1649 Maryland law that made restricting the religious rights of Christians a crime; the first law guaranteeing religious freedom to be passed in America. **82**

Tonkin Gulf Resolution (1964) Congressional measure that gave President Lyndon B. Johnson the authority to wage war in Vietnam. **879**

totalitarianism Political system in which the government controls every aspect of citizens' lives. **751**

total war Type of war in which an army destroys its opponent's ability to fight by targeting civilian and economic as well as military resources. **502**

totems Images of ancestors or animals; often carved onto tall poles by Native American peoples of the Pacific Northwest. **12**

town meeting Political meeting at which people make decisions on local issues; used primarily in New England. **94**

Townshend Acts (1767) Laws passed by Parliament placing duties on certain items imported by the colonists. **139**

trade deficit An imbalance in which a nation imports more than it exports. **911**

trade unions Workers' organizations that try to improve pay and working conditions. **365**

Trail of Tears (1838–39) An 800-mile forced march made by the Cherokee from their homeland in Georgia to Indian Territory; resulted in the deaths of thousands of Cherokee. **347**

transcendentalism Idea that people could rise above the material things in life; philosophy shared by some New England writers and thinkers in the mid-1800s. **392**

transcontinental railroad Railroad that crossed the continental United States; construction began in 1863 and was completed in 1869. **555**

Transportation Revolution Rapid growth in the speed and convenience of transportation; in the United States this began in the early 1800s. **366**

Treaty of Brest-Litovsk (1918) Peace agreement between the Central Powers and Russia that removed Russia from World War I. **683**

Treaty of Dancing Rabbit Creek (1830) Agreement in which the Choctaw gave up more than 10 million acres of land in Mississippi and accepted removal to Indian Territory. **346**

Treaty of Fort Laramie (1851) The first major treaty between the U.S. government and Plains Indians; allowed U.S. citizens to travel across Indian homelands. **547**

Treaty of Ghent (1814) Treaty signed by the United States and Britain ending the War of 1812. **319**

Treaty of Greenville (1795) Agreement between American Indian confederation leaders and the U.S. government that gave the United States Indian lands in the southeastern part of the Northwest Territory and guaranteed that U.S. citizens could safely travel through the region. **284**

Treaty of Guadalupe Hidalgo (1848) Treaty that ended the Mexican War and gave the United States much of Mexico's northern territory. **436**

Treaty of Medicine Lodge (1867) Agreement between the U.S. government and southern Plains Indians in which the Indians agreed to move onto reservations. **548**

Treaty of Paris (1763) Peace agreement that ended the French and Indian War. **130**

Treaty of Paris of 1783 Peace agreement that officially ended the Revolutionary War and established British recognition of the United States. **181**

Treaty of Tordesillas (1494) Treaty signed by Spain and Portugal in which both countries agreed to move the Line of Demarcation 800 miles farther west. **36**

Treaty of Versailles (1919) Treaty ending World War I that required Germany to pay billions of dollars of war costs and established the League of Nations. **688**

Tredegar Iron Works Large iron factory that operated in Richmond, Virginia, in the early to mid-1800s. **375**

trench warfare World War I military strategy of defending a position by fighting from the protection of deep ditches. **672**

Triangle Shirtwaist Factory Fire Accident at a New York City factory in which 146 workers died after a fire broke out in the building; helped spur legislation to improve factory safety standards. **616**

triangular trade Trading networks in which goods and slaves moved among England, the American colonies, the West Indies, and West Africa. **100**

Triple Alliance Military alliance formed by Austria-Hungary, Germany, and Italy in the late 1800s. **669**

Triple Entente Military alliance formed by Britain, France, and Russia in 1907. **669**

Truman Doctrine (1947) President Harry S Truman's policy stating that the United States would provide economic aid to any country fighting against communism. **801**

trust Legal arrangement grouping several companies under one board of directors to eliminate competition and to regulate production. **582**

Twelfth Amendment (1804) Constitutional amendment that created a separate ballot for president and vice president. **292**

Twenty-first Amendment (1933) Constitutional amendment that ended national prohibition by repealing the Eighteenth Amendment. **707**

Twenty-sixth Amendment (1971) Constitutional amendment that lowered the federal voting age from 21 to 18. **891**

U-boats German submarines; stands for undersea boat. **673**

unalienable rights Basic human rights such as life, liberty, and the pursuit of happiness. **159**

Uncle Tom's Cabin (1852) Antislavery novel written by Harriet Beecher Stowe that showed northerners the violent reality of slavery and drew many people to the abolitionists' cause. **455**

Underground Railroad Network of people who helped thousands of slaves escape to the North by providing transportation and hiding places. **410**

Underwood Tariff Act (1913) Act that significantly lowered U.S. tariff rates and introduced the first modern personal income tax. **629**

United Farm Workers (UFW) Union formed by César Chávez to improve pay and working conditions for migrant farm workers. **863**

United Mine Workers (UMW) Union of coal mine workers that went on strike in 1946. **806**

United Nations (UN) International organization formed in 1945 to resolve conflicts between nations. **799**

Universal Negro Improvement Association (UNIA) Association founded by Marcus Garvey in 1914 to end imperialism in Africa and discrimination in the United States. **709**

urban renewal Program launched by the federal government to improve life in U.S. cities through better public services and new housing projects. **828**

utopian communities Places where people worked to establish a perfect society; such communities were popular in the United States during the late 1700s and early to mid-1800s. **392**

vaqueros Mexican cowboys in the West who tended cattle and horses. **560**

vertical integration Ownership of businesses involved in each step of a manufacturing process. **582**

veto To cancel. **223**

Vietcong Communist guerrilla force that fought against the government of South Vietnam. **876**

Vietminh Group of Vietnamese nationalists organized by Ho Chi Minh and dedicated to Vietnamese independence. **875**

Vietnamization Policy followed by the Nixon administration of gradually turning over all the fighting in the Vietnam War to the South Vietnamese Army. **888**

Vietnam Veterans Memorial Memorial in Washington, D.C., dedicated in 1982 to honor Americans who died in or went missing in the Vietnam War. **893**

Virginia Plan (1787) Plan for government proposed at the Constitutional Convention in which the national government would have three branches—executive, judicial, and legislative; representation in the legislature would be determined by state population. **201**

Virginia Statute for Religious Freedom (1786) Legislation that gave people in Virginia freedom of worship and freedom to speak their opinions about religion. **188**

Voting Rights Act of 1965 Law that ensured every eligible U.S. citizen's right to vote. **858**

Wade-Davis Bill Reconstruction plan that imposed two conditions for a former Confederate state to rejoin the United States; it had to outlaw slavery, and majority of adult males had to take a loyalty oath; those who had supported the Confederacy could not vote or hold office. **515**

War Hawks Members of Congress who wanted to declare war against Britain in the early 1800s. **312**

War Industries Board (WIB) Agency created by President Woodrow Wilson during World War Ito oversee the production and distribution of goods manufactured by the nation's war industries. **680**

War on Drugs President George Bush's continuation of the government effort to stop illegal drugs from entering the United States. **933**

War on Poverty Name given to President Lyndon B. Johnson's programs assisting poor Americans. **852**

War Powers Act (1973) Legislation that required the president to get congressional approval before committing U.S. troops to an armed struggle. **893**

War Production Board (WPB) World War II agency that oversaw the conversion of factories to war production. **768**

Warren Commission Special group appointed by President Lyndon B. Johnson to investigate the assassination of President John F. Kennedy. **851**

Warsaw Pact A military alliance of eastern European nations formed by the Soviet Union in 1955. **803**

Washington Conference (1921) Meeting among the United States and the world's major nations to discuss disarmament. **704**

Watergate Scandal in which President Richard Nixon authorized a cover-up of a break-in at the Democratic National Committee headquarters; led to Nixon's resignation in 1974. **907**

Whig Party Political party formed by opponents of Andrew Jackson in 1834 who supported a strong legislature. **342**

Whiskey Rebellion (1794) Protest by small farmers in Pennsylvania against new taxes on whiskey and other alcohol. **284**

wigwams Small circular huts in which some northeastern Native American peoples lived. **16**

Wilderness Campaign (May–June 1864) A series of battles between Union and Confederate forces in northern and central Virginia that stretched Confederate resources to their limit. **501**

Wilmot Proviso (1846) Proposal to outlaw slavery in the territory added to the United States by the Mexican Cession; passed in the House of Representatives but was defeated in the Senate. **451**

Wisconsin Idea Governor Robert La Follette's program of reforms for Wisconsin in the early 1900s; became a model for other state governments. **612**

Woman's Christian Temperance Union Women's reform organization founded in 1874 to fight alcohol abuse. **620**

Woodstock (1969) Concert that took place near Woodstock, New York; became a symbol of the counterculture's idealistic spirit. **869**

Worcester* v. *Georgia (1832) Supreme Court ruling that the Cherokee Nation was a distinct territory over which only the federal government had authority; ignored by both President Andrew Jackson and the state of Georgia. **347**

Works Progress Administration (WPA) (1935) New Deal agency created to put American men and women to work constructing and repairing bridges, roads, buildings, and parks. **740**

World Trade Center A large business and financial office complex in New York City; the Twin Towers of the complex were destroyed by a terrorist attack on September 11, 2001. **944**

World Trade Organization Organization that supervises international trade; has some 140 members, including the United States. **942**

writs of assistance Special search warrants that allowed tax collectors to search for smuggled goods. **139**

xenophobia Fear and hatred of foreigners. **701**

XYZ affair (1797) Incident in which French agents attempted to get a bribe and loans from U.S. diplomats in exchange for an agreement that French privateers would no longer attack American ships. **289**

Yalta Conference (1945) Meeting of U.S. president Franklin D. Roosevelt, British prime minister Winston Churchill, and Soviet leader Joseph Stalin during World War II to plan for the postwar world. **798**

yellow journalism The use of sensational, often exaggerated new stories in newspapers or other publications to attract readers. **646**

yeomen Small landowning farmers. **376**

Zimmermann Note Telegram sent by Germany's foreign minister to Mexico during World War I proposing an alliance between the two countries. **677**

zoot-suit riots (1943) Attacks by U.S. sailors against Mexican Americans in Los Angeles. **770**

Glossary/Glosario

This Glossary contains terms you need to understand as you study American history. After each key term there is a brief definition or explanation of the meaning of the term as it is used in *Call to Freedom*. The page number refers to the page on which the term is introduced in the textbook.

ABC Powers/potencias ABC Argentina, Brasil y Chile. **663**

abolition/abolición Dar por terminada la esclavitud. **407**

Adams-Onís Treaty/Tratado Adams-Onís (1819) Acuerdo en el que España cede el territorio de Florida a Estados Unidos. **330**

Alamo/Álamo Misión española en San Antonio, Texas. Sitio de una famosa batalla durante la Revolución texana de 1836. La victoria del ejército mexicano dio como resultado la muerte de todos los texanos defensores del edificio. **425**

Albany Plan of Union/Plan de Unión Albany (1754) Plan redactado por Benjamin Franklin y otros delegados para pedir a las colonias que se unieran bajo un gobierno común. **128**

Alien and Sedition Acts/Leyes de extranjería y sedición Leyes aprobadas por un Congreso con mayoría federalista que hizo ilegal publicar mensajes orales o escritos en contra del gobierno; fueron utilizadas para combatir al Partido Demócrata Republicano. **290**

Allied Powers/potencias aliadas Alianza creada en la Primera Guerra Mundial por Gran Bretaña, Francia, Rusia y más tarde Estados Unidos, y en la Segunda Guerra Mundial por Gran Bretaña, Francia, Estados Unidos y otros países para combatir a los países del Eje de Potencias. **671, 763**

amendments/enmiendas Cambios, correcciones o agregados que se hacen de manera oficial a la constitución de un país. **210**

American Anti-Slavery Society/Sociedad Estadounidense contra la Esclavitud Grupo fundado en 1833 por William Lloyd Garrison y otras personas para la abolición inmediata de la esclavitud y la igualdad racial de los afroestadounidenses. **409**

American Civil Liberties Union/Unión de Libertades Civiles Estadounidenses (ACLU, por sus siglas en inglés) Organización formada en 1920 para proteger los derechos civiles. **701**

American Colonization Society/Sociedad Estadounidense de Colonización Sociedad organizada en 1817 para establecer en África Occidental una colonia llamada Liberia como hogar para los afroestadounidenses libres. **408**

American Expeditionary Force/Fuerza Expedicionaria Estadounidense (AEF, por sus siglas en inglés) Tropas de apoyo que sirvieron fuera de Estados Unidos durante la Primera Guerra Mundial. **682**

American Federation of Labor/Federación Estadounidense del Trabajo (AFL, por sus siglas en inglés) Uno de los primeros sindicatos del trabajo en Estados Unidos; fundado en la década de 1880 por Samuel Gompers para agrupar varios sindicatos de obreros calificados. **587**

American Indian Movement/Movimiento Indígena Estadounidense (AIM, por sus siglas en inglés) Organización formada en 1968 para proteger los derechos de los indígenas estadounidenses. **864**

Americans with Disabilities Act/Ley de Estadounidenses con Discapacidad (ADA, por sus siglas en inglés) (1990) Ley que garantiza a las personas con discapacidad igual acceso a servicios públicos, transporte y oportunidades de empleo. **933**

American System/Sistema estadounidense Plan de alza de impuestos creado por Henry Clay para realizar mejoras internas como la reparación de caminos y canales. **334**

amnesty/amnistía Perdón oficial del gobierno por un acto ilegal. **515**

anarchists/anarquistas Personas que se oponen a cualquier forma de gobierno. **587**

annex/anexar Tomar control de un territorio para incorporarlo a un estado, país, etc. **426**

Antifederalists/antifederalistas Personas que se oponían a la ratificación de la Constitución. **206**

Anti-Imperialist League/Liga Antiimperialista Grupo de estadounidenses que se oponían al tratado que daba por terminada la guerra entre Estados Unidos y España porque creían que Estados Unidos tenía intenciones de crear un imperio colonial. **650**

apartheid/apartheid Sistema de leyes sudafricanas que fomentaban la segregación racial. **916**

appeasement/pacificación Acción de ceder ante una agresión para mantener la paz. **763**

Appomattox Courthouse/Corte de Appomatox Lugar en el que el general del ejército de la unión Ulysses S. Grant aceptó la rendición del general confederado Robert E. Lee, dando por terminada la Guerra Civil. **503**

apportionment/adjudicación Uso de la población para determinar el número de legisladores que cada zona del país debe tener en la Cámara de representantes. **222**

apprentices/aprendices Personas que aprenden un oficio de un experto en la materia. **105**

arbitration/arbitraje Encuentros formales para analizar y solucionar desacuerdos. **626**

archaeology/arqueología Estudio científico del pasado no escrito. **5**

armistice/armisticio Tregua entre grupos o países en guerra. **685**

Army-McCarthy hearings/audiencias Ejército-McCarthy Audiencias de las investigaciones del senado en el caso de supuestos brotes de comunismo en el ejército de Estados Unidos denunciados por el senador Joseph McCarthy, que fueron televisadas en la década de 1950. **815**

Articles of Confederation/Artículos de la Confederación (1777) Documento que creó el primer gobierno central de Estados Unidos, mismo que fue reemplazado por la Constitución en 1789. **189**

artifacts/artefactos Restos de objetos fabricados por el hombre. **5**

assembly line/línea de ensamble Sistema que cuenta con una línea móvil en la que cada obrero ensambla una parte para acelerar la producción. **711**

astrolabe/astrolabio Instrumento usado por los navegantes en algún tiempo para determinar la posición de una embarcación con base en la posición de las estrellas. **33**

Atlanta Compromise/Compromiso de Atlanta (1895) Discurso en el que Booker T. Washington criticó a los afroestadounidenses enfatizando que deberían mejorar su educación y situación económica en lugar de crear revueltas en contra de la discriminación y segregación racial. **622**

Atlantic Charter/Carta del Atlántico (1941) Pacto firmado por el presidente de Estados Unidos Franklin D. Roosevelt y el primer ministro de Inglaterra Winston Churchill comprometiéndose a luchar por la paz mundial. **765**

atomic bomb/bomba atómica Arma nuclear que produce una gran explosión mediante la separación de los núcleos atómicos de un elemento; Estados Unidos lanzó dos bombas de este tipo sobre Japón en la Segunda Guerra Mundial. **785**

automation/automatización Uso de máquinas en la producción industrial. **826**

Axis powers/potencias del Eje Alianza militar formada por Italia y Alemania en 1936 a la que más tarde se unieron Japón y otros países para combatir a las potencias Aliadas durante la Segunda Guerra Mundial. **752**

baby boom/auge de los bebés Aumento significativo en la tasa de natalidad, especialmente en Estados Unidos, en los años posteriores a la Segunda Guerra Mundial **828**

backcountry/backcountry Región fronteriza de Virginia y las Carolinas, localizada entre la costa y los montes Apalaches. **131**

Bacon's Rebellion/rebelión de Bacon (1676) Ataque encabezado por Nathaniel Bacon en contra de los indígenas estadounidenses y el gobierno colonial de Virginia. **69**

balance of power/equilibrio de poder Situación generada cuando la lucha entre países rivales no se inclina a favor de ninguno. **669**

balance of trade/balanza de intercambio Relación entre los bienes que un país adquiere de otros países y los que les vende. **98**

Bank of the United States/Banco de Estados Unidos Banco nacional rentado por el Congreso en 1791 para ofrecer seguridad a la economía de Estados Unidos. **277**

Bataan Death March/marcha de la muerte de Bataan (1942) Marcha obligada, durante la Segunda Guerra Mundial, de miles de prisioneros estadounidenses y filipinos hacia los campos de trabajos forzados en la península de Bataan. **779**

Battle of Antietam/Batalla de Antietam (1862) Victoria del ejército de la unión en Maryland que es recordada como la batalla de un solo día más sangrienta de la historia de Estados Unidos. **486**

Battle of Britain/Batalla de Bretaña (1940-41) Combate entre las fuerzas aéreas británicas y alemanas por el control del espacio aéreo de la Gran Bretaña. **764**

Battle of Brandywine Creek/Batalla de Brandywine Creek (1777) Batalla de la Revolución en la que las fuerzas británicas arrasaron con los patriotas en Pennsylvania. **172**

Battle of Bunker Hill/Batalla de Bunker Hill (1775) Batalla de la Guerra Revolucionaria realizada en Boston en la que los colonos demostraron que tenían la capacidad de enfrentar al ejército británico. **156**

Battle of El Alamein/Batalla de El Alamein (1942) Victoria de las tropas británicas que impidió el avance de las Potencias del Eje en el norte de África durante la Segunda Guerra Mundial. **773**

Battle of Fallen Timbers/Batalla de Fallen Timbers (1794) Batalla entre las tropas estadounidenses y una confederación indígena estadounidense que se resistía al establecimiento de personas de raza blanca en el noroeste de Estados Unidos; esta batalla condujo al Tratado de Greenville. **284**

Battle of Gettysburg/Batalla de Gettysburg (1863) Victoria del ejército de la Unión en Gettysburg, Pennsylvania, que inclinó la balanza en contra de los confederados durante la Guerra Civil. **499**

Battle of Goliad/Batalla de Goliad (1836) Victoria del ejército mexicano durante la Guerra de Texas en la que el general Antonio López de Santa Anna ordenó la ejecución de soldados texanos después de su rendición. **425**

Battle of Horseshoe Bend/Batalla de Horseshoe Bend (1814) Victoria del ejército estadounidense durante la Guerra de 1812 en la que las tropas de Andrew Jackson obligaron a los indios creek a ceder gran parte de su territorio en el sur del país. **317**

Battle of Lake Erie/Batalla del Lago Erie (1813) Victoria en la que, comandado por Oliver Hazard Perry, el ejército estadounidense puso fin al control británico del Lago Erie. **316**

Battle of Leyte Gulf/Batalla del Golfo de Leyte (1944) Batalla de la Segunda Guerra Mundial que tuvo lugar en Filipinas y que es recordada como el combate naval más largo de la historia. **781**

Battle of Midway/Batalla de Midway (1942) Batalla de la Segunda Guerra Mundial en la que la fuerza aérea estadounidense causó serios daños a la armada japonesa. **780**

Battle of New Orleans/Batalla de Nueva Orleáns (1815) La mayor victoria del ejército en estadounideuse la guerra de 1812; este combate tuvo lugar dos semanas después de la firma del tratado de paz que dio por terminada esta guerra. **318**

Battle of Pea Ridge/Batalla de Pea Ridge (1862) Batalla de la Guerra Civil en la que el ejército confederado establecido en Missouri y al que se habían unido algunos indígenas estadounidenses, fue derrotado en el noroeste de Arkansas. **491**

Battle of Princeton/Batalla de Princeton (1777) Batalla de la Revolución en la que los patriotas hicieron retroceder a las fuerzas británicas en Nueva Jersey. **171**

Battle of San Jacinto/Batalla de San Jacinto (1836) Batalla final de la Guerra de Texas en la que fue derrotado el ejército mexicano y Texas obtuvo su independencia. **425**

Battle of Saratoga/Batalla de Saratoga (1777) Batalla de la Guerra Revolucionaria realizada en Nueva York que marcó la victoria más importante de los patriotas hasta ese momento. **172**

Battle of Shiloh/Batalla de Shiloh (1862) Batalla de la Guerra Civil realizada en Tennessee en la que el ejército de la Unión adquirió mayor control sobre el Valle del Mississippi. **489**

Battle of Stalingrad/Batalla de Estalingrado (1942–43) Victoria fundamental de las fuerzas aliadas encabezadas por las tropas soviéticas en contra del ejército alemán durante la Segunda Guerra Mundial. **774**

Battle of the Atlantic/Batalla del Atlántico Intensa y larga batalla naval de la Segunda Guerra Mundial por el control de las rutas marítimas del océano Atlántico. **765**

Battle of the Bulge/Batalla del Bulge (1944–45) Combate de la Segunda Guerra Mundial en el que las fuerzas aliadas finalmente impidieron al ejército alemán contnuar con su plan ofensivo de guerra. **777**

Battle of the Coral Sea/Batalla del Mar de Coral (1942) Combate de la Segunda Guerra Mundial en el que las tropas aliadas detuvieron el avance del ejército japonés en el Pacífico. **779**

Battle of the Little Bighorn/Batalla de Little Bighorn (1876) "Útimo puesto de Custer"; lucha entre las tropas federales al mando del general George Armstrong Custer y los guerreros de la tribu sioux encabezados por Toro Sentado que marcó la derrota más importante del ejército estadounidense en territorio del oeste. **549**

Battle of the Thames/Batalla del Támesis (1813) Victoria del ejército estadounidense al mando de William Henry Harrison que puso fin a la alianza de indios y británicos durante la Guerra de 1812. **316**

Battle of Tippecanoe/Batalla de Tippecanoe (1811) Victoria del ejército estadounidense sobre la confederación india que intentaba evitar el establecimiento de poblaciones de blancos en el noroeste. Esta batalla aumentó las hostilidades entre Gran Bretaña y Estados Unidos. **311**

Battle of Trenton/Batalla de Trenton (1776) Batalla de la Revolución que tuvo lugar en Nueva Jersey y en la que las fuerzas de los patriotas capturaron a más de 900 soldados hesianos. **171**

Battle of Vincennes/Batalla de Vincennes (1779) Batalla de la Revolución librada en el oeste, en la que los patriotas retomaron de manos de los británicos el poblado de Vincennes, de población mayoritariamente francesa y localizado en la ribera del río Wabash. **178**

Battle of Yorktown/Batalla de Yorktown (1781) Última batalla importante de la Guerra Revolucionaria; sitio de rendición del general británico Charles Cornwallis ante los patriotas en territorio de Virginia. **180**

Bear Flag Revolt/Revuelta de Bear Flag (1846) Revuelta iniciada por colonos estadounidenses en contra del gobierno de México para declarar al territorio de California como una república independiente. **434**

bear market/tendencia a la baja Tendencia a la baja en el precio de las acciones en el mercado de valores. **732**

beats/beats Grupo de jóvenes escritores que criticaban el estilo de vida estadounidense en la década de 1950 mediante artículos y una conducta opuesta; también conocidos como beatniks. **830**

benevolent societies/sociedades de beneficencia Organizaciones que brindaban ayuda a los inmigrantes en caso de enfermedad, desempleo y muerte. **591**

Berlin Airlift/ayuda aérea de Berlín (1948) Esfuerzo conjunto de Estados Unidos y Gran Bretaña para llevar alimentos y suministros a Berlín Occidental por vía aérea durante un bloqueo soviético de todos los accesos terrestres. **803**

Berlin Wall/Muro de Berlín Muro construido en 1961 para separar las dos áreas en que se dividía Berlín y evitar que los residentes de la parte oriental emigraran a la parte occidental. **849**

Bessemer process/Proceso Bessemer Método fácil y económico de fabricación de acero, inventado por el británico Henry Bessemer en la década de 1850. **579**

bicameral legislature/legislatura de cámara dual Cuerpo de legisladores compuesto por las dos Cámaras. **93**

Bill of Rights/Ley de Derechos Primeras 10 enmiendas hechas a la Constitución de Estados Unidos que fueron ratificadas en 1791. **211**

Black Codes/códigos negros Leyes aprobadas en los estados del sur durante la Reconstrucción para restringir los derechos de los afroestadounidenses. **521**

blacklisting/lista negra Personas a las que se les negaban los empleos; actitud común en contra de cualquier persona bajo sospecha de actividades comunistas en la década de 1950. **813**

Black Power/poder negro Movimiento político y social de la década de los sesenta que hacía un llamado para ofrecer mayor poder económico y político a los afroestadounidenses. **859**

Blackshirts/camisas negras Grupo de italianos encabezados por Benito Mussolini que llegaron al poder a principios de los años veinte. **751**

Blitzkrieg/Blitzkrieg "Guerra relámpago"; rápido avance militar usado por las tropas alemanas contra Polonia en 1939. **763**

bonanza/bonanza Gran veta de algún mineral precioso. **553**

bonds/bonos Certificados que representan el dinero de los ciudadanos tomado en préstamo por el gobierno. **273**

Bonus Army/ejército de la bonificación Grupo de veteranos de la Primera Guerra Mundial que realizaron una marcha hacia Washington, D.C., para exigir el pago inmediato de las bonificaciones de guerra que les había prometido el gobierno. **735**

boomtowns/pueblos en explosión Comunidades del oeste que crecieron rápidamente gracias a la minería, pero que desaparecieron tan pronto como surgieron. **554**

bootleggers/contrabandistas Personas que introducían ilegalmente licor proveniente de Canadá y México a Estados Unidos en la época de la prohibición. **707**

borderlands/territorio fronterizo Región dominada por España que abarcaba el norte de México, Florida y partes de los actuales estados de Arizona, Nuevo México y Texas donde vivían algunos europeos. **46**

border states/estados fronterizos Delaware, Kentucky, Maryland y Missouri. Estados ubicados entre el norte y el sur en los que se practicaba la esclavitud y que no se adhirieron a la Confederación durante la Guerra Civil. **480**

bosses/caciques Líderes políticos corruptos que usaban sobornos y favores especiales para ganar votos en las elecciones. **607**

Boston Massacre/matanza de Boston (1770) Incidente en el que soldados británicos abrieron fuego contra un grupo de colonos matando a cinco personas. **140**

Boston Tea Party/Motín del Té (1773) Protesta en contra de la ley del té en la que un grupo de colonos abordó los barcos británicos que transportaban té y echaron al mar alrededor de 340 cofres con este producto. **142**

Boxer Rebellion/rebelión de los Boxers (1900) Ataque de un grupo de nacionalistas chinos conocidos como Boxers a un grupo de extranjeros que dio por terminada la participación de China en asuntos externos; la revuelta fue controlada por las tropas navales de Estados Unidos después de dos meses. **292**

boycott/boicot Rechazo a la compra de bienes específicos. Método usado con frecuencia como protesta contra determinados movimientos. **137**

braceros/braceros Trabajadores mexicanos autorizados por el gobierno de Estados Unidos para trabajar en este país durante la Segunda Guerra Mundial. **770**

Brain Trust/asesores de confianza Grupo de expertos políticos que trabajaron con el presidente Franklin D. Roosevelt para terminar con la Gran Depresión en la década de 1930. **737**

brinkmanship/política arriesgada Política de la administración del presidente Eisenhower que declaraba una guerra abierta a la expansión del comunismo. **823**

Brown v. Board of Education/Brown vs. Consejo de Educación (1954) Decreto de la Suprema Corte que declara ilegal la segregación en las escuelas públicas; esta ley anuló la doctrina de igualdad y separatismo racial Plessy vs. Ferguson establecida en 1896. **834**

bull market/tendencia al alza Mercado de valores cuyos precios muestran una tendencia al alza. **732**

Bull Moose Party/Partido del Alce Sobrenombre dado al Partido Progresista formado por Theodore Roosevelt y sus simpatizantes en 1912. **628**

Bureau of Indian Affairs/Oficina de Asuntos Indígenas Agencia creada por el gobierno en el siglo XIX con la finalidad de hacer llegar las políticas federales a territorios habitados por tribus indígenas. **346**

business cycle/ciclo comercial Patrón económico en que los comercios pasan de periodos de prosperidad a momentos de depresión. **734**

buying on margin/compras al margen Compra a crédito de acciones del mercado de valores. **732**

cabinet/gabinete Grupo de líderes del sector ejecutivo que brinda asesoría al presidente de una nación. **224**

California Gold Rush/fiebre del oro de California (1849) Migración de miles de personas a California al saber que se había descubierto oro en la zona. **437**

California Trail/Camino de California bifurcación sureña del Camino de Oregón que atravesaba Sierra Nevada y terminaba en California. **430**

Californios/californianos Colonos españoles que habitaron en California. **431**

Camp David Accords/Acuerdos de Campo David (1978) Acuerdos de paz entre Israel y Egipto negociados por el presidente Jimmy Carter. **916**

caravel/carabela Barco rápido y fácil de maniobrar diseñado por los portugueses. **33**

carpetbaggers/carpetbaggers Republicanos del norte que se mudaron al sur en la época de la Reconstrucción. **527**

cash crops/cultivo para la venta Nombre dado a los productos cosechados con la finalidad de obtener ganancias económicas y no para consumo personal. **103**

casualties/bajas Personas asesinadas, heridas, capturadas o extraviadas durante una guerra. **129**

cattle drive/arreo de ganado Largos recorridos en los que un grupo de vaqueros llevaba ganado a los mercados del norte o a zonas de pastizales. **561**

Cattle Kingdom/reino del ganado Zona de las Grandes Planicies que se extendía de Texas a Canadá en la que muchos ganaderos establecieron sus ranchos a finales del siglo XIX. **559**

Central Intelligence Agency/Agencia Central de Inteligencia (CIA, por sus siglas en inglés) Organización creada por el gobierno federal en 1947 para conducir operaciones de investigación secretas. **823**

Central Powers/potencias centrales Alianza creada en la Primera Guerra Mundial por el imperio austro-húngaro, a la que también se unieron Bulgaria y el imperio otomano. **771**

charter/carta Documento oficial que garantizaba a una persona o grupo el derecho de establecer una colonia. **51**

checks and balances/revisión y balance Sistema establecido por la Constitución para evitar que cualquier rama del gobierno adquiera demasiado poder. **205**

Chicano movement/movimiento chicano Esfuerzo de un grupo de jóvenes activistas de origen hispano para terminar con la discriminación y fomentar el orgullo por su herencia cultural. **863**

Chinese Exclusion Act/Ley de Exclusión de Chinos (1882) Ley que prohibió la inmigración de los chinos a Estados Unidos por un periodo de 10 años; dicha ley fue extendida a principios del siglo XX. **592**

Chisholm Trail/sendero Chisholm Ruta establecida por Jesse Chisholm en 1867 para conectar San Antonio, Texas con Abilene, Kansas, en el arreo del ganado. **561**

circumnavigate/circunnavegar Hacer una navegación completa alrededor de algo. **40**

Civil Rights Act of 1866/Ley de Derechos Civiles de 1866 Ley que otorgaba a los afroestadounidenses los mismos derechos que a los habitantes de raza blanca. **522**

Civil Rights Act of 1875/Ley de Derechos Civiles de 1875 Ley que permitía a los afroestadounidenses demandar a cualquier negocio que mostrara una actitud de discriminación racial. **530**

Civil Rights Act of 1964/Ley de Derechos Civiles de 1964 Ley que hacía ilegal la segregación racial en lugares públicos y prohibía a empleadores, sindicatos y universidades ejercer discriminación de raza, género, religión u origen étnico. **857**

Clayton Antitrust Act/Ley Antimonopolios Clayton (1914) Ley que fortaleció las leyes federales antimonopolio. **630**

Clermont/Clermont Primer barco comercial de vapor de grandes dimensiones, diseñado por Robert Fulton y probado en 1807. **366**

Cold War/Guerra Fría Lucha de poderes entre Estados Unidos y la Unión Soviética desde el final de la Segunda Guerra Mundial y hasta 1991. **800**

collective bargaining/negociación de contrato colectivo Proceso en el que los líderes de un sindicato negocian con los dueños de las industrias, con la finalidad de obtener mejores salarios y condiciones de trabajo para los obreros. **586**

Columbian Exchange/intercambio colombino Intercambio de plantas, animales e incluso enfermedades producido al iniciarse el contacto entre América, África, Asia y Europa. **41**

Committee on Civil Rights/Comité de Derechos Civiles (1946) Comité creado a iniciativa del presidente Harry S. Truman para investigar la discriminación racial y plantear soluciones a nivel federal. **833**

Committee on Public Information/Comité de Información Pública (CPI, por sus siglas en inglés) Departamento creado en 1917 por el presidente Woodrow Wilson para fomentar la ayuda pública en tiempos de la Primera Guerra Mundial. **678**

Committees of Correspondence/comités de correspondencia Comités creados por la Cámara de Representantes de Massachusetts en la década de 1760 para que poblados y colonias compartieran información que los ayudara a enfrentar las leyes británicas vigentes. **137**

common-school movement/Movimiento de Escuelas Comunes Reforma social iniciada a mediados del siglo XIX para fomentar la idea de que todos los niños recibieran educación en un mismo lugar sin importar su origen o clase social. **403**

Common Sense/Common Sense (1776) Folleto escrito por Thomas Paine en el que criticaba a las monarquías con la finalidad de convencer a los colonos estadounidenses de la necesidad de independizarse de Gran Bretaña. **158**

Commonwealth of Independent States/Federación de Estados Independientes (CIS, por sus siglas en inglés) Alianza formada por antiguas repúblicas soviéticas en diciembre de 1991. **934**

Communists/comunistas Personas que buscan la distribución igualitaria de la riqueza y el fin de cualquier forma de propiedad privada. **683, 700**

Compromise of 1850/Compromiso de 1850 Acuerdo propuesto por Henry Clay para permitir a California el ingreso a la Unión como estado libre y dividir el resto de la cesión mexicana en dos territorios donde la aprobación o abolición de la esclavitud fuera decidida por voluntad popular; el acuerdo también definía los límites de Texas y Nuevo México, además de abolir el comercio de esclavos en Washington y establecer una nueva ley para la protección de esclavos fugitivos. **453**

Compromise of 1877/Compromiso de 1877 Acuerdo creado para resolver la disputa de las elecciones presidenciales de 1876; en él, los demócratas aceptaban al republicano Rutherford B. Hayes como presidente a cambio del retiro de las tropas federales del sur. **531**

Comstock Lode/veta de Comstock Gran yacimiento de oro y plata encontrado por Henry Comstock en 1859. **553**

concurrent powers/poderes concurrentes Poderes compartidos por el gobierno federal y los gobiernos estatales. **221**

Confederate States of America/Estados Confederados Nación formada por los estados del sur el 4 de febrero de 1861; también conocida como Confederación. **472**

Congress of Industrial Organizations/Congreso de Organizaciones Industriales (CIO, por sus siglas en inglés) Asociación nacional laboral formada en 1938 para agrupar sindicatos industriales. **741**

conquistadores/conquistadores Soldados y exploradores españoles que encabezaron las expediciones militares en Estados Unidos y reclamaron territorios en nombre de España. **42**

conservation/conservación Protección de la naturaleza y sus recursos. **626**

constitution/constitución Conjunto de principios básicos que determina los poderes y las obligaciones de un gobierno. **188**

Constitutional Convention/Convención Constitucional de Filadelfia (1787) Encuentro realizado en Filadelfia en el que delegados de los estados redactaron la Constitución de Estados Unidos. **201**

Constitutional Union Party/Partido Unido de la Constitución Partido político formado en 1860 por habitantes del norte y del sur en apoyo de la Unión, sus leyes y la Constitución. **469**

containment/represión Política exterior seguida por Estados Unidos durante la guerra fría para prevenir la expansión del comunismo soviético. **802**

Continental Army/Ejército Continental Ejército creado por el Segundo Congreso Continental en 1775 para defender las colonias estadounidenses del dominio británico. **154**

contrabands/contrabando Esclavos que escapaban o eran capturados por el Ejército de la Unión durante la Guerra Civil. **494**

Contract with America/Contrato con Estados Unidos Reforma republicana de diez puntos propuesta a mediados de la década de 1990 para incluir, entre otras modificaciones, enmiendas de presupuesto equilibrado y de cobro de impuestos. **937**

Contras/Contras Grupo de rebeldes antisandinistas surgido en Nicaragua. **930**

Convention of 1818/Convención de 1818 Acuerdo entre Estados Unidos y Gran Bretaña para definir los derechos de pesca y establecer las nuevas fronteras al norte. **329**

Copperheads/copperheads Demócratas del norte que se oponían a la abolición de la esclavitud y simpatizaban con las creencias sureñas durante la Guerra Civil. **495**

corporations/corporaciones Compañías que venden parte de las mismas en forma de acciones del mercado de valores para recaudar fondos. **581**

cotton belt/región algodonera Región que se extendía de Georgia al este de Texas en la que se producía la mayor parte del algodón cosechado en Estados Unidos a mediados del siglo XIX. **374**

cotton diplomacy/Diplomacia del algodón Esfuerzos de la Confederación por aprovechar la influencia de la industria textil británica del sur para convencer a Gran Bretaña de apoyar su causa durante la Guerra Civil. **482**

cotton gin/trilladora de algodón Dispositivo inventado por Eli Whitney en la década de 1790 que revolucionó la industria algodonera al facilitar la separación de las semillas de las fibras en las plantas de algodón. **373**

Council of the Indies/Consejo de Indias Grupo de funcionarios de la realeza establecido en 1524 para vigilar las acciones del gobierno y la aplicación de las leyes españolas en América. **44**

counterculture/contracultura Cultura alternativa que apoya valores en contrapartida de la sociedad común. **867**

covenant/pacto Acuerdo sagrado. **76**

covert operations/operaciones encubiertas Misiones secretas. **823**

creditors/acreedores Personas que prestan dinero. **197**

Crusades/cruzadas (1096-1221) Serie de guerras iniciadas por los cristianos europeos para recuperar posesión de las Tierras Santas. **25**

Cuban missile crisis/Crisis de los Misiles en Cuba (1962) Crisis militar que estuvo a punto de provocar una guerra nuclear cuando barcos de guerra estadounidenses sitiaron a Cuba hasta que las autoridades soviéticas decidieron retirar sus misiles de la isla a cambio de que Estados Unidos no invadiera la zona y retirara parte de sus misiles instalados en Europa. **849**

culture/cultura Valores y tradiciones compartidas por una sociedad, como la familia, el gobierno, el idioma y las creencias religiosas. **6**

Cumberland Road/Camino Cumberland Primer proyecto federal de construcción de carreteras, iniciado en 1815 para crear caminos entre Cumberland, Maryland y el poblado en el que actualmente lleva el nombre de Wheeling, West Virginia. **335**

Daughters of Liberty/Hijas de la Libertad Grupos de mujeres que realizaron boicots y adoptaron otras medidas para apoyar la resistencia de las colonias al dominio británico. **139**

Dawes General Allotment Act/Ley de lotificacíon de Dawes (1887) Ley aprobada por el Congreso con la finalidad de reducir la influencia de las tribus indígenas al dividir su territorio en varias reservas y ofrecerles la ciudadanía estadounidense. **552**

D-Day/Día D 6 de junio de 1944; fecha de la invasión aliada a territorio francés durante la Segunda Guerra Mundial. **774**

debtors/deudores Personas que deben dinero. **197**

Declaration of Independence/Declaración de Independencia (1776) Establecimiento del Segundo Congreso Continental que definió los derechos de los colonos, expresó sus reclamos en contra de la Gran Bretaña y declaró la independencia de las colonias. **159**

Declaration of Sentiments/Declaración de sentimientos (1848) Declaración redactada y firmada por varias personas en apoyo de los derechos de las mujeres durante la Convención de Seneca Falls en la que se describía con detalle su punto de vista sobre las injusticias sociales en su contra. **415**

deficit/déficit Deuda que resulta cuando un gobierno gasta más dinero del que tiene. **929**

delegated powers/poderes delegados Poderes otorgados exclusivamente al gobierno federal por la Constitución. **220**

Democratic Party/Partido Demócrata Partido político formado por los simpatizantes de Andrew Jackson después de las elecciones presidenciales de 1824. **339**

Democratic-Republican Party/Partido Demócrata-Republicano Asociación política formada en la década de 1790 con la finalidad de preservar el poder de los gobiernos estatales y promover la agricultura. **288**

deport/deportar Enviar a inmigrantes ilegales de vuelta a su lugar de origen. **255**

depression/depresión Descenso considerable en la actividad económica, combinado con un alza del desempleo. **197**

détente/détente Periodo de la década de 1970 en el que disminuyeron las hostilidades entre Estados Unidos y la Unión Soviética. **906**

direct primary/elecciones primarias Método de elección en el que los votantes eligen a sus candidatos a los cargos públicos. **611**

Disabled in Action/Discapacitados en Acción (DIA, por sus siglas en inglés) Grupo formado en 1970 para proponer reformas legales en beneficio de las personas con discapacidades. **865**

disarmament/desarme Reducción del número de armas nucleares. **704**

dissenters/opositores Personas que están en contra de las opiniones oficiales, sean religiosas o políticas. **75**

Dixiecrats/Dixiecrats Integrantes del Partido de los Derechos de los Estados, formado en 1940 por demócratas sureños inconformes con el reducido apoyo que brindaba el presidente Harry S Truman a los derechos civiles. **806**

dollar diplomacy/Diplomacia del dólar Política creada por el presidente William Howard Taft para influir en los gobiernos de América Latina mediante la intervención económica y no militar. **658**

domestication/domesticación Proceso de reproducción de plantas y animales para consumo humano. **6**

Dominion of New England/Dominio de Nueva Inglaterra (1686-1698) Unión poco popular de colonias del norte bajo el mandato del rey James II. **95**

domino theory/teoría del dominó Creencia común en el periodo del presidente Dwight D. Eisenhower que explicaba que si una nación del sudeste de Asia caía presa del comunismo, las demás naciones del sudeste de Asia también caerían. **875**

Donner party/partida Donner Grupo de viajeros del oeste extraviados en la Sierra Nevada durante el invierno de 1846-1847. Sólo 40 de los 98 viajeros sobrevivieron. **430**

double jeopardy/doble riesgo Ley que indica que una persona no puede ser enjuiciada dos veces por el mismo motivo. **251**

doves/palomas Ciudadanos que pedían el retiro de las tropas estadounidenses de Vietnam. **883**

draft/reclutamiento Sistema obligatorio de elección de soldados en las fuerzas armadas de Estados Unidos. **257**

Dred Scott decision/Decisión Dred Scott (1857) Decreto en el que la Suprema Corte declaraba que los afroestadounidenses no tenían derecho a ser ciudadanos estadounidenses, que la restricción de la esclavitud acordada en el Compromiso de Missouri era anticonstitucional y que el Congreso no tenía autoridad para abolir la esclavitud en territorio federal. **464**

dry farming/cultivo de sequía Método agrícola usado en las Grandes Planicies en la década de 1890 para cultivar ciertos productos con muy poca agua. **566**

due process/proceso debido Aplicación justa de la ley. **251**

Dust Bowl/Cuenca del polvo Nombre dado a una parte de las Grandes Planicies en la década de 1930 debido a la intensa sequía que se vivía en la región. **746**

duties/aranceles Impuestos pagados por la importación de bienes. **99**

Earth Day/Día de la Tierra Día celebrado mundialmente el 22 de abril a partir de 1970 para fomentar el cuidado del medio ambiente. **921**

Eighteenth Amendment/Decimoctava enmienda (1919) Enmienda constitucional que prohibió la producción, venta y transporte de bebidas alcohólicas en Estados Unidos; fue anulada en 1933. **620**

elastic clause/Cláusula elástica Artículo I, sección 8 de la Constitución que otorga al Congreso autoridad para ampliar sus poderes delegados en asuntos no especificados en la Carta Magna; también conocida como "cláusula propia y necesaria". **221**

electoral college/Colegio electoral Grupo elegido en cada estado para reunir votos en las elecciones presidenciales. El número de electores inscritos en cada estado debe ser proporcional al número de representantes y senadores en el Congreso. En cada estado, los electores deben votar por el candidato elegido por su partido. **269**

emancipation/emancipación Liberación de la esclavitud. **407**

Emancipation Proclamation/Proclama de emancipación (1863) Decreto emitido por el presidente Abraham Lincoln en 1862 otorgando la libertad a los esclavos residentes de las regiones no ocupadas que se rebelaran contra la Unión; el decreto tomó efecto el 1 de enero de 1863. **493**

embargo/embargo Prohibición de los tratados de comercio con un país. **309**

Embargo Act/Ley de embargo (1807) Ley que prohibía a los comerciantes estadounidenses realizar intercambios con otros países. **309**

Emergency Quota Act/Ley de Cuota de Emergencia (1921) Ley que limitaba el número de inmigrantes a Estados Unidos a 357,000 al año. **709**

eminent domain/dominio eminente Derecho del gobierno a tomar propiedades privadas para extender los bienes públicos. **251**

empresarios/empresarios Personas contratadas por la República mexicana para establecer poblaciones en Texas a principios del siglo XIX. **423**

encomienda system/Sistema de encomienda Sistema adoptado en Hispanoamérica para que los colonos tuvieran derecho de cobrar impuestos a los indígenas o exigirles trabajo a cambio de protección o la enseñanza de oficios específicos. **44**

Endangered Species Act/Ley de Especies en Peligro de Extinción (1966) Ley que protege a los animales en riesgo de desaparecer. **921**

energy crisis/crisis energética Situación generada en la década de 1970 por el aumento de los precios de los combustibles y la disminución de reservas. **904**

English Bill of Rights/Cesión Inglesa de Derechos (1689) Cambio del poder político de la monarquía británica al parlamento inglés. **97**

Enlightenment/Ilustración Era de la razón. Movimiento iniciado en Europa en el siglo XVIII cuando las personas empezaron a adquirir más conocimientos sobre la naturaleza, la sociedad y el gobierno. **113**

entrepreneurs/emprendedores Personas que inician nuevos negocios. **581**

Environmental Protection Agency/Departamento de Protección del Medio Ambiente (EPA) Agencia creada por el Congreso en 1970 con la finalidad de reforzar las leyes de protección ambiental. **921**

environments/medio ambiente Clima y paisaje donde habitan seres vivos. **6**

Equal Rights Amendment/Propuesta de Igualdad de Derechos Propuesta constitucional emitida para garantizar los derechos de las mujeres prohibiendo la discriminación por género; fue aprobada por el Congreso en 1972 pero no fue ratificada por suficientes estados para convertirse en una enmienda constitucional. **864**

Erie Canal/canal de Erie Canal que corre de Albany a Búfalo, en el estado de Nueva York. Su construcción se completó en 1825. **335**

escalation/intensificación Política propuesta por el presidente Lyndon B. Johnson para fomentar la intervención de Estados Unidos en la guerra de Vietnam. **880**

Espionage Act of 1917/Ley de espionaje de 1917 Ley creada para castigar a las personas que ayudaran al enemigo o no cumplieran con el servicio militar obligatorio durante la Primera Guerra Mundial. **679**

European Union/Unión Europea (EU, por sus siglas en inglés) Grupo de 11 naciones europeas fundado en 1991 con la finalidad de crear un mercado, una moneda y un banco comunes que les permitiera desarrollar su potencial económico a nivel mundial. **942**

executive branch/Poder Ejecutivo Parte del gobierno federal que incluye al presidente y los departamentos administrativos; su función es aplicar las leyes de la nación. **204**

executive order/orden ejecutiva Orden no aprobada por el Congreso emitida por el presidente en ciertas circunstancias; una orden ejecutiva tiene la fuerza de una ley aprobada por el congreso. **223**

executive privilege/privilegio ejecutivo Derecho del presidente de mantener en secreto cierta información para proteger la seguridad nacional. **908**

Exodusters/Exodusters Extenso grupo de afroestadounidenses sureños que se establecieron en los nuevos territorios del oeste a finales del siglo XIX. **565**

expatriates/expatriados Personas que abandonan su lugar de origen para vivir en un nuevo lugar. **719**

exports/exportaciones Productos que un país vende a otros países. **98**

fads/moda Gran interés en cierta actividad durante un tiempo breve. **715**

Fair Deal/Trato justo Serie de programas de reforma creados por el presidente Harry S Truman. **807**

Fair Employment Practices Committee/Comité de Prácticas Justas en el Empleo (FEPC, por sus siglas en inglés) Comité creado durante la Segunda Guerra Mundial con la finalidad de prevenir la discriminación en las industrias de guerra y en los empleos ofrecidos por el gobierno. **770**

Farmers' Alliances/Alianzas de Agricultores Grupos políticos formados por agricultores a finales del siglo XIX para elegir candidatos a cargos públicos que favorecieran sus intereses. **600**

fascism/fascismo Teoría política que demanda la creación de un gobierno fuerte encabezado por un solo individuo donde el estado sea más importante que el individuo. **751**

federalism/federalismo Sistema de gobierno cuyo poder se distribuye entre una autoridad central y varios estados individuales. **204**

Federalist Papers/Federalist papers Conjunto de documentos que defienden y explican la Constitución con la finalidad de que los ciudadanos sepan que las leyes federales no deben sobreponerse a las de los estados. **208**

Federalist Party/Partido Federalista Asociación política creada en la década de 1790 siguiendo las ideas de Alexander Hamilton con la finalidad de fortalecer al gobierno federal y fomentar la industria y el intercambio comercial. **288**

Federalists/federales Personas que apoyaban la ratificación de la Constitución. **207**

Federal Reserve Act/Ley de la Reserva Federal (1913) Ley que creó el sistema bancario nacional para ayudar al gobierno a regular la economía del país. **629**

Federal Trade Commission/Comisión Federal de Comercio (FTC, por sus siglas en inglés, 1914) Comisión que se creó en 1914 para investigar y prevenir las adtividades comerciales y de negocios injustas y desleales. **630**

feudalism/feudalismo Sistema de gobierno surgido en la Edad Media en el que los habitantes de una región ofrecían lealtad absoluta a un terrateniente a cambio de tierras de labranza o protección. **19**

Fifteenth Amendment/Decimoquinta enmienda (1870) Enmienda constitucional que dio a los afroestadounidenses el derecho al voto. **526**

54th Massachusetts Infantry/54avo Batallón de Infantería de Massachusetts Regimiento de la Guerra Civil formado por soldados afroestadounidenses que tuvo un papel determinante en el ataque al Fuerte Wagner en Carolina del Sur. **494**

fireside chats/charlas de chimenea Pláticas del presidente Franklin D. Roosevelt transmitidas por radio para toda la nación. **738**

First Battle of Bull Run/Primera Batalla de Bull Run (1861) Primera batalla importante de la Guerra Civil. El ejército confederado obtuvo la victoria. En esta batalla se demostró que ninguno de los bandos ganaría la guerra con facilidad. **484**

First Battle of the Marne/Primera Batalla de Marne (1914) Batalla de la Primera Guerra Mundial en la que fuerzas francesas lograron detener el avance de las tropas alemanas cerca de París. **771**

First Continental Congress/Primer Congreso Continental (1774) Encuentro de delegados de las colonias en Filadelfia para decidir cómo responderían al cierre del Puerto de Boston, al alza de impuestos y a los abusos de las autoridades británicas. Los delegados hicieron una serie de peticiones al rey George III, incluyendo los derechos que consideraban justos para los colonos. **152**

flappers/flappers Grupo de mujeres jóvenes creado en la década de 1920 que desafiaba las tradiciones sociales con su conducta y vestimenta. **699**

folktales/cuentos populares Narraciones orales que con frecuencia ofrecen una moraleja. **380**

Fort Sumter/Fuerte Sumter Base federal de Charleston, Carolina del Sur, cuyo ataque por los federales en abril de 1861 dio origen a la Guerra Civil. **478**

forty-niners/gambusinos Buscadores de oro que emigraron a California durante la fiebre del oro. **437**

Fourteen Points/Plan de Catorce Puntos (1918) Plan del presidente Woodrow Wilson para reconstruir Europa después de la Primera Guerra Mundial y evitar futuras guerras. **687**

Fourteenth Amendment/Decimocuarta enmienda (1868) Enmienda constitucional que, entre otras cosas, ofrecía todos los derechos de un ciudadano a cualquier persona nacida o nacionalizada estadounidense, con excepción de las tribus indígenas. **523**

free coinage/acuñación libre Sistema monetario en el que se acuñaban monedas de oro y plata, y papel moneda cuyo valor estaba respaldado por una cantidad específica de oro o plata. **599**

Freedmen's Bureau/Departamento de Personas Liberadas Agencia creada por el Congreso en 1865 para brindar ayuda a personas pobres del sur del país. **518**

Freedom Rides/viajes de libertad (1961) Recorridos en autobús que realizaban los líderes del movimiento en favor de los derechos civiles en los estados del sur para protestar por la segregación racial en los autobuses. **856**

free enterprise/libre empresa Sistema económico en el que los comercios compiten sin restricciones importantes del gobierno. **99, 581**

Freeport Doctrine/Doctrina de la libertad (1858) Declaración hecha por Stephen Douglas durante los debates Lincoln-Douglas en la que fomenta el uso de la soberanía popular para aprobar o rechazar la esclavitud. **466**

Free-Soil Party/Partido de la libertad de suelo Asociación política formada en 1848 por habitantes de los estados del norte que apoyaban la abolición de la esclavitud y que habían abandonado al Partido de Whig y al Partido Demócrata porque ninguno de los dos apoyaba esta causa. **451**

French Revolution/Revolución francesa Rebelión francesa iniciada en 1789 en que la población francesa se rebeló ante la monarquía y tomó el país para convertirlo en una república. **278**

Fugitive Slave Act/Ley de Esclavos Fugitivos (1850) Ley que calificaba como un crimen ayudar a un esclavo a escapar de su amo, además de permitir la captura de esclavos fugitivos incluso en zonas donde la esclavitud era ilegal para devolverlos a sus dueños. **454**

Fundamentalism/fundamentalismo Movimiento religioso protestante que explica que el contenido de la Biblia es en esencia verdadero. **708**

Fundamental Orders of Connecticut/Decretos Fundamentales de Connecticut (1639) Primeros principios del recién creado gobierno de Estados Unidos presentados por escrito. **77**

Gadsden Purchase/Compra de Gadsden (1853) Compra de territorio mexicano por parte de Estados Unidos; la adquisición incluía parte de los actuales estados de Nuevo México y Arizona. **436**

General Amnesty Act of 1872/Ley General de Amnistía de 1872 Ley que rechazaba la Décimo Cuarta enmienda y prohibía a los antiguos confederados ejercer cualquier cargo público. **530**

generation gap/brecha de generación División entre dos generaciones de individuos. **867**

Geneva Accords/Acuerdos de Ginebra (1954) Acuerdo que dividió temporalmente a Vietnam como Vietnam del Norte y Vietnam del Sur, además de llamar a elecciones libres en 1956 para reunir nuevamente al país. **875**

genocide/genocidio Asesinato deliberado de todo un grupo de personas. **788**

Gettysburg Address/Discurso de Gettysburg (1863) Pláticas en las que Abraham Lincoln reconocía el valor de los soldados de la unión y renovaba su compromiso de triunfo en la guerra civil. **500**

Ghost Dance/Danza de los Espíritus Movimiento religioso de los indígenas estadounidenses que se extendió con rapidez en las Grandes Planicies durante la década de 1880. **550**

Gibbons v. Ogden/Gibbons Ogden (1824) Decreto de la Suprema Corte que establece que la ley federal tiene prioridad sobre las leyes estatales equivalentes; definición ampliada del comercio interestatal. **368**

GI Bill of Rights/Declaración de Derechos GI (1944) Ley de reajuste para hombres en servicio que ofrecía a los veteranos de guerra beneficios educativos y préstamos para construir granjas, casas o negocios. **805**

glasnost/glasnost Campaña soviética establecida en la década de 1980 que promovía la apertura política y libertad de expresión. **931**

global warming/calentamiento global Amenaza potencial al medio ambiente por el aumento de la temperatura de la Tierra debido al calor atrapado en la atmósfera. **941**

Glorious Revolution/Revolución gloriosa (1688) Revuelta ocurrida en Inglaterra contra el rey católico James II que condujo a su destitución y al levantamiento de los protestantes Mary y William de Orange como nuevos monarcas. **96**

glyphs/glifos Símbolos o imágenes, especialmente aquellos tallados en una superficie o grabados en relieve. **6**

gold standard/estándar del oro Sistema monetario en el que el valor de una moneda está respaldado por una reserva de oro. **599**

Good Neighbor policy/política del buen vecino Política de asuntos externos aplicada por el presidente Franklin D. Roosevelt para promover las buenas relaciones con América Latina mediante la influencia económica en lugar de la fuerza militar. **750**

Great Awakening/Gran Despertar Movimiento cristiano evangélico que se extendió rápidamente en las colonias durante las décadas de 1730 y 1740. **109**

Great Compromise/El gran compromiso (1787) Acuerdo firmado durante la Gran Convención en el que se indicaba que la población de cada estado determinaría el número de representantes asignados en la cámara baja, mientras que el número de representantes en la cámara alta sería el mismo para todos. **202**

Great Depression/la gran depresión Severa disminución del desarrollo económico global que inició con el quebranto el mercado de valores estadounidense en 1929. **733**

Great Migration/la gran migración Migración masiva de 500,000 afroestadounidenses a ciudades del medio oeste y del norte de Estados Unidos durante y después de la Primera Guerra Mundial. **76, 701**

Great Society/La Gran Sociedad Ley presentada por el presidente Lyndon B. Johnson con la finalidad de crear programas de ayuda para terminar con la pobreza y el racismo. **852**

guerrilla warfare/guerrilla Tipo de guerra en la que los soldados realizan ataques y escapes rápidos contra el enemigo, por lo general detrás de la trinchera. **179**

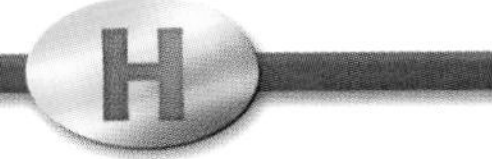

habeas corpus/Habeas corpus Protección constitucional contra los arrestos ilegales. **495**

Harlem Renaissance/Renacimiento de Harlem Periodo de desarrollo artístico de la comunidad afroestadounidense de la década de 1920; nombrado así por haber surgido en el barrio de Harlem, en Nueva York. **718**

Hartford Convention/Convención de Hartford (1815) Encuentro de federales en Hartford, Connecticut, para protestar por la Guerra de 1812. **319**

hawks/halcones Estadounidenses que apoyaban la idea de aumentar el gasto militar y la intervención de Estados Unidos en la guerra de Vietnam. **884**

Hay-Bunau-Varilla Treaty/Tratado Hay-Bunau-Varilla (1903) Acuerdo entre Estados Unidos y Panamá que dio a Estados Unidos una concesión de 99 años para operar un canal de 10 millas de largo que cruzara el istmo de Panamá. **654**

Hay-Herrán Treaty/Tratado Hay-Terrán (1903) Acuerdo entre Colombia y Estados Unidos que proponía dar a Estados Unidos una concesión de 99 años para operar el canal construido en el istmo de Panamá; este acuerdo fue rechazado por el senado colombiano. **654**

Haymarket Riot/Revuelta de Haymarket (1886) Incidente en el que murieron varios oficiales de policía al explotar una bomba durante una protesta laboral realizada en la Plaza Haymarket de Chicago. **587**

headright/concesión Sistema creado por la London Company en el que se otorgaban 50 acres de tierra a los colonos que pagaran el viaje para establecerse en Virginia. **67**

Highway Act/Ley de Carreteras (1956) Ley que otorgó cierta cantidad de dinero para la construcción de un sistema interestatal de carreteras. **827**

hippies/hippies Integrantes de la contracultura desarrollada en la década de 1960 que experimentaron diversas formas de vida y conducta. **867**

Ho Chi Minh Trail/Sendero Ho Chi Min Red de senderos, caminos y túneles que conectaban el norte de Vietnam desde Laos y Camboya hasta Vietnam del sur y que sirvieron como la ruta más importante hacia el Vietcong. **879**

Holocaust/Holocausto Matanza sistemática de más de 6 millones de judíos y alrededor de 3 millones de personas de otras razas que realizaron los nazis durante la Segunda Guerra Mundial. **787**

Homestead Act/Ley Homestead (1862) Ley aprobada por el Congreso que fomentaba la migración al oeste cediendo territorios federales a los pequeños agricultores. **564**

Homestead strike/Huelga Homestead (1892) Huelga iniciada en la fábrica de acero de Andrew Carnegie en Pennsylvania que dio como resultado un violento enfrentamiento entre manifestantes y policías. **588**

horizontal integration/integración horizontal Posesión de todos los negocios de una rama particular del comercio. **582**

House of Burgesses/Casa de los burgueses Asamblea colonial electa en Virginia. **94**

House Un-American Activities Committee/Comité de Actividades Externas (HUAC, por sus siglas en inglés) Comité creado por el Congreso en 1938 para investigar a los ciudadanos acusados de realizar actividades comunistas. **813**

Hudson River school/Escuela del Río Hudson Grupo de artistas creado a mediados del siglo XIX cuya obra muestra diversos paisajes del territorio estadounidense. **352**

Hull House/Hull House Casa de acuerdos fundada por Jane Adams y Ellen gates Satrr en Chicago en el año de 1889. **595**

hunter-gatherers/cazadores personales Personas que cazaban animales y recolectaban plantas para satisfacer sus necesidades. **5**

hydrogen bomb/bomba de hidrógeno Tipo de bomba nuclear. **821**

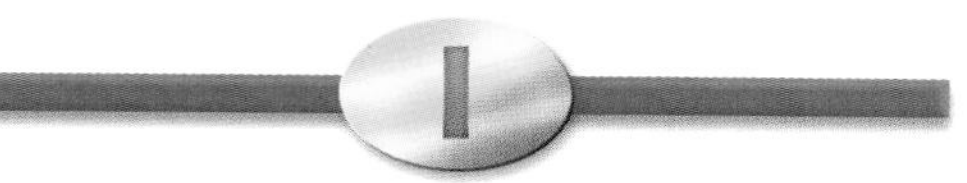

igloos/iglúes Casas construidas con bloques de hielo por los habitantes de las tribus inuit y aleut en el territorio que actualmente ocupan Alaska y Canadá. **12**

immigrants/inmigrantes Personas que abandonan su país para establecerse en un país diferente. **71**

Immigration Restriction League/Liga de Restricción de Inmigración Organización formada en 1894 por nativistas con la finalidad de reducir la inmigración; esta ley exigía a los inmigrantes que demostraran que sabían leer y escribir antes de entrar a Estados Unidos. **592**

impeach/inculpar Levantar cargos en contra de alguien. **223**

imperialism/imperialismo Construcción de un imperio mediante el establecimiento de colonias o la conquista de otras naciones. **640**

imports/importaciones Productos que un país compra a otras naciones. **98**

impressment/Leva Práctica británica que obligaba a los colonos, incluidos los ciudadanos estadounidenses, a servir en las fuerzas armadas británicas, lo cual aumentó las fricciones entre Gran Bretaña y Estados Unidos a principios del siglo XIX. **309**

indentured servants/sirvientes por contrato Colonos que recibían pasajes gratuitos a América del Norte a cambio de trabajo sin salario por varios años. **68**

Indian Removal Act/Ley de Expulsión de Indígenas (1830) Ley aprobada por el Congreso para retirar a los indígenas estadounidenses del este del Valle del Mississippi y restablecerlos en el territorio que les había asignado el gobierno. **345**

Indian Territory/Territorio indígena Área que abarcaba la mayor parte del actual estado de Oklahoma en la que muchas tribus indígenas del sureste fueron obligadas a establecerse durante la década de 1830. **345**

indict/acusar Levantar cargos formales en contra de alguien que haya cometido un crimen. **251**

Industrial Revolution/Revolución Industrial Periodo de rápido crecimiento industrial debido al uso de maquinaria en los procesos de fabricación que inició en la Gran Bretaña a mediados del siglo XVI y se extendió poco después a Estados Unidos. **363**

Industrial Workers of the World/Trabajadores Industriales del Mundo (IWW, por sus siglas en inglés) Organización socialista formada en 1905 para agrupar a los obreros en un gran sindicato. **618**

inflation/inflación Alza de los precios de los bienes y servicios en combinación con la disminución del valor del dinero. **48, 196**

Information Revolution/revolución informativa Rápido aumento del acceso e intercambio de información iniciado en la década de 1990 con la popularización de las computadoras. **943**

initiative/iniciativa Ley que permite a los votantes proponer nuevas leyes mediante la reunión de firmas en una petición colectiva. **612**

installment plans/planes de pago Programas de compra de bienes en los que el cliente realiza un pequeño pago inicial y una serie de pagos mensuales con una tasa de interés específica hasta pagar el total de la compra. **713**

interchangeable parts/partes intercambiables Proceso desarrollado por Eli Whitney en la década de 1790 para que las partes fundamentales de todas las máquinas similares fueran exactamente iguales. **364**

Intermediate-Range Nuclear Forces Treaty/Tratado de Fuerzas Nucleares de Medio Alcance (INF, por sus siglas en inglés, 1987) Tratado firmado por el presidente Ronald Reagan y el líder soviético Mikhail Gorvachev para eliminar las armas nucleares de alcance medio en Europa. **931**

Internal Security Act/ley de seguridad interna (1950) Ley que exigía el registro de los grupos bajo sospecha de ser partidarios del comunismo y que otorgaba al gobierno la facultad de arrestar a todo sospechoso de deslealtad durante las emergencias nacionales. **814**

International Space Station/Estación Espacial Internacional Estación espacial que Estados Unidos, Rusia y otros países construyeron conjuntamente después de terminada la guerra fría. **941**

Internet/Internet Sistema mundial de redes de computadoras. **943**

internment/internado Reubicación obligada de prisioneros. **771**

interstate commerce/comercio interestatal Intercambio comercial entre estados. **196**

Interstate Commerce Act/Ley de Comercio Interestatal (1887) Ley que ofrece reglamentos uniformes de comercio entre estados. **598**

Interstate Commerce Commission/Comisión de Comercio Interestatal (ICC, por sus siglas en inglés, 1887) Comisión creada por la Ley de comercio interestatal para que las compañías ferrocarrileras cobraran el precio justo por sus servicios. **598**

Intolerable Acts/Ley de Actos Intolerables (1774) Leyes aprobadas por el Parlamento para castigar a los colonos que habían participado en el Motín del Té; esta ley cerró el puerto de Boston y canceló los derechos de la colonia de Massachusetts. **143**

Iran-contra affair/Asunto Irán-Contras Nombre dado al escándalo en el que participó el gobierno de Estados Unidos al vender armas en secreto a Irán y usar las ganancias para patrocinar a los contras en Nicaragua en 1986. **930**

Iran hostage crisis/Crisis de los rehenes en Irán Situación delicada en la que 53 estadounidenses fueron capturados en la embajada de Estados Unidos en Teherán, Irán y mantenidos como rehenes durante 444 días a partir de 1979. **917**

ironclads/acorazados Buques de guerra fuertemente armados con elementos de hierro. **487**

Iroquois League/Liga de iroqueses Confederación política formada por cinco naciones del noroeste del país: Cayuga, Mohawk, Oneida, Onondaga y Seneca. **16**

Islam/Islam Credo que surgió en el Oriente Medio en al año 600 d.C., bajo la guía de Mahoma; su libro sagrado es el Corán. **23**

island-hopping/islas importantes Estrategia desarrollada en la Segunda Guerra Mundial para conquistar solamente aquellas islas del Pacífico que representaban puntos estratégicos en el avance contra Japón. **781**

isolationism/aislamiento Política de evitar cualquier tipo de intervención en los asuntos de las demás naciones. **641**

Jay's Treaty/Tratado de Jay (1794) Acuerdo negociado por John Jay para resolver los problemas entre Gran Bretaña y Estados Unidos en relación con los tratados del oeste, la incautación de barcos estadounidenses por las autoridades británicas y las deudas con los comerciantes británicos. **281**

Jazz Age/época del jazz Término con el que se conoce a la década de 1920 debido a la enorme popularidad que adquirió un nuevo tipo de música llamada jazz. **718**

Jim Crow laws/Leyes de Jim Crow Leyes que fomentaban la segregación en los estados del sur. **531**

John Brown's raid/Ataque de John Brown (1859) Incidente en el que el abolicionista John Brown y 21 hombres más se apropiaron de un arsenal federal en Harpers Ferry, Virginia, con la esperanza de iniciar una rebelión de esclavos. **467**

judicial branch/Poder judicial División del gobierno federal conformada por las cortes nacionales; su función es interpretar la ley, castigar el crimen y resolver disputas entre estados. **204**

judicial review/Revisión judicial Decreto que otorga a la Suprema Corte el poder de declarar anticonstitucional una acción del Congreso en caso necesario. **301**

Judiciary Act/Ley judicial (1879) Ley aprobada por el Congreso para crear un sistema federal de justicia. **271**

kamikaze/kamikaze Táctica usada durante la Segunda Guerra Mundial por los pilotos japoneses al lanzarse en picada contra el enemigo con aviones cargados de explosivos. **783**

Kansas-Nebraska Act/Ley Kansas-Nebraska (1854) Ley que creó los territorios de Kansas y Nebraska y permitió a los votantes decidir por cuenta propia si la esclavitud debería ser abolida o aceptada. **459**

kayaks/kayaks Canoas casi completamente cerradas, con capacidad para una persona, fabricadas con pieles de animales. **12**

Kellogg-Briand Pact/Pacto Kellogg-Briand (1928) Pacto firmado por Estados Unidos y otras 14 naciones para dar a la guerra carácter de ilegalidad. **704**

Kentucky and Virginia Resolutions/Resoluciones de Kentucky y Virginia (1798-1799) Documentos republicanos que argumentaban el carácter anticonstitucional de las Leyes de no intervención. **290**

Khmer Rouge/Khmer Rouge Ejército comunista camboyano. **889**

kitchen cabinet/gabinete de cocina Grupo informal de consejeros del presidente Andrew Jackson. Fue llamado así porque en ocasiones se reunían en la cocina de la Casa Blanca. **340**

kivas/kivas Cámaras ceremoniales circulares usadas en las actividades religiosas de los indígenas estadounidenses del suroeste. **14**

Knights of Labor/Knights of Labor Primer sindicato del trabajo en Estados Unidos; fundado en 1869 para agrupar a trabajadores de distintas razas, géneros y capacidades. **586**

Know-Nothing Party/Partido de "no sé nada" Organización política fundada en 1849 con la finalidad de dificultar a los inmigrantes de otros países la adquisición de la ciudadanía estadounidense y su nombramiento en cargos públicos. **397**

Kristallnacht/Kristallnacht "Noche de los vidrios rotos"; 9 de noviembre de 1938; noche en que los nazis atacaron muchas propiedades judías ocasionando la muerte de miles de judíos e hiriendo a muchos otros. **752**

Ku Klux Klan/Ku Klux Klan Sociedad secreta creada por sureños de raza blanca en 1866 y que usó el terror y la violencia para restringir los derechos de los afroestadounidenses. **529**

Land Ordinance of 1785/Ordenanza de territorios de 1785 Decreto aprobado por el Congreso en el que se autorizaba el uso de encuestas y la división de territorios públicos del oeste del país. **190**

League of Nations/Liga de las Naciones Congreso internacional de naciones formado en 1919 para resolver disputas y mantener la paz y la seguridad colectiva. **687**

legislative branch/Poder Legislativo División del gobierno que propone nuevas leyes y decide cuáles de ellas deben ser aceptadas. **204**

Lend-Lease Act/Ley de Préstamos del Gobierno (1941) Ley que permitía a Estados Unidos prestar armas y otros suministros de guerra a la Gran Bretaña y más tarde a la Unión Soviética para combatir a las potencias del eje durante la Segunda Guerra Mundial. **764**

Levittown/Levittown Uno de los primeros ejemplos de planeación y construcción en masa de casas habitación, creado por William Levitt en Long Island, Nueva York. **827**

Lewis and Clark expedition/expedición de Lewis y Clark Expedición encabezada por Meriwether Lewis y William Clark que partió en 1804 con la finalidad de explorar el territorio comprado por Estados Unidos a Francia en la región de Luisiana. **306**

libel/libelo Declaración falsa, generalmente impresa, que daña la reputación de una persona. **94**

***Liberator*, The/*Liberator*, The** Periódico abolicionista publicado por William Lloyd Garrison a partir de 1831. **408**

Liberty bonds/Bonos Liberty Bonos emitidos por el gobierno estadounidense durante la segunda guerra mundial para recaudar fondos de ayuda para los aliados. **680**

limited government/gobierno limitado Principio político que establece que el gobierno debe estar confinado por leyes que limiten su poder. **188**

Limited Nuclear Test Ban Treaty/Tratado de Prohibición de Pruebas Nucleares (1963) Acuerdo internacional de prohibición de pruebas nucleares sobre la superficie de la tierra firmado por Estados Unidos y la Unión Soviética. **849**

Lincoln-Douglas debates/debates Lincoln–Douglas Serie de siete debates entre el republicano Abraham Lincoln y el demócrata Stephen Douglas durante la campaña de 1858 para el senado por Illinois. **465**

Line of Demarcation/Línea de demarcación Límite establecido por el papa Alejandro VI en 1493 a aproximadamente 300 millas de las Islas Azores. Según el documento, los territorios no reclamados al oeste del límite pertenecían a España y los del oeste a Portugal. **36**

Little Rock Nine/Los nueve de Little Rock Los primeros nueve estudiantes afroestadounidenses inscritos en la secundaria de Little Rock, Arkansas en 1957. **835**

longhouses/grandes viviendas comunes Edificaciones rectangulares construidas en Irak, en las que habitan varias familias. **16**

Long March/La Gran Marcha (1934) Retirada de un grupo de comunistas chinos para escapar del ejército nacionalista chino. **808**

loose construction/construcción libre Interpretación de la Constitución que permite al gobierno federal adoptar medidas que la Carta Magna no prohibía de manera específica. **276**

Lord Dunmore's Proclamation/Proclamación de Lord Dunmore (1775) Declaración emitida por el gobernador real de Virginia con la promesa de otorgar su libertad a los esclavos que participaran en la lucha contra el ejército británico durante la Revolución de Independencia. **167**

Lost Generation/generación perdida Grupo de escritores estadounidenses cuya obra criticaba severamente a la sociedad de la posguerra en rechazo de la destrucción y la muerte provocadas por la Primera Guerra Mundial. **719**

Louisiana Purchase/compra de Luisiana (1803) Compra de territorio francés localizado entre el río Mississippi y las montañas Rocosas que aumentó las posesiones de Estados Unidos a casi el doble. **304**

Lowell system/sistema Lowell Aprovechamiento de los molinos de agua en la industria textil, medida que dio empleo a muchas mujeres jóvenes solteras en el siglo diecinueve. **365**

Loyalists/leales Colonos que siempre apoyaron la causa británica durante la Revolución de Independencia. **160**

Lusitania/Lusitania Barco de pasajeros británico hundido por un submarino alemán en mayo de 1915 en el que murieron 128 estadounidenses; ésta fue una de las razones por las que Estados Unidos decidió tomar parte en la Primera Guerra Mundial. **676**

Maginot Line/Línea Maginot Línea de defensas fortificadas construida por Francia a lo largo de su frontera con Alemania después de la Primera Guerra Mundial. **763**

Magna Carta /Carta Magna (1215) Carta real. Acuerdo firmado por el Rey John de Inglaterra en el que se otorgaba mayores derechos a los individuos, estableciendo que incluso la nobleza y el rey debían obedecer la ley. **22**

maize/maíz El cultivo más importante de los indígenas estadounidenses en América del Norte y América Central. **6**

Manhattan Project/Proyecto Manhattan Proyecto secreto de los aliados creado en 1942 para desarrollar la bomba atómica. **785**

manifest destiny/destino manifiesto Creencia popular de muchos estadounidenses a mediados del siglo XIX de que Estados Unidos estaba destinado a expandirse hasta la costa del Pacífico. **432**

manors/feudos Estados de mayor tamaño gobernados por reyes y nobles en la Edad Media. **19**

Marbury* v. *Madison*/*Marbury* versus *Madison (1803) Caso de la Suprema Corte que dio origen a las revisiones judiciales. **300**

March on Washington/Marcha de Washington Manifestación masiva en favor de los derechos civiles que tuvo lugar el 28 de agosto de 1963 en Washington D.C. **857**

Marshall Plan/Plan Marshall Programa de apoyo económico a los países europeos para ayudarlos a reconstruir su economía después de la Segunda Guerra Mundial. **802**

Massacre at Wounded Knee/Masacre de Wounded Knee (1890) Matanza por parte del ejército estadounidense de un grupo de 150 indígenas de la tribu sioux en Wounded Knee, Dakota del Sur, que dio por terminada la guerra en las Grandes Planicies entre estos bandos. **550**

massive retaliation/represalias masivas Estrategia que consistía en lanzar amenazas de uso de armas nucleares para detener las **agresiones comunistas. 823**

mass production/producción en masa Producción eficiente de grandes cantidades de productos idénticos. **364**

Mayflower Compact/Pacto de Mayflower (1620) Acuerdo redactado por los colonos en el que establecían sus propias normas de gobierno. **71**

McCarthyism/macartismo Método de acusaciones sistemáticas sin la presentación de pruebas; nombrado así por ser el senador Joseph McCarthy, quien lo utilizó. **815**

McCulloch* v. *Maryland*/*McCulloch* versus *Maryland (1819) Caso de la Suprema Corte que declaraba que el Segundo Banco de la Nación era una empresa constitucional y que al ser una institución federal Maryland no podía intervenir en sus operaciones. **341**

McKinley Tariff/Arancel McKinley (1890) Ley que permitía a cualquier país vender azúcar a Estados Unidos sin pagar aranceles. **642**

Medicaid/Medicaid (por su abreviatura en inglés) (1965) Programa federal de seguros médicos a personas de escasos recursos. **852**

Medicare/Medicare (por su abreviatura en inglés) (1965) Programa federal de atención médica a personas mayores de 65 años. **852**

mercantilism/mercantilismo Creación y conservación de riquezas mediante un control minucioso de intercambios comerciales. **98**

mercenaries/mercenarios Soldados extranjeros contratados por un salario. **167**

Mexican Cession/cesión mexicana Territorio cedido por México a Estados Unidos mediante el Tratado Guadalupe Hidalgo que incluía los actuales estados de California, Nevada y Utah, así como parte de Arizona, Nuevo México, Colorado, Texas y Wyoming. **436**

Mexican Revolution/Revolución Mexicana Revolución iniciada en 1910 por Francisco Madero para derrocar al dictador mexicano Porfirio Díaz. **661**

MIAs/MIAs (por sus siglas en inglés) Soldados desaparecidos en combate. **892**

Middle Ages/Edad Media Periodo de la historia europea entre el 500 y el 1500 D.C. **19**

middle class/clase media Estrato social y económico ubicado entre la clase rica y la clase pobre. **398**

Middle Passage/travesía media Viaje de los esclavos africanos a través del Océano Atlántico para llegar a América del Norte y a las Indias Occidentales. **101**

migration/migración Desplazamiento de un grupo de personas de un lugar a otro. **5**

militarism/militarismo Política de control militar del gobierno. **669**

militia/milicia Fuerzas armadas formadas por civiles que sirven de manera temporal como soldados. **126**

minutemen/milicianos Miembros de la milicia en la época de la Colonia que estaban preparados para combatir en cualquier momento si la situación lo requería. **153**

missions/misiones Poblaciones establecidas por sacerdotes en Hispano América con la finalidad de convertir a los indígenas al catolicismo. **44**

Missouri Compromise/Acuerdo de Missouri (1820) Acuerdo propuesto por Henry Clay que permitía a Missouri su ingreso a la Unión sin abolir la esclavitud en su territorio y a Maine como estado libre, además de abolir la esclavitud en los estados localizados al norte del meridiano 36°30′. **333**

mobilize/movilizar Preparar fuerzas militares para la guerra. **670**

Model T/modelo T Automóvil de precio accesible fabricado por Henry Ford en 1908, también conocido como Tin Lizzie. **711**

monopoly/monopolio Control económico absoluto de un bien o servicio. **32**

Monroe Doctrine/Doctrina Monroe (1823) Declaración del presidente James Monroe en la que advierte a las naciones europeas su rechazo contra cualquier futura expansión o intervención en América. **331**

Montgomery Bus Boycott/Boicot de autobuses de Montgomery (1955–56) Boicot de afroestadounidenses a los autobuses de la ciudad de Montgomery, Alabama, que condujo a cambios en los reglamentos discriminatorios de los autobuses. **836**

Montgomery Improvement Association/Asociación de mejoramiento de Montgomery Organización formada en 1956 por residentes afroestadounidenses de Montgomery, Alabama, para consolidar el boicot de autobuses y coordinar las protestas de afroestadounidenses; estaba encabezada por Martin Luther King Jr. **836**

Mormons/mormones Miembros de la Iglesia de Jesucristo de los Santos de los Últimos Días. **440**

Mormon Trail/Camino Mormón Ruta que siguieron los mormones del oeste hasta Utah. **441**

Morrill Act/Ley de Morril (1862) Ley federal que cedió terrenos a los estados del oeste para fomentar la construcción de nuevas universidades. **565**

Morse code/clave Morse Sistema desarrollado por un asistente de Samuel Morse en el que las letras del alfabeto son representadas por combinaciones de puntos y rayas para transmitir mensajes telegráficos. **369**

Motown Records/Motown Records Primera compañía discográfica importante propiedad de un afroestadounidense; fundada por el hombre de negocios Berry Gordy en 1959. **868**

mountain men/montañeses Hombres contratados por compañías occidentales para atrapar animales y obtener pieles en las montañas Rocosas y otras regiones del oeste de Estados Unidos. **427**

muckrakers/muckrackers Periodistas que escribían artículos acerca de la corrupción en los negocios y la política para originar una reforma. **611**

mugwumps/*mugwumps* Reformadores republicanos que abandonaron al partido para apoyar al candidato demócrata Grover Cleveland en las elecciones presidenciales de 1884. **608**

Munich Conference/Conferencia de Munich (1938) Reunión de líderes de la Gran Bretaña, Francia y Alemania donde acordaron ceder a Alemania control de la región de Sudetenland a cambio de que Adolfo Hitler no invadiera otros territorios europeos. **763**

National Aeronautics and Space Administration/Administración Nacional de Aeronáutica y Espacio (NASA, por sus siglas en inglés) agencia establecida por el Congreso en 1958 para realizar investigaciones sobre el espacio. **822**

National American Woman Suffrage Association/Asociación Nacional Estadounidense para el Sufragio Femenino (NAWSA, por sus siglas en inglés) grupo formado en 1890 por Elizabeth Cady Stanton y Susan B. Anthony para luchar por el derecho al voto de las mujeres. **621**

National Association for the Advancement of Colored People/Asociación Nacional para el Progreso de la Gente de Color (NAACP, por sus siglas en inglés) grupo formado en 1909 por W. E. B. Du Bois y algunos simpatizantes con la finalidad de ofrecer a los afroestadounidenses igualdad económica, educativa y social tomando como inspiración el movimiento del Niágara. **623**

national debt/deuda pública Cantidad de dinero que un país debe a sus acreedores. **273**

National Grange/National Grange Organización social y educativa fundada en 1867 para dar a los agricultores mayor representación política y así mejorar su calidad de vida. **598**

National Industrial Recovery Act/Ley Recuperación Industrial Nacional (NIRA, por sus siglas en inglés) (1933) Ley federal creada para fomentar el desarrollo económico mediante la suspensión de las leyes antimonopolio y la eliminación de las prácticas ilegales de competencia entre empleadores: esta ley fue declarada anticonstitucional en 1933. **739**

nationalism/nacionalismo Creencia de que una nación, idioma o cultura es superior a los demás. **668**

National Labor Relations Act/Ley de Relaciones Laborales Nacionales (NLRA) (1935) Ley federal que legalizó a los sindicatos y las negociaciones del contrato colectivo de trabajo. **741**

National Liberation Front/Frente Nacional de Liberación (NLF, por sus siglas en inglés) Organización formada para combatir al gobierno de Ngo Dinh Diem en Vietnam del Sur. **876**

National Organization for Women/Organización Nacional de Mujeres (NOW) Grupo formado en 1966 por Betty Friedan y otras feministas para lograr que la mujer obtuviera mayor poder político. **864**

National Origins Act/ley nacional de procedencia (1924) Ley que redujo la inmigración a Estados Unidos y que detuvo por completo la entrada de inmigrantes japoneses; estableció un cupo que favoreció a los inmigrantes procedentes del norte de Europa. **709**

National War Labor Board/Junta Nacional Laboral para la Guerra Agencia creada en la administración del presidente Woodrow Wilson para resolver disputas entre trabajadores y los directivos de las compañías. **681**

National Woman's Party/Partido Nacional de la Mujer (NWP, por sus siglas en inglés) Organización fundada por Alice Paul en 1913 que usó métodos controvertidos para obtener el derecho al voto femenino. **621**

nativists/nativistas Ciudadanos estadounidenses que rechazaban la inmigración porque no confiaban en los inmigrantes y temían que éstos les quitaran sus empleos. **397**

Nat Turner's Rebellion/Rebelión de Nat Turner (1831) Revuelta en la que Nat Turner y un grupo de esclavos de Virginia asesinaron a varias familias en diversas plantaciones en un intento frustrado por acabar con la esclavitud. **381**

naturalized citizen/ciudadano naturalizado Persona nacida en otro país a quien se le otorga la ciudadanía. **255**

Navigation Acts/Leyes de Navegación (1650–96) Leyes británicas que regulaban el comercio en las colonias. **99**

Nazis/nazis Partido Nacional Socialista Grupo político encabezado por Adolfo Hitler que asumió el poder en Alemania en la década de 1930. **752**

Neutrality Acts/Leyes de Neutralidad Grupo de cuatro leyes aprobadas a finales de la década de 1930 para mantener a Estados Unidos al margen de incidentes internacionales. **280**

New Deal/New Deal Programas creados por el presidente Franklin D. Roosevelt para restablecer la economía de Estados Unidos durante la Gran Depresión. **738**

New Federalism/Nuevo federalismo Sistema de repartición de ingresos propuesto por el presidente Richard Nixon para que los estados dispusieran de los fondos otorgados por el gobierno federal como mejor les pareciera. **903**

New Frontier/Nueva frontera Conjunto de propuestas internas y externas anunciado por el presidente John F. Kennedy en su discurso de toma de posesión de 1961. **847**

new immigrants/nuevos inmigrantes Inmigrantes que llegaron a Estados Unidos durante y después de la década de 1880; en su mayoría eran del sur y occidente de Europa. **590**

New Jersey Plan/Plan Nueva Jersey Propuesta de creación de un gobierno con una sola cámara con representación de cada estado, pero no de la población. La propuesta fue rechazada en la Convención Constitucional de Filadelfia. **202**

nickelodeons/nickelodeons Teatros donde se exhibían las primeras películas con imágenes en movimiento; llamados así porque la entrada generalmente costaba una moneda de cinco centavos, es decir, un níquel. **716**

Nineteenth Amendment/Decimonovena enmienda (1920) Enmienda de la Constitución que otorgó a las mujeres el derecho al voto. **622**

no-man's-land/tierra de nadie Franja territorial entre las trincheras de ejércitos enemigos en el frente occidental durante la Primera Guerra Mundial. **673**

nominating conventions/convenciones de nominación Encuentros en los que los partidos políticos eligen a sus candidatos a la presidencia y la vicepresidencia. Se realizaron por primera vez en la década de 1820. **338**

nonagression pact/Pacto de no agresión Acuerdo entre las naciones para no atacarse entre sí. **763**

Non-Intercourse Act/Ley de no interacción (1809) Ley que reemplazaba a la Ley de embargo, restableciendo el intercambio comercial con todas las naciones, excepto Gran Bretaña y Francia. **310**

nonviolent resistance/resistencia de no violencia Método de protesta pacífico que rechaza el uso de la violencia incluso en casos de defensa propia. **855**

North American Free Trade Agreement/Tratado de Libre Comercio de América del Norte (NAFTA, por sus siglas en inglés) (1993) Tratado de Libre Comercio entre Estados Unidos, Canadá y México. **937**

North Atlantic Treaty Organization/Organización del Tratado del Atlántico Norte (NATO, por sus siglas en inglés) Alianza militar formada en 1949 por Estados Unidos, Gran Bretaña y 10 países más con la finalidad de defenderse entre sí en caso de ataque. **803**

Northwest Ordinance of 1787/Ordenanza del Noroeste de 1877 Decreto aprobado por el Congreso para establecer una estructura política en el territorio del noroeste y crear un sistema de admisión de nuevos estados. **190**

Northwest Passage/pasaje del noroeste Pasaje de agua inexistente que los primeros exploradores de América del Norte buscaron con insistencia para cruzar el continente. **49**

Northwest Territory/Territorio del Noroeste Organización del territorio que incluía los actuales estados de Illinois, Indiana, Michigan, Ohio, Wisconsin y parte de Minnesota. Creado por la Ordenanza del Noroeste en 1787. **190**

nullification crisis/crisis de anulación Disputa entre Carolina del Sur y el gobierno federal, a finales de la década de 1820, por el derecho del estado para anular o cancelar un arancel impopular. **341**

Nuremberg Trials/Juicios de Nuremberg (1945) Juicios de crímenes de guerra para oficiales nazis de alto rango que el Tribunal Internacional Militar realizó en la ciudad de Nuremberg, Alemania. **799**

Ohio Gang/Banda de Ohio Grupo de allegados políticos del presidente Warren S. Harding en Ohio, muchos de los cuales se involucraron en diversos escándalos relacionados con el gobierno. **703**

old immigrants/antiguos inmigrantes Inmigrantes que llegaron a Estados Unidos antes de la década de 1880; en su mayoría eran del norte de Europa. **590**

Olive Branch Petition/Petición de la rama de olivo (1775) Paz solicitada por el Segundo Congreso Continental al Rey George III de Gran Bretaña, quien decidió rechazarla. **154**

Open Door Policy/Política de puertas abiertas (1899) Declaración del secretario de estado John Hay de que todas las naciones deben tener el mismo acceso al intercambio comercial con China. **644**

open range/pradera abierta Terrenos públicos usados como tierras de pastoreo. **559**

Operation Desert Storm/Operación Tormenta del desierto (1991) Invasión de las Naciones Unidas encabezada por Estados Unidos para obligar a Irak a retirar sus tropas de Kuwait. **935**

Operation Rolling Thunder/Operación Trueno envolvente Ataques aéreos de Estados Unidos a las industrias para la guerra de Vietnam del Norte durante la guerra de Vietnam. **879**

Oregon Trail/Sendero de Oregón Camino de 2,000 millas que se extendía desde el este de Missouri al territorio de Oregón. **429**

Organization of Petroleum Exporting Countries/Organización de Países Exportadores de Petróleo (OPEC, por sus siglas en inglés; OPEP, en español) Alianza formada por las principales naciones productoras de petróleo en 1960 para mantener los precios elevados valiéndose de la regulación de la producción y venta de este producto. **904**

ozone layer/capa de ozono Capa delgada de gas en la atmósfera superior, que evita que los rayos solares perjudiciales lleguen a la superficie de la Tierra. **940**

pacification/pacificación Política de funcionarios de Estados Unidos y de Vietnam del Sur con la finalidad de proteger a los aldeanos mediante la creación de áreas civiles resguardadas por tropas del gobierno. **881**

Pacific Railway Acts/Leyes del Ferrocarril del Pacífico (1862, 1864) Conjunto de dos leyes aprobadas por el gobierno federal que ofrecían préstamos económicos y cedían terrenos a las compañías ferrocarrileras con la intención de promover la construcción del ferrocarril transcontinental. **555**

Paleo-Indians/paleoindígenas Primeros estadounidenses que cruzaron de Asia a América del Norte entre el año 38,000 y el 10,000 A.C. **5**

Palmer raids/redadas de Palmer (1920) Redadas ordenadas por el fiscal general A. Mitchell Palmer contra supuestas organizaciones radicales. **700**

Panama Canal/Canal de Panamá Canal que Estados Unidos construyó en el istmo de Panamá para enlazar el Océano Atlántico con el Océano Pacífico; el canal entró en operación en 1914. **656**

Panama Canal treaties/Tratados del Canal de Panamá (1977) Acuerdo realizado entre Estados Unidos y Panamá para transferir a Panamá el control del canal a partir del año 2000. **915**

Panic of 1837/Pánico de 1837 Crisis financiera de Estados Unidos que provocó una importante depresión económica. **342**

Panic of 1873/Pánico de 1873 Crisis financiera estadounidense; inicio de una depresión económica que debilitó al Partido Republicano. **530**

pardon/perdón Anulación de un castigo. **223**

Paris Peace Accords/Acuerdo de Paz de París (1973) Acuerdo entre los líderes del Frente de Liberación Nacional, Vietnam del Norte, Vietnam del Sur y Estados Unidos para terminar con la guerra de Vietnam; convocado para el retiro de las tropas estadounidenses de la región, la liberación de los prisioneros estadounidenses de guerra y el establecimiento de una zona restringida desmilitarizada para separar a Vietnam del Norte de Vietnam del Sur. **891**

Parliament/Parlamento Órgano británico de legislación. **93**

patents/patentes Derechos de exclusividad para la fabricación o venta de un invento. **580**

Patriots/Patriotas Colonos estadounidenses que lucharon para independizarse de Gran Bretaña durante la Revolución. **160**

Peace Corps/Cuerpos de paz Programa del presidente John F. Kennedy que envía voluntarios estadounidenses a otras naciones para apoyar a naciones en desarrollo mediante proyectos de mejoramiento. **847**

Pendleton Civil Service Act/Ley de Servicio Civil Pendleton (1833) Ley que estableció un sistema de méritos para otorgar empleos en el gobierno federal. **609**

Pentagon/Pentágono Enorme complejo arquitectónico ubicado en Arlington, Virginia, que es la base de la dirección militar de Estados Unidos; su nombre se debe a su forma geométrica de cinco lados. **945**

perestroika/perestroika Política soviética de la década de 1980 que inició reformas políticas y económicas. **931**

petition/petición Solicitud formal. **249**

Pickett's Charge/Ataque de Pickett (1863) Ataque fallido del ejército confederado, al mando del general George Pickett, durante la Batalla de Gettysburg. **499**

Pilgrims/peregrinos Miembros de una secta separatista puritana que emigró de Inglaterra a principios del siglo XVII para establecerse en América. **71**

Pinckney's Treaty/Tratado de Pinckney (1795) Acuerdo entre Estados Unidos y España que modificó los límites de Florida y facilitó a los barcos estadounidenses el uso del puerto de Nueva Orleáns. **282**

pioneers/pioneros Primeras personas que llegan a poblar una región. **131**

plantations/plantaciones Grandes granjas que por lo general se especializan en un cultivo específico. **45**

planters/hacendados Agricultores acaudalados dueños de grandes plantaciones. **69, 375**

Platt Amendment/Enmienda Platt (1902) Enmienda de la constitución cubana que daba a Estados Unidos el derecho de involucrarse en los asuntos internos y externos de Cuba; esta ley perdió efecto en 1934. **650**

***Plessy* v. *Ferguson*/Plessy vs. Ferguson** (1896) Caso de la Suprema Corte que estableció la doctrina de igualdad separatista para negros y blancos en las instalaciones públicas. **532**

political action committees/comités de acción política (PAC, por sus siglas en inglés) Organizaciones que recaudaban fondos para patrocinar a los candidatos políticos que apoyaban las mismas causas que los contribuyentes. **258**

political machines/maquinaria política Organizaciones políticas que usaban métodos legales e ilegales para asegurar la victoria de sus candidatos en las elecciones. **606**

political parties/partidos políticos Grupos de personas que participaban en la elección de los funcionarios del gobierno e influían en las políticas adoptadas. **287**

poll tax/impuesto de capitación Impuesto especial que debía pagar una persona para votar. **531**

Pontiac's Rebellion/Rebelión de Pontiac (1763) Intento fallido del Jefe Pontiac de la tribu Ottawa y sus aliados por retirar a los colonizadores europeos de la frontera noroeste. **133**

Pony Express/Pony Express Sistema de mensajeros a caballo creado en 1860 para entregar la correspondencia por todo Estados Unidos. **555**

pop art/arte pop Movimiento artístico que desafió los valores tradicionales mediante el uso de imágenes y objetos populares y triviales. **868**

popular sovereignty/soberanía popular Idea de que la autoridad política pertenecía al pueblo. Principio que en una época permitió a los votantes de una región aceptar o rechazar la esclavitud. **204, 451**

Populist Party/Partido Populista Partido político nacional creado en 1891 que apoyaba las reformas a la acuñación de plata, las restricciones de migración y la expropiación de los sistemas de ferrocarriles, de teléfonos y de telégrafos. **600**

potlatches/ofrendas Ritos ceremoniales en que los invitados de los indígenas del noroeste del país entregaban sus posesiones de valor para ganar respeto. **12**

Potsdam Conference/Conferencia de Postdam (1945) Reunión del presidente de Estados Unidos Harry S Truman, el primer ministro de la Gran Bretaña Winston Churchill y el líder soviético Joseph Stalin después de la rendición alemana en la Segunda Guerra Mundial, en la que dividieron Alemania y Austria en cuatro zonas de ocupación. **799**

Pottawatomie Massacre/Matanza de Pottawatomie (1856) Incidente en el que el abolicionista John Brown y siete hombres más asesinaron a los habitantes de Kansas que apoyaban la esclavitud. **461**

Powhatan Confederacy/Confederación de Powhatan Poderosa alianza de indígenas algonquinos al mando de Wahunsonacock. **66**

precedent/precedente Acción o decisión que más tarde sirve como ejemplo. **270**

presidios/presidios Bases militares españolas localizadas en América. **44**

privateers/corsarios Barcos privados autorizados por una nación para atacar a sus enemigos. **280**

Privy Council/Consejo Privado Grupo de consejeros reales que definían las políticas de las colonias de Gran Bretaña en América. **92**

Proclamation of 1763/Proclamación de 1763 Proclamación británica que prohibía el establecimiento en el futuro de colonias al oeste de los montes Apalaches y ordenaba a las colonias ya establecidas en ese lugar que se establecieran en otro lugar. **134**

progressives/progresistas Grupo de reformadores que propugnaba la solución de problemas sociales y políticos, creado a finales del siglo XIX. **610**

propaganda/propaganda Historias e imágenes diseñadas para apoyar un punto de vista particular. **140**

proprietors/propietarios Dueños. **82**

prospect/prospector Buscador de oro. **438**

protective tariff/tarifa de protección Impuesto sobre artículos importados que eleva su precio con la finalidad de que los habitantes prefieran los productos locales. **275**

Protestant Reformation/Reforma protestante Movimiento religioso iniciado por Martín Lutero y sus seguidores en 1517 para reformar la Iglesia Católica. **47**

Protestants/protestantes Reformistas que protestaban por la realización de ciertas prácticas de la Iglesia Católica. **47**

pueblos/pueblos Poblaciones españolas establecidas en América. **44**

Pullman Strike/huelga de Pullman (1894) Huelga ferrocarrilera de trabajadores de la compañía Pullman's Palace Car que paralizó a varias líneas de ferrocarril hasta que las cortes federales les ordenaron que regresaran a sus labores. **589**

Pure Food and Drug Act/Ley de Alimentos y Drogas Puros (1906) Ley que prohibía la fabricación, venta y transportación interestatal de alimentos y medicamentos contaminados o mal envasados. **626**

Puritans/puritanos Protestantes que querían reformar la Iglesia Británica. **70**

Radical Republicans/republicanos radicales Integrantes del Congreso que pensaban que los estados sureños necesitaban grandes cambios sociales para volver a ser admitidos en la Unión. **521**

range rights/derechos a las praderas Derechos sobre las fuentes de agua en las Grandes Planicies; los ganaderos compraban estos derechos para poseer control exclusivo del agua y las tierras en las que ésta se encontraba. **560**

range wars/guerras de praderas Disputas entre ganaderos acaudalados, pequeños ganaderos y agricultores de las Grandes Planicies por el uso de las praderas abiertas. **563**

ratification/ratificación Aprobación formal. **190**

realpolitik/realpolitik Palabra de origen alemán que significa "prácticas políticas"; sistema propuesto por Henry Kissinger e implantado por el presidente Richard Nixon para anteponer los intereses de la nación a las ideas políticas o morales en la toma de decisiones sobre asuntos exteriores. **905**

recall/recordatorio Medida que, de ser necesario, permitía a los votantes destituir a un funcionario de su cargo antes de que su periodo de funciones terminara. **612**

Reconstruction/Reconstrucción (1865-77) Periodo posterior a la Guerra Civil en que el gobierno de Estados Unidos concentró sus esfuerzos en la restauración de los estados del sur y en la reunificación de la nación. **515**

Reconstruction Acts/Leyes de Reconstrucción (1867-68) Leyes que pusieron a los estados del sur bajo supervisión militar y les exigieron la creación de una nueva constitución basada en la Decimocuarta enmienda. **524**

Redcoats/casacas rojas Soldados británicos que lucharon contra los colonos en la Revolución Estadounidense. Llamados así por el color rojo brillante de sus uniformes. **154**

Redeemers/redentores Grupo de demócratas sureños que ayudó al partido demócrata a recuperar su poder durante la Reconstrucción y trató de limitar los derecho de los afroestadounidenses. **531**

Red Scare/temor rojo Ola de terror anticomunista que arrazó Estados Unidos después de la Segunda Guerra Mundial. **700**

referendum/referendo Medida que permite a los ciudadanos votar por propuestas de ley. **612**

rendezvous/Rendevouz Reunión anual realizada por personas que habitaban en las montañas para intercambiar pieles y socializar. **427**

reparations/indemnización Pago de los daños y gastos ocasionados por una guerra. **688**

repeal/rechazar Abolir. **138**

representative democracy/democracia representativa Gobierno de representantes elegidos por el pueblo. **220**

republicanism/republicanismo Apoyo a un sistema de gobierno representativo. **188**

Republican Party/Partido Republicano Partido político formado en 1854 para detener la diseminación de la esclavitud al oeste del país. **462**

Republic of Texas/República de Texas Nación independiente que existió de 1836 a 1845 cuando finalmente Texas se anexó a Estados Unidos. **426**

reservations/reservaciones Territorios federales separados para los indígenas. **548**

reserved powers/poderes reservados Poderes exclusivos de los gobiernos de los estados o de los ciudadanos. **221**

revivals/restauraciones Reuniones públicas eclesiásticas en las que los ministros daban sermones ante grandes cantidades de personas. **108**

Rhode Island System/Sistema de Rhode Island Sistema desarrollado por Samuel Slater a mediados del siglo XIX con la finalidad de contratar a familias completas para laborar en la industria textil. **365**

right of deposit/derecho de depósito Derecho de transferir bienes a otro destino sin pagar cuotas alguna. **281**

Roosevelt Corollary/Corolario Roosevelt (1904) Agregado del presidente Theodore Roosevelt a la Doctrina Monroe; declaraba que Estados Unidos vigilaría los asuntos del hemisferio occidental para evitar que los países europeos intervinieran en la región. **657**

roundup/rodeo Acción de reunir al ganado en círculo para formar una sola manada. **560**

Rush-Bagot Agreement/Acuerdo de Rush-Bargo (1817) Acuerdo que limitaba el poder naval en los Grandes Lagos a embarcaciones de Estados Unidos y Canadá. **328**

sanctions/sanciones Multas económicas. **916**

Sandinistas/sandinistas Partido político revolucionario fundado en Nicaragua que en 1979 derrocó a un dictador que favorecía los intereses de Estados Unidos. **930**

Santa Fe Trail/Camino de Santa Fe Ruta que va de Independence, Missouri, a Santa Fe, en lo que hoy es Nuevo México; principalmente utilizada por comerciantes. **431**

Saturday Night Massacre/Masacre de la noche del sábado Nombre dado a la serie de sucesos que incluyeron el despido de un investigador especial del caso Watergate y a la renuncia del fiscal y su asistente por rehusarse a despedir al investigador mencionado. **909**

scalawags/scalawags Nombre que los demócratas dieron a los republicanos blancos del sur durante la reconstrucción; en términos literales, este calificativo significa "malos camaradas". **528**

scientific agriculture/agricultura científica Uso de técnicas científicas para mejorar la producción agrícola. **374**

scientific method/método científico Observación y experimentación con sucesos naturales que permiten elaborar teorías con el propósito de predecir otros sucesos o comportamientos. **113**

Scientific Revolution/Revolución científica Periodo de gran aprendizaje iniciado en el siglo XVII, en el que científicos, matemáticos y astrónomos europeos trataron de obtener explicaciones acerca de los misterios del universo. **112**

Scopes trial/juicio de Scopes (1925) Enjuiciamiento de John T. Scopes, un profesor de secundaria arrestado en Dayton, Tennessee, por enseñar la teoría de la evolución de Darwin en su clase de ciencias. **708**

sea dogs/Sabuesos de mar Marineros ingleses patrocinados por la Reina Elizabeth I para robar los tesoros de los navíos españoles a finales del siglo XVI. **48**

search-and-destroy missions/misiones de búsqueda y destrucción Estrategia de Estados Unidos en la guerra de Vietnam en la que patrullas estadounidenses buscaban campamentos y depósitos de suministros ocultos para destruirlos mediante potencia de fuego y ataques aéreos masivos. **880**

search warrant/orden de cateo Orden de un juez que autoriza entrar a la propiedad de una persona para buscar evidencias que lo relacionen con un delito. **250**

secession/secesión Retiro formal de una organización (un país, por ejemplo). **471**

Second Battle of Bull Run/Segunda Batalla de Bull Run (1862) Batalla de la Guerra Civil en la que el Ejército Confederado obligó a gran parte de las tropas de la Unión a abandonar el territorio de Virginia. **485**

Second Battle of the Marne/segunda Batalla de Marne (1918) Última ofensiva del ejército alemán en la Primera Guerra Mundial y momento decisivo en la guerra para los aliados. **684**

Second Continental Congress/Segundo Congreso Continental (1775) Reunión de delegados de la colonia realizada en Filadelfia para tomar decisiones acerca de la lucha en Lexington y Concord. **154**

Second Great Awakening/Segundo Gran Despertar Periodo de evangelización religiosa iniciado en la década de 1790 y difundido rápidamente en todo Estados Unidos en la década de 1830. **390**

Second Industrial Revolution/segunda Revolución Industrial Periodo de crecimiento explosivo de la industria estadounidense a finales del siglo XIX. **578**

sect/secta Grupo religioso. **70**

Sedition Act of 1918/Ley de Sedición de 1918 Ley aprobada durante la Primera Guerra Mundial que prohibía a los estadounidenses hacer declaraciones desleales sobre el gobierno, la constitución o la bandera. **679**

segregation/segregación Separación obligada de personas de diferentes razas en lugares públicos. **531**

Selective Service Act/Ley de Servicio Selectivo (1917) Ley que obligaba a los hombres entre 21 y 30 años de edad a registrarse en la lista de disponibilidad de las fuerzas armadas. **679**

Selective Training and Service Act/Ley de Instrucción y Servicio Selectivo (1940) Primer reclutamiento estadounidense de la historia que se hiciera en tiempos de paz. **767**

self-determination/autodeterminación Derecho de las personas a decidir su propia condición política. **687**

Seneca Falls Convention/Convención de Seneca Falls (1848) Convención nacional por los derechos de la mujer; lugar donde se redactó la Declaración de sentimientos. **415**

separation of powers/separación de poderes División del poder de un gobierno en diferentes ramas que ejercen distintas acciones legales; evita que cualquiera de ellas tenga demasiado poder. **221**

Separatists/separatistas Grupo radical de puritanos que tenía como propósito eliminar cualquier relación con la Iglesia Británica. **70**

settlement houses/casas de las colonias Centros comunitarios creados en la década de 1890 para ofrecer educación, recreación y actividades sociales a inmigrantes y personas de escasos recursos. **595**

Seven Days' Battles/Batallas de los Siete Días (1862) Serie de batallas de la Guerra Civil en las que el Ejército Confederado obliga a las tropas de la Unión a retirarse de Richmond, Virginia, la capital confederada. **485**

Seventeenth Amendment/Decimoséptima enmienda (1913) Enmienda constitucional que permite a los votantes elegir de manera directa a los senadores de la nación. **611**

sharecropping/cultivo de intercambio Sistema adoptado en las granjas del sur durante la guerra civil en el que los campesinos cultivan tierras ajenas a cambio de una pequeña parte de la cosecha. **533**

Shays's Rebellion/Rebelión de Shay (1786–87) Levantamiento de los agricultores de Massachusetts, encabezados por Daniel Shay, para protestar por los altos impuestos, el aumento de sus deudas y el cierre de las granjas. **198**

Sherman Antitrust Act/Ley Sherman Antimonopolio (1890) Ley que prohibía la creación de monopolios o fideicomisos que restringieran el libre comercio. **584**

Sherman Silver Purchase Act/Ley Sherman de la Compra de Plata (1890) Ley que incrementó la cantidad de plata adquirida por el gobierno de Estados Unidos para acuñar monedas. **599**

siege/sitio Bloqueo militar de una ciudad o fuerte. **155**

Siege of Vicksburg/Sitio de Vicksburg (1863) Bloqueo de seis semanas realizado por el ejército de la Unión en Vicksburg para forzar la rendición de esa ciudad durante la Guerra Civil. **490**

silent generation/generación silenciosa Nombre dado a los adolescentes y estudiantes universitarios en la década de 1950 debido a que la mayoría de ellos parecía conformarse con las expectativa sociales sin protestar. **831**

Silent Majority/mayoría silenciosa Término usado por el presidente Richard Nixon para designar a un gran grupo de electores conservadores que rechazaban los cambios adoptados en la década de 1960. **902**

Silk Road/ruta de la seda Ruta comercial de varios miles de millas que conectaba a China con el Mar Negro. **25**

sit-down strike/huelga de brazos caídos Tipo de huelga en la que los empleados se rehusan a trabajar y a abandonar las instalaciones de trabajo para evitar que los patrones los reemplacen. **741**

sit-in/plantón Demostración de protesta en la que un grupo de personas acude a un lugar específico y se niega a abandonarlo. **855**

Sixteenth Amendment/Decimosexta enmienda (1913) Enmienda constitucional que permite al gobierno federal aprobar impuestos directos como el impuesto sobre el trabajo. **629**

slave codes/códigos de esclavos Leyes aprobadas por las colonias para el control de los esclavos. **104**

socialism/socialismo Sistema económico en el que el gobierno o los trabajadores son propietarios de los medios de producción. **618**

Social Security Act/Ley de Seguridad Social (1935) Ley que creó un organismo de seguridad social que ofrece pensiones de retiro y seguro de desempleo a los trabajadores, personas de edad avanzada y discapacitados. **740**

societies/sociedades Grupos de personas que viven juntas y comparten una misma cultura. **6**

sodbusters/buscadores de tepe Nombre dado a los agricultores de las planicies y al tipo de arado que usaban para romper el duro suelo de la región como preparación para el cultivo. **566**

Sons of Liberty/Hijos de la libertad Sociedades secretas formadas a mediados del siglo XVIII por los colonos para protestar por la creación de nuevos impuestos y para atemorizar a los recaudadores. **137**

southern strategy/estrategia del sur Intento del partido republicano por ganar el apoyo de los demócratas del sur y quienes se oponían a las reformas de los derechos civiles mediante la restricción de toda ley sobre la materia. **903**

Spanish Armada/Armada Española Gran flota naval española derrotada por la armada británica en 1588. **48**

speakeasies/speakeasies Clubes ilegales encubiertos en los que se vendían bebidas alcohólicas en la época de la prohibición. **707**

speculation/especulación Inversión económica en un negocio de alto riesgo con la esperanza de obtener grandes ganancias. **732**

speculators/especuladores Inversionistas que compran artículos a precios bajos con la esperanza de que aumente su valor. **273**

spheres of influence/esferas de influencia Áreas de un país, especialmente de China, cuyos recursos naturales y comercio eran controlados por otras naciones; práctica común a finales del siglo XIX. **644**

spirituals/espirituales Canciones religiosas cantadas con gran emotividad por los esclavos del sur que combinaban elementos de origen africano y europeo para expresar sus creencias religiosas. **380**

spoils system/sistema de mimos Práctica política de ofrecer empleos a los partidarios de una causa. **340**

Sputnik/Sputnik (1957) Primer satélite artificial de la historia; lanzado al espacio por la Unión Soviética. **822**

stagflation/stagflation Situación económica caracterizada por una elevada inflación y altos índices de desempleo. **903**

stalemate/estancamiento Situación en la que ninguna de las partes en conflicto obtiene una victoria decisiva. **674**

Stamp Act/Ley del timbre (1765) Ley aprobada por el Parlamento británico para aumentar la recaudación fiscal en las colonias con impuestos como el de la compra de papel y estampillas postales, licencias y documentos legales. **137**

staple crops/cultivos básicos Productos de demanda constante. **106**

states' rights/derechos de los estados Creencia de que el poder de los estados debía ser mayor que el del gobierno federal. **340**

steerage/tercera clase Área inferior del casco de un barco en la que muchos inmigrantes viajaban a Estados Unidos para ahorrar dinero. **591**

strait/estrecho Paso angosto y serpenteante en el mar. **39**

Strategic Arms Limitation Talks/Pláticas de reducción de armamento estratégico (SALT, por sus siglas en inglés, 1972) Pláticas entre el presidente de Estados Unidos Richard Nixon y el líder soviético Leonid Brezhev que condujeron a la firma de un tratado que limitaba el número de misiles nucleares de largo alcance de ambos países. **906**

strict construction/construcción estricta Interpretación especial de la Constitución que permite al gobierno federal adoptar solamente aquellas medidas que la carta magna no prohíba de manera específica. **276**

strike/huelga Negativa de un grupo de empleados a laborar hasta que sus empleadores satisfagan sus demandas. **365**

Student Nonviolent Coordination Committee/Comité de Coordinación Estudiantil por la No Violencia (SNCC, por sus siglas en inglés) Organización estudiantil formada en 1960 para coordinar las protestas en favor de los derechos civiles y ofrecer capacitación a los protestantes. **856**

Students for a Democratic Society/Sociedad de Estudiantes por una Sociedad Democrática (SDC, por sus siglas en inglés) Grupo estudiantil que protestó activamente contra las estrictas reglas universitarias y la intervención de Estados en la guerra de Vietnam. **866**

subsidy/subsidio Pago de una bonificación. **642**

suburbs/suburbios Vecindarios residenciales en las afueras de una ciudad. **594**

Suez Crisis/Crisis de Suez Crisis internacional iniciada en 1956 cuando la Gran Bretaña, Francia e Israel invadieron la región del Canal de Suez en Egipto. **824**

suffrage/sufragio Derecho al voto. **188**

Sugar Act/Ley del azúcar (1764) Ley aprobada por el Parlamento británico que establece el pago de impuestos sobre la remolacha y el azúcar importada por las colonias. **135**

Sunbelt/Sunbelt Estados del sur y del sudoeste que atrajeron a muchas personas y comercios en la década de 1950 con el ofrecimiento de menores impuestos, un mejor clima y más oportunidades de trabajo. **827**

supply-side economics/supply side economics Teoría económica según la cual la disminución de impuestos permiten aumentar la actividad económica, la recaudación y la adopción de un presupuesto equilibrado. **929**

Sussex pledge/plegaria de Sussex (1916) Promesa de los líderes alemanes en la Primera Guerra Mundial de no atacar a barcos mercantes sin previa advertencia. **676**

Sutter's Fort/Fuerte Sutter Colonia del norte de California fundada por el inmigrante suizo John Sutter en 1839, que se convirtió en un popular destino para los inmigrantes. **431**

Taft-Hartley Act/Ley Taft-Hartley (1947) Ley que otorgaba al gobierno federal mayor autoridad para terminar con las huelgas y exigía a los líderes de los sindicatos que realizaran juramentos en contra del comunismo. **806**

talkies/cine hablado Películas con sonido o diálogos. **716**

Tariff of Abominations/Arancel de abominaciones (1828) Sobrenombre dado a cada nueva tarifa de impuestos rechazada por los habitantes del sur. **340**

tariffs/aranceles Impuestos pagados por los bienes importados o exportados. **196**

Tea Act/Ley del té (1773) Ley aprobada por el Parlamento británico que permitía a la Compañía British East India vender té a bajo costo a las colonias sin intermediarios, afectando a los comerciantes locales de té. Esta decisión dio origen al Motín del Té de Boston. **141**

Teapot Dome scandal/escándalo Teapot Dome Escándalo que afectó a la administración del presidente Warren G. Harding cuando el secretario de asuntos internos Albert Fall fue acusado de la venta ilegal de reservas petroleras a cambio de favores y préstamos personales. **703**

technology/tecnología Herramientas usadas para producir bienes o realizar un trabajo. **363**

Tejanos/texanos Colonizadores españoles que habitaban en la región que actualmente es el norte de Texas. **423**

telegraph/telégrafo Máquina inventada por Samuel Morse en 1837 para enviar mensajes a grandes distancias mediante impulsos eléctricos transmitidos por cables. **369**

Teller Amendment/Enmienda Teller (1898) Enmienda de la resolución en la que Estados Unidos declaraba que no tenía la intención de invadir y apropiarse de Cuba. **647**

temperance movement/movimiento de abstinencia Reforma social emprendida a finales del siglo XIX para fomentar la restricción en el consumo del alcohol. **402**

tenements/barracas Viviendas pobremente construidas en las que habitaban grupos de inmigrantes. **399**

Tennessee Valley Authority/Autoridad del Valle de Tennessee (TVA, por sus siglas en inglés) Programa del Nuevo Tratado que proponía la construcción de presas para suministrar energía hidroeléctrica y contar con un medio de control de inundaciones en el valle del río Tennessee. **738**

Ten Percent Plan/Plan del Diez Por Ciento Plan de reconstrucción en el que el presidente Abraham Lincoln pedía a 10 por ciento de los votantes de un estado como mínimo que juraran lealtad a Estados Unidos y aceptaran la abolición de la esclavitud para ser aceptado en la Unión. **515**

terrorism/terrorismo Uso de ataques violentos por individuos o pequeños grupos con el propósito de conseguir ciertas metas políticas. **938**

Tet Offensive/Ofensiva del Tet (1968) Ataque de las tropas de Vietnam del Norte y el Vietcong al ejército de Vietnam del Sur en el Tet (la celebración de año nuevo en Vietnam) que demostró que Vietnam del Norte aún tenía suficiente poder militar. **885**

Texas longhorn/cuernos largos Raza vacuna de gran tamaño criada por los ganaderos del oeste de Texas. **558**

textiles/textiles Ropa. **363**

Thirteenth Amendment/Decimotercera enmienda (1865) Enmienda constitucional que abolió la esclavitud. **516**

38th parallel/paralelo 38 Línea de latitud que separa a Corea del Norte de Corea del Sur. **809**

Three-Fifths Compromise/Compromiso de las Tres Quintas Partes (1787) Acuerdo de la Convención Constitucional que estipula que en cada estado deben incluirse tres quintas partes de los esclavos en el conteo de la población para determinar el número de representantes de ese estado en la cámara baja del Congreso. **203**

Toleration Act of 1649/Ley de tolerancia de 1649 Ley de Maryland que calificaba como crimen la restricción de los derechos religiosos de los cristianos; fue una de las primeras leyes en proteger la libertad de credo religioso que se aprobó en las colonias inglesas. **82**

Tonkin Gulf Resolution/Resolución del Golfo de Tonkin (1964) Medida constitucional que dio al presidente Lyndon B. Johnson autoridad para declarar la guerra a Vietnam. **879**

totalitarianism/totalitarismo Sistema político en el que el gobierno controla todos los aspectos de la vida de los habitantes. **751**

total war/guerra total Tipo de guerra en la que un ejército destruye la capacidad de lucha de su oponente mediante ataques a la población civil, la economía y los recursos militares. **502**

totems/tótems Imágenes de antepasados o animales talladas en troncos de árboles cortados por los indígenas del noroeste de la costa del Pacífico. **12**

town meeting/asamblea popular Encuentro político iniciado en Nueva Inglaterra en los que los residentes tomaban decisiones sobre los problemas locales. **94**

Townshend Acts/Leyes de Townshend (1767) Leyes aprobadas por el Parlamento británico para cobrar impuestos en la importación de ciertos productos a las colonias. **139**

trade deficit/déficit comercial Desequilibrio que surge cuando un país importa más productos de los que exporta. **911**

trade unions/sindicatos de intercambio comercial Organizaciones formadas por los trabajadores para mejorar su salario y sus condiciones laborales. **365**

Trail of Tears/Sendero de las lágrimas (1838–1839) Marcha de 800 millas que realizó de manera obligada la tribu cheroqui de su territorio natal en Georgia al nuevo territorio, en la que perdieron la vida miles de estos indígenas. **347**

transcendentalism/trascendentalismo Creencia de que las personas podían elevarse sobre los objetos materiales en vida. Movimiento popular entre los escritores y pensadores de Nueva Inglaterra a mediados del siglo XIX. **392**

transcontinental railroad/ferrocarril transcontinental Ferrocarril que cruzaba la parte continental de Estados Unidos conectando el este con el oeste. **555**

Transportation Revolution/revolución del transporte Rápido aumento de la velocidad y comodidad de los medios de transporte que inició en Estados Unidos a principios del siglo XIX. **366**

Treaty of Brest-Litovsk/Tratado Brest-Litovsk (1918) Acuerdo de paz firmado entre las Potencias Centrales y Rusia para que esta se retirara de la Primera Guerra Mundial. **683**

Treaty of Dancing Rabbit Creek/Tratado de Dancing Rabbit Creek (1830) Acuerdo en el que la tribu choctaw cedió más de 10 millones de acres de su territorio a Mississippi y aceptó reubicarse en el nuevo territorio indígena. **346**

Treaty of Fort Laramie/Tratado del Fuerte Laramie (1851) Primer tratado importante entre el gobierno de Estados Unidos y los indígenas de las Grandes Planicies que permitió a los ciudadanos estadounidenses viajar por territorio indígena. **547**

Treaty of Ghent/Tratado de Ghent (1814) Tratado entre Estados Unidos y la Gran Bretaña que dio por terminada la Guerra de 1812. **319**

Treaty of Greenville/Tratado de Greenville (1795) Acuerdo entre la Confederación Indígena Estadounidense y el gobierno de Estados Unidos que otorgó a la nación la parte sudeste del territorio indígena ubicado al noroeste del país y garantizó la seguridad a los ciudadanos estadounidenses que viajaran por esas tierras. **284**

Treaty of Guadalupe Hidalgo/Tratado de Guadalupe Hidalgo (1848) Tratado que dio por terminada la guerra entre Estados Unidos y México en el que éste cede a Estados Unidos gran parte de su territorio norte. **436**

Treaty of Medicine Lodge/Tratado de Medicine Lodge (1867) Acuerdo entre el gobierno de Estados Unidos y los indígenas de las Grandes Planicies en el que éstos últimos aceptan vivir sólo en el territorio asignado a sus reservas. **548**

Treaty of Paris/Tratado de París (1763) Acuerdo de paz que dio por terminada la guerra de los franceses contra los indígenas estadounidenses. **130**

Treaty of Paris of 1873/Tratado de París de 1783 Acuerdo de paz que oficialmente da por terminada la Revolución y en el que la Gran Bretaña reconoce legalmente a Estados Unidos. **181**

Treaty of Tordesillas/Tratado de Tordesillas (1494) Acuerdo firmado por España y Portugal en el que ambos países se comprometían a desplazar la línea de demarcación 800 millas al oeste de su posición original en relación con las Islas Azores. **36**

Treaty of Versailles/Tratado de Versalles (1919) Tratado con el que finaliza la Primera Guerra Mundial y en el que se exige a Alemania el pago de varios miles de millones de dólares como gastos de guerra, además de establecer la Liga de las Naciones. **688**

Tredegar Iron Works/Tradegar Iron Works Gran fábrica de acero que operaba a mediados del siglo XIX en Richmond, Virginia. **375**

trench warfare/guerra de trinchera Estrategia militar de defensa de una posición desde las trincheras, comúnmente usada en la Primera Guerra Mundial. **672**

Triangle Shirtwaist Factory Fire/Incendio de la fábrica de camisas Accidente ocurrido en una fabrica de la ciudad de Nueva York en el que murieron 146 trabajadores al incendiarse el edificio; este suceso obligó al Congreso a crear nuevos estándares de seguridad en las fábricas. **616**

triangular trade/acuerdo triangula Redes de intercambio de esclavos entre Inglaterra, las colonias estadounidenses y África Occidental. **100**

Triple Alliance/Triple Alianza Alianza militar formada por el imperio austro-húngaro, Alemania e Italia a finales del siglo XIX. **669**

Triple Entente/Triple Entente Alianza militar formada en 1907 por la Gran Bretaña, Francia y Rusia. **669**

Truman Doctrine/Doctrina Truman (1947) Campaña en la que el presidente Harry S. Truman ofrece ayuda económica a cualquier país que ayude a Estados Unidos a combatir el comunismo. **801**

trust/monopolio Acuerdo legal que agrupa a varias compañías bajo el mando de un solo consejo directivo para eliminar la competencia y reglamentar la producción. **582**

Twelfth Amendment/Décimosegunda enmienda (1804) Enmienda constitucional que creó una boleta por separado para los votos de presidente y vicepresidente. **292**

Twenty-first Amendment/Vigesimoprimera enmienda (1933) Enmienda constitucional que dio por terminada la prohibición mediante la anulación de la Decimoctava enmienda. **707**

Twenty-sixth Amendment/Vigesimosexta enmienda (1971) Enmienda constitucional que redujo la edad mínima de los electores en las votaciones federales de 21 a 18 años. **891**

U-boats/barcos U Submarinos alemanes. **673**

unalienable rights/derechos inalienables Derechos básicos de la humanidad, como el derecho a la vida, a la libertad y a la búsqueda de la felicidad. **159**

Uncle Tom's Cabin/La cabaña del tío Tom (1852) Novela abolicionista escrita por Harriet Beecher Stowe que mostró a los habitantes del norte del país la cruda realidad de la esclavitud e hizo que muchos de ellos se adhirieran a la causa del abolicionismo. **455**

Underground Railroad/ferrocarril clandestino Red de personas que ayudó a miles de esclavos a escapar al norte ofreciéndoles transporte y lugares para ocultarse. **410**

Underwood Tariff Act/Ley de Reducción de Aranceles (1913) Ley que redujo de manera significativa los aranceles e introdujo la primera reforma moderna de impuestos personales. **629**

United Farm Workers/Unión de Trabajadores Agrícolas (UFW, por sus siglas en inglés) Unión formada por César Chávez para mejorar el salario y las condiciones de trabajo de los campesinos inmigrantes. **863**

United Mine Workers/Unión de Trabajadores Mineros (UMW, por sus siglas en inglés) Unión de trabajadores de las minas de carbón que estalló una huelga en 1946. **806**

United Nations/Organización de Naciones Unidas (UN, por sus siglas en inglés; ONU, en español) Organización internacional creada en 1945 para promover la paz mundial y resolver conflictos entre las naciones. **799**

Universal Negro Improvement Association/Asociación Universal por el Mejoramiento de la Raza Negra (UNIA, por sus siglas en inglés) Asociación fundada por Marcus Garvey en 1914 con el propósito de terminar con el imperialismo en África y la discriminación en Estados Unidos. **709**

urban renewal/renovación urbana Programa lanzado por el gobierno federal para mejorar el nivel de vida en Estados Unidos mediante la creación de mejores servicios públicos y nuevos proyectos de vivienda. **828**

utopian community/comunidad utópica Lugar en el que un grupo de personas trabaja para establecer una comunidad perfecta, como las que se popularizaron en Estados Unidos a finales del siglo XVIII y de principios a mediados del XIX. **392**

vaqueros/vaqueros Rancheros mexicanos del oeste que cuidaban manadas de ganado y caballos. **560**

vertical integration/integración vertical Propiedad de los medios implícita en cada paso de un proceso de manufactura. **582**

veto/veto Cancelación de una ley. **223**

Vietcong/Vietcong Fuerza comunista de guerrilla que operaba con el ejército del Frente Nacional de Liberación para derrocar al gobierno de Ngo Dinh Diem, en Vietnam del Sur, durante la década de 1950. **876**

Vietminh/Vietminh Grupo de nacionalistas vietnamitas organizados por Ho Chi Minh que dedicaron sus esfuerzos a la obtención de la independencia de Vietnam. **875**

Vetnamization/vietnamización Política adoptada por la administración del presidente Nixon para delegar gradualmente la lucha de la guerra de Vietnam al ejército de Vietnam del Sur. **888**

Vietnam Veterans Memorial/Monumento a los Veteranos de Vietnam Monumento construido en Washington, D.C., para honrar a los estadounidenses que murieron en la guerra de Vietnam. **893**

Virginia Plan/Plan de Virginia (1787) Plan del gobierno propuesto en la Convención Constitucional para dividir al gobierno en tres ramas: El poder ejecutivo, el poder legislativo y el poder judicial. También establecía que la representación de cada estado en la legislatura debía ser determinada por la población de ese estado. **201**

Virginia Statute for Religious Freedom/Estatuto de Virginia para la libertad religiosa (1786) Ley que otorgaba a los habitantes de Virginia la libertad de elegir y practicar cualquier religión, además de expresar sus opiniones religiosas. **188**

Voting Rights Act of 1965/Ley de derecho al voto de 1965 Ley de protección del derecho de los ciudadanos al voto. **858**

Wade-Davis Bill/Proyecto Wade-Davis Plan de reconstrucción que imponía dos condiciones a los estados que querían reintegrarse a la Unión: que abolieran la esclavitud y que la mayoría de hombres adultos hicieran un juramento de lealtad; quienes apoyaran a los Confederados no podían votar ni ejercer cargos públicos. **515**

War Hawks/halcones de guerra Integrantes del Congreso que tenían la intención de declarar la guerra a Gran Bretaña a principios del siglo XIX. **312**

War Industries Board/Consejo de Industrias de Guerra (WIB, por sus siglas en inglés) Agencia creada por el presidente Woodrow Wilson durante la Primera Guerra Mundial para supervisar la fabricación y distribución de productos de las industrias de guerra del país. **680**

War on Drugs/guerra contra las drogas Esfuerzo del gobierno para terminar con la venta y consumo ilegal de drogas tanto en Estados Unidos como en el extranjero. **933**

War on Poverty/guerra contra la pobreza Nombre dado por el presidente Lyndon B. Johnson a la serie de programas de ayuda a los necesitados. **852**

War Powers Act/Ley de Poderes de Guerra (1973) Ley que exige la aprobación del Congreso a cualquier iniciativa militar presidencial antes de iniciar una lucha armada. **893**

War Production Board/Consejo de Producción de Guerra (WPB, por sus siglas en inglés) Agencia creada durante la Segunda Guerra Mundial para supervisar la producción de las industrias de guerra. **768**

Warren Commission/Comisión Warren Grupo especial asignado por el presidente Lyndon B. Johnson para investigar el asesinato del presidente John F. Kennedy. **851**

Warsaw Pact/Pacto de Varsovia Alianza militar entre los países del este de Europa convocada por la Unión Soviética en 1955. **803**

Washington Conference/Conferencia de Washington (1921) Encuentro entre los líderes de Estados Unidos y las naciones más importantes para analizar el tema del desarme. **704**

Watergate/Watergate Escándalo en el que se vio involucrado el presidente Richard M. Nixon al autorizar el acceso de un grupo secreto al cuartel general del Partido Demócrata; este suceso provocó la renuncia del presidente Nixon en 1974. **907**

Whig Party/Partido Whig Asociación política formada por oponentes de Andrew Jackson en 1834 para demandar una legislatura más fuerte. **342**

Whiskey Rebellion/Rebelión del Whiskey Protesta de los campesinos de Pennsylvania contra los nuevos impuestos aplicados a la producción de whiskey y otras bebidas alcohólicas. **284**

wigwams/wigwams Pequeñas habitaciones circulares en las que vivían los indígenas estadounidenses del noreste del país. **16**

Wilderness Campaign/Campaña en despoblado (mayo-junio de 1864) Serie de batallas entre la Unión y los Confederados al norte y al centro de Virginia que estuvo a punto de agotar los recursos del Ejército Confederado. **501**

Wilmot Proviso/Propuesta Wilmot (1846) Propuesta de abolición de la esclavitud en el territorio adherido a los Estados Unidos por la cesión mexicana. Fue aprobada por la Cámara de representantes, pero rechazado por el Senado. **451**

Wisconsin Idea/Idea de Wisconsin Programa de reformas creado por el gobernador de Wisconsin Robert La Follete a principios del siglo XX que se convirtió en modelo a seguir para otros estados. **612**

Woman's Christian Temperance Union/Unión de Mujeres Cristianas por la Abstinencia Organización de mujeres reformistas fundada en 1874 para luchar contra el abuso en el consumo del alcohol. **620**

Woodstock/Woodstock (1969) Concierto de rock realizado cerca de Woodstock, Nueva York, que se convirtió en símbolo del espíritu idealista de la contracultura. **869**

Worcester v. Georgia/Worcester versus Georgia (1832) Caso en que la Suprema Corte declaró a la nación cheroqui como un territorio distinto sobre el que sólo el gobierno federal tenía autoridad. Fue ignorado por el presidente Andrew Jackson y por el estado de Georgia. **347**

Works Progress Administration/Administración del Progreso Laboral (WPA, por sus siglas en inglés) (1935) Agencia creada con el New Deal para invitar a hombres y mujeres estadounidenses a colaborar en la construcción y reparación de puentes, caminos, edificios y parques públicos. **740**

World Trade Center/Centro Mundial de Comercio Gran complejo de instalaciones comerciales y financieras en Nueva York; las Torres Gemelas de este complejo quedaron destruidas luego de un ataque terrorista el 11 de septiembre de 2001. **944**

World Trade Organization/Organización Mundial de Comercio Organización que supervisa el comercio internacional; cuenta con 140 integrantes, incluido Estados Unidos. **942**

writs of assistance/mandato de asistencia Garantías que permitían a los recaudadores de impuestos buscar bienes ocultos por los contribuyentes. **139**

xenophobia/xenofobia Temor y odio hacia los extranjeros. **701**

XYZ affair/asunto XYZ (1797) Incidente en el que funcionarios franceses intentaron obtener sobornos de diplomáticos estadounidenses a cambio de favorecer las relaciones entre ambos países, provocando una guerra no declarada entre las fuerzas navales de las dos naciones. **289**

Yalta Conference/Conferencia de Yalta (1945) Encuentro del presidente de Estados Unidos Franklin D. Roosevelt, el primer ministro de la Gran Bretaña Winston Churchill y el líder soviético Joseph Stalin durante la Segunda Guerra Mundial para planear el mundo de la postguerra. **798**

yellow journalism/amarillismo Publicación de historias sensacionalistas y con frecuencia exageradas en los periódicos para atraer la atención de los lectores. **646**

yeomen/pequeños terratenientes Pequeños agricultores. **376**

Zimmerman Note/Nota Zimmermann Telegrama enviado por el ministro de asuntos exteriores al gobierno de México durante la Primera Guerra Mundial para proponerle una alianza entre ambos países. **677**

zoot-suit riots/Revueltas zoot-suit (1943) Ataques de marinos estadounidenses a mexicano estadounidenses que residían en Los Ángeles. **770**

Index

Key to Index
c = chart
f = feature
m = map
p = photo

F

G

S

U

V

W

X

Y

Z

Acknowledgments

Arte Público Press: "Brindis: For the Barrio" from *Arise, Chicano! and Other Poems* by Angela de Hoyos. Copyright © 1975 by Angela de Hoyos and Mireya Robles. Published by M & A Editions, San Antonio.

HarperCollins Publishers Ltd.: From "Stalingrad: December 1942, A German Infantryman's View" from *In Their Shallow Graves* by Benno Zieser, translated by Alec Brown. Copyright © 1956 by Elek Books.

Harvard University Press, Cambridge, Mass.: "World, in Hounding Me" by Sor Juana Inés de la Cruz from *A Sor Juana Anthology,* translated by A. S. Trueblood. Copyright © 1988 by the President and Fellows of Harvard College.

Harvard University Press and the Trustees of Amherst College: From "This is my Letter to the World" from *The Poems of Emily Dickinson,* edited by Thomas H. Johnson. Copyright © 1951, 1955, 1979, 1983 by the President and Fellows of Harvard College. Published by the Belknap Press of Harvard University Press, Cambridge, Mass.

The Heirs to the Estate of Martin Luther King, Jr., c/o Writers House, Inc. as agent for the proprietor: From "I Have a Dream" by Martin Luther King, Jr. Copyright © 1963 by Martin Luther King, Jr.; copyright renewed © 1991 by Coretta Scott King.

Pathfinder Press: From "OAAU Founding Rally" and from "Short Statements: Fight or Forget It" from *By Any Means Necessary: Speeches, Interviews, and a Letter* by Malcolm X. Copyright © 1970, 1992 by Betty Shabazz and Pathfinder Press.

Putnam Berkley, a division of Penguin Putnam Inc.: Quote by Winona Espinosa from *The Homefront: America During World War II* by Mark Jonathan Harris, Franklin D. Mitchell, and Steven J. Schechter. Copyright © 1984 by Mark Jonathan Harris, Franklin D. Mitchell, and Steven J. Schechter.

Random House, Inc.: From "On the Pulse of Morning" from *On the Pulse of Morning* by Maya Angelou. Copyright © 1993 by Maya Angelou.

Simon & Schuster Books for Young Readers, an imprint of Simon & Schuster Children's Publishing Division: From *My Brother Sam is Dead* by James Lincoln Collier and Christopher Collier. Copyright © 1974 by James Lincoln Collier and Christopher Collier.

Texas A&M University Press: From *With a Black Platoon in Combat: A Year in Korea* by Lyle Rishell. Copyright © 1993 by Lyle Rishell.

Viking Penguin, a division of Penguin Putnam, Inc.: From *The Crucible* by Arthur Miller. Copyright 1952, 1953, 1954 and renewed © 1980, 1981, 1982 by Arthur Miller. From *The Grapes of Wrath* by John Steinbeck. Copyright 1939 and renewed © 1967 by John Steinbeck.

Sources Cited:

Quote by Colin Powell from *The American Statesman,* 1997.

Quote by Gale Kaplan from "Just a Housewife" from *A History of Women in America* by Carol Hymowitz and Michaele Weissman. Published by Bantam Books, 1978.

Quote by an Aztec messenger from *The Broken Spears: The Aztec Account of the Conquest of Mexico,* Expanded and Updated Edition, edited by Miguel León-Portilla. Published by Beacon Press, Boston, 1992.

Quote by Sgt. Dave Richardson from "Battle above the Solomons" from *Yank: The Story of World War II as Written by the Soldiers* by the Staff of Yank, the Army Weekly. Published by Brassey's, Inc., McLean, VA, 1984.

From "Across the Plains in a Prairie Schooner" by Catherine Haun from *Ordinary Americans,* edited by Linda R. Monk. Published by Close Up Publishing, 1994.

From "Record Smasher" by Tom Verducci from *Sports Illustrated,* September 9, 1998. Published by CNN/SI Time Warner, 1998.

Quote by Clara Hancox from *The Century* by Peter Jennings and Todd Brewster. Published by Doubleday, New York, 1998.

From *When Heaven and Earth Changed Places: A Vietnamese Woman's Journey from War to Peace* by Le Ly Hayslip. Published by Doubleday, 1989.

Quote by 'Abd al-Latif from *The Rise of Colleges: Institutions of Learning in Islam and the West,* translated by G. Makdisi. Published by Edinburgh University Press, 1981.

Quote by Dan Carpenter from *You Must Remember This: An Oral History of Manhattan from the 1890's to World War II* by Jeff Kisseloff. Published by Harcourt Brace & Co., San Diego, 1989.

Quote by Guy Owen from *The Private Side of American History: Readings in Everyday Life,* edited by Thomas R. Frazier. Published by Harcourt Brace, Orlando, FL, 1983.

Quote by Bartolomé Las Casas from *The Conquest of America: The Question of the Other* by Tzvetan Todorov, translated by Richard Howard. Published by HarperCollins Publishers, Inc., New York, 1984.

From *Yesterday: A Memoir of a Russian Jewish Family* by Miram Shomer Zunser, edited by Emily Wortis Leider. Published by HarperCollins Publishers, New York, 1978.

From "Recantation of the women of Andover, 1692" from *The History of the Colony and Province of Massachusetts Bay* by Thomas Hutchinson, edited by Lawrence Shaw Mayo. Published by Harvard University Press, Cambridge, 1936.

From *My People the Sioux* by Luther Standing Bear. Published by Houghton Mifflin Company, Boston, 1928.

Quote by Shawnee chief Tecumseh from *Indian Wars* by Robert M. Utley and Wilcomb E. Washburn. Published by Houghton Mifflin Company, Boston, 1977.

Quote by Mary Smith from "The Woman Worker Speaks" by Ruth Young and Catherine Filene Shouse from *Independent Woman,* vol. 24, October 1945.

Quote by Joseph Brant and Little Turtle from *The Ohio Frontier: Crucible of the Old Northwest, 1720-1830* by R. Douglas Hurt. Published by Indiana University Press, Bloomington, 1996.

From "Interview with Ngyugen Huu Tho" by Christine Pelzer White from *Journal of Contemporary Asia,* vol. 11, no. 1, 1981.

Quote by Karlsevni from *Voyages To Vinland: The First American Saga,* translated and interpreted by Einar Haugen. Published by Alfred A. Knopf, Inc., New York, 1942.

Quote by Juan Chanax from *Strangers Among Us* by Roberto Suro. Published by Alfred A. Knopf, Inc., New York, 1998.

Quotes by Thomas Minehan and by an anonymous teenager from *The Great Depression: America in the 1930s* by T. H. Watkins. Published by Little, Brown and Company, New York, 1993.

From *Remembering America: A Voice from the Sixties* by Richard N. Goodwin. Published by Little, Brown and Company, Boston, 1988.

From *The Great Crusade and After, 1914-1928* by Preston William Slosson. Published by Macmillan Company, 1930.

Quote by Sam Rayburn from *Sam Johnson's Boy: A Close-up of the President from Texas* by Alfred Steinberg. Published by Macmillan, New York, 1968.

Quote by Jessie Lee Brown Foveaux from *The Manhattan (Kansas) Mercury,* March 1, 1998.

Quote by Juanita "Skeeter" Maxey from *America Goes to the Movies: 100 Years of Motion Picture Exhibition* by Barbara Stones. Published by the National Association of Theatre Owners, North Hollywood, 1993.

Quote by an assembly-line worker from *Who Built America? vol 2, From the Gilded Age to the Present,* edited by Joshua Freeman, et al. Published by Pantheon Books, 1992.

Quote by Ibn Battuta from *A Short History of Africa* by Roland Oliver and J. D. Fage. Published by Penguin Books Ltd., 1962, 1966.

Quote by George Robinson from *Listening to Radio, 1920-1950* by Ray Barfield. Published by Praeger Publishers, Westport, CT, 1996.

From *The Spirit of St. Louis* by Charles Lindbergh. Published by Scribner's Sons, New York, 1953.

Quote by Esther Clark from *Pioneer Women: Voices from the Kansas Frontier* by Joanna L. Stratton. Published by Simon & Schuster, Inc., New York, 1981.

Quote by Ethel Noland, friend of Harry Truman, from *Oral History Transcripts from Truman* by David McCullough. Published by Simon & Schuster, New York, 1992.

From *Ancient North America: The Archaeology of a Continent* by Brian M. Fagan. Published by Thames and Hudson Inc., New York, 1991, 1995.

From interview with Barbara Baisley from "Man and Woman of the Year: Middle Americans" from *Time,* January 5, 1970.

Quote by Barbara Langsam from "Letters to the Editor" from *Time,* March 27, 1992.

Quote by Eloina Ortega from "The Nation" section from *Time,* July 5, 1976.

Quote by a Victorio follower from *In the Days of Victorio: Recollections of a Warm Springs Apache* by Eve Ball. Published by University of Arizona Press, Tucson, 1970.

Quote by Chester Copeland, and from interview with Paul and Pauline Griffith from *Like a Family: The Making of a Southern Cotton Mill World* by Jacquelyn Dowd Hall, et al. Published by the University of North Carolina Press, 1987.

From interview with Madge Alford from *Indian-Pioneer Papers,* University of Oklahoma, Norman, OK.

From an Aztec poem from *Aztec Thought and Culture: A Study of the Ancient Nahuatl Mind* by Miguel León-Portilla, translated by Jack Emory Davis. Published by the University of Oklahoma Press, Norman, 1963.

Quote by John Howard Lawson from *Thirty Years of Treason: Excerpts from Hearing Before the House Committee on Un-American Activities,* edited by Eric Bentley. Published by Viking Press, New York, 1971.

Quote by Leona Marshall Libby and Richard Nixon from *The Fifties* by David Halberstam. Published by Villard Books, New York, 1993.

Quote by Moritz Vegh from *The Boys* by Martin Gilbert. Published by Weidenfeld & Nicolson, London, 1996.

Quote by Michiko Yamaoka, interviewed by Mitsuru Ohba, from *"Voices of A-Bomb Survivors"* web site, October 13, 1998. Available on the World Wide Web at http://www.csi.ad.jp/ABOMB/Hibakusha/h03.html.

Photography Credits:

Abbreviated as follows: (t) top, (b) bottom, (l) left, (r) right, (c) center.

Cover and Title Page: Image Copyright ©2003 PhotoDisc, Inc.

Table of Contents and Front Matter:

Page iv Jerry Jacka/Courtesy Dennis Lyon Collection; v(t), The Granger Collection, New York; v(b), Musee des Beaux-Arts, Orleans, France/Bridgeman Art Library, London/New York; vi North Wind Picture Archives; vii The Granger Collection, New York; viii(b), Carl Socolon/The Landis Valley Museum; viii(tr), Kim Neilsen/Smithsonian Institution, Washington, DC/ PRC Archive; ix(bc), Bettmann/CORBIS; ix(br), The Granger Collection, New York; x Bettmann/CORBIS; xi The Granger Collection, New York; xii(tl, tc), Archive Photos; xiii(b), HRW; xiii(t), Doug Mills/AP/Wide World Photos; xiv Independence National Historical Park Collection; xiv National Archives (NARA); xvii Jeffrey Brown/Liaison Agency; xviii(tl), Paul Conklin; xviii(tc), Independence National Historical Park Collection; xx The Granger Collection, New York; xxi(cr), Image Copyright © 2003 PhotoDisc, Inc./ HRW; xxi(br), Sam Dudgeon/HRW; xxvii(br), HRW Photo; xxviii, from THE CIVIL WAR: FORWARD TO RICHMOND, Photograph by Al Freni, xxviii(c)1983 Time-Life Books, Inc. Courtesy, Troiani Collection; xxx, Courtesy CNNfyi.com; xxxi(tl), Annie Griffiths Belt/ CORBIS; xxxi, Ruth Fremson/AP/Wide World Photos; xxxii(bl), ©Image Ideas, Inc.; xxxii(tl), Derek P. Redfearn/ The Image Bank; xxxii(r), Culver Pictures, Inc.; xxxiii(br), HRW Photo; xxxiv(l), Bob Daemmrich/Stock Boston; xxxiv(tr), The Granger Collection, New York; xxxiv(br), Ken Cobb/Library of Congress; xxxv, National Museum of American Art, Smithsonian Institution, lent by the U.S. Department of the Interior/Art Resource, NY; S0(bl, cl), Annie Griffiths Belt/CORBIS; S0(bc), Karen Blier/AFP/CORBIS; S1 (bl), USPS; S1(r), The Granger Collection, New York; S2(cr), Library of Congress; S2(br), Sam Dudgeon/HRW; S2(bl), Hulton-Deutsch Collection/CORBIS; S3(br), Sam Dudgeon/HRW; S3(tl), The Granger Collection, New York; S4, S5, S6(t, c), S8(bl, t, c), HRW Photo; S8(br), Peter Newark's Western Americana; S9, S12, S17(br), HRW Photo.

Unit One: Page 1 The Granger Collection, New York; 1(r), Tate Gallery, London/Art Resource, NY. **Chapter One:** Page 2(tl), Sam Dudgeon/HRW; 2(tr), Werner Forman Archive, British Museum, London/Art Resource, NY; 2(bl), CORBIS/Roger Ressmeyer; 2(bc), Stone/Adrian Neal; 3(tr), Michael Holford; 3(tl), ©Robert Frerck/Woodfin Camp & Associates; 4 George Lepp/Stone; 6 Dean Conger/Corbis; 7(t), Bodleian Library, Oxford, image MS Arch. Sheldon A.1 folio 37R; 7(b), Alain Keler/Art Resource, NY; 8 Laurence Parent; 9 Superstock; 10 Jerry Jacka/Courtesy Dennis Lyon Collection; 12(t), National Museum of Natural History, Smithsonian Institution, Washington, D.C./Peter Harholdt/ SuperStock; 12(tc), Peter Newark's American Pictures; 13 Lawrence Migdale/Photo Researchers, Inc.; 14(tr), Werner Forman/Art Resource, NY; 14(tl), Ray Manley/ SuperStock; 15 National Museum of American Art, Washington DC/Art Resource, NY; 16 Library of Congress; 17 Viking Ship: The Gokstad Ship, Science Museum, London, UK/Bridgeman Art Library, London/New York; 18 *Vikings Attacking a Greenland Eskimo Camp,* Nationalmuseet, Copenhagen, Denmark/Bridgeman Art Library, London/New York; 19(br), Greenwich suit of armor, C. 1550, Christie's Images/Bridgeman Art Library, London, UK/New York; 19(bl), Musee Conde, Chantilly/Giraudon; 20 Michael Holford; 21(t), Portrait of William the Conqueror (1027-87)/Philip Mould, Historical Portraits Ltd, London, UK/Bridgeman Art Library, London/New York; 21(b), Nik Wheeler/CORBIS; 22 The British Library; 23 AKG Photo, London; 24 Ancient Art & Architecture Collection Ltd.; 25 E.T. Archive; 27 CORBIS. **Chapter Two:** Page 30(tl), *Gambling Patoli and the God, Xochipilli,* from Codex Maghabecciano, Aztec manuscript, Private Collection/Bridgeman Art Library, London/New York; 30(tr), Stock Montage/SuperStock; 30(bl), 31(tl), The Granger Collection, New York; 31(cr), James Stevenson/National Maritime Museum; 32 The Metropolitan Museum of Art, Gift of J.Pierpont Morgan, 1900. (00.18.2) Photograph copyright 1979 The Metropolitan Museum of Art.; 33 COMEX/DRASSM/Xavier Desmier/ Rapho Agency/Liaison International; 34 Robert Frerck/Odyssey/Chicago; 35 Bettmann/ CORBIS; 36 The Granger Collection, New York; 37 Victoria & Albert Museum, London/Art Resource, NY; 38 AKG Photo; 39 The Granger Collection, New York; 41 C. Chesek/ J.Becket/Negatives/Transparencies #4051, Courtesy Department of Library Services, American Museum of Natural History; 42 Bettmann/CORBIS; 43 *The Taking of Tenochtitlan by Cortes,* 1521, British Embassy, Mexico City/Bridgeman Art Library, London/New York; 44 Mark Nohl/New Mexico Magazine; 45 Art Resource, NY; 46 Bob Daemmrich Photo, Inc.; 47 Scala/Art Resource, NY; 48 The Granger Collection, New York; 49 American Museum of Natural History/Photo by Lynton Gardiner; 50, 51 The Granger Collection, New York; 54(tl), National Maritime Museum/E.T. Archive; 54(cr), Image Copyright © 2003 PhotoDisc, Inc./HRW.; 55(br), Richard Weiss/Peter Arnold, Inc.; 56(tc), Image Copyright © 2003 PhotoDisc, Inc./HRW Photo.; 57(bc), ©Scott Camazine/Photo Researchers, Inc.; 59 Sam Dudgeon/HRW.

Unit Two: Page 60 The Granger Collection, New York; 61(c), *Sioux ball player Ah-No-Je-Nange,* "He who stands on both sides", 19th century litho, Private Collection/Bridgeman Art Library, London/New York. **Chapter Three:** Page 62(tr, tc), The Granger Collection, New York; 62(bl), American Bible Society; 63(t), Penn's Treaty with the Indians (1771-72) by Benjamin West, oil on canvas, Courtesy of the Museum of American Art of the Pennsylvania Academy of the Fine Arts Philadelphia. Gift of Mrs. Sarah Harrison (The Joseph Harrison, Jr. Collection).; 63(tr), Layne Kennedy/CORBIS; 64 The Granger Collection, New York; 65 Colonial Williamsburg Foundation; 67 Detail from the National Portrait Gallery, Smithsonian Institution, Washington, DC/Art Resource, NY; 68(cl), Archive Photos; 68(bl), Colonial Williamsburg Foundation; 69 North Wind Picture Archives; 71 Detail, Courtesy of the Pilgrim Society, Plymouth, Massachusetts; 72 The Granger Collection, New York; 73 Private Collection/Bridgeman Art Library, London/New York; 74, 75 The Granger Collection, New York; 76 North Wind Picture Archives; 78, 79 The Granger Collection, New York; 80 CORBIS; 81 Courtesy St. Ignatius Church; 82 Enoch Pratt Free Library; 83-85 The Granger Collection, New York; 86 Stock Montage, Inc.; 87 The Granger Collection, New York. **Chapter Four:** Page 90(tr), Peter Newark's American Pictures; 90(bl), Fitzwilliam Museum, University of Cambridge, UK/ Bridgeman Art Library, London/New York; 90 Library of Congress; 91(tl), Stock Montage, Inc.; 91(tr), Science & Society Picture Library; 93 State Capitol, Commonwealth of Virginia, Courtesy Library of Virginia, image altered.; 94 ©Daniel MacDonald/Stock Boston; 95-97 The Granger Collection, New York; 98 Detail, *Portrait of King James I and VI of Scotland,* by John Whitehead Walton, (1831-85), (after Paul van Somer), The Crown Estate/Institute of Directors, London, UK/Bridgeman Art Library, London/New York; 98 David Muench/CORBIS; 98 Royal Albert Memorial Museum, Exeter, Devon, UK/ Bridgeman Art Library, London/New York; 100 Courtesy of the John Carter Brown Library at Brown University; 102 Hulton Deutsch Collection Ltd./Stone; 103 Maryland Commission on Artistic Property of the Maryland State Archives. MSA SC 1545-1106; 104(tl), The Granger Collection, New York; 104(t), Bettmann/CORBIS; 104(t), 105 The Granger Collection, New York; 106 Rare Book Department, The Free Library Of Philadelphia; 107 Maryland Historical Society, Baltimore; 108 Ken Lax, Courtesy of American Bible Society; 109 George Whitefield Preaching, by Collett/National Portrait Library, Londµon/Bridgeman Art Library, London/New York; 110 The Granger Collection, New York; 111 Culver Pictures; 112 Scala/Art Resource, NY; 113 Culver Pictures; 114(b), The Granger Collection, New York; 115 Musee des Beaux-Arts, Orleans, France/Bridgeman Art Library, London/New York; 116 Detail from The Pierpont Morgan Library/Art Resource, NY; 117 Private Collection/ Bridgeman Art Library, London/New York;120-121(bc), *British Ships of War Landing Their Troops,* 1768, Private Collection/Bridgeman Art Library, London/New York; 120(t), Image Copyright © 2003 PhotoDisc, Inc./HRW; 120(c), Image Copyright © 2003 PhotoDisc, Inc./HRW; 121(tr), Jas. Townsend & Son, Inc.; 123(b), *The Slave Market,* by Amadeo Preziosi, (1816-82), Victoria & Albert Museum/Bridgeman Art Library, London, UK/New York. **Chapter Five:** Page124(tl), Bettmann/CORBIS; 124(tr), The Granger Collection, New York; 124(bl), CORBIS; 125(tr), Courtesy the Bostonian Society, The Old State House; 125(tl), North Wind Picture Archives; 126 Archive Photos; 127 North Wind Picture Archives; 128 The American Revolution: A Picture Sourcebook, Dover Publications, Inc.; 129 Medal commemorating the British capture of Quebec, 1759, Private Collection/ Bridgeman Art Library, London/New York; 131 The Granger Collection, New York; 132(t), Courtesy of the Hunt Institute for Botanical Documentation, Carnegie Mellon University, Pittsburgh, PA; 132(b), Chief Pontiac, attributed to John Mix Stanley, Detroit Historical Society; 133, 134 The Granger Collection, New York; 135 Archive Photos; 136(b), Deposited by the City of Boston, Courtesy, Museum of Fine Arts, Boston; 137(br), Colonial Williamsburg Foundation; 138 Courtesy of the John Carter Brown Library at Brown University; 139 Jas. Townsend & Son, Inc.; 140 Corbis; 141 Peter Newark's American Pictures; 143 Bequest of Winslow Warren, Courtesy Museum of Fine Arts, Boston MA. Reproduced with Permission. © 2000 Museum of Fine Arts, Boston. All Rights Reserved; 144 Colonial Williamsburg Foundation.

Unit Three: Page148 *Patrick Henry Before the Virginia House of Burgesses* (1851) by Peter F. Rothermel. Red HIll, The Patrick Henry National Memorial, Brookneal, Virginia.; 148 Sam Dudgeon/HRW; 149(c), Bettmann/CORBIS. **Chapter Six:** Page150(tl), Peter Newark's American Pictures; 150(tr), Independence National Historical Park Collection; 150(bl), North Wind Picture Archives; 150(c), Larry Stevens/Nawrocki Stock Photo; 151(tl), SuperStock; 151(tr), Colonial Williamsburg Foundation; 152 The Granger Collection, New York; 153(t), Gift of Joseph W. Revere, William B. Revere, and Edward H.R. Revere, Courtesy, Museum of Fine Arts, Boston; 153(b), The Granger Collection, New York; 154 CORBIS; 155 Photograph courtesy of the Concord Museum, Concord, Massachusetts and the Lexington Historical Society, Inc., Lexington, Massachusetts. Photograph by David Bohl; 156 The Granger Collection, New York; 157 Courtesy, Scholastic Inc.; 158(cl), The Granger Collection, New York; 158(bl), Library of Congress/ HRW; 159 Archive Photos; 160 Peter Newark's American Pictures; 161 Culver Pictures; 162 Larry Lee/CORBIS;166 Mount Vernon Ladies' Association; 167(tr), Christie's Images; 167(b), Benninghoff Collection of the American Revolution; 168 The Granger Collection, New York; 169(l), Collection of The New-York Historical Society; 169(r), Collection of The New-York Historical Society; 170 Anne S.K. Brown Military Collection, Brown University Library; 171 Art Resource, NY; 172 The Granger Collection, New York; 174(tl), Erich Lessing/Art Resource, NY; 174(cl), The Historic New Orleans Collection, Museum/ Research Center, color added; 175, 176(tl), The Granger Collection, New York; 176(tr), Peter Newark's American Pictures; 177 Courtesy of The Library of Virginia; 178(b), The Granger Collection, New York; 178(tl), CORBIS/William James Warren; 180 *The Battle of Yorktown* from Janice Meredith by Paul Leicester, Ford, Dodd, Mead & Co., 1899/ Delaware Art Museum, Howard Pyle Collection; 181 CORBIS. **Chapter Seven:** Page 184(tr), SuperStock; 184(c), Johns Hopkins University, Larry Stevens/Nawrocki Stock Photo Inc.; 184(bl), Prado, Madrid/Bridgeman Art Library, London/New York; 185(t), Virginia Museum of Fine Arts, Richmond, VA. Detail of Washington as Statesman at the Constitutional Convention by Junius Brutus Stearns. Gift of Edgar William and Bernice Chrysler Garbisch. Photo: Ron Jennings. ©2003 Virginia Museum of Fine Arts; 185(l), Joseph Sohm/Chromosohm Inc./CORBIS; 186(cl), Independence National Historical Park Collection; 187(t), Art Archive, London/SuperStock; 187(cr), Stock Montage, Inc.; 188 The Granger Collection, New York; 189(b), Rare Books and Manuscripts Division, The New York Public Library, Astor, Lenox and Tilden Foundations; 190 Ted Spiegel; 191 North Wind Picture Archives; 192(t), CORBIS; 192(b), British Library/The Art Archive; 194(cl), Jas. Townsend & Son, Inc.; 195(t), Courtesy, Winterthur Museum; 196(b), Eileen Tweedy/ The Art Archive; 197(c), The Granger Collection, New York; 197(t), Courtesy of the Massachusetts Historical Society; 198(t), The Granger Collection, New York; 198(l), North Wind Picture Archives; 199(t), Stock Montage, Inc.; 200(cl), 201(b), The Granger Collection, New York; 201(t), Joseph Sohm/Stock Boston; 202(b), Nebraska State Historical Society; 202(t), Courtesy Winterthur Museum; 203(t), The Library Company of Philadelphia; 205(t), National Archives (NARA); 206(cl), Library of Congress; 207 PRC Archive; 208(t), 210, 211 The Granger Collection, New York; 214(t), Image Copyright © 2003 PhotoDisc, Inc./HRW; 214(c), Image Copyright © 2003 PhotoDisc, Inc./HRW; 215 H. Abernathy/H. Armstrong Roberts; 216 Reuters NewMedia Inc./CORBIS; 216(t), Image Copyright © 2003 PhotoDisc, Inc./HRW; 217(cr), HRW Photo by Lance Schriner; 217(tr), Lance Schriner/HRW; 217(bc), Lance Schriner/HRW; 217(bl), Lance Schriner/HRW; 217(tl), Lance Schriner/HRW. **Chapter Eight:** Page 218(tr, tl), The Granger Collection, New York; 218(bl), ©Hulton Getty/Liaison Agency; 218(br), Wally McNamee/Corbis-Sygma; 219(tr), Bob Daemmrich/Stock Boston; 219(tl), Lisa Quinones/Black Star; 219(bl), Woodfin Camp & Associates; 220 Bernard Boutrit/Woodfin Camp & Associates; 221(br), Paul S. Conklin; 221(t), PICTOR; 222 Stock Montage, Inc.; 223 The Granger Collection, New York; 224 Collection, the Supreme Court of the United States, courtesy The Supreme Court Historical Society; 225 Paul Conklin; 226 The Granger Collection, New York; 227 H. Armstrong Roberts; 228 Independence National Historical Park Collection; 248 Independence National Historical Park Collection; 249 The Granger Collection, New York; 250 Jeffrey Brown/Liaison Agency; 251 Bob Daemmrich Photo, Inc.; 253 Louie Psihoyos/Woodfin Camp & Associates, Inc.; 254 Sandra Baker/Liaison Agency; 255 Paul Sakuma/AP Photo/Wide World Photos; 256 Spencer Grant/PhotoEdit; 257 Jeff Greenberg /PhotoEdit; 258(tl), Joe Marquette/AP/Wide World Photos; 258(bl), Richard B. Levine; 259 Bob Daemmrich/Stock, Boston; 263 Sam Dudgeon/HRW.

Unit Four: Page 264 Christie's Images; 265(c), Courtesy Oregon State Archives, Mural located in Oregon State Capitol by Frank H. Schwartz c. 1938. **Chapter Nine:** Page 266(tl), The Granger Collection, New York; 266(b), Gianni Dagli Orti/CORBIS; 266(tr), Bettmann/CORBIS; 267(tl), Daniel Huntington 1816-1906, *The Republican Court* 1861, Oil on Canvas, 167.6 x 277.0 (66 x 109), The Brooklyn Museum 39.536.1, Gift of the Crescent-Hamilton Athletic Club ; 267(tr), The Art Archive/Yale University New Haven/ Album/Joseph Martin; 268(cl), Courtesy of the John Carter Brown Library at Brown University; 269(t), The Granger Collection, New York; 270 Bettmann/CORBIS; 271(t), The Granger Collection, New York; 272(cl), National Portrait Gallery, Smithsonian Institution, Washington, DC, Gift of Henry Cabot Lodge/Art Resource, NY; 273(c), Museum of American Financial History; 274(tl), The Granger Collection, New York; 274(tr), R. Foulds/ Washington Stock Photo; 275 Library of Congress; 276(t), ©Laurie Platt Winfrey Inc./ Woodfin Camp & Associates; 277(tr), Larry Stevens/Nawrocki Stock Photo; 277(tl), The Granger Collection, New York; 278(cl), Mansell Collection/TimePix; 279(cr), Giraudon/Art Resource, NY; 279(t), Giraudon/Art Resource, NY; 280 Michael Nicholson/CORBIS; 281 The Granger Collection, New York; 282(t), The Historic New Orleans Collection; 283(c), New York State Historical Association, Cooperstown, New York; 284 The Metropolitan Museum of Art, Gift of Edgar William and Bernice Chrysler Garbisch, 1963. (63.201.2); 285 HRW Photo Research Library; 286(t), ©Laurie Platt Winfrey Inc./Woodfin Camp & Associates; 287(cr), The Granger Collection, New York; 288(b), Sally Anderson-Bruce/ The Museum of American Political Life, University of Hartford, West Hartford,CT; 288(t), McAlphin Collection, Miriam and Ira D. Wallach Division of Art, Prints and Photographs, The New York Public Library, Astor, Lenox and Tilden Foundations; 290 The Granger Collection, New York; 292 The Granger Collection, New York; 293 The Granger Collection, New York; 295(t), The Granger Collection, New York. **Chapter Ten:** Page 296(tr), The Granger Collection, New York; 296(bl), Giraudon/Art Resource; 296(tl), North Wind Picture Archives; 297(tl), Peter Newark's American Pictures; 297(tr), CORBIS; 298(c), Collection of the American Numismatic Society; 298(c), Collection of the American Numismatic Society; 299 *View of the West Front of Monticello and Garden* (1825) by Jane Braddick Peticolas (1791-1852) watercolor on paper, courtesy of the Thomas Jefferson Memorial Foundation, Inc., Photographer: Edward Owen.; 300(tl), National Archives negative 68-2488-2 G1945-22; 300(b), Stock Montage, Inc.; 301 North Wind Picture Archives; 302 North Wind Picture Library; 303 The Granger Collection, New York; 304 Fred J. Maroon; 305 Charles M. Russel, Lewis and Clark Expedition, oil on canvas, 1918, 0137.2267, From the Collection of Gilcrease Museum, Tulsa; 306 North Wind Picture Archives; 307 The Granger Collection, New York; 308 Courtesy of The Mariners' Museum, Newport News, VA; 309 North Wind Picture Archives; 310 ©The Field Museum, Neg #A93851.1c, Chicago.; 311(t), The Granger Collection, New York; 312 National Portrait Gallery, Smithsonian Institution/Art Resource, NY; 313 HRW; 314 Courtesy of The Mariners' Museum, Newport News, VA; 315(t), North Wind Picture Archives; 315(cr), Mickey Osterreicher/Black Star; 316, 317(bl), The Granger Collection, New York; 317(br), ©Laurie Platt Winfrey Inc./Woodfin Camp & Associates, Inc.; 318, 319 The Granger Collection, New York; 322(r), HRW; 323(tr), Christie's Images; 323(tl), Christie's Images; 323(ad), HRW Photo Research Library; 323(b), Abby Aldrich Rockefeller Folk Art Museum; 324(t), Image Copyright © 2003 PhotoDisc, Inc./HRW. **Chapter Eleven:** Page 326(tr), (Detail) Collection of the New-York Historical Society, neg #34684; 326(br), North Wind Picture Archives; 326(tr), Larry Stevens/Nawrocki Stock Photo; 326(tl), Larry Stevens/Nawrocki Stock Photo; 326(bl), Victoria & Albert Museum, London/Art Resource, NY; 327(tl), The Granger Collection, New York; 327(tr), The Museum of American Political Life, University of Hartford, West Hartford,CT; 328 National Portrait Gallery, Smithsonian Institution, Washington, DC/Art Resource, NY; 329 Historical Society of Pennsylvania, Fourth of July Celebration in Center Square by John Lewis Krimmel (Bc 882 K897); 330 National Archives (NARA); 331 ©Laurie Platt Winfrey Inc./ Woodfin Camp & Associates, Inc.; 332 © Shelburne Museum, Shelburne, Vermont, detail of the painting *Conestoga Wagon* by Thomas Birch; 333 The Granger Collection, New York; 335 Maryland Historical Society, Baltimore, Maryland; 337 ©Laurie Platt Winfrey Inc./Woodfin Camp & Associates, Inc.; 338 Woodfin Camp & Associates; 339 National Portrait Gallery, Smithsonian Institution, Gift of the Swedish Colonial Society through Mrs. William Hacker/Art Resource, NY; 340 Karen Blier/AFP/CORBIS; 341 [neg. #42459] ©Collection of The New-York Historical Society; 342, 343 The Granger Collection, New York; 344 Bettmann/CORBIS; 345 Peabody Museum-Harvard University/Photograph by

Hillel Burger; 346(b), The Granger Collection, New York; 346(cl), Robert D. Rubic/Rare Books and Manuscripts Division, the New York Public Library, Astor, Lenox and Tilden Foundations; 347 WOOLAROC MUSEUM, BARTLESVILLE, OKLAHOMA; 348 North Wind Picture Archives; 349 Patrick Henry, (1736-99), pictured on a decorative pendant, Carnegie Institute, Pittsburgh, PA, USA/Bridgeman Art Library, London/New York; 350 Detail of The Headless Horseman Pursuing Ichabod Crane, by John Quidor, 1858, Smithsonian American Art Museum, Washington DC/Art Resource, NY; 351 The Granger Collection, New York; 352 The Granger Collection, New York; 353 Courtesy Barnes & Noble Publishing; 355 The Granger Collection, New York; 356 Sam Dudgeon/HRW.

Unit Five: Page 358, 359(c), The Granger Collection, New York. **Chapter Twelve:** Page 360(tl), Kim Neilsen/Smithsonian Institution, Washington, DC/PRC Archive; 360(tr), SuperStock; 360(b), The Granger Collection, New York; 361(tl), Library of Congress, Washington DC/SuperStock; 361(tr), Smithsonian Institution neg. #75-2984; 361(cl), Gianni Dagli Orti/CORBIS; 362 The Granger Collection, New York; 363 Bettmann/CORBIS; 364 The Granger Collection, New York; 365 © Bettmann/CORBIS; 366 Archive Photos; 369 Bettmann/CORBIS; 370(br), National Museum of American History 1999 /Smithsonian Institution; 370(bl), Bettmann/CORBIS; 372(c), Colonial Williamsburg Foundation; 373 Library of Congress/ PRC Archive; 374(bl), CORBIS/Richard Hamilton Smith; 375 The Granger Collection, New York; 376(b), Culver Pictures, Inc.; 377 Stock Montage, Inc.; 378 Private Collection, Photograph Courtesy of Kennedy Galleries, NY; 380 Chicago Historical Society, X.1354; 381 North Wind Picture Archives; 384(t), Image Copyright © 2003 PhotoDisc, Inc./HRW; 384(c), Image Copyright © 2003 PhotoDisc, Inc./HRW; 386(t), Culver Pictures; 386(b), The Museum of the Confederacy, Richmond, Virginia, Photography by Katherine Wetzel; 387(b), Stock Montage, Inc. **Chapter Thirteen:** Page 388(b), The Granger Collection, New York; 388(tl), Courtesy of the Massachusetts Historical Society; 388(tr), The Granger Collection, New York; 389(tr), HRW Photo by Maria Paraskevas, courtesy Historical Documents; 389(tl), Peter Newark's American Pictures; 389(cl), National Army Museum, Chelsea, UK; 390(c), Bettmann/CORBIS; 391(b), The Granger Collection, New York; 391(t), George Goodwin/United Methodist Church; 392 Courtesy of Massachusetts Historical Society; 393 Bettmann/CORBIS; 394 Brown Brothers; 395(c), Courtesy of the Bostonian Society/Old State House, photo by Mark Sexton; 397 The Granger Collection, New York; 399 North Wind Picture Archives; 400(c), The Granger Collection, New York; 401(b), Culver Pictures; 401(t), National Library of Medicine /PRC Archive; 402 Archive Photos; 403(tr), The Granger Collection, New York; 403(tl), Winslow Homer, *Country School,* 1873 oil on canvas, 1928.56, gift of anonymous donor, Addison Gallery of American Art, Phillips Academy, Andover, MA; 404 Anonymous, Girls Evening School, American. Pencil and watercolor, 13 1/2 x 18 1/8 in. Gift of Maxim Karolik for the M. & M. Karolik Collection of American Drawings and Watercolors, 1800-1875. Courtesy, Museum of Fine Arts, Boston.; 405(t), The Granger Collection, New York; 405(c), The Mount Holyoke College Archives and Special Collections; 406 ©Roger-Viollet; 407 Courtesy of the Illinois State Historical Library; 408 Photographs and Prints Division, Schomburg Center for Research in Black Culture, The New York Public Library, Astor, Lenox and Tilden Foundations; 409 The Granger Collection, New York; 410 Victoria Smith/HRW; 411(cr), North Wind Picture Archives; 412, 413 The Granger Collection, New York; 414 Archive Photos; 415 Bettmann/CORBIS; 416 The Granger Collection, New York; 417 HRW. **Chapter Fourteen:** Page 420(tl), Missouri Historical Society, St. Louis; 420(bl), The Art Archive/National History Museum Mexico City/Dagli Orti; 420(tr), Joseph Drayton, Indians and Trappers at Fort Walla Walla, Oregon Territory, 1841, Oregon Historical Society, Negative number OrHi 959; 421(cl), The Metropolitan Museum of Art, The Helena Woolworth McCaan Collection, Winfield Foundation Gift, 1958. (58.52); 421(t), Library of Congress/PRC Archive; 421(tr), Courtesy of the Oakland Museum of California; 422 Bettmann/CORBIS; 423 Bob Daemmrich Photography; 424(t), Daughters of the Republic of Texas Library; 425(b), Bettmann/CORBIS; 425(t), Texas State Library and Archives Commission; 426 Texas State Library and Archives Commission; 427 Harcourt Brace Photo; 428(cl), Culver Pictures; 428(b), PRC Archive; 429 Carl Socolon/The Landis Valley Museum; 430 Stock Montage, Inc.; 431 The Granger Collection, New York; 432 Courtesy Cornell University Library, Ithaca, New York; 434(cl), Collection of David J. and Janice L. Frent /PRC Archive; 434(t), Stock Montage, Inc.; 435 Society of California Pioneers; 436 National Archives; 437 Courtesy of The Bostonian Society, Old State House; 438 Wells Fargo Bank; 439 Courtesy of the California History Room, California State Library, Sacramento, California; 440(tr), *Handcart Pioneers* by C.C.A. Christensen, © by Intellectual Reserve, Inc. Courtesy of Museum of Church History and Art, Used by Permission.; 441(tl), Bettmann/CORBIS; 445 Sam Dudgeon/HRW.

Unit Six: Page 446 The Granger Collection, New York; 447(c), Library of Congress. **Chapter Fifteen:** Page 448(tl, tr), The Granger Collection, New York; 448(bl), AKG London; 449(tr), The Granger Collection, New York; 450 Bettmann/CORBIS; 451(b), Steven Laschever/Museum of American Political Life, University of Hartford, West Hartford, CT; 451(t), Library of Congress; 453 The Granger Collection, New York; 454 Natinonal Archives (NARA); 455(c, t), The Granger Collection, New York; 456 Nancy Gewitz/ Antique Textile Resources; 457 Collection of Janice L. and David J. Frent/PRC Archive; 459 Kansas State Historical Society; 460(t, b), 461, 462-464 The Granger Collection, New York; 465 Illinois Secretary of State; 466 National Portrait Gallery, Smithsonian Institution, Art Resource, NY; 467 Library of Congress; 468 The Metropolitan Museum of Art, Gift of Mr. and Mrs. Carl Stoeckel, 1897. (97.5) ©1982 by The Metropolitan Museum of Art; 470 The Granger Collection, New York; 471 Library of Congress; 471 National Gallery of Canada, Ottawa, Gift of the Massey Collection of English Painting, 1946.; 473 The Granger Collection, New York. **Chapter Sixteen:** Page 476(tl), The Granger Collection, New York; 476(bl), The Art Archive/Palazzo Pubblico Siena/Dagli Orti; 476(c), Ken Cobb/Library of Congress; 477(tl), National Geographic Image Collection; 478 Library of Congress; 478(tr), Museum of the Confederacy, Richmond, VA. Photo by Katherine Wetzel; 480 Bettmann/CORBIS; 481(br), The Museum of the Confederacy, Richmond, Virginia, Photography by Katherine Wetzel; 481(t), The Granger Collection, New York; 482 Library of Congress; 483 from THE CIVIL WAR:FORWARD TO RICHMOND, Photograph by Al Freni, ©1983 Time-Life Books, Inc. Courtesy, Troiani Collection; 484 Bettmann/CORBIS; 485 Virginia Historic Society; 487 Bettmann/CORBIS; 488 U.S. War Dept. General Staff photo/National Archives (NARA) negative 165SB75/LCB81841055; 489 Bettmann/CORBIS; 491 Woodfin Camp & Associates; 491(b), The Granger Collection, New York; 492 North Wind Picture Archives; 494 The Historical Society of Pennsylvania; 495 The Granger Collection, New York; 496 National Portrait Gallery, Smithsonian Institution, Washington DC/Art Resource, NY; 497 Bettmann/CORBIS; 498 Anne S. Brown Military Collection, Brown University; 499 State Museum of Pennsylvania; 500 Virginia Historical Society; 501 Collection of the Mercer Museum of The Bucks County Historical Society; 502(tl), Lloyd Ostendorf Collection; 502(t), Atlanta History Center; 503 Tom Lovell / National Geographic Image Collection (detail); 504 Library of Congress; 505 North Wind Picture Archives; 508(t), National Archives (NARA), negative 615.00A.004 ; 508(t), Image Copyright © 2003 PhotoDisc, Inc./HRW; 508(br), SuperStock; 509(br), Stock Montage, Inc.; 510 Library of Congress, Manuscripts Division. **Chapter Seventeen:** Page 512(tl), The Granger Collection, New York; 512(tr), Louisiana Collection, Howard Tilton Memorial Library, New Orleans, LA 70118; 512(bl), The Granger Collection, New York; 513(tl), Library of Congress; 513(tr), H. Armstrong Roberts; 514 The Valentine Museum; 516 Library of Congress; 517 North Wind Picture Archives; 518 © William Taufic/The Stock Market; 519 Peter Newark's Pictures; 520 Stock Montage, Inc.; 521(t), The Granger Collection, New York; 521(b), Bettmann/CORBIS; 522 SuperStock; 523, 525 The Granger Collection, New York; 526 North Wind Picture Archives; 527 Courtesy of South Carolinian Library, University of South Carolina, Columbia.; 528(b), The Granger Collection, New York; 528(t), Private Collection/PRC Archive; 530 U.S. Senate Collection; 531(b), The Granger Collection, New York; 531(t), Bettmann/CORBIS; 533 The Metropolitan Museum of Art , Morris K. Jesup Fund, 1940. (40.40). Photograph © 1985 The Metropolitan Museum of Art.; 535 The Granger Collection, New York; 536 Jubilee Singers, Courtesy of Fisk University Library, Special Collections; 537 North Wind Picture Archives; 539 The Granger Collection, New York; 541 Sam Dudgeon/HRW.

Unit Seven: Page 542 Denver Public Library Western History Collection; 543(c), Buffalo Bill Historical Center, Cody, Wyoming. **Chapter Eighteen:** Page 544(tl), Alfred Jacob Miller, Fort Laramie. Beinecke Rare Book and Manuscript Library, Yale University.; 544(tr), Courtesy Wells Fargo Bank; 544(bl), AKG Photo, London; 544(c), Michael Freeman/CORBIS; 545(tr), Iris & B. Gerald Cantor Center for Visual Arts at Stanford University; 1998.115/Gift of David Hewes; 545(bl), Mary Evans Photo Library, England; 545(tl), Christie's Images; 546 The Granger Collection, New York; 547 Werner Forman Archive, Pohrt Collection, Plains Indian Museum, BBHC, Cody Wyoming, USA/Art Resource, NY; 548, 549 The Granger Collection, New York; 550 The Field Museum, #A111822-2c; 551 Bettmann/CORBIS; 552 The Granger Collection, New York; 553 E.R. Degginger/Color-Pic, Inc.; 554 The Granger Collection, New York; 555 Peter Newark's Western Americana; 556(b), Peter Newark's Western Americana; 556(t), Union Pacific Historical Collection; 557 Union Pacific Historical Collection; 558 ©Laurence Parent; 559(t), Peter Newark's Western Americana; 559(b), Montana Historical Society, Helena; 560(bl), Peter Newark's Western Americana; 560(cl), Solomon D. Butcher Collection, Library of Congress; 562 ©2003 PhotoDisc; 563 The Granger Collection, New York; 564, 565 Peter Newark's Western Americana; 566 Nebraska State Historical Society; 567 ©Collection of the New-York Historical Society, negative #41800; 568 Batavia Depot Museum, Batavia, Illinois/Courtesy, Chicago Historical Society; 568(t-bkgd), ©PI/Photo © David Hardwood/Panoramic Images, Chicago 1998; 568(tl), Peter Newark's Western Americana; 568(tr), The Granger Collection, New York; 569 Library of Congress; 572(t), Image Copyright © 2003 PhotoDisc, Inc./HRW; 572(b), Colorado Historical Society; 572(cr), Image Copyright © 2003 PhotoDisc, Inc./HRW; 574 National Archives (NARA) negative 30.20.E.079; 575 Image Copyright © 2003 PhotoDisc, Inc./HRW. **Chapter Nineteen:** Page 576(tl), Property of AT&T Archives. Printed with permission of AT&T.; 576(bl), © Collection of the New-York Historical Society, negative #51392; 576(bc), Leonard de Selva/CORBIS; 576(tl), The Granger Collection, New York; 577(tl), Library of Congress #LCUSZC4-4637 DLC Detroit Publishing Co. Photo Collection; 577(cr), Chermayeff and Geismar, Inc./MetaForm, Inc.; 577(cl), Bettmann/CORBIS; 578 Archive Photos; 579 The Granger Collection, New York; 580 Science Museum, London, UK/Bridgeman Art Library, London/New York; 581(br), Culver Pictures, Inc.; 583 National Portrait Gallery, Smithsonian Institution, Washington D.C./ Art Resource, NY; 584 Culver Pictures, Inc.; 585 Bettmann/CORBIS; 586 The Granger Collection, New York; 587 Bettmann/CORBIS; 589(tc), Chicago Historical Society, neg. no. ICHi-30421; 589(t), Bettmann/CORBIS; 591 Frank Driggs Collection; 592, 593 The Granger Collection, New York; 594 Lake County (IL) Museum/Curt Teich Postcard Archives/Museum/PRC Archive; 595 National Gallery of Art, Washington, D.C./SuperStock; 596 Kansas State Historical Society ; 597 C Squared Studios/Photodisc/Picture Quest; 598(cl), Randy Leffingwell; 598(tl), The Granger Collection, New York; 599(tr), Courtesy of the Museum of the American Numismatic Association ; 599(b), Library of Congress; 600 ; 601 Bettmann/CORBIS. **Chapter Twenty:** Page 604(tr), The Granger Collection, New York; 604(tl), Collection of Janice L. and David J. Frent/PRC Archive; 604(b), Ann Ronan /Image Select, Inc.; 605(tr), Bettmann/CORBIS; 605(tl), The Granger Collection, New York; 605(cl), Knudsens Fotosenter, Oslo; 605(br), Sam Dudgeon/HRW; 606 Photo Courtesy of The Newberry Library, Chicago; 607 The Granger Collection, New York ; 608(cl), Collection of Janice L. and David J. Frent / PRC Archive; 609 The Granger Collection, New York; 610 Brown Brothers; 611(b), Bettmann/CORBIS; 611(bc), Culver Pictures, Inc.; 612 Library of Congress; 613(bc), Everett/CSU Archives; 613(br), CORBIS; 613(bkgd), SuperStock; 615 Bettmann/CORBIS; 616 The Granger Collection, New York; 617 Brown Brothers; 618 The Granger Collection, New York; 619 Library of Congress; 620, 621 Bettmann/CORBIS; 622 The Granger Collection, New York; 623(cr), Library of Congress; 623(tr), Courtesy of the Crisis Publishing Co., Inc., the publisher of the magazine of the National Association for the Advancement of Colored People. General Research and Reference Division; Schomburg Center for Research in Black Culture; The New York Public Library; Astor, Lenox and Tilden Foundations; 624 Private Collection/PRC Archive; 625 Library of Congress; 626 Theodore Roosevelt Collection, Harvard College Library; 627 Library of Congress /PRC Archive; 628(b), The Granger Collection, New York; 629 Bettmann/CORBIS; 630 Stock Montage, Inc.; 631 Laurie Platt Winfrey/Woodfin Camp & Associates; 635 Sam Dudgeon/HRW.

Unit Eight: Page 636 National Archives (NARA) negative 165-WW2885-2; 637(c), The Granger Collection, New York. **Chapter Twenty-One:** Page 638(tl), Anchorage Museum of History and Art, Gift of Mr. and Mrs. John M. Sorenson; 638(tr), The Granger Collection, New York; 638(bl), Library of Congress; 639(cl), Brown Brothers; 639(t), Library of Congress; 640 Stock Montage, Inc.; 641 Courtesy of the U. S. Naval Academy Museum /PRC Archive; 642(t), UPI/Bettmann/CORBIS; 643 Bishop Museum, The State Museum of Natural and Cultural History; 644 Peabody Essex Museum, Salem, Massachusetts; 645 Trustees of the British Museum ; 646 The Granger Collection, New York; 647 Library of Congress; 648 National Guard Bureau/PRC Archive; 649 USPS; 651 Keystone-Mast Collection #X6637, UCR/University of California at Riverside/California Museum of Photography; 652 The Granger Collection, New York; 653 U.S. Naval Institute Photo Archives; 654 Courtesy of The Mariners' Museum, Newport News, VA; 656, 657 The Granger Collection, New York; 659 Bettmann/CORBIS; 660, 661(b), The Granger Collection, New York; 661(t), UPI/Bettmann/CORBIS; 663(t), 665, The Granger Collection, New York. **Chapter Twenty-Two:** Page 666(tr, tl), The Granger Collection, New York; 666(c), Collection of Colonel Stuart S. Corning. © Rob Huntley/Lightstream/Courtesy of PRC Archive; 666(bl), Bettmann/CORBIS; 667(tr), Bettmann/CORBIS; 667(tl), The Granger Collection, New York; 667(bl), Rykoff Collection/CORBIS; 668 Culver Pictures, Inc.; 669 Reproduced with permission of Punch, Ltd.; 670 The Granger Collection, New York; 671 The Art Archive/Royal Automobile Club London/NB Design; 672 Lunch at Chatillon camp for the 8th Battalion, August 1918 (oil on canvas) by Joseph Felix Bouchor (1853-1937), Musee Franco-Americaine, Blerancourt, Chauny, France/Roger-Viollet, Paris/Bridgeman Art Library, London/New York; 673 Culver Pictures, Inc.; 676 The Granger Collection, New York; 677 Hulton Deutsch Collection/Woodfin Camp & Associates, Inc.; 678 Lance Schriner/HRW; 679 UPI/Bettmann/CORBIS; 680(tl), Archive Photos; 680(t), Collection of Colonel Stuart S. Corning/Photo © Rob Huntley/Lightstream/PRC Archive; 681(tr), The Granger Collection, New York; 681(tc), 682 The Granger Collection, New York; 683 Bettmann/CORBIS; 684(all), Eric Beggs/HRW; 685(tr), Archive Photos; 685(cr), ©Dorling Kindersley Ltd./Courtesy of Spink & Son Ltd., London; 686 UPI/Bettmann/CORBIS; 687 Bettmann/CORBIS; 688 © Laurent Van Der Stockt/Liaison Agency; 689 Collection of Janice L. and David J. Frent; 690(cr, cl), Eric E. Beggs/HRW; 691 Bettmann/CORBIS; 693 The Granger Collection, New York; 694 HRW. **Chapter Twenty-Three:** Page 696(tl), Archive Photos; 696(tr), Laurie Platt Winfrey Inc./Woodfin Camp & Associates, Inc.; 696(bl), AKG Photo, London; 697(tl, tr), The Granger Collection, New York; 697(cl), Mary Evans Photo Library, England; 698 Super-Stock; 699 Corbis/Pemco-Webster & Stevens Collection; Museum of History & Industry,

Seattle; 700 Stock Montage, Inc.; 701 UPI/Bettmann/CORBIS; 702 Lance Schriner/HRW; 703(br), 704(tl), The Granger Collection, New York; 704(bl), Underwood & Underwood/CORBIS; 705 Herbert Hoover Presidential Library/Corbis; 706 ED Archive, London/SuperStock; 707(cr), Negative number 66859, ©Collection of The New-York Historical Society; 708 The Granger Collection, New York; 709 Photography by Karen Yamauchi for Chermayeff & Geismar Inc./Metaform Inc.; 710 Bettmann/CORBIS; 711 The Granger Collection, New York; 712 Detail, Mural: Detroit Industry, South Wall, by Diego M. Rivera, Gift of Edsel B. Ford, Photograph ©1994, The Detroit Institute of Arts; 714 Corbis/Pemco - Webster & Stevens Collection; Museum of History & Industry, Seattle; 715 Brown Brothers; 716 SuperStock; 717 Culver Pictures, Inc.; 718 Philadelphia Museum of Art: The Alfred Stieglitz Collection; 719 ©Catherine Karnow/Woodfin Camp/Picture Quest; 721 The Granger Collection, New York; 722(t), Image copyright ©2003 PhotoDisc, Inc./HRW; 722(c), Image copyright ©2003 PhotoDisc, Inc./HRW; 723(b), Library of Congress/Corbis; 724(tr), Image copyright ©2003 PhotoDisc, Inc./HRW; 724(b), Photographs & Prints Division, Schomburg Center for Research in Black Culture, The New York Public Library, Astor, Lenox and Tilden Foundations; 725(b), Brown Brothers.

Unit Nine: Page 728 American Red Cross; 729(c), The Granger Collection, New York. **Chapter Twenty-Four:** Page 730(bl), Bettmann/CORBIS; 730(tr), National Museum of American Art, Smithsonian Institution, Washington, D.C./Art Resource, NY; 730(tl), 731(tl) The Granger Collection, New York; 731(tr), Sam Dudgeon/HRW; 731(cl), Bettmann/CORBIS; 732 John Held Jr., LIFE Magazine, © TIME Inc./Courtesy of the general libraries, The University of Texas at Austin/HRW photo by Victoria Smith; 733(b), The Granger Collection, New York; 733(cr), FPG International; 734(cl), PRC Archive; 735(b), Culver Pictures, Inc.; 736(t), Brown Brothers; 737 Franklin D. Roosevelt Library; 738 National Portrait Gallery, Smithsonian Institution/Art Resource, NY; 740(b), Albro, Maxine: California Agriculture (detail). Coit Tower, San Francisco, 1934. Photo by Lito, courtesy Masha Zakheim; 741 Library of Congress/Courtesy of PRC; 742(bl), 743 The Granger Collection, New York; 744 Brown Brothers; 745 Southern Historical Collection, University of North Carolina, Photo by Louise Boyle; 746 Franklin D. Roosevelt Library; 747 Library of Congress; 748(tl), Archive Photos; 749 The Granger Collection, New York From THE GRAPES OF WRATH by John Steinbeck. Copyright 1939 renewed © 1967 by John Steinbeck. Used by permission of Viking Penguin, a division of Penguin Putnam, Inc.; 750 Sam Dudgeon/HRW; 751 Culver Pictures, Inc.; 752(t), Nawrocki Stock Photo; 752(bl), © Copyright Chicago Tribune Company. All rights reserved. Used with permission; 753 The Granger Collection, New York; 756(tl), Classic PIO Partners; 756(c, br), Image copyright ©2003 PhotoDisc, Inc./HRW; 757 Hulton-Deutsch Collection/Corbis; 758(t), Image copyright ©2003 PhotoDisc, Inc./HRW; 758(b), FPG International; 759(bc), Brown Brothers; 759(t), Charles Apple. **Chapter Twenty-Five:** Page 760(bl), Ria-Novosti/Sovfoto; 760(tr), The Granger Collection, New York; 760(cl), National Archives/PRC Archive; 761(tl), Hulton-Deutsch Collection/CORBIS; 761(tr), National Archives/PRC Archive; 762 CORBIS; 763 National Gallery of Canada, Ottawa, Gift of the Massey Collection of English Painting, 1946.; 764 Brown Brothers; 766(tl), Dana Edmunds/Pacific Stock; 766(cl), Courtesy of Joseph Rygiel/PRC Archive; 767 Sam Dudgeon/HRW, stamps courtesy Kristen Darby; 768 The Granger Collection, New York; 769 FSA-OWI Collection, Library of Congress; 770 Bettmann/CORBIS; 771 Library of Congress, FSA/OWI Collection; 772 The Art Archive / Eileen Tweedy ; 773 Courtesy Sen. Daniel Inouye ; 774 AKG Photo; 776 Naval Historical Foundation; 777 Library of Congress, FSA/OWI Collection; 778 National Archives; 779 United States Marine Corps; 780 Division of Political History, Smithsonian Institution, Washington, D.C.; 781 AKG Photo; 783 Bettmann/CORBIS; 784 Photri; 785 Archive Photos; 786(b), U.S. Air Force/ National Geographic Society Collection/PRC Archive; 786(cl), Philip Jones-Griffiths/Magnum Photos; 788 Hulton/Archive; 789 Bettmann/CORBIS; 793 ©Robin L. Sachs/PhotoEdit.

Unit Ten: Page 794 ©Willinger/FPG International; 795(c), Photofest. **Chapter Twenty-Six:** Page 796(tr), UPI/Bettmann/CORBIS; 796(c), Archive Photos; 796(bl), UPI/Bettmann/CORBIS; 796(tl), Veterans Administration Photo; 796(bl), Franklin D. Roosevelt Library; 797(tl), CORBIS; 797(tr), Archive Photos; 798 Copyright © 1945 by The New York Times Co. Reprinted by Permission; 799 UPI/Bettmann/CORBIS; 801 Editorial cartoon by Tom Little, 1948; courtesy of the Nashville Tennessean.; 802 Woodfin Camp & Associates, Inc.; 803 Victoria Smith/HRW; 804 USPS; 805 Bettmann/CORBIS; 806 The White House Collection, copyright White House Historical Association and The National Archives and Records Administration, negative 590.0042 c.03.08; 806(tl), The White House, Courtesy Harry S. Truman Library; 807 Bettmann/CORBIS; 808 The Granger Collection, New York; 809(tr), Photri; 809(c), Collection of Col. Stuart S. Corning, Jr./PRC Archive; 811 Bettmann/CORBIS; 812 Syracuse University Library Department of Special Collections. Syracuse, New York; 813 Everett Collection ; 814 Michael Barson/Archive Photos; 815 The Granger Collection, New York. **Chapter Twenty-Seven:** Page 818(tc), David Spindel/SuperStock; 818(tl), Bettmann/CORBIS 818(bl), National Portrait Gallery, Smithsonian Institution, Washington, DC, Gift of TIME Magazine/Art Resource, NY; 818(tr), Hulton/Archive; 819(t), Index Stock Imagery, Inc.; 819(tr), © 1954/TIME Inc. Reprinted by Permission; 819(cl), © Sovfoto/Eastfoto; 820 Bettmann/CORBIS; 821 Reuters/HO /Archive Photos; 824 FPG International; 825 Lockheed Martin Corporation; 826 The Power of Positive Thinking © 1952, 1978 by Prentice-Hall, Inc. Courtesy the Norman Vincent Peale Center for Christian Living. Sam Dudgeon/HRW; 827(b), Tom Kelly/Archive Photos; 827(br), © L.P. Winfrey/Woodfin Camp & Associates, Inc.; 828 Index Stock Imagery, Inc.; 830 © CNAC/MNAM/Dist Réunion des Musées Nationaux/Art Resource, NY; 831 CORBIS; 832, 833(t), Bettmann/CORBIS; 833(cr), Collection of David J. and Janice L. Frent/PRC Archive; 834 Black Star; 835(b), UPI/Bettmann/CORBIS; 835(tr), Library of Congress; 836 AP/Wide World Photos; 837 Brown Brothers; 840(t), Image copyright ©2003 PhotoDisc, Inc./HRW; 840(c), UPI/Bettmann/CORBIS; 841 Library of Congress/CORBIS; 842(t), Archive Photos; 842(r), Image copyright ©2003 PhotoDisc, Inc./HRW; 843(l), ©N/A/Chicago Historical Society/Picture Quest. **Chapter Twenty-Eight:** Page 844 © 1978 Matt Herron/Take Stock; 844(bl), Topham Picture Service; 844(cr), Sovfoto; 844(tr), Owen/Black Star; 845(tl), NASA; 845(c), © 1969 Time, Inc. Reprinted by Permission.; 845(tr), Bob Rowan/CORBIS; 846(tc, cl), Victoria Smith/HRW; 847(tl), AP/Wide World Photos; 849 Les Immel/Peoria Journal Star; 850, 851 AP/Wide World Photos; 854(tl), Alfred Eisenstaedt/ Life Magazine © Time Inc.; 854(cl), SILENT SPRING courtesy Houghton Mifflin Company; 855 © 1976 Bill Pogue c/o MIRA; 856 HRW; 857 UPI/Bettmann/CORBIS; 858(tl), UPI/Bettmann/CORBIS; 858(bl), ©1998 John Launois/Black Star; 859(cr), Sam Dudgeon/HRW; 859(tr), AP/ Wide World Photos; 861 Woodfin Camp & Associates, Inc.; 862 Dr. Hector P. Garcia Papers, Special Collections & Archives, Texas A&M University-Corpus Christi Bell Library; 863 Archive Photos; 864(l), Corbis/Reuters; 864(tr), Richard Pasely/Stock Boston; 865 Paul Fusco/Magnum Photos, Inc.; 866 Ted Cowell/Black Star; 867 Henry Diltz/CORBIS; 868 Bettmann/CORBIS; 869(tr, cr), Archive Photos; 871(tl), Sarge O'Neill/John F. Kennedy Library. **Chapter Twenty-Nine:** Page 872(tl), West Point Museum, U.S. Military Academy, West Point, NY. Photo by Josh Nefsky; 872(c), Bettmann/CORBIS; 872(tr), Tim Page/CORBIS; 872(bl), Woodfin Camp & Associates; 873(tr), Sam Dudgeon/HRW; 873(tl), CORBIS/AFP; 874 ©Harlingue-Viollet/Liaison Agency; 875(tr), Victoria Smith/HRW; 876(tl), Woodfin Camp & Associates, Inc.; 876, 877 Bettmann/CORBIS; 878 Max Scheler/Black Star; 879, 882 Bettmann/CORBIS; 883 Sara Matthews/Swarthmore College Peace Collection; 884 Tim Page/CORBIS; 885 Bettmann/CORBIS; 885(cr), CORBIS/Nathan Benn; 886 Steve Schapiro/Black Star; 887 Eddie Adams/Time Magazine © 1972 Time, Inc.; 888 AP/Wide World Photos, Inc.; 889(t), UPI/Bettmann/CORBIS; 889(cr), Bettmann/CORBIS; 890 John Filo; 891 Jean Claude Fracolon/Liaison Agency; 892 Arthur Grace/Sygma; 893(tr), UPI/Bettmann/CORBIS; 893(cr), Sam Dudgeon/HRW, Courtesy of Lyndol Descant; 895 Sam Dudgeon/HRW, Courtesy Gene Rumann; 896 Victoria Smith/HRW, Courtesy Cynthia H. Luongo; 897 Sam Dudgeon/HRW.

Unit Eleven: Page 898 R. Krubner/H. Armstrong Roberts; 899(c), Stephen Frisch/Stock Boston. **Chapter Thirty:** Page 900(tl), Archive Photos; 900(tr), Erich Hartmann/Magnum Photos; 900(b), AP/Wide World Photos; 901(bl), Photri; 901(tl), Wally McNamee/Woodfin Camp & Associates; 901(tr), HRW; 901(b), Sam Dudgeon/HRW; 902 AP/Wide World Photos; 903 CORBIS; 904(b), Image copyright ©2003 PhotoDisc, Inc./HRW; 904(br), Digital Stock Corp./HRW; 904(bl), Richard Haynes/HRW Photo; 905(t), AP/Wide World Photos; 906(tl), Liaison Agency; 907 ©1999 Dennis Brack/Black Star; 908 AP/Wide World Photos; 909 Margulies/Rothco; 909(b), The Granger Collection, New York; 910(br), UPI/Bettmann/CORBIS; 910(bl), Photri; 911(tc), Bettmann/CORBIS; 911(tr), Rose Skytta/Jeroboam; 912 Hulton/Archive; 913 Ted Hardin/Black Star; 914 Wally McNamee/Woodfin Camp & Associates, Inc.; 915 ©Ron Kimball Studios; 916(b, t), Bettmann/CORBIS; 917 © Alain Mingham/Liaison Agency; 918 Richard B. Levine; 920 Paul Barton/The Stock Market; 921 Jason Laure/Woodfin Camp & Associates, Inc.; 922(tl), Image copyright ©2003 PhotoDisc, Inc./HRW; 922(bl), Photo courtesy of Apple Computer, Inc.; 923 © 1997 Lucasfilm Ltd./ Photofest; 925 Draper Hill/ © 1974 The Commercial Appeal, Memphis; 926(tc), Novosti/SIPA Press; 926(tr), Bill Gentile/SIPA Press; 926(bc), Wally McNamee/CORBIS; 926(bl), Robert Maass/CORBIS; 927(cl), Premium Stock/CORBIS; 927(tr), NASA; 927(tl), Doug Mills/AP/Wide World Photos; 927(br), Sam Dudgeon/HRW; 928 © Michael Evans/Sygma; 929 Bettmann/CORBIS; 930(t), AP/Wide World Photos. **Chapter Thirty-One:** Page 931 ©1984 Department of Defense from Black Star; 932 Sam Dudgeon/HRW; 933(c), 934 AP/Wide World Photos; 935 Woodfin Camp & Associates, Inc.; 936 SuperStock; 937 Chuck Burton/AP/Wide World Photos; 938; AFP/CORBIS; 939 CORBIS/Reuters NewMedia, Inc.; 940 Peter Van Steen/HRW; 941 Woodfin Camp & Associates; 944 Daniel Hulshizer/AP/Wide World Photos; 945 Thomas E. Franklin/The Record (Bergen County, NJ)/Corbis SABA; 946 Shannon Stapleton/REUTERS/TimePix; 948 Spencer Platt/Getty Images; 949 Lucy Nicholson/AFP/CORBIS; 951 John Trever/Albuquerque Journal; 952(tl), Image copyright ©2003 PhotoDisc, Inc./HRW; 952(tr), Image copyright ©2003 PhotoDisc, Inc./HRW Photo; 953(l), Jim Sugar Photography/Corbis; 953(c), © Bob Strauss/Woodfin Camp & Associates, Inc.; 953(r), Vince Streano/Corbis; 953(b), ©Phil Schofield/AllStock/Picture Quest; 954(t), Michael Howell/Photonica; 955(br), Bob Daemmrich/Uniphoto Picture Agency; 955(tr), Mark Godfrey/The Image Works; 956 HRW; 957 Michelle Bridwell/HRW.

Back Matter: Page 958(bkgd), Maps Division, The New York Public Library, Astor, Lenox and Tilden Foundations; 958(tr), HRW Photo by Sam Dudgeon, stamps courtesy Kristen Darby; 958(tc), Independence National Historical Park Collection; 958(br), William Johnson/Stock/Picture Quest; 958(bc, bl, tl), Image copyright ©2003 PhotoDisc, Inc. R1-R4(all), R5(all except bc, br), White House Collection, copyright White House Historical Association; (bc, br), The White House; R6 Image copyright ©2003 PhotoDisc, Inc.; R7 The Granger Collection, New York; R9-R12(border), Jay Mallin Photos.

Feature Borders:

Young People in History: Pages 1, 61, 149, 265, 359, 447 543, 637, 729, 795, 899, (cap, marbles, thread, soldier), Images copyright ©2003 PhotoDisc, Inc./HRW; (cameo, buttons, umbrella), Sam Dudgeon/HRW.

Connecting To Geography: Pages 54, 57, 120, 123, 214, 217, 322, 325, 384, 387, 508 511, 572, 575, 772, 775, 756, 759, 840, 843, 952, 955, Victoria Smith/HRW/Courtesy National Geographic/MapQuest.

Illustrator Credits:

All maps created by MapQuest.com, Inc.

Unit One: Chapter One: Page 5 (b), Nenad Jakesevic; 28 (t), Kenneth Batelman. **Chapter Two:** Page 52 (t), Kenneth Batelman; 53 (tl), Leslie Kell.

Unit Two: Page 121 (tl), Dave Merrill/Steven Edsey & Sons; 146 (cr), Greathead Studios, Inc. **Chapter Three:** Page 88 (l), Kenneth Batelman. **Chapter Four:** Page 99 (b), Argosy; 118 (l), Kenneth Batelman; 119 (tl), Greathead Studios Inc. **Chapter Five:** Page 136 (t), Argosy; 142 (t), Leslie Kell; 144 (t), Kenneth Batelman; 145 (tl), Charles Apple.

Unit Three: Page 217 (c), Steven Stankiewicz. **Chapter Six:** Page 182 (l), Kenneth Batelman; 183 (tl), Karen Minot. **Chapter Seven:** Page 209 (b), Leslie Kell; 212 (t), Kenneth Batelman. **Chapter Eight:** Page 247 (b), Karen Minot; 252 (t), Karen Minot; 256 (b), Argosy; 260 (t), Kenneth Batelman.

Unit Four: Page 323 (tr), Dave Merrill/Steven Edsey & Sons. **Chapter Nine:** Page 273 (tr), Saul Rosenbaum/Deborah Wolfe Ltd.; 293 (b), Nenad Jakesevic; 294 (l), Kenneth Batelman. **Chapter Ten:** Page 320 (l), Kenneth Batelman. **Chapter Eleven:** Page 334 (b), Argosy; 336 (t), Nenad Jakesevic; 354 (t), Kenneth Batelman.

Unit Five: Page 387 (t), Karen Minot. **Chapter Twelve:** Page 367 (b), Nenad Jakesevic; 382 (t), Kenneth Batelman. **Chapter Thirteen:** Page 398 (t), Argosy; 418 (l), Kenneth Batelman; 419 (tl), Dave Merrill/Steven Edsey & Sons. **Chapter Fourteen:** Page 433 (t), Argosy; 442 (l), Kenneth Batelman.

Unit Six: Page 508 (bl), Charles Apple. **Chapter Fifteen:** Page 459 (t), Argosy; 469 (t), Saul Rosenbaum/Deborah Wolfe Ltd.; 474 (t), Kenneth Batelman. **Chapter Sixteen:** Page 486 (b), Nenad Jakesevic; 506 (t), Kenneth Batelman; 507 (tl), Charles Apple. **Chapter Seventeen:** 534 (t), Argosy; 538 (l), Kenneth Batelman.

Unit Seven: Chapter Eighteen: Page 557 (tr), Saul Rosenbaum/Deborah Wolfe Ltd.; 568 (t), Charles Apple; 570 (t), Kenneth Batelman; 571 (tl), Charles Apple. **Chapter Nineteen:** Page 582 (b), Argosy; 602 (t), Kenneth Batelman; 603 (tl), Charles Apple. **Chapter Twenty:** Page 632 (t), Kenneth Batelman; 633 (tl), Charles Apple.

Unit Eight: Page 404 (bl), Ken Mowry; 406 (t), Ken Mowry. **Chapter Twenty-one:** Page 664 (l), Kenneth Batelman. **Chapter Twenty-two:** Page 674 (b), Nenad Jakesevic; 694 (t), Kenneth Batelman. **Chapter Twenty-three:** Page 713 (b), Argosy; 720 (l), Kenneth Batelman.

Unit Nine: Page 756 (c), Charles Apple; 759 (t), Charles Apple. **Chapter Twenty-four:** Page 742 (t), Leslie Kell; 754 (t), Kenneth Batelman. **Chapter Twenty-five:** Page 774 (t), Argosy; 790 (l), Kenneth Batelman.

Unit Ten: Page 842 (c), Charles Apple. **Chapter Twenty-six:** Page 802 (b), Argosy; 816 (l), Kenneth Batelman **Chapter Twenty-seven:** Page 828 (tl), Charles Apple; 829 (b), Nenad Jakesevic; 838 (t), Kenneth Batelman. **Chapter Twenty-eight:** Page 853 (b), Craig Attebery/Jeff Lavaty Artist Agent; 864 (t), Charles Apple; 870 (l), Kenneth Batelman. **Chapter Twenty-nine:** Page 881 (b), Argosy; 894 (t), Kenneth Batelman.

Unit Eleven: Page 946 (c), Charles Apple; 947 (l), Charles Apple; 949 (tl), Charles Apple. **Chapter Thirty:** Page 909 (b), Leslie Kell; 924 (t), Kenneth Batelman. **Chapter Thirtyone:** Page 942 (t), Argosy; 944 (t), Kenneth Batelman.

Epilogue: Page 953 (l), Kenneth Batelman.